D0026203

NEW PERSPECTIVES IN ABNORMAL PSYCHOLOGY

New Perspectives in Abnormal Psychology

Edited by

Alan E. Kazdin
DEPARTMENT OF PSYCHOLOGY
PENNSYLVANIA STATE UNIVERSITY

Alan S. Bellack
DEPARTMENT OF PSYCHOLOGY
UNIVERSITY OF PITTSBURGH

Michel Hersen
WESTERN PSYCHIATRIC INSTITUTE AND CLINIC
UNIVERSITY OF PITTSBURGH SCHOOL OF MEDICINE

New York / Oxford
OXFORD UNIVERSITY PRESS
1980

Library of Congress Cataloging in Publication Data
Main entry under title:

New perspectives in abnormal psychology.

Bibliography: p.
Includes index.
1. Psychology, Pathological. 2. Psychotherapy.
I. Kazdin, Alan E. II. Bellack, Alan S.
III. Hersen, Michel.
[DNLM: 1. Psychopathology.
WM100.3 N532]
RC454.N48 616.8′9 79-15431
ISBN 0-19-502652-7

Printed in the United States of America

PREFACE

Abnormal psychology is a topic that touches everyone in some way. The field encompasses a wide diversity of deviant behaviors and psychological problems. The disorders range from difficulties in adjusting to the common stresses of everyday life to the more severely disordered reactions that result in a person's inability to function. The topics of abnormal psychology are of wide interest for other reasons. Abnormal psychology is concerned with behavior in general, not with just severely disturbed behavior. The field draws upon many disciplines within the biological and social sciences, owing to the manifold influences that contribute to behavior.

This book is designed to provide the undergraduate and beginning graduate students with an introduction to the many different topics within abnormal psychology. The field is now so broad that no one individual is able to be an authority in all areas, issues, and topics. Therefore, we have chosen to have a multi-authored text with each of the chapters written by a recognized authority in the field. The contributors have prepared chapters that detail the current developments, major theoretical issues, and research findings for each topic that is addressed.

The book is divided into four Parts. Part I raises fundamental issues about abnormal psychology and is an introduction to, and a background for, the topics that follow. Fundamental issues include definitions of what abnormal behavior actually is, the history of abnormal psychology and the identification of abnormality, and the methods of studying topics within the field. Part II examines the determinants of behavior. Behavior is the product of many influences that span prenatal development to old age. This Part introduces the range of influences that contribute to behavior in general and illustrates specific determinants that lead to psychological disorders. Part III, the largest section of the book, discusses a variety of different disorders. In each chapter, the basic clinical disorder is discussed along with theoretical and research developments that have helped clarify the disorder. Finally, Part IV discusses treatment of the various abnormalities discussed in the previous unit. Treatment encompasses a variety of techniques both for outpatient and institutional treatment. Part IV discusses treatment alternatives derived from a variety of different conceptual positions.

We are very grateful to the contributors for their efforts, tolerance, and patience during the course of this difficult project. We thank our editor, Marcus Boggs, for his encouragement and assistance. Finally, but hardly least of all, we thank Lauretta Guerin, Mary Newell, and Michele R. Shawver for their secretarial assistance.

University Park, PA — Alan E. Kazdin
Pittsburgh, PA — Alan S. Bellack
Pittsburgh, PA — Michel Hersen

February 1980

CONTENTS

CONTRIBUTORS

David B. Abrams
Department of Psychology
Rutgers University

Jack S. Annon
Department of Psychology
University of Hawaii

David Balla
Department of Psychology
Yale University

Alan S. Bellack
Department of Psychology
University of Pittsburgh

Edward G. Carr
Department of Psychology
State University of New York
at Stony Brook

Alan F. Fontana
Veterans Administration Hospital
West Haven, Connecticut

Cyril M. Franks
Department of Psychology
Rutgers University

Sol L. Garfield
Department of Psychology
Washington University

James H. Geer
Department of Psychology
State University of New York
at Stony Brook

Gerald Goldstein
Department of Psychology
University of Pittsburgh

Donald W. Goodwin
Department of Psychiatry
University of Kansas Medical Center

Diana Hartley
Menninger Foundation

Michel Hersen
Western Psychiatric Institute and Clinic
University of Pittsburgh
School of Medicine

William A. Hunt
Department of Psychology
Loyola University of Chicago

Edward S. Katkin
Department of Psychology
State University of New York
at Buffalo

Alan E. Kazdin
Department of Psychology
Pennsylvania State University

Gisela Labouvie-Vief
Department of Psychology
Wayne State University

G. Alan Marlatt
Department of Psychology
University of Washington

Joseph Mendels
Department of Psychiatry
University of Pennsylvania
School of Medicine

Asher R. Pacht
Department of Psychology
University of Wisconsin

Hayne W. Reese
Department of Psychology
West Virginia University

Craig H. Robinson
Department of Psychology
University of Hawaii

Francine Rose
Department of Psychology
University of Washington

Richard J. Rose
Department of Psychology
Indiana University

Alan O. Ross
Department of Psychology
State University of New York
at Stony Brook

Kurt Salzinger
New York State Psychiatric Institute

David Shapiro
Department of Psychiatry
University of California
at Los Angeles

Stephen Stern
Department of Psychiatry
University of Pennsylvania
School of Medicine

Eugene H. Strangman
Department of Psychology
University of Wisconsin

Hans H. Strupp
Department of Psychology
Vanderbilt University

Ralph R. Turner
Department of Psychology
West Virginia University

Peggy M. Zaks
Department of Psychology
Wayne State University

Edward Zigler
Department of Psychology
Yale University

NEW PERSPECTIVES IN ABNORMAL PSYCHOLOGY

FUNDAMENTAL ISSUES

Assumptions and views about abnormal behavior vary markedly among lay persons and professionals alike. Considerable debate exists about what constitutes abnormality and whether many specific forms of deviance should be included at all. The different views about abnormal behavior have important implications for the kinds of questions that research asks and the kinds of answers that are sought. The present chapters raise several fundamental issues about the nature of abnormal behavior, the types of disorders that should be included, and the ways in which scientific research investigates abnormality.

Alan E. Kazdin (Chapter 1) provides an introduction to the basic concepts, definitions, and misconceptions of abnormal psychology. The models or general approaches to the study of abnormal psychology are presented. William A. Hunt (Chapter 2) discusses the different conceptualizations of abnormal behavior that have developed over the course of history. In addition, the types of disorders and the need to develop a systematic way of classifying them are elaborated. Michel Hersen (Chapter 3) discusses scientific research methods used to study abnormal psychology. Abnormal psychology is bascially an area of scientific study where the interplay between theory and research yields information about how and why disorders arise and the manner in which these disorders can be ameliorated. Hersen presents different research methods that are used to investigate fundamental questions about the causes of abnormal behavior, the distribution of disorders according to social and cultural variables, and the diagnosis and treatment of disordered behavior.

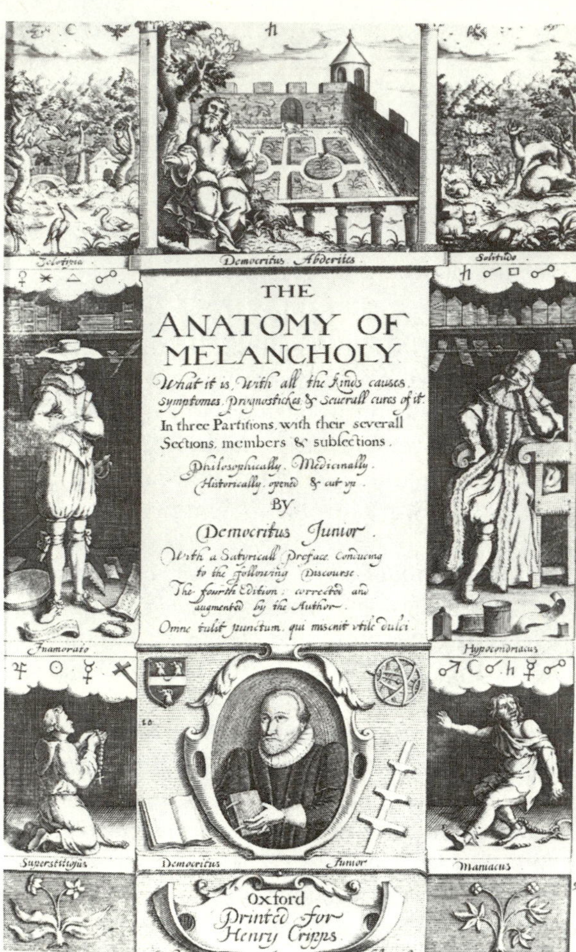

Zelotipia

Democritus Abderites

Solitudo

THE
ANATOMY OF
MELANCHOLY

What it is, With all the kinds causes,
symptomes, prognostickes, & severall cures of it.
In three Partitions, with their severall
Sections, members & subsections.
Philosophically, Medicinally,
Historically, opened & cut up.

BY

Democritus Junior.

With a Satyricall Preface, conducing
to the following Discourse.
The fourth Edition, corrected and
augmented by the Author.
Omne tulit punctum, qui miscuit utile dulci.

Inamorato

Hypocondriacus

Superstitiosus

Democritus Junior

Maniacus

Oxford
Printed for
Henry Cripps.

Borago

Blon fe.

Helleborus

Title page to the
1628 edition of Burton's
The Anatomy of Melancholy.

Benjamin Rush (1745–1813),
physician, humanitarian,
signer of the Declaration of Independence,
teacher, dogmatist.

Philippe Pinel (1745–1826) at the hospital of the Salpêtrière, Paris.

Emil Kraepelin (1856–1926),
psychiatrist, scientist,
and clinical systematist.

Sigmund Freud (1856–1939),
posing for his portrait
by the sculptor Oscar Nemon.

1

BASIC CONCEPTS AND MODELS OF ABNORMAL BEHAVIOR

ALAN E. KAZDIN

Abnormal psychology is the study of deviant behavior and psychological dysfunction. As an area of study, abnormal psychology is often fascinating. Many of the problems discussed are familiar because they resemble characteristics of one's own psychological functioning and everyday experiences. Such problems as stress, depression, anxiety, frustration, and uncertainties about one's own adjustment are part of ordinary living. For many people, the pressures of ordinary living are enough to lead them to seek help. In addition to problems of ordinary living, there are severe forms of maladjustment that may seem especially bizarre or aberrant. Some individuals may stop eating, they may believe that they are instructed by God to harm others, or they may be sexually attracted to inanimate objects. In any case, there seems to be a natural curiosity about psychological problems and how they come about, in part because of their resemblance to our own reactions and in part because of the seemingly bizarre reactions.

As traditionally formulated, the field of abnormal psychology considers problems that have been referred to by such terms as mental illness, emotional problems, deviance, bizarre behavior, and nervous breakdown. These terms are used popularly and are not entirely adequate in clarifying the domain of the field and the wide range of problems included. Actually, any problem individuals may have in adjusting to their environment may be discussed in terms of abnormal psychology, thus leaving almost no limits to the behaviors addressed.

The study of abnormal psychology is directed to basic questions about deviant and maladaptive behavior. Major questions are:

1. What types of maladaptive behaviors and psychological disorders are there?
2. What are the causes of these disorders and with what characteristics (e.g., social, physiological) are they correlated?
3. What can be done to ameliorate these disorders?
4. What can be done to prevent maladjustment?

These and the questions that could be derived from them are primarily the domain of clinical psychology and psychiatry. These disciplines seek to define and explain psychological disorders and to provide methods to ameliorate them.

Traditional conceptions of abnormal behavior have been closely tied to medicine. Of course, psychiatry is that branch of medicine that studies abnormal behavior. The ties of abnormal psychology to medicine are evident in the terminology commonly used to refer to abnormal or deviant behavior. The notions of mental illness, mental health, and psychopathology all reflect this orientation. Individuals who are mentally ill may be seen in "treatment" or "therapy' and are placed in a psychiatric "hospital" where they remain until they are "cured." Each of these terms and indeed the way in which individuals identified as abnormal are handled by the mental health professions reflect the traditional and contemporary medical orientation.

The medical orientation also has implied that there are psychological diseases identifiable in much the same way as medical diseases. These "diseases" are looked upon as qualitatively distinct states that differ from normal behavior and psychological functioning. At the outset of the book, it is important to emphasize that the domain of abnormal psychology is not merely identifying clear psychological disorders referred to as "mental illnesses." There are very few disorders that can be so readily identified. The vast majority of maladaptive behaviors and problems of adjustment cannot be identified by objective indices in the way that many physiological disorders can be identified. With some psychological problems, there are organic symptoms or causes that facilitate identification. Yet, these are exceptions. The rest of abnormality is defined primarily in relation to a social context where judgments about what is adaptive and maladaptive need to be made. These judgments require laypeople as well as "mental health" professionals to decide whether the behavior in question is reasonable or deviant in light of an individual's circumstances. This also makes the domain of abnormal psychology somewhat difficult to specify.Identifying discrete disorders would simplify the field greatly.

This chapter will discuss the nature of abnormality and the problems of defining the field. Definitions and criteria for identifying abnormal behavior will be reviewed. The many different definitions available are important here because they reflect considerations that go into deciding whether behavior is abnormal. Although one might debate a theoretical definition of abnormality, in practice researchers have relied upon several different definitions to investigate and understand the development and amelioration of abnormal behavior.

Research investigations and definitions of abnormal behavior proceed from a particular conceptual approach toward the subject matter. There are many such approaches used in the study of abnormal behavior. These approaches or models have made scientific research extraordinarily rich in breadth. For example, for a given psychological disorder, research may evaluate influences derived from genetics, physiological functioning, personality theory, family interaction, and social living conditions. These different areas of study are encompassed by major conceptual approaches, which are highlighted in the present chapter.

Abnormal behavior is by no means solely an area of scientific research. Because most of us are familiar with some forms of deviant behavior or problems of adjustment, we may already have views about what constitutes abnormality and what individuals identified as deviant or "mentally ill" are like. This chapter also discusses some commonly held misconceptions about abnormal behavior.

Identifying and defining abnormality

Basic criteria

Diverse definitions can be used to identify mental illness, psychological impairment, or behavioral disorders that are to be treated in abnormal psychology. Four possible categories of criteria for defining abnormality are: statistical, social, medical, and legal. Each of these is helpful in detecting abnormal behavior.

Statistical definition. A statistical definition of abnormal behavior is based upon the notion of the relative frequency of behaviors in the population at large. Abnormality could be defined as those behaviors that are relatively infrequent or are atypical of the population. Essentially, a statistical definition denotes behaviors that are numerically rare in the culture.

In the population, one can discuss the frequency of behaviors or the number of individuals who display a particular behavior. As with most behaviors, traits, and physiological characteristics, it is useful to conceive of the distribution of specific characteristics in terms of a bell-shaped curve. For example, Figure 1.1 illustrates a bell-shaped curve to represent the standing of the population on a hypothetical measure of anxiety. If everyone were tested on a questionnaire that measures anxiety, one would expect the distribution to resemble Figure 1.1, where most individuals are in some middle range of anxiety. As one moves away from the middle of the distribution in each direction, a decreasing number of individuals evince the extreme values on the measure.

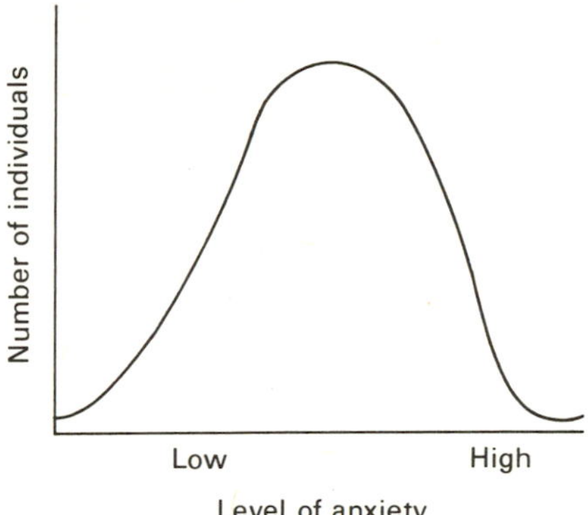

Fig. 1.1. A hypothetical representation of the distribution of anxiety in the population as measured by a psychological inventory. The results are represented by a bell-shaped curve that shows the relative number of individuals with various levels of anxiety.

Individuals at the low end of the scale (left side) would be considered to show little or no anxiety, even in the face of danger. Individuals at the high end of the scale (right side) would be considered to show high anxiety. At the extreme would be a few individuals of very intense anxiety, constantly anxious in their everyday lives. They might be anxious all of the time, independent of their specific situation. A general pervasive anxiety that cannot be traced to specific events is termed "free floating" anxiety and might characterize individuals at the high extreme of the distribution.

In any case, the extremes of the distribution for a given trait or behavior are defined as abnormal in this definition. In the above example, the absence of anxiety as well as extreme levels of anxiety might be maladaptive for everyday functioning. Individuals who show these levels of anxiety might be selected purely on a statistical basis in light of their extreme standing.

There are several problems with defining abnormality this way. Initially, it is unclear what dimensions are relevant for deciding that an individual has psychiatric impairment or is "mentally ill." There are many dimensions where extremes of the distribution are quite valuable. Unusual abilities, by definition, are statistically rare yet are not usually regarded as relevant to one's psychiatric status. Extremely high intelligence, musical ability, inventiveness, or creativity would not be regarded by most individuals as abnormal in the sense of psychological aberration. For a statistical definition of abnormality, the specific dimensions relevant for determining psychopathology of an individual need to be delineated. Of course, once they are, one already has some notions about the nature of abnormal behavior and its detection.

If a dimension were agreed upon as relevant, there might be a problem in deciding whether extremely high or low scores or both were to be included in the notion of abnormality. There are no clear guidelines specified by the statistical definition alone that dictate whether extremely high or low scores should be part of abnormality. For example, extremely high intelligence is usually not included in the realm of psychiatric diagnosis and abnormality despite the fact that high intelligence is rare. On the other hand, extremely low intelligence is included under mental retardation and is well within the realm of abnormal psychology. Also, for social behaviors, only one side of the extreme scores may be relevant for abnormality. Severe withdrawal often is considered to reflect psychiatric impairment. On the other side of the continuum might be excessive gregariousness. A person who is gregarious to the extreme might be regarded as very friendly or simply obnoxious but not psychologically impaired. As a general rule, determining which end of the extremes on a dimension would constitute abnormality or psychological dysfunction requires information beyond statistical criteria. Even if this information were available, a related problem is deciding the cutoff point beyond which individuals would be considered abnormal.

The statistical definition oversimplifies the nature of abnormal behavior. Abnormal behavior is not a matter of one dimension such as anxiety, along which individuals could be classified. Rather, there may be several dimensions including how the individual functions socially, the manner in which the problem is manifested, and how an individual meets obligations and expectations of others. The different dimensions that would be relevant to a statistical definition and their relative weight in deciding whether one is abnormal are not clear.

As a final problem, the statistical definition implies that being average (near the mean of the distribution) is desirable or healthy. While behaving like others no doubt plays a role in ascriptions of normality and abnormality, conformity with a particular pattern of behavior represents a constricted view of ideal behavior. Also, there is the problem of deciding the standard for conforming. Standards for acceptable performance vary markedly as a function of socioeconomic standing, cultural and ethnic ties, race, sex, age, and other demographic variables. Conforming with one's peer group might be used to justify criminal acts, if one's peer group consisted of a gang that frequently committed such acts. For some subcultures, deviance would be adhering to the law.

Despite the problems of a statistical definition of abnormality, it does reflect an important part of identifying psychological disorders. In fact, many problems are statistically infrequent and represent extremes of a distribution of behavioral patterns and traits. However, statistical rarity also characterizes behaviors not viewed by professionals or the public as the proper domain of abnormal psychology. Thus, other criteria are needed as well.

Social definition. The social definition indicates that abnormality is not simply a matter of the relative frequency of behavior but rather a consensual agreement: abnormality is whatever society says is mental illness or psychological impairment. Unacceptable behaviors are defined by people in everyday life who decide what is sufficiently deviant to single out as mental illness. The social definition recognizes that the behaviors viewed as dangerous or disruptive or merely beyond comprehension are likely to be singled out as deviant.

Behaviors that violate social norms are likely to be those labeled as abnormal. The norms refer to rules of social behavior rather than laws that define criminal behavior. The norms and social rules may be implicit standard role expectations that people have of others. Individuals who violate role expectations are likely to be labeled as deviant or mentally ill (Scheff, 1966). For example, individuals who violate role expectations by not going to work for prolonged periods, by engaging in excessive drinking in a way that interferes with ordinary functioning, and by exhibiting extreme moodiness might violate the expectations of others and so be labeled abnormal.

The social definition recognizes the importance of the people in contact with the person labeled as abnormal. Indeed, those who identify an individual as behaving abnormally play a major role in defining and detecting deviant behavior. Someone usually has to be bothered by the behavior to identify that behavior as deviant. To convey this point, Ferster (1965) has noted that behavior is not *disturbed* but *disturbing* to someone. Thus, identification of deviant behavior and "mental illness" may involve others who interact with the individual whose behavior is deviant. Deviant behavior is defined socially in light of the behavior of the individual relative to standards for behaviors and expectations of those with whom the individual functions. These standards are not absolute, but they vary according to the social reference group to which the individual belongs.

There are a few problems with the social definition of abnormality. First, it does not meet the characteristics of many mental health professionals who believe that mental illness is more than mere violation of social norms. To be sure, behavior labeled as mental illness in fact is likely to be deviant and violate expectations. Yet, there is much more than violation of social norms for many behaviors referred to as psychiatric disorders. For example, in organic psychoses there may be deviant behavior involving delusions, hallucinations, and irrational speech. Although these behaviors represent violations of social norms, the disorders are much more inclusive.

A social definition is basically a conformity view of abnormal behavior. Individuals in society look for adherence to widely accepted standards of behavior. Conformity to these standards defines normal behavior whereas deviation from these standards defines abnormal behavior. This is tantamount to saying that adjustment or mental health is engaging in behavior that is relatively frequent, and contains all of the problems of the statistical definition.

Overall, the social definition captures an important part of the notion of abnormality. There is clearly a social component in identifying abnormality. Being identified and hospitalized for psychiatric treatment is not just a matter of showing particular symptoms or types of deviant behavior. Many individuals in everyday life suffer from extreme withdrawal, lengthy bouts of depression, intense temper reactions, debilitating anxiety, and similar behaviors, but are not labeled as mentally ill or psychologically impaired. For example, in a classic study on individuals in the general population, Srole, Langner, Michael, Opler, and Rennie (1962) sampled people from Midtown Manhattan in New York City. Over 1600 individuals completed detailed questionnaires about their physical and mental conditions as well as details about their past and present. Evaluation of these questionnaires revealed that 23.4 percent were considered to be psychiatrically impaired with some form of recognized psychiatric disorder. These data suggest specific forms of deviance may be relatively pervasive in the population at large although the individuals manifesting them are not identified by mental health professionals as abnormal.

The findings also suggest that factors other than deviance may be relevant to a diagnosis of abnormality. Factors such as holding a job, having others who are interested in caring for the person with deviant behavior, and socioeconomic standing may be important determinants of how abnormal behavior is defined and viewed.

Medical definition. A medical definition holds that the presence of specific symptoms defines abnormality. Symptoms reveal that the individual suffers from some underlying disorder or state. Two variations of the medical definition might be distinguished depending upon whether the disorder or symptoms are viewed as organically or psychologically based. The medical definition as it applies to organic disorders refers to symptoms as reflecting a diagnosed biological disorder. Many disorders in abnormal psychology are known to have a biological basis, and the medical definition is completely adequate for identifying these. The medical definition as it applies to psychological or behavioral disorders refers to symptoms as having a psychological basis. The problem is a psychological disturbance or a "mental illness."

There are many disorders that are part of psychiatry and abnormal psychology that have no known organic basis. These disorders are referred to as *functional disorders* and are distinguished from the *organic disorders*.The medical definition as applied to functional disorders is the issue addressed here, and refers to identifying psychological symptoms in terms of traits, moods, attitudes, behaviors, etc., and tracing these to underlying psychological disturbances. Thus, symptoms such as delusions, hallucinations, sharp changes in mood, and prolonged depression might be viewed in the medical definition as signs of mental disease.

An obvious difficulty with the medical definition of functional disorders has been in deciding what the symptoms are and tracing them to the underlying disorders. Currently, there is a commonly used system of psychiatric classification that descirbes a wide range of psychological disorders. This system is published as a manual by the American Psychiatric Association and is referred to as the *Diagnostic and Statistical Manual.* (The system described in the manual will be discussed in Chapter 2.) Essentially, the manual specifies the symptoms that define various disorders. The medical definition can be employed by referring to the manual and determining whether the descriptions of various syndromes (groups of symptoms) characterize a given client.

Guidelines for deciding what constitutes symptoms and what these symptoms reflect have been provided by theories of personality and behavior as well as research on patients who are diagnosed as mentally ill. These theories hypothesize psychological processes that account for normal or abnormal psychological development and psychological dysfunction. Certainly, the most influencial theoretical account of psychological development was the theory of psychoanalysis by Sigmund Freud. Freud developed a theory of personality and a method of psychotherapy based upon his own clinical work with neurotic patients. As discussed in more detail later in the chapter, Freud provided an account of how a child's personality develops and the problems that may arise as the child's instincts and impulses are gratified or thwarted. Concepts from psychoanalysis can be used to describe how normal and abnormal behaviors of an adult reflect the individual's early psychological development. Symptoms were viewed as reflecting the overt expression of psychological drives, conflicts, and defensive reactions. From the standpoint of the medical definition, Freud contributed greatly to the notion that abnormal behavior could be traced to disturbed psychological processes.

A problem with the medical definition is that so-called mental disease differs considerably from physical disease, and the approach of medicine is not easily applied to many types of disordered behavior. Many physiological disorders can be detected through symptoms that clearly depart from normalcy. Fever, swelling, persistent vomiting, elevated white blood-cell count, and similar bodily reactions are symptomatic of many physical disorders. Also, a specific pathogen may be identified such as bacteria, virus, or toxic agent. Breakdown of a system (e.g., kidney dysfunction) or trauma (e.g., external injury) can also be identified as the precipitating agent. On the other hand, in psychiatry and clinical psychology, the symptoms of a large number of disorders are a matter of degree that cannot be easily identified or distinguished from normalcy. Perhaps a greater difference is that with psychiatric disorders the precipitating agent or original cause of the problem rarely can be identified. The nature of psychiatric disorders, their identification, and etiological bases are a matter of great debate.

Another problem with the medical definition is that it fails to recognize that the presence of symptoms alone, however defined, is not the sole basis for identifying abnormality or mental illness. As noted earlier, many social factors contribute to whether an individual is identified as deviant in the first place. Designation of psychological impairment is very much related to the reactions of others and hence is relative to social norms and desired behaviors. Indeed, some authors have taken the extreme position that symptoms of many so-called mental illnesses are simply problems of living, the result of individuals trying to adapt to situations that commonly arise in everyday life (Szasz, 1961). According to Szasz, the problems of adjustment are inappropriately labeled "mental illness" when they merely reflect individuals trying to adapt.

Overall, the medical definition attempts to define abnormality by the presence of symptoms that reflect some more pervasive underlying disorder. The definition is used in the case of many organic psychoses where the presence of a particular symptom can be traced to specific forms of brain damage resulting, for example, from excessive consumption of alcohol over a prolonged period. In fact, the medical definition is used to identify individuals who are being considered for psychiatric hospitalization or discharge. Individuals responsible for such decisions look for such signs as delusions, hallucinations, and depression. Thus the medical definition, although incomplete as an adequate criterion for deciding abnormality, enjoys wide use already.

Legal definition. Although one might debate the appropriate definition for identifying abnormal behavior based upon statistical, social, or psychological considerations, a legal definition is used by the courts as a basis for their decisions. The definition of mental illness or psychiatric impairment arises primarily in cases where the court is trying to determine whether the individual should be held criminally responsible for an illegal act.

The major definition of criminal responsibility was developed from a famous trial in England of Daniel M'Naghten, who committed murder. The court ruled that M'Naghten was not guilty for reasons of insanity because he did not know what he was doing at the time of the murder. M'Naghten was sent to a psychiatric institution where he remained until his death over 20 years later. The case has been a landmark decision and its ruling has since been referred to as the M'Naghten Rule. The rule denotes that persons are insane if they do not know the nature of what they are doing or whether the act is right or wrong. Of course, determining whether these conditions are met is a matter for experts and a jury to decide since there are no generally accepted objective measures.

The M'Naghten Rule was developed in 1843 and many other rulings have followed. One ruling given in New Hampshire in 1869 has specified more carefully the relationship between the individual's psychological state and the criminal act in cases where criminal responsibility is under dispute. With the New Hampshire Rule, a person is not considered responsible for a criminal act if the act *results* from the presence of mental illness or a mental defect. An individual is absolved from criminal prosecution only if it can be shown that the crime in some way relates to the psychological condition or defect.

Legal definitions of abnormal behavior vary depending upon the purpose of the decision or whether there is evidence of psychological impairment. For example, the process of committing individuals to a hospital, determining whether they are ready for release, and whether an individual is competent to make decisions all require specific rulings. The requirements for meeting legal definitions for these different purposes and the procedures for processing individuals whose psychological status is under scrutiny vary from state to state.

The definitions specify boundaries for handling social problems and designating types of behavior as psychiatric rather than criminally based. Hence, they are not necessarily based upon understanding or clarifying the nature of abnormal behavior. In short, legal definitions do not help in determining what type of behavior is normal and what is not. Indeed, legal definitions are likely to follow scientific insights into abnormal behavior rather than reflect them. This is not necessarily a criticism of legal definitions, but rather a recognition of their purpose in making practical decisions about the legal status of individuals. The legal definitions of psychiatric impairment or mental illness are directed at reaching specific decisions that alter the status of individuals and determine the rules under which they will be treated. For example, whether a person should be hospitalized or should lose certain individual liberties such as voting or entering into contracts are the specific end results of legal definitions.

Legal decisions depend upon judgments by professionals about individuals whose psychiatric status is in question. In addition, relatives of the individual, a jury, and others who have contact with the client may be involved in testimony affecting the legal status of the individual. Professional judgments that tend to be influencial in legal decisions involve subjective evaluation of the individual's competence and behavior patterns. Expert testimony is notoriously variable. It is not especially difficult to obtain experts within a given discipline such as psychiatry or clinical psychology to make opposing claims. The differences in opinions that arise in legal situations only show that clear definitions of abnormality are not available in many cases. In any case, the legal definition often is based upon judgments of others. These judgments only hide an implicit definition that professionals and others in decision-making positions hold. It is very likely that these judgments are based upon other definitions, such as the social and medical definitions mentioned earlier.

Definitions for research

The basic definitions outlined above portray components of what constitutes abnormal behavior. The definitions are not very specific and would be difficult to apply with consistency to the study of abnormal behavior. For purposes of research, slightly narrower definitions usually have been used.

It is important to mention the definitions used in research for a number of reasons. First, scientific knowledge about abnormal behavior is based upon these definitions so that any limitations of the definitions must be remembered in interpreting findings from research. Also, general concepts such as mental illness or psychopathology need to be defined concretely so they can be studied. This allows others to understand exactly what is meant by the term and what was studied. It is also important for interpreting research findings, and it permits others to conduct research along the same lines to corroborate and expand upon the scientific findings.

Several different definitions have been used in research on abnormal psychology. Scott (1958) described the types of definitions used in research as a way of delineating mental illness. These include exposure to psychiatric treatment, maladjustment, psychiatric diagnosis, subjective criteria, and the presence of psychiatric symptoms on objective measures. Two final definitions are maladjustment and positive striving as a sign of mental health; these are not as concrete or popular as the other definitions.

Exposure to psychiatric treatment. One definition useful for research purposes is defining mental illness as being exposed to psychiatric treatment. In many studies, mental illness is defined as being treated in a psychiatric facility, usually as an inpatient in a hospital. For research this is very useful because of the availability of hospital files, so that large groups of patients can be studied on the basis of information in their files even after they have left the institution or have died. Also, for research, patients represent a captive population who are readily available for investigation.

Of course, there are obvious limits in restricting the definition of mental illness to individuals who are hospitalized. The criteria for hospitalization are not standardized at all, so that patients within one hospital do not necessarily resemble patients at another hospital. Criteria for admitting patients depend upon the availability of beds, financial resources, state laws concerning confinement, and several other factors that may have little bearing on the psychological status of the individual. In addition, as noted earlier, many individuals who suffer from psychiatric impairment are not hospitalized. This suggests that other variables identify individuals as prospective patients and distinguish those who are institutionalized from those who are not. It cannot be assumed that individuals who are hospitalized are more severely disturbed than many who are not. Hospitalization itself is a function of such factors as social class, whether an individual has a job, and whether he or she lives with someone who is interested in keeping them out of the hospital.

Studying individuals who are institutionalized has other limitations such as introducing possible artifacts in research. For example, several years ago, research purported to identify physiological differences between hospitalized schizophrenic patients and normal control subjects (Angel, Leach, Martens, Cohen, & Heath, 1957). Schizophrenic patients were found to differ in the metabolization of adrenaline in the blood. This finding stimulated great interest and hope in identifying an agent that perhaps was somehow related to the cause of schizophrenia. However, it was found later that different intake of vitamin C (lower amount for schizophrenic patients) caused the differences in the biochemical analyses. The hospital diet of the institutionalized schizophrenic patients accounted for the results. In general, the possibility exists that by focusing on institutionalized patients, extraneous factors including social class, education, dietary differences, or living in an institution may influence the results.

Psychiatric diagnosis Another definition used in research that relates to hospitalization is psychiatric diagnosis. Diagnosis refers to classifying individuals into one of many different types of psychiatric disorders. In everyday life, neurotic, psychotic, and schizophrenic are commonly used diagnosic terms, although there are many different variations of each of these categories and other categories that are unfamiliar to those outside of the mental health professions. Using psychiatric diagnosis as a definition of mental illness in research has the advantage of allowing finer analysis of psychiatric problems. Rather than the global classification of hospitalized or not, implied by the definition mentioned above, investigators can distinguish different types of populations within the hospital and study differences in behavior, · physiological reactions, background variables, and responsiveness to treatment.

Assigning individuals to various diagnostic categories would seem to be a very useful research approach. However, there have been some limitations. A major one is that professionals frequently disagree about assigning psychiatric diagnoses to patients. Very general categories of diagnosis lead to more reasonable levels of agreement. However, as finer diagnoses are attempted agreement drops off considerably (see Hersen, 1976; Zubin, 1967).

Part of the problem is that symptoms comprising a given diagnosis are not unique. Patients across different diagnostic categories often share similar symptoms. Also, individuals within a given diagnostic category may show different symptoms (Katz, Cole, & Lowery, 1964). Thus, assigning patients to diagnostic categories is not as straightforward a task as one might believe. Nevertheless, assigning patients to categories and refining procedures for this assignment have occupied major research efforts in the field. The generally accepted view is that different forms of abnormal behavior can be understood by delineating specific types of behavioral patterns and intensively studying these separately. Thus, psychiatric diagnosis has been used extensively in research.

Subjective criteria. A person's own feelings of unhappiness or inadequacy have been used occasionally as a means of measuring psychological impairment. Presumably, individuals who are subjectively distressed often seek help. Distress is a major part of initiating treatment and obviously plays a major role in defining abnormal behavior. For example, dissatisfaction with one's personal achievements or marriage, depression, and excessive worrying all might be forms of subjective distress. However, there are many serious problems that may be outside of an individual's immediate awareness. For example, delusions of persecution and excessive consumption of alcohol may not be associated with subjective distress that the individual considers as such. Indeed, some behaviors included in the realm of psychiatry such as drug addiction occasionally may even be associated with euphoria.

In any case, subjective distress is an important criterion for research, particularly in outpatient research where clients seek therapy in light of feeling that something is wrong with their lives. Psychotherapy studies often implicitly employ this criterion because clients are included only if they have sought treatment. Yet, for many populations, particularly those institutionalized in psychiatric facilities, subjective discomfort is not necessarily a distinguishing characteristic.

Another problem with subjective criteria as a definition of psychological disorders is that they depend upon the situation in which the individual normally functions. For example, one might expect individuals from impoverished living conditions to be unhappy. The unhappiness is not necessarily abnormal or a sign that there is psychiatric impairment. The unfortunate living conditions, when appraised from a realistic perspective, could well yield unhappiness.

In general, a medical analogy may convey the limitations of subjective evaluation as the sole criterion for identifying disorders. With physical illness the presence of discomfort on the part of patients may be a signal of their illness. Indeed, many—perhaps most—physical disorders are first signalled by discomfort in the patient. However, there are other disorders such as arteriosclerosis, many forms of cancer, and diabetes where the disease can be identified long before symptoms develop and before the patient experiences discomfort. Thus, although subjective discomfort is an important ingredient in defining a problem, by itself it is not a reliable cue for detecting the range of physical disorders.

Presence of symptoms on objective measures. Assessment of a wide range of psychological characteristics and behaviors with objective measures has been used in research to define abnormality. Objective measures such as questionnaires, structured interviews, or tests designed to reveal personality attributes have been used to identify specific symptoms. For example, assessment devices can measure the extent to which an individual experiences anxiety or withdraws from social situations. On some measures, the individual may report specific symptoms such as chronic insomnia, bed wetting, or headaches. In cases where the individual reports the symptoms, this definition resembles subjective discomfort. However, objective assessment of symptoms may reveal behaviors or personality characteristics that are viewed by professionals as symptoms, but are not a source of subjective discomfort to the individual.

The advantage in using psychological measures to define abnormality is that they can be scored in a standardized fashion. There are many questionnaires and inventories that clients can complete that are scored in a consistent fashion so subjective judgment of the professional may not intrude to decide whether a symptom is present. Also, with objective assessment, professionals can obtain normative data from the population to assess where most people stand with respect to a given personality characteristic. Essentially, objective assessment of specific symptoms combines features of the statistical, social, and medical definitions outlined earlier.

There are problems with assessing psychological impairment on the basis of psychological measures that are well known in the field of clinical psychology. Performance on psychological measures does not invariably have a counterpart in a person's actual behavior. For example, on a given psychological device, a client may show signs that are scored as very high in aggression and suspiciousness, relative to others in the culture. However, performance on the measure does not necessarily mean that the individual behaves aggressively or is overly suspicious of others in his or her everyday life. Yet, research in clinical psychology attempts to assess performance of individuals on specific objective measures as well as the behaviors in everyday life with which such performance is correlated.

The lack of correspondence between performance on psychological measures and performance in real-life is part of a larger assessment problem. Responses on different measures are not always related even if the measures attempt to assess the same characteristic. Several measures of a given symptom or psychological characteristic do not always correlate highly. For example, performance on different measures of anxiety are not highly related. Even measures such as physiological arousal are not always related. Heart rate, pulse, blood pressure, and galvanic skin responses, all of which have been used as a measure of arousal, are not necessarily highly correlated for a given subject.

Maladjustment. Maladjustment as a general concept has been used infrequently as a direct measure of psychological impairment or abnormal behavior. Maladjustment refers to dealing inadequately with one's surroundings and may encompass many other definitions used in research, such as subjective discomfort or the presence of specific symptoms. The notion of maladjustment implies a failure in adapting to the situation in which one normally functions. Thus, maladjustment is tied to social behavior, expectancies for performance, and perhaps unique demands of the situation in which one is functioning. After all, the means of adjusting to one situation may not be appropriate to other situations where codes of behavior vary.

People may show visible signs of maladjustment in many ways. Presumably specific behaviors such as attempting suicide, performing delinquent acts, and constantly quitting one's job are often considered to reveal maladjustment. However, for each of these behaviors, the judgment of maladjustment presupposes a particular value system, usually middle-class values. For example, areas of sexual deviance are prescribed by prevailing social mores rather than by objective measures of psychological impairment. Homosexuality, long considered in psychiatry as a disorder, has been removed from the list of disorders because of contemporary changes in views about homosexual behavior. Similarly, other categories of behaviors once considered as deviant or reflecting maladjustment may vary. As a general concept, maladjustment is too general to be of great use for research in abnormal psychology. Thus, more specific measures are likely to be used such as the presence of specific symptoms, subjective discomfort, or psychiatric diagnosis.

Mental health as positive striving. Another general definition focuses on signs of mental health rather than mental illness. Jahoda (1955, 1958) advocated looking for signs that an individual is positively striving, developing, seeking, and finding fulfillment in life as a means of defining health. Presumably, individuals who are well adjusted are adapting to crises and stressful situations. In addition, they may be actively growing and developing. Such development might be evident in flexible behavior across constantly changing situations, and actively seeking out experiences rather than passively accepting events as they occur. Many theorists have posed definitions of adjustment that stress psychological growth. For example, Carl Rogers (1951) and others have emphasized that self-actualized individuals are growing, developing, and seeking new experiences. They are flexible rather than rigid and can integrate diverse features of the world and themselves into their personality.

The search for measures of mental health rather than illness has merit because it recognizes that individuals may not be abnormal but still are unsatisfied with their life and where it is leading. However, measures of striving and goal-directed behaviors might be as nebulous and heavily value-based as an overall basis for evaluating adjustment. For scientific research, more concrete measures and well anchored concepts are needed. Objective measures indicating that individuals are self-actualizing or striving can be developed, but they would need to be very specific to be useful.

General comments. Overall, Scott (1958) noted that many definitions used in research tend to stress adjustment of the individual to social situations. Whether an individual is subjectively distressed or is hospitalized, the basis for this can often be traced to the individual's social behavior. Thus, the social context in which the individual is functioning appears to be "lurking in various shapes" behind nearly all definitions of mental illness (Scott, 1958, p.41).

Social values dictate which is desirable behavior in many cases, particularly with behaviors defined as abnormal. A given behavior may not be identified as problematic unless other aspects of the individual's social functioning are somehow affected. For example, consumption of drugs and alcohol may not be viewed as abnormal and under the jurisdiction of psychiatry until they influence social behavior or become dangerous in some way. Similarly, conduct problems (e.g., delinquent acts), anxiety, and daydreaming are not considered as abnormal until they have social impact and interfere with the individual's social functioning or the functioning of others.

Commonly used criteria for identifying abnormality

The criteria for deciding whether someone is abnormal or mentally ill in everyday life differ from those used in research. Identification of abnormality in everyday life is a prior stage. Behavior may first be identified in everyday life as deviant, for example, by one's relatives or by law enforcement agencies, before the mental health professional intervenes for diagnosis or treatment. Thus, it is important to discuss major criteria that seem to account for identifying people's behavior as abnormal. Buss (1966) has identified three criteria used in everyday life to identify abnormality: discomfort, bizarreness, and inefficiency.

Discomfort. Individuals who identify their own behavior as abnormal or worthy of psychological intervention may experience some discomfort or a felt problem that leads to seeking help. The individual may seek help on his or her own or be prompted by others. All sorts of problems may account for discomfort such as the death of a loved one, onset of insomnia, sexual dysfunction, and diagnosis that a seemingly physical problem may not have an organic basis, or problems such as unhappiness or dissatisfaction with one's job. The discomfort may be anticipated rather than experienced at the time treatment is sought. Impending events ranging from taking a new job, flying on an airplane, or getting married may lead individuals to seek aid. Any event that leads to excessive worry or depression, as determined by the individual or others in their environment, may lead one to seek treatment.

Although it is difficult to point to a general principle that characterizes the possible sources of discomfort that lead to treatment and labeling the problem as abnormal, there are general dimensions that may characterize such problems. In general, the source of discomfort may be *chronic* or *acute.* Many problems, such as depression, can be either. A depressed patient may not be able to recall ever really being happy or elated, and this report might be corroborated by others. Alternatively, acute depression may be precipitated by such events as death of a relative.

The source of discomfort can be either *circumscribed* or *general.* Circumscribed problems may be very specific, such as phobias, tics, and inadequate social behaviors in dating and interacting with the opposite sex. Alternatively, problems may be much more general such as "free-floating" anxiety, unhappiness, dissatisfaction with one's life, and "existential crises."

Finally, discomfort may entail psychological problems alone or in conjunction with physical symptoms as well. For example, problems such as anxiety and unhappiness may not be associated with physical symptoms. On the other hand, these problems may be related to physical symptoms such as hypertension or loss of appetite. Psychosomatic problems such as certain types of asthma, allergic reactions, and ulcers illustrate the interaction of psychological and physical symptoms.

Discomfort that the individual experiences is usually considered as the source of the problem that leads one to seek treatment. However, the discomfort may be experienced by others who interact with the individual. These other individuals who are affected by the prospective client may recommend, insist on, or procure treatment for the individual. This can be seen clearly in cases with conduct problem children. The children may not experience discomfort at all. Rather, the parents may seek help because of what they perceive as problems in handling their children.

Bizarreness. The second criterion that is relevant for deciding whether an individual's behavior is abnormal is the extent to which it deviates from acceptable levels of behavior. Engaging in specific behaviors that reflect delusions, hallucinations, loss of memory, intense anxiety, compulsive rituals (e.g., constant handwashing), obsessive thoughts, and so on are likely to be regarded as abnormal.

It is not easy to characterize the behaviors that are invariably viewed as abnormal. The evaluation of behavior often depends upon the setting and context in which it occurs. For example, repeated undressing would be viewed as normal and even expected of an entertainer as part of burlesque entertainment in a night club but as deviant and a sign of psychological disturbance if it were performed in the middle of a downtown intersection. Also, the extent to which a behavior is bizarre may be a matter of degree. For example, most individuals experience some anxiety. One can point to extreme cases where the amount of anxiety might clearly be abnormal. However, there is an ambiguous area where the normality of various shades of anxiety can be readily debated.

Some behaviors regarded as abnormal do not seem to be a matter of degree. Rather their occurrence at all usually is viewed as sufficiently bizarre to diagnose abnormality. Self-injurious behavior such as repeatedly cutting oneself or attempted suicide, visual and auditory hallucinations, and bizarre sexual practices such as pedophilia (sexual attraction to children) are not commonly practiced and are almost invariably regarded as signs of psychopathology. Of course, one can easily conceive of exceptions where the context changes and these behaviors are not viewed as bizarre. For example, visual and auditory hallucinations at a seance, attempted suicide when experiencing a painful terminal illness, and bizarre sexual practices in cultures where these are not regarded as deviant are only some examples of exceptions.

Bizarreness as a criterion for abnormal behavior reflects the role of society in deciding the nature of abnormality. Changing standards over time produce many inconsistencies in the behaviors that are regarded as tolerable so that behaviors viewed as deviant at one point or as sources of discomfort either for the individual or others with whom the individual interacts may be acceptable at other times. This is dramatically illustrated in legal standards, which have changed for such behaviors as the consumption of alcohol and marijuana.

Inefficiency. The extent to which an individual functions adequately in his or her normal role is the third criterion for identifying behavior as abnormal. Performance of role behaviors refers to completing one's responsibilities and daily activities. These may entail adequately functioning on the job, taking care of others (e.g., children), or managing one's own life. In general, the extent to which an individual meets expectations in daily living is relevant for deciding whether behavior is abnormal.

The criterion of inefficiency is most easily invoked where there is an abrupt change in how well the individual handles his or her life. If an individual stops going to work or engaging in ordinary self-care behaviors (e.g., grooming, bathing, eating) after years of responsible behaviors in these areas might be identified as exhibiting some disturbance. On the other hand, a history of irresponsibility, tardiness at work, and overall sloppiness, if within the range of toleration for the particular job and life style the individual has adopted, may well go unlabeled as abnormal.

Probably, the greater an individual's responsibilities, including the greater the number of demands for efficient performance and the complexity of these demands, the easier it is to detect inefficiency and inadequate performance. When role requirements are not clear, it is difficult to assess whether there is inefficient completion of role behavior. For example, the inefficiency of individuals who have few obligations for self-care or for going to work, as might be the case of a retired tycoon whose personal and business affairs are managed in great detail by others, would be difficult to evaluate.

Inefficiency as a criterion for evaluating the abnormality of an individual's behavior is dependent upon many factors other than what the individual is actually doing. Age might help decide whether one's behavior is viewed as abnormal. For example, a young adult failing to manage his or her own affairs and becoming very negligent in meeting the demands of a professional position might be viewed as abnormal. If the same behaviors were performed by a professional person well past the age of retirement, the behaviors might be viewed as an expected or understandable process of aging.

General comments. Discomfort, bizarreness, and inefficiency should not be viewed as independent criteria that dictate whether an individual's behavior will be labeled as deviant. These criteria may operate together or separately, depending upon the specific problem and who identifies the individual as deviant. For example, discomfort alone may be sufficient to lead an individual to seek treatment and later to receive a diagnostic label. An individual who is anxious or depressed, overly self-critical, or generally unhappy may for these reasons alone seek treatment. Yet, the discomfort may be the only criterion if he or she has not been identified as bizarre and maintains ordinary work and personal role behaviors.

In other cases, meeting one criterion may not be sufficient to identify the individual as abnormal unless other criteria are met as well. For example, many bizarre behaviors are tolerated if the individual functions reasonably efficiently. Talking to oneself, irrational statements, and strange, idiosyncratic but innocuous behaviors may be tolerated if the individual functions well otherwise. Indeed, idiosyncratic, bizarre behaviors may be regarded merely as eccentric or weird but not a sufficient basis for labeling the individual as abnormal if normal daily activities are performed adequately.

Models of abnormal behavior

Within the field of abnormal psychology, several different models can be identified. *Model* refers to the overall way of ordering or conceptualizing the area of study. It represents an orientation in explaining abnormal behavior, conducting research, and interpreting experimental findings. The overall conceptualization of abnormal behavior dictates the kinds of questions an investigator will ask and the type of answers that will be sought in research.

A model of abnormal behavior is distinguished here from a theory that explains behavior. A theory tends to be a more specific explanation of a particular phenomenon. It poses a particular set of propositions or statements that can be tested. In contrast, a model is a much broader orientation that reflects one's basic position in conceptualizing the problems. For example, some investigators adhere to a biological model of abnormal behavior, which means that they believe the underlying basis of abnormality should be sought by investigating the organic underpinnings of behavior. Yet, among several different investigators who adhere to this general approach, there are many different theories to explain specific disorders and their biological bases. Even though the investigators may be working within the same model, they may differ greatly in the theories to which they adhere and the type of questions asked in their research.

It is important to provide an overview of basic models to understand the general orientations that pervade the many topics of abnormal psychology. Research throughout the remaining chapters can be viewed from the standpoint of different approaches or models. Knowing the types of models that serve as the basis of the bulk of research provides a conceptual framework in which areas of research can be placed. The present discussion highlights general characteristics and samples of research questions addressed by four major models of abnormal behavior, namely, the biological, intrapsychic, behavioral, and social-interpersonal models.

Biological model

Overview. The biological model views abnormal behavior as having an organic basis. Research on the biological model brings to bear techniques of diverse biological sciences to study organic factors that may relate to abnormal behavior. Physiology, biochemistry, pharmacology, neurology, genetics, nutrition, and several other areas have been studied with respect to psychological dysfunction and mental illness. Research within each of these areas takes the view that aberrant behavior is likely to result from some sort of impairment or variation at the biological level. Understanding psychological impairment may be achieved by looking at the biological underpinnings of behavior.

Background. Historically, the biological model has been recognized as a prevailing model of abnormal behavior. Its only competitor was a demonological model, in which deviant behavior was attributed to demons and evil spirits that were assumed to possess afflicted individuals. The history of psychiatry can be traced by examining the waxing and waning of biological and demonological models and whether treatment in a particular period was controlled by the equivalent of physicians or religious leaders (see Zilboorg & Henry, 1941).

In modern times, the scientific approach toward physical illness extended to abnormal behavior. The plausibility of the biological model was increased greatly by showing that select behaviors regarded as abnormal could be traced to biological disorders. Most prominent among these findings was the discovery of the cause of general paresis, a neurological disorder with both physical and psychological symptoms. Prior to death, which may result from paresis in its late stage, psychological symptoms may be evident such as intellectual impairment, distorted perceptions, and bizarre ideation. In the late 1800s and early 1900s a series of breakthroughs demonstrated that general paresis was caused by the syphilitic spirochete. Along with this discovery, effective treatments were found. Thus, syphilis was shown to be the biological basis for behaviors considered to reflect on a form of "mental illness." The successful isolation of syphilis as a biological disorder with psychological and physical repercussions was followed by many similar findings with other disorders. These successes offered promise that abnormal behavior in general could be traced to underlying physical disorders.

Contemporary research. Current research on abnormal behavior within this model examines the biological bases of behavior in far too many ways to begin to enumerate here. This research has been stimulated by the many disorders already shown to have an organic basis. Variations of psychoses and mental retardation, for example, are known to have a clear organic basis. Down's syndrome (mongolism) is a condition associated with severe or moderate retardation and is characterized by various physical features such as slanting eyes, flat and broad face and nose structure, appearance of an elongated tongue, short neck, and stubby fingers. Although many biological differences have been found between Down's syndrome children and normal children, researchers have demonstrated that mongoloid children are characterized by specific anomalies in their chromosomes (Lejeune, 1970). And different types of anomalies can distinguish different patterns of mongolism. Down's syndrome is only one of many different forms of mental retardation found to have a biological basis.

Extensive research has been conducted to investigate the genetic and biochemical bases of psychotic reactions. For years, investigators have attempted to isolate physiological differences between normal humans and various diagnostic groups (e.g., psychotics, sexual deviates) to try to understand the basis of disordered behavior. Indeed, similar work has been conducted with criminals to understand the nature of aggressive and antisocial behavior. The investigations do not necessarily mean that all behaviors can be traced to biological causes in the same sense as general paresis or Down's syndrome. Rather, the investigations reflect the application of biological techniques to understand the bases of behavior.

Intrapsychic model

Overview. The intrapsychic model views abnormal behavior as resulting from underlying psychological processes. Attention is shifted to such psychological processes as conflicts, frustrations, internal strivings, and similar attributes of internal functioning of the personality. Abnormal behaviors are considered to reflect aberrations in psychological development and personality functioning. Amelioration of the problem behaviors can result from addressing the internal processes from which they are assumed to be derived.

Background. The intrapsychic model of abnormal behavior owes its origin largely to the biological model. In medicine and psychiatry, the orientation of the biological approach has been to look for organic causes of overt symptoms. This approach has been greatly profitable in medicine. Also, there have been many successes, alluded to earlier, in the search for organic pathology for psychological aberrations. Despite the multiple successes of the biological approach, for a major portion of disorders referred to as "mental illness," no evidence of organic pathology exists.

In the late 19th century, the biological model was not particularly helpful in explaining the basis of abnormal behavior in cases where no clear organic cause could be isolated. Individuals began to look for psychological factors that might cause abnormal behavior. Although there were several advances leading to this orientation, important work was stimulated by demonstrations of effective psychotherapy procedures based upon hypnosis and various forms of suggestion. Select demonstrations indicated that techniques of suggestion could ameliorate psychological symptoms such as hysterical paralysis (paralysis not caused by an underlying organic basis).

Other techniques also were found to ameliorate aberrant behaviors. For examples, neurotic anxiety and obsessions were found in clinical practice to be relieved by catharsis, i.e., having the individual express their feelings, memories, and conflicts about particular events. Patients were often relieved of their psychological problems, at least temporarily, be merely discussing them and recalling events related to their development. The efficacy of suggestion, catharsis, and similar methods indicated that the basis of the disorders might be in the individual's psychological rather than biological functioning. Hence, there was a need to explain what the psychological processes were, how they developed, and how they led to abnormal behavior.

The greatest single influence that stimulated an intrapsychic model of abnormal behavior was the work of Freud. Freud's theory of psychoanalysis posited a complex network of psychological mechanisms, structures, impulses, and developmental stages that explained overt behavior. His theory filled the void by providing an account of psychological functioning. Although specific features of the theory are beyond the scope of the present chapter, a few general characteristics warrant mention.

Freud conjectured that personality development can be traced to the expression of biological or sexual energy (libido) and the sources of gratification toward which that energy is directed. He believed that psychological processes unfold in early childhood when instinctual gratification focuses upon different sources of stimulation. Freud explained psychological development as passing through a series of psychosexual stages. The stages were determined primarily by the focus on the expression of libidinal energy on various parts of the body (i.e., oral, anal, and genital areas) as a source of gratification as well as by the psychic mechanisms he assumed to be operative during those stages.

Freud accounted for neurotic behaviors or symptoms, the focus of his own therapy, as substitute gratifications for unconscious impulses that had been denied expression. He believed that sexual themes, related to early childhood, were implicated in the problems of his patients. The goal of therapy was to uncover the sources of repressed impulses and unconscious processes that would eliminate problematic behaviors. Essentially, the psychological energy that was manifest in symptomatic behaviors needed to be eliminated or rechanneled to more constructive and socially acceptable ways of behaving. Although this sketchy account does not begin to elaborate the complexity of processes involved, the purpose here is merely to indicate the approach and orientation of Freudian theory as a representative of the intrapsychic model.

Actually, Freudian theory is only one of many views that are subsumed under an intrapsychic approach to psychopathology. Aside from many revisions of psychoanalytic theory that modified various tenets of Freud's original views, a variety of competing theories of personality have been advanced that can account for abnormal behavior (see Hall & Lindzey, 1970). For example, Carl Rogers, a clinical psychologist, developed a phenomenological theory, or self-theory, of personality (Rogers, 1942, 1951). The theory of personality advocated by Rogers is an intrapsychic view but can be readily distinguished from orthodox psychoanalysis. Rogers's theory focuses an individual's self-concept and perceptions of the environment to account for the development of symptomatic behavior. The client's problems stem from not accepting him- or herself and failing to assimilate various portions of experience that are threatening. Treatment is directed at altering self-perceptions and opening the person to various sources of experience.

Contemporary research. Research within the intrapsychic approach has proceeded along several lines, only a few of which can be mentioned here. The different theoretical positions within the model have posited a wide range of processes that might account for behavior. Various needs, traits, internal strivings, sources of psychological energy, concepts about oneself and others, and other intrapsychic processes have been proposed to account for behavior and investigated as such. For example, research within the different theories attempts to measure intrapsychic processes and to identify individuals who show different levels of these processes. Another line of research is to relate psychological processes, as measured by various inventories and psychological tests, to specific psychiatric diagnoses. This research attempts to understand the different processes that might underlie psychiatric disorders and account for differences in behaviors associated with each. Other research attempts to relate underlying psychological processes to characteristics of the parents or the home situation.

Behavioral model

Overview. The behavioral model views abnormal and normal behavior as a function of specific learning experiences. Behavior is referred to as abnormal or normal largely on the basis of social and subjective criteria rather than any inherent characteristics of the behavior itself. Independently of how behavior is labeled, the behavioral model views it primarily to be the result of one's learning experiences. The focus of the behavioral model is to provide relevant learning experiences that can alter maladaptive behavior. Although the behavioral model conceptualizes behavior in terms of learning, its primary focus is on developing therapeutic procedures to alter behavior.

Background. Until relatively recently, psychology as an independent science had contributed little directly to the study and treatment of abnormal behavior. The dominant approaches have been the biological and more recently the intrapsychic models. Over the last 25 years, there has been a growing dissatisfaction with a disease approach to psychiatric disorders. Questions have been raised about whether most forms of so called abnormal behavior are appropriately conceptualized as a psychological or biological "disease." The dissatisfaction with orthodox psychoanalysis, in part, has contributed to behavioral conceptualizations of abnormal behavior. Psychoanalysis as a theory of personality has been subject to criticism because many of its propositions are not readily amenable to scientific investigation. Also, in cases where research has been conducted, many of the basic propositions, for example the role of child development on adult behavior, have not been well supported (Caldwell, 1964; Hovey, 1959; Sewell, 1952).

The behavioral model represents a psychological interpretation of abnormal behavior in terms that eschew the notions of disease and intrapsychic conflict as the basis for abnormal behavior. The behavioral model approaches behavior from the standpoint of learning theory in psychology. The three types of learning relied upon are classical conditioning, operant conditioning, and observational or vicarious learning.

Classical conditioning refers to the process whereby new stimuli gain the capacity to elicit reflex responses. Reflex reactions, referred to as *respondents,* include such behaviors as flexion of a muscle in response to pain, startle reactions in response to an aversive event presented rapidly, and salavation in response to presence of food in one's mouth. *Operant conditioning* refers to procedures whereby the frequency of various behaviors is increased or decreased because of the consequences that are provided for responding. Behaviors that are influenced by the consequences, referred to as *operants,* include those acts individuals normally engage in such as walking, talking, and smiling. Operants are not elicited by stimuli in the way that respondents or reflexes are. *Observational learning,* also referred to as modeling or vicarious learning, refers to learning from observing someone else perform a behavior. Specific behaviors can be learned from merely observing another person (referred to as a model) without the observer actually performing the act. Observational learning can influence both respondent and operant behaviors.

The above types of learning, well investigated in experimental laboratory research, have been used to understand the development of abnormal (and normal) behavior. In addition, and of greater emphasis for the behavior model, theories and findings in the psychology of learning and other areas of psychology as well have helped generate therapy techniques to alter diverse forms of behaviors viewed as abnormal. For example, anxiety-reduction techniques have been developed from classical condtioning interpretations of fear. Incentive systems based upon operant conditioning have influenced the behaviors of psychotic patients, hyperactive children, mentally retarded residents, and other populations to bring them to levels of more adequate functioning. Similarly, therapy techniques based upon observational learning have been used to overcome fears and to develop interaction in children and adults.

Contemporary research. Research in the behavioral approach has focused primarily upon techniques to alter behavior. Relatively little work has elaborated how abnormal behavior such as psychotic acts, sexual deviance, and intense anxiety develop. Yet, independent of the manner in which they have developed, many behaviors have been amenable to change through treatment techniques derived from the standpoint of the behavioral model. Techniques have effectively altered conduct problems in children and adolescents, specific psychotic behaviors (such as irrational talk, delusions, and hallucinations), anxiety, compulsions, and obsessions of neurotics, enuresis, and other disorders (Kazdin & Wilson, 1978).

Social-interpersonal model

Overview. The social-interpersonal model is based upon the notion that deviant behavior is a function of interpersonal processes. An individual's personality and behavior, normal or abnormal, develops from interactions with others. The level of interaction of interest may vary across versions of approaches within the model. A major view is that a child's interactions with his or her parents account for adaptive or maladaptive behavior. The relationship with one's parents is viewed as central to developing feelings of self-regard, trust, independence and dependence, and other psychological characteristics. Another level of analysis of interpersonal interactions is the relation of the individual to society more generally, in terms of normative standards of behavior.

Background. Much of impetus for the social-interpersonal model derives from dissatisfaction with orthodox psychoanalysis as a model of psychiatric disorders. Psychic impulses that guide an individual's development, according to orthodox psychoanalytic theory, unfold much the same way that biological characteristics seem to unfold, namely, on a predetermined schedule. Psychoanalytic theory stresses internal (intrapsychic) processes of the individual as determinants of behavior. Such a focus deemphasizes the social components of development and the influence of the interactions of others. A social-interpersonal model shifts attention to the relationship of the individual to others and the impact of social variables.

Another major influence on the development of a social-interpersonal model was sociology. Theoretical accounts as well as empirical research in sociology have pointed out the influence of social roles, norms, social class, and other variables that characterize an individual's relations to others and to society as a whole. For example, Emile Durkheim, an extremely influencial sociologist, discussed the relation of a breakdown of social structures, goals, and cultural norms in a social system on suicide rates (Durkheim, 1964). A number of variables of sociological interest have been shown to relate to psychiatric disorders, deviance, and criminality including social class, occupation, religion, and ethnic ties. The impact of these variables has been to suggest overall that biological, intrapsychic, and behavioral factors alone are not sufficient to account for maladaptive behavior in society.

Although different levels of explanation have been offered within the social-interpersonal model, psychologists have given considerable attention to the importance of a child's interactions with his or her parents. Many different accounts have been offered to explain characteristics of mothers, fathers, or families as a whole that may contribute to disordered behavior of the child and later the adult (cf. Fontana, 1966). Communication patterns among family members have received attention and illustrate the overall orientation of the social-interpersonal model. One view is that a child's disordered behavior may be traced to faulty communication. Parents may communicate conflicting messages that confuse a child (Bateson, Jackson, Haley, & Weakland, 1956). For example, a parent's words, intonations, and gestures may give conflicting information about the parent's intentions, feelings, and love. The child's own views about himself may be confused and he or she may simply withdraw emotionally as a maneuver to adapt to a family situation.

Different views and levels of analysis within the social-interpersonal model may embrace or eschew intrapsychic concepts. For example, according to some theories, social interactions are important because they influence intrapsychic processes such as self-concept or feelings of personal worth. Yet, a social-interpersonal account of maladaptive behavior can be made by looking at social factors that affect an individual. This level of analysis, more likely to characterize the interests of sociologists, focuses upon social rather than intrapsychic factors as the source of an individual's problems.

Contemporary research. Many different theories and research areas exist within a social-interpersonal model. One line of research focuses on interaction patterns that may distinguish families of individuals identified as abnormal from those who are viewed as normal. This research attempts to isolate factors that may cause or develop pathology in the family of disturbed individuals. Another is social factors that contribute to abnormal behavior. Epidemiological studies attempt to identify the characteristics of individuals who are diagnosed as deviant. Several sociological variables such as education, social mobility, occupation, urban or rural residence, and religion all influence the incidence of disordered behavior and even the type of disorders that will develop.

General comments

The biological, intrapsychic, behavioral, and social-interpersonal models represent the major approaches in abnormal psychology. There are other approaches that conceptualize abnormal behavior from other perspectives. For examples, humanistic and existential models have been proposed that provide a different focus in accounting for the development and amelioration of abnormal behavior. However, they have not been as widely embraced nor are they as amenable to scientific research as the models mentioned above. The bulk of contemporary research on the central topics of abnormal psychology related to the measurement, causes, treatments, and outcome of deviant behavior are embraced by the above models.

In discussing the models generally, it is important to reiterate that many theories exist within each model. For example, within the intrapsychic model alone, many theories have been advanced to account for the basis of neurotic anxiety. Conflicting theories within a given model or across separate models serve as impetus for experimentation. Subsequent chapters will review research for problem areas that convey the different theoretical positions.

Conceptions and misconceptions about psychopathology

Many misconceptions are held by the public about individuals whose behaviors are identified as abnormal. The attitudes and conceptions widely held about mental illness are very important. The public's view about psychiatric disorders influence those behaviors that are identified as problematic and influence the decision either by the individual whose behavior is deviant or those in contact with them whether or not to seek treatment. The present section considers the public's attitudes, conceptions, and misconceptions about mental illness.

Public attitudes toward the psychiatrically impaired

The misconceptions that the public holds about "mental illness" can be introduced by first looking at how the psychiatrically impaired are viewed. Several investigations and inquiries into how the public views different forms of abnormal behavior and what ingredients account for labeling individuals as abnormal have been reported (Wechsler, Solomon, & Kramer, 1970). One of the most extensive and widely cited set of investigations was conducted by Nunnally (1961) who surveyed hundreds of individuals considered to be representative of the United States population at large in terms of education, ratio of males to females, income, religious affiliation, and age. Several different questionnaires were used to assess attitudes toward individuals labeled as mental patients, neurotic men and women, insane individuals, and so on.

As might be expected, the results indicated that the mental illness is viewed very negatively by the public. The public sees the mentally ill as worthless, dirty, dangerous, and unpredictable, and it distinguishes severity of disorders such as psychoses and neurosis. Of course, psychoses are more severe than neuroses and usually impede the individual's ability to function in normal social, intellectual, and occupational roles. Although the public reacts to both types of disorders very negatively, psychoses are viewed much more negatively. The greatest single area of distinction pertains to the public's view of the predictability of behavior. The public tends to view psychotic patients as much less predictable than neurotic patients.

The negative attitudes indicate the public's general reaction to psychiatric impairment. Aside from these attitudes, there are a number of specific conceptions that appear to be common in the culture. Many of these represent misconceptions that are simply refuted by evidence or represent overgeneralizations of characteristics of individuals diagnosed as psychiatrically impaired. The misconceptions pertain to specific characteristics of the mentally ill and are consistent with the overall attitudes in pointing to pejorative attributes. Elaboration of a few of the major misconceptions sheds light on many stereotypes about psychiatric disorders.

Misconception 1: behavior of the mentally ill is bizarre and dangerous

Many people believe that the mentally ill are bizarre and dangerous. This view may be understandable in light of some of the influences on the public. For example, research has shown that the mass media tend to present a distorted view of mental illness (Nunnally, 1961). References to abnormal behavior in television, radio, newspapers, and magazines, although generally infrequent, tend to present more extreme views of deviance than in fact are likely to be found. The media emphasize dramatic and bizarre behaviors that are not necessarily characteristic of most individuals diagnosed as having psychiatric problems.

The media, in reporting factual material, often make implicit assumptions that foster misconceptions about individuals with a history of abnormal behavior. For example, newspaper articles frequently draw a connection between bizarre murders or acts of sexual deviance and psychiatric impairment if the person described has had any association with psychiatric treatment. A by-line might read, "Ex-patient murders. . . ." In the public's exposure to such material, the salience of the act in terms of bizarre or dangerous characteristics may be sufficiently dramatic to foster or confirm stereotypic notions about psychiatric patients and their expected behaviors.

In fact, the behavior of many individuals with psychiatric impairment is not particularly bizarre or greatly different from that of individuals not identified as impaired. Many behaviors defined as abnormal are a matter of degree such as anxiety, mood states, inability to function adequately under stress, or excessive alcohol consumption. While extremes of these areas may differ markedly from that of ordinary behavior, they are not necessarily bizarre. The few bizarre behaviors that appear among those diagnoses as mentally ill—such as irrational talk, delusions, hallucinations, self-injury—by no means characterize most individuals with psychiatric disorders.

The view that psychiatric patients, in general, represent a dangerous class of people is a particularly outstanding misconception. Evidence has shown that individuals with no previous arrest record who are hospitalized are not especially violent after their subsequent release. Indeed, patients who are discharged and functioning in society at large are much less likely than the ordinary public to commit violent crimes (see Scheff, 1966).

The view that patients are dangerous to themselves or to others is not merely a misconception held by the public, but also by many professionals involved in the process of hospitalization. In many states a major basis for hospitalizing individuals whose behavior is abnormal is that they would be dangerous to themselves or to others. Yet, research has suggested that only a small fraction of the patients considered for admission show signs of representing a danger of any sort (Scheff, 1966).

Overall, the belief that the behavior of the mentally ill usually is bizarre or dangerous is not based upon the evidence. This is not to say that psychiatric patients do not occasionally do bizarre or dangerous things. However, the frequency of these types of behaviors do not seem commensurate with the extent of the view held by the public.

Misconception 2: mental illness is incurable

A commonly held view is that psychiatric impairment is not curable and that once an individual is afflicted with a diagnosed abnormality, it will remain for the rest of his or her life. Actually, a great many different disorders have been identified in psychiatry. These differ greatly in their responsiveness to various forms of available treatment. Thus, distinctions have to be drawn about the different types of behavior and the extent to which they can be altered.

Different lines of evidence illustrate that manifestations of abnormal behavior are not necessarily permanent. In fact, for many disorders there is even a relatively high rate of improvement without formal treatment, a change referred to as *spontaneous remission.* For example, neurotic reactions often improve without formal psychological treatment (e.g., Sloane, Staples, Cristol, Yorkston, & Whipple, 1975). Although the bases for these changes are not well understood, they refute the belief that psychiatric conditions are permanent.

Spontaneous remission is not the only source of relevant information. There are many different therapy techniques, discussed in later chapters, that address a wide range of clinical problems. For example, specific treatments are available for anxiety, compulsions and obsessions, symptoms of psychoses, conduct disorders, enuresis, and several other problems as well. It is difficult to say whether treatments "cure" individuals, partly because professionals greatly debate the notion of a "cure" and whether it is relevant to treatment evaluation.

The problem of defining cure and the goals of treatment can readily be seen in the case of alcoholism. For years, it was assumed that the goal of treatment for alcoholics was complete abstinence. Whether an individual was cured was defined by whether he or she consumed alcohol after treatment. Yet, recent research has suggested that alcoholics can be trained to drink moderately or engage in controlled social drinking (Nathan, 1976). Thus, the notion of what constitutes the goal alters how treatment will be evaluated. Independent of the definition about the end result of treatment and whether the result would qualify as a "cure," it is clear that many treatments return individuals to normal or socially acceptable levels of behavior (Kazdin, 1977).

Misconception 3: mental illness is a sign of personal weakness

It is often believed that mental illness results from a weakness of character or some other personal trait of the individual. Thus, individuals who manifest abnormalities are to be held responsible, at least partially, for their condition. This view implies that people should be blamed for their situation because they have not been able to control themselves or handle life's stresses.

Actually, the bases of most forms of abnormality are not well understood. Yet, there is agreement among professionals that individuals are not to be blamed or held responsible for their situation. Many factors including one's living situation, hereditary predisposition, family background, and socioeconomic status are implicated in the diagnosis of psychiatric disorders. Attributing psychiatric impairment to a personal weakness simply ignores the multiple sources of influence on behavior over which the individual has no clear control.

Blaming individuals for their mental illnesses and viewing psychiatric impairment as a character weakness is a carryover of anachronistic views. In the middle ages, it was believed that mental illnesses resulted from the possession of demons or evil spirits of the afflicted individual's soul. The spirits were considered to have entered the individual's soul because of the sins of the individual. Relating the notion of mental illness to sin may underlie the contemporary stereotype of personal weakness in mental illness, since immoral behavior presumably should be under the individual's own control.

Misconception 4: mental illness is inherited

Many individuals believe that mental illness is inherited and that people are vulnerable or protected on the basis of their genetic background. Actually, the hereditary basis for most psychiatric disorders is unclear. There are some disorders with a well established genetic basis including specific forms of retardation (e.g., phenylketonuria, Tay-Sachs disease) and neurological deterioration (e.g., Huntington's chorea). Research also has shown a relationship between the incidence of psychotic disorders and heredity. For example, studies of monozygotic and dizygotic twins have been viewed as particularly strong evidence demonstrating a genetic component in schizophrenia (e.g., Ban, 1973; Mosher & Gunderson, 1973). However, even here, there has been some debate about the extent of genetic influence.

One of the major problems in studying genetic influences is separating them from environmental influences. Merely tracing psychological disorders along family lines does not distinguish whether a psychiatric disorder or propensity for the disorder was due to inheritance or the home environment. It could well be that parents foster psychiatric disorders and pass along abnormalities in this way rather than through heredity. Research has devised ways of examining the relative impact of different influences. For example, studies of children of schizophrenic adults have looked at whether the children acquire schizophrenia even though they are raised by foster parents outside of the home of their biological parents. Even when such children are adopted and reared in other homes, they tend to acquire much higher rates of schizophrenia than do adopted children whose biological parents have no diagnosed disorder (e.g, Heston, 1966; Kety, Rosenthal, Wender, & Schulsinger, 1971). This research has played an important role in illustrating the genetic influences on schizophrenia. However, the precise manner by which a predisposition toward schizophrenia is transmitted remains to be demonstrated. And, the genetic basis does not demonstrate that schizophrenia is caused merely by a particular type of gene action. Actually, nongenetic factors appear to be implicated in schizophrenia as well.

Overall, there is no clear evidence that heredity directly underlies any more than a few disorders. Similarly, there is no evidence that individuals are invariably protected by their heredity. Many social factors dictate who is likely to suffer from forms of psychiatric impairment, suggesting that even if a genetic predisposition were demonstrated, a number of other considerations would be relevant for determining whether the condition became manifest.

Misconception 5: mentally ill individuals are irrational and incompetent

A commonly held view is that the mentally ill are irrational and lose all powers of controlling their own behavior. This view is generally restricted to the more severe forms of psychiatric impairment such as psychotic reactions rather than habit disorders, neurotic reactions, and conduct disorders. Research has demonstrated that psychotic disorders such as schizophrenia are associated with certain deficiencies in thinking and abstraction (see Salzinger, 1973). However, it is one thing to say that specific cognitive deficits have been noted in research and quite another to say that individuals are irrational.

There are distinct irrational aspects to psychotic disorders including irrational speech. For example, expression of delusions or descriptions of hallucinations may be illogical and refer to events that violate consensual information. However, irrational expressions alone are not signs that the individual is always irrational. Research with psychotic patients has demonstrated that they can indeed plan and make decisions in practical situations (e.g., Greenberg, Scott, Pisa, & Friesen, 1975). A particularly interesting line of research has suggested that hospitalized psychotic patients can greatly control their behavior to achieve particular ends in the hospital (Braginsky, Braginsky, & Ring, 1969). Specifically, patients can manage the impressions that the staff have of them to maintain their position in the hospital and to avoid a change in status (e.g., placed in a back ward).

General comments

Some of the major misconceptions held about the mentally ill are illustrated above. More could be enumerated. For example, people sometimes believe that psychiatrically impaired individuals are mentally retarded or that mental illness is associated with extremely high levels of intellectual functioning. These and other misconceptions seem to be traceable to a basic assumption; namely, that individuals with psychiatric impairment or abnormality are fundamentally different from those who are regarded as normal. Certainly, at the extremes of a distribution for a given behavior, the distinction between acceptable and deviant behavior can be readily discerned. However, deviant behavior and abnormality are a matter of degree and very often are defined socially. Thus, it is difficult to make qualitative distinctions for many disorders and to reasonably suppose that the laws controlling behavior differ from those that apply to and account for normal behavior.

Summary

Abnormal psychology refers to the study of deviant behavior and psychological dysfunction. The major questions addressed in scientific research in the field pertain to identifying the various types of disorders, the factors that may cause or correlate with these disorders, and techniques for treatment and prevention.

Although it seems straightforward to describe the domain of abnormal psychology, as the study of maladaptive behavior and psychological dysfunction, there is great ambiguity in identifying the criteria for classifying behavior as deviant or maladaptive. Basic definitions use *statistical, social, medical,* and *legal* criteria for identifying abnormalities. Each criterion by itself is inadequate and does not provide a principle to identify the range of abnormal behaviors. Researchers have relied upon such definitions as exposure to psychiatric treatment, psychiatric diagnosis, subjective criteria, and the presence or absence of symptoms on objective measures. Each of these too has limitations about including and excluding the range of behaviors commonly viewed as deviant.

Independently of the specific definitions, three characteristics seem to be important for identifying psychological dysfunction: comfort, bizarreness, and inefficiency. Clients or those with whom they have contact may identify behavior as abnormal and worthy of treatment because of subjective discomfort. Bizarre behaviors may deviate greatly from accepted performance in everyday living and are important in identifying abnormality.

Finally, inefficiency or a breakdown in meeting role expectations also may serve as the basis for identifying abnormality. These three criteria alone or in combination are central in defining abnormal behavior.

Within abnormal psychology, different models or conceptual approaches can be distinguished. These models refer to the way of ordering the area of study, the types of questions asked, and the manner in which the answers are sought. The *biological* model looks for an organic basis of abnormality and encompasses several different biological sciences such as genetics, physiology, biochemistry, neurology, and others. The *intrapsychic model* looks for the basis of abnormal behavior in psychological processes that may have gone awry. The *behavioral model* views abnormal behavior as a function of learning experiences and seeks to develop techniques based upon this assumption to alter behavior. Finally, the *social-interpersonal model* looks at interpersonal and sociological variables as they influence abnormality. Each of these models embraces major areas of research in the field which will be evident throughout subsequent chapters.

Most people are familiar with deviant behavior and psychological dysfunction through personal experience, friends, literature, and the media. Such familiarity is not necessarily an advantage in understanding the scientific disciplines included in abnormal psychology. The public's view of psychological disorders appears to consist of negative attitudes and misconceptions. Several misconceptions were discussed, including the belief that the mentally ill are invariably bizarre or dangerous, that they are incurable, that mental illness is a sign of personal weakness, that it is inherited, and that individuals diagnosed as mentally ill are irrational and incompetent. Overall, the misconceptions seem to derive from the view that individuals diagnosed as have psychiatric impairment are fundamentally different from those who are not. Subsequent chapters will elaborate the nature of specific types of disorders and their treatment and present contemporary research and theory in abnormal psychology.

GLOSSARY

Behavioral model: The approach toward abnormal behavior that emphasizes the role of learning in the development and alteration of behavior. This approach focuses primarily upon developing procedures to alter behaviors.

Biological model: The approach toward abnormal behavior that searches for the biological bases of behavior. This approach stresses the role of such areas as genetics, pharmacology, biochemistry, neurology, and other areas of the biological sciences.

Classical conditioning: The learning process whereby new stimuli gain the capacity to elicit reflex responses (respondents). New stimuli gain this capacity by being paired with stimuli that automatically elicit these responses.

Functional disorders: Those psychological disorders with no known biological basis.

Intrapsychic model: The approach toward abnormal behavior that emphasizes the role of psychological processes inside the individual's personality that may account for the development of abnormal behavior. This approach stresses such factors as unconscious processes and unresolved psychic impulses.

Legal definition of abnormal behavior: Definitions used by the courts to make specific decisions such as whether an individual should be responsible for a criminal act or should be hospitalized. Different definitions are applied depending upon the specific purpose under consideration and the laws of individual states.

Medical definition of abnormal behavior: A definition based upon the notion that the presence of specific symptoms defines abnormality. The specific symptoms reveal that an individual is suffering from some underlying disorder.

Observational learning: Learning based upon observing someone else perform a response. The observer need only watch a model to learn the response.

Operant conditioning: Learning based upon providing consequences that alter the frequency of behavior (operants). Consequences may be provided that increase or decrease the probability that a response is performed.

Organic disorders: Those psychological disorders known to have a biological basis.

Social definition of abnormal behavior: A definition based upon the notion that society defines what behaviors are regarded as abnormal. Behaviors that violate norms, social rules, and role expectations are likely to be defined as abnormal.

Social-interpersonal model: The approach toward abnormal behavior that emphasizes the role of the interpersonal processes such as family interaction and sociological variables such as social class in abnormal behavior.

Statistical definition of abnormal behavior: A definition that is based upon the notion that certain behaviors are relatively rare and that this criterion defines behaviors that are abnormal.

2

HISTORY AND CLASSIFICATION

WILLIAM A. HUNT

The deviant behaviors commonly called mental disorders have been with us since the beginning of history. Often bizarre, peculiar, and personally and socially inappropriate, they disturb the health and happiness of the individual concerned and at times may pose a threat or at the least an irritation to the fixed and orderly social life of the community. Thus, when a dishevelled man suddenly stops on a busy city street corner, turns his head to the sky, and begins personally addressing God in a loud and angry voice, it is upsetting and a source of uneasiness to those passing by. Some may be incensed by what they feel is a sacrilege, some may be afraid of bodily harm, and some may feel sympathy and concern for what they feel is a person ill and in trouble. In any case, it is behavior they camnot overlook but cannot understand, and therefore they feel powerless to intervene. As a result, humanity has puzzled over what these mysterious and disturbing behaviors were, how they cane about, what course they would follow, and what could be done about them.

In current practice these are the common problems of *diagnosis* (recognizing and classifying the deviant behaviors), *etiology* (understanding their causes), *prognosis* (predicting their course), and *therapy* (the institution of some indicated method of treatment). The explanations vary and the answers are seldom final, but they always reflect the available knowledge and the dominant cultural influences of the time. Thus, their study is intimately connected with history and with the development of the medical and behavioral sciences.

The chapter will begin by dealing with the basic principles of taxonomy—the technique of identifying, naming, and classifying phenomena—and will then apply these principles to the problems of diagnosis in psychopathology. Too often we narrowly associate science only with the exercise of experimental techniques in the laboratory and in the field, and forget that a long process of observing, identifying, and classifying behavior must precede the experimental process itself.

Thus, if we wish to study the effect of some new drug on schizophrenic behavior, we must first observe a common class of related deviant behaviors to which we may attach the class label "schizophrenia," identify the behavior of each patient as belonging to this class, and so identify the patient as a schizophrenic. Only then can we proceed with the experiment proper, in which we administer the drug and observe its effects on the patient's behavior. In the biological sciences we speak of taxonomy; in the field of psychopathology we speak of diagnosis. In both cases we are involved in the establishment of distinct classes of like phenomena and the interrelationships between them. These behaviors and their interrelationships are the information given us by the class name, label, or diagnostic category involved.

In the case of the man on the street corner shouting at God, his behavior would probably be classed as schizophrenic and diagnosed as suffering from schizophrenia. This diagnosis would tell us that his behavior is probably buttressed by delusions that he can speak directly to the Lord, and by false sensory experiences or hallucinations that he hears the voice of the Deity answering him. The diagnosis also would tell us that he were one of a larger class labeled "psychotic" whose behavior might become sufficiently extreme to necessitate some form of social restraint such as custodial care in a mental hospital.

But above and beyond this complex informational communicative function, there is a simple satisfaction in being able to name this puzzling, mysterious behavior. Over the centuries people have found that to be able to name an unfamiliar thing robs it of some of its power to arouse uneasiness and fear in the observer. Everyone who at sometime has been ill and has worried about some unexplained fever or bodily pain has experienced the relief attendant upon a doctor's diagnosis of influenza or indigestion or whatever. The apprehension lightens, as does the fear of the unknown. A character in Saul Bellow's *Mr. Sammler's Planet* (p. 111), a moonlighting academic botanist who prospers by identifying and mapping the trees and shrubs on the estates of wealthy landowners, comments: "I'm convinced that knowing the names of things braces people up. . . . You can make dough by becoming a taxonomist." But one can also make mistakes—no diagnostic system is perfect nor are the clinicians that use them.

The next section is a discussion of the history of psychopathology, relating it to diagnosis and to the cultural influences of the times. It will become apparent that as our knowledge of deviant behaviors increases, so does the difficulty of identifying and classifying them. It has been said that the purpose of diagnosis is to communicate information about etiology, prognosis, and therapy. But as our knowledge of each of these grows so do our problems.

The discussion of history will be divided into four rough periods. Approaches before the 18th century reflected the undeveloped state of medicine. There were some descriptions of mania, depression, and dementia, but the main stress was on demoniacal possession, exorcism, and the punitive treatment of the patient. The late 18th and early 19th century saw the beginnings of some medical understanding, but adequate therapy was missing. The patient was largely neglected or remanded to custodial care of a primitive and cruel sort. The middle 19th to early 20th century saw the beginnings of two powerful influences—the development of the dynamic, psychoanalytic approach as represented by Janet and Freud, and the beginnings with Kraepelin and Bleuler of a scientific descriptive psychiatry. The modern period, from the middle of the 20th century on, is marked by the development of behavioral dynamics, psychopharmacology, heredity, and an emphasis on environmental factors. We no longer seek a single cause for disturbed behavior but realize it is the result of the interaction of many factors all of which play a part in the final outcome. All of this complexity makes new problems for classification and diagnosis.

The chapter will close with a summary of the case for and against diagnosis. Diagnosis will be defended as a necessary technical process but in need of increased sophistication. Contemporary diagnostic approaches are pictured as a necessary supporting structure for the further development of a scientific psychopathology but flexible enough to accommodate our growing knowledge of psychopathology.

Classification

Taxonomy refers to the theoretical study of the rule and principles governing classification. Classification refers to the arranging or ordering of any collection of things into classes or sets possessing some common property or properties. They may be defined *extensionally* by simply enumerating the members of the class or *intensionally* by listing the characteristics necessary for inclusion in the class. *Monothetic* classes are those in which some common property is shared by every member of the class. *Polythetic* classes comprise groups of members that share large numbers of common properties but not necessarily all of them. The simpler the relationship, the more apt the classification is to be monothetic; the more complex, the more apt it is to be polythetic.

In the case of psychopathology, the entities to be classified are the deviant behaviors that form the realm of abnormal psychology. And, the class names constitute the familiar diagnostic labels such as psychosis, schizophrenia, neurosis, character disorder. Thus a person exhibiting withdrawn behavior accompanied by reality distorting hallucinations and delusions would be classed as schizophrenic. But this is a polythetic class since there are many sorts of schizophrenic behaviors, and no schizophrenic patient will exhibit all of them. On the other hand, the type of phobic neurosis called acrophobia (fear of high places) is monothetic because to be called acrophobic the person must exhibit this unique, specific type of behavior.

Commonly, the various classes of deviant behavior or diagnostic entities may be organized hierarchically. The specific phobias such as acrophobia, agoraphobia (fear of open spaces), and claustrophobia (fear of closed spaces) may all be placed together under the common class of phobic behavior, which in turn may be classed with other deviant behaviors such as obsessive compulsive, hysterical, and anxiety under the common designation, neurosis. Just so, the term psychosis covers several different types of psychotic behaviors, such as schizophrenia, manic-depressive or affective psychoses, and paranoia, with each of these again divisible into several specific subtypes under each psychosis.

This hierarchical organization illustrates two general characteristics (inclusiveness and specificity), which affect the breadth and depth of a diagnostic category as a carrier of information. The more inclusive a category is, the more objects or class members it will tell you something about. The more specific the category is, the more it will tell you about the class it subsumes, but the class will be smaller.

To state it more simply, the broader the diagnostic category, the *more things* it will convey some information about; the more specific the category, the *more information* it will convey about any one thing. There is a reciprocal relationship implied here in that the breadth of application of a diagnostic category is achieved at the expense of depth. It is an example of the old adage about the specialist being a man who knows more and more about less and less. Since the basic function of a diagnostic label is as a carrier of information, these matters are important.

They also concern the question of reliability in diagnosis. Any number of studies have shown that psychiatrists often disagree with one another in their use of diagnostic labels, but all the studies agree that the reliability shown is a function of the specificity of the diagnosis. Illustrative of this is a study (Hunt, Wittson, & Hunt, 1953) that was essentially a reliability study involving a comparison of the diagnoses given 794 Naval enlisted men at a training station wtih the subsequent diagnoses given them at a Naval Hospital to which they were transferred. The training station diagnosis was not entered in the health record and the men were transferred under the neutral category "Diagnosis Unknown, Observation." The standard reliability study would simply compare specific diagnoses. Thus, a diagnosis of schizophrenia subsequently classified as manic depressive would be considered a disagreement to be tabulated as an instance of unreliability. Viewed in this fashion, the results were distinctly unimpressive with category reliabilities ranging from 0 percent to 63 percent and an average agreement of only 33 percent. However, at a practical level we might reasonably conclude that some clinicians were in agreement on some patients. The functional value of the amount of agreement remains in doubt. Yet, whether the guilt rests on the diagnostic system or should be shared with its practitioners is an open question, although certainly a desirable characteristic of any technique is its resistance to misuse.

Suppose, however, we say that the specific disorders involved, such as schizophrenia, hysteria, anxiety neurosis, paranoid personality, and emotional instability, can be grouped under the larger, more inclusive categories of psychosis, psychoneurosis, and personality disorders. Doing this increases the average agreement to 54% and still offers information, although there is an informational loss. Thus, to say a patient is psychotic tells us something, but saying he is schizophrenic tells us more. However, it restricts the number of people that can be included in the class.

We can go further in this situation and say that the basic function of diagnosis was to separate from the Navy persons who for reasons of personality disorder would be unable to render acceptable service. This creates a still broader class, "unsuitable for service," under which are subsumed the classes of psychosis, psychoneurosis, and personality, with specific categories in turn subsumed under these. Viewed in *this* fashion, agreement on unsuitability was 94 percent, a very respectable performance.

It should be noted that where hierarchical organization exists in any category system, the problem of reliability and validity becomes complicated. Therefore, any subclass carries not only its own special characteristics, but by implication the characteristics of the larger class under which it is subsumed. To call a patient manic may indicate a surface tension and press to action quite unlike schizophrenic, but it implies the mutual participation of both in a class of people called psychotic who raise common problems of social difficulty quite unlike those of psychoneurosis. In such a case, reliability depends on the level at which it is estimated, and such unlike diagnoses as schizophrenic and manic depressive nevertheless implicate the commonality of psychosis. On this level they are congruent diagnoses. What from one aspect seems a hopelessly inadequate classificatory schema turns out to have served the Navy's purposes rather well.

We have just spoken of hierarchical classifications and their relation to the problem of reliability. The classes in any system need not of necessity be related. Provided only that the members of a class be related by some common property or properties, each class may be separate and distinct and not related to any other class. When a relationship is present between classes and is abstract and theoretical, as it often is in psychiatry, we speak of *nosology*. If we say that psychosis involves a separation *from* reality, with the schizophrenic withdrawing into his own personal world, while the manic patient bursts into a wild exhibition of senseless and irrational behaviors (a flight *into* reality), then we are proposing a nosological classification.

Customs of taxonomy will differ in different disciplines. When a new entity is placed in its proper class in biology, this is referred to as identification. In psychopathology, it is referred to as diagnosis. While taxonomy in biology stresses information, understanding, and the comprehension of the present and historical aspects of the phenomenon and its relation to other phenomena, diagnosis in psychiatry tends to stress the prediction of future developments, the anticipation of later symptomatology to be expected, the future course of behavior, and the possibility of and means for its control.

The class names or diagnostic categories that have been mentioned are common ones, most of them recognizable to the layperson. Professionally, they would be called Kraepelinian or neo-Kraepelinian terms after Emil Kraepelin (1855–1926), the German psychiatrist whose differentiation between schizophrenia and manic-depressive psychosis is often regarded as the beginning of modern descriptive, classificatory psychiatry. In dealing with the history of the 19th and 20th centuries, more attention will be given to his work and its gradual development into the *Diagnostic and Statistical Manual of Mental Disorders* sponsored by the American Psychiatric Association. Familarly known as DSM, the manual has been revised once (DSM II) and another revision (DSM III) will soon be published.

Diagnoses are carriers of information, and they should be viewed as such. They should be evaluated in terms of the economy with which they transmit information, the extent and accuracy of the information transmitted, and the functional importance or relevance of this information in the particular diagnostic situation. The information conveyed by diagnosis will always be distorted by the perceptual biases and limitations of the professional individuals practicing it. In any age classificatory categories will be interpreted and elaborated in the context of the level of knowledge, the cultural milieu, even the needs and desires of the group using them. But such interpretations are not of necessity inherent in the diagnostic process itself. Excellent summaries have been given from the taxonomic side by Sokal (1974) and from the diagnostic side by Blashfield and Draguns (1976).

We have already seen that unreliability or the inability of clinicians to agree among themselves is a serious problem for diagnostic practice. Blashfield and Draguns point out four factors that contribute importantly to reliability:

1. The exactness with which the diagnostic rules are presented in the intensional definition of the category involved. In other words, how carefully the definition is spelled out.
2. The training, background, and experience of the diagnostician.
3. The amount and nature of the information the clinician uses. Research has shown that the relationship between amount of information used and the reliability of the diagnosis is curvilinear; that is, the diagnostician performs best when the amount of information is moderate. He or she is worst with either too little or too much information.
4. The clinician's own consistency in diagnostic usage. Reliability may be affected by a personal mood, the diagnostic setting, and the emotional distance between the clinician and the patient.

In their discussion they make a telling comparison between the DSM II definition of schizophrenia, which lists 13 major symptoms but makes no mention of how many are necessary for a diagnosis of schizophrenia, and a study by Feighner, Robins, Guze, Woodruff, Winokur, and Munoz (1972), which states very specific rules under three groupings:

A. *Both* a history of at least six months of symptoms and an absence of depressive or manic symptoms sufficient for an affective disorder.

B. *Either* delusions or hallucinations without significant perplexity or disorientation, or verbal production that lacks logical or understandable organization.

C. At least *three* of the following: must be single, have a poor premorbid adjustment, have a family history of schizophrenia, an absence of substance abuse within the year previous to onset, and onset before 40.

Incidentally, this is a nice example of a polythetic class category, since all the members of the group must share some properties but not necessarily all of the properties. This also highlights nicely the use of very specific rules in Feighner et al. as compared with the ambiguity of DSM II.

Little is said specifically about the problem of validity, or the correctness of a diagnosis because most of it is subsumed under the discussion of reliability. How can one measure validity if diagnosticians cannot agree on the diagnosis, and how can one check validity against some external criterion if this is not carefully defined and easily recognizable? There are few longitudinal studies in which diagnosed subjects are followed over an extended period of time to see whether their diagnosis is congruent with their subsequent behavior. One Navy study, however, meets the requirements of inter-judge agreement on diagnosis, specific and easily identifiable behavioral criteria, and an extended period of study (Hunt, Wittson, & Hunt, 1952).

The subjects were some 628 Naval recruits who had been studied intensively on the psychiatric ward of a large naval training station. Roughly, 100 each were selected from the following six categories: normal controls, neurotics, schizoid personalities, alcoholics, low intelligence, and asocial psychopaths. To be included in the study each recruit (including the normal controls):

1. Had to have been studied by at least two staff members and had the diagnosis agreed upon by every staff member seeing the case.
2. Had to have been adjudged "marginal" and sent to duty as capable of rendering military service.
3. Had to have successfully completed three years of service with subsequent honorable discharge.

This is obviously a highly selected group since each of these "marginal" men served three years without discharge for medical or disciplinary reasons. Interest in the behavior of the men stemmed from two sources: 1. Did they show deviant behaviors that reduced the efficiency of their performance? and 2. Were these behaviors congruent with their original diagnosis? As criteria, two clearly defined criteria were selected: 1. Were they ever admitted to a naval hospital? and 2. Had they ever had a court martial? (ranging in severity from a captain's mast or deck court to a general court martial). The disciplinary charges were then broken down into three categories: 1. Absent over leave or without leave (AOL and AWOL), 2. misuse of alcohol (drunk on duty), and 3. insubordination.

The results are summarized in Table 2.1. They illustrate both the good and the bad side of our common diagnostic categories. In general there is a group picture of behavior congruent with the diagnosis, but individual prediction is difficult. Again, we must remember that these subjects constituted a very select group.

The figures for hospitalization show the psychosomatic involvement typical of the mental disorders. The psychopathological subjects were hospitalized from 4 to 7 times as often as the normal controls. Incidentally, only one alcoholic was hospitalized for alcoholism. The wide range of medical problems exhibited and the small number of cases in each psychiatric category make it impossible to establish any correlation between illness pattern and diagnostic category.

On the disciplinary side, however, some clear relations appear between type of disciplinary infraction and diagnosis, and they fit the common interpretation given our clinical categories. The neurotic subjects are no more of a disciplinary problem than the normal controls, but they show six times as many infractions for misuse of alcohol. Schizoid personalities show more leave difficulties and also more insubordination, but had no record of alcoholic abuses. The alcoholics, as one might predict, are outstanding in all categories. Those individuals of low intelligence (mental age from 9 years, 6 months to 12 years, six months, with a mean mental age of 11 years) are frequent abusers of leave privileges and show some insubordination but little trouble with alcohol. This seems more a matter of misunderstanding and lack of comprehension than any deliberate social transgression. The psychopaths, of course, are outstanding in every category but are most marked for leave difficulties and insubordination. Their difficulties spring not only from lack of comprehension of and disregard for the social proprieties but from an overt and deliberate rebellion against them as well.

Within the narrow limits of this study, the criterion behaviors followed fit the accepted clinical picture of the diagnoses used. In this sense, the results validate the diagnostic system. The various groups, as groups, do what they might be expected to do. From the standpoint of individual prediction, however, the picture is not as bright. Even with the group conforming most to the accepted

Table 2.1 Hospital and Disciplinary Records of Marginal Psychiatric Cases

N	Classification	Hospital cases %	Disciplinary cases %	Leave difficulties %	Alcoholic abuse %	Insubordination %
91	Normal controls	4.4	12.2	7.7	1.1	1.1
120	Neurotics	17.5	10.0	6.7	6.7	1.7
97	Schizoid personalities	24.7	26.8	13.4	0.0	4.1
102	Alcoholics	27.5	41.6	33.3	10.8	7.8
121	Low intelligence	24.0	45.0	32.2	2.5	7.4
97	Psychopaths	20.8	62.0	50.0	10.3	22.7

Adapted from Hunt, Wittson, & Hunt (1952).

clinical picture—the asocial psychopaths—for every man who can be expected to get into disciplinary trouble there will be one who will not, and for every one who does, only 1 out of 2 of them will have leave difficulties, and 1 out of 4 of them be guilty of insubordination. This is the old problem in measurement of translating group differences into meaningful individual prediction.

The uniformity of mental illness seems cross-cultural as well. Drawing particularly from her experience among the Eskimos and the Yoruba (an African tribe), Jane Murphy (1976), speaking of schizophrenia says, "Almost everywhere a pattern composed of hallucinations, delusions, disorientations, and behavioral aberrations appears to identify the idea of 'losing one's mind.' even though the content of these manifestations is colored by cultural beliefs (p. 1027).

Language difficulties are illustrated by her failure to find words that could be translated as a general reference to neurosis, or as parallels to our use of anxiety or depression. Interestingly, however, there is a large vocabulary of words for emotional responses that we might classify as manifestations of anxiety or depression. And these manifestations are considered illnesses treatable by a shaman or witch doctor. This leads her to conclude that symptoms of mental illness are manifestations of an affliction shared by virtually all mankind.

Opposition to this idea of the universality of symptoms comes from the proponents of so-called labeling theory or societal reaction theory. Labeling theory views the supposed manifestations of mental illness as deviations from the type of behavior accepted as normal in a particular sociocultural group, with the definition of normality differing from group to group. Diagnosis becomes the application of a cultural stereotype referring to a residue of deviant behavior, which each society defines differently. These labels convey social disapproval and thus stigmatize the labeled individual as undesirable. The label tends to become fixed and like a self-fulfilling prophecy is accepted by the individual who perpetuates the stigmatized behavior. The use of the labeling process throughout the social agencies in modern industrialized society often creates problems rather than alleviating them for the people they treat.

Unfortunately, the socially less powerful individuals in any group are more vulnerable to such treatment. There is always a danger that the diagnosis of mental illness can become a means of social control over any individual exhibiting behavior contrary to the dominant social code. An example would be the practice in some totalitarian countries of treating political dissidents as mentally ill and confining them in mental hospitals. Supposedly, the political opinions of such a dissident might well change after a series of electroshock treatments or even after confinement on a locked hospital ward full of disturbed patients. It is this use of diagnostic labeling backed by a prescribed course of treatment that furnishes the motif for Ken Kesey's novel, *One Flew Over the Cuckoo's Nest.*

While labeling theory per se developed in sociology, it has been popular in psychiatry for some time. Szasz's (1961) book, *The Myth of Mental Illness,* has been among the most influential books in the mental health field in the last twenty years, and his *Law, Liberty, and Psychiatry* (1963) particularly concerns itself with the injustices done by diagnosis within our legal system. The English psychiatrist R. D. Laing (1967) also has had a great influence here with his *The Politics of Experience.*

Szasz (1961) claims that a definition of mental illness demands some established deviation from a clearly defined behavioral norm, and not one in terms of the psychological, ethical, and legal concepts currently dominating the psychiatric field. It should not depend upon the imposition of value judgments external to the behavior being studied. In discussing schizophrenia, Laing (1967) calls it a label given to a deviant person in any society to justify ignoring him. He calls for treating such individuals as human beings with rights and privileges as such.

Townsend (1977), in answering Murphy (1976) and defending labeling theory, points out that the major psychoses such as schizophrenia and manic-depressive disorder appear to be found universally. He does, however, endorse the views of Szasz and Laing by stressing that many people who have "problems in living" and cannot get along in the normal social routine cause trouble and embarrassment for society and may be diagnosed as mentally ill. The mental hospital, then, becomes a means of housing "the indigent, rootless, and helpless who have nowhere else to go." The fault here lies not with diagnosis but with inadequate social planning.

Unfortunately, such misuse of an administrative diagnosis, however well intentioned, may unwittingly carry serious consequences for the individual concerned. Such a diagnosis not only labels the person in his own eyes but burdens him with a role he may accept and attempt to fulfill. More importantly, it may result in his being declared legally incompetent and even in his being involuntarily committed to custodial care. Worst of all, within the hospital the diagnosis itself may entail a prescribed course of treatment involving shock treatment or serious medication that may not be in his best interest if the diagnosis is incorrect.

Diagnosis has been called the central activity of psychiatry and the organizing principle of most of its text books and institutions. With its practice so basic to the mental health professions and to the supportive social agencies as well as our legal system, both civil and criminal, it is inevitable that mistakes and abuses should occur; but one can legitimately ask whether the diagnostic system or the diagnostician using it is at fault.

Stainbrook (1953) has attributed much of our difficulty to three influences:

1. The insistence on a monistic, single factor etiology. We can no longer look for single univariate causes of mental disorder but must cope with a complex, multivariate etiology involving the interaction of many individual factors. No single-minded espousal of deviant behavior as based solely on neurological anomaly, pharmacological dysfunction, Pavlovian or operant conditioning, or the dynamic machinations of a Freudian unconscious will serve. As Stainbrook says, "The essence of all these etiological constructions was not that they were all wrong, but that they were all proposed as exclusively right.

2. The nosological rigidity imposed by the acceptance of the concept of disease as a fixed entity, leading to morbidity. We must accept the fact that disease is an individual's reaction to pathogenic conditions, and since pathogenic conditions are infinitely variable and human adaptive reactions limited, we must expect similar adaptive reactions to different stress situations.

3. An overly rapid attempt on the part of psychiatry to reduce the findings of psychology and the social sciences to medicine. Something may be lost in too hasty and too complete a reductionism. As he says, "Toleration and understanding of other worlds of discourse and the ability to accept the frames of reference of the logical languages of other sciences without the sacrifice of his own conceptual systems would seem to be, for the contemporary psychiatric scholar, an historically substantiated attitude" (pp. 17–18). And, we might add, for any member of the other mental health professions.

Any present day etiologically-oriented diagnostic system must deal with deviant behavior that has its roots in such diverse areas as heredity, pharmacology, pre- and postnatal experience, and physical as well as social environment. There is a real question whether any classificatory system based solely on symptomatic behaviors can satisfy the complexity of factors involved. Witness our previous comparison of the DSM II definition of schizophrenia with that of Feighner et al. The first consisted solely of a listing of symptomatic behaviors, while the latter included such diverse bits of information as age of onset, marital history, premorbid work and social history, and heredity.

Meehl's (1962) classic paper "Schizotaxia, Schizotypy, and Schizophrenia" was an early recognition of the need for a multivariate or polythetic definition of schizophrenia. Under schizotaxia, he discusses the constitutional, hereditary, and genetic (or as he says *poly*genetic) factors underlying schizophrenic behavior. Under schizotypy, he deals with the developmental and social factors molding schizophreniclike behavior. Putting these together in the varying necessary amounts of each and under stress results in the decompensation called clinical schizophrenia. Unfortunately, the specific information necessary for putting forward a predictive formula for the individual person is lacking (and will be for some time to come), but Meehl's conceptualization of the problem offers a basis for understanding the complexity of schizophrenia.

Meanwhile, as we survey the history of the mental disorders, it will become evident that in a time like the present, when our knowledge of deviant behavior is increasing so rapidly, the prime requisite of any diagnostic system would seem to be the flexibility and the adaptability necessary if the system is to grow as our knowledge and understanding of deviant behavior grows. As Kety has said, discussing current issues in psychiatric diagnosis before the Sixty-Seventh Annual Meeting of The American Psychopathological Association in New York City, March 3–4, 1977, there is no harm in adopting diagnostic conventions. The danger comes when a change in conception is necessary. We might paraphrase: To adopt is human, to adapt divine.

In closing this section a quotation from John Barth's novel, *The End of the Road* (pp. 165–166), is appropriate. "Assigning names to things is like assigning roles to people. It is necessarily a distortion, but it is a necessary distortion if one would get on with the plot, and to the connoisseur it's all good clean fun."

History

We have seen how people first attempt to understand and control these strange, disturbing, deviant behaviors called mental disorders by describing them, sorting them into classes, and giving them names. These classes, then, may be related and organized into a nosological or theoretical system having implications for etiology and treatment. The implications then are interpreted through the state of knowledge and the mores and customs of the culture at the moment and translated into action.

Through all these actions run three general themes of interest to us:

1. Where do these behaviors come from? Do they originate from outside or from within the individual? Are patients possessed by outside influences, by devils or by gods, or does the seat of trouble lie within the individual, in his mind or in his brain? This is the conflict between the supernatural or mystical explanation and a scientific one, usually represented in history by the development of medicine. Sometimes they are mixed as in the *Talmud* where insanity is recognized as illness and given to the doctor and not the rabbi for treatment. Such treatment, however, is based upon the use of charms and amulets rather than upon the use of drugs.
2. What are the patient's limits of personal responsibility? At what point does control of his behavior pass from the individual and at what point is he absolved from responsibility for his actions? This is not only a legal matter of concern to forensic or court psychiatry, but rises in psychotherapy in terms of so-called will power (ego strength) involving the marshalling and use by the patient himself of his own resources.
3. What is the attitude of society to the behavior? Does it accept it or reject it? Are the insane accepted as the "darlings" of the gods and viewed as seers and soothsayers as they sometimes were in ancient Greece, or are they viewed as misfits and potential miscreants and isolated in chains in prisons? Or is the attitude one of ambivalence as it is today in our humanitarian attempt to take the mentally ill out of their isolation in large custodial hospitals where they are denied many of the niceties of normal living? They are then returned to the local community in smaller, halfway houses located in residential areas, only to find the local community loath to have such a facility located within its own boundaries!

Pre–eighteenth century

Very little is known about mental disorders in prehistoric man and that little is largely extrapolation from the knowledge of primitive peoples collected by anthropologists. The investigation of human and animal remains has established that disease existed and there is no reason to believe that psychiatric disorders were excluded. It was a magical world inhabited by evil spirits, ghosts, and other supernatural beings who vengefully and sometimes wantonly punished both the tribal transgressor as well as the innocent tribal member by visiting calamity upon him (today we speak not quite objectively of "bad luck"). At times this was done by entering and possessing his body, thus disrupting his thoughts and gaining control of his behavior. Such therapy as was practiced seems to have been by exorcistic ritual to drive the intruding spirit from the body of the possessed. Such rituals were often primitive and would seem to have been as hard on the patient as they were on the evil spirit.

There is evidence that *trepanation,* the removal of a portion of the skull, was practiced by the early Incas in Peru. But whether this was designed to provide an opening through which the offending spirit could escape form the afflicted person's head or whether it simply represented a crude technique for treating traumatic damage to the skull is not certain. There is a somewhat battered Mayan fresco in a small ruin near Mexico City that seems to depict a health spa, but whether disorders were treated there is unclear. In any case, our anthropological material on primitive people is much more reliable and much more extensive.

The world of primitive people was a threatening, anxiety-ridden world. They had little understanding of the natural forces around them and interpreted these in terms of their own feelings, endowing them with human attributes. Where this animism failed to satisfy, they created gods, spirits, ghosts, and demons to fill the gap. Under these circumstances there was little tolerance for the mentally ill. Apparently, they were abandoned to perish or even deliberately put to death. As Zilboorg and Henry (1941) state in discussing primitive man,"His psychological energies were dedicated more to the problem of getting rid of the uncertainty and fear generated by illness than to realistic efforts to eliminate the illness itself (p. 28).

In such a system of magical thinking (theurgic mysticism) there rapidly developed a type of individual, priest, medicine man, or shaman who served as middle man between the people and their gods. They were the keepers of the temple, the guardians of the mystic rites, or, as we might say, the keepers of the keys. Their duty was to communicate with the beneficent deities and to appease the harmful ones.

The primitive shaman or medicine man was a nice example of this. He administered the treatment of both physical and mental illness. His authority lay in his own vulnerability to possession by the spirits, a possession that enabled him to communicate with them. Present opinion is that he himself was probably a neurotic or hysteric. He usually performed his "seance" before a small group. He would work himself into a frenzy by an elaborate ritual involving smoking, drinking, and drug taking, accompanied by rhythmic music usually on drums, and ritualistic movements. The spirits would then reveal themselves through the voice of the shaman, much like a present day seance. The shaman, or the patient himself (if he were able), might then attempt to appease the spirits and request relief from the patient's difficulty.

There was some rough classification and naming of deviant behaviors but nothing approaching formal diagnosis. The etiology was interference from the outside by evil spirits, and the universal therapy was exorcism. While the intrusion by evil spirits in one sense relieved the patient of responsibility for his behavior, often it was assumed that the demoniacal possession represented punishment for some evil or unfortunate act. In *Deuteronomy,* among the numerous curses listed for failing to obey the word of the Lord is the following (28:28): "The Lord will smite thee with madness." Final judgment was in the hands of the gods, and either the illness, mental or physical, disappeared or you perished by illness, abandonment, or outright murder. As *Leviticus* says (20:27), "A man also or a woman that hath a familiar spirit, or that is a wizard, shall surely be put to death; they shall stone them with stones; their blood shall be upon them."

The Bible is replete with mention of mentally disordered behavior, as in this story of David, an early example of the social rejection of madmen (I Samuel 21:12–15): "And he [David] changed his behavior before them, and feigned himself mad in their hands, and scabbled on the doors of the gate, and let his spittle fall down upon his beard. Then said Achish . . . Shall this fellow come into my house?" And in the New Testament (Luke 8:28–32) there is a story about the transfer of evil spirits from a possessed man to a herd of swine.

This belief in demoniacal possession persevered throughout the Greco-Roman period down into the Middle Ages when the church conducted its crusade against witches. In 1478 the infamous *Malleus Maleficarum,* a guide book for the detection and punishment of witches, was published.

As befitted the increased cultural level of the times, both practices and practitioners become more sophisticated. Plato's *Phaedo* mentions the use of incubation in which the patient, both physical and mental, after ritual purification, was required to sleep in corridors under the temple of Asklepios. These corridors were constructed in the form of a maze to the center of which the patient symbolically could work his or her way. Asklepios would come to the patient in a dream and touch the affected part in healing. If he or she recovered, the patient was expected to make votive offerings to the god.

There was an increasing recognition of some possessions as "good" as in seers, soothsayers, and priests. Such were felt to be possessed by the gods and were recognized as divine. As Judith Neaman (1975) says in discussing the medieval church, "Both the mystic and the demonical are situated at the fringes of insanity, for, in the eyes of the medieval church, the mystic was divinely sane despite and even because of the fact that ordinary sinners considered him irrational" (p. 61). This differentiation between bodily illness, mental illness, and possession was a constant problem for church law, and was often misused and misapplied in a way that would certainly alarm Szasz and Laing today.

The beginnings of modern medicine are often attributed to Hippocrates in the fourth century B.C. He took a firm stand against epilepsy as a sacred disease and claimed it was no more sacred than any other disease and saying it had specific characteristics and a definite cause. He is best remembered perhaps for his introducing the concept of hysteria as a female disorder associated with the womb. As described by Plato (Timaeus, 1971): "Whenever the matrix, or womb, as it is called—which is an indwelling creature desirous of child bearing—remains without fruits long beyond the due season, it is vexed and takes it ill; and by straying all ways through the body and blocking up passages of the breath and preventing the respiration it casts the body into the uttermost distress, and causes, moreover, all kinds of maladies until the desire and love of the two sexes unite them" (p. 120), a conception, however romantic, hardly popular today.

Hippocrates was preeminently a clinician, busy observing and treating patients. He wrote many interesting case histories, and accurately described the manias, the melancholias, and mental deterioration. He had a great influence on Plato but less on other philosophers. As Zilboorg and Henry (1941) state, both theurgic mysticism and abstract philosophy were so potent that "medicine from the very beginning was forced to enter the field of psychopathology not as a welcome, benevolent brother in search of the truth, but as a belligerent who at once had to combat opposition and conquer the right to heal" (p. 41).

Plato considered the soul to be in two parts, the rational and the irrational, and madness resulted when the proper balance between them was not maintained. He recognized two kinds of madness, one a result of disease, the other a gift of the gods. Here he differs from Hippocrates and continues the confusion between "good" and "bad" possession.

One of his interesting conceptions was the idea of a "sophronesterion" or "house of sanity" to which individuals whose thinking was disturbed could be sent for a period of five years to have their thoughts corrected through teaching and intellectual exercise. At regular intervals, they would be interviewed by judges and if thought to be improved would be released. The fate of the poor patient who did not improve after this or other "therapies" was dubious. He might be imprisoned, turned over to the custody of his family, exiled, or turned loose to wander through the countryside, an object of abuse and humiliation.

After the enlightenment of the Greco-Roman period there began the gradual decline into the intellectual impoverishment of the middle ages. In a world once more beset by fear and anxiety, man turned from reason to faith for comfort, and belief in the supernatural once more became a powerful social force. Toward the end of the period there was an increasing revolt against traditional thinking and the accepted body of knowledge, and it seemed necessary to both the temporal and spiritual forces that they consolidate their power. The church made a determined attack on heresy. Church or "canon" law, a combination of church pronouncements grafted onto the Roman law or *Corpus iuris civilis,* seemed to recognize the difference between physical illness, mental illness, and possession, as it did the crime of heresy. But in the passion of consolidating its power over the people, the church overlooked these differentiations. Consequently, magician, sorcerer, heretic, and mentally disordered were caught in the same net and suffered together. As Alexander and Selesnick (1966) point out, "The mentally ill were caught up in the witch hunt. Theological rationalizations and magical explanations served as foundations for burning at the stake thousands of the mentally ill as well as many other unfortunates" (p. 70). While the "diagnoses" of canon law were not completely clear, it is doubtful that clarification could have saved the mentally disordered from the hysteria of the times. The *Malleus Maleficarum,* for instance, recommends that if a doctor cannot find a reason for a disease, and if drugs do not alleviate it, it is clearly caused by the devil.

Eighteenth to early nineteenth century

As we move into the nineteenth century, two English names should be mentioned as portending the progress to come. They are Robert Burton (1577–1640), the clergyman and scholar, and Thomas Sydenham (1624–1689), the physician. Burton, starting to write *Anatomy of Melancholy,* expanded his goal and dealt with the psychological and social causes of insanity. He rejected the supernatural and placed his emphasis on the emotional causes of mental illness.

Although Sydenham was a physician not especially interested in mental disorders, he noticed the frequency of neurotic and hysteric symptoms among his patients, paying particular attention to the wide range of physical symptoms through which they manifested themselves. He was among the first to describe the neuroses, and distinguished himself by pointing out that hysteria was not limited to women but occurred in many of his male patients.

Despite the increasing enlightenment of society, little was done for the insane. They wandered the countryside like werewolves, mocked, beaten, and tortured. If taken into custody, they were placed in hospitals like Bethlehem (Bedlam) in London or the Bicêtre in Paris, where they were placed in chains beside common criminals. People would even come and for a small admission fee be allowed to observe their strange behavior.

In the early eighteenth century, however, some attempt was made to better their lot. Britain in 1744 established rules for their commitment. St. Luke's Hospital was opened in Moorsfield, England, in 1750, and later in the United States through the influence of Benjamin Franklin the Pennsylvania Hospital was opened, the first public hospital in the United States to admit the mentally ill.

There was a new spirit in the air, a new humanitarian regard for the dignity and rights of all people, including the insane. Prominent among the innovators was Phillipe Pinel (1745–1826), who managed to keep his balance (and his head) through the turmoil of revolutionary France at that time. In 1793 he was appointed physician-in-chief at the Bicêtre (for male patients) and later of the Salpêtrière (the woman's hospital). These institutions housed criminals, the mentally retarded, and the insane, all of them kept in chains under cruel and inhuman conditions. One of Pinel's first administrative steps was to free the mentally ill from their chains, and to institute a new humanitarian treatment regimen. This was based upon Aristotle's view that sanity demanded a balance between reason and the passions. Pinel felt the physician must dominate the patient and direct his activities, but with a firmness mixed with kindness. There was a discussion of religious and personal values, and exercise and recreation in a structured environment. Pinel also instituted the keeping of records and case histories, a novel procedure for the times, but a necessary prerequisite for any obejctive study of mental illness.

He classified the mental disorders under four categories—melancholia, mania, dementia, and idiocy—and analyzed and classified the symptoms adding greatly to the descriptive psychiatry of the period. However, he refused a more specific set of categories as he felt that the medical science of his time was not sufficiently developed to merit change.

Pinel's humanitarian practices had an international influence upon some of his more enlightened colleagues, and his "moral treatment" was introduced in Italy, England, and the United States. In Florence, Italy it was introduced by Vincenzo Chiarugi at the Hospital Bonifacio, whose regulations specifically stated that: "It is the supreme moral duty and medical obligation to respect the insane individual as a person."

In England, William Tuke, a Quaker, became interested in the lot of the mentally ill after he visited the Lunatick Asylum in York, where he was appalled by the sadistic treatment given the inmates. He was successful in raising money for reform, and in 1796 founded the York Retreat. He did not believe in the prevalent treatment of patients by bleeding and purges, which resembled the exorcistic practice of an earlier date. To the contrary, he substituted the moral treatment of Pinel using firmness, friendliness, and respect in addition to providing sanitary conditions, good food, exercise, and religious values.

Benjamin Rush, a signer of the Declaration of Independence and recognized as the father of American psychiatry, had his early training in Edinburgh where he incorporated many of the progressive English and French ideas. A humanitarian thinker supportive of social reform, he introduced moral treatment methods at the Pennsylvania Hospital. He did not, however, surrender his belief in the bloodletting, emetics, and purgatives so popular at that time.

Also prominent was Eli Todd (1762—1823), a Yale-trained country physician in Connecticut whose interest in mental disorder was sharpened by family involvement as his father died insane and his sister suffered from depression. Todd moved to Hartford and gathering support from his Connecticut colleagues founded the Hartford Retreat (now known as The Institute of Living) in 1824. He provided "moral management" using the basic ideas of Pinel.

A number of other private institutions were started at this time, famous among them being the McLean Asylum (1818) near Boston, and the Bloomingdale Asylum in New York in 1821. Subsequently some ten state hospitals were founded including the State Lunatic Hospital at Worcester, Massachusetts, under Samuel Woodward and the New York State Hospital at Utica, New York, under Amariah Brigham.

In 1844, thirteen of the directors of such hospitals got together and founded the Association of Medical Superintendents of American Institutions for the Insane, the oldest medical society in the United States. That same year the *American Journal of Insanity* (now the *American Journal of Psychiatry*) was begun.

Before leaving the period, some mention should be made of Franz Mesmer (1743–1815), although one hesitates to put him in the mainstream of psychiatry. Mesmer had the idea that man possessed some magnetic fluid that, when liberated, usually by physical contact, has healing effects. He claimed to have great success with this "animal magnetism," but it roused great controversy among his fellow medical men. This caused him to leave Vienna and go to Paris in 1778. Here he aroused even greater controversy, but not before securing the support of many prominent people who believed in his power. What mesmerism contributed undoubtedly lay solely in the increased understanding it provided of the neuroses and the added interest it ultimately directed toward the mechanisms of suggestion and hypnosis.

To summarize, the period was marked by its humanitarianism and attention to the problems of the mentally ill rather than any great increase in understanding of the illnesses themselves. But this attention and effort was necessary to establish a base for the burgeoning descriptive and theoretical advances coming in the last half of the century.

Middle nineteenth to early twentieth century

The moral treatment advocated by Pinel, Chiarugi, Tuke, Rush, and Todd did not last long, particularly in America where Dorothea Dix devoted her energies to forcing the state legislatures into building more and larger hospitals. Here the mentally ill were collected and separated from family and society. Under these conditions the small groupings and personal solicitude that marked moral treatment were impossible. Treatment became impersonal and mental illness was considered a physiological problem rather than a psychosocial one.

There were some innovations but they arose more from administrative problems rather than any direct therapeutic interest. Tuberculosis was a constant threat in any of the large, crowded institutions, and there were attempts to handle the necessary isolation of tubercular patients by erecting tents to house them. This added the benefits of fresh air, a popular treatment for tuberculosis at that time. When such a program was started at the Manhattan State Hospital on Ward's Island, the staff noticed improved patient behavior. There was less soiling, less violence, and more social interaction. So tent cities had some popularity for a while, but when winter came and the patients went inside they regressed and the improvement was lost. Also, superintendents (i.e., hospital directors) started constructing pavilions rather than erecting tents, and as the pavilions increasingly resembled buildings, tent treatment lost its distinctive features.

There was some discussion of two complementary types of hospital, one for custodial care of chronic cases, the other structured around an active therapy program. There were boarding-out programs. A cottage program was started at the McLean Hospital, and Adolph Meyer, a proponent of treating the whole person, advocated a community oriented program that anticipated today's community mental health programs. However, as Ruth Caplan (1969) says in her fascinating *Psychiatry and the Community in Nineteenth-Century America,* "As in the past, however, such proposals for integration were succeeded, during the following decades, by the retreat of psychiatrists with their patients into the sactuary of their clinics and professional offices" (p. 309).

The period really belonged to experimental and theoretical psychology as Charcot, Janet, and Freud pushed their investigations into the dynamics of neurotic behavior. As Freud's title *The Psychopathology of Everyday Life* so aptly testifies, it was the period that set the stage for the twentieth century, when the average man was admitted to the sanctity of the psychiatrist's office without the stigma of insanity being attached to him. This entry of psychiatry into the field of normal human behavior provided the roots for many of the jurisdictional problems that beset the mental health professions today.

In his laboratory at the Salpêtrière, Jean Charcot was studying the hysterias by using hypnosis both as a research tool and therapeutic technique. As a neurologist, however, he had little interest in the psychological mechanisms involved and remained firmly convinced that hysteria was a diseased condition of the nervous system. He was also convinced that only hysterics could be hypnotized, an argument he ultimately lost.

Freud came to study in Charcot's laboratory in 1885 when he received a traveling fellowship from Vienna. While he considered himself a fellow neurologist and accepted Charcot's orientation, he became interested in the psychological aspects of hysterical behavior. Freud proposed to study hysterical versus organic paralyses as he felt the former conformed to the popular idea of their demarcation and the latter the anatomical one. Charcot gave his permission but had no enthusiasm for Freud's psychological interpretation.

Pierre Janet (1859–1947) was the last of the great representatives of the French school. Like Charcot, he had a neurological bias and considered hysteria the result of a constitutional weakness of the mind. While he is sometimes quoted as mentioning the unconscious as a dynamic factor, at a latter date in an argument with Freud he denied using the words in any serious fashion. In any case, they seem to have made an impression on Freud, as did the cathartic use of hypnosis in enabling the patient to remember and relive the precipitating experiences back of his symptoms and to get subsequent relief from them.

Freud returned to Vienna and for a while worked with Breuer, using hypnosis as a therapeutic technique and subsequently for dream interpretation and free association. As Freud became more involved in the sexual interpretation of the neuroses, he broke away from Breuer and continued alone. Freud drew upon all the emerging knowledge of the neuroses, added innumerable observations and conceptualizations of his own, and orchestrated it into the complex theoretical system we know as psychoanalysis. With him the classification of neurotic behaviors achieved a broad nosological underpinning. His concept of sexual libido as the basic, instinctual driving force; of infantile sexuality and its development through oral, anal-sadistic, and phallic stages; the id, ego, and superego evolving in the gradual shift from pleasure principle to reality principle; the topological concepts of unconscious, preconscious, and conscious; and the defense mechanisms such as repression, displacement, rationalization, isolation, projection, and denial have all been incorporated into our twentieth century culture and have been reflected in the vocabulary of the educated Western man. The defense mechanisms in particular (apart from their special Freudian connotations) furnish an almost universal base for any contemporary understanding of human personality. To echo Stainbrook's earlier comment, one can criticize Freud not for being all wrong, but for insisting on being exclusively right.

Many of Freud's early psychoanalytic colleagues split off with their own interpretations: Adler with his stress on inferiority as a motivating force, Jung with his insistence on the importance of archaic memories or predispositions of the psyche based upon universal human experiences, and Rank highlighting the trauma of birth. At a later date, Erickson and Anna Freud stressed the development of the ego, Horney the use of self-effacement, expansiveness, and resignation as modes of defense, Sullivan introduced social and interpersonal factors, and Fromm the problem of social conformity and loss of freedom.

Among the nonanalytically oriented schools of the first half of the twentieth century, the nondirective or client-centered movement led by psychologist Carl Rogers (1951) is of particular interest since it played down the role of diagnosis. Rogers believed in the patient's ability to solve his problems through the use of his own inner resources. The therapeutic interview offered him a chance to think about and express his feelings in an accepting, permissive environment, without being offered advice or direction. The therapist's role was merely to clarify and reflect the patient's statements. While not recommended for psychotics or the mentally retarded, it was regarded as a universal technique applicable in all other cases. With such a universal common approach, diagnosis becomes unnecessary. This is a popular criticism of diagnosis. If no specific therapy of choice exists, why diagnose? The argument overlooks the fact that diagnosis may offer valuable assistance in making a prognosis.

The psychoses also received some attention during this period. It was a period of improved description and awakened interest in classification. Emil Kraepelin (1855—1926), often overenthusiastically considered the father of descriptive psychiatry, pulled together catatonia, hebephrenia, and the dementias under the concept of dementia praecox. Subsequently, Eugen Bleuler substituted the term schizophrenia, but Kraepelin's description of it was retained, as was his differentiation and description of manic-depressive psychosis. While this marks the beginning of the modern interest in classification, the neuroses and personality disorders were yet to be included.

In 1917 the American Medical Psychological Association prepared a statistical classification of mental disorders, and later in 1928 when the American Medical Association moved toward a standard nomenclature of morbidity and death, psychiatry prepared the section on mental disorders. Only after World War II did the American Psychiatric Association issue its *Diagnostic and Statistical Manual* as a complete catalogue of the mental disorders.

To conclude, the period was marked by a tremendous increase in our knowledge of the mental disorders, particularly the neuroses, with a consequent increasing interest in the problems of classification. With the advent of the dynamic defense mechanisms of the unconscious, the concept of demoniacal possession by an outside influence, deity, or devil gave way to the concept of internal possession by unconscious dynamisms, and man was literally possessed by himself. The rites of exorcism gave way to the techniques of psychotherapy. The use of these dynamic concepts for the interpretation of normal personality mechanisms marked the increasing participation in the field of psychopathology of the behavioral sciences, particularly psychology, sociology, and anthropology.

The modern period

The insistence with which Charcot and Janet clung to their belief that the neurotic behaviors seen in hysteria were attributable to some disease or degeneration in the brain or nervous system, and their resistance to Freud's interpretation of them as dynamic mechanisms through which the organism was seeking some compensatory adjustment began the long controversy between the organic and functional schools. This conflict lasted well into the twentieth century.

In the middle thirties, the organic approach was reinforced by the introduction of several radical pharmacological and surgical treatments. Sakel tried treating schizophrenia by inducing an insulin coma. On the grounds that schizophrenia was rarely found in epileptics, Meduna proposed the use of metrazol to induce artificial seizures. Cerletti and Bini introduced electroshock, a treatment that in its milder forms is still used. Finally, Moniz proposed leucotomy, a type of psychosurgery in which the fibers connecting the prefrontal lobes of the brain with the thalamus were severed. While a clear rationale was not present for any of these techniques, some psychotic patients did show some improvement. The presence of conflicting results, the severe insults to the nervous system involved, and the often irreversible damage done led to their gradual decline in popularity.

Just as with the older controversy over heredity versus environment, we have come to realize the absurdity of an either-or solution and to accept the fact that mental disorder is a function of the interaction between both organic and functional factors. There might be some agreement that the organic factors weight more heavily in the psychoses while the functional are more important in the neuroses. (During World War

II the Navy's discharge rate for psychosis remained relatively stable while that for neurosis rose steadily as the conflict continued.) Actually, deviant behavior exhibited is a function of the interaction of both factors with the final weighting varying from individual to individual and from situation to situation.

The complexity of the etiological picture is illustrated by Zubin (1975), who presents six popular etiological models all currently in use and supported by research. They range from the field theory approach exemplified by the ecological model to the atomistic approach of the genetic model. They are:

1. *Ecological model,* stressing deviant environments and environmental stressors such as socioeconomic status.
2. *Developmental model,* stressing the failure to adjust at transitional points in life.
3. *Learning theory model,* stressing the acquisition of ineffective behaviors.
4. *Internal environment model,* stressing biochemical and metabolic factors.
5. *Neurophysiological model,* stressing deviant brain functions.
6. *Genetic model,* stressing atomistic hereditary factors.

Zubin concludes that the common element in all this is the production of some kind of vulnerability in mental patients. When they are subjected to sufficiently stressful situations, an episode of illness results. In depressive and manic patients these episodes are time limited; in schizophrenics they may or may not be since some schizophrenics seem never to recover. He resolves the seeming paradox by appealing to the prognostic literature that suggests that patients with a good premorbid history improve, while poor premorbids after the episode is over still cannot cope with life. It is obvious that any classificatory system with prognostic value must take account of the patient's history.

World War II gave a tremendous impetus to all the mental health professions. Drawing on the lessons of World War I, the military realized the tremendous psychiatric problem it would face if and when hostilities broke out, and consequently began planning. A great increase in hospital facilities, outpatient clinical services, and front-line treatment was necessary. Moreover, it would be possible to alleviate some of the burden if psychiatric selection were used at the draft board and training level to weed out the obvious misfits before they were sent to combat. It was realized that the problem was not psychiatry's alone, but that psychology and social work were also involved.

The direct benefits from the resulting comprehensive program involved the improved efficiency of the military services, the humanitarian avoidance of unnecessary psychic trauma for those obviously unable to cope with the pressures of military service, and a reduction of the inevitable financial burden imposed on the country by the subsequent provision of psychiatric care for the veterans.

There were indirect benefits as well. The intimate collaboration demanded that the different mental health professions familiarized themselves with the contributions of the other, and taught the value of professional cooperation. There was an increased knowledge of and sensitivity to psychiatric problems on the part of nonpsychiatric medical personnel, many of whom took advantage of the brief training courses in psychiatry offered to general pactitioners and members of other specialties. Some of these have remained in psychiatry. There was an attendant arousal of interest in the psychiatric problem among the general public and an increased support for programs in the mental health area.

As was to be expected, the preventive action did help, but inevitably the end of hostilities left a sizeable number of psychiatric casualties for which the country had to provide treatment. The Veterans Administration (VA) was reorganized to meet the increased demands upon it. New hospital and outpatient clinic facilities were provided, but there was a glaring need for professional staff to operate them. The VA met this lack by funneling training funds to medical schools and universities to help them meet the increasing manpower demands for mental health professionals.

At the same time, these efforts were supplemented by the National Institute of Mental Health (NIMH), established under the wise direction of Robert Felix. NIMH also provided training funds of a freer nature, not under the "work and learn" restrictions of some of the VA grants. Perhaps more important that its broad training effort has been its encouragement of research. Not only were in-house research facilities set up within NIMH itself, but funds were granted to researchers in universities and hospitals outside NIMH. Such funding has been a primary resource for research, not only in basic research, but for the trial investigation of new treatment programs. Nothing has been as important for the development of mental health services in these postwar years as NIMH.

The result of this interest and support has been a tremendous increase in knowledge of the mental disorders and the ability to understand and control them. To return to Zubin's six etiological models, much has been learned about the ecology or environmental aspects of deviant behavior, the socioeconomic factors that influence it, the effects of sudden changes in living and life style brought about by unemployment or change of employment, by promotion, bereavement, divorce, retirement, and changes in residence, and the stresses they produce. Information has increased about developmental stages, both biological and psychological. Advances in learning, both classical Pavlovian conditioning and Skinnerian operant conditioning, have given us behavior modification, perhaps the most important psychological contribution to psychotherapy since psychoanalysis.

Even more dramatic have been the advances in psychopharmacology, the use of the phenothiazines in the control of schizophrenia, and the discovery of the importance of monamine metabolism in the pathogenesis of the vital depressions (endogenous). In this last case, we have a disorder (depression) apparently produced by two separate and distinct deficiencies, one a deficiency in serotonin, the other a deficiency in norepinepherin, yet both show the same clinical psychopathology. While psychopharmacology has not as yet yielded any final insight into the etiology of the mental disorders, it has contributed much to the control of psychotic behavior and the alteration of its prognosis.

Our study of the neurophysiology of psychopathological behavior, as instanced by advances in electroencephalography and in the study of signal detection, information processing, and reaction time, has given us further insight into cerebral function. Last but not least, great progress has been made in our understanding of the genetics of mental disorders, in schizophrenia, depression, alcoholism, and the personality disorders. As yet, there are few specific chromosomal markers such as in Down's syndrome (mongolism), but regular genetic patterns are emerging with more clarity than ever before.

This proliferation of information has made the task of classification and diagnosis increasingly complex. Nowhere is this better reflected than in the development of the *Diagnostic and Statistical Manual of Mental Disorders* (DSM) sponsored by the American Psychiatric Association. Originally produced in 1952 in an attempt to introduce some guidance and order in the field of diagnosis and to bring it into line with the International Classification of Diseases (ICD) widely used throughout the world, it has been revised in 1968 (DSM II) and has undergone another recent revision (DSM III). While the DSM remains basically symptomatically oriented in the clinical observations of psychopathological behavior (in the Kraepelinian tradition), both revisions increasingly face the need of introducing other dimensions into the diagnostic picture, a trend previously mentioned in the study by Feighner et al.

DSM II altered DSM I by dropping the term reaction in most cases, encouraging the concomitant diagnosis of more than one disorder in some cases, and abandoning some overall groupings and using independent subgroupings instead (e.g., involutional psychotic reaction was dropped, involutional melancholia was placed among the major affective disorders, and involutional paranoid states were placed under paranoid states).

DSM III offers a better reflection of our current knowledge of psychopathology and only secondarily will an attempt be made to render it compatible with the International Classification of Diseases. The commission drawing it up stated four main purposes:

1. To facilitate professional communication,
2. To serve as a guide to differential treatment,
3. To furnish information about likely outcomes,
4. To reflect our knowledge of etiology.

Thus a fourth goal, communication, has been added to the classic trio of etiology, prognosis, and treatment. This mirrors the increasing professional organization within the mental health professions and the lessening individual isolation of its practicioners.

The commission heralds the DSM III as the first national classificatory system in psychiatry to use operational criteria. While the hard core remains the clinical observation of symptomatic behavior, the necessity of using other information in the diagnostic picture is recognized by the use of adjunctive "axes" on which the patient may be rated for such things as the severity of psychosocial stressors and the highest level of adaptive functioning during the previous year. It got extensive pretesting in the field before being released, but its debut is expected in 1980.

While behavior modification and psychopharmacology have made the most important and innovative contributions to the current therapeutic picture, the more conventional psychotherapies have also played an important part. By conventional, we mean the various combinations of catharsis and reeducation that have been the benchmark of classical psychotherapy since the early days in Greece. The specific techniques of encouraging catharsis and facilitating reeducation have proliferated so much since World War II that it is impossible to deal with each of them here.

Catharsis ranges from the relatively gentle ventilation typical of most client-centered, nondirective approaches, through the often highly charged interaction of "encounter" groups, to the primitive fury of the "primal scream" in primal therapy. Play therapy, role playing, and psychodrama are used to facilitate the expression of feeling. These last verge into insight and reeducation, which in turn ranges from the self-education of the nondirective approach to the directed education of formal psychoanalysis. The goals may vary from superficial insight into immediate surface problems to deeper insight into basic personality dynamics.

The techniques range from individual treatment as in classical psychoanalysis to group methods. Originally proposed as an economic means of handling large numbers of patients with limited therapeutic manpower, group therapy rapidly developed its own rationale based upon the use of the dynamic interactions developing between the members of a group. Groups may be unselected or selected with a definite purpose in mind as in group family therapy. Today most of the current therapeutic orientations can be adapted to group use.

This proliferation of therapies has been accompanied by many administrative innovations. The use of psychotropic drugs has made possible a greater control of disturbed patient behavior so that custodial care is easier and psychotherapy is possible in many cases where it was impossible before. The seventies have seen a determined effort to minimize the importance of custodial care, to decrease the use of large hospitals, and wherever possible to return the patient to the community. Without the new drugs this could not have been accomplished. The program has been assisted by the use of family care, nursing homes, halfway houses, and day care centers. Decentralization has been aided by the establishment of regional Mental Health Centers each responsible for a specific geographical area. Each center has an outpatient clinic and facilities for emergency hospitalization. All of these innovations fit into the current humanitarian focus on improved patient care, increased therapeutic intervention, and more attention to the patient's constitutional rights as a human being.

Summary

Primitive people lived in a magical world inhabited by ghosts, spirits, and supernatural beings who visited punishment upon the unlucky member of the tribe. There was no understanding of the nature of mental illness, and madness was attributed to possession of the person's mind and body by an evil spirit who must be driven out by exorcistic rites and rituals performed by a shaman, medicine man, or priest. If exorcism did not work, the patient was abandoned, left to die, or sometimes deliberately murdered. Later it was recognized that some possession was divine, and such a possessed person was recognized as being favored by the gods.

With the development of Greek culture, there was increased interest in medicine and some recognition of the medical nature of mental disorder. In the fourth century B.C., Hippocrates described the manias, depression, and the dementias. He classed hysteria as a female disorder attributed to dysfunction of the womb. Despite these beginnings, the general public clung to the supernatural explanation. In the intellectually impoverished Middle Ages, these beliefs in demoniacal possession flourished, leading to extensive witch hunts in which heretics and the mentally ill were all treated alike and persecuted as social criminals. In the absence of any adequate descriptive psychiatry as a basis for classification and diagnosis, the decision was left up to the courts and church authority.

With the beginnings of enlightenment in the seventeenth century some interest was again aroused in the mentally ill. Sydenham noticed the frequency of neurotic behavior among his patients and pointed out that hysteria occurred in males as well as females. Despite the increasing cultural level of society, little was done for the disordered person until the eighteenth century when a new humanitarian interest began with the appointment of Pinel as director of the Bicêtre and Salpêtrière hospitals in Paris. Pinel literally struck the chains from his patients and introduced a new "moral treatment" that respected them as human individuals. His ideas were carried to England by Tuke, to the United States by Rush, and to Italy by Chiarugi. Pinel also was interested in descriptive psychiatry but felt the time was not ripe for an extended classificatory system.

Great progress was made in the latter part of the nineteenth century when the work of Charcot and Janet with hypnosis drew attention to hysteria and the neuroses. While Charcot and Janet still held to their belief that these phenomena were organic in their origins, Freud insisted on viewing them as dynamic mechanisms of the unconscious, the result of unrecognized life conflicts in the individual. Thus, psychoanalysis opened psychiatry to an understanding of neurotic behavior and extended the findings to an interpretation not only of psychopathology but to normal behavior as well.

At the same time Kraepelin, with his description of dementia praecox as an inclusive category covering the phenomena of catatonia, hebephrenia, and paranoisis, gave a needed impetus to descriptive psychiatry. The added information and interest contributed by Freud and Kraepelin highlighted the need for a more adequate classificatory system for psychopathology.

World War II added to this pressure and resulted in an aroused public interest in mental health, which was expressed in the reorganization of the Veterans Administration and the creation of the National Institute of Mental Health. The increased clinical practice and burgeoning research activity and the resulting preoccupation with diagnosis in the mental health area demanded further attempts to establish an adequate taxonomy and classificatory system for psychopathological behavior to meet the increased importance of diagnosis in the clinical, legal, and social service areas.

In 1952 the American Psychiatric Association sponsored its *Diagnostic and Statistical Manual* (DSM) to provide the needed guidance. This was revised in 1968 and then again, producing DSM III. Adequate diagnosis is necessary for the research investigation of etiology, for the understanding of prognosis, and in some areas for the selection of treatment of choice. Diagnosis is not as yet a perfect system, which is as it must be in a still young, developing discipline. Reliability and validity still remain problems. One might paraphrase that you can diagnose all the patients some of the time, some of the patients all of the time, but not all patients all of the time. Flexibility of any classificatory system still is necessary, and the cost of flexibility is some lessening of reliability and validity. This is the price one pays for eventual maturity.

Glossary

Affective Psychosis: Any of a group of psychoses marked either by extreme elation or depression, sometimes alternating. There is a tendency to remission and recurrence.

Delusion: A false fixed belief.

Diagnostic and Statistical Manual of Mental Disorders (DSM): Official guidelines for the classification and diagnosis of the mental disorders. Sponsored by the American Psychiatric Association.

Etiology: The cause or origin of an illness.

Exorcism: Delivering a person from evil spirits by the performance of mystical or religious rites and rituals.

Hallucination: A false sensory perception in the absence of a concrete external stimulus.

Labelling Theory: Views supposed mental illness as merely deviant behavior that varies in definition from culture to culture.

Monothetic: Any class in which every member shares a common property with the others.

Neurosis: A mental disorder characterized by anxiety but without overt distortion of reality, also known as *Psychoneurosis*.

Nosology: A taxonomic (diagnostic) system in which the classes have a theoretical relation to one another.

Paranoid: Behavior that is marked by suspicious self-reference often accompanied by feelings of persecution.

Phobia: Pathological fear of some specific stimulus or situation.

Polythetic: Any class the members of which share some common properties but not all of them.

Prognosis: A prediction of the probable course of an illness.

Psychopharmacology: The study of drugs that affect the mental and behavioral processes.

Psychosis: A mental disorder characterized by interference with normal thinking, emotion, and communication accompanied by a distortion of reality.

Psychotropic Drug: A drug that affects mental functions and behavior.

Schizophrenia: A psychotic mental disorder characterized by disturbances in thinking, mood, and behavior.

Taxonomy: The theoretical study of the rules and principles governing the necessary classification system underlying diagnosis.

Theurgic: Characterized by the intervention in human affairs of a divine or supernatural agency.

3

EMPIRICAL METHODS IN THE BEHAVIOR DISORDERS

MICHEL HERSEN

The empirical method in abnormal psychology is devoted to separating fact from fiction. Throughout the ages, numerous theories concerning abnormal behavior have abounded. Not only have many of these theories proven to be false, but many of them led to practices that today could only be considered as inhuman. A case in point is the attribution of witchcraft to some "deranged" individuals in Europe during the Middle Ages and in seventeenth century America, leading to their persecution and death.

Although most incorrect notions about abnormal behavior have not resulted in such dire consequences, the range of inaccuracy is extensive. Undoubtedly, even some of our cherished notions about abnormal behavior of the late 1970s will ultimately be laughed at by later generations. Nonetheless, the difference between the contemporary approach to psychopathology and that of an earlier age is today's valiant attempt to examine issues scientifically. Indeed, the entire purpose of this chapter is to outline the scientific method as it is now applied to the field of abnormal psychology.

To have a full appreciation of the material in succeeding chapters, it is recommended that the presentation herein be given careful attention, as the areas of abnormal behavior that have been empirically examined are considerable. Equally extensive are the specific experimental techniques that have been used for such study.

In this chapter we will first examine some of the basic tenets of the scientific method as they apply to abnormal psychology. Such concepts as testability, reliability, standardization, and validity are to be defined. Next, we will describe the means through which the behavioral scientist is able to gather information about abnormal phenomena (e.g., self-reports of the individual being studied, direct observation of motoric behavior, and assessment of physiological functioning). Third, we will look at the kinds of experimental strategies that are used by scientists concerned with abnormal behavior. And finally, we will discuss and illustrate with specific examples the types of studies that have been performed. Included are studies that involve diagnosis, treatment, and the evaluation of genetic predispositions toward certain kinds of disorders.

The scientific method

We already have referred to the scientific method on several occasions in the introductory section to this chapter. But what exactly is the scientific method as it applies to abnormal phenomena? And how does the scientific method differ from mere casual observation of abnormal behavior and attempts at theorizing?

Testability

Perhaps the most distinguishing feature of the scientist, in general, is his willingness to subject his theories, hunches, ideas, and speculations to systematic evaluation in a rigorous and standardized fashion. Thus, the scientist examining abnormal behavior would and should be unwilling to make a definitive assertion based on a few random observations he has made. However, such random observations can eventually serve as the basis for forming and testing specific hypotheses. Consider, for example, the psychotherapist who has had initial success treating depressed patients with a new technique. On the basis of his own observations and experience, the therapist might be certain that an important discovery has been made. However, the scientific world obviously will not accept the assertion on faith alone that he has developed an "effective psychotherapy for depressed patients." To convince the scientific world, the therapist will be required to demonstrate that the new treatment is better than none at all, and then perhaps to show that the treatment is better than one currently accepted and practiced by most other psychotherapists. Only then can there be scientific approval of the new treatment for depression.

In any event, one might say that the attitude of the true scientist is one of *skepticism* and *doubt,* unless data point to the contrary. Moreover, any new treatment, theory, hunch, or speculation must be tested before it will receive "scientific approval." (Consider the public and scientific controversy over the drug "laetrile" during the late 1970s as to its presumed powers in controlling cancer in the absence of any experimental studies with humans.) Also, the proposition should be one that *is* amenable to legitimate experimental test in a public manner. Going back to our earlier example of witchcraft, one would be hard-pressed to say that the proposition that "mental illness" is a result of "demonic possession" is a testable hypothesis. On the other hand, the comparative evaluation of two minor tranquilizers in reducing anxiety level is certainly subject to experimental test.

Reliability

Reliability is a second key tenet of the scientific method. Basically, a reliable observation or event is one that can be reproduced at will under standardized conditions. However, if the observation obtained under standardized conditions is limited to one individual, to one specific psychological laboratory, or in one psychiatric hospital, this observation cannot be labeled as reliable. For example, if a particular type of psychotherapy said to be effective for the reduction of anxiety is only effective in the hands of its originator, then the reliability of that therapy is questionable. Similarly, if a given antidepressant medication works only when prescribed by one particular physician, but no other physician prescribing it at a similar dosage and with similar depressives obtains the same effect, then the reliability of the drug has not been established. In the preceding case, it may very well be that the drug in itself is not the critical factor bringing about change. To the contrary, any change occurring may simply be a function of the "personality" of the prescribing physician. (Elsewhere this has been called a "placebo" cure.)

Thus, returning to what reliability means, it is clear that the observation or effect must be one that can be reproducible under standardized conditions by many individuals, in many different laboratories, hospitals, or cities. Of course, there obviously will be degrees of reproducibility, ranging from 0 percent to 100 percent. Generally, however, a reliability ratio of 80% or more is considered to be acceptable by the scientific community.

Standardization

Standardization is another basic tenet of the scientific approach, and it is clearly related to the notion of reliability. Indeed, in order to have an accurate assessment of a given procedure's reliability (be it diagnostic or therapeutic), the particular procedure must be clearly specified such that it could be carried out within similar time, setting, distance, and instructional constraints by different individuals in different locations. Thus, when we refer to a standardized psychological test such as the Wechsler Adult Intelligence Scale (Matarazzo, 1972), we mean that it is administered on different occasions to the same or different individuals with identical instructions, in a similar setting (e.g., well-lit room, comfortable surroundings), and that the subjects' reponses (across different administrations) are recorded and scored in an identical fashion. If the instructions were to be varied from subject to subject, or if the scoring criteria were to differ from one subject to another, the test could not be said to have been administered in a standardized fashion.

Turning to a different example, if one were interested in assessing the reliability of a particular antipsychotic drug in decreasing hallucinatory behavior in schizophrenic patients, that drug would have to be administered under standardized conditions. Included in the standardization procedure might be the time of day the drug is administered, how frequently it is administered, the specific dosage at which it is given, and whether it is administered orally or injected intra-muscularly. Again, the point to be emphasized is that precise conditions are followed to ensure standardization and comparability from one administration to the next within and across patients.

Validity

A fourth tenet of the scientific approach to abnormal behavior is the issue of validity. In general, validity refers to the quality of being true, correct, or factual. However, when we say that a psychological test is valid, what exactly do we mean? Of course, a multifaceted answer will be needed to respond to this question as there are several types of validity.

Let us first consider "face" validity. Face validity is present if the test or technique appears to be measuring or functioning in direct relation to its presumed purpose. Thus, in the case of a test assessing degree of depression (such as the Beck Depression Inventory—Beck, Ward, Mendelsohn, Mock, & Erbaugh, 1961), face validity is said to be present if the items comprising the test *seem* to be measuring the various features associated with depression. Such items might touch on: sadness, guilt, crying, decreased appetite, or suicidal thoughts. In contrast, a question about sexual behavior would not appear to be relevant (i.e., face valid), although it might provide important information. Similarly, a psychotherapeutic technique might be described as having high face validity if it seems to deal with the problem at hand. For example, a psychotherapeutic technique designed to teach anxious patients how to better relax obviously has face validity.

A second type of validity is known as "concurrent" validity. For example, if an intelligence test is able to differentiate with a high degree of regularity students who are doing well or poorly in their classes (as based on *current* teachers' ratings), then it would appear that the test has concurrent validity. That is, the test serves to differentiate students as matched with a currently available external criterion (i.e., teachers' ratings).

A third type of validity is known as "predictive" validity. And, as the term suggests (once again using our example of a psychological test), the psychological test should be able to predict an individual's subsequent behavior with a high degree of regularity. For example, if a personality test such as the Minnesota Multiphasic Inventory (MMPI) (Hathaway & McKinley, 1967) were to be administered regularly to all armed forces recruitees, one could assess to what degree their responses on that test would be predictive of successful adaptation to military life. If indeed responses to the MMPI clearly differentiated successful versus unsuccessful adaptation to military life, then the test would be credited with "predictive" validity. Thus, at least in the case of our psychological test, responses to the test are matched with an outside behavioral criterion at some future date.

Ethics

One of the unwritten tenets of the "true" scientist is his scrupulous reporting of data, irrespective of whether they do or do not confirm his favorite hypotheses. It may be a truism that any scientist (behavioral or otherwise) is bound by professional integrity to report his results in an honest and unbiased fashion. However, there are ample data showing that behavioral scientists may be unaware of how their biases are affecting, in subtle fashion, the outcome of their experiments (cf. Rosenthal, 1966). Rosenthal (1966) clearly shows that in both animal and human research, communication of the experimental hypothesis to the research assistants can result in data favorable to that hypothesis. In addition, there are those few "scientists" who, due either to personal or professional pressures (e.g., the publish or perish pressure of the academic department in the large university), consciously have distorted their data (e.g., the researcher at the Sloan-Kettering Cancer Institute in New York who attempted to falsify the results of his experiments on immunology with mice in the mid-1970s). This researcher specifically falsified his data by painting the backs of his experimental mice with a black felt-tip pen.

Given that this volume is devoted to the study of abnormal behavior, such lapses in scientific integrity can be put into context. Yet, there is no doubt that these are reprehensible acts (although isolated) that serve to retard rather than advance a particular area of study. On the other hand, data reported in journals and books by investigators are almost never challenged on ethical grounds, inasmuch as the great majority of researchers are automatically presumed to be honest.

Another ethical concern faced by the researcher in the field of abnormal behavior involves the welfare of his subjects (animal or human), clients, and patients during the course of study. Numerous institutional and governmental precautions (e.g., guidelines developed by the Department of Health, Education, and Welfare) have appeared in order to protect the rights of subjects involved in research. Indeed, informed consent and the right to terminate participation in any research project without the risk of suffering repercussions are the norms in today's research enterprise. That is, the benefits and possible risks of being involved in a given research project are clearly indicated to the prospective subject.

Although at times these precautions have been viewed as excessive by some experimental and clinical researchers, on the whole, the clear criteria outlining the rights of the research subject, client, or patient have not retarded the advancement of knowledge nor have they hampered the majority of research operations. More importantly, however, the dignity of the subject and the research endeavor has been enhanced.

Methods of assessment

Before we begin our discussion of specific research strategies used in evaluating abnormal behavior, we will first carefully examine the various methods of assessing behavior that have been employed by researchers in the field. In discussing these methods of assessment, a clear distinction will be made between the use of casual observations and those that are conducted under standardized conditions, have acceptable levels of reliability, and are valid. In the absence of standardization, reliability, and validity, the opportunity for inter-study comparisons is limited. Moreover, as noted in the previous section, standardization, reliability, and validity are the cornerstones of the scientific approach.

Self-reports

There are many ways a selected individual's behavior can be assessed and evaluated (Hersen & Bellack, 1976). Obviously, one of the simplest procedures is to ask the individual to make a self-assessment. For example, the responses to typical questions such as: "How are you doing?" or "How are you feeling today?" are representative of an individual's self-assessment. Of course, self-assessment methods followed in the study of abnormal behavior tend to be more specific (i.e., focused on a particular area or on a particular disorder) and are administered in much more rigorous fashion than the casual: "How are you?" As the reader might readily imagine, hundreds and thousands of self-report paper-and-pencil scales and tests have been developed by researchers to assess a wide variety of problem areas. These include but are not limited to the assessment of: anxiety, depression, fear, marital satisfaction, sexual functioning, health, paranoia, schizophrenia, neroticism, psychoticism, extraversion, ego strength, assertiveness, social skill, and the potential for violent behavior.

Motoric responses

A second approach to measurement is to observe the individual's actual behavior under standardized conditions. It is possible to automate the procedure, as in the case of a voice-activated relay system.[1] In other instances, a permanent product of the behavior (e.g., dieting) can be assessed using gauges (e.g., weight loss as measured on a scale). Naturally, the automated and permanent products measures are most reliable as human judgment is not involved. However, other behaviors, usually of an interactive nature, require human judgment.[2] For example, the cooperative play of retarded children in a free play situation might be scored on a presence or absence basis in 30-second intervals during a total recording period of 15 minutes. In this case 30 observations can be made within the 15-minute limitation. Usually when this type of observation is made the reliability of the first observer's recordings are independently checked by a second observer.This is referred to as the percentage of agreement score. Using our above-mentioned example of cooperative play evidenced by retarded children, let us assume that Observer A records 20 instances of cooperative play. On the other hand, Observer B records only 16 instances of cooperative play within the same 15-minute time span. To obtain the percentage agreement score, one divides the smaller sum (16) by the larger sum (20). In this case the percentage of agreement between independent raters is 80 percent.

When making direct observations of motoric behavior it is generally preferable to make them in the individual's natural environment. Also, if possible, it is better if the observations can be done in an unobtrusive fashion. However, often it is difficult to assess behavior in the natural situation either because of logistical difficulties (e.g., access to the environment) or because of ethical limitations (e.g., observing sexual behavior). When these two restrictions are present a frequently employed alternative has involved measurement in analogues of the actual situation. Such analogue situations tend to involve role playing. For example, instead of observing a shy male actually telephone a girl for a date, the analogue situation might involve his *playacting* the scene with an attractive female partner (the role model) under role played conditions.

Physiological responses

A third approach to measurement is to examine the individual's physiological responses under standardized conditions. By physiological, we are referring primarily to responses of the autonomic nervous system. Included in this category are such responses as: heart rate, pulse rate, finger blood volume, galvanic skin respones (GSR), respiration rate, electromyogram (EMG) level, penile blood volume, and alpha, beta, delta, and gamma waves from the brain (evaluated with an electroencephalograph).

Generally, monitoring of physiological reponsibility requires complicated electronic equipment (e.g., polygraph, electroencephalograph). Usually, the subject of study must remain relatively immobile, as movement tends to interfere with the recording process. However, telemetric devices capable of long distance transmission have been developed (albeit at considerable cost), thus permitting assessment of physiological responses at greater range while also allowing the subject some freedom of movement within the environment. Although as we have previously stated, most recordings of physiological responses require electronic equipment, a simple response such as pulse rate can be recorded by hand with the additional assistance of a stopwatch (e.g., Miller, Hersen, Eisler, & Hilsman, 1974).

The relationship of physiological responding to abnormal behavior has been a subject of considerable inquiry over the last three decades. In spite of the fact that often this relationship is unclear, there are some disorders in which arousal of physiological responses is intensified. For example, with increased anxiety, there is a tendency for an increase in heart rate and respiration rate. Also, during states of high tension (the classic "tension" headache), EMG levels, reflecting actual muscle tension, are higher.

One of the difficulties associated with evaluating the relationship of physiological responses to abnormal behavior is that different individuals tend to respond with different physiological systems when stressed (Lacey & Van Lehn, 1952). That is, when stressed, some individuals may respond with an increased heart rate, others with heightened respiration, and still others with elevated EMG levels. This clearly makes inter-individual comparisons in studies difficult. Indeed, evaluation of whether an individual is a heart-rate or an EMG responder has been made with very young children including newborn babies (Lacey, 1956). However, being fully aware of the limitations, it still is possible to obtain reliable and valid data when monitoring physiological responses. This is especially true when the subject serves as his own control in a given experiment.[3]

Informant ratings and observations

A fourth approach to measurement is directed toward obtaining information about the research subject (often a psychiatric patient) from those in the environment who know him best or who are in a good position to observe him directly. Depending on the subject's status at the time of the study, a wide range of informants is possible. Thus, for the patient who has been hospitalized for some time, one might ask nurses and nursing assistants to observe and record his behavior while on the psychiatric ward. For a newly admitted psychiatric patient, one might question his closest relatives or friends as to his work, social, educational, and marital adjustment just prior to developing serious psychiatric symptoms. Similarly, a patient's post-hospital discharge work, social, educational, and marital adjustment might be assessed by a relative or friend.

An individual's psychiatric status (i.e., mental status) might be evaluated before, during, and after a short or lengthy psychiatric hospitalization. Also, an individual's status with regard to a particular psychiatric syndrome (e.g., depression) might be carefully assessed by a responsible professional (e.g., psychologist, psychiatrist, psychiatric nurse, psychiatric social worker) using a structured interview format. These types of assessments can be made both by professionals who have just met the subject and by those professionals who have known him longer. In either case, ratings are to be made on the basis of a structured interview (i.e., specified questions that are posed in a given order).

In the case of children who are seen on an outpatient basis or for those who are hospitalized, parents and guardians tend to be the primary source of information. The same holds true for those individuals who are incapable of being reliable informants themselves (e.g., the retarded, severely psychotic, organic, or senile). Information obtained from parents and guardians can be far ranging. Indeed, the range may extend from prenatal history, to developmental milestones, to health history, to current functioning.

The strategies for obtaining relevant information from significant others (i.e., informants) are quite varied. In some instances unstructured interviews might be carried out. In other cases, structured interviews may better serve the purpose. And in still other cases, the informant may be asked to fill out paper-and-pencil rating scales, yielding numerical scores. Of course, in the carefully designed research investigation, structured interviews and rating scales that are reliable and valid are generally employed for comprehensive reviews (see Hogarty, 1975; Spitzer & Endicott, 1975).

Biochemical measures

In the last two decades, with the increased attention that has been given to biological psychiatry (see Chapter 20), greater interest has been directed toward examining the biochemical status of the abnormal subject. Also, with the continued and expanded use of pharmacological agents (drugs) in treating various manifestations of abnormality, methods for measuring blood and urine levels of some of the drugs have been developed by psychopharmacologists.

Although a detailed discussion of the specifics of the biochemical procedures (whereby such assessments are made) is well beyond the scope of this chapter, the student ought to be aware of some of the more important developments in the field. For example, lithium carbonate is a drug commonly prescribed for treating the manic phase of manic-depressive disorder. However, above certain levels in the blood (more than 1.5 milli equivalents per liter) the drug may have toxic effects. Thus, when administering lithium carbonate, repeated monitoring of lithium levels in the blood is required.

Another example of a biochemical assay is the "drug screen," used to determine presence of narcotics, amphetamines, barbiturates, and sedatives in the subject's urine. The expression "dirty urine" refers to the presence of elevated levels of a drug (e.g., heroin) in the urine analysis. This kind of assessment is certainly critical in evaluating effects of various treatment programs for drug addicts, particularly as the verbal report of the drug addict cannot be accepted at face value (i.e., it often is unreliable and invalid).

A third example of a biochemical measure has been used by state police in many parts of the country to evaluate whether an arrested driver is intoxicated. Colloquially known as the "balloon test," a sample of the individual's breath is obtained by asking him or her to blow into a tube that then fills a balloon. The composition of this air is subsequently analyzed via gas chromatography, resulting in an approximation of a blood/alcohol concentration level. This approximation deviates only slightly from true levels obtained from actual blood samples. The utility of this measurement system in doing treatment and in conducting research with alcoholics should be obvious to the reader. Here too the objectivity of measurement far surpasses the questionable reliability and validity of the alcoholic's typical subjective estimate as to whether and how much he has had to drink.

Population statistics

Although population statistics cannot be strictly regarded as a method of assessment, they do represent an orderly way of organizing data about abnormal individuals. And there is no doubt that such statistics prove important in terms of assessment, treatment, and research. Subsumed under population statistics are several subcategories. *First* are the so-called demographic characteristics of an individual or group. Included may be various social statistics such as age, sex, marital status, professional status, financial status, race, ethnic origin, and prior hospitalizations. *Second* may be the incidence statistics of a particular disorder. That is, what is the rate of new cases of a given disorder within a circumscribed place and time? Thus one might refer to the incidence of suicide in New York following the Christmas holidays. *Third* may be the prevalence statistics of a particular disorder. That is, what percentage of a population under study has that particular disorder at a given time. For example, if in a population of 1000, 100 are classified as having disorder X, then the prevalence of disorder X in that population is said to be 10 percent.

Illustrations

In this section we will describe a few of the specific measurement techniques that are subsumed under the previously described categories. For the student's interest, we will also present selected items from self-report inventories and will illustrate how some of the measurement techniques were used in actual research studies.

Self-report inventories. Table 3.1 lists some of the frequently used self-report inventories in clinical research. Sample items from the inventories, the number of items per inventory, and the particular scoring format used for each are presented in this table. In addition, a reference is included for each inventory for the interested reader concerned about normative, reliability, and validity data.

The prototype of the self-report inventory, of course, is the extensively studied MMPI. Thousands of studies have been carried out during the course of validating the entire inventory and independent portions of it. Because of the vast number of items (566) comprising this inventory, many subscales have been developed. However, in most clinical and research work the 10 main scales have been used: 1. hypochondriasis, 2. depression, 3. hysteria, 4. psychopathic deviate, 5. masculinity-femininity, 6. paranoia, 7. psychastenia (i.e., anxiety), 8. schizophrenia, 9. hypomania, and 10. social introversion. In addition, there are three so-called validity scales (1. L=lie, 2. F=fake, 3. K=defensiveness) that can be used as checks on the reliability and validity of the subject's responses. Because of the widespread use of this inventory, several computer programs have been developed to both score the results and to interpret the scale patterns.[4]

Motoric behavior. An example of an automated technique for measuring motoric behavior was divised by Mills, Agras, Barlow, and Mills (1973). This measure was developed to record frequency of handwashing episodes in hospitalized obsessive-compulsives. A 6x8 foot wooden board surrounded by a fence was placed in front of the wash basin in the patient's room. Whenever the patient walked on the board to approach the wash basin, switches wired in sequence underneath the board activated a cumulative recorder placed in an adjoining room. Thus, total frequency of handwashing on a daily basis was recorded. This automated measure correlated very highly with nurses' independent observations of handwashing episodes.

A clear example of a permanent products measure (i.e., weight) appears in a study conducted by Elkin, Hersen, Eisler, and Williams (1973). In this study the investigators were interested in varying caloric presentation in an anorexia nervosa patient.[5] The two measures of interest were daily caloric intake and weight. Weight was monitored daily at a specified time and under specified conditions (i.e., the patient was weighed with his back turned to the gauges of the scale while wearing underwear). Thus, standardized conditions were met over succeeding measurement days.

A good example of a motoric measure requiring direct observation and reliability checks appears in Liberman, Teigen, Patterson, and Baker (1973). The investigators in

Table 3.1. Examples of Self-Report Inventories

Inventory	Sample Items	No. of Items	Scoring Format	Reference
MMPI	My soul sometimes leaves my body.	566	True—False	Hathaway & McKinley (1967)
Beck Depression Inventory	3. I hate myself 2. I am disgusted with myself 1. I am disappointed in myself 0. I don't feel disappointed in myself	21 sets of 4 items	0–3 Subject endorses 1 of 4 choices.	Beck et al. (1961)
Fear Survey Schedule II	Hypodermic needles	51	1 — — — —7 None — — Terror	Geer (1965)
Wolpe-Lazarus Assertiveness Scale	Do you usually keep your opinions to yourself?	30	Yes—No	Wolpe & Lazarus (1966)
Lubin Adjective Check List	wilted, miserable, fine active, sunny, droopy	32	Number of positive and negative adjectives endorsed by subject.	Lubin (1965)

this study were concerned with percentage of delusional and rational talk in four schizophrenic patients. Each of the four patients was interviewed four times daily for 10-minute periods by a member of the nursing staff. Appropriate topics for conversation previously had been prepared if prompting were to be necessary for beginning or maintaining a conversation. While conversing with the patient, the nurse recorded (using a stopwatch in unobtrusive fashion) the amount of time the patient engaged in rational talk. A second member of the nursing staff served as the reliability check, yielding reliabilities ranging from 0.75–0.95 (mean=0.82) across measurement sessions.

Physiological response. An example of the measurement of a physiological response is provided in a single case study conducted by Epstein, Hersen, and Hemphill (1974). In this biofeedback experiment, the patient was a 39-year-old male who had suffered from tension headaches for some 16 years. Tension levels (i.e., EMG) were recorded from his frontalis muscle (a muscle located above the eyebrows running through the forehead). During the course of a typical "tension headache" this muscle tends to become extremely tense (i.e., heightened EMG levels). EMG levels were obtained by placing the electrodes one inch above the eyebrow directly above the middle of each eye. EMG activity was amplified with a Grass 7P-3 hi gain preamplifier. During measurement sessions the patient sat on a comfortable chair in a room adjoining the recording chamber where the electronic equipment was kept. Prior to each measurement session there was a 10-minute adaptation phase.[6] Recording of baseline levels of EMG took place during the next 10 minutes.

Informant rating. The Katz Adjustment Scale-Relative Form (KAS-R) (Katz & Lyerly, 1963) is an example of an inventory used to obtain information from the relative or close associate of the patient. Questions, administered by an interviewer, focus on the informant's direct observation of the patient for a three-week period prior to the actual interview. The items of the KAS-R cover several main areas: 1. ratings of symptoms and social behavior, 2. performance of socially expected behaviors, 3. relative's expectation for the performance of socially expected behaviors, and 4. satisfaction with free time activities. The KAS-R consists of 127 items, with items rated on a 1–4 point basis: 1. almost never, 2. sometimes, 3. often, 4. almost always. Listed below are two sample items from the KAS-R: No. 9 "Acts as if he doesn't have much energy;" no. 73 "Behavior is childish." A review of the literature by Hogarty (1975) indicates that both the reliability and validity of the scale are satisfactory.

Biochemical measure. Blood/alcohol concentration levels were assessed by Miller, Hersen, Eisler, and Watts (1974) by obtaining alveolar breath samples of their outpatient chronic alcoholic during the course of his experimental treatment for alcoholism. Throughout the research project the patient was telephoned at random intervals each week in order to determine his whereabouts. When located, a research assistant was sent to the patient's home or place of employment to administer the breath test. The patient's breath sample was collected at this time with an SM-7 Sobermeter (manufactured by Luckey Laboratories in San Bernadino, California), and was subsequently analyzed via gas chromatography in the hospital laboratory. During the study the patient's blood/alcohol concentration ranged from 0.00 to 0.27. To have an idea of the range, let us consider the following. If the patient were to drink seven ounces of whiskey in one hour, a blood/alcohol concentration of 0.11 percent would be attained (i.e., 110 mg. of alcohol/100ml. of blood).

Population statistics. An example of the demographic (i.e., background) characteristics of two groups of day hospital patients (Austin, Liberman, King, & DeRisi, 1976) appears in Table 3.2. An examination of the specific data in this table suggests that the patient composition of the Oxnard DTC and

Table 3.2. Background Characteristics of Patients at Oxnard DTC and DTC II Who Were Evaluated by Goal Attainment Scaling

Characteristics	Oxnard DTC (N = 30) %	DTC II (N = 26) %
Diagnosis[a]		
Schizophrenic	40.0	34.6
Manic-depressive	13.3	7.7
Neurotic (anxiety and depression)	36.7	46.2
Personality disorder	10.0	3.8
Substance abuse	0	7.7
Sex		
Male	43.3	46.2
Female	56.7	53.8
Education		
College	30.0	23.0
High school graduate	36.7	46.2
Some high school	26.7	23.1
No high school	6.6	7.7
Age		
16–30	53.3	61.5
31–40	16.7	15.5
41 and above	30.0	23.0
Marital status		
Single	53.3	57.7
Married	36.7	23.1
Divorced & separated	6.6	11.5
Widowed	3.4	7.7
Income		
Dependent (govt. support, family support)	86.7	80.8
Self-supporting	13.3	19.2
Previous hospitalization		
Yes	53.3	73.0
No	46.7	27.0
Median attendance		
Days in day treatment program	39.0	27.5

[a]Diagnoses were made by the clinical staff at the time of intake.
From Austin et al. (1976) (Table 1).

DTC II was similar, although obviously not identical. Close similarity of this kind is important, especially when the efficacy of two programs (as is the case here) is being contrasted. Therefore, any differences in outcome can be attributed to the superior efficacy of the one program and not patient differences in the two programs (see next section on Experimental Strategies).

Experimental strategies

Now that we have looked at the basic principles underlying the scientific method and have outlined some of the ways to measure abnormal behavior, an examination of experimental strategies used in the field of abnormal psychology is warranted. Although there are countless variations in strategy for evaluating abnormal phenomena, there are two basic methods that have been followed. One is the experiment in which cause-and-effect relationships can be determined. These experiments can answer questions such as: 1. Is Psychotherapy A more effective than Psychotherpay B for treating phobia? 2. Is Drug X better than Drug Y for reducing hallucinations? 3. Does introduction of a behavioral technique in a classroom for retardates decrease their out-of-seat behavior? 4. Does increase of stress level increase perceptual distortion in a laboratory task?

The second type of experiment is one in which the relationship or extent of correlation is ascertained. For example: 1. Is there a relationship between social class level and mental illness? 2. Is there a relationship between level of depression and degree of unexpressed hostility? 3. Is there a relationship between mental health of parents and that of their offspring? 4. Is there a relationship between anxiety and depression in those suffering from neurotic depression? 5. Are depressives more prone to suicide attempts than persons in other diagnostic categories?

In discussing the two basic experimental strategems, we will consider the issues of experimental design, confounding variables, statistical significance, and clinical significance. First, however, let us examine the basic features of experiments in which cause-and-effect relationships can be evaluated.

Cause-and-effect

In the cause-and-effect experiment, the investigator is able to demonstrate unequivocally that as a function of his procedure, some change in his abnormal subject has taken place. For example, the administration of antidepressant medication in a depressed patient should lead to a decrease in his depression over the course of several weeks.

Independent variable. In the above example, the *procedure* involves giving the patient antidepressant medication. In the language of experimental psychology, the procedure is commonly referred to as the *independent variable.* That is, the *independent variable* is the one that is under the *direct control* (manipulation) of the experimenter. He or she does or does not give the depressed subject antidepressant medication over the six-week study period.

Dependent variable. In our example, the change in depression in our patient is referred to as the *dependent variable.* It measures the effectiveness of the manipulation of the independent variable (e.g., the antidepressant drug). Following our example, a score on the Beck Depression Inventory is representative of a *dependent variable.* (As indicated in the previous section on Methods of Assessment, *dependent* measures include self-reports, motoric behavior, physiological responses, informant ratings and observations, and biochemical indices.)

Experimental hypothesis. Now that the reader is familiar with some of the basic language of experimental psychology, it will be useful to trace the history and development of a given experimental project. In so doing, we will continue with our example of antidepressant medication for the depressed patient.

Usually, an experiment is born out of an investigator's hypothesis that a given procedure will work in a particular way. In the field of abnormal psychology, this could come about as a result of theoretical speculation, follow-up of the work of others, or on the basis of clinical observation and practice. In our example, the investigator may have had success treating a number of depressed patients with a new antidepressant drug, but is interested in obtaining experimental confirmation of clinical impressions.

Experimental design

The objective of a good experimental design is to eliminate bias and to ensure that *valid* cause-and-effect conclusions are arrived at by the investigator. Thus, attempts are made to eliminate or control for possible confounding variables.

Let us, then, continue with our hypothetical study involving drugs. Our investigator now is ready to test the antidepressant with a larger group of depressives (20). To promote reliability, the drug should be administered under standardized conditions and to depressives who share common characteristics. To examine the effects of the drug, our investigator might compare Beck Depression Inventory (BDI) scores before and six weeks after treatment has started. However, even if major improvements (i.e., a decrease in BDI scores) are noted after six weeks, our investigator still could not, at this point, make unequivocal statements about the drug's efficacy. The reason for this is that other factors in the environment may have contributed to improvement. Mere passage of time could have led to improvement in addition to various life circumstances experienced by our 20 depressives. These kinds of factors are referred to as experimental confounds and interfere with the validity of the conclusions that can be reached (at this point the experiment is considered *internally invalid*).

Control groups. To improve the internal validity of this experiment, a control group of untreated patients bearing similar characteristics (e.g., age, sex, type, and duration of the depression) would have to be included. This group, then, would provide a six-week baseline period against which the experimental group might be contrasted. Thus, the control group would be given the BDI at the same time as the drug treatment group (comparable periods to pretreatment and six weeks posttreatment).

To further ensure comparability of the treated (experimental) and untreated (control) patients, one of two strategies might be followed. One might be to match the two groups of 20 depressed patients on each of the relevant demographic variables. Of course, this approach is time-consuming, tedious, and often costly. A second approach might involve randomly assigning the 40 depressed patients to the two groups by a flip of the coin. This is known as *random assignment,* whereby possible confounding factors are presumed to distribute equally between the two groups.

At this point in our experiment, even if there were significant differences between the two groups in favor of the experimental group, the validity of the conclusions reached might still be challenged. Indeed, there are at least two confounds remaining in this experiment. The *first* concerns the fact that patients in the experimental group are ingesting a substance. The simple act of ingesting a substance is often sufficient to lead the subject to expect improvement. This is known as a "placebo" effect (how often have we felt better immediately after taking an aspirin before its actual chemical effect could conceivably take place?). In all drug research and in most psychotherapy research, in addition to an untreated control group, a second control group known as a "placebo" control is added.

In our drug study, an additional 20 depressives would be assigned to the placebo group (either matching or relevant demographic variables or randomly assigned to this group and the other control and experimental groups). The placebo subjects would receive the same number of pills (with identical coloring, markings, and shape), with the exception that an inert (inactive) substance would be substituted for the drug. Thus, the placebo condition serves as a control for the patient's expectation of improvement unrelated to the active ingredients in the treatment proper.

A final confound remaining in our experiment, as it stands now, is that both the investigator and the patients are aware of the fact that they are or are not receiving an active drug. Therefore, it is possible that either the expectation of the investigator or the expectation of the patients may serve to bias the results. To counteract this kind of bias, a "double-blind" procedure is followed. Here, both the individual administering the drugs or placebos and the patients themselves are purposely kept *unaware* as to whether an *active drug* or *placebo pill* is being administered.

Given all the aforementioned controls and procedures, now we have an *internally valid* experiment that is capable of yielding useful data and, of course, valid conclusions.

Group comparison studies. Our hypothetical drug treatment investigation is representative of research generally categorized as the group comparison approach. In these studies experimental hypotheses are evaluated by contrasting relatively large groups of subjects (usually at least 10 or more per group). However, it might be misleading to the reader if an impression is left that only treatment (psychotherapy or drug) is evaluated in the group comparison method. Quite to the contrary, evaluation of treatment represents only a very small fraction of the studies in abnormal psychology involving group comparisons. Indeed, most evaluations of cognitive, behavioral, attitudinal, physiological, and perceptual processes in psychopathology typically are made by contrasting various groups of subjects. Included are comparisons of different abnormal populations (e.g., Hersen, Levine, & Church, 1972), comparisons between abnormals and normals (e.g., Saccuzzo & Miller, 1977), comparisons within abnormal populations but at differing levels of psychopathology (e.g., Hersen, 1971a), and sex differences in psychopathology (e.g., Katkin & Hoffman, 1976). The aforementioned are just a few of the numerous research possibilities in which the group comparison approach has been carried out.

Statistical significance

We previously have referred to the term statistical significance, but have not defined it. This is an important term, as statistical procedures are carried out in group comparison studies to determine which of the groups showed the greatest effect. Many kinds of statistical procedures have been developed by statisticians, depending on the nature of the research problem and the particular experimental design employed. However, for comparing the magnitude of the difference between two groups (e.g., experimental versus control), a *t* test is typically used. For the evaluation of differences among three contrasted groups (e. g., experimental, no treatment control, placebo control), an analysis of variance procedure is often followed (see Winer, 1962).

When the results of research investigations are presented in journal articles, we often see the following sentence: "There were *significant differences* between the experimental and control groups in favor of the experimentals." This means that there was a low probability that the difference obtained between experimentals and controls were due to chance. There is always a possibility, even in the best experiment, that the results were accidental, or due to chance. The lower the probability of chance results (as determined by statistical analyses), the greater the probability that the results were produced by the independent variable. The convention in psychological research is that a difference is considered statistically significant if the likelihood is less than 5 in 100 that it was a function of chance. In journal articles, this is referred to as the .05 level of significance and is presented as $p<.05$.

Clinical and social significance

There is an important distinction that needs to be made between the concepts of statistical significance and that of clinical and social significance. For example, it is quite possible that the differences between two groups might be small (e.g., 2–3 points on the BDI), but nonetheless are significant when evaluated statistically. However, despite the presence of statistical significance, the clinical and/or social significance of this small difference is minimal. Thus, this kind of difference that is statistically significant yet clinically insignificant represents little of practical value (see Kazdin, 1977). Indeed, the important research findings in the field of abnormal psychology tend to be those that are both statistically significant and clinically and socially meaningful.

Clinically significant results have been reported in studies where clients whose behaviors represent severe excesses or deficiencies are brought to within acceptable or "normal" levels of performance after treatment. For example, O'Connor (1972) developed social interaction in withdrawn nursery school children using modeling or modeling combined with reinforcement. Prior to treatment, the children were well below the level of their nonwithdrawn peers in such behaviors as proximity and visual and verbal contact with peers. After treatment, social interaction of the trained children surpassed the level of their nonwithdrawn peers, an effect that was maintained up to six weeks of follow-up. Bringing the withdrawn children to normal levels of interaction suggests that a truly important change was made in treatment.

External validity

One additional point needs to be made in terms of group comparison designs. This is in reference to the *external validity* of the experiment. We already have discussed the importance of achieving internal validity in experimental work by including relevant control conditions in an investigation. External validity, on the other hand, refers to the generalizability of the results of any given experiment. For example, is there a relationship between results obtained under laboratory conditions and those seen in the subject's natural environment? Also, can the results in one experiment in a given laboratory be replicated in a second experiment in a different laboratory? In the absence of such generalization of results, a specific study cannot be said to have external validity. Under these circumstances, the conclusions reached on the basis of one study would not enjoy wide applicability.

Single case research

Cause-and-effect relationships can also be demonstrated in single case research designs. In this type of research strategy the subject serves as his own control. That is, baseline[7] phases are contrasted to phases in which treatment is administered. Baseline phases are labeled as A, and treatment phases are labeled as B. Although single case research is primarily devoted to evaluation of treatment techniques (see Hersen & Barlow, 1976), other aspects of psychopathology can be investigated (e.g., Hersen, Miller, & Eisler, 1973).

A-B-A-B designs

The A-B-A-B design is the prototype of single case research. During baseline (A), several repeated measurements (usually three or more) are made of the behavior targeted for change. Then in phase B, treatment is introduced. In this phase, several additional measurements of the targeted behavior are taken. If the targeted measure is one that is slated for decrease and shows that trend in the B phase, then there is a *suggestion* that treatment is having its desired effect. However, to *confirm* the fact that treatment is causing the decrease (rather than some other factor), baseline conditions are reinstated in the next phase. If indeed treatment initially caused the decrease, then a reversed trend should appear when it is withdrawn in the second A phase. (This procedure is often referred to as a reversal or withdrawal phase.) Next, treatment is reinstated in the second B phase, thus providing a second confirmation of its controlling effects over the targeted behavior if once again it decreases.

An excellent illustration of the A-B-A-B design appears in a study conducted by Hall, Fox, Willard, Goldsmith, Emerson, Owen, Davis, and Porcia (1971). Here the effects of contingent teacher attention (i.e., the treatment) were examined on the "talking-out" behavior of a 10-year-old retarded boy attending special education classes.

Number of "talk-outs" in class during five daily 15-minute sessions was the targeted measure for change (i.e., the dependent variable). Examination of Figure 3.1 indicates that "talk-outs" ranged from three to five in baseline. In the B phase (Contingent Attention 1) the teacher ignored "talk-outs" but paid more attention to the boy's positive

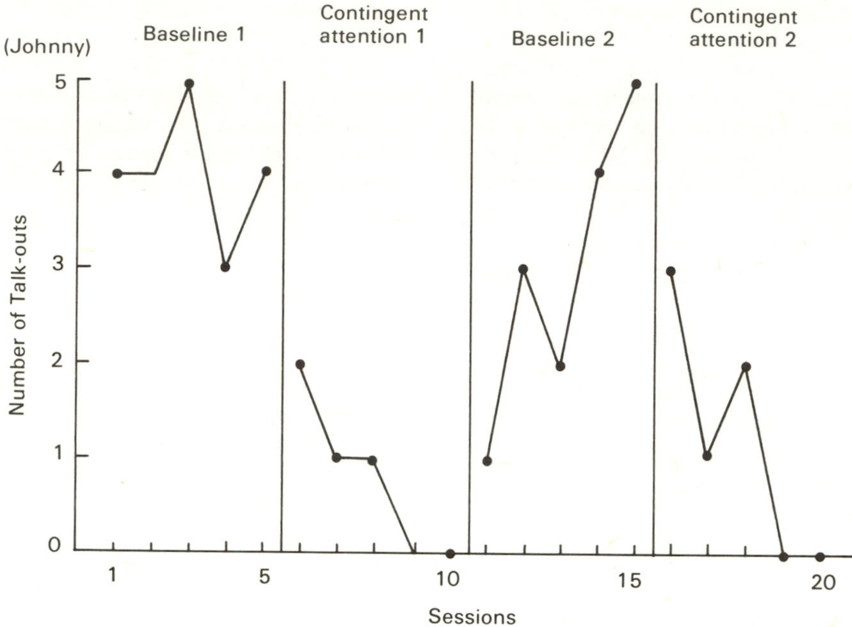

Fig. 3.1. A record of talking-out behavior of an educable, mentally retarded student. Baseline_1, before experimental conditions. Contingent Teacher Attention_1, systematic ignoring of talking-out and increased teacher attention to appropriate behavior. Baseline_2, reinstatement of teacher attention to talking-out behavior. Contingent Teacher Attention_2, return to systematic ignoring of talking-out and increased attention to appropriate behavior. (From Hall et al., 1971, Figure 2.)

behaviors, resulting in a decrease in "talk-outs" to 0 in sessions 9 and 10. In the subsequent return to A (Baseline 2), the teacher once again responded as she did in the initial baseline (i.e., paid attention to "talk-outs"). Data in sessions 11–15 evidence a marked increase in "talk-outs" to a high of five. However, reinstitution of Contingent Attention 2 (second B) once again led to a decrease in "talk-outs" to 0 in sessions 19 and 20. Hersen and Barlow (1976), commenting on this study, point out: "Thus, application and withdrawal of teacher attention clearly demonstrates its controlling effects on "talk-out" behavior. This is twice-documented as seen in the decreasing and increasing data trends in the second set of A and B phases" (p. 183).

We might note that in most single case research, especially when the data are as clear as those in Hall et al. (1971), results are analyzed by visual inspection. However, when the trends in the data are not as apparent, statistical techniques developed for single case analyses are employed (see Kazdin, 1976).

Multiple baseline design

There are instances when A-B-A-B designs are not feasible. One such instance is when self-injurious behavior (e.g., head-banging in psychotic children) is being treated, as withdrawal in the second A phase poses a moral dilemma. A second instance is when treatments are used involving irreversible procedures such as therapeutic instructions. Once instructions are given, they really cannot be withdrawn or reversed as in the case of "contingent attention."

The multiple baseline design, however, serves to circumvent the above mentioned limitations. In this design, several (usually three or more) independent (unrelated) behaviors within an individual are targeted for treatment. Following initial baseline (A) assessment, treatment (B) is then applied to the first targeted behavior. After treatment appears to have taken effect, but no changes are noted in the remaining untreated baselines, then the same treatment is applied to the second targeted behavior. The study continues until all of the targeted measures have been treated in turn. Elsewhere, the multiple baseline design has been described as follows: "Baseline and subsequent treatment interventions for each targeted behavior can be conceptualized as separate A-B designs, with the A phase further extended for each of the succeeding behaviors until the treatment variable is finally applied . . . the effects of the treatment variable are inferred from the untreated behaviors" (Hersen & Barlow, 1976, pp. 226–227).

Let us now illustrate the use of this design in a study in which social skills treatment was applied to an unassertive eight-year-old girl (Bornstein, Bellack, & Hersen, 1977). During the baseline assessment, the child's responses to role-played scenes requiring assertive responses were videotaped. Examination of Figure 3.2 shows that eye contact was very low, as was loudness of speech, number of requests, and ratings of overall assertiveness.

Social skills treatment, consisting of instructions, feedback, rehearsal, and social reinforcement (encouragement) from the therapist was first directed to increasing eye contact. As the reader will see, eye contact improved substantially when treatment was applied. However, *no changes* in the untreated behaviors were noted. Next, treatment was directed to increasing loudness of speech. Again, improvement for this behavior appeared, but no change in number of requests was seen. Finally, treatment was specifically directed to increasing the child's number of requests in role-played scenes. Overall assertiveness, not specifically treated, increased as each of the targeted behaviors was treated in sequence. Also, two and four week follow-ups after completion of treatment indicated that improvements were maintained.

As should be apparent, the graph shows that when, and only when, treatment was applied to the targeted behavior, then improvements in that behavior were observed. It is highly unlikely that some other factor affected each behavior when and only when treatment was applied. Thus, the controlling effects of social skills treatment over the targeted behaviors was demonstrated in this single case analysis.

Other design strategies

There are dozens of other design strategies used during the course of single case research. However, the A-B-A-B and multiple baseline strategies are the two most frequently followed by investigators. The reader interested in becoming familiar with the other design strategies is referred to the monograph by Hersen and Barlow (1976).

Advantages and limitations

We should point out that single case research designs are somewhat limited by the fact that there are no control conditions (other than baseline) and that the effects may be limited to one subject (unless the study is replicated with additional subjects). Nonetheless, they are useful. Indeed, very powerful and dramatic treatment effects have been noted during the course of single case research.

The following are some of the advantages of the single case approach to research. *First,* single case research is useful in showing the controlling effects of various treatments. *Second,* the single case research approach has proven advantageous in pilot work, particular in generating hypotheses that can later be tested in large-scale group comparison designs. *Third,* in contrast to the group comparison approach, the single case strategy is economical. *Fourth,* the single case approach is flexible inasmuch as

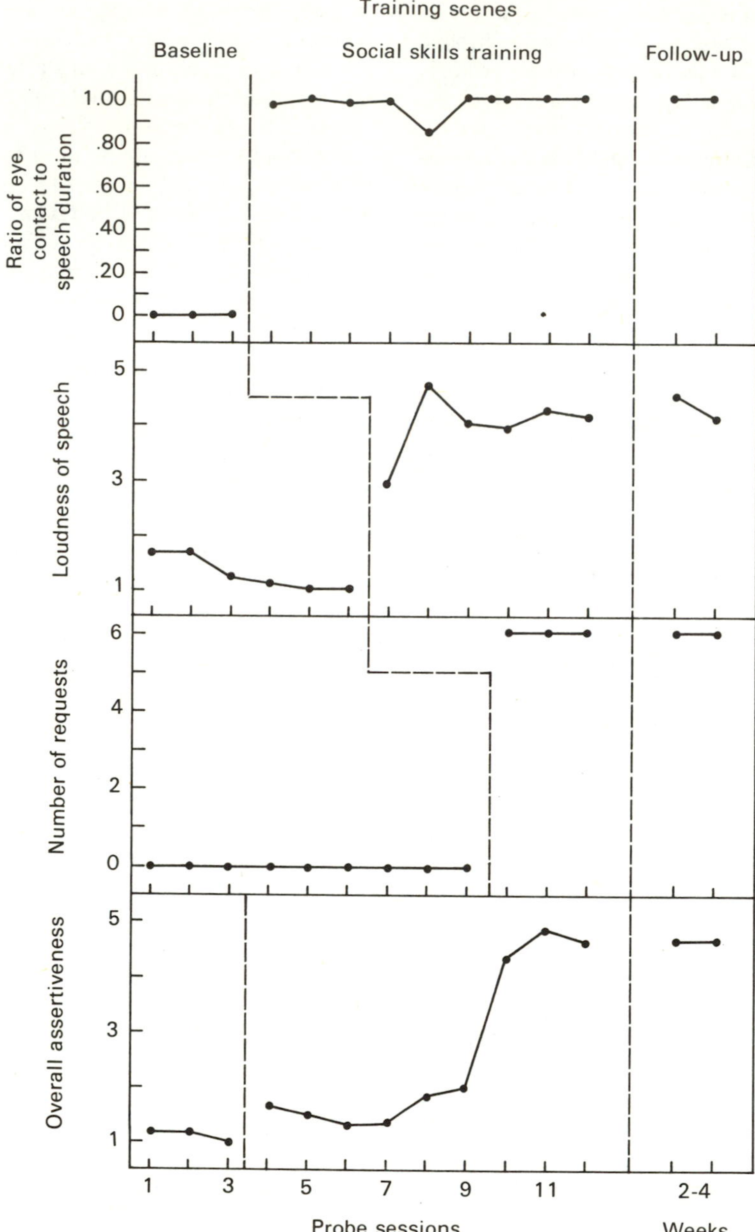

Fig. 3.2. Probe sessions during baseline, social skills treatment, and follow-up for *training* scenes for Jane. A multiple baseline analysis of: ratio of eye contact to speech duration, loudness of speech, number of requests, and overall assertiveness. (From Bornstein et al., 1977, Figure 1.)

changes in treatment can easily be instituted without interfering with a predetermined research plan, as would be the case in group comparison designs. *Fifth,* the clinical import of changes is easily depicted through the graphic analysis in single case work. And *sixth,* the single case research approach permits the investigator to evaluate treatments for the rare disorders, where insufficient numbers of subjects are available for study in group comparison designs (e.g., Turner, Hersen, & Alford, 1974).

Correlational analyses

A totally different approach to research is the correlational method. Here, instead of examining cause-and-effect relationships and manipulating independent variables, the investigator is concerned with the extent of relationship between two variables.

There are several statistical procedures for evaluating the correlation between variables. One of the most frequently used techniques is known as the Pearson Product-Moment Correlation Coefficient. This statistic permits an evaluation of both the extent of strength relationship (r = 0.00 to 1.00) and the direction or nature of the relationship (+ = positive, − = negative). An r of 0.00 indicates there is *no* relationship between the two variables. An r of 0.25 indicates that there is a low relationship between the two variables. An r of 0.90 indicates that there is a very high relationship between the two variables. Finally, an r of + 1.00 indicates a perfect positive relationship. A positive relationship is one in which an increase in one variable is associated with an increase in the other (e.g., height and weight). With a negative correlation, an increase in one variable is associated with a decrease in the other (e.g., obesity and longevity).

For the sake of clarity, we will present a hypothetical example of a perfect positive and a perfect negative correlation. In Table 3.3 the reader will note that 20 subjects took tests A, B, C, and D. An evaluation of the relationship between scores on A and B indicates a perfect positive correlation (r = +1.00). By contrast, an evaluation of the relationship between scores on C and D indicates a perfect negative correlation (r = −1.00).

Table 3.3. Positive and Negative Correlations

Subject	Test A	Test B	Test C	Test D
1	60	70	89	60
2	61	71	88	61
3	62	72	87	62
4	63	73	86	63
5	64	74	85	64
6	65	75	84	65
7	66	76	83	66
8	67	77	82	67
9	68	78	81	68
10	69	79	80	69
11	70	80	79	70
12	71	81	78	71
13	72	82	77	72
14	73	83	76	73
15	74	84	75	74
16	75	85	74	75
17	76	86	73	76
18	77	87	72	77
19	78	88	71	78
20	79	89	70	79
	r = +1.00		r = −1.00	

As is the case for all statistical procedures, the significance of the correlation can be computed. Once again, the reader will recall that the convention in psychological research is that significance is defined by a probability of less than 5 in 100 that the relationship was due to chance ($p < .05$). It should be noted that in correlational work, given the same correlation coefficient (e.g., r = +0.50), the greater number of cases, the higher the likelihood that the correlation will be significant. Thus, although a correlation of +0.50 *is not significant* with five cases, the same correlation with 15 cases *is significant* ($p < .05$).

At times, the researcher may be interested in looking at how several variables correlate with one another. This was the case in a study conducted by Hersen (1971b). In this study, male and female psychiatric patients were administered several psychological tests (1. Ego-Strength Scale,

2. Taylor Manifest Anxiety Scale [TMAS], 3. Fear of Death Scale, 4. Fear Scale, and 5. Fear Inventory). The relationship of the scores obtained is presented in Table 3.4. This table is referred to as a correlational matrix. For example, in Table 3.4, the relationship between Ego-Strength and the TMAS for males is −0.72. The relationship between the Fear Scale and Fear Inventory for females is +0.81. Examination of the table reveals both positive and negative correlations, with all relationships attaining statistical significance ($p < .01$).

When interpreting a correlation, the reader should be aware that a given relationship between two variables *does not* imply causation. This is an important concept to keep in mind, as a given correlation between two sets of data might be accounted for by a third or yet fourth variable not controlled in the correlational analysis. Let us consider the following example. If in a large city there is a high relationship between number of crimes committed per year and the proportion of the population belonging to a given ethnic group, does it mean that being a member of that ethnic group causes criminality? Absolutely not! It may very well be that because of a third variable (e.g., low socioeconomic status) associated with that particular ethnic group, there then is an increased rate of crime. Any correlation coefficient must be interpreted with extreme caution in order to avoid erroneous conclusions.

Finally, it must be pointed out that even though a study is evaluated in a group comparison design with group comparison statistics (e.g., *t*-tests, analyses of variance procedures), it does not automatically imply that a cause-and-effect relationship has been established. For example, consider the experiment where a group of depressives and a group of normals are contrasted on a simple motor task. Let us also assume that the normals do better on this task. Often, with this type of experiment, both the investigator and/or the reader do not recognize that this is an example of correlational research. That is, the investigator has not directly manipulated the "presumed" independent variable (depression vs. normality). To the contrary, depression and normality are givens in this experiment. Subjects were so classified before they entered the psychological laboratory for their evaluations on the motor task. Thus, this study really indicates the specific correlation between depression and the motor task and normality and the motor task through the use of noncorrelational statistical analyses.

Types of studies

As the reader should recognize by now, the field of abnormal psychology is extensive. There are many theoretical, clinical, and empirical issues that are repeatedly tackled by dedicated investigators. Many of these issues will be evaluated in greater detail in the following chapters. However, at this point, we wish to acquaint the student with some of the representative areas that researchers have considered by describing one study in each of the following areas: 1. epidemiology, 2. behavioral assessment, 3. psychiatric diagnosis, 4. genetic determinants of psychiatric disorder, and 5. psychotherapeutic treatment of abnormal behavior.

Epidemiology

Epidemiology in the field of abnormal psychology refers to the study of a particular disorder (e.g., schizophrenia, phobia, depression) within a specific population (e.g., town, section of a city, city). As we previously noted in the section on population statistics, the researcher may be concerned with *incidence* and/or *prevalence* statistics.

Since epidemiological studies generally are extremely time-consuming and are difficult to accomplish for technical reasons, most epidemiologists tend to canvass a small portion of a given population. An excellent example of this is the classic Midtown Manhattan Study (Langer & Michael, 1963), in which a representative sample of New York City was assessed for the presence and ex-

Table 3.4. Intercorrelations Among Scales for Males (N = 160), Females (N = 191), and Total Group (N = 231)

Variable	2	3	4	5
1. Ego-Strength				
Males	−.72	−.40	−.41	−.41
Females	−.77	−.56	−.58	−.51
Total	−.75	−.49	−.51	−.48
2. TMAS				
Males		.45	.46	.42
Females		.61	.60	.52
Total		.54	.52	.46
3. Death Scale				
Males			.54	.48
Females			.54	.43
Total			.53	.44
4. Fear Scale (FSS-11)				
Males				.78
Females				.81
Total				.81
5. Fear Inventory (FSS-111)				

$p < .01$ for all data shown
From Hersen (1971b) (Table 1).

tent of psychological disturbance. Another example of epidemiological research appeared in the equally well-known Hollingshead and Redlich (1958) study. There, the relationship of mental illness and social class was examined in the city of New Haven, Connecticut.

A somewhat more recent epidemiological investigation was conducted by Agras, Sylvester, and Oliveau (1969) in Burlington, Vermont. In this study the objective was to determine the incidence and prevalence of common fears and phobias in a segment of the population. It was decided to interview a probability sample of the households in the Burlington area. Institutionalized individuals, of course, were excluded from the sample. Of the attempts to interview the representative sample (1/193 of the households in Burlington), 94 percent of the interviews proved successful, yielding a final total of 325 people.

An interview schedule was constructed that listed 40 commonly feared situations. Included were questions concerning the duration and intensity of the feared situation, as well as queries related to attempts at seeking treatment for those fears that reached phobic dimensions. Each of the 325 respondents was interviewed at length by a well-trained interviewer.

Although many interesting findings emerged from this excellent study, the most critical finding was that involving prevalence. Indeed, contrary to other findings, total prevalence of phobia turned out to be considerably greater than previously estimated. Agras et al. (1969) estimate total prevalence at 76.9 per 1000 population. Of this number, 74.7 per 1000 population were described as "mildly disabled." The number was much smaller for those labeled "severely disabled" (2.2 per 1000 population). Absence from work for those employed and inability to carry out household duties for housewives and the unemployed served as the operational definition of "severely disabled." Agras et al, (1969) concluded that similar to other studies concerned with neurotic populations, "the bulk of the population is affected by the mildest condition, namely common fears, while mild phobias affect a significant but lesser portion of the population, and severe disabling phobias are much less common" (p. 154).

Behavioral assessment

The study conducted by Eisler, Hersen, Miller, and Blanchard (1975) on situational determinants of assertive behavior is an example of a behavioral assessment investigation. It also is an illustration of analogue assessment in that behavioral observations were made on the basis of role played responses rather than on observation of behavior in the natural environment. Specifically, 60 hospitalized male psychiatric patients were asked to respond via role playing to 32 situations designed to elicit assertive responses. The 32 situations were varied such that one-half involved female role partners and one-half invovled male role partners. In addition, the situational context was varied by having role partners portray familiar and unfamiliar individuals.

Responses to the 32 situations were videotaped and rated by one set of judges on seven nonverbal measures (e.g., duration of eye contact, number of smiles) and five verbal content measures (e.g., praise, compliance). A second set of judges rated all the responses to the role partners' prompts on the basis of overall assertiveness, using a 1–5 point scale. High and low assertive groups (top third; bottom third) were then contrasted with respect to the 12 measures of interpersonal behavior. None of these 12 measures yielded significant differences between the two groups. More importantly, however, results of several analyses of variance indicated that behavior in the 32 situations was largely a function of the interpersonal context (i.e., positive versus. negative, male versus. female role partner, unfamiliar versus. familiar individual). Also, high and low assertive subjects, differentiated on the basis of behavioral ratings, were significantly different with respect to their self-reports of assertive behavior. That is, there was a significant relationship between self-reports of assertiveness and actual responding in the role played behavioral task.

Psychiatric diagnosis

As should be apparent from Chapter 2, there has been difficulty in developing a universally accepted diagnostic scheme that is both functional and reliable. The imprecision of psychiatric diagnosis has been particularly troublesome to researchers in the field of abnormal psychology. However, there have been some more recent attempts to minimize human error in classifying patients by relying on objective correlates of the various diagnostic categories. One promising strategy uses motor activity as an indicator of affective states such as depression and mania (e.g., Kupfer, Foster, Detre, & Himmelhoch, 1975). Another approach has consisted of monitoring all night electroencephalographic (EEG) sleep patterns of patients bearing different diagnostic labels (Coble, Foster, & Kupfer, 1976; Reich, Weiss, Coble, McPartland, & Kupfer, 1975). Indeed, the latency of total rapid eye movement (REM)[8] sleep has proven to be particularly useful in differentiating categories of patients and subcategories within specific diagnostic entities.

Let us now consider one such study. Coble et al. (1976) assessed 40 outpatients referred for 2 consecutive nights of sleep diagnostic studies with respect to their depressive symptoms. Each of the 40 outpatients was interviewed and given a number of self-report scales to fill out. Six months following this evaluation, the patients were divided into categories of primary (N = 15) and secondary (N = 25) depressives on the basis of independent follow-up diagnoses. Primary depression meant that there was no previous psychiatric disorder other than the possibility of depression or mania. Secondary depression meant that the current depression was "superimposed on a preexisting" psychiatric or medical diagnosis other than mania or depression.

The results of this study appear in Table 3.5 and reveal the following: 1. REM latency

Table 3.5. Electroencephalographic Sleep in Primary and Secondary Depressives Differences between Means of Nights 1 and 2)

Sleep		Primary (n = 15)	Secondary (n = 25)
Time spent asleep total recording period (percent)	75.6 ± 4.2	84.1 ± 2.2	NS*
Time spent asleep (min)	304.6 ± 17.8	330.6 ± 10.6	NS
REM latency (min)	48.9 ± 5.7	78.4 ± 4.8	< .0001
Stage 1 REM (percent)	20.9 ± 1.4	18.3 ± 0.9	NS
REM activity/time spent asleep (ratio)	0.42 ± 0.1	0.26 ± 0.02	< .002
REM activity/REM time (ratio)	2.0 ± 0.1	1.4 ± 0.1	< .002
Stage 1 (percent)	7.9 ± 0.8	8.9 ± 1.3	NS
Stage 2 (percent)	65.8 ± 2.6	67.0 ± 1.9	NS
Stage 2 REM (percent)	1.0 ± 0.2	0.5 ± 0.1	< .05
Delta (percent)	4.4 ± 2.1	5.3 ± 1.4	NS
Clinical ratings			
Depression	24.8 ± 2.9	24.0 ± 2.8	NS
Anxiety	13.5 ± 2.7	11.0 ± 1.5	NS

*Not significant
From Coble et al. (1976) (Table 1).

was significantly greater for primary depression, 2. The REM activity/time-spent-asleep ratio was significantly greater for primary depressives, 3. The REM activity/REM-time ratio was significantly greater for primary depressives, and 4. Stage 2 sleep REM percent was significantly greater for primary depressives.

These findings have particular import as there were no significant differences in clinical ratings of depression and anxiety between the primary and secondary depressives (see Table 3.5). In summary, this study shows that "the delineation of primary versus. secondary depression was greater than 80 percent on the basis of only two nights of sleep" (Coble et al, 1976, p. 1126).

Genetic determinants

In recent years, the old nature-nurture (genetic vs. environment) controversy has been revived as a result of the increased attention given to the study of genetic determinants of psychiatric disorder. In several studies, evidence for the genetic transmission of schizophrenia (e.g., Holzman, Kringlen, Levy, Proctor, Haberman, & Yasillo, 1977), depression (Allen, 1976), and alcoholism (Goodwin, Schulsinger, Hermansen, Guze, & Winokur, 1973) has appeared. Investigators concerned with genetic factors have followed a number of research strategies (see Stabenau, 1977, for an excellent review).

One strategy involves comparing the concordance rates (i.e., correlations) in monozygotic (identical) twins, dyzygotic (nonidentical) twins, siblings, and other family relationships. A given disorder such as schizophrenia is selected. Evaluation of psychiatric histories of the index case (the case so afflicted) and that of the relatives is accomplished. If indeed there is a genetic factor, the closer the genetic ties (e.g., monozygotic versus dysygotic twins), the greater the concordance rates. For example, if there is presence of schizophrenia in one monozygotic twin, presence of schizophrenia in the second monozygotic twin should occur more frequently than in the case of dyzygotic twins. Although such evidence is interesting, the reader should be aware that this is an example of correlational research. Obviously, no independent variable (i.e., genes) was experimentally manipulated.

A second method is to study rare cases where one twin or other sibling has been raised by his biological parents, while the other one has been raised by adopted parents. Presumably, if the disorder has a genetic basis, incidence rates should not differ significantly for those raised by biological and adopted parents.

A third strategy is to study the offspring of biological parents who have a given disorder raised by adopted parents who do not have the disorder. These offspring should then be contrasted to different, but matched adoptees whose biological and adopted parents *do not* have the given disorder. If there is genetic transmission, the presence of the disorder should be greater in those offspring of the biological parents who had the disorder themselves than in the control subjects. This is exactly the type of study that was conducted by Goodwin et al. (1973). They contrasted 55 men who had at least one biological parent diagnosed alcoholic with a matched group of 77 men where neither biological parent was an alcoholic. Both groups of men had been adopted out early in life.

Evaluation of many variables in these two groups revealed the following: 1. Children of alcoholics had four times the alcoholism rate of children of nonalcoholics, 2. children of alcoholics had three times the divorce rate of children of nonalcoholics, 3. and aside from the aforementioned, none of the differences was significant for any of the other demographic variables studied.

Although these differences are interesting, and they do suggest the *possibility* of genetic transmission, the data represent the product of correlational research. Again, it should be underscored that no variable was experimentally manipulated. Caution should be exercised in making cause-and-effect statements.

Psychotherapy outcome

Sloane, Staples, Cristol, Yorkston, and Whipple (1976) compared the effects of psychotherapy (N = 30), behavior therapy (N = 30), and a waiting list condition (N = 34) for 94 neurotic and personality disordered patients. Assignment to these three groups was done on a random basis. Patients in each of the two active treatment conditions were seen for four months. Therapists for each of the treatment conditions were matched on the basis of experience (ranging from 6 to 20 years), with three therapists assigned to each treatment condition. Each therapist treated 10 patients.

The psychotherapy condition involved short-term, time-limited, analytically oriented treatment. Behavior therapy, also time-limited, involved the administration of a variety of standard behavioral strategies (e.g., desensitization, assertive training) at the discretion of the therapist. Waiting list patients were simply placed on a waiting list and periodically contacted by a research assistant.

Each of the 94 patients was assessed initially at four months and then at one year by one of three experienced psychiatrists not directly involved with treatment aspects of the study. These psychiatrists (i.e., assessors) were "blind" as to which treatment group a given patient was assigned. Patients were evaluated as to target symptoms, MMPI, Eysenck Personality Inventory, and the California Psychological Inventory.

In general, both of the treatment groups showed significantly more improvement than the waiting list controls. Psychotherapy yielded the greatest effect with patients of higher socioeconomic status and for those who evidenced lower levels of psychopathology on the MMPI. On the other hand, behavior therapy seemed most effective with patients who were high on Hysteria and Mania scales of the MMPI.

Sloane et al. (1976) conclude in part that: "These results suggest that patient selection may be less critical for success in behavior therapy than in psychotherapy. The behavioral approach may be suitable for a broader range of patients. . . . Thus, for certain patients, psychotherapy may be more effective than behavior therapy. . . . Behavior therapy may be the treatment of choice for patients with acting-out tendencies and more severe pathology" (p. 338).

Summary

This chapter has considered empirical methods in the study of the behavior disorders. The student was first presented with a description of the scientific method as applied to abnormal psychology. Definitions and examples of testability, reliability, standardization, and validity were given in addition to a brief discussion of ethical practices in the field. Next, the methods for assessing abnormal behavior were reviewed. Specific examples of self-reports, motor responses, physiological responses, informant ratings and observations, biochemical measures, and population statistics followed a more general description of these categories. Then, we considered the two basic strategies followed in conducting research in abnormal psychology: 1. cause-and-effect experiments and 2. correlational analyses. With respect to cause-and-effect experiments, issues related to group comparison studies and single case research were outlined. The questions of control groups and statistical and clinical significance also were given some attention. Particular concern was directed to the limitation of conclusions that can be made on the basis of correlational analyses. Finally, examples were presented of the different types of studies carried out by investigators in the field of abnormal psychology. Included were studies categorized as: 1. epidemiological, 2. behavioral assessment, 3. diagnostic, 4. genetic determinants of psychiatric disorder, and 5. psychotherapy outcome.

NOTES

1. In this system, the individual's speech electronically triggers the recording mechanism, thus permitting a reliable assessment of number of speech sequences and total speech duration within an allotted time segment.
2. Interactive behaviors describes a situation where two or more individuals are engaged in verbal or physical interaction with one another.
3. In this type of study, responses in several physiological systems may be monitored concurrently during alternating baseline and experimental (e.g., stress conditions) phases in one subject.
4. Scores are obtained for each of the scales, but the pattern of scores (i.e., pattern analysis) is important for an accurate interpretation of the results.
5. As noted by Elkin et al. (1973), "Anorexia nervosa, a disorder characterized by extensive weight loss preceded by disgust for food and a marked decrease in caloric intake, is found in the absence of contributing physical antecedents. Vomiting and diarrhea frequently are part of the clinical syndrome or result when food is forced, thus making further caloric intake even more aversive" (p. 75).
6. In most work involving physiological assessments, adaptation periods are required in order to acclimate the subject to his or her surroundings and to the electronic equipment attached to him or her.
7. Baseline refers to the natural frequency of the targeted behavior observed and recorded before treatment is introduced.
8. REM sleep has been associated with episodes of dreaming during which time rapid eye movements are evident. Such REM periods recur approximately every 90 minutes during the course of normal sleep.

GLOSSARY

Blood/alcohol concentration (BAC): A biochemical measure that determines the mg. level of alcohol per 100 ml. of blood. This can be approximated by taking breath samples and analyzing the contents via gas chromatography.

Correlational analysis: An experimental strategy whereby the relationship of two or more variables can be determined. Positive and negative relationships are possible, with values of the correlation ranging from 0.00 to 1.00.

Demographic variable: Refers to the background characteristics of a given population under study. Included are age, sex, diagnosis, marital status, income, socioeconomic status, etc.

Dependent variable: The target behavior measured (e.g., motoric, self-report, physiological) as a function of a manipulation in the independent variable.

Double-blind: A procedure followed in drug research whereby neither the patient nor the physician in aware of whether the pill given contains active medication or an inert substance. Thus, the experimental confounds of doctor and patient expectancy for improvement can be controlled.

Dyzygotic twin: A genetically nonidentical twin (i.e., developed from two fertilized eggs).

Epidemiology: The study of incidence and prevalence of a particular disorder in a circumscribed population.

Incidence: The rate of *new cases* of a given disorder within a circumscribed place and time.

Independent variable: The variable that is manipulated and is under experimental control in a cause-and-effect experiment.

Inter-observer agreement: The relationship or reliability of observations of a targeted behavior by two independent observers. Computed by dividing the smaller sum by the larger sum and expressed as a percentage score.

Lithium carbonate: A naturally occurring element (no. 3 on the periodic table) effectively used in the treatment of manic-depressive disorder and in some of the depressions.

Minnesota Multiphasic Personality Inventory (MMPI): A 566-item, true-false inventory used in determining an individual's psychiatric diagnosis. Scores are evaluated on the basis of a pattern analysis.

Monozygotic twin: A genetically identical twin (i.e., developed from the same fertilized egg).

Multiple baseline: A single case research strategy in which independent behaviors within an individual are targeted for treatment on a sequential basis.

Permanent products measure: A measure obtained by reading a gauge (e.g., pounds on a scale), which represents a definitive change as a result of some procedure (e.g., weight change directly due to dieting).

Placebo group: In drug research a group (receiving an inert substance) that controls for the effect of ingesting a substance in the active drug treatment condition. In psychotherapy research a group (receiving an inert therapy) that controls for the attention obtained in the active treatment condition.

Prevalence: The percentage of a population under study that has a particular disorder at a given time. If in a population of 1000, 100 are classified as having disorder X, then the prevalence of disorder X is 10 percent.

Reliability: The extent to which an observation or effect can be reproduced under standardized conditions (e.g., at different times, by different individuals, in different laboratories, in different hospitals). Degrees of reproducibility range from 0 to 100 percent.

Reversal phase: The second A (baseline) phase in A-B-A-B design during which time the active treatment is withdrawn.

Standardization: One of the basic tenets of the scientific method whereby precise conditions of a procedure (e.g., test, therapy) are specified in order to ensure complete comparability from one administration to the next.

Statistical significance: In psychological research refers to a finding that has less than a 5 percent probability that it was due to chance. Usually expressed as follows ($p < .05$).

Testability: In psychological research an hypothesis that is capable of being confirmed or disconfirmed through an experimental analysis.

Validity: The degree or extent to which the results of a given test or procedure can be attributed to its administration. There are several types of validity including "face," "concurrent," and "predictive" validity.

DETERMINANTS OF BEHAVIOR

Behavior is determined by many different factors. The range of factors and the manner in which they interrelate are by no means resolved even in understanding normal development and behavior. Yet, before discussing different forms of psychopathology, it is important to convey the determinants of behavior more generally. Understanding abnormal behavior requires familiarity with complex and multiple influences that span prenatal development to old age.

The present chapters focus on the major determinants of behavior and serve as a foundation for later material that elaborates the concrete forms of psychopathology. A range of factors are introduced in the present chapters including prenatal, genetic, physiological, social, cultural, and psychological influence on behavior. In the process of conveying the different determinants of behavior, the present chapters introduce a variety of forms of abnormal behavior and hence serve as a preview of material to follow in Part III.

Richard Rose (Chapter 4) provides an introduction to genetic factors and the mechanisms of heredity that influence behavior. Genetic influences are illustrated with a number of disorders that entail both physiological and psychological manifestations. James H. Geer (Chapter 5) elaborates physiological factors of the organism that influence behavior. The functions of the nervous and endocrine systems as well as the influence of drugs are discussed. Hayne W. Reese and Ralph R. Turner (Chapter 6) describe psychological factors that emerge through child development, beginning with infancy and extending through adolescence. A wide range of influences on behavior and theories of development are discussed in relation to the emergence of cognitive and behavioral patterns and social, moral, and language development. Finally, Gisela Labouvie-Vief and Peggy M. Zaks (Chapter 7) elaborate factors that influence performance in the aging adult. Aging is a development stage with its own biological, social, and cultural determinants.

Late eighteenth-century etching depicting the fascination of the social world with phrenology.

Franz Anton Mesmer (1734–1815), physician and enunciator of the theory of animal magnetism.

The three worlds of the mind—sensation, imagination, intellectuality. Seventeenth-century engraving.

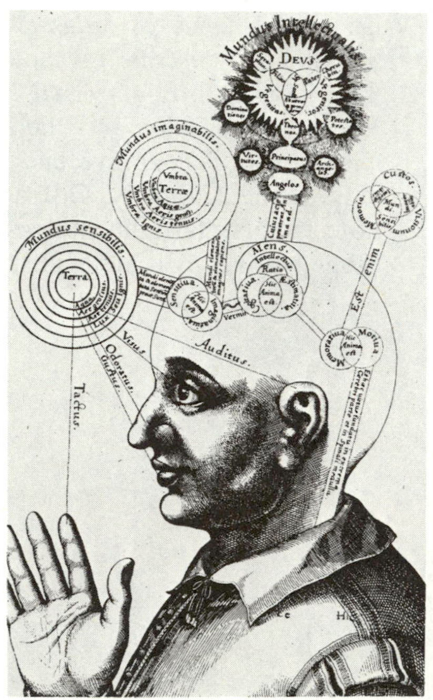

"The sleep of reason produces monsters."
Francisco Goya (1746–1826).

Lifespan.

4

GENETIC FACTORS

RICHARD J. ROSE

In 1788, King George III, then fifty years old, suffered two attacks of acute abdominal pain accompanied by constipation, nausea, and generalized weakness. Soon, the king was further afflicted with insomnia and headache. Progressively failing, he experienced convulsions and stupor, and the Royal physicians concluded that his life was endangered. Then, suddenly, the King's physical condition dramatically improved, but mental confusion and behavioral irrationality remained:

> Delerious all day . . . impressed by false images . . . continually addressed people dead or alive as if they were present . . . engrossed in visionary scenery . . . his conversation, like the details of a dream in its extravagant confusion. (Macalpine & Hunter, 1966, from records of the royal physicians)

Because episodes of delirious excitement alternated with periods of lucidity and calm, the King was diagnosed as suffering from mania; he was placed in restraint, reviled in the press of colonial America, and treated as a madman in his own country.

The two contemporary researchers (Macalpine & Hunter, 1966) have now established that the King suffered not from mania, but from porphyria, a metabolic disorder that is hereditary in origin. The most important of the King's symptoms was the dark coloration of his urine during the acute attacks—a discoloration due to the presence of porphyrin, a pigment contained in hemoglobin. Because porphyrin is normally metabolized by body cells, its presence in the urine indicates metabolic abnormality.

Porphyria is a familial disorder whose chronic course is marked by episodes in which abdominal pain, constipation, and vomiting become intense, and neurological symptoms occur. Mental symptoms—excitement, confusion, paranoid ideas—are common during the acute attacks.

What was a mysterious "madness" is now understood as an inborn error of metabolism, attributable to the action of a single gene. This understanding reflects two features of porphyria: (1) The disease exhibits familial aggregation consistent with a model of genetic transmission, and, (2) the mechanism from gene to behavior is largely understood.

To establish that George III suffered from

porphyria, it is necessary to document the disorder in his family history. If the King suffered from a metabolic disease that is transmitted across generations, one or more of his living descendants should exhibit abnormal metabolites in urine. And, in fact, a living member of the family of George III was found to suffer from porphyria (Macalpine, Hunter & Rimington, 1968). The finding led to a thorough search of the King's descendants for other cases. The search led from Mary Queen of Scots to living family members through 13 generations spanning 400 years. The search convincingly documents the familial transmission of porphyria from the Stuart family and Mary Queen of Scots, to the Royal Houses of Hanover and Prussia. Four of the King's sons and his granddaughter, Princess Charlotte, suffered from the disorder. We now know that this history of familial resemblance reflects the transmission of genetic material across generations.

Our knowledge of porphyria extends beyond evidence of heritable transmission, however. In the porphyrias, the gene- behavior mechanism is understood; the effect of the gene is a failure of body cells to convert porphyrin, due to the absence of the necessary enzyme. The inability to properly metabolize porphyrin produces abnormalities of the autonomic and central nervous systems and ultimately leads to the dramatic symptoms exhibited by King George: agonizing pain, wild and delerious confusion, excitement, and inappropriate behavior.

Porphyria provides an historical illustration of a physical/behavioral disorder caused by an inborn error of metabolism. Such genetic errors are one mechanism by which genes influence behavior. Although individually rare, such genetic errors assume substantial social significance in the aggregate.

This chapter provides an introduction to genetic factors in behavior disorders. The different mechanisms by which genes influence behavior will by surveyed with selected examples. Behavior disorders that, like porphyria, reflect the action of single genes will be illustrated by Huntington's disease, a progressive and fatal disorder transmitted by a dominant gene; by phenylketonuria, a form of mental retardation arising from an inborn error of metabolism transmitted by a recessive gene; and by one form of mental retardation attributable to genes located on the X-chromosome.

Individual genes are arranged on paired chromosomes, and errors in the structure or number of chromosomes produce behavioral disorders. To illustrate, the chapter will review Down's syndrome, a severe form of mental retardation in which the affected individual carries an extra chromosome in each cell, and by Turner's syndrome, an instructive disorder due to the absence of a sex chromosome.

The most complex and least understood genetic effects on behavior arise from the joint action of multiple genes coacting with multiple effects of environmental experience. A number of important conditions—e.g., the schizophrenias, affective disorders, alcoholism, criminality, hypertension—exhibit familial resemblance that is difficult to explain solely by environmental causes, but that does not fit simple patterns of genetic transmission, either. Adequate explanation of such conditions calls for a multifactorial model in which the additive action of many individual genes provides a predisposition to the disorder, which is precipitated and maintained by environmental effects. Patterns of heritable transmission based on the action of multiple genes will be reviewed in the third section of the chapter through a review of twin-family studies of intelligence. The final section of the chapter selectively surveys behavior-genetic analysis of schizophrenia to illustrate principles of multifactorial transmission.

The material reviewed in this chapter has been selected to illustrate representative methods and findings. Of necessity, emphasis was placed on certain disorders and certain methods to the exclusion of others. (Readers interested in a more exhaustive review may wish to consult D. Rosenthal's *Genetic Theory and Abnormal Behavior,* or *The Genetics of Mental Disorders* by E. Slater and V. Cowie.)

Chromosomes and behavior

Down's syndrome

The most common serious problem in newborns is a condition we now call Down's syndrome. Each 600–650 live births include a mentally retarded child with a set of symptoms first described by an English physician, Langdon Down. The physical symptoms include: 1. an unusual form of the upper eyelid that creates an oriental appearance and gave rise to the earlier name for the syndrome, mongolism; 2. a high prevalence of heart malformation, which contributes to 3. very reduced life span; 4. a single fold across the palm of the hand instead of the usual pattern of several folds; and, 5. the primary psychological symptom of severe mental retardation. While some individuals with Down's syndrome have tested IQs near normal, about one-third test below an IQ of 25, and most of the remainder test between 25 and 50. Down's syndrome accounts for 10 percent of the residents in public institutions for the mentally retarded, and it is the most frequent single diagnosis of severe retardation, characterizing about 30 percent of all severely retarded children in the country.

A decade after Down described the syndrome that now bears his name, it was observed that the risk of bearing an affected child steadily increased with maternal age. After age 30, the likelihood of bearing a Down's syndrome baby approximately doubles in each successive 5-year period. Combining data, the risk is about 1/1500 below age 30, but risk rises to 1/65 after age 45.

Why should this be so? What does the dramatic maternal age effect mean? To understand, we shall make a brief excursion into the process of cell division that underlies human reproduction. Cell division is the mechanism of sexual reproduction in all complex organisms. The human organism starts out as a single-celled *zygote* formed from the fusion of a sperm and an egg. Incredibly complex multiplications of that single cell lead to the mature human. The nuclear division of the cell occurs through two processes. In *mitosis,* the materials divide so that each daughter cell is identical. Mitosis occurs in all cells except those destined to become *gametes,* or sex cells. In the formation of gametes, another form of nuclear cell division occurs: *meiosis.* Meiosis is the cell division involved in sexual reproduction. It accounts for the shuffling of parental genetic material during formation of the gametes.

The hereditary material, DNA, is carried by the chromosomes, the darkly stained bodies in the nucleus of the cell. Humans have 23 pairs of chromosomes; 22 of these are corresponding (homologous) pairs of autosomes. The 23rd pair is comprised of the sex chromosomes, XX in females, XY in males.

During the process of mitosis, when the cells are rapidly dividing, the division may be arrested, and under a stain, the individual chromosomes in the nucleus of a cell become visible. The chromosomes can be distinguished one from another by length and shape, and organized into a standard sequence. The sequence defines the *karyotype.* The karyotype of the normal human female is designated as 46, XX, to indicate the human female has 46 chromosomes, two of which are the sex chromosomes, both X. The karyotype of the normal male is 46, XY. The Y chromosome is very much smaller than the X, and can be readily distinguished from it.

A number of nonlethal chromosome errors can and do occur as a consequence of accidents in mitosis or meiosis. If a pair of chromosomes fail to separate during meiosis in the egg, the resulting gamete may carry an additional chromosome. United with a normal sperm, the zygote will contain three chromosomes—a condition called *aneuploidy.* Nearly a century after Down described the syndrome, it was discovered that affected individuals had 47 chromosomes rather than the usual number of 46. The extra chromosome is one of the smallest *autosomes,* or nonsex chromosomes, conventionally called number 21. As a consequence, Down's syndrome is also called *trisomy-21.*

Nondisjunction, failure of chromosomes to properly separate during cell division, increases in frequency with the age of the mother. It is this fact that explains the increased incidence of Down's syndrome with increased maternal age. A woman is born with all the oocytes she will ever produce. Each remains in an arrested early stage of meiosis from birth until ovulation, which occurs at the rate of one per menstrual cycle from menarchy until menopause. Thus, a given ovum may remain in a state of suspended development for 12–40 years or so. Nondisjunction is thus a function of senescence of the oocytes. This may be due to a breakdown of chromosomal fibers, or it may be a response to a virus or to radiation, and, of course, the greater the age of the mother, the longer such agents will have acted on her oocytes.

Recently, with improved medical care during childhood, some Down's syndrome females do live to reproductive age. In cases studied to date, about one-half of the offspring of Down's syndrome women are themselves affected. But such cases in which the extra chromosome is indirectly transmitted from mother to child are rare; in the usual case, both parents of a Down's syndrome child are themselves normal, and the cause or etiology of the syndrome in the child is a nondisjunction of the chromosome material during meiosis. Thus, while Down's syndrome is obviously genetic, it is not usually transmitted from parent to child.

Turner's syndrome

Multiple behavioral effects of a chromosome abnormality are evident in Turner's Syndrome, in which the usual karyotype is 45, XO. Females with the karyotype lack a second X chromosome due to nondisjunction. Their ovaries are nonfunctional, there is gross sexual immaturity, menstruation does not occur, and affected women are sterile. About one-half of all Turner's are 45, XO; the other half have various abnormalities of the X chromosome in some or all of their body cells. All females with the syndrome exhibit short stature and sexual immaturity; many have other congenital anomalies, as well. Figure 4.1 illustrates a typical case.

Three features of the syndrome are of special interest here. First, despite absence of functioning ovaries with consequent loss of estrogen and failure to menstruate, Turner's girls are unmistakably feminine in interests and actions. They participate in gender-expected games and exhibit usual interests in dress and cosmetics; their fantasies of love and marriage are definitely feminine; they are described as good, responsible babysitters and effective foster mothers (Hampson, 1965; Money, 1965, 1968). Apparently, neither femininity nor female gender role is dependent on functioning gonads or normal levels of sex hormones.

Second, a specific defect in cognitive ability is common in Turner's syndrome (Money, 1968). The defect, a relative inability to mentally visualize spatial relations, is evident in performance scales of standard intelligence tests, in drawing geometric designs or constructing patterns with cubes, and in a perceptual style called field dependency, in which the dependent individual cannot easily distinguish a percept from the context in which it is embedded. The perceptual style is often tested with the rod-and-frame test, in which the subject's task is to align a tilted rod until it is physically vertical; the rod lies within a frame whose tilt is controlled by the experimenter. The subject's field dependence is measured by her inability to ignore the strong distraction of the frame when attempting to align the rod to vertical. Relative to their sisters and to control subjects, Turner's girls are reported to be unusually field-dependent in this task (Nielsen, Nyborg, & Dahl, 1977). Further analyses (Nyborg & Nielsen, 1977) suggest that the differences are due to response inconsistencies among the Turner's girls.

Third, certain personality characteristics are associated with Turner's Syndrome. These women are described clinically as passive-dependent, docile, readily accepting of authority (Hampson, Hampson, & Money, 1955). The passivity and docile dependency may, however, be an indirect consequence of short stature and sexual immaturity: Turner's girls are the brunt of frequent teasing by school peers, and their

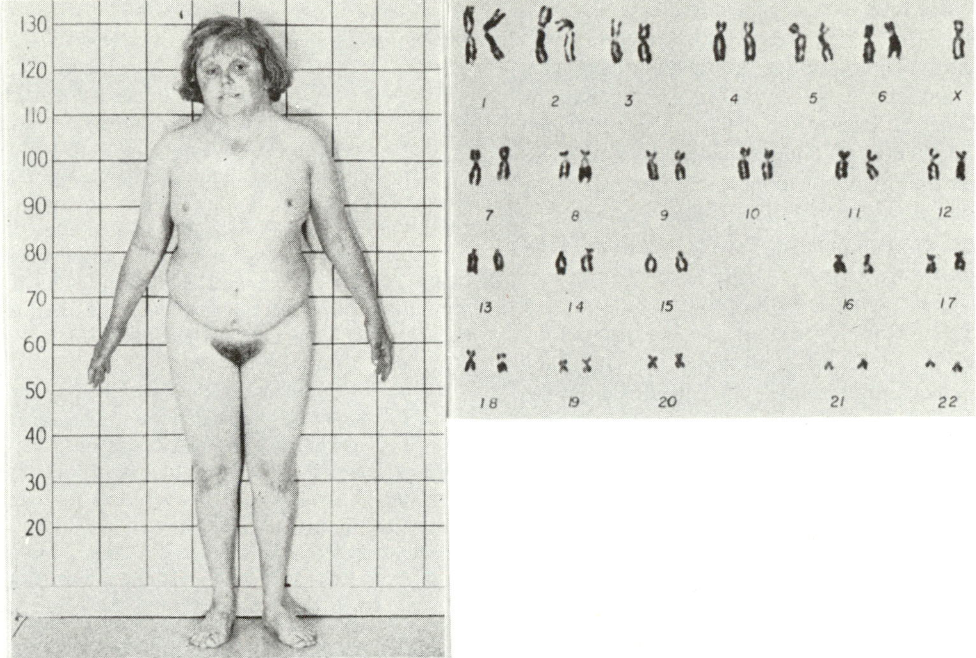

Fig. 4.1. The Turner syndrome. (*left*) The features are female external genitalia, short stature, webbed neck, low-set ears and typical facies, broad shieldlike chest with widely spaced nipples and underdeveloped breasts, small uterus, and ovaries represented only by fibrous streaks. In some cases coarctation of the aorta (a marked narrowing just beyond the mouth of the left subclavian artery) leads to severe hypertension in the upper part of the body. Such has been corrected surgically in the patient illustrated here; note the surgical scar on the left side of the thorax. (*right*) The karotype of this patient, with 45 chromosomes and an XO sex-chromosome constitution.

delayed sexual development and infertility may affect their personality style. A direct test of these clinical impressions has been reported (Baekgaard, Nybord, & Nielsen, 1978) in a Danish study with careful controls. The Maudsley Personality Inventory was administered to 45, XO Turner's, to Turner's with partial deletions/translocations of the X chromosome in some cells, to sisters of Turner's patients, to nonsiblings with growth retardation and primary amenorrhea (failure to menstruate), and to normal controls. Test scores from all groups were compared to norms with results that the 45, XO groups scored significantly lower on the neuroticism scale. Turner's girls with chromosome abnormalities other than 45, XO had scores within normal limits. The emotional stability reflected in the low neuroticism scores is consistent with clinical impressions of Turner's girls; it is suggested that it is a concomitant of total absence of the second chromosome.

Other sex chromosome aneuplodies

Two additional syndromes, due to excessive sex chromosomal material, are of special interest to students of abnormal behavior. Both syndromes affect males. One involves an additional X chromosome, the other an extra Y chromosome.

In Klinefelter's syndrome the karyotype is 47, XXY. The effects of the additional X chromosome include a slight but significant reduction in intellectual functioning. Surveys of penal institutions reveal a much higher prevalence of Klinefelter's males than expected from incidence of the syndrome among newborns; there is little question that the syndrome is associated with behavior disorder (Federman, 1967).

The other syndrome involves an extra Y chromosome, yielding the karyotype 47, XYY. Most affected males are tall, and many exhibit mental retardation. Perhaps as a consequence, the syndrome is unusually frequent among men in security institutions for the mentally retarded.

Early reports suggested a direct effect of the extra Y chromosome on antisocial behavior, mediated, perhaps, by a double dose of male hormones. However, recent studies, which have carefully controlled for both height and IQ (Witkin & Mednick, 1976), cast doubt on the hormonal hypothesis. Intellectual dysfunction is an important mediating variable in criminality of XYY males. The association of the YY karyotype and aggressiveness appears to be attributable to an indirect effect: individuals who are tall and retarded are much more likely to be institutionalized.

Single gene transmission

About one in 50 newborn infants has a disorder caused not by a chromosomal aberration, but by action of single genes. The genes occur in pairs, one on a maternal chromosome, the other on the homologous paternal chromosome. The two genes in each pair occupy a certain position or locus on homologous chromosomes. A gene at any locus may have variant forms called *alleles*.

Single gene disorders are caused by one or two homologous alleles that are altered or *mutated* from the normal state. Single gene disorders are classified as autosomal dominant, autosomal recessive, or X-linked, according to their patterns of transmission within families.

An autosomal dominant disorder: Huntington's Disease

The fear of losing one's mind and the fear of losing control over one's body are among the most profound fears known to mankind. Both losses occur in Huntington's disease, a hereditary and terminal brain disorder which begins insidiously, usually in middle age. Men and women affected grow irritable or hostile; their personalities change. Some become manic, some apathetic, some suicidally depressed. Powers of reason, memory, and judgment fade, leading inevitably to dementia.

Physical symptoms accompany the mental changes. Patients may appear clumsy or fidgety at first. They may grimace or smile in a peculiar way. As the disease progresses they may have difficulty in talking or swallowing; they lose control over normal body functions. Their restless movements become exaggerated and incessant. They twist, writhe, and lurch; they make flailing movements of head, trunk, or limbs, ever on the verge of falling.

These symptoms describe what Huntington's disease looks like in someone who has struggled 10 or 20 years with it. It may explain why a woman now known to have had Huntington's disease was hanged as a witch in 17th century Salem. Or why the late composer and folk singer, Woody Guthrie, was considered an alcoholic and was in and out of mental hospitals for years before the true diagnosis of Huntington's disease was made. (DHEW Publ. No. (NIH) 78–1501, 1977, p. xvii)

The tragedy of Huntington's disease is compounded by its late age of onset. Most affected individuals develop no symptoms until after age forty, after they have conceived children, thereby transmitting the inherited basis for the disease to the next generation.

Children of an affected parent have a 50–50 chance of inheriting the disease themselves. At present, tragically, there is no basis by which one can distinguish those who are at risk from those who are not. Thus, there is no way to identify who will develop the disease until its symptoms begin. Children of an affected parent know that they are at risk, but must make decisions about career, marriage, and childbearing in fearful uncertainty.

How can I adequately convey to you what the pressure of being threatened by Huntington's disease is like? Let me try by telling you about two possessions I keep.

One is a picture, a photograph from a newspaper clipping. It is one of those rare photographs that captures a scene so pathetic, so utterly piteous that you try to tell yourself that such a thing cannot possibly be real. But it is, undeniably real. It shows a woman in her forties. She is strapped into a wheelchair. She is obviously out of control; legs flung high, knees to her chin, her feet high over her head, hands clutching. Her face is a study in anguish; lips stretched, teeth bared, jaws pulled wide and strangely askew, tongue out-thrust, eyebrows leaping. Her body is emaciated to the point where every bone and tendon is visible through her clinging skin. She is dressed in a diaper. The caption on the photograph tells us that the woman is a victim of Huntington's disease. I keep it as a ready and infallible reminder of what Huntington's disease really has to offer me should it become my lot.

My other possession is a pistol, a .38 caliber police special. It is my insurance that I will never end up like the lady in the photograph.

One aspect worth mentioning is the memory I have to live with; the memory of my childhood home being turned into a complete shambles by the mother I loved growing steadily more crazy and debilitated. I can still feel the horror that gripped me the first time I saw my mother's urine run down her leg and across the kitchen floor. My heart sinks to recall all the fighting, the yelling, and the crying. And there was the agonizing over the painful decision finally to have her committed. All of this due to Huntington's disease, and at the time none of us even knew why. It is a bitter memory to live with. (DHEW Publ. No. (NIH) 78–1501, 1977, p. 13)

What does it mean to state that Huntington's disease is inherited? It means that the cause of the disease is physically transmitted in the hereditary material, the genes.

The transmission of genes across generations is known by their observable effects. The effects of some genes can be observed when they are present on one chromosome although the homologous chromosome carries the normal gene at that locus. This condition is called the *heterozygote* state, and an allele that can be recognized in heterozygotes is called *dominant.*

Several principles of inheritance, discovered by Gregor Mendel, characterize dominant gene action: 1. All heterozygotes are affected, since the expression of dominant conditions requires only one mutant gene; 2. each affected individual has a 50 percent chance of passing the condition onto each of his children, since the affected parent may, with equal likelihood, transmit either the normal gene or the mutant gene to any one of his children; 3. because the gene is carried on one of the autosomes, rather than the X or Y chromosome, sons and daughters will be affected with equal likelihood; 4. the condition will be transmitted in vertical fashion and will appear in every generation.

Huntington's disease (HD) has been traced back to Bures St. Mary, Suffolk, England (Myrianthopolus, 1966). Among the villagers who sailed to the American colonies in 1630 were three young men who left Bures because their antisocial behavior had become too extreme. Among the descendants of these three men, seven daughters and granddaughters were treated as witches (Porter, 1968), and in the fifth generation of the Bures family, there is a clearly diagnosed case of HD. From that case, the disease can be traced through ten generations to the present. HD must have been present in the original ancestors of the Bures family, and behaviors identified as antisocial misconduct or witchcraft must, in fact, have been Huntington's Disease.

The pattern of transmission of Huntington's confirms that the disease is caused by a single, dominant gene. But how can a single gene initiate an irreversible course of physical and behavioral symptoms ending in dementia and death?

As early as 1895, it was proposed that inheritance is accomplished by physical transmission of chemical compounds from parent to child. The heriditary material we now know consists of deoxyribonucleic acid (DNA). The structure of DNA was identified, in 1953, in the Nobel-prize-winning work of Watson and Crick. Genes differ in the sequence of the nucleotides that are strung along the DNA chains, and DNA carries genetic information across generations. DNA mediates the synthesis of proteins. The behavioral effects of genes must result from biochemical reactions within cells, since these biochemical reactions require enzymes, which are proteins.

Thus, an individual gene controls the metabolism of an enzyme or a protein or regulates other genes that do so. If HD is caused by a single gene, that gene must involve protein abnormality.

The fundamental symptoms of HD—progressive disturbances in movement, feeling, and thinking—reflect abnormality in inhibitory control. A possible cause of the disease, therefore, is a change in brain chemistry—specifically a loss of a neural transmitter that inhibits nerve action. Analysis of brain tissue from HD patients reveals low levels of a substance which inhibits nerve action; the substance is gamma-amino-butyric acid (GABA), and an intensive search is underway for an agent that will increase functional brain levels of GABA, in the hope that such an agent will provide treatment for HD.

The search for effects of the gene is not limited to cellular biochemistry. Behavioral scientists can search for the effects of the HD gene in integrated behavioral acts. To illustrate, it has been shown (Potegal, 1971) that patients with Huntington's exhibit impairments in compensating for self-produced movements in tests of spatial localization. Similar impairments have been demonstrated in animals with surgical lesions in the caudate nucleus of the brain.

Of the 2,300 known genetic diseases, more than 1,000 are autosomal dominants, for which the specific nature of the gene-disease pathway remains uncertain. Huntington's has been proposed as a model for research study of genetic disease. And psychologists are playing an increasingly important role in research on HD; e.g., a prerequisite for effective genetic counselling and clinical intervention is the ability to identify carriers of the mutant gene; recent evaluation of psychometric test signs within the kinships of HD patients (Lyle & Gottesman, 1977) may be an initial step toward that goal.

An autosomal recessive disease: PKU

Inborn errors of metabolism, illustrated earlier with porphyria, constitute an important area of behavior genetic study. Perhaps the best known example of such an error is phenylketonuria, or PKU. The typical patient is small in stature and in weight, tends to have blue eyes, blonde hair, and very fair skin. There is often mild to moderate microcephaly, and abnormal EEGs occur in about 60 percent of the cases. Severe temper tantrums are often evident in very early life. During the first few weeks following birth, vomiting, irritability, and perhaps epileptic seizures occur. By about the fifth to sixth month of life, mental retardation becomes evident (Hsai, 1967). The frequency of PKU is about 5/100,000; it accounts for about 1 percent of those who are institutionalized for mental retardation. The familial aggregation of the disorder provides evidence of recessive-gene transmission: 1. both parents are normal; 2. most other family members are also normal, but one in four of the siblings are affected; and 3. the prevalence of the condition markedly increases if the parents are genetically related.

PKU is a defect of amino acid metabolism. The defect is in the enzyme that converts phenylalanine, an essential amino acid, to tyrosine. The metabolic error leads to an increase in phenlpyruvic acid in the urine and provides for the initial clinical identification of the disorder. With appropriate tests the condition can be identified at birth or soon thereafter. That fact has led to an effective prevention program. The IQ level of PKU children can be raised to near normal levels if they are placed on a diet low in phenylalanine from a very early age. While the evidence is somewhat controversial, it illustrates the important fact that a condition with genetic etiology can often be treated and/or prevented.

X-linked transmission: mental retardation

There are some traits whose pattern of inheritance fits neither dominant nor recessive transmission. These traits exhibit significant familial aggregation, but with two unusual characteristics: 1. There is no father-to-son transmission: the union of an unaffected father with a normal mother produces affected daughters, but normal sons; 2. such traits show a sex difference in the frequency of occurrence among males and females, and some find expression only in males.

Common examples of traits with these characteristics include hemophilia or bleeding disease and several forms of color-blindness. These traits are known to be transmitted by a recessive gene located on the X chromosome. Because the gene for color-blindness is recessive in character, women will not express the trait; if they do inherit the abnormal allele on one of their X chromosomes, its effect will be masked by the normal gene at the homologous locus on their other X chromosome. But a male who inherits the mutant gene will be color-blind, since he has no homologous gene to counteract its effect. Most women therefore will be normal, but some will carry the gene, transmit it to their sons who will be color blind and to their daughters who, in turn, may transmit the gene to their sons in the next generation. Affected males can transmit the mutant gene only to their daughters, who also become carriers. Sons of affected fathers must receive the gene from their mothers, since from their fathers they receive a Y chromosome, which does not code genetic information for color vision.

There are many other behavioral traits that exhibit patterns of inheritance suggesting X-linkage. Some, like hemophilia, are definitely established as X-linked recessive. For others, including several forms of mental retardation, the possibility of X-linked inheritance remains only a hypothesis.

Since the turn of the century there have been repeated suggestions that tested intelligence is more variable in males than in females. In public institutions, the percentage of male excess among institutionalized retardates is consistently above 10 percent (Lehrke, 1978), and community surveys of the prevalence of mental retardation have frequently reported an excess of males—a finding that complements findings from institutional surveys. This phenomenon is consistent with the hypothesis of X-linkage in mental retardation (Lehrke, 1978). Males who lack a homologous chromosome for genes on their single X chromosome will have a trait expressed at the frequency with which the gene exists. If a recessive gene on the X chromosome has a population frequency of .05, the trait will appear in 5 percent of all males.

The hypothesis of X-linked transmission in mental retardation has recently been tested, and, using new techniques in cytogenetics, evidence to support the speculation has begun to appear. A survey of mildly retarded institutionalized males (Harvey, Judge, & Wiener, 1977) identified four individuals who had a structurally abnormal X-chromosome. One of the patients was a 20-year-old man who had been in an institution for the retarded since the age of 11. Blood samples were collected from all available members in three generations of this patient's family. The samples were analyzed for abnormalities of the X chromosome. One hundred metaphases were analyzed in each case, and the number of metaphases exhibiting the abnormality was counted.

Figure 4.2 shows the pedigree of this family. The patient is identified in the figure as case III.1 and is designated by the arrow. His maternal half-brother, case III.2, is a nine-year-old boy functioning at a moderately retarded level; while living at home, he was attending a day center for retarded children. The patient and his half brother exhibited the abnormal X chromosome in 35–35 percent of their cells. Their mother, case II.1, exhibited the abnormality in 24 percent of her cells, and her affected brother, case II.3, showed it in 40 percent of his cells. Finally, case I.4, the maternal grandmother of the patient, exhibited the abnormality in 6 percent of her cells.

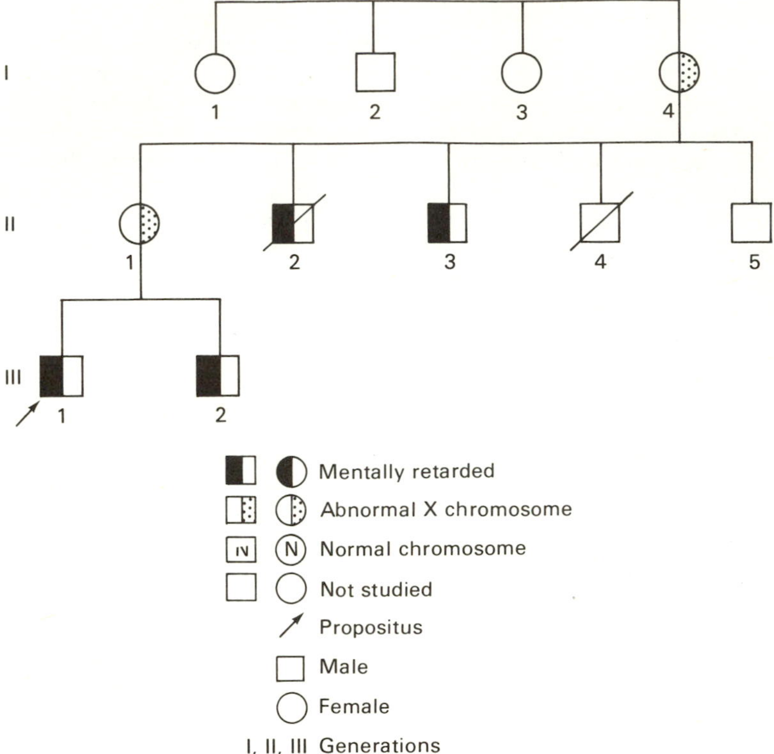

Fig. 4.2. Pedigree illustrating familial X-linked mental retardation.

Data from this pedigree and others would explain the higher incidence of mental retardation in males, and, in particular, reports within families that only males are affected. The transmission pattern strongly suggests X-linked inheritance.

Polygenic transmission

Traits that are quantitatively continuous cannot be explained by the action of single genes. Such traits can, however, represent the cumulative effects of many genes at many different chromosomal loci. The effects of such polygenes are not individually distinguishable, for each male makes a small contribution to the trait's expression. Polygenic transmission applies to such obviously quantitative traits as height, weight, or intelligence, and, in addition, mental states and personality traits assumed to be present or absent, may, in fact, represent an underlying continuum. For example, schizophrenia and depression, often conceptualized as qualitative states that are present or absent in all-or-none manner, may represent the extreme tail of an underlying distribution created by polygenic action.

Variability in polygenic traits will usually exhibit a normal, bell-shaped distribution. Of course, the mere fact that a behavior exhibits a normal distribution does not establish its polygenic transmission. How can we test the validity of a polygenic model? Predictions from a simple polygenic model of inheritance are based on the expectation that resemblance between relatives will correspond to the proportion of genes they share in common. Given certain simplifying assumptions, familial resemblance will be a direct function of the number of genes identical by descent from a common ancestor. There is an obvious complication, however. A behavioral trait determined by a large number of small, independent environmental factors will also exhibit a normal distribution, and such environmentally determined traits will exhibit resemblance between relatives who share common environments. The closer the environmental similarity, the greater the behavioral resemblance. Thus, the effects of shared environments can mimic that of shared genes.

To distinguish effects of common genes from those of common experience, we can compare individuals who share the same proportion of genes but differ in the amount of shared experience; conversely, we can study individuals who share common experiences, but differ in genetic overlap. In this way, we can partition the total variation in behavior into that portion attributable to environment and that portion attributable to heredity. The techniques to do this, which comprise the field of biometrical genetics, are rather complex, but the principles are easily understood.

To illustrate, consider the genetic and environmental similarity of twins and siblings. Fraternal twins are formed from two separate ova released at about the same time and independently fertilized by two separate sperm. Since fraternal twins are derived from two zygotes, geneticists call them dizygotic (DZ). Like ordinary brothers and sisters, DZ twin pairs share, on the average, 50 percent of their genes, and one-half of DZ twin pairs will be of opposite sex. Thus, fraternal or DZ twins are no more alike than ordinary siblings. They are, however, much more likely to share experiences. Two brothers may be born years apart, separated by the births of two sisters; they occupy very different positions in the family—one is firstborn, the second is last and influenced by his two older sisters; the brothers are born into changed family circumstances, and, if the family has moved, the two brothers attended different schools and spend the formative years of childhood in different neighborhoods. By contrast, DZ twin brothers will share a common intrauterine environment, are of identical age and occupy the same position within the family, share common friends, attend school together, and graduate in the same year. Thus, comparison of DZ twins with ordinary nontwin siblings measures effects of environmental variation on behavior. The two groups are genetically equivalent, but both prenatal and postbirth environment are more similar in the twin brothers.

Another estimate of additive, environmental affects can be obtained from the comparison of fraternal twins of like sex with those of opposite sex. In our society, perhaps no factor more systematically creates differences in experience than does gender role. Consequently, for behavioral traits influenced by the additive influence of many independent environmental effects, fraternal twins of opposite sex will be less similar than fraternal twins of like sex.

A third estimate of additive environmental influence can be obtained from a comparison of resemblance of parents and their children with the similarity of siblings. If all genes are merely additive—if there is no dominance—both groups have a genetic resemblance of .5, but there is an entire generation difference in experience.

To assess the polygenic model—the additive effects of independent genes, we can contrast resemblance of like-sex DZ twins with that of genetically identical twins. As the reader probably knows, identical twins are derived from a single zygote that divides within the first days of pregnancy. Such monozygotic (MZ) twins have all their genes in common and, are, therefore, always of the same sex. If the polygenic model holds, i.e., if all behavior differences are attributable to the additive effects of independent genes, MZ twins, who are genetically identical, will show a perfect resemblance to one another (limited only by unreliability in measurement of the trait). The resemblance of DZ twins, who share half their genes, will be .5, and since in this simple polygenic model the environment has no effect, siblings, like DZ twins, will also exhibit a resemblance coefficient of .5.

Further, if the polygenic model holds, we can predict the similarity of more distant relatives. Second-degree relatives (e.g., half-brothers or sisters, an uncle and his niece, or a grandmother and her grandchild) share 1/4 of their genes, and, if age, sex, and other sources of variation in experience have no effect, all second-degree relatives will exhibit a resemblance of .25.

To summarize: We can test for additive effects of independent environmental influences by comparing relatives who share the same proportion of genes but who differ in the amount of common experience—fraternal twin sisters compared to their much older nontwin sister. Conversely, we test for additive effects of independent genes by comparing relatives who are approximately matched for the amount of common experience but who differ in the proportion of shared genes—the classic comparison of MZ and like-sex DZ twins.

To illustrate these principles, three study designs, particularly useful in assessing polygenic traits, will be reviewed. The designs study: 1. twins and siblings, 2. adopted children, and 3. kinships of adult MZ twins. The illustrations will focus on the resemblance between relatives for several traits, including IQ, height, and fingerprint ridge count. The latter is a classic example of a polygenic trait: the ridges on the dermal surfaces of the hand are formed by the twelfth week after conception, and are not influenced by any postbirth experience. As a consequence, ridge count serves as a guide for the interpretation of behavioral traits.

Twin-sibling studies. In a study of 320 pairs of London twins and their available nontwin siblings, aged 5–15, resemblance for ridge counts was compared to that for IQ, height, and social maturity (Huntley, 1966). The sample included 85 monozygotic twin pairs, 135 like-sex dizygotic pairs, and 100 dizygotic pairs of opposite sex. Verbal intelligence was assessed with a composite of four vocabulary tests known to be culturally influenced. In addition to the vocabulary measures, fingerprint ridge count, height, and social maturity were assessed. These four traits were chosen in the expectation that they would reflect differing degrees of genetic influence. The results are shown in Table 4-1.

The first column reminds the reader of the genetic correlation based on the proportion of genes identical by descent. The remaining columns report the observed correlations for each of the four traits in twins and siblings. We note that the correlations for ridge count very nearly match the genetic correlations. For height, the correlation of MZ twins is slightly lower, and it is lower yet for IQ. Since all differences between MZ twins must be nongenetic, we can conclude that nongenetic factors pay an increasingly important role in the development of height and IQ. The measure of social maturity is based on an assessment of the degree to which children and adolescents look after themselves and participate in activities leading to social independence. Note that for this measure, DZ twins are almost as similar as are MZ twins, while age-separated siblings resemble one another much less. This pattern is inconsistent with the expectations of a genetic model.

From the observed twin correlations, we can estimate *heritability,* defined as the proportion of behavioral variation attributable to variation in genes. The comparative heritability estimates for ridge count, height, social maturity, and vocabulary suggest that, as expected, the four traits can be ordered according to degree of genetic influence. Variation in ridge count is adequately explained by a simple model of polygenic transmission. The assumptions necesary for that simple model are fully met for ridge count: 1. only genetic effects occur, 2. the genes are simply additive, with no dominance, and 3. mating is random with respect to the trait. The last assumption is clearly false for height and IQ, since for both traits we tend to marry those similar to ourselves.

For ridge count, variation in genes fully accounts for measured variation in the trait, and estimated heritability approaches 100 percent. Most of the variation in height can

Table 4.1.

	Genetic Correlation	Fingerprint Ridge Counts	Height	IQ	Social Maturity
MZ twins	1.0	0.96	0.90	0.83	0.97
DZ twins (like-sex)	0.5	0.47	0.48	0.53	0.89
DZ twins (total)	0.5	0.49	0.49	0.45	0.82
Siblings	0.5	0.51	0.41	0.45	0.32
$h^2 = 2(r_{MZ} - r_{DZ})$		98%	84%	60%	16%

For height and IQ, the correlations for DZ twins and siblings have been adjusted for effects of nonrandom mating. From Huntley (1966).

also be attributed to additive genetic effects, but some nongenetic contribution (here estimated at 16 percent) is evident. For verbal intelligence, estimated heritability remains substantial, but 40 percent of the total variation in the vocabulary test data is attributable to nongenetic influences. Finally, for social maturity, genetic factors play a small role, and most of the variation appears due to age-specific experiences common to siblings who are reared in the same home.

Adoption studies. Studies of adopted children provide a powerful technique to disentangle effects of shared heredity from those of shared experience. To assess environmental influences on behavior, one can study the resemblance of genetically unrelated individuals who are reared together—e.g., an adopted child and his foster parents; conversely, to isolate genetic effects, one can study the resemblance of genetically related individuals who are reared apart—e.g., a foster child separated at birth from his biological parents.

Adoption is, of course, a social convention, not a scientific experiment. Neither the children given up for adoption nor the married couples who adopt them are representative of the general population. Adopted children tend to be born to very young unmarried mothers. The foster parents will be screened on social and occupational characteristics. Further, adopted children are not randomly allocated to applicants for foster parenting; instead, adoption agencies follow selective placement practices attempting to match characteristics of the foster and biological parents, and such selective placement creates resemblance between foster child and foster parent. Thirdly, the biological father is rarely available for study, and, often, nothing is known of him.

Despite these methodological problems, however, the study of adopted children has provided convincing evidence of genetic effects on complex social behaviors, including the schizophrenias, the affective disorders, alcoholism, criminality, early infantile autism, and hyperactivity. The adoption data are so persuasive that they have forced researchers of all orientations to include genetic ideas into their theoretical and clinical positions.

The earliest applications of the adoption method were in studies of IQ, and a brief summary of the latest and largest adoption study of IQ will illustrate the method. The study, directed by Horn, Loehlin, and Willerman (1977, 1978), is in progress at the University of Texas.

The Texas Adoption Study is unique in that IQ data are available for both adoptive parents and biological mothers, and the children were, in nearly every case, permanently separated from their natural mother in the first 72 hours of life. The children were identified through an agency that provides live-in care for "out-of-wedlock" pregnancies; the agency charges a fee for the care, with the consequence that the biological mothers tend to come from a higher socioeconomic background than that of the population at large. The adoptive parents

Table 4.2. IQ Correlations from the Texas Adoption Study

	Correlation	Pairs
Biological mother and adopted child	.29	342
Adoptive mother and adopted child	.18	451
Adoptive father and adopted child	.12	454
Adoptive mother and natural child	.23	165
Adoptive father and natural child	.26	166
Adoptive mother and biological mother	.15	336
Adoptive father and biological mother	.12	338

From Horn, Loehlin, and Willerman (1978).

have an average tested IQ of 108, and some selective placement is revealed in the small but significant correlation between tested IQs of adoptive parents and the biological mothers. Summary results are given in Table 4.2. The critical finding is that the adopted children show a greater resemblance to their natural mother, from whom they have been separated, than to their foster parents with whom they have spent their lives. In fact, the correlation between foster child and natural mother slightly exceeds that between foster mother and her natural children.

These data are consistent with other reports (Munsinger, 1975), which document genetic effects on the development of intellectual abilities. It should be apparent, of course, that the magnitude of parent-child correlations reveals that nongenetic factors also play a substantial role in cognitive development (i.e., the correlations are not very high).

Kinships of MZ twins. The families of adult identical twins provide another methodology for partitioning the sources of variance in quantitative traits. The multiple parent-offspring relationships found within these families are illustrated in Figure 4-3. Children in each of the two nuclear families diagrammed in part A of the figure obtain half their genes from their twin mother, but also share half their genes with their twin-aunt, who is their mother's monozygotic twin. Of course, the children do not live in the home of their aunt, so the common household environment of a nuclear family will not affect the resemblance of a nephew or niece to their mother's twin. This unique relationship provides a parallel to that between children separated from their biological mother and reared in a different home. However, the children's mother and their aunt are identical twins, and their genetic identity may lead them to create similar households, thereby providing an environmental explanation for the resemblance between nephew or niece and twin-aunt.

The unrelated wives of identical twin brothers provide an evaluation of this environmental effect. We can compare the resemblance between nephew or niece and their nontwin-aunt in the families of male twins, shown in Figure B, with the corresponding relationshp of nephew/niece to twin-aunt illustrated in Figure A. Because children share neither common genes nor a common household with the nontwin-aunt, resemblance between them can arise only through environmental factors common to both households. In contrast, children are genetically related to their twin-aunt as closely as they are to their biological mother, and a simple polygenic model predicts that they will resemble their aunt as closely as they do their mother.

Finally, note that the multiple relationships of children to their mothers and twin- or nontwin-aunts are directly paralleled in kinships of male twins by relationships between children and their father and twin- and nontwin-uncles.

To illustrate the method, data will be reported (Rose et al., 1978) for the Block Design sign Test, a standardized measure of nonverbal intelligence, and for total ridge

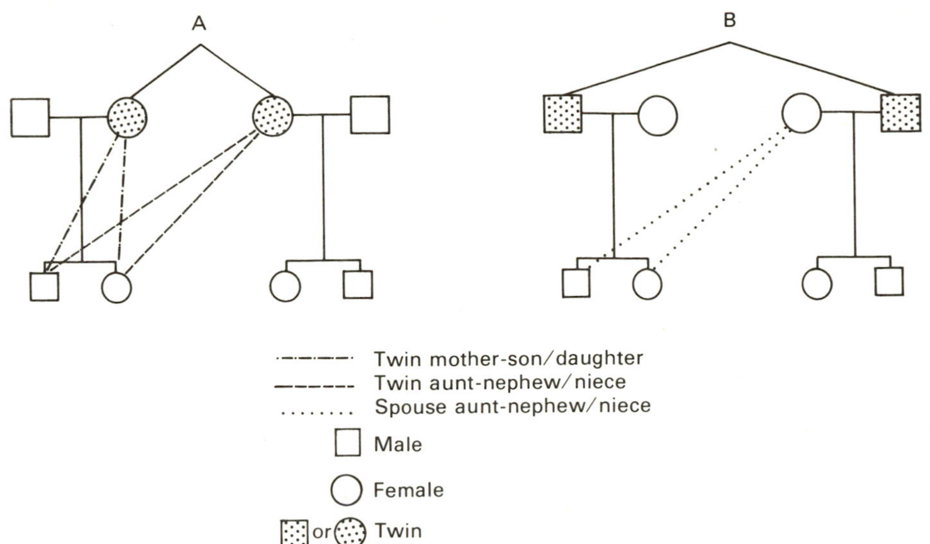

Fig. 4.3. Parent-offspring relationships in families of identical twins. (From Rose et al., 1979.)

count measured in 550 members of the families of 65 adult MZ twins. Selected results are summarized in Table 4.3. The upper portion of the table reports the resemblance of children to their parents, aunts, and uncles. Note that for both ridge count and Block Design, children resemble their twin-uncle or -aunt as closely as they do their own father or mother while showing no resemblance to their nontwin-uncle or -aunt. The results suggest that for both measures, parent-child similarity is a function of additive gene effects; for neither traits is there evidence of an environmental effect due to shared household experience.

Since their twin parents are monozygotes, children of identical twins are genetically related as half-siblings who share $^1/_2$ of their genes. Socially, they are reared in separate homes as ordinary cousins. In the lower part of Table 4.3 the resemblance of these half-siblings is compared to that of ordinary brothers and sisters sharing $^1/_2$ their genes, and to their identical-twin-parents. For both traits, the resemblance of full siblings is of the same order of magnitude as is that between parent and child, and the similarity of half-siblings is about one-half that of full siblings. Both results are in accordance with expectations of polygenic transmission.

Heritability estimates can be obtained from the resemblance coefficients reported in Table 4.3. The estimates are based on the proportion of shared genes, so that the resemblance coefficient of siblings, who share $^1/_2$ of their genes, is doubled, while that for half-siblings, who share $^1/_4$ of their genes is quadrupled. Table 4.4 reports the heritability estimates for both traits. Two conclusions can be drawn: First, ridge count is much more heritable than is Block Design; second, neither trait is significantly influenced by common environment. Heritability estimates from genetic half-siblings living in different households are as high as those of full siblings reared together.

Genetic analysis of schizophrenia

The methods and ideas illustrated for IQ will now be applied to the study of schizophrenia, the major disorder of abnormal psychology.

Twin, adoption and MZ half-sibling studies will be reviewed to provide evidence

Table 4.3. Regression and Correlation Analyses of Block Design Test Scores and Fingerprint Ridge Counts

	Block Design		*Ridge Count*	
	value	N	value	N
Regressions				
Son/daughter on father/mother	.28	572	.42	564
Nep/niece on twin-uncle/aunt	.23	318	.37	310
Nep/niece on spouse uncle/aunt	−.01	254	−.06	247
Correlations				
Monozygotic twins	.68	65	.96	60
Full siblings	.24	297	.36	296
Half-siblings	.10	318	.17	310

From Rose et al. (1979).

of polygenic transmission of schizophrenia, and the chapter will conclude with an example of efforts to identify the genetic predisposition among fostered children who are at risk for the disorder.

In 1916, Ernst Rudin reported the results of his pioneering effort to apply Mendel's rediscovered principles of genetics to schizophrenia. A half-century later, Rudin's daughter, Edith Zerbin-Rudin, published a comprehensive summary of hereditary factors in endogeneous psychoses (Zerbin-Rudin, 1967). Based largely on her review, Table 4.5 summarizes the expectancy-risk of schizophrenia for relatives of schizophrenics.

Contained within the data of Table 4.5 are three findings that implicate genetic factors in the transmission of schizophrenia. First, expectation of schizophrenia in the general population is quite constant. The incidence of 0.86 is based on pooled findings from six countries for more than three decades; neither continuing changes in health services nor national variations in cultural organization and familial practices significantly affect population incidence. This finding "is difficult to explain . . . without hypothesizing a genetical pre-disposition fairly evenly distributed over Europe and very likely over the world" (Slater, 1968, p. 16). Secondly, relatives of schizophrenics are at an increased risk for the disorder: Risk is about ten times higher in siblings and children than in the population at large, and risk remains significantly elevated among more distant relatives. Thirdly, magnitude of risk corresponds to degree of genetic relationship: Risk is clearly higher for first degree relatives than those in second degree relationships, and the risk for genetic relatives is much higher than that for spouses who share no genes identical by descent. The lowered risk reported for parents is more apparent than real: schizophrenia tends to be incompatible with effective marriage and child-rearing; an adjusted procedure for calculating risk in parents of schizophrenics yields an estimate of about 11 percent, a figure comparable to that found for siblings and children.

The major finding in Table 4.5, a constant population risk that is elevated in relatives according to degree of genetic relatedness, establishes the folklore that madness runs in families, and, as such, provides evidence necessary for implicating genetic transmission in schizophrenia. But, while necessary, that evidence is not sufficient: Families share common experiences as well as common genes. That schizophrenia "runs in families" cannot, itself, establish the causal role of genetic factors. To do so requires new data based on a new conception of the role of genes in behavior disorders. The new conception was articulated by P. E. Meehl, who, in a presidential address to the American Psychological Association, argued that "schizophrenia, while its content is learned, is fundamentally a neurological disease of genetic origin" (1962, p. 387). The new data are recent studies of twins and foster-reared

Table 4.4. Heritability Estimates for Block Design Test Scores and Total Ridge Count (TRC)

Relationship	*Estimated h^2* Blocks	TRC
Parent-offspring	.56	.84
Twin-uncle/aunt-nephew/niece	.46	.74
Full siblings	.48	.72
Half-siblings	.40	.68

From Rose et al. (1979).

children, and it is to these studies we now turn.

Twin studies

The classic method in behavior-genetic analysis of schizophrenia is the use of twins. A summary of 11 major twin studies of schizophrenia is reported in Table 4.5. A detailed and critical review of these studies concluded that "we are dealing with replications of the same experiment. . . . It seems reasonable to postulate that genetic factors are largely responsible for the specific nature of most of the schizophrenias and that these factors are necessary but not sufficient for the disorder to occur" (Gottesman & Shields, 1966, p. 80).

This conclusion, of course, does not deny that sharing trait-relevant experiences will increase the similarity of behavioral outcome in twins. The data of Table 4.5 provide clear evidence of this fact: similarity of twins is measured by the percentage of pairs who are alike, or *concordant,* and we note that the pooled concordance for DZ twins of the same sex is twice that for opposite-sex fraternal pairs. The twofold difference must arise from differential sharing of relevant social experiences, and, as such, it provides direct evidence of the impact of social learning upon concordance of twins.

Quite obviously, environmental factors are always operating in the genesis of complex behavior. No set of genes appears to be sufficient for the development of schizophrenia. Twin studies reveal that MZ concordance is well below unity—perhaps below 50 percent; yet, it remains 3–6 times that of same-sexed DZ pairs, and the most reasonable explanation for this well-replicated finding is a genetic one (Pollin, 1972).

Adoption studies

Compelling evidence for that conclusion comes from clinical assessment of psychiatric disorders among foster-reared relatives of schizophrenics. In natural families, the sharing of common experiences inevitably confounds the sharing of common genes. How, then, can we evalute the disturbed offspring of a schizophrenic parent? Are the cognitive and affective disorder of the parent and his aberant child-rearing behaviors the manifestation of a genetic disorder in the parent? Or are they the psychological cause of the illness in the child? Because the deviant psychological experiences have usually been received at the hands of the patient's biological relatives, traditional family data are compatable with either a genetic or social transmission hypothesis.

The use of adoption to resolve this issue was independently conceived by a number of different investigators. Their techniques differ both in intent and design, but all involve the study of individuals adopted in infancy. We shall review results from two of these studies not only because they establish a genetic factor in the schizophrenias, but also because they reveal the complexity of genetic-experiential interaction and the diversity of adult outcomes.

As here described, both studies are directed to the question: Do genes play a role in the etiology of schizophrenia? The first technique used evaluates the adult personality of individuals born to a schizophrenic parent but reared from infancy in foster or adoptive homes. The second technique starts with schizophrenic adults who were adopted in infancy, and assesses the prevalence of schizophrenic disorder in both adoptive and biological relatives.

Table 4.5. Expectation of Schizophrenia in the General Population and in Relatives of Index Cases: Pooled Data

No. of investigations	No. of countries	Relationship to index case	No. of relatives investigated (age corrected)	Expectation of schizophrenia
19	6	unrelated general population	330,752.0	0.86
14	8	parents	6,622.0	5.07
12	7	siblings	8,484.5	8.53
6	2	children	1,226.5	12.31
4	4	uncles/aunts	3,376.0	2.01
5	4	nephews/nieces	2,315.0	2.24
4	4	first cousns	2,438.5	2.91
		Twins	Concordance	
		DZ pairs		
6	5	opposite sex	24/430	5.6%
9	7	same sex	71/593	12.0%
10	8	*MZ pairs*	252/437	57.7%

Table adapted from Shields and Slater (1967); data other than for twins from Zerbin-Rudin (1967); data are age-corrected, but only cases of definite schizophrenia are included; twin data from Gottesman and Shields (1966): no age corrections, but some doubtful cases of schizophrenia are included; Kallman's study of childhood schizophrenia is omitted.

L. L. Heston's study. The first study to use adoption as a technique for unraveling the role of genes and experience in the genesis of schizophrenia was initiated by L. L. Heston, who at that time was a resident in psychiatry at the University of Oregon Medical School. Heston evaluated the life outcomes of "97 persons who through accident of birth and rearing were eligible for inclusion in a natural experiment bearing on the etiology of schizophrenia." (Heston & Denney, 1968, p. 363)

Experimental subjects. The 47 experimental subjects were individuals born to schizophrenic mothers institutionalized in an Oregon State Psychiatric Hospital. All experimental subjects, as children, were discharged from the State Hospital within the first three days of birth to the care of either family members or foundling homes.

Control subjects. Selected from records of the same foundling homes that received experimental subjects, the controls were matched for sex, type of eventual placement, and length of time in child care institutions.

Grouping of subjects. About half of the children born to schizophrenic mothers went to foundling homes, while the remaining half went directly to families; a similar distribution was found among Control subjects. This fortuitous, natural grouping of subjects introduced a second major variable into Heston's research: institutional care during childhood. Table 4.6 illustrates how the Experimental and Control subjects are subdivided to form two new groups, the Family and Institutional groups.

Institutional group. Subjects in the Institutional groups spent an average of two years in group care, but that gross figure may underestimate the actual period during which the Institutional sample underwent disruption of their home environment: 10 of the 47 subjects were readmitted to the same or another institutional home, and several changed homes a numer of times.

Family group. Among the children who did not go to foundling homes, or who spent less than three months in them, most started life in a foster family composed of biological

Table 4.6. Grouping of Adoptees According to Genetic and Experiential History

Genetic History	Early Environmental History: Child care institution	Early Environmental History: Family rearing	
Schizophrenic mother	25	22	Experimental group N = 47
Mother with no psychiatric illness recorded	22	28	Control group N = 50
	Institutional group: N = 47	Family group: N = 50	

From Heston and Denny (1968).

relatives. The children were, of course, shifted about, but environmental disruptions within the Family group were significantly less than those of the Institutional sample.

Follow-up methods. All of the original subjects, except five females, were located or accounted for. A rich amount of information of psychiatric import was obtained. Records of subjects known to police agencies were examined; retail credit reports were obtained; school records, civil and criminal court actions, and newspaper files were reviewed; the records of all public psychiatric hospitals in the three west coast states were screened for names of the subjects and all records located were carefully reviewed; inquiries were directed to other psychiatric facilities serving areas where the subjects were living, to private physicians, and to various social service agencies with which the subjects were involved. Families, relatives, and employers were routinely contacted.

In addition to the public information obtained from such sources, subjects were contacted by letter when located, and asked to participate in a personal interview. This standardized interview was structured as a medical questionnaire and social history exploring all dimensions in considerable depth. Most subjects were interviewed in their homes, where the setting provided additional observations.

Evaluation of subjects. The dossier compiled on each subject, excluding all information referring to genetic background or foundling home history, was evaluated blindly and independently by two psychiatrists. Two evaluative measures were used: In the first, the Mental Health Sickness Rating Scale, a numerical score ranging from 100 to 0, with increasing psychosocial disability, was assigned; secondly, where clinically warranted, the raters assigned a psychiatric diagnosis. Results, summarized in Table 4.7, were striking and clear-cut: psychiatric disability was predominately concentrated in the experimental group. About one-half of the total sample born to schizophrenic mothers exhibited major psychosocial disability. Five subjects were independently diagnosed schizophrenic by all three raters. All five were members of the experimental group. No schizophrenia was found among controls. But, in addition to this central finding, mental deficiency, psychopathy and conduct disorders, delinquency, and generalized evidence of adjustment difficulties (such as failure to marry and psychiatric discharge from the Armed Services) were also significantly more frequent in the experimental subjects. One analysis of these results is that schizophrenia is a polygenic disorder in which a subcritical dosage of the implicated genes predisposes to disorders other than schizophrenia.

Heston's central find is that 5 of the 47

Table 4.7. Comparison of Adoptees Differing in Genetic History

	Control	Experimental	Probability
Number	50	47	
Males	33	30	
Age (mean)	36.3	35.8	
Adopted	19	22	
MHSRS (mean)	80.1	65.2	0.0006
Schizophrenia	0	5	0.024
Mental deficiency	0	4	0.052
Character disorder	2	9	0.017
Neurotic personality	7	13	0.052
Felons	2	7	0.054
Persons spending more than one year in psychiatric or penal institution	2	11	0.006

From Heston and Denny (1968).

Experimental subjects, born to schizophrenic mothers, themselves adopted the disorder. The age-corrected morbidity-risk for these foster-reared children is 16.6 percent—a finding wholly consistent with the risk for children born to a schizophrenic parent and reared by that parent. Parallel findings have been reported by Karlsson (1966) for an Icelandic sample and by the NIMH investigators working in Denmark (Rosenthal et al., 1968). The Danish study is particularly important, since it eliminates the intrauterine environment as a factor in these results. Of 69 parent-child pairs in the Danish study, only 11 (16 percent) were instances where the parent was psychiatrically hospitalized before the child's birth, and in 6 of these 11 cases the father was the schizophrenic parent.

One final comment on Heston's study: The environmental variable of foundling home care has no demonstrable effect. Table 4.8 compares the Institutional and Family groups by collapsing the genetic history of the subjects; all group differences are eliminated. In short, there is no evidence here that wide variation in childhood care affects psychosocial adjustment in adulthood. Of that, more later.

A Danish adoption study. A second use of adoption to assess genetic factors in schizophrenia examines the prevalence and nature of psychopathology in both biological and adoptive relatives of individuals who, following minimal contact with their biological families, were adopted and later developed schizophrenia. To illustrate, the work of Seymour Kety and his colleagues in Denmark (Kety et al., 1968) will be reviewed.

The study was made possible by three Danish registers: an Adoption Register containing records of all adoptions granted in Denmark together with relevant information on the biological parents; a population register maintained in each community and containing name and address changes; and the Psychiatric register at the Institute of Human Genetics at the University of Copenhagen, which maintains a record of all hospitalized psychiatric disorder.

The Adoption register yielded a sample of about 5,500 individuals born between 1924 and 1947—a period selected to maximize the yield of index cases within or beyond the period of maximum risk for schizophenia. From this sample 507 adoptees were found who were later admitted to a psychiatric facility. In 33 of the 507 cases, a diagnosis of

Table 4.8. Comparison of Adoptees Differing in Environmental History

	Institutional	Family
Number	47	50
Males	31	32
Age (mean)	34.1	38.0
Schizophrenic Mother	25	22
MHSRS (mean)	73.0	72.7
Schizophrenia	3	2
Mental deficiency	2	2
Character disorder	5	6
Neurotic personality	9	11
Felons	6	3
Persons spending more than one year in psychiatric or penal institution	8	5

From Heston and Denny (1968).

schizophrenia could be agreed upon by independent judges using an abstracted case history. These were carefully matched with control adoptees who had no record of mental hospitalization. A search of the Danish population registers yielded 306 identified biological parents, siblings, and half-siblings, and 157 adoptive relatives of the same relationships. Of these 463 relatives, 67 had a history of admission to a psychiatric facility; these records were abstracted and edited to remove biasing information and independent diagnoses were then made.

If schizophrenia is, in part, genetically transmitted, there should be a higher prevalence of schizophrenic disorders among the biological relatives of the index cases than in the biological relatives of matched controls. Data testing that hypothesis are presented in Table 4.9. Of 150 biological relatives of index cases, 13 (8.7 percent) had a diagnosis of schizophrenia, border-line schizophrenia, or inadequate personality. That figure compares to three cases among the 156 biological relatives of matched controls (1.9 percent) with similar diagnoses. Prevalence of these disorders in the adoptive families was significantly lower and randomly distributed between relatives of index cases and controls.

The high frequency of schizophenia-related disorders in the natural relatives of foster-reared schizophrenics could be due to shared familial risk to damaging agents in early life—e.g., to malnutrition, viruses, or toxins. Even the 19 cases who were separated in the first few weeks of life (cases shown in the lower half of Table 4.9) do not eliminate possible prenatal factors. However, the large number of half-siblings in these data do permit us to effectively rule out intrauterine and paranatal experiences. Of the 13 biological relatives with schizophrenia-related disorders, many were half-siblings, and 5 were paternal half-siblings. These, of course, do not share the intrauterine environment; they share only a portion of the common gene pool. Thus, the prevalence of schizophrenic disorder in the paternal half-siblings makes it most unlikely that significant environmental factors are influencing these data.

More recently (Kety et al., 1975) interview evaluation of mental illness in the relatives of the two groups of adoptees has been reported. Ninety percent of the living relatives (parents, siblings, and half-siblings; biological and adoptive) cooperated in psychiatric interviews from which diagnoses

Table 4.9 Distribution of Schizophrenic Disorder in the Biological and Adoptive Relatives of Index Cases and their Matched Controls

Results for total sample of 33 adopted schizophrenics		
	Biological Relatives	Adoptive Relatives
Index cases	13/150	2/74
Matched controls	3/156	3/83
probability	<.007	n.s.
Results for subsample of 19 index cases and 20 controls who were separated from biological relatives in early life		
	Biological Relatives	Adoptive Relatives
Index cases	9/93	2/45
Matched controls	0/92	1/51
probability	<.002	n.s.

Entries in the Table are the number of relatives with schizophrenia or schizophrenialike disorders as a fraction of the total number of identified relatives.

From Kety, Rosenthal, Wender, and Schulsinger (1968).

were made independently by three raters. Results confirm that schizophrenia and related disorders are significantly concentrated in the biological relatives of the schizophrenic adoptees. Prevalence of schizophrenic disorder in their adoptive relatives was no higher than in control populations.

Kinships of MZ twins

Using the Danish Twin Registry, M. Fischer (1971) has applied to schizophrenia the study of MZ twin kinships, earlier illustrated in Figure 4.3. Fisher identified adult MZ twins disconcordant for schizophrenia, and she then assessed the prevalence of the disorder in children of both ill and normal twins.

Frequency of schizophrenia was assessed among 47 children whose MZ twin-parent was schizophrenic; that result was compared to the prevalence of schizophrenia found in 25 children of the discordant (nonschizophrenic) co-twins. Since the twin-parents are monozygotes, both groups of children have inherited genes for schizophrenia, but children in the first group were also exposed to the social influence of a schizophrenic parent sharing the same home. However, the two groups do not differ in age-corrected prevalence for schizophrenia. The results are 12.3 percent for children of schizophrenic twins and 9.4 percent for the children of the normal twins.

Fisher's data suggest it is not social exposure to a schizophrenic parent, but, rather, transmission of the parent's genes that increases risk of schizophrenia in a child. Fisher's novel results parallel findings from adoption studies and provide further evidence implicating genes in the genesis of schizophrenia.

Biometrical Genetics and Schizophrenia

Given convincing evidence that genetic factors are important, the next step is to specify how the genes work. What kind of genetic-environmental model fits the data on familial transmission of schizophrenia? The biometrical genetic approach, introduced earlier in analysis of IQ, partitions the observed variation in behavior into components that reflect genetic effects on one hand and diverse environmental influences on the other. Gene action can be distinguished as additive or dominant, and, on the environmental side, the effects of common family experience can be distinguished from the idiosyncratic experiences of each individual.

As previously described, estimates of additive genetic effects can be obtained from

Table 4.10. Concordance for Schizophrenia

	MZ Twins reared together	DZ Twins reared together	Parent-Offspring reared apart
N	102	260	101
% Concordance	29.4	7.41	7.92
Correlation	0.76 ± 0.04	0.35 ± 0.01	0.37 ± 0.02

From D.W. Fulker (1973, p. 272).

the proportion of genes identical by descent for various family groupings (e.g., MZ twins, ordinary siblings, half-siblings). The effects of common environmental variance (the experiences shared within the household of a nuclear family) can be estimated from contrasts of twins reared together with those reared apart, or from parents and their offspring reared together compared to parents and offspring reared apart, as a consequence of adoption. Finally, recall that for MZ twins reared within a common household, differences must arise through the idiosyncratic experiences of one twin—experiences not shared with the co-twin. Thus, effects of experiences unique to an individual can be estimated by subtracting from unity the correlation of MZ twins, reared together.

D. W. Fulker (1973) has applied these ideas to pooled concordance data from four recent studies comparing MZ and DZ twins, all reared together, and to results of two adoption studies that provide unique data on risk of foster-reared children of a schizophrenic parent. The pooled data include 102 MZ twin pairs, 260 DZ twins, and 101 fostered children of a schizophrenic parent. Fulker's analysis is summarized in Table 4.10. A simple gene-environment model was shown to adequately fit these data. The maximum likelihood estimates attribute 73 percent of the variation to additive gene effects, and 27 percent to idiosyncratic experience. All genetic effects are additive; there is no evidence of dominance effects. Further, there is no evidence of influences arising from common family experience.

The absence of a common environmental effect is especially to be noted. Table 4.10 reveals the similarity of the concordances and, therefore, the correlations, for DZ twins reared together and for parent-offspring reared apart. Both groups share 50 percent of their genes, and a simple additive gene model therefore predicts the similar correlations shown in Table 4.10.

These reports provide no evidence that common environment plays a causal role in schizophrenia. That unexpected conclusion reflects the fact that risk for a child born to a schizophrenic, but foster-reared, is no less than that of a child born to and raised by a schizophrenic. Recall also that risk for a child of a schizophrenic MZ twin is no higher than that of children of the normal co-twin (Fischer, 1971).

Schizotaxia, schizotypy, schizophrenia

Given compelling evidence of genetic factors in schizophrenia, we now return to the conceptualization of the disorder offered by Meehl (1962). Meehl distinguished the social content of schizophrenia from its underlying genetic predisposition. The behavioral content of the disorder is, of course, socially learned. What is inherited, then, must be in the form of a predisposition that renders some individuals more likely to acquire the behavioral symptoms. Meehl suggested the term schizotaxia for the unlearned consequence of genetic transmission. Schizotaxia provides the specific etiology for the disorder—it is necessary, but not sufficient, for schizophrenia to develop. Individuals who inherit schizotaxia develop a "schizoid"' personality characterized by social withdrawal and shy aloofness. Some of these schizotypes become schizophrenic. Whether, when, and how they do so depends on other genetic factors and on the social experiences to which they are exposed. In short, the relationship between schizotaxia- schizotypy-schizophrenia is an inclusive one: no schizotaxia, no schizophrenia. But schizophrenia is not an inevitable consequence of genes. Only a minority of those at risk ever develop clinical symptoms, and whether they do or not depends, in large part, on environmental factors.

A critical question then becomes: How does one search for schizotaxia? Meehl suggested that we conceptualize it as a neural integrative defect. Since distractability is a symptom characteristic of acute schizophrenic patients, we might assume that the consequence of schizotaxia is an inhibitory defect, which makes the individual susceptible to distraction and underlies the cognitive symptoms of schizophrenia.

Distractibility can be measured experimentally by the effect of distractors on error-rate in visual discrimination. So measured, distractability characterizes acute schizophrenics and reliably differentiates them from nonschizophrenic controls (Neale et al., 1969). In addition, studies with normal MZ and DZ twins (Rose, 1978) suggest that the behavior is significantly influenced by genetic variation. The crucial test, then, is whether the behavior distinguishes children at risk for schizophrenia from matched controls. A recent report (Asarnow et al., 1977) that assessed distractibility in foster children born to a schizophrenic biological mother suggests that some of the children do exhibit significant deficits. The study is based on a very small sample, and it is cited not as definitive research but as illustrative of the conceptual logic of current studies on schizophrenia. With persistence, ingenuity, and luck, the approach may ultimately permit identification of the etiology of the disorder.

Genetic analyses of other behavior disorders

Genetic predispositions play a role in autism, reading disability, affective disorders, criminality, alcoholism, hypertension, hyperactivity, and anxiety neuroses. Research in these disorders parallels that just reviewed for schizophrenia. Twin and adoption data establish that genetic factors play a causal role, but adequate explanation of any of these disorders requires a multifactoral model. Accordingly, in each case, as in schizophrenia, the critical task is to elucidate the nature of the genetic predisposition through longitudinal study of individuals at risk.

Most common human disorders occur as a result of the interaction of polygenes with multiple environmental influences. These multifactorial disorders include cleft lip, hypertension and coronary artery disease, diabetes, familial mental retardation, and schizophrenia; in total they affect one of every two of us.

Twin, family, and adoption studies of schizophrenia establish its genetic predisposition. Intensive research efforts are now underway to identify the nature of the genetic effect. Such high-risk research holds eventual promise for primary prevention of schizophrenia, and illustrates the challenge, excitement, and hope of behavior-genetic studies in abnormal psychology.

Summary

Packed into dense bodies called chromosomes, genes are segments of DNA molecules that regulate protein synthesis in the cells. Effects of genes on the development of disordered behavior are evident at several levels.

Nondisjunction during meiotic cell division produces abnormalities of chromosome number and structure. Among newborn infants, the total frequency of such chromosome abnormalities is about 5.5 per 1000. Most are associated with mental retardation, growth deficiencies, infertility, or other congenital anomalies. The best known chromosome abnormality is Down's syndrome, due to aneuploidy of a small autosome; severe mental retardation, reduced lifespan, and distinct physical characteristics result. Nondisjunction of sex chromosomes is illustrated by Turner's syndrome, a disorder of short stature and sexual immaturity with correlated cognitive and personality characteristics. Aneuploidy of sex chromosomes results in two syndromes in males: Klinefelter's and the YY syndrome.

Effects of single mutant genes constitute the specific etiology of several important behavior disorders. Huntington's disease, a degenerative and fatal disorder often accompanied by personality change, is the result of an autosomal dominant gene. Autosomal recessive genes cause a number of metabolic diseases with behavioral symptoms; an illustration is PKU. Sex-linked recessive disorders include forms of severe mental retardation estimated to affect 8/1000 newborn males.

Differences in the normal range of tested intelligence are also, in part, due to genetic variation, but the genetic effects are attributable to the additive effect of many genes. Such polygenic transmission can be predicted from the proportion of genes shared among relatives. For tested intelligence, resemblance between relatives closely parallels proportion of shared genes, thus providing a compelling and important example of polygenic transmission.

GLOSSARY

Deoxyribonucleic acid (DNA): The chemical compound in genes responsible for hereditary transmission.

Dizygotic (fraternal) twins: Twins produced by the simultaneous fertilization of two separate ova.

Down's syndrome (trisomy-21): A severe form of mental retardation in which the affected individual carries an extra chromosome in each cell.

Heritability: The proportion of behavioral variation that is attributable to variation in genes.

Huntington's disease: A genetic disorder whose first symptoms appear in middle age, it gradually causes increasingly severe personality and physical disturbances ending in death.

Monozygotic (identical) twins: Twins produced by the fertilization of a single ovum.

Phyenylketonuria (PKU): A form of mental retardation arising from an inborn error of metabolism transmitted by a recessive gene.

Schizotoxia: The genetically determined susceptibility to develop schizophrenia given certain environmental experiences; it is necessary but not sufficient for the disorder to occur.

PHYSIOLOGICAL FACTORS

JAMES H. GEER

The material contained in this chapter is designed to give the reader an appreciation of the complex systems that provide the foundation upon which behavior depends.[1] We shall not be describing the physiological bases of disordered behavior. Rather, we shall describe the systems that play a major role in integrating behavior, only alluding to how they play a role in abnormal behavior. Other chapters will refer to the specific changes and functioning that may characterize certain disordered states. The presence of this chapter in the book reflects the position that, in order to appreciate behavior and its complexities, a knowledge of the physiological mechanisms upon which it rests is imperative. While a behavioral science can be developed that relegates physiological mechanisms to a minor role, a full and complete understanding demands that the physiological basis of behavior be recognized. Since certain alterations in physiological mechanisms result in disordered behavior an appreciation of those processes is necessary. We shall restrict our description of physiological processes to consideration of the nervous system and the endocrine system. These systems provide the immediate substrate upon which behavior depends. It is the nervous system that receives stimulation, performs integrating operations upon the impulse, and then provides outputs that initiate and control behavior. The endocrine system produces chemicals that have regulatory action upon behavior; typically, these chemical effects are slower acting and less specific than nervous system activity. The endocrine system also provides an integrative role in organizing body processes and behavior.

Central nervous system

The central nervous system (CNS) is divided into two major components: the brain and the spinal cord. Let us first describe the

The author wishes to acknowledge the assistance of Ms. Beth Murphy and Ms. Stacey Nathan who helped compile information for this chapter.

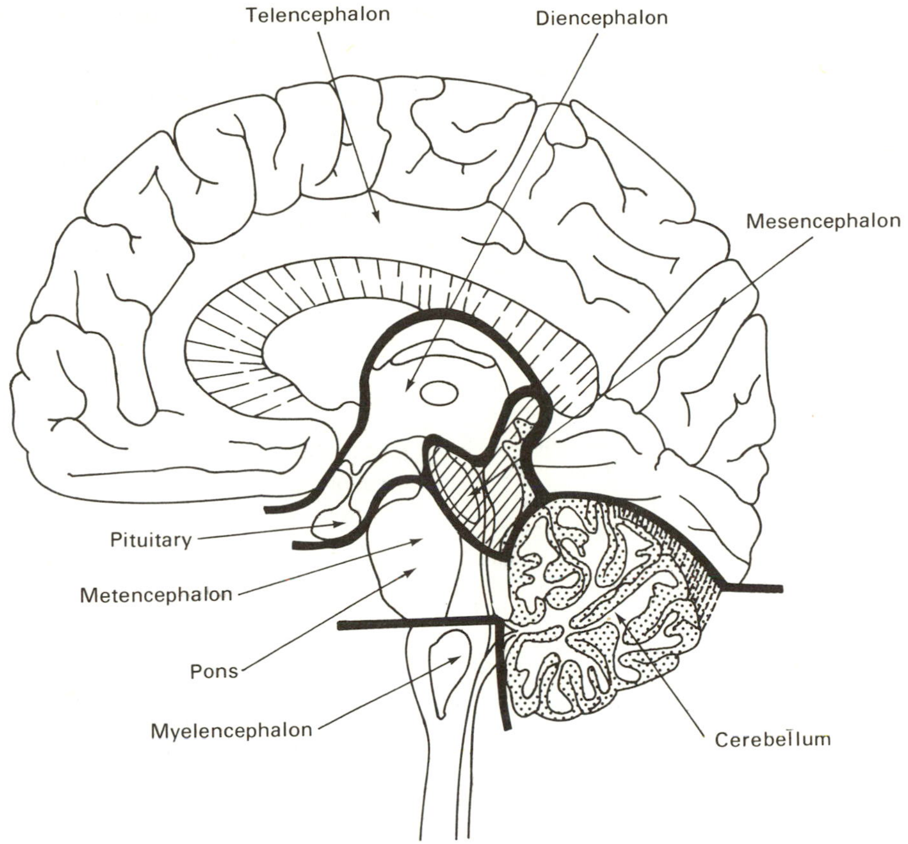

Fig. 5.1. Cross section of the brain.

organization of the brain. While there are several ways in which the brain could be divided, we shall present a five-division system widely used by neuroanatomists. The five divisions, each of which contains subdivisions, are easily followed through embryological development. Figure 5.1 is a schematic drawing of the brain in cross section that shows the five divisions and some of their structures. It is not a faithful representation of the human brain, but is intended to present the general scheme in a simplified manner. We shall describe the five divisions beginning from the closest to the spinal cord and proceeding to the most distant.

Myelencephalon

This portion of the brain serves as the junction between the brain and the spinal cord. The major structure in the myelencephalon is the medulla. The myelencephalon has several important roles in the structure of the nervous system. One of these is that the medulla is the place at which some of the cranial nerves enter and exit the central nervous system. A second is that in the medulla lie clusters of cell bodies that are concerned with the regulation of certain vital body functions. These include regulation of blood pressure, cardiac activity, and respiration.

Thirdly, many nervous tracts pass through the medulla to and from the cord and higher centers of the brain. Portions of the reticular activating system are contained in the medulla.

Metencephalon

This division of the brain lies immediately above the myelencephalon and has the first structure within it that is clearly differentiated from the spinal cord. The major structures in the metencephalon are the cerebellum and the pons. The cerebellum plays a crucial role in smoothing and coordinating muscular movements. The cerebellum has gray and white matter, which is characteristic of the rest of the brain. The pons is principally a transmission area that connects the two halves of the cerebellum and also contains tracts of both ascending and descending nerve fibers to and from other parts of the brain. There are several clusters of nerve cell bodies in the pons, one of the more important of which is the nuclei for the fifth cranial nerve, important in controlling sensation and movement in the face and mouth.

Mesencephalon

This division is relatively small and functions primarily as a passageway between higher and lower portions of the nervous system. The mesencephalon is divided into the roof (tectum) and the floor (tegmentum). The roof has sensory functions relating to vision and hearing. The floor is composed principally of sensory tracts running upwards, and descending motor tracts. The floor also has a portion of the reticular formation that extends into other portions of the brain.

Diencephalon

The principal components of the diencephalon are the thalamus, the hypothalamus, and the pituitary. The pituitary is a gland that regulates much of the body's activities and will be discussed later in this chapter when we consider the endocrine system. The thalamus is the major relay station in the brain. There are three major types of thalamic nuclei that we can describe. The first are subcortical or intrinsic nuclei. These do not connect to the cerebral cortex, but rather link subcortical structures. Sensory relay nuclei, on the other hand, connect sensory input to the cerebral cortex. We might note that sensory input can indirectly reach the cortex through connections in the reticular formation, thus bypassing the thalamus. The third class of thalamic nuclei are the association nuclei. They receive inputs from within the thalamus, but in turn send their projections to the cortex, thus directly influencing cortical events.

The hypothalamus, with its associated pituitary stock and gland, make up the other principal structures in the diencephalon. The major function of the hypothalamus is to integrate and control activity in the autonomic nervous system. While other centers in the brain have effects upon autonomic activity, the hypothalamus seems to be particularly important in integrating that activity with much of behavior. Research has shown the hypothalamus to play a role in temperature regulation, hunger, thirst, sexual functioning, and other motivational states. It is known to regulate the production of hormones by the pituitary.

Telencephalon

This last division of the brain is the most advanced division and in humans makes up most of the mass of the nervous system. It is estimated to contain over nine billion of the approximately twelve billion cells that make up the human brain. The telencephalon consists of the olfactory bulb and tracts, the basal ganglia, and the cerebral hemispheres. The olfactory bulb and tracts are made up of all bodies connecting the olfactory receptors to the brain. The basal ganglia lie below the cortex and consist of phylogenetically old nuclei that appear to be important in the control of motor functions.

The largest structures in the telencephalon are the cerebral hemispheres. They are made

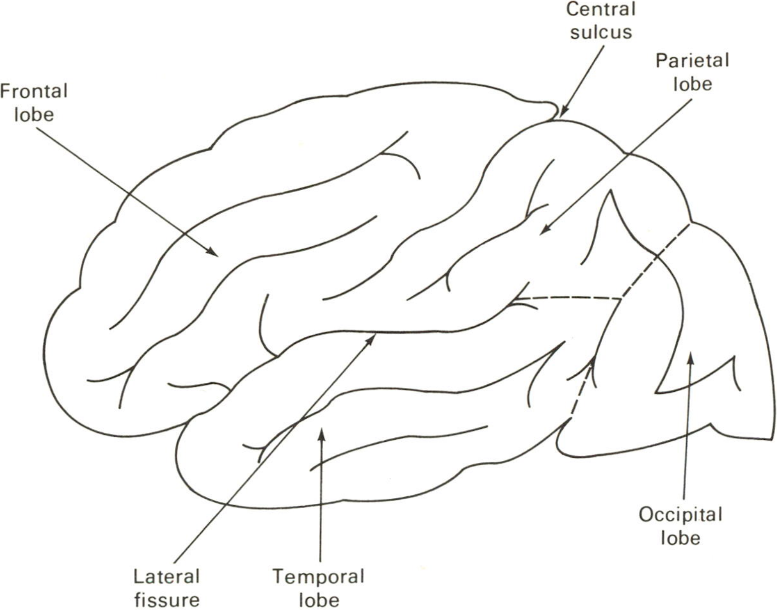

Fig. 5.2. Side view of brain.

up of the gray matter of the cerebal cortex, the white matter (primarily fiber tracts to and from lower portions of the brain) lying below, and the corpus callosum, which contains the connecting fiber tracts between the left and right cerebral hemispheres. The cerebral cortex is quite convoluted with many ridges and valleys. Apparently, the convolutions or folds function to greatly enlarge the cortical area. There are fissures that break up the cerebral cortex into divisions or lobes. Figure 5.2 shows a simplified side view of the human brain with the lobes and some of the fissures labeled for identification. The cerebral cortex is made up of many neurons and their connections. Studies have demonstrated that many cortical nerve cells connect only with other cells in the cortex, providing an immensely rich and complex network for receipt and transmission of nervous system activity. There are three varieties of fibers in the cerebral cortex. One type, commissural, are those associated with connecting the hemispheres through the corpus callosum. A second type, association, are those that connect one portion of the cerebral cortex to another. The third, projection, are those fibers that deliver impulses to and from the cortex to another component of the brain. Our very brief, simplified picture of the cerebral cortex we hope will permit the reader to begin to appreciate the immensely complex structure that is so important in determining behavior.

Spinal cord

The spinal cord serves two major functions. One is the conduction of neural impulses between the brain and various inputs and outputs of the spinal nerves. The second is that the spinal cord serves an integrative function and, in some instances, functions to operate reflexes without much if any help higher in the CNS. Those within-the-spinal cord reflexes are simply called spinal reflexes. Figure 5.3 is a schematic cross-sectional view of the spinal cord. The cord is

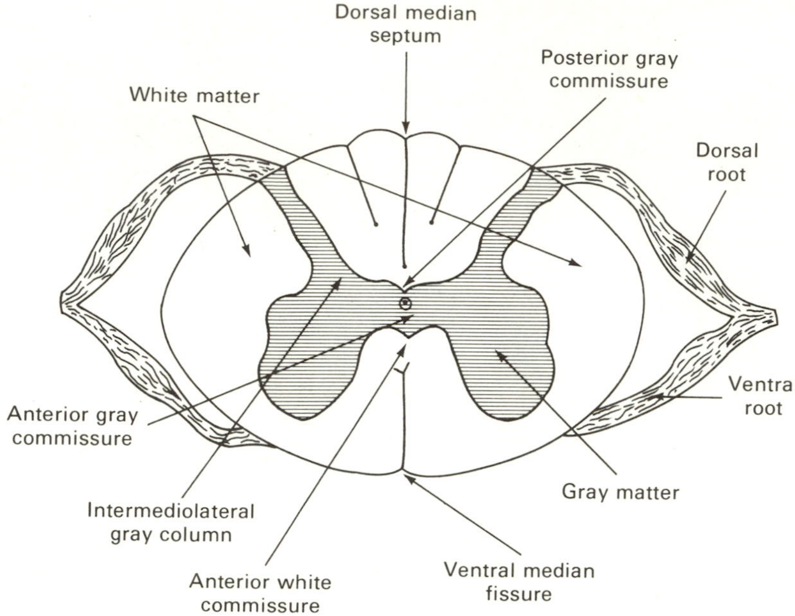

Fig. 5.3. Cross section of spinal cord.

divided into halves by the dorsal and ventral fissures. The halves are connected by the gray and white commissures. Incoming impulses enter through the dorsal root fibers, and the gray matter of the dorsal horn. From the ventral horn of the gray matter, fibers emerge to leave the cord via the ventral roots and form the pathways that operate various components of the body. All descending fibers terminate upon motor neurons in the cord, which in turn act to stimulate activity somewhere in the body. Ascending fiber systems convey sensory information up the cord to higher structures. Those fibers that terminate within the cord are termed intersegmental tracts and are often involved in spinal reflexes. Crossover is a general principle in the CNS. That means that incoming signals from the right side of the body are delivered to the left side of the brain, and similarly, descending fibers from the left side cross over and go down the right side of the spinal cord.

Although its mode of operation is not well known, the CNS has been equipped with a defense against chemical assault. The blood-brain barrier acts to restrict the passage of substances to the brain. This protective mechanism is very important in keeping the chemical environment in the brain relatively constant. Without such a protective system, the CNS would be much more readily effected by the ingestion of various substances than is the case.

The CNS and its role in emotion

Emotions are central to the understanding of abnormal or disturbed behavior. Certain structures in the CNS have been identified as being particularly important in emotion. We shall briefly consider some of these findings. It must be noted that our understanding in this matter is severely limited and suggestions that are offered here must be viewed as tentative and preliminary.

First of all, the evidence suggests that the cerebral cortex plays an organizing role in emotion. Much of the evidence comes from research with animals in which the cortex is surgically removed, or connections with the rest of the brain are severed. Animals with the cortex removed have a lower rage threshold, suggesting that one function of the cortex is to inhibit lower centers. A second cortical function seems to be the control of direction or focus of emotional responses. Decorticated animals often show complete rage responses, but not directed toward the specific stimuli that elicit the rage. For example, if the stimuli is pinching the tail, the animal may attack straight ahead. The third function attributed to the cortex is timing of emotional responses. The animal without a cortex is not only more easily aroused, but also recovers more rapidly. Thus, the cortex seems to be involved in the timing of emotional reactions by providing limiting and smoothing functions.

As is obvious from the above discussion, brain structures other than the cerebral cortex are involved in emotional responding. It is likely that, to some degree, most of the brain plays some role in emotion. Research, however, has identified a group of structures that seem to be very involved in emotion. This group of structures is called the limbic system. It includes the hippocampus, hypothalmus, amygdala, portions of the basal ganglia, septum, optic area, paraolfactory area, and epithalamus among subcortical structures; and the portion of the cortex called the limbic cortex, which includes hippocampal gyrus, pyriform area, uncus, cingulate gyrus, and the orbitofrontal area. This complex system is involved in controlling many of the body's automatic systems such as blood pressure and body fluid balance. Emotional responses also seem very dependent upon various parts or combination of portions of the limbic systems. To describe all of the proposed relationships would be beyond the scope of this presentation. However, the limbic system has been demonstrated to be involved in pleasure, pain, rage, alertness, sleep, sexual activities, and aggression. While it would be incorrect to state that emotion resides in these structures, clearly they play a crucial role.

Another CNS system that deserves mention is the reticular activating system. This system seems to be central in determining the overall activity level of the CNS. Thus, its activity has implications for wakefulness and sleep as well as for attentional mechanisms. The reticular formation begins in the upper end of the spinal cord and extends into the hypothalamus and the thalamus. It is made up of many diffuse neurons that are closely interrelated, along with small nuclei that have both motor and sensory functions. When the reticular system is quiet the individual sleeps; when sensory input arrives the system activates and arouses the individual. As you can imagine, sensory inputs vary in their ability to produce the arousal reaction—for example, pain is particularly effective as an arousing stimulus. Lesions in the reticular formation can result in coma and lack of responsiveness to stimuli.

Brain waves

By placing sensitive electrodes on the surface of the head, it is possible to record some of the electrical activity of the brain. The electrical potentials (i.e., changes) recorded are called brain waves, and the printed record of these waves is known as an electroencephalogram (EEG). These recordings apparently reflect the activity of many nerve cells in the cerebral cortex lying beneath the recording electrode. The record does not show activity in single or just a few cells, but seems to reflect synchronized neuron activity. It is believed that much of the cortical activity seen in the EEG reflects activity in portions of the reticular formation. Brain waves are classified principally on the basis of their regularity, amplitude or strength, and their frequency. The EEG can be used to diagnose certain clinical conditions with a fair degree of accuracy. In particular, epilepsy and brain lesions or tumors can often

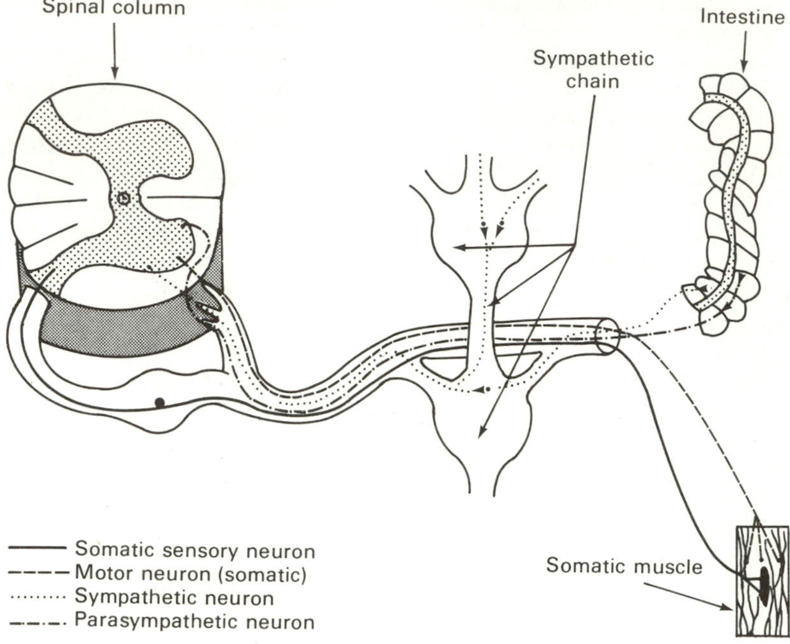

Fig. 5.4. Section of peripheral nervous system.

be recognized by distinct brain waves. It is also possible to make statements concerning wakefulness or sleep stage on the basis of EEG recordings. Finally, the EEG is used in the determination of "brain death" in those cases of individuals who have become comatose as a result of injury to the brain from any one of numerous reasons. While some people feel that they can distinguish "personalities" on the basis of EEGs, the evidence for this is not well established.

Peripheral nervous system

Those parts of the nervous system that lie outside of the brain or spinal cord are labeled the peripheral nervous system. The peripheral nervous system consists of both ganglia (groups of cell bodies) and nerves (neuron fibers). The system has been divided into two divisions: the autonomic and the somatic. Both the autonomic and somatic have components within and outside of the CNS. What makes their separation meaningful is the portions of the body they serve. The autonomic system controls the smooth muscles of the blood vessels and other internal organs, some of the endocrine glands, and the heart. In a general way, the autonomic system controls the internal milieu of the body. The somatic system conveys impulses to and from the skeletal musculature and the sense organs. We will find that outside the CNS the autonomic and somatic systems differ quite distinctively, but within the CNS they are not readily distinguished.

The peripheral autonomic system is differentiated in part by the fact that many of its nerve junctions (synapses) and clusters of cell bodies (ganglia) lie outside the CNS. Figure 5.4 shows an idealized view of the peripheral nervous system. Some of these ganglia form a chain (the sympathetic chain) lying just outside the spinal cord. These ganglia are connected to each other in addition to the cord and the glands or smooth muscles that they activate. This arrangement results in a more or less unitary system that

Table 5.1. Some Effects of the Sympathetic and Parasympathetic Systems

	Parasympathetic Effect	Sympathetic Effect
Heart	Beat slower and with less strength	Beat faster and with increased strength
Sweat glands	No effect	Increased sweating
Adrenal gland	No effect	Increased production of hormones
Pupil of eye	Constrict	Dilate
Bowels	Increased peristalsis	Decreased peristalsis
Blood pressure (via effect on blood vessels)	Decrease	Increase
Sexual response (males)	Erection	Orgasm and ejaculation
Sexual response (females)	Blood volume increases in genitals (probable)	Orgasm (probable)

operates much more as a whole than does the somatic division of the peripheral nervous system. The autonomic nervous system is further divided into two subdivisions: the sympathetic and the parasympathetic. The division is based on both anatomical and physiological differences. In the sympathetic division, about 90 percent of the motor pathways originate in the spinal cord, then synapse (connect) with a neuron or nerve cell in the sympathetic ganglia, which in turn stimulate the end organ. In the parasympathetic division the motor pathway is from the cord directly to the end organ. At that point a synapse is made with the neuron that operates upon the end organ. An additional anatomic distinction between the sympathetic and parasympathetic divisions is the fact that the nerves for the parasympathetic come from regions of the spinal cord that lie above and below the sympathetic division.

A major distinction between the sympathetic and parasympathetic division that has very important consequences is the fact that they typically secrete a different chemical at their nerve endings. The parasympathetic motor neurons secrete acetylcholine. Such nerves are variously called either cholinergic or adrenergic. A few of the sympathetic nerve endings also secrete acetylcholine, but most secrete norepinephrine (also called noradrenalin). In general, acetylcholine (parasympathetic) acts to reduce activity in an end organ and norepinephrine (sympathetic) acts to increase activity. It also appears that the action of norepinephrine lasts only a few seconds, whereas outside of skeletal muscles, acetylcholine seems to act over longer periods of time. The time differences result from different mechanisms being responsible for the removal of the chemicals from their sites of action. Table 5.1 lists the effects of the sympathetic and parasympathetic divisions upon various end organs. The reader should note that many of the effects are those that accompany emotional behavior (see the discussion of anxiety in chapter 8). It is for this reason that the autonomic nervous system was covered in detail.

One final point needs to be discussed in relation to the sympathetic and parasympathetic divisions. For a long time it was popular to think of the sympathetic and parasympathetic systems as operating in an antagonistic relationship: the sympathetic system involved in increasing activity and the parasympathetic in decreasing activity in the end organs. While there is some validity to that formulation, it very quickly breaks down upon careful analysis. One of the reasons is that both the sympathetic and parasympathetic systems are continually active, with the nerve endings secreting acetylcholine or norepiniphrine. This activity is called "tone," and describes the continuous activity of the system. Because of tone, both sympathetic and parasympathetic divisions can increase or decrease activity in an

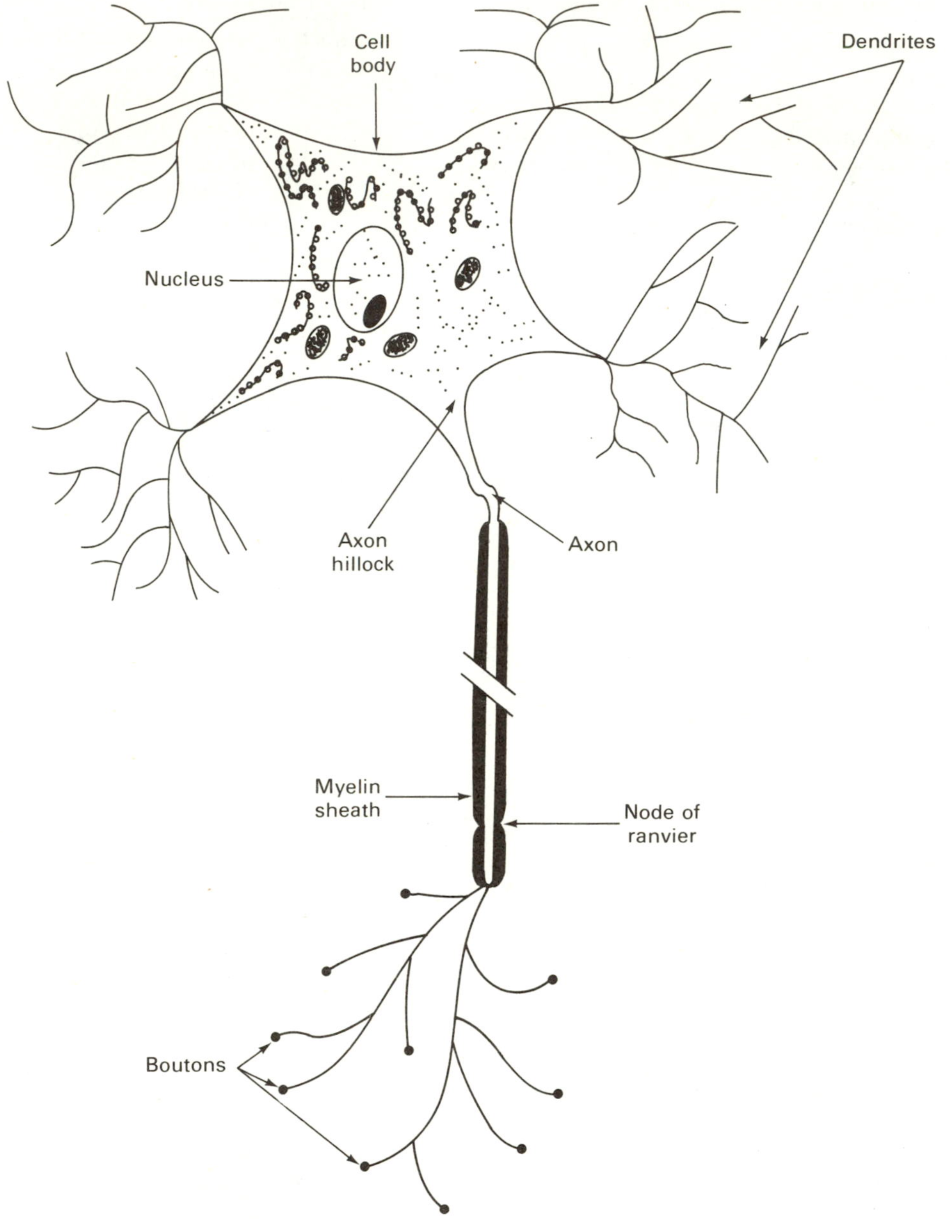

Fig. 5.5. The nerve cell.

end organ by either increasing or decreasing the rate of stimulation. When the added complication occurs that a few of the sympathetic division's neurons secrete acetylcholine, we see that the distinction between divisions as being antagonistic loses some of its validity. In our subsequent discussion of drug effects we shall return to considerations of the autonomic nervous system and its operation.

The nerve cell: structure and function

Neurons are the name given to nerve cells. Neurons have three major parts called the cell body, the axon, and the dendrites. The cell body contains a nucleus and many other components such as mitochondria, fibrils, and robosomes. The dendrites are the receiving parts of the neuron and are generally short, heavily branched structures close to the cell body (see Figure 5.5). The axon is often a long, single structure that delivers the nervous impulse. Neurons often have many dendrites, but only one axon, although the axon may have branches. At the site on the cell body where the axon originates is a small bump called the axon hillock where the nerve impulse arises. Figure 5.5 must be viewed as diagrammatic since neurons vary dramatically in their complexty. One neuron can stimulate many others and in turn be stimulated by many others, while in other instances one neuron may effect only one other. In part, it is this complexity that allows the incredibly rich and varied behavior of humans.

The nerve impulse

What actually occurs in a nerve cell and how the activity in one cell affects another are questions of fundamental importance in understanding the nervous system. The first of these questions deals with the nerve impulse, its nature, and the mechanism by which it is transmitted within the neuron.

The inside of a nerve cell has an electrical charge, compared to the fluids that immediately surround the cell. This charge is called the membrane potential, and results from an accumulation of negative ions (potassium) inside and positive ions (sodium) just outside the membrane border between the cell and the intercellular fluids. This means that a resting membrane is much more permeable to potassium than to sodium ions. Secondly, there is a physiological mechanism called a "sodium pump" that actively removes sodium ions from the inside of the cell. When some event causes the membrane to suddenly become permeable to sodium ions, a series of events occur. The basic event is the rapid flow of ions (particles with electrical charges) through the membrane. This flow of charges is an electrical current and is called the action potential.

By carefully measuring the electrochemical events we can describe the steps in the development and spread of the action potential or nerve impulse. When the membrane become permeable to the sodium ions and the current flow begins, the effect typically occurs at one spot in the neuron. It has been shown that the membrane breakdown (depolarization) can be caused by electrical, chemical, mechanical, or temperature stimulation. Immediately after the depolarization, the depolarized section starts reinstituting its resistance to sodium ion flow. However, typically the membrane immediately adjacent to the original place of depolarization, apparently being affected by the current flow, starts to depolarize while the original spot begins repolarization. In this manner the action potential travels from the site of original depolarization to other parts of the cell. The repolarization follows along behind the spreading action potential, and it prevents the depolarization from spreading back upon itself. Under most conditions this action potential is in all-or-none effect. That means that the neuron either fires or it does not, but once it fires the nerve impulse occurs at full strength regardless of the strength or quality of the stimulus that initiated the firing.

There is a good deal of knowledge concerning the details of the nature of the action potential. These need not concern us here; however, there is one factor concerning the propagation of the impulse that should be noted. The speed of the impulse as it travels down the axon toward its final destination is affected by whether or not the neuron's axon is *myelinated.* The myelin sheath that surrounds some axons is a white liquid substance and acts to speed propagation or spread of the action potential. At points about every millimeter along the myelinated axon there are interruptions in the myelin sheath called nodes of Ranvier (see Figure 5.5). The nerve impulse in a myelinated axon jumps from node to node, and thus moves more rapidly

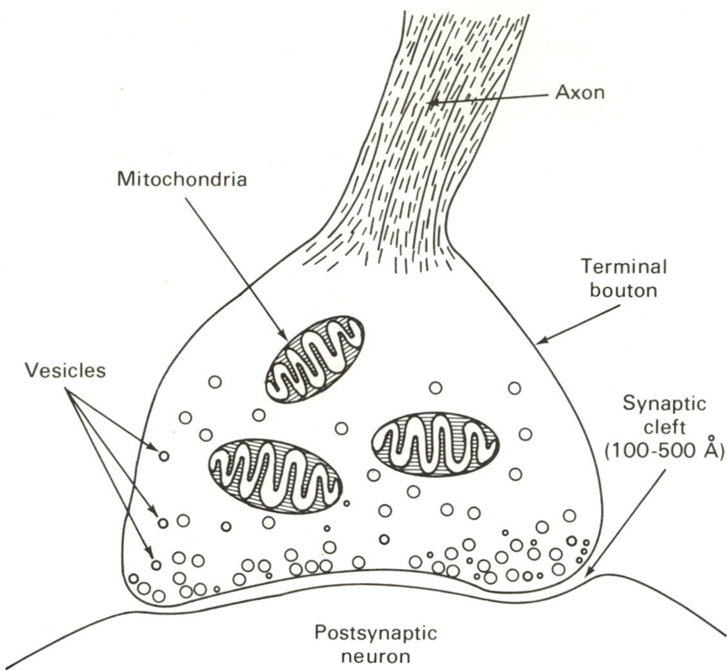

Fig. 5.6. The synapse.

along the axon than in an unmyelinated neuron where the skipping does not occur. It is felt that the jumping of the impulse not only speeds up the propagation of the impulse, but also is an energy saving device, since not all of the membrane depolarizes and nor must it then repolarize (a process that requires energy expenditure by the neuron). The white matter in the CNS is made up of a heavy concentration of myelinated neurons.

As we have noted, there are numerous stimuli that can produce an action potential in a nerve cell. There also are factors that can increase the nerve cell's sensitivity to stimulation, thus making it so reactive that it fires with no apparent external stimulation. In general, any substance that increases membrane permeability has that effect. One of the most potent substances that increases neuron excitation is acetylcholine. We have already learned that acetylcholine is produced by neurons in the sympathetic nervous system. We also know that reduced concentration of calcium ions increases the excitability of neurons. On the other hand, there are substances that reduce the excitability or produce inhibition of neuron activity. These act by increasing the membrane's resistance to the flow of ions. As low levels of calcium ions increase permeability, high levels decrease permeability. Also, low potassium concentration reduces membrane permeability. As we shall learn, many psychoactive drugs have their effect upon nerve cell excitability or irritability (ease of stimulation).

Synapse

The action potential travels from the point of excitation throughout the nerve cell and along the axon to its junction with another neuron or an end organ. This junction is called a synapse. Since neurons are surrounded by their membranes, they are not directly connected. Rather, there is a small space (synaptic cleft) between the end of the axon, typically divided into many small collateral fibers each ending with a small enlargement called a terminal bouton, and the dendrite or cell body of the next neuron. The mechanism by which the action potential from one neuron acts to stimulate another is of fundamental importance in understanding how the nervous system operates and how it can be disrupted.

The effect of a presynaptic neuron upon the postsynaptic neuron can be one of two varieties; one excitatory and the other inhibitory. Let us first consider the excitatory effect. At the synaptic junction the terminal bouton of the presynaptic neuron has vesicles that contain a transmitter substance. When the action potential reaches the terminal bouton, the depolarization of the membrane results in some of the vesicles emptying their contents into the synaptic cleft. The excitatory transmitter acts to increase the permeability of the membrane of the postsynaptic neuron. If sufficient numbers of terminal boutons stimulate a postsynaptic neuron, it will develop its own action potential. One excitatory transmitter substance, at least in the parasympathetic division of the autonomic nervous system, is acetylcholine. We also know that norepinephrine is an excitatory transmitter in the sympathetic division of the autonomic nervous system. There is considerable controversy over the nature of transmitters in the CNS. It is generally accepted that acetylcholine, norepinephrine, dopamine, and serotonin act as central neural transmitters. It is likely that there are others as well.

As noted, some synapses act to inhibit or reduce the likelihood of the postsynaptic neuron from developing an action potential. This inhibition can occur from an inhibitory transmitter that acts to decrease membrane potential. Very little is known about the nature of inhibitory transmitters other than their effect. It appears that presynaptic neurons are either inhibitory or excitatory, but not both. Inhibition in the CNS plays a central role in selecting among responses and preventing generalized excitation from spreading throughout that would immobilize the individual.

We should not forget that neurons not only stimulate other neurons, but they also act upon end organs. Transmitters act to stimulate the end organs such as skeletal or smooth muscles in a manner like that occuring within the nervous system. For the smooth muscles we find that both acetylcholine and norepinephrine act as transmitters. What is complicating is that acetylcholine excites some and inhibits other smooth muscles and the same is true for norepinephrine. It does seem that these two substances act antagonistically regardless of the direction that either one takes. Some factor in the end organ determines the action of the transmitter. At skeletal muscle neuron synapses, acetylcholine acts as the excitatory transmitter. Acetylcholine acts very rapidly to stimulate muscle cells into action and a second substance, cholinesterase, acts to rapidly break down the acetycholine to prevent it from acting too long. We shall learn later of drugs that act to affect acetylcholine and cholinesterase.

Hormones and behavior

The endocrine system, along with the CNS, are the two major systems in the body whose role is to integrate processes and regulate behavior. The endocrine system consists of various glands in the body that produce chemicals, known as hormones, that are released into the bloodstream and are transported to distant parts of the body where they have their effects. As we shall see, hormones sometimes act directly upon behavior and at other times provide setting conditions that place constraints or limits upon behavior. Our knowledge of hormones and their role in behavior is in its infancy. However, since there are some very important known relationships, we present the information in a summary form. We also shall present some of the information currently available concerning the interaction between the CNS and the endocrine system. For our purposes we do not need to discuss all of the endocrine glands; we shall limit ourselves to those glands whose hormones are known to be associated with behavioral effects.

In general, hormones act to control metabolic activity at their sites of action. Because hormones are chemicals and are present in the bloodstream, their actions follow time courses that differ from that of nervous system activity. While many people assume that hormone effects are necessarily slow acting and of relatively long duration, such is not always the case. Some effects may take months or years to be noticeable, while others occur in seconds. The circulating levels (not always related to their effect) of some hormones many change only very slowly while for others the concentration in the bloodstream may change from minute to minute. Some hormones act at sites nearby their location of production, while others act at some distance from their place of manufacture. For example, acetylcholine produced by a neuron acts on the structure across the very tiny synaptic junction. FSH (follicle stimulating hormone), a hormone from the pituitary, has its action upon the gonads.

All hormones probably affect behavior, although many do so indirectly. For example, ADH (antidiuretic hormones) decrease water excretion by the kidneys. Water balance in the body is crucial in the health of the individual, but ADH's effect upon behavior is more indirect than hormones that regulate nervous system activity. We shall only consider the hormones with relatively direct effects.

Adrenal medulla

One endocrine gland whose hormones have direct effects upon behavior is the adrenal medulla. The adrenal gland is composed of two independent parts: the cortex and the medulla. The adrenal medulla, under stimulation from the sympathetic nervous system, secretes two hormones directly into the bloodstream. They are epinephrine and norepinephrine, the same substance secreted by the neurons of the sympathetic nervous system. The effects of norepinephrine from the adrenal medulla is the same as that produced by direct action of norepinephrine at the sympathetic nervous system synapse, except that the duration of action is much longer. Epinephrine, the second adrenal medulla hormone, has effects quite similar to norepinephrine with certain exceptions. These include the important difference that epinephrine has a much greater effect in increasing all metabolism, and thus increasing generalized activity. The adrenal medulla generally secretes three times more epinephrine than norepinephrine. As can be readily understood, the adrenal secretions have a much broader effect upon behavior than the sympathetic systems, since all cells are reached by the circulation and not just the ones ennervated by the sympathetic nervous system. Thus, hormones from the adrenal medulla stimulate all cells in the body. As noted, the adrenal medulla's control comes from the sympathetic nervous system fibers that directly stimulate the hormone secreting cells. Therefore, in two ways (directly upon end organs and indirectly through the adrenal medulla), the sympathetic system can increase the amount of energy expended by the activity of the body. Both reflect activity of hormones upon cellular activity.

It has been suggested that these effects prepare the body for coping with stresses of both physical and psychological origins. Thus, the adrenal medulla, through the production of epinephrine and norepinephrine, has powerful effects upon behavior. The system is circular and in part self-activating. That is, the sympathetic system stimulates the adrenal medulla to secrete epinephrine and norepinephrine, which in turn stimulates all cells, including the sympathetic nervous system, to increase activity thus stimulating more activity in the adrenal medulla. It has been suggested that this self-stimulating system accounts, in part, for the relatively long-term effects of frightening events.

Sex hormones

Most people know of the existence of sex hormones and many assume that they control much of sexual behavior. Certainly that is true for lower animals; however, for humans, the hormonal control of sexual behavior is rather relaxed. It appears that the sex hormones play limiting roles rather than specific directing functions as is the case in many other species. There are two types of hormones that are related to sex. The first include the gonadotrophic hormones produced by the pituitary that have the effect of stimulating the sex glands (ovaries and testicles) into producing the male and female sex hormones. Thus, we have hormones that stimulate the production of other hormones in a complex and fascinating manner. There are three different gonadotrophic hormones secreted by the pituitary gland that have pronounced effects upon the functioning of the gonads. They are: 1. FSH (follicle stimulating hormone), 2. LH (luteinizing hormone) also known in the male as ICSH (interstitial cell-stimulating hormone), and 3. LTH (lactongenic hormone or prolactin).

These hormones, while secreted by the pituitary, have their production controlled by the hypothalmus; thus, the CNS has control over the production of sex hormones. The effects of the gonadotrophins differ in males and females since the target organs differ between sexes. FSH in males stimulates the testicles to produce sperm cells. In females FSH stimulates the ovaries to prepare for ovulation. For males LH stimulates cells in the testes to produce the principal male sex hormone, testosterone. In females, in combination with FSH, LH stimulates the ovaries to allow ovulation. LH also stimulates the corpus leutium, the ovarian cells that remain after ovulation, to produce large quantities of female sex hormones. Finally, LTH is not known to play a role in males, but in females it acts upon the ovaries probably to stimulate the corpus leutium and also promotes secretion of milk in the breast. In women, the gonadotropic hormones operate upon a feedback system that results in the monthly menstrual cycle. There is no known counterpart for men. The fact that stress can effect menstrual cycles probably reflects the CNS control over gonadotropic hormone production.

As we noted, the gonadtrophic hormones operate upon the gonads to stimulate them into activity. One of the major functions of the gonads is the production of the male and female sex hormones. We now turn to a discussion of the principal sex hormones. In women there are two major types of sex hormones: the estrogens and progesterone. Let us first consider the estrogens. There are at least six estrogens that have been identified although only three are present in large amounts. They are produced principally by the ovaries, except during pregnancy when the placenta secretes much more than the ovaries. The estrogens acts to cause the growth of tissues and cells. Table 5.2 summarizes the effects of both the estrogens and progesterone upon target structures. The estrogens act to develop both primary and secondary sex organs. The changes that occur at puberty in the sexually maturing female are caused primarily by the estrogens. The estrogens are also responsible for maintaining many of the changes once they are established. Progesterone has the principal role of preparing the uterus for implantation by a fertilized ovum. It also aids in milk production by preparing the breasts for lactation.

Male sex hormones are called androgens, and the principal ones are testosterone and 4-androstene-3, 17, -dione. Both are manufactured in the testes. The adrenal glands in both sexes are known to normally produce small quantities of at least five different androgens. Testosterone is the most responsible for the development of male genitals and secondary sex characteristics, playing a role analogous to estrogen in females. Table 5.3 summarizes testosterone's effects seen at puberty. During embryonic development testosterone is responsible for the development of male genitals. It should be noted that testosterone and the estrogens are quite similar in chemical structure. In fact, small amounts of the estrogens are formed from the chemical breakdown of testosterone, and it also is known that the testes secrete

Table 5.2. Effects of Estrogens and Progesterone

Estrogen

Changes at puberty:
Increase in size of vagina and uterus
Increase in breast size due to fat deposits
Increase in hips and thigh size due to fat deposit
Smoothing and softening of skin
Pubic and underarm hair development
Increased blood supply to skin
Increased rate of skeletal growth followed by process that stops growth of long bones
Increased activity by sebaceous glands possibly causing acne

Postpuberty effects:
Slight increase in metabolism level
Maintenance of feminine fat distribution
Maintenance of smooth skin texture
Major role in preparing uterus for implantation by fertilized ova
Play a role in menstrual cycle

Progesterone

Changes at puberty:
Increase in breast size
Important role in beginning menstrual cycling

Postpuberty effects:
Major role in preparing uterus for implantation by fertilized ova
Plays a role in menstrual cycle
Helps prepare body during pregnancy for various changes

Table 5.3. Effects of Testosterone

Changes at puberty:
Increase in size of penis and testicles
Increase in size of prostate and other internal sex organs
Growth of hair on face, trunk, underarms, and pubic area
Larynx grows and voice deepens
Muscles develop
Skin thickens and becomes tougher
Increased secretion rate of sebaceous glands sometimes causing acne
Increased size and strength of bones followed by process that stops growth of long bones

Postpuberty effects:
Maintenance of masculine muscle development
Baldness when combined with genetic factors
Considerable increase in metabolism level

estrogens. The role, if any, of estrogens in males is not known.

What, if any, are the behavioral effects of the sex hormones? The answer lies in two parts. First, they prepare the body by developing genitals and secondary sex characteristics. Anomalies in the development of sexual characteristics may have pronounced effects upon sexual behavior through either or both biological or cultural factors. Certainly maldeveloped genitals affect sexual behavior.

The second part of the answer lies in considering the role of sex hormones in sex interest and performance. Many people assume that sex hormones are the factors underlying human sex drive or interest. In fact, the evidence for such a belief is sparse. It may be briefly summarized by reporting that some researchers feel that there is a hormone basis to sex drives and that it likely derives from the androgens.

Recall that even though the androgens are male hormones, some are produced in limited quantities in women. Thus, this so-called libido hormone is available to both sexes. The evidence for androgens being the sex drive or libido hormone is derived almost exclusively from uncontrolled case studies that we shall not present. If there is an effect of hormones on sexual interest and preferences, it appears to be very slow acting and relatively free of levels or amounts of the hormones. A great deal of research is needed before any precise statements can be made about the relationship between hormones and sexual interests or preferences in humans. At the present time we can only describe the role of sex hormones in the development of tissues and note their role in conception and pregnancy. While there are many hormones other than those produced by the adrenal medulla and the sex hormones, their relationship to behavior is not well established and, thus, we shall not consider hormones further.

Drug effects

The study of the effects of drugs upon behavior is very complex and is not yet well understood. Psychopharmacology is in its infancy; yet, we can briefly point out some of the more important ideas and findings. A very difficult problem in the examination of drug effects is to present a system of classification. Classification can be based upon many different points of view. We could group drugs as to their effect upon the nervous system and so on until we had an imposing and confusing list. Not only would our list be long, but it would have to be quite confusing. For example, some drugs energize behavior at one dose level and inhibit at another; how would we classify those if our categories included behavioral excitation and inhibition? We shall describe drug effects using classifications based upon both clinical and applied usage and in some instances upon their effect on the nervous system.[2]

CNS depressants

Some drugs have their behavioral effects apparently through their ability to depress activity in the nervous system. They seem to have their effect through the mechanism of reducing cell metabolism. Recall we spoke earlier of this effect when discussing the neuron. There is considerable variation in location in the brain that may be affected by different drugs as well as the exact manner by which cell excitability may be affected. We can only briefly note some of these depressant drugs and their effects. The major categories of CNS depressants are: 1. alcohol, 2. analgesics, 3. antidepressants, 4. general and local anesthetics, 5. sedative-hypnotics, and 6. tranquilizers. We shall briefly discuss each category.

Alcohol has a depressant effect on CNS activity and was at one time used as an anesthetic, probably because of this effect. Alcohol is rapidly absorbed into the bloodstream when ingested and quickly reaches the brain. It appears to have an early effect upon inhibitory centers; thus at low doses it looks like an excitant, since it inhibits inhibitions. With increased amounts, the depressive effects upon motor coordination, respiration, etc., may be seen and at sufficiently high levels death will result from the depressive effect.

Analgesics (morphine, codeine, and heroin) are drugs that reduce pain but do not result in general anesthesia. Morphine has the ability to reduce the psychological effect of pain while apparently having only a slight effect upon the pain sensation. Heroin, in addition to affecting pain, may yield a sense of elation bordering on rapture. This effect upon feeling tone is the basis for its abuse. Interestingly, heroin, after crossing the blood-brain barrier, is converted back into morphine in the brain. Apparently very little is needed in the brain to produce the effects noted above.

Antidepressive drugs are administered to individuals experiencing depression. There are two major variations: the monoamine oxidase (MAO) inhibitors and the tricyclic antidepressants. The MAO inhibitors block the activity of monoamine oxidase, which depletes norepenephrine, dopamine, and serotonin in the brain. These CNS transmitters thus increase in their concentration, apparently resulting in the clinical effect upon depression. The MAO inhibitors often have adverse side effects, so that they have been replaced by the tricyclic antidepressants such as Elavil and Tofranil. They appear to affect norepenephrine, although exactly how is a matter of dispute. The classification of the antidepressive drugs as CNS depressants is not well established at this time.

General anesthetics are broken down into two groups, the volatile and the nonvolatile. Volatile anesthetics, such as ether and chloroform, are inhaled; the nonvolatile, such as Pentothal and Brevital, are administered intravenously. The volatile general anesthetics seem to work by decreasing the neuron's tendency to respond to stimulation. They seem to be particularly effective in depressing activity in the reticular activating system. The nonvolatile general anesthetics seem to have the same effect; however, they block sensory input less than the volatile. Local anesthetics, such as procaine and novocaine, also act to depress neuron excitability. They interfere with transmission of pain simulation more readily than sensory and motor impulses. Cocaine is a local anesthetic, but it also has effects in the CNS. Apparently it inhibits inhibitory centers, thus acting like alcohol in producing altered feeling states.

The sedative-hypnotics are drugs that are supposed to reduce neural activity without producing sleep. In reality, in large enough quantities, they do produce sleep. Barbituates fall in the classification of sedative-hypnotic and in small does yield antianxiety effects that may lead to abuse. It is felt that they operate by inhibiting the cortex, thus releasing cortical control of the reticular system. There are many barbituates that differ on the basis of speed of onset and duration of effective activity. Chloral hydrate, the principal ingredient in the "Mickey Finn," is a sedative-hypnotic whose clinical use has been abandoned because of adverse side effects.

The tranquilizers comprise a large group of drugs that are effective in treating anxiety and other psychological disturbances. They are usually classified by their effect as antipsychotic and antineurotic drugs. The antipsychotic are also known as the major tranquilizers, and antineurotic tranquilizers are also known as the minor tranquilizers. The differences between the classes include the following. They apparently work either on psychotic or neurotic disorders, but typically not both. The major tranquilizers affect lower brain centers more than the minor tranquilizers. The major tranquilizers affect autonomic nervous system activity more pronouncedly, and there are often side effects upon muscle control with the major tranquilizers. Also, the minor tranquilizers appear to be more likely to develop addiction or addictivelike effects. While there are other differences, these reflect those of principal interest in this chapter. The major tranquilizers fall into three major types: the phenothiazine derivatives (e.g., Thorazine), the rauwolfia alkaloids (Serpasil-reserpine), and the butyrophenones (e.g., Haldol). The mechanism for their effects are disputed, but they often have markedly positive effects upon the seriously disturbed behavior of psychotics. The minor tranquilizers include meprobamate (Miltown), chlordiazepoxide (Librium), and diazepam (Valium). The minor tranquilizers act as muscle relaxants. This may be how they act to reduce anxiety although it is still a matter of debate since they also have CNS effects. The minor tranquilizers are actually depressants, since their effects appear to be to reduce activity in the CNS.

CNS stimulants

Those drugs that increase the tendency of neurons to be excited are stimulants. The amphetamines comprise most drugs placed in this category. They have been used to increase alertness and reduce lethargy. They often result in increased muscle activity and have been associated with feelings of euphoria and well being. While their mode of action is not well known, they do result in the increase in cortical acitvity often associated with changes in attention and fatigue.

Psychotominetics

This class of drug acts to produce reactions that mimic psychotic states. The best known psychotominetics are LSD, mescaline, and psilocybin. It has been speculated that they act by affecting amines that occur in the CNS. Their effects are often dependent upon past experience and may last for widely differing periods of time. LSD is the most widely studied of these drugs, and it is felt to have its effect upon the reticular activating system. LSD is known to be an antagonist to the CNS transmitter serotonin, but how that relates to the behavioral effects of LSD is unclear. Some researchers classify marijuana in this category. It does not have properties that resemble the psychotominetics; however, the effects of marijuana upon feeling states are well established.

Drug effects at the synapse

It is well known that some drugs affect synaptic transmission. The mechanisms behind the effects are complicated, and we present them here to illustrate the complexity of drug effects upon the nervous system. We have already discussed the fact that acetylcholine is a synaptic transmitter. We know it acts that way at the preganglonic synapses in the sympathetic and parasympathetic nervous system, at the end organ in the parasympathetic system, and at the neuromuscular junction in the skeletal or voluntary muscles. It also appears to be a transmitter in the CNS, although that evidence is less clear. There are a number of ways that drugs can effect the synapse where acetylcholine is the transmitter. First, there can be an interference with the production of acetylcholine by the cell. Second, drugs may interfere with the release of the transmitter. Third, there can be a stimulation of the receptor reaction to acetylcholine, making the postsynaptic cell act as if the transmitter is either not present or, in the mirror image case, as if there are great amounts of acetylcholine present. Finally, there can be an interference with the process that removes acetylcholine. Research has shown that various chemical agents act in each of the manners described above. For example, nicotine stimulates the receptors and thus acts like acetylcholine at the synapse. The point to be made is that there are a wide variety of ways in which drugs can effect transmission at the synapse and the outcomes may be similar though the mechanisms may widely differ.

Norepinephrine operates as the transmitter at the end organ in the sympathetic nervous system. That synaptic transmission may be effected in the same ways that were described for acetylcholine. For example, the tranquilizer reserpine depletes norepinephrine stores and results in inactivation of the synapse. We wish to note an additional complication. In both cholinergic (acetylcholine) and adrenergic (norepinephrine) synapses, there are two types of transmitter receptors labeled alpha and beta. They are reactive to different drugs and thus can be used for more selective effects upon synaptic transmission. This, for example, has great practical value in the treatment of high blood pressure where the drug Inderol (propranolol) blocks only beta adrenergic receptors. By selective blocking it appears that some adverse side effects can be reduced, thus making the treatment more widely acceptable. As with synaptic effects with acetylcholine, the basic point is that drugs can have complex effects upon synaptic transmission where norepinephrine is the transmitter. It is reasonable to anticipate that similar effects will be found with other transmitters.

Summary

This chapter should make several points clear to the student of abnormal behavior. First of all, behavior relies upon a foundation of highly complex physical events. We have only a limited knowledge of those events, yet our knowledge has provided insights into both the nature of disordered behavior and its treatment. To ignore the physiology and structure of the body, and particularly of the nervous system, invites not only incomplete understanding, but errors in conceptualizing abnormal behavior. The second point that this chapter should make clear concerns the many areas at which individuals are vulnerable to breakdown. The complexity of the neuron, with the many ways that its functioning can be affected, must make the point clear. In fact, it may seem incredible that the system operates at all. In spite of the bewildering complexity, the system is robust. It operates well under a wide range of conditions, and functions efficiently even though there are portions working under duress or perhaps completely disabled through physical damage or genetic default.

GLOSSARY

Acetylcholine: A transmitter substance in the parasympathetic nervous system and the CNS.

Action potential: The impulse in a nerve cell.

Androgens: The name given to male sex hormones, principally, but not exclusively testosterone.

Autonomic nervous system: The section of the nervous system that controls the visceral activities in the body.

Axon: The part of the nerve cell that transmits the nerve impulse to the next neuron or end organ.

Central nervous system (CNS): The part of the nervous system contained within the brain and spinal cord.

Dendrite: The part of a nerve cell that receives stimulation from other neurons.

Endocrine gland: Those glands that secrete their products (hormones) directly into the bloodstream.

Epinephrine: A substance produced by the adrenal medulla that increases the activity levels of cells.

Fiber: A neuron's axon.

Ganglion: The cluster of cell bodies of neurons found outside the CNS.

Gonad: The general term for testicles and ovaries.

Gonadotropic hormones: Hormones produced by the pituitary whose effects are to stimulate the gonads into activity.

Gray matter: The name given to the area of the CNS whose neurons are unmyelinated and have a gray appearance.

Limbic System: Composed of parts of the brain that seem to be particularly important in emotion.

Myelin: A while fatty liquid substance (a limpid) that surrounds some axons and speeds the nerve impulse.

Nerve: A group of neuron fibers found outside the CNS.

Neuron: Nerve cells.

Norepinephrine: A transmitter found in the sympathetic nervous system and the CNS also produced by the adrenal medulla.

Nucleus: A cluster of cell bodies of neurons found within the CNS.

Parasympathetic Nervous System: A division of the autonomic nervous system characterized by secretions of acetylcholine at their nerve endings.

Reticular Activating System: A diffuse collection of neurons in the lower brain that seems to be particularly important in attention and sleep.

Seratonin: A substance believed to be a transmitter in the CNS.

Sympathetic Nervous System: A division of the autonomic nervous system characterized by secretion of norepinephrine at their nerve endings.

Synapse: The junction between a nerve cell and another nerve cell or end organ.

Transmitter: The chemical substance released at the synapse that affects the next cell's activity.

White matter: Those areas of the CNS whose neurons appear white because of their myelin sheath.

NOTES

1. Since the material in this chapter represents the work of many scientists over a long period of time, we shall omit references to each concept or finding. Rather, we list several seminal works in the reference section that the reader may consult for more detailed information. These references were important sources in the compilation of this chapter and rightfully deserve citation as such.
2. For a discussion of drugs and their effect, we strongly recommend Abel (1974), who provides an excellent survey of the field. We have relied heavily upon his classification scheme in this section.

DEVELOPMENTAL FACTORS: CHILD

HAYNE W. REESE
RALPH R. TURNER

Developmental psychology is concerned with *changes* in psychological processes that occur over part or all of the life span. Surveys of those changes, such as this chapter, can be organized by process or by age period. In a process-oriented organization, a specific process such as perception is surveyed across the entire age span under consideration, such as birth through adolescence. Then another process such as personality is surveyed across this age span, and so on. In an age-oriented organization, the age span under consideration is separated into periods or stages, such as infancy, early childhood, late childhood, and adolescence. All processes are surveyed within one age period, then within the next age period, and so on.

The major advantage of the process approach is that it clearly reveals age changes. A major disadvantage is that the interrelations among the processes are hard to see. It is difficult to see the whole child when his or her psychological processes are considered separately. The major advantage of the age-period approach is that the interrelations among psychological processes are more clearly revealed. But, a major disadvantage is that age changes are hard to see. The age-period approach is used in this chapter, to provide normative information about children of a particular age so that comparisons with abnormal development can more easily be made. (For a relatively brief, introductory level use of the process approach, see Lipsitt & Reese, 1978.)

Stages of child development

Child development covers the age range from conception to the end of adolescence. It is convenient to divide this range into five age periods, beween which major transitions occur in various psychological processes. The periods are the prenatal period (conception to birth), infancy (birth to 2 years), early childhood (2 to 6 or 7 years), late childhood (6 or 7 to 11 or 12 years), and adolescence (age range discussed later). The normal functioning of children in each of these periods is described in this chapter. Before proceeding to these descriptions, however, it will be useful to survey the major theoretical orientations found in contemporary developmental psychology. These serve to organize the information available and, as will be shown, each emphasizes a different primary source of change in the individual. Understanding these sources of change will help you further understand how, and whether, intervention techniques should be effective.

Theories of development

Theories of development can be grouped into two broad classes, behavioristic and cognitive. Within each class several specific theories are encountered.

Behavioristic approaches. The two major behavioristic approaches are those derived from formal learning theory, most notably the Hull-Spence learning theory (White, 1970), and those derived from the Skinnerian approach. The latter approach, which is considered to be more empirical than theoretical, has been labeled in various ways, including Skinnerian psychology, operant psychology, the experimental analysis of behavior, and the functional analysis of behavior. When applied to developmental psychology the last term is the most apt (Etzel, LeBlanc, & Baer, 1977).

Both behavioristic approaches agree in asserting that behavioral development is primarily attributable to learning, but they disagree in the way they characterize the learning process and in their characterization of the conditions that influence the learning process. In the learning-theory approach, a key concept is *mediation.* In this context, mediation means that a stimulus and response are associated because each is associated with an intervening mechanism, called a mediator. The mediator is usually considered to be an internal response. For example, individuals form stereotypes by labeling objects or other persons. The label then arouses particular responses acquired previously. Stereotyping is efficient because it eliminates the need to learn a new set of responses to every object or person, but it is often inappropriate because the new object or person is not responded to on its own merits but rather on the basis of its label. Nevertheless, it should be made explicit that stereotyping and classifying are the same processes, theoretically, except that "stereotyping" is likely to be malignant and "classifying" benign.

According to the learning-theory view, development consists largely of learning and using more and more complex kinds of mediators. Labels are not the only kinds of mediators assumed by developmental psychologists who use the learning-theory approach. Another kind of mediator is the attentional response, which controls the kinds of information received by the individual. It is selective, in that it leads the person to focus on some aspects of a situation and to ignore others. Research interpreted within this kind of theory has shown that the number of available attentional responses increases developmentally, as does the speed of switching from inappropriate attentional responses to appropriate ones. For example, it appears that the major deficiency in simple learning by retarded children is in the speed of acquiring the appropriate attentional response. Once they have acquired this mediating response, they solve the learning task as rapidly as mentally normal children, but they acquire the mediating response more slowly (Eimas, 1970).

The basic model in the learning-theory approach involves stimulus-response associations. The association may result from either classical or instrumental conditioning procedures, but in any case the focus is upon a stimulus and the response it evokes. In the functional-analysis approach, in contrast, the basic model involves free-operant responses. A distinction is made between respondent behaviors, which are *elicited* by stimuli, and operant behaviors, which are *emitted* rather than elicited. In the functional-analysis approach it is this distinction, rather than the different procedures, that differentiates classical from instrumental conditioning.

In the functional analysis of development, it is anticipated that most and perhaps all developmentally important phenomena will involve operant behaviors. To investigate these phenomena, according to Baer (1973), the researcher should: First, select a behavior for analysis; second, study the behavior in the psychological laboratory to determine whether it is respondent or operant by attempting to control it through application of operant conditioning procedures; third, if the second step shows that the behavior is operant, determine by observation in the natural environment whether nature seems to mimic the operant conditioning procedures; and finally, if the third step is affirmative, intervene in the natural environment to make sure that the apparent conditioning procedures observed there in the third step are in fact controlling the behavior.

According to the functional-analysis approach, development involves primarily the acquisition of operant behaviors. Acquisition is assumed to result from the same processes as those used in the psychological laboratory—conditioning, shaping, fading, and discrimination training (Baltes, Reese, & Nesselroade, 1977; Reese, 1976). In the real world the parent, teacher, or other caregiver is not always available to "consequate" (reward or punish) the target behavior, but the natural environment contains "ecological" reinforcers (and punishers), which are automatically produced when a person interacts with certain objects (e.g., Baer, Rowbury, & Goetz, 1976; Bijou & Baer, 1965). For example, if an infant pounds on a table, a sound is produced and the sound functions as a reinforcer—an ecological reinforcer—that maintains pounding. (For the parents, it may be a punisher of behavior that would maintain proximity to the infant.) The availability of ecological reinforcers would eliminate the necessity of having all reinforcers provided by a caregiver.

Ecological reinforcers will not be available for some behaviors, and the consequences of these behaviors may be irregular because of the irregular availability of a caregiver. However, learning will not be prevented, only slowed down. Thus, development in the natural environment is slow because of inefficient programming of reinforcers.

Cognitive approaches. In the behavioristic view, the stimulus-response association is mechanical; the response will inevitably occur if the appropriate setting conditions are present (including a stimulus and an appropriate state of the organism). In the cognitive view, the stimulus-response association reflects a mental activity that determines the response. Even if the appropriate setting conditions are present, the response will occur only if the person selects from his or her repertoire the appropriate mental activity and applies it. That is, the occurrence of the response depends not only upon the external stimulation and the state of the organism, but also upon evocation and utilization of the appropriate mental activity. This mental activity is labeled in various ways by different theorists, but the words *rule, operation,* and *strategy* are widely used and can be interpreted as synonyms. They are not necessarily verbal; for example, the rules (operations) involved in unconsciously scratching an itch or swatting a mosquito are motoric.

Knowing a rule and using it are not the same thing and, hence, cognitive theorists make a distinction between competence and performance. Many persons know the rules for hitting a baseball, but only a few become home-run champions. Similarly, most persons know the rules required for mental arithmetic, but few can apply these rules effectively. In the case of mental arithmetic, a major problem is the memory requirement. Memory is required for the effective use of any except perhaps the most simple rules, and when the memory requirement is beyond the person's capability, the rule cannot be used effectively. Memory capability is itself a product of the use of rules, such as rehearsal or frequent repetition. Thus, the use of a rule may actually involve the use of a whole system of rules, some subordinated to or serving others. For example, naming the items presented in a list is an operation (rule) that serves the operation of rehearsing, and rehearsing is an operation that may serve the operations of mental arithmetic, which in turn may serve complex operations involved in solving an engineering or accounting problem.

Two major kinds of cognitive theory can be identified. One includes the so-called information-processing theories and computer simulations, which are typically specific to a relatively narrow domain. For example, separate theories of this type have been developed for such domains as memory, discriminative learning, concept identification, and problem solving (in specific tasks). Usually, no attempt is made to relate the specific operations assumed for one domain to operations assumed for others. The other approach, usually called cognitive developmental, is more frankly mentalistic and is generally broader in scope. Thus, for example, Piaget's theory is intended to deal with all kinds of problem solving, but the focus is on the child's logical organization rather than behavior in a specific task.

Comparison of the approaches. In all four approaches, the interest is not so much in describing the child's behavior as in determining what produces the behavior. In the functional-analysis approach, the causes of development are sought in the environment—the stimuli that are contingent on the child's behavior and that maintain or modify the occurrence of the behavior. In the learning-theory approach, the environmental variables are conditions of development but not causes, although the causes are related to environmental events. In the cognitive approaches, environmental variables are conditions rather than causes of development, as in the learning-theory approach, but the causal variables are mental rather than physical. Like the behavioristic approaches, the information-processing approach involves a focus on the behavior observed. The question asked is, what mental operations could produce this specific behavior? In the cognitive developmental approach, the observed behavior is of no special interest except insofar as it provides information about the child's mental activities.

These characterizations of the four approaches are, to be sure, general and intended to provide only an overview. They should indicate the orientation of a particular approach, the kinds of things a developmentalist will find interesting from that approach, and the way observations will be used. Specific applications will be discussed in the remaining sections of this chapter, in which the five periods of childhood are described.

Prenatal period

At first glance, one might assume that psychological influences begin at birth. However, a wide range of influences present in the prenatal environment can alter the course of development, sometimes quite drastically, even before the first breath is drawn.

Prenatal periods

The organism develops through three general prenatal periods. During the *germinal period* (from fertilization to 2 weeks), the organism is called a zygote. It undergoes very rapid cell division, while moving down the fallopian tube into the uterus. Once in the uterine cavity, it implants itself in the uterine wall. Most spontaneous abortions occur during this period, usually because of improper implantation. The *embryonic period* (2–8 weeks), during which the major organs develop, meets the biological definition of a "critical period" in that certain environmental factors have influences that they do not have earlier or later. The mother is often not sure she is pregnant at this time and therefore may not take appropriate precautionary measures to avoid these influences, discussed in the next subsection. The *fetal period* is the longest prenatal period, lasting from 8 weeks after conception until birth, normally at 9 months. Generally, it is a period of "fine tuning" during which the major systems develop and behavior begins.

Prenatal environmental influences

Maternal nutrition. One of the important influences on prenatal development may be the amount and quality of maternal nutrition. The pattern of influence is complex, however. Large-scale intervention programs with malnourished populations indicate increased birthweights and advancement on some early developmental abilities but the effects on later cognitive development are mixed (Herrera, 1978, in Columbia; Klein, 1975, in Guatemala). Although many other studies support the importance of adequate nutrition for proper prenatal development, the question of timing is still unanswered. Some studies show greater effects when starvation occurs early (Vore, 1971) while others show greater effects later (Naeye, Blanc, & Paul, 1973). Still other studies have shown no effects; for example, in one study 125,000 Dutch men who were conceived during a famine did not differ in IQ from a similar group not exposed to famine (Stein, Susser, Saenger, & Marolla, 1972).

Maternal drug intake. Drugs may have severe and long-lasting effects on development (Bowes, Brackhill, Conway, Steinschneider, 1970). A clear example can be seen in the *thalidomide* babies born with severe defects during the early 1960s. Addictive drugs and halucinogenic compounds have severe effects, but so also do more commonly used drugs such as hormones (birth control pills), tobacco, and alcohol. For example, smoking mothers are twice as likely to have low-birthweight babies as nonsmoking mothers.

Maternal illness. Several illnesses have been implicated in abnormal prenatal development. For example, if the mother contracts rubella (German measles) during the first 3 months of pregnancy, the child has a 3 to 1 chance of being born with visual and auditory defects, mental retardation, central nervous system damage, heart defects, and growth retardation (Papalia & Olds, 1975). The diseases resulting in abnormal prenatal development also include *toxoplasmosis,* resulting in brain damage, blindness, or death; *tuberculosis;* and *congenital syphilis.*

Maternal emotions. Mothers who are anxious about their pregnancies are more likely to have problem deliveries and to bear abnormal babies than those who are not so anxious. In addition, maternal stress has been implicated in birth defects such as cleft palate and harelip (Strean & Peer, 1956).

Infancy

Age range

Infancy extends from birth at full term to about two years of age. The reason for specifying birth *at full term* is that premature babies (born much earlier than nine months of gestation) are apparently abnormal in certain ways (Braine, Heimer, Wortis, & Freedman, 1966; Moore, 1970). Infancy ends when the child is capable of relatively independent action, including well-developed locomotion, good facility at communication, good (though still very limited) reasoning powers, and a clear sense of self. In the present section we will consider how accomplishments such as these come about.

Learning

The behavior of the newborn infant is reflexive and controlled by excitatory processes. For example, at birth and during the neonatal period (the first few weeks after birth), visual exploration is involuntary, controlled by an orienting reflex that is automatically elicited by stimulation. During this period, orienting movements are gross and poorly directed. At about one-and-one-half months of age the infant begins to make gross movements in the direction of the stimulation, and with continued development the exploration becomes more precisely directed. It also becomes better organized, developing from detection of edges at birth to systematic scanning after two months of age. Developmentally, visual exploration becomes more organized and more precise: it changes from an involuntary reflex to voluntary, systematic behavior (see Reese & Porges, 1976).

Early research on classical conditioning in infants, conducted before about 1930, suggested that conditioning does not occur before the infant is several months old. For example, Krasnogorski studied the responses of salivation and swallowing, and concluded that conditioning is impossible before the fourth or fifth month after birth (see Razran, 1933; Siqueland, 1970a). Similarly, researchers were unsuccessful in attempts to condition such responses as the eye blink in response to a puff of air to the eye, and leg flexion in response to electric shock to the foot. Subsequent research, however, appeared to demonstrate classical conditioning in younger infants, even those less than a week old. Apparently, the early experiments were unsuccessful because the conditions were less than optimal—time intervals between the conditioned and unconditioned stimuli were too long, for example—and the responses selected for study were ill-chosen (see Siqueland, 1970a).

Modern researchers have successfully conditioned such responses as sucking and head-turning, responses involved in feeding. Less successful are attempts to condition defensive reactions. The concept of *preparedness* (Seligman, 1970) has been invoked to explain these successes and failures with different responses (as contrasted with successes and failures due to different procedures). Preparedness means that conditioning will not occur unless the conditioned and unconditioned stimuli are "associable," even if both the stimuli are of sufficient intensity to be perceived by the organism and the conditioned stimulus reliably elicits an unconditioned response. It seems that evolution and maturation prepare the organism to associate some stimuli more readily than others. Preparedness clearly demonstrates the important relationship between biological maturation of the child and learning conditions present in the environment, both of which must be optimal for efficient learning to occur.

Classical conditioning has been demonstrated in the newborn infant. It may be easier to establish in older infants (Siqueland, 1970a), but the evidence for this age trend is uncertain (Fitzgerald & Brackbill, 1976). Such a trend could result from age differences in preparedness, but it could also result from age differences in motivation, effectiveness of the unconditioned stimulus in eliciting the unconditioned response, or state of the infant at the time of testing (Siqueland, 1970a).

Operant conditioning has been obtained as early as the first day after birth (Kron, 1966), but it appears to be easier to obtain in older infants than in younger ones. Again, however, the cause of the age trend may be procedural rather than related to the learning process itself. The most success has been obtained when infants are forced to use their heads, in the sense that the operant response systems involve sucking, head-turning, vocalizing, and smiling (Siqueland, 1970b). Later in life, peripheral response systems involving reaching, touching, and kicking can be used. This trend is consistent with developmental trends of maturation (Gesell, 1954): development proceeds in a cephalo-caudal direction and a proximo-distal direction—from head to tail and from central axis outward.

The studies of learning show that the human infant is equipped with an extensive repertoire of reflexive responses (Siqueland, 1970b, p. 122), but is also active and adaptive from the first days of life. If development proceeds normally, the infant's adaptive capacity continues to increase and to come increasingly under voluntary control. However, if the environment is unstimulating and restricted in the stimulus-response regularities and behavioral contingencies that promote learning, both physical and mental development will be delayed, at best. If the deprivation is severe and prolonged, the result is irreversible retardation (Lipsitt & Reese, 1978).

Memory

The occurrence of conditioning in infancy does not necessarily indicate thought or understanding, because conditioning can reflect merely the establishment of habitual action patterns involving only recognition memory, a very primitive kind of cognitive process.

Even newborn infants are capable of recognition memory, as shown by research on "habituation" (Flavell, 1977). Habituation is studied by repeatedly presenting a stimulus and observing the response it arouses. If the response becomes progressively weaker, habituation of the response is said to have occurred. Habituation has been demonstrated in newborn infants (Kaye, 1970), and they are therefore to be judged capable of recognition memory.

Recognition-memory ability, which seems to be required for conditioning is demonstrated by the research on habituation. But habituation would prevent the occurrence of conditioning. Fortunately, evolution has determined that habituation of responses to conditioned stimuli does not occur, or occurs slowly.

A more advanced type of memory is required for recall than is required for recognition. Recall, or "evocation" as Piaget (1968) called it, requires the prior formation of some kind of symbolic representation of an event and entry of the representation into memory storage, then retrieval of the representation from storage for recall. According to Piaget, evocative memory is not possible before the age of about $1\frac{1}{2}$ to 2 years; that is, as we shall discuss later, it is not possible before the beginning of the "preoperational" period, when the capacity for symbolic representation appears.

"Evocative memory" is not the same as "elicited behavior." The first author's younger son, Brad, knew the locations of various objects in the pantry by the age of 15 months, seeming to violate Piaget's general age norm for evocative memory. For example, when his dad took the watering can from its hook, Brad would point to the plastic pail used to catch the water; at the cocktail hour when dad gathered the cocktail shaker and glasses Brad would to go the liquor shelf and point, and after the cocktails were made would go to the location of his unsalted crackers and point. The father's actions with certain implements—and similar actions by the mother—seemed to serve as retrieval cues for the locations of associated implements. However, according to Piaget, behaviors like Brad's do not require symbolic representations, they require only overt motoric imitation. Pointing is a curtailed form of reaching, and therefore Brad's pointing was an imitation of his father's and mother's reaching. During infancy, according to Piaget, absent events are "re-presented" by imitation stimulated by sensory input. In contrast, a symbolic representation would signify the event that was imitated, but would not be the imitation itself (Phillips, 1975, pp. 64–65).

Cognition

Piaget suggested that cognitive development represents a movement from "wired-in" reflexive responses present at birth toward a highly symbolic, flexible, efficient system of hypothetico-deductive logic that is capable of being applied to a wide range of problems and settings. It is this capability, in Piaget's view, that makes the human the most highly adapted species.

In Piaget's analysis of cognitive development, the infant is in the sensorimotor period, which is divided into six stages. Table 6.1 shows these stages, together with the later periods of cognitive development. The cognitive organizational units that underlie behavior are called *schemes*. In Stage 1, the available schemes are reflexes. "Later schemes are more complex—more 'mental'—and it becomes increasingly appropriate to think of them as 'strategies,' 'plans,' 'transformation rules,' 'expectancies,' etc." (Phillips, 1975, p. 12). A scheme includes a particular set of actions (physical or mental) and the set of events or objects that trigger these actions. For example, the "sucking scheme" includes the organized set of acts involving the mouth, throat, tongue, and breathing apparatus, and includes the set of objects that can be sucked (Flavell, 1977, p. 17).

Schemes can be combined to form more

Table 6.1. Stages of Cognitive Development in Piaget's Theory

Period	*Age range*[a]	*Major characteristics*
Sensorimotor	Birth to 2 years	Includes 6 stages.
Stage 1	Birth to 1 month	Innate, reflexive schemes. No understanding of object permanence.
Stage 2	1–4 months	Coordination of schemes, particularly visual and manual schemes.
Stage 3	4–8 months	By using coordinated schemes, infant becomes object explorer; true imitation begins. Object permanence depends on infant's perception of object.
Stage 4	8–12 months	Intentional behavior appears. Object permanence still dependent on actions.
Stage 5	12–18 months	Active, purposeful, trial-and-error exploration of objects and their properties. Object remains permanent if given visible displacements but not invisible ones.
Stage 6	18–24 months	Transition from sensorimotor to symbolic schemes. True object permanence; symbolic representation.
Preoperational	2–6 years	Symbolic representations permit deferred imitation. Language development.
Concrete operational	7–11 years	Planful, "cognitive" approach to problems; reality oriented.
Formal operational	11 years[b]	Understands all types of analogies; able to reason from counterfactual and referent-free premises. Formal logic.

Adapted from Elkind (1970); Flavell (1977); Phillips (1975).
a. Age ranges very approximate.
b. Begins at 11 or 12 to 15 years of age.

complex units. For example, the older infant has coordinated the grasping scheme, the mouthing scheme, and the sucking scheme, and consequently can suck anything that can be grasped and moved to the mouth.

Schemes are related to inputs through the processes of *accommodation* and *assimilation.* Essentially, accommodation is a change in a scheme so that it accords more closely with the input, and assimilation is a change in the input so that it fits the scheme more closely. Flavell (1977) has suggested that accommodation is a discovery process and assimilation is an interpretive process. When an infant begins to suck a rattle, the rattle is assimilated to the sucking scheme—that is, the rattle is interpreted as something that can be sucked. Simultaneously, the sucking scheme is accommodated to the rattle—that is, the sucking behavior must be altered somewhat to permit sucking of the rattle.

Accommodation and assimilation are assumed to occur together, but one may be dominant over the other. When they are more or less in balance, the child is exhibiting "adapted intelligence"; he or she is adapting to the environment, learning about it, and interpreting it appropriately. When accommodation is dominant, the child is exhibiting imitation; schemes are being modified to accord with the input from a model. When assimilation is dominant, the child is exhibiting play. For example, pretending that a stick is a doll requires ignoring the "blatant physical differences between stick and doll" (Flavell, 1977, p. 18).

Knowledge and skill increase through accommodation and assimilation, but in Piaget's analysis the progress toward maturity involves reorganizations of the structure of schemes. These reorganizations result in new and different systems, each more efficient than the preceding one. The transition process is called equilibration; it results from conflict between what the child sees and what he can interpret. That is, because younger children's cognition is relatively primitive, they cannot have a complete, full understanding of phenomena. Their understanding is accomplished largely by ignoring much of the input; they neither assimilate (interpret) it nor accommodate to it (notice new features of it). There is consequently a discrepancy between input and cognitive structure. When discrepancies become widespread and not too large in magnitude, equilibration occurs and reorganizes thought processes to a higher level. This reorganization results in a reduction of the discrepancy.

A major, and basic, concept that develops during infancy is that of object permanence. While it is obvious to the adult that objects exist, and exist permanently, Piaget's research revealed that this knowledge is not uniform but rather needs to be acquired through experience. This acquisition, furthermore, takes place in a universal, fixed sequence of developmental stages. In Stage 1 (Table 6.1), infants will follow an object visually until it disappears and will then lose interest in the object. None of their behavior suggests that they have any mental representation of the object's continuing existance. Later, in Stages 2, 3, and 4, infants become competent at visual searching (peeking over a crib at a fallen object, for example) but will not search manually even though they have the competence to do so. Still later, in Stage 5, infants show adeptness at manual searching, even if the object was fully hidden (while they watched) prior to their reaching for it. But if an object is hidden under cover *X* several times, and then hidden under cover *Y*, Stage 5 infants will try first under *X* and then abandon the search. Finally, Stage 6 infants can coordinate visual evidence, representational competence, and manual ability and successfully search for hidden objects.

Language

Nonverbal communication. In its broadest sense, language includes all forms of communication and is not limited to speech. It includes, for example, the facial expressions and intonation patterns that accompany speech and modify the meanings of individual words. In fact, these gestures or "paralinguistic" features can often replace words with no loss of meaning. Viewed in this way, it is apparent that even the very young infant possesses "language," in that its cries communicate needs and its quiet cooing and gurgling communicate satisfaction, or a lack of insistent need. (However, it seems that young infants do not communicate different needs with different cries. Parents who believe otherwise are apparently reacting not to differences in crying but to the setting or timing of the cries—for example, a cry 3 or 4 hours after a feeding is likely to signal hunger [Risley, 1977, p. 91].)

Steiner (in press) has shown that facial expressions vary with the pleasantness of odors and tastes. For sweet smelling and sweet tasting stimuli, the mouth is drawn back a little at the corners and sucking and licking movements occur. For sour stimuli, the lips are pursed, the nose is wrinkled, and the eyes blink. For putrid and bitter, the corners of the mouth are depressed, the middle part of the upper lip is raised, and retching or spitting may occur. The facial reactions indicating aversion (to sour, putrid, and bitter) are more vehement and dramatic than those indicating acceptance, perhaps because there is greater urgency in rejecting aversive stimulation. For present purposes, Steiner's most significant conclusion is that these facial reactions are innate; they are present at birth and perhaps even earlier. Their form is the same in normal newborn infants, anencephalic infants (lacking all but the primitive structures of the brain), hydrocephalic infants, deaf and blind individuals, mentally retarded adolescents and adults, and normal adolescents and adults. In short, the expressions do not require any learning, are not imitative, are mediated by primitive brain structures, and are pervasive throughout life.

The differential facial expressions have an obvious adaptive function in the young infant, who needs to communicate with the caregiver about acceptance and rejection of foods. Later, it may be similarly useful to provide such signals to the social group, but through learning these signals could come to symbolize other conditions than acceptance and rejection of foods. Steiner quoted Darwin's descriptions of the facial expressions representing good spirits, contempt, low spirits, and disgust, and noted the essential similarity of the expression of good spirits to the reaction of sweet, contempt to sour, and low spirits or disgust to putrid or bitter.

Language development proceeds on other fronts as well as the paralinguistic: phonological, semantic, and syntactic.

Phonology. Phonology deals with the ways sounds are produced and discriminated. Studies by Eimas and others (Eimas, 1975; Eimas & Tartter, 1978) have shown that even very young infants can make some of the phonological discriminations that human adults can make. Production, however, lags far behind.

Semantics. The child's productive language, or speech, begins with the first utterance of a word that is recognized by listeners as meaningful. It may not have been in the listener's vocabulary, but its meaning may be recognized from context. For example, "muk-a-muk" seems to be a fairly common word for "milk" among infants in English-speaking countries. "Kee" may be "Kitty," "Ee" may be "Eat," and so on. The first recognizable word can be expected, on the average, at about one year of age, although individual differences are large (Palermo, 1970). The productive vocabulary is smaller than the receptive vocabulary. That is, persons use fewer words than they know. By the age of $1\frac{1}{2}$ to 2 years, the child's productive vocabulary exceeds a hundred words, and may be as large as two or three hundred words (Palermo, 1970).

Syntactics. Syntax refers to the structure of language. In the first stage of syntactic development, the child's "grammar" consists of one-word sentences. That is, single words are uttered with the force of complete sentences. For example, "Car" may mean "This is my car," "Give me that car," "There is a car," or "There are cars going by." The specific meaning is usually detectable from the context of the utterance and its inflection.

When the productive vocabulary has reached perhaps a hundred words, the child begins to exhibit a more complex grammar, in which sentences are characteristically two words long. Research on the "grammar" of these simple sentences began in the 1960s, and at first it appeared that the syntax was relatively simple, reflecting "telegraphic speech," or reflecting the direct expression of deep structures that underlie the surface manifestations found in adult speech, or reflecting combinations of fixed-position ("pivot") words with a variety of other words (Bloom, Lightbrown, & Hood, 1975; Braine, 1976). By the early 1970s, however, it became apparent that even the two-word utterances have a complicated grammar, and now there is considerable controversy about its composition (Bloom et al., 1975; Braine, 1976). Braine (1976), for example, argued that the child at this level has considerably less grammatical competence than had been thought, and that in fact the "grammar" consists of a set of formulas or rules that are relatively specific in applicability—each used to express a narrow range of meanings. The rules fix the positions of words in the sentences, and are acquired independently rather than fitting into some abstract, organized system. Examples are given in Table 6.2.

In the next stage, the child produces three-word sentences such as "There man coat," "Baby see mommy," "Daddy push it," and "No play that." This stage may begin near the age of 2 years, or may not begin until the age of $2\frac{1}{2}$ years or later; individual differences are large. In any event, the subsequent stages become more and more complex in syntactical structure, which comes more and more to approximate

Table 6.2. Examples of Two-Word Sentences

	Actor/action	
Kimmy bite	Mommy sleep	cow moo
Kimmy eat	Mommy read	doggy bark
	Identification	
that Kimmy	Mommy lady	hair wet
that hole	Kurt boy	Kendall monkey
	Location	
there cow	mess here	towel bed
here mess	sit there	ear outside
	Possession	
Kendall pail	Papa door	doggy hole
Kendall dinner	Kimmy bike	pig tail
	Other combinations	
more lotion	hat on	look Kendall
poor doggy	shoe off	see running

Classification often depends on knowing the context of the utterance. E.g., "Kendall monkey" is known from context to mean "Kendall is a monkey" rather than "Kendall's monkey." Adapted from Braine (1976, Table 3, p. 19). Used by permission.

adult syntax not only in the production of declarative sentences but also in the production of negations ("I won't eat it"; "He is not a girl") and questions ("Can't you get it?"; "Why you caught it?") (examples from Palermo, 1970).

In about two or three years, then, the child can be expected to progress from a being whose communication is simple, reflexive, and automatic, as is his or her attention and other behavior, to one whose communication is complex, flexible, and deliberate, again like attention and other behavior.

Developmental disabilities. Severe disruptions in language acquisition are called *aphasias.* Various kinds of aphasia are identified, depending on the nature of the disorder, but all involve problems in speech production or in the understanding of speech. They usually result from brain damage. Less severe delays in development are more common but their causes are less well understood. Delayed speech may reflect mental retardation, brain damage, or deficient stimulation. Language delay is common in institutionalized children, for example.

Social behavior

It is believed that, "although there is no one-to-one relationship between specific childrearing practices and particular personality characteristics, a close emotional and affectionate relationship with an adult (not necessarily the mother) during the first few years of life is an essential ingredient for normal personality development" (Endler, Boulter, & Osser, 1976, p. 144). This relationship begins in infancy, appearing first at 3 to 6 months of age, and is called *attachment.* Attachment at this age is reflected by a "brightening" at the appearance of a familiar person, or a few familiar persons. At about the same age or somewhat later, the infant shows distress when such a person leaves. This distress has been interpreted as reflecting attachment, separation anxiety, or dependency, which are interrelated but not identical (see McCandless & Trotter, 1977; Mussen, Conger, & Kagan, 1974).

Later, the infant begins to react to the appearance of a stranger. The reaction may be extreme distress or may be merely a "sobering," a wariness. Whether extreme or mild, the reaction was formerly interpreted to reflect "stranger anxiety," but now is more commonly interpreted to reflect "stranger apprehension," because the emotion aroused seldom seems to be extreme enough to be called anxiety (Rheingold & Eckerman, 1973). Not all babies exhibit it; but those who do usually begin to show it in the last third of the first year. It has no known pathological implications, in spite of the individual differences, and therefore parents should not be concerned if their baby seems to be shy or fearful of others (or if their baby seems *not* to be shy or fearful of others). Until around the middle of the second year, stranger apprehension is exhibited toward strange adults but not toward other children, but in the second half of the second year the infant may show apprehension toward strange children, particularly age peers, and not toward strange adults.

These processes are not well understood at present, but their origins may appear very early in life. In fact, there is reason to believe that the groundwork is laid down in the first few days after birth; optimal development after that period may depend on regular interaction with a warmly receptive caregiver during that period. The interaction is usually between the infant and its mother, and includes, especially during feedings, mutual visual regard or eye contact. The importance of eye contact as a mutual signaling system for other social behaviors has been well established in adults (Argyle & Dean, 1965), but its importance is also seen as early as the first three days. For example, Wolff (1963) noted that mothers who had previously spent little time playing with their infants suddenly began to do so when eye contact became established.

The effects of eye contact may be inborn and reflexive, but learning is also involved to some extent. Some other social behaviors are similarly interpreted. For example, smiling upon social contact with strangers appears in subhuman primates as well as in human adults (Andrew, 1963). It is generally a signal of submissiveness; a grinning ape looks ferocious to a human but apparently looks harmless to one of its own species. The genetic origin of smiling is seen in human infants, since the smiling behavior of blind infants is very much like that of infants with normal vision (Watson, 1965, p. 174).

Regardless of genetic origins, however, eye contact, smiling, and other social behaviors also involve learning—learning when, where, and to whom the behaviors should be made. Although there are "wired-in" properties of the eye that may serve to "capture" the infant's attention (high contrast, movement, bull's-eye pattern) and thus increase social responsivity, a two-person behavioral system is also established. The infant's visual regard of the mother can be interpreted as a reinforcing stimulus for the mother, and maternal visual regard can be viewed as the response to, and a reinforcing stimulus for, the infant's social behaviors. Contingent mutual responsiveness sets the stage for the learning of mother as a positive reinforcing agent (Arco, 1977).

In short, some social behaviors may originate as automatic reflexes, but later they become independent of the initial eliciting stimuli and become operant. Operant conditioning of smiling and vocalizing has been demonstrated experimentally (e.g., Brackbill, 1958; Rheingold, Gewirtz, & Ross, 1959), and one author has suggested that the conditioning of social behaviors may be easiest when the reinforcing stimulus is also social (Millar, 1976). Given that social behaviors such as these are operant, it follows that restrictions in the opportunities for learning, such as those mentioned in the section on conditioning, will disrupt social development. The disruption could be that a desirable behavior occurs too infrequently, perhaps because a competing behavior was learned instead, or because the desirable behavior was never learned; or the disruption could be that an undesirable behavior occurs too frequently. For example, a child may have difficulty learning to wait his or her turn to speak at the dinner table because the outbursts and interruptions produce the desired consequences—parental attention.

Table 6.3. Stages of Moral Development in Kohlberg's Analysis

Level	*Stage*	*Major characteritics*
Preconventional	0	Premoral: The good is what I want and like.
	1	Punishment/obedience orientation.
	2	Instrumental hedonism and concrete reciprocity.
Conventional	3	"Good child" morality: maintain approval by others.
	4	Law and order; maintenance of social order, fixed rules and authority.
Postconventional	5A	Social contract; utilitarian law-making perspective.
	5B	Higher law and conscience orientation.
	6	Universal ethical principal orientation.
	7	Cosmic or infinite orientation.

Adapted from Kohlberg (1973, Table 1, p. 187 and text).

Moral development

Socialization refers to the acquisition of socially accepted behaviors. An important part of socialization is moral development. "Morals" are internalized standards and beliefs that have some control over one's social behavior. Researchers are primarily concerned with three questions: How are the standards internalized? Do the standards in fact control behavior in specific settings? How does a person make moral judgments or decisions?

The last question has received the most attention from developmental psychologists. Piaget and, later and much more extensively, Kohlberg proposed theories based on the assumption that moral development is linked directly with cognitive development. Thus, Kohlberg has proposed a stage model of moral development (Table 6.3) that represents the kinds of standards that control moral judgments (and, according to Kohlberg, other moral behavior).

In Kohlberg's analysis, the earliest stage—Stage 0—is premoral, and is characteristic of the first year of infancy. The individual in this stage is completely hedonistic; that is, "the good is what I want and badness is preventing me from getting it immediately." Delay of satisfaction is "bad." In Freud's system, the individual in this stage is described as operating under the pleasure principle, which means demanding immediate satisfaction of desires (McCandless, 1970).

In the second year of infancy, the child enters Kohlberg's Stage 1 (see Table 3). In this stage the motivation of moral action—the reason for conforming to moral rules—is to avoid punishment.

Early childhood

Age range

The period identified as early childhood extends from 2 to 6 or 7 years of age, covering the range from the end of infancy to an age characterized by many transitions (as we shall see later). In Piaget's system this is the *preoperational* period.

Learning

The learning-task performance of young children until the age of about 5 years, is characteristically more associative than cognitive. That is, an associative account in purely behavioristic terms explains most of their behavior. They are learning stimulus-response associations, either between eliciting stimulus and respondent behavior or between discriminative stimulus and operant behavior.

After the age of about 6 or 7 years, children's performance in learning tasks is explained more easily as cognitive than as associative. That is, older children often perform as though their actions were controlled by cognitive operations, or rules. Thus, the last part of the preoperational period, like the last part of the sensorimotor period (Stage 6), is a time of transition.

In early childhood, learning processes are more like those in infancy than like those in later childhood. The 4-year-old and the infant are more alike than the 4-year-old and the 6-year-old. The reason is that during early childhood a new learning ability develops, the ability to base learning on language and other symbolic representations such as gestures and images. This new learning process is *mediation* (discussed in the introductory section on behavioristic approaches): Instead of directly associating stimuli and responses, the child acquires the ability to associate symbolic representations of stimuli and responses.

Table 6.1 shows that the development of true symbols marks the end of infancy and the beginning of early childhood. However, having a repertoire of symbols—a "vocabulary" including symbolic gestures and images as well as words—is not the same as *using* symbols. As Titchener pointed out long ago (1909, p. 202), *having* images is not the same as *using* images. Images of past experiences may come spontaneously to mind, but deliberately using images as aids to memory, for example, is a different thing altogether. Thus, although children *have* symbols from the beginning of early childhood, they cannot use symbols effectively until later.

The use of symbols as mediators will facilitate performance in a wide variety of learning tasks. Children obviously cannot use a potential mediator if they do not have it in their repertoire; they would be in a state of ignorance. In a psychologically more interesting stage, children have the potential mediator in their repertoire but fail to use it. This is called a state of *production deficiency* (Flavell, 1970), because the children fail to produce the potential mediator even though it is in their vocabulary. Even if they know the required mediator and produce it, it may fail to have any control over their behavior. This problem is identified as a *control deficiency*—a failure of the potential mediator to control other behavior (Kendler, 1972).

Production deficiencies are frequent in early childhood and occur even in adulthood, though rarely. They are more common at all ages than control deficiences, which have pretty much disappeared normally by the end of later childhood (Kendler, 1972). Control deficiencies are relatively rare even in childhood, but *inefficiencies* in the use of mediators are fairly common.

Theoretically, the developmental sequence should run like this: 1. At an early age, mediation does not occur because the child does not have the required mediators. 2. Later, mediators are produced and used inefficiently. The child does not spontaneously use mediators, but if appropriately trained or instructed will use them. However, even if appropriately trained and instructed, the child in this stage uses the mediators with less than full efficiency. Furthermore, when no longer prompted to use the mediators, the child ceases to use them. 3. In the next stage, the child still does not use mediators spontaneously, but if appropriately trained or instructed will use them, and with full efficiency. The child is likely to continue to use them after the prompting is removed—even a week later (Yuille & Catchpole, 1974). 4. In the final stage, the child uses mediators spontaneously and efficiently.

The above analysis is behavioral, but the concepts of production and control deficiencies and inefficiencies are also encountered in cognitive analyses (Flavell, 1970). In a cognitive analysis, instead of referring to mediators, the concepts refer to rules, operations, or strategies, and the names of the concepts may be changed. Production deficiency, with respect to cognitive operations, is sometimes called "evocation" deficiency, to indicate that the appropriate operation is not evoked in a task (hence, cannot be utilized); and control deficiency is sometimes called "utilization" deficiency, to indicate that the operation fails to have the expected outcome. However, "utilization" deficiency is also used to refer to inefficiencies—the operation is evoked but used inefficiently.

In short, the period of early childhood is one in which the spontaneous and efficient use of mediators or cognitive operations develops.

Memory

Just as mediators or cognitive operations usually facilitate learning, so they usually also aid memory. Thus, memory also improves during the period of early childhood. Early in the period, memory is largely automatic, but the child may use some primitive kinds of memory aids. Automatic memory—also called "involuntary" or "nonstrategic" (Brown, 1975)—does not require the use of special memory aids. An example is recognition memory. The child, like the infant, can recognize familiar persons, objects, and scenes; but recognition memory does not require any special memory aids. However, recognition memory can be improved under certain conditions by the use of memory aids. For example, attaching a verbal label can aid recognition when the old and new items are very similar.

Young children have verbal labels (symbols) available, but generally fail to use them as memory aids. Indeed, young children are likely to be blithely unaware of the memory requirement in situations, and even if aware of the memory requirement, they are likely to be unaware that memory may require special effort. Thus, they are often unaware that memory is expected or needed, and are often unaware of how to bring about memory when they do know it is needed. No wonder, then, that they are deficient in the production and utilization of memory aids (Brown, 1975; Hagen, Jongeward, & Kail, 1975, Myers & Perlmutter, 1978).

Actually, however, if the memory task is put in the context of a game, children may exhibit the use of memory aids that they will seem to be incapable of using when the task appears to be an academic exercise (Zaporozhets & Elkonin, 1971). Very early in early childhood, nevertheless, the aids are likely to be primitive and little more advanced than memory aids exhibited by animals. For example, in the "delayed-reaction test," the subject watches the experimenter place bait of some kind in one of several locations that are identical except for position, then after a delay the subject is allowed to try to find the baited location. Rats, dogs, and children as young as 2-years-old can bridge the delay only by remaining oriented toward the baited location; as long as they keep looking at it, they can "remember" the location of the bait. If they look away, or if their orientation is disrupted otherwise, they "forget" (Hunter, 1913; Wellman, Ritter, & Flavell, 1975). Human adults might have no problem. They could simply label the locations, for example, by using clock or compass points as codes for locations in a circular array. However, even college students benefit from instructions to use such codes, indicating a production deficiency for this strategy (McAllister, 1953).

The end of early childhood is marked by a transition to a stage in which the child uses memory strategies efficiently, although the sophistication and complexity of strategies continue to improve during late childhood (Butterfield, Wambold, & Belmont, 1973).

Cognition

Flavell (1977) has characterized early childhood as a period in which the child becomes increasingly aware of "consistencies, invariants, regularities, and other 'predictables' in his everyday world. That world just becomes a more predictable, orderly, and coherent place when one knows that *X* will continue to retain its *X*-hood over time and transformations . . . and that *Y* will continue to happen every time *X* happens" (p. 78). Central to this increasing awareness is an increasing ability to represent the "predictables."

By the end of infancy, the child has acquired the concept of *object permanence.* However, the concept for the young child refers to qualitative permanence and not to quantitative permanence. That is, the object retains its basic identity, but does not necessarily remain the same in quantity.

For example, in the standard "transposition" task, two stimuli different in size (or brightness, or some other dimension) but otherwise identical are presented, and choice of one is rewarded. Suppose the larger one is designated as correct. After the child has learned to choose the large one consistently, the experimenter surreptitiously removes the smaller stimulus and substitutes one larger than the correct size. Typically, children—and animals tested in the same task—choose the new size, which is now the "larger" one, rather than the stimulus which is correct in absolute size. Similarly, if the experimenter presents the originally incorrect size with one still smaller, making the originally incorrect size the "larger" one in the test pair, subjects will choose it even though it is the size they avoided during the acquisition phase. The new larger stimulus may be chosen for various reasons: the children learned about relative size and not about absolute sizes; or they learned about absolute sizes but believe that between presentations the two stimuli changed in size—the correct object has *this* absolute size but has magically increased in size and is therefore still correct: It's the same object somehow grown larger (Reese, 1968, pp. 138, 140).

Cognitive developmental researchers use this task and "conservation" tasks to gain evidence about the nature of the logical structures that underlie the observed behavior. Central to cognitive development is the knowledge that objects or substances retain an identity even though subjected to certain transformations. For example, the weight of a ball of clay does not change when its shape is changed. Table 6.4 lists some of the conservation tasks used in this kind of research. The transition from failure to success on tasks such as these occurs at the end of early childhood, making the end of the period of preoperational thought and the beginning of "concrete operational thought" (Piaget & Inhelder, 1969).

Table 6.4. Examples of Piagetian Conservation Tasks

Concept	Sample Task
Number	Two rows of regularly spaced pennies; same number of pennies in each row, same spacing in each row; child agrees the number of pennies is the same in the two rows. Examiner elongates one row by increasing the spacing, and asks whether the rows still have the same number of pennies.
Mass	Two identical balls of clay, which the child agrees are identical. Examiner deforms one ball (rolling it into a sausage, flattening it into a pancake, or breaking it into a number of little pellets), and asks whether the amount of clay is the same as in the undeformed ball.
Length	Two identical rods, which the child agrees are identical; rods displayed horizontally, with ends aligned. Examiner displaces one slightly to the right (ends no longer aligned), and asks whether the lengths are still the same.
Area	Two green boards, representing pastures; boards identical in size; each contains a cow and the same number of identical "houses." The houses are placed together in a square on one board and scattered on the other. The child is asked whether the cows have the same amount of grass to eat.

After the child makes his judgment in a conservation task, he or she is asked to explain this judgment. (This is the best procedure according to Reese and Schach [1974], but Brainers [1973, 1974] disagrees.) The preoperational child does not realize that the number, mass, length, or area is the same in spite of the transformation performed. The concrete operational child realizes that the transformation does not change these attributes, and explains that "nothing was added and nothing was taken away" (or, for example, "the number of houses is the same so they take up the same space"). The child who is in transition between these stages may get the right answer, but for the wrong reason. For example, such a child may say that the number is the same only after verifying this fact by counting, thus using an empirical, trial-and-error, preoperational approach. The concrete operational child, in contrast, bases the answer on logic.

Another characteristic of cognition in early childhood is the absence of insight. Insight means that previously learned behaviors are combined into a new sequence to meet the demands of a task, or previous experiences are combined in a novel way to solve a problem. If the new combination comes about gradually, it is a product of learning rather than insight. Insight does not occur with much frequency before the age of about 10 years (Kendler & Kendler, 1967). Another kind of behavior that has been called insight occurs in early childhood. It involves choosing from among several previously learned behavior sequences the one that is appropriate for the task at hand. No new combination of behaviors or experiences occurs, only a new application of previously learned combinations. This kind of "insight" is evidently primitive, because it occurs in rats as well as young children (Kendler & Kendler, 1967).

Theoretically, in true insight symbolic representations of behaviors (or experiences) are combined mentally and—of utmost importance for true insight—the results of the combination are correctly anticipated. The young preoperational child can neither perform the mental combinations nor anticipate their results. Later in the preoperational period, the child can do the combinations mentally, as shown by the ability to generate "elaborations" (new combinations of experiences) in paired-associate tasks (Reese, 1977); but he or she still cannot anticipate the results of these combinations, as shown by a deficiency in "anticipatory imagery"—the use of imagery to figure out the results of hidden actions (Piaget & Inhelder, 1969).

Language

Semantics and syntactics. Language development proceeds rapidly during early childhood; one estimate put vocabulary size at about 270 words at 2 years of age and about 2,560 at 6 (McCandless & Trotter, 1977, p. 343). Basic adult syntax is acquired by the end of the period of early childhood, although complex sentence forms are imperfectly understood until late childhood. For example, 6-year-olds understand passive sentences much better than 5-year-olds do, but much worse than 9-year-olds (Hayhurst, 1967).

Stuttering. Speech disruptions or nonfluencies are normal during the period of early childhood, reaching a peak at about 3 to 5 years of age. They are more frequent in boys than girls, perhaps because girls have larger vocabularies and speak at a slower rate than boys. Both the larger vocabulary and slower speaking would make finding the wanted word easier for girls than for boys, hence reduce the number of hesitations and repetitions in speech. Stuttering—abnormal speech disruption—also begins at about this time, and is also more frequent in boys than in girls.

Although stuttering is not well understood (Jonas, 1977), a causal connection has been assumed to exist between the normal and abnormal types of disruptions. Specific assumptions vary somewhat, but the theories essentially say that a significant person, such as the mother or father, overreacts to normal disruptions, probably believing that they are abnormal, and communicates distress to the child. The child learns to associate distress with the very act of speaking, and the distress causes stronger disruptions, which produce stronger distress, etc. Distress (anxiety) will disrupt the performance of any act that is not well-learned. Abnormal stuttering emerges just before the time when speech should have become well-learned, hence the distress would be expected to interfere with speaking. Also, the performance of even a mechanical, habitual act is disrupted if the actor's attention is focused on the act. For example, walking becomes an automatic, habitual activity by the age of 3 years, certainly, but if you are walking normally and begin to attend to your movements, your gait will change. So in speech it is possible that the act of speaking, which should become fluent when it becomes automatic and habitual, is disrupted when attention is focused on it. The child who has learned to be distressed by speaking is likely to focus attention on the act of speaking, hence is likely to exhibit the disruptions identified as stuttering.

Role in cognition. Another aspect of language is its role in cognition. Piaget has emphasized that *language* is not synonymous with *thought,* but he admits that language provides most of the symbols used in thought. The early behaviorists interpreted thought as subvocal speech, a view similar to that of the Soviet psychologists Vygotsky and Luria. According to the Soviet view, a major accomplishment of early childhood is the development of verbal self-regulation. The verbal control of behavior begins when an adult's verbalizations can control the child's behavior. The child's own verbalizations in this stage may parallel his/her own motor activities, but do not control them. Later, the child's own verbalizations will acquire the regulative function, but only when these verbalizations are overt, or spoken out loud. By the end of early childhood, the child's speech becomes internal and retains the regulative function (Flavell, 1977).

Social behavior

An important aspect of social development during early childhood is "sex typing" or sex-role identification—the learning of the sex roles characteristic of a culture. In America, the traditional sex roles are changing, but culture changes slowly and differentiated sex roles are still prevalent. In early infancy, the sex roles are often differentiated by the color of the clothes (pink for girls, blue for boys) and by the reaction of adults. In one study, women were found to react differently to a baby boy depending on whether he was dressed and introduced as a boy or as a girl (Will et al., 1976). Thus, the occasions for learning differential sex roles begin in infancy. In later infancy and thereafter, the clothing is different; even if little boys and girls both wear blue denim pants, the pants are likely to be decorated differently. In addition, according to the stereotypes, little boys are not supposed to play with dolls (but stuffed animals are permissible), little girls are not supposed to play rough-and-tumble games; little boys can get dirty but little girls should stay clean; little boys should be physically active, little girls should be talkative; and so on.

Theorists have disagreed about the relative influence of parental responses during sex-role acquisition, but they agree that the parents serve as socializing *agents.* The parents reinforce those behaviors they consider to be appropriate, and either ignore or punish those they consider inappropriate. As a result, the child learns which behaviors are approprite for each sex.

During early childhood, the differentiation between the sex roles refers largely to play activities and toys. Because different activities and toys are promoted for the two sexes, their interests begin to diverge and they begin to segregate into same-sex play groups. At this time, the level of play is relatively advanced, in that a degree of mutual interest and cooperation is implied within a play group.

Once the child has entered the levels of play characterized by interactions with other children, the peer group acquires the capacity to control his/her behavior (Baer et al., 1976). It is possible that although parents initiate much of the training involved in socialization of the child, the peer group is primarily responsible for maintaining the socialized behaviors. After all, the adult caregiver cannot be available all the time to dispense contingent stimuli to maintain the behavior. However, the peer group

Table 6.5. Sample of Transitions Occuring between Five and Seven Years of Age

Younger child	*Older child*
Classical conditioning increases	Classical conditioning decreases
Little direct inference	Frequent direct inference
Simple discrimination improves	Simple discrimination declines
Prefer tactual exploring	Prefer visual exploring
No left-right sense	Personal left-right sense
Form, word, and letter reversals	Decline in reversals
Easily disoriented	Resists disorientating
Increasing prediction of adult IQ	Maximal prediction of adult IQ
Speech expressive and instrumental	Speech internalized
Little planning before drawing	Planning before drawing
Reinforced by praise	Reinforced by correctness

Adapted from White (1965, Table III, p. 209). White's table includes 10 additional transitions.

will be available and will serve that function much of the time. Materials—"ecological reinforcers"—can also take on this function (see the introductory section on behavioristic approaches).

Moral development

The child begins early childhood in Kohlberg's Stage 1 of morality (see Table 6.3); but a transition to Stage 2 morality occurs at about 3 years of age. The reasons for conforming in Stage 2 are to obtain rewards and to have favors returned. The end of early childhood is marked by a transition to Stage 3 morality.

Late childhood

Age range

The age range covered by the period identified as late childhood extends from about 7 to about 11 years of age. In Piaget's system it is the period of concrete operations (see below). The period begins with the completion of many transitions, some of which are summarized in Table 6.5, and it ends at the beginning of adolescence.

Learning and memory

Learning and memory become more efficient with increasing age during late childhood, but both are essentially "adult" throughout the period in that they are mediated by deliberately selected mental operations (rules, strategies) that are often tailored specifically for the task at hand. The child does not become increasingly "cognitive" during this period, but becomes increasingly efficient in selecting, developing, and applying cognitive operations (Hagen et al., 1975).

Flavell (1977) has suggested that the late-childhood mind, in contrast with the early-childhood mind, "has a better general understanding that certain inputs do and certain inputs do not constitute 'problems,' that problem-type inputs require reasoning, measurement, or other forms of intellectual activity, and also that the right sort of intellectual activity could produce a satisfactory, possibly unique solution to the problem. In other words, the older child has a much better sense of what a conceptual problem is, of what a problem solution is, and of the fact that it normally takes more than a quick perceptual judgment to get from the former to the latter" (p. 86).

This is not to say that during this period the child is a miniature adult. Rather, like the adult the child has the *will* to be cognitive, but unlike the adult the child often lacks the *skill*. Late childhood can be characterized as a period in which cognitive skills are perfected, although as we shall see in the section on adolescence there is still one major cognitive advance to be made before cognition is fully mature (the advance from "concrete" to "formal" operations).

One of the transitions at the beginning of late childhood is entry into the formal education system. Even for the child who has attended nursery school and kindergarten, the curriculum of the first grade (begun about the age of 6 years in the United States) presents new problems and demands, emphasizing learning and memory. Brown (1978) has suggested that the development of learning and memory skills during late childhood is largely a product of this schooling. As soon as formal education is completed, a person can usually use notes as memory aids—reminders on calendars, shopping lists, lists of things to do. Sometimes pure memory, unaided by external prompts, must be relied on, as in taking a driving license examination and perhaps examinations in one's profession, or remembering a telephone number long enough to dial it. However, the requirement of relying on memory without external aids is much more characteristic of formal education than of everyday life.

It is not that memory without external aids is absent from everyday life, but that it is not a *requirement* of everyday life as often as it is of formal education. However, what we remember without external aids is likely to be different in these two situations. For example, we remember in everyday life the theme or gist of a movie or television program, while in school we must remember dates, sequences of events, and formulas. Technically, the difference is between memory for meanings, or "semantic" memory, and memory for specific contents, or "episodic" memory. An example would be remembering what a particular poem is about (semantic memory) versus memorizing the poem (episodic memory). It follows that students are likely to develop a larger bag of tricks for episodic memory than for semantic memory, hence they have memory tricks that are not particularly useful in everyday life.

Cognition

During the relatively long period of late childhood, we see the initial molding and later solidification of concrete logical operations. According to cognitive developmentalists, children who have acquired concrete operations are able to deal with the environment in a flexible, efficient, and symbolic manner. Such children have at their disposal a set of operations or rules that are logical, although *concrete*. In order to deal with objects these children must manipulate them, either physically or in imagery, and in this sense these children are tied to a concrete understanding of phenomena. The conservation tasks are used to detect development of the structures underlying this level of understanding.

We noted in the section on cognition in early childhood that in the period of concrete operations (late childhood), the child makes correct judgments and gives correct reasons for them in tests of conservation of number, mass, length, and area. Number tends to be passed earliest, but all are likely to be passed by the age of 7 years. Two other conservation tasks, however, are not likely to be passed until later in the period of concrete operations, even though both involve the same basic logic: nothing was added and nothing was taken away. The conservation of *weight* does not appear until the age of about 9 years, and the conservation of *volume* appears only at the end of the period, at 11 or 12 years of age. This *décalage* (French for "separation" or "displacement") has been assumed to reflect the difficulty of the concepts involved rather than any differences in mental operations.

True conservation is demonstrated only when the child indicates that it is based on logical necessity rather than empirical fact. Hence, as noted in the section on cognition in early childhood, number conservation based on counting is not true conservation, because in verifying the equality by counting the child demonstrates a belief that the equality is an empirical fact rather than a logical necessity. To test for the recognition of logical necessity, some researchers have used a "disconfirmation" design: after the child gives the correct conservaton response the examiner surreptitiously changes the material so that conservation is apparently violated. For example, after the child says the ball and sausage weigh the same, the examiner secretly pinches off a piece from the sausage and demonstrates on a balance scale that they do not weigh the same. The test is to see whether the child accepts the disconfirmation. Success may depend on the examiner's skill at sleight of hand in keeping the trick hidden from the child; a better disconfirmation procedure would be to rig the scale with a hidden magnet to indicate imbalance (Miller, 1976).

The disconfirmation studies have generally shown that a recently acquired operation is more likely to be rejected upon disconfirmation than is an operation that has been consolidated into the child's whole system of operations. However, if the disconfirmation is strong enough even well-integrated operations may be rejected. In one study with children from a parochial school, the disconfirmation was much more effective when demonstrated by a "priest" or "scientist" than when demonstrated by a "magician" (Chandler et al., 1977).

Language

Vocabulary increases during late childhood, to an estimated 7,200 words at 12 years of age (Thorpe, 1955, p. 244), and syntax continues to become more complex. However, the child comprehends much more complex forms than he or she typically produces. This distinction between competence and performance is also seen in adults, who like the child may speak in sentence fragments even though they know correct grammar. The rules of complex syntax, such as for generating negative passives (e.g., "The flowers are not being watered by the girl"), are acquired during late childhood; that is, the older child can understand the meaning of sentences with complex syntax. However, even toward the end of late childhood, the child has difficulty *constructing* sentences with complex syntax (Palermo 1970), illustrating another aspect of the competence-performance distinction.

Social behavior

The tendency for the sexes to segregate continues in late childhood, culminating in active antagonism that reaches a peak at about the end of the period. Girls have been shown to be more antagonistic toward boys than boys are toward girls, perhaps because at the time the studies were done the male role was much more desirable than the female role and the girls were perhaps envious or resentful (Reese, 1966).

During late childhood, the peer group becomes increasingly important as an agent of socialization, although the parents remain the primary agents. Accompanying the increasing importance of the peer group is an increasing ability to place oneself in another's position—the ability to understand another's point of view, to empathize the feelings and cognitions of others. However, Chandler (1977) concluded from a review of the research that overgeneralizing one's own viewpoint and information, attributing it inappropriately to others, occurs not only in early and late childhood, but also, often, in adolescence and adulthood. Nevertheless, the ability to adopt another's position is greater in late childhood than in early childhood, and it influences not only social behavior but also cognition and morality (Chandler, 1977).

Moral development

Kohlberg's Stage 3 morality is characteristic throughout the period of late childhood. Stage 3 is "good child" morality, aimed at maintaining good relations with others and obtaining their approval. The motivation for moral action is to avoid dislike or disapproval by others.

Adolescence

Age range

Adolescence is a transitional stage between childhood and adulthood and, as such, presents some peculiar definitional problems for the psychologist. Although the beginning of adolescence should be easily marked as the onset of puberty, there are difficulties in actually determining that point. The problem is that the external manifestations of puberty—breast development and the beginning of menstruation in girls, growth of the testes and penis and nocturnal emissions in boys—lag behind the internal hormonal changes that produce them (White & Speisman, 1977). It is generally accepted that adolescence begins, on the average at 10 or 11 in girls and 11 or 12 in boys. Individual differences are large, however (Katchadourian, 1977).

The problem is even more pronounced when one attempts to establish an end point. While agreeing that adolescence ends when the individual is grown up—at adulthood—researchers have found that not all physical and psychological structures mature at the same rate. Sexual maturity is attained before adult height is reached; and cognitive maturity is reached in early adolescence, but personality development continues into old age.

Early and late adolescence

An often used organizing theme for adolescent development is Erikson's (1963) notion of identity formation. Erikson viewed adolescence as a period during which this single psychosocial crisis—identity versus role confusion—is dominant. However, Newman and Newman (1975) made a convincing case that adolescence involves two different periods, each with its own set of issues. During early adolescence the psychosocial crisis concerns group identity versus alienation. Later, after 18, the personal identity versus role confusion discussed by Erikson seems more appropriate. While the crises themselves are only mentioned here, a review of the developmental tasks undertaken during each period should be a useful overview of development during this period.

Development tasks in early adolescence

Physical maturation. During early adolescence, both males and females undergo physical changes, both in height and weight and in primary and secondary sex characteristics, that alter their self-perceptions and may affect their interpersonal relations. These changes sharpen their images of themselves as adults and strengthen their sex-role identification.

Learning, memory, and cognition. During early adolescence, the individual usually reaches the period of formal operations. The adolescent can now deal with the abstract and the hypothetical. Cognition becomes "relatively independent of concrete reality [in] that the *content* of a problem has at last been subordinated to the *form* of relations within it" (Phillips, 1975, p. 134). Thus, the individual in the period of formal operations can deal with the possible as well as the real, and can understand and appreciate metaphor, irony, satire, proverbs, parables, and "analogies of all kinds" (Phillips, 1975, p. 132).

In studies of learning and memory, adolescents (and adults) sometimes exhibit production deficiencies (Kendler, 1972), but they are capable of using extremely sophisticated memory aids (Paivio, 1971) and problem-solving strategies (Levine, 1975).

Membership in the peer group. Upon entering the more heterogeneous environment of high school, the adolescent may find a reordering of students according to different kinds of skills, abilities, and characteristics (e.g. good looks, athletic ability, social class, academic performance). Peer group membership requires learning the group's structure and norms, including expectations for behavior that shape the adolescent's attitudes and beliefs. Although the friendships of this period may change, the social skills acquired during this process provide a foundation for functioning in mature social groups (Newman & Newman, 1975).

Heterosexual relationships. The development of primary and secondary sex characteristics interacts with societal expectations for flirting and dating to produce new importance in heterosexual relationships. Recent data show that intimate sexual activity is occurring during this time and at a higher rate than in the past. For example, 44 percent of the boys and 30 percent of the girls surveyed had reported that they had had sexual intercourse before age 16 (Sorensen, 1973).

Developmental tasks in late adolescence

Autonomy from parents. Leaving the home involves the acquisition of skills for maintaining one's own household (e.g., handling money, cooking, driving) as well as psychological skills involved in taking independent action. Internalized values permit recognition and selection of appropriate behavior. The ability to leave home is also linked to the role of the peer group in satisfying needs for closeness and support, heretofore provided by the family. Finally, cognitive maturity provides a storehouse of information, problem-solving skills, and capacity for planning (Newman & Newman, 1975).

Sex-role identity. Beginning in early childhood with identification with the same-sexed parent, a person goes through a sequence of experiences that consolidate sex-role identity. The early peer group affiliation teaches intimacy between equals. Early adolescent experiences involve incorporation of a maturing physique; and late adolescence interactions lead to encounters with expectations from adults and peers for mature sex-role behavior (Newman & Newman, 1975).

Internalized morality. Moral development during late adolescence involves the application of moral judgment to matters much more complex than those contemplated by the school-age child. The change from conventional to postconventional morality (see Table 6.3) involves "a reorientation toward traditional moral principles, a recognition of the subcultural bias that persists in existing moral values, and a degree of conflict over which values have personal meaning" (Newman & Newman, 1975, p. 227).

Career choice. Although the choice of a career sets the tone for later adult life style, the adolescent often makes the decision with little or no actual experience. The choice reflects the emerging conception of identity. For some adolescents the choice parallels or extends the parental identity; for others, it is a decision based on actual experience, introspection, and fact-finding. The environment plays an important role by providing or not providing the appropriate information concerning options at the appropriate time (Newman & Newman, 1975).

Summary

This chapter is an overview of the kinds of psychological changes that normally take place during each of the periods of childhood. Emphasis is on change in major processes and on theoretical explanations of why these changes occur.

Two general kinds of theories used to account for the child's development are: 1. those relying primarily on environmental influences and associative learning, and 2. those positing internal mental activities.

Prenatal development occurs during the germinal, embryonic, and fetal periods. The first three months are considered to be a *critical period* during which the organism is susceptable to a variety of environmental influences that may have serious implications for further development.

Infancy is a period during which reflexive behaviors are refined, hierarchically organized, and integrated. Sensory and attentional processes are fine-tuned but cognition is relatively primitive. Recognition memory and operant and classical conditioning involving relatively large-scale, diffuse responses exemplify the infant's cognitive activity. Social responsivity is largely nonverbal and involves reciprocal signaling systems between the infant and the primary caregiver. An example is mutual gazing during feedings.

During early childhood the move toward cognitive efficiency accelerates. Yet, although young children are able to represent the environment internally, most of their capabilities are still associative. Their symbolic activity suffers from production and control deficiencies and inefficiencies. For example, they have verbal labels available for use as memory aids, but often fail to use them properly or even to use them at all. Nevertheless, they become increasingly aware of the regularities in the world, and increasingly able to represent them adequately. Language is in full bloom at this time and serves not only cognitive development but social development as well. Sex-role identity, initiated in infancy, is developed and maintained through play and parental reinforcement.

Rather than becoming *more* "cognitive" in late childhod, the individual becomes increasingly *efficient* in selecting, developing, and applying cognitive operations in a variety of problem situations. The child now has much of the adult's competence in learning, memory, and problem solving. What is lacking is the adult's skill. The child is able to solve concrete problems but cannot hypothesize efficiently about possible outcomes. Socially, this is a period of increased activity with the same-sexed peer group.

The adolescent is equipped, physically and mentally, with many adult-level skills and abilities. Change during this period is characterized by an integration of these skills and abilities into a conceptual whole—a sense of self-identity. In early adolescence the developmental tasks center around social issues, group membership, heterosexual relations, and the like. In later adolescence, these skills are used to ready the individual for eventual emancipation from the parents and maintenance as an independent individual in the adult world.

GLOSSARY

Accommodation: In Piagetian theory, the need to adjust or modify one's schemas because new information fails to fit them.

Assimilation: In Piagetian theory, the process of making new information part of one's existing schemes or framework of experience.

Attachment: An affectional bond between the infant and the primary caregiver. It is reflected by such behaviors as following the caregiver and crying when the caregiver is absent.

Competence-performance distinction. A distinction made in cognitive theories: Potential ability (competence) may be more or less realized in a specific situation; performance may underestimate actual ability.

Conservation: In Piagetian theory, it refers to the understanding that qualities (amount, length, weight) remain the same when only the form of the object changes.

Control deficiency. A potential mediator is produced, but fails to have any control over other behavior.

Critical period. A period of time during which the organism is particularly susceptible to the influence of certain kinds of stimulation, for example, drugs during the embryonic prenatal period.

Decalage: In Piagetian theory, the inability of a child to perform some tasks within a cognitive stage while being able to perform others that require the same cognitive operations.

Ecological reinforcers and punishers: "Natural" consequences of behavior that increase or decrease the probability of its recurrence; for example, a young child's yelling to startle a flock of pigeons.

Equilibration: In Piagetian theory, the process of obtaining balance between assimilation and accommodation. Equilibration is the propelling force behind cognitive development in this theory.

Insight: Previously learned behaviors are combined into a new sequence to meet the demands of the task, or previous experiences are combined in a novel way to solve a problem.

Maturation: A genetically linked developmental process that operates similarly across individuals given the minimum level of necessary stimulation.

Mediation: A key concept in learning theory, it means that a stimulus and response are associated because each is associated with an internal response called a mediator.

Object permanence: The knowledge that objects continue to exist when they are no longer directly perceived.

Operation: Generally, an operation is an organized, logical set of mental activities that are used to acquire some information or to produce an apropriate response.

Preparedness: In conditioning theory, it means that conditioning will not occur unless the conditioned and unconditioned stimuli are "associable," even if both the stimuli are of sufficient intensity.

Production deficiency: A potential mediator is not produced, or used, even though it is in the person's repertoire.

Scheme: In Piagetian theory, it refers to any organized pattern of behavior; for example, a baby's "grasping scheme."

Sex-role identification: Refers to a socialization process, starting in infancy, by which the individual acquires behaviors considered to be appropriate for his or her sex.

Stranger anxiety or apprehension: Wariness and uneasiness shown by an infant in the presence of a stranger, usually an adult.

Symbolic representation: Developing near the end of the sensorimotor period; refers to the ability to form and utilize mental representations of events or objects in their absence.

ADULT DEVELOPMENT AND AGING

GISELA LABOUVIE-VIEF
PEGGY M. ZAKS

Most theories of development addressed to earlier parts of the life-span (see Chapter 6) have taken as one primary aim the identification of "maturity"—that presumed state in which the organism achieves an equilibrium sometime between the early rush of childhood changes and later deteriorative biological processes signifying eventual death. Yet paradoxically, a definition of adulthood proper has been a rather neglected topic of the various theories of development. Concern about the lack of an appropriate view of adulthood changes has recently been expressed by scientists, but appears to be shared by the public alike. Sheehy's (1976) book *Passages,* for instance, has ranked top among nonfiction books during the summer of 1977, resonating to the search of many adults for an affirmative answer to the question: "Is there life after youth?"

While change has come to be accepted as an integral and positive aspect of child developmental theories, the same posture has been less general when talking about adulthood. With the exception of a few attempts at presenting theories of life-span development (see Baltes, 1977), postmaturational change in many theoretical frameworks often carried negative overtones (see Riegel, 1959): There appeared to be a tendency to pathologize postmaturational change and couch it in terms of regression toward earlier, infantile modes of functioning. Thus at best, adulthood appeared as a static suspense of earlier development; often, however, it evoked somewhat sad images captured in such colloquialisms as "Going through a second childhood," or "can't teach an old dog new tricks."

Some might want to write off this state of affairs as an embarrassment to the scientific audience. We favor a more positive interpretation, however. The recency of the interest in adults, we believe, indicates several dra-

Preparation of this chapter was facilitated by a grant to the senior author from the Institute of Gerontology at Wayne State University.

matic and unprecedented changes in our society, which have changed the very fabric of adult life, and indeed are forcing upon developmental psychologists new ways of looking at life-span development. The still-prevalent, somewhat static view of adult development may have been a fairly appropriate one when referring to past, highly stable cultures, in which development could be equated with the individual's socialization into a predictable set of tasks and a static set of roles (Mead, 1970). In such societies, changes in adult roles often appear to have been initiated by changing biological capacities of the organism (Neugarten & Hagestad, 1976). Recent advances in science and technology, however, have created new phenomena—a lengthening of the life span and with it, a "greying" of the population; the "empty nest" phenomenon; career mobility; marital instability—that affect the lives of many adults and that are a testimony to the assertion that change has become an intrinsic aspect of adult development.

Recent attempts to formulate theoretical models that speak directly to the activities and adaptations required of middle-aged and older adults have focused on two major issues. First, there is an increased concern with the fact that standards of "maturity" in adulthood can no longer be solely borrowed from theories aimed at child development. Second, there is an emerging realization that development cannot be defined any longer in a cultural and historical vacuum; it is inevitably embedded in a flow of historical events. To the reader not intimate with the literature on adulthood and aging these may be rather obvious points. Researchers and theory builders often are in a more difficult position insofar as they become constrained by the conceptual tradition of their discipline. Some of the questions that are at the theoretical forefront of a psychology of adult development and aging have, indeed, been strongly shaped by this heritage.

Historically, conceptualizations of adult development have emanated from two rather disconnected bodies of literature. Some theories of adulthood change have emerged from attempts to extend primarily child-centered developmental models, such as those of Freud and Piaget. Such theories have taken their metaphor from evolution and biological growth models and proposed to use the term development in referring to growth processes that are directed toward a mature endstate, that are universal, and that are essentially organized by irreversible processes of maturation. At the other end of the life span, the young discipline of geropsychology launched only in the post–World War II era emanated from a variety of then existing orientations: anthropometric and psychometric assessments, laboratory studies of decision making and reaction time, learning and memory, and abstract problem solving, as well as the bio-medically oriented study of changes relating to senility and imminent death (see Riegel, 1977). The fusion of these various approaches led to an early view of adulthood and aging as primarily controlled by inner biological and maturational changes; adulthood merely appeared to be a period somewhat delicately suspended between adolescent maturation and frailty in later life.

When talking about adult development, therefore, much of the literature has been guided by a biologically oriented, decremental view. The first part of this chapter will survey and evaluate some of this research. In the second and third part, however, we will turn toward a consideration of emergent lines of research and theory that suggest that this somewhat pessimistic picture, although valid in part, may not be truly representative of the full range of adult competencies, nor may it truly aid us in comprehending the dynamics of development in adulthood and aging.

Inner biological changes and development in later life

Primary manifestations of aging

The fusion of the two different theoretical traditions—child development and gerontology—has imparted a particular theoretical meaning on conceptualization of aging and growing older. Aging, in the context of this fusion, is often juxtaposed to the notion of development. On the one hand, theories of child development focused on those universal and directive processes that resulted in an organism's efficient and adaptable functioning. Aging theorists, on the other hand, were primarily interested in determining how and explaining why life eventually terminated in death. Essentially, the former perspective presumed a positive and forward direction, while the latter implied a gradual process of regression and deterioration in functioning throughout adulthood. Thus aging, at least in part, connoted processes opposite to those implied in development. As Comfort (1956) put it, "aging" was used to refer to a "change in behavior of the organism with age, which leads to a decreased power of survival and adjustment" (p. 190).

Much of the earlier research into developmental changes in adulthood (see Riegel, 1977) similarly was directed at isolating behavioral changes that paralleled this universal and irreversible biological process; or, in Birren's (1970) words, at identifying those "primary manifestations of aging" that, on a level of behavioral organization, paralleled the biological pattern of stability and decline after maturity.

Biological changes indicating a slow but steady decline in physiological functioning throughout adulthood (e.g., Shock, 1977; Weg, 1975) are often cited as corroborating evidence for the deterioration of psychological functions with advancing age. Ultimately, such changes leave the aging organism more vulnerable to disease and mortality. Significantly, age-related changes in biological and physiological functioning do not merely affect the various isolated systems (e.g., cardiovascular, pulmonary, immunological), but the coordination between different systems as well (Shock, 1977). As a result, the aging organism has come to be seen as less adaptable on a physiological level.

Many theories propose micro-level, cellular mechanisms to account for the aging individual's higher physiological vulnerability (see Finch & Hayflick, 1977). What is most significant is that aging organisms appear to have a defective control of homeostatic mechanisms. Thus, deficits may be less apparent when the organism is at rest. However, the rate of readjustment to normal equilibrium in the old individual is slower when equilibrium is disrupted (Selye, 1956; Shock, 1977). A lessened ability to readjust to changes in temperature, or to regulate blood sugar levels, for example, are instances of such reduced homeostatic balance. Presumably such disturbances imply a decreased ability to respond to a wide variety of not only physical stressors (such as exercise, temperature, glucose intake), but personal, social, and emotional stresses as well (Selye, 1956). Thus there is some justification to conclude that on a biological level, aging may be equated—at least, in part—with reduced adaptability.

Cognitive functioning. It comes as no surprise, then, that conceptualizations of cognitive and social changes have suggested a similar picture of increased vulnerability of the aging individual to an environment that places demands on change and readaptation. For instance, the current beliefs about intellectual changes through life has been expressed in the theory of fluid and crystallized intelligence of Cattell (1963) and Horn (1970, 1976; Horn & Cattell, 1966, 1967). According to this two-factor model, crystallized intelligence refers to those cognitive processes that are embedded in a context of cultural meaning and that are relatively "age-insensitive" (Botwinick, 1973). Fluid intelligence, by contrast, typically concerns the processing of information in a context of low meaningfulness and exhibits profound age differences between younger and older adults. The prediction of different decline rates in crystallized and fluid intelligence subsumes an enormous body of empirical evidence (for summaries, see Baltes & Labouvie, 1973; Botwinick, 1973, 1977; Horn, 1970, 1976) and offers one explanation for the established finding that the elderly perform well on tests of stored information, while experiencing difficulty with tests of immediate memory, spatial relations, and abstract reasoning. Both these performance changes, as well as the changes in structural organization on which they are thought to rest, are said to reflect the interplay between life-long cumulative learning on the one hand and "normal," maturational aging on the other.

The fluid-crystallized model has been a rather accurate and integrative one. The generalizations have been derived from a number of similar models, such as the verbal-performance distinction inherent in research based on the Wechsler scales (e.g., Botwinick, 1967; 1977) and the information-psychomotor speed dichotomy made in Jarvik's (e.g., Jarvik & Cohen, 1973) and Birren's (1968, 1970) research. It is also indirectly related to research on verbal learning and memory processes (Botwinick, 1973; Horn, 1976), cognitive operations of Piaget (e.g., Papalia & Bielby, 1974), as well as a variety of neurophysiological findings (e.g., Jarvik, Eisdorfer, & Blum, 1973). In sum, then, the generalization that emerged out of this literature was that aging adults are quite able to operate in their accustomed settings and their concrete living situations. In contrast, they were seen as slow to respond, and especially slow to process new information; as embedded in their own concrete viewpoints; and as impaired in their adaptation to new settings.

Social and interpersonal processes. The bulk of the aging literature until the past decade concerns the developmental course of more impersonal activities as those discussed above. There has been a belief, nevertheless, that such activities may have far-reaching implications for more personal and interpersonal behaviors. Thus, the older person's decreasing ability to utilize novel information from the environment and to modify his or her behavior in accordance with changing demands, his or her dependence on concrete experience, and his or her slowing of behavior may set limits on general adaptive skills in later life. Early research on personality and social functioning suggested that development in later life paralleled the deteriorative process reflected in fluid measures of intelligence.

One trait often associated with intellectual decrement is rigidity. Elderly individuals have a tendency to perseverate and resist conceptual change, to refuse to relinquish old and established behavior patterns, and to resist the acquisition of new patterns of behavior (Chown, 1961; Schaie, 1958; Schaie & Labouvie-Vief, 1974). Accompanying rigidity may be an increase in dogmatism (Monge, 1972; Riegel & Riegel, 1960), which may interfere with flexible social functioning. However, as noted by Chown (1961), it is not clear whether rigidity is a normal behavior to be expected in older samples, or whether it can be accounted for by the older person's lower level of education and, therefore, measured intelligence.

One interesting approach to potential implications of higher levels of rigidity has been research relating to egocentrism in older adults. Socially effective behavior often demands that one consider the attitudes and feelings expressed by other people, or that one monitor one's verbal behavior so as to deliver meaningful messages to the partners of interpersonal interactions. In this sense, Looft and Charles (1971) found that old adults, unlike young adults, performed more egocentrically on measures of social and communicative competence, although as noted by Zaks and Labouvie-Vief (1977), such egocentrism may constitute a response to a socially impoverished environment.

On a more general level, social and personality changes indicated a restriction of growth-expansion motives, a decline in happiness, a loss of self-confidence, and higher levels of anxiety (see Kuhlen, 1964), together with reduced levels of social participation (Cumming & Henry, 1961). All of these changes appeared to parallel a biological expansion-restriction curve (Buehler, 1933; Kuhlen, 1964). Neugarten (1965, 1977) referred to these changes as an "increased interiority of the personality" in later life. In her sample, based on the Kansas City Study of Adult Life, "40-year-olds seemed to see themselves as possessing energy congruent with opportunities presented in the outer world; while 60-year-olds seemed to see the environment as complex and dangerous, tend to see the self as conforming and accommodating to outer world demands" (Neugarten, 1965, p. 11). This change or shift in ego style was described as a movement from active to passive mastery. While typical of individuals in their sixties, this pattern also appeared in a more subtle turning inward of the middle-aged adult. These individuals expressed an increased concern with health problems and energy conservation, and appeared to reorient their subjective time perspective from time since birth to time left until death.

Perhaps the most widely known framework to integrate these various changes in personality and social behavior is the disengagement theory (Cumming & Henry, 1961). Although it became controversial soon after its propagation, the original interpretation was to see the process of disengagement as an intrinsic and adaptive part of growing older, and a way for the aging person to withdraw from the pressures of social participation that came to be increasingly taxing on his or her weakening physical abilities. As Eisdorfer (1970) put it, "since the homeostatic mechanism in the aged may be more vulnerable . . . it may simply be physiologically more sound for him to remain uninvolved" (p. 66).

Biological determinism versus interactive viewpoints

Although, as we have shown above, there is rather overwhelming empirical evidence to support the contention of age-related limitation of the aging individual's ability to adapt to new settings, a number of authors (e.g., Baltes & Labouvie, 1973; Labouvie-Vief, 1977; Schaie, 1974) recently have expressed concern about the adequacy of such a generalization. The last decade has accumulated much research suggesting a number of possible amendments to such a simplistic picture, and raising the possibility that those psychological parameters showing strong relations to biological decline may either be an overly specific (i.e., not fully representative of the range of behavioral repertoire of adult and aging individuals) kind of behavioral restriction, or may be rather poorly related to age or time or both.

Methodological issues. In the first place, a direct linkage between biological causes and psychological consequences often appears less than compelling. Baltes and Labouvie (1973) and Labouvie-Vief (1977) have extensively reviewed the pertinent literature and pointed out a number of methodological pitfalls that make such a connection tenuous at best. It is often based, for instance, on mere surmise or correlative evidence, or it represents an explanatory hypothesis superimposed on behavioral descriptive evidence—such as measures of abstract reasoning and short-term memory (see Horn, 1976), psychomotor speed (e.g., Jarvik & Cohen, 1973), or Piagetian tasks (e.g., Papalia & Bielby, 1974)—in the absence of corroborating biological data. It is often, moreover, contaminated by the fact that elderly samples differ from younger ones on criteria other than age or maturation (e.g., education, institutionalization), and it is such nondevelopmental sampling factors that often may allow for powerful alternative or supplemental interpretations (e.g., Papalia & Bielby, 1974).

Discontinuity between normal and pathological development. Apart from such general considerations, it is not at all clear at present whether a general tendency toward *individual* deterioration can be inferred by *group-average* data. On both psychological (see Baltes & Labouvie, 1973) and biological levels (see Comfort, 1956) gradual individual decline may result from an increase in the probability of precipitous decline to be expected at each successive age level. Thus cognitive deterioration in later life appears to have well-demonstrated biological correlates only in those cases where it is secondary to the development of advanced pathology (Eisdorfer & Wilkie, 1973, 1977; Riegel & Riegel, 1972; Wang, 1973). Such relationships are rather exceptional in individuals who are living in a community and are in relatively good health (Birren, 1970; Eisdorfer & Wilkie, 1973, 1977; Hertzog, Gribbin, & Schaie, 1975). Or, as Birren (1963) has suggested, the relationship between biological variables and cognitive functioning may be a discontinuous one in the sense that it holds only if certain pathological limits are exceeded. In the absence of such conditions, many authors have doubted the usefulness of a model that relies on age or age-correlated maturational factors as an organizational principle for variability in adult cognition (see also Flavell, 1970; Reese, 1973).

Biological aging as cause versus outcome. With the above considerations in mind, many authors (e.g., Woodruff, 1975) have tried to conceptualize aging as a more interactive process in which biological as well as psychological aging processes themselves are seen as embedded in a flow of intrapersonal and broader historical events. Much attention has been given, for instance, to the effect that faulty dietary and/or exercise habits may have on disease processes—such as cardiovascular disease, disease of the colon, or diabetes (see Weg, 1975, for discussion). Many psychological changes of the fluid type often appear to be related to certain life styles rather than age. Botwinick and Thompson (1971) noted that age differences in psychomotor speed appeared to reflect differences in physical exercise habits rather than age. Labouvie-Vief (1977) has summarized similar evidence, with particular attention to research indicating that presumed deficits in cognitive functioning may often be helped with various interventive programs.

One such interactive model of particular promise is derived from Selye's (1956) model of aging as reduced homeostatic capacity. The lessened ability to respond to stress, in Selye's conceptualization, is itself a consequence of a cumulation of life-long stresses that exhaust the homeostatic reservoir. Thus, a cumulation of dramatic changes (e.g., death of a spouse, illness, loss of friends and relatives, decrease in income, institutionalization) within a short period of time could possibly induce a decline in health as well as psychological capacities (e.g., Dohrenwend & Dohrenwend, 1977; Holmes & Masuda, 1974; Holmes & Rahe, 1967; Rowland, 1977).

Yet the differences between individuals in their reaction to such stressors are pronounced, and as a result, researchers are now proposing to make finer distinctions than a mere listing of presumed stresses. For instance, is stress anticipated or does it strike unexpectedly? Is it valued positively or negatively? Why is something a stress for one individual but not for another? Without doubt, the individual's cognitive posture vis-à-vis stress enters as a powerful moderator into the stress-adaptation equation (for excellent discussions of this issue, see Eisdorfer & Wilkie, 1977; Lowenthal & Chiriboga, 1973).

Direct versus indirect effects of biological changes. Not only may an individual's cognition determine biological adaptation to an internal or external event, but it is also true that behavioral changes correlated with certain biological changes may be influenced by the person's interpretation of such events. A good example is sexual changes in later life. In aging men, physiological changes in general mean an increased need for continuous stimulation to achieve erection, and a much prolonged refractory period before another full erection (see Masters & Johnson, 1968). To aging males (as well as their sexual partners) who measure themselves against a youthful ideal of sexual prowess, such changes may create a threat that in turn is a deterrent to adequate sexual performance. On the other hand, the notion of aging as eroding sexuality in later life (e.g., Botwinick, 1973) is less pervasive in other societies where the ideals of sexually successful performance are defined more in accordance with the aging man's characteristic pattern of sexual expression (that is, less ejaculatory urgency, more capacity for long-continued stimulation; see Sheehy, 1976).

Similar considerations hold for aging females. As Masters and Johnson (1968) point out, female sexual capacity has often been related in a direct manner with endocrine starvation, and treated with the administration of estrogen or estrogenlike products. However:

> Estrogenic compounds frequently do improve sex drive in an indirect contribution above and beyond the original intended purpose of insuring a positive protein balance in the aging female. A woman previously experiencing a healthy libido may become relatively asexual while contending with such menopausal discomforts as excessive fatigue, flushing, nervousness, emotional irritability, occipital headaches, or vague pelvic pain. This individual's personal eroticism may be restored to previously established response levels following the administration of estrogenic preparations. The obviously increased sex drive well may have developed secondary to relief of the woman's multiple menopausal complaints, rather than as a primary or direct result of the actual adjustment of the individual's sex-steroid imbalance. (Masters & Johnson, 1968, p. 270)

Thus, seemingly direct psychological consequences of menopause in women may often be indirectly affected by the expectations, stereotypes, and folklore surrounding it (Lehr, 1966).

Biological vs. psychological adaptation. Our final criticism of a simplistic biological interpretation is much more theoretical, but of extreme importance. A decline in functions of the fluid type has often been arbitrarily equated with reduced behavioral adaptability. It is true, however, that reduced *biological* plasticity does not have a necessary bearing on reduced *psychological* adaptability. In fact, it is possible to see the process of development as a successive restriction of physiological plasticity in favor of more highly structured, conceptual (i.e., psychological) modes of functioning (Brent, 1977; Werner, 1948). Thus, the developing child's loss of adaptability to different linguistic environments is not usually termed a deficit. Similarly, the embryonic process of sex-role differentiation from undifferentiated gonads through successive stages to an irreversible and differentiated gender identity (Money & Ehrhardt, 1972) is not usually understood as a "decremental" process—despite the fact that at each turning point a choice is made that later on cannot be renegotiated. In this sense, development is synonymous with a progressive restriction of plasticity. But a too strongly biological concept of development relies too heavily on the fluid abilities of the adult and aging individual.

The above interpretation carries two important implications. First, it expands on Birren's (1963) discontinuity hypothesis and suggests a theoretical rationale for such discontinuity. That is, the rather uniform course of development in childhood or terminal pathological conditions may permit us to view time-related processes of biological growth or regression as a meaningful principle for the organization of early development. During much of adulthood, however, experience no longer will operate in concert with the constraining process of biological growth (Flavell, 1970); hence, as more fully discussed below, psychosocial events deserve our fuller attention in an attempt to understand adult development. Second, the proposition also suggests that a full understanding of adult development may elude us by concentrating on biological criteria of adaptability—such as speed, short-term memory, and certain forms of abstract problem solving. We will return to this point in the next section.

Continuities and discontinuities of development in adulthood

While on the surface much descriptive evidence points to social constriction and cognitive decline as a function of increasing age, can such changes indeed be called decremental? What is to be called growth or decrement, progression or regression is the result of the application of a standard that defines optimal functioning. As long as such standards are derived from primarily biological notions of adaptation, or from theoretical frameworks that are primarily youth-oriented, age-related variability in behavior is forced into an unilinear model, with the resulting implication of lower and higher levels of functioning. Juxtaposed against the achievements of youth, then, adulthood is inevitably marked by failures. To avoid such a foregone conclusion, it becomes essential to examine: 1. if earlier, or more biological, modes of functioning are superseded by new, adult-specific modes, and/or 2. if the diverse forms of adult adaptation can be forced into one unilinear scheme. It is this dual question that stands at the forefront of some refreshing lines of thinking currently emerging in the area of adult development, and although some of this material is still tenuous, we feel it is promising enough to deserve brief attention in this section.

Youth- versus adult-oriented standards of maturity

The problem of judging the progress of development against standards appropriate to the requirements of a particular stage of the life cycle is best shown by a discussion of cognitive changes, although, as we will demonstrate shortly, it also has a bearing on social adaptation.

Cognition. From the perspective of cognitive development, the basic task is to offer a satisfying interpretation for the older individual's difficulty with cognitive tasks of the fluid type (e.g., resistance to apply abstract modes of thought out of a concrete, day-to-day context, or for the demonstrated difficulty with memory tasks). In traditional cognitive-developmental theory, for instance, two interpretations have been used to account for this finding (e.g., Piaget, 1972). First, the general quality of environmental stimulation will affect both the rate of progression through stages and the final stage attained: Older adults, with their lower educational achievement, may never have reached their optimal level of competence. A second, less stringent interpretation is based on the observation that, with maturity, development becomes more specialized. At any time, the individual does not function at *one* stage only, but is characterized by a degree of multilevel operation in which the highest level of competence is achieved only under optimal circumstances (e.g., when well motivated or when in one's area of professional competence).

Both of these postures have affected research on adult development by placing less emphasis on regressive notions and enforcing instead a clear distinction between competence and performance. Thus, a person's level of competence is no longer thought to be inevitably expressed in a one-shot testing situation, but only after optimal variations of task format, motivational conditions, and with appropriate experience. Research of this type has been reviewed by Goulet (1973) and Labouvie-Vief (1977), and it has in general supported the notion that many of the tasks constituting the usual battery of cognitive assessments may be rather poor indicators of the elderly individual's cognitive repertoire. In fact, poor scores may often be the result of such inhibiting factors as high levels of anxiety, uninteresting and meaningless tasks, cautiousness and reluctance to guess, or lack of familiarity.

A yet more radical interpretation of fluid-type deficits is possible. This position might hold that those tests on which older adults do most poorly may not have any bearing at all on adult cognitive competence, either because more fluid forms of adaptation constitute a developmentally prior (i.e., youth-appropriate) mode of adaptation, or because the kinds of reasoning processes under investigation constitute only one possible and highly specialized mode of reasoning (see Labouvie-Vief & Chandler, 1978), or both. In this interpretation, the focus of study is being redirected from a priori defined criteria of cognitive maturity to an examination of the adult and aging individual's ability to cope with the unique, developmentally salient issues encountered in day-to-day adult life.

It is significant that most current measures of intellectual performance have been validated against criteria of academic success of young people involved in educational settings. Thus, although the picture of intellectual maturity derived from such tests may be relevant to that setting and that stage of life, it may lack validity if applied to more mature adults and to new, nonacademic situations.

What is this youthful image of cognitive maturity? Adolescence, according to Piaget (1972), brings the movement from the concrete to the hypothetical, permitting the young person to operate in a world of possibility rather than just reality. The result is a high degree of flexibility; rather than being embedded in their own concrete viewpoint, youth are able to approach any subject matter from multiple perspectives. New possibilities and viewpoints alien to the youth's background can not only be comprehended, but also generated by permutation; problems can be examined in a purely abstract, formal way for their logical cohesiveness, apart from judgments of personal likes and dislikes.

It is possible that this ability to engage in abstraction (out of the context of pragmatic considerations) is particularly relevant in youth who are involved in exercising these newly acquired skills, and in carving out a sense of personal and professional identity (Erikson, 1968). Here the ability to maintain flexibility and to avoid a premature channeling of energies and interests may be highly adaptive. As Schaie (1977) put it, this is an "acquisitive" phase, a phase of taking in, a time of perfecting one's skills while reserving judgment as to their concrete value or utility.

While the theme of youth is flexibility, the hallmark of adulthood is commitment and responsibility. Careers must be started, intimacy bonds formed, children raised. In short, amidst a world of a multitude of possible logical alternatives, there is a need to adopt one course of action. This commitment to one pathway and the disregard of other logical alternatives may indeed mark the onset of adult cognitive maturity (Perry, 1970; Riegel, 1973). At the same time, commitment brings a return to pragmatic necessities. Playful exercise of cognitive schemes, endless generating of 'ifs' and "whens," may no longer be adaptive; the task becomes instead to best utilize one's knowledge toward the management of concrete situations. Cognition becomes constrained by pragmatic necessities: Strategic control of one's life, managing time, conserving energy (Birren, 1969; Schaie, 1977). This phase may bring a relinquishment of the earlier emphasis on resolving contradictions: Contradiction must be accepted as part and parcel of adult life, giving rise to a new form of "contradictive cognition" (Clayton, 1975) that accepts, and even thrives on, imperfection, compromise, and failure.

Whatever the dimension that defines a more appropriate mode of adult cognition (the flexibility-commitment dimension just discussed, or the biological-psychological dichotomy mentioned earlier), these comments remind us that it may no longer be possible to write off the adult's difficulty with many tasks as regression. Take, for example, the notion that aging brings an impairment in memory. Whether or not this statement bears on regressive or progressive change is not as obvious as it first appears. Most of the tasks used to assess adult mnemonic competence deal with the relatively meaningless recall of such isolated items as words or word pairs: A mechanical recording of events that may be appropriate at early developmental stages but is unlike the kinds of mnemonic feats that adults perform in everyday life: What little evidence we have on such skills (Loewe, 1977; Reese, 1976; Walsh & Baldwin, 1977) suggests that decrements may be altogether lacking. Again, this observation reminds us of the earlier statement that notions of progressive or regressive change in adulthood must be related to a theory specifying the adaptive function of different modes of organization at different times in life. Jenkins (1971) has framed this point clearly:

> If we give (the head) higher order things to do, it retains the analysis of the higher order relations it extracts and uses these relations to generate products related to the initial activity. It seems to function very efficiently in pursuing such tasks. If,

on the other hand, we give the head stupid things to do by "brute force" it can only do relatively stupid things with the task and in the normal case it functions relatively inefficiently. (p. 285)

Identity development. Much as the adoption of a youthful ideal of maturity may have blurred a proper understanding of cognitive development, so may it also have misrepresented the process of social and emotional development in adulthood. Even among those theorists who have explicitly adopted a life course perspective (e.g., Buehler, 1933; Erikson, 1968; Kuhlen, 1968), development was usually seen to culminate late in one's adolescence or early adulthood. Even Erikson's (1968) theory of identity development, which has become most widely known for its propagation of specific postadolescent stages of personality development, nevertheless conceived adolescence as the pivotal stage in identity development. It is here, according to Erikson, that the young person attempts to carve out a sense of self by locating him- or herself on a conscious level, in an age-peer group, a sex role, an anticipated occupation, an ideology. The success with which this task is accomplished is thought to have a decisive bearing on how future crises are met. The adolescent who has succeeded in defining his or her identity is more likely to succeed in intimacy, generativity, and final ego integrity. A diffused sense of identity, in contrast, foreshadows a sense of isolation, stagnation, and an eventual inability to accept one's life as a meaningful whole.

In contrast to Erikson's somewhat placid view of adulthood there is a growing attempt to look at adulthood, not as the culmination of identity development, but as the very battlefield on which questions of identity explode. This is a view already anticipated by Jung (1933), who agrees that adolescence marks a revolution—one, however, that merely *starts* with the conscious differentiation from family and authority. At that time, one's self-understanding still may be limited and geared to the immediate demands of the future. It is only temporarily valid and is followed by a deeper, full-blown crisis of midlife that, according to Jung, is truly pivotal.

More recently, Sheehy (1976) has proposed a similar perspective, influenced by the work of Levinson and his colleagues (e.g., Levinson et al., 1974). Adolescent identity, in her view, is achieved in a preliminary and foreclosed way, and primarily defined by the "should's" of the outside world: family authority, cultural pressures, and peer models. Through most of one's midlife, further crises are centered around confronting these external should's, and such crises may find their expression in a review of one's life's goals, in abandoning current lifestyles (e.g., careers, marriages), in a redefinition of priorities. And it is that time, according to Sheehy, that may foreshadow how one is to face the last half of life:

If one has refused to budge through the mid-life transition, the sense of staleness will calcify into resignation. One by one, the safety and supports will be withdrawn from the person who is standing still. Parents will become children; children will become strangers; a mate will grow away or go away; the career will become just a job—and each of these events will be felt as an abandonment. On the other hand. . . .

If we have confronted ourselves in the middle passage and found a renewal of purpose around which we are eager to build a more authentic life structure, these may well be the best years. . . . At 50, there is a new warmth and mellowing. Friends become more important than ever, but so does privacy. Since it is so often proclaimed by people past mid-life, the motto of this stage might be "No more bullshit." (Sheehy, 1976, pp. 31–32)

Multilinear views of adulthood

The above comments remind us of the need to judge the progress of development against criteria validated specifically for adults. A similar but even more general reorientation of research in the area of adult development and aging is exemplified by the impact that Cumming and Henry's (1961) formulation of the disengagement theory exerted on the subsequent conduct of research in later life. In brief, the lesson learned from this research was that not only need one grapple with the issue of defining adult appropriate modes of functioning, but one also needs to be aware of the fact that there may not be just one such mode.

Immediately after publication of the Cumming and Henry book (1961) a tremendous controversy rose around the presumed adaptive nature of disengagement. As argued by Havighurst, Neugarten, and Tobin (1968), there was no valid a priori way to opt for disengagement; or, for that matter, for its negation, the "activity" theory (see Bengtson, 1973), which proposed that maintenance of high levels of activity, despite societal pressures to the contrary, constituted a more adaptive pattern. Thus, a distinction would have to be made between disengagement as a modal developmental event or process, and disengagement as a theory of optimal aging.

To tackle this question, Havighurst et al. (1968), working with the Kansas City Sample, developed a measure of what they thought reflected adaptive coping. This index, the life satisfaction rating, assessed the general affective quality of the adult subjects. Specifically, ratings were obtained of the degree to which these adults: (a) took pleasure in their daily round of activities, (b) regarded their life as meaningful, (c) felt that they had successfully achieved their life goals, (d) held a positive self-image, and (e) maintained, in general, happy and optimistic moods. Other measures assessed the degree of engagement these subjects maintained, such as: the amount of time they spent interacting, their involvement in and variety of roles (e.g., as spouse, parent, grandparent, workers, club-members), as well as how their perceived role changed since age sixty or, if subjects were younger, over the last ten years.

The results of this study warn us not to simplify disengagement. Overall, Havighurst et al. found that, as people reduced or relinquished their previous role involvements, they also tended to suffer a decrease in positive affect. Maintenance of activity was correlated with life satisfaction ($r = .46$). This finding has since been replicated (see Atchley, 1977, for a review) and, in general, it is fair to conclude that a majority of elderly people fare better if they continue to maintain high levels of activity and involvement.

It was obvious at the same time, however, that there were large individual variations from this general pattern, and the relationship between engagement and life satisfaction appeared to be moderated by the particular adaptational styles of different individuals. In a further analysis of a subsample of 70–79-year-old Kansas City subjects (Neugarten, Havighurst, & Tobin, 1968), there was some indication that life satisfaction and disengagement was related differently in different personality types.

For a subgroup called the "integrated" (all characterized as mellow, flexible, well-functioning adults), for instance, life satisfaction appeared high regardless of role activity. Some of these people disengaged from social participation and focused instead on a new, absorbing activity (e.g., a hobby). For these elderly, adaptation to late life may be excellent as long as one close relationship with a confidant is maintained (see Lowenthal, 1977). Yet a second group, the "armored-defended," appeared to reach high levels of satisfaction only as long as they were able to maintain fairly high levels of activity—a finding that appeared to be related to their previous life styles as striving, ambitious, achievement-oriented adults who appeared to ward off anxiety through tight defense systems.

Similar findings attesting to the diversity of ways in which adults may come to function well and adaptively have been reported in other research (Maas & Kuypers, 1974; Neugarten, Crotty, & Tobin, 1964), and the moral of such findings is clear: As yet, we have no overall theoretical framework for the multitude of ways in which individuals adapt to their particular life situations. However, it is unlikely that all of adult development can be described by one unilinear model that specifies one possible developmental sequence only and thereby holds up *one* singular mode of mature adult adaptation. Indeed, as Lowenthal (1977) has suggested, it is altogether possible that current notions of *the* developmental course (e.g., the significance of the mid-life transition, or the presumed shift from active to passive mastery in later life) are merely representative of restricted samples (e.g., upper-class individuals in the former, men in the latter case) and their specific ways of adapting to adulthood.

Transitions and catalysts

As developmental psychologists interested in the second half of life are coming to reject a unilinear, youth-oriented model of development, they certainly do more justice to the wide variability of behavior displayed in adulthood. At the same time, however, it becomes an essential task to spell out the factors that determine whether and when an individual moves forward or regresses, or why a person embarks on one particular developmental path but not another. Having rejected uniformity, a concomitant of biological change, it is then necessary to define those transition mechanisms that are catalysts in directing individuals to one or another developmental path. What, then, are some of the critical events that relate to change in adulthood?

Culture and cultural change

One of the most decisive aspects that structures the life course may well be the time at which we are born into a culture, with its particular technology, mores, and adaptive demands. Yet this fact is often neglected by developmental psychologists who attempt to expose developmental laws by cross-sectional comparisons of people differing in age and, therefore, cultural conditioning (Baltes, 1968; Kuhlen, 1964; Schaie, 1965). To illustrate the problems of such assessment, consider the results of a hypothetical study in which 20–60-year-olds were measured in terms of their height. Such results would indicate an age-related decrease in height which, however, could not be interpreted as individual shrinkage. Rather, due to the recent increase of about an inch per generation (Tanner, 1972), they would reflect a cultural change process that has affected each generation, or birth cohort, in the study population. Thus it is necessary to make a distinction between mere age *differences* and true age *changes* (i.e., individual development).

In a similar way, it appears now that past research on adult cognitive development may not have assessed decrements (i.e., age changes), but rather reflected the fact that each cohort or generation may differ according to their specific levels of functioning. These levels, though higher for younger than older cohorts, are maintained for each cohort at a stable level throughout most of adulthood and may display a drop only in the sixties or later (e.g., Schaie & Labouvie-Vief, 1974).

Research on personality processes in adulthood has also indicated that cohort flow may make a substantial imprint on the individual. Schaie and Parham (1976), for instance, offered data to suggest that age differences in rigidity reflected cohort change rather than individual development. Similarly, Woodruff and Birren (1972), in a study covering 25 years, found that cohort differences were larger than age differences for an assortment of personality variables.

Once again, findings such as these remind us that the variability among adults cannot be contained in one single standard. At any time, cultural change and subcultural heritage create tremendous diversification, and it is this basis, from which adult development emerges, that needs elucidation just as the changes in behavior themselves.

Ultimately, of course, it would be desirable to have a better understanding of those basic conditions of life that cause individuals to cope in their characteristic ways with their unique developmental events. Thus, changes in technology, education, economics and demography all create a changing background against which development is portrayed (for a summary, see Baltes, Cornelius, and Nesselroade, 1976). Two of these conditions, those of age and sex-linked roles and expectations, are discussed in the remainder of this chapter.

Age-linked sequencing of events

Cultural change also has a profound bearing on the occurrence, timing, and sequencing of events. At any historical time, the adult life span is, in part, regulated by a system of culturally imposed "prods" and "brakes." There is, for instance, an appropriate time for leaving home, for marriage, parenthood, professional maturity, and retirement (Havighurst, 1972; Neugarten & Hagestad, 1976).

The consequences of and adjustments to various life changes may well vary according to the way in which people judge such events—whether they are early, on time, or late. Women are aware of an "appropriate" time to marry (Neugarten, Moore, & Lowe, 1965); men judge their career development according to an internal clock prescribing where they "should" be at any given age (Sofer, 1970). Older women may expect widowhood and even "mentally rehearse" for it, while younger women or older and younger men may fail to do so (Neugarten, 1977; Treas, 1975; Watson & Kivett, 1976). As a result, older women may actually be more resilient, experiencing less dramatic disruption of their life when the spouse dies.

Such social time tables, of course, are themselves modified by cultural change. The effect of cultural change appears to have been to create a strong differentiation between biological, psychological, and social clocks. In earlier, more stable cultures, age-related changes in roles—such as those associated with the period of adolescence—may have been defined in accordance with an individual's biological maturation. In more complex, rapidly changing societies, however, the synchronization of biological, psychological, and social maturity has become disrupted (Conger, 1973). Or, to paraphrase Conger (1973), in present-day culture maturity merely starts in biology, but ends in culture.

Just as the transition from childhood to adulthood has changed in meaning, new differentiations have also been made in later life. Middle-age has become clearly delineated and new stages of old age have emerged—the young-old and old-old (Neugarten & Hagestad, 1976). Middle-aged individuals are, for instance, experiencing a relatively long period of physical vigor, of diminished family responsibilities as a result of the empty nest, and of heightened commitment to work. Similarly, due to increased longevity, the historically changing rhythm of events in the family and work cycle, and better education, the young-old are experiencing an interval of relatively good health and vigor, of freedom from the traditional responsibilities of both parenthood and work, and of security in terms of economic concerns (Neugarten, 1977).

With respect to old age, cultural change has altered the very fabric of life. Some have argued that, as the percentage of older people has increased in modern societies, the older population may have moved to a position less respected: their prestige and power has become lowered, as well as the quality of their life (Cowgill & Holmes, 1972).

One potential result of this recent change in the status of the older population is that age norms regarding appropriate behaviors for the elderly have become less important. With such a lack of positive normative guidelines, many older people appear to age in a context surrounded by stereotype (see, Bennett & Eckman, 1973). Thus, they get caught up in a vicious cycle of "social breakdown," where social, emotional, and financial supports are missing and where they are labelled as deficient (Bengtson, 1973). Such an aura of social neglect and negative stereotyping often leads to a withdrawal of appropriate reinforcements necessary for competent behavior (see Baltes & Labouvie, 1973). Many elderly individuals—especially those institutionalized—are cast in a "sick-role" that results in an encouragement of dependency and helplessness (MacDonald & Butler, 1974). Thus, decremental changes in later life may often be ushered in by the social system.

Not all authors accept this "victim view" of the elderly. The vulnerability of the older individual will likely depend upon his or her resources (Dowd, 1975). A loss of norms and roles may even represent a gain in freedom from societal constraints for those who choose and have the resources to exploit it (Bengtson, 1973). Thus the lack of clearly defined age roles may imply, for some elderly, more flexibility or a greater range of personal choice in structuring their lives.

Sex roles

Few areas demonstrate the need for a multilinear, life course perspective more clearly than that of sex roles. As recently as 1970, a survey of this topic was likely to convey the impression that sex role development largely occurred in early life and culminated in the adolescent's adapting an "appropriate" (masculine or feminine in accordance with the youth's biological sex) sex role (Urberg & Labouvie-Vief, 1976). Only a few isolated writings expressed the conviction that a polarized sex role, while important in the adolescent, might be less adaptive either later on (Mussen, 1962) or for those pursuing careers unusual to their sex (Heilbrun, 1970; Horner, 1970). This decade, in contrast, has experienced a vigorous attack on the view that sex role development ends when polarized masculine and feminine roles are learned, asserting instead that a complex modern society requires one to move back and forth with flexibility between "masculine" and "feminine" poles of behavior (Bem, 1974; Block, 1973). Thus, a few authors recently have proposed that this "sex role transcendence" or "androgeny" constitutes the truly mature way of functioning and an advancement beyond adolescent sex role polarization (e.g., Block, 1973; Hefner, Rebecca, & Oleshansky, 1975).

Much as the propagation of androgeny as *the* new mature end to sex role development may resonate to the current *zeitgeist,* it may also fail to account for the complexities involved in an adult's continuing sex role adaptation. As is true for other aspects of development in adulthood, the particular mode, as well as its adaptive value, must ultimately be related to the current demands placed on the individual.

The success with which individuals may be able to integrate traditionally masculine-instrumental and feminine-nurturant qualities may vary according to their stage in life or may be expressed in a sequence of multiple roles. Although some authors have claimed that androgenous women display better mental health characteristics (see Conger, 1973, for review), it is likely that such a relationship does not universally hold. It may not be characteristic, for instance, of women involved in the rearing of several children and the management of a career (Pearlin, 1975). Similarly, early entry into parenthood may create strain for men (Jaccoby, 1969), while "late" fathers may find it easier to synchronize parental and career roles (Nydegger, 1973), presumably, because the demands associated with establishing two new careers (parental vs. occupational) do not coincide. It is not surprising to find that the development or suppression of androgenous characteristics is often closely interwoven with stages of the parenting cycle: Pregnancy in young marriages may cause a polarization of instrumental and nurturant characteristics (Feldman, 1978), while the empty nest period frees women to cultivate their instrumental needs and men to develop their expressive characteristics (Gutmann, 1975). It is possible, of course, that this particular pattern is itself time-linked and may abate in the future as the still predominant role division in marriages comes to be more equitably distributed between wives and husbands (Hoffman, 1977).

At the present time, however, it is true that most adults still have been socialized into traditional roles, and whether or not they move out of them may be entirely dependent not upon their age, but the time at which they experience a crisis initiating a role shift. For some, this may be divorce (Sedney, 1977); for others, the empty nest; for some, widowhood (Lopata, 1975); for others yet, their particular course of early socialization which has created a sense of being trapped in traditional but ill-fitting roles (Livson, 1975). It also appears that such a role shift may be more likely in women, possibly due to the fact that current sex roles permit greater flexibility for women (Lynn, 1969; Maas & Kuypers, 1974). A good example is offered by Maas and Kuypers's forty-year follow-up of young couples. Here, high stability both of behavior and context was observed in men. This was not true of women, however. One group of women, in particular, early in their adulthood were highly dissatisfied with their marriages, unhappy in their parenting roles, socially withdrawn, and in general poorly adapted. As older and no-longer-married women, however, they were highly satisfied, dividing their time between rewarding involvements with friends, children, and occupations.

Those adults who do venture out of their traditional roles, moreover, often appear to do so at some significant but temporary psychological cost. (Livson, 1975; Sedney, 1977). In later life, those earlier conflicts may bear fruition and ease the transition to widowhood (Lopata, 1975; Treas, 1975) and, for some, adaptation to retirement (Atchley, 1977; Maas & Kuypers, 1974).

Summary

As a society changes, so does the way its members experience and conceptualize the process of development. We have made an attempt in the present chapter to convey some understanding not only of the process of individual aging, but of that of theorizing about aging, as well. At present, the field of adult development and aging is in the middle of a developmental crisis akin to those confronting the individual throughout his or her life. Past interpretations are being reevaluated, new ones are tentatively being put forward. It is easier, of course, to tell the outcomes of any crisis after it has happened, since only time tells the value of emerging positions. Nevertheless, a certain pattern already appears to be establishing itself.

As the synchrony between biological, psychological, and social aspects of aging has become disrupted, so, too, notions of aging that are based on a purely biological basis are being challenged. This is not to deny, of course, that behavior has biological manifestations on some level. It is merely to state that, as far as the process of adult development is concerned, it is difficult to isolate general patterns that might make intelligible the changes adults experience. Nor is there *one* such pattern with which to judge the achievements of adults. At any age level, there is marked heterogeneity, and this diversity can only be understood if we attend to the sequence of concrete tasks and events that make up the life course.

As a result, there is less and less concern with attempting to isolate some natural process of aging tied to chronological age. Still, adult development is not mere chaos, either. Patterns may be discerned, but they often vary according to the contexts in which developmental demands are made. Many of these contexts are dictated by cultural change with its still poorly explained effects on educational systems, intergenerational cohesion, technological participation, and sex role specialization. Some of them may also be less transient and tied to the rhythms of work, intimacy, and parenting as they are established and coordinated over the life cycle.

This emerging posture is already exerting an effect on the interpretation of adult development. Incremental or decremental transitions often are no longer seen as natural concomitants of growing older. Rather they may result from the way in which experience is structured through certain social dynamisms and settings. Thus with regard to sex role changes, transitions in adulthood may be ushered in by such events as work or parenting, which themselves are profoundly affected by cultural change. Adaptation to life-after-marriage will greatly vary according to one's prior life style and the resulting unequal availability of resources in reestablishing an independent life style. Those changes surrounding the retirement period, also, may not necessarily be natural in the sense of being inevitably linked to aging. The institutionalization of retirement often brings changes in resources, status, and opportunities that often imply a drastic impoverishment of social context and hence a greater likelihood for reduced competence.

This view has created a surging concern with influencing, rather than merely describing, the process of development, based upon a realization that the adult's assessed level of behavior (performance) does not necessarily reflect his or her level of competence. The emphasis on cognitive intervention (see Labouvie-Vief, 1977), change in such settings as housing and institutions (lawton & Nahemow, 1973), therapeutic intervention programs (Eisdorfer & Stotsky, 1977), and a new concern with the diversity of patterns of coping (Coelho, Hamburg, & Adams, 1974) all are instances of this new direction.

The emergent view of adults and the elderly as ideally effective and competent copers with their particular developmental tasks is indeed a welcome event and it is in contrast to a predominant concern with deficit characteristic of the field until recently. Once we are willing to think of development in later life as potentially multidirectional and context-bound, it will be possible to gain an unbiased representation of the potentialities, as well as limitations, of middle and later life.

GLOSSARY

Age norms: A system of norms or expectations that govern age-appropriate behaviors and interactions.

Aging: A broad process of change in the structural and functional properties of the biological, psychological, and social aspects of living organisms.

Biological aging changes: A slow but steady decline in physiological functioning throughout adulthood.

Biological growth model: A model stating that the organizing principles of developmental and age changes are biologically based and that these changes are universal, irreversible, and inevitable.

Cognitive development: A process of change in the mental process involved in knowledge acquisition and utilization.

Cohort: A group of persons who were born in the same historical time period and/or who share a similar socialization history.

Competence-performance: The difference between an individual's potential level of performance (competence) and the actual performance itself.

Cross-sectional method: Observation of samples of different age levels at one point in time.

Crystallized intelligence: Cognitive processes presumed to be embedded in a context of cultural meaning, and which are "age insensitive": tests of information, vocabulary, etc.

Cultural change: The changing context in which generations or cohorts grow and age.

Discontinuity childhood-adulthood: A position stating that the standards of maturity in adulthood can not merely be borrowed from theories aimed at child development and that adulthood change can not be fully understood by extending primarily child-centered developmental theories.

Discontinuity pathology-normal development: A position stating that while in pathology there may be a relationship between biological deterioration and behavior, such as senility, this relationship does not necessarily hold up in a "normal" or healthy range of individuals.

Disengagement: Descriptively, the increased interiority and decreased social participation in later life; theoretically, the normative mutual withdrawal between individual and society in later life.

Fluid intelligence: Cognitive processes that are presumed to exhibit a developmental pattern closely related to biological growth and decline curves and reflect an individual's ability to process novel, low-meaningful information.

Identity development: Working out a viable sense of who one is as a sexual being, in a sex role, in an age peer-group, as an independent, unique person, in an occupation, and in an ideology; a process by which the individual develops a sense of continuity between past, present, and future, and a sense of integration and continuity across various social contexts.

Intellectual development: See *Cognitive development.*

Life-span development: A position stating that the states or changes of an individual are best understood in the context of the *whole* life span.

Longitudinal method: Observation of one sample (cohort) repeatedly over an extended time period.

Maturity: In a particular theoretical framework, *maturity* refers to the achievement of an optimal level of functioning. This level varies from theory to theory, and thus when making comparisons one must be aware of the theory that furnishes a standard—in particular, whether one looks at youth or adult standards of maturity.

Mid-life transition: Considered a normative turning point in middle adulthood where adults may face such issues as failing physical powers, the feeling that time is running out, and a redefinition of purpose in one's work or parenting role.

Multilinear developmental models: Rather than implying that all individuals can be compared on the basis of the same standard, this position holds that different developmental pathways will be found, depending upon the kind of adaptation required.

Regression: A disintegration of structural and functional properties of the biological, psychological, and social aspects of living organisms.

Sex roles: Individuals internalize or adopt a masculine and feminine role in accordance with their biological sex. Sex roles may be polarized or androgenous—androgenous individuals may be able to synchronize traditionally masculine-instrumental and feminine-nuturant qualities according to their stage in life or in a sequence of multiple roles.

Standards of maturity: See *Maturity*.

three

DYSFUNCTIONAL BEHAVIORS

The material in this section examines specific forms of dysfunctional behavior or psychopathology. The chapters illustrate the tremendous range of human behavior patterns. In addition to describing the predominant symptom patterns of each dysfunction, research and theory on their causes will be presented. Considerable controversy exists over the identification of several of the disorders; for example, experts disagree about what depression is and how different forms of depression should be categorized. Hence, the student should not be surprised that there is little agreement about the causes of many of the disorders. In general, the chapters in this section are primarily based on the current research literature rather than on any particular theory about human behavior (e.g., psychoanalytic theory).

The two most pervasive forms of psychological distress are anxiety and depression. In Chapter 8, Alan S. Bellack describes anxiety and its effects, and then discusses the neuroses—a series of disorders in which anxiety plays a central role. Stephen L. Stern and Joseph Mendels then consider depression in Chapter 9 on affective disorders. The broad range of affective disturbances and the disagreement about the various ways in which depression and mania occur are highlighted in this chapter. David Shapiro and Edward S. Katkin present psychophysiological disorders in Chapter 10. These are disturbances in which there is substantial physiological involvement, such as asthma and ulcers. Kurt Salzinger discusses schizophrenia in Chapter 11. This severe disturbance has been especially difficult to understand and treat. Salzinger contrasts historical conceptions of the disorder with current research on schizophrenic behavior.

Chapter 12, by Gerald Goldstein, deals with organic brain syndromes and related disorders. The various causes of neurological impairment and the often subtle effects are described. In Chapter 13 G. Alan Marlatt and Francine Rose discuss addictive disorders, focusing on alcoholism and heroin addiction. Sexual disorders are considered in Chapter 14 by Jack S. Annon and Craig H. Robinson. The importance of group values and social mores in defining "normal" and "abnormal" sexual behaviors is clearly emphasized in this Chapter. Chapter 15, by Asher R. Pacht and Eugene H. Strangman, deals with crime and delinquency. In addition to material on causes and treatment of these disorders, the authors highlight the difficulty of labeling and classifying "criminal" behavior. Alan O. Ross and Edward G. Carr discuss childhood disorders in Chapter 16. This chapter covers a variety of disturbances including childhood schizophrenia, school problems, aggressive behavior, and withdrawal or isolation. The final chapter in this unit (Chapter 17), by David Balla and Edward Zigler is on mental retardation. These authors describe the reciprocal impact of retardation on the individual and his/her family, as well as discussing the causes and nature of retardation.

The Pilgrimage of the Epileptics to the church of Molenbeeck-Saint Jacques. Seventeenth-century engraving after P. Brueghel.

A teenage girl afflicted with anorexia nervosa. Wood engraving in *Lancet,* 1888.

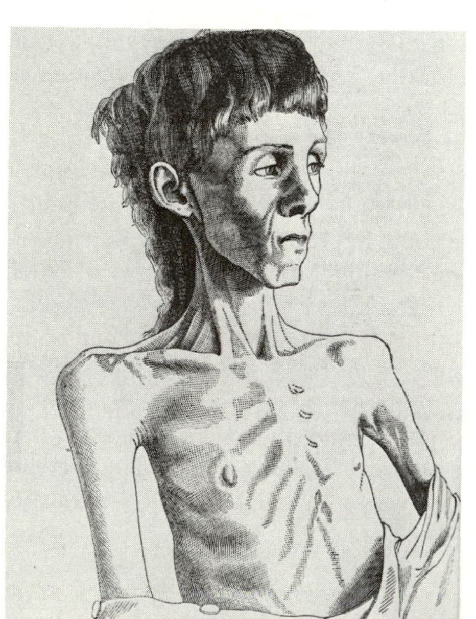

"Madness," an early nineteenth-century English engraving.

A Chinese opium palace, San Francisco.
Harper's Weekly, April 1880.

A state mental hospital in California, 1978.

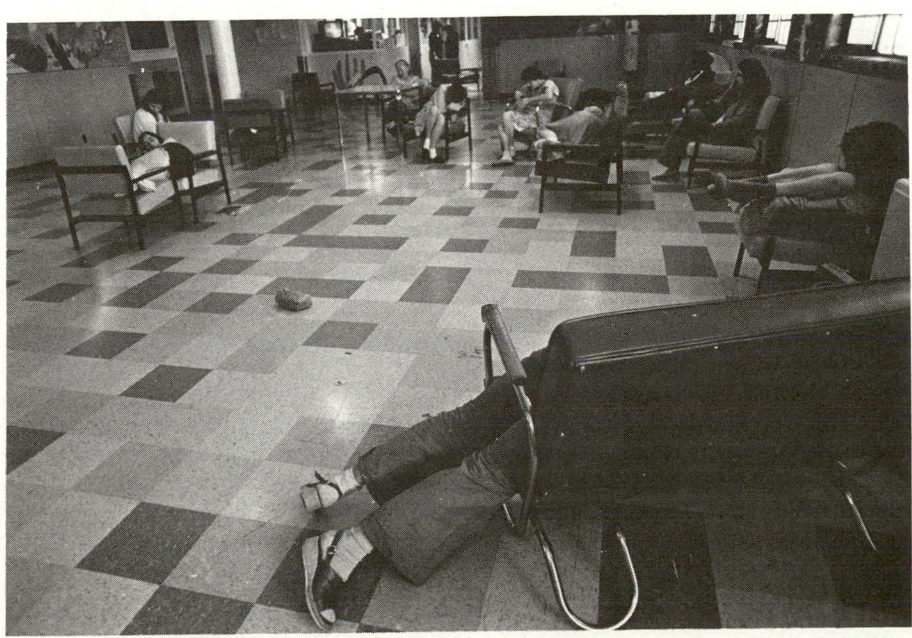

ANXIETY AND NEUROTIC DISORDERS

ALAN S. BELLACK

The mid–twentieth century has been referred to as the "Age of Anxiety." Vietnam, Watergate, the assassinations of the Kennedys and Martin Luther King, the Middle East crises, détente with the Soviet Union, nuclear proliferation, the energy crisis, inflation, and crime have all contributed to widespread apprehension about the future, concern over personal safety, and other forms of distress. These environmental stresses are all superimposed on other sources of distress typical of daily living in any era, as well as those difficulties that are the result of some maladaptive or abnormal aspect of the individual. The result of this virtual bombardment of stressors is that anxiety has become the most widespread form of psychological distress and pain. While anxiety would thus be a critical mental health problem in and of itself, it is especially a problem in that it has been implicated as a major factor in many forms of psychopathology, including: neuroses, schizophrenia, psychosomatic disorders, alcoholism, crime and delinquency, and sexual deviation. Because of the central role accorded to anxiety in so many disorders, it is necessary to understand what anxiety is, what causes it, and what effects it has, before examining the specific types of psychopathology.

In addition to discussing anxiety, this chapter will also cover neurotic disorders: a group of extreme anxiety disturbances. Neuroses, as a group, account for the largest proportion of individuals who can be classified as having psychiatric problems. Characteristically less severe than psychotic disorders, neuroses are a group of disorders that produce intense suffering and interfere with the normal behaviors of everyday life. Our discussion of neuroses will follow the section on anxiety: the most critical factor in their development. We will first consider some general issues about neurotic disorders and then examine the specific types of neuroses and their etiology. It should be pointed out that certain individuals whose primary disorder is depression are categorized by some mental health experts as having depressive neurosis. This labeling is subject to controversy; consequently, this group will be considered later in chapter 10, on affective disorders.

Anxiety

Imagine yourself in each of the following situations:

1. It is 1:30 A.M. and you are in the midtown area of a large city. You turn off of a main street and begin walking down a dark side street where your car is parked. The further you walk, the fewer people you see. The doorways are all dark, and you enter the shadows where a street lamp has burned out. As you reach for your car keys, you hear a noise behind you.

2. You have always been healthy, but in the past few weeks you have begun having persistent headaches and periodic dizzy spells. Aspirins and other pain relievers have been of no help, so you finally go to a physician. After a series of questions and tests, he informs you with a somewhat grave tone that he is not yet sure of what is wrong, and that he wants to take some x-rays of your head. You are now waiting in his office to receive the results of the test. Then, the door opens.

These two situations are, obviously, quite different in most respects. Yet, there is one critical similarity that should be readily apparent if you actually imagined yourself in them: they both produced uncomfortable feelings (which would undoubtedly be a lot more uncomfortable if you were really in the situations). The specific nature of those feelings differs for different people. They might include sweaty palms, a knot in the stomach, heart palpitations, headache or tension in the back of the neck, or simply a psychological feeling of tension or distress. If you were really in one of the situations, you might also have taken a sudden sharp breath, "jumped" in the direction of the noise or door, or broken out in a "cold sweat." You probably would have been unable to think clearly or react quickly, and you might well have stammered if you had to speak. You might use any of a number of terms to describe your feelings: tense, nervous, worried, frightened, up tight. However, regardless of the specific nature of your reaction or the term you use to describe it, a single label sums up your experience: *anxiety*.

The nature of anxiety

If you describe the situation in the physician's office and your feelings to a group of mental health professionals, nine out of ten would probably agree that you were anxious. However, if you asked them to define anxiety, you would probably receive ten different definitions. All of the definitions would probably include some mention of the fact that anxiety is an unpleasant emotion characterized by feelings of threat or danger, but the elaborations of this basic view would be quite different. The reason for this lack of agreement is that anxiety is neither a discrete response that occurs in the same manner under the same conditions for everyone (such as the knee-jerk reflex), nor is it a concrete, observable phenomenon (such as a broken bone). Rather, anxiety is a summary term that describes a complex and variable set of reactions to a variety of situations. Further, the reactions themselves do not equal anxiety, but anxiety is the presumed *factor* that produces the reactions. Hence, *anxiety is a construct or a hypothesized mediating* variable (Lang, 1971). This is a critical point to understand.

When people are exposed to some types of situations (e.g., the physician's office described above), certain responses occur (e.g., emotional distress, pounding heart). In an effort to explain why these responses occur and to predict when they will occur again, we hypothesize that there was some internal process or response that ties the situations and reactions together: anxiety. Hence we can presume that the reactions occurred because the situation *must have been* anxiety arousing, and we predict that the reactions will occur in the future in other anxiety arousing situations. Anxiety is not, itself, observed or measured, but it is a convenient and logical concept for predicting and explaining behavior.

However, because anxiety is neither observable nor directly measurable, a concrete definition is elusive. Definitions can be categorized along several dimensions. *Stimulus definitions* emphasize the stimulus conditions that produce anxiety, and typically presume that there are different types of "anxiety" responses that vary with the stimulus. For example, Freud differentiated "objective anxiety" from "neurotic anxiety." Objective anxiety is a response to a real or realistic threat (e.g., a lion), while neurotic anxiety is an irrational response to an internal conflict (e.g., fear of aggressive impulses), which has no basis in fact.

A related distinction that has been the subject of considerable controversy in the scientific literature is whether or not "fear" should be differentiated from "anxiety." Some writers (cf. Szpiler & Epstein, 1976) regard fear as a response to an identifiable threat from which the individual is impelled to flee. In contrast, anxiety is viewed as a response to an unidentifiable threat (as with the college student who is anxious in social situations), for which no specific response can be initiated (i.e., you don't know what to flee).

Others argue that this distinction is not useful for two reasons (Martin, 1971). *First,* there does not appear to be a clear and reliable difference between the subjective feelings, physiological responses, and overt motor actions that occur in response to vague and specific threats. *Second,* it has been argued that a specific threatening stimulus can, in fact, always be identified with careful assessment. Hence, the semantic distinction between the two emotional states does not allow for greater explanatory and predictive power.

The term anxiety has also been used to identify stable personality characteristics. Karen Horney (c.f. Hall & Lindzey, 1970) coined the phrase basic anxiety to describe underlying feelings of vulnerability and helplessness, which she presumed were the basis of all neurosis. Spielberger (1966) has suggested that a distinction be made between "trait anxiety" and "state anxiety." Trait anxiety is a stable characteristic of the individual that makes him/her more or less susceptible to becoming anxious at any moment. High trait anxious people become anxious very easily, under a host of different circumstances. State anxiety, on the other hand, is a short-term emotional experience akin to the reaction produced by the two situations described at the beginning of this section. The high trait anxious person would experience high state anxiety very frequently.

Given this diversity of perspectives, why would nine of our ten mental health experts agree that the person in the physician's office was anxious? Surprisingly, there is little disagreement about how to *identify* anxiety; the disagreement pertains to what it is that has been identified! Anxiety can best be conceptualized as a *response pattern* rather than a single discrete response. The pattern is generally assumed to involve some combination of: 1. cognitive reactions and 2. physiological reactions. In the following sections we will consider what these reactions are and how they are associated with anxiety.

Cognitive reactions. The term cognitive as used here refers to thinking and feeling. Perhaps the most critical aspect of anxiety is that it is associated with subjective distress. Feelings of tension, threat, danger, vague unease, and impending harm or disaster are all commonly associated with anxiety. Sometimes the feelings are amorphous, and are reflected by such descriptions as "jittery," "on edge," or "up tight." At other times, very specific thoughts and images flash through the mind. For example, in a recent experiment (Wade, Malloy, & Proctor, 1977) college students were requested to approach as close to a harmless snake as they could, including touching it if possible. Students who independently described themselves as fearful of snakes reported having mental images of themselves being bitten as they attempted to approach the snake. The specific versus vague nature of the unpleasant feelings associated with anxiety probably vary across people, as well as across situations for the same people. That is, some people (e.g., obsessive-compulsive neurotics) are more likely to experience specific thoughts than are others (e.g., anxiety neurotics), but everyone is likely to have

Table 8.1. Sample Items from Two Anxiety Scales

State-Trait Anxiety Inventory (Spielberger et al., 1970)	Almost Never	Some-times	Often	Almost Always
I am "calm, cool, and collected"	1	2	3	4
I lack self-confidence	1	2	3	4
I feel blue	1	2	3	4
I am a steady person	1	2	3	4

Manifest Anxiety Scale (Taylor, 1953)
(answers indicate anxiety)
I cannot keep my mind on one thing. (True)
I sweat very easily even on cool days. (True)
I am easily embarrassed. (True)
I am happy most of the time. (False)

vague feelings at some times and specific thoughts at others. An important factor in this regard is whether or not some specific danger is apparent in the situation or is somehow suggested to the person. For example, the nonspecific tension before a major exam can be suddenly focused on a specific potential question after one student says, "You don't think he will ask us about————————, do you?"

Subjective distress cannot be assessed directly by an objective observer (you cannot see someone's thoughts and feelings). Consequently, this aspect of anxiety is evaluated by self-report. The simplest and most common way of securing self-report is simply to ask the individual how he/she feels, and what he/she is experiencing. For example, "What were you feeling while you were waiting for the doctor?" "What was that experience like?" "What was going through your mind?" "Do you often get those feelings?" The specific interview style and the types of questions asked will vary with the theoretical persuasion of the interviewer, and what he/she feels is the most important type of information to secure. Thus, the psychoanalytic interviewer would probe for unconscious conflicts that produce anxiety, the client-centered interviewer would try to elicit an expression of feelings, and the behavioral interviewer would probe for specific details about the experience (e.g., exactly what it was like, the circumstances preceding the experience, etc.).

A second technique for gathering information about subjective feeling states is the use of self-report inventories or tests. Interview material is often ambiguous and requires the interviewer to interpret the person's responses (people use the same words to mean different things). Testing secures a standardized and objective account, and also provides a quantitative summary of the person's status, allowing for easy comparison with some reference group (e.g., how anxious is this student in comparison to other students at his school?).

Anxiety inventories fall into three general categories: trait, state, and specific situations. The trait measures focus on anxiety as a general characteristic or personality disposition. Questions reflect the person's general tendency to be anxious in a variety of situations. Sample questions from two representative inventories, the State-Trait Anxiety Inventory (Spielberger, Gorsuch, & Luschene, 1970), and the Taylor Manifest Anxiety Scale (Taylor, 1953), are presented in Table 1. State anxiety inventories are designed to assess momentary feelings, rather than general dispositions. These tests can employ the same questions as trait inventories by simply altering the initial instructions. Thus, a trait inventory would direct the person to respond according to his/her typical feelings, while a state inventory would request answers that reflect feelings right at that moment.

Tests have been developed to measure anxiety in a host of specific situations including: speech anxiety, test taking anxiety, heterosocial anxiety, and anxiety about being evaluated by others. Rather than asking the test taker to make a cross-situational statement about anxiety (as on trait measures), these devices examine reactions to specific types of situations. As we suggested above in regard to the lack of distinction between fear and anxiety, anxiety tends to be *situation specific*. That is, people become anxious in response to certain identifiable stimuli. The term stimulus here means anything that precedes and precipitates anxiety. The stimulus could be a thought (e.g., a bad memory), a physical reaction (e.g., a chest pain), or something in the environment (e.g., an impending speech in a class). Some people do become anxious more easily or frequently than others. Nevertheless, specific anxiety provoking events can be identified even for the most anxiety-prone individual. Trait measures appear to be useful for measuring anxiety-proneness, but they are not very efficient at predicting *when* the anxiety will occur. Situation specific measures, on the other hand, are useful for predicting behavior in the situations covered by the test items (e.g., giving speeches, taking tests).

Examples of situation specific anxiety measures are illustrated in Table 8.2. Both tests were developed by Watson and Friend (1969) to assess separate aspects of interpersonal anxiety. The Social Avoidance and Distress Scale was designed to measure level of distress and tendency to avoid social situations. The Fear of Negative Evaluation Scale measures anxiety about being viewed in a critical light by others. While these two scales are both related to social anxiety, they focus on slightly different sources or stimuli for the anxiety. It is quite possible that one person could be anxious in many social situations without specifically fearing negative evaluations, while another person could be anxious only when he/she believed that he/she was being judged by others. Used together, the two tests allow for better prediction of behavior and feelings than either scale used alone. Better prediction implies, in part, that a treatment plan could be devised more effectively.

Table 8.2. Sample Items from the Social Avoidance and Distress Scale and the Fear of Negative Evaluation Scale (Watson & Friend, 1969)[a]

Social Avoidance and Distress Scale
I feel relaxed even in unfamiliar social situations. (False)
I often find social occasions upsetting. (True)
I am usually nervous with people unless I know them well. (True)
I find it easy to relax with other people. (False)
Fear of Negative Evaluation Scale
I rarely worry about seeming foolish to others. (False)
I am often afraid that I may look ridiculous or make a fool of myself. (True)
If someone is evaluating me I tend to expect the worst. (True)
When I am talking to someone, I worry about what they may be thinking about me. (True)

[a]Answers indicate anxiety.

Physiological reactions. We saw in Chapter 5 that the nervous system has two major subsystems: the autonomic and the central. The autonomic nervous system, itself, has two subsystems: the sympathetic and the parasympathetic. The sympathetic nervous system (SNS) is frequently referred to as the "fight or flight" system, because of its crucial role in preparing the organism for action. Not coincidentally, from an evolutionary perspective, anxiety also plays a key role in preparing the organism for action. Anxiety is a signal of impending danger, which prepares the organism for "fight or flight." Consequently, it should not be surprising that the SNS plays a central role in anxiety.

In general all SNS responses are associated with anxiety. Heart rate and blood pressure increase to provide more nutrients and oxygen to muscles. Blood flow to the extremities (e.g., fingers and toes) decreases, and blood flow to the brain increases via changes in diameter of blood vessels. Digestive and sexual processes are suppressed, and respiration increases. The electrical conductance properties of the skin (e.g., palms) increase in conjunction with increased sweat gland activity. There are also a variety of changes in endocrine gland secretions, as well as increased muscle tension (a central nervous system response), especially in the neck and shoulder region. These physiological processes provide the basis for many of the physical symptoms reported by people experiencing anxiety: heart palpitations (increased heart rate), sweaty palms (increased sweat gland activity), dryness of the mouth, and knots in the stomach (suppression of digestive processes), inability to catch one's breath (increased respiration rate), headache (a result of pressure produced by dilated cerebral blood vessels), and coldness or chills (loss of body heat due to constriction of blood vessels in the extremities).

This list of responses describes the *range* of physiological reactions associated with anxiety. Each individual has an idiosyncratic response style that is superimposed on this general pattern (cf. Sternbach, 1966). Thus, one individual might respond primarily with large increases in heart rate, moderate increases in respiration rate, and very slight changes in blood pressure. Another person might experience strong increases in neck muscle tension and slight changes in heart rate and blood pressure. A third person might, in fact, experience minimal changes in physiological activity while still experiencing high levels of subjective distress. Finally, a fourth person might even respond with some parasympathetic nervous system reactions, such as urination and stomach distress (e.g., "butterflies in the stomach") (Martin, 1971).

Relationship between cognitive and physiological reactions. The picture we have presented above is one of great variability among people. Cognitive responses can entail specific thoughts and images or vague apprehension and distress. Physiological responses usually involve SNS activity, but the pattern of that activity varies with the individual, and some people can respond primarily with parasympathetic or central nervous system activity. This picture is made even more complex by the fact that the two response systems do not always act in synchrony. Some people are primarily cognitive responders, having little physiological reaction, while others are primarily physiological responders, having little cognitive reaction (cf. Franks & Wilson, 1976, p. 218). How then can we ever identify anxiety? The following two criteria seem logical: 1. If the person reports that he/she is anxious or tense even in the absence of physiological arousal, he or she should be presumed to be anxious (unless there is reason to suspect a purposefully false report); 2. If there is physiological arousal in conjunction with overt behavior typically associated with anxiety (see below), presume the person is anxious even if there is no subjective distress.

The effects of anxiety

Anxiety can be experienced at varying levels of intensity ranging from mild "jitters" to extreme panic. High levels of anxiety and persistent occurrence of moderate levels of anxiety can result in a variety of forms of psychopathology. In addition to these "larger" consequences, anxiety is associated with a number of specific, short-term effects. In this section we will consider the effects of anxiety on: a. learning and performance and b. avoidance behavior.

Learning and performance. The discussion thus far has emphasized the painful aspect of anxiety, and has suggested that anxiety is an undesirable response. However, this is not necessarily the case. The tension and apprehension associated with the end of a close football game, mountain climbing, automobile racing, and movie thrillers (e.g., *Jaws)* can all be experienced as positive sensations, which are actually sought out by

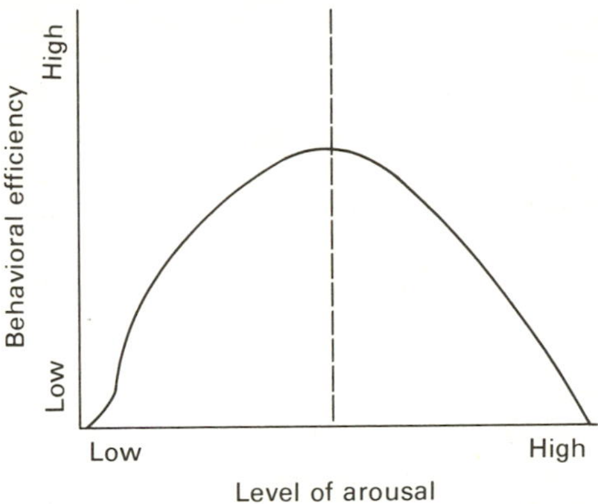

Fig. 8.1. The "inverted U shaped curve" shows the relationship between arousal and behavioral efficiency. As arousal increases, efficiency first increases, and then begins to decrease.

many people. Enthusiasts of such objectively dangerous sports as scuba diving and sport parachuting often report the experiences to be ennervating.

The effects of anxiety on learning and performance can also be either positive or negative. Low levels of anxiety frequently increases learning and performance ability, while high levels of anxiety typically result in reduced ability. This relationship is generally represented by the *inverted U shaped curve* shown in Figure 8.1. The term arousal refers to the degree to which the organism is physiologically and neurologically activated or energized: a process closely related to anxiety. Behavioral efficiency is low with very low levels of arousal. As arousal increases, so does efficiency, which reaches a maximum level with moderate arousal. As arousal continues to increase beyond that point, efficiency begins to decrease and behavior becomes disorganized. This phenomenon is exemplified by the behavior of athletes, who try to "psych themselves up" before a big game in order to perform well, but who can get *too* "psyched up" and make numerous careless errors (e.g., fumbles and penalties in football).

A partial list of responses that have been shown to be affected by high anxiety includes (Martin & Sroufe, 1970): 1) increase in restlessness, tics, gesturing, stuttering, and slips of the tongue; 2) decrease in short-term memory, ability to make perceptual discriminations, motor dexterity, reaction time, and ability to learn complex material; and 3) increase in old (i.e., well-learned and habitual) responses and decrease in new (i.e., not yet well-learned) responses. This is adaptive if the old response is correct or appropriate, but maladaptive if the new response is correct. In sum, high anxiety can lead to confusion, lack of coordination, slowness, increased errors, inefficiency, and lack of flexibility.

Avoidance behavior. A considerable amount of research has demonstrated that animals and humans will work to reduce aversive stimulation and will repeat behaviors that lead to this goal. This is referred to as "negative reinforcement." This principle explains one of the most significant effects of anxiety: the development of avoidance responses leading to anxiety reduction. This phenomenon is demonstrated by a classic study conducted by Neal Miller (1948). The subjects were rats, although related studies have since been conducted with humans. The experimental setting was a box containing a white compartment and a black compartment, separated by a wall containing an open doorway. The floor of the white compartment contained a grid, through which an electric shock could be administered. The rat was first placed in the white compartment, and after a short while, the shock was administered. Before long, the rat found the doorway and escaped shock by entering the black compartment. This procedure was repeated until the escape response was well-learned and quickly performed. The rat was then placed in the white compartment again, but no shock was delivered. However, the animal still ran directly to the black compartment. Further, on subsequent trials the doorway was closed and the rat showed a host of behavioral signs of anxiety. The animal had learned to fear the white compartment. Miller then installed a small wheel that could be turned by the rat to open the door. After a few trials, still without shock, the rat managed to turn the wheel and quickly ran into the "safe" black compartment. On further trials, the rat quickly and reliably turned the wheel and fled from the white compartment.

This experiment demonstrates a number of important facts about anxiety. *First,* anxiety can be learned (in this instance, by classical conditioning). *Second,* anxiety is not simply a response, but it can also be a powerful stimulus that leads to further responses (in this case, it served as a cue for escape). In humans, both the cognitive reactions and the proprioceptive (i.e., internal) feedback from the physiological changes are perceived as signs of danger, and stimulate further action. *Third,* the reduction of anxiety is reinforcing and will promote (operantly) conditioned avoidance responses. In Miller's experiment, the rat first fled to reduce the pain from the shock, but continued to run and learned to turn the wheel in order to reduce anxiety.

Once the shock was turned off, Miller's rats fled from a nonexistent danger. Their behavior would have seemed highly "irrational" to someone who did not know their history (i.e., the fact that they were responding to conditioned anxiety cues). Many people engage in seemingly "irrational" behaviors that are also maintained by anxiety reduction. Physical avoidance is a major component of phobias (see below). People who are afraid of flying will travel by automobile or bus, despite the inconvenience, and even quit jobs that require flying. Claustrophobics, people who are afraid to be in small enclosed spaces, will not work in buildings that require riding in an elevator, and will drive extended distances in order to avoid tunnels. Students with public speaking anxiety will avoid any course that requires an oral presentation. In general, anything that can be feared can produce avoidance behavior, and the more intense the fear, the more extreme will be the avoidance.

Physical avoidance is far from the only means to reduce anxiety. One common alternative is to engage in behaviors that produce positive feelings, such as eating or smoking cigarettes. Eating to reduce anxiety is frequently a factor in obesity. A number of people learn to fear some of their own responses, such as anger or sexual arousal. In these cases, avoidance can entail inhibiting those responses or performing incompatible responses (e.g., being "super nice"). Finally, certain drugs, such as alcohol, can be consumed for their sedative effects.

In contrast to animals, whose behavior is highly susceptible to automatic conditioning processes, much of human behavior is mediated or affected by the way events are perceived or understood. In regard to fear, this means that our *perception* of events is often as important as the reality of the events themselves. If we think a stimulus is dangerous (or safe), we may be fearful (or unafraid) regardless of the actual physical danger. This is illustrated by a recent study of the behavior of snake-fearful college students (Carver & Blaney, 1977). A microphone was attached to the subject's chest, under the pretense that heart rate was to be measured. The student was then requested to approach as close as possible to a caged snake. While the student walked forward, the experimenter played a tape recording (which the subject could hear) of either a constant heart beat or a rapidly increasing heart beat. The students who heard the constant beat were able to get considerably closer to the snake than the group hearing the increasing beat. Apparently, the constant rate group was led to believe that they were not anxious, while the increasing rate group was led to believe that they were becoming more anxious.

Just as anxiety can be reduced by external manipulations of what we think, we can reduce our own anxiety by learning to alter our perceptions or cognitions. An example of this is provided by an experiment designed to test procedures for reducing children's fear of the dark (Kanfer, Karoly, & Newman, 1975). Fearful 5- and 6-year-old children were first requested to stay in a small dark room for as long as they could. They were then assigned to one of three groups. Children in each group were instructed to practice saying one of three things to themselves: 1) "I am a brave boy (girl). I can take care of myself in the dark"; or 2) "The dark is a fun place to be. There are many good things in the dark"; or 3) "Mary had a little lamb. Its feece was white as snow." All children were then requested to again spend as much time in the room as they could and to use a control dial to keep it as dark as they could. The children rehearsing competence statements (I am brave) showed the most improvement in ability to remain in the dark, followed in order by the "dark is fun" group and the nursery rhyme group.

Thus, simply thinking did not help the children much, but certain specific types of thinking were effective in reducing anxiety. A variety of strategies appear to be effective for different people. Several of the psychoanalytic "defense mechanisms" are, in essence, cognitive avoidance strategies. *Denial* (e.g., "I'm not angry") involves refusing to recognize threatening stimuli. *Rationalization* (e.g., "I didn't want to win anyway") can be accomplished by changing beliefs or goals. *Intellectualization* (e.g., "That was an interesting test, and I learned a lot even though I failed") entails focusing in elaborate fashion on nonthreatening aspects of experience. Such techniques can all be learned in the same manner as physical avoidance, and once learned, can occur almost automatically to reduce anxiety. When used in moderation, avoidance strategies can be quite adaptive. However, as will be shown in the discussion of neuroses, when used excessively they can severely restrict activity and distort experience.

The etiology of anxiety

Jane and Susan are in the same tenth grade class. They come from similar homes, and their parents are good friends. Jane has always been an active, outgoing girl. She likes sports, is on the swim team, and is president of a sorority. Susan has always been described as a "sensitive" child. She was afraid to sleep in the dark for several years, and had to be withdrawn from kindergarten because she cried when her mother dropped her off. She has never learned to swim, as she is afraid of water. She is shy, doesn't date much, and does not participate in extracurricular activities.

Jane and Susan live very different lives, in large part because Susan experiences anxiety in many situations and Jane does not. What could cause such a difference? There are two general factors which appear to account for the development of anxiety: physiological make-up, and learning.

Physiological factors. Newborn babies and infants seem to look and act alike to most people who have little experience with them. However, experienced observers, such as maternity room nurses, often report large differences between children. Some are described as active and alert, while others remain relatively still and quiet. Some are excitable, easily disturbed, and have sleep and eating difficulties (often called "colic"). Others are viewed as placid and happy, and appear to be relatively undisturbed by slight noises, lights, and activity around them. Systematic research on infants supports many of these observations (cf. Thomas, Chess, Birch, Hertzig, & Korn, 1963). Most importantly, children do seem to differ in their physiological sensitivity to stimulation, or their arousability. It seems likely that a child who is easily aroused could either be on edge much of the time, or highly susceptible to becoming anxious in a large variety of situations (recall our previous discussions of trait anxiety and of the effects of level of arousal on behavior).

Research on adults also points to the existence of differences in physiological functioning. Chronically anxious adults have been found to differ from "normal" adults and adults with other forms of psychological disturbance on three types of factors (Martin, 1971). 1. They show greater physiological arousal to stress. This means that they tend to become very anxious to what should be mildly stresstul events, and they also become anxious to more types of stimuli. 2. They do not *adapt* to stress as easily. That is, they continue to react to a repeated stimulus, while the other groups react less on successive trials (i.e., normals get used to mild stresses and anxious people don't). 3. Anxious people do not *habituate* as quickly as normals. This means, essentially, that it takes them a lot longer to calm down once they have become anxious.

The causes of these differences are not known. The differences between infants might be due to genetic factors, but they might also be due to some prenatal factors (such as maternal consumption of alcohol or cigarettes), problems occurring during birth or shortly thereafter, or even diet. In regard to the anxious adults, it is unclear if their difficulties existed from early childhood, or if they developed later on. Thus, the physiological responsiveness might be a result of learned anxiety responses, or a factor that produced the high anxiety. In any case, some people do have overly sensitive physiological systems, and this sensitivity probably plays an important role in the development and persistence of anxiety reactions.

Learning. Genetic makeup and physical structure do not determine the specific ways in which organisms behave. Rather, these factors interact with experience to shape behavior. Physiological sensitivity might make people overly susceptible to becoming anxious, but what they are anxious about and the way in which they deal with anxiety are a function of learning.

One way in which anxiety can be learned we have already seen in the study by Miller (1948). The rat came to fear the white compartment after it was repeatedly associated with pain (i.e., electric shock). This process, in which an initially neutral stimulus becomes aversive after being paired with an aversive stimulus, is a form of *classical conditioning*. The Miller experiment also illustrates one way in which avoidance behavior is learned. The rat was reinforced for avoidance by anxiety reduction, and so avoidance was repeated. This process is referred to as *operant conditioning*.

Because it would be unethical to develop significant fears in humans, there is no clear evidence to show that human fears can be developed in the same way. However, there have been numerous laboratory demonstrations of similar effects in humans, and these processes seem to fit the self-reports many people provide about how their fears began. For example, a child might become afraid of water (an initially neutral stimulus) after almost drowning (as aversive event), and so avoid swimming. Adults have reported becoming afraid to enter small, enclosed places after being trapped on elevators or in subways. Some people who are afraid to be assertive or express anger report that their parents punished them for such responses during childhood. The combination of classically conditioned anxiety and operantly conditioned avoidance is referred to as the "two factor" theory, and until recently, it had been thought to explain the development and maintenance of all fears. It is now considered to be only one of several possible factors (cf. Rachman, 1976b).

One of the difficulties of the two factor theory is that it suggests that fears develop *only* if the individual has had some aversive experience with the feared stimulus. This is not the case. Many people are afraid of things they have never encountered, let alone had aversive experience with. Few airplane phobics have been involved in crashes. Most people would be frightened by a lion running loose without ever having been bitten, and many people would be afraid to make a parachute jump without ever having fallen from a great height. The learning process which is probably involved in the development of these fears (possibly most fears) is observational learning, also called vicarious learning or modeling (Bandura, 1969).

There is substantial research showing that people have the capability to learn by observing others as well as by trial and error or direct experience. This capability includes learning by simply watching other people, by watching movies or television shows, by reading, and by receiving instructions or information from others. In regard to fear, we can learn to be afraid of something by watching someone being hurt (e.g., get bitten by a dog), by reading that something is dangerous, or by being told that something is dangerous. How many people became afraid of sharks and shark attacks after seeing the movie *Jaws?* How many elderly people have become afraid to go outside their homes after reading newspaper reports and watching television shows about mugging and other crimes?

It appears that many human fears are learned in childhood by modeling (i.e., observing) the fearful behavior of parents. The following hypothetical case history illustrates how this might happen:

> Robert is a ten-year-old who is terrified of dogs. His mother was bitten by a dog when she was a child and is also afraid of dogs. She reacted fearfully whenever she saw a dog on the street. When Robert was young enough to be carried, she would pick him up to shelter him whenever a dog passed by; he became frightened upon feeling her sudden tension. When he was older, she would quickly rush him across the street or into a doorway to avoid a dog. When he was old enough to play outside by himself, she warned him to beware of stray dogs, and not to play near the home of a neighbor who owned a dog. When he asked for a pet dog at the age of seven, she told him about her childhood experience, providing vivid details about the teeth marks, ripped skin, and pain. When Robert was eight years old, he became friendly with a boy who owned a dog, and his mother forbade him playing at the friend's house, again reminding him of her bite. By age nine, Robert exhibited all of his mother's fear behavior, and could describe her bite as vividly as if it had happened to him.

A final note

Human beings seem to be extremely susceptible to developing anxiety responses. It has been hypothesized that this susceptibility is the result of evolution and natural selection (cf. Morris, 1967). Survival in the prehistoric environment depended on great sensitivity to signs of danger: precisely the role of anxiety. Those prehistoric people who survived to pass on their genes might well have been those who developed anxiety reactions most readily. There is also some suggestion that modern man has not only inherited a general propensity to learn anxiety, but that we are biologically *prepared* to develop some specific types of fears (Seligman & Hager, 1972). For example, fears of animals, heights, darkness, enclosed places, open spaces, sudden loud noises (e.g., thunder), and angry faces are very common (especially in children), and, apparently, easily learned. On the other hand, fears of such things as grass, sand, eggs, and houses are relatively rare. The prepared fears (supposedly) had survival value for our ancestors, and by now, the propensity to develop them is transmitted genetically. While we could become afraid of grass given some very unusual circumstances, prepared fears would develop very easily.

An example of how this process, referred to as "preparedness," might work is provided in the following anecdote. "A four-year-old girl was playing in the park. Thinking that she saw a snake, she ran to her parents' car and jumped inside, slamming the door behind her. Unfortunately, the girl's hand was caught by the closing car door, the results of which were severe pain and several visits to the doctor. Before this she may have had a fear of snakes, but not a phobia. After this experience a phobia developed, not of cars or car doors, but of snakes" (Marks, 1977, p. 192).

The preparedness concept not only accounts for some problems of two-factor theory (e.g., why the girl did not learn to fear the source of pain), but also seems to add to our knowledge about modeling effects. For example, some parents dislike television, refuse to allow television sets in the house, and inform their children of the evils of watching television. While their children might learn to share the parents' attitudes, they do not become *afraid* of television sets. In contrast, similar negative attitudes about snakes, insects, or dogs can frequently produce childhood fears. We do not yet have enough information about preparedness to be sure that the concept is valid (i.e., true). However, it is a compelling notion that might well explain much about human anxiety.

Neurotic disorders

The term neurosis has become a part of our everyday vocabulary. To say, "He is neurotic," can be anything from a complaint about someone whose behavior is consistently annoying, to a term of sympathy for someone who is frequently distressed and is somehow unable to work or relate effectively. Surprisingly, there might well be more agreement about the colloquial use of the term than there is among mental health experts about its technical meaning. Not only do experts disagree about what neurosis is, but they cannot regularly agree about what neuroses look like. Thus, while nine of ten experts might agree when they have seen anxiety, only six of ten are apt to agree about whether or not a particular individual has a neurosis (Zubin, 1967).

The concept of neurosis as a type of emotional disturbance was popularized by Freud. He viewed neurosis as a pattern of behavioral and psychological disturbance produced by conflict within the personality structure. The overt manifestations of disturbance, such as fears or compulsions, were presumed to be symptoms of some underlying problem. According to Freud, the neurotic individual fails to successfully pass through one of the critical developmental stages of childhood. The residue of this failure remains buried in the unconscious, to reappear in adulthood. At that time, the individual experiences intense conflict over the expression of impulses (e.g., anger, sex), and the symptom erupts as a means to reduce the conflict.

From this perspective, neurosis is a relatively specific disorder, with a clearcut etiology. The different types of neuroses (e.g., phobic or hysterical) simply reflect variations of the disorder, classified according to the predominant symptom. However, this viewpoint has not been supported by research, and it does not adequately explain or describe the actual behavior of so-called neurotic individuals.

There appear to be only two things about neurosis that are generally accepted. *First,* the term refers to a number of behavior disturbances that are either based on or accompanied by relatively intense anxiety. Consequently, neurotic individuals experience acute distress, and engage in a variety of behaviors designed to avoid or reduce the distress. These avoidance behaviors frequently interfere with everyday functioning. Thus, the neurotic might be unable to relate well to others, or might perform poorly on the job, or might have some sexual impairment. Frequently, the avoidance behaviors and their effects are more disturbing than the anxiety itself. This aspect of neurosis, in which the individual is driven to perform behaviors which are painful, is referred to as the *neurotic paradox.*

The *second* aspect of neurosis involves the severity of the disorder. Psychological disturbance can be viewed as a continuum ranging from little or none (i.e., normality) to severe (i.e., psychotic). Neurosis falls somewhere between these two extremes. Thus, the neurotic is under stress and cannot perform up to capacity, but is still typically able to meet most of the demands of daily living. Unlike psychotics, most neurotics are not so incapacitated that they require in-patient care (e.g., psychiatric hospitalization). However, the student should be aware that some people called neurotic are so mildly impaired that they hardly deserve a psychiatric label, while others are more dysfunctional than some psychotics.

Because the neurotic label tells us little more than that the person is probably very anxious and only moderately disturbed, the term is not very useful, and may well be dropped from psychiatric terminology. The *Diagnostic and Statistical Manual of Mental Disorders* is the official diagnostic guide of the American Psychiatric Association. The 1952 (DSM-I) and 1967 (DSM-II) versions both listed neuroses as a distinct set of disorders, defined essentially according to the Freudian model. However, the third edition (DSM-III), which (at the time of this writing) is currently being developed, will probably not include neurosis as a disorder (Spitzer, Sheehy, & Endicott, 1977). The major symptom patterns (e.g., phobias, compulsions) that were previously listed as types of neuroses will be called "disorders," and either be listed separately or clustered with related dysfunctions (e.g., anxiety disorders).

With this general background, we can proceed to the specific disorders themselves. In the following sections we will consider: phobic disorders, generalized anxiety disorders, obsessive-compulsive disorders, and hysterical disorders.

Phobic disorders

A case of airplane phobia. Mr. L. is a 33-year-old salesman who is married and has two young children. He was referred to a local mental health center by his family physician because of an intense fear of airplanes. He reported having no psychological difficulties aside from this fear, which developed 9 months ago during a business trip. This was the first time he had ever been in an airplane, and like most other people who have never flown, he was somewhat apprehensive about the flight. The airplane flew through a heavy rainstorm, and Mr. L. became somewhat nauseous due to the bumping and up and down motion of the plane. As the flight continued, he broke out into a "cold sweat," and felt generally uncomfortable. He began to feel some relief as the plane came in for a landing, when it suddenly lurched to one side, and began to swerve off the runway with a flat tire. It eventually came to rest in the grass, and he breathed a great sigh of relief when he finally got off. As he conducted his business over the next two days, he hardly thought about his negative experience. However, on the morning he was to return home, he read a newspaper story about a plane crash. He suddenly became terrified, felt his heart pounding, and again broke out in a cold sweat. He cancelled his airline reservation and took a train home. His reaction had no effect on his daily life for the next several months. However, his boss recently told him that he was scheduled for another trip by plane, and he became panicky and felt that he would have to quit his job rather than fly. He now becomes anxious when he reads about airplanes, sees them on television or in the sky, and when he thinks about the upcoming trip.

A case of agoraphobia. Susan R. is 24 years old, married, and has a 2-year-old son. She came for treatment in desperation, feeling that her life was becoming intolerable. She reported that she had numerous intense fears, which were getting worse and worse. She was constantly afraid that she was going to lose control of her breathing and that "something terrible" would happen. She could not leave her house alone without experiencing intense anxiety; she either called a friend or waited for her husband in order to go out. Even with company, she could not go into a room or building which was small or dimly lit. She could remain in a large room or building only if she had a clear path to the exit. Crowds made her very uncomfortable, and she could not tolerate driving her car, going through tunnels, or being stuck in traffic. Recently, she was also becoming nervous when at home alone, and when waking up at night in the dark. She reported first experiencing many of these difficulties as a teenager. She was never comfortable in crowds, or enclosed places, and she always requested to sit near the door in classes and movie theaters. However, her problem did not become severe, until an incident when she was 21. She was driving to a social engagement that she did not want to attend. As she drove, she became more and more tense and irritable, and began breathing shallowly and irregularly. She became stuck in traffic and the tenseness increased, when she suddenly felt as if she was unable to breathe. In a panic, she pulled off the road, got out of her car, and remained there, for what seemed a long time, until her panic subsided. She finally drove home with great difficulty. From that point, she began to worry increasingly about being unable to breathe, her fears became more widespread and intense, and she became less and less able to carry out her daily activities.

Definition

The two case histories presented above are illustrative of phobic disorders. Phobias are intense, recurrent fears that are irrational in the sense that they are highly out of proportion to the reality of the situation. Some phobic individuals have single specific fears and little or no other psychological disturbance. Such isolated fears can be minimally disruptive to everyday life if the feared stimulus is rarely encountered. At other times, as with the salesman described above, the fear can cause major problems by preventing the person from engaging in important activities. Many individuals suffer from multiple fears, and their lives are almost dominated by fear and avoidance of those things that provoke it (e.g., the agoraphobic woman described above). In such cases, diffuse anxiety and panic attacks are not uncommon.

Types of phobias

It appears that phobias can be developed in response to an almost infinite variety of stimuli. Rachman and Seligman (1976) described one woman who was afraid of chocolate and avoided anything brown, and another woman who was deathly afraid of vegetables and plants. Phobias are generally divided into three categories: specific phobias, social phobias, and agoraphobia. Specific phobias are fears of distinct objects, animals or situations. Common examples include fear of: dogs, insects, injections, water, elevators, flying, heights, enclosed places, thunderstorms, and dentists. Social phobias involve fear of a variety of different types of social situations, such as: public speaking, crowds, interacting with members of the opposite sex, sexual activities, small group situations, eating in public places, and using public restrooms. Agoraphobia is probably the most stressful and incapacitating phobia. While it can be limited to fear of open spaces, it typically includes multiple fears of open spaces, crowds, enclosed spaces, travel, being alone, and fear of "losing control," fainting, or being unable to breathe. Panic attacks and diffuse anxiety are also common elements. Probably as a result of the pervasiveness and severity of their difficulties, many agoraphobics experience feelings of hopelessness and depression.

The prevalence (frequency of occurrence) of fears and phobias in the general population is difficult to determine because most people do not seek treatment, and they differ in their willingness to call themselves "fearful." The best current estimate of prevalence comes from a study of residents of Vermont (Agras, Sylvester, & Oliveau, 1969). About 7.69 percent of the population reported having a phobia; 7.47 percent had phobias that were mildly disabling, and 2.2 percent suffered from severely disabling phobias (i.e., they were unable to manage daily responsibilities). Table 8.3 presents a breakdown of the specific fears most commonly reported. The data indicate that mild fears are relatively common, while prevalence decreases as intensity increases.

One of the findings of this study was that age of onset of fears (i.e., incidence) and frequency of occurrence vary with the type of fear. The most common patterns are presented in Figure 8.2. Fears of snakes and injections both develop very frequently in childhood, while fear of crowds continues to develop throughout adult life. The patterns for prevalence give some suggestion about how long phobias tend to persist without treatment. Fear of injections has a sharply declining prevalence, which means they are relatively short-lived. Fear of snakes, on the other hand, apparently tends to persist for a long time. Interestingly, neither the course of untreated phobias nor the intensity of fear is predictive of how treatable a phobia is. In general, isolated phobias are highly responsive to treatment, while individuals with multiple phobias and generalized anxiety are more difficult to treat.

Etiology

Before considering how phobias develop and persist, we must first consider their paradoxical nature. In the course of living, almost everyone has had numerous aversive experiences: falling off bicycles, automobile accidents, dog bites, near drowning, being lost in a crowd as a child, social embarrassments. However, as shown in the Vermont study, very few people become phobic. Of those who do develop phobias, most are afraid of only one or a few of the many

Table 8.3. Prevalence of Common Fears, Intense Fears, and Phobias (per 1000 person population)

Common Fears			Intense Fears			Phobia			
Snakes	390	(m 199) (F 547)	Snakes	253	(M 118) (F 376)	Illness injury	31	(M 22) (F 39)	42%
Heights	307	(M 278) (F 333)	Heights	120	(M 109) (F 128)	Storms	13	(M 0) (F 24)	18%
Storms	211	(M 95) (F 311)	Flying	109	(M 70) (F 144)	Animal	11	(M 6) (F 18)	14%
Flying	198	(M 105) (F 274)	Enclosures	50	(M 32) (F 63)	Agoraphobia	6	(M 7) (F 6)	8%
Dentist	198	(M 174) (F 215)	Illness	33	(M 31) (F 35)	Death	5	(M 4) (F 6)	7%
Injury	182	(M 185) (F 179)	Death	33	(M 46) (F 21)	Crowds	4	(M 2) (F 6)	5%
Illness	165	(M 122) (F 203)	Injury	23	(M 24) (F 22)	Heights	4	(M 7) (F 0)	5%
Death	161	(M 129) (F 184)	Storms	31	(M 9) (F 48)				
Enclosures	122	(M 99) (F 140)	Dentists	24	(M 22) (F 26)				
Journeys alone	74	(M 67) (F 101)	Journeys alone	16	(M 0) (F 31)				
Being alone	44	(M 17) (F 64)	Being alone	10	(M 5) (F 13)				

Adapted from S. Agras, D. Sylvester, & D. Oliveau, *Comprehensive Psychiatry*, 1969, *10*, 152.

things that were associated with pain or aversion during the course of their lives. Could it be that people only develop phobias when they have had traumatic experiences? Apparently not. Few people who have what would appear to be traumatic experiences (e.g., being in an airplane crash) become phobic. Further, most phobics report that the beginnings of their fears were not associated with traumas. Perhaps phobias are modeled from parents? This is not the general case either. While there is a relationship between the incidence of phobias in parents and children, most phobics do not have parents with the same fears.

It appears that no single factor is sufficient to explain the development of all phobias. In fact, there is probably no one factor that is *solely* responsible for the development of *any* phobia. Rather, there are a number of factors which are involved, and phobias can develop when any of several combinations of the factors occur.

Learning. Phobias are extreme forms of mild fears and anxieties. Thus, it should not be surprising that the same learning processes discussed above in regard to anxiety should be important with phobias as well. Three learning processes seem to be involved: a) classical conditioning, in which a neutral stimulus elicits fear after being associated with an aversive experience, b) operant conditioning, in which avoidance behavior is reinforced by fear reduction, and c) observational learning.

The role of observational learning requires special comment, in that we stated above that phobics and their parents do not frequently have the same fears. It appears that parents can teach their children to be fearful without teaching specific fears. For

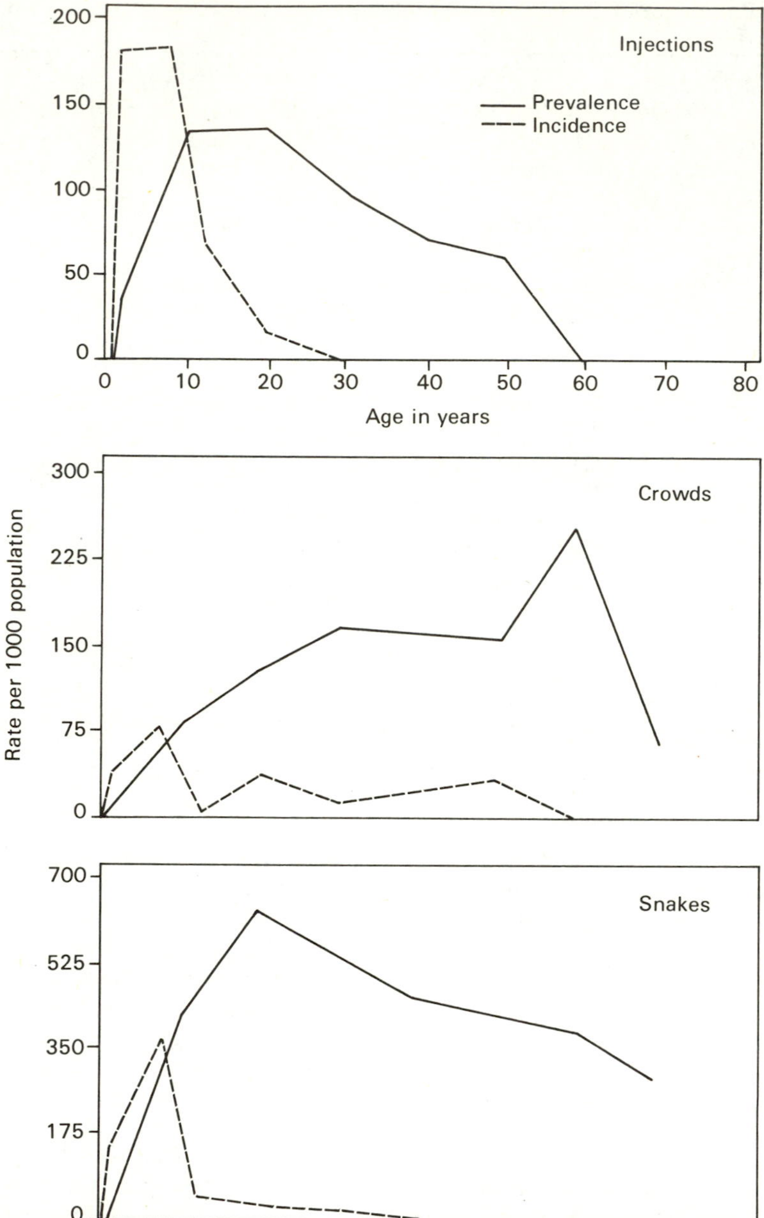

Fig. 8.2. Three different patterns of incidence and prevalence rates for common fears. Fear of doctors, darkness, and strangers followed pattern shown for injection. Fear of death, injury, illness, and separation followed that shown for crowds; fear of animals, heights, storms, enclosures, and social situations followed that shown for snakes. (Reprinted with permission from S. Agras, D. Sylvester, & D. Oliveau, *Comprehensive Psychiatry*, 1969, *10,* 153.)

example, if the parents are generally timid or fearful, the child can learn that it is wiser to avoid dangerous or uncomfortable situations and that he or she must be on guard against a world full of dangers. Such a child might then be especially susceptible to becoming phobic if he/she ever does have an aversive experience.

Physiological factors. We have already indicated that some people are easily aroused, do not easily habituate or adapt to stressful stimuli. Such people might well develop conditioned fears easily and/or over-respond to what would otherwise be a mild annoyance. In addition to this general pattern, physiological differences have been found between people with different types of fears (cf. Marks, 1970). Thus, phobics might not only be physiologically predisposed to become phobic, but they might be predisposed to develop some fears and not others.

Preparedness. We have already considered this factor in regard to anxiety in general. Simply put, the human species might be genetically prepared to develop certain specific types of fears.

Exposure to the feared stimulus. One reason why phobias persist is that the individual continually avoids the feared stimulus and, therefore, never learns that it is really safe (recall that Miller's rats never learned that the shock was turned off). Whether or not phobias develop in the first place is partially a function of whether or not the person is reexposed to an aversive stimulus before a major fear and avoidance pattern can develop. Reexposure can fail to occur due to coincidental circumstances, as when a child almost drowns on the last swimming day of summer. Or, parents or others can reinforce the incipient fear by preventing reexposure and demonstrating great concern and distress about a near-accident. Also, an individual who has learned to quickly avoid potentially dangerous situations in general might be unlikely to reexpose himself or herself. The importance of reexposure is reflected in a common folk remedy for preventing fears, which involves quickly placing a child back into the situation after an accident (e.g., back on the bicycle or into the water). Interestingly, the most effective treatment for phobias is systematic exposure to the feared stimulus (cf. Bellack & Hersen, 1977, Chapter 3).

Cognitive factors. We have already discussed the role of cognitive factors in mild fear and anxiety. Essentially, the person's perception of the situation and his experience is frequently as important as the reality of the situation. Even the development of "conditioned" responses is apparently not entirely automatic. Rather, learning is affected by whether or not the person perceives some relationship between events.

One additional cognitive factor is the degree to which the individual feels capable of coping with events, and of maintaining some degree of control over his/her behavior. Albert Bandura (1977) has referred to this perception or feeling as *self-efficacy*. In general, we tend to become anxious when we feel a loss of control or an inability to cope effectively. Situations which signal a loss of control are, thus, anxiety provoking. This process is especially relevant in agoraphobia. Many agoraphobics report that their fears began under some circumstance in which they hyperventilated. Hyperventilation is a temporary breathing problem that occurs when the blood contains too high a concentration of oxygen. It results in breathing irregularity, lightheadedness, and a feeling of being unable to catch one's breath. While this experience is somewhat frightening to everyone, most people focus on efforts to regain control of their respiration, and have little, if any, aftereffects. In contrast, agoraphobics frequently panic and as a result, have more difficulty regaining control. They then tend to become progressively more anxious about losing control again. Much of the avoidance behavior of severe agoraphobics appears to be centered around being in a "safe" place or near family members, in case respiratory control is lost again.

It might well be that people who fail to

become phobic have learned to interpret their experiences on logical or objective grounds, and have confidence in their ability to cope with or control their environment. Phobics, on the other hand, might often fail to make such logical explanations, and conclude that they cannot cope with their experience. For example, a child who is bitten by a dog might conclude that he or she should not tease dogs, or that he or she should stay away from one particular dog or dogs without collars. However, if the child failed to make such a discrimination, it would be reasonable to be apprehensive about and avoid all dogs. The tendency to objectively analyze experience, and to feel confident in one's ability to cope with the environment could certainly be learned, or not learned, as in the case of some phobics.

Generalized anxiety disorder

Case example. Linda R. is a 26-year-old single woman. She works as a file clerk for a small company, although she has a Master's degree in English. She would like to be a reporter, but feels that it would be "too much to handle." She lives with her parents, has several female friends, and dates men infrequently. She had been a somewhat shy and timid child, and was described by others as "sensitive." She reported that her life had been satisfactory until about $1\frac{1}{2}$ years ago. Since then, she has become almost chronically tense and anxious. She described the feelings as a sense of being constantly on edge, or waiting for something terrible to happen. At times, she can feel her heart start to pound and becomes "breathless." Her hands seem to always be sweating and she jumps at the slightest sound. She seems never to be able to relax, and sleeps fitfully. Two or three times a week she is overwhelmed by panic: she becomes confused, dizzy, and feels like she is going to "split apart." She feels an urge to get up and run, but she doesn't know where to go. The panic attacks are accompanied by severe headaches, stomach tightening, trembling, and her heart feels like it will burst out of her chest. The attacks can last for minutes or hours. They come and subside with no apparent reason or warning. Linda cannot think of anything which might have caused her difficulty initially, and she does not know what sets off the panic attacks. She is desparate for some relief.

Definition

Generalized anxiety disorder is a chronic disturbance, characterized by two types of symptoms: 1. persistent, diffuse anxiety, and 2. panic attacks. Like Linda, most people suffering from this disorder report that they are frequently tense, anxious, and fearful. They live much of their lives with a sense of "impending doom." While tension does sometimes subside, especially in mild cases, most people with the disorder are unable to relax and really enjoy themselves. Typically, the subjective distress is accompanied by a variety of physical symptoms and autonomic nervous system reactions, including: heart palpitations, sweating, respiratory difficulty, headaches, chest pains, trembling, dizziness, faintness, and lack of energy or weakness. A common complaint is, "I feel like there is always a band around my head (or chest), squeezing."

Panic attacks are specific episodes in which the anxiety, sense of dread, and physical symptoms are suddenly and acutely magnified. As might be imagined, these attacks interrupt all other activity and thought. Frequently, the individual feels like he/she is being smothered, and is going to die. Panic attacks can occur from once or twice a year, to several times each day. They can last from a few minutes to a few hours, and often appear to occur and vanish with no apparent reason.

The two types of symptoms (panic and diffuse anxiety) can be found in varying combinations, ranging from recurrent mild anxiety, to chronic anxiety with occasional panic attacks, to frequent panic attacks interspersed with mild or severe anxiety. Some mental health experts argue that the disorder is only present if panic attacks occur, while others use the category to describe any nonspecific anxiety dysfunction. The identification problem is further confused when patients report having specific fears. Many individuals cannot identify any specific stimulus for their distress. Others can describe situations which make them more uncomfortable. In fact, generalized anxiety disorders are often very hard to differentiate from agoraphobia: both are accompanied by panic attacks, fear of losing control or dying, and a variety of avoidance behaviors.

Etiology

There are three major factors or explanations which can be offered in regard to how generalized anxiety disorders develop.

Phobias It has been argued that generalized anxiety is not a unique disorder at all, but that it is based on the existence of phobias. The majority of people who exhibit this dysfunction cannot (initially) identify specific feared stimuli. This does not mean that such precipitating factors do not exist. Few if any people are *always* anxious. If anxiety comes and goes, there might well be identifiable factors that are responsible. Phobias can produce a clinical picture of chronic anxiety if the feared stimulus is frequently present in the person's environment. Multiple phobias, fear of losing control or of being unable to breathe, fear of having a heart attack, and agoraphobia can all result in behavior patterns very similar to generalized anxiety disorder. If the feared stimulus is an idea or a feeling (e.g., anger), the person would essentially carry the stimulus around with him, be continually exposed to it, and appear to be anxious all the time with no external stimulation. Panic attacks could occur when the idea or feeling becomes intense or persistent. If specific phobias could be identified, the diagnosis of "generalized anxiety disorder" would be inappropriate, and the etiologic factors discussed above (in regard to phobias) would be sufficient to explain the pattern of symptoms.

Physiological sensitivity A second factor in the development of generalized anxiety is physiological sensitivity or overreactivity. We have previously discussed the fact that the autonomic nervous system functioning of *people with chronic anxiety differs from normals and phobics.* People with generalized anxiety disorders are more easily aroused, remain aroused longer, and continue to become aroused to familiar stimuli longer than do the other groups. It is possible that chronic anxiety somehow changes the nervous system to produce these differences. On the other hand, nervous system sensitivity can precede and result in chronic anxiety.

This latter possibility seems quite plausible. Animals can certainly be bred for timidity or aggressiveness; German shepherds are quite different from poodles. Research with anxiety patients suggests that there is a high correspondence between the occurrence of generalized anxiety disorders in children and their parents. In addition, identical twins (who inherit the exact same gene pool) are much more likely to *both* have (or not have) this disorder than are fraternal (nonidentical) twins or nontwin siblings. These findings suggest that propensity to develop generalized anxiety disorder might be genetically transmitted. Further research is needed before this hypothesis can be confirmed.

Learning The third possible explanatory factor is, of course, learning. There are a number of parental behaviors that might lead to timidity, fearfulness, and generalized anxiety. We have already considered modeling of these behaviors and reinforcement of avoidance behavior. A more general pattern is "overprotection." Some parents hover over their children, preventing exploration, insuring that they are always "safe" and happy, quickly intervening in minor disputes, and prohibiting any activity that might remotely be dangerous. Such parents also frequently overrespond to any distress their children report. Children growing up overprotected often do not learn how to cope with their environment, how to handle stress or minor pain and illness, how to be assertive with other people, or how to function without the parent as a go-between. Consequently, as adults, they would continually be faced with situations that they had not learned how to handle, and they might well lack feelings of self-efficacy or competence. Life would consist of a never-ending series of threat-producing situations.

Anxiety, as a response to threat, would thus be ever present.

Obsessive-compulsive disorder

Case example. George P. was a 38-year-old engineer who was married and had two children. He came for treatment at the urging of his wife, who could no longer tolerate his bizarre behavior. George reported that he was deathly afraid of being "contaminated" by germs. The germs were carried around on the soles of peoples' shoes, and he felt that he could be contaminated by touching the soles of shoes, or by touching anything that was touched by someone who had touched the soles of their shoes.

George performed an elaborate series of rituals to avoid contamination, or to uncontaminate himself if he did come in contact with germs. When he got dressed in the morning, he put on his shoes by holding them with tissues, so as to avoid touching them. If he did accidentally touch them, he was compelled to wash his hands. Washing could only remove the germs if performed in a specific manner. Each part of the washing routine was carried out in a series of seven repetitions. The water was turned on, and the left hand was immersed seven times. Soap was then placed on a washcloth with seven rubs. Each finger was individually washed by seven strokes of the washcloth, and then rinsed seven times. The same routine was then followed with the other hand. Drying then also involved a series of seven rubs of each finger. If George were interrupted during this sequence or otherwise lost count, he was forced to begin the entire sequence over again. The routine was performed slowly and carefully, and often took 1 hour to complete. George reported that on one occasion, it took him $3^1/_2$ hours to finish washing.

Once he left the house for work, George was constantly on guard to avoid touching other people, or anything touched by others. He used tissues to open doors, pick up the telephone at his office, and handle mail or papers. He avoided shaking hands with other people whenever possible, and refused to eat in restaurants. He kept his office locked, and carefully examined it each time he entered to see if anything had been touched. The examination involved visual checking of the office contents. He would stand in the doorway and look at everything seven times. If he "sensed" that anything had been touched, he used tissues to systematically clean the item using seven strokes to clean each section. Consequently, it took George anywhere from 10 minutes to 2 hours to get into his office and get to work in the morning, as well as *every time* he left the office during the day. Of course, anytime he touched something contaminated he had to wash his hands. George reported that he had spent up to 6 hours checking, cleaning, and washing while at work.

In addition to his behavior in relation to contamination, George was compelled to complete many other activities in sequences of seven repititions, including: combing his hair, brushing his teeth, shaving, and completing such household chores as washing dishes and mowing the grass. These activities, thus, all took a great deal of time, and were repeated whenever the sequence was broken. Before retiring each night, George thoroughly checked the entire house to make sure everything was locked, the stove was off, and no water was dripping. The entire house was checked seven times, and each door and window was tested seven times during each of the checks. On some nights, he experienced doubts that everything was satisfactory even after checking, and so he was forced to repeat the entire sequence. This routine took anywhere from 45 minutes to 4 hours to complete each night.

George could offer no explanation for his behavior. He recognized that it was irrational, and wished that he could stop, but could not resist the urge once it was aroused. He reported that as a child he was always neat and orderly, and felt highly uncomfortable when he got dirty, or if his possessions were left in disarray. He began to perform his current rituals several years ago, when the firm he worked for merged with another company. He was afraid he would lose his job, and became very depressed. He now continues to become depressed every few months, and his compulsions intensify at those times.

Definition

Obsessive-compulsive disorder is a distressing disturbance, which can include any of several interrelated symptoms. *Obsessions* are repetitive, irrational thoughts or ideas which intrude into consciousness. They are aversive, unwanted, and reappear despite the fact that the individual knows they are irrational. Obsessions can be so bizarre that they would be difficult to distinguish from the delusions of paranoid schizophrenics, were they not perceived as irrational and aversive by the individual. The most common obsessions involve thoughts of being harmed or of harming others. George was "obsessed" with the idea that he might become contaminated. Other common obsessions are: a young mother's feeling that she will stab or cut her baby, or inadvertently put poison in its food, and a person's feeling that he or she will drive his or her car into a crowd of people. Obsessions such as these are often very much like phobias; the individual does not have an *urge* to do harm so much as a *fear* that he/she will harm himself or others. Another common theme involves feelings of responsibility for protecting others from harm. Thus, George's nighttime checking behavior might have been motivated by repetitive thoughts about protecting his family from some threat (e.g., a gas leak, burglars).

Compulsions are repetitive behaviors that are somehow tied to the obsessions (we will discuss this below under Etiology). Compulsions are stereotyped behaviors that have a ritualistic quality: they must be performed in a very specific manner. Like obsessions, they are viewed as irrational and unwanted, but the compulsive person is driven to perform them. Compulsions commonly take two forms (Rachman, 1976a): corrective activity and checking. Corrective activity most frequently involves cleaning or hand washing to undo the effects of contamination. Checking appears to be aimed at preventing something from happening. Thus, the woman afraid of harming her baby might spend hours and hours systematically folding and unfolding her laundry to make sure that no pins or needles were left in the diapers or sheets.

Obsessions are sometimes differentiated from *ruminations*. Ruminations are also repetitive thought patterns, which can include anything from inability to stop thinking about a problem or a song, to continually reciting a phrase or counting numbers over and over and over again. These activities rarely have the phobic quality of true obsessions, and may or may not result from the same process. The counting or reciting type of rumination appears to be a variant of compulsive checking, in which the individual is preventing something from happening or avoiding some aversive thought by a ritualistic cognitive activity.

Obsessive compulsive disorder is frequently marked by several other manifestations. The symptoms often appear first during bouts of depression. Periods of relatively severe depression seem to recur more frequently than is the case with many other disorders, and the obsessive-compulsive symptoms typically become more acute during those times.

In addition to specific obsessions and compulsions, many obsessive-compulsives exhibit what is referred to as a "compulsive personality." This is a general style of behavior that involves excessive orderliness and neatness, and a meticulous overattention to details (they typify the expression about being "unable to see the forest for the trees"). These individuals often have extreme difficulty making decisions, ruminating endlessly about the pros and cons of even small matters (e.g., which movie to attend, or what to order in a restaurant). The term obsessive doubting is used to describe the decision making process, which might proceed as follows, "Should I order chicken or steak? I like steak better, but chicken is less expensive. But they usually don't cook it right. But steak has too much cholesterol. But I can always get chicken at home. But I don't know how good the steak is here. But what vegetables go with chicken," etc.

This general style of thought and behavior produces another common characteristic: *primary obsessional slowness* (Rachman, 1974). Obsessive-compulsives often appear to be living in slow motion, taking excessive amounts of time to perform such simple activities as washing and dressing. The following is a description of how two obsessive-compulsive men shaved each morning:

> After gathering their shaving equipment and carefully placing each piece in a set position, they would then carry out some preliminary face-washes. A lather would then be worked up using an inflexible regular motion involving a set number of movements. Some lather was then placed on the face and one small region of the face shaved, involving a vast number of small and

precise movements of the razor. Thereafter another small region of the face received some lather and was in turn shaved in a precise and ordered manner. It was as if they were shaving hair by hair. (Rachman, 1974, p. 11)

Etiology

Obsessive-compulsive disorders are among the most perplexing to explain. While they seem to share common features (and, hence, common explanations) with such other disorders as phobias and depression, they are sufficiently unique that they defy simple explanations. Why do obsessive thoughts persist in the absence of external stimulation if they are really aversive? Why do they so frequently pertain to the same themes? If compulsive behavior is basically an anxiety reducing response, why is it so ritualistic in character, in contrast to the relatively informal avoidance behavior of phobics? The answer to these questions are, admittedly, quite tentative, and come from two lines of inquiry: clinical observation of obsessive-compulsives, and research with animals.

In observing (and talking with) obsessive compulsives, a common thread seems to run through their lives: they are continually on guard against making errors or doing something wrong. They are not particularly incompetent or error-prone; they are generally intelligent and ultra-cautious. Rather, they seem to have learned to fear making errors in general. Full-blown obsessions appear to be phobias about certain types of errors. Furthermore, the consequences of the error (e.g., harming someone) appear to be of less concern than a feeling of *being responsible* for the error. Thus, in treatment, compulsive checkers can often be persuaded to curtail checking rituals of 20 or 30 years duration if told that the therapist will be responsible if someone is harmed (of course, the ritual is again performed as soon as "responsibility" is returned to the patient). Simply put, these people appear to be extremely sensitive to *guilt*.

A possible explanation for how this sensitivity develops and leads to obsessive-compulsive disorder is presented in Figure 8.3 (Rachman, 1976a). The individual begins with a constitutional sensitivity to aversive stimulation, punishment, and anxiety. As a child he is exposed to parental over-concern and over-control. This over-control can take either of two general forms, which can lead, ultimately, to either compulsive cleaning or compulsive checking (or both, if both types of control are present). We have already considered parental over-protectiveness in a previous section. It tends to produce fearfulness, which can be manifested as fear of harm to oneself (e.g., contamination), and results in compulsive cleaning. The reason why some children of over-protective parents become phobic and others become compulsive is unknown. It is possible that the two seemingly different disorders are basically the same.

The over-critical parent is rarely or never satisfied with the child's behavior or accomplishments. The child is not praised and encouraged for his efforts, and never seems to meet parental expectations or receive approval. Such a child is apt to believe that he is error prone, and because errors result in punishment (e.g., criticism), he becomes fearful of making errors. This is later manifested as a fear of harming others, which results in compulsive checking. This pattern may also explain another common set of obsessions: fear of doing something horrible or sinful, such as screaming obscenities in church, or performing some distasteful sexual act. These obsessions are often paired with such preventive compulsions as ruminative counting, and ritualistic hand movements.

It is interesting that obsessive-compulsive disorder is frequently intertwined with depression. The symptoms often begin and become more acute during depressive episodes. Depression is typically accompanied by negative self-evaluations, self-criticism, lowered belief in one's competence, and excessive guilt. These perceptions and beliefs might all exaggerate the obsessive-compulsive's existing tendency to feel guilty, have self-doubt, and feel vulnerable and error prone. The development of full-blown obsessions would then be a logical consequence.

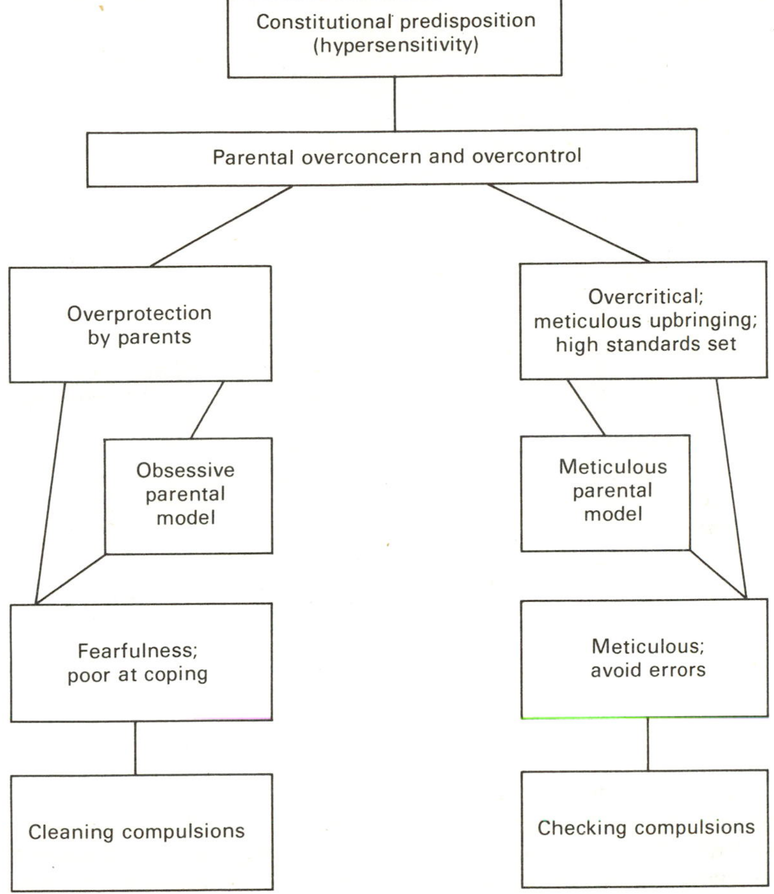

Fig. 8.3. A proposed schema for the development of compulsive cleaning and compulsive checking. (Reprinted with permission from S. Rachman, *Behaviour Research and Therapy,* 1976, *14,* 271.)

While this model appears to explain how obsessions develop, it does not indicate why they are so persistent. There is little doubt that they are aversive; they produce both subjective discomfort and physiological arousal (as do any feared stimuli). Why do they not cease to occur like other punished or aversive responses? *First,* they are at least partially based on fact. Our young mother *could* accidentally stab her child with a pin, and someone *could* become infected by germs carried on shoes. *Second,* the consequences of the feared event are believed to be so great that they could not be tolerated. In this sense, the aversive quality of the obsession is less than the aversiveness of the feared event, which could, conceivably, occur. Essentially, the obsessive behaves as if he is better off obsessing than taking a chance on not obsessing.

Compulsions are responses that reduce the anxiety produced by obsessions. Checking and cognitive compulsions reduce anxiety by preventing something from happening. Compulsive cleaning reduces anxiety by correcting or undoing something that has already

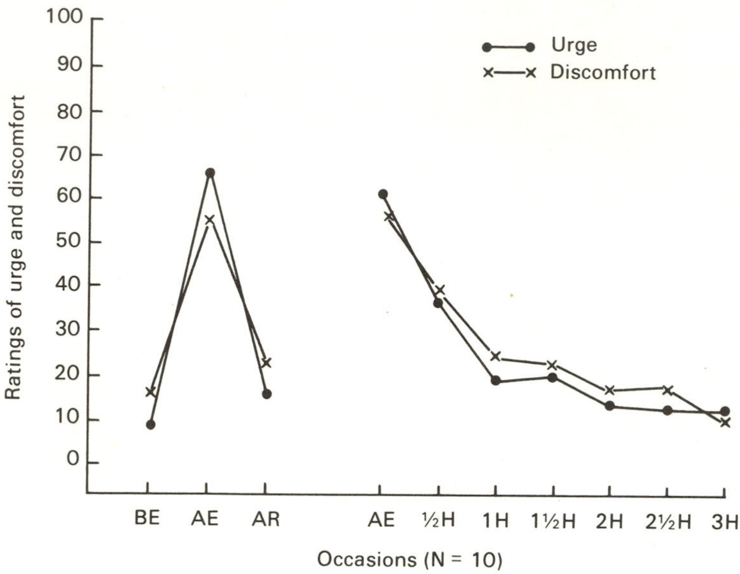

Fig. 8.4. Mean ratings for urge and discomfort across occasions (n=10). The measurement occasions plotted on the horizontal axis are: BE-before exposure to provoking stimulus; AE-after exposure; AR-after ritual; AE-after second exposure; and half-hourly intervals up to 3 hours. (Reprinted with permission from S. Rachman, P. DeSilva, & G. Röper, *Behaviour Research and Therapy,* 1976, *14,* 448.)

occurred (e.g., contamination). This process is illustrated in Figure 8.4. A group of severe obsessive-compulsives were exposed to an item that stimulated their obsessions (e.g., dirt), and then allowed to perform their compulsive ritual (Rachman, DeSilva, & Roper, 1976). They were then reexposed and prevented from performing the ritual. Exposure resulted in a dramatic increase in discomfort and an urge to perform the ritual. Both the urge and discomfort dropped quickly after the ritual. When the ritual could not be performed, the urge and discomfort decreased very gradually over a three-hour period. This finding suggests that compulsions are maintained by the same processes that maintain phobic avoidance behavior: the reinforcing effects of anxiety reduction.

The ritualistic quality of compulsive behavior is more difficult to explain. A number of experiments with animals have shown that highly persistent, ritualistic responses can be developed under certain special conditions. One procedure involves forcing the animal to respond to an unsolvable problem, when the wrong response results in electric shock. Another strategy is to produce intense conflict, such as by periodically shocking the animal while it is eating. In both situations, the animal adopts a stereotyped behavior pattern in response to the unpredictable occurrence of an aversive stimulus. Human compulsions might be developed in a similar manner. Obsessions certainly revolve around unpredictable and highly aversive situations (e.g., the mother *might* harm her baby). It could also be that the fear produced by obsessions is so intense that once an effective anxiety reducing response is identified, the individual cannot risk varying that response. The highly meticulous response style of the obsessive-compulsive would lend itself to adopting such a methodical and consistent response.

Hysterical disorders

The label hysterical disorders loosely describes a number of specific dysfunctions including: Briquet's disorder, conversion disorder, amnesia, fugue, and multiple personality. There is considerable disagreement about whether or not these dysfunctions are related subtypes of one disorder (as specific phobias are subtypes of Phobic Disorders), or if they are independent. DSM-III categorizes Briquet's disorder and conversion disorder together as somatoform disorders, and amnesia, fugue, and multiple personality together as dissociative disorders. We will follow this grouping in our discussion.

Somatoform disorders

A conversion disorder. "Jennifer, an attractive, stylishly dressed 17-year-old, had a chief complaint of incessant coughing, except during sleep, at the rate of 40 to 50 per minute. The coughing cycle consisted of a deep inhalation, a brief pause, then a burst of 4 to 5 coughs in diminishing loudness, which was repeated with mechanical precision. The barking cough, nonproductive and audible at a distance of several meters, had been unremitting for the past 4 years. Jennifer recalled that approximately 2 years earlier, after the last of three bronchoscopies, her speech became unintelligible. She then progressively supplanted speaking with writing until she stopped talking entirely. From then on she claimed to be unable to make any sounds in spite of repeated and intense efforts. During the early stages of her mutism, she was heard to vocalize occasionally and even to speak while sleeping. However, her parents reported no other sounds than coughing for the past year. She communicated entirely by writing, carrying paper, which she skillfully concealed behind her purse, with her at all times in public. Her existence, by this time, was essentially reclusive" (Munford, Reardon, Liberman, & Allen, 1976, p. 1009). Over the preceding 3 years, Jennifer had received an exhaustive series of medical examinations: no organic reasons for her difficulty could be identified.

Jennifer was reported to be a nervous child, and her mother frequently held her during meals in order to calm her down. "When she was 10 years old, she began her menses. Jennifer reported that her periods were frequent and heavy, causing her embarrassment and anxiety, especially since she believed herself to be the only girl in her class who was menstruating. She recalled when her period occurred, she would simultaneously contract a sore throat, thereby necessitating her absence from school" (p. 1009). Intensive medical examinations, including several extended hospitalizations, began when she was 13. She was forced to miss a great deal of school, and received increasing amounts of attention and solicitation from her parents. Her symptoms seemed to get worse, and more frequent after each hospitalization, until she finally became totally mute.

Definition

Somatoform disorders are psychological dysfunctions characterized by physical disturbances for which there are no organic causes. *Briquet's disorder* involves a long history of recurrent ailments and complaints. There are two aspects of this pattern that are generally considered to be critical for diagnosis. *First,* over a period of years, the individual complains about a host of different illnesses affecting many different parts of the body. *Second,* the manner in which the complaints are presented is unusual. They are often vague in regard to onset and duration. On the other hand, they are typically presented in a dramatic manner, in which the severity and pain are exaggerated. "When first seen . . . , the typical patient is a married woman in her thirties. Her history is often delivered in a dramatic, complicated fashion. She usually presents with multiple vague complaints to her general physician, and the straitforward history of a present illness is diffult to elicit. Frequently, the physician has trouble deciding when the present illness began, or even why the patient came" (Woodruff, Goodwin, & Guze, 1974, p. 263). The disorder is also characterized by sexual difficulties (e.g., frigidity), marital discord, and depression. The most serious complication is that people with this disorder often demand and receive numerous unnecessary surgical operations.

Phobias and obsessive-compulsive disorders can be identified by the presence of specific symptoms. This does not appear to be the case with Briquet's disorder. In fact, many patients receive this label by default.

That is, if they report many physical illnesses and pains for which organic causes cannot be found, the complaints can be explained away by calling the patient an "hysteric." There are two counter-arguments about the importance of this disorder. On the one hand, it has been suggested that a tremendous number of needless surgical procedures are performed each year because Briquet's disorder has not been identified (Woodruff et al., 1974). Alternatively, it has been argued that many people with real organic illnesses are misdiagnosed as hysteric, and thus do not receive adequate medical attention, because their illnesses are not identified (cf. Slater & Glithero, 1965). Maltreatment results in either case. Research is needed to resolve this important controversy.

Conversion disorders are characterized by specific physical symptoms which mimic some organic disorder, but have no organic basis. Conversion symptoms primarily involve loss of sensory or motoric abilities, such as: blindness, deafness, mutism, paralysis of arms or legs, and loss of sensation in some part of the body (anasthesias). False pregnancy, coughing, vomiting, and severe tics are also common. In contrast to the recurrent, multiple, vague complaints of patients with Briquet's disorder, those patients with conversion reactions typically have one or two flamboyant symptoms that periodically come and go. These symptoms are also usually disabling, rather than simply painful or distressing.

As in the case of Jennifer, conversion symptoms are generally very difficult to identify. These patients have an uncanny ability to portray the real organic parallels of their symptoms. Several clues to the hysterical nature of the disability can sometimes be found after careful observation and medical evaluation. Conversion patients frequently display less concern about their symptom than would ordinarily be expected of someone who has suddenly become disabled. In its classic form, this reaction entails a bland, impersonal "who, me?" attitude, which is called *la belle indifférence*.

While conversion symptoms are good copies, they are nevertheless copies, and are not perfect. In some cases, the symptoms are neurologically impossible. For example, sensation is lost in one part of a limb and retained in another part served by the same nerve tissue. In other cases, the symptoms are selective. A patient might report blindness at only certain times or in the presence of certain people. Or, the person might somehow walk around an object on the floor despite reporting total blindness. It should be emphasized that the conversion patient is not consciously feigning illness or malingering. The disability is real, even though not organic, and is not under the patient's voluntary control.

Etiology

Conversion disorders are considerably more common among women than men, and they are manifested most frequently by individuals with little education or low intelligence. The first symptom episode occurs most often during the teenage years. The disorder was apparently much more common during the Victorian era, when it was studied and highlighted by Freud, than it is today. This is partially a function of the increased education and medical sophistication of our modern society. In addition, the symptoms are frequently reactions to unacceptable impulses, such as sexual desires and anger. Our more open society has made such feelings less reprehensible.

Three factors appear to be important in the development and maintenance of conversion disorders. First and foremost, the symptoms seem to be anxiety reducing responses. They typically begin and recur under conditions of high stress and anxiety. Once they occur, they prevent the individual from engaging in some activity or perceiving something that is anxiety provoking. In many respects, the symptoms are massive and naive responses. The patient essentially concludes: "If I can't see it, it won't harm me," or "If I can't move my legs, I can't have intercourse." These responses, in mild and conscious form, are common in childhood (e.g., "I can't go to school, I have a cold.") However, recall that this disorder occurs primarily in young and uneducated people, who would be less able to develop more sophisticated anxiety reduction strategies.

The conversion patient almost invariably receives special treatment from the environment. He/she is excused from many responsibilities, receives considerable attention from family members and physicians, and is often waited on. This response from the environment is highly reinforcing, and plays a major role in maintaining symptomatic behavior (Blanchard & Hersen, 1976). Freud has referred to this phenomenon as *secondary gain,* to distinguish it from the primary gain of anxiety reduction.

The third factor in the development of the disorder is observational learning of sick role behavior (Martin, 1971). The symptoms are such good copies of physical disorders that in most cases, it is unlikely that the portrayal could occur without prior exposure to someone with the real illness. In addition, it seems likely that the advantages of sick role behavior were also learned by observing someone else. For example, Munford et al. (1976) report that Jennifer (described above) was able to describe several experiences in which she observed someone receive considerable benefits from being sick. One instance involved her being impressed by a sick friend's "ability to summon her mother at will by ringing a little silver bell" (p. 1013).

Dissociative disorders

A case of multiple personality (Ludwig, Brandsma, Wilbur, Bendfeldt, & Jameson, 1971). Jonah was a 27-year-old man, who sought treatment because of severe headaches and periods of memory loss: "Though his problem was apparently of a long-standing nature, his behavior during the recent lapses in memory resulted in separation from his wife and 3-year-old daughter, thereby upsetting and frightening him sufficiently to seek out psychiatric help. He had been told that three weeks prior to admission he attacked his wife with a butcher knife and beat her, running both her and his daughter out of the house. . . . The patient denied any recollection of these episodes, but his wife informed him that during these times he referred to himself as Usoffa Abdulla, Son of Omega. According to other information provided by a friend, Jonah also revealed that on the night prior to admission he apparently tried to stab a man and was chased by the police and fired upon" (p. 299). Through interviews and observation of his behavior on a psychiatric ward, it soon became apparent that Jonah's behavior would periodically change in dramatic fashion. He reported no awareness of these changes, only that they seemed to coincide with severe headaches and memory lapses. It was finally determined that Jonah had four distinct personalities: Jonah, Sammy, King Young, and Usoffa Abdulla. The last three personalities existed independent of Jonah, and appeared when Jonah was under great stress and threat.

"*Jonah.* Jonah may be regarded as the primary personality; . . . he claims to be unaware of the existence of any other identity. He describes himself . . . as shy, retiring, sensitive, polite, passive, and highly conventional.

Sammy. Sammy describes himself as purely intellectual, rational, and legalistic. It is his function to get what he wants by legal means and to talk his way out of any difficulties; . . . he displays no emotion.

The avowed reason for Sammy's initial appearance, when Jonah was about 6 years old, is clinically revealing. According to Sammy, Jonah's mother and stepfather had a violent altercation, during which the mother stabbed her husband. . . . On the very first occasion when the parents got together at home again, Sammy emerged and calmly informed them that they had behaved irresponsibly and that it was unwise for them to fight in front of their children.

King Young. This entity . . . replaces Jonah completely on occasions whenever Jonah cannot find the right words to say in order to gratify his sexual desires with a woman.

King Young views himself as pleasure-oriented and as quite a ladies man. He enjoys good times, especially with women, is a glib talker, and cannot take "no" for an answer.

According to King Young, he made his first appearance when Jonah was 6 or 7 years old. Jonah, whose mother used to dress him in girl's clothes at home, was described as being very confused about his own sexual identity. This confusion and anxiety became aggravated one day at school when Jonah experienced a great deal of difficulty in connecting the names of Jerry and

Alice with pictures of a boy and a girl in his first grade book. At that point, King Young intervened and set Jonah straight and has looked after his sexual interests ever since.

Usoffa Abdulla. . . . Usoffa may be described as a cold, belligerent, and angry person. He is generally sullen, silent, occasionally sarcastic, and primed to respond aggressively to any threat or challenge. He viewed himself as physically powerful and immune to pain. . . .

When Jonah was 9 or 10 years old, a gang of white boys decided one day to beat him up. . . . They proceeded to pummel Jonah with their fists, and he became absolutely terrified. . . . Jonah lost consciousness and Usoffa Abdulla emerged. Usoffa fought so viciously and vehemently that he purportedly almost killed a couple of the boys. From that moment on Usoffa has maintained a constant vigilance over Jonah to insure his safety" (p. 300).

Definition

Dissociative disorders are, essentially, cognitive disturbances in which some aspect of thinking, feeling, or behaving is denied access to consciousness. *Amnesia* is a loss of memory about certain past events. It can be limited to memory of some specific experience, or extend to one's total identity. In the latter case the individual forgets his name, address, family, occupation, etc. The memory loss can last from a few minutes to many years, and it can occur once or recur chronically. Amnesia characteristically is limited to memory of stressful information and events. Even with "total" amnesia, the patient can usually remember such impersonal things as language, world history, and current events. Dissociative amnesia is differentiated from amnesia produced by organic disease and head injury. Organic amnesias result from neurological damage to information storage capability, rather than from psychological stress.

Fugue states are amnesic conditions in which the individual physically flees from his normal environment, as well as forgets it. Fugue patients are sometimes found wandering aimlessly hundreds or thousands of miles away from home. In other cases, the individual begins a new life: picking a new name, remarrying, and beginning a new career. Some individuals falsely claim to have amnesia, as an excuse for some behavior. However, true amnesia victims really cannot remember.

Multiple personality is a related disorder, in which certain patterns of thought and behavior are regularly split off from consciousness. In this rare disorder, the individual seemingly lives two or more different lives to express behavior patterns which are anxiety provoking. As exemplified by the case of Jonah, the personalities are usually dramatically different. Each personality can be totally unaware of the others, or have partial awareness of one or more of the others. Thus, Jonah was amnesic for the three alter-personalities, while they were each aware of Jonah, and partially aware of each other.

This case is especially interesting as Ludwig et al. administered a variety of tests to the different personalities, verifying their independence. While each personality performed the same on intelligence tests, they gave dramatically different patterns on personality tests. As one of their measures, the authors recorded physiological arousal (i.e., anxiety) during a word association test. The words which were presented were selected so as to be anxiety provoking to only one of the personalities. Amazingly, each word produced arousal only with the appropriate personality. It would be most unlikely for anyone to fake this pattern of results.

Etiology

Dissociative disorders are relatively rare, and there is little research on their development. Like conversion disorders, they appear to be massive responses to stress and anxiety. The source of stress is often conflict over the expression of impulses. The individual has a strong urge to make some response, while at the same time experiencing guilt or anxiety about the impulse or its expression. The dissociative symptoms resolve the conflict by forgetting it, by fleeing from the site of the conflict, or by blanking out any awareness of its expression. In each case, the symptom is maintained by its effectiveness in reducing distress. These disorders have parallels in the behavior of most children. A child can often escape punishment by persistently denying he/she did something or heard a parental rule. This denial is more than a simple lie; the child can often become convinced that he/she really did not do the misdeed or hear the rule. Children also have active fantasy lives, in which they act out such things as aggression against parents. These fantasies also have a very real quality. Dissociative disorders might well be extensions of these childhood techniques for reducing threat and expressing forbidden impulses.

Summary

The focus of this chapter has been anxiety: what it is, how it affects us, how it develops, and some of the extreme disruptions in behavior produced by excessive anxiety. Anxiety is a physiological and subjective (cognitive) reaction to real or imagined threat. The specific things that make people anxious are learned. But, there appear to be substantial individual differences in susceptibility to anxiety and inherited predispositions to become anxious to certain types of stimuli. Anxiety can increase behavioral efficiency if it is moderate, but extreme anxiety is disruptive and aversive.

Neurosis is an ill-defined term that refers to a series of anxiety-based disorders. Phobias are intense, irrational fears, accompanied by extreme forms of avoidance behavior. Generalized anxiety disorder is a disturbance involving chronic levels of high anxiety and panic attacks. Obsessive-compulsive disorders are characterized by repetitive phobiclike thoughts, and ritualistic behaviors that serve to reduce the fear. Briquet's disorder consists of a chronic pattern of complaints about pain and illness. Conversion disorder is a disturbance marked by loss of function of some part of the body in the absence of an organic cause. Amnesia and fugue are memory losses in response to stress. Multiple personality is a disorder in which stress and anxiety are handled by splitting the personality into two or more independent identities and behavior patterns. Like anxiety, these disorders are all learned patterns of feeling and behavior, which probably develop in people having some physiological sensitivity to stress and anxiety.

GLOSSARY

Amnesia: A partial to complete loss of memory for recent events. It occurs in response to high levels of anxiety and stress.

Anxiety: An aversive emotional state, which can include feelings of threat or danger, and physiological arousal.

Briquet's disorder: An anxiety disorder marked by excessive complaints of physical disturbance and pain, for which no organic cause can be found. The complaints are recurrent and highly elaborate.

Compulsion: A highly stereotyped response that is typically performed over and over again in an effort to reduce anxiety stimulated by obsessions.

Conversion disorder: A disturbance characterized by loss of function in some part of the body despite the absence of an organic cause.

Fugue: A form of amnesia characterized by physical flight from home and family.

Generalized anxiety disorder: A pattern of chronic anxiety often accompanied by panic attacks.

Multiple personality: A disorder in which two or more distinct identities and patterns of behavior are maintained as a method of dealing with stress and anxiety.

Neurotic paradox: The mystery surrounding why people can continue to perform highly aversive behaviors despite their desire to resist.

Obsession: A recurrent thought or thought pattern that provokes intense fear.

Phobia: An intense irrational fear that typically results in extreme avoidance behavior.

Preparedness: A species-wide genetic predisposition to develop certain fears quite easily.

Two-factor theory: A theory about the etiology of phobias stating that fears are developed by classical conditioning, and avoidance behavior is maintained by operant conditioning.

AFFECTIVE DISORDERS

STEPHEN L. STERN
JOSEPH MENDELS

The affective disorders are a group of conditions characterized by an abnormality of mood or feeling—affect. In depression the primary mood is one of sadness or apathy; whereas in mania, euphoria or irritability predominates. "Affect" (pronounced with the accent on the first syllable) is used to connote emotional feeling and the outward manifestations of that feeling. Although some persons do make distinctions among the terms affect, mood, emotion, and feeling, there is no clear agreement as to the shades of meaning of these terms. In this chapter, they are used interchangeably. Affect is usually distinguished from cognition, or the processes involved in thinking; this distinction is not always easy to make.

Patients suffering from affective disorders manifest a variety of other signs and symptoms in addition to the abnormality of mood. These constitute the depressive or manic "syndrome." Mania and depression are considered together here because they frequently occur in the same individual, either at different times or together, and may share common causes and respond to some of the same treatments.

Literary descriptions of clinical depression go back at least as far as Homer and the Book of Job. The first author formally to describe depression as a clinical entity may have been Hippocrates, the father of medicine, who coined the term melancholia; he attributed it to the influence of black bile and phlegm on the brain. Artaeus, in the second century A.D., first recognized that melancholia and mania frequently occur in the same individual. In 1851, a French psychiatrist, Jules Falret, described "circular insanity" in considerable detail; the clinical syndrome he delineated is very similar to what we would now call *bipolar illness*. In 1896, Emil Kraepelin, an eminent German psychiatrist, separated the major functional (or nonorganic) psychiatric syndromes into dementia praecox (later termed schizophrenia) and manic-depressive psychosis. He made this distinction chiefly on the basis of outcome: patients with dementia praecox nearly always had a chronic downhill course, whereas those with manic-depressive illness tended to recover. Kraepelin's concept of manic-depressive psychosis was a very broad one, including most of the syndromes we now designate as affective disorders.

The development in the late 1930s of electroconvulsive therapy constituted a major breakthrough in the treatment of both depression and mania. In the late 1950s the first effective antidepressant drugs were introduced, followed a decade later by lithium carbonate, the first specific antimanic medication. During the past twenty years there has been a major expansion of research into the affective disorders, with investigators exploring psychological and interpersonal aspects of depressed and manic patients on the one hand and their genetic and biochemical characteristics on the other.

The term depression has multiple meanings both in everyday usage and in the field of mental health. Some of these are: 1. depression as a relatively transitory feeling of sadness that is an entirely appropriate response to a disappointing event. For example, a college student might say, "I really feel depressed tonight. I sure messed up that exam." Rather than "depressed," he or she might have said, "terrible." 2. Depression as the profound feeling of sadness and hopelessness that many persons experience after the loss of a loved one—grief or mourning. Whereas these two examples of depression may be regarded as normal responses to life circumstances, those that follow reflect the abnormal. This distinction is sometimes difficult to make and may at times be based on subjective judgment rather than firm scientific criteria. 3. Depression as used to describe the intensely painful feelings of patients who suffer from "depressive illness"—depression as a symptom. 4. Depression as the collection of signs and symptoms that accompany depressed mood in pathological states, such as poor appetite, early morning awakening—the syndrome of depression. 5. Depression as the term for a specific disease entity (or perhaps a group of diseases). Given these multiple uses of the term depression, it is not surprising that considerable confusion surrounds its use. Some authors have suggested the use of alternative terms such as melancholia to refer to the disease entity. Although a persuasive case can be made for the introduction of such a term, none has been widely accepted. Accordingly, in this chapter we shall continue to use "depression" in its multiple meanings.

Clinical features

Clinical depression can be defined as a condition characterized by a persistent and abnormal lowering of mood (feeling sad, blue, unhappy) and/or a loss of interest in usual activities, accompanied by a variety of characteristic signs and symptoms (Mendels, 1970). This depressed mood differs from normal sadness or unhappiness by its inappropriateness to the situation, its intensity, its duration, and the effect it has on the life of the person who experiences it—it interferes with normal living. No two cases of depression are identical, but a typical depressed individual might present as follows:

Mrs. Joan Smith is a 43-year-old woman, the mother of two children, who works as a secretary for a large law firm. Normally she is a productive, happy person who enjoys her family and her job. Six weeks ago she noticed that her work, which she had always found enjoyable, was becoming more difficult and more of a burden to her. She began worrying about her job, her family, and her health, although there was no apparent cause for concern. Feeling increasingly unhappy, she began to cry frequently; often she was not sure why. She started having difficulty falling asleep, would toss and turn during the night, and would awaken in the early morning darkness and be unable to get back to sleep. These early morning hours, as she lay awake in bed, were the time of day she came to dread the most. Her taste for food diminished and she began to lose weight. She found that she no longer derived any satisfaction from the activities that she used to enjoy. She became extremely self-critical and blamed herself for her misfortunes. Formerly a calm person, she now felt tense and irritable nearly all of the time. She began to feel that her troubles would never go away and started to think of suicide as the only way out. Alarmed by the changes that he saw in his wife, her husband urged her to consult the family physi-

A Case of Depression

Miss R. is a 32-year-old single white female, who was employed as a social worker. She came to a psychiatric clinic on her own initiative, for treatment of anxiety and sleeping problems. Miss R. reported that she experienced both free-floating anxiety and periodic anxiety attacks, which "come and go with no apparent warning." The anxiety states were also frequently associated with "black moods." These moods were described as horrifying periods of helplessness in which she felt as if the world was closing in around her. Miss R. reported that her sleeping difficulties had begun at least 10 or 12 years ago. She indicated that on a "good night" she slept for 5 to 6 hours. Frequently when she did fall asleep, she had nightmares and woke up intermittently throughout the night. She could not remember the last time she woke up in the morning feeling rested.

Miss R. indicated that her childhood had been characterized by fearfulness and anxiety. Her parents had a "bad" marriage, in which her father would frequently get drunk and beat her mother. Miss R. was terrified by these fights, and often had nightmares about them. She currently has a poor relationship with her family and feels quite guilty about this.

Miss R. reported that she has few friends, and is generally uncomfortable in interactions with other people. She has felt somewhat isolated since she began high school. She does not date men, and reports only one serious heterosexual relationship during her life. That relationship ended when the man started dating Miss R's roommate. Essentially, her current life is characterized by isolation and despondency. She is very concerned about what the future holds in store for her, and fears spending the rest of her life alone. She has never attempted suicide, but has thought about it often during the past few years, especially during the "black moods." She indicated that she does not want to kill herself, but is afraid that she might if she felt sufficiently hopeless.

cian, who referred her for psychiatric treatment. With antidepressant medication and supportive psychotherapy, her mood lifted and within a few weeks she felt markedly improved. By the end of two months, she felt physically and emotionally like her old self.

This example illustrates many of the important signs and symptoms of depression, listed in Table 9.1. It should be emphasized, however, that not all cases of depression will present with all of these symptoms.

The signs and symptoms of depression can be divided into four groups: affective, cognitive, somatic, and behavioral.

Affective symptoms

The most prominent feature of depression, usually, is the abnormally lowered mood. This may be associated with crying or a feeling of wanting but being unable to cry. Not all depressed patients report feeling unhappy; some may be bothered by feelings of apathy, of "not caring any more." There is often anhedonia, an inability to derive satisfaction from activities that are usually pleasurable. Most depressed patients complain as well of feeling nervous, anxious, or irritable. They may also experience feelings of guilt (disproportionate to reality and perhaps quite irrational), which may be intimately associated with thoughts of self-blame and worthlessness.

The feelings of depression may be worse at certain times of the day, characteristically the early morning hours. This fluctuation of mood, which may be associated with early morning awakening and with fluctuations in the other symptoms of deprssion, is referred to as diurnal variation, and suggests that normal biological rhythms may be disturbed in some cases of depression.

Table 9.1. Signs and Symptoms of Depression

Affective	Psychomotor retardation
Sadness	Agitation
Apathy	*Somatic*
Anhedonia	Sleep disturbance
Anxiety	Loss of appetite and weight
Guilt	Constipation
Cognitive	Decreased energy
Impaired concentration	Loss of libido
Indecisiveness	Menstrual changes
Self-blame	Aches and pains
Low self-esteem	*Suicidal Behavior*
Hopelessness	Thoughts
Helplessness	Threats
Behavioral	Attempts
Neglect of personal appearance	
Social withdrawal	

Cognitive symptoms

Depression is associated with a number of characteristic cognitive changes, or abnormalities in thinking. Difficulty in concentrating and thinking clearly are common, as is indecisiveness. Beck (1973) has delineated the "depressive triad": a negative view of the self, a negative view of the world, and negative expectations for the future. Depressed patients frequently feel helpless; that is, unable to take any action that would improve their predicament. Thoughts of self-blame, worthlessness, and hopelessness may become so severe as to be delusional. For example, a depressed man may feel that he has been a total failure at supporting his family and is penniless, when in fact he is quite wealthy. Depressed patients frequently believe that they will never recover. Several authors, including Beck and Bibring, have postulated that these cognitive changes are at the core of depression.

Behavioral symptoms

Appearance. Depressed patients frequently neglect their personal appearance; they may give little attention to hygiene, and dress in somber colors.

Social withdrawal is common and in some severe cases may lead to total isolation. Some behavior theorists feel that depressed individuals characteristically fail to perform behaviors that would elicit positive feedback from their environment. This lack of support from others may tend to make the depressed patient feel more depressed, which leads to further withdrawal.

Psychomotor retardation refers to the slowing down of thoughts and physical activities, leading to a "slow motion" appearance. Conversation may be difficult or, at times, impossible. There is usually difficulty in concentrating and in thinking clearly. In an extreme and rare form, psychomotor retardation may lead to depressive stupor, in which the patient is mute and does not move at all.

Agitation. The depressed patient may be agitated rather than retarded. Agitation is defined as a subjective feeling of anxiety, tension, or restlessness associated with physical hyperactivity. The mildly agitated patient will fidget and have difficulty sitting still. More severely agitated patients will pull at their clothes, wring their hands, bite their lips, pace up and down, and constantly complain and appeal for help and reassurance.

Somatic symptoms are common. They include:

1. *Sleep disturbance:* Although complaints of decreased sleep are most characteristic, some depressed patients may report that they "sleep all the time." Those complaining of insomnia may describe difficulty falling asleep or staying asleep, as well as early morning awakening—the most characteristic sleep change in depression. Patients complain of not feeling rested on awakening and describe low energy and easy fatigability throughout the day.

2. *Loss of appetite and weight* are common, although some patients report increased appetite and weight gain. It is not clear whether the weight loss in depression is due merely to decreased food intake or to other factors as well. Gastrointestinal complaints including constipation, dry mouth, and heavy feelings in the abdomen are also common.

3. *Loss of libido:* Both men and women may complain of decreased interest in and satisfaction from sex, and men may complain of impotence. Women may also experience menstrual irregularity.

4. *Aches and pains:* Depressed patients may have a number of other somatic complaints, such as upset stomach, lump in the throat, and miscellaneous vague complaints. Pain may be quite persistent and on occasion may be the most prominent symptom. Depressed patients may become preoccupied with their physical complaints. These somatic or hypochondriachal concerns may become so severe as to be delusional. For example, a depressed patient may believe that his bowels are rotting away.

Masked depression

Some depressed patients may present with complaints of physical problems such as insomnia, constipation, weight loss, poor appetite, fatigability, or aches and pains rather than with a disturbance of mood. These patients are usually seen by their family physician who may, after a diagnostic work-up proves negative, simply tell them that, "There is nothing to worry about," or "You just need to go away and relax a while." Most patients with these "masked depressions" (also referred to as hidden depressions or depressive equivalents) will admit to a feeling of sadness and/or a loss of interest when questioned *directly,* although they may well attribute this to their physical complaints. However, some patients suffering from masked depression may not be aware of feelings of sadness or apathy. The diagnosis of depression is difficult in these cases, though it may be suggested by the history of a recent loss, the presence of various other symptoms of depression, and/or a personal or family history of affective disorder. It is extremely important that these patients be properly diagnosed and treated for the underlying depressive disorder.

Depression in children

Although the classical syndrome of adult depression is not very frequently seen in prepubertal children, masked depressions appear to be common. These may involve somatic complaints, as in adults, or other kinds of behavioral problems, such as tantrums, bedwetting, separation anxiety, school difficulties, or antisocial behavior. After puberty, depressions resembling those of adults are common.

Depression in the involutional period

The ages of 45 to 55 in women and 50 to 60 in men are marked by a number of hormonal and psychosocial changes. Endogenous depressions occurring during this period are often said to be characterized by agitation, guilt, and hypochondriachal concerns; individuals with this type of depression, called "involutional melancholia," are said to have a premorbid personality of the obsessive-compulsive type. Recent research, however, has indicated that this type of depression is no more common during the involutional period than at other ages over 40. Thus, there does not appear to be a good rationale for a separate diagnosis of "involutional melancholia."

Depression in the elderly

During the later years, depressed patients frequently present with physical complaints or with symptoms of memory loss or confusion. The distinction between depression and senile dementia may be very difficult to make.

Course

The outcome is usually favorable in depressive disorders, provided the patient does not commit suicide. The vast majority of depressions will remit spontaneously, with a median duration for the untreated episode of approximately six months. Moreover, many patients suffer only a single episode of depression. In some cases, however, the patient goes on to develop a chronic depression, while other patients may have such frequent recurrence that their ability to lead a normal life is severely hampered.

Variability of symptoms

The signs and symptoms of depression may fluctuate considerably. For example, a young man who has become depressed because of an unhappy love affair may feel much better when his girlfriend begins to show signs of attention to him again. This tendency for depression to vary according to changes in the patient's environment is known as reactivity. At the other extreme are patients for whom the depressed mood is autonomous. In these cases, the mood varies little if at all and the patients will show no improvement in spirits despite, for example, learning of good news.

Severity

The severity of a depressive episode may vary widely. Some patients may continue to function well; in some cases only the patient himself knows that something is amiss. At the other extreme are individuals who are totally incapacitated and who require hospitalization because of their inability to care for themselves or because of their suicidal intentions. The severity of the depression has little to do with the eventual outcome. Frequently, patients who are extremely depressed with virtually all of the signs and symptoms of depression in severe form may respond rapidly and well to somatic treatment, such as electroconvulsive therapy or antidepressant drugs. In contrast, some patients with mild or moderate depression may not respond to treatment and may go on to chronic illness.

Suicidal behavior

Approximately 25,000 suicidal deaths are reported each year in the United States, making suicide the eleventh most common cause of death. Among persons of college age, it is the second leading cause of death. The official statistics severely underestimate the true suicide rate, perhaps by two or three times or more. For a variety of personal, social, and religious reasons, many suicidal attempts are not officially recorded. Also, a number of persons who die through apparently accidental means, such as automobile accidents, may have killed themselves deliberately.

Many individuals who take their lives are suffering from a depression or, if ill with schizophrenia or alcoholism (the two diagnoses next most highly correlated with suicide), are suffering from an associated depression at the time they take their lives. Robins, Gassner, Kayes, Wilkinson, and

Table 9.2. Characteristics that Make a Depressed Person a Serious Risk for Suicide

Age over 40 years
Male sex
Urban residence
Unmarried status
Absence of social supports
Chronic physical illness
Lack of employment
Alcoholism
High degree of hopelessness
History of previous suicide attempts
Aquaintance with someone who has committed suicide

Modified from D. Schuyler. *The Depressive Spectrum.* New York: Jason Aronson, 1974.

Murphy (1959) have estimated that 14 percent of persons with a diagnosis of manic-depressive illness will eventually take their own lives. Thus depression is a potentially lethal disease.

Depressed patients may be so hopeless that they view suicide as the only means of escape from an intolerable situation, or they may be obsessed by ideas of guilt and desire punishment. Not all depressed patients are suicidal. Some may think that life is not worth living or even wish that they were dead, yet still not plan to take their own lives.

Depressed patients may be especially likely to make a suicide attempt after they have started to recover from the depression. At that time, they may still feel despondent, but may be less retarded and have the energy to carry out a suicide plan.

Table 9.2 lists variables associated with an increased risk of suicide. Suicide rates have recently been tending to equalize among various demographic groups: for example, the rate is increasing among the young and women. Women make many more suicide attempts than men, but men are much more likely actually to succeed in taking their lives. This may be in part because men are more likely to use relatively irreversible methods of taking their lives, such as firearms, whereas women are more likely to choose potentially remediable methods such as an overdose of pills.

Classification of depression

Accurate classification and diagnosis are essential to improving our ability to understand and treat the affective disorders. We will first discuss some of the traditional approaches to the classification of depression and then describe several more recent approaches.

Traditional approaches to classification

When Kraepelin coined the term manic-depressive psychosis in 1896, he included "the whole domain of the so-called periodic and circular insanities, mania, and a greater part of the morbid states termed melancholia." He later expanded the concept to include all cases of "affective excess" that did not lead to deterioration. Kraepelin viewed manic-depressive psychosis as an endogenous illness (i.e., due to factors arising within the individual). "Manic-depressive psychosis," he wrote, "is to an astonishing degree independent of external influences."

Kraepelin was a perceptive observer whose separation of schizophrenia and manic-depressive psychosis was a landmark in the development of modern concepts of mental illness. Unfortunately, his concept of manic-depressive psychosis was so broad as to limit its usefulness in making classifications *within* the affective disorders. Moreover, his assumption that manic-depressive psychosis is entirely endogenous in origin has led to considerable controversy and misunderstanding.

The term manic-depressive psychosis or manic-depressive illness is generally used today to refer either to bipolar affective disorder or to bipolar disorder together with unipolar illness. Because of this ambiguity, it is probably best not to use this term in diagnosis.

Following Kraepelin, a number of authors sought to establish classifications within the field of depression. Most of these tended to view depression in terms of dichotomies.

Endogenous and reactive depression

Some authors have used the word endogenous to describe a depressive episode arising in the absence of precipitating events. This is the sense in which Kraepelin used the term. Others have used it to refer to a depression characterized by a group of largely somatic signs and symptoms, including poor appetite, weight loss, constipation, early morning awakening, retardation or agitation, self-blame, and diurnal mood variation, with the depressed mood most severe in the early morning, but nonreactive to environmental changes.

What is the evidence for the existence of endogenous depression as a separate condition? Several factor analytic studies have shown that many of the signs and symptoms ascribed to endogenous depression tend to occur in the same individuals and that these individuals frequently have a family history of affective disorder and respond well to somatic treatments. In contrast, the distinction between precipitated and nonprecipitated depressions is often difficult to make in practice, and does not appear to define subgroups that are homogeneous with regard to clinical features, family history, or treatment response. Thus, it seems most appropriate to reserve the term endogenous depression for a depressive illness marked by certain characteristic signs and symptoms, without necessarily making any inferences with regard to etiology. Because of the etiological implications that have been associated with the word endogenous, some authors have suggested the use of a new term, endogenomorphic, for this condition. Since it is not yet in wide use, we will continue to use endogenous.

The term reactive depression is usually used in contrast with endogenous depression to describe a depression in which the low mood fluctuates in response to changes in the environment, or to describe a depression that was precipitated by an environmental event. Adolf Meyer and his followers also used the term reaction to indicate virtually any functional psychiatric disorder—for example, schizophrenic reaction, anxiety reaction, depressive reaction—because they felt that all psychiatric disorders could be understood as reactions to an individual's life experiences.

Given the current state of our knowledge, it would seem unwise to classify an episode of depression solely on the base of the reactivity of the mood. As noted above, the presence or absence of precipitating events also does not in itself seem to be useful for the purpose of classification (cf. Mendels & Cochrane, 1968).

Psychotic and neurotic depression

The term psychotic depression is best used to describe a depression characterized by disordered reality testing, which is usually manifested by hallucinations or delusions. Unfortunately, many authors use this term simply to indicate a severe illness, one in which there is marked interference in the individual's ability to function. Still others, particularly in Britain, have used the term interchangeably with endogenous depression.

"Neurotic depression" also has many meanings: 1. a disorder in which reality testing is intact; 2. a relatively mild disorder; 3. a disorder characterized by intrapsychic (neurotic) conflict; 4. a disorder that is precipitated by an environmental stress; or 5. a disorder that is *not* characterized by the signs and symptoms of endogenous depression.

It is clear that the multiple meanings of the terms endogenous, reactive, psychotic, and neurotic have led to considerable confusion. A reasonable approach for the present would seem to be to retain the concept of "endogenous depression," since this appears to be a relatively well-defined entity, and to refer to the heterogeneous group of all other depressions as nonendogenous.

More recent approaches

As a result of the difficulties with the old system of classification, a number of proposals for modification have been made.

DSM-III. The American Psychiatric Association (1977) is currently preparing a new system of classification of the affective and other mental disorders, the *Diagnostic and Statistical Manual,* third edition (DSM-III). DSM-III includes operational criteria for each of the affective and other disorders. Table 9.3 lists the proposed operational criteria for an episode of "Depressive Disorder." Individuals with an endogenous depression, it will be seen, would easily meet these criteria. Those with a nonendogenous depression might or might not; those who do not would probably be diagnosed as having an "adjustment disorder with depressed mood" or an "atypical depressive disorder."

The proposed system of classification of the affective disorders in DSM-III is shown in Table 9.4. Two other very useful distinctions that have recently been proposed are between primary and secondary depressions and between unipolar and bipolar illness.

Primary and secondary depression

In this system, originally proposed by Robins and Guze (1972), an episode of primary depression is one that occurs in a patient who has had no previous psychiatric disorders, with the exception of mania or a prior episode of depression. An episode of secondary depression is one that has been preceded at some time in the patient's life by a nonaffective mental disorder; for example, schizophrenia, alcoholism, or obsessive-compulsive neurosis. This system has considerable utility, in that a schizophrenic patient who becomes depressed is likely to be very different from a patient with primary depression, in terms of biological parameters, clinical picture, family history, and response to treatment. Individuals with depressions secondary to some other conditions, however, such as obsessive-compulsive or phobic neurosis, might not necessarily differ greatly from primary depressives. Clearly, more research is needed comparing individuals suffering from primary depression with those whose depressions are secondary to a variety of other conditions.

Unipolar and bipolar depression

In this classification, originally proposed by Perris (1966), depressed patients with a history of depression only are referred to as unipolar, whereas those with a history of mania or hypomania (a less severe form of mania) are referred to as bipolar (cf. Wolpert, 1977). Table 9.5 lists some of the reported differences between unipolar and bipolar patients. It is likely that the group of unipolar depressions is in itself heterogeneous. For example, Winokur (1973) divides it into pure depressive disease and depressive spectrum disease. Other subtypes of depression within the broadly based unipolar group are likely to emerge with future research. Bipolar depressions may also consist of more than one type.

Both unipolar and bipolar depressives are considered to have primary depressive illness. Individuals who experience periods of mild elation and periods of mild depression are often disgnosed as having cyclothymic personality. This is probably a variant of bipolar affective disorder.

"Normal" depression

An additional issue in the classification of depression concerns the relationship between "normal" and clinical depression. Normal depression refers to a condition in which the individual's unhappy mood, though relatively persistent, is an appropriate response to his/her life situation. The distinction between normal and clinical depression is often not easy to make. The prototype of normal depression is mourning. Loss of a loved one may lead to a condition

Table 9.3. Proposed Operational Criteria for an Episode of Depressive Disorder in DSM-III

A. Dysphoric mood or pervasive loss of interest or pleasure. The disturbance is characterized by symptoms such as the following: depressed, sad, blue, hopeless, low, down in the dumps, "don't care anymore," irritable, worried. The disturbance must be prominent and relatively persistent but not necessarily the most dominant symptom. It does not include momentary shifts from one dysphoric mood to another dysphoric mood, e.g., anxiety to depression to anger, such as are seen in states of acute psychotic turmoil.

B. At least four of the following symptoms:

1. Poor appetite or weight loss or increased appetite or weight gain (change of one pound a week or ten pounds a year when not dieting).
2. Sleep difficulty or sleeping too much.
3. Loss of energy, fatigability, or tiredness.
4. Psychomotor agitation or retardation (but not mere subjective feelings of restlessness or being slowed down).
5. Loss of interest or pleasure in usual activities, or decrease in sexual drive (do not include if limited to a period when delusional or hallucinating).
6. Feelings of self-reproach or excessive or inappropriate guilt (either may be delusional).
7. Complaints or evidence of diminished ability to think or concentrate such as slow thinking, or indecisiveness (do not include if associated with obvious formal thought disorder).
8. Recurrent thoughts of death or suicide, or any suicidal behavior, including thoughts of wishing to be dead.

C. The period of illness has had a duration of at least one week from the time of the first noticeable change in the patient's usual condition.

D. None of the following, which suggests schizophrenia is present:

1. Delusions of being controlled or delusions of thought broadcasting, insertion, or withdrawal.
2. Hallucinations of any type throughout the day for several days or intermittently throughout a one-week period unless all of the content is clearly related to depression or elation.
3. Auditory hallucinations in which either a voice keeps up a running commentary on the patient's behaviors or thoughts as they occur, or two or more voices converse with each other.
4. At some time during the period of illness delusions or hallucinations for more than one month in the absence of prominent affective (manic or depressive) symptoms (although typical depressive delusions, such as delusions of guilt, sin, poverty, nihilism, or self-deprecation or hallucinations of similar content are permitted).
5. Preoccupation with a delusion or hallucination to the relative exclusion of other symptoms or concerns (other than delusions of guilt, sin, poverty, nihilism, or self-deprecation, or hallucinations with similar content).
6. Marked formal thought disorder if accompanied by either blunted or inappropriate affect, delusions or hallucinations of any type, or grossly disorganized behavior.

E. Not due to any specific known organic mental disorder.

F. Not superimposed on schizophrenia, residual subtype.

G. Excludes simple bereavement following loss of loved one if all of the features are commonly seen in members of the subject's subcultural group in similar circumstances.

---

closely resembling clinical depression, with low mood, loss of interest, hopelessness, and various somatic symptoms such as poor appetite and sleep disturbance. Low self-esteem and suicidal ideation are, however, uncommon (cf. Clayton, Halikas, & Maurice, 1972).

Epidemiology

Scope of the problem. Depression is a major public health problem (Silverman, 1963). In the United States in 1970, 251,000 persons were admitted to hospitals with a diagnosis of depression. This constituted 23.8 percent of the psychiatric admissions during that

Table 9.4. Proposed Classification of the Affective Disorders in DSM-III

Episodic Affective Disorders
Manic disorder
single episode
recurrent
Depressive disorder[1]
single episode
recurrent
Bipolar affective disorder
manic
depressed
mixed
Intermittent Affective Disorders[2]
Intermittent depressive disorder (depressive character)
Intermittent hypomanic disorder (hypomanic personality)
Intermittent bipolar disorder (cyclothymic personality)
Atypical Affective Disorders[3]
Atypical depressive disorder
Atypical manic disorder
Atypical bipolar disorder
Reactive Disorders[4]
Adjustment disorder with depressed mood

1. Equivalent to the category of "unipolar depression."
2. Disorders characterized by brief periods of abnormal mood with associated signs and symptoms, separated by periods of normal mood, which are usually of longer duration.
3. Disorders that cannot be characterized as episodic or intermittent affective disorders or as reactive disorders.
4. Not classified under Affective Disorders in DSM-III.

year, and was the largest single diagnostic category. An additional 200,000 depressed persons are estimated to receive outpatient treatment annually, and many others are either misdiagnosed or receive no treatment at all. The annual cost to the affected individuals, their families, employers, and society in terms of health care costs and lost earnings runs in the billions of dollars. The cost in terms of human suffering is incalculable.

In a thorough study in Iceland, where very detailed psychiatric records are kept, Helgason (1964) estimated that the total lifetime prevalence for what would now be called primary depressive illness was approximately 9 percent in women and 5 percent in men. These figures represent the chance that any one individual will have an episode of clinical depression some time during his or her lifetime. The corresponding figure for schizophrenia is only 1 percent. In view of the tendency for depressive disorders to be underdiagnosed, some authors have suggested that the lifetime risk for developing an episode of depression may in fact be twice as great. The majority of these cases are thought to be of the nonendogenous type. Of the endogenous depressions, most are unipolar rather than bipolar.

There are differences in the distribution of depression across groups in society. Some of these are noted below.

Sex. Depression is more common in women than in men (cf. Weissman &Paykel, 1974). The female-to-male ratio is nearly 2:1 for most forms of depressive disorder, though in bipolar disorder the sex distribution is approximately equal. The reasons for this difference are not always clear. Some of it may be due to hormonal factors. For example, depression appears to be more common at the time of ovulation, premenstrually, during menstruation, and during the several months after the birth of a child. These are all times of hormonal flux. Also, after age 55, when women are postmenopausal, the incidence of depression is about the same in women and men.

Psychosocial factors also seem likely to play a role. Social, legal, and economic descrimination against women may make it difficult for them to achieve job satisfaction. Housewives may be plagued by boredom. Moreover, women have traditionally been taught that it is not "ladylike" to be assertive, which may increase their risk of becoming depressed. The rate of depression is higher in married than in single, divorced, or widowed women, whereas in men the reverse is true.

Some authors have also suggested that

Table 9.5. Differences Between Patients with Bipolar and Unipolar Depression

	Bipolar	Unipolar
Personal history of mania (defining characteristics)	Yes	No
Family history of mania	Yes	No
Family history of depression	Yes	Yes
Sex ratio (female:male)	~1:1	~2:1
Median age of onset	25–30	35–40
Psychomotor state during depression	More retarded	More agitated
Personality characteristics (as measured by psychological tests)	Fairly normal	Abnormal
Probability of response to Li_2CO_3 during acute depression	Greater	Lesser
Prophylactic response to Li_2CO_3	Yes	Yes
Evoked EEG potential	Abnormal	Normal
Divorce rate	Greater	Lesser
Risk of postpartum depression	Greater	Lesser
Number of episodes of affective disorder	Greater	Lesser

alcoholism, which may be genetically linked to some types of depressive disorder, may be a "depressive equivalent" in men. If the statistics for alcoholism were included, the rates for depression in men and women might be more nearly alike.

Age. Depression is apparently uncommon in children; at least it is seldom recognized in its classic form. Following puberty, a variety of depressive disorders are seen. The median age of onset is 25 to 30 years for bipolar affective disorder, and 35 to 40 years for unipolar illness. The first episode of affective disorder may occur at any time from adolescence through old age. In contrast, onset after age 40 is unusual in schizophrenia, the neuroses, or the personality disorders.

Transcultural studies. The incidence of depression, particularly endogenous depression, appears to be fairly constant worldwide. There do seem however, to be some cultural differences in the way depression is manifested. Patients in non-Western countries may be more likely to express their depression in somatic terms, rather than to complain of feeling sad. Guilt also is less common in non-Western societies.

Causes of depression

We do not yet know what causes depression. Indeed, given the many forms of depression, it is probable that a number of factors are involved. It must also be recognized that some of these factors may interact with each other. For example, an individual may be genetically predisposed to develop a depression, but may never do so unless exposed to some specific stressful stimuli. Many such interactions are possible. For convenience, the major theories will be considered in several groups.

Psychological theories

Affective (psychoanalytic) theories. In 1911, Abraham (1911) proposed that the crucial difference between grief and depression is that the bereaved person is concerned with a lost love object, whereas the depressed patient is preoccupied with himself and his own feelings of loss, guilt, and low self-esteem. In his initial psychoanalytic formulation of depression, Abraham suggested that the depressed patient redirects feelings of hostility that he had previously felt toward the lost person and channels them toward his self. In "Mourning and Melancholia," Freud (1917) developed Abraham's theories by emphasizing the paramount role of loss of self-esteem in depression. Freud emphasized that depression may result from a symbolic loss and not necessarily the actual loss of a loved object. He suggested that the withdrawal of love and support by a significant figure (usually a parent) during a crucial stage in development prediposes an individual to depression later in life.

In subsequent work, Abraham postulated that when this withdrawal of love occurs during the oral stage of psychosexual development, the individual becomes fixated at that stage of development and tends, as an adult, to become very dependent on other people, as well as to seek oral types of gratification.

Although Abraham and Freud made major contributions to the understanding of depression, their formulations have not proved to be applicable to all kinds of depression. For example, in some depressed patients anger may be directed toward others rather than the self.

A number of psychoanalysts have made further contributions to these ideas. Spitz (1946), observing hospitalized infants separated from their mothers, noted an initial stage of angry protest, followed by a stage of withdrawal and seeming despair. He termed this "anaclitic depression." Bowlby (1973) reported similar, though less marked, phenomena in older children separated from their parents. Maternal separation in infant monkeys has also been shown to produce a similar picture. These studies indicate clearly that as Freud and Abraham postulated, loss of parenting can have profound effects on the young organism. The relationship between these experiences and adult depression remains to be elucidated, however.

One of the most influential of the modern psychoanalytic theorists is Edward Bibring (1953), who emphasized that the loss of self-esteem in depression is usually the result of a consciously perceived disparity between an individual's desires and reality. He focused on the important role that the feeling of helplessness has in the development of depression. Bibring's ideas were the starting point for subsequent cognitive theorists.

Cognitive theories. The cognitive changes in depression have traditionally been viewed as being secondary to the primary disturbance of affect. However, Beck (1976) has proposed that the abnormal mood is a consequence of characteristic abnormal patterns of thinking (i.e., a cognitive disturbance). These include tendencies toward low self-esteem, excessive self-criticism, frequent self-commands, and exaggerated concepts of duty and responsibility. Frequent "automatic thoughts"—for example, "I made a stupid mistake. I must be incompetent,"—lead to intensification of the depressed mood. Beck also delineated a number of errors in thinking that depressed patients habitually make. An example is "overgeneralization": depressed patients tend to draw sweeping conclusions, frequently of a self-deprecatory nature, based on vary scanty data.

Seligman (1975), drawing on data from animal experiments, has proposed a theory of depression based on "learned helplessness." This is a phenomenon in which animals, after being exposed to an unavoidable noxious stimulus, show a persistent decreased ability to escape from avoidable noxious stimuli. This phenomenon was initially observed in dogs treated with electric shock, but has subsequently been demonstrated in a variety of other species, including humans, using a variety of unpleasant stimuli (Maier & Seligman, 1976).

A feeling of helplessness is a well-known concomitant of clinical depression. Seligman has suggested that it may be at the core of depression. The ability to escape from an unpleasant situation may generate a depressed mood, which makes the person less able to cope with the situation, and so a vicious cycle is set up.

Behavioral theories. Behaviorists have sought to understand depression by attempting to quantify and analyze the observable behaviors of depressed persons. At the core of depression, according to Lewinsohn (1975), is a decrease in the rate of response-contingent reinforcement. That is, the depressed person is unhappy because he does not obtain sufficient satisfaction from his environment. This may be due to a variety of factors, such as decreased participation in pleasurable activities, a tendency to rate the pleasantness of activities lower than do nondepressed individuals, inadequate social skills, and/or living in an unfavorable environment in which positive reinforcement is difficult to obtain. Another aspect of the behavioral approach to depression is the analysis of the precipitants and consequences of depressed feelings and behavior. Learning that a patient's depressed behaviors are exacerbated in certain situations or that certain of his depressed behaviors are reinforced by his environment may have important implications for treatment.

Overview

These psychoanalytic, cognitive, and behavioral theories have been of value in providing a rationale for useful psychotherapeutic approaches to depression. However, there is an urgent need for studies designed to test these theories empirically. It should be kept in mind that the presence of unconscious conflicts, cognitive distortions, or abnormal behaviors in depression does not necessarily mean that these abnormalities *caused* the depression.

Social theories

Many authors have suggested that social and psychological factors may interact in causing depression (cf. Bart, 1974). For example, discrimination and inadequate education may make it difficult for persons in lower socioeconomic groups to obtain positive reinforcement from their environment. This may engender feelings of helplessness and hopelessness. Middle-class persons with aspirations for advancement may be especially vulnerable to a loss in self-esteem if their expectations are not fulfilled.

One way of understanding the relationship between social environment and the likelihood of developing depression is to study the role of life events in precipitating depressive illness. Considerable attention has been directed to this area in recent years. Paykel and associates (Paykel, Myers, Dienelh, Klerman, Kindenthal, & Pepper, 1969), classifying events as either exits or entrances, found that exits such as deaths and losses tended to be associated with the onset of depression. Not all authors have reported similar associations, however. (See the review by Schless and Mendels [1977] for a further discussion of the issues in this field of research.)

Biochemical theories

In recent years, prompted by the development of effective drug treatments, there has been a major expansion of research into biochemical aspects of the affective disorders. This is clearly an important endeavor, since regardless of whether depression in a particular individual is primarily biological or psychological in origin, changes in mood, cognition, and behavior must necessarily be expressed through biochemical mechanisms.

A variety of biochemical theories of depression have been proposed, all of which await validation (cf. Mendels, 1975). Included among these are:

1. The hypothesis that there is a deficiency of important neurotransmitters called *biogenic amines* in certain areas of the brain. This is known as the biogenic amine hypothesis. The development of this

hypothesis was stimulated by the discovery that acute administration of all of the effective antidepressant drugs increases the amount of biogenic amines in the brain, and that decreasing brain levels of these amines can in some (but not all) instances lead to depression. Although this hypothesis is probably not true in its simplest form, it has had great value in stimulating fruitful research.

2. The hypothesis that there is an abnormality in the functioning of the brain systems that normally regulate hormonal secretion and other important biological activities. For example, there are extensive abnormalitites in the mechanisms controlling the release of the hormone cortisol by the adrenal cortex. This may reflect a dysfunction in the diencephalon, at the base of the brain. The diencephalon exercises control over the pituitary gland and, through it, the rest of the endocrine system. The changes in mood, sleep, appetite, and sexual function in depression are considered by many to reflect an abnormality in diencephalic function.

3. The hypothesis that nerve cell function is disturbed due to an alteration in the distribution of certain cations, such as sodium and potassium, across the nerve cell membrane, leading to a state of unstable hyperexcitability of the central nervous system. The development of this hypothesis was stimulated in part by the discovery that the lithium ion—a monovalent cation like the sodium and potassium ions, which play a major role in nerve cell function—is an effective treatment for certain types of affective disorders. Abnormalities in cation transport across the cell membrane have also been reported in some patients with bipolar illness.

Genetics There is considerable evidence that genetic factors play an important role in the development of at lease some forms of affective disorder (Slater & Cowie, 1971).

Twin studies. Most investigators have found that in endogenous affective disorders the concordance rate (the tendency for both members of a set of twins to suffer from a given psychiatric disorder if one does) is higher for monozygotic (identical) twins than for dizygotic (fraternal) twins. The average concordance rate for the monozygotic twins in these studies was approximately 70 percent whereas the rate for the dizygotic twins was only 20 percent. The converse of these data indicate that 30 percent of the time, individuals with identical genetic make-up *did not* both develop affective disorder. This indicates that environmental factors do play an important role in the development of affective illness even in the presence of a significant genetic predisposition.

Family studies. Affective disorder tends to run in families, more for bipolar than for unipolar illness. Patients with bipolar disorder may have relatives with either depression or mania, whereas the only affective disorder that relatives of unipolar patients tend to suffer from is depression. Winokur (1973) has reported data indicating that there may be at least two kinds of unipolar depressive illness. In pure depressive disease, characteristically seen in men over 40, the relatives of these individuals either have depressive disorders or no psychiatric illness. In depressive spectrum disorder, the prototype of which is a young woman, the family members may suffer from alcoholism or sociopathy, as well as from depression.

Mode of transmission. Little is known about the mode of genetic transmission for affective disorder. In certain families a gene for bipolar illness may be located on the X chromosome and segregate with color blindness or with a certain blood type. This would be an X-linked dominant form of transmission with incomplete penetrance. Other data inconsistent with this mode of transmission have, however, also been reported, leaving the matter unresolved. There are also claims for a polygenic mode of inheritance for unipolar depressive disorder. It is entirely possible that different genotypes could produce the same phenotype, namely depression.

Psychophysiology

A number of investigators have studied the electrical activity of the brain in affective disorders by use of the electroencephalograph (EEG). Although consistent abnormalities have not been reported in resting EEGs obtained while patients are awake, certain abnormalities have been found utilizing special techniques. Studies of sleep EEGs have revealed that, in comparison to normal subjects, depressed patients take longer to fall asleep, have more spontaneous awakenings, have less Stage 4 or deep sleep, and tend to wake earlier in the morning. Although it is difficult to study hypomanic or manic patients, preliminary evidence indicates that they have similar sleep abnormalities.

Several investigators have studied evoked potentials, in which the EEG changes in response to a stimulus such as a bright light or a loud noise are evaluated. Manic and bipolar depressed patients have both been shown to produce evoked potentials that are significantly different from normal; unipolar depressed patients do not appear to differ consistently from normals in this regard.

The electromyograph (EMG), which measures the electrical activity of muscles, has also been used to study depressed patients. Most investigators have reported a generalized increase in muscle tension in depression, as measured by the EMG. Schwartz, Fair, Salb, Mandel, and Klerman (1976) have found that EMGs of the facial muscles of depressed patients frequently reflect an unhappy facial expression, even when their faces do not appear sad to the observer.

Psychological tests and rating scales

A number of general psychological tests and especially developed rating scales are used for diagnosing depression, for measuring its severity, and for following its course over time.

General psychological tests

Self-rating. Among the general psychological tests, the MMPI (Minnesota Multiphasic Personality Inventory) is the most widely used self-rating scale. It consists of 566 items that the patient scores as either true or false. A number of subscales are derived from the test scores, including the D-Scale, which measures the depth of clinical depression. Recently, the SCL-90 (Symptom Checklist–90) has been developed for studying psychiatric outpatients. It consists of 90 symptoms that the patient rates on a scale from 0 to 4, in which 0 indicates that the symptom in question did not bother the patient at all and 4 means that he or she was bothered very much by the symptom. Nine subscales, including one for depression, are derived from the SCL–90.

Projective tests. Projective tests, such as the Rorschach and the Thematic Apperception Test (TAT) may provide indications of the extent of an individual's depression and the dynamics underlying it. Word association tests may also be useful in the assessment of depression.

Depression rating scales

Self-rating. The Beck Depression Inventory and the Zung Self-Rating Depression Scale are two instruments commonly used in the evaluation of depression. The Beck Inventory consists of 21 sets of statements, each set containing 4 or 5 sentences; the patient is instructed to select the one statement he or she feels is most applicable to him. The Zung Scale consists of 20 items that the patient scores as being present a little of the time, some of the time, part of the time, or most of the time.

Observer-rating

The Hamilton Rating Scale for Depression is the most widely used of the observer-rating scales. This is a 17-item test in which the interviewer rates a variety of signs and symptoms of depression on a scale from 0 to 2 or 0 to 4, including depressed mood, guilt, sleep disturbance, and anorexia. This test has been shown to be a highly reliable instrument for rating the severity of depression. The Raskin 3-Area Scale is an instrument by which the observer rates a depressed patient globally on a scale from 1 to 5 in each of 3 areas: verbal behavior, appearance, and secondary symptoms of depression.

Personality and depression

One interesting use of psychological tests has been to examine the question of premorbid personality in depressive disorder. Recent studies indicate that persons who develop unipolar depression are more likely than normal to have a personality characterized by obsessiveness (orderliness, conscientiousness, achievement orientation), dependency, introversion, pessimism, low self-confidence, and low levels of assertiveness and social adroitness. In contrast, the premorbid personality of bipolar depressives has been reported to resemble closely that of normals, except perhaps for increased obsessiveness.

Treatment of depression

Depression is, in most cases, a self-limiting process. What, then, are the goals of treatment? To help the patient recover as rapidly as possible, to minimize suffering, and, of course, to reduce the risk of suicide. Once the clinician makes a diagnosis of depressive disorder, he or she is faced first with the decision of whether or not to recommend hospitalization. Hospitalization may serve a number of functions: to place a suicidal patient under close supervision, to remove him from a stressful home situation, and, perhaps, to facilitate the establishment of a therapeutic relationship. In addition, if electronconvulsive therapy is indicated, treatment can generally be performed most easily in a hospital setting. There is, however, an increasing tendency to treat depressed persons on an outpatient basis. This is due to economic considerations as well as to the desire of most patients to remain with their families and at work.

After a decision has been made with regard to hospitalization, the clinician then must decide whether psychotherapy alone or in combination with somatic therapies is indicated.

Psychotherapy

In treating of the severely depressed patient, supportive psychotherapy is generally combined with somatic therapies. Key elements in this type of psychotherapy are to establish a positive, accepting relationship with the patient; to pressure him or her that he/she very likely will get better; and to caution him/her against making any important decisions in his/her life, since he/she may not be able to view circumstances objectively while depressed. Involving the patient's family in the treatment and helping the patient to structure daily activities may also be extremely helpful.

For mildly and moderately depressed individuals who are considered suitable for psychotherapy, the approach is somewhat different. In these cases, the goals of therapy are to help the patient to recover from the depression as rapidly as possible, to help him or her understand insofar as possible why he/she became depressed, and to help him make changes in his/her personality and behavior designed to lessen the likelihood of future recurrences. Some of the more psychotherapeutic approaches used with depressed patients are described below:

Psychoanalytic psychotherapy. The goals of this kind of therapy are to help the patient become aware of unconscious conflicts and their roots in childhood experiences and to help him or her learn to resolve them himself. Aiding the patient in understanding his/her feelings toward the therapist is an important element in this approach (Hollender, 1965; Mendelson, 1974).

Cognitive therapy. In this type of treatment, as in the approaches that follow, the therapist is generally more active and directive than in psychoanalytic psychotherapy. The goal here is to help the patient become aware of the cognitive distortions and negative thoughts that may be contributing to the depressed mood, to aid him/her in dealing with them appropriately, and to help him/her learn to think in a distortion-free manner.

Behavior therapy. The behavior therapist seeks to help the patient identify the possible environmental precipitants and consequences of his/her depressed feelings and behavior. The goal is to encourage the patient to obtain more positive reinforcement from the environment. This may entail instruction in social skills, such as assertiveness (Lewinsohn, Biglan, & Zeiss, 1976).

Couples, family and group therapy. Frequently, marital or family problems may cause or contribute to a patient's depression. In these cases, treating the couple or the family as a unit may be a necessary part of the treatment program. Group therapy can be quite helpful in individuals who have significant interpersonal problems.

Somatic therapies

Electroconvulsive therapy. Among the somatic therapies, electroconvulsive therapy (ECT) has the highest rate of effectiveness: up to 90 percent in endogenous depression. It is much less effective in nonendogenous illness. ECT may be given either bilaterally, with electrodes placed on both sides of the patient's head, or unilaterally. Unilateral treatments seems to result in less memory impairment and seems to be just as effective. A significant advantage of ECT is that it works very rapidly. Severely depressed patients may show dramatic improvement after as few as two treatments, given at the rate of one every other day. In most cases, ECT is continued after the patient shows an initial response, up to a total of six to ten treatments, in order to decrease the risk of relapse.

Although ECT does have some disadvantages—brief periods of disorientation and confusion may be seen after each treatment and short-term-memory impairment lasting for several months after the course of ECT may also occur—it is a very safe and effective treatment when properly administered to appropriate patients. Generally, it is used in patients who have failed to respond to antidepressant drugs or in severely ill, suicidal patients, for whom it may be life-saving.

The mode of action of ECT is unknown (Fink, Kety, McGaugh, & Williams, 1974). The occurrence of a seizure in the diencephalon, a part of the brain that may be dysfunctional in depression, does seem to be essential to the therapeutic effect.

Antidepressant drugs. Antidepressant medication, first introduced 20 years ago, has become one of the most important methods for treating depressed patients (Cole & Davis, 1975). Of the three groups of drugs listed in Table 9.6, the tricyclic antidepressants are the most widely used and generally the most useful. They have been reported to work most effectively in endogenous depressions, although they may be helpful in some patients with nonendogenous depressions as well. The monoamine oxidase (MAO) inhibitors are also effective antidepressant drugs, although somewhat less helpful than the tricyclic antidepressants. Since there is a risk of more severe side effects with these agents, they are seldom the drugs of initial choice for most depressed patients. There have, however, been reports that patients characterized as suffering from "atypical depressions" or "hysterical dysphorias" are more likely to respond to the MAO inhibitors than to the tricyclic antidepressants.

The mechanisms of action of the tricyclic antidepressants and the MAO inhibitors have not been determined, although it has been proposed that these drugs may work by

Table 9.6. Antidepressant Drugs[1]

Category	Genetic Name	Trade Name
Tricyclic antidepressants	Amitriptyline	Amitriptyline HCl
		Elavil
		Endep
	Desipramine	Norpramin
		Pertofrane
	Doxepin	Adapin
		Sinequan
	Imipramine	Imavate
		Imipramine HCl
		Imipramine hydrochloride
		Janimine
		Presamine
		SK-Pramine
		Tofranil
	Nortriptyline	Aventyl HCl
		Pamelor
	Protriptyline	Vivactil
Monoamine oxidase (MAO) inhibitors	Isocarboxazid	Marplan
	Phenelzine	Nardil
	Tranylcypromine	Parnate
Lithium carbonate	Lithium carbonate	Eskalith
		Lithane
		Lithium carbonate
		Lithonate

1. Drugs included are those currently being marketed in the United States.

increasing the amount of the neurotransmitters serotonin and/or norepinephrine at certain synaptic sites in the brain. The validity of this proposal is uncertain. In general, the response to the antidepressant drugs is not so rapid as to ECT.

Lithium carbonate has been shown to be an effective drug in the treatment of acute mania and in the prophylaxis of recurrent manic and depressive episodes. Several studies suggest that it may also be effective in certain acutely depressed patients, particularly those with bipolar illness. The discovery that lithium is useful in the treatment of both mania and depression has contributed to the development of new ideas regarding the relationship between these two disorders. As noted above, the close resemblance among the lithium, sodium, and potassium ions has also suggested that abnormal cation transport may play a role in the genesis of certain affective disorders.

It must be emphasized that psychotherapy and somatic therapies can be very successfully combined. For example, an endogenously depressed patient with interpersonal difficulties might respond well to antidepressant medication combined with cognitive and behavioral treatment in a group setting. It is extremely important that the treatment approach be individualized.

Mania

Mania can be defined as a condition marked by a prominent and persistent feeling of elation or irritability, accompanied by a variety of characteristic signs and symptoms:

1. *Increased Activity*. The manic patient usually is extremely active physically and reports boundless energy. This physical hyperactivity is distinguished from the agitation that may be seen in depression by the purposeful nature of the manic's actions.

Manic individuals may also be unusually active in a variety of other ways. For example, they may join a number of clubs and organizations and spend their time making extensive and impractical plans for the future, often involving financial matters or career advancement. Increased sociability is another characteristic sign of mania. The manic person frequently will call old friends by long distance at odd hours of the day or night. He/she may give unsolicited advice to strangers, and in general acts in an intrusive, demanding, and domineering manner.

2. *Talkativeness.* Manic patients are nearly always more talkative than usual. Frequently they speak very rapidly or, even if their speech is at a normal rate, they may tend to keep on talking without making normal pauses; this is called pressure of speech. A person talking with a manic patient may find it very hard to make himself heard.

3. *Flight of Ideas.* This is the term used to express a manic's tendency in his conversation to jump from one topic to another. A logical connection between the various thoughts is usually apparent to the observer, in contrast to the idiosyncratic associations of schizophrenia. Puns and playful use of words are also common in mania. Manic patients are easily distracted by external stimuli and may change their topic of conversation based on random stimulation.

4. *Inflated Self-Esteem.* Manic patients frequently show evidence of inflated self-esteem, (grandiosity). They may believe that they have unusual abilities and can accomplish anything that they set their mind to.

5. *Decreased Need for Sleep.* Sleep disturbance in mania resembles that in depression, with decreased total sleep time and early morning awakening. In contrast to the depressed patient, however, the manic awakens feeling rested and full of energy.

6. *Poor Judgment and Lack of Insight.* Manic individuals frequently become involved in activities without recognizing their high potential for negative consequences. For example, during a manic episode a normally careful driver may drive 120 m.p.h. without thinking that he might become involved in an accident or be stopped by the police. Buying sprees, sexual indiscretions, and foolish business investments are common. The manic individual characteristically has no insight into the nature of the illness. Indeed, he/she does not usually recognize that there is anything wrong with him/her.

Additional features

As noted above, a manic patient's mood may be either euphoric or irritable. Although in some cases these moods are characteristic for the particular patient, in others the patient's mood may vary between euphoria and irritability depending on the situation. A manic may be elated when he is able to get his/her way, but become markedly angry when frustrated.

Manic patients may occasionally have hallucinations or delusions, especially paranoid or grandiose delusions. The content of the hallucinations is characteristically related to the elevated mood. For example, a manic may hear voices telling him that he/she has extraordinary powers and can save the world from destruction.

Relationship with depression

Most manic patients have a history of clear-cut episodes of depression. Manic episodes are also frequently preceded and/or followed by brief mild depressive mood swings. Transitory periods of depressive mood, lasting for hours or even days, may occur during the course of the manic episode itself. Mixed states may also be seen; for example, an individual may show pressured speech and grandiose ideas along with depressed mood and suicidal ideation.

The coexistence and temporal proximity of symptoms of depression and mania suggest that the traditional view of mania as the mirror image or polar opposite of depression is inaccurate. Not only do symptoms of depression and mania frequently coexist in the same individual, but there is also evidence that similar physiological and biochemical changes may be seen in mania and in depres-

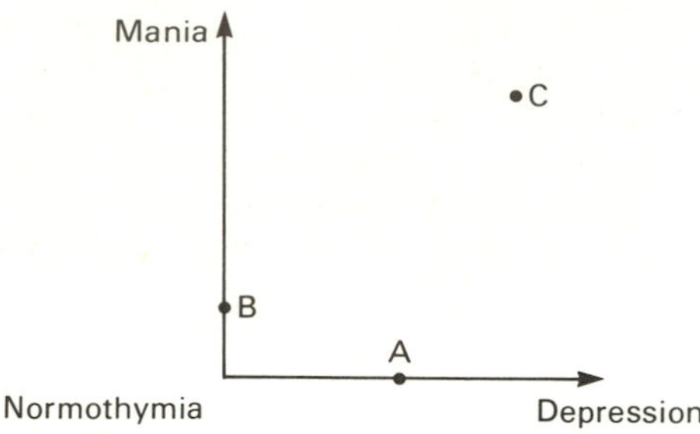

Fig. 9.1. Relationship between mania and depression. A represents moderate depression with no mania. B represents mild hypomania and no depression. C represents severe depression *and* severe mania.

sion, particularly bipolar depression. There is, in addition, good evidence that lithium carbonate is effective in the treatment of some episodes of depression, as well as manic episodes. These and other findings suggest that mania and depression might more usefully be conceptualized as shown in Figure 9.1, in which depression is the abscissa and mania the ordinate. In this view an individual with bipolar affective disorder may be anywhere within the quadrant. For example, in Figure 9.1 at A the patient is moderately depressed with no admixture of manic symptoms, while at B she is mildly hypomanic but without depression. At C she is severely ill, suffering from a mixed syndrome with features of both states. From this model it is clear that the signs and symptoms usually associated with depression or mania may occur together in a wide range of combinations.

Classification of mania

Little attempt has been made so far to distinguish among different individuals with mania, as has been done in the case of depression. It is generally assumed that mania is an endogenous or a biological illness, in that individuals with this disorder respond well to somatic treatments and usually have a family history of affective disorder. Some individuals, particularly those over 40, do not, however, have a family history of depression or mania. Taylor and Abrams (1973) have suggested that these individuals may, in fact, be suffering from a different disorder.

Hypomania is a term frequently used to describe a less severe episode of mania. The distinction between mania and hypomania is often subjective.

Treatment

The key to treatment of the manic patient is to obtain his/her cooperation. This may require considerable effort and skill, since manic individuals traditionally deny that there is anything wrong with them. Hospitalization is often useful, not only for the markedly manic patient, but also for the hypomanic individual, whose lack of judgment may lead to considerable difficulties for the patient and the patient's family.

Manic patients, with their hyperactivity and lack of insight, are poor candidates for psychotherapy, at least during the manic episode itself. Fortunately, mania generally shows an excellent response to somatic treatments. The introduction of ECT marked a major advance in the treatment of mania. Prior to its development it was not uncommon for manic individuals to die from overexertion and dehydration. The subsequent development of the neuroleptic drugs and lithium carbonate, however, has made the use of ECT rarely necessary today. Neuroleptic agents—used primarily to treat schizophrenia—are also an effective treatment for mania, but the manic patient often complains of feeling sluggish. Lithium carbonate is the treatment of choice in mania. It is effective in about 80 percent of manic patients and is well tolerated. Approximately 7 to 10 days after the institution of lithium therapy, the manic patient's behavior and mood tend to rapidly return to normal. Because of this lag period, most clinicians recommend using neuroleptics along with lithium initially. As the lithium begins to work, the dosage of neuroleptics is gradually decreased and finally discontinued. Neuroleptics are effective in most cases that do not respond to lithium.

Summary

While we have learned a great deal in recent years about the affective disorders, there remains much that we still do not understand—about predisposition, causes, treatment, and prevention. Only through combined study of psychological, social, and biological factors and their interrelationships are we likely to arrive at a comprehensive understanding of the nature of these troubling disorders.

GLOSSARY

Affect: Emotional feeling and the outward manifestations of that feeling. Frequently used interchangeably with "mood," "emotion," and "feeling."

Affective disorder: A disorder marked by a persistent abnormality of mood and associated with a variety of other characteristic signs and symptoms.

Agitation: A subjective feeling of anxiety or tension accompanied by physical restlessness or hyperactivity.

Anhedonia: Inability to experience pleasure.

Bipolar affective disorder (bipolar illness): A disorder marked by episodes of both mania and depression. An episode of depression occurring in a person with this disorder is referred to as a bipolar depression.

Cyclothymic personality: A chronic condition, marked by periods of mild elation and mild depression. Probably a variant of bipolar affective disorder.

Depression: Used in this chapter principally to refer to:

1. A feeling of persistent sadness that is abnormal in terms of its inappropriateness to the situation, its duration, its intensity and its interference with normal living;
2. A disorder marked by abnormally lowered mood and/or a loss of interest in usual activities and accompanied by a variety of characteristic signs and symptoms.

Endogenous depression: A depression characterized by the presence of certain largely somatic signs and symptoms: poor appetite, weight loss, constipation, early morning awakening, self-blame, and depressed mood that is worse in the morning but nonreactive to environmental events. Also used to refer to a depressive episode that was not precipitated by life stress.

Flight of ideas: Rapid shifts in conversation or thought from one topic to another related topic.

Grandiosity: Inflated self-esteem, which may be delusional.

Hypomania: Less severe form of mania.

Involutional melancholia: A depression occurring in the involutional period (approximately 45 to 55 years of age in women and 50 to 60 years in men) that is marked by agitation, guilt, and hypochondriacal concerns.

Mania: A disorder marked by a persistent feeling of euphoria or irritability, accompanied by a variety of characteristic signs and symptoms.

Manic-depressive illness (manic-depressive psychosis): A term used by Kraepelin to refer to most types of affective disorder. Others have used it synonymously with bipolar affective disorder or to refer to both unipolar and bipolar disorders together.

Masked depression: A depression in which the presenting complaint is of a physical nature rather than a disturbance in mood. Depression may also be masked by other kinds of emotional and behavior problems, especially in children.

Neurotic depression (depressive neurosis):

1. A depression in which reality testing is intact;
2. A relatively mild depression;
3. A depression characterized by intrapsychic (neurotic) conflict;
4. A depression precipitated by an environmental stress;
5. A depression that is *not* characterized by the signs and symptoms of endogenous depression;

Pressure of speech: Used to describe speech in which normal pauses are lacking.

Primary depression: An episode of depression that occurs in a patient who has never had a nonaffective mental disorder. (He or she may have had a prior episode of mania or depression.)

Psychomotor retardation: A condition in which

thinking, speech, and physical activity are slowed down.

Psychotic depression: A depression characterized by disordered reality testing; this is usually manifested by hallucinations or delusions. Also sometimes used to indicate any severe episode of depressive illness or as a synonym for "endogenous depression."

Reactive depression: A depression in which the low mood fluctuates in response to changes in the environment. Also used to describe a depression that was precipitated by an environmental event.

Secondary depression: An episode of depression that was preceded at some time in the patient's life by a nonaffective mental disorder.

Unipolar depression: A disorder marked by the occurrence of one or more depressions, without the occurrence of mania or hypomania.

PSYCHOPHYSIOLOGICAL DISORDERS

DAVID SHAPIRO
EDWARD S. KATKIN

Psychophysiological disorders, sometimes referred to as psychosomatic disorders, present great conceptual challenges to psychology and medicine. Understanding them requires attention to behavioral, biological, and social determinants of illness. Indeed, after decades of research, there is still considerable disagreement concerning their proper definition (Lipowski, 1977b). Some investigators feel that all medical diseases are influenced by behavioral and social factors, whether the common cold or cancer. Others claim that there is no such thing as psychophysiological disorders and that the term is simply based on ignorance of their biological causation. Our purpose in this chapter will be to give an overview of the current state of knowledge concerning psychophysiological disorders, to evaluate the extent to which psychological and behavioral factors play a role in their development, maintenance, and alleviation, and then describe some strategies of research for their investigation. Let us begin with a consideration of a general definition.

Definition

The *Diagnostic and Statistical Manual of Mental Disorders* (2nd ed. DSM-II) of the American Psychiatric Association defines psychophysiological disorders as those "characterized by physical symptoms that are caused by emotional factors and involve a single organ system, usually under autonomic nervous system innervation" (1968, p. 46). There are three aspects of this definition that deserve close scrutiny: first, psychophysiological disorders manifest *physical symptoms;* second, they are presumed to involve a *single organ system;* and third, they usually, but not always, occur in organ systems under the control of the *autonomic nervous system.*

The definition states that in order to be considered a psychophysiological disorder, the symptoms reported by the patient must involve actual changes in the structure or function of the affected organ system. Thus, these disorders are quite different in character from conversion reactions or hysterical syndromes, discussed elsewhere in this book. Conversion reactions do not involve obvious structural or functional changes in organs or organ systems, but are more akin to "imaginary" ailments. Psychophysiological disorders are most decidedly not imaginary and can even be life-threatening.

The definition states that a psychophysiological disorder affects a single organ system, such as the cardiovascular system or the gastrointestinal system. Inasmuch as more than one system in a given patient may be affected, by definition the patient could be said to suffer from more than one disorder. A psychophysiological disorder of the skin, for instance, is not expected to "spread" to the heart or the lungs. The importance of this distinction will become apparent later in the chapter when we discuss some mechanisms involved in the development of these disorders. Thus, one explanatory model takes as its point of departure the observation that psychophysiological disorders usually affect one organ system only (Engel, 1972). Another conception emphasizes the more general effects of stress in all bodily systems (see Hinkle, 1977).

The definition states that psychophysiological disorders usually affect organ systems under the control of the autonomic nervous system. The autonomic nervous system is that division of the peripheral nervous system that regulates the function of smooth muscles, cardiac muscle, blood vessels, and glands. Organs and functions regulated by the autonomic nervous system are generally described as being free of conscious control. Try to instruct your kidneys to decrease the rate at which they are forming urine, or try to direct your heart to beat at precisely 85 beats per minute. You may realize that you do not, in fact, have much direct control of these major life functions of your body, for, in the natural state, these functions are virtually autonomous. For that reason the organ systems that function in this manner are said to be autonomically innervated or under the control of the autonomic nervous system. In most, but not all, cases, such autonomically innervated organs are the sites of psychophysiological symptoms. As we shall see later, the potential for self-regulation of various internal bodily responses can be enhanced through various means such as biofeedback, suggestion, or meditation.

Variety of psychophysiological disorders

The American Psychiatric Association officially recognizes nine categories of psychophysiological disorders, but bear in mind that these categories are controversial. Some investigators believe that the list is overly restrictive, while others believe that it is unnecessarily broad. Nevertheless, the list gives us an idea of the wide range of disorders considered to be psychophysiological in nature, and it makes an excellent starting point for a presentation of important issues.

1. *Psychophysiological skin disorders.* This group includes neurodermatitis (an inflammation of the skin presumed to be a result of emotional stress, hyperhydrosis or excessive sweating, nonspecific rashes, and eczema.
2. *Psychophysiological respiratory disorders.* This category contains bronchial asthma (nonallergic), hyperventilation (overbreathing), and chronic hiccups (a rare but debilitating disorder).
3. *Psychophysiological cardiovascular disorders.* Essential hypertension (high blood pressure), cardiac rate disorders, and migraine headaches (caused by cerebral vascular changes) are included in this category.
4. *Psychophysiological hemic (blood) and lymphatic disorders.* This refers to emotionally caused changes in the functioning of the blood and lymph systems.
5. *Psychophysiological gastrointestinal disorders.* This category includes ulcers, gastritis, colitis, and various forms of chronic indigestion.
6. *Psychophysiological genital-urinary disorders.* These include sexual dysfunction, menstrual disorders, and urinary dysfunction of emotional origin.
7. *Psychophysiological endocrine disorders.* These are disorders of endocrine or ductless glands that are integrally related to proper functioning of the autonomic nervous system (e.g., adrenals, pituitary, and gonads).
8. *Psychophysiological disorders of a sense organ.* Some cases of retinal disease and occasional inner ear problems are thought to be psychological in origin.

9. *Psychophysiological musculoskeletal disorders.* Tension headaches, muscle cramps, and low back pains are most prominent among this group.

Note that the last category is not consistent with the DSM-II definition, for the musculoskeletal system is not under the control of the autonomic nervous system. Moreover, there is little evidence to support the classifications of psychophysiological hemic, lymphatic, endocrine, and sense organ disorders, and the diagnosis of such disorders as psychophysiological in origin is rare. Of the remaining categories, most attention has focused on the study of cardiovascular, gastrointestinal, and respiratory disorders. In fact, so much popular attention has been given to these three areas that it is commonly accepted by the layman that high blood pressure, ulcers, and asthma are disorders that are actually caused by stress or emotionality. The next section will deal with the role of psychological factors in psychophysiological disorders, examining some relationships of these disorders to personality, learning, cognition, life stress, and sociocultural factors.

Psychological factors

It is frequently the case in medical diagnosis that a syndrome is identified by a process of elimination. That is, when a physician is presented with a set of symptoms that could be caused by a variety of factors, he or she proceeds systematically to try to rule out each possible cause by performing some specific test. The cause that cannot be ruled out is often labeled as the basis of the symptoms. Sometimes the physician can apply a direct test to identify positively the specific underlying cause of the symptom, but there remain a number of diseases for which clear cut positive tests do not exist. Virtually all psychophysiological disorders are in that category, and proper diagnosis invariably requires ruling out specific physiological bases. For example, a patient with excessively high blood pressure may be manifesting the symptom because of a narrowing of arteries in the kidney, narrowing of the aorta (the major artery leaving the heart), tumors of the adrenal glands, or other specific physical changes (Freis, 1974).

If the physician can find evidence for the existence of one of these forms of so-called curable hypertension, then he labels the high blood pressure a *secondary* phenomenon. However, if renal, blood vessel, or adrenal gland abnormalities can be completely ruled out, the physician, finding no "specific disease," labels the hypertension as *primary,* or essential, inferring either that the disease is caused by psychological factors or that the cause is unknown. Thus, in virtually all cases, the psychological basis of a disorder is inferred from the absence of specific observable physical causes. This fact leads to two alternative approaches to conceptualization of and research on psychophysiological disorders. One strategy assumes that there are always specific and sufficient biological causes. It attempts to find them and thereby ultimately eliminate the category of psychophysiological disorders from medical dictionaries. A second strategy is to pursue research that will enable positive identification of psychological causes or correlates of physical symptoms manifested in psychophysiological disorders. To be sure, the latter strategy has been quite popular and has led to a variety of approaches ranging from psychodynamic methods to the evaluation of the effects of life stress and cultural processes on disease. A number of these approaches will be discussed below.

To a large extent, these two strategies represent the polarities of mind and body or psyche and soma. A third, more sophisticated and more demanding strategy involves the search for explanatory mechanisms that directly link environmental and behavioral processes with biological processes. Psychophysiological researchers have proposed certain concepts and methods that may provide an effective scientific framework for examining their interaction. A discussion of this viewpoint will follow the presentation of psychological factors.

Personality and individual difference factors

The study of personality factors in psychophysiological disorders has been dominated by psychoanalytic approaches that lean heavily on the notion that each syndrome results from a specific unconscious emotional conflict. The foremost proponent of the analytic view is Franz Alexander (Alexander, 1950; Alexander, French, & Pollock, 1968). Briefly, Alexander's theory suggests that current conflicts are related to unconscious symbolic conflicts associated with earlier stages of psychosexual development, and that these earlier stages are associated with specific organ systems that develop symptoms when the conflict cannot be satisfactorily resolved. For example, if a patient feels a strong need to ask for help, but has developed defenses that make him unable to do so, this situation is likely to trigger unconscious experiences of early infancy in which the patient may have wanted to cry for mother, but stifled the cry. This stifling of the cry, according to the analytic view, may be expressed in adulthood in the form of wheezing, and constitutes the psychological basis for asthma.

Similarly, an inability to express hostile feelings may lead to a damming up of emotion, which is symbolic of the inability of the child to aggress against the powerful parent. According to the analytic view, such damming up of feeling may lead to generalized bodily increases in tension, reflected in systematic increases in blood pressure.

The development of the analytic approach to psychophysiological disorders is based upon speculations about early childhood experiences that cannot be readily examined in a neat, scientific manner. Consequently, like so many other psychoanalytic approaches, the validation of the theory rests upon some degree of uncontrolled reporting of clinical patients, and some degree of blind faith. For these reasons, other approaches to personality assessment have been developed.

Among the more empirical approaches to the assessment of personality is the use of psychological tests administered to patients suffering from various psychophysiological disorders and to control groups for comparison. The objective is to determine specific measurable personality factors that might differentiate different disorders. For example, the "hypertensive personality" has been described as marked by a "characteristic inability to express anger . . . and indeed at times by an obsequious type of behavior as a retreat from potentially hostile expression" (Shapiro, Redmond, McDonald, & Gaylor, 1975, p. 300). Can this pattern be objectified in self-rating scales or projective tests?

Although many studies have found factors in the Rorschach test or the Minnesota Multiphasic Personality Inventory that can differentiate patient groups from normal controls, the results have had very little serious impact because of two major problems. First, the findings have been relatively vague, suggesting only that patients are more disturbed or neurotic than normals; and second, the studies cannot determine if the "neurosis" found among patients is the cause or the result of the psychophysiological disorder. The personality pattern of hypertensive patients may stem from their physiological hyperreactivity rather than the hyperreactivity arising from their personality (Shapiro et al., 1975). Such patients may try to behave in a certain characteristic fashion so as to deliberately avoid excessive physiological response. Would similar personality profiles be found in other groups of clinically ill patients who do not have high blood pressure? Proper delineation would also require comparisons with control groups that are emotionally disturbed but do not have psychophysiological symptoms (Davison & Neale, 1974).

Although research on personality correlates of specific syndromes has failed to come up with reliable or easily interpretable findings, there has been a recent surge of interest in a behavior pattern that may be associated with heart diseases. This pattern, designated Type A by its discoverers (Friedman, 1969; Friedman & Rosenman, 1959, 1974), is characterized by intense competitive striving for achievement, a pervasive sense of time urgency, and an easily elicited trait of aggressiveness. The Type A pattern, according to its observers, is not a chronic manifestation; rather, it represents a constellation of behaviors that may be evoked by challenging situations. Empirical research on the Type A personality has been facilitated by the development of an objective scale of measurement (Jenkins, Zyzanski, & Rosenman, 1971). Although the data are not entirely clear, it appears from early findings that men who are diagnosed as having the Type A behavior pattern are twice as likely to develop coronary heart disease than a similar group of men diagnosed as having Type B, which is the polar opposite type with respect to achievement motivation, time urgency, and hostile responsiveness.

Conditioning and learning

Generally speaking, the conditioning and learning approach to psychophysiological disorders takes as its point of departure the idea that the symptom has been learned through some process of reinforcement, either of the classical or of the instrumental conditioning type. Until the 1960s, most theories of autonomic learning leaned heavily upon the Pavlovian or classical conditioning model, because it was widely believed that autonomic functions could not be learned through instrumental conditioning (Katkin & Murray, 1968). Recent research, however, has demonstrated that instrumental autonomic learning is a bona fide phenomenon, although it remains unclear whether the laboratory demonstrations can be carried over effectively into clinical practice (Katkin, Fitzgerald, & Shapiro, 1978).

Pavlovian conditioning. The basis of the Pavlovian approach to psychophysiological disorders rests upon the assumption that the patient must first show a biologically invariant symptomatic response to an environmental stimulus, the unconditional stimulus. Through repeated associations of this unconditional stimulus with a "neutral" stimulus, the neutral stimulus becomes capable of eliciting the symptomatic response. A specific example of this notion may serve to clarify the phenomenon. Suppose that a child has a biologically determined severe allergic response to roses, such that he or she experiences bronchospasms in their presence, and shows a genuine asthma response when so exposed. Suppose further that before this allergy was discovered, the child was visited regularly by a relative who always brought roses, and thus always caused the child to suffer an attack. Pavlovian theory suggests that the relative becomes a conditional stimulus in a classical conditioning paradigm; the relative is paired with the roses and eventually comes to elicit an asthma attack, with or without the roses.

Attempts to demonstrate classical conditioning of asthmatic reactions have generally resulted in failure (Dekker, Pelse, & Groen, 1957; Purcell & Weiss, 1970). Recently, however, Hill (1975) showed that motion picture films of allergic substances were capable of eliciting bronchoconstriction among allergic children. His experiment is impressive, in that the children were exposed randomly to films of all the substances to which they were collectively allergic, but each child showed bronchoconstriction only to the film of the specific substance to which he was allergic.

Aside from this, there have been few positive demonstrations of specific conditioning of a psychophysiological symptom. Instead, as they attempt to develop a clearer understanding of the basic psychophysiological mechanisms underlying autonomic learning, researchers have devoted their energies almost entirely to basic demonstrations of the conditionability of nonpathological autonomic responses.

Although it has been known since Pavlov's early demonstrations that autonomic responses can be conditioned, serious flaws persist in the Pavlovian model of symptom formation. As was described earlier, this model requires that the patients who develop symptoms in response to neutral stimuli (such as relatives or other persons) must have had a preexisting biologically determined unconditional response to some substance. This model, therefore, does not explain the cases of asthma that occur among people with no clear allergic response; nor does it deal adequately with the wide array of syndromes that do not necessarily show specific stimulus-response relationships. Furthermore, the Pavlovian model implies that a learned symptom should be extinguishable; yet, there are no good experimental demonstrations of the successful extinction of a psychophysiological disorder through Pavlovian procedures.

The failure of the strict Pavlovian model has generated considerable effort within the behaviorally-oriented research establishment to develop more comprehensive learning theoretical approaches to the understanding of symptom development and symptom alleviation. Two prominent recent developments have been Lachman's (1972) automatic learning theory, and the operant or biofeedback model of psychophysiological disorder.

Lachman's autonomic learning theory. Lachman has developed an approach to psychophysiological disorders that is based upon behavioral learning theory, but retains a focus on biological predisposing factors. The basic feature of Lachman's theory is the assertion that there are certain "original" or "native" stimuli that invariably elicit emotional behavior, and that the elicited emotional behavior consists of both overt, observable patterns and covert, implicit changes in visceral functions, such as heart rate and blood pressure. Through a process of stimulus substitution, or classical conditioning, new cues become conditioned to serve as effective elicitors of the overt and covert components of the emotional response. A second tenet of Lachman's theory is that the visceral component of the elicited emotional patterns is characterized by resistance to extinction. In other words, repetition of certain eliciting stimuli will continually elicit the visceral responses, with no sign of habituation or, in Pavlovian terms, extinction. Lachman's third premise is that the overt elements of the emotional behavior are more easily controlled than the covert elements. Thus, the patient may appear to have learned to control irrational emotional responses, but nevertheless remains reactive at the visceral level. According to Lachman, "Emotional behavior—intense internal reactions that initially in the history of the organism are aroused via receptor stimulation—may lead to conditions of chronic physiological activation or may produce more or less permanent structural changes—psychosomatic manifestations" (1972, p. 65).

In addition to this description of the development of "emotional-stimulus learning," Lachman has discussed the concept of "autonomic response learning," introducing important concepts of operant or instrumental conditioning to his model. Autonomic response learning, according to Lachman, implies that specific autonomic responses are selectively learned on the basis of differential reward or reinforcement. He gives the example of a child who may complain of gastrointestinal pain and be "rewarded" with permission to skip school, plus an abundance of nurturance. Theoretically such rewards may lead to an increased probability of increased gastric acid levels resulting in more frequent belly aches. This aspect of Lachman's autonomic learning theory provides a bridge to the next area of discussion, the role of instrumental conditioning in the development of psychophysiological disorders.

Instrumental learning. The operant approach to psychophysiological disorders has become much more popular during the past few years because of the proliferation of basic research in the general area of biofeedback, or instrumental autonomic conditioning (Katkin & Murray, 1968; Shapiro & Surwit, 1974). Basically, the operant view of these disorders states that a symptom may be reinforced if its expression is consistently instrumental in obtaining reinforcement. Historically, an operant conceptualization such as this was ignored because of the widely held belief that autonomically mediated responses could not be conditioned in the operant manner (Skinner, 1938). During the 1960s, however, a number of laboratories began to demonstrate that autonomically mediated responses could be conditioned instrumentally (Kimmel & Kimmel, 1963; Miller, 1969; Shapiro, Crider, & Tursky, 1964). These and other demonstrations led to the development of biofeedback, a technique that uses instrumentation to provide a person with immediate and continuing signals concerning bodily functions of which that person is not normally aware.

Miller (1975) pointed out that learning to control visceral responses may be likened to learning to shoot a basketball. Whereas muscles used to shoot baskets provide the learner with immediate and usable feedback, the smooth muscles, glands, and blood vessels that are the typical target organs for psychophysiological disorders do not provide readily usable feedback. With electronic interfaces, such feedback can be obtained, and the learner can use it to modify previously uncontrollable functions, according to the same principles used to increase one's field goal percentage. These principles were applied first to the regulation of autonomic functions in normal subjects, and later to the regulation of pathological autonomic functions in patients suffering from psychophysiological disorders (see Katkin, Fitzgerald, & Shapiro, 1978; Shapiro & Surwit, 1976).

A discussion of the use of biofeedback for the treatment of psychophysiological disorders will be presented later in this chapter. One consequence of this research effort was the concurrent evolution of a model of etiology of psychophysiological disorders based upon instrumental learning. From the numerous studies demonstrating that autonomic functions could be modified instrumentally, there emerged a growing interest in the idea that psychophysiological symptoms may be developed through a process of instrumental learning. In a series of investigations carried out on baboons, Harris and his colleagues (Harris & Brady, 1977; Harris, Findley, & Brady, 1971; Harris, Goldstein, & Brady, 1977) have demonstrated that baboons can learn to elevate their blood pressure in order to avoid shocks or receive food: "Large magnitude elevations in diastolic blood pressure, 50 to 60 mmHg above resting levels, could be generated under conditions which made shock-avoidance and food-acquisition contingent upon the required pressure elevations. Furthermore, these experiments confirmed that such instrumentally-conditioned circulatory changes could be brought under explicit exteroceptive environmental stimulus control and that they could be produced on a relatively acute basis (i.e., intervals up to 5 minutes in duration) seventy or more times each day over the extended course of these initial studies" (Harris, Goldstein, & Brady, 1977, p. 206).

Studies such as these form the empirical basis for a growing interest in the idea that psychophysiological symptoms may be instrumentally learned patterns of autonomic response. If such a model is to be fruitful in the future, careful research will be required to discover the nature of effective reinforcers and the extent to which there are response-reinforcement specificities that can be identified and then interrupted by preventive intervention.

Attitudes and cognitive processes

The idea that specific attitudes play a role in psychophysiological disorders derives from basic psychophysiological research indicating that cognitive processes have an influence on physiological functioning. A hypothesis has been proposed that a specific attitude characterizes all individuals with a particular psychophysiological disorder and that each disorder is characterized by a different attitude. This hypothesis was developed and tested in numerous ways by David Graham and his associates in research summarized extensively by Graham in 1972. Delineation of the specific attitudes evolved originally out of interviews with patients in different diagnostic categories. An attitude was defined as a statement containing two elements: (a) what the person feels is happening to him, (b) what the person wishes to do about it. Some selected examples are taken from Graham (1972).

1. Urticaria (hives): felt he was taking a beating and was helpless to do anything about it.
2. Ulcerative colitis: felt he was being injured and degraded and wished he could get rid of the responsible agent.
3. Asthma and rhinitis: felt left out in the cold and wanted to shut the person or situation out.
4. Duodenal ulcer: felt deprived of what was due him and wanted to get even.
5. Essential hypertension: felt threatened with harm and had to be ready for anything.
6. Migraine: felt something had to be achieved and then relaxed after the effort.
7. Raynaud's disease: wanted to take hostile gross motor action.
8. Low backache: wanted to run away.

The "specificity-of-attitude hypothesis" was also tested experimentally in a number of ingenious experiments. Using hypnosis procedures, certain of the above specific attitudes were suggested to subjects to see whether physiological changes associated with the particular disorder could be elicited in this way. By and large, the resulting evidence supports the theory. For example, suggesting the Raynaud's attitude resulted in a decrease in skin temperature; suggesting the hives attitude resulted in an increase in skin temperature; suggesting the hypertension attitude resulted in a rise in blood pressure. Similar suggestions to nonhypnotized subjects also yielded evidence in support of the theory. It is even more significant that physiological changes unrelated to the particular illness did not change in the same direction as did the predicted physiological response associated with the symptom.

In many respects, this research on specific attitudes has been unique in suggesting a specific link between cognitive and physiological processes in disease. However, the research is not without methodological difficulties, such as in the selection, definition, and assessment of the appropriate attitudes and in the determination of specific physiological consequences of such attitudes. Moreover, we do not have as yet a good notion about the physiological pathways through which specific attitudes are transformed into specific physiological responses and symptoms.

Life stress and sociocultural factors

The concept of stress is one of the most overworked terms in the study of psychophysiological disorders. It has been used to refer to the stimuli or events that are the presumed source of maladaptive behavioral and physiological reactions as well as to the specific and nonspecific effects of the stimuli on the individual.

It is difficult to catalogue the large variety of stimuli or events that can elicit or trigger excessive reactions. One can point to stimuli or events involving pain, punishment, demanding mental effort, sustained work, or behaviors requiring continuous adjustments. However, even relatively commonplace behaviors such as exercise, postural change, feeding, and sexual activity can have a potent influence on cardiovascular and other functions (Cohen & Obrist, 1975). More complex reactions of the individual, labelled "integrated behavioral patterns" (Cohen & Obrist, 1975), have also been singled out for study. These are the "defense reaction," a pattern involving "fright, flight, and fight" occurring in reaction to noxious and life-threatening events, and a pattern characterized by motivated sensory intake behavior or heightened attention or vigilance on the part of the individual.

Clearly, it is difficult to separate out the stimulus from the response components in these conceptions of stress. We are also not able to establish for sure which maladaptive reactions of the individual are linked specifically to which eliciting events. More importantly, noxious environmental events may not inherently determine adverse reactions. Rather, the outcome often depends upon other factors, namely how the person perceives the source of the stress, and how the person sees his own capacity to cope with the stress. Lazarus (1977) has advanced the concept of *cognitive appraisal* to characterize the psychological context of the emotion arising from adaptive transactions between the individual and the environment. Cognitive appraisal "expresses the evaluation of the significance of a transaction for the person's well-being and the potentials for mastery in the continuous and constantly changing interplay between the person and the environmental stimulus configuration" (Lazarus, 1977, p. 15).

At the level of the individual or of the social group, numerous writers and investigators have attempted to examine these complex interactions as they may occur in psychophysiological disorders (Hinkle, 1977; Lazarus, 1977). For example, Moos (1977) proposed that measurement of the "perceived social climate" is a promising way of investigating the effects of particular social settings. He differentiates three sets of factors that distinguish different social and environmental settings: relationship dimensions, personal development dimensions, and system maintenance and system change dimensions. Relationship dimensions mean whether people like one another and care about one another; personal development means whether people take on roles of leadership and responsibility in groups in carrying out required tasks and organization activities; system maintenance and change means work pressure, time pressure, stability of the organization's goals, and the like. Moos speculates that perceived social climate may relate to physiological activation and possibly to the genesis of psychophysiological disorders. He speculates that social environments can be made "healthier," for example, by improving the fit between individual and group characteristics.

The family itself has been taken as a model of a social system that may lead to the development or maintenance of psychophysiological disorders. Minuchin, Baker, Rosman, Liebman, Milman, and Todd (1975) describe three conditions considered necessary to produce such disorders in general: 1. a certain type of family organization that encourages somatization (somatization means a tendency to focus on and form physiological symptoms); 2. involvement of the child in parental conflict; and 3. physiological vulnerability. The authors postulate that the family as a social system may actually "trigger the onset or hamper the subsidence of psychophysiologic processes," and the resulting psychosomatic symptoms may be reinforced as a means of regulating family interactions. To put it in simpler terms, a sick child may be used by the family in different ways as a means of preserving or protecting itself, avoiding conflict, pitting one subunit against another (parent with child against the other parent), or maintaining status quo and avoiding conflict resolution.

Perhaps the simplest and most direct approach to the study of life stress and its effects is offered by epidemiology. Epidemiology is the study of distribution of disease frequency, according to various environmental, social, and other characteristics (Eastwood, 1977). Rahe's (1977) study of *recent life change* has been among the most productive in this area. This research has employed two questionnaires as a means of investigating how life stress is correlated with disease frequency. The first is the *Social Readjustment Rating Questionnaire,* which attempts to scale the significance of life events in terms of their intensity and the length of time necessary to readjust to them. The second is the *Schedule of Recent Experience,* which gathers data on actual recent life changes in such categories as health, work, home and family, personal-social, and financial events. The life change questions were revised into a recent questionnaire called the *Recent Life Changes Questionnaire.* Individual subjects may be requested to rate the degree to which their life changes involved readjustment on their part.

Using these methods, a large number of studies have shown clear relationships between life change units and various diseases, including psychophysiological disorders as well as other diseases. Increases in life change often precede illnesses and, the more the change, the more severe the illness. For example, Rahe (1977) has summarized a number of studies showing that recent increases in life change are correlated significantly with myocardial infarction and sudden death from coronary heart disease. Similar conclusions may be drawn from earlier anecdotal accounts of the role of stressful life circumstances in disease (see Eastwood, 1977) and from numerous social-cultural correlational studies (see Gutmann & Benson, 1971).

Significant life change events, by the way, are not limited to those that we would think of as negative or aversive in and of themselves. In the personal-social area, for example, "engagement to marry" or a "vacation" may be as potent as "sexual difficulties" or "legal troubles resulting in your being held in jail." The critical factor is that the event necessitates a major readjustment in life pattern and behavior on the part of the individual.

We have reviewed several major areas of investigation of psychological factors and mechanisms involved in the development of psychophysiological disorders. It should be obvious that, in our present state of knowledge, we can only point out the various psychological processes that appear to play a significant role. In any given disease or person, the particular interplay of forces cannot be specified with any degree of certainty. In the next section, we will try to sketch out a few psychophysiological concepts that may be useful in examining the interaction of the various factors. To complicate matters, many other processes presumably come into play in determining the pathogenesis of a particular disease, e.g., genetic and constitutional factors, diet, physical aspects of the environment (air, water quality), particular individual susceptibilities and vulnerabilities. Many of these may in turn be affected by psychosocial processes and life style.

Psychophysiological models

Psychophysiology is a field of basic research concerned with relationships between psychological and physiological aspects of behavior. "Psychophysiology is a research area which extends observation of behavior to those covert proceedings of the organism relevant to a psychic state or process under investigation and which can be measured with minimal disturbance to the natural functions involved" (Ax, 1964, p. 1). Because of its theoretical emphasis and experimental orientation, psychophysiology may be considered a basic science of psychosomatic or psychophysiological medicine, although it must be obvious that a whole gamut of basic disciplines contribute greatly to this complex field of basic investigation and clinical research (e.g., general, clinical, social, and experimental psychology, general physiology and neurophysiology, pharmacology, biochemistry, epidemiology, and sociology, in addition to various fields of medicine such as psychiatry, internal medicine, and physical medicine) (Lipowski, 1977a).

Several basic concepts have been proposed in psychophysiology that involve the phenomena of psychophysiological disorders. First is the concept of *stimulus-response specificity,* which means that "a given stimulus consistently evokes the same pattern or hierarchy of physiological responses (sometimes referred to as stereotypy) among most subjects" (Roessler & Engel, 1977, p. 51). An example of stimulus-response specificity is the increase in blood pressure, which follows immersion of the hand in ice water.

A second type of specificity is called *individual response specificity,* which accounts for "idiosyncratic" responses of the group under study. Engel (1972) gives the following example: A group of hypertensive patients showed more blood pressure reactions to *all* stimuli than did patients with rheumatoid arthritis. The latter showed more reactions in muscles surrounding symptomatic joints. This type of specificity is also referred to as "symptom specificity." Both stimulus-response specificity and individual response specificity are involved in psychophysiological disorders, although it is obvious that individual response specificities are critical. To the extent that susceptibility to a particular disease may be related to the tendency to overreact in one given physiological modality related to that disease, then we can explain the adverse consequences of environmental pressure and stress for the development of specific disorders (see Ader, 1977).

Examples exist for such individual response specificity in psychophysiological disorders, although more comprehensive data are needed to define the role of individual susceptibilities in disease in interaction with stimulus response specificity as well as other factors such as prior experience and learning, cognitive appraisals and attitudes, and other individual differences (Roessler & Engel, 1977).

A step in this direction has been taken by Miller and Dworkin (1977). They distinguish between physiological symptoms that are primarily learned through social reinforcement, such as the "secondary gains" of attention and sympathy of others, and symptoms that are primarily organic in nature. Miller and Dworkin also point out that the fact that the symptom is primarily organic does not mean that a particular *behavioral* response cannot be learned that will control its recurrence or frequency. For instance, learned alterations in breathing or heart rate can alter the frequency of organically caused premature ventricular contractions (described as the heart skipping a beat).

Miller and Dworkin (1977) have advanced a psychophysiological hypothesis about the reinforcement of increases in blood pressure in essential hypertension. Their theory is based on two pieces of psychophysiological evidence. First, it has been shown that baroreceptor stimulation has an inhibitory effect on the reticular formation and therefore on cortical arousal. The baroreceptors are pressure sensitive nerves in major blood vessels, such as the carotid artery, that are stimulated by alterations in blood pressure and heart rate. Second, animal experiments show that large increases in blood pressure can be learned by instrumental conditioning. That is, animals (such as baboons) will learn to increase their blood pressure if such an increase results in a reward or the avoidance of noxious stimulation. Taking these two facts together, Miller and Dworkin hypothesized, "in a situation in which a person is suffering from aversive stimulation, an increase in blood pressure will stimulate the carotid sinus and produce an inhibition of the reticular formation which, in turn, should decrease the strength of the aversiveness. Then this decrease in the strength of aversiveness should serve as a reward to reinforce the learning of the increase in blood pressure" (p. 139). This hypothesis has not been subject to test, although it has the virtue of being testable, particularly in animals. The proponents of this hypothesis point out that other ingredients in the individual need to be considered in relation to the hypothesized process: unusual sensitivity to aversive stimulation, unusually strong inhibition of the reticular formation from a given increase in blood pressure, and unusual ability to learn increases in blood pressure. They believe that the vulnerability to this process would be increased to the degree that the environment has subjected the individual to levels of aversive stimulation that can be reduced via inhibition of the reticular formation but not by other means.

Whether or not this particular hypothesis is confirmed, the thinking behind it is commendable in that it embodies a multiplicity of interacting physiological and psychological properties, each of which is cogent. It should stimulate further hypotheses about possible psychophysiological bases of other disorders.

Finally, we should call attention to another basic psychophysiological concept, that of general *activation* or *arousal*. Broadly defined, activation refers to a general state of the organism as reflected in the dimension of extreme alertness through drowsiness to sleep, and also as indicated by certain changes in the brain and central nervous system functions, somatomotor and autonomic nervous system phenomena, and gross behaviors. However, changes in the various processes are not always patterned in a consistent fashion (Kiely, 1977; Roessler & Engel, 1977). Inasmuch as general physiological activation may be involved in various psychophysiological disorders, it is important to consider such activation processes for their own sake. However, as we have already pointed out, various specificities (individual response, stimulus response) complicate the orderliness of the phenomena of activation.

One particular example can exemplify the possible usefulness of the activation concept. There is good evidence that the autonomic nervous system is specifically involved in some patients with borderline essential hypertension, although it is not clear whether the autonomic activation is primary or secondary to the disease (Julius & Esler, 1975; Julius & Schork, 1971). Some abnormality of the autonomic nervous system may predispose certain individuals who are otherwise susceptible to having increases in blood pressure to develop hypertension on a chronic basis. Increased sympathetic nervous system activity has been thought to be implicated in other disorders as well. By delineating the role of physiological activation of this sort in particular subgroups of patients, it may be possible to fashion behavioral therapies directed toward decreasing sympathetic nervous system tone: for example, by the use of relaxation, meditation, or biofeedback.

It should be clear from the above sections that we have many hypotheses about the psychological sources of psychophysiological disorders. The more we know about the etiology and pathogenesis of such disorders, the more rational we can be in fashioning methods of prevention and treatment. Unfortunately, the specificity of our knowledge is less than optimum so that our efforts at treatment are still relatively trial-and-error in nature. But a great deal of clinical medicine is no more empirical. Let us turn our attention to the various psychological methods devised to help people with psychophysiological disorders.

Prevention and treatment

Treatment of psychophysiological disorders is a highly complex and often confusing affair, owing to the complexity of the symptoms. Since the manifest symptoms of these disorders are physical, one frequent component of competent treatment involves the use of drugs. For example, hypertensives are given specific drugs that reduce blood pressure (e.g., vasodilators, autonomic nervous system blocking agents) and asthmatics are given bronchodilatory drugs. Yet, as we have seen, the disorders may involve psychological determinants, and it has become common to prescribe psychological treatment for them. Alternatively, the possibility that psychological methods may be used to gain control over symptoms, whatever their etiology, has also been suggested as another strategy.

The nature of psychologically oriented treatment is usually determined by the predisposing belief system of the physician prescribing it. Thus, if one believes that patterns of personality adjustment are critical to the disorder, one might prescribe psychodynamic or other personality oriented psychotherapy. On the other hand, if one is behaviorally oriented, the treatment of choice might be biofeedback or some other form of behavior modification. A theory that places primary emphasis on environmental stress might lead to a prescription for environmental change, sometimes referred to as milieu therapy, or some form of relaxation or meditation as a means of inhibiting adverse reactions to stress. It is common for one or another form of psychological treatment to be used simultaneously and in conjunction with chemotherapy or other medical treatments. Moreover, different forms of psychological treatment may be combined simultaneously (e.g., relaxation and desensitization, biofeedback and psychotherapy, relaxation and hypnosis).

Psychotherapy

The dominant form of psychodynamic treatment for psychophysiological disorders has been the psychoanalytic and neoanalytic approach, a development that followed rather naturally from the early emphasis on psychoanalytic explanations of such disorders (Alexander, 1950). The fundamental approach of psychodynamic treatment is to help the person to achieve insight about the unconscious conflicts that are the determinants of the anxieties that lead to symptom formation. In general, patients are expected to develop more effective ways of dealing with anxiety through the therapeutic process of insight into its source, and the expected result will be a gradual disappearance of the physical symptoms. Although this theoretical approach has some appeal on its face, reviews of the effectiveness of such approaches have indicated that psychodynamic therapy has been relatively unsuccessful (Solomon & Patch, 1971).

Some theorists have focused on the role of family interactions in the treatment of psychophysiological disorders (Minuchin et al., 1975), particularly when dealing with childhood asthma. A commonly held belief is that asthma may be exacerbated or maintained by faulty parent-child relationships. Consequently, it is not uncommon for children with asthma to be treated in family therapy together with parents and siblings. Although there has been some empirical research to suggest that family disturbance may be an important factor in the maintenance of asthma (Rees, 1963), there remains virtually no substantial evidence that family therapy is successful in reversing asthma. Definitive research on the question is hampered by extremely difficult problems in selecting appropriate control groups.

Milieu therapy

For those theorists who place primary emphasis on environmental determinants of psychophysiological disorders, it is only natural that treatment should consist of prescription for a change in milieu. Thus, it is common for psychotherapists to recommend that executives "slow down" or in some cases radically change their life styles. Extended vacations or leaves of absence are often prescribed, but these are usually seen as temporary palliative treatments, and it is recognized that returning to previous stress-inducing patterns may result in a recurrence of symptoms.

An interesting environmental approach to treatment was carried out by Purcell, Brady, Chai, Muser, Molk, Gordon, and Means (1969), who investigated the therapeutic effects of removing certain asthmatic children from their parents. In their study, which was a fairly well-controlled experimental procedure, evidence was obtained that for certain nonallergic asthmatic children, separation from the parents (but not their home) resulted in significant reductions in frequency and severity of asthma attacks. The implications of these findings are complex, for it is unlikely in our society that parents and children can be readily separated from each other for extended periods of time. The study suggests, rather, that there is a strong family effect on asthma symptoms and that research must be focused on ways to alter the relationships so that symptoms may be reduced without imposing separations on the family. There has been little research on the effects of such separation for other psychophysiological syndromes.

Relaxation and meditation

Relaxation and meditation have been proposed as treatments for psychophysiological disorders for various reasons. If excessive reactions to the stresses of life are presumed to play a role in such disorders, then relaxation may help the individual reduce his actual levels of physiological activation (muscle tension levels, excessive autonomic nervous system activity) or reduce his tendency to react excessively to situations involving stress.

Relaxation may be achieved in different ways. One method is Progressive Relaxation, based on the early work of Edmund Jacobson (1938). This practice involves specific exercises in tensing and relaxing various muscles and muscle groups in order to achieve an awareness of muscle tension and to bring about complete muscular relaxation. The individual can practice relaxation exercises on a regular basis or as needed in everyday life situations. A number of studies support the value of this practice for psychophysiological disorders (e.g., Davis, Saunders, Creer, & Chai, 1973; Haynes, Moseley, McGowan, 1975).

A second systematic approach to relaxation has been developed by Herbert Benson. The procedures are derived from transcendental meditation, but they exclude the spiritual features associated with that popular practice. Benson gives the following rationale for what he calls the relaxation response (Benson, Greenwood, & Klemchuk, 1977): The pathogenesis of several major diseases such as hypertension is associated with an integrated hypothalamic response triggered by situations requiring continuous behavioral adjustments. This response is comparable to the emergency reaction, defense reaction, or fight-flight response—patterns of behavior and physiological response described by many investigators. According to Benson, this hypothalamic response is mediated by increased sympathetic nervous system activity and is associated with increases in adrenaline and noradrenaline levels, oxygen consumption, heart rate, respiratory rate, arterial blood lactate, and increased muscle blood flow. Hypertension may result from frequent elicitation of this reaction, according to Benson.

The effects of the relaxation response are completely opposite to the emergency reaction and can be achieved by a variety of relaxation methods. It is assumed that by frequent elicitation of the relaxation response, diseases correlated with occurrence of frequent emergency reactions can be prevented and treated. The basic elements common to such relaxation are: a mental device or mantra, a passive attitude, decreased muscle tonus, and a quiet environment. The Relaxation Response method involves sitting quietly in a comfortable position with eyes closed, keeping one's muscles deeply relaxed, breathing through the nose and saying the word "one" during each breath cycle, and continuing the practice for 20 minutes each time. One is instructed to maintain a passive attitude, not to worry whether one is achieving a deep level of relaxation, to ignore distracting thoughts, and to continue repeating the word "one." A number of clinical studies have been carried out by Benson and associates that suggest a positive benefit for patients with essential hypertension and for other disorders, although the evidence is of a limited nature at this time.

Aside from progressive relaxation, transcendental meditation, and the relaxation response, we should mention other disciplines that involve similar elements. These derive primarily from Eastern cultures and involve methods that have been around for centuries, such as various forms of yoga and Zen practice. Although there is an empirical literature on the various practices, there is still relatively little agreement among researchers about the physiological and psychological mechanisms involved and in what respects the various practices differ from one another and from other forms of self-regulation and relaxation (see Woolfolk, 1975).

Biofeedback

Biofeedback as a method of treatment is derived from basic research in man and animals on the regulation of various physiological responses by means of operant conditioning methods. In human applications, the term biofeedback can be thought of in terms of its component meanings. "Bio" means biological, and "feedback" means that some output of a system is put back into the system so as to regulate it. In biofeedback, biological information recorded from an individual is transformed into some form of visual, auditory, or other sensory display, and presented back to the individual at the same time or at nearly the time of actual occurrence of the physiological changes. The biofeedback may be said to augment existing internal feedback from the viscera to the central nervous system through an external sensory pathway. Utilizing biofeedback, the individual may gain some degree of voluntary control over certain physiological responses or patterns of responses usually considered involuntary (e.g., heart rate changes, brain wave activities, and subtle motor nerve activity).

The feature of biofeedback that most distinguishes it from other methods of self-regulation is its capability of modifying very specific responses or patterns of response. Several basic research studies suggest that very specific patterns of visceral activity (blood pressure and heart rate) can be regulated by the individual (Schwartz, 1972; Shapiro, Crider, & Tursky, 1964; Shapiro, Tursky, & Schwartz, 1970).

The literature on biofeedback consists of a huge number of demonstrations, case studies, and semi-controlled observations. A rationale for the clinical use of biofeedback is clear if the symptom of the psychophysiological disorder is quite specific. Examples of the latter are the reduction of blood pressure or other critical cardiovascular parameters in essential hypertension (Shapiro, Mainardi, & Surwit, 1977), increase or decrease of activation of particular muscles in various neuromuscular disorders (Brudny, Korein, Grynbaum, Friedmann, Weinstein, Sachs-Frankel, & Belandres, 1976; Budzynski, Stoyva, Adler, & Mullaney, 1973), control of cardiac arrhythmias that are dependent on either increases *or* decreases in heart rate (Engel & Bleecker, 1974), control of migraine symptoms by reducing the dilatation of particular blood vessels (Friar & Beatty, 1976), control of epileptic symptoms through the facilitation of certain central nervous system inhibitory processes (Sterman, 1977), and the control of asthma through decreases of respiratory resistance (Vachon & Rich, 1976). Other clinical potentials and related research in biofeedback are discussed in Shapiro and Surwit (1976), Schwartz and Beatty (1977), and Beatty and Legewie (1977).

Aside from the above uses to control specific symptoms, biofeedback methods are often seen as a means of achieving muscular and general relaxation or of facilitating "low-arousal states" that may be useful in counteracting stress or in facilitating decreased levels of physiological activation (see Stoyva, 1976).

Other therapeutic procedures

In the previous sections on prevention and treatment, we have discussed a number of selected major psychological approaches to the amelioration of psychophysiological disorders. Elsewhere in this volume are chapters describing other procedures that may be effectively applied as well. For example, the behavior therapies (Chapter 19) involve procedures that may facilitate dealing with excessive reactions of the individual to particular life stresses, or that may engage the individual in appropriate behaviors that offer alternative means of responding to particular events.

Hypnosis is another procedure that may prove beneficial, particularly for patients who are prone to go into a hypnotic trance and accept suggestions readily. Frankel (1977) has described three aspects of the clinical use of hypnosis. The first involves the element of relaxation as a means of reducing tensions and minimizing external and internal stimuli that interfere with the experience. The second concerns symptom removal or habit control in which "the patient is persuaded to distort sensory perception, to obscure pain, to achieve control over smooth muscle or to permit autonomous or dissociated activity in the voluntary muscles" (p. 368). The third element involves the use of hypnosis as a means of facilitating recall and insight. Barber (1970) gives a comprehensive review of research on the physiological effects of hypnosis. There are numerous papers recounting the degree to which suggestions can alter sensory-perceptual processes, labor contractions, circulatory functions, metabolic and gastrointestinal functions, cutaneous functions, asthma, secretory functions, cold-stress, narcotic drug effects, and emotional states. However, clinical studies evaluating the usefulness of hypnosis in treating various psychophysiological disorders are not comprehensive or satisfactory in research design (Frankel, 1977). Finally, it should be emphasized that the benefits of hypnosis are limited to those patients who are susceptible to accepting suggestions readily. However, it is likely that no single procedure is suitable for all patients and that greater attention should be paid to determining the proper fit between patient and treatment method. Comparative studies of different treatment methods in different disorders and in different subgroups of patients defined by various individual characteristics are sorely needed.

Conclusion

In this chapter, we have tried to present some modern perspectives on the topic of psychophysiological disorders. It is an area of basic and clinical research involving many theoretical and empirical complications. Rather than emphasizing the various specific disorders that are often selected for special discussion, our purpose was to give an overview of the thinking and strategies of inquiry in this area of investigation. It should be obvious that there is a great diversity of concepts, methods, and research strategies, and that no single theory or viewpoint has emerged or is likely to emerge that can simply order the various phenomena. There is no question, however, that social, psychological, and behavioral processes are involved in various diseases, although our understanding of their relative roles in interaction with biological processes is still quite limited. Moreover, lumping the various disorders thought to be psychophysiological into a single category may not facilitate the uncovering of essential elements. Perhaps we need to search for a new taxonomy of psychophysiological disorders based on functional, social, and psychological characteristics.

Unfortunately, theorizing in this field of medicine is still relatively undeveloped, and the polarities of mind and body still abound. The DSM-II definition of psychophysiological disorders, discussed at the beginning of this chapter, exemplifies what we mean. To assert that psychophysiological disorders are "characterized by physical symptoms that are *caused* by emotional factors" (our italics) is not any more or less tenable than to assert that such disorders are caused by *biological* factors. The latter position, however, is probably more acceptable to many researchers and clinicians coming out of training in the traditions of physiological medicine and who are uncertain about and unfamiliar with the concepts and methods of behavioral sciences and psychophysiology. Similarly, behavioral scientists are often deficient in their knowledge of the basic biological processes essential in physical medicine. Only through greater interdisciplinary training and communication will there be an improvement in the thoroughness and completeness of our conceptualizations and investigations in this important area.

Can we offer a better definition of psychophysiological disorders? Our approach is to modify the previous definition by eliminating the concept of specific "emotional" causation, the restriction to a single organ system or to the autonomic nervous system. Our definition is: A psychophysiological disorder is a disorder of bodily organs and organ functions, significantly influenced by psychological, behavioral, or sociocultural factors in its predisposition, causation, development, or maintenance.

The definition that we have offered will hopefully broaden the perspective of investigation and clinical efforts in this area. We need to reexamine the range of phenomena involved. Can we determine new ways of ordering the data in terms of truly psychophysiological and psychobiological concepts and methods? Greater attention should also be paid to study of predisposition, initiation, and maintenance of the particular diseases, inasmuch as different psychophysiological interactions may be operative in the different phases (Weiner, 1976). Despite the complexities, the phenomena of psychophysiological disorders should provide an intellectual and practical challenge to us all for years to come.

Summary

The standard psychiatric definition of psychophysiological disorders defines them as disorders characterized by physical symptoms that are caused by emotional factors and that involve a single organ system, usually under autonomic nervous system innervation. Included under this definition are a variety of disorders of the skin, respiration, cardiovascular system, blood, gastrointestinal system, genital-urinary system, endocrine glands, sensory systems, and musculoskeletal system. A variety of psychological factors have been found to be associated with the development and maintenance of such disorders. These include the role of personality and individual difference factors, influences resulting from conditioning and learning, and the effects of attitudes and cognitive processes. Life stress and sociocultural factors are also associated with psychophysiological disorders.

Psychophysiological models have been useful in conceptualizing and studying these disorders. These are discussed in terms of the concepts of stimulus response specificity, individual response specificity, and activation.

Various methods of prevention and treatment are described: psychotherapy, milieu therapy, relaxation and meditation, biofeedback, and other treatment procedures. The chapter concludes with a discussion of the limitations of the psychiatric definition of psychophysiological disorders and offers a new, broader definition.

GLOSSARY

Activation (or arousal): a general state of the organism varying from extreme alertness to sleep, indicated by changes in various physiological functions.

Biofeedback: A method of achieving voluntary control or self-regulation of specific physiological responses or patterns of responses (e.g., visceral, electrocortical, and covert somatomotor). The method involves presentation to the individual of a sensory display of his ongoing physiological activity as it is occurring in time.

Cognitive appraisal (Lazarus): The individual's evaluation of the impact of situations or stress for his own well being and for his ability to cope with the stress.

Individual response specificity (or symptom specificity): The tendency for individuals or groups to respond physiologically in a stereotyped or idiosyncratic way to certain stimuli or stress.

Perceived social climate (Moos): The individual's perception or appraisal of characteristics of his social or work setting.

Progressive relaxation (Jacobson): A procedure used to achieve total muscular relaxation, involving tensing and relaxing of muscles.

Psychophysiological disorder: A disorder of bodily organs and organ functions, significantly influenced by psychological, behavioral or sociocultural factors in its predisposition, causation, development, or maintenance.

Psychophysiology: A field of basic research concerned with relationships between psychological and physiological aspects of behavior.

Recent life change (Rahe): Significant events in one's life that necessitate major readjustments in life pattern and behavior.

Relaxation response (Benson): A procedure used to achieve complete relaxation, involving a mental device or mantra, a passive attitude, decreased muscle tonus, and a quiet environment.

Specificity-of-attitude hypothesis: States that patients having a given psychophysiological disorder tend to have idiosyncratic attitudes defined by what they feel is happening to them and what they wish to do about it. The specific attitude is believed to be associated with a specific physiological process associated with the disorder.

Stimulus response specificity: The tendency for certain stimuli to elicit the same pattern or hierarchy of physiological responses in all people.

Type A behavior pattern (Friedman & Rosenman): A pattern of behavior associated with heart disease, involving intense competitive striving for achievement, a pervasive sense of time urgency, and an easily elicited trait of aggressiveness.

SCHIZOPHRENIA

KURT SALZINGER

Just as we say that beauty exists in the eye of the beholder, we might also say that schizophrenia exists in the mind's eye. Not that schizophrenia is *only* in the mind's eye; but to fully understand the tragic phenomenon that strikes about 2 percent of all Americans at one time or another (Center for Studies of Schizophrenia, 1972), we must make clear how the labeling process itself takes place. Uninitiated readers may well throw their arms up in despair at a puzzle that requires that we discover both the method and the object of the method's search simultaneously. And yet it is this very puzzlement that has engaged scientists from so many fields over the years. It would be fair to say that schizophrenia, whatever it is, has been the focus of research in fields ranging all the way from biochemistry to anthropology and sociology, stopping off at neuropathology, even dentistry, and of course the subject matter of this chapter, psychology.

In his introduction to a very recent comprehensive review of research and therapy in schizophrenia, Romano (1978) talked of what he called the nonunderstandability of the behavior of the patient as a diagnostic criterion for the disorder of schizophrenia. To illustrate that nonunderstandability of the schizophrenic patient, Romano related the story of a patient of his who would not eat and had, therefore, to be tube-fed. The patient had to be tube-fed twice for each meal because he regularly vomited the first such feeding, retaining only the second. Romano decided to question the patient on this matter. The patient explained that he vomited "because I have no stomach." When Romano pursued the matter by asking where the second feeding goes in that case, the patient replied, "It goes to the upper peninsula." All efforts to understand this statement were to no avail even after Romano interviewed the patient and his family, made tests of various kinds, and studied the dreams of the patient.

But what are some of the other characteristics of the people who earn the diagnosis of

---

The author wishes to thank Richard S. Feldman who, as usual, helped to make my writing more understandable.

schizophrenia? According to one study by Smith, Pumphrey, and Hall (1963), it was found that some 53 percent of a sample of patients who found their way to a hospital got there because they committed a violent act, or threatened to commit one; 38 percent of the patients exhibited socially unacceptable behavior such as shouting, nudity, irrational talk, and otherwise inexplicable behavior; and the remaining 9 percent were brought to the hospital because of a self-asserted need for treatment.

What are the patients like who are diagnosed as schizophrenic? Landis and Bolles (1950) describe a catatonic schizophrenic patient, a 27-year-old laborer who led what appeared to be a relatively normal life until for a period of 3 weeks before being hospitalized, he became seclusive, sloppy in dress, and had difficulty sleeping. At a bar he accused a long-known acquaintance of talking behind his back and became very excited. He was brought home while continuing to shout and to spit at the people "who were trying to get" him. In the hospital he was first monosyllabic and slow and then became mute and refused to eat. After some 5 weeks of such a severe behavior disorder, including incontinence and standing in peculiar positions, he became a little more cooperative. After one year he was somewhat more cooperative but showed himself to be disoriented, was limited in conversation, showed auditory hallucinations, and occasionally became assaultive.

O'Kelly and Muckler (1955) describe a case history of a paranoid schizophrenic patient. The patient in question entered the hospital after failing to find a body for his "experiment in restoring life." He had been in the army for more than 16 months, acting in psychotic ways without being hospitalized. For about 8 years he had suffered from delusions, including one that people had been trying to kill him. He also believed that he was turning into a woman and would soon be able to bear children. It is interesting to note that this patient was able to survive in society with rather bizarre ideas without being hospitalized or even offered mental health aid.

These are the kinds of case histories one is likely to encounter when asking for a description of what a schizophrenic patient is like. Again we have to point out that the essential part appears to be a certain amount of inexplicableness, behavior that is hard for an outsider to understand.

The classical description

The classical description of schizophrenia is based on the work of Bleuler (1950), a Swiss psychiatrist. According to Bleuler, four primary symptoms usually need to be present to make a diagnosis of schizophrenia. Bleuler's four A's, as they are sometimes called by those who work in psychiatric settings, are: 1. loosening of association, 2. inappropriate affect, 3. marked ambivalence, and 4. autistic thinking.

Let us briefly look at each of these symptoms in turn. *First,* loosening of associations is often reflected in the speech of the schizophrenic patient. At times the logic of the conversation and the train of thought are extremely difficult, if not impossible, to follow. Consider the following example of schizophrenic speech: "My father was here. I stepped back into my shoes. No, stop it! I'm sorry I can't be in touch with her. I don't like the look of the red phone outdoors."

Second, inappropriate affect refers to an emotional reaction that is not consistent with the nature of its stimulus. Examples include silly giggling in response to a serious question, crying in reaction to an innocuous question, or hysterical laughing in response to the announcement of a tragic event.

Third, marked ambivalence refers to the extreme changes in decisions and nonverbal behavior in relation to a specific event or situation. What is particularly striking about such ambivalence is the relatively rapid alternation of positions taken by the patient within a relatively short time (e.g., sometimes within the course of a single interview). To illustrate, consider this patient's ambivalence toward his mother when ques-

Paranoid Schizophrenia

Olive W., a married fifty-seven-year-old mother of three children, was committed for the second time to a state hospital in the South. Poorly educated, she was the wife of an unskilled laborer working at a menial municipal job. Her family had always been in very modest financial circumstances. . . . In her early forties she was involved in an automobile accident and sustained minor injuries. Soon afterward she began to express the idea that someone was following her with the intention of doing her harm. She noted that people passed her house in groups of threes and felt that this had special significance for her. Finally, she began to experience auditory hallucinations and lost interest in caring for herself or her home. When she became very disturbed and assaultive toward members of her family and accused them of plotting her demise, it was necessary that she be hospitalized. After a stay of four months, she was discharged to care of the family. (From Zax & Stricker, 1963, p. 86)

Catatonic Schizophrenia

Franz G., a twenty-one-year-old single man, was referred to a state hospital in a large eastern city by the police, and was entered on the hospital rolls as "John Doe," because he had no identification and did not respond, verbally or nonverbally, to questions. . . . Franz was found at a race track standing motionless, staring straight ahead, and not speaking. He was taken to a hospital, and when physical examination revealed no physical basis for this mutism, he was transferred to the state hospital under the name of John Doe. He followed instructions at the hospital but, left to himself, would just sit and stare into space, and did not respond to any queries about his behavior. His sleep was fair and appetite undisturbed during this period. When a doctor asked him some questions in German he suddenly snapped out of his mute state to say that he had been very depressed and worried and added, "I lost money at the race track. I am worrying and I am afraid that my mother would punish me for that." He then lapsed back into mutism and remained mute for the following week, except for sporadic violent outbursts against other patients. After a week he suddenly became quite talkative, indicating that he was well aware of the events of the preceding week, and reiterating that he had lost his mother's money at the race track. When Franz identified himself it was discovered that he had escaped from a nearby institution, and he was then returned. (From Zax & Stricker, 1963, pp. 78, 79–80)

tioned about her: "I hate that bitch; she likes to treat me as a child. My mother was so good to me; she used to feed and hold me whenever I fell down and cried. I'm going to leave that damn place where she plays queen." Again, not only is there ambivalence in speech, but, ambivalent nonverbal *behavior* typically accompanies and/or follows the verbal utterance.

Fourth is the patient's autism. Austistic thinking is governed by the patient's needs and wishes, and is not consistent with the reality of the situation. In normals, dreams and fantasies are representative of autistic processes. In schizophrenics, the more dramatic manifestations include delusions and hallucinations. Much of the schizophrenic's waking life is pervaded by autistic thinking and behavior (e.g., peculiar posturing or grimacing).

Although these are the original four A's listed by Bleuler as cardinal symptoms of schizophrenia, in the last 20 to 30 years three additional A's have been referred to in the literature. One is termed *anhedonia* and reflects the schizophrenic's inability to derive

Hebephrenic Schizophrenia

Robert A., a twenty-four-year-old single man, was transferred to a mental institution in a large eastern city from a local municipal hospital because of his bizarre behavior. . . . He entered the municipal hospital with a self-inflicted mutilation of his penis, done in order that he could get his girlfriend pregnant at a distance. While being treated for this wound he discussed, at great length, the special symbolism of words and numbers, interrupting himself to laugh inappropriately at times. He also volunteered the information that he was sick because dwarfs had stuck him with green needles. He was soon transferred to a nearby mental institution.

Upon his admission Robert was overactive and very noisy, frequently threatening people around him, but never actually assaulting them. He indulged in open, frequent, and prolonged masturbation, and would give sexual connotations to inanimate objects on the ward. Robert answered many questions relevantly and coherently but, even so, his speech was scattered with delusional material. His speech was spontaneous and continuous, but if interrupted he would respond with relevant, albeit predominantly delusional, material. (From Zax & Stricker, 1963, pp. 64–65)

Simple Schizophrenia

Charleton C., a thirty-six-year-old single man, was committed for the first time to a midwestern state hospital after being arrested for vagrancy. . . . He never remained at any job longer than a year, and frequently left otherwise satisfactory jobs because he felt that he had stayed in one place too long a period of time. He traveled from area to area seeking various migrant and transient employments, and was thus able to support himself, albeit at a rather low level.

Two years before his commitment to the hospital he began to have difficulty with even the minimally demanding jobs he usually obtained. He became suspicious of his co-workers, and rather than isolate himself from them, as he previously had done, began to accuse them of various crimes. In an attempt to avoid contact with others, he neglected any semblance of work unless it became necessary to satisfy his basic needs. In the year before he was committed, Charleton was arrested for vagrancy on nine different occasions in the southwest, the midwest, and the northeast. Finally, when he seemed confused and was unable to follow instructions, the police had him examined, certified, and committed to a state institution. (From Zax & Stricker, 1963, pp. 57–58)

pleasure from life's usual satisfactions (particularly the interpersonal). A second is the schizophrenic's *social aversiveness* to those interpersonal situations that for most people seem positively reinforcing. The third is difficulty in maintaining *attention.* Because of the schizophrenic patient's cognitive distortion (i.e., hallucinations, delusions), they are unable to focus and concentrate, thus responding to a multitude of stimuli simultaneously.

A later section of this chapter will describe several other classification schemes to account for the different symptom pictures evidenced by schizophrenic patients. Indeed, as time goes on, the list for a given classification scheme may either grow larger or smaller. Also, it should be noted that there are drug-induced psychoses (LSD, Amphetamines, PCP—"angel dust") that appear to mimic many of the symptoms of schizophrenia. However, drug-induced psy-

Table 11.1. Signs and Symptoms of Four Schizophrenic SubTypes

Paranoid	Catatonic	Hebephrenic	Simple
auditory hallucinations	stuporous immobility	shallow affect	shallow emotional
delusions	occasional uncontrolled excitement	inappropriate emotional reactions	lack of drive
thought disturbance	uncommunicativeness	silly giggling	unconcern about life changes
ideas of reference*	muteness	extreme looseness of associations	general absence of bizarre behavior
misinterpretation of reality	preoccupation	posturing	life style of vagrant, tramp, hermit, or prostitute
	weight loss	word salad†	
		hallucinations	
		delusions	

*Persistent impression that unrelated conversation, smiling, or action of others is related to oneself.
†Words of the patient's own making juxtaposed in bizarre fashion.

choses that give the appearance of schizophrenia are not included under the schizophrenia label.

Following Kraeplin (1919) and Bleuler (1950), four subtypes of schizophrenia were originally designated: 1. paranoid, 2. catatonic, 3. hebephrenic, and 4. simple type. Each of these subtypes has a cardinal symptom associated with it (delusions with paranoid schizophrenia, bizarre motor behavior with catatonic schizophrenia, disturbance in association and affect with hebephrenic schizophrenia, and social inadequacy and withdrawal in simple schizophrenia). More comprehensive signs and symptoms of these four schizophrenic subtypes appear in Table 11.1. It should be noted that in most instances the signs and symptoms of schizophrenia make their first appearance in the late teens and early twenties. In paranoid schizophrenia the actual onset of the symptoms is a bit later.

The concept of schizophrenia

The medical model. At this time, the label schizophrenia is officially conferred by those who follow the medical model. The diagnosis of schizophrenia is also given by nonpsychiatrists, but never with the same official sanction nor with the same frequency. From the point of view of these practical considerations, it is important to realize, therefore, since the power to render such diagnoses at present resides in the psychiatrists, that even though the label is given only on the basis of a *model* of behavior, it is nevertheless treated as a fact once applied to real people. Furthermore, whether or not many professionals question the diagnosis, and many others are successful in pointing out various kinds of flaws in the diagnosis, there is nonetheless a real group of people who are so labeled and to whom others respond in a particular way, thereby fortifying the label placed on them. Before going into the details of the attributes that constitute the diagnosis of schizophrenia, it is important to make explicit the assumptions that go into making a diagnosis in the first place.

Various terms, once used by a restricted group of professionals only, have a way of creeping into the general vocabulary and so establishing themselves as fact. The term symptom is a good example of such a word. Even some behavior therapists, who certainly ought to know better, are willing to say that their treatment is restricted to mere symptoms. What is wrong with such a statement? "Symptoms" assumes the behavior to which it refers is not as important as the underlying cause, and implies that the therapist had better study the cause rather than mere indicators of sickness. Some central cause—for example, an invading organism such as a virus—is considered to be the important fact in diagnosis. On the basis of such a fact, one can decide to treat a patient suffering from a physical malady; treatment based on symptoms like headaches or nausea is indequate. Thus while one might try to lower temperature, a mere sign of an illness, by giving a patient a cold bath, nobody would consider that to be a treatment for the cause of the illness. Those who take seriously the medical model of abnormal behavior make the same assumption about the centrality of such causes as anxiety, as opposed to such a relatively unimportant fact as a person's tic even if consisting of a facial grimace occurring several times a minute.

In psychiatry, the central cause—the etiology, as opposed to the symptom—used to be identified in terms of such "psychological" factors as anxiety, and that practice is not dead even now with respect to schizophrenia. However, in the main, the pendulum has swung to another extreme of presumed etiology, so that not only schizophrenia and other psychoses, but many other forms of maladjustment are being searched for the biochemical origin.

From the acceptance of the medical model comes the assumption that the treatment of mere symptoms is not only ineffective, but that when it eliminates the treated symptom, the underlying cause will surface once again in the form of another symptom. Another associated assumption of this model is that one should look for the causes of disease within the person who is a potential patient, rather than outside, in the patient's physical and/or social environment. It is important to note that the choice of the model into which we cast what facts we garner will determine to a great extent where we look for additional facts and how we go about the business of finding them out (which will be discussed later).

We are now ready to look over the kinds of criteria used to decide whether the person being examined is schizophrenic or not.

The Diagnostic and Statistical Manual of the American Psychiatric Association. Although classification of all sorts became quite prominent during the period of the renaissance and again in the eighteenth century when systems of classifications of mental maladies were also tried out (Alexander & Selesnick, 1966), struggles for uniformity in the classification are still being waged. This is evident in the differences of diagnostic practices at this time between the United States and the United Kingdom (Professional Staff of the United States–United Kingdom Cross-National Project, 1974; Zubin & Gurland, 1977).

The Committee on Nomenclature and Statistics (1952) described the more recent history of classification in this country, pointing out that in 1917 the Committee on Statistics of the American Medico-psychological Association had formulated a plan for uniform statistics for mental diseases in hospitals. Nevertheless, according to the Chairman of the Committee on Nomenclature and Statistics, by 1948 the psychiatric nomenclature situation "had deteriorated almost to the point of confusion which existed throughout medical nomenclature in the twenties" (p. vii). In that year three different systems of classification were extant: the Standard form, which was primarily suited for hospitalized patients; the Armed Forces classification, which sprang up because of new kinds of psychiatric casualties produced during the second world war; and finally the Veterans Administration classification system, which resembled but was not the same as the Armed Forces classification. None of these classification systems fell neatly into the International Statistical Classification System. That confusion resulted in the 1952 classification system, which was then later revised in 1968, the system being used now in many hospitals and compiled in the *Diagnostic and Statistical-Manual of Mental Disorders* (DSM-II).

Since September 1973, a new Task Force on Nomenclature and Statistics (1977) of the

American Psychiatric Association has been constituted; this task force is generating DSM-III. Although it is now undergoing field trials and so has not yet been finally accepted, it will no doubt be accepted as it now stands, with only minor changes. For that reason, we will describe the diagnostic entity of schizophrenia as defined by DSM-III, a draft dated 4/15/77. It should be noted that by no means is there unanimity of acceptance of the new classification system, as can be shown in the papers by Salzinger (1977, 1978a), Schacht and Nathan (1977), and Zubin (1977–1978).

The new system of classification has several advantages over the older systems. It is more specific, it provides more detailed guides for making each decision, and it is more systematic in instructing the user in making the diagnosis. Section C of DSM-III is called "Schizophrenic Disorders." The schizophrenic disorders are said to consist of a general disorganization of the previous level of functioning, one which cannot be explained by any of the specific conditions listed under the Organic Mental Disorders. Schizophrenia as defined in DSM-III involves at least one of the following: *delusions* (an unwarranted belief that someone else is controlling the patient, that insignificant events are somehow related personally to them, that other people can hear their thoughts); *hallucinations* (a typically auditory sensation in which the patients here voices talking to them in the absence of appropriate external stimulation, sometimes in some insulting fashion); or *formal thought disorder* (the use by the patient of what seem to be incidental, noncontextually determined associations, vague statements, and obscure or stereotyped phrases). It is interesting to note that the earlier used characteristic of shallowness or inappropriateness of affect is missing among the primary characteristics of schizophrenics. The drafters of DSM-III admit that the importance of an affective disturbance in schizophrenia is outweighed by the difficulty of making a reliable judgment except when present in extreme form; they also admit that the use of antipsychotic drugs is so prevalent, and results so often in flattening of affect, that it is not possible to differentiate the drug effect from the disorder.

Other characteristics of schizophrenia are also listed. Surprising to a psychologist is the lack of evidence for any significant degree of influence from the field of experimental psychology in the use of terms and on the matter of how one may determine the patient's difficulties. For example, the very use of the out-dated term volition is surprising. The explanation for a disturbance in volition is also not very clear, or at least not specific enough, in telling the user how to look for an instance of a disturbance is self-initiated goal-directed activity. Nor is there any mention of how many such instances one must find, when, with whom, and under what conditions; that is, whether the conditions make such activities appropriate or not (as in the contrast of behavior in the army when the person is on maneuvers, or at a party in civilian life). Nor is there any attempt to specify how the user is to come by the information for judging this category.

Perhaps most disturbing to the experimental psychologist is the lack of any reference at all to the plethora of objective experimental measures that have been developed by psychologists for testing the various functions that the diagnosis asks for (e.g., the disturbances in motor behavior and perception said to characterize schizophrenia). The experimental psychology literature is replete with examples of reliable methods for the measurement of functions such as these and many more. Specific, objective measures of the functioning of patients could be obtained just for the asking. Furthermore, the findings of behavior theory provide the schema within which one can place the examination of the functions of interest, for these diagnoses are ignored in DSM-III, its protestations about its radical innovations notwithstanding.

A point needs to be made about the use of the Research Diagnostic Criteria (RDC), a new development in DSM-III, which state that to be called schizophrenic, patients must have at least one of the three classes of symptoms listed above, namely delusions, hallucinations, or formal thought disorder. They must have shown signs of the illness (the word used to describe schizophrenia here, although in the main the word disorder is used) for at least two weeks; and finally, the illness (again) must not seem to be due to any Organic Mental Disorder listed in DSM-III. The fact that the criteria—even though at one time incorrectly called operational, and even now not that well specified—nevertheless are explicit for the first time in having the diagnostician looking for specific kinds of difficulties before assigning the label of schizophrenia, is certainly an improvement over previous practices in which an attempt was made to match a general picture found in the Manual to the general impression of a patient.

The new DSM also classifies each patient in terms of what it calls the phenomenology (the categories being quite similar to what they were in preceding manuals) and in terms of the course of illness. The latter axis classifies the disorder with respect to suddenness of onset (i.e., whether it took less than three months from the first signs of increasing psychopathology to the first full-blown psychotic schizophrenic symptoms or whether it is chronic [having been going on for at least the last two years], with various grades in between). Along the same dimension there is also the category of "in remission." No precise guidelines are furnished for differentiating that diagnosis from the "no mental disorder" diagnosis except for some vague statements about the period of time since the last episode of disorder and the number of episodes before. This is an example of a potential troublespot with all sorts of practical implications (cf. a recent vice-presidential election in which a question was raised about a diagnosis of affective disorder in the candidate's past).

The phenomenological axis in schizophrenia consists of the *disorganized* (earlier called hebephrenic) schizophrenic and characterized by so-called silly affect and incoherence; the *catatonic* schizophrenic who is dominated by a marked decrease in reactivity to the environment, muteness, or bizarre postures; and the *paranoid*, whose behavior is dominated by false beliefs of being persecuted or of being able to accomplish incredible things. Another subclassification of schizophrenia is *undifferentiated* (once called mixed) and means that the criteria for any specific subclassification mentioned above do not fit the patient or that a number of different subclassifications all fit the patient's disorder equally well. The subclassification *residual* is used for patients who once had an episode of schizophrenia but whose present picture contains no prominent psychotic symptoms. There are two other related diagnoses: Schizo-affective disorder, manic, and Schizo-affective, depressed. They were considered part of schizophrenia in the March 15, 1977, edition but were separated from Schizophrenia in the June 15, 1977, Research Diagnostic Criteria. The reason for the separation of these two categories from schizophrenia was apparently the uncertainty or at least disagreement that psychiatrists had on whether to place these kinds of patients among the affective disorders or among the schizophrenic ones. Both categories have characteristics belonging to the affective disorders and to the schizophrenic ones. The manic subtype is characterized by greater verbal and nonverbal activity than "usual," inflated self-esteem, and a smaller need for sleep, in addition to some to the schizophrenic symptoms mentioned above. The depressed subtype is characterized by being sad, blue, and "depressed" plus some of the characteristics mentioned for schizophrenia.

The behavioral model. Clearly the definition of schizophrenia stems from the medical model. Nevertheless, it is impossible to leave out entirely a behavioral model since, after all, the information on the basis of which the psychiatric diagnosis is made is behavioral. Much of it is verbal behavior, but a good part of it is nonverbal. Thus, it requires that we have a behavioral model for the determinants of schizophrenia. We will return to a formal consideration of the behavioral model, since a number of theories describe schizophrenia in such terms. Cultural, social, general environmental, and family factors in addition to the more usual learning factors are included in the rubric, the behavioral model.

The question to be considered with respect to applicability of the behavioral model is not the question of whether the disorder is caused, in some ultimate sense, by biochemical factors or by environmental factors. The question is rather one of determining which factors (environmental, genetic, or a combination) are acting on each particular response class under consideration. The problem to which the behavioral model addresses itself is that of locating or identifying the behavioral mechanism that mediates a particular "symptom." Thus, the behavioral mechanism is useful in specifying the way a posited biochemical fault produces hallucinations. Are the hallucinations due, for example, to the parts of the environment that become important, or does the person respond to private stimuli as if they were public ones? Is the individual who has hallucinations more easily conditionable to new stimuli (those only associated with the appropriate stimuli, such as a grimace being associated with a threatening remark)? The role of the concept of the behavioral mechanism in explaining the psychopathological phenomenology is more fully developed in a paper by Salzinger (1978b). The behavioral mechanism plays a role in understanding the causes of schizophrenia, the factors that maintain it, and the factors that could be applied to change that disorder. In other words, no matter what may be the mixture of magnitudes of cause in producing schizophrenia, the near cause is always a behavioral one. Furthermore, there is no guarantee that the factors that "caused" schizophrenia are the same as those that presently maintain it or that could be used to eliminate or attenuate it.

Although not specific to the diagnostic entity of schizophrenia—in fact, independent of such classifications—behavioral analysis techniques have in recent years (Hersen & Bellack, 1976a; Salzinger in Zubin et al., 1975) sprung up to produce objective measures of the functioning of patients. These measures provide information that one can use to judge the current state of the patient as well as the usefulness of various intervention procedures, since they allow one to evaluate change in the patient's behavior when it occurs. Also important to note is that unlike the old tests that psychologists constructed to evaluate psychodynamic theories and that are useless now either for the drug treatments or the behavior modification techniques, these new behavioral assessment techniques are for the most part cognizant of the variables that behavior theory has found to be significant. The information the techniques provide is not simply whether a particular patient engages in a given behavior, but also when, in what place, on what occasion, how frequently, and with what consequence. Since these kinds of information are still not asked for in the classical psychiatric diagnosis, the behavior model approach will continue to provide information that the medical model cannot.

Methodological problems

The discussion so far has already suggested a number of methodological problems with which one is confronted when dealing with schizophrenia. The diagnosis itself is presently in a state of flux. That may be all the good news to tell about it. Certainly, earlier studies have made it quite clear that the reliability of the category (i.e., the extent to which two experts agree that someone is schizophrenic) was not very high at all (Zubin, 1967). In fact that author felt moved to describe the general situation at that time as "chaotic." A more recent paper by Spitzer and Endicott in Zubin et al. (1975) reported the amount of agreement for major diagnoses based on case records (so that much of the variability usually found when there is disagreement between two different interviewers has been eliminated) to be .48 using the DSM-II criteria. We have to note here that this low index of agreement was obtained by computing an index called "kappa," which varies from 0 (least) to 1 (most agreement). When the same case records were analyzed by trained research analysts who used the new research diagnostic criteria or at least one form of them, the reliability increased to .84 for the category of schizophrenia. Unfortunately, that result answers only part of the question of reliability. It only tells us about the agreement to be expected between two trained researchers when someone has already decided, by interviewing the patient and writing up the record, what information is relevant.

But what about the real situation, namely the agreement when two different clinicians each do their own interviews? Let us look at a reliability study that examines such a test-retest reliability situation directly. Helzer, Clayton, Pambakian, Reich, Woodruff, and Reveley (1977) interviewed 101 psychiatric patients independently using a structured interview (in which the areas about which questions are asked are specified and the interviewer must cover those topics). Although this kind of interview is not typical for clinical work (i.e., it is more commonly used for research), the results of this study are nevertheless almost identical with earlier studies summarized by Spitzer and Fleiss (1974), namely a kappa of .58. Low as the amount of agreement is, we must note that it might be an overestimate since the interviewers were allowed to make multiple diagnoses. At best therefore we can conclude that the diagnosis of schizophrenia explains 58 percent of the variance when the interviews are done under research conditions. The implication is that most of the results that stem from patients diagnosed clinically will include other types of patients who should not have been diagnosed as schizophrenic. We shall talk of the implications of this later on.

What is the reason for the low reliability? The answer lies, in part, in the system of classification itself, in part in the lack of standardization of the inquiry procedure, although the structured interview eliminates part of that problem, and in part in the most intractable problem of all, the uncertain source of information used to arrive at a diagnosis. As long as one insists on getting all of the relevant information by interviewing the potential patient, who must serve simultaneously as a source of aberrant behavior to be observed by the interviewer and as a source of information reporting to the interviewer on his/her state, past behavior, etc., the reliability of the results must be open to question.

Finally, we must ask a question about the conduct of the interview itself. Here, as we have already pointed out, the interviewer exerts some control by asking about a particular list of topics; in some cases, even the wording of the question is suggested, although not absolutely specified. A variable remains, though, that is not controlled even in the structured interviews now in use in the research context of diagnosis. That variable is the behavior of the interviewer *after* the patient's response, namely the reinforcers. Several experiments have shown that the reinforcing behavior of the interviewer can modify the verbal behavior of the patient even in periods of time as short as ten minutes (Salzinger & Pisoni, 1958, 1960, 1961; Salzinger, Portnoy, & Feldman, 1964). Under these circumstances, interviewers are unfortunately in the position of modifying the very phenomenon that they are supposed to be merely observing. Furthermore, it is interesting to note that the response class that was successfully conditioned was that of affect, the absence or inappropriateness of which is supposed to typify schizophrenic patients and, what is more, is supposed to be prognostic of schizophrenia (that is, allow us to determine how long the person will continue to be abnormal).

All of this discussion can be summarized by saying that there are many conditions that produce the kind of low reliability of diagnosis that characterizes this area of abnormal behavior. We must add to this another set of methodological problems intrinsic to research on diagnosis. Obviously, when a particular category includes patients not constituting a homogeneous group, then we would

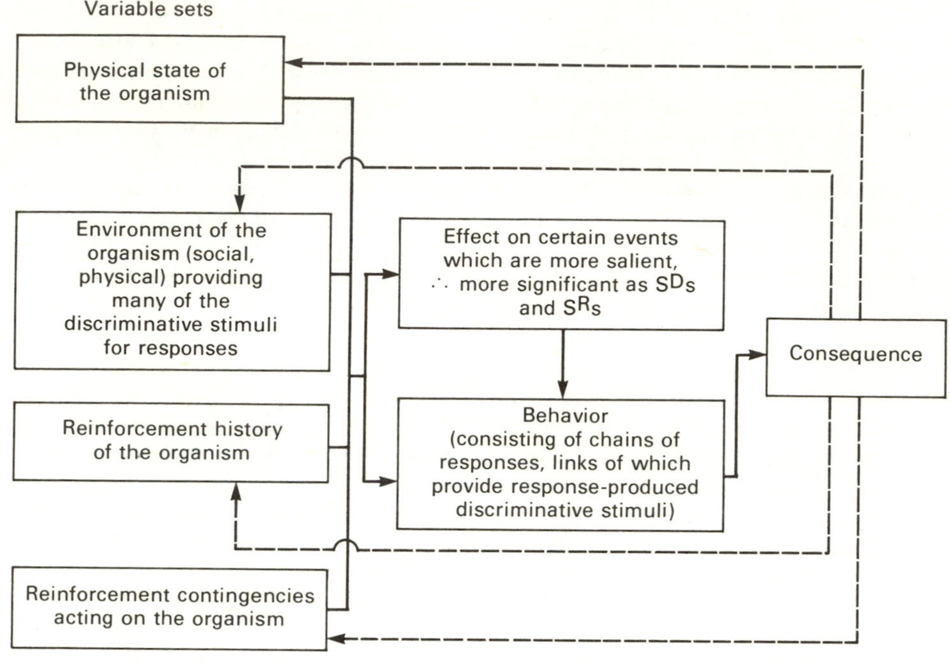

Fig. 11.1. The behavioral mechanism seeks to explain the various ways in which behavior is controlled by variables that precede or follow it. (From paper presented by Salzinger, Portnoy, & Feldman, 1978b.)

expect to find difficulty in replicating experimental results. In addition, however, there is the question of whether a universal kind of disturbance is to be found in the behavior of schizophrenics. If so (and such an assumption would seem to be mandatory), we will have to look not only for a biochemical basis for that general disturbance but also for a behavioral basis. The latter requires the concept called the behavioral mechanism (Salzinger, 1978b). Essentially, the behavioral mechanism explains the kind of control exerted over behavior under varying circumstances. It asks: Under what conditions does a given response class occur and what are the consequences of that behavior when it occurs on that occasion (see Fig. 11.1)? It allows us to discover why a patient labeled schizophrenic responds more slowly than normals, or extinguishes more rapidly, or talks about things in a way that is difficult to understand.

We will examine the phenomenon of difficulty of understanding schizophrenic speech in greater detail later on, but for now let us speculate about what the different underlying behavioral mechanisms could be. The speech of the schizophrenic could be called forth by a larger range of stimuli than that of the listener (which might explain the schizophrenic's flitting from topic to topic). Another behavioral mechanism might be that the patient is responding to physical stimuli to a greater degree than to social and verbal ones of other interlocutors as normal people usually do (which might account for the schizophrenic's appearing to be unresponsive to people). The patient could have a deficit in response-produced stimulus control, that is, the very last thing that the patient said might have more control over what he/she will say next than the entire context calls for. Or the conditioning history of the speaker could be such that peculiar patterns of words and sentences were conditioned by factors other than those now impinging on the speaker—for example, the patient might have been specifically reinforced for speaking ambiguously. The point is that the same phenomenon could have a whole host of different behavioral mechanisms underlying it. Unless we learn to understand those underlying mechanisms, we will not be able to make statements of any generality or to explain the vast range of aberrant behaviors which characterize any given diagnostic category.

To give an example from a more clear cut situation, let us look at a blind person who has an obvious stimulus deficit. Such a person might flourish in an environment in which all the stimuli are auditory and tactual and none visual, as in a dark environment. Under these circumstances, it would not be possible to find a deficit in the blind person. On the other extreme where all the critical stimuli are visual, such a person would require help from others and thus would give an obvious picture of complete dependency on other individuals. Between these extremes is the familiar situation of the blind person in our society. The behavior of these people is at least as different from person to person as that of seeing individuals. The person who has been trained to listen to various kinds of sounds or who is living in a place where the sounds are predictable would fare much better, and would give evidence of being happier than the person who was exposed to an ever-changing environment so that he or she would have to learn over and over again about the significance of various sounds.

There is one case in which the behavioral mechanism is very badly needed to elucidate the behavior of the schizophrenic patient, and that is the variable of cooperation. Shakow (1946) was very much aware of this potentially confounding variable and made an attempt to measure it independently whenever he was examining other variables such as the schizophrenic's reaction time, to take a classical measure of the behavior of the patient. Shakow measured cooperativeness, defined roughly as the extent to which the patient seemed to try to follow directions, by means of a rating scale. That approach has some obvious weaknesses, such as the confounding of the behavior of interest with the estimate of the cooperativeness. What one needs to do is measure the degree to which different variables determine the outcome of each experiment. Thus, even though such a phenomenon as reaction time, particularly in response to a simple single stimulus, seems to measure something very basic, it turns out that a number of different variables do in fact determine it. The classical reaction time experiment has no particular consequence following the responses.

We may well ask, however, what would happen if there were a positive or negative reinforcer contingent on a reaction time less than some predetermined length. One might expect that the subject "will try harder" to respond as fast as possible. In fact, experiments have shown (Goodstein, Guertin, & Blackburn, 1961; Klein, Cicchetti, & Spohn, 1967; Rosenbaum, MacKavey, & Grissell, 1957) that the classical difference in reaction time between the schizophrenic and the normal person can be virtually eliminated by using a reinforcement contingency. Note that the vaguer concept of cooperativeness has now been modified into the more precisely measurable variable of response to a reinforcement contingency. We can then actually match normals and schizophrenics with respect to the variable of cooperativeness; then if we still find a difference between the populations, we can attribute it to aspects of the stimulus or the motor response, variables that can be further examined and analyzed. By means of the concept of the behavioral mechanism, psychologists can make an important contribution to the understanding of abnormal behavior. We do not need ever more precise descriptions of phenomenology of schizophrenia. As we discover the behavioral mechanisms underlying the abnormal behavior, we can review the functional relationships between the environment and the patient's genetic predisposition.

Stimulus control

As explained above, one source of difficulty for an individual might well stem from the way that person responds to stimuli. Let us look at how schizophrenics are drawn to stimuli. The drawing power of stimuli is a problem in many cases. Thus, for example, in learning tasks set before children, or for that matter for anyone trying to study something that is not a pure joy, there are obviously two not unrelated problems. The first is how to keep the relevant stimuli controlling one's behavior so as to be able to study as efficiently as possible, and the other is to keep irrelevant stimuli from taking over control of other responses available to one at the time the studying is supposed to be taking place.

This first spate of research in schizophrenia is subsumed under the concept of distractibility. The typical finding is that schizophrenic patients are more easily drawn to stimuli that are not relevant to the task at hand than are normal individuals or patients in other diagnostic categories. Most recently, Oltmanns and Neale (1978) called our attention to that phenomenon again, suggesting that distractibility might well be the underlying factor for the supposedly characteristic thought disorder. Andreasen (1978) has recently been making a valiant attempt to be explicit in the instructions for rating speech samples with respect to thought disorder. Furthermore, she provides examples for the different ratings that are to be assigned for each speech sample. This is an obvious improvement over previous judgment procedures; unfortunately, the detection of thought disorder is nevertheless subjective and will therefore remain difficult to replicate from one study to another, or even from one patient to another, when studies are done in different hospitals or even by different clinicians who have not been carefully trained to make these judgment. Objective techniques that psychologists have been working on for years are clearly superior to clinical judgments. However, even such rating scale results can help in the search for behavioral mechanisms. Oltmanns and Neale (1978) report a correlation of .55 ($p < .05$) between a measure of distractibility and a clinically derived measure of thought disorder. They suggested that their concept of distractibility is an underlying mechanism of schizophrenia.

Let us briefly look at their experimental measure of distractibility. It consists of having subjects respond to different numbers of digits in the presence and absence of different numbers of distracting digits. In the report by Oltmanns, Ohayon, and Neale (in press) it was found that persons diagnosed as schizophrenic by the hospital and also given that same diagnosis according to the RDC (research diagnostic criteria) were definitely distractible, whereas the other schizophrenics (those given different diagnoses according to the RDC) and the normals were not distractible on the tasks in question.

The notion of distractibility as a basic deficit in schizophrenia is not a new one. Chapman (1956), using a technique that Payne (1966) contends is similar to the concept of overinclusiveness, found that schizophrenic patients were increasingly more distracted as the number of extraneous stimuli in a card-sorting test increased. Overinclusiveness, of course, simply means that subjects respond to more stimuli than they ought to, as determined by the task at hand. The point is that these concepts are basically ideas about stimulus control, and when we get to the theory section we will compare these concepts with others in order to explain the behavior of schizophrenic patients responding to stimuli.

We have already talked about the classical measure of response to external stimuli, namely, the reaction time technique. Let us look at some additional experiments in this area. Zubin (1975) supplies a useful summary of experiments in reaction time. Increase in the intensity of the stimulus to which the subject is instructed to respond reduces reaction time in both normal and schizophrenic subjects. More interesting, however, are the results in reaction time when the subject is required to respond to an unspecified sequence of different stimuli. The subject is always supposed to respond in the same way (e.g., to release a key when a stimulus comes on—whether that stimulus is, say, a sound or a light). The only unknown facts in such experiments for the subject are exactly when the next stimulus will occur and what kind of stimulus it will be. Sometimes the stimuli that follow each other are of the same stimulus modality (both sound or both light) and sometimes of different stimulus modality. When the stimuli that follow one another are of different modality (crossmodal), then the reaction time to the second stimulus is longer than when it follows a stimulus of the same modality (ipsimodal); this phenomenon, which is called the crossmodal shift, increases the reaction time more for the schizophrenic patients than for normals (Sutton, Hakerem, Zubin, & Portnoy, 1961; Sutton & Zubin, 1965; Waldbaum, Sutton, & Kerr, 1975). In addition, the uncertainty of the kind of stimulus that is to occur on any trial also increases the reaction time independent of the modality shift phenomenon (Kristofferson, 1967; Waldbaum et al., 1975).

Finally, Zahn, Rosenthal, and Shakow (1961, 1963) showed the importance of the effect of the preparatory interval on reaction time. The preparatory interval is the time that the subject has to get ready to respond to the next stimulus; not only the interval on any given trial but the preceding interval has an effect on reaction time, with the schizophrenic patients being more influenced by having an immediately prior interval that is longer than the current one than when the successive intervals are equal or the current interval is longer than the prior one. Such results are interpreted as showing a deficit in attention in the schizophrenic patient. That is, the schizophrenic has some difficulty in processing stimuli. We shall see later the different kinds of theories that such data give rise to. But before leaving this interesting kind of experiment, it will be worthwhile to point out that not only do these data suggest theories that might explain the more complex behavior of schizophrenics that seems to defy understanding, but despite their simplicity, such data can also reflect such intuitively understandable facts as the length of the previous maladjustment (premorbid state) and outcome of illness of patients tested in their reaction to stimuli. Crider, Maher, and Grinspoon (1965) showed that those patients who had a poorer premorbid history were slower in their reaction times. Another study (Weaver & Brooks, 1964) showed a relationship between reaction time and outcome of illness after two years.

King (1975) used not only the reaction time measures mentioned above, and obtained similar results, but included, in his attempts to study the patient, the whole gamut of what he called psychomotor behavior. Some examples of these psychomotor tests, in addition to simple reaction time tasks, are tapping tests (in which the subject is instructed to tap a plate or two plates as rapidly as possible), and finger dexterity tests (in which the subject must do such tasks as place nails into small holes). King has been able to show that such tests differentiate schizophrenics from normals and that they relate to degree of disturbance in the schizophrenics. His reasoning with respect to the use of psychomotor tests is that they probably best reflect the functioning of the brain, being somewhere between the neurological reflex and the more conceptually based tests usually employed by the clinical psychologist. In a certain sense, these psychomotor tests do not belong under the heading of simple stimulus control, since they require that the subjects respond not only to the external stimuli but also to their own last response; certainly the finger dexterity task or the continuous problem solving tasks are of that nature. King's assumption that the use of simple motor tasks will reveal something about the functioning of the brain is supported by his finding that brain damage and other altered functioning of the nervous system are reflected in the psychomotor tests he uses for testing the schizophrenic patients.

Stimulus control is measured in psychology by some of its oldest techniques, namely, the psychophysical methods that go back to the first experimental psychology laboratory. Perceptual constancy experiments have shown that schizophrenics have difficulty in this area as well. Unfortunately, the results are not as consistent as one might wish. Results are not easily replicated, possibly because of the diagnostic problems already explained. In addition, some studies have already shown that where the experiment allows response bias to enter (e.g., Clark, 1966; Clark, Brown, & Rutschmann, 1967), the difference in performance between schizophrenics and normals may well be attributable to the response tendency rather than to the way in which the stimulus is reacted to.

On the other hand, some psychophysical techniques have generated clearer results. In 1957, Salzinger showed that schizophrenic patients tend to respond more to the immediate stimulus of the effect of the anchor weight preceding the weight being judged than to a warning verbal stimulus to take into account the effect of the anchor weight. The actual procedure of the experiment is as follows. Subjects were instructed to judge the heaviness of a series of weights by lifting each and rendering a judgment in terms of "very light," "light," "medium," "heavy" and "very heavy." After the subjects established a frame of reference, they were required to lift an extremely heavy weight (the anchor, which is more than twice as heavy as the heaviest test weight), told not to judge that weight and to try to counteract its effect on judging the other stimuli. The schizophrenics tended to have their judgments affected by the anchor weight; that is, they judged the test weights to be lighter after lifting the anchor weight than the normals did when they were exposed to the same conditions. This shows the greater susceptibility of the schizophrenics to the more immediate physical stimuli than to the more remote verbal stimuli. This result was corroborated by a further experiment by Wurster (1965), who used anchors as Salzinger did. In another condition, however, Wurster employed an anchor weight only once in a while, finding that this time it was the normals who were influened by the anchor stimulus rather than the schizophrenics. In other words, the schizophrenics were influenced by stimuli when they occurred at the time when their judgments were being made, but this effect was not spread out over all the stimuli, whereas the normals showed a more general effect on their whole frame of reference in rendering judgments.

Some investigators have concentrated on the use of physiological responses as indices of the response to stimuli. Hakerem, Sutton, and Zubin (1964) and Hakerem and Lidsky (1975) found pupillary size to be smaller initially and to give rise to a smaller contraction in response to light in schizophrenics than in normal subjects. An attempt was made to interpret these results in terms of the functioning of the autonomic nervous system, but certain possible artifacts due to the cumulative effects of drug intake in the patients could not be totally discounted. It is obviously of interest to try to take direct measure of physiological functioning in order to infer underlying physiological deficits, but the results so far have not been as clear as investigators had hoped (see, for example, Shagass & Overton, 1975) with respect to the slower recovery of evoked potentials in schizophrenics.

In summary, responses to simple stimuli in reaction time experiments and in some psychophysical experiments show differences between normals and schizophrenics that might serve as a basis for the identification of behavioral mechanisms; those appear to be of a nature allowing one to measure the relative performance of the subject at more than one time, that is, the difference in performance under more than one condition. Zubin (1975) tries to explain this phenomenon in terms of the concept of shift of attention, according to which the difficulty enters not so much in terms of where the schizophrenic pays attention but rather in terms of those moments that require a shift in that attention. One of the theories that he feels might explain this deficit in schizophrenia is the immediacy hypothesis (Salzinger, 1973), discussed later.

Language behavior

In our society, nothing so reveals us as the way we speak and otherwise interact with our fellow human beings. Many of us, like the authors of this book, make a living with our speech and writing. Through the language behavior we emit, people get to know us, and this is true not only of the content of our speech and writing but also of the forms we employ for our communications. In some cases, it is the use of certain expressions; in some, it relates to our pause patterns; in still others, to our intonation patterns, rate of speech between the pauses, the sentence structure, etc.

In other words, we provide people with a kind of signature through our language behavior. This is so because, although some aspects vary with audience (Salzinger, in press), many aspects of language behavior that have been well conditioned and overlearned are stable over many different situations. In addition to revealing the speaker or writer, language has two important functions; the first is that of regulating one's own behavior and the second is that of communicating with and influencing other people.

Regulatory function of language behavior

Let us first look at the problem of regulating one's own behavior. Here we are referring to the planning and problem-solving function of language. Obvious examples of this language use are planning a trip, setting up a schedule, and writing oneself a note about remembering to do something. Another function of language is to solve problems, in such obvious cases as arithmetic problems, crossword puzzles, or examination questions, but also in less obvious cases, such as how to increase one's income, how to influence the passage of legislation, how to get a better office or a better job, how to provide one's children a more interesting summer vacation, how to obtain a better program of education, how to get a bigger apartment, how to deal with the problem of an older person who keeps too much to himself and doesn't eat regularly, and so on. In fact, we all solve problems of varying magnitudes all day long and we all use verbal behavior to do so. Some have suggested that we use language more than we should, that we ought to try to use pictures or at least to imagine solutions in the form of pictures to various problems better solved in that way. It has often been said that Einstein's theory of relativity could not have originated without a spatial picturization including an outside observer viewing objects in motion. Be that as it may, language behavior plays a major role in our problem-solving behavior, whether we think aloud or to ourselves.

The difficulty that schizophrenic patients seem to encounter with respect to thinking has for some time been expressed by the concept of thought disorder. Both DSM-II and DSM-III consider thought disorder to be critical in the diagnosis of schizophrenia—despite the fact that recent research suggests that thought disorder in the usual loosely defined way is characteristic of manic as well as of schizophrenic patients. Without getting into too great detail about this controversy, it is instructive to note that Andreasen finds with her rating scales that both schizophrenic and manic patients show a positive formal thought disorder consisting of such qualities as tangentiality and incoherence related to great pressure of speech, whereas only schizophrenics show a negative thought disorder, which she describes as "laconic speech" and "poverty of content of speech." Whatever the particular definition given to thought disorder in schizophrenia, there is still agreement that some such concept is appropriate to characterize it.

Two investigators were most identified with early experimental study of thought disorder in schizophrenia: Vigotsky (1934) and Goldstein (1944). Essentially their approach consists of sorting objects into various categories or along various dimensions; the inability to accomplish such a task was taken by them as evidence of a defect in abstraction ability. The basic idea was of course to find what this author now refers to as a behavioral mechanism, that is, to find some underlying behavioral explanation for the difficulties that schizophrenics manifest in much of their behavior. Essentially, Vigotsky's and Goldstein's point was that schizophrenic patients had lost their ability to think abstractly. Benjamin (1944), using a somewhat different approach, asked subjects to interpret proverbs and found that schizophrenics tended to interpret them in a very concrete fashion. Take the proverb "A rolling stone gathers no moss" and the interpretation "Nothing can grow on a stone that's always moving" as an example of concrete thinking. It is instructive to examine the book by Kasanin (1944), who presented an early and seminal summary of the abstract-concrete dimension analysis of thought disorder in schizophrenic patients. A plethora of further studies resulted, many of them well summarized in Chapman and Chapman (1973).

Another paper from the Kasanin book ought to be referred to explicitly, since it too has had a wide influence, at least in the conceptualization of the basic fault in schizophrenia. Von Domarus (1944) discussed the so-called schizophrenic laws of logic. He accused schizophrenics of indulging in paralogical thinking, which according to him consists of concluding identity of concepts on the basis of identity of predicates. He gives a dramatic example in which Jesus, cigar boxes, and sex are considered to be identical; the patient's reasoning is that all three are encircled—Jesus by a halo, the cigar boxes by the tax band, and women by sex glances of men. This sounds too good. In fact, it is often the dramatic but unique example that comes to be passed on from textbook to textbook so that students come to think that this is what the typical schizophrenic patient is like. The truth of the matter is that all of the dramatic examples so often cited in the literature are but rare occurrences. They are useful only if we can abstract from them some principle that describes typical patients along a dimension on which the dramatic example constitutes one extreme and presumably normal behavior constitutes the other.

Even the Kasanin (1944) book already contained interpretations that differed from the abstract-concrete interpretation of the basic deficit of schizophrenia. Cameron (1944) attributed the errors in sorting that schizophrenics make to their overinclusiveness, or their inability to draw proper boundaries in the problem they are trying to solve. Over twenty years later, Payne (1966) took this concept of overinclusiveness to mean "an impairment of some central filtering process whose function it is actively to inhibit external sensations, and internal thoughts which are not relevant to whatever is the focus of attention at a given time" (p. 95).

In a very interesting follow-up experiment by Chapman (1956), it became clear that the sorting of cards in terms of concepts became materially worse in the case of schizophrenics when the cards contained distracting stimuli. Furthermore, this distraction took place equally when they were concretely or conceptually related to the main stimuli, suggesting that the schizophrenics were able to abstract sufficiently to be distracted by conceptually related stimuli. Clearly some other concept is called for in interpreting this kind of behavior. The advantage of objective and repeatable experiments is that one can interpret the data of any one experiment restricted only by the data of further experiments. In other words, once people such as Goldstein and Vigotsky reduced their theories to specific experimental tasks, their work had value even when their theoretical speculations seemed not entirely warranted. Whatever one thinks of their theories, therefore, the fact that they used specific techniques has made their contribution the start of a significant change from the more traditional speculative approach to describing schizophrenic patients—a practice no longer as popular as it once was.

The regulatory function of language has been investigated in still another way, through the technique of word association. Here the patient is presented a series of words one at a time and asked to "give the first word that comes to mind." Word association experiments have over the years suggested such characteristic schizophrenic responses as clang associations, where the critical determinant seems to have been the sound of the stimulus word rather than its meaning, and idiosyncratic associations, which are responses unique to the person rather than being the common responses that are found in word association norms. A study by Peastrel (1964) can be used to bolster the clang-association results. He found that schizophrenics tended to generalize more to homonyms of the conditioned stimulus in a classical conditioning experiment, whereas normal subjects tended to generalize more to synonyms than to homonyms. Nevertheless, the word association approach presents a number of problems in supplying an understanding of schizophrenics. Thus, Moon, Mefferd, Wieland, Porkony, and Falconer (1968) contend, on the basis of their experimentation, that schizophrenic patients actually mishear the words they appear to respond to with a "distant" (farfetched) association. When these investigators corrected for mishearing, no significant difference in distant associations was found between normals and schizophrenics.

Communicative function of language behavior

The matter of stimulus control comes up in another context in which a variant of word association forms the basic technique of studying schizophrenic deficits. This technique is also the bridge between the regulatory and the communicative functions of language behavior. Cohen (1976, 1978) has summarized a series of experiments directed at studying what he calls referent communication—that is, the ability of people to transfer specific information to one another. The technique involved allows one to gauge not only the ability to send information but also the ability to receive it.

Referent communicability. Let us look at the basic paradigm. Cohen and Camhi (1967) paired schizophrenic patients and normal hospital employees in all possible ways, so that some pairs consisted of two normals, some of two schizophrenics, and some of a normal and a schizophrenic in which the information was, in some cases, sent by the normal to the schizophrenic, and in some by the schizophrenic to the normal person. Each sender was shown a list of word-pairs and asked to provide clues for one of the words—the referent—in the form of other words that might lead a listener to choose the referent word. To take an actual example, the subjects might be shown the word pair "cure-remedy"; one word would be underlined and the sender's task would be to provide a clue for the referent. The only restriction on the sender was that the clue could not rhyme or be spelled like the referent word. The results were very interesting, as Table 11.2 indicates. The table shows quite clearly that although schizophrenics are less accurate than normal speakers in sending a message, they do not differ from normals in their ability to profit from the communications sent to them when they are listeners. Moreover, the table shows that there is no special interaction: the schizophrenic communication is equally difficult for the normal and the schizophrenic listeners.

Table 11.2. Communication Accuracy: Average Proportion Correct Referent Choices in Each Speaker-Listener Group

Speaker	Listeners	
	Schizophrenic	Normal
Schizophrenic	.66	.67
Normal	.72	.74

From Cohen & Camhi (1967) (Table 2).

This fascinating technique addresses itself to a very important function in everyday living, but it reduces the situation to its bare essentials and allows one to extract an objective measure from it. It also suggests a behavioral mechanism for the schizophrenic deficit, namely an inability to reject a sampled response (loosely speaking, a thought that's come to mind); in the experimental situation discussed above, the speaker has the task of looking at the referent and the nonreferent word, and, after thinking of a possible cue word, of deciding whether to use that word or not. Cohen's theory states that this stage gives the schizophrenic patient trouble. It is an interesting theory to explain a number of schizophrenic phenomena, and as will be seen later in the section on theory, it resembles a number of theories that discuss the schizophrenic's deficient ability to reject stimuli that are not relevant. Here the point is not to decide whether this theory is the best one, but rather to demonstrate how a particular approach to the study of schizophrenia can both be socially relevant and provide information on a possibly basic deficit that might explain not only this class of schizophrenic behavior but other response classes as well.

Before leaving this technique, we must take note of one difficulty. Patients are likely to view such an experimental technique as artificial. This makes it similar to techniques such as reaction time experiments which, because the patients know they are participating in an experiment, are therefore subject to the whole range of confounding variables involved in cooperation.

Samples of "schizophrenic" speech. Examination of continuous samples of schizophrenic speech samples have traditionally been verbatim transcriptions of psychiatric interviews that made little attempt at experimental control. Woods (1938) used the verbatim speech samples collected from some 125 schizophrenic patients. Although he reported that he kept examiner influence at a minimum, no exact description of his procedure is available. Nevertheless, he presents a good number of samples of what has come to be called typical schizophrenic speech when, as already pointed out earlier, these are at best examples of rather extreme peculiarities of schizophrenic speech (Woods, 1938, p. 308):

Examiner: Can people receive messages from others when these people are not near?

Patient: Yes.

E: How?

P: By radio, telephone.

E: Any other way?

P: By writing letters, by wire, by water.

E: Did you say water?

P: By some code or by, or by flowers, by old plays, by true lovers.

This conversation is given as an example of tangential speech, but one can't help wondering about the context of this exchange. It seems that the examiner takes very little interest in what the patient says until, at last, he says something somewhat bizarre and then the next question begins to elicit the kinds of peculiarties of speech (thinking?) thought to be characteristic of schizophrenia. The reader is reminded of the studies by the author and his colleagues (Salzinger & Pisoni, 1958, 1960, 1961; Salzinger, Portnoy, & Feldman, 1964a), which have shown how the reinforcing behavior of the interviewer affects the very phenomenon that is merely supposed to be observed. Interestingly enough, in the example given, even after being prompted to increasingly more remote associations, the responses are still somewhat related to the question until they begin to sound odd, although one can see some sense even in the response of "by water," meaning that the message might be sent by boat mail; the notion of sending messages by code is not quite right although obviously still related, and even the idea of sending a message "by flowers" is acceptable since advertisements suggest that approach—a message is implicit in the act of sending flowers. The question is always to analyze carefully the conditions under which some of the bizarre things that schizophrenics say, occur. If there is a moral to be drawn from the above, it is that nobody is bizarre all of the time, that for all patients there appear to be some conditions under which the behavior observed seems quite normal (cf. Salzinger & Salzinger, 1973). This is not a trivial point, for it warns us that no behavior is simply a function of the person emitting it; behavior is always also a function of the conditions under which the person is behaving, including the reinforcement contingencies as well as the physical and social conditions related to the person at any given time (cf. Fig. 1, The behavioral mechanism).

Content analysis. What about the objective analysis of continuous verbal behavior of patients? Content analysis began in abnormal psychology when nondirective therapists such as Carl Rogers decided that the therapeutic hour ought to be submitted to detailed analysis, and in that context they recorded the speech of patients, typed it up, and then decided to do content analysis of the typescripts. Meadow, Greenblatt, Levine, and Solomon (1952) made use of a fairly simple content analysis, restricting their categorization to the units that could be categorized as showing comfort, discomfort, or neutrality of feeling; they then calculated the DRQ (discomfort-relief quotient), which consisted of the number of discomfort statements divided by the total number of statements. They found that the less seriously ill patients had the higher DRQ. They interpreted that to mean that those patients had more insight into their condition than the schizophrenic patients who lacked the insight to realize they were suffering discomfort. These results are perhaps not quite as intuitively obvious as one might wish, but similar results have been obtained by Maher, McKean, and McLaughlin (1966), who found lower DRQs in those schizophrenics described as obviously thought disordered (this is related to being worse off in the previous study).

Laffal (1960, 1961, 1965) did a much more elaborate content analysis on many hours of psychotherapy with a schizophrenic patient; he called his method contextual analysis because his analysis concentrated on the varying contexts in which the different categories of verbal behavior occurred at different stages of therapy. Gottschalk and colleagues (1967; Gottschalk & Gleser, 1969), obtaining three- to five-minute speech samples from patients, constructed a rather elaborate content analysis complete with rating scales. Although the authors showed adequate reliability of scoring, the categories were constituted on the basis of a psychodynamic theory of behavior, thus reducing the general usefulness of a content analysis that might otherwise be more concerned with the manifest content. Finally, in the context of content analysis, we might mention Maher, McKean, and McLaughlin (1966), who did a rather elaborate survey (in addition to their DRQ analysis just mentioned) of written schizophrenic materials collected from all over the country. Making use of the general inquirer program, they arrived at a computer-analyzed approach to the analysis of language.

Formal analysis. Another approach to schizophrenic speech has gone a different route—one that is formal, whose objectivity is obvious, and where quantification is easy. Formal measures of this kind were first promulgated by Whitehorn and Zipf (1943) in a classic paper based upon the analysis of the rate of repetition of words. Their basic hypothesis was that speech is a compromise between minimizing the effort of the speaker (by using the same word to cover many different meanings and therefore having a high rate of repetition) and minimizing the effort of the hearer (using a new word every time a new concept is called for, resulting in a low rate of repetition). They found that schizophrenics repeat more than normals. Mann (1944) compared schizophrenics and normals on their written productions and Fairbanks (1944) compared them on their speech. Both found that schizophrenics had lower rates of repetition (TTRs) than the normal controls. Unfortunately the significance of this result is attenuated by the fact that the schizophrenic and normal groups were not equated in terms of education and speech community. Feldstein and Jaffe (1962) repeated the comparison in two groups generally equated on education and failed to obtain a significant difference. However, the Feldstein and Jaffe study used small samples of speech (twenty-five words) to calculate TTRs. Obviously a small sample limits the variation of TTRs. Furthermore, their study obtained speech samples from schizophrenic patients being treated with tranquilizing drugs. The importance of that variable is clear in a study by Salzinger, Pisoni, Feldman, and Bacon (1961), who showed, albeit in one normal subject only (over extensive samples of verbal behavior), that an increase in dose of chlorpromazine increases TTR. A later study by Hammer and Salzinger (1964) compared normals and schizophrenics who had received no drugs. The subjects were matched on the basis of speech community and education, and it was found that the TTR, although affected by these variables, was greater in schizophrenic than in normal speech. Furthermore, application of other indices of repetition resulted in larger differences between the normals and schizophrenics and weaker association to social variables. We conclude that there is at least some evidence for greater repetition in the speech of schizophrenics than in that of normals.

Another approach to language behavior is to examine its temporal characteristics. In 1953, Chapple, an anthropologist, decided to design a standardized interview. In one part of the interview, he encouraged (reinforced?) the interlocutor to continue to speak, in another he paused for a long time before speaking again, and finally in another, he interrupted the interviewee an inordinate number of times. Chapple (1960) and Saslow and Matarazzo (1959) later adapted this interview to the study of schizophrenic patients. The measures of the effect of the various interventions were the duration of the patient's utterances, latencies between the interviewer's remarks and the patient's, and the duration of the patient's continued speech while being interrupted. One of the more interesting findings was the patient's slower reaction time to the interviewer's remarks. Schizophrenics show a slower reaction time not only in what may appear to be an artificial situation (the usual reaction time experiment in which the subject is instructed to respond as fast as possible to the onset of a sound or visual stimulus), but also in a more natural situation such as an interview.

General communicability. We have already discussed referent communication measures as one way of determining how efficiently schizophrenics communicate. Here we shall present a more general measure of communicability. Language is very redundant; that is, contained in the same sentence or even word is information also present in other words and other sentences. When you mishear a word or two, you can frequently figure out what you missed. This very important property of language has been used in what has come to be called the cloze procedure.

It was originated by Taylor (1953), although to be sure techniques like it were used before and afterwards. The procedure consists of the following: Every *n*th (usually every 5th) word of a text is left out. A group of subjects is then instructed to guess the missing words. The procedure is called "cloze" because the subject has the task of completing something, akin to completing a circle drawn only partially to completion; gestalt psychologists call this inclination to complete incomplete figures "closure." Whether that is the proper way of describing such a phenomenon as filling in blanks is not as important as the fact that subjects do rather well in this task.

Salzinger, Portnoy, and Feldman (1964b) decided to make use of a number of monologues collected for another purpose (Salzinger, Portnoy, & Feldman, 1964a—as already indicated above—namely that of investigating the conditionability of speech in schizophrenic patients. Monologues obtained under the control condition, in which the patients received no reinforcement, were the speech samples used in this study. The first two hundred or so words of each of a number of monologues were then prepared in cloze procedure form, that is, with every fifth word deleted, and they were presented to a group of college students whose task it was to guess the words that were missing. Figure 2 presents the cumulative number of schizophrenic and normal samples as a function of the proportion of correct guesses to total guesses. S-1 refers to the first 100 words emitted by the schizophrenic patients, S-2 refers to the second 100 words emitted by the schizophrenics, N-1 and N-2 refer respectively to the first and second 100 words emitted by the normal control subjects. The

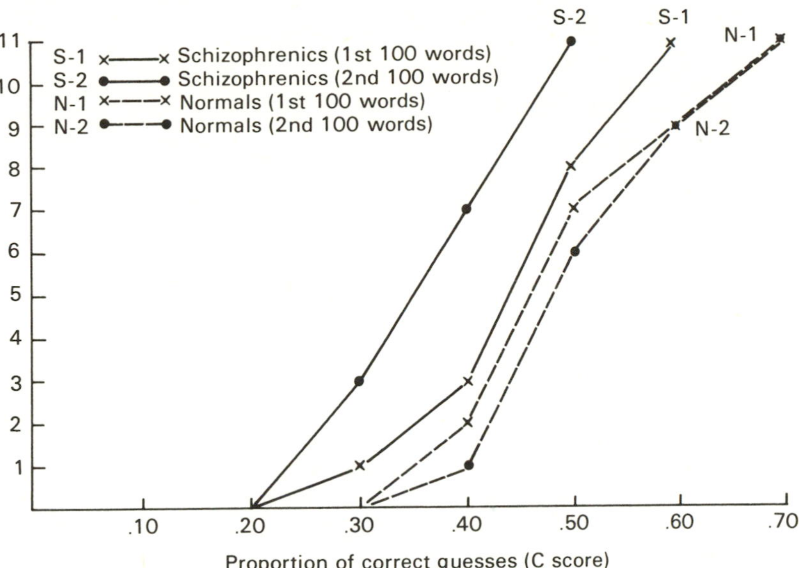

Fig. 11.2. Cumulative frequency of schizophrenia and normal subjects as a function of proportion of correct guesses to total guesses (C score). The two chronic schizophrenics and their normal matches are not included. S-1 and S-2, and N-1 and N-2 refer respectively to the first and second 100 words of the schizophrenic and normal passages. (From Salzinger, Portnoy, & Feldman, 1964b.)

results show that the two groups of normal speech samples are more communicable (defined by the number of exactly correct guesses for each of the blanks) than are the schizophrenic ones. Moreover, whereas the normal samples remain stable, the schizophrenic speech samples become less communicable from the first to the second 100 words. The authors interpreted this to mean that as the external stimulus control (exerted by the experimenter's instructions) becomes weaker from the first to the second 100 words, the schizophrenic patients must rely on their own self-produced speech to guide further speech and that the response-produced stimulus control makes manifest the difficulties characteristic of schizophrenic speech that we cited earlier.

The cloze procedure provides an objective technique of measuring an obvious critical aspect of social behavior. In addition, it lends itself to theoretical interpretation by the immediacy hypothesis (Salzinger, 1971a, b, 1973; Salzinger, Portnoy, & Feldman, 1978). We shall say more about it in the section on theories. The theory states that schizophrenic patients tend to respond to stimuli closer to them in time than do normal subjects. The cloze procedure is sensitive to the immediacy of the stimulus controlling the speaker not only with respect to the external stimulus but also with respect to the response-produced stimulus that is so important in language behavior. The immediacy hypothesis was tested directly in the following way by Salzinger, Portnoy, Pisoni, and Feldman (1970). Using the results of the cloze procedure study cited above (Salzinger, Portnoy, & Feldman, 1964b), they matched blanks of the cloze procedure protocols (from pairs of schizophrenic and normal subjects of the same age, sex, education, and speech community) on part of speech and probability of guessing the words in the cloze procedure form. These blanks were then presented to a new group of normal subjects who were asked to guess the

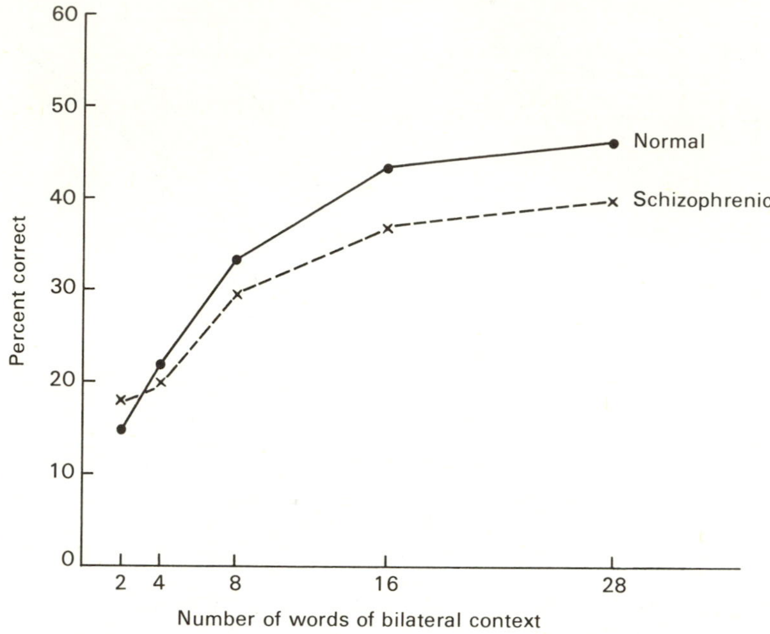

Fig. 11.3. Percent of correct words guessed to schizophrenic and normal speech segments as a function of the number of words of bilateral context. (From Salzinger, Portnoy, & Feldman, 1978.)

deleted words under different conditions of context: with only one word before and one after each blank, two before and two after, four before and four after, eight before and eight after, and finally, fourteen before and fourteen after. Figure 3 shows an increase in the proportion of correct guesses for both normal and schizophrenic speech, but the normal speech keeps increasing at the point where the schizophrenic speech has already reached a plateau. Schizophrenic speech is more influenced by the closer words than is the normal speech, since the "clozers" continued to profit from having more remote words available for normal but not for schizophrenic speech.

One might expect that a measure that taps a socially significant variable would also relate to such partially socially determined phenomena as time spent in a psychiatric hospital. And indeed we (Salzinger, Portnoy, & Feldman, 1966) found a correlation of −.47 between the number of days spent in the hospital and the cloze procedure score for a monologue emitted at time of admission. This means that the higher the cloze score (the better the communicability), the shorter the stay in the hospital.

Language perception. So far, only Cohen's referent communication has dealt with the schizophrenic way of receiving information. The other techniques, although obviously influenced by the way in which schizophrenics receive information, nevertheless concentrated on the production of language. Here we will present some studies that try to assess how well schizophrenics perceive language. An old technique for the assessment of language perception consists of testing the immediate or even the delayed recall for verbal material organized in different ways. Generally speaking, schizophrenics do not remember as well when recall as opposed to recognition is measured (see Salzinger, 1973, for a review of experiments). Perhaps more interesting, however, is the question of how well schizophrenics seem to be able to take advantage of context in remembering. As just pointed out, schizophrenics take advantage of close context primarily in language production. In general, studies that test memory as a function of context find that schizophrenics are less able to take advantage of the context than are normals.

A number of studies have examined the question of immediate vs. remote context using a method very much like that of the production studies, particularly that of Salzinger, Portnoy, Pisoni, and Feldman (1970). To take but two recent examples, Blaney (1974) found that, whereas normals profited from having additional context, schizophrenic patients did not, in the process of guessing a word deleted from a segment of verbal behavior. De Silva and Hemsley (1977) did a similar experiment using longer verbal behavior samples to which the schizophrenics and normals had to respond by guessing the missing words; deleting every fourth, every seventh, or every tenth word, they showed that normal subjects profited from the sparser deletion patterns, whereas schizophrenics appeared to deteriorate in their performance with increasing amounts of context available. In general, one can conclude that schizophrenics do better with immediate than with remote context. We will discuss below the implications of these findings for the immediacy hypothesis. Here we merely present findings consistent for production and perception of language.

Schizophrenic language—its perception and production—continue to attract investigators. The interested reader should consult Chapman and Chapman (1973), Rochester and Martin (in press), Salzinger (1973), and Vetter (1968, 1975) for further studies in this area.

Theories

Those who are weary of theories have long ago suggested that the excess found in the area of schizophrenia are to be attributed to the paucity of data. In defense of current theories, however, it is fair to say that they have become much more testable than they used to be.

The very concept of schizophrenia is a theoretical one based on the assumption that the medical model is the proper perspective from which to view the behavior of interest. This theory is biologically focused, although all the dependent variables are usually measured in semibehavioral ways, through interviewing techniques buttressed by rating scales. The origin of the idea of a biological fault to explain the bizarre behavior of schizophrenia is its seeming resistance to psychological intervention techniques plus the evidence for a genetic component. The classical studies were done by Kallmann (1946), who found that monozygotic (from one egg and therefore having identical genetic endowment) twins have higher concordance (the same diagnosis in both twins) rates than dizygotic (from two different eggs and therefore having different genetic endowment) twins—a finding often but not always repeated in subsequent studies (Rosenthal, 1970); in some of the studies Rosenthal reports the dizygotic twins have greater concordance than monozygotic twins; furthermore, it is difficult to explain that the concordance rates vary from study to study among monozygotic twins all the way from 0 to 86.2 percent.

Genetic studies have been extended to following up children of schizophrenic mothers, some of whom were adopted and raised by normal parents, and comparing them to two groups of children born to normal parents, some of whom were raised by normal and some by schizophrenic adoptive parents. The results showed that 18.8 percent of those born to schizophrenic parents (although not raised by them) were judged to be schizophrenic or "near-schizophrenic," whereas only 10.7 percent of the normal children raised by schizophrenic adoptive parents and 10.1 percent of the normal children raised by normal adoptive parents were so judged. Once again we have some difficulty with the exact definition of schizophrenia (cf. the matter of broadening vs.

narrowing definitions discussed in the first section of the chapter). Whatever the evidence for the genetic factor, there is evidence that one exists, and although exactly what it is behaviorally still needs to be studied, there is nevertheless enough evidence in its favor to have encouraged a search for a biochemical fault.

A number of biochemical theories of schizophrenia have been suggested. They are well summarized in Snyder (1974). A favorite today is the dopamine theory of schizophrenia. Beginning with the observation that amphetamine produces schizophreniclike behavior, knowing that it releases norepinephrine and dopamine into the synaptic cleft, and adding to that the observation that the so-called antipsychotic drugs block dopamine receptors, we have the makings of a biochemical theory that states essentially that schizophrenics have an excess of dopamine in certain sites of the brain.

Another biologically related theory of schizophrenia is based on the recent research on the asymmetry of cerebral hemispheric functioning. This research states that the right hemisphere deals in a nonsequential way with spatial and emotional phenomena. The left hemisphere, on the other hand, deals with language functioning and other sequential phenomena. On this basis, such investigators as Flor-Henry (1976), Yozawitz (1977), and Shimkunas (1978) suggest that schizophrenia is mainly due to a lesion or at least some neuronal disorganization of the dominant (usually left) hemisphere, whereas the affective disorders have basic problems in the right or nondominant hemisphere.

As already pointed out, it is critical while positing biological causes to state what the behavioral mechanisms are that intervene between the biological faults and the ultimate bizarre behavior that brings people to the attention of the mental health authorities.

Despite what might seem to be the final blow to notions of environmentally caused schizophrenia by the adoption study alluded to above, such theories continue to exist. Ullmann and Krasner (1975), for example, view schizophrenia as the product of the extenction of attending responses, particularly to the social stimuli to which other people in our society are likely to respond. This formulation suggests a basic mechanism to account for an underlying problem whose interaction with other aspects of living produces the bizarre behavior that we characterize as schizophrenia. Wynne (1977), coming at the problem from an entirely different point of view, also stresses the importance of behavioral mechanisms in the etiology of schizophrenia. Influenced by Bateson et al.'s [1956] double-bind idea of functioning under contradictory instructions, Wynne shows that communication deviances in the family members are very much involved in schizophrenia. The double-bind theory is most enticing; nevertheless, it has been encouraged by a disappointingly small number of confirming studies. One study (Salzinger, Portnoy, & Feldman, 1973), which produced an experimental analogue of the double bind by asking normal subjects to write essays in favor of political candidates of whom they did not approve, showed at least some signs of communication difficulties regularly found in schizophrenic patients. The essays written in favor of candidates the writers disapproved of had lower communicability, as measured by the cloze score, than the essays written in favor of candidates they did approve of. In other words, even normal subjects, given a situation in which they had to say something they did not really believe in, took the route of communicating in ways that were more difficult to understand.

A learning theory that took into account the genetic factor was promulgated by Mednick (Mednick & Schulsinger, 1968, 1973), who found that the population of high-risk children (those born to a schizophrenic mother) showed faster conditioning and more generalization but a faster recovery from arousal. Mednick maintains that schizophrenics are more generally aroused and therefore are more likely to be avoidance conditioned since the reinforcer is the elimination of, or prevention of, an aversive event. The idea (first explored by Mednick) of using high-risk children to learn about schizophrenia before the secondary influence of society responding to the peculiar behavior of the high-risk child has become more popular in recent years (e.g., Erlenmeyer-Kimling, 1975). It has probably also influenced such ideas as the vulnerability concept in conjunction with time-limited episodes of schizophrenia (Zubin, 1976). The latter idea once more brings back the importance of critical life events in the production of schizophrenia (Dohrenwend & Dohrenwend, 1974).

Shakow (1962) maintains that the principal difficulty of the schizophrenic is an inability to maintain a major set; that is, a readiness to respond some time in the future. Chapman and Chapman (1973) believe that schizophrenic behavior can be explained by merely looking at the response biases of normal subjects since schizophrenics emit those responses that have the generally highest probability of occurrence independent of the context. Garmezy (1966) hypothesizes that schizophrenics are governed in large measure by overresponding to aversive stimuli, accompanied by a lessened responsiveness to social stimuli. A number of theorists in this area have viewed the responsiveness to stimulation as the source of basic difficulty. We have already mentioned Ullmann and Krasner in this context. Silverman (1967), Venables (1964), and Yates (1966) speak of a stimulus control problem, and the latter concentrates on the stimulus *processing* (within the person) as the major problem.

Two other theories will be briefly mentioned, the disattention theory of Cromwell and Dokecki (1968) and the immediacy hypothesis of Salzinger (Salzinger, 1973; Salzinger, Portnoy, & Feldman, 1978). The latter theory states that schizophrenics tend to pay more attention to those stimuli that are currently acting on them than do normal subjects. The study on communicability showed that schizophrenics' speech is primarily governed by closely neighboring words as they speak them but not by more remote ones (Salzinger, Portnoy, Pisoni, & Feldman, 1970). A conditioning study (Salzinger & Pisoni, 1960) found that schizophrenics' behavior shows faster extinction than normals', demonstrating that then the critical stimulus, the reinforcer, is no longer present, normal subjects are still affected by its earlier presence, whereas the schizophrenics react only to the current conditions—the lack of reinforcement—and therefore their responses extinguish more rapidly. Although the Cromwell-Dokecki theory is similar to the immediacy hypothesis, it requires a two-stage model to explain the schizophrenic's tendency to remain in the present. Furthermore, it does not state, if the schizophrenic has difficulty in letting go of a stimulus, how that eventually happens. In contrast, the immediacy concept says that the specific stimuli currently acting on the individual will have a greater probability of controlling that individual's behavior than other stimuli more remote. It is interesting to note in this context that Shimkunas (1978) thought that the research on left hemisphere dysfunction—disorganization of sequential processing, with a consequent right-hemisphere take-over of functioning—would result in schizophrenic behavior as described by the immediacy hypothesis. For further descriptions of theories in this area, the interested reader is advised to look at Chapman and Chapman (1973) or Salzinger (1973).

Treatment

There has not been much optimism about the success of treatment of schizophrenia despite the fact that two parallel developments of new treatments have taken place. The first is the revolution in psychopharmacology (Segal, 1975). The importance of this revolution was in fact two-fold. It removed some of the florid symptoms and thus changed the attitude of those who took care of schizophrenics from one of hopelessness to one of being able to do something. And for the first time the number of inpatients went down. It also gave rise to biochemical theories of the origin of the problem. In terms of treatment, the more recent socially and financially motivated attempts to empty the state hospitals have raised the question of maintenance of treatment, of long-range side effects, and of long-range effectiveness (Davis, 1975; Gardos & Cole, 1976; Tobias & MacDonald, 1974).

The second treatment mode has been social, family treatment (Beels, 1975), and—related in practice if not in theory—behavior modification (Hersen & Bellack, 1976a; Kazdin, 1976; Liberman, 1974; Paul & Lentz, 1977). There is not sufficient space here to compare the various methods of treatment; however, we can say that behavior modification treatment will need to be used with schizophrenics whether the primary use is to teach social skills, as shown by Hersen and Bellack (1976b), or whether the interest is to reconstruct the lives of chronic patients long ago consigned to institutionalization but who apparently can be helped, given the proper conditions of treatment, surveillance, and evaluation, as in Paul and Lentz (1977). Furthermore, the application of drugs, while in some ways effective, does not solve the problem, especially in the cases of those living in the community, since it is not known whether the drugs are causing harm and whether at some stage the treatment can be discontinued or at least reduced.

Summary

The object of this chapter has been to examine the disorder called schizophrenia in as much detail as is possible, limited only by the known facts and by space considerations. If no hard and fast conclusions about the disorder have been formulated, that is simply a reflection of the state of research at this time. Beginning with considerations of the medical model in contrast to the behavioral model, and then going on to methodological problems inherent first in the definition and diagnosis of the disorder and then going on to show their role in research as well, this chapter reviewed the research in stimulus control and language behavior. This kind of organization reflects the ways in which the behavior of normal people is controlled also. Thus stimulus control is an organizing factor because normal behavior is controlled in this way. Language behavior is important because of its significance in society. Finally, there was a brief section about theories of schizophrenia and about treatment. These are important topics, much in need of further work.

GLOSSARY

Clang association: A response in the word association test that is determined by the sound of the stimulus.

Cloze procedure: A method for the measurement of a person's ability to communicate.

Communicative function of language: Transferring information to, and influencing the behavior of, others.

Delusion: A belief not warranted by the facts, such as being controlled by others, or having one's thoughts heard by others.

DSM: Diagnostic and Statistical Manual, issued by the American Psychiatric Association as the official classificatory system of psychiatric disorders.

Etiology: Cause of a disorder, especially as conceptualized according to the medical model.

Hallucination: Report of sensory stimulation in the absence of appropriate stimulation, such as hearing someone's voice in its absence.

High-risk children: Children likely, because of genetic or environmental reasons, to fall victim to some form of psychopathology.

Major set: Readiness to respond sometime in the future.

Overinclusiveness: Responding to a more stimuli than the task at hand requires.

RDC: Research diagnostic criteria, a part of the DSM-III according to which some subset of a list of symptoms must be present to apply a given diagnosis.

Regulatory function of language: Planning and otherwise regulating one's own behavior.

Reliability of diagnosis: Agreement independently arrived at between two or more people in the assignment of a particular diagnosis.

Shallowness of affect: Dearth of emotional expression.

Symptom: The manifestation, rather than the cause, of the disorder.

12

ORGANIC BRAIN SYNDROMES AND RELATED DISORDERS

GERALD GOLDSTEIN

There is frequently a distinction made in the field of psychopathology between "functional" disorders, that have no apparent physical basis, and "organic" disorders, or those conditions that can be more or less definitely associated with some physical process. In most cases, the physical process associated with the organic disorders is some impairment of brain function.

This chapter is devoted to a discussion of the patient with brain dysfunction, or the "organic" patient. It begins with a brief history of how brain-damaged patients were studied over the years, followed by a review of some of the modern concepts of brain dysfunction. There are many things that can go wrong with the brain, and there is a relationship between what goes wrong and the fate of the patient in regard to behavioral consequences, morbidity, and mortality. Therefore, some material on neuropathology, or the pathological processes that may afflict brain tissue, is presented.

Aside from the matter of what various pathological processes can do to the brain, there are also the questions about what brain-damaged patients look like clinically and how brain damage is diagnosed. The clinical appearance of brain damage turns out to be a complex matter depending on such considerations as type of pathological process, the location in the brain in which the pathology exists, and a number of factors having to do with the patient, such as age and premorbid personality. To illustrate the clinical appearance of brain-damaged patients, a number of vignettes of different kinds of brain damage are presented. The chapter concludes with a section on the variety of methods for detecting brain damage.

One of life's mysteries concerns how the physical processes going on in our central nervous systems are translated into mental events such as thinking, remembering, engaging in purposeful behavior, and perceiving. Many years ago this mystery was named the mind-body problem and became the subject of extensive writings by philosophers and later by psychologists. In recent years, the phrase mind-body problem has been more or less replaced by brain-behavior relationships, and the study of such relationships has become an object of empirical scientific inquiry. Individuals engaged in such studies are called neuropychologists, and neuropsychology has become a broad field of scientific inquiry and clinical application. The fields of neuropsychology and abnormal psychology meet when the object of inquiry is the brain-damaged patient. The term brain-damaged patient will not be defined at this point except to say that we will be referring to individuals with deviations in behavior that can reasonably be associated with identifiable, structural damage to the brain. This chapter will provide a summary of some of the things that are known about such patients.

The basic phenomenon to be discussed here is that damage to the brain is often associated with alterations of behavior. The basic problem is that of gaining some systematic understanding of what aspects of damage are associated with particular behavioral consequences. For example, one aspect of brain damage is the location of the damage in the brain. Brain damage at one location may result in behavioral consequences that are quite different from those associated with damage to other locations. Damage to one area of the brain may lead to paralysis, while damage to some other area may produce blindness or loss of the ability to speak. As will be seen later, location is not the only aspect of brain damage that contributes to the behavioral result. The *type* of damage is most crucial. There has been an unfortunate tendency among behavioral scientists to treat brain damage as a single entity. It is not. We do not treat all damage to other organs of the body as single entities. For example, we rarely talk about "lung damage" or "the lung damaged" patient. Rather, we more commonly talk in terms of tuberculosis, emphysema, or lung cancer. Yet we glibly continue to talk about "brain damage" and "the brain-damaged patient" rather than about patients with brain infections, brain wounds, or circulatory disorders of the brain. It is important to appreciate from the beginning that "damage" or "lesion" are broad terms that cover a number of pathological entities, and that the brain, like other organs of the body, is subject to impairment by a variety of pathological processes. The brain may become infected, or damaged by trauma; it may be impaired by oxygen deprivation or introduction of various toxic substances; it can be afflicted with cancer and a variety of degenerative processes, some of which are not fully understood.

Without definitive knowledge of how the brain really works, we are forced to construct scientific fictions, known as models. As these models are supported by scientific evidence they become less fictional and more concordant with the manner in which the phenomenon under study actually functions. Certain models may be found to be more useful and congruent with the experimental findings than are other models.

If one had to choose a date to mark the beginning of modern human neuropsychology, it would probably be 1861. During this year the neurologist Paul Broca reported on the case of a patient who had sustained marked loss of the ability to speak. An autopsy revealed that the patient had sustained serious damage to the third frontal convolution of the left cerebral hemisphere, an area in the anterior (forward) position of the left side of the brain. So was the center for speech discovered, and to this day the third frontal convolution of the left hemisphere is known as Broca's area. Later, the neurologist Wernicke located the area that mediates comprehension of speech, and other investigators localized various sensory and motor functions either through stimulation of animal brains or autopsy studies of humans. During the period initiated by Broca's discovery there was a great deal of investigation of patients with focal brain lesions marked by a major effort to localize various functions and abilities. Various syndromes were discovered, and the centers and pathways whose damage or interruption produced these syndromes were mapped out.

At the time of the peak period for localization theory, the roots of a counter-theory were already present in the work of Pierre Flourens. Flourens was not a strict believer in the idea of various brain centers, but rather suggested that while each part of the central nervous system may have its own specialized functions, there is nevertheless a unity to the system as a whole and this unity dominates the entire system. As years went by and scientific knowledge accumulated, increasingly impressive evidence was generated attesting to the view that all brain function could not be explained on the basis of precise localization of function. This evidence is crucial to our understanding of brain-damaged patients in various clinical situations, and so will be briefly reviewed here.

The neurologist Hughlings Jackson proposed a distinction between primary and secondary symptoms of brain damage. The primary symptoms are the direct consequences of the lesion, while the secondary symptoms are those changes that take place in the *unimpaired* stratum. Thus, brain damage produces effects not only at the site of the lesion, but throughout the brain. Another neurologist of Jackson's time, Henry Head, pointed out that localization in the cerebral cortex was more variable and complex than seemed to be the case originally. He formulated the significant proposition that the response obtained from a particular locus is not absolute, but rather is a momentary phenomenon depending upon what has happened previously.

The American physiological psychologist Karl S. Lashley delivered perhaps the most telling blows to early localization theory through his studies involving generating brain lesions in animals. In essence, Lashley found that behaviors such as discrimination learning or performance in a maze are less dependent on the location of preserved tissue than they are on the amount of preserved tissue. This finding was formulated in the form of two principles, equipotentiality and mass action. The principle of equipotentiality states that an intact part of a functional area of the brain can carry out functions lost by the destruction of other parts. Mass action is a qualification of the equipotentiality principle, indicating that efficiency of performance can be reduced in proportion to the extent of brain injury. In essence, the amount of destroyed tissue may be a more important consideration than the location of that tissue in regard to determining the behavioral outcome (Beach, Hebb, Morgan, & Nissen, 1960.)

Evidence from the clinical realm that strikingly paralleled the findings of Lashley was obtained by two of the modern pioneers of human neuropsychology, Kurt Goldstein and Martin Scheerer. Goldstein was a psychiatrist who had the opportunity to intensively study soldiers who sustained brain wounds during World War I. He was later joined by Martin Scheerer, a psychologist, and the collaboration of the two resulted in a major contribution to our knowledge of brain damage in humans (Goldstein & Scheerer, 1941). These investigators were strongly influenced by Hughlings Jackson and by the developments and theoretical formulations of gestalt psychology, which were emerging at about the same time as they were studying their brain-damaged patients. Goldstein and Scheerer's studies led them to conclude that many of the symptoms of brain damage could be viewed not as specific manifestations of damage to particular loci, but as impairment of a more general function that they called the "abstract attitude." The abstract attitude is not localizable in any region of the brain, but depends upon the functional integrity of the brain as a whole. Thus, to Goldstein and Scheerer, brain damage is not a matter of the functional consequences of destruction of centers for various abilities and the communication pathways among them. They, in fact, represent a point of view that is antithetical to "diagram making." To them, the functional consequences of brain damage are best described in terms of a total personality change in the patient that involves not only the whole brain, but the whole patient as a person. The key to this change is seen as impairment of the abstract attitude.

In summary, scientific studies of the consequences of brain damage have been characterized in the past by controversy concerning how the brain works. To some, it is a matter of localization of various functions in centers, while to others it is some form of integrative activity involving the system as a whole. While the controversy still exists to some extent, it has become less extreme in nature. No one now believes that there is no localized function in the brain, nor would anyone deny that there are some forms of behavior that cannot be localized to some particular area. There has been a synthesis of localization and mass action theories.

Concepts of brain dysfunction

A systematic understanding of what may happen to an individual when he sustains brain damage has to be based on some model of how the brain works. We seem to have gone from the early or classical period of localization theory to mass action theory and from there to a more sophisticated theory that represents a kind of compromise between the two views, a theory that better accommodates the actual facts. In essence, the brain appears to be capable of highly localized control of certain functions, and of controlling certain other functions through means other than geographically localized centers. Thus, in cases of brain damage, there may be symptoms that are highly localizable and other symptoms that cannot be localized at all. There are, then, specific and nonspecific effects of brain damage, both of which may appear in the same individual at the same time. Evidence for this point of view has probably been presented the most clearly by the Teuber group (Teuber, 1959). These investigators were able to show that subjects with lesions involving very discrete and specific portions of the brain had symptoms that could be directly attributed to the lesion site, but they also had other symptoms that were shown by essentially all of the patients studied, regardless of the location of the lesion. For example, a subject may have had a lesion in the part of the brain that controls vision. Such a subject would have an area of blindness corresponding to the location of the destruction produced by his brain wound. But like all other patients studied, he would also have difficulty with such tasks as placing blocks into a formboard while blindfolded. All of Teuber's brain-wounded subjects had difficulties with the formboard and other complex tasks, regardless of where their brain wounds were located. In clinical settings, many of the brain-damaged patients seen have various combinations of specific and nonspecific symptoms, while other patients have only nonspecific symptoms.

An old principle of brain function that has held up well and that has been incorporated into modern neuropsychology is the principle of contralateral control. Many bilaterally symmetrical, higher organisms have crossed nervous systems, such that the right side of the brain controls the left side of the body and vice versa. While this principle is not absolutely consistent, it is true that most of the motor, auditory, and sensory pathways cross over. The major exception to the rule is vision, in which only the connections from the inner or nasal halves of the retina cross over while the outer or temporal halves go straight back. For example, the nerves leading from the inner half of the right retina go to the left hemisphere, while those leading from the outer half of that retina go to the right hemisphere. The contralateral control principle explains why many brain-damaged patients have difficulties on only one side of the body. Perhaps the most familiar example of this phenomenon is the stroke patient, typically paralyzed on one side or the other. If he/she is paralyzed on his right side, the major brain damage is likely to be in his left cerebral hemisphere, while the reverse is true if the paralysis is on the left side. Even the extremest advocates of mass-action type theories would have to accept the level of localization produced by contralateral control.

Since the time of Broca, and perhaps before, it was recognized that the human brain has one functional feature that distinguishes it sharply from the animal brain. Humans have what is called a "dominant hemisphere" and a "minor hemisphere." The dominant hemisphere, which is the left hemisphere in most people, controls language functions; it is the "talking" hemisphere of the brain. The minor, or right, hemisphere has little to do with language, and only has some minimal capacity to comprehend speech. It is now thought that the right hemisphere controls a number of nonverbal functions, many of which require spatial relations abilities. We therefore speak of the functional asymmetry of the cerebral hemispheres, in that while the two hemispheres in humans are anatomically quite similar, they do different things. Brain-damaged individuals typically show some loss of language abilities when the left hemisphere contains the major brain damage, while individuals with right hemisphere brain damage often have difficulty with spatial orientation and related nonverbal skills.

Each hemisphere of the brain is anatomically divided into four sections or lobes. The frontal lobe takes up a great deal of the anterior portion of the brain. The temporal lobe constitutes the side of the brain, while the parietal lobe makes up the portion of the top of the brain that lies to the rear of the frontal lobe. The occipital lobe forms the rear of the brain. Figure 12.1 contains a simple diagram of the brain. Most authorities agree to some form of regional localization, in which each of these lobes have a relatively distinct function. The frontal lobes have to do with regulation and control of motor functions. The parietal lobes mediate the various body senses such as touch and pain. The temporal lobes control hearing, while the occipital lobes control vision. If we combine this regional localization principle with the functional asymmetry principle, we get a pretty good, rough map of brain function. For example, it can be seen that the left temporal lobe would control hearing of language, while the right temporal lobe would handle hearing of nonverbal sounds. If there is brain damage that is restricted to a particular lobe, the patient will usually have fairly specific symptoms associated with the function of that lobe. For example, the patient with a left temporal lobe lesion would have difficulty in comprehending speech, while the patient with a right occipital lobe lesion would be expected to comprehend speech well, but might have trouble recognizing objects, or seeing at all, in a portion of his left visual field.

As we have already indicated, the behavioral consequences of brain damage do not depend entirely on localization. They depend on a number of factors, the kind of brain damage being perhaps the most important of them. We therefore speak of a principle of type-locus interaction, which simply means that the consequence of any brain lesion is produced by an interaction between the location of the lesion and the type of pathology that produced it. In addition to type-locus interaction, there are a number of other significant factors such as how long the patient had the brain damage, the age at which he or she was brain damaged, and the premorbid personality. A brain lesion sustained by a child during the preschool years may have very different consequences from what would follow the acquisition of the same lesion later in life. Indeed, the neuropsychology of children is a specialized area with its own research literature and conceptual systems. One might, for example, think about the status of cerebral dominance in the preverbal child. Premorbid personality enters primarily into the adjustment picture. The severity, persistence, and response to treatment of neurological symptoms often has an apparent relationship with the motivation and premorbid level of functioning of the patient.

In summary, the concepts of specific and nonspecific symptoms, contralateral control, functional asymmetry, regional localization, and type-locus interaction are basic considerations regarding our current understanding of brain-damaged patients. These concepts reflect a synthesis of the earlier, more extreme, views of localization and mass action, and provide a level of sophistication sufficient to cope intelligently with the complexities of this field.

Neuropathological considerations

The brain may suffer from most of the diseases and injuries that afflict the other organs and organ systems. What follows is a brief outline of some of the major kinds of brain damage, with an emphasis on clinically significant features of the various conditions. The pathological process producing the brain lesion can have highly significant implications not only for the diagnosis, but also for the treatment and management of the patient. Some brain lesions, for example, are terminal illnesses. In some cases death is rapid, while in others there is a slow but inexorable course of deterioration. In other instances, the damage can be repaired, and there can be unfortunate consequences if this is not recognized. Hence, the type of lesion is a crucial consideration in the assessment and treatment of patients with brain disorders.

Head trauma

Despite the substantial protection afforded to the human brain by the skull, the brain is often injured by accident or by intention, as in the cases of fighting and warfare. It is useful to distinguish between two major types of head injury: closed-head and open-head injury. The popular term concussion is a type of closed-head injury. In closed-head injury the vault of the skull is not penetrated, but the brain is shaken around violently, and may become damaged through banging against the skull. The term concussion is generally used when there is no permanent brain damage, but only a transient set of symptoms such as dizziness, confusion, and double vision. In the case of open-head injury, the skull is penetrated and brain tissue is destroyed by the penetrating object. Brain wounds produced by bullets or shell fragments that enter the brain through the skull are common forms of open-head injury. In these cases, there is permanent, structural brain damage that often results in symptoms that may also persist permanently. Head injury of both types involves a number of phases. While not always the case, the victim frequently loses consciousness and may remain unconscious for a substantial length of time. As a rule, the length of time that the patient remains unconscious is associated with his prognosis; the longer the time unconscious, the poorer the outcome. After consciousness is regained, there is an acute phase in which the patient demonstrates a number of neurological symptoms. His speech may be impaired, he may be partially paralyzed or blind, and he may be generally confused and disoriented. Often, he will be amnesic for events that took place from shortly before his injury to the present time. Sometimes these patients have seizures and must be treated with anticonvulsant drugs. This acute period generally resolves, and the patient enters a more quiescent phase. Many of the symptoms disappear, the confusion and amnesia abate, the seizures frequently stop, and the patient is generally left with residual dysfunction that may be severe or minimal, but is generally less severe than was the case shortly after regaining consciousness. Depending on the severity of the injury, the residual deficits may range from barely detectable to broad ranging and devastating.

Head injury is probably the most frequently seen type of brain damage in a young adult population. If it occurs in a brain that is otherwise reasonably healthy, and if it is not devastatingly severe, the probability of recovery is reasonably good, relative to that of the other brain disorders. The open-head injured patient commonly has a combination of specific and nonspecific symptoms, while the closed-head patient generally has only nonspecific symptoms such as impairment of intellectual abilities in general, memory difficulties, and relatively minor perceptual and motor losses on both sides of his body.

Brain tumors

Cancer can exist in the brain, just as it does in other organs. Tumors of the brain and head are of several types, and the type is important with regard to both the patient's behavior and survival. The so-called intrinsic tumors attack the brain substance itself, and progress fairly rapidly. The extrinsic tumors lie outside of the brain tissue and exert their pathological influence mainly by pressure on the brain or on the blood vessels supplying the brain. The extrinsic tumors are generally nonmalignant and often may be removed surgically. The intrinsic tumors, while treatable surgically, are often fatal, and when not so, generally leave the patient with substantial impairment. Sometimes tumors that start elsewhere in the body spread or metastasize to the brain. The symptoms associated with tumors depend largely on their type and the part of the brain affected, but in the case of intrinsic tumors in particular, symptoms are usually very severe and may increase in severity quite rapidly. However, extrinsic tumors which go undiagnosed for many years may also produce severe neurological symptoms.

In the case of brain tumors, the psychologist is often a supportive observer while the surgeons, chemotherapists, and radiologists make often heroic efforts to save the patient. When the patient does survive, there are many ways in which the psychologist may become involved in his or her recovery and rehabilitation. In the case of surgically treated patients, there is often dramatic recovery that appears quite rapidly. Clinically, these patients look much like individuals who have sustained open-head wounds, perhaps because their lesion has been converted, in a manner of speaking, from a cancerous, spreading mass of tissue to a stable and nonmalignant wound. The treatment issue generally involves whether or not the malignant tissue has been entirely removed, and whether or not it might recur in some other area.

Brain malformations

During the course of embryonic development of the brain and skull, numerous things can go wrong to result in a maldeveloped brain at birth. The brain itself may not develop properly, or a malformation of the skull can exert pressure on the brain, thereby damaging it. Sometimes genetic factors are at work, as in the case of Down's syndrome, while in other cases diseases acquired during pregnancy are the responsible agents. Many children born with congenital brain malformations are mentally retarded, but sometimes the defects are quite subtle and only become detectable during the school years when these children often develop learning difficulties. Occasionally, congenital brain malformations are accompanied by some anomaly in the appearance of the body. Usually, the head and hands are the affected areas. The head may be too large or too small; the eyes may be spaced too widely apart, or the ears may be asymmetrically placed; the fingers may be thin and "spiderlike." The basic reason for this association between brain malformation and maldevelopment of the external surface of the body is that the structures involved come from the same layer of embryonic tissue, and if the damage occurs before they are differentiated, then the damage will occur in what later becomes the brain and the tissue constituting the external body surface.

There is one obvious and significant difference between individuals with congenital brain malformations and other brain-damaged patients. While brain-damaged patients for the most part have achieved skills that they subsequently lose because of their brain damage, the congenitally brain-damaged individual has difficulty in ever acquiring these skills. Typically, these individuals have difficulty throughout their lives in adapting to their environment. They often do not reach the landmarks of infant development at the appropriate times, nor do they do well academically. When they become adults, their vocational success is usually quite limited. They generally do not have physical-health problems, and with the exception of certain conditions like Down's syndrome, they have a normal life expectancy. Their major problems are psychological, and they are less able to cope as the demands of the environment become increasingly complex.

From a behavioral standpoint, it is difficult, if not impossible, to distinguish between individuals who have congenital brain malformations and those who sustain brain injury around the time of birth. Cerebral anoxia or head trauma during the birth process can give rise to the same sorts of developmental difficulties as are seen in individuals with congenital brain malformations. It may, therefore, be more useful to think in terms of early life brain damage as an entity, than in maintaining a distinction between congenital brain malformations and other forms of early life brain damage.

Blood vessel disease

It is in the area of blood vessel, or vascular, disease that one becomes most keenly aware that the brain is a part of the body. The status of the heart and the circulatory system has a strong relationship to the functioning of the brain, since the brain requires oxygen and oxygen is supplied by blood. The heart must be functioning well and the vessels must remain reasonably unclogged for the system to work normally. Cerebral vascular disease, or blood vessel disease involving the brain, is perhaps the commonest cause of brain damage. Indeed, nearly everyone seems to acquire some degree of this illness, but for most of us it does not become clinically significant. Apparently, nature has provided us with a great deal of tolerance in the system. There can be substantial clogging of a vessel without serious functional consequences.

There are two major forms of cerebral vascular disease, but it is generally felt that both of them are produced by the same process. The process is called atherosclerosis, and involves the slow deposition of fatty tissue along the inner walls of arteries. When there is atherosclerosis throughout the system of cerebral arteries with no clear focal point, we speak of diffuse or generalized cerebral atherosclerosis. Sometimes, the fatty tissue produces a complete or near complete blockage of an artery. When this occurs the person generally loses consciousness and when he regains it there is frequently a paralysis of one side of the body and a number of other associated symptoms. In this case, we say that the person had a stroke, or more technically, a cerebral vascular accident. If the stroke involves the left hemisphere, the patient typically is paralyzed on the right side of his body and may have aphasia (inability to use or understand language). If it involves the right hemisphere, paralysis is on the left side, and there are difficulties with spatial relationships and orientation.

Clinically significant cerebral vascular disease is generally seen in older people, but may be seen in middle-aged people or even young adults, particularly when certain medical conditions occur. If the person has diabetes or high blood pressure, he or she is more susceptible to cerebral vascular involvement than are people who do not have these conditions. There are some genetic conditions that promote greater production of the fatty material than is normal. Some people have genetic defects in the blood vessels of the brain that make conditions less stable than usual and increase the possibility of stroke. Therefore, while strokes in young adults are rare, they do occur.

Behaviorally, the stroke patient is quite different from the patient with diffuse cerebral vascular disease. First of all, a distinct physical handicap is present: paralysis or weakness of one side of the body. Second, there are generally distinct symptoms of language disturbance or of impaired spatial relations abilities. Third, the illness has a rapid onset from which there is often some degree of recovery. The patient with diffuse cerebral vascular disease is generally not grossly physically handicapped. He has use of his arms and legs, although both sides of the body may function somewhat less well than normal. Generally, there is no aphasia and no specific disturbance of nonverbal abilities, but rather a more generalized intellectual deficit affecting a number of areas including perception, memory, abstract reasoning, problem solving, and speed of thought and action. There is really no clear concept of recovery in the case of diffuse atherosclerosis, since the illness constitutes a slowly progressive and irreversible process. Efforts may be made to slow down the process, or to restore as much function as possible to the compromised blood vessels. Exercise, weight reduction programs, low fat diets, and reduction of stress may slow down the process somewhat, but whether they do so or not remains a controversial matter. Drugs called vasodilators are sometimes used to expand the narrowed blood vessels and restore some degree of cerebral blood flow, and drugs called anticoagulants are sometimes used to prevent excessive thickening of the blood that may lead to clotting. The effectiveness of these drugs is also controversial.

Degenerative and demyelinating diseases

In certain illnesses, the brain or the entire central nervous system gradually wastes away for reasons that are not clear. In the case of the degenerative diseases, the wasting or atrophy resembles what is seen in very old people, but it occurs substantially earlier than the senile period. For that reason, these conditions are called presenile dementias. The brain ages at a rate much more rapid than normal. The most common of these diseases are called Alzheimer's disease and Pick's disease. In another form of degenerative disease, the atrophy not only produces intellectual deterioration, but a disorder characterized by involuntary, spasmodic movements. This disease is known as Huntington's chorea. Huntington's chorea has been well established as an inherited illness, but the origins of Alzheimer's disease and Pick's disease remain unclear. They may be inborn metabolic defects.

Multiple sclerosis is the most common form of demyelinating disease. It is described as a demyelinating disease because its pathology involves the erosion of the white sheaths of myelin that enclose the nerve fibers. Nerve conduction takes place along the myelin sheath, and when it erodes, conduction cannot take place normally. As is well known, multiple sclerosis is a disease of young adults. It may be rapidly or slowly progressive, and there is no known cure for it. While for many years it was thought to be a genetic disorder, the recent evidence suggests that it is caused by some form of virus.

Perhaps the most cogent yet obvious thing to say about the degenerative and demyelinating diseases is that they are catastrophic. They can reduce normal, functioning individuals in a relatively brief time to severely mentally and physically handicapped patients. Suicide is not uncommon among multiple sclerosis and Huntington's chorea patients. Treatment generally consists of nursing care and certain medications that have minimal capacity to slow the progression of the illness. Rehabilitation can be seen only in terms of making the best of the years remaining.

Alcoholism

There seems little doubt that chronic alcoholism can produce significant damage to the central nervous system as well as to other parts of the body (Goldstein & Neuringer, 1976). The pathological process itself is much like the degenerative diseases, except that in the case of alcoholism it is self-induced. Apparently, the direct effect of alcohol itself is not the only contributor to the brain pathology. Alcoholics typically do not maintain good nutrition, and it appears that a serious thiamine (vitamin B_1) deficiency can produce degenerative changes in certain portions of the brain. Most alcoholics who develop brain damage have a diffuse condition that affects a wide variety of perceptual and intellectual abilities. However, some develop specific syndromes. One of these is called Korsakoff's disease, and is marked by a striking inability to remember. The other condition is called Wernicke's syndrome. These patients have difficulty in walking and in controlling the movement of their eyes.

For the most part, the neurological consequences of alcoholism are reflected in impaired psychological functioning. There are difficulties with memory, judgment, abstract reasoning ability, and coordination. While these difficulties are most pronounced dur-

A Case of Korsakoff's Syndrome

Korsakoff's syndrome is a disorder in which the patient cannot recall recent events and cannot learn new things. It is generally associated with a long history of alcoholism and malnutrition. The patient in question here was a 50-year-old man with 14 years of education. He had been in the army following World War II, and later was employed as an accountant. He apparently began abusing alcohol in his late teens, and so had a drinking history of over thirty years duration when we saw him. He had been repeatedly hospitalized for alcoholism, gradually losing all attachments to his work and family.

On the ward, the patient could not recall events that had taken place a few minutes previously. He maintained that relatives long deceased were still alive, and had no idea of how long he had been in the hospital. When questioned, he indicated that he had been there for a brief period of time (actually several years) and was soon to return to live with his mother, who had actually died some time ago. It was not clear that he was in a hospital, and he had no knowledge of time. His mood was generally agitated, and he would typically become irritable when requested to perform some task.

When given a battery of neuropsychological tests, the patient demonstrated apparent general deterioration from what he had been in the past. As is characteristic of Korsakoff's syndrome, he retained information he had acquired in the past, but did very poorly on tasks requiring the ability to deal with novel situations. Thus, for example, he had the vocabulary level of an average adult, but when asked to solve problems involving abstract thinking or working with puzzlelike material that was unfamiliar to him, he demonstrated severe impairment. He therefore did not only have a memory problem but a more global difficulty with processing information. Considering that he had been an accountant, it was particularly telling to note that his score on an arithmetic achievement test was mid fifth-grade level.

ing states of intoxication, in the chronic alcoholic they are also present when sober. Thus, the pathology of alcoholism appears to involve some permanent changes in the brain. These changes are conceptualized by some authorities as premature aging. While progression of the condition can be arrested through abstinence from alcohol and maintenance of adequate nutrition, the impaired judgment and reasoning abilities that result from the alcoholism may prevent the patient from dealing logically and effectively with his or her condition. Therefore, many of these patients continue to drink and may die of complications of alcoholism at relatively young ages if the process is not arrested. The treatment of alcoholism is largely psychiatric and behavioral. Efforts are made to motivate the patient to abstain from drinking or to reduce consumption, and to maintain adequate nutrition.

There is no specific treatment for Korsakoff's syndrome, but usually thiamine is given every day in the hope of preventing further brain damage. Sometimes these patients are given psychotropic drugs if they are particularly anxious or depressed. This particular patient was given lithium, which seemed to reduce his agitation but did not improve his memory or other mental problems. He remains in the hospital, without significant improvement, with the hope that he can eventually be sent to a nursing home in which he may have a less restricted life. Because of the permanent brain damage produced by some combination of the effects of alcohol and thiamine deficiency, the prognosis for this patient is extremely poor. Since he no longer has alcohol available, he will probably not deteriorate further, but no significant recovery can be anticipated either.

Toxic and infectious illnesses

The brain may be poisoned or infected. Sometimes this happens with such severity that the person dies, but more often there is survival with or without residual neurological dysfunction. While alcohol is the most popular toxic agent, excessive use of other drugs such as barbiturates and bromides may seriously affect brain function. Some of the more common consequences of ingesting excessive amounts of these substances are convulsions, delirium, tremors, and lethargy. Frequently, these symptoms are temporary and disappear after a brief period, but sometimes there are permanent residuals. A fairly frequently seen type of toxic disorder is carbon monoxide poisoning. It is generally seen in depressed patients who survive a suicide attempt by inhaling carbon monoxide in a closed area. In such cases, there is often permanent brain damage, and patients with this condition may be exceedingly impaired intellectually and physically. Toxic states are sometimes mistaken for acute episodes of functional psychiatric disorders in that the patient is frequently confused and disoriented, and may engage in some forms of apparently bizarre behavior. For example, in delerium tremens, a toxic state associated with alcohol withdrawal, the patient may hallucinate.

Brain infections are generally associated with epidemics, but are also sometimes seen even when there are no epidemics at large. The terms commonly used to describe these conditions in a general way are encephalitis and meningitis. Encephalitis refers to inflammation of the brain itself, while in meningitis the infection is in the meninges or membranous tissue that lines the brain. Infections, of course, are caused by microorganisms that invade tissue and produce inflammation. During the acute phase of the condition the patient may be seriously ill and survival may be problematic. Often there are headaches, fever, and a stiff neck. There may be confusion or alteration of the state of consciousness ranging from drowsiness, to excessive sleeping to the extreme of coma. Some forms of encephalitis are popularly known as "sleeping sickness."

As psychologists, we most frequently see patients who have had infections leaving them with residual neurological damage. This group is variable with regard to degree and type of impairment. There may be a variety of neurological problems associated with the postinfectious state, and it is difficult to make any firm generalizations. The irritability, restlessness, and aggressiveness of postencephalitic children are well known phenomena. Likewise, the delusions of grandeur and the maniclike behavior of patients with general paresis, or cerebral syphilis, constitutes a commonly observed syndrome. Individuals with focal infections may be left with paralysis of one side of the body or other severe, specific neurological disorders.

The relative absence of epidemics and the discovery of the antibiotics have turned primary cerebral infections into a relatively rare class of diseases. We do see some patients who develop encephalitic conditions secondary to general systemic infections such as typhoid fever, yellow fever, mumps, and Asian influenza. However, general paresis and the epidemic encephalitic conditions are quite uncommon.

Epilepsy

Unlike all of the conditions described thus far, epilepsy is not a particular neuropathological condition, but rather is a manifestation of many of those conditions. In effect, it is a symptom and not a disease. We generally think of epilespsy in terms of fits. But this is only one type of epilepsy. There are other types in which there is no observable motor abnormality, and there are still other types in which the motor activity resembles purposeful behavior. What all of these conditions have in common is that there is always a sudden or paroxysmal episode of brain dysfunction. One way of putting this is that if you were looking at a recording of an epileptic person's brain waves, you might see a sudden and dramatic change in the pattern of these waves. You would not have to be looking at the person, and even if you were you might not notice anything. At times, this alteration may be associated with an episode of jerky movements, but other things may happen as well. In petit mal epilepsy, the person may simply lose contact with the environment for a brief period of time, and then go back to what he or she was doing as if the pause never took place. The person may exhibit threatening behavior, or smell peculiar odors or have visions. The last two phenomena are examples of a condition called psychomotor or temporal lobe epilepsy. Sometimes the brain wave pattern, or electroencephalogram, has characteristics seen in epileptic patients, but there is no behavioral evidence for epilepsy. Whether or not individuals with this condition should or should not be called epileptics is a matter of divided opinion.

There are several ways of classifying epilepsy. One clinically useful method involves making a distinction between epilepsy with known and unknown etiology. If the cause of the epilepsy is known, it may be directly treatable. For example, it may be caused by a surgically removable brain tumor. If the cause is unknown, as is the case for a great deal of epilepsy, the treatment can only be symptomatic. There is some association between various classes of epilepsy and the presence of accompanying intellectual impairments. Klove and Matthews (1974) found that individuals with psychomotor or temporal lobe epilepsy tend not to have significant intellectual impairment, while individuals with major motor seizures are likely to have some degree of impairment. These investigators also suggested that early age of onset of major motor seizures of unknown etiology is associated with greater intellectual impairment during later life than is the case for early age of onset major motor seizures of known etiology. For practical purposes, it might be fair to say that one may expect to see intellectual deficit in individuals with major motor seizures, particularly if the seizures started relatively early in life. However, do not expect to see intellectual deficits in patients with temporal lobe epilepsy.

The epileptic patient may have a variety of difficulties. An incomplete account is offered here. The disease still has some social stigma attached to it, and some people continue to maintain superstitious beliefs about it. Epileptics often cannot obtain licenses to drive a car, or insurance that allows them to work around potentially dangerous equipment. During a temporal lobe seizure a patient can commit an antisocial act over which he had no control and which he honestly cannot recall. Seizures may be symptoms of life-threatening neurological diseases. Epileptics may injure themselves while having a seizure. Children with petit mal epilepsy may have school difficulties because of their lapses of attention. Improper treatment of a patient undergoing a seizure may do harm to the patient as well as to the individual giving the treatment. In this regard, when a person is having a motor seizure, two rules should be followed: Try to protect the patient's head, and try not to hurt yourself. Do not try to physically restrain the patient's motor activity and do not try to put a padded tongue depressor or other implement into the patient's mouth. Despite folktales to the contrary, it is very difficult to swallow your tongue, even while having a motor seizure, and an attempt to put an implement into the mouth during a motor seizure may result in a nasty bite.

Fortunately, several good treatments for epilepsy exist. Anticonvulsant drugs, when administered in proper dosages, are often effective in reducing the frequency of seizures, and sometimes will render the person completely seizure-free. For certain types of epilepsy, if the patient is not responsive to the various drugs, there are surgical procedures that control the epilepsy and leave the patient with very little neurological residual. Some success has been reported in the use of biofeedback and behavior modification techniques for the control of seizures. In general, there is good reason to be optimistic about treatment outcome in the epileptic patient.

The clinical picture

Thus far, the matters dealt with consisted largely of general considerations related to concepts of the brain and brain damage, and to the different pathological processes that may produce brain damage. While these issues are useful in gaining a conceptual grasp of the area of psychopathology under discussion, it is difficult to achieve an understanding of brain-damaged patients without some knowledge of the clinical phenomenology of the various conditions that come under the category of brain damage. In this section, an attempt will be made to present some descriptive material that will provide some information about what brain-damaged patients look like in real life.

In their *Diagnostic and Statistical Manual,* the American Psychiatric Association (1968, 1978) places brain-damaged patients into the category "Organic Brain Syndrome." We have avoided this term throughout this chapter, primarily because of its vagueness. However, it may be useful to use the concepts underlying the term in a discussion of the clinical phenomenology of brain damage, because they do pertain to certain aspects of the grossly observable behavior of many brain-damaged patients. According to the 1968 manual, patients with organic brain syndromes have the following symptoms: (a) impairment of orientation; (b) impairment of memory; (c) impairment of all intellectual functions such as comprehension, calculation, knowledge, and learning; (d) impairment of judgment; (e) lability and shallowness of affect. While not all of these symptoms appear in all brain-damaged patients, one or more of them commonly appear in patients with structural brain lesions.

Indeed, the 1978 manual (DSM-III) represents a major attempt to refine the concept of organic brain syndrome by distinguishing among a number of subtypes (e.g. amnesic syndrome, organic delusional syndrome). When we meet and talk to brain-damaged patients, we are ordinarily struck by their poor memory and orientation, or by their inability to conceptualize, organize, and plan. In hospital settings, they can generally provide little information concerning the reason for their being there, and often can express no future plans. The concreteness described by Goldstein and Scheerer (1941) is often apparent.

While all brain-damaged patients may have in common some of the characteristics of the organic brain syndrome, these characteristics vary greatly in degree and pattern. Some patients may have dramatic intellectual deficit, but minimal impairment of memory. Some may have shallow affect, but others may have an intense emotional tone ranging from euphoria to deep depression. There is great variability with regard to intellectual functions. While one could probably find all forms of intellectual impairment in brain-damaged patients when treated as a group, individual patients more typically have patterned intellectual performance in which certain functions are impaired while others are preserved. What is impaired and what is preserved depends on a number of factors that vary greatly among individual patients. In the following sections we will present some descriptions that characterize individuals with various types of brain lesions.

The patient with bilateral brain damage

Before going on with the description of patients with bilateral (diffuse static or slowly progressive) brain damage, it may be worthwhile to make some brief remarks concerning the incidence of this type of lesion, and of other lesion types, in the population of brain-damaged individuals. The bilateral type of brain damage is by far the most commonly seen type of lesion. Individuals with unilateral and focal lesions are much less common. The point is made here because there is a disproportionality between the quantity of research and clinical literature, and the incidence of various types of brain disorder. The bulk of the literature has to do with patients with unilateral and focal lesions. Such patients are thought to be of more interest in terms of teaching and research value than are patients with diffuse brain damage. This attitude is akin to the academician's preference for writing at length about some rare disease while paying little or no attention to such mundane concerns as the common cold. The diffuse lesion is the common cold of brain damage.

The patient with diffuse brain damage comes closer than any group to the general description given of the organic brain syndrome. These patients rarely have specific symptoms. They generally do not have physical disabilities such as paralysis or perceptual difficulties, but there are many exceptions to this rule. The multiple sclerosis patient may become blind, and the patient with Huntington's chorea does have a substantial movement disorder. There are two characteristics that describe the great majority of these patients: generalized intellectual deficit and slowness. The slowness is quite pervasive and involves both motor activity and thought processes. One general rule is that it takes these patients substantially longer to complete some activity than it takes the normal person. They require more time to eat a meal, take care of their personal hygiene, and to perform almost any activity of daily living. Even speech may be slowed down.

The intellectual deficit seen in patients with diffuse lesions may vary substantially in degree. Sometimes orientation is affected, such that the patient does not know who he is, where he is, and when it is. However, disorientation is not all that common, except perhaps for time. The patient, when asked, may not know the exact date or may give a poor estimate of the time of day. Since many normal people do not always know the date, a failure to report accurately is not necessarily abnormal. Most brain-damaged patients know who they are and where they are, with the major exception of the amnesic patient, to be discussed below.

There is typically a major difference in level of performance between tasks learned and mastered in the past and those involving new situations. Old motor habits are retained and many of these individuals can continue to work if they need do no more than routine, familiar tasks. Long-term memory is generally very well preserved. Since language is learned during childhood, these patients do not typically have difficulties with speech or with understanding the speech of others. These patients can often provide detailed information about their childhood, their work, and other aspects of their past lives, as in normal conversation. Therefore, they remember words, how to put sentences together, and other aspects of language. The major difficulty lies in their impairment in regard to capacity to record and consolidate new information. This defect is sometimes characterized as a short-term memory problem, but our observations suggest that the real problem is in new learning. These patients can generally recite back to you what was just said, indicating that they can recall the material given, if it is not too complex. What they have great difficulty in doing is incorporating this new material into their repertoire of behaviors or fund of knowledge.

Patients with diffuse brain damage appear to have a common motivational problem, or what looks like a motivational problem. They have great difficulty in initiating purposeful action. Rarely do they initiate a conversation or engage in some activity on their own. People working with brain-damaged patients generally report that they have to be led into activities, and reminded to do things. Some brain-damaged patients can be mistaken for schizophrenic patients because of their apparent apathy and indifference. As many clinicians phrase it, they lack sparkle or enthusiasm. It is easy to interpret this phenomenon as representing reactive depression related to the patient's perception of his progressive illness. This interpretation might make some sense if the patient has the capability of conceptualizing the nature of his illness and its ultimate consequences. However, many brain-damaged patients lack the mental capacity needed to evaluate their conditions and are, so to speak, spared from suffering through the often long progression of their deteriorating conditions.

The emotional life of the brain-damaged patient is not at all well understood, since these patients can rarely communicate about their thoughts and feelings. It is a mistake to generalize from how we would react to their circumstances. Their reaction, in view of their altered mental status, may be substantially different from ours. Our impression is that the motivational lag of the brain-damaged patient is protective in nature and prevents him from getting into difficulty in a bewildering world. It may aid in warding off what Kurt Goldstein called a "catastrophic reaction": a state of severe anxiety resulting from an inability to cope with the demands of the environment.

There are a number of features that are unique to particular types of diffuse, bilateral brain damage. While the remarks made above apply more or less to all types, there are also a number of problems that are specific to particular types. We will outline some of them here.

The alcoholic patient. These patients frequently have multiple problems. There are the psychiatric and social difficulties associated with their drinking behavior as well as their neurological problems resulting from a long history of excessive alcohol ingestion. The third problem involves the general medical difficulties that are frequently associated with alcoholism. Diseases of the liver, pancreas, and gastrointestinal system are quite common among chronic alcoholics. The neurological problems not only involve the cerebral hemispheres but the cerebellum and the peripheral nerves as well. They may have irritable, painful legs from peripheral neuritis, or inflammation of the nerves supplying the legs. They may have problems with balance and gait. Some alcoholic patients have profound memory difficulties. This kind of patient will be discussed later under the topic of amnesic disorders. Typically, there is little insight concerning the source and nature of their illness. Because of the substantial intellectual impairment found in these patients they are generally not good candidates for the verbal, insight-oriented treatments commonly used with alcoholic patients. Prevention of additional drinking is usually provided by environmental restraints.

The multiple sclerosis patient. It was thought at one time that there was no intellectual impairment in multiple sclerosis until the terminal stages of the illness. While this may be true in some cases, recent research suggests that the progression of intellectual decrement roughly parallels the physical changes characteristic of this illness (Reitan, Reed, & Dyken, 1971; Goldstein & Shelly, 1974). Perhaps the major problem of the multiple sclerosis patient is that while the first symptoms of the illness may appear during young adulthood, the life span may be close to normal. In other words, the patient may live for many years with a progressively debilitating disease. The progression often occurs in plateaus, such that there may be stability for some time followed by a rapid worsening. In comparison with the Huntington's chorea patient, who has a similar situation, the multiple sclerosis patient tends to be less intellectually impaired, and for many years may remain very aware of his gradually worsening condition. The multiple sclerosis patient is generally characterized by the number of his neurological symptoms. Paralysis, incoordination, double vision, blindness, and difficulties in bladder control and in swallowing are some of symptoms that may develop.

The Huntington's chorea patient. Since Huntington's chorea is a hereditary illness, when someone is born to a family with a history of the disease there is naturally great concern over whether the child will acquire it as an adult. Thus, children born into families with histories of Huntington's chorea grow up in an atmosphere of apprehension over a questionable future. If the disease is acquired, it is manifested by both substantial intellectual deterioration and a movement disorder characterized by flailing movements of the arms, facial grimacing and twisting, and lashing movements that may be accentuated by walking. The movements are constant, except during sleep. They may be partially controlled by tranquilizing drugs, but cannot be abolished.

The patient with Alzheimer's or Pick's disease. These diseases are characterized almost completely by mental deterioration. There is generally no motor disorder, no convulsions, and little else in the way of visible, physical manifestations of the illness. The person may be asymptomatic until middle age, at which time a process of rapid deterioration begins. Patients with Alzheimer's disease rarely live for more than four years following the onset; Pick's disease patients may live somewhat longer. These two diseases are difficult to diagnose. Not only are they hard to tell from each other, they are both hard to distinguish from other diffuse processes, particularly cerebral vascular disease. It is often said that the diagnosis is only determined at autopsy. In any event, if it is determined that an individual has Alzheimer's or Pick's disease, the tragic consequences of rapid deterioration and a short remaining life must be anticipated.

The patient with unilateral brain damage

Patients with brain damage mainly in one or the other cerebral hemisphere are in many ways quite different from patients with diffuse lesions. They may have some of the characteristics of an organic brain syndrome, but they generally do not have them to the extent seen in patients with bilateral lesions. More often they have specific symptoms associated with the side of the brain involved. It should be emphasized from the beginning that the distinction between unilateral and bilateral is a matter of degree. The disease processes that produce brain damage do not respect the longitudinal fissure that divides the two hemispheres as a border that cannot be crossed. It is difficult to imagine a person having a cerebral vascular accident in one hemisphere without some degree of atherosclerosis in the other hemisphere. It is also unlikely that a head injury can produce a lesion in one restricted portion of the brain without affecting other parts indirectly. As an object moves through the brain it may create pressures that can produce damage in many unpredictable places in addition to the site of the obvious damage. There are no doubt cases in which brain damage is truly unilateral, but they are the exception rather than the rule. Bearing this in mind, we will nevertheless go on to discuss the nature of unilateral lesions. However, one should think of the term unilateral as implying the area of maximal involvement rather than the area to which the brain damage is restricted.

The left hemisphere. As suggested in the discussion of concepts of brain function, patients with left hemisphere lesions should have two prominent symptoms: an impairment of language abilities, called aphasia, and loss of function of the right side of the body. Sometimes there is complete paralysis of the right side, a condition called hemiplegia, or the right side is substantially weakened, in which case the disability is called hemiparesis. Sometimes sensation is involved such that the patient cannot sense touch or pain on the right side. Vision is also affected in certain instances, and the patient cannot see one side of visual space. If the lesion is in the left hemisphere, the right visual field would be the one involved. Such a condition is known as the hemianopia.

Aphasia, right hemiplegia or hemiparesis, and a right hemianopia is a combination of symptoms that is quite commonly seen among patients with left hemisphere brain damage. However, not all parts of the combination need be present at any particular time. Each symptom can appear independently. Actually, the combination appearing as an entity occurs almost exclusively in the case of patients who have recently had left hemisphere cerebral vascular accidents. While changes in body sensation, vision, and motility were mentioned, nothing was said about hearing. Lateralized impairment of hearing does occur, but in a rather subtle way. It may occur as a part of the aphasia, since some patients with left hemisphere brain damage lose some of their ability to comprehend the speech of others. Careful testing may also reveal that the patient may not attend to sounds received by the right ear. Most interesting are the findings from a newly developed procedure called dichotic listening. In dichotic listening, the patient listens to a stereophonic tape that sends different messages to each ear simultaneously. If the stimuli are words, the normal person will do better at identifying words transmitted to the right ear as compared with the left ear, a phenomenon known as the right-ear advantage. However, the patient with left hemisphere brain damage loses this advantage and may in fact do worse with his right ear than with his left.

While the problem of aphasia is a complex matter that has received extensive study, we can make some brief remarks about it here. The essence of the disorder is that there is some disturbance of language associated with structural damage to the brain, generally to the dominant or left hemisphere. The disturbance can involve speaking, the comprehension of speech, or both. Some investigators distinguish among the different types of aphasia along these lines. The aphasia is classed as expressive, receptive, or mixed. Others go by the speech output and distinguish between fluent and nonfluent aphasias. Those that prefer this system feel that the term expressive aphasia is misleading because it may imply that patients with other kinds of aphasia do not have difficulties in expression (Goodglass & Kaplan, 1972).

Aphasia is a severely disabling and frustrating disorder. The patient may know what he or she wants to say, but is unable to formulate his intentions into a meaningful sentence. The patient may know what an object is, but cannot come up with the name for it. He or she may require long and repeated explanations of what others are trying to communicate. Frequently, the abilities to read, write, and tell time are lost. The speech of the patient may be rambling and circumlocutory or it might be primitive and extremely limited. Sometimes, the rambling, empty speech of the fluent aphasic may be mistaken for the bizarre language of the schizophrenic patient. It is important to understand that aphasia is not an emotional or "psychogenic" disorder, nor is it an indication of low intelligence. The emotional problems of aphasic patients are generally secondary to the aphasia, and represent the frustration and irritation that frequently come from being unable to communicate. Some aphasic patients may have no significant impairment of general intelligence, but cannot demonstrate that this is the case because of their communication difficulty.

Aphasia is often not a permanent condition and recovery from it is not at all uncommon. While recovery may be greatly aided by speech therapy, at least some of it appears to be spontaneous. The mechanism by which this happens is of great interest to neurologists and neuropsychologists, but is not clearly understood. Either there is a reorganization of the entire brain, or of a speech area in the right hemisphere that becomes operative following destruction of the primary area in the left hemisphere. In our experience, failure to recover from aphasia suggests that the patient's neurological condition has not stabilized and some active pathological process may be at work. The existence of recovery from aphasia implies that not all patients with left hemisphere brain lesions will demonstrate that condition. They may have had it at one time, but it is no longer present. In these cases, the unilateral motor dysfunction may persist even though the aphasia has disappeared.

The right hemisphere. The functions of the right hemisphere are not as well understood as are those of the left hemisphere. When a patient sustains a right hemisphere lesion, the sensory and motor deficits are the same as those found in patients with left hemisphere lesions, except that they are on the other side. Therefore, left hemiparesis or hemiplegia, left-sided sensory loss, and left hemianopia would constitute the set of sensory and motor symptoms that could occur. However, there is no aphasia. What happens instead appears to be an impairment of a number of spatial relations abilities. The condition is technically known as constructional apraxia, but this term does not really describe what actually occurs. Terms like spatial orientation and sense of direction are also insufficient. The condition is identified primarily on the basis of loss of the ability to construct assemblies or copy designs. Benton (1969) pointed out, however, that performance on these two types of tasks are not very highly related to each other. Furthermore, the association between constructional apraxia and right hemisphere disease is not as strong as is the association between aphasia and left hemisphere disease.

Aside from the constructional apraxia, patients with right hemisphere lesions sometimes demonstrate a group of bizarre symptoms that Weinstein and Kahn (1955, 1959) interpret in terms of denial of illness. Most prominently, these patients deny that there is anything wrong with the left side of their body or with their head. They may also report strange experiences such as the feeling that they have two heads or three legs. These patients may also have a symptom called prosopagnosia: an inability to recognize familiar faces. Underlying this disability may be a problem in recognizing nonverbal stimuli in general (Newcombe, 1974). Sometimes these patients have difficulty in dressing themselves and are said to have "dressing apraxia." These varied difficulties may or may not have a single underlying basis, but they all can be seen as having something to do with spatial relationships, some involving the body and others space in the external world. While the denial syndromes do not quite fit into this concept, they may be based, at least in part, on a defect in the mechanism that provides the normal person with a spatial image or map of his or her own body. Schilder (1932) recognized this mechanism some time ago, and called it the "postural model" component of the body image.

Clinically, patients with right hemisphere disease are often felt to have poorer prognoses than patients with left hemisphere brain damage. The reasons for this are not clear, but may have something to do with the treatments available. An equivalent of speech therapy does not seem to exist for the right hemisphere. As far as we can tell, the patient with right hemisphere brain damage finds the world to be a very bewildering place. Attempts to perform some task or go to some distant location causes confusion and the patient does not achieve what was intended. In some cases, even relatively simple nonverbal tasks such as dressing cannot be properly accomplished. It may be mentioned that the dressing difficulty is apparently not necessarily associated with the loss of function of the left arm. The difficulty may appear even when significant loss of motor function is absent.

Table 12.1. Major Characteristics of Hemispheric Lesions

Left Hemisphere Lesions
Contralateral Control Disturbances
right hemiplegia or hemiparesis
right hemisensory loss
right hemianopia
right auditory inattention
Aphasic Disturbances
impairment of fluent speech
impairment of auditory comprehension
loss of "right ear advantage" on dichotic listening
impairment of reading ability
impairment of writing ability
impairment of calculation ability
impairment of right-left orientation
Right Hemisphere Lesions
Contralateral Control Disturbances
left hemiplegia or hemiparesis
left hemisensory loss
left hemianopia
left auditory inattention
Spatial Relations Disturbances
impaired ability to construct assemblies
distortions in copying figures
loss of "sense of direction"
Other Disturbances
loss of ability to recognize faces
body image distortions
dressing Apraxia

Table 12.1 (adopted from an article by Levy, 1974) summarizes some of the major characteristics of left hemisphere and right hemisphere brain damage.

The patient with a focal brain lesion

Sometimes brain damage is restricted to a very limited area, with little or no demonstrable diffuse pathology or involvement of some other area. In such cases, the patient has a focal lesion. There are a relatively limited number of things that can produce focal lesions. The most common cause is open-head injury. The most extensive studies of focal lesions took place following the major wars, because of the number of servicemen who sustained bullet or shell fragment wounds of the head. Vascular accidents involving small blood vessel branches can produce focal lesions as can certain types of brain tumors. Psychosurgery, a group of surgical procedures used to treat severely disturbed psychiatric patients and terminal patients in chronic severe pain, also produces focal brain lesions. However, the issues involved in this latter area are so complex that they cannot be reasonably treated here.

In the case of the patient with a focal lesion, it is necessary to call on the principle of regional localization, as well as on the principles of contralateral control, functional asymmetry, and type-locus interaction, to explain the symptoms. Thus, a patient with a left frontal lobe lesion may have difficulties with motor regulation of the right side of his body as well as with speech. He should not have body-sense, auditory, or visual difficulties. If the lesion is restricted to the third frontal convolution (Broca's Area), the difficulty may be in the speech area only. Depending on the area of the brain involved, nonprogressive focal lesions can leave the patient with very circumscribed deficits. For example, a small lesion in the occipital lobe can result in a limited area of blindness.

In general, patients with focal brain lesions have specific and nonspecific symptoms. The specific symptoms relate primarily to the site of the lesion, as in the examples given above. The nonspecific symptoms are unrelated to the lesion site, and are apparently seen in the vast majority of brain-damaged patients, regardless of site or type of lesion. They generally have to do with failure to efficiently perform some complex task that is usually done quite readily by nonbrain-damaged individuals. As we have already mentioned, Teuber (1959) showed that one of these tasks involves the ability to place blocks into a formboard while blindfolded. Another task of this type has to do with being able to find simple figures hidden in backgrounds forming complex, irregular patterns.

While there are always many exceptions to the generalizations made here, they are true often enough to be useful. Individuals with focal brain lesions are generally quite intact and capable of independent living. Their neurological disorders only produce major adaptive difficulties when the specific area of deficit is challenged. It is interesting to note that Teuber's subjects with penetrating missile wounds consisted largely if not entirely of individuals living in noninstitutional settings. Some of them are quite successful at their careers. Some patients with focal brain lesions have problems with epilepsy. For example, scar tissue from a head wound can form an irritative focus that could generate seizures. Some focal lesions are static and reasonably quiescent, but progressive focal lesions also occur. A brain tumor may start as a small focal lesion and then expand. A cerebral infection such as a brain abscess can start in a circumscribed area and then grow larger. With the exception of progressive focal processes, notably brain tumors, patients with focal lesions tend to go through acute and chronic stages of their illness. In the case of head injury, there is often a period of unconsciousness followed by confusion, amnesia, and prominent signs of neurological dysfunction related to the site of the lesion. As this situation resolves, the patient does not completely recover but the confusion and amnesia generally abate, and the localized symptoms diminish in intensity. In our experience, some of these patients show only relatively subtle residual symptoms that require special tests to elicit.

The patient with focal brain damage has traditionally been the prime "teaching case" for neuropsychology. These cases are of particular interest because they provide invaluable data concerning what various areas of the brain do. It is as if an act of nature has provided in humans an analog to what the physiological psychologist can produce through surgical techniques in experimental animals. The literature is filled with case reports describing the symptoms and lesion localization of patients with focal brain damage. The degree of specificity of these symptoms is sometimes quite remarkable: an inability to appreciate music, or to recognize visual stimuli despite the presence of normal visual acuity; loss of the ability to read without any other associated deficits; an inability to recall recent events accompanied by average general intelligence and normal long-term memory. All of these symptoms and numerous others are possible with focal lesions. It should be pointed out, however, that a characteristic difficulty with the case studies of patients with these kinds of disorders is an insufficient examination. While the more prominent symptoms of the type just mentioned are perhaps of major interest, there is generally a failure to even give a screening examination for nonspecific symptoms, some of which may be providing significant adaptive difficulties for the patient.

The amnesic patient

The patient who cannot remember presents unique assessment and treatment problems. While most brain-damaged patients show some impairment of memory, there are certain groups of patients in which the memory impairment is extremely profound and the most prominent symptom. Patients with this kind of disorder have been carefully studied in recent years by Butters and Cermak (1975, 1976) and by Milner (1966, 1970). These investigators make a distinction between the kind of memory disorder seen in the patient with Korsakoff's disease and the patient with damage to the temporal lobes. In the case of the Korsakoff patient, the major brain damage is felt to be in the frontal lobes and its underlying structures in the base of the brain. Behaviorally, the similarities between these groups are probably greater than the differences. The memory defect seen in most brain-damaged patients is an anterograde amnesia—an inability to recall recent events. While there is often some degree of retrograde amnesia, or inability to recall remote events, recent memory is generally much worse. What is generally most striking is the patient's inability to learn anything new or to record new experiences. In the case of the Korsakoff patient there is a marked tendency to make up things to fill in for the missing memories.

Amnesic patients typically can relate little about their recent past life, but they may recall details of their childhood. If institutionalized, they generally cannot tell you for how long or provide accurate information concerning current events. Typically they are not oriented in time, often not knowing the correct year. Longitudinal observation of these patients may produce striking findings. For example, if a relative visits a patient on some particular day, the next day the patient may not recall that such a visit took place. If asked what he or she did yesterday, the patient may create a story or produce some brief answer like "nothing" or "what I do every day." Experimental studies have shown that these patients have encoding defects in that they do not analyze incoming information on the basis of categories formed from the material's physical, semantic, or other features. Failure to encode information effectively makes the memories of this material unstable and highly susceptible to interference. From an affective standpoint, these patients are typically extremely apathetic and unmotivated. In our observation, there is a strong tendency for them to be irritable, sometimes to the point of verbal abusiveness.

In many ways, the patient with temporal lobe damage is much like the Korsakoff patient. However, if only one temporal lobe is involved, the memory loss may be material specific. If the left temporal lobe is damaged, then the patient may be amnesic for verbal material only, while patients with right temporal brain damage may only have difficulty in the recall of nonverbal material. The temporal lobe patient also does not appear to have the encoding defect seen in Korsakoff patients. Their problem seems to be largely one of registration or forming new associations, in contrast to the Korsakoff patient whose problem seems to be mainly the inability to form efficient strategies for processing new information.

The amnesic patient presents a particularly difficult clinical problem in that most of the information transmitted on some particular occasion will not be recalled at a later time. One can imagine the consequences of this difficulty for such treatments as verbal counseling or psychotherapy. The disorders are usually permanent, and little spontaneous recovery of memory can be expected. The spontaneous recovery of memory through being hit on the head or some other means, as depicted in movies and novels, is rarely if ever seen in real life.

Acute brain syndromes

The medical use of the term acute can be misleading. While the term seems to have implications for severity or seriousness, its major technical meaning in the present context is temporary or reversible. Thus, an acute brain syndrome is a disorder of brain function that may not be associated with permanent brain damage. This particular phraseology is used because what appears to be an acute brain syndrome may sometimes leave the patient with permanent, residual damage. Sometimes neurologists refer to acute multiple sclerosis. This terminology does not imply that the multiple sclerosis is reversible, but that the patient has undergone a rapid flare-up of symptoms. Such episodes may in fact produce significant permanent damage over a relatively brief period of time.

Acute brain syndromes have a number of common characteristics. The onset is sudden. The patient may be perfectly normal until certain changes in his behavior occur. He may start to speak with slurred speech, or there may be an unexplained change in mood or in motor behavior. As the condition develops there may be increasing impairment in intellectual functioning, memory, and judgment. In its full-blown form the patient may become delerious, stuporous, or may go into coma. Typically these patients are confused, disoriented, and have limited consciousness of what is happening around them. If the condition is indeed an acute brain syndrome, it may last up to a month. Sometimes the patient pulls out of it with no apparent aftereffects, while in other cases there may be some degree of permanent neurological residual.

While many pathological conditions can be chronic or acute, acute brain syndromes are most frequently caused by cardiac, toxic, or traumatic problems. An acute brain syndrome can follow serious disturbance of heart function, or after ingesting some poison or following a head injury. In a sense, alcohol intoxication is a form of acute brain syndrome. The staggering gait, confusion, memory lapses, and slurred speech of the inebriated person are all symptoms that commonly appear in other types of temporary brain dysfunction as well as in alcohol intoxication. Following head injury, some individuals develop a combination of symptoms called a posttraumatic syndrome that has some resemblances to an acute brain syndrome. The associated symptoms are some combination of headache, dizziness, ringing in the ears, nervousness, irritability, diminished concentration, impaired memory, easy fatiguability, difficulty in sleeping, uncertainty, and sexual difficulties. It is clear that this syndrome represents a combination of psychiatric and neurological symptomatology or both the direct consequences of the head trauma and the patient's affective reaction to it. This combination of symptoms often resolves as the patient recovers and becomes more sure of himself.

Diagnosis of brain damage

While interest in psychiatric diagnosis has waxed and waned, there has always been a keen interest in diagnosing brain dysfunction. In this area, diagnosis is of a somewhat different nature from diagnosis of psychopathology in general. First of all, in the field of brain dysfunction it is possible to detect some visible lesion that is producing the disorder. It may be a tumor or an infection, or a softening of tissue produced by vascular disease, or many other tangible entities. This situation clearly does not hold in conditions such as schizophrenia or the anxiety disorders. A related difference is that there is currently available a whole battery of machines and devices designed to diagnose brain damage. Aside from behavioral tests, the technology of electrophysiology, radiology, nuclear medicine, computer science, and many other specialty areas have been brought to bear on the problem of the diagnosis of brain damage. Neurological diagnosis is no longer strictly neurological, but is truly a multidisciplinary enterprise. In this section we will briefly review some of the major diagnostic procedures.

There are essentially two major methods of diagnosing brain disorders: looking at the brain and looking at what the brain does. Generally, we do not have the opportunity to look at the brain directly, and must do so with X-rays of various types. However, we may also look at a product of the brain, the cerebral spinal fluid, through various laboratory techniques. We may also examine the brain's electrical activity with the electroencephalogram (EEG). In the case of the EEG we do not really look at the brain directly, and our distinction breaks down a bit here. Logically, the EEG is really a "looking at the brain" procedure because the brain waves tell more about the status of nervous system structures than they do about the capability of the individual to function in various ways. Thus, our discussion of the "looking at the brain" methods will include the EEG and various radiological or X-ray techniques.

The electroencephalogram (EEG)

The electroencephalogram machine is used to record the electrical activity of the brain through electrodes pasted to various areas of the scalp. The electrodes are placed over the major lobes of the right and left hemisphere, and so there are usually frontal, temporal, parietal, and occipital lobe electrodes. A tracing of the activity recorded is made on a continuously moving sheet of paper, with each electrode represented by a line or channel. Conventionally, there are eight or sixteen channels used. The usual procedure calls for the patient to remain relaxed with eyes closed while the recording is being made. Sometimes it is useful to make a recording while the patient is asleep, and so a sleep-inducing medication is sometimes administered prior to making the recording. The standard procedure generally lasts about a half hour, but sometimes all-night recordings are taken.

When the recording is completed, the output is "read" or interpreted by a neurologist or electroencephalographer. Without going into detail, there is a range of normal brain activity representing various states of consciousness ranging from waking to deep sleep. Some individuals with brain disorders demonstrate deviations from the normal. As we are dealing with wave forms, the deviations are generally in frequency or amplitude. The waves may be coming faster or slower, or they may be larger or smaller than normal. Sometimes the abnormalities are seen throughout the record, but at other times they are only seen on certain channels while the remainder of the record is normal. In the EEG report, the interpreter will generally state that the record is normal, abnormal, or borderline. If it is abnormal or borderline, the deviant findings will be mentioned such as "bursts of diffuse, fast activity" or "left temporal lobe spikes." A spike is a high voltage, sharp wave of 3 msec. to 25 msec. duration that generally connotes the presence of epileptic activity in the brain, although it does not necessarily mean that the patient has had or will have actual seizures of any kind.

The EEG is clearly at its best in the diagnosis of epilepsy. Seizure disorders can frequently be identified with regard to type, and sometimes even the locus of the brain lesion producing the seizures can be accurately predicted. It would probably be fair to say that the EEG does not do as well in the diagnosis of nonepileptic brain damage. Normal EEGs can be obtained by patients with a wide variety of types of brain damage. Therefore, a positive or abnormal EEG is quite likely to mean that the patient has some neurological difficulty. However, a negative EEG means nothing. It doesn't even necessarily mean that the patient does not have epilepsy. Some epileptics only develop abnormal electrical activity during a seizure episode, and if they are not tested during such an episode the EEG may be normal. There is a misleading piece of popular information that something like 15 percent of the normal population has an abnormal EEG. The basis for this belief is not clear, but even if true it is misleading. All it may really mean is that 15 percent of the normal population has brain dysfunction that happens to be detectable by the EEG but not by other neurological diagnostic methods. However, this could simply be an artifact of the EEG procedure rather than a true indicator of abnormal brain function.

Radiological methods

The radiological methods used for diagnosis of brain damage range from very simple procedures to extremely complex and sophisticated ones. In order to see any soft tissue (the brain) inside of the skull, it is necessary to use special procedures. One of these procedures is called the pneumoencephalogram, and the other major one is called cerebral angiography. These procedures involve injecting contrast material into the brain so that certain structures can be seen in the x-ray films. In the case of the pneumoencephalogram, air or other gas is used. The air serves as a contrast medium against which the ventricles and other spaces in the brain can be seen. The brain is not seen directly, but changes in the size, shape, and position of the spaces indicate corresponding changes in the brain itself. In the case of cerebral angiography a dye is injected, usually into one or both carotid arteries in the neck, and x-rays of the head are taken as the dye flows through the cerebral blood vessels. Again, the brain is not seen but the status of the arteries can be evaluated, and the presence of space occupying lesions can be inferred. For example, if an artery is lying in an abnormal position it may be because a tumor, cyst, or blood clot is pressing on it. While these pathological structures cannot be seen, they must be there or the artery would be defying the law of gravity.

A recent development in radiology has made the above mentioned techniques as well as the brain scan, a method of visualizing the brain using radioisotope material, more or less obsolete. The new technique is called computerized transaxial tomography, or computer augmented tomography. Through computer assisted organization of a series of x-rays, this technique can localize brain damage in three dimensions, although it does not actually produce a three-dimensional picture. Almost any kind of visible brain damage can be seen using this procedure, with the exception of lesions located deep in the base of the brain. It is particularly good for visualizing brain atrophy, but it can also localize brain tumors, traumatic lesions, and other disorders. Computerized tomography appears to be very close to the long-sought-after procedure that can directly visualize the brain.

The neurological examination

The neurological examination is a procedure that assesses what the nervous system can and cannot do. A full examination is a rather extensive survey covering the spinal cord and the peripheral nerves as well as the brain. It is actually an extension of the general physical examination that emphasizes the nervous system. Most of us are familiar with the part of the neurological examination given in the routine physical. The doctor may tap you on the knees with a hammer, or look into your eyes with an ophthalmoscope. The neurological examination places great stress on elementary sensory and motor functions. Many outlines are available for this examination, but they all cover essentially the same areas. As in most examinations, the first step is to take a history, when possible, from the patient first-hand. This step is generally followed by a physical examination. Usually, the patient is first asked to walk with eyes open and closed, and to perform other tests of gait and balance. As this is taking place and during other occasions, an inspection is made of the patient's general appearance: the shape of the head; body proportions; the condition of the skin; the presence of scars or other external indicators of disease or injury. The head and spine may be examined in some detail. The remainder of the examination is divided into four major components: the cranial nerves, the motor system, the sensory system, and mental status. The cranial nerves are the nerves that supply the head. They control such things as movement of the tongue and eyes, opening and closing of the eyes, sense of smell, contraction of the pupils, and related functions. Usually the neurologist looks directly into the eyes with an ophthalmoscope during this part of the examination. The sensory system examination involves testing of the patient's ability to perceive light touch and pin pricks over various parts of his body. Sense of vibration is also tested with a tuning fork. The motor system examination includes testing reflexes, and evaluating strength, speed, dexterity, and muscle tone throughout the body. The mental status examination is a clinical examination of various cognitive and perceptual abilities. It varies a great deal depending upon the examiner and the nature of the case. Language function and memory may be briefly evaluated and cognitive abilities may be tested by asking the patient to perform such tasks as solving arithmetic problems or interpreting proverbs. Generally, the examiner determines if the patient is oriented in regard to time, place, and person, and tries to find out what level of comprehension he may have. Often this step is accomplished by asking questions concerning why the patient is in the hospital, who the people on the ward are, and related matters. Where available, examiners tend to leave a more thorough evaluation of mental status to the psychologist, who can administer certain tests specifically designed for assessment of brain-damaged patients. Such procedures are called neuropsychological tests, discussed briefly in the following section.

Neuropsychological tests

Neuropsychological tests are used to diagnose brain damage, assess functioning in a number of areas, and are used as an aid in treatment and rehabilitation planning. A psychological test is a neuropsychological test if it is sensitive to the condition of the brain. Most such tests evaluate cognitive, perceptual, and motor skills, since it is in this area of behavior that brain damage seems to have the greatest influence. Many such tests are available, and a good description of a wide variety of them is contained in a book by Lezak (1976). In current practice, it is more customary to administer a battery of tests than it is to administer only a single test. These test batteries assess a wide variety of abilities such as general intelligence, language skills, spatial relations skills, perception, memory, and motor function. The more comprehensive batteries map out the brain using the concepts of contralateral control, functional asymmetry, regional localization, and specific and nonspecific symptoms.

Some authorities feel that behavioral tests are often more sensitive to brain dysfunction than are other diagnostic procedures, and that sometimes a brain lesion can be detected by neuropsychological tests before it is picked up by the EEG, neurological examination, or x-rays. With the advent of computerized tomography, the case for this point of view has been weakened somewhat, but there is still no substitute for behavioral testing as a means of assessing functioning. While computerized tomography is probably the best method of "looking at the brain," neuropsychological testing is probably the best method of "looking at what the brain does."

Treatment and rehabilitation

There is an undeserved aura of pessimism regarding working with brain-damaged patients. The anatomical fact that central nervous system tissue does not regenerate seems to have led to the unfortunate and inaccurate conclusion that the functions originally controlled by the destroyed tissue cannot return. As we now know, there can be substantial recovery from many of the functional impairments associated with several kinds of brain damage. While some of this recovery may be spontaneous, there seem little question that restitution of function can be promoted by various forms of treatment. It would, for example, be fair to say that the prognosis for recovery from stroke is probably better than it is from several of the functional psychiatric disorders such as schizophrenia and alcoholism. While certain traditional methods of treating brain-damaged patients have been available for some time, newer methods also have been introduced.

Traditional methods

The traditional methods tend to be more applicable to the patient with specific deficits. For example, if the patient is aphasic, the treatment of choice is speech therapy, a well established, effective, and generally available treatment. Likewise, if the patient has a physical disability such as a hemiparesis, physical therapy is often effective. If the patient has epilepsy, there is good reason to be optimistic about obtaining seizure control through the use of a number of pharmaceutical agents. Various surgical techniques are often effective in the treatment of brain tumors, diseased blood vessels, and increased intracranial pressure produced by blocks to the circulation of cerebral spinal fluid.

With the exception of the treatment of epilepsy, the success of medication has been mixed. Numerous attempts have been made to synthesize "memory pills" that can be shown to be helpful to brain-damaged patients. Usually, after some initial successes, further research has turned out to be disappointing. Sometimes, attempts are made to treat patients with cerebral vascular disease by dilating the blood vessels or thinning the blood. While certain drugs can sometimes produce the desired physical effects, there is little evidence that doing so significantly improves mental functioning. There is even some question as to whether these medications can dilate severely atherosclerotic blood vessels. Sometimes psychotropic medications including tranquilizers, antidepressant drugs, and antianxiety drugs are tried on these patients, but our experience indicates that they are generally not very effective. In general, the traditional approach of administering medicine has not shown much promise with regard to the treatment of patients with brain damage.

Innovative methods

Perhaps the key to innovation in the treatment of the brain-damaged patient has to do with attempting to fit the treatment to the pattern of deficits and preserved abilities of the patient, rather than trying to fit the patient into some preestablished treatment regime. There is no single ideal "treatment for brain damage." The appropriate treatment is the one that meets the patient's needs. One method of determining what the appropriate treatment program should be is neuropsychological testing. Neuropsychological tests can delineate the patient's assets and liabilities, and thus form the basis for a rational treatment plan. There is also a great need for treatment programming for the patient who "falls between the cracks." We are referring to the vast majority of brain-damaged patients who are not aphasic, do not have major physical disabilities, and do not have epilepsy. What these patients do have is impairment of a variety of cognitive, perceptual, and motor skills, for which there is little in the way of established treatment methods. However, the behavioral assessment, including neuropsychological testing, of such patients can identify the deficit patterns and encourage us to be innovative in planning and implementing retraining programs. In this regard, behavior modification programs oriented toward cognitive, perceptual, and motor retraining show much promise. As in other areas, it is not only important to offer the proper directions or instruction, but it is perhaps equally important to motivate the patient to participate in the treatment. The point of this approach is not to write off the traditional methods but to use them in a maximally effective manner. In our view, maximal effectiveness can be worked toward in two ways: 1. by doing a comprehensive evaluation of the patient so that treatment needs are clearly identified, and 2. by attempting to motivate the patient to participate in his or her rehabilitation.

Summary

This chapter was devoted to a discussion of patients with structural brain damage. The point of view taken was that such patients are best understood in terms of current theory of brain function in humans. For the present purposes, these theories were summarized in the form of a number of principles, as follows.

1. Certain functions are mediated by geographically localized centers in the brain, while other functions do not appear to be localizable.
2. With some exceptions, the right cerebral hemisphere controls functioning of the left side of the body, while the left hemisphere controls the right side.
3. In most people, the left cerebral hemisphere controls language functions, while the right cerebral hemisphere controls spatial relations abilities.
4. There is good evidence for a principle of regional localization. The frontal lobes mediate motor regulation, the temporal lobes hearing, the parietal lobes body senses and the occipital lobes vision.
5. In the event of brain damage, the type of damage interacts with its locus in determining the behavioral outcome.

In view of the significance of the principle of type-locus interaction, a brief survey was made of the features of some of the more commonly occurring types of brain damage. In addition, a series of descriptions roughly characterizing various kinds of brain damaged patients was offered. Such descriptions were made for patients with diffuse, unilateral and focal brain damage, as well as for patients with amnesic disorders and acute brain syndromes. Electroencephalographic, radiological, neurological, and neuropsychological methods for diagnosing brain damage were briefly reviewed, as were some of the traditional and innovative methods of treatment and rehabilitation of brain-damaged patients.

GLOSSARY

Abstract attitude: A level of cognitive function, generally involving conceptual reasoning, that is commonly impaired in brain-damaged individuals.

Aphasia: An impairment of language abilities associated with structural brain damage, usually involving the left cerebral hemisphere.

C-T scan; CAT scan: A computer assisted x-ray technique that allows for determination of the location of brain lesions in three dimensional space.

Chorea: A disorder characterized by involuntary flailing, twisting, and lashing movements.

Constructional apraxia: A disturbance of spatial relations abilities often associated with right hemisphere brain damage.

Convolution: A folded-in, prominent, rounded mass of tissue on the surface of the brain constituting an identifiable structural unit. Also known as a gyrus.

Degenerative disease: A group of diseases characterized by progressive atrophy of the brain, generally beginning during middle age.

Demyelinating disease: Multiple sclerosis and a group of rarer diseases in which there is erosion of the myelin sheaths that coat nerve cells.

Dominant hemisphere: The side of the brain, usually the left side, that mediates language.

Electroencephalogram (EEG): A recording of the electrical activity of the brain.

Equipotentiality: The capacity for unimpaired brain tissue to take over functions lost by destruction of other tissue within the same functional area.

Hemianopia: Blindness of one-half of the visual field associated with damage to the visual system pathways in the brain.

Korsakoff's syndrome: A severe disturbance of recent memory, generally associated with alcoholism and thiamin deficiency.

Lesion: A general term describing any kind of tissue damage or other pathology.

Neuropsychology: The study of relationships between the brain and behavior.

Ophthalmoscope: A device for seeing the inside of the eye.

Organic brain syndrome: A chronic or acute mental disorder associated with impairment of brain tissue function.

Petit mal epilepsy: A seizure disorder characterized by episodic lapses of consciousness.

Prosopagnosia: Inability to recognize familiar faces.

Psychomotor/temporal lobe epilepsy: A seizure disorder characterized by episodes of a number of involuntary but apparenty purposive, organized motor behaviors or hallucinatory sensory experiences.

13

ADDICTIVE DISORDERS

G. ALAN MARLATT
FRANCINE ROSE

The study of addictive disorders is one of the most exciting areas of contemporary abnormal psychology. Not only do we know very little about the underlying mechanisms of addiction, but we also lack sufficient knowledge about how to successfully treat individuals who experience serious problems with such drugs as alcohol or heroin. Our purpose is to kindle the spark of intellectual curiosity about the nature and treatment of addictive disorders and to prompt a more active interest in this compelling and fascinating problem.

If we look up the verb "to addict" in *Webster's New Collegiate Dictionary* (1974 edition), we find two somewhat contradictory definitions: "1: to devote or surrender (oneself) to something *habitually* or obsessively . . . 2: to cause (a person) to become *physiologically* dependent upon a drug" (our italics).

These two definitions encompass the primary riddle of addiction. Is addiction a learned habit, or a disease mediated by physiological dependence? Asked in another way, and leading to a host of related questions, to what extent is addiction based on psychological factors such as learning, cognition, and response to environmental determinants, and to what extent is it based on such physiological factors as heredity, the physical effects of various drugs, or related pharmacological and biochemical processes? What are the differences, if any, between physical and psychological dependence on drugs? Is the "root" of addiction to be found in the drug or in the user? Are there different "kinds" of addiction associated with each of the "addictive" drugs? How much do we really know about the underlying physiological nature of addiction? Are there "opiate receptors" in the brain, and if so, how do these relate to heroin addiction? How do such "physical" phenomena such as tolerance to drug effects and withdrawal contribute to the addictive cycle? What does it mean to get "high"—what do we know about the physical and psychological effects of intoxication? Does the "placebo effect" imply that we can get high on our own expectations of the effects of a particular drug, or are such effects explained in terms of classical conditioning, a model which downplays the importance of awareness and cognitive mediation?

When we turn to the arena of treatment intervention, a parallel set of questions arises. Can an "addict" ever really be "cured" of his or her addiction? Can an alcoholic ever drink again in a normal manner? Must a heroin addict always rely on a substitute drug such as methadone to "maintain" adjustment? Why are paraprofessional organizations such as Alcoholics Anonymous or therapeutic communities such as Synanon sometimes successful in caring for alcoholics or heroin addicts when traditional professional treatment programs have often fared so poorly? What new and innovative treatment procedures show the most promise? And, perhaps the most exciting question of all, can people learn to "turn themselves on" without the aid of chemical assistance? Can such techniques as biofeedback and meditation provide an alternative high to drugs?

In the following pages, we will review theories and evidence touching on many of these perplexing questions. By the end of the chapter, some tentative answers to a few of these questions will be discussed, while others will go unanswered. Given space limitations, we have chosen to focus on only two addictive disorders: alcoholism and heroin addiction. This narrow focus is justified on two counts. *First,* alcoholism and heroin addiction have the greatest significance among addictive disorders because of their impact as human problems in our society. *Second,* the study of these two disorders alone allows us to discuss most of the key issues and assumptions involved in the entire addictions field. We shall return to a discussion of some of these important issues in the concluding section of the chapter.

Alcoholism

Some facts and figures about alcohol and drinking

Along with caffeine and nicotine, alcohol is one of the three most widely consumed drugs in contemporary society. Concurrent with this extensive use, unfortunately, there exists a wide range of misuses and abuses associated with alcohol. In a recent question-answer column in the weekend magazine section of our local newspaper, the extent of these problems was stated in a nutshell:

> Q. I've got to give a talk on booze and how it affects U.S. lifestyles. Can you give me any background information?
>
> A. In 1975 we guzzled 49 billion bottles of beer and 781 million gallons of wine and alcohol. Almost two-thirds of all murders and nearly one-third of all suicides involve alcohol abuse, as do roughly half of all fire deaths, fatal car accidents and drownings. Not incidentally, cirrhosis of the liver is killing 67 percent more people today than in 1956. (From "People Etc.," *The Seattle Times Magazine,* Sept. 18, 1977)

The National Institute on Alcohol Abuse and Alcoholism (NIAA) has issued a series of reports (1971, 1974, 1977) to the U.S. Congress concerning the use and abuse of alcohol in American society. Drawing from a number of national surveys and public polls, these reports indicate that in the mid-seventies approximately 68 percent of adults (18 and older) drink alcoholic beverages at least occasionally. An extensive national survey conducted by Cahalan and his associates (Cahalan, Cisin, & Crossley, 1969) provides a more concise breakdown of American drinking practices. This report shows that 77 percent of adult men and 60 percent of adult women are drinkers, with the highest proportion of drinkers occurring in the younger age categories (age 21–24). Recent surveys show a substantial amount of drinking among the teenage population as well. An aggregation of surveys indicate that from 71 percent to 92 percent of high school students have had at least some drinking experiences.

Statistics for the "average" drinker can be misleading, however, since not everyone who drinks alcohol drinks the same amount each year. The average male drinker, for example, consumed 3 times as much as the average female drinker; and the average alcoholic person consumes about 11 times as much as the average social drinker. Drinking rates also vary considerably in accordance with one's age, ethnic background, religious affiliation, and socioeconomic status (Cahalan et al., 1969). Cahalan's survey also shows that among adults of both sexes, 32 percent are total abstainers (1 out of 3 abstainers used to drink but have stopped), 15 percent are infrequent drinkers (those who drink at least once a year, but less than once a month), 41 percent are light or moderate drinkers (drinking at least once a month, but with no more than about 3 or 4 drinks per occasion), and the remaining 12 percent are heavy drinkers (drinking nearly every day or weekly, frequently consuming 5 or more drinks per occasion). How many heavy drinkers (21% of the men and 5% of the women in Cahalan's sample) experience problems with their use of alcohol?

In other surveys, Cahalan and his colleagues (Cahalan, 1970; Cahalan & Room, 1974) attempted to assess the extent of drinking-related problems among American drinkers. Here, Cahalan adopted the position stated by the Cooperative Commission on the Study of Alcoholism (Plaut, 1967), defining *problem drinking* as the "repetitive use of beverage alcohol causing physical, psychological, or social harm to the drinker or to others" (a definition widely accepted in the field). The problems assessed in the Cahalan and Room report included, for example, psychological dependence (drinking to alleviate depression or nervousness or to escape from the problems of everyday living), frequent intoxication, problems with spouse or relatives or with one's employers related to drinking, health problems, and problems with law, police, and accidents. Based on this analysis, a surprisingly high proportion of the total sample (31%) had experienced at least one of these drinking-related problems in the three years preceding the survey (43% of the men and 21% of the women). When more severe involvement was evaluated (high problem score), 15 percent of the men and 4 percent of the women could be said to have problems or potential problems with drinking. Estimating the number of "alcoholics" in the population is a hazardous undertaking (estimates range from 5 to 15 million alcoholics in the United States), because there is little agreement among professionals as to the criteria for defining or diagnosing alcoholism as a discrete disorder. Because of this ambiguity in terminology, many contemporary professionals prefer the term problem drinking to alcoholism, although some would argue that the term addictive drinking should be reserved for those who have the most serious and involved physical problems with alcohol (cf. Keller, 1978). Regardless of the semantics involved, there is little doubt that the problems associated with the abuse of alcohol are very real indeed.

Problem drinking: a case study

Before moving on to a discussion of various theories relating to alcohol abuse, let us pause to focus on an individual who has experienced a variety of problems with alcohol (for further details concerning this case, see Marlatt, 1978). Liane was a recent client in our Center for Psychological Services at the University of Washington. A thirty-year-old single woman, who lived in a self-contained apartment in her parent's home in Seattle, Liane was a senior undergraduate student majoring in psychology. In the months prior to our first contact, Liane's drinking began to interfere with her studies. Rather than devoting time to her assignments, Liane would spend most of her evenings alone, sipping vodka and watching television. She did not have a steady boyfriend, and spent most of her free time either alone or with her parents, claiming that she could not relate comfortably to most people unless she had been drinking.

A two-week daily diary of her alcohol intake revealed that she was consuming almost a full quart of vodka each day, along with a variety of tranquilizers. When we confronted her with the seriousness of her condition, she agreed to undergo a period of voluntary hospitalization to provide medical supervision for her detoxification from both alcohol and the other drugs she had been

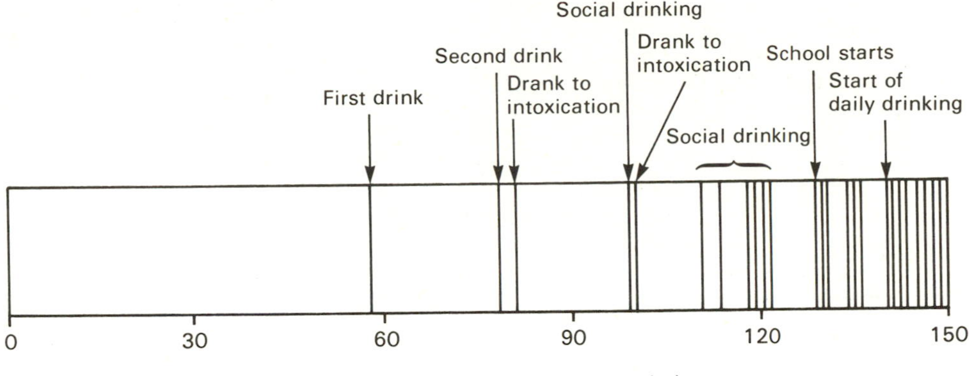

Fig. 13.1. Relapse pattern of the client discussed in the case study. Vertical lines refer to drinking episodes during the first 150 days following her discharge from the hospital.

taking. Before she was released from the hospital, she committed herself to complete abstinence from alcohol for a period of at least one year. All went well for the first few weeks, and she was able to maintain abstinence during this initial period.

On the 58th day following her discharge from the hospital, however, Liane experienced a "slip" and consumed one drink during a luncheon date with a female friend. On the 78th day, she repeated this experience. Finally on the 81st day, Liane drank to the point of intoxication during a weekend evening alone in her apartment. The course of her drinking during the first 150 days after her hospitalization is presented in Figure 13.1. An examination of this figure shows the pattern of a typical relapse. After becoming intoxicated on the 81st day, Liane again refrained from drinking for about two weeks, followed by another occasion of "social drinking" (limiting herself to no more than two drinks), and shortly thereafter, another bout of intoxication. With the start of classes in the fall, her drinking began to increase again until it almost equalled the rate of intake she reported prior to treatment. Currently, Liane has shown considerable improvement and is continuing treatment in our program.

We asked Liane to keep a running account of her experiences during the period following her discharge from the hospital. With her permission, we quote from her description of the circumstances surrounding her first intoxication experience:

August 9, 81st day after leaving the hospital. I got up early, and I felt content and at ease. I put some records on, which I hadn't done since I came home from the hospital. Unfortunately, as I recollect now, the records started my change in mood. As I played some records and sang along, my mood became melancholy and I began feeling sorry for myself. The point at which I noticed my "free floating anxiety" came around 4:00 in the afternoon. I have my little fantasies. This is not easy to write, and I don't know how to write it without sounding like I belong in a mental institution. My fantasy is to take a real person (male) whom I don't know personally, but through TV, etc., and, well, to imagine that we are together. So, suddenly, abut 4:00, his face just popped into my mind. This really affected my mood, because, well, I was alone in the house, it was Saturday, and I knew I was going to be alone for the evening. After a while, I began to feel more and more anxious about this. At first, I thought I would feel better if I could take a tranquilizer, so I searched all over the house for the pills my mother had hidden. I couldn't find them, which made me all the more upset. What I did find, though, was two bottles of scotch, miniature bottles like you buy on a plane, hidden in a teapot in the kitchen. I also found three bottles of beer in the fridge upstairs. At first, I tried to ignore them, but I couldn't. Finally I took out the two bottles of scotch and put them on the table. I just looked at them for a long time, without even touching them. After about half an hour, I finally opened one of the bottles and poured it into a glass with some ice. I sipped the drink but didn't feel anything at first, so I poured in the other one and drank that too. After that, I drank the bottles of beer in the fridge and then I don't remember what happened. I woke up later that night with a hangover, and I felt terrible about what I had done.

Explanatory models of alcoholism

Just as there is little agreement about the diagnostic criteria used to identify someone as an "alcoholic," considerable disagreement exists concerning the underlying causes and determinants of alcoholism as a discrete disorder. This disagreement reflects the absence of established empirical evidence supporting one theory over another. We know surprisingly little about how alcohol induces intoxication, let alone how alcohol can become "addictive" at the physiological level. As the 1974 NIAAA report to congress concludes, "It seems obvious that without a firm understanding of the mechanism responsible for alcohol intoxication, theories attempting to explain alcohol addiction or withdrawal stand on even less certain ground" (p. 93). Despite the lack of supporting data concerning the nature of the addictive process, numerous theories have been advanced to explain the "causes" and effects of alcoholism (Siegler, Osmond, & Newell, 1968; Tarter & Schneider, 1976). Currently, a great deal of controversy has flared up among adherents of the various theoretical models. One such controversy has to do with the implications for treatment derived from opposing theories: Can some alcoholics ever be taught to regain control over their drinking behavior? On the one hand, we have the proponents of the disease concept of alcoholism, who claim that the only "cure" for the disease involves total and absolute abstinence from alcohol use. On the other hand, some investigators (who prefer the term problem drinking), have argued that it is a learned, behavioral disorder, and that controlled drinking is indeed a useful goal for at least some alcoholics.

This debate goes to the heart of the question raised at the beginning of this chapter: Is alcoholism a physiologically based disease, or can it best be described as an acquired, behavioral disorder (or some combination of the two approaches)? The answer to this question, yet to be determined on the basis of experimental evidence, will have profound implications for the prevention and treatment of alcohol-related problems in the years to come. Let us examine in some detail the basic assumptions and existing evidence for both the disease theory (the medical model), and the behavioral disorder theory (the social-learning model).

The medical model

Prior to the emergence of the medical model, individuals who had serious problems with alcohol were often treated as moral degenerates, persons who lacked the "moral fiber" or "will" to control their drinking or abstain from alcohol. Often spurred on by religious beliefs, many people thought of drinking and particularly drunkenness as a sin or moral failing. These atitudes, still present in many sectors of society, reached their peak in 1919 with the passing of the Volstead Act (Prohibition), forbidding the manufacture and sale of alcoholic beverages. Even though Prohibition was repealed in 1933, in many "dry" counties in the United States (chiefly in the South), the sale of alcoholic beverages is still prohibited by law. The moral approach created more problems than it attempted to solve. Persons suffering from drinking problems often perceived themselves as moral outcasts and misfits; their guilt and stigma probably served to exacerbate their difficulties with alcohol. Public intoxication was treated as a criminal offense, contributing to the "revolving door" cycle in which many alcoholics (particularly those inhabiting the skid row sections of most cities) were repeatedly arrested, released, and arrested again following another drinking episode. In recent years, the adoption of the Uniform Alcoholism Act by many states has led to the development of policies in which the publicly intoxicated individual is taken to a local detoxification and treatment center instead of being thrown in the "drunk tank" at the nearest jail.

Opposition to the moral model provided one impetus for the development of the currently popular disease model of alcoholism. In the United States, Dr. Benjamin Rush was among the first to refer to the intemperate use of distilled spirits as a "disease" in his classic 1785 essay entitled, *Inquiry Into the Effects of Ardent Spirits on the Human Body*. It was not until the middle of the twentieth century, however, that the disease model of alcoholism became accepted on a popular level. The late E.M. Jellinek of the Rutgers Center for Alcohol Studies is often credited with having advanced the disease concept of alcoholism in this country (Jellinek, 1960). Based on his experiences working with alcoholics (and on questionnaire surveys), Jellinek proposed an elaborate theory to show that alcoholism could be construed as a disease. Among other propositions, he outlined four "types" of alcoholism, including *gamma alcoholism,* considered by him to be the predominant form of alcoholism in North America. Jellinek characterized the gamma type of alcoholic as someone who was physically dependent on alcohol, as evidenced by the appearance of physiological withdrawal symptoms upon the cessation of excessive drinking. The gamma alcoholic also was thought to exhibit loss of control—an inability to voluntarily control or stop one's drinking after the consumption of the first drink or two, presumably mediated by physiological addiction. As we shall see later, this concept of loss of control is an essential assumption of the classic disease model.

Jellinek also proposed that alcoholism was a progressive disease, with insidious onset and development. In 1952, he proposed an oft-cited model of the phases in the development of alcoholism: 1. The *proalcoholic symptomatic phase*—in which the drinker begins to experience relief from tension with repeated use of alcohol; 2. the *predromal phase*—where the drinker begins to experience blackouts or lapses in memory for events that occurred during a drinking episode, along with a greater preoccupation with alcohol and associated feelings of secrecy, guilt, and denial of drinking as the source of one's difficulties; 3. the *crucial phase*—in which loss of control is the paramount symptom, along with behaviors such as increased rationalization about drinking, morning drinking, hiding and sneaking drinks, loss of friends and/or family, and other problems; and 4. the *chronic phase*—characterized by exclusive preoccupation with drinking, drinking binges or sprees often lasting for days at a time, decreased tolerance to alcohol's effects, and a general moral and physical deterioration—the "rock-bottom" stage. Jellinek believed that these stages developed sequentially, and that the entire process might take many years to unfold. The phases described by Jellinek appear to parallel the orderly development of many other physical diseases—a parallel no doubt intended to emphasize the applicability of the disease model to explain alcoholism.

While the description of Jellinek's phases may have some basis in reality, the available evidence to date suggests that this model applies only to some alcoholics, and not to others. Cahalan's survey data, reviewed earlier, shows that the most serious problems associated with drinking tend to appear very early in the drinker's career—often before age 25 among men. The recent public outcry about the so-called growth of "teenage alcoholism" suggests that the idea of progressive stages that take many years to develop is outmoded. Recent research has shown that not all alcoholics experience blackouts, and that frequently such experiences occur much later in the drinker's history than Jellinek suggests (Goodwin, Crane, & Guze, 1969). Other studies have shown that although there may be some progression of symptoms as dependence on alcohol increases, the ordering of these effects does not correspond to Jellinek's model (Orford & Hawker, 1974).

Furthermore, there is little empirical evidence to support the notion that most alcoholics experience loss of control, considered by Jellinek to be the crucial symptom of the crucial phase of gamma alcoholism.

One of the most significant implications of the disease model of alcoholism is the treatment required of total abstinence. An alcoholic can never drink again, according to this analysis, because of the strong probability that the first drink will trigger the symptom of loss of control, presumably mediated by alcohol's triggering effect on some unspecified physiological processes. This physiological triggering mechanism is subjectively perceived by alcoholics as a physical "craving" for alcohol, in which "one alcoholic drink sets up a chain reaction so that they are unable to adhere to their intention to 'have one or two drinks only' but continue to ingest more and more—often with quite some difficulty and disgust—contrary to their volition" (Jellinek, 1960, p. 41). Loss of control can thus be construed as the pathognomonic symptom of alcoholism—the very basis of the addiction itself. As the capacity for loss of control is often considered as the hallmark symptom of alcoholism (Keller, 1972), and is said by these theorists to be maintained at a physiological level even though the alcoholic has been abstinent for some time, the requirement of total abstinence has become the sine qua non of the traditional alcoholism treatment programs.

Recent research on the loss of control phenomenon has challenged the validity of this basic assumption. In brief, these studies have shown that increased drinking and/or reported craving for alcohol can be induced in alcoholics who *believe* they are consuming a drink containing alcohol, even though there is in fact no alcohol whatsoever in the beverage. In these studies, alcoholics were presented with drinks supposedly containing alcohol (eg., vodka and tonic): some subjects actually received drinks containing alcohol, while others received drinks containing no alcohol. In other conditions, alcoholics were told they would be consuming nonalcoholic drinks, even though some actually received drinks containing alcohol. The findings of these studies were clear cut. Alcoholic subjects consumed more drinks (representative of the "loss of control" effect) when they believed they were drinking alcohol, regardless of the actual content of the drinks (Engle & Williams, 1972; Maisto, Lauerman, & Adesso, 1977; Marlatt, Demming, & Reid, 1973). The finding that psychological expectancy factors play an even greater role than the physiological effects of alcohol in determining alcohol consumption in these studies casts a serious shadow of doubt over the validity of the disease model assumption of loss of control drinking.

To date, no existing evidence has pinpointed the physiological basis of addiction to alcohol. Numerous mechanisms have been postulated, including endocrinological dysfunction (Tintera & Lovell, 1949), brain cell dysfunction (Lemere, 1956), and a disorder of appetitive regulation (Randolph, 1956). Similarly, the evidence in support of a genetic determinant of alcoholism is equivocal and often contradictory (Tarter & Schneider, 1976). Although there is considerable evidence to show that alcoholism tends to occur more frequently in some families than others, and other evidence suggests an inherited predisposition in some animal research (see reviews by Cruz-Coke, 1971; Cadoret, 1976; McClearn, 1973), the available data are not yet sufficient to rule out the overriding potency of environmental factors. Recent research, on the other hand, has highlighted the potency of observational learning and modeling as determinants of alcohol consumption (Caudill & Marlatt, 1975; Lied & Marlatt, 1978).

To say that the basis of the disease model of alcoholism is seriously in doubt by no means implies that medical complications associated with alcohol abuse are minimal or nonexistent. Quite the contrary, in fact: Excessive use of alcohol has been found to be related to a whole host of disorders and maladies. While the moderate use of alcoholic beverages may be relatively harmless, excessive and prolonged chronic use is far from benign in its effects. While a complete description of these associated disorders is beyond the scope of the present chapter, the reader should note that excessive abuse of alcohol has been found to associated with disorders of the hepatic system, particularly cirrhosis of the liver (Korsten & Liever, 1976; Lieber, 1973), certain cardiac disorders (Myerson, 1971), some forms of cancer (NIAAA, 1974), some sleep disorders (Gross & Hastey, 1976), and selected congenital disorders including the 'fetal alcoholism syndrome" in which the offspring of mothers who consumed large quantities of alcohol during pregnancy are often malformed or retarded in development (Jones, Smith, Ulleland, & Streissguth, 1973; NIAAA, 1974, 1977).

Perhaps the most serious and striking effects of alcohol abuse are those involving the nervous system (Davies & Walsh, 1971; Freund, 1976). Considerable evidence exists to show that chronic use of alcohol is associated with a variety of forms of brain damage (Tarter, 1976), including destruction of brain cells and cerebral dysfunction. One chronic dysfunction sometimes associated with alcohol abuse (particularly in association with vitamin deficiency) is *Korsakoff's syndrome,* characterized by disorientation, mental confusion, loss of recent memory, and confabulation (falsification of events to conceal memory loss). Psychoticlike symptoms are also sometimes attributed to prolonged, chronic use of alcohol. In *acute alcoholic hallucinosis,* the main symptoms are auditory hallucinations, although the precise etiology of this disorder remains unclear. Finally, psychoticlike symptoms (which may include disorientation, valid hallucinatins of the "pink elephant" variety, acute fear, marked tremor, and occasional seizures) are often associated with the condition known as *delirium tremens* (the "DTs"), an acute withdrawal reaction that may occur when some alcoholics stop drinking. In some cases, this withdrawal syndrome can have fatal consequences. It should be mentioned, however, that the withdrawal "syndrome" associated with alcohol use is a widely variable phenomenon, ranging in severity from a mild case of hangover and the "shakes," to severe physical and psychological dysfunction.

The social-learning model

In the past decade, a number of criticisms of the medical model and the conception of alcoholism as a disease have been raised. Most of these criticisms have been voiced by profesionals in the general field of mental health, particularly from behavioral scientists (Hershon, 1974; Pomerleau, Pertschuk, & Stinnet, 1976; Verden & Shatterly, 1971; among others). Briefly summarized, the arguments critical of the disease model have included the following points: 1. The focus on alcoholism as a disease has emphasized the exclusive importance of internal, physiological, and biochemical factors, and has paid little attention to the role of psychological, environmental, and behavioral determinants; 2. in the absence of empirical evidence demonstrating the existence of the underlying addictive or disease mechanism, the medical model has not led to the development of adequate prevention or treatment programs for alcohol dependence, other than promoting the requirement of total abstinence from alcohol use; 3. paradoxically, those who advocate the disease model (including the influential position of Alcoholics Anonymous) have relied upon moral and semi-religious principles to encourage abstinence as the only acceptable treatment goal (while at the same time, labeling any drinking behavior following treatment as "relapse" or treatment failure); 4. many alcoholics who accept and believe the medical model may come to see themselves as helpless victims of a disease, thus absolving themselves of any personal responsibility or motivation to change their behavior, perhaps encouraging the use of the disease theory as an excuse for continuing their abuse of alcohol; and 5. the slogans derived from the disease model (e.g., "one drink leads to a drunk," 'once a drunk, always a drunk") may come to act as self-fulfilling prophecies, leading to even more drinking. The disease model, with its exclusive emphasis on abstinence, offers few incentives to seek help or volunteer for treatment for the problem drinker who will not or cannot accept this absolute requirement to never drink again.

In recent years, an alternative approach to understanding alcohol problems has received increased attention. Derived from the principles of behaviorism and experimental social psychology, the social learning model makes a number of assumptions that differ markedly from the disease model. Problem drinking (a term that avoids defining drinking problems as indicative of an underlying alcohol*ism* disease) is viewed by advocates of the social position as a learned, behavioral disorder. Drinking problems, as with problems involving eating (obesity), smoking, or sexual behaviors, can best be understood within a theoretical framework derived from learning theory, cognitive psychology, and related behavioral science disciplines. From this perspective, all drinking behavior (from social drinking to problem drinking) is assumed to lie on a continuum, rather than being defined as a dichotomy (normal drinking vs. alcoholism). The parameters of the continuum focus on the observable aspects of drinking behavior, including the frequency and duration of drinking episodes, amount of alcohol consumed and degree of intoxication, and the problems (if any) associated with excessive use.

Social learning theorists are very much concerned with the *determinants* of drinking behavior, including environmental and situational antecedents, cognitive expectations, and the individual's own past learning experiences with alcohol. They are also interested in discovering the *consequences* of drinking, so as to uncover both the reinforcing effects that may contribute to increased drinking, and the negative consequences that may serve to inhibit rates of consumption. These consequences range from the specific physical effects of alcohol to the interpersonal and social reactions experienced by the drinker. Because problematic drinking is assumed to be the consequence of maladaptive learning, treatment is often construed as an educational or "relearning" process. Consistent with this assumption, some therapists have investigated the possibility of training some problem drinkers to moderate or control their alcohol intake, in marked contrast to the dictums of the disease model. We shall again discuss some of these behavioral treatment programs (including controlled drinking) at the end of this section.

If drinking is a learned behavior, what are the reinforcing consequences associated with the acquisition and maintenance of alcohol consumption? This key question has prompted a great deal of speculation and research among social learning theorists. For many years, behavioral investigators have evaluated the validity of the "*tension reduction*" *hypothesis* (TRH) as a possible explanation of the reinforcing effects of alcohol. Initially based on research with animals (e.g., Conger, 1951, 1956), the TRH states that drinking is reinforced through the tension-reducing properties of alcohol. In terms of this hypothesis, alcohol is viewed as a tranquilizing agent, reinforcing the act of drinking by the reduction of anxiety or arousal it provides the drinker. But does alcohol actually reduce tension? Do drinkers consume more alcohol when they are tense or anxious? The available research evidence with both animal and human subjects suggests that there is no unambiguous answer to these questions (see reviews by Cappell, 1975; Marlatt, 1976a). Research with alcoholics whose drinking behavior has been observed over long periods of time in an experimental ward setting has found, contrary to the predictions of the TRH, that many subjects report an *increase* in tension, dysphoria, and depression over prolonged drining (e.g., Nathan & O'Brien, 1971). Does this mean that alcohol serves to increase rather than decrease tension? To date, there is still no clear resolution of these issues.

Recent research, however, has led to the development of an alternative to the TRH. Experiments on the effects of alcohol on physiological response systems suggest that the effects of alcohol may be *biphasic* in nature (Marlatt, 1976a; Mello, 1968; Russell & Mehrabian, 1975). Rather than the consumption of alcohol producing a linear decrease in arousal or tension as predicted by the TRH, alcohol seems to have two physical effects, producing a biphasic response: the immediate and initial effects may be to *increase* arousal, followed by a delayed "depressant" effect, experienced as a rather unpleasant or dysphoric reaction by the drinker. The initial increase in excitation, at low levels of alcohol concentration in the blood, may be experienced by the drinker as a "high"—subjective feelings of excitement, increased energy, and perceptions of the self as more powerful (cf. McClelland, Davis, Kalin, & Wanner, 1972). Physiological responses such as heart rate are increased during this phase. As blood-alcohol concentration rises, however, the body seems to react in quite the opposite way. Feelings of fatigue, stupor, nausea, and an overall increase in dysphoria may ensue; all of these effects are those traditionally associated with alcohol as a depressant drug. Thus, instead of tension reduction, alcohol may produce two quite different effects: first an upper followed by a downer.

If the validity of the biphasic hypothesis is supported by future research, some of the apparent contradictions in our current knowledge about alcohol and problem drinking may be resolved. Consider the following line of reasoning. Most people who drink do so because they like the effects—they like to get high, at least occasionally. Prior to taking a drink, the drinker's *expectations* of the effects are positive: If I drink this, I will feel good. This expectation may be based on one's past experience with the initial excitatory phase of the biphasic response, an effect that provides the most *immediate* reinforcement for drinking (in contrast with the *delayed* effects of the second, dysphoric stage). Behavioral science has established the finding that immediate reinforcement has a much stronger effect than delayed reinforcement. Under appropriate conditions of setting, mood, dose level, and positive expectations, the drinker will probably experience the euphoric effects of alcohol. But, what then? As time passes, and/or as the consumption level increases, the positive effect begins to turn sour as the second, dysphoric stage develops. Unfortunately, many drinkers attempt to deal with this increase in dysphoria by drinking still more alcohol. For some problem drinkers who have developed *physical tolerance* to the effects of alcohol (more and more alcohol is required to produce the desired effect), the initially sought-after positive effects may be short-lived or absent altogether.

The conditions for "loss of control" drinking, according to this theoretical model (Marlatt, 1978) are as follows: positive expectancies for the effects of alcohol, increased physical tolerance (which acts to dampen the initial euphoric effects), coupled with the delay in time it takes for any consumption of alcohol to be absorbed into the blood stream. The result may be that the drinker begins to gulp down several drinks in rapid succession, much like a gambler in Las Vegas pulls the lever of the slot machine in anticipation of hitting the jack pot. But for the excessive drinker, the reward (if any) is quickly followed by the costs of the dysphoric physical effects that follow. Rather than exhibiting loss of control, the drinker may be behaving in a manner similar to any organism placed under a variable-interval reinforcement schedule (where reinforcement may or may not follow a particular time interval). In line with this view, we would like to suggest a new term to replace loss of control: the *Rapid Alcohol Consumption Effect* (RACE). The so-called addictive drinker who shows this effect may be exhibiting behavior best understood in terms of the principles of learning and reinforcement theory, in contrast with the position that labels rapid drinking as a symptom of an underlying disease. Once caught in this vicious circle, the problem drinker may attempt to escape or avoid the negative consequences by more and more drinking, behavior that is strongly resistant to extinction.

Social drinking

Social learning theory can apply to the understanding of normal or social drinking, as well as to problem drinking. By focusing on the determinants and consequences of moderate drinking, behavioral scientists can gain insight into how problem drinking may develop in some individuals, while the vast majority of others show few if any problems associated with their drinking. This information can then be used in the establishment of innovative programs of prevention and treatment intervention. In our own research program we have conducted a series of studies designed to investigate determinants of social drinking, particularly among younger, college-age drinkers.

While still underway, our experiments have provided some important initial findings. In most of the studies conducted in our laboratory, drinking rates are assessed directly by having subjects take part in a *taste-rating task*. This task, presented to subjects as a procedure whereby they are asked to make comparative taste-ratings among various alcoholic beverages, actually serves as an unobtrusive index of alcohol consumption (Marlatt, 1977). Subjects vary widely in the amount of alcohol they consume in the process of making their taste-ratings, allowing us to observe individual differences in overall consumption and styles of drinking as a function of our experimental manipulation.

In our early studies, we attempted to assess the validity of the TRH by exposing drinkers to several stress manipulations to determine if the increased "tension" increased alcohol consumption in the taste-rating task. In a preliminary study (Higgins & Marlatt, 1973), we induced stress in matched groups of male social drinkers and problem drinkers by the use of a standard procedure often used in stress research with human subjects; we threatened them with the possibility of a painful electric shock. Although no shock was actually delivered, half the subjects were led to believe they would receive a shock following participation in the taste-rating task. The other half of the subjects did not expect to receive a painful shock. The findings showed that even though problem drinkers consumed significantly more alcohol in the task than social drinkers, the groups anticipating the stressful shock did not drink any more than the control condition subjects.

In a follow-up study, Higgins and Marlatt (1975) investigated the effects of a *social* stress procedure on drinking rates among male social drinkers. In this experiment, the high-stress group was led to believe that following participation in a taste-rating task, they would be evaluated by a group of college women who would be rating the men on a number of dimensions, including personal attractiveness. The subjects in the evaluation threat condition consumed significantly more alcohol than subjects in the control condition (who did not anticipate being rated). The results of this study suggest that one factor that may increase drinking is the anticipation of evaluation by others—particularly if the evaluation is interpersonal in nature. These findings may help explain why some people drink heavily at the beginning of a social gathering (or who belt down a drink or two before going to a party). Rather than providing evidence for the TRH, the results are consistent with the biphasic theory described above: subjects may have attempted to deal with the impending evaluation by fortifying themselves (getting high and feeling stronger or more in control) by drinking.

In a related study, we investigated how feelings of anger and frustration affect rates (Marlatt, Kosturn, & Lang, 1975). We hypothesized that if social drinkers were angered by someone who unfairly criticized and belittled them while they were working on a difficult task (unscrambling anagrams in a task presented to them as a test of their intelligence), they would subsequently consume more alcohol in a taste-rating task. We also hypothesized that if some subjects who were angered in this manner were given the opportunity to retaliate, they would drink less than subjects who were deprived of this opportunity. Both male and female heavy social drinkers served as subjects in this experiment. The results supported our predictions. Angered subjects drank significantly more alcohol in the taste-rating task than control subjects who were not angered; and, more importantly, subjects in the retaliation condition drank the least of all three conditions. This study suggests that if drinkers are provided with an alternative to drinking (engaging in assertive behavior) when they are feeling angered and frustrated, their drinking may be reduced as a result.

Finally, we have conducted two studies to assess the effects of social modeling (observational learning) on social drinking behaviors. We are all aware of the pervasive number of inputs we are constantly exposed to associated with alcohol and drinking: the influence of liquor, wine, and beer advertising; the portrayal of drinking in television and motion pictures; the drinking behavior of our friends and members of our family. How do all of these drinking "models" affect our own drinking behavior? To provide an initial answer to this important question, we decided to start with a rather simplified experimental analogue. The first study (Caudill & Marlatt, 1975) involved having males classified as heavy social drinkers take part in a taste-rating task in the presence of a confederate "subject" who played the role of either a heavy drinker (guzzling down the equivalent of a full bottle of wine during the taste-rating task), or a light drinker (consuming only one-seventh of a bottle). Control subjects took part in the task without a partner. Results showed a significant modeling effect: those subjects who were paired with a heavy drinking model drank significantly more than subjects who drank alone, or subjects who were paired with a light drinking model.

In a subsequent study (Lied & Marlatt, 1978), using a similar design, we found that the modeling effect was most pronounced in male heavy drinkers who were paired with a heavy drinking model of the same sex. Female heavy drinkers, and both male and females who were classified as *light* social drinkers, did not show such an increase in drinking when paired with a same-sex model. Subsequent studies by other investigators have also demonstrated the potency of modeling as a determinant of both increased and decreased drinking rates.

Clearly, social drinking is strongly influenced by social factors. The influence of such social factors as interpersonal evaluation, anger, and modeling (including social pressure) have also been found to be important determinants of relapse among problem drinkers (Marlatt, 1978). These findings have important implications for programs of prevention and treatment, as reviewed below.

Assessment of alcohol abuse

The basic differences between the assumptions of the medical model and the social learning model concerning the nature and origins of alcohol abuse are also reflected in the various approaches to assessment of alcohol abuse endorsed by each model. Disease model theorists search for the diagnostic signs of alcoholism, whereas behavioral scientists are interested in assessing behaviors associated with alcohol use and abuse. We shall briefly review some of the most prominent assessment procedures deriving from both approaches.

Traditional diagnostic tests for alcoholism have been reviewed recently by Jacobson (1975). The National Council on Alcoholism (NCA), an organization that strongly endorses the disease concept of alcoholism, has published their "Criteria for the Diagnosis of Alcoholism" (NCA, 1972), consisting of three pages of critical symptoms supposedly indicative of alcoholism. The diagnostic procedure consists of a physical examination and a medical-social interview designed to assess the level and severity of each of the "major criteria" (physiological and clinical signs) and "minor criteria" (behavioral, psychological, and attitudinal symptoms).

No data on the reliability and validity of the NCA Criteria have been published, because as noted in Jacobson's review, "The Criteria are valid because, in effect, the medical profession has unanimously decided that, based on their collective knowledge, experience, and expertise, the symptoms listed are definitive and diagnostic of alcoholism at some stage and to some degree of certainty" (Jacobson, 1975, p. 29).

Traditional diagnostic procedures have often made use of checklists and questionnaires of the *Reader's Digest* variety to determine whether or not a respondent can be classified as an alcoholic. Typically, these questionnaires contain a list of questions or items (e.g., "I would rather drink alone than with others," "I drink because it takes away my shyness"), which the respondent endorses with a yes or no answer. A critical score or cutoff is then used to identify potential or actual alcoholics. The simple items cited above are taken from one such instrument, the Alcadd Test (short for *Alc*ohol *Add*iction) (Manson, 1949). A similar test frequently used for screening purposes is the Michigan Alcoholism Screening Test, or MAST, devised by Selzer (1971). Sample items from the MAST include, "Have you gotten into fights when drinking?" and "Do you ever drink before noon?" Screening tests for alcohol or drug addiction have been with us for a long time, yet evidence for their reliability and differential validity is inconclusive at best (W.R. Miller, 1976). To appreciate some of the difficulties one encounters in interpreting the meaning of screening tests, we offer one of our own in Table 13.1 (Miller & Marlatt, 1977).

Behavioral assessment procedures are widely used by proponents of the social learning model of alcohol abuse. Rather than searching for critical diagnostic signs or symptoms of alcoholism, behavioral procedures attempt to provide a descriptive analysis of the individual's drinking behavior. Some of these procedures rely on verbal self-report or written descriptions, while others provide a direct, observational assessment of actual drinking behavior. Perhaps the easiest procedure to use is to ask the individual to provide a detailed daily account of his or her drinking behavior (self-monitoring), including such factors as time of drinking, amount consumed (including the type and alcohol proof level for each beverage), the environmental and interpersonal context in which drinking occurs, and the emotional and physical antecedents and consequences for each drinking occasion. A great deal of information can be obtained from a self-monitoring drinking diary, including estimates of peak daily blood-alcohol levels, situational determinants of moderate and immoderate consumption, and so forth. In addition to self-monitoring data (or in instances where this information cannot be obtained), a structured, behaviorally oriented questionnaire called the Drinking Profile has been developed (Marlatt, 1976b). Many items are included in the Drinking Profile, designed to gather information concerning the individual's demographic background, drinking patterns and behavior, beverage preferences, and the antecedents and consequences of drinking. While the Drinking Profile is not designed to "diagnose" alcoholism, it can provide assistance in the planning of behavioral treatment strategies for problem drinkers.

Direct observational measures of alcohol consumption are often more exact and reliable than instruments and qustionnaires dependent upon self-reported information. Several unique procedures have been developed by behavioral investigators, and have been reviewed in detail in a number of recent publications (Briddell & Nathan, 1976; Marlatt, 1977; P.M. Miller, 1973; W.R. Miller, 1976; Nathan, 1976; Nathan & Briddell, 1977). Research with problem drinkers who are observed over various time intervals in research wards often makes use of operant assessment procedures, in which the drinker must perform some response (such as bar presses) to earn points to "purchase" alcoholic beverages. Patterns of consumption can then be observed directly by the investigators. The taste-rating task, described earlier, is an example of a "choice" assessment procedure, providing assessment of consumption rates and patterns in a relatively unobtrusive fashion. Other investigators have made use of a simulated bar setting, to

Table 13.1. The Banff Skiism Screening Test: An Instrument for Assessing Degree of Addiction

YES	NO		YES	NO	
_____	_____	1. Do you often find yourself thinking about skiing?	_____	_____	11. Have you ever gone on skiing binges lasting for two days or more?
_____	_____	2. Have you spent more money on skiing than you should?	_____	_____	12. Do you ever drive immediately after skiing?
_____	_____	3. Do you ever ski alone?	_____	_____	13. Have you ever found, when you stop skiing after prolonged indulgence, that your body is uncomfortable (e.g. aches and pains, sweating, shakes)?
_____	_____	4. Do you ever ski in the early morning?	_____	_____	14. Have you ever experienced a white-out?
_____	_____	5. Do you ever find that once you start skiing you are unable to stop?	_____	_____	15. Do you take your slopes straight down?
_____	_____	6. Has skiing ever separated you from your family?	_____	_____	16. Do you prefer your substance in white powder form?
_____	_____	7. Does your spouse (or other family member) ever complain or worry about your skiing?	_____	_____	17. Do you find that it takes progressively steeper slopes to satisfy you?
_____	_____	8. Do you find yourself skiing instead of meeting obligations?	_____	_____	18. Have you ever been hospitalized because of skiing?
_____	_____	9. Do you ski when depressed, to feel better?			
_____	_____	10. Do you find that one run almost always leads to another?			

Scoring and Interpretation. The Banff Skiism Test is scored simply by counting the number of "Yes" responses. Initial normative data suggest the following diagnostic criteria:

Score	*Diagnosis*
0–2	Flat affect
3–4	Latent skiism (Cross-Country Syndrome)
5–6	Prodromal (Beginning) Skiism
7–9	Intermediate Skiism (Downhill Syndrome)
10–12	Advanced Skiism (Skizoid)
13–18	Skizophrenia

From Miller & Marlatt (1977) (Table 1). This test was hatched during the Eighth Banff International Conference on Behavior Modification, Banff, Alberta, March 1976.

provide a semi-naturalistic environment in which to observe drinking behavior. The direct observation of drinking in natural settings in the environemnt (e.g., in bars and taverns) has also been used increasingly in recent years (Reid, 1977). Behavioral assessment methods have also been used as pre-post measures to evaluate treatment effectiveness.

Traditional treatment methods

Until recently, the basic treatment approach to alcoholism has been based almost exclusively on assumptions deriving from the disease model (Blum & Blum, 1972). While all such programs have accepted total abstinence as the only acceptable goal of treatment, the procedures used to attain this goal have varied considerably. Many treatment programs are geared to the philosophy of Alcoholics Anonymous, and are often staffed by counselors who are themselves recovered alcoholics. Many disagreements exist in the working relationships between the professional treatment workers (psychiatrists, psychologists, and social workers) and the A.A. oriented paraprofessionals, with the latter group rejecting the "mental health" model adopted by many professionals. Despite the fact that A.A. members embrace the disease concept (their view is that some people are physiologically "allergic" to alcohol, and are thus susceptible to alcoholism), the A.A. approach to treatment is based primarily on moral and semi-religious principles. The A.A. group programs do seem to be effective with many alcoholics, particularly those who will accept the group support and encouragement offered by the "fellowship" of other members. The high success rate acclaimed by A.A. is based only on those individuals who have accepted the program and does not include the large number of drop-outs. Because A.A. is very reluctant to have its programs evaluated by outside professionals and research evaluators (Bebbington, 1976), any claims made for their success must be judged with caution.

Inpatient programs for alcoholism in hospitals and private clinics are often patterned after A.A philosophy. A typical program might last from 14 to 60 days, and include such treatment components as detoxification, group therapy and A.A. group meetings, lectures about the effects of alcohol and the disease model, along with occupational and vocational rehabilitation programs. When the patient is ready to be discharged, he or she may be asked to take Antabuse (disulfiram), a drug that combines with alcohol to produce a very unpleasant physiological reaction (including dizziness, nausea, and tachycardia) when alcohol is consumed. To be effective, Antabuse must be taken orally on a daily basis. While first thought to be a panacea drug in the treatment of alcoholism, Antabuse programs have not proved to be very effective. Relatively few patients will continue to take the drug for more than a few days at a time. The success of inpatient programs and of outpatient psychotherapy methods based on traditional insight-oriented therapy procedures has been disappointing, with a relapse rate of from 70 percent to 90 percent within ninety days of the completion of treatment (Armor, Polich, & Stambul, 1976). Relapse, as defined within the disease theory of alcoholism, consists of *any* drinking following treatment.

Behavioral treatment methods

Within the past few years, a number of innovative treatment procedures have been developed by investigators who are identified with the social-learning and behavioral approaches to alcohol abuse. These procedures include techniques designed to produce abstinence (e.g., aversion therapy), but many of the treatments can be used in programs where the treatment goal may be to produce a significant reduction in alcohol consumption—controlled-drinking programs. A brief review of some of the major treatment methods developed by behavior therapists and related investigators is presented below. The reader who wishes further information on these procedures is referred to a number of recent books on this topic: Marlatt and Nathan (1977); P.M. Miller (1976); P.M. Miller and Mastria (1977); W.R. Miller and Munoz (1976); Nathan, Marlatt, and Løberg (1978); and Sobell and Sobell (1978).

Among the first behavioral treatment procedures to be used extensively is *aversion therapy* (see review by Wilson, 1977). The purpose of aversion therapy is to produce a conditioned aversion to alcohol by pairing it frequently with a noxious stimulus, such as electric shock or an emetic drug (e.g., emetine) that produces nausea and vomiting. Recent outcome studies have suggested that while electrical aversion therapy seems to have rather limited success in the treatment of problem drinkers, chemical aversion therapy seems to offer greater promise (Wilson, 1977). Although chemical aversion has been used for years at such clinics as Seattle's Schick Shadel Hospital, fully controlled outcome studies evaluating this procedure have yet to be reported. The chief limitation of aversion therapy as a single treatment technique is that it fails to provide for an alternative response to drinking. Considerable research evidence exists to show that punishment alone (including aversion), unless an alternative response is established, usually produces only a temporary suppression of the target behavior.

Other behavioral programs have been developed that are designed to teach problem drinkers *alternatives to drinking* as a means of coping with stressful events. The most promising methods seem to be those that teach the drinker alternative ways to relax (including deep muscle relaxation, systematic desensitization, biofeedback, and meditation), or procedures that teach basic social skills. A number of studies (reviewed by P.M. Miller, 1976) have found that alcoholics or problem drinkers may be deficient in the expression of assertive behavior, such as learning to express anger, refuse drinks, or resist social pressures to drink. Marlatt (1978) has found that the inability to cope with feelings of anger or to resist social pressures to drink are two situations frequently associated with relapse among treated alcoholics who were trying to maintain abstinence. Programs designed to teach social skills, including assertiveness training, have been quite successful in initial studies (Chaney, O'Leary, & Marlatt, 1978; P.M. Miller, 1978). The basic aim of programs designed to teach alternatives to drinking is to develop a self-control model in which the problem drinker first learns to recognize situations that may lead to urges to drink or increased consumption, and then is taught to engage in an appropriate alternative response.

Controlled drinking treatment programs include a number of intervention techniques, including those reviewed above. The aim of such programs is to teach the problem drinker skills that may enable the individual to exert control over his or her drinking, and to limit consumption to relatively moderate amounts of alcohol. One such technique that has received considerable attention is *blood-alcohol discrimination training* (cf. Caddy, 1977; Nathan, 1978). In this procedure, the drinker is taught to discriminate the level of alcohol in the bloodstream, using both external cues (monitoring alcohol intake over time) and/or internal cues (monitoring the physiological effects of alcohol) as prompting devices. Some investigators (e.g., Lovibond & Caddy, 1970) have attempted to set upper limits for blood-alcohol concentration with problem drinkers by administering electric shocks whenever this limit has been exceeded. Drinkers who have learned to discriminate their own blood-alcohol levels may be able to exercise this ability and know "when to stop" so as to moderate their consumption.

Other controlled drinking investigators have made use of a multi-faceted or "broad spectrum" approach to treatment intervention, drawing on a number of specific components (Hamburg, 1975). Perhaps the most ambitious program of this type has been developed by the Sobells (Sobell & Sobell, 1973, 1976, 1978). The Sobells evaluated the effectiveness of a controlled drinking program (compared with a conventional program) with a group of chronic alcoholics who chose either controlled drinking or abstinence as their treatment goal. The controlled-drinking program consisted of a number of components, including behavioral self-analysis, self-management training, social skill training, aversive conditioning, and videotape feedback of both drunken and sober behavior. All patients were followed up carefully for a period of two years following completion of the program.

The results of this study have been quite encouraging for the behavioral approach. For those patients who selected the controlled drinking goal, 78.90 percent of those who received the behavioral treatment program were functioning well (either abstinent or drinking in a controlled manner on at least 80% of all days), compared to only 23.50 percent of the group receiving conventional treatment. For subjects who chose abstinence, 53.87 percent of the patients who received the behavioral program were functioning well, while only 31.43 percent of the control group patients were doing as well. It should be noted that a relatively high proportion of alcoholics who receive traditional abstinence-oriented treatment can be classified as moderate or controlled drinkers following treatment (Armor et al., 1976). When specific treatment programs designed to attain the goal of controlled drinking are introduced, the results are even more impressive (Lloyd & Salzberg, 1975). Although these results have created considerable controversy among adherents of the disease model of alcoholism, the viability of nonabstinence as a treatment goal can no longer be ignored (Miller & Caddy, 1977; Pattison, 1976).

Heroin Addiction

Introduction

The origin of opium has been traced back to at least several thousand years B.C. The method of obtaining opium from the poppy has essentially remained the same as it was then. Harvesters cut the ripened seed pod, allowing the sap to flow to the surface, where it is left to stand in the sun until forming a gummy substance, which is then collected. As it is effective in removing both physical and emotional pain, opium constituted the main therapeutic agent of medical men for more than two thousand years, through the nineteenth century.

In 1804, morphine was developed by a German chemist, Friedrich Serturner, from an alkaline base in opium meconic acid. It was hoped that this new compound would provide the same relief as opium without containing the same habit-forming propensities. Unfortunately, this discovery contributed greatly to the development of the type of drug addiction that became prevalent in the West. In the years that followed, other opium derivatives were developed in hopes of finding one that was not habit-forming. Finally in 1898, heroin was developed. It turned out to be about three times as potent as morphine and just as habit-forming. This was the last opiate derivative to be praised by medical men as nonhabit-forming (Lindesmith, 1968).

When one speaks of opiate narcotics, it is generally in reference to derivatives of opium. Among these are morphine, heroin, dionin, dilaudid, apomorphine, metopon, and codeine. Methadone is a synthetic equivalent of opiate narcotics. Its effects are similar to morphine, but they develop more slowly and persist longer. It is used in the treatment of withdrawal distress inasmuch as its effects are similar to other opiates with subsequent milder withdrawal. However, methadone has also been found to be addicting (Maurer & Vogel, 1973).

There is some speculation that, aside from the addicting quality of these drugs themselves, there may be a psychological component to the process of becoming addicted to opiate narcotics. The following is a case study from Alfred Lindesmith's book *Addiction and Opiates* (1968).

Mr. Q., a professional criminal, began to use drugs about 1925, when his wife died. He drowned his sorrows in liquor, and one night, as he was coming home after considerable indulgence, he was accosted by an addict who had often begged money from him before. Knowing that the man was an addict because he had been pointed out as such, Mr. Q. decided to play a joke on the beggar by pretending to arrest him. Then dropping this pose, he decided on the spur of the moment to try some morphine. They went to the beggar's regular agent, and the purchase was made. Mr. Q. took a very small injection and gave the rest to the addict. He greatly enjoyed the sensation produced by the drug. Several weeks later, the addict looked up Mr. Q. in order to get help in obtaining a supply, offering to share the returns fifty-fifty. Mr. Q. had had no intention of using the drug, but agreed to help, so the addict insisted that Mr. Q. accept his share. He first refused, then accepted the drug and took it home, forgetting about it for a while. He had no means of administering it at this time. One day a friend who ran a small business establishment moved into new quarters where he found an all-metal syringe concealed behind the molding. Mr. Q. took it home and, finding that it worked, began to use his little supply of morphine. When it was exhausted, he noticed that he wasn't feeling entirely right, and, remembering that morphine had helped him before when he felt depressed, he decided to buy some more. He went to the place where he and the beggar had first purchased some, and there, by sheer accident, met a man who had a large bottle of the stuff which he was willing to sell cheap. Mr. Q. commented, "Well I took it home and really got hooked on that stuff. Before it ran out I knew that I would have to have more, so I went out and made connections." When asked how he knew that he was addicted, he explained, "I used to take a couple of shots a day of the stuff, and then I noticed that I was beginning to depend on it, so I thought I'd do without it one day and didn't take my morning shot. Well, along in the afternoon, I was with some of the fellows in a saloon somewhere, and I was feeling rotten and yawning all the time. One of the fellows was an addict and he asked me if I had a yen.

'What the hell's a yen?' I asked, and he said it came from having a drug habit. He asked me if I was taking morphine at home, and I said I was, about two times a day.

'When did you have your last shot?'

'Yesterday afternoon.'

'And you didn't have any this morning?'

'No.' He asked me if my legs hurt and they did.

'Why, Jesus Christ!' the man said, 'You've got a habit and don't know it.'

"I went home and on the way I thought I could hardly make it because my legs were so wobbly. Well, when I got home, naturally I was feeling bad and wanted to feel better, so I fixed up a shot and thought I would see if the fellow was right. In a few minutes I was all right, feeling as lively as a spring chicken. Naturally I began to find out what I could do about this habit by talking to addicts and by reading." (Lindesmith, 1968, pp. 92–94)

Of all the drugs used in this country, heroin has gained the reputation as being the most addictive and the most destructive to both the individual and to society. As Mattison (1894) once wrote:

The subtly ensnaring power of morphia [morphine] is simply incredible to one who has not had personal observation or experience. . . . I make bold to say that the man does not live who, under certain conditions, can bear up against it. . . . Let him not be blinded by an underestimate of the poppy's power to ensnare. Let him not be deluded by an over-confidence in his own strength to resist, for along this line history has repeated itself with sorrowful frequency, and as my experience will well attest, on these two treacherous rocks hundreds of promising lives have gone awreck." (pp. 187–188)

Such statements have greatly influenced public sentiments toward heroin, some founded on fact, some on misconceptions. In the forthcoming section, current issues on heroin addiction will be presented in hopes of reconsidering some of the myths surounding this topic.

Some facts and figures about heroin addiction

While opiate narcotics have been used in this country for over a century, it was originally customary to administer these drugs orally (smoking or eating). This method less often leads to addiction than when an opiate is hypodermically injected. The introduction of federal legislation to control the flow of drugs (e.g., the Harrison Act of 1914) and to penalize the user (the Jones-Miller Act of 1922) drastically altered the use of opiate narcotics in the United States. While these restrictions did prevent further spread of the habit, they also increased illicit drug traffic, demoralized the addict, and stimulated crime.

Recently there has been a marked increase in the nonmedical use of opiate narcotics, especially heroin and methadone. In 1971, there were an estimated 560,000 heroin addicts in this country, or 27 per thousand population, as compared to 315,000, or 15.6 per thousand population in 1969. It is estimated that the total cost to society in terms of treatment, hospitalization, etc. was $7.1 billion in 1971, and $4.3 billion as the value of thefts by addicts in that year. In the United States, three states (New York, California, and Illinois) account for about 77 percent of known opiate addicts. It should be noted that statistics of this sort tend to be unreliable. For example, in 1964, federal statistics estimated there were 6,624 known addicts in California, while that state officially listed some 17,109 addicts during that same year (Maurer & Vogel, 1973).

Some experts feel that the incidence of deaths directly related to heroin has been relatively constant over a number of years at about 1 percent to 2 percent of the addiction population (DuPont, 1971). In 1972, New York City reported 1,409 deaths attributable to addiction (Ray, 1974). Contrary to popular belief, however, there appears to be little direct permanent physiological damage from the chronic use of pure opiate narcotics. Complications arise mainly from impure street samples, infections from unsterile needles, and improper techniques of venipuncture. There is even some doubt that heroin overdose, the most frequent cause of addiction related death, is due to a simple excess of opiate narcotics. It is reported that most overdose cases in North America result from a rapid toxic reaction to the intravenous injection of an illicit mixture containing heroin (Commission of Inquiry into the Non-Medical Use of Drugs, 1973). Quinine, for example, which is frequently found in New York heroin, may be a significant factor in fatal drug reactions. Overdose of quinine alone can produce rapid pulmonary edema and death. Since respiratory failure is also the cause of death in an overdose of pure opiate narcotics, it is difficult to distinguish which drug could have been the actual cause of death.

Perhaps the most perplexing and still unresolved question in the area of drug abuse is drawing the line between the state of using a drug on a habitual or continuous basis and the state of being addicted to the drug. Most authors would agree that the general state of addiction to any drug, including alcohol or heroin, is clearly one in which the individual has lost the power of self-control with reference to a drug and is no longer able to exercise choice over the amount of intake. This loss of control phenomenon could be founded on either a physiological or psychological basis, or both. This definition of "loss of control" is very similar to the notion of loss of control drinking in the disease model of alcoholism.

Addiction is usually associated with the following: 1. An increase in *tolerance,* or diminishing effects upon repetition of the same dose of the drug. This causes the individual to increase his dosage in order to obtain equivalent effects to the original dose; 2. *physical dependence,* an altered physiological state or body equilibrium brought about by the repeated administration of the drug over a long period of time. This necessitates the continuation of the drug to avoid withdrawal distress; 3. *craving,* or an overpowering subjective desire or need to continue taking the drug and to obtain it by any means; 4. *psychological dependence* on the drug, consisting of the substitution of drug use for other types of adaptive behavior; and 5. the tendency to *relapse,* even after a period of prolonged abstinence (Himmelsbach & Small, 1937; World Health Organization, 1950).

While it is possible to conceive of almost any drug as addictive, because the user may develop a certain amount of craving, psychological dependence, and perhaps even tolerance toward the drug, heroin is typically seen as a highly addictive drug because of its reputation for disrupting physiological equilibrium and causing severe withdrawal distress upon its removal. It is difficult to estimate, from secondhand reports, just how severe heroin withdrawal is. One reads passages such as:

> I bore my suffering as well as I could until the end of the fourth day, and then I had to yield. . . . And in all subsequent trials that I made, I could never hold out against these gastric symptoms beyond the fourth day. (Layard, 1874, p. 707)

> I have never seen a withdrawal reaction from heroin that came anywhere near the stereotype promulgated by Hollywood. In fact, I have never seen anyone have as much physical trouble giving up heroin as I have seen many people have giving up cigarettes. . . . The subjective experience of kicking heroin, like all subjective experiences associated with drugs, seems to be more directly the result of set and setting than of the drug. In a supportive setting, with proper suggestion, a heroin addict can withdraw without medication other than aspirin and have little more discomfort than that of a moderate cold. I saw this in San Francisco in 1968 in men with $70-a-day habits. (Weill, 1972, p. 42)

Another interesting fact is that withdrawal distress is most common among street users, whose heroin contains far less opium than that administered to hospital patients. However, the latter do not appear to show signs of withdrawal. Furthermore, hospital patients receiving opiates for medicinal purposes rarely become addicted. So it does appear that the situational factors surrounding drug use play an important role in addiction.

To illustrate this point, Robins (1976) conducted a survey of Vietnam veterans. The availability and widespread use of heroin in Vietnam caused considerable apprehension in the U.S. that soldiers would return with irreversible heroin addiction that would amplify the existing epidemic in this country. Some 470 men, consisting of addicts and nonaddicts, were randomly selected from the population of returnees. The results of this study contradicted traditional preconceptions surrounding the use of heroin. To begin with, while 43 percent of the veterans had used heroin in Vietnam, only 20 percent had been addicted there. In the 8 to 12 months between their return from Vietnam and the first interview, 10 percent of this population had used narcotics, and only 1 percent were addicted. These data are important inasmuch as they demonstrate that more than half the veterans who used narcotics never became addicted, and that heroin addiction is not necessarily chronic and irreversible.

It should be noted that the situational factors surrounding the drug use of Vietnam veterans differs substantially from that of the street addict. For one thing it is quite possible that heroin use in Vietnam was largely based on self-medication (i.e., it provided relief of pain or anxiety). Upon their return to civilian life, these individuals suffered less of the symptoms that might have driven them to heroin in Vietnam. Perhaps more important, however, is the fact that their return to the U.S. drastically reduced the availability of heroin. In order to continue its use, these veterans would have had to make new and probably less legitimate contacts to obtain a continuous supply. However, these findings are striking considering the myths about heroin's power to physically "hood" the individual. If in fact heroin is as physically addictive as it is reported to be, one might expect the proportion of veterans who remained addicted after their return from Vietnam to be much higher than 1 percent.

Theoretical models of heroin addiction

Probably still the most widely held belief is that addicts as individuals differ in personality from nonaddicts. It is not unusual to read passages in respectable journals such as:

> The authors like the concept that some people who feel inadequate to meet the demands of society are addiction prone, while others have adequate strength to meet the demands upon them, perhaps with minor psychoneurotic adjustments but without becoming addicted to the use of chemicals or drugs. (Maurer & Vogel, 1973, p. 35)

Most individual-factor theories of opiate dependence are psychiatric or psychoanalytic in nature, resting on the assumption that addicts suffer from some psychological or personality malfunction or inadequacy. Heroin addicts are described as "frustrated," "paranoid," "dependent," "rebellious," "escapist," "aggressive psychopathic." Unfortunately, most of the studies from which these psychopathological diagnoses are derived are the result of clinical observations that have not been empirically tested and have one or more of the following four imperfections in design (Commission of Inquiry into the Non-Medical Use of Drugs, 1973). The *first* problem is that the evaluation of addicts is often conducted after the individual has been addicted for a period of time, thus making it difficult to determine whether the diagnosed maladjustment was a cause of the opiate dependence or a result of it. *Second,* if this maladjustment is not a result of addiction it is also possible that it was caused by long periods of hospitalization or incarceration. For example, Hill, Haertzen, and Davis (1962) found that institutionalized addicts were, on the whole, more psychopathic than the nondependent general population, but were no more psychopathic than institutionalized inmates or alcoholics. A *third* problem is the bias of psychiatrists conducting the interviews, or their own preconceptions about heroin addicts, which undoubtedly influence their evaluations. *Finally,* the lack of standard objective measures and the use of vague diagnostic categories have made it difficult to replicate such studies.

A very new and astonishing development in the area of drug addiction is the finding that the brain is capable of manufacturing its own narcotics. This discovery began with the finding of highly specific opiate receptors in the limbic system, a part of the brain concerned with the emotional reaction to pain. It is unlikely that such highly specific receptors were developed by nature just to bind with the substance found in opium poppies. Thus the search began for morphinelike substances occurring naturally in the body. In 1975, Hughes and Kosterlitz were able to isolate sustances from the brain of a pig that, when placed directly on the pig's opiate receptors, were found to produce effects similar to morphine. These natural opiates (*enkephalins* and *endorphins*) have been located throughout the brain, but are particularly concentrated in the midbrain and pituitary (Restak, 1977).

This new discovery has implied several ways in which enkephalins and endorphins may play a role in opium addiction. One model suggests that administration of morphine overloads the opiate receptors, which in turn convey a message to the enkephalin neurons to stop firing and releasing enkephalin. When this happens, opiate receptor cells can tolerate more morphine to make up for the enkephalin they are no longer receiving. Thus, tolerance to morphine develops (Snyder, 1977). When the administration of morphine is stopped, the opiate receptors are now receiving neither morphine nor enkephalins, and the withdrawal sequence begins. Similarly, when the brains of rats are repeatedly injected with enkephalin or endorphin, they develop symptoms of tolerance and physical dependence (Snyder, 1977).

There is some speculation that the effectiveness of acupuncture as analgesic may lie in its ability to release endorphins in the midbrain and thus reduce pain. In Trainor's report, Pomeranz is cited as saying: "Needling activates deep sensory nerves which cause the pituitary (or midbrain) to release endorphins. These endorphins block signals from getting through the nerve chains in the pain pathway carrying messages from spinal cord to the higher brain centers" (Trainor, 1977).

To summarize, scientists view the discovery of enkephalins and endorphins as one of the most promising lines of research for the etiology and treatment of drug addiction. Much future work is needed to ascertain the exact function of these substances and their relationship to opiate narcotics.

Another approach to drug addiction is that, like other behaviors, it is learned through conditioning (e.g., Lindesmith, 1968). In much the same way that Pavlov's dog salivated at the sound of a bell, it has been reported that stimuli associated with withdrawal, such as people or places present during the withdrawal experience, can produce some signs of withdrawal in the addict when presented alone. Similarly, stimuli associated with the administration of an opiate narcotic, such as the sight of a hypodermic needle, may temporarily relieve withdrawal symptoms (Commission of Inquiry into the Non-Medical Use of Drugs, 1973). Thus, there is some evidence that a conditioning or learning component could be involved in physical dependence and the withdrawal syndrome.

A well known learning theory of addiction was introduced by Lindesmith (1968). He distinguished drug addiction from drug habit on the basis that addiction is learned through negative reinforcement from the relief of withdrawal, rather than positive reinforcement from the pleasurable effects of the drug, which is more closely associated with the habitual use of nonaddictive drugs, such as cocaine, marijuana, and LSD. Behavior can be learned by pairing a response with positive reinforcement (reward) or by removing an aversive event. According to Lindesmith, heroin addiction is conditioned by the individual's experience of withdrawal. Another determining factor of addiction is the cognitive experience of withdrawal. Whether withdrawal distress leads to readdiction or not depends on the individual's apparaisal of the distress. If the addict realizes that his discomfort and misery are caused by the absence of the drug and can be dispelled by another dose, he is more likely to become readdicted. Those who experience withdrawal distress without understanding the cause of it typically do not relapse. Referring back to the case of Mr. Q., his conversation with a fellow addict seemed to influence his appraisal of withdrawal distress: "I was feeling bad and wanted to feel better, so I fixed up a shot and thought I would see if the fellow was right. In a few minutes I was all right." Unfortunately, no one can assess what might have happened had that conversation not taken place.

A curious fact about relapse is that many addicts become readdicted to heroin even after prolonged abstinence. It is apprently not just the immediate relief from withdrawal distress, then, that drives the ex-addict back to heroin. Lindesmith's theory of addiction does not adequately account for this phenomenon, although he does attempt to explain relapse after prolonged abstinence in terms of the withdrawal experience. According to Lindesmith, the knowledge that heroin can relieve withdrawal distress leads to a desire or "yen" for the drug. In this respect, withdrawal elicits desire. In a similar fashion, desire has been found to elicit withdrawal. Addicts who have been off drugs for long periods of time frequently experience pseudo-withdrawal symptoms on occasions when they are strongly tempted to resume use. This explanation does not appear wholly satisfactory, since one might expect the potency of both withdrawal and desire to dissipate after a prolonged abstinence period.

While Lindesmith's theory cannot stand up as the singular explanation for heroin addiction, he does point to one very important fact (i.e., the physiological effects of heroin itself do not appear to override the individual's own appraisal of his drug experience as a determining factor of addiction).

Treatment

Methadone maintenance was originally developed by Dole and Nyswander in 1966. Since the prognosis for the average heroin addict is poor, there has been growing support for methadone maintenance programs as the most effective means of managing opium dependence. On the positive side, methadone maintenance attracts a larger number of addicts than would a program advocating total abstinence. It allows these individuals to be removed from dependence on the illicit market and from drug-related crimes; and to a large extent, it affords an increase in gainful employment, and in social and personal adjustment.

There are, however, many criticisms of this system (Commission of Inquiry into the

Non-Medical Use of Drugs, 1973). For one thing, it is debatable that the goal of a treatment should be to take the drug dependent person off drugs altogether. In addition, there are various hazards connected with the administration of methadone including: 1. The danger of making patients dependent on methadone when they do not yet have an opiate dependence; 2. the diversion of legal supplies of methadone to an illegal market, particularly in cases where the drug is prescribed rather than administered on the premises; 3. the experimentation with heroin that will be encouraged by the erroneous belief that methadone offers a "cure" for heroin dependence; 4. heavy reliance on methadone that might discourage the individual from the more difficult goal of abstinence; and 5. the lack of information on the long-term effects of methadone.

One might ask why methadone is preferred over heroin for the purpose of treatment since they are both associated with opium. Methadone produces less of an instantaneous euphoria and generally has longer lasting effects (Maurer & Vogel, 1973). In addition, methadone is effective when administered orally, and many feel that it is important to wean the addict from the hypodermic needle for both hygienic and psychological reasons (e.g., Coombs, 1975). Furthermore, tolerance develops to heroin much more readily than to methadone. It could be argued, however, that more addicts could be attracted to maintenance programs were heroin offered, rather than methadone. Some programs have proposed offering heroin maintenance just long enough to lure the addict into the program, at which point he might be persuaded to try methadone.

While heroin maintenance was originally employed in Great Britain and with striking success (the population of known addicts appears to have stabilized in recent years), the British have gradually been shifting their emphasis from heroin to methadone, although a high proportion of methadone is administered in intravenous form. The reason for that, they argue, is that it is easier to wean an addict from intravenous methadone to oral methadone than from heroin to oral methadone. On the other hand, it could be argued that administering methadone intravenously greatly reduces its advantage over heroin.

In any case, the apparent success of the "British System" lies less in the method of drug administration than in their multifaceted approach to treatment including social workers, vocational guidance and training, counseling, psychiatric care, and housing facilities. It is well known that addicts who can escape their previous drug-centered social environment stand a much better chance for rehabilitation. It is often mentioned that in addition to being hooked on a drug, the individual becomes addicted to his life-style of the pursuit of narcotics and interactions with other drug users (Commission of Inquiry into the Non-Medical Use of Drugs, 1973; Coombs, 1975; Maurer & Vogel, 1973).

The therapeutic community

One approach directed toward the rehabilitation of the addict is the long-term, live-in, family surrogate program such as Synanon, and Daytop. These programs provide a supportive yet challenging environment where the drug offender can attempt new life-styles and new self-concepts among others who understand his or her problems. The self-help philosphy common to these programs is designed to produce beneficial and long-term behavioral changes.

Signs of positive changes, such as confessions, positive remarks, task performance, and drug avoidance are rewarded in a variety of ways. These include social rewards, such as approval and affection, material rewards, such as better living quarters, and an increased amount of freedom to engage in preferred activities. Another purpose of Synanon is to remove the addict from the environment associated with his previous drug-taking life. Former friends are separated, and members are not allowed to talk with new members without supervision, since these conversations are likely to revolve around drugs.

Unfortunately, while these programs claim to have an 80 percent to 90 percent cure rate, this figure includes only those who complete the program. The majority of addicts who enter these programs (75% to 85%) leave before the program is completed (Commission of Inquiry into the Non-Medical Use of Drugs, 1973; Coombs, 1975). It could also be argued that few addicts are attracted to such treatment programs to begin with. The cost of these programs, both in terms of manpower and funding, appears to greatly outweigh the benefits.

Behavioral treatment

The assumption of a behavioral approach to the treatment of drug addiction is that addiction, like any behavior, is learned and can subsequently be unlearned through the application of cognitive and behavioral principles (e.g., Copemann, 1975; Droppa, 1973). One such approach is the use of aversive conditioning. This is accomplished in a variety of ways, including the injection of nausea-inducing substance, apomorphine, which is timed to produce undesirable effects shortly after the patient injects himself with heroin. Another method of aversive conditioning is the electric needle, which administers intermittent shocks upon the injection of a narcotic substance. This was developed by Blachly (1970) to break the needle habit for methadone maintenance patients.

Aversive conditioning is most successful when paired with adequate reinforcement for nonaddictive behavior patterns. Simply eliminating old behavioral responses to certain situations is not as effective as providing and reinforcing new behavioral responses to these same situations. For example, the individual should be provided with new ways of dealing with stress, new means for social contacts, and a new method of income.

In summary, regardless of the type of treatment used, ex-addicts stand a much better chance of avoiding relapse if they are no longer functioning in the same environment that supported their drug-taking habit. It appears as if the goal of any therapy should include a means by which the individual can develop a new self image as a nonuser. The tendency to lapse into the old lifestyle appears to hinge on the success of the new lifestyle. Therefore it would seem that an obligation of any treatment program would be to provide the necessary social and vocational skills to ensure this goal.

Conclusion

This chapter has focused on alcohol and the opiates as two examples of drugs frequently associated with abuse. Along with the barbituates and many tranquilizers, alcohol and the narcotics (including opium, morphine, heroin, and methadone) fall into the general class of *depressant* drugs. Other drugs of potential abuse include *stimulants* (amphetamines, cocaine), and the *hallucinogens* (LSD, mescaline, psilocybin). Other drugs, such as marijuana, are more difficult to categorize (marijuana is sometimes classified as a depressant and sometimes as a hallucinogenic drug). While most of our comments apply to the depresant drugs, the key issues and questions we have discussed may also be raised in connection with other drug categories. In traditional usage, the term addictive has been applied only to those drugs that, if used excessively, may lead to *physical dependence.* Physical dependence is said to occur when both of the following conditions hold: there is evidence of increased *tolerance* to the effects of the drug (increasing doses are needed to maintain or achieve a given effect); and the user experiences clearly defined physical symptoms of *withdrawal* when the drug is removed. Both alcohol and heroin are capable of eliciting physical dependence under conditions of repeated excessive use. Other drugs, although they do not seem to lead to physical dependence, may be used habitually, sometimes to the point of abuse (creating a number of physical, personal, or social problems for the user). The term *psychological dependence* is sometimes used to describe the habitual use of drugs in the absence of physical dependence. Marijuana, cocaine, and the hallucinogenic drugs, among others, may lead to psychological dependence, even though they do not seem to produce physical dependence. In practice, however, both physiological and psychological factors interact as determinants of drug use, and it is often difficult to disentangle the two sets of factors.

One theory that attempts to integrate the physical and psychological factors associated with the addictive disorders has been proposed recently by Solomon and his associates (Solomon, 1977; Solomon & Corbit, 1974). Termed the *opponent-process theory,* this position holds that addiction may be viewed as a form of acquired motivation, sharing characteristics with other similar behaviors such as love and attachment. Stated briefly, this theory purposes that any drug that produces changes in the affective or emotional state of the user operates in a biphasic manner. For drugs such as alcohol or heroin, the first stage (the "A state") is marked by positive affect or pleasurable hedonic consequences (the "high"). The body soon reacts to this initial shift in affect (perhaps through homeostatic balancing mechanisms) through the arousal of an "opponent process" stage, which opposes and suppresses the emotional strength of the "A state." This second phase (the "B state") is of opposite affective and hedonic quality (the "down" following the initial "upper").

In contrast with the immediacy of the "A" state, the "B" state is hypothesized to have a longer and more sluggish onset, taking longer to build to a maximum level of intensity, and longer to dissipate after the drug is removed. When a drug is first used, the "A" state is much stronger and exerts greater influence than the opposing "B" state, which may acount for the initial reinforcing effects of alcohol or heroin.

After repeated administrations and a corresponding increase in tolerance develops, however, the opposing "B" state builds in magnitude and intensity until it almost begins to overshadow the pleasurable effects of the "A" state. Since the user's expectations may still be geared toward achieving the pleasurable "A" state, the elicitation of the dysphoric "B" state may prompt the user to increase or prolong use of a drug in a vain attempt to escape or avoid the noxious consequences, attempting the regain access to the pleasurable "A" state. The analysis of the biphasic response to alcohol reviewed earlier in this chapter is consistent with Solomon's opponent-process theory, as is Lindesmith's theory of heroin addiction. Future research may show that the opponent-process theory provides a comprehensive account of the motivational processes underlying addictive behavior.

In addition to providing clarification of the physiological, motivational, and behavioral correlates of the addiction process, future research may also tell us more about the role of *cognitive factors* in the use and abuse of drugs. Until recently, cognitive mediating factors have largely been ignored in this area, perhaps because of the primary focus on the pharmacological and physiological effects of drugs. Research showing the potency of expectation and placebo effects as determinants of drug use and its associated correlates strongly suggests that cognitive factors are extremely important and can no longer be ignored. The power of expectancy as an antecedent of the use and effects of alcohol (Marlatt, 1978) has already been alluded to in this chapter. Similar research showing that both the initial effects of heroin and the withdrawal syndrome may be greatly influenced by conditioning processes (cf., Davis & Smith, 1976; O'Brien, 1976) also can be interpreted as showing the importance of environmental and psychological factors in the use of narcotic drugs.

Finally, some authorities have recently suggested that we have already expended too much effort and research in an attempt to pin down the addicting properties of *drugs,* and that by doing so, we have often neglected the *person* who uses drugs as a result. In a recent influential book called *The Natural Mind,* Weil (1972) has argued convincingly that most drugs produce an altered state of consciousness in the user, and that there may even exist an innate, natural "drive" that motivates people to alter their consciousness by using drugs or some other mind altering technique. From this perspective, many people "need" drugs not because they are physiologically addicted to them, but because they are strongly motivated to experience "nonordinary" forms of consciousness, and drugs provide a relatively easy access to this state. According to Weil:

> Morphine does not cause relief of pain any more than marihuana causes a high; it serves as a trigger for an altered state of consciousness in which pain is perceived differently from usual. Neither does morphine cause dependence; it becomes the object of dependent behavior arising from the misunderstanding of cause and effect characteristic of materialism and straight thinking. In other words, analgesia and dependence are mixed up in people, not in drugs, and there is no point in trying to separate them by playing with molecules. The search for the nonaddicting narcotic is as fanciful as the search for gold that materialistic alchemists carried out in their laboratories instead of in their minds. (Weil, 1972, p. 172)

Society may eventually decide that the way to solve the "drug problem" does not lie in legislative prohibitions, moral harangues, or in the search for nonaddictive drugs. The track record for these traditional methods has been notoriously poor at best (Szasz, 1974). If Weil's thesis is correct, perhaps we should invest more time and energy in developing nondrug alternatives as means of altering consciousness, including such possibilities as meditation, yoga, and biofeedback (cf. Marlatt & Marques, 1977). If successful, the practice of such techniques may enable the individual to get high without getting hooked.

Summary

An important question raised throughout this chapter was the extent to which addictive disorders are mediated by physiological factors associated with the physical effects of various drugs, as opposed to the mediating effects of psychological factors such as learning, cognition, and environmental determinants. In the first section, current issues in the field of alcoholism were discussed, with an emphasis on the recent controversy concerning the nature of alcoholism as either a physiologically based disease or as an acquired behavioral disorder. Advocates of the disease model view alcoholism as an irreversible physiological dependence on alcohol, characterized by withdrawal symptoms and "loss of control" drinking. From this point of view, the only goal for treatment is to insist upon total abstinence from alcohol use. Those who support the social-learning model, on the other hand, emphasize the importance of psychological and environmental factors as determinants of problem-drinking behavior. The importance of cognitive mediating processes (in contrast with physiological factors) is also emphasized within the social-learning approach. Adherents of this position argue that learning to control one's drinking behavior is an alternative goal in the treatment of alcohol-related problems.

The second section of the chapter reviewed the topic of heroin addiction. Issues were raised to question the validity of long-standing beliefs suggesting that addiction to heroin and other opiate derivatives is based almost entirely upon the addictive properties of the drug used. It was noted, for example, that out of all the Vietnam veterans who reported using heroin while overseas, only a small percentage continued use of this drug upon their return to the United States. The role of psychological and environmental determinants of addictive behaviors was stressed throughout this discussion. While methadone maintenance programs are still the most common treatment methods (along with the abstinence-oriented therapeutic community approach) for heroin addiction, the recent discovery that the brain manufacturers its own opiatelike substances has given rise to hopes for new forms of treatment. In the concluding section, the opponent-process theory was described as an attempt to integrate the physiological and psychological factors associated with the addictive disorders. Finally, it was emphasized that cognitive mediating factors in the drug user may play as important a role in the development of addiction as do the physical properties of the drug itself.

GLOSSARY

Acute alcoholic hallucinosis: A psychoticlike disturbance sometimes is associated with chronic excessive use of alcohol; auditory hallucinations sometimes occur.

Biphasic response: Describes the reaction to alcohol as a two-stage process: an initial excitatory stage, followed by a delayed depressant effect.

Blood-alcohol discrimination training: A procedure designed to teach drinkers to monitor their blood-alcohol level, based on feedback from external and/or internal (physiological) cues.

Controlled drinking: The learned ability to exercise control (setting limits on the frequency and amount of drinking) over one's consumption of alcohol.

Delerium tremens: An acute and sometimes fatal withdrawal reaction associated with the cessation of alcohol consumption; psychoticlike hallucinations and delusions may occur.

Enkephalins and *endorphins:* Morphinelike substances that have been found to occur naturally in the body. The production of these substances is, for the most part, localized in the midbrain.

Gamma alcoholism: A type of alcoholism defined within the disease model, characterized by physical dependence on alcohol and loss of control drinking; considered by Jellinek to be the predominant form of alcoholism in North America.

Korsakoff's syndrome: A chronic condition associated with prolonged, excessive use of alcohol coupled with vitamin deficiency; symptoms include disorientation, loss of recent memory, and confabulation (falsification of events).

Loss-of-control drinking: A key symptom of alcoholism as viewed by the disease model; an ability to voluntarily limit one's consumption of alcohol following the ingestion of one or two drinks. Alternative term: Rapid Alcohol Consumption Effect (RACE).

Opponent-process theory: A theory hypothesizing a biphasic reaction to drugs that produce an affective or emotional response: the initial effects (e.g., euphoria) are followed by an opposing process of opposite hedonic quality (e.g., dysphoria).

Physical dependence: Dependence on a drug as defined when there is evidence of increased tolerance and physical symptoms of withdrawal when the drug is removed from the system.

Problem drinking: Drinking that produces or is associated with significant problems for the drinker (personal, social, physical); sometimes used as an alternative for alcoholism as a descriptive term.

Tension-reduction hypothesis: The TRH holds that the act of drinking is reinforced by the tension-reducing effects of alcohol.

14

SEXUAL DISORDERS

JACK S. ANNON
CRAIG H. ROBINSON

In a chapter on sexual disorders in an abnormal psychology text, it is first important to examine the too commonly used term abnormal. Who is applying the label? From what viewpoint? What does it mean? There are many possible uses of the term abnormal which confuse its possible meaning. Is it a medical definition? A legal definition? A psychiatric definition? A self definition? This term and similar terms such as deviate and pervert have strong negative connotations and do not provide any information that would be helpful in attempts to understand a particular behavior or to assist people who engage in a particular behavior and who wish to change it.

In dealing with sexual disorders in this chapter, the authors will avoid the use of value-laden terms and use descriptive terms to enable the reader to more fully understand what is involved in sexual disorders and their treatment. To lay the groundwork for this approach, we will first briefly take a look at this "normality" issue in relation to biological and sociocultural influences on sexual behavior in general.

Sexual behavior

Biological Influences

There is no question that biological factors influence human sexuality. The question is, to what degree and in what form? Comparative studies across species, such as those of nonhuman primates, point out possible evolutionarily acquired characteristics in common with humans. Although humans are not apes, both share common ancestors. While there are obviously major differences between human and nonhuman primate sexuality, there are also some interesting similarities in behavior. Beach (1976) has provisionally defined "masturbation" as a basic primate trait that is probably traceable to shared mammalian origin.

Cross-species comparisons further highlight the difficulties associated with the "normal-abnormal" distinction. For example, Chevalier-Skolnikoff (1976), reporting on her observations of stumptail monkeys, described sexual behaviors that, if they were engaged in by humans, would be variously labeled as: cunnilingus, fellatio, analism, promiscuity, exhibitionism, voyeurism, heterosexuality, bisexuality, lesbianism, tribadism, and pedophilia, among others. Are these "abnormal" monkeys in need of therapy?

On the other hand, surface similarities by themselves do not justify theoretical inferences. That certain species engage in similar behaviors does not *prove* that the behavior is "biologically normal." The conclusion may or may not be correct, but it cannot be based upon minimal comparative evidence. As Beach (1976) has pointed out, knowledge of the causes and functions of behavior *within* a species is first essential to the interpretation of resemblances or differences *between* species. Thus, much work is being devoted to other possible factors, such as endocrinology, that influence the elemental sexual functions within a species.

Most psychological learning theorists and clinicians do not deny human biological origins, and they recognize the influence of genetic, biochemical, or physiological factors in human sexuality. But the *form* and *direction* that these behaviors take is principally attributed to sociopsychological influences.

Socio-cultural influences

The influence of culture on what is to be considered "normal" sexual behavior versus "abnormal" sexual behavior or a sexual "disorder" can hardly be overstated. Anthropological research has repeatedly shown that wide variation in patterns of sexual behavior exists between different cultural groups. There can also be tremendous variability between subgroups in a given culture, depending on such factors as socioeconomic level and political or religious beliefs. In short, both the range of sexual behaviors considered appropriate and/or deviant cross-culturally encompasses virtually the entire range of observed sexual responses (Ullmann & Krasner, 1975). Even the powerful influence of culture on sexual behaviors thought to be sex-linked or gender specific has been frequently demonstrated. In her famous study of three tribes regarding commonly held notions of masculine and feminine traits, Margaret Mead (1935) concluded that whatever role human instincts and biological factors play, they appear relatively minor compared to the cultural factors shaping an individual's sexual role and responses.

An example from the anthropological literature may illustrate the role culture may play in controlling frequency and type of certain sexual behaviors and responses. The Ford and Beach (1951) study of 76 societies revealed striking cultural variations regarding sexual activities between same-sex partners. Data from about one-third of the societies suggested that same-sex involvement was either most unusual, nonexistent, or highly secretive. By contrast, in 68 percent of the societies studied, same-sex activity was accepted to varying degrees for certain members of the society. However, common to all societies studied, same-sex activity was more acceptable when occurring between adult females rather than males, though the frequency of such activity was higher for males than for females, and more common in adolescents than in adults.

Wide variation concerning permissiveness or restrictiveness on sexual behavior between children exists. In general, American parents typically attempt to suppress, or at least vigorously discourage, sex play between children as well as adolescents. By contrast, many African and Oceanic cultures allow children a great deal of sexual freedom. It is not uncommon in such cultures for children to engage in a variety of sexual activities, including intercourse, with no adult prohibitions.

Regardless of whatever sexual behaviors its members engage in, each culture has a code for "appropriate" sexual behaviors; individuals engaging in activities not endorsed by the code are considered "deviants." It is relevant to note that many behavioral scientists consider "deviance" as a convenient label to be placed upon individuals who violate a society's rules of conduct rather than as an inherent property of the individual.

A striking example of effects that culture (in this case changing social viewpoints) can have on sexual attitudes is seen in the American Psychiatric Association's (APA) recent position on sexual behavior between members of the same sex. In December 1973, the trustees of the APA voted to remove homosexuality from its lists of mental disorders. In his review of Person's book on *Deviant Imagination,* Miller (1976) emphasizes the sociopolitical influence on attitudes regarding "deviant" sexual behavior by pointing out that the homosexual has moved from evil, to sick, to normal in just a few decades. Further, in alluding to the APA decision, MIller cites the following caustic comment by the editor of *Mental Health:* "In one great medical 'breakthrough,' some 12,000,000 formerly 'sick' citizens have become 'well'—by fiat" (Miller, 1976, p. 804).

A psychological learning viewpoint

The major influences that biology and one's culture and social milieu play in setting the stage for possible sexual problems is only too obvious. However, *how* and *what* an individual learns sexually within a given culture extends far beyond social norms and codes of sexual conduct. In discussing the role of learning in human sexual behavior, Ullmann and Krasner (1975) note that the range of biological stimuli and acts a person can be involved with far exceed that which a given culture would select as appropriate. Of course, environmental conditions also affect the probability of an individual being exposed to sexually related stimuli or activities.

The more opportunity a person has to be exposed to sexual stimili, whether or not such stimuli are considered culturally "appropriate," the higher the probability some form of sexual activity may be learned. In looking for a possible explanation of how and what individuals learn about sex within a given culture, consider the following: Unlike nonhuman primates and mammals, the human at birth has relatively few "built-in" responses (other than those such as the startle response to loud noises or loss of support). On the other hand, the human infant does have basic needs for air, nourishment, water, and sleep in common with all animals. Of course, if these are not met the infant (or the adult) will die. Sex is not such a need. If an individual human or animal does not engage in sex, it will not cease to live. Yet animals must mate in order for the species to survive. From an evolutionary viewpont, genital intercourse and mating patterns must exist because they are essential for species survival. Beach (1976) suggests that the possibility remains that behaviors essential for reproduction are built up through learning from a *core* of unlearned stimulus-response patterns that are mediated by genetically controlled mechanisms. What does this core consist of?

Again consider the newborn human. There are reports that about 50 percent of males are born with erections and approximately the same number of females with vaginal lubrication (the counterpart of the arousal-erection response in males). We also know that in a natural sleep state, the average healthy adult male normally may experience an erection on the average of about one every 90 minutes, usually during rapid eye movement sleep. Comparably, the average healthy adult female may lubricate approximately every 90 minutes in a sleep state. From these data, it appears that sexual arousal is a natural physiological process, like respiratory, bladder, and bowel functions. However, as Masters and Johnson (1970) have pointed out, although sexual functioning is a natural physiological process, it is unique, as sexual responsivity can be functionally denied for a lifetime or be delayed indefinitely.

In looking at cross-species comparison, Beach (1976) has concluded that one aspect of sexual behavior that does *not* depend on learning is the positive or reinforcing effect of sexual climax. From a learning point of view such sexual responses may be seen as natural or unconditioned reinforcers that can potentially shape a wide range of sexual behaviors and attitudes through classical and/or operant conditioning principles.

Another important cross-species comparison by Beach (1976) says: "The self-stimulatory activities of male monkeys and apes are so similar to autogenital behavior in human males that we are justified in provisionally defining male masturbation as a basic primate trait" (p. 484). Beach goes on to point out that though female masturbation among primates has been observed it is reported much less frequently and that the evidence is less convincing. The male genitals are external to the body and arousal leading to erection may be more easily discovered through accidental handling or fondling or friction against materials and objects than in the female where the genitals are primarily internal. When such random behavior results in sexual arousal, then the chances that the animal may engage in similar behaviors increases in probability according to operant conditioning principles. The more such behaviors increase in frequency, the more the animal may begin to systematically pair up sexual arousal responses with specific previously neutral stimuli. Eventually, sensory contact with these stimuli alone may involuntarily evoke an arousal response and behavior. Hence, classical and operant learning principles may account for animals pairing sexual responses and behaviors with "unusual" stimuli such as that described by Beach (1976) concerning a cat and it sexual behavior with its food dish.

If such behavior can be learned by nonhuman animals, it is not difficult to see that such principles may also apply to human responses and behaviors as well. For example, in American culture it is common during toilet training for small boys to receive positive consequences for handling their genitals appropriately (i.e., aiming directly into the toilet), while little girls learn to sit and "not to touch down there" and if they do, such as during a bath, "only briefly—no lingering." With their external genitals and natural arousal responses to friction, it is easy to see that masturbation in males may begin at a very early age and even lead to orgasm if prolonged. Orgasm has been observed in boys as early as five months of age (Kinsey et al., 1953). Though the overall incidence may be lower, orgasm for girls has also been described as occurring at as young as 4 months of age (Kinsey et al., 1948). Kinsey and his colleagues conclude that masturbation is an essentially normal and frequent phenomenon among many children, both male and female. In possible contrast to nonhuman animals, human masturbation may also be evoked and/or accompanied by fantasy and imagery, which may relate to specific sexual behaviors with partners or other object choices.

McGuire, Carlisle, and Young (1965) have suggested that continual masturbation to a fantasy may play an important role in the formation and shaping of sexually "deviant" behaviors. Orgasm experienced during masturbation may provide the critical reinforcing event for the conditioning of the fantasy preceding or accompanying masturbation. They argue that what particular fantasy is used may be arbitrarily determined by a random experience to which the individual was subjected at some point in life.

There have been numerous case descriptions from a learning-oriented view that have supplied grounds for the masturbatory conditioning hypothesis (Annon, 1971; McGuire et al., 1965). Although direct experimental testing of the theory is not ethically possible, successful clinical use of such masturbatory conditioning principles has been widely reported (e.g., Annon, 1971, 1973) although there have been occasional failures (Conrad & Wincze, 1976).

Experimentally, Rachman (1966), and Rachman and Hodgson (1968) demonstrated that it is possible to experimentally condition arousal in males to previously neutral stimuli (slides of black boots) by pairing their presentation with sexually arousing stimuli (color slides of nude women).

In summary, the psychological learning viewpoint holds that there are no separate principles for "deviant" or "abnormal" and "normal" sexual behavior. As Ullmann and Krasner (1975) have argued, rather than trying to define what is "normal," "perverted," or "deviant," the question is: How is any behavior learned, or how does anybody come to like or value anything?

Sexual disorders

Indirect and direct approaches

The eventual goal of all therapeutic systems is change in the client, and the major difference is how to do this. Depending upon the theoretical system involved, there are two conceptually different approaches to treatment: *direct* and *indirect*. In the former the presenting problem is generally dealt with directly, while in the latter it may only be seen as a symptom of an underlying problem. The indirect approach aims first to alter certain assumed intrapsychic systems that then result in the symptom being resolved. These approaches have been variously called "evocative" or "psychodynamic," and are represented by such systems of therapy as the psychoanalytic, client-centered, or Gestalt viewpoints. The direct approaches are represented by such therapeutic systems as the rational-emotive, reality, or psychological learning viewpoints. A brief outline of one representative system from each approach will give the reader an example of the two contrasting approaches to treatment.

Psychoanalysis: an indirect approach. This system was developed by Freud and it is built on a basic biological drive theory. Freud postulated that each person has a limited amount of *libido,* or psychic energy, and certain innate biological needs that cause tension. He believed that each person progressed through sequential stages of psychosexual development (called *oral, anal, phallic, latency,* and *genital*) in order to gratify basic drives. This progression saw the development of the *id, ego,* and *superego.* If a person did not receive sufficient gratification in one of these stages, due to various causes, such as traumatic events, the person would become *fixated* at a certain stage, and that person's adult behavior would be seen as attempts to gratify such fixated needs (e.g., fixation at the oral stage might lead to preoccupation with kissing, smoking, drinking, eating). Perhaps most well known were his concepts of the *conscious* and *unconscious.* If relevant material that was unconscious were made conscious, through *insight,* then the person could possibly resolve his or her fixation. Some therapeutic procedures developed by Freud for resolution of conflicts were the techniques of *free association, dream analysis,* the analysis of the *transference* relationship between the clinician and the client, and direct psychoanalytic *interpretations* by the clinician.

Many of Freud's followers, such as Carl Jung, Alfred Adler, and Otto Rank, rejected the theoretical notion of a basic *biological* drive, but continued to use many of the therapeutic procedures based on their own revised theories. They also followed one of the basic tenets of Freud in that if patients could cognitively recall and understand the importance of the origin and maintaining of their *repressed* or *suppressed* experiences through *insight,* they would be "cured." However, it was not until the late 1950s when some clinicians began to experimentally test this hypothesis that many psychoanalysts began to question that such an assumption was always necessary or sufficient for cure. This led to the current expansion of modified or reformed psychoanalytic practice.

Psychological learning theory: a direct approach. This system has emerged in relatively recent years, and it derives its theoretical constructs from psychological learning theory and bases its therapeutic procedures on experimentally established principles of learning. The basic assumption underlying this system is that "neurotic" or other maladaptive behaviors are acquired or learned, and therefore are subject to the normal laws of learning as are nonneurotic, adaptive behaviors. Learning is defined in a broad sense generally as a *relatively permanent change in behavior that is acquired as a result of practice,* and excludes any behavior that results from direct intervention in the functioning of the nervous system or from maturation. In its early formulations, "behavior" referred to *overt* behavior that could reliably be observed and/or measured by another. More recently, many learning-oriented clinicians have moved away from what is seen by them as a limitation in working exclusively with overt behaviors, and now deal with *covert* behaviors such as cognitions and feelings. These behaviors are assumed to follow the same principles of learning.

By "practice" it is generally assumed that behavior is acquired through two, possibly three, basic types of learning. One type of learning is *classical conditioning,* first formulated by Pavlov, who demonstrated that the continued presentation of a rung bell immediately followed by meat powder could eventually result in a dog salivating and making chewing movements to the sound of the bell alone. This type of conditioning is seen as involuntary and it has been demonstrated that many emotional and sexual responses may be learned through conditioning.

The second type of learning is *operant conditioning,* most clearly described by Skinner who demonstrated that when a certain voluntary behavior on the part of a pigeon or rat was consistently and immediately followed by a food pellet, the frequency of that behavior increased.

A possibly third principle is seen by Bandura as *vicarious learning.* This is a broad term that covers any learning process whereby the person changes or acquires a behavior as a result of observing the behavior of another person, either directly, or through the use of films, videotapes, or through the reading of books or magazines. There is a growing body of experimental literature behind this principle to discover what elements are necessary and sufficient to enable such learning to take place.

There are numerous therapeutic procedures based upon learning theory such as *systematic desensitization, behavior rehearsal, contingency contracting, assertive training, covert* and *overt reinforcement, covert sensitization,* and *guided imagining.* Some of these procedures such as systematic desensitization have considerable empirical evidence as to their efficacy for certain problems, while others are of too recent origin to have accumulated as much experimental verification.

As may be seen by this very brief overview of only two systems, each has its own explanation for "deviant" sexual behavior. For example, sexual arousal and behavior associated with inanimate objects, labeled fetishism, would be seen in the psychoanalytic view as either a defense against homosexuality or as arising from anxiety resulting from oedipal and preoedipal factors during the phallic stage of development. On the other hand, the psychological learning view would assert that many such behaviors may be the result of masturabatory conditioning experieces.

Because of different theories, each system also would generally use a different set of therapeutic strategies and procedures. For example, the psychoanalytic clinician might view an erection problem as resulting from an unresolved oedipal situation and proceed indirectly by leading the individual to understand and gain insight as to this probable cause, which would then bring about the resolution of the problem. By contrast, the psychological learning clinician might attempt to help the client increase approach responses to the anxiety provoking situation either covertly through such procedures as systematic desensitization, guided imagining, or covert reinforcement; or overtly with a carefully graded series of behavioral suggestions for gradual sexual contact based on successive approximation principles; or possibly various combinations of suggestions depending upon the particular client.

All of the above procedures have worked with some individuals at some time. The important question is, What procedure works most effectively with which client under what circumstances? If all had equal outcomes, then economics would suggest using those that take the least amount of client time and money. In addition, some of the procedures have had empirical support while others have never been open to experimental verification. In general, the strongest theory is the one that directly generates empirically testable therapeutic procedures. Those systems with testable hypotheses are open to change. Consequently, they can more closely approximate an accurate view of human behavior and behavior change.

These are but two of over 300 psychotherapy systems that have been identified (Herink, in press). (For a more detailed comparison of other systems in general and sex therapy models in particular, see Annon & Robinson, in press a.) No one system appears to have the support of a majority of clinical practitioners, though probably most clinicians subscribe to one of perhaps a dozen major systems. Some clinicians, who call themselves *eclectic,* do not subscribe completely to any one approach, but rather borrow freely from many approaches if they appear to be helpful.

Systems of classification

There currently are a number of systems for categorizing problem sexual behaviors. Buss (1966) suggests two categories: deviant object and deviant response, the former for appropriate behaviors to wrong stimuli, and the latter for deviant responses regardless of appropriateness of partner. Eysenck and Rachman (1965) use three classifications: 1. inability to make an adequate sexual response to appropriate stimulation, 2. sexual response to inappropriate stimuli, and 3. combinations of both. Lester (1975) adopted a fourfold classification of deviant sexual behavior: variation in mode, object, or strength of sexual response, and a miscellaneous category. Staats and Staats (1963) proposed a more extensive system, which includes behavioral deficits, inappropriate behavior, inadequate or inappropriate stimulus control, defective discriminative stimulus control of behavior, and inadequate or inappropriate reinforcing systems.

Merely placing a label on a particular sexual activity does not provide much useful information. Table 14.1 contains a partial list of terms that have been used in the literature, with varying degrees of frequency and understanding, for assumed and/or possible sexual disorders. There are undoubtedly many more in existence. Even a casual glance at the list will reveal that one would have to be either an expert in sexual terminology or a Latin-Greek scholar to make any sense of what some of the labels mean. To further confuse the matter, different "experts" may define the same term in a different manner.

Labeling a person or their behavior is no longer an acceptable approach for understanding and assisting people with complex human problems, sexual or othewise (Annon, 1976). Labeling does not give any clinically useful information about a person's thoughts or feelings in relation to their particular problem. Furthermore, labeling a person leads to assumptions about thoughts or behaviors that may simply not be true about a particular individual. Persons so labeled tend to be viewed as having many behavioral characteristics that may in fact be seldom or never exhibited in their actual behavior. Additionally, labeling tends to imply that a person responds or acts in the same way under all conditions. However, it is well known that how a person behaves in any given situation is greatly influenced by past situations involving circumstances similar to the present one. Finally, labeling sexual problems or behaviors does not dictate treatment.

While it is recognized that human behavior is rich, complex, and overlapping, classification systems could offer a tentative method for understanding sexual problems. However, what is needed is a system that does not use labels, but one that describes the behavior of concern without value judgments being placed on the "appropriateness of inappropriateness" of the behavior and that offers some notion as to the relative clinical incidence of the behavior in question.

As a step in this direction, the authors propose a scheme comprising four possible areas of concern: Response, Object, Behavior, and Identity (ROBI). The ROBI descriptive classification scheme for assumed or possible sexual disorders may be seen in Table 14.2.

This scheme has a number of advantages. By using the referencing between Tables 14.1 and 14.2, readers should be able to have

Table 14.1. Traditional Labels for Assumed or Possible Sexual Disorders

1. Adamism III B2
2. Adultery II A2
3. Algolagnia III A5a&b
4. Analingus III A2
5. Analism III A2
6. Anorgasmia I A1
7. Apotemnophilia IV C
8. Autoanalism II
9. Autoeroticism II A1
10. Autofellatio II A1
11. Axillism II A4
12. Bestiality II A10
13. Bisexuality II A3
14. Bondage III A4; III A5a&b
15. Coprolalia III B3, 4 & 5
16. Coprophagy II B1
17. Coprophilia II B1
18. Cunnilingus III A1
19. Dyspareunia I B1
20. Ejaculatio Praecox I A2
21. Ejaculatio Retardata I A1
22. Ejaculatory Incompetence I A1
23. Erectile dysfunction I B1
24. Exhibitionism III B2
25. Fellaire III A1
26. Fellatio III A1
27. Femoralism II A4
28. Fetishism II A4, II B
29. Flagellation III A4; III A5a&b
30. Fornication II A2
31. Frigidity I A1; I B1; I C1
32. Frottage III A6
33. Gerontophilia II A7
34. Graophilia II A7
35. Gynandry II A3
36. Group sex II A6
37. Heterosexuality II A3
38. Homosexuality II A3
39. Hyperaesthesia I A2; I B2; I C2
40. Hypolibido I C1
41. Impotence I A1; I B1; I C1
42. Incest II A8
43. Inunctionism III A3
44. Inversion II A3
45. Ipsation II A1
46. Irrumation III A1
47. Kleptolagnia III A8
48. Klismophilia II A1; II B
49. Koprolagnia II B1
50. Lesbianism II A3
51. Low Libido I C1
52. Lust murder III A4; III A5a
53. Mammaeism II A4
54. Masochism III A5b
55. Masturbation II A1
56. Ménage à trois II A6
57. Metatrophism IV B
58. Mixoscopia III B1
59. Mysophilia II B
60. Narcissim II A1
61. Natelism II A4
62. Necrofetishism II B3
63. Necrophilia II B3
64. Necrosadism II B3; III A4; III A5a
65. Nymphomania I A2; I B2; I C2; II A5
66. Onanism II A1
67. Oralism III A1; III A2
68. Orgasmic dysfunction I A1
69. Orgasm II A6
70. Osmolagnia II B2
71. Osphresiophilia II B2
72. Ozolagnia II B2
73. Paedophilia II A9
74. Partialism II A4
75. Pederasty II A9; III A2
76. Pedophilia II A9
77. Piquer III A5a
78. Pluralism II A6
79. Pornolagnia II A2
80. Premature ejaculation I A2
81. Promiscuity II A5
82. Prostitution II A2; II A5
83. Pygmalionism II B
84. Pyrolagnia III A9
85. Rape III A4; III A5a
86. Retarded ejaculation I A1
87. Sadism III A5a
88. Sado-Masochism III A5
89. Saliromania III A10
90. Sapphism II A3
91. Satyriasis I A2; I B2; I C2; II A5
92. Scatology II B1
93. Scopophilia III B1
94. Scoptophilia III B1
95. Scrotilinctus III A1
96. Sodomy II A3; II A9; II A10; II B3; III A1; III A2
97. Transsexualism IV A
98. Transvestism II B; III A7
99. Tribadism II A3
100. Troilism II A6
101. Undinism II B1
102. Uranism II A3
103. Urolagnia II B1
104. Urophilia II B1
105. Vaginismus I B1
106. Vampirism II A4; III A5a
107. Voyeruism III B1
108. Wife swapping II A2; II A6
109. Zooerasty II A10
110. Zoophilia II A10

some general understanding of what type of sexual behaviors are associated with the traditional labels used in the literature. The descriptions are not intended to be precise, particularly since there is little agreement even among experts as to what the labels mean. For example, the term sodomy has been and continues to be defined in numerous ways, ranging from sexual contact with animals or children to oral genital stimulation between two adults of the same or opposite sex. The multiplicity of cross-refer-

Table 14.2. A Descriptive Classification Scheme For Assumed or Possible Sexual Disorders

Sexual problems related to:

- I. *Response* (with opposite and/or same sex) involving:
  - A. Orgasm
    - 1. None, infrequent, or delayed 6, 21, 22, 31, 41, 68, 86
    - 2. Too soon 20, 39, 65, 80, 91
  - B. Arousal
    - 1. None or low, 19, 23, 31, 41, 105
    - 2. High 39, 65, 91
  - C. Desire
    - 1. None or low 31, 40, 41, 51
    - 2. High 39, 65, 91
- II. *Object choice* involving;
  - A. Animate contact associated with:
    - 1. Self 8, 9, 10, 45, 48, 55, 60, 66
    - 2. Married or unmarried partners, 2, 30, 79, 82, 108
    - 3. Same sex partners 13, 35, 37, 38, 44, 50, 90, 96, 99, 102
    - 4. Parts of a partner 11, 27, 28, 53, 61, 74, 106
    - 5. Many partners 65, 81, 82, 91
    - 6. More than one partner at the same time 36, 56, 69, 78, 100, 108
    - 7. Older partners 33, 34
    - 8. Relatives 42
    - 9. Children 73, 75, 76, 96
    - 10. Animals 12, 96, 109, 110
  - B. Inanimate contact (28, 48, 59, 83, 98) associated with:
    - 1. Urine and/or feces 16, 17, 49, 92, 101, 103, 104
    - 2. Odors 70, 71, 72
    - 3. Corpses 62, 63, 64, 96
- III. *Behavior* involving:
  - A. Direct contact associated with:
    - 1. Oral-genital intercourse 18, 25, 26, 46, 67, 95, 96
    - 2. Oral-anal or anal intercourse 4, 5, 67, 75, 96
    - 3. Oiling or lathering 43
    - 4. Force or coercion 14, 29, 52, 64, 85
    - 5. Pain 88
      - a. Giving 3, 14, 29, 52, 64, 77, 85, 87, 106
      - b. Receiving 3, 14, 29, 54
    - 6. Touching strangers 32
    - 7. Cross dressing 98
    - 8. Stealing 47
    - 9. Burning 84
    - 10. Soiling or destroying 89
  - B. Indirect contact associated with:
    - 1. Seeing 58, 93, 94, 107
    - 2. Being seen 1, 24
    - 3. Talking 15
    - 4. Telephone calling 15
    - 5. Writing 15
- IV. *Identity* involving:
  - A. Gender 97
  - B. Role 57
  - C. Body image 7

enced categories in Table 14.2, where the traditional labels fall, illustrates the definitional prolems involved.

The categories presented describe in behavioral terms a variety of sexual activities that people across cultures are known to engage in. While the descriptions are admittedly rather general, they at least offer a way of viewing sexual behaviors for what they are while attempting to minimize the "rightness or wrongness" or "pathology" denoted by a label for a complex set of behaviors.

The vast majority of sexual problems known to the authors appear to fall within one of the four major headings in Table 14.2. Category I includes all those problems that are commonly referred to as dysfunctions with sexual *response*. Concerns in this area are usually viewed as a problem by the individual and his or her partner, and generally include some type of inadequacy or dissatisfaction on the part of the individuals involved.

Problems in Category II may nor may not be viewed by the individual as a problem. However, they may be viewed as a problem by various segments of a given society or a culture. This category of object choice is further subdivided into animate and inanimate objects that an individual interacts with to produce sexual responses. Here it is not so much what the individual does as with *whom* or *what* they do that leads to societal and/or legal sanctions.

Category III lists a number of sexual *behaviors,* some of which also have direct legal or societal prohibitions. The problems listed here are further divided into direct or indirect contact and are primarily concerned with the behaviors themselves that the individual engages in for the purpose of facilitating sexual arousal. The concern in this category is not so much with the object choice the individual has made, but rather with the *way* that he or she goes about interacting with the object for purposes of sexual gratification. As with Category II, the individuals involved with Category III type behaviors may or may not necessarily consider their behavior to be a problem.

The "problems" listed in Category IV are mainly listed in that they typically are discussed in chapters on sexual disorders. The authors do not necessarily view concerns regarding identity as a sexual problem, per se. An individual who feels that he or she is a person trapped in the body of the "wrong" sex is struggling with an entirely different type of dilemma than, say the person who experiences intense sexual arousal, and hence legal retaliation, when exposing him or herself to children.

The two tables are cross referenced so that a behavioral description in Table 14.2 may be found for each label in Table 14.1, and vice versa.

In general, the behaviors described within each subcategory and between the categories themselves are presented in Table 14.2 in approximately their order of incidence: the larger the number of the category, the less frequent the occurrence.

The three subcategories of orgasm, arousal, and desire in category I on response are particularly interesting. Not only are these problems related to incidence, but clinical observations suggest that they are possibly hierarchical for the individual. That is, people with concerns about orgasm (such as none for a female or too quickly for a male) may eventually experience difficulty in the next category of Arousal (resulting in perhaps lack of lubrication and pain for females and erection concerns for males), which then could lead to problems of desire (either low or none). This would be predicted from an operant viewpoint, which states that behavior followed by negative consequences decreases in probability. The natural sexual response usually follows from desire to arousal to orgasm. If all these are functioning to the satisfaction of one partner, then the probability of that partner engaging in the same sexual behavior is increased. On the other hand, if the other partner has concerns in one of the areas, then the probability of their wishing to engage in such sexual activity decreases. This then leads to stated differences that are blamed on different "sex drives," instead of looking at the consequences of sexual behavior on the parts of each partner. The rankings of incidence for various behaviors are only approximate. For those sexual behaviors that are seldom reported in the literature, the authors admit to highly subjective judgments regarding their ranking as to frequency of complaint.

In an attempt to emphasize the importance of description as well as to attenuate the possible emotional reactions associated with many traditional labels, none of the term from Table 14.1 will be used when describing these problems and their treatment in the following section.

Treatment

Space limitations do not allow more than an overview of treatment for the sexual concerns described in Table 14.2. (For a much more extensive review of the psychological learning approach to treatment for each of these problem areas, see Annon, 1975, 1976.) In discussing treatment, emphasis will be placed on empirical findings where available in order to point out theoretical ambiguities and positions. Numbers that appear in parentheses throughout the remainder of this chapter refer to the traditional labels found in Table 14.1.

Sexual problems related to response

Concerns over some aspect of sexual response, either with opposite and/or same sex partners, are among the most prevalent in the American culture. Most problems in this area may be seen as some form of sexual incompatibility between partners who are experiencing difficulty in initiating or achieving mutual satisfaction and pleasure in sexual relations.

Orgasm

There is some evidence to indicate that the experience of orgasm for males and females is essentially the same (Proctor, Wagner, & Butler, 1973; Vance & Wagner, 1976). Males and females have also been known to continue to experience orgasm even though their genitals have been removed or reconstructed, such as in sex change surgery, provided that they have learned to experience orgasm prior to such surgery. Masters and Johnson (1966) provide evidence to indicate that males and females are more similar in their capacity for, and experience of, sexual responsiveness than they are dissimilar. However, when it comes to treatment, males and females with identical sexual problems in response are approached as if they were separate and distinct. It is the authors' opinion that treatment procedures that work for sexual response concerns of one sex may be equally effective in treatment of similar problems of the other sex. For that reason the ROBI classification scheme does not present distinctions between the two except when relevant.

None, infrequent, or delayed. The reported incidence of not having learned to experience orgasm or experiencing it only on infrequent occasions is much higher for females (6, 31, 68) than males (21, 22, 41, 86). This might be the result of the males' early experience of stimulation of their external genitals as described previously. Though there may be many biological, chemical, or organic factors that influence desire or arousal patterns, there is little evidence to indicate that these factors play any direct role in a person's ability to experience orgasm. In other words, it is generally assumed that all healthy males or females have the potential to learn how to experience orgasm.

Prior to the advent of the more direct therapeutic approaches, these problems had long been considered refractory to treatment. For females, psychological learning approches to treatment are generally directed at reducing the anxiety that has become associated with certain sexual behavior, or assisting the female to learn new behaviors conducive to the experience of arousal and orgasm through some form of successive approximation to sexual response such as that described by the Masters and Johnson (1970) approach, or a combination of both.

There now exist many procedures that have been described in the literature that help females achieve orgasm, as well as several research studies demonstrating the efficacy of more novel approaches. For example, Robinson (1974a, b), in a controlled study with no therapist contact, demonstrated that women exposed to observational learning (modeling) through the use of videotapes, both acquired novel sexual behaviors and/or significantly increased sexual activities that had been occurring only rarely at the time that they entered the program. His procedures were also effective in promoting more favorable attitudes toward specific sexual activities presented in the videotapes. This study offers an illustration of procedures that are designed to assist a female to change her attitudes as well as learn new behaviors through vicarious learning. (For a more detailed presentation of the use of vicarious learning in the treatment of sexual concerns, see Annon & Robinson, 1978b.)

As previously stated, male difficulty in experiencing orgasm, particularly during intercourse, is relatively rare. Past indirect approaches to treatment sometimes took up to six years of ongoing therapy (Ovesey & Meyers, 1968). Masters and Johnson (1970) have reported success in their two-week intensive therapy program by using procedures that can best be described by successive approximation principles. Failure to achieve orgasm during genital intercourse is the most infrequent problem reported by males, and, conversely, these same problems are the most frequently reported by females. Most interesting is to note that this picture reverses itself with the next category.

Too soon. A male feeling that he has reached an orgasm too soon (20, 39, 80, 91) is one of the most commonly reported male sexual response concerns in American culture. However, for females (39, 65) it is extremely rare, as it is for males who engage in same-sex behavior. What is meant by "too soon" is plagued with different opinions, and ranges from "anytime before the male (or the female) is ready" to "after the completion of four strokes." Apparently, the two necessary elements in order to experience this as a problem are the male's penis in the vagina and a stopwatch.

Unlike erections concerns, this problem during the sexual life of an otherwise healthy male does not have any known common physical cause. Some believe that it is probably normal and natural for a healthy male to ejaculate quickly. Other feel that it is a learned response through masturbation or being rushed when in a highly aroused situation. However, knowing whether such behavior is "natural" or "learned" is not much immediate help to the male or female who sees it as a problem.

Direct approaches to treatment are usually based on discrimination learning and successive approximation procedures, with the main objective of helping the male to learn a new response. Semans's (1956) technique of a series of extended sessions of stimulation of the penis by the male's partner; or Masters and Johnson's (1970) "squeeze" technique, where the female partner applies pressure in the glans of the penis just prior to the male's report of impending ejaculation have both been equally successful.

Annon (1976) suggested that the necessary and sufficient conditions underlying these approaches may not necessarily be the "squeeze" or the "stop and start," but may be the *increased frequency* of contact leading to orgasm and ejaculation that is usually incorporated into these techniques.

To the best of the authors' knowledge there are no reports of treatment for this concern in females.

Arousal

The arousal response in males and females may be elicited by overt tactile stimulation or sensory input to the eyes, ears, nose, and mouth, and/or by covert stimulation such as dreams, thoughts, and fantasies. The arousal response appears to be a natural physiological process that in males induces blood volume and pressure pulse changes in the penis during erection. The comparable response in females is vaginal blood volume and pressure pulse changes and lubrication. Researchers have been able to measure their responses through the use of penile strain gauges and photoplethysmographs in order to discover what factors elicit and influence arousal. Again, the data suggest that what elicits arousal in males and females may be more similar than dissimilar (Heiman, 1975).

From a psychological learning point of view, what the arousal response may become associated with through classical and/or operant principles is unlimited. Of course, a great deal of research has been devoted to discovering what people have learned to respond with sexual arousal to (e.g., pictures, slides, films and audio- and videotapes related to opposite sex, same sex, children, inanimate objects, rape). Such objective measurement of arousal can be very useful in treatment for initial ongoing and posttherapy assessment.

None or low. There are many possible factors that may interfere with the arousal response in males (23, 41) and females (31). For example, engaging in continued painful intercourse by a female (19) may eventually lead to an involuntary contraction of the vaginal outlet (105—a classically conditioned response) that may even prevent penile entry. As Roen (1965) has suggested, there are numerous possible organic diseases (e.g., anatomic abnormality, neurologic disease, systemic disease, trauma, either accidental or surgical, and hormonal deficiencies) as well as chemical or medicinal factors (e.g., drugs of a narcotic or sedative nature, morphine, alcohol) that may interfere with the natural arousal response. However, what is most interesting is that, say, for two men with exactly the same organic problem, one may have erection problems and the other none at all.

Even some castrated, estrogen-treated males with prostatic cancer may perform sexually with litle problem (Belt, 1973). Despite the large number of known possible organic causes, most authorities seem to agree that from 90 percent to 95 percent of the possible causes are psychological, and may include such factors as orgasm concerns, fatigue, preoccupation, jet lag, over-drinking, criticism from a partner, boredom with a partner, having an unattractive partner, worry over disease or pregnancy, guilt over masturbation, same-sex responses, unfaithfulness, or anxiety associated with expected performance by one partner or the other. (Such events may precipitate thoughts about the next sexual encounter, which in turn produce a great deal of anxiety and worry, commonly called "fear of performance." Such a fear effectively blocks the normal arousal system and thus results in another failure. Once this chain starts to function, it may be difficult to break. Learning-oriented approaches generally see such problems as the result of conditioned anxiety, and treatment is largely aimed at reducing the anxiety associated with the approach to sexual relations.

Direct approaches to treatment of males with arousal-erection concerns usually are graded sexual responses to the actual sexual situation if some degree of arousal is reported, or covert systematic desensitization if no arousal is present. For males, reports of pain associated with sexual intercourse interfering with arousal are rare relative to such complaints from females.

For female pain during sexual relations, there are obviously many possible physical causes that require a careful gynecological examination and appropriate medical treatment. As mentioned before, if pain continues to be associated with sexual intercourse, there is a possibility that this may result in a classically conditioned response of an involuntary spastic contraction of the vaginal outlet (105), which prevents penile entry. This condition occurs in otherwise normal genitalia and may last for years (Friedman, 1962). Up to the advent of direct approaches to treatment, this condition was considered highly refractory to most forms of intervention. The direct approaches are usually aimed at reducing anxiety associated with the response, and helping the woman to learn a new response by using principles of successive approximation. Haslam's (1965) use of a series of graded dilators inserted in the vagina until the woman is able to retain one the size of a normal penis and then subsequent slow insertion with her partner's penis has become a standard approach. Most techniques, such as those of Masters and Johnson (1970), where the couple take the dilators home with them, or where the couple use fingers or successive approximation of penile entry over time (Annon, 1976) are variations of this basic approach.

High. A high or continual degree of arousal in males (39, 91) and females (39, 65) is seldom reported in the literature except in connection with injuries or diseases of the spinal cord, which, for example in males, may cause persistent erection of the penis without sexual desire. In such cases medical treatment is obviously required.

Desire

None or low. Although the physiological ability to experience arousal and orgasm may be present, the cognitive *desire* to engage in such experiences on the part of the male (40, 41, 51) or female (31, 40, 51) may be partially or complete absent. Usually those who complain of this problem avoid sexual encounters. However, if they do engage in such activities, many do go on to experience some level of arousal and possibly orgasm. As with arousal problems, constitutional or organic factors may play some role in inhibition of desire, as well as such factors as anxiety, or depression, interpersonal conflict, intrapersonal conflict, traumatic sexual experiences, unwelcomed fantasies, or generalized sexual inhibition. Treatment is usually seen as difficult, although hypnosis and direct approaches, such as suggestion that the person temporarily refrain from any form of sexual activity for a period of time, have been successful in resolving such concerns. There are virtually no empirically based studies on exactly what factors influence desire or what particular forms of treatment are most efficient. Many such problems may originate because of negative consequences occuring in connection with arousal and/or orgasm experiences, and perhaps dealing directly with these aspects may influence the cognitive desire difference.

High. Problems in a high degree of desire in males (39, 91) and females (39, 65) are often discussed in the clinical literature, but no empirical studies on relevant factors in etiology or treatment appear to be available.

Sexual problems related to object choice

Unlike problems of arousal, object choice concerns may not be viewed by the individual as a problem, though they may be viewed as such by various sized segments of a given society or culture. Here it is not so much what the individual does sexually as with whom or what they do that leads to societal and/or legal sanctions.

Animate choices

Self. Sexual self-choice has been variously described as self-love (9, 60), self-stimulation of the genitals (45, 55) or anus (8, 48), oral self-stimulation of the penis (10), or withdrawal of the penis from the vagina prior to orgasm (66). Cultural and medical acceptance of the practice of self-stimulation designed to elicit arousal and orgasm has been slow in evolving. Initially it was "sinful," then "perverted," followed by "possibly normal, but nasty." Next, it was considered to be "normal and natural" as long as it was "not done to excess." Unfortunately, no one has ever been able to define what "excess" means. From what has been written earlier, it may be concluded that from the authors' viewpoint such behavior is not only considered "natural and normal," but may be therapeutically helpful in treating a wide range of sexual problems (for examples, see Annon, 1973).

Married or unmarried partners. Various cultural and legal systems restrict choice of partners and may not condone sexual behavior between unmarried partners (30), or between married and unmarried partners (2), or exchanging married partners (108), or the selection of married or unmarried partners by married or unmarried individuals on a monetary basis (79, 82). Treatment, if it is requested, is usually aimed at assisting the particular individual to accept or reject such choices without undue anxiety.

Same-sex partners. It appears that all cultures, past and present, generally condone an adult experiencing desire, arousal, and orgasm with another adult of the opposite sex (37) within a restricted framework of time, place, manner, and situation. However, an adult male engaging in such behavior with another adult male (38, 44, 96, 102) or an adult female with another adult female (35, 38, 44, 50, 90, 99, 102), or an adult engaging in such behavior with the opposite and the same sex simultaneously (13) may be looked at quite differently depending upon the culture.

Another controversial issue has been whether such behavior is to be considered "neurotic," "psychotic," or not necessarily "mentally ill." Numerous studies have been done in attempts to find differences. In general, those who do engage in same-sex behaviors do not differ from others who do not, and they are not psychologically disturbed or more "mentally ill" than the general population. Where reported findings of differences have been found, they usually do not appear to hold up under replication, as there are an insufficient number of studies of adequately defined samples under properly controlled conditions to provide definitive answers.

Probably the most disputed area concerns possible etiology of such behavior, which of course leads to whether treatment is called for or what treatment to offer if it is. Many researchers and therapists have carefully examined the evidence for hormonal, genetic, or constitutional factors and found it lacking. Others feel that such factors may provide a predisposition to male or female gender orientation. The American Medical Association Committee on Human Sexuality (1972) has stated that such behavior does not have any known genetic or hormonal basis. Barnett (1973) reviewed the scientific evidence and concluded that there is little evidence that genetic, hormonal, or constitutional factors play a *direct* role in sexual disorder in general, and same-sex behavior in particular. As has been stated before, most workers in the area generally agree that such behavior is acquired. They disagree as to how it is acquired.

Whether to treat or not depends upon whether such behavior is viewed as an illness. As has been mentioned previously from a psychological learning point of view, such questions are not any more relevant than asking if engaging in opposite-sex behavior is an illness. The current trend is to talk of "change" rather than "cure" for those who desire it. Until the advent of the psychological learning approach, treatment for those who requested a change in sexual preference had been largely psychoanalytically based and aimed at uncovering the assumed preoedipal origins of the problem. Such treatment was generally not seen as very successful (Curran & Paar 1957). When first confronted with client's requests for change in orientation from same sex to the opposite sex, early learning-oriented treatment methods used aversion therapy with shock or drugs. As theoretical and experimental sophistication increased, simple classical conditioning procedures gave way to conditioned aversion. Some therapists found the use of only one procedure to be effective; others reported failures with only one approach such as aversion to same-sex stimuli, or systematic desensitization to opposite-sex stimuli. Because of positive results, a number of clinicians and researchers proposed various standard models and programs for treatment. However, whether or not the present state of knowledge about treatment warrants the use of such models or programs for all people who wish change orientation is questionable.

An example of controlled laboratory research in the area of developing heterosexual arousal is provided by Barlow, Abel, Agras, and their associates. They have done some excellent work in systematically demonstrating the conditions most helpful in developing heterosexual arousal by altering masturbatory fantasies (Abel, Barlow, Blanchard, 1973) using biofeedback and reinforcement to increase heterosexual arousal. (For a more detailed overview of some of their work in this area, see Abel and Blanchard, 1973.)

Well controlled studies, such as these, are essential to the advancement of a psychological learning-oriented therapy based upon empirical evidence. However, the clinician faced with immediate client problems cannot always wait for extensive laboratory research on each procedure before treatment is offered. Conversely, the indiscriminate use of one or many procedures without any systematic plan for the ordering of techniques may also do disservice to clients. Treating only one aspect of the situation such as assisting a person to learn to enjoy opposite-sex relationships does not necessarily mean that the person will not continue to respond with arousal to members of the same sex. This may be one reason that past reports talked about clients leaving therapy who responded equally to both same and opposite sex partners (e.g., 13). Most workers now stress the use of multiple procedures for different aspects of the presenting problem based on intensive initial, ongoing, and follow-up assessment. Whether such treatment is "necessary" or should be made available to those who request it will be discussed later when examining legal and ethical issues in treatment.

Parts of a partner. Desire, arousal, and/or orgasm associated with various parts of a partner (74) such as a partner's breasts (53), buttocks, (61), thighs (27), armpits (11) or even blood (106) have been reported since the start of recorded literature. The possible etiology and treatment for such sexual choices will be covered when discussing inanimate object choices.

Many partners. The sexual choice of many partners (81) on the part of either a male (91) or female (65), or on a monetary basis (82) has been extensively described in the clinical literature with litle controlled empirical support as to etiology or appropriate treatment if requested.

More than one partner at the same time. This behavior is usually described as the choice of sexual activity with either two others at the same time (56, 100), two couples at the same time (108), or group sexual activity (38, 69, 78). While there are a considerable amount of descriptive studies of such behavior, there again is extremely little empirical research as to etiology and treatment.

Older partners. Whether the choice of a partner considerably older than oneself is seen as a problem or is condoned or punished appears to depend upon the culture within which such choice are made. For example, a female making such a choice is much more socially accepted in American culture than is a male making a similar choice.

Relatives. There is a great deal of anthropological literature on the choice of a relative for a sexual partner (42). As Sagarin (1977) has noted, research into the pertinent factors determining such object choice is hampered by definition and frequency problems. For example, in the United States, the penal codes of the various states do not distinguish a relationship between stepfather and stepdaughter from one between father and daughter. On the other hand, such a distinction may not be as relevant as how a particular individual may have learned such behavior and how they might learn to change it.

Children. Research on those who have learned to experience sexual arousal and engage in sexual behavior with young children of either the same or opposite sex (73, 75, 76, 96) is comparatively rare. Exceptions to this are studies on the effects of different drugs on such behavior (Tennent, Bancroft,

Case Description of Sexual Deviation

Paul reported a five-year history of incestual behavior with his oldest daughter, beginning when she was 13 years old. Incestual activity consisting primarily of kissing, fondling, and mutual masturbation continued until she was 18. He also noted that during sexual intercourse with both his previous and present wife, the daughter served as object of his fantasies. When his daughter was 16 years old, Paul's first wife learned about the ongoing incestuous relationship. This resulted in separation and divorce.

Paul's early sexual history provides a *possible* model for deviant sexuality. Between the ages 9 and 10 years, he observed an uncle playing strip poker with a neighbor's wife. He witnessed mutual fondling between the same uncle and a waitress at the drive-in restaurant and was instructed by the uncle to fondle his young female cousin. Between the ages of 14 and 15 years, he engaged in mutual manipulation with a sister and her girlfriend. His older sister then married an alcoholic who later raped his own eldest daughter.

Other aspects of Paul's early sexual history might have contributed to his present difficulties, but are typical for some male populations. At the age of 18, his brother-in-law brought him to a prostitute where he first experienced sexual intercourse. Subsequent visits to prostitutes were unsatisfactory as he tended to ejaculate prematurely. While in the armed services overseas, Paul and his friends had sexual relations with girls as young as 13 years of age.

Paul's sexual relationship with his first wife was extremely poor and was characterized by her rejecting attitude and his premature ejaculation. Following the birth of his oldest daughter, sexual intercourse occurred infrequently, with Paul having occasional intercourse with other women. When his wife reached the age of 36 years, she expressed an interest in resuming a normal sexual relationship, but was rejected by Paul. By this time he had begun his incestuous relationship with his daughter.

Adapted from Harbert et al. (1974, p. 80).

& Case, 1974) or blood volume changes in response to pictures or slides of children (Quinsey, Steinman, Bergersen, & Holmes, 1975).

Indirect forms of treatment have not been too successful (Shoor, Speed, & Bartelt, 1966). One of the first reports of a psychological learning-oriented approch was that of Stevenson and Wolpe (1960), who described successfully using assertive training procedures. Others have moved away from using only one or two treatment modalities, such as Feingold's (1966) use of reeducation, systematic desensitization, and assertive training, or Annon's (1975) use of systematic desensitization, masturbatory conditioning, social behavior training, and covert aversion conditioning.

Animals. Sexual behavior between humans and animals (12, 96, 109, 110) has been referenced since the Bible, and incidence appears to depend upon the culture and the availability of such contacts. For example, Kinsey et al. (1948) reported that close to 40 percent to 50 percent of American farm youth had some type of sexual contact with animals at some point in their histories. More recently, others (Thayler, 1977) have suggested that sexual contact with dogs by women who live alone in city apartments may be more prevalent than is usually known. People requesting treatment for such behavior are relatively rare and therefore there is little empirical support for one form of treatment over another.

Inanimate choices

This behavior may be described as desire, arousal, and/or orgasm associated with inanimate objects (28, 59) that may range from rubber, shoes, purses, baby buggies, sculpture (83), underwear and clothing (98), to enemas (48), urine and/or feces (16, 17, 49, 92, 101, 103, 104), odors (70, 71, 72), or corpses (62, 63, 64, 96).

In regard to etiology, there are a few that hint at a possible connection with brain damage (Bethell, 1974), but the more common psychoanalytic viewpoint suggests that the object is symbolic in nature and usually represents displaced arousal (Epstein, 1975). Of theoretical interest from a psychological learning theory framework were the experiments previously of Rachman and Hodgson (1968) in which they were able to condition sexual arousal responses to slides of a pair of knee length boots, and the report of McConaghy (1970) who conditioned penile volume changes to the presentation of slides with red circles or green triangles. These studies, in conjunction with the masturbatory conditioning hypothesis of McGuire, Carlisle, and Young (1965), suggest how such responses may be learned in connection with a potentially endless variety of stimuli.

Indirect approaches to treatment have usually reported difficulty (Shenken, 1964). However, there is a great mass of psychological learning oriented literature that has reported successful elimination of such responses. Generally, early treatment procedures involved some form of aversion therapy that pairs the object (or pictures of it) with either noxious drugs or shock.

Sexual problems related to behavior

The behaviors in this category are divided into direct and indirect contact and are primarily concerned with the activity that the individual engages in for purposes of facilitating sexual arousal, desire, and/or orgasm. The concern here is not so much the object choice of the individual but rather the way in which the person goes about interacting with the object choice for purposes of sexual gratification. As with the previous category on object choice, the behaviors themselves may or may not necessarily be considered a problem by the person who engages in them, though they often are considered as problems by sizeable segments of society.

Direct contact

Oral-genital intercourse. Oral-genital contact, (67) whether it be given by a male or female to a female (18) or to a male's penis (25, 26, 46, 96) or scrotum (95), is one form of behavior whose acceptance and practice appears to have increased dramatically in the United States in the past 25 years (Hunt, 1974). However, despite the reported incidence, such behavior is in violation of the legal codes in numerous states, even between consenting married adults.

Oral-anal or anal intercourse. Oral-anal (4, 5, 67) or anal intercourse (75, 96) between partners also has increased in reported incidence. For example, Hunt's (1974) survey of married males and females under 35 in the United States indicated that half of them had experienced manual anal foreplay, and more than 25 percent had experienced oral-anal foreplay.

Oiling or lathering. The behavior of obtaining sexual gratification by having oil, ointment, or other unguents rubbed over and into the body probably started with ancient Rome, but it is still considered a "perversion" by some when carried to "extreme" (Smithfield, 1970). It is interesting to note that the suggestions to engage in such behaviors are incorporated in a great many sexual therapy programs at the present time.

Force or coercion. This behavior is generally described as sexual desire, arousal, and/or orgasm associated with binding (14), whipping or beating (29), raping (85) or even murdering (52, 64) an unwilling partner. As Abel, Barlow, Blanchard, and Guild (1975) have pointed out, treatment for such behavior has typically not been available. The few programs that do exist have been lengthy, lasting at least two years. Also, recidivism rates after simple incarceration are alarmingly high (e.g., 35%), while recidivism after treatment is variable (e.g., 6%–35% depending upon the program and length of follow up).

With the recent development of measurement studies with cooperative patients (Abel & Blanchard, 1976), we can currently separate rapists from nonrapists on the basis of their penile responses to rape versus nonrape cues. Erection calibration is the most accurate measure, because this is the only physiologic variable in males that occurs exclusively during sexual arousal and not through other emotional states. Abel and his coworkers (Abel, Barlow, Blanchard, & Mavissakalian, 1974) have also found that audio descriptions of sexual activities are more useful than slides or movies for generating arousal to complex sexual stimuli such as rape. Since this measurement capability is now available, it becomes more appropriate to treat this group of people who formerly were excluded from psychological assistance.

Pain. This behavior is similar to the above and is usually described as sexual desire, arousal, and/or orgasm associated with inflicting pain (3, 87) on either a willing or unwilling partner by binding (14), beating or whipping (29), biting and sucking (106), puncturing (77), raping (85), or murdering (52, 64).

Abel, Barlow, and Blanchard (1973) conducted the first controlled study of altering masturbatory fantasy in a multiple-baseline, single-case experimental design with a young male who was referred because he could no longer control his urges to mutilate females. Abel et al. elected to work with his thoughts and fantasies, and used masturbatory conditioning to specific fantasies that were changed in a systematic fashion from purely "deviant" to completely "nondeviant." By the end of the treatment, the client reported losing interest in the fantasies until they no longer appealed to him. The data indicated that masturbation was responsible for arousal to previously nonarousing descriptions. Using masturbtory latency as a dependent measure of sexual arousal could prove very helpful in this type of research and treatment.

On the surface it would appear the sexual desire, arousal, and/or orgasm associated with self-infliction of, or receiving, pain (3, 14, 29, 54) would be a glaring exception to the reinforcement theory of learning. However, several theorists have outlined how such behaviors may be acquired and maintained according to general learning principles (e.g., Brown, 1965; Sandler, 1964; Ullmann & Krasner, 1975). Fantasies of this behavior have been treated successfully by shock aversion (McGuire & Vallance, 1964; Marks, Rachman, & Gelder, 1965). Abel, Levis, and Clancy (1970) have reported good results in treating the behavior itself with shock aversion applied to taped sequences of descriptions of the behavior. Pinard and Lamontagne (1976) have also described good results with the use of electrical aversion and aversion relief in conjunction with increased heterosexual retraining.

Touching strangers. Sexual response associated with touching or rubbing against strangers (32), usually in crowded public places, has often been reported in the clinical literature, but seldom does the person request treatment. Serber (1970) has announced good results by using shame aversion therapy in which the patient is asked to perform the behavior in front of a number of observers.

Cross dressing. This is usually seen as sexual arousal and behavior associated with wearing the clothing of the opposite sex (98). There have been many dynamic and biological theories to account for this behavior. However, none has been empirically established. A psychological learning model suggests how such behavior may be acquired through the operant and classical learning principles, similar to the behavior associated with inanimate object choice (28). There have been well over thirty cases describing successful treatment by behavioral techniques such as aversion therapy with drugs, electrical shock, desensitization, shame aversion therapy; or various combinations of procedures such as thought stopping, covert sensitization, and shock avoidance.

Stealing. Sexual response and behavior involved with stealing (47) may be associated with the actual behavior itself regardless of the object stolen, or with a combination of both as when the person repeatedly steals the same objects (e.g., women's underclothes from clotheslines). Such behavior is often described as being accompanied by masturbation at some point (which would account for the classically conditioned response of arousal to such behavior).

Burning. Sexual response associated with the burning of objects or dwellings (84) has occasionally been reported in the literature. As above, such behavior is usually followed by the person secretly observing the fire and masturbating, which could explain the behaviors associated with arousal and its reinforcement.

Soiling or destroying. There are a few reports of people who have learned to respond with sexual arousal to the act of soiling, damaging, or destroying the property of others (89), which illustrates once again the wide range of actions (or objects) that may potentially come to elicit sexual arousal and behavior through classical and/or operant principles.

Indirect contact

Seeing. This is generally described as sexual arousal and behavior associated with secretly observing the nude body or genitals of others (93, 94, 107) or watching others engage in sexual behavior (58). Whether such behavior is culturally condoned or legally sanctioned depends upon whether it takes place in a nightclub or a movie theater or in the backyard of a neighbor. Stoudenmire (1973) has described good results with a client who engaged in such behavior for twenty years by suggesting contingent masturbation instructions. Gaupp, Stern, and Ratliff (1971) had equally good success with the application of electrical aversion-relief procedures. Ferinden and Tugender (1972) used the Premack principle of placing higher probability behavior contingent on lower probability behavior, by having their client imagine himself engaging in such behaviors only after he first imagined himself engaging in social activities such as parties.

Being seen. This behavior usually involves sexual desire, arousal, and/or orgasm, associated with the voluntary exposure of genitals to others in what is typically referred to as "inappropriate" situations. As with many other categories, "inappropriate" is determined by cultural norms, time, place, and situation (e.g., it may be considered "appropriate' for a female to engage in this behavior in a nightclub, but not at the zoo; or a male in a locker room, but not at a public park).

An explanation of how such behavior may be developed through learning has been available for over half a century (Smith & Guthrie, 1922). However, over thirty years passed before psychological learning oriented treatment reports began to appear. Since those early reports of Wolpe (1958) and Bond and Hutchison (1960), using systematic desensitization, a deluge of successful clinical reports has emerged using electrical shock aversion to emotive images, urges to exposure, slides of statements of the behavior, as well as various combinations. A relatively new and apparently highly effective approach to treatment is a procedure based on the patient exhibiting himself in highly controlled conditions designed to greatly increase his feelings of shame.

Treatment is beginning to move away from the application of only one procedure to the use of many interventions with one person, such as hypnosis, covert sensitization, role playing, social skills training, aversive shock, and sexual reeducation and treatment.

Talking, telephone calling, and writing. Sexual responses associated with the use of sexually seductive or obscene language such as talking or through telephone calls and letter writing to anonymous persons (15) is frequently commented upon in the popular press but people who engage in this behavior are seldom seen in clinical practice. Usually such behavior is accompanied by masturbation or leads to arousal and masturbation, which serves to reinforce the behavior.

Sexual problems related to identity

Gender

The majority of the literature dealing with those people who feel that they are "trapped in the wrong body" and who wish to have their sex surgically changed to that of the opposite sex (97) confines itself to descriptions of possible etiological factors in gender identity or procedures for carrying out such surgery (Green & Money, 1969; Money & Ehrhardt, 1972). While most reports describe cases where the male wishes to change his sex to female, Pauly (1974a, b) carried out an exhaustive review of the world literature and reported extensive findings on eighty cases of females who wished to change their sex. Articles are usually limited to interviews, children's toy preferences, geriatric clients, or case reports such as those describing the occurrence of two persons with such identity problems in the same family.

Descriptions of therapy are generally confined to counseling the person before, during, and after surgery. On the other hand, Barlow, Agras, and Reynolds (1972, 1973) have reported what appears to be the first successful attempt to change gender identity in an adult through the application of learning-based procedures. Abel (1975) further reports that he and his associates have had similar success with a number of other adult cases.

Working along similar lines, Rekers and Lovaas (1974) have described excellent results in treating a young male child whose extreme feminine dress and behaviors suggested irreversible neurological and biochemical determinants. Rekers and Varni (1977) have further reported success in teaching a 6-year-old boy to self-monitor his own sex-role behavior, and then to self-reinforce gender appropriate responding.

These excellent studies demonstrate the careful application of a psychological learning oriented approach to assessment and treatment, and they will undoubtedly lead to further efforts to develop effective clinical procedures that may offer an additional alternative to surgery should they choose it.

Role

This behavior is seen by some (De River, 1958) as the conversion of certain sexual and erotic attitudes that appear as masculine in females and feminine in males without leading to overt sexual behavior with the same sex (57). However, in the current American culture with its move toward androgyny and unisex apparel, such sex-role-typing concerns are seldom for treatment in clinical practice.

Body image

The relationship between sexual attraction and amputated limbs is a little known phenomenon (7) that is seen with those who are erotically obsessed with getting themselves amputated, or who exhibit an erotic obsession for amputated limbs or digits (Money, Jobaris, & Furth, 1977).There is no agreed upon method of treatment.

Difficulties associated with treatment

Whether or not a psychological learning approach to treatment is effective is not an appropriate question. Its effectiveness with some clients with certain problems has been well documented. A more appropriate question is: Which set of procedures is most effective for what specific problem presented by what type of client to which therapist from what orientation? Similar questions have long been put forth by many others, but answers have been slow in coming. This section will attempt to examine some of the variables that not only make comparative evaluation difficult, but also make therapeutic success less probable.

Response problems

After Masters and Johnson (1970) first published the successful results of their two-week intensive treatment program, a number of centers across the nation began to work along similar lines and to report similar results. Masters and Johnson have been reported as saying that perhaps only 50 out of the estimated 3,500 to 5,000 sex therapy clinics operating in the United States can be considered legitimate (*Medical World News,* May 10, 1974). In many cases these treatment centers and programs may or may not derive their therapy procedures from a theoretically sound basis supported by empirical research. Although most of these centers report good results, few provide detailed descriptions of client problems or treatment procedures and follow-up. This makes it difficult to compare the necessary elements for treatment. For some of the reports it appears that treatment included techniques of reeducation, encouragement, expectancy, and insight. Without further research on the importance of these cognitive and social aspects and how they relate to the basic therapeutic procedures, necessary and sufficient interventions will be difficult to determine.

Object choice and behavior problems

Definitions

It is obviously difficult to evaluate the appropriateness or effectiveness of a specific procedure on a given population, or to compare its effectiveness with another, if the only description of the client given is, say, "The patient has been a practicing transvestite for four years," or "impotent for two years," or "a confirmed transsexual." There is an obvious need for assessment procedures that provide for a clear *description* of the problem behavior in operationally defined terms, rather than the indiscriminate use of labels.

Assessment

As the psychological learning approach has become more widely known, as a broader range of clients with a broad range of problems have been referred for such treatment. Without careful assessment procedures, the danger exists that many people with superficially similar problems may be treated by inappropriate procedures.

Initial, ongoing, and pre-post assessment. While most learning-oriented therapists and researchers strongly advocate a thorough behavioral analysis prior, during, and after planned interventions, in actual practice little support exists for a clear and systematic behavioral diagnosis. Even when there is agreement that such assessment is needed, there is disagreement as to exactly what form the assesment should take. There is the problem of developing and standardizing reliable and valid measures that the majority of learning-oriented therapists and researchers could use so that comparative evaluations might be made. A second problem is the ethical problem that is involved in attempting to develop and use such measures with sexual behaviors.

Treatment procedures

As has been described previously, a wide range of treatment procedures have been used by learning-oriented therapists. However, a considerable number have not resulted in successful outcomes. There are a number of possible reasons in addition to faulty assessment for these reported failures that deserve individual attention.

Aversion treatment. Barker (1965) and Rachman (1965) have both noted that chemical aversion is usually highly unpleasant for the patient as well as for the staff, and the drugs do not allow for tight control of time factors known to be important in conditioning procedures. Many investigators feel that it is better to use electrical conditioning rather than chemical to control for these and other confounding factors.

The incorrect selection and use of stimulus materials, as well as the use of different shock intensities, may also be factors in determining successful outcomes with aversion techniques. In general, the restrictive use of aversion therapy without proper assessment may be one of the most likely causes of failure.

Restricted problem treatment. Another possible reason for failure in treatment is the therapist's limited approach to only one aspect of the presenting problem. Many learning-oriented therapists now feel that most cases require a combination of therapeutic procedures that will help the client to learn alternate responses. However, there is no common agreement as to how one determines which procedures to use in what order for what aspect of the problem.

Restrictive treatment problems. The restrictive use of one particular treatment procedure for many different presenting problems has also been criticized by a number of therapists and researchers. For example, Lazarus and Serber (1968) have noted that at one time, the terms behavior therapy and systematic desensitization were synonymous. More recently, the teaching of "assertion training" similarly seems to be used for a wide range of presenting problems. When such procedures gain in popularity the boundaries for their specific application may become hazy, like firing a shotgun without taking aim (Lazarus & Serber, 1968). The same criticism applies to those who use electrical aversion treatment procedure for many different presenting sexual problems.

Lazarus (1967) along with many others have long advocated a broad spectrum approach to learning therapy in place of the automatic use of one or a few techniques. However, it should also be made clear that the current stress by many learning-oriented therapists on a broad spectrum approach to treatment has no virtue unless there is some theoretically based plan for ordering their various interventions.

Annon has subsequently developed an overall scheme, called the P-LI-SS-IT model (Annon, 1975, 1976), for use by a range of professionals from a variety of disciplines; it aids in determining the complexity of the intervention procedure that will be required to alter the problem. As Gambrill (1977) has pointed out, this is an important distinction to make, for such a plan not only ensures that clients with more complex problems receive intervention programs suited to them, but it also ensures that a problem that can be altered by a rapid procedure is not addressed by an expensive, long-term program. Barlow (1977) has advanced a multidimensional model for assessment of sexual behavior. This model describes three major components of sexual behavior (sexual arousal, heterosexual social skills, and gender identity or gender role deviations) and the three response systems (verbal, behavioral, and physiological) as they may be assessed in either the natural environment or in contrived situations.

These models are of too recent origin to have had extensive application, so their theoretical and practical utility cannot be judged. However, they appear to be steps in the right direction, and further clinical trails and empirical research will be necessary to see how closely they approximate an accurate view of human sexual behavior and behavior change.

Ethical and legal considerations

A body of literature already exists on the ethical problems associated with the application of psychological learning principles (e.g., behavior modification, behavior therapy) to the treatment of sexual concerns (e.g., Begelman, 1975; Halleck, 1976). Such ethical problems are probably not any different from those inherent to other therapeutic orientations. Yet, clinicians practicing from a psychological learning orientation have been especially sensitive, perhaps even overly defensive, regarding moral questions involving which client goals they will or will not accept, and which treatment procedure should be employed. (A concise overview of the most common misconceptions about behavioral methods may be found in Gambrill, 1977.)

The fact that behavioral procedures evoke

a disproportionate number of ethical and legal questions (in contrast to other therapeutic means) is in part due to the specificity regarding goals and behavior change behavioral approaches require. In discussing ethical issues involving behavioral control, Bandura (1969) notes that any influence over another person's behavior that is accidental or unplanned seems to be acceptable. However, if such influence is *preplanned,* though the effects may be identical as to that observed under chance conditions, it is suspect. Bandura (1969) further suggests that treatment objectives and goals that remain vague or unspecified, and the process of relabeling the client's concern, conveniently allow therapists to minimize these ethical decisions with which they may be confronted.

Several peculiar ethical and/or legal issues confront clinicians who attempt to assist people with sexual problems. For example, as recently as 5 years ago, more than 80 percent of the states in the United States had laws against a variety of sexual activities beween mutually consenting adults (e.g., Table 14.1, items 2, 30, 96, 18, 26). While admittedly many of these "crimes" were not always vigorously prosecuted (depending of course on the value system of both the legal authorities and the people in a given locale), the fact that they remain technically illegal can present an ethical dilemma for the therapist who is aware of them.

The changing mores in our culture regarding sexual freedom suggest many sex therapists would have no ethical problem in assisting an unmarried couple who are living together to improve their sexual relationship, despite possible laws against "cohabitation." On the other hand, how many clinicians would agree to assist an adult male change his sexual preference from young boys to adult *males,* especially if the latter activity was also considered illegal, not to mention its personal and social desirability as perceived by the therapist? There seems to be much consensus regarding the appropriateness of treating, be it court imposed or self-sought, individuals who have sexual problems that impinge on the rights of others (e.g., Table 14.1, items 15, 47, 52, 64, 84, 85). However, what about sexual behaviors between consenting adults that may do no more than offend the value system of the therapist?

Much of the present literature regarding sex therapy and ethical issues involves the treatment of individuals who have sexual preferences for members of the same sex. For purposes of clarity and ease of communication, the labels heterosexual and homosexual will be used, though reluctantly.

The controversy over whether treatment should be given to a person wishing to change his or her sexual orientation has been most prominent within the behavior therapy camp. Ironically, it appears to be the higher potential effectiveness of psychological learning principles in modifying same-sex behaviors (e.g., Feldman & MacCulloch, 1971) in contrast with other treatment approaches (e.g., classic psychoanalysis; Bieber, 1976) that finally give rise to the controversy.

Many therapists have frequently asserted that social learning theory does not equate same-sex behavior with "abnormality" nor opposite-sex behavior with "normality." The right of the person to choose a different sexual orientation has long been explicitly or implicitly acknowledged (e.g., Ullmann & Krasner, 1975). This position is in sharp contrast with that taken by some of the more militant gay alliances that have appeared to deny such an individual's right to receive treatment if the goals were toward opposite-sex reorientation. Further confusion has been undoubtedly fostered by the American Psychiatric Association's elimination from its diagnostic manual "homosexuality" as a "mental disease." Of particular relevance here is the recognition that psychiatric diagnoses are established and maintained by *consensus,* and not validation (Gambrill, 1977). (E.g., by a "voting" procedure, "homosexuality" lost its status as an illness.)

The ethical implications of assisting people to change their sexual orientation was most dramatically illustrated by Gerald Davison's presidential address at the 1974 Annual Convention of the Association for

Advancement of Behavior Therapy. Davison argued that the very existence of change of sexual orientation approaches probably served to strengthen societal prejudices against same-sex behavior that in turn are the motivating factors for these individuals wanting therapy to change their orientation (Davison, 1976).

Begelman (1975) has advanced the argument even further. He points out that "the problem of homosexuality" does not even exist in the psychiatric or behavioral dictionary. He then stresses the point with the following illustration: "When a heterosexual has a problem, it is because he is impotent; when a homosexual has a problem, it is because he is a homosexual" (p. 179). Another illustration is: "Homosexuals are homosexuals because of anxieties concerning heterosexual relationships," which however logically invites the converse statement: "Heterosexuals are heterosexuals because of anxieties concerning homosexual relationships" (p. 179). We, of course, would not find much acceptance for this latter assertion within the psychiatric community (e.g., Bieber, 1976).

Regardless of how empirically or theoretically sound any treatment procedure may be, the value system of the therapist will inevitably come into play. The present authors find themselves leaning toward a "middle of the road" approach that neither denies nor asserts a person's right to receiving assistance for changing sexual orientation. The idealized clinical scenario described by Halleck (1976) concisely illustrates this position whereby the individuals who are considering changing their sexual orientation should be given information as to current biological and psychological theories of homosexuality and how they relate to them. Furthermore, they should have some idea as to the extent to which their present discomfort probably is related to oppressive environmental stress, particularly that stress generated by society's intolerance of same-sex preference. They should also be aware of the possible hazards of any treatment they might undertake and should know all the therapist's concerns regarding the possible gains or *losses* for them if treatment is successful.

Thus, it should be clear that there are numerous complex ethical and legal issues in dealing with individuals who have, or are labeled as having, sexual problems. At present there are few clear ethical and legal guidelines for those in the helping professions. Recognition of this shortcoming plus increasing dialogue and debate suggests forthcoming change in long-held values that have undoubtedly served more to inhibit than facilitate the process and outcome of therapy.

Summary

This chapter has attempted to illustrate a variety of issues pertaining to the diagnoses, evaluation, and treatment of those behaviors commonly referred to as sexual disorders. Some of the more relevant biological and sociocultural influences or determinants of sexual behavior were described, followed by a discussion of the role that learning plays in the development and maintenance of sexual behavior. Examples of empirical evidence supporting the influence of psychological learning principles were given. Both indirect and direct treatment approaches were described, with more emphasis given to the latter. Following discussion of the many problems involved when labels are used in reference to sexual problems, an alternative classification scheme (i.e., ROBI) was proposed, which describes a multitude of sexual "disorders" confronting the clinician. The four major areas of classification within the scheme include sexual problems involving response, object choice, behavior, and identity. A review of treatment procedure, based on psychological learning theory, was presented along with comments as to the efficacy of the procedures when such conclusions seemed justified by the available data. Some problems involving definition, assessment, and treatment were described, followed by a review of some of the current ethical and legal considerations regarding the treatment of sexual problems.

GLOSSARY

Assertive training: Any of several procedures designed to help the client learn to outwardly express his or her own thoughts and feelings in interpersonal relationships. The usual goal is to enable the client to stand up for, and exercise, his or her rights without denying the rights of others. The assumption underlying the procedure is that assertive behavior is antagonistic to anxiety, and therefore, when the client learns to become appropriately self-assertive, he or she will no longer be anxious in such interpersonal situations.

Aversion therapy (aversion conditioning, avoidance conditioning): Any of a wide number of procedures where the performance of an unwanted, undesirable, or inappropriate behavior is immediately followed by the application of an aversive stimulus (e.g., electric shock, nauseating drugs, shame, imagined vomiting). The usual goal is to aid the client in learning how to avoid certain behaviors that he or she no longer wishes to engage in (e.g., sexual behavior with young children, arousal to animals). The underlying assumption is that repeated association of the behavior with the negative stimulus will eventually result in the behavior acquiring some of the strong aversive properties of the negative stimulus, and the client will ultimately learn to avoid the behavior as one would the negative stimulus.

Behavior: In strict behavioral terms, any movement through space—meaning that the activity must be observable by another person. In broad terms, any activity of the client. In its use today by behavioral clinicians, the term also includes such covert or internal activity as thoughts and emotions. All views agree on the one point that such behavior must be *readily* and *reliably* identified by at least one person, even if that one is the client.

Behavioral rehearsal: A special form of role playing that enables the client to practice certain situational behaviors with the clinician before engaging in such behaviors in the actual situation. Often the procedure includes the clinician's modeling appropriate behaviors for the client to rehearse. It is assumed that much of the client's anxiety associated with the behavior will be desensitized during such rehearsal. See also *Role playing.*

Classical conditioning (Respondent conditioning, Pavlovian conditioning): One of the basic processes of learning. If the presentation of one stimulus (which does not elicit any particular response from the individual) is closely and repeatedly followed by the presentation of a second stimulus (which does elicit a specific response), eventually the presentation of the first stimulus *alone* will elicit a response similar to that which is elicited by the second stimulus alone (e.g., continued association of ringing a bell immediately followed by presentation of meat to a dog will eventually result in the dog salivating to the sould of the bell alone). In such conditioning it is said that the stimulus *elicits* a response from the individual, and such a response is called a *conditioned response.* This type of conditioning is usually seen as involuntary, and it has been demonstrated that many emotional responses are learned through such conditioning. See also *Extinction, Operant conditioning.*

Counter conditioning: A process whereby one response to a stimulus gradually becomes weaker because the client learns a new response to the same stimulus that is incompatible with the previous response (e.g., learning relaxation responses to heterosexual behavior gradually eliminates the former anxiety response).

Covert reinforcement: A procedure, based upon operant conditioning principles, designed to increase the probability of the occurrence of a certain behavior or response that the client wishes to engage in. The term covert is used because the reinforcement for the response is presented to the client in *imagination.* See also *Reinforcement, Operant conditioning.*

Covert sensitization: An aversion therapy procedure, based upon operant conditioning principles, where the *imagined* performance of an unwanted behavior is immediately followed by the application of an *imagined* aversive stimulus (e.g., vomiting, ridicule, accidents). The term sensitization denotes the attempt to build up an avoidance response to the undesirable behavior. See also *Aversion therapy, Operant conditioning.*

Desensitization: Any process that attempts to decrease an avoidance response in a desirable behavior, or situation. Usually this involves procedures designed to reduce anxiety associated with the performance of the desirable behavior, or remaining in a situation. See also *Systematic desensitization.*

Discrimination learning: A process that involves the client's learning to respond differently to somewhat similar stimuli (or situations). If the client's response to one situation is consistently followed by positive consequences (reinforcement), while the same response to a nearly similar situation is consistently followed by negative (punishment) or neutral consequences, then discrimination would be expected to eventually occur. This process is complimentary to generalization. See also *Generalization, Reinforcement.*

Extinction: A process that decreases the probability of the occurrence of a certain behavior or response that the client no longer wishes to engage in. In operant conditioning terms, extinction refers to the removal of the positive consequence (reinforcement) that has been following the undesirable behavior. When the reinforcer is removed or no longer given, the behavior will eventually weaken and finally disappear. In classical conditioning terms, extinction refers to the continued presentation of a stimulus without pairing it with presentation of a second stimulus with which it has been paired in the past (e.g., in the case of a dog who has been classically conditioned to salivate at the ringing of the bell, *continued* presentation of the bell alone without the pairing of the second stimulus, meat will eventually result in the dog's no longer salivating to the ringing bell). See also *Classical conditioning, Operant conditioning; Reinforcement.*

Generalization: A process whereby the client responds in much the same way to somewhat similar, but different, stimuli (or situations). If the client who has learned to respond in a certain way to one particular situation responds in the same way to a second but somewhat similar situation, generalization is said to have occurred (e.g., the child who calls *all* moving vehicles "cars"). It is expected that the response will be less likely when the second stimulus is quite different from the original stimulus (e.g., the child may or may not call an airplane a "car"). This process is complementary to discrimination. See also *Discrimination learning.*

Learning: Learning may be defined as a relatively permanent change in behavior potentiality that occurs as a result of reinforced practice, and *excludes* any behavior that results from direct intervention in the functioning of the nervous system or from maturation. Learning is usually regarded as a more general concept than conditioning. Conditioning is most often limited to classical and operant forms, whereas learning is seen by many as including vicarious and modeling processes in addition to conditioning. However, there is some disagreement between learning theorists who believe thal all learning follows from the simple conditioning forms, and those who feel that additional principles are required to explain the more complex forms of learning.

Modeling (Imitation learning): A procedure of vicarious learning designed to help the client learn new behaviors that he or she wishes to engage in. One such procedure involves the clinician's first demonstrating the behavior to be learned then immediately guiding the client through an imitation of the performance. Other procedures involve the use of filmed or videotaped models. See also *Behavior rehearsal, Role playing, Vicarious learning.*

Operant: Any voluntary behavior or class of behaviors that generally first appear as a random movement on the part of the individual. The term means that certain behaviors "operate" on the environment to produce consequences. Strictly speaking such behaviors are called "emitted" behaviors, as contrasted with *respondents,* which are called "elicited" behavior. See also *Operant conditioning, respondent.*

Operant conditioning (Instrumental conditioning, Skinnerian conditioning: One of the basic processes of learning, which states that the consequences immediately following a certain behavior will affect the future occurrence of that behavior. When a certain behavior (or operant) is followed by positive consequences (positive reinforcement, or "reward"), then the probability of the occurrence of that behavior in the future is increased, depending upon the number of times such consequences follow the behavior. Conversely, when a certain behavior (or operant) is followed by negative consequences (an aversive stimulus, or "punishment"), then the probability of the occurrence of that behavior in the future is decreased, depending upon the number of times such consequences follow the behavior. Generally speaking, operant conditioning implies that the consequence is *contingent* upon the response and not just a random happening. See also *Classical conditioning, Contingency, Operant, Punishment, Reinforcement.*

Premack principle: A principle stating that frequently occurring behaviors are self-reinforcing, or rewarding and desirable in themselves, and that they can be used to reinforce and increase the occurrence of other behaviors that occur with less frequency. In practice, such frequency occuring behaviors are made *contingent* upon the client first engaging in the lower frequency behavior that the client wishes to increase. See also *Contingency; Operant conditioning; Reinforcement.*

Reinforcement: In operant conditioning terms, any event or consequence that follows a behavior (or operant) and increases the probability of the behavior occuring in the future. Any stimulus or event whose immediate *presentation* after a behavior *increases* the probability of the future occurrence of that behavior, is called a *positive reinforcer* (e.g., a man kissing his lover immediately after she has presented him with a gift may increase the probability of her gift-giving in the future, *if* she considers the kiss a positive consequence). Any stimulus or event whose immediate *withdrawal* after a behavioral *increases* the probability of the future occurrence of that behavior is called a *negative reinforcer* (e.g., if the man immediately stops being cold and argumentative with his lover when she presents him with a gift, this may increase the probability of her gift-giving in the future, *if* she views his cold and argumentative behavior as negative).

On the other hand, any stimulus or event whose immediate *presentation* after a behavior *decreases* the probability of the future occurrence of that behavior is called an *aversive stimulus* or *punishment* (e.g., if the man becomes argumentative and cold immediately after his lover presents him with a gift, this may decrease the probability of her gift-giving in the future, *if* she views his cold and argumentative behavior as negative). It should be clear from the foregoing that negative reinforcement and punishment are not the same and operate in different ways. In sum, reinforcement refers to events that *increase* the probability of a response, and punishment refers to events that *decrease* the probability of a response. Whether a specific stimulus or event is positive or aversive can be determined only by its effect on the behavior of the individual (i.e., does it increase or decrease the probability of a future response?). In classical conditioning terms, the pairing of the second stimulus that elicits a response with the first stimulus that initially does not elicit a response is referred to as reinforcement. See also *Classical conditioning, Contingeny, Extinction, Operant conditioning.*

Successive approximation (Shaping Approximation conditioning): An operant conditioning procedure designed to enable the client to learn new behaviors or responses by initially reinforcing those existing behaviors in the client's repertoire that most closely resemble the final desired behavior. Gradually, reinforcement is made contingent upon closer and closer approximations of the final desired behavior, until such time as the desired behavior itself is engaged in and reinforced. See also *Operant conditioning, Reinforcement.*

Systematic desensitization: A procedure designed to eliminate maladaptive anxiety. The procedure typically involves three basic steps: 1. Training the client in deep muscle relaxation; 2. creating a written hierarchy of anxiety-producing behaviors or stimuli associated with the problem situation; and 3. having the client imagine engaging in the behaviors, while being in a deeply relaxed state. Desenstitization begins with the least anxiety-provoking imagined behavior, which is repeatedly presented until the client reports no associated anxiety. Subsequently, each item is treated in a similar fashion until the hierarchy is complete. See also *Counter conditioning, Desensitization, Emotive imagery, Guided imagining, Implosive therapy, Successive approximation.*

Vicarious learning: A broad term that covers any learning process whereby the client changes or acquires a behavior as a result of observing the behavior of another person, either directly, or through the use of films or videotapes, or through reading books or magazines. Many of the procedures have been variously labeled observational learning, imitation, identification, modeling or social facilitation. See also *Behavior rehearsal, Modeling, Role playing.*

CRIME AND DELINQUENCY

ASHER R. PACHT
EUGENE H. STRANGMAN

A chapter on crime and delinquency in an abnormal psychology book is rare. Despite the impact that crime has on our everyday lives, such texts often treat criminal and delinquent behavior briefly and inadequately, usually under the rubric of conduct or character disorders. Since such treatment focuses on antisocial personality disorders, sexual deviations, and the addictive disorders, the majority of criminal and delinquent activities are ignored, making an integrated discussion of crime and delinquency impossible.

In spite of the magnitude of the problems created by criminal and delinquent behavior, crime has only recently begun to receive much consideration from psychologists. Basic knowledge about criminal and delinquent behavior is minimal. The complexity of the issue slows an understanding of such behavior, and is complicated by questions such as : What constitutes criminal or delinquent behavior: Who defines it? What is considered a crime? How do we identify a criminal? What characterizes a criminal? Are criminals distinguishable by demographic, psychological, emotional, educational, and/or socioeconomic variables? What is the etiology of crime? Are crimes, criminal behaviors, or criminals influenced by the prevailing social, moral, or economic climate? There are no simple answers to these questions, and there is no consensus about how to address them. For example, unlike the study of dysfunctional behaviors described elsewhere in this book, criminal and delinquent behaviors are seldom defined by clinical professionals or by behavioral researchers. Although these behaviors are studied by a variety of disciplines including sociology, biology, criminology, and psychology, they are primarily defined by the criminal justice system using a legalistic base. Understanding is further hampered by the emotional and moral attitudes generated by public discussion of crime.

Before proceeding, it is essential that we clarify what constitutes criminal and delinquent behavior. These behaviors are defined by state and federal statutes that are ostensi-

Case History

Thomas L., a sixteen-year-old high-school student, was admitted to a northeastern metropolitan hospital on the order of the juvenile court, following conviction for juvenile delinquency. He had been charged with illegal possession of a pistol, resulting in the fatal shooting of a neighbor's child. He lived in a lower-middle-class neighborhood with his adoptive parents.

According to the court record, Thomas was an illegitimate child who was abandoned by his mother at birth and brought up in a large orphanage until he was seven.

. . . Thomas attended many different schools, and got into difficulty over his behavior in each. He was extremely disrespectful to teachers, restless and overactive in the classroom, frequently involved in fights, and truanted frequently. Fighting and generally destructive behavior were also characteristic of him outside of school, although whenever he broke and otherwise marred articles at home he attempted to conceal his responsibility by lying and blaming others. He often stole small articles from stores and, if apprehended, lied about how he happened to have the objects in his possession.

. . . Shortly before his current difficulty began, when staying with a neighbor while his parents were at work, he rummaged through their closets and happened upon an old German Luger and a box of bullets. He took these and went to the school playground in order to show off his new acquisition. The first person he met was a neighbor's daughter who was much younger than he, and who didn't believe the gun was real. In order to prove it Thomas loaded the gun. His stories as to what ensued were variable. According to one version of the story there was a noise which startled both children, and in turning rapidly the gun was discharged, hitting the child in the temple and killing her instantaneously. However, Thomas told other versions in which he claimed that he didn't reaize the gun was loaded. . . . There were no witnesses to the accident, but after the shot a number of people saw Thomas riding away, and called the police. Thus, when Thomas returned, the police were already on the scene and looking for him. He first told them that another boy had done the shooting, fully described this imaginary boy, and claimed he had just arrived for the first time. He appeared very calm and composed and continued to alibi, frequently changing the story in repetition. When his parents arrived on the scene he broke down and admitted he had done the shooting, but insisted that it was accidental. He took the police to the abandoned weapon and explained that he had been too frightened to tell the truth earlier. His mother said, "Tommy never tells the truth even when it's easier." He was convicted by the juvenile court and referred to a psychiatric clinic for observation.

Reprinted with permission from M. Zax & G. Strickler. *Patterns of psychopathology: Case studies of behavioral dysfunction.* New York: Macmillan, 1963 (pp. 238–240).

bly based on the needs and wants of their contituents. It is these legal definitions that answer the question of what constitutes criminal or delinquent behavior, rather than the conceptualizations of behavioral experts. The police officer, as gatekeeper of the criminal justice system, decides whether or not to make an arrest. This judgment is critical in determining whether or not an individual is engaging in criminal behavior. A final disposition may be made by a prosecutor who decides to drop or press charges, or by a judge or jury ruling on guilt or innocence. While behavioral science experts may get involved in various ways between arrest and conviction or release, they do not directly define criminal behavior or determine whether or not the individual is guilty of engaging in such behavior.

Because legal definitions are politically created, they differ from one jurisdiction to another. An individual may be arrested and convicted for the crime of gambling in Wisconsin, an activity which is legal in Nevada.

Similarly, society's definition of deviant behavior changes over time, and modification of our law tends to follow those changes (albeit at a slower pace). Drinking alcohol, a violation of the law during prohibition, is now perfectly legal for adults. Some states have made efforts to decriminalize victimless crimes, e.g., common drunkenness, homosexuality between consenting adults, and possession of small amounts of marijuana. Such efforts will continue since victimless crimes comprise a large portion of arrests and require a significant expenditure of criminal justice energy and funds. Criminal behavior, then, is any behavior that violates the criminal statutes of a particular jurisdiction. It must be emphasized that the focus of the definition is on the criminal activity itself, rather than on the psychological state of the individual. The latter may be a "mitigating circumstance" when determining the specific charge and/or sentence.

In defining criminal behavior a distinction should be made between felony offenses and misdemeanors. Misdemeanors are less serious offenses, usually of the nuisance type. Thus, an individual might be charged with disorderly conduct, a misdemeanor, for verbally abusing another person and with assault, a felony, or for physically attacking an individual. Similarly, in most jurisdictions theft of a small amount of money is considered a misdemeanor while theft of a larger amount is a felony.

Another important distinction is that between criminal and delinquent behavior. Although all criminal behavior is considered delinquent, behaviors labeled delinquent do not necessarily involve violation of criminal statutes. In common usage, delinquent behavior is associated only with juvenile offenses. Juveniles are always considered delinquent if found guilty of anything defined as illegal for adults. Under the guise of protecting juveniles, however, many jurisdictions adjudicate them as delinquent for committing acts that are not criminal for adults. These "status offenses" include chronic truancy, incorrigibility, and sexual promiscuity. It is ironic that the juvenile may spend more time incarcerated for the offense of truancy than an adult might spend following a conviction for robbery, manslaughter, or even some degrees of sexual assault. Fortunately, an increasing number of states are moving in the direction of removing status offenses from their juvenile codes or trying to find alternatives to incarceration that deal more effectively with juveniles.

In sum, criminal behavior is any behavior defined as illegal by state or federal statutes rather than by behavioral science. It is, however, the judgment of the arresting officer, the prosecutor, judge, or jury that determines disposition in each individual case. Thus, behaviors defined as criminal not only vary from state to state but also from situation to situation. Illegal behaviors are described as either misdemeanors or felonies. Finally, although all criminal behavior is usually considered delinquent behavior, delinquent behavior includes juvenile status offenses as well as violations of criminal statutes.

Explanations of criminal behavior

For a variety of reasons, there is no satisfactory theory of criminal behavior. One obvious problem in developing useful explanations is the heterogeneity of behaviors labeled criminal. Theorists must account not only for acts of murder and rape, but also for tax evasion and check forgery. To date, this problem remains unresolved.

Another problem affecting research in general that has an even greater impact on criminologic research involves human biases, attitudes, and feelings that distort the data. This is particularly true when researching such acts as murder and rape. Even beyond this, however, given the nature of criminal behavior, there are serious limitations on methodology and design. Ethical considerations prevent us from creating a laboratory experiment to isolate the variables involved in many criminl acts, e.g., murder and assault. Furthermore, it is impossible to control many important variables in the field study of criminal behavior.

Another major obstacle to the explanation of criminal behavior is the selection of the population to be studied. Halleck (1967) notes that in our system of criminal justice, two peole may engage in the same behavior with one being defined as a criminal and the other not, i.e., one may be arrested and convicted and the other may not even be arrested or else found not guilty. The question for the scientist in this instance is, which population should be studied, even assuming there is the choice to study the latter group? Megargee highlights the problem by concluding, "It can be seen that prisoners, who are the subjects typically studied, represent a very small and highly biased sample of the population of people committing illegal acts. The more intelligent, skilled, and experienced criminals are most likely to avoid detection; of those identified by the police, those with the best connections, the greatest financial resources, the most stable work and family backgrounds, the fewest prior offenses, and the whitest skins are most likely to avoid arrest, conviction, and imprisonment" (1975, p. 4). Much of the data for theory building has unfortunately come from this "highly biased sample" of imprisoned criminals.

If the dilemmas faced in the study of criminal behavior are ever to be resolved, the solutions are unlikely to emanate from a single discipline. As a research discipline, psychology has not given the study of criminal behavior much attention nor has it engaged in interdisciplinary research. Historically, psychologists have not found the field very attractive. Consequently, the volume of well designed psychological research on criminal behavior is small. Most departments of psychology do not have specific programs dealing with crime and delinquency, and only in recent years, as federal funding of research has become available, has there been an increasing interest in psychological research related to criminal behavior. In terms of research, teaching, and theory building, the discipline that has attended most closely to the areas of crime and delinquency has been sociology. Since only a few universities have schools of criminal justice or departments of criminology, most criminology efforts are still carried out within departments of sociology. Social work and, to a much lesser extent, psychiatry have generally focused on applied rather than theoretical aspects of the field.

In light of the many obstacles to research on criminal behavior, it is not surprising that much of the work is plagued with methodological problems. A number of theories from different disciplines have, nevertheless, been advanced. The earliest theorizing about the etiology of criminal behavior attributed the cause of crime and delinquency to a biological defect. In the last quarter of the 19th century, Lombroso (1918) advanced the theory of criminal atavism. Based on his examination of skulls, brains, and pathological anomalies of convicted offenders, he became convinced that they resembled those of primitive man. He concluded that criminals must, therefore, possess instincts preventing them from adjusting adequately to an advanced, civilized society. Goring (1913) rejected Lombroso's theory while retaining a base of physical and mental inferiority for criminality. Hooten (1939), a physical anthropologist, basing his conclusions on a large samle of male criminals, advanced the notion that criminal behavior stemmed directly from inherited biological inferiority. There are sufficient methodological flaws in all three studies to make the conclusions untenable.

More recently Sheldon (1949), a psychiatrist, devised a method of measuring physique in order to classify people into one of three basic body types: endomorphs (round, soft, fat bodies), ectomorphs (lean, delicate bodies), and mesomorphs (muscular bodies). He found a high degree of mesomorphism among the 200 delinquent boys that he sampled. Like his predecessors, his research has also been criticized for inadequate sampling and analysis of the data. The Gleuck's (1956), in their monumental study of delinquency, offered some support for Sheldon's theory by their finding that mesomorphs were overrepresented in their sample of delinquents. It is possible, however, to explain this overrepresentation on other grounds.

Other theorists focused on the inheritance of criminality. One technique for investigating the role of heredity is to conduct twin studies. Ashley Montague (1941) reviewed studies of criminality in twins. Such studies reveal that monozygotic (identical) twins show concordance for criminal behavior two thirds of the time, while dyzyotic (fraternal) twins both manifest criminal behavior approximately one third of the time. These findings would appear to support the conclusion that criminality is inherited. There are, however, major criticisms of such studies since they do not control for the similarity in treatment afforded identical twins. Such twins are not only more likely to be exposed to similar environments but they also are more likely to be treated similarly by family and friends than are fraternal twins. While these criticisms do not rule out the role of heredity in crime, they do point out that alternative explanations must be considered.

Other biological explanations for crime have linked crime with mental deficiency, neurological disorders, endocrine deficiencies, chromosomal abnormalities, and even eating chocolate. Neither this nor any of the others have proved definitive for crime in general or for specific crimes. For every offender who possesses a particular biological or genetic trait, there is another offender of the same type who does not. It is highly unlikely that any purely biologic theory would suffice to encompass the heterogeneity of behavior called criminal. We cannot, however, discount totally the role of biology in the development of criminal behavior. Some current theorists believe that behavioral predispositions and potentialities are inherited, but are highly dependent upon the appropriate socioenvironmental conditions for emergence. This thinking exemplifies a trend toward multidisciplinary approaches to understanding criminal behavior.

Sociologists have severely criticized theories focusing on biology and other individual deficits as being too narrow to adequately explain criminal behavior. Instead they have offered explanations that attempt to account for the influence of the environment upon the individual. One of the most influential of the sociological theories was developed by Sutherland (1947). His theory of *differential association* attempts to explain criminal behavior as the result of a series of natural occurrences. The criminal is not sick or deficient, but rather learns criminal behavior through intimate association with others who are engaged in criminal activity. In other words, a series of socialization experiences shape the nature and direction of the individual's activities by permitting, if not actively encouraging, illegal behavior.

Another variety of sociological theorizing highlights culture or value conflict. Merton (1938) has focused attention on the values clash he has observed in American society. He would argue that the major orientation of American society is success, and further, that success is defined largely in material terms. Thus, while individuals are pushed in the direction of desiring wealth, opportunities for reaching that goal arc not equal for everyone. When opportunities to reach goals are incongruent with the goals themselves "anomie" results, and the conditions are ripe for the development and expression of socially deviant behavior. In a similar vein, Cloward and Ohlin (1960) have theorized that where legal avenues to material success do not exist but illegal ones do, the latter will be used to achieve what is perceived as a legitimate goal.

A problem with these as well as other sociological approaches is that none answers the question of why only some persons commit crimes given the large number of people who "fit" the theories, and would therefore be predicted to commit crimes. Sociological theories are, unfortunately, no closer to an all encompassing theory of criminal behavior than are the biological theories. One problem has been the lack of attention to individual differences in favor of explanations that emphasize poor companions, poverty, broken homes, or bad neighborhoods.

In contrast to sociological explanations that focus on societal elements, the few attempts made by psychological theorists have emphasized the individual elements that contribute to the development of criminal or delinquent behavior patterns. Most of those attempts have resulted from the efforts of clinicians working with delinquents. The early explanations focused on internal dynamics that predisposed the individual to criminal or delinquent behavior. In the 1930's Aichhorn, a Viennese educator trained in psychoanalysis, argued that elements in the individual's environment were highly unlikely to cause criminal behavior unless the condition of "latent delinquency" existed within the individual. Latent delinquency was characterized by an inability to wait for need gratification, an inability to gain satisfaction of personal needs from relationships with other people, and a distinct lack of guilt. Development of these particular characteristics was attributed to the lack of a strong positive relationship with the mother during the early formative years.

Like Aichhorn, others (Redl & Wineman 1951; Friedlander, 1967) have focused on the contribution of intrapsychic dynamics to the development of delinquent behavior. In essence, they postulate that defective character development is responsible for most delinquent activity. With this emphasis on the personality structure of the individual, little attention has been paid by dynamic theorists to environmental events. For this and their general disregard of sociological variables, they have been criticized by other criminologic theorists.

Social learning theorists have offered their own explanation of delinquent or antisocial behavior. According to this theory, criminal or delinquent behavior is developed just like any other behavior. Bandura (1973) argues that behavior is acquired through direct experience as a result of rewards and punishments and by observation and consequent modeling. Acquired behavior is maintained by such things as a recognition of the probable consequences of the behavior, the reinforcement of the behavior through rewards and punishments, and by cognitive processes, which permit the individual to recognize the relationship between the behavior and its consequences. Efforts to change behavior (e.g., delinquent activities) must therefore involve strategies to deal with those factors that maintain the behavior. Social learning theorists have attempted to integrate the influence of the larger society, the local community, and the family on the development of delinquent behavior (Bandura & Walters, 1959; Eysenck, 1960; Ullmann & Krasner, 1975). Although much work needs to be done, the social learning approach offers the best hope to date for the development of an integrated theory of criminal and delinquent behavior.

Hare (1970) offers another psychological explanation of deviant behavior through his studies of *psychopathy*. Although often misused, the term psychopath is not synonymous with the term criminal. Some convicted criminals are indeed psychopaths, but not all. Similarly, some, but not all, psychopaths are not criminals. Indeed some psychopaths may be successful merchants or hold high political office. Hare examines clinical, psychometric, physiological, learning, and socialization data that appear to be associated with psychopathy and offers some tentative conclusions. For example, his data suggest that diagnosed psychopaths appear to have a higher threshold of cortical arousal than nonpsychopaths. It follows that psychopaths may seek highly stimulating activities since "run of the mill" events neither interest or excite them. For psychopaths, then, seeking of excitement may become the overriding need, with the result that little attention is paid to the consequences of the behavior. Similarly, Hare examines the other data and offers tentative explanatory hypotheses and suggests directions for further research. The limits of this approach for theory building are evident from its narrow focus on a single diagnostic entity.

The most recent and to date most comprehensive and explicit attempt to apply psychological theory and research to the explanation of criminal behavior is that of Feldman

(1977). In the preface to his book, *Criminal Behavior: A Psychological Analysis,* Feldman states:

> In recent years the extensive and well-supported findings of the experimental psychology of learning have been applied to a number of areas of applied psychology, most notably to those behaviors labeled abnormal. This book is in part an attempt to extend such an analysis to criminal behavior by reviewing, inevitably incompletely, the recent upsurge of research activity in both laboratory and field settings relevant to the explanation and control of criminal behavior. (1977, p. vii)

For the student interested in a more detailed and up-to-date review of psychological as well as biological and sociological determinants of criminal behavior his book is an ideal reference.

This brief discussion of the biological, sociological, and psychological contributions to understanding the etiology of criminal behavior makes it clear that no grand theory encompassing all aspects of criminal behavior will ever be developed. More likely is the development of several mini-theories explaining various types of categories of criminal behavior. From a clinical vantage point, it appears that some criminals offend as a result of psychological or emotional imbalance while others are more highly influenced by the sociocultural environment in which they live. For some, the particular economic circumstances of the moment exert the most powerful influence on their behavior while for others biological or neurological dysfunctions are the key factor. Progress in understanding and explaining the various criminal behaviors will be slow and will require a truly interdisciplinary effort.

Classification of offenders

Real progress in understanding delinquent and criminal behavior, will require that some system be developed for grouping those behaviors in an orderly manner. At present, no agreed-upon classification or taxonomic system exists. Various approaches have been attempted including classification by specific offense or offense clusters and by psychological type. The former have been used primarily by persons in the criminal justice system, while typologies have been favored by behavioral scientists and clinicians who are seeking to relate classification systems to treatment.

Classification of offenders based upon their specific offense is virtually useless. In most jurisdictions this would amount to a hundred or more specific categories of crimes. Somewhat less cumbersome is the FBI Uniform Crime Report, which lists 29 different crimes. This still remains, however, a very unwieldly and complex classification system of limited usefulness other than for informational purposes.

Other general systems attempt to cluster specific criminal acts into broad offense categories. Such a system might consist of a tripartite division of criminal behavior such as 1. crimes against property, 2. crimes against persons, and 3. victimless crimes. Crimes against property include all unlawful behaviors that involve damage to or unlawful possession of property belonging to others. Specific examples are burglary, larceny, criminal damage to property, and white collar crimes such as embezzling. The factor common to all these behaviors is that the offender and victim do not usually have direct contact.

Crimes against persons involve some degree of personal assault by one person upon another. They may be premeditated and deliberate, as in first degree murder, or result from an unrelated activity, as causing the death of a person when driving an auto while drunk. Unlike property offenders, crimes against persons involve face to face contact between aggressor and victim. Murder and sexual assault incur the greatest amount of public wrath, with those convicted of these crimes not only receiving the longest sentences but also typically serving a larger percentage of their sentence than those convicted of property crimes.

The third category, victimless crimes, refers to those criminal behaviors in which no other party is involved or that assume the mutual consent of the parties involved. Such behaviors as prostitution, homosexual acts, smoking marijuana, and public drunkenness fall into this category. There are current efforts in several states to decriminalize some of these behaviors and a number of jurisdictions have already done so.

The offense-based classification approaches say nothing about the personality of the offender and how to deal with him/her. Classification of offenders by type of offense assumes a homogeneity within offense types, which is not usually the case. For example, Megargee (1966), in a study of men convicted of violent crimes, found at least two vastly different personality types requiring different treatment interventions. Unfortunately offense-based systems are static and, unlike the taxonomic systems of biology or geology, are of limited usefulness. Corrections administrators and others responsible for offender programming are not interested in complex classification systems unless they provide specific direction for dealing effectively with the various types of offenders.

Over the years numerous efforts to develop functional systems have been made by sociologists, psychiatrists, and psychologists. As might be expected, the systems proposed by members of the latter two disciplines have focused on personal characteristics of offenders or delinquents. An early effort along those lines was that of Jenkins and Hewitt (1944) and confirmed by Jenkins (1966). These studies identified five groups of children sharing common symptoms: shy-seclusive, overanxious-neurotic, hyperactive, undomesticated, and socialized delinquents. Another breakdown is between *social* delinquents and *neurotic* delinquents. Neurotic delinquents were also found to be more responsive to adult influence, in contrast to social delinquents who responded more readily to peer pressures. Recent attempts to develop classification systems have been both more sophisticated and more ambitious in scope than these early efforts. The paragraphs below discuss three of the better known current approaches.

In the early 1960s Warren (1966), along with colleagues in the California Youth Authority, began work on what became known as the Interpersonal Maturity Level Classification System. The theoretical base for this system was formulated by Sullivan, Grant, and Grant (1957) and postulates seven successive stages of maturity ranging from the least mature (i.e., the interpersonal interactions of the new born infant—Level 1) to an ideal of social maturity (Level 7), which is seldom reached. Fixation can occur at any age. In their view, stages two to four characterize the juvenile delinquent population. Following are descriptions of the way persons classified at these three levels perceive the world:

Maturity Level 2 (I_2): The individual whose interpersonal understanding and behavior are integrated at this level is primarily involved with demands that the world take care of him. He sees others primarily as "givers" or "withholders" and has no conception of interpersonal refinement beyond this. He is unable to explain, understand, or predict the behavior or reactions of others. He is not interested in things outside himself except as a source of supply. He behaves impulsively, unaware of the effects of his behavior on others.

Maturity Level 3 (I_3): The individual who operates at this level is attempting to manipulate his environment in order to get what he wants. In contrast to level 2, he is at least aware that his own behavior has something to do with whether or not he gets what he wants. He still does not differentiate, however, among people except to the extent that they can or cannot be useful to him. He sees people only as objects to be manipulated in order to get what he wants. His manipulations may take the forms either of conforming to the rules of whoever seems to have the power at the moment ("If you can't lick them, join them") or of the type of maneuvering characteristic of a "confidence man" ("Make a sucker out of him before he makes a sucker out of you"). He tends to deny having any disturbing feelings or strong emotional involvement in his relationships with others.

Maturity Level 4 (I_4): An individual whose understanding and behavior are integrated at this level has internalized a set of standards by which he judges his and others' behavior. He is aware of the influence of others on him and their expectations of him. To a certain extent, he is aware of the effects of his own behavior on others. He wants to be like the people he admires. He may feel guilty about not measuring up to his internalized standards. If so, conflict produced by the feelings of inadequacy and guilt may be internalized with consequent neurotic symptoms or acted out in anti-social behavior. Instead of guilt over self-worth, he may feel conflict over values. Or, without conflict, he may admire and identify with delinquent models, internalizing their delinquent values. (Warren, 1966, pp. 1–2)

From these three maturity levels the research group headed by Warren identified nine delinquent subtypes that represent an attempt to classify the individual's response to his/her view of the world. The determination of the subtype is made on the basis of information obtained during a semi-structured interview conducted by a highly trained interviewer. Detailed lists of behavioral items describe each of the nine subtypes, defining the way in which the individual perceives and responds to the world and is in turn responded to by others. Of greatest importance is the use of these descriptions as the basis for the treatment approach to be used.

For those charged with the responsibility of caring for delinquents, this system is very useful. Not only does it classify, but it also denotes the type of treatment approach to be used with a particular subtype. The empirical work designed to test the validity of this system, however, has been equivocal. Research carried out by the California Youth Authority staff has been generally supportive of the system (Palmer 1973). Research results on populations elsewhere have been mixed (Lerner 1971).

A second major attempt by a researcher to develop a psychological classification system has been carried out by Quay and his associates (Quay 1964; Quay & Peterson, 1967; Quay & Parsons, 1970). In contrast to the theoretically derived system of Warren et al., Quay used an empirical approach to classification and employed the technique of factor analysis to develop his dimensions of juvenile delinquency. His sources of data included behavioral ratings, case history ratings, and self-report questionnaire responses. From these data he isolated a varying number of factors, which he describes as personality dimensions. The factor dimensions are: 1. inadequate-immature delinquency; 2. neurotic-disturbed delinquency; 3. unsocialized-psychopathic delinquency; 4. social-subcultural delinquency; 5. family dissension; and 6. school maladjustment. The greatest weakness of this approach appears to be an inconsistency resulting from the use of different data sources, which produce different sets of dimensions. It should also be noted that the dimensions produced by the factor analyses are not "pure" although the first four are believed to be relatively pure factorial types.

One exciting aspect of Quay's approach has been the application to the development of treatment programming at the Federal Bureau of Prisons' Robert F. Kennedy Youth Center at Morgantown, West Virginia. Here, youthful offenders are grouped into homogeneous living units and specially selected staff are trained to work in programs developed to meet needs based on the Quay dimensions. The program is being researched and final results are not yet available. Early results are sufficiently encouraging so that Quay has been asked to develop a similar approach for adult offenders. Empirical analysis over time, however, will be necessary to determine the ultimate worth of the program.

The third and most recently developed system is that of Megargee and his associates (1977a,c) at Florida State University. This approach is based on personality characteristics, using a profile analysis of the Minnesota Multiphasic Personality Inventory. Ten types of offenders have been delineated. Research conducted to date indicates that there are highly significant differences among the ten subgroups with respect to behavior, social histories, life styles, and personality patterns. Furthermore, assignment of an individual to one or another of the subgroups implies a differential treatment approach. To avoid the problems associated with premature closure, the researchers have chosen to use nondescriptive terms (e.g., Group How, Group Item) rather than the psychological classifications. They believe that further analysis is necessary on other populations before descriptive labels can be applied to the subgroups.

Megargee (1977c) has delineated seven criteria by which he says a taxonomic system would be judged with respect to its usefulness in a criminal justice setting. The system should: 1. be sufficiently complete so that most of the offenders in an agency an be classified; 2. reduce ambiguity through the use of clear operational definitions; 3. be reliable; 4. be valid; 5. be dynamic, so that changes in an individual will result in a change in classification; 6. provide implications for treatment for each classification; and 7. be economical, so that large numbers of offenders can be classified with minimal expense and personnel. Megargee (1977c) notes that their system meets the first five criteria and that research is currently being conducted to determine whether the treatment implied by the classification is in fact effective. The approach suggested by this typology has considerable merit and should be pursued by other investigators.

Regardless of the typology involved, research must demonstrate that the specific system can be generalized to offenders in other settings who differ in age, sex, offense patterns, cultural backgrounds, etc. When this is accomplished we will have taken a crucial step in the development of an adequate, reliable and valid predictive assessment system, which is essential to our understanding and treatment of criminal and delinquent behavior.

Crime among women*

It is striking but not surprising that female criminality in the United States has been almost completely ignored by criminologists, lawyers, sociologists, psychologists, and others involved in the criminal justice system. Even in criminology textbooks the topic of female criminality has been covered in a chapter or less. There are at least three major reasons for including a section on women in crime in an abnormal psychology text. One is to deal with the popular myth that increased criminality among women involves more violent and aggressive crimes. The second is to dispel the belief that any increase in female crime is a product of the women's rights movement. The third is to describe the theories about the nature of female criminality and the disservice of those theories to the treatment of women in our criminal justice system from time of arrest to point of release.

"Traditionally, most writers on the subject of women in crime have traced female criminality to biological and/or psychological bases, with virtually no discussion of such social-structural considerations as the state of the economy, occupational and educational opportunities, divisions of labor based on sex roles, and differential association" (Simon, 1975, p. 4). Explanations have been relatively simplistic and often suggestive of single cause-effect relationships in which women are divided into normal or "good" women, and criminal or "bad" women.

Such adjectives as devious, deceitful, emotional, intellectually dull, passive, lonely, dependent, and pathetic are used by various writers to describe female criminals and delinquents. At the turn of the century, Lombroso (1918) described the "born female crinimal" as "excessively erotic, weak in maternal feeling, inclined to dissipation . . . who also has the worst qualities of woman: namely, an excessive desire for revenge, cunning, cruelty, love of dress, and untruthfulness, forming a combination of evil tendencies which often results in a type of extraordinary wickedness" (1918, pp. 187–88). Women criminals often are not even considered worthy of the grudging respect

*The authors are indebted to Ms. Barbara Van Horne for her significant contributions in the preparation of this section.

given male felons, who are at least seen as a threatening force.

Although the theorists differ on specific rehabilitation programs, ranging from sterilization to psychoanalysis, the basic focus is on individual change, rather than a modification of environment and/or social roles. Thus, the correctional system has theoretical justification for treating women as deviant, mentally unbalanced, or inferior and in need of control and modification for their own good.

A current question about the pattern of women's crime asks if there is a trend toward violent and aggressive offenses. The yearly FBI *Uniform Crime Reports* are offered as supporting evidence of an increase. The latest report (U.S. Dept. of Justice, 1977) shows a 58 percent increase in arrests of females between 1968 and 1977, compared with a 13 percent increase for males. The percent change for violent crimes for the same period was 72 percent for women and only 49 percent for men.

Without closely examining these figures, such rates can cause alarm. They are, however, misleading. For example the comparison of 1968 and 1977 statistics show a 100 percent increase in arrests of females for robbery (considered a violent crime in the FBI report), compared with a 45 percent increase for males. This figure is less alarming when it is noted that it results from an increase of 2663 females arrested compared to an increase of 20,252 males. These statistics, therefore, cannot be cited as proof of a significant trend toward increased violence among women. Since women have always been a minority in the criminal justice system, any increase in arrests results in a substantially higher percent change over time. An examination of the FBI data also indicates that the greatest arrest increases for women were in the property crime category, while for men the greatest increase was in violent crimes. Females constituted approximately 10 percent of the arrests for violent crimes in 1960 and that figure has remained constant through 1977.

Considering an even longer historical perspective, some important patterns become even clearer. A restrospective study (Rans 1976) reviewed the records of 3,000 inmates admitted to an Iowa Women's Prison between 1918–1975. The data on violent crimes indicated that in Iowa, at least, more women were sent to prison for assault between 1945–49 than during any other time before or since. Figures for murder also lend no support to the notion of increased violence among women criminals. Over 10 percent of new admissions to the Iowa facility carried a murder conviction in the early 1920s. Between 1970–75 the figure has risen to 11 percent, hardly a statistically significant increase.

Economic crimes, however, do show a sharp increase. Since 1960 crimes involving money, such as forgery, embezzlement, and larceny, have shown a 40 percent increase. Rather than being tied to the women's movement, however, women's criminal activities appear to be more related to the economic forces of inflation, depression, unemployment, and family responsibilities than to any other factor. The population of women at the Iowa Reformatory was highest in the early 1930s, during the height of the Great Depression. The second highest population peak was reached during the economic slump of the early 1960s.

These findings suggest that women's crimes reflect women's status in society. Women react to economic forces, to social roles, and to psychological needs. Historically women have not been in a position, economically, socially, or psychologically, to be aggressive leaders in crime. Traditionally, they have been subservient to males in crime as well as in the rest of their lives. For the most part they are petty offenders who shoplift, use illicit drugs, pass bad checks, and become involved in prostitution. They may act as accomplices to men in offenses such as robbery. They also commit "crimes of passion" primarily against husbands and lovers, but sometimes against children. Women's lack of participation in "big time" crime has reflected their role in the larger social class structure. As that is slowly changing with more women gaining positions of control and power in the legal marketplace, they might be expected to attain similar positions in the illegal world.

Following arrest, adult women appear to fare better than their male counterparts in court. Despite the increase in the number of arrests, the number of women incarcerated has shown only a minimal change. Women also tend to receive lighter sentences than men. Women who are sent to prison tend to come disproportionately from poor whites, blacks, and other minorities. "A recent national survey of female offenders found that 64 percent of the institutionalized women are minorities. Findings are also confirmed that incarcerated adult women are most often poor, uneducated, come from a racial minority, and usually have the responsibility for themselves and their children.

Despite the leniency shown to adult women offenders, juvenile courts have traditionally given girls more severe treatment than boys. Girls are more frequently brought to the attention of the courts for status offenses. The Juvenile Delinquency and Youth Crime Task Force Report of the President's Commission on Law Enforcement and the Administration of Justice (1967) noted a major discrepancy in court referrals between girls and boys. Over half the girls, in contrast to one-fifth the boys, were referred for noncriminal delinquent activities. Despite the generally less serious nature of the offenses by girls, they are usually detained longer than their male counterparts (Klein & Kress, 1976).

For both girls and women, it is likely that the roles of women in our society along with the prevalent theories of female criminality influence police officers, case workers, judges, and juries to treat female offenders as being inferior and childlike and, therefore, in need of special protection. Along with the changing status of women in our society, we also need a fresh conceptualization of female criminality that avoids the stereotypical thinking of the current theories.

Methods of dealing with offenders

We have discussed the difficulties in explaining, classifying, and predicting criminal behavior. We have also noted that incarcerated criminals represent a biased population for research, theory building, and developing strategies to prevent crime. The remainder of this chapter will be devoted to a discussion of what to do with those who are arrested and convicted.

Throughout human history, society has sought ways to deal with law breakers. These have ranged from the ingenious to the brutal and have often been ingeniously brutal. Physical punishment, public ridicule, capital punishment, and imprisonment have all been used. In the book of Genesis, Joseph was imprisoned for allegedly dallying with another man's wife. Socrates was incarcerated and ultimately put to death for allegedly corrupting Athenian youth. For much of our history, flogging was a standard punishment for offenses against the public morality. In early colonial times the pillory and stock were also used for such infractions. Man's inhumanity to man is nowhere better demonstrated than in our treatment of criminals. While an "eye for an eye" standard still prevails in some cultures, most civilized societies rely almost exclusively on imprisonment as the major way of dealing with those found guilty of serious crimes.

In a democracy, depriving an individual of the freedom to move and speak freely is no small punishment, and society must have some defensible reasons for such action. What are society's reasons for incarceration? Most institutions today are referred to as "correctional" institutions, a name that seems to imply an underlying philosophy. It may be inferred that the purpose of the correctional institution is to "correct," or to rehabilitate. Rehabilitation, has long been a stated purpose for incarcerating individuals and the basis for investment of psychological services in correctional settings. Other purposes of incarceration, however, have been proposed by various experts in the field. They fall into four general categories: punishment, deterrence, incapacitation, and rehabilitation. Despite the primary interest of psychologists in rehabilitation, we would like to examine briefly the three other reasons for imprisonment.

The loudest voices heard these days belong to those declaring that the purpose of imprisonment should be punishment. While not a new point of view, the pendulum is once again swinging in the direction of increased emphasis on punishment as the primary purpose of imprisonment. According to this view, the message of imprisonment should be "because we don't approve of your behavior, you will have to suffer by giving up your freedom." It is unclear, however, whether persons are sent to prison *as* punishment or *for* punishment. If the public and correctional administrators hold the latter attitude, it justifies the brutal and inhuman condition all too frequently found in places of detention. Many prisons are truly the outhouses of society and, for many, prisoners are the last remaining "good" scapegoats. Despite efforts in many jurisdictions to institute more humane conditions, society will continue to incarcerate criminal offenders both *as* punishment and *for* punishment.

Deterrence is closely related to punishment as a reason for incarceration. The proponents of punishment argue that imprisonment deters individuals from committing further crimes when they are released and maintain that those who have not yet committed a crime are deterred from doing so because they know the consequences of such behavior. The evidence of the deterrent value of imprisonment, however, is equivocal. For example, statistics comparing states and countries with capital punishment to those which do not show no significant difference in murder rate per 100,000 population. The murder rate may even be higher in those jurisdictions with capital punishment. There are no significant data, however, with respect to the number of individuals who are dissuaded from committing criminal acts because of the possibility of imprisonment if caught. If punishment is to be an effective deterrent it must be both swift and certain. Neither of these adjectives can be applied to the criminal justice system as it currently functions within the United States.

Confinement of the incarcerated individual thus preventing further criminal activity is known as incapacitation, and is the third reason given for incarceration. Regardless of the deterrent effect of imprisonment, at least he/she is prevented from engaging in criminal behavior in society while confined. For a small number of offenders, incapacitation may be the only way of protecting society. These offenders have a history of confinement and repeated criminal activity. Since for them incarceration has no deterrent effect, the only recourse may be to confine them as long as legally possible.

Any one of these reasons may be considered a legitimate basis for incarceration from society's point of view. Punishment serves the dual purpose of allowing society its "pound of flesh" while also serving as a deterrent of further criminal behavior. Incapacitation may be seen as necessary for those relatively few who seem unable to avoid serious criminal activity.

Is rehabilitation a legitimate reason for incarceration? Of major significance to psychologists is the antitreatment stance that appears to be gaining momentum. Much of the impetus for this stance has come from the writings and speechs of Robert Martinson. He and his colleagues (Lipton, Martinson & Wilks, 1975) analyzed some 231 studies of treatment about which Martinson concludes: "*With few and isolated exceptions, the rehabilitative efforts that have been reported so far have had no appreciable effect on recidivism.* Studies that have been done since our survey was completed do not present any major grounds for altering that original conclusion" (Martinson, 1974). Although a careful examination of the Martinson research reveals a number of inconsistencies, and although he has been taken to task by a number of correctional researchers (Adams, 1976; Palmer, 1975), his "nothing works" (a phrase which, by his own admission, he uses as a "shocker") is having a significant impact on correctional administrators. Norman Carlson, Director of the Federal Bureau of Prisons, has expressed his skepticism about the correctional philosophy of the past decade, which was based on the belief that offenders could be rehabilitated. There appears to be some evidence that, combined with this movement away from a philosophy of rehabilitation, a "hard line" attitude toward offenders is being adopted. Spokesmen for this point of view (e.g., Wilson, 1975) urge increased incarceration. It is noteworthy that the current trend follows closely on the heels of the most recent reform movement after the 1971 insurrection at Attica. During this period there was a declared moratorium on the building of new correctional institutions and an emphasis on the development of community programs for offenders. One result, although not necessarily related, was increased crime rate and a burgeoning of institution populations far beyond their capacities.

The criticism of offender rehabilitation and in particular psychological treatment for the offender is certainly not new. It was most clearly raised by Judge David Bazelon at a 1972 Conference on correctional psychology in an address titled "Psychologists in Corrections—Are They Doing Good for the Offender or Well for Themselves?" He suggested that psychologists "initiate a process of self-criticism and re-examination" and concluded that "psychologists have not produced any remarkable successes in the corrections field" (Bazelon, 1973, pp. 150–151).

This criticism is deserved. Psychologists (and their psychiatric colleagues) are responsible for much of the current confusion about treatment in the criminal justice system. As a group, correctional clinicians have embraced a medical (disease) model for understanding crime and delinquecy. In selling themselves and their services, they often acted as if they not only knew the causes of crime but, even more importantly, the cure. Correctional psychologists forgot what they knew about individual differences and, with few exceptions, failed to discriminate among offender needs. They assumed that most offenders were "sick" and, therefore, in need of some kind of treatment. It is particularly unfortunate that clinicians seldom bothered to check the efficacy of their programs. Despite the efforts of those few clinicians who showed imagination and creativity, who refused to accept a prescriptive disease model and who insisted on program evaluation, many of the treatment programs instituted in correctional settings have had limited effectiveness.

It is no wonder that Martinson claims that "nothing works" and that Bazelon asks whether correctional psychologists can justify their existence. It is not, in our judgment, treatment approaches per se that have failed but rather the uncritical and indiscriminate use of these approaches that has failed. In 1966 the senior author wrote, "Mental health programs have not made a significant impact on the correctional field as a whole. Both the shortcomings of the correctional environment, which has been stressed, and the shortcomings of the mental health approach in corrections, which has been ignored, have contributed to this failure. Despite these inadequacies mental health personnel can make useful contributions in the correctional setting if traditional concepts are modified and new roles are developed" (Pacht & Halleck, 1966, p. 1). Mental health personnel have still not made a significant impact on the correctional field and have been reluctant to move away from traditional approaches. It should be even clearer today that clinicians cannot generalize their knowledge about the treatment of middle-class neurotics to their work with offenders and expect it to be effective. By and large, offenders are not mentally ill and clinicians have no right to treat them as though they were. To utilize the services of clinicians effectively requires the development of intervention programs geared to helping the individual offender meet his/her goals rather than the goals the clinician or society has set for him/her. It must also be recognized that most offenders may not need nor be able to use what correctional clinicians have to offer.

A number of factors must be examined in

order to understand treatment failures and contribute to rehabilitation success. We have already noted that not all offenders are "sick" nor do all need clinical services. What then comprises the target population? The commonly used label emotionally disturbed offender usually refers to the categry of offender whose symptoms imply an internal psychological conflict. The most common example of such behavior is the psychotic individual. Terms such as emotionally disturbed or mentally ill are not applicable to the majority of offenders. There are very few offenders who could be accurately described as emotionally or mentally ill. Such labels have little utility in describing offender populations and serve only to reinforce the viability of the disease model, which has failed to prove its value in the criminal justice setting. Indeed, they fail to identify those offenders whose behavior is incapacitative both to themselves and to the community and who may be in need of clinical intervention.

A more appropriate label for the population in need of clinical intervention is 'behaviorally disordered" offenders. The primary characteristic of such persons is that they attempt to handle the anxiety generated by their conflicts by externalization rather than internalization. For example, a juvenile who was experiencing anxiety about parental rejection might manifest that anxiety in psychotic delusions and/or hallucinations (internalizations) that may require hospitalization. The same anxiety, however, may also lead to acting out against society (externalization) and result in commitment to a correctional institution as a "bad kid." Halleck (1962) has pointed out that the distinctions made between and resultant placements of individuals classified as "sick" or "bad" are often quite arbitrary. In the latter case, when the person is sent to a correctional institution the disorder is no less serious and no less in need of clinical attention.

There is an unfortunate tendency among many correctional clinicians to retain their traditional conceptualization of offenders in classical psychiatric and psychological terms. Most offenders are labeled as emotionally disturbed and prescriptive treatment programs are established to deal with their "sickness." While there are some selected types of offenders for whom traditional diagnostic and treatment programs are appropriate (Pacht, Halleck, & Ehrmenn, 1962), such approaches are wasteful and inappropriate for most offenders. It is little wonder, therefore, that many traditional programs have failed.

The basic issue facing the clinician in corrections is to determine what psychological and social mechanisms underlie the incapacitating illegal behaviors and to define strategies, in concert with the offender, for dealing with those behaviors. A model that looks at the total socialization of the individual in his/her unique surroundings and attempts to define collaboratively those areas in which his/her behavior is inadequate and/or inappropriate is preferred to the more archaic "disease" model. The use of such a model allows clinicians to include in their target population offenders who are not usually seen as being mentally disturbed. Included are persons whose primary problem may involve difficulties in impulse control, alcohol abuse, drug addiction, etc.

While it is difficult to generalize, data from the Wisconsin system would indicate that approximately one-third of all Wisconsin offenders are in need of some kind of specialized clinical intervention (Pacht 1972). That figure appears to be consistent among all offenders including juveniles and adults who are on probation, in institutions, or on parole. The crucial conclusion is that while one-third need help, as many as two-thirds of the correctional population may not need clinical intervention. To force clinical treatment on those individuals, as has been routinely done in many instances, is not only wasteful but also a disservice to the individual, the clinician, and the public. Possibly, the poor results reflected in outcome studies on correctional treatment programs may be related to established patterns of offering programs to offenders who are not in need, and inappropriate to those in need.

Since a majority of offenders may neither need nor be able to benefit from treatment programs, differential assessment is essential. Simply because individuals in the criminal justice system belong to subclasses (e.g., sex offenders) of a larger class called criminal offenders, it cannot be assumed either that they need treatment or that the treatment needs, for those who do, are the same. Although routine assessments are done in most correctional jurisdictions, they have been relatively useless. Only recently has there been a renewed emphasis on the necessity for careful assessment if we are to answer the question, "Which methods work best for *which* types of offenders and under *what* conditions or in what types of settings?" (Palmer, 1975, p. 151). To develop meaningful goal oriented strategies for treatment, offender needs and deficits in both psychological and social areas must be systematically and validly assessed.

Goal oriented strategies imply that the needs of the individual must be assessed in terms of his/her model and cultural background rather than that of the clinician. People with middle-class backgrounds are accustomed to a somewhat orderly procedure of seeking assistance when they encounter problems. They are able to postpone attention long enough to make appointments and arrange transportation. They are verbal enough to describe their difficulties to a middle-class professional. Indeed, many of them fit the YAVIS description of patients eagerly sought by psychotherapists. They are *y*oung, *a*ttractive, *v*erbal, *i*ntelligent, and *s*ensitive. By contrast, most correctional clients are PAISL. They are *p*oor, *a*ngry, *i*nadequate, *s*uspicious *l*osers. A sample profile of adult offenders is shown in Table 15.1

People with backgrounds of poverty, those from slum and transitional areas of larger cities and minority groups, particularly those discriminated against, do not accommodate to the middle-class pattern of help-seeking. They do not trust the authority figures that typically staff clinics and correctional institutions. They do not see clinicians as being sympathetic toward the kinds of crises situations that they face. Unfortunately, many clinicians have done little to dispel those perceptions. They are unwilling to give up middle-class models and adapt to the treatment requirements of their offender clients. Far too many mental health professionals see delinquents and criminals as untreatable, uncooperative, and not worth the time and effort. That stereotype establishes another block to treatment of offenders. A critical difference between prescriptive programming mandated by the disease model and treatment that follows a social systems model is the requirement that the offender be involved in planning. Treatment in correctional settings is difficult at best, and is virtually impossible if the treatment is seen as delivered by middle-class authority figures in a coercive fashion.

From the foregoing discussion, a natural question would be: Is effective clinical treatment possible in a correctional setting? In our judgment, the answer is yes providing that: (a) there is a reduction in the total dependence upon the disease model; (b) there is increased use of goal oriented assessment and treatment; (c) only those clients who need and can benefit from treatment are offered treatment; (d) an entire continuum of treatment techniques including both traditional and innovative approaches are available; and (e) a specific treatment plan is developed in concert with the client, from the available continuum. The remainder of this chapter will be devoted to describing some of the clinical as well as nonclinical treatment approaches being used in an effort to reintegrate offenders into the larger society.

Intervention strategies

The 1950s and 1960s could be called the Golden Age of Rehabilitation in criminal justice settings, particularly with respect to the use of clinicians in correctional institutions. Treatment staff and consequently treatment programs proliferated. Some of the treatment efforts were novel and appeared to achieve some success, often because of the unique efforts of the person

Table 15.1.

Adult Profile Data		*Male*	*Female*
Admitted for a violent crime		43%	31%
% of above with a prior violent conviction		30	17
Admitted for a property crime		36	8
Sentence length: less than 2 years		6	14
2–4 years		27	35
4–6 years		24	8
More than 6 years		43	43
Having a prior felony conviction		32	39
Having previous prison experience (not jail)		27	20
Prior probation experience		39	58
Having no juvenile institution experience		71	82
Current age			
18–19		11	11
20–24		36	34
25–29		25	30
30 +		28	27
Age at first offense less than 20		64	45
Race: Nonwhite		41	57
Grade completed:			
less than eighth		15	13
ninth or tenth		34	29
mean grade		7.2	7.4
Achievement:			
less than sixth grade		31	9
sixth to eighth		25	24
eight to tenth grade		23	26
mean grade		6.4	6.1
Intelligence defective or borderline defective		6	15
Region in which convicted	I	11	12
	II	13	6
(Milwaukee County)	III	51	66
	IV	14	11
	V	11	5
Months at latest job:	0	28	38
	1–5	46	38
	6–12	15	22
Percent of time employed the year prior to incarceration	0–24%	39	47
	25–49%	18	6
History of problems with alcohol		50	26
History of hard nicotine use		25	21
History of emotional or mental problems		34	33

From Flad & Associates (1976).

innovating the program. A majority, however, had only face validity and failed for many of the reasons noted in the preceding section.

In general, correctional clinicians have utilized the prevailing treatment techniques with little or no modification for the specialized needs of delinquent and criminal populations. Just as in more typical mental health settings, intervention strategies have included chemotherapy and virtually every mode and method of psychotherapy. Initially, the traditional individual and group psychotherapies were predominant. More recently, family and couples therapy approaches have been introduced. Individual therapsists have worked, as they do in most settings, from their own, unique theoretical framework, whether it be behavioral, psychoanalytic, gestalt, transactional analysis, client-centered, milieu, or eclectic.

From these various perspectives, some experimental programs, designed to meet specialized correctional needs, have been developed. Examples include institutional approaches like the Asklepieion Community and the CASE project, community based programs like Achievement Place and Meridian House, and exit programs like the Wisconsin Alcohol Education and Treatment Program. Other programs, less directly related to psychological treatment, are the prerelease programs that attempt to facilitate reentry into the community and Mutual Agreement Programming that directly involves the offender in release planning. Although not usually considered nor specifically designed as psychological treatment approaches, they serve as viable intervention strategies in the area of correctional rehabilitation. These approaches as well as the psychological treatment interventions are discussed in more detail below.

Chemotherapy has been the treatment of choice for a relatively small group of offenders. Included are those who have been diagnosed as borderline psychotic, psychotic in remission, severely depressed, and those with high levels of anxiety. The stress endemic to correctional institutions often exacerbates these conditions and a period of hospitalization may be necessary.

Traditional individual and group psychotherapies have been used in the criminal justice setting with varying degrees of success. By traditional we mean the verbal, psychodynamically based psychotherapies, i.e., the talk therapies, usually offered in the context of the disease model. Of the two, group therapy has had the greater popularity because it is more economical of staff time, reaches more clients, and makes greater use of peer rather than authoritarian pressure to encourage positive change. There is also some evidence that it is effective with selected offender groups (Pacht et al., 1962).

An important treatment approach, particularly for juveniles and adult offenders, is family therapy. This approach requires that the entire family be treated. It is based on a social systems model in which the family is viewed as operating in a dysfunctional or maladaptive fashion. Although the offender may have the most easily identified "symptom," the entire family must be treated in order to establish the requisite social climate for offender rehabilitation. This is difficult since most correctional institutions are located at great distances from offenders' home communities. The current trend toward community based treatment will provide increased opportunities for employing family therapy.

Treatment interventions based on milieu principles have been used in mental health settings for many years. Basically a group approach, they depend on peer pressure to effect changes in the behavior of patients. Milieu therapies per se have not been widely used in correctional settings. Three that have been developed for such use are guided group interaction, Aslepieion Community and resident programs for drug abusers. The first was developed specifically for use with juvenile delinquents. Based on the commonly accepted observation that adolescents are more influenced by their peers than by adults, the guided group interaction technique attempts to break down the "we" versus "them" attitude that develops between correctional institution residents and staff. When the peer culture is negative, the display of negative behavior toward staff is reinforced by peers, which serves to escalate the conflict between staff and residents. Through daily cottage meetings involving all residents and staff, guided group interaction seeks to turn the cottage peer culture into a positive force in the individual residents' lives. Proponents of the technique claim good results.

The second program, based on the principles of transactional analysis, has been introduced into at least two federal correctional institutions. It is known as the Asklepieion Community and consists of a unit of the prison (e.g., a cell block) operated entirely by the members of the community. Entrance into the community is governed by rigid criteria and continued residence in the community is dependent upon participation according to specific community rules. All members are expected to exhibit continuous growth in personal responsibility, autonomy, and community concern. To achieve this, both transactional analysis techniques and the Asklepieion "game" are used. In the latter, members of the group take turns making direct verbal attacks on each other in an attempt to break down defenses permitting the individual to take a careful look at him/herself in order to deal directly with the problems.

Residential drug treatment programs, located outside correctional institutions have served many former or potential correctional clients. Most were developed in the belief that the most effective way to assist drug abusers to "kick their habit" is through the direct influence and association with former drug abusers. Well known programs such as Synanon and Day Top Village are based on this principle and use confrontation games as a primary technique. Despite claims for the success of all these programs, their results remain equivocal because little well designed research has been done.

A related approach developed for problem drinkers is the Wisconsin Alcohol Education and Treatment Program (Goodrick, Vigdal, & Sutton, 1976). It was designed to be a voluntary, six-week program, available just prior to release, for adult male offenders whose history showed abusive use of alcohol. The program combines direct educational programs about alcohol, social skills, and assertiveness training, and more traditional group and individual counseling. Specific interventions are worked out jointly between the individual and the program staff and may include such elements as involvement in Alcoholics Anonymous and the use of Antabuse. A key feature of the program allows the resident, with staff consultation, to decide whether his individual goal will be controlled drinking or complete abstinence. Analysis of the early follow-up data supports the value of the program.

Behavior therapies are currently very popular in most mental health settings. Among the general public, however, there is often an unfortunate confusion between these therapies and the more specific aversion therapy that uses electric shock or various drugs as negative reinforcers. With offenders particularly, there is an association with the movie *Clockwork Orange,* in which the misuse of this technique had detrimental results for the client. The aversive approaches represent a type of behavior therapy used very infrequently in criminal justice systems at the present time because of their negative reputation, and the possibility that their use would be labeled "cruel and inhuman punishment" by the courts. There are, however, many behavioral approaches that, when used by trained persons, are effective without being dehumanizing. Essentially, the techniques of behavior therapy are intended to facilitate improved self-control by reducing tension and expanding the skills, abilities, and independence of individuals. Thus, individuals who have problems in controlling certain impulses can be taught socially appropriate ways in which to deal with those impulses.

A behavioral technique that appears to offer great promise to criminal justice clients is social skill training. This technique assumes that the individual lacks certain skills necessary for effective social functioning. Without these skills the individual is severely handicapped since he/she may not have socially acceptable alternatives available, and will continue to get into difficulty within both the institution and the community (Freedman, 1974). Social skills training begins with a detailed assessment of the individual's deficiencies, followed by teaching the necessary skills. Behavioral techniques utilized to teach social skills include assertiveness training, modeling, behavioral rehearsal, and relaxation. Meridian House represents an effort currently underway to use and systematically evaluate this approach with delinquent boys (McFall, 1977).

Because the nature of any prison system is conducive to the production of extreme stress, headaches, high blood pressure, anxiety, gastrointestinal problems, and other stress related symptoms occur in a significant proportion of the population. Stress management involves the application of such techniques as deep muscle relaxation and various forms of meditation. A new approach in correctional institutions is biofeedback therapy, which attempts to increase the offender's ability to self-regulate his/her own physiology to reduce tension. None of these approaches represent panaceas and clinicians will continue to search for ways to reduce institutional stress.

A number of experimental and creative approaches to treatment have been developed in juvenile settings. One such program was the "Contingencies Applicable to Special Education" or CASE project (Cohen & Filipczak, 1971). Their subject population consisted of forty-one incarcerated teenage delinquents who had engaged in crimes ranging from auto theft and house breaking to rape and homicide. Most were school dropouts who had been equally unresponsive to the educational programs offered at the National Training School for Boys. The objective of the program was to expand "the academic and social repertoires . . . through the use of operantly formulated contingency systems and the design of a special environment" (Cohen & Filipczak, 1971, p. xix). Through the use of a completely planned and controlled token economy, they were able to increase the academic growth rate two to four times the average for American public school students. Follow-up data on recidivism, often used to gauge the value of programs, showed that the CASE program delayed but did not prevent delinquents' return to incarceration. Although two-thirds less than the norm were returned during the first year, the total recidivism rate for CASE students was near the norm by the third year.

Phillips, Wolf, Fixsen, and Bailey (1976) developed the "Achievement Place Model," aimed at preventing delinquency in a sample of adolescent boys. Achievement Place is a community based, community directed, family style treatment program staffed by professional teaching parents. The purpose of Achievement Place is to educate youths in a variety of social, self-care, academic, and prevocational skill areas. Specific behavioral goals are worked out for each child, frequent feedback sessions are offered, and the whole range of educational and personal behavior is examined. The approach appears promising and is being replicated in various places around the country. Final research results are not yet available.

There are a number of intervention programs that are not primarily psychological in nature. Because they are intimately associated with offender rehabilitation, they will be briefly described. One such category of programs are the "release" programs. Most professional corrections workers would agree that the most critical period for the incarcerated resident is just prior to and just after release from an institution. In an attempt to help bridge the chasm from prison to streets, a variety of prerelease or reintegration programs have been developed. The goal of these programs is to prepare the offender for his/her adjustment to the community.

The prerelease center was a popular concept that is still used in some jurisdictions.

Typically, a few weeks before release, the offender is sent to a minimum security facility and provided with a series of classroom and field experiences designed to help him/her deal with the realities of release. Included are such things as: conditions of parole; how to get and keep a job; educational opportunities available; welfare department information; wardrobe tips; motor vehicle operation, including how to get a license and/or buy a car; budgeting and borrowing money; how to deal with legal problems; job interviews. Little effort has been expended in evaluating the effectiveness of prerelease centers and there has been a decline in their usage, although the specific reasons for the decline remain unknown.

Work release programs are another way of bridging the gulf from incarceration to release. From a financial standpoint, the period immediately following release is the most difficult for the parolee. The typical parolee is poor and does not have a readily available source of money. Finding a job is, therefore, critical for the released offender and some jurisdictions have developed work release programs for selected offenders. He/she is allowed to leave the institution to work during the day and return at night. While working, he/she is paid the going wage, which is used both to pay the institution for room and board and for a savings account to be released when parole is granted. Ideally, the work release job will be one that will continue after full release from the institution. Practically, this has been very difficult because very few offenders live in the rural communities in which most institutions are located. As community based correctional centers are developed in urban areas, the probability that a work release job can be continued after parole will be enhanced.

The halfway house programs represent still another release approach. They have been defined as "a temporary residence facility for released offenders located in the community and offering various programs assisting the re-entry of the individual into a society which has systematically excluded him. The halfway house serves to assist the released offender in successfully accomplishing the transition from the highly regimented and artificial environment of prison life to the world of daily decision-making, competition, and responsible, acceptable social conformity and interaction" (National Institute of Mental Health, 1971, p. 15). Diverse programs are operated from halfway houses and include: counseling programs for juveniles, special training for employment problems, and general survival skill training. Disparate populations, varying lengths of stays, inconsistent programming, and minimal attention to evaluation have all limited knowledge about the general success of these programs. Inconclusive data suggest, however, that halfway house programs may be very effective, but only for selected categories of offenders.

Mutual Agreement Programming (MAP) is an exciting new approach that attempts to involve the offender more collaboratively in the development of his/her treatment program. Experimental programs, initially funded in several states to test the idea, have been expanded in some jurisdictions. The basic concept is very simple and represents a dramatic move away from programming by authority. In exchange for a fixed parole date that the individual knows in advance, the offender agrees, in a written contract, to participate in and finish various treatment or training programs. After a mutual review of the offender's needs, strengths and weaknesses, a contract is negotiated between the offender and the Parole Board. The contract may include such goals as learning to read and write, attending group psychotherapy, or learning basic or advanced welding. When both the paroling authority and the individual offender are satisfied with the contract, it is signed by both and becomes legally binding. If the resident fulfills the terms of the contract, he/she must be released on or before the agreed-upon date. If the State fails to deliver the requisite programs, the parole date must still be honored since the resident was not at fault. If, however, the offender fails some aspect of the program, the contract becomes void and the State is no longer bound to release the individual on the agreed date. The contract may be renegotiated and a new date established. MAP programs are designed both to assess and meet the needs that both the individual and the institution feel are important to rehabilitation goals. Data are being collected but are not yet sufficient for evaluation of these programs.

The number and variations of treatment programs that have been attempted are almost limitless. This has been a brief and rather cursory attempt to examine some of the current efforts directed toward offender rehabilitation. Although some of the emerging programs are exciting, they all suffer from a lack of outcome data with which to judge their effectiveness. It should be obvious that no treatment program, whether it be old or new, traditional or innovative, should ever be established without built-in, rigorous evaluation. Fortunately during the past few years, there has been a marked increase in the technology available for criminal justice evaluation. The behavioral scientist and clinician working in the corrections area has a number of evaluation models from which to choose (e.g., Glaser, 1974). There is no longer any excuse for ignoring the need for and value of program evaluation. Only through the results of such evaluations can effective programs be nurtured and expanded and worthless programs abandoned.

Summary

The authors have attempted to present an introduction to some of the issues involved in the study of crime and delinquency. A cursory examination of the status of current explanations of crime and methods of classifying criminal behavior reveal that the explanations lack universality and classification systems are in their infancy. A multi-disciplinary approach to the etiology and classification of criminal behavior, which pays more than lip-service to the needs of women offenders, must be developed.

While a myriad of intervention strategies have been used, there are few data available which attend to their effectiveness. Of primary need is the development of evaluation systems that will permit useful treatment approaches to be retained and ineffectual approaches discarded. Only then might it be possible to have a significant impact on the direction of criminal justice programs.

GLOSSARY

Anomie: A condition or personal attitude of an individual that reflects a lack of purpose; a rootlessness and paucity of ethical values or personal identity.

Antabuse: A prescription drug used in the treatment of alcohol abuse. It produces a violent vomiting reaction if alcohol is ingested following its use.

Concordance: The term used in genetics to denote when both members of a twin pair possess or lack a particular characteristic or trait.

Correctional System: That part of the criminal justice system responsible for the care and supervision of an individual from conviction to discharge from sentence. Usually consists of the correctional institutions, probation, and parole.

Criminal Justice System: The entire system with which an accused lawbreaker may become involved: police, courts, and correctional system.

Dyzygotic: Fraternal or two-egg twins.

Face validity: Being plausible at a glance; "common sense" validity that is of little scientific value.

Milieu: Immediate environment both physical and social.

Mitigating Circumstance: In a criminal act, any feature of that act that would either decrease or increase its seriousness. Also referred to as extenuating circumstance.

Monozygotic: Identical or single-egg twins.

Parole: The portion of the criminal sentence served under supervision in free society following a period of incarceration.

Prerelease: The time just before release from incarceration, commonly accepted to be the period 6–8 weeks prior to release.

Probation: A method of allowing a person to

serve their sentence under supervision in free society.

Psychopath: Often used synonymously with sociopath. An individual characterized by impulsiveness, lack of guilt, and an inability to feel any genuine concern for others.

Recidivism: Repeated juvenile or adult offending.

Reintegration: To return a person to free society equipped to participate successfully in that society.

Status Offense: Behavior that is an offense when committed by a juvenile but not considered an offense when committed by an adult, e.g., truancy.

Taxonomic: Classification of like events, characteristics, or traits into descriptive categories.

CHILDHOOD DISORDERS

ALAN O. ROSS
EDWARD G. CARR

The classification of a child's behavior as abnormal or disordered depends on certain value judgments made by adults (such as parents and teachers) significant in the child's social environment. Such judgments are made in relation to developmental and situational expectations that form the basis for what society considers as *normal* behavior.

Over a period of years, a child's motor, social, and language behaviors change in a predictable and orderly fashion. Because of this orderliness, it is possible to judge whether a child's behavior is deviant with respect to a set of *developmental norms*. For example, by two years of age, most children can speak in phrases and understand simple directions. Therefore, a five-year-old child who can do neither is judged to be deviant with respect to developmental norms.

A given behavior may be considered deviant in one situation but not in another. Thus, *situational norms* are also a basis for judging whether a child's behavior is normal or abnormal. These situational norms, in turn, are influenced by a variety of cultural, subcultural, setting, and individual factors. *Cultural norms* are particularly apparent in judgments of aggressive behavior. Boys of the Dani tribe in New Guinea frequently practice the tactics of aggressive warfare against each other. Dani adults do not consider these behaviors problematic and, in fact, actively encourage such fighting (Gardner & Heider, 1969). In contrast, Polynesian adults of the Society Islands would label the same behaviors as extremely aggressive and dangerous and would take steps to suppress such activity (Levy, 1969).

Within a given culture one can find a variety of *subcultural norms*. Thus, stealing and fire-setting may be considered normal, valued behaviors in the subculture of a youth gang while at the same time these behaviors are judged as delinquent by the dominant, middle-class subculture.

Setting norms also play an important role. A boy who shouts and runs wildly in a playground setting may be labeled healthy and active but if this child should behave similarly in a classroom setting, he may well be labeled hyperactive or disruptive.

Finally, there are a number of *individual*

norms that vary from one adult to another. Thus, one mother may label the occasional crying of her infant as a tantrum and seek professional help, whereas a different mother might label the same behavior as a mild upset not deserving any special consideration.

This discussion highlights the fact that no behavior is deviant in and of itself. A child's behavior is not judged to be abnormal according to some absolute standard but only in relation to a host of developmental and situational norms.

Once the decision is made to label a child's behavior as disordered, one typically has to deal with two kinds of problems. Some child disorders involve an *excess* of a particular maladaptive behavior; for example, the child may exhibit a frequency of tantrums or aggression judged to be too high. Here the psychologist's task is to discover what factors are maintaining the behavior and then to eliminate those factors. Other child disorders involve a *deficiency* in a particular set of behaviors; for example, the child may never have learned how to talk or how to get dressed without help. Here the psychologist's task is essentially educational; that is, ways must be found to teach the child those skills that have not yet been acquired.

In trying to deal with the above problems, behaviorally oriented psychologists have focused their efforts on trying to answer one fundamental question: "Under what conditions does a given behavioral phenomenon occur?" When this question can be answered, the controlling conditions can often be changed so as to *prevent* the occurrence of a problem behavior or to *change* the frequency, intensity, or topography of a given behavior in a socially desirable direction.

In what follows, we shall examine a number of theories and studies pertinent to understanding the conditions under which a variety of childhood disorders occur. One prominent childhood disorder, mental retardation, will not be examined, however, as it is discussed in detail in another chapter of this volume.

Childhood psychosis

The two major categories of childhood psychosis, the most profound form of psychological disorder, are *early infantile autism* and *childhood schizophrenia.* Autism is a relatively rare disorder that characterizes approximately 4 children n 10,000. As implied by the word "early," autism is detectable within the first two years of life and is frequently apparent almost from the moment of birth. Autistic infants, unlike normal infants, do not show anticipatory movements when their mothers go to pick them up; instead they lie passively in their cribs. Furthermore, when they are picked up or cuddled, they may struggle or arch their body away from their mother rather than fit comfortably against her body as a normal baby would. Autistic children exhibit an *extreme aloneness* in their social behavior. For example, they do not exhibit a social smile, appear not to recognize members of their own family, and do not develop play relationships with other children. Contrasting with the absence of social attachments is the fact that these children will often form strong attachments to inanimate objects such as spray cans or pipe cleaners and spend endless hours manipulating them.

Autistic children have severe problems with speech and language. About 50 percent of them are mute, never having learned to speak. Those who do speak exhibit many peculiarities including *echolalia* and *pronominal reversal.* Echolalia has two forms. In *immediate echolalia,* the child simply parrots the adult's speech. Thus, when an adult asks, "How are you?" the child answers, "How are you." In *delayed echolalia,* the child repeats things that were said hours or even weeks before. It is not uncommon for such children to repear verbatim a lengthy television commercial heard several days previously. In pronominal reversal, an autistic boy will refer to himself as "you" rather than "I." Thus when the child wants a glass of water, he will ask for it by saying, "Do you want a glass of water?" Pronominal reversal is closely linked to echolalia as is evident from this example. The child simply repeats a question that had been addressed to him in the past when he appeared thirsty.

Another characteristic of autism is an *obsession to preserve sameness.* The child may have a tantrum following minor changes in routine such as a slight alteration in the path of a daily walk. Another child may become very upset if a door is left open and will spend much time moving about the house closing doors.

Several other characteristics of autistic children are worth noting. A number of these children exhibit *self-injurious behavior.* They may bite themselves until they bleed or bang their head against a wall. Such behavior is not only dangerous but it also makes it almost impossible to work with such a child in any constructive fashion. Many autistic children engage in *self-stimulatory behavior.* They spend great amounts of time rocking back and forth or engaging in repetitive hand movements, activities that seem to serve no other function than providing the child with sensory stimulation. Finally, despite the many problems noted above, medical examinations reveal no obvious signs of brain damage or other physical impairment.

Childhood schizophrenia differs from autism along a number of important dimensions. First, the incidence is somewhat higher, being 6 to 7 per 10,000 children. Second, and most importantly, the condition appears to have a much *later onset,* typically appearing after age 5. Prior to this age the child is described as having developed normally in most areas of functioning. Like autistic children, schizophrenic children often appear socially withdrawn but, unlike the autistics, these children may develop an extreme *symbiotic relationship* with their mother wherein the child may persistently cling to her while at the same time she focuses almost all of her attention on the child.

The language problems of schizophrenic children differ from those of autistic children. Schizophrenic language typically contains much distorted content, bizarre fantasies, and meaningless phrases such as "100 percent cherry sauce impeachment." Perceptual distortions such as delusions and hallucinations, though common among schizophrenic children, are rarely observed among autistic children. Finally, schizophrenic children exhibit a number of peculiar movements such as body whirling and toe walking, not commonly seen in autistic children.

Although there are apparently a number of features distinguishing childhood schizophrenia from autism, considerable terminological confusion exists in the field. Some investigators, for example, claim that schizophrenic children also display an insistence for preservation of sameness as well as echolalic speech. Other investigators routinely include children with clear-cut signs of brain damage under the rubric of autism. Notwithstanding this confusion, researchers continue to make a distinction between childhood schizophrenia and autism and several theories have been advanced to explain the etiology of these two disorders.

One prominent theory of autism holds that the condition results from the child's "turning away" from the parents who are described as being cold, mechanical, and insensitive (Kanner, 1949). There is little evidence to support this theory. In fact, parents of autistic children frequently raise other, perfectly normal children, something that would not be expected if their hypothesized "coldness" were a direct cause of autism. In addition, the observation that autism is essentially present from the moment of birth would tend to rule out parental behavior as a cause since such behavior would presumably have to act over some period of time in order to produce any long-term damage. Unfortunately, despite the paucity of scientific evidence to support this theory, it is still being espoused in some quarters (cf. Bettleheim, 1967). The net effect of this theory has been to place a tremendous and unnecessary amount of guilt on parents who are already burdened with the difficult task of raising an autistic child.

Zaslow and Breger (1969) proposed a *diathesis-stress model* of autism. According to them, a constitutional predisposition (the diathesis) produces a child who has an aversion to being held. This predisposition then interacts with a psychological stress, such as parental detachment, to produce the various behaviors characteristic of autism. Some infants do in fact seem to be born with a predisposition to be much less "cuddly" than the average baby. If a mother reacts to her infant's physical aloofness by reducing the amount of contact, serious consequences may ensue. For example, a mother's physical contact with her infant is frequently associated with a reduction in aversive conditions such as hunger, thirst, and the discomfort of wet diapers and cold. Such contact forms the crucial basis upon which social attachment is built. Thus, it is speculated that a mother who drastically reduces contact with her noncuddly infant may produce a child who is socially aloof, and this characteristic in turn prevents the development of the social smile, language, and the ability to deal adaptively with the human environment, all of which require at least some minimal level of social attachment. Lacking the stability and security of human relationships, the child becomes attached to a variety of inanimate objects whose removal or alteration in any way sets off a rage reaction, a fact that leads adults to describe such a child as having an obsessive desire to preserve sameness. Zaslow and Breger's hypothesis remains speculative. An adequate test of their hypothesis would entail, at a minimum, the systematic observation of autistic infants to determine if they are in fact less cuddly than normal infants together with a detailed longitudinal study of the interaction between mother and infant to see if the mother does reduce physical contact with her child over time.

A *biological hypothesis* of autism has been put forward by Rimland (1964). He speculated that an excess of oxygen shortly after birth produces damage to the reticular formation, an area of the brain stem thought to be responsible for the integration of memory with current perceptions. The result of such damage would be to produce a specific cognitive impairment, namely an inability to relate new stimuli to remembered experience. A child with such an impairment would be unable to associate the mother, for example, with such positive past experiences as feeding and being comforted and would therefore lack a basis for affectionate or stable interpersonal relationships. Further, the deficit would greatly retard the development of language since most abstractions involving symbols and concepts require that a child be able to relate past experiences to current perceptions. Finally, the severe inability to integrate new stimuli with previous experiences suggests that the autistic child would function with least difficulty in a static environment and this might explain why the child reacts with such distress and anxiety to any attempt to alter the surroundings or change routines. Rimland's hypothesis is thus quite robust with respect to explaining how the major behavioral problems of autism might arise, but as yet there is no extensive body of research that adequately tests the hypothesis. Further, one implication of Rimland's theory, that autistic children might be unable to learn very much because of their basic cognitive impairment, seems considerably overstated. Under special conditions, these children *are* able to learn a great deal.

Lovaas and his colleagues have proposed a *stimulus overselectivity model* of autism. This model is based on the results of an experiment conducted in 1971 by Lovaas, Schreibman, Koegel, and Rehm. These investigators presented a complex stimulus consisting of visual (a bright light), auditory (a tone), and tactile (a pressure cuff) elements to different groups of autistic, retarded, and normal children in a discrimination paradigm. Each child was reinforced for pressing a lever when the stimulus complex was present but not when it was absent. Once the discrimination had been mastered, the investigators introduced test trials in which only one of the three elements of the stimulus complex was presented in order to determine which of the elements each child had been attending to. In general, what they found was that the normals had learned to attend to all three elements, the retarded to only two, and the autistics to only one of the elements. Some of the autistic children behaved as if they saw the stimulus but did not hear or feel it; others behaved as if they heard the stimulus but did not see or feel it. Given that none of the children had physical impairment in their auditory, visual, or tactile senses, the results of this study provide a clue to the understanding of autism. In learning the meaning of words, for example, a child is required to pair an auditory stimulus (the spoken word) with a visual stimulus (the referent of the word). If the child were unable to attend to both the auditory and visual stimuli at the same time, language learning would become impossible. Likewise, in the formation of social attachments, an infant must be able to associate tactile stimuli (such as stroking and rubbing) with visual stimuli (the sight of the mother). A failure to make this association could prevent the formation of social attachments. Thus, given the existence of stimulus overselectivity, one can account for the language retardation and social aloofness characteristic of autistic children.

Recent data, however, suggest that the model described above may not be as comprehensive as was originally thought. Schover and Newsom (1976) demonstrated that overselectivity was directly correlated with a child's level of functioning as measured by mental age (MA). High functioning (high MA) autistic children were unlikely to display overselectivity whereas low functioning (low MA) autistics were very likely to display this deficit. The proposed model thus appears most powerful in explaining the deficits of low functioning autistic children but is unable to account for autism in higher functioning children. Lovaas's model, then, like the other models discussed, appears to account for only some of the facts. A more adequate account may well have to deal with the possibility that *several* different combinations of factors might be acting together to produce the condition we label as autism, if "autism" is indeed a single entity and not a term that covers a variety of profound behavior disorders.

Several theories have also been advanced to explain the etiology of childhood schizophrenia. Among the most popular of these theories is the *psychogenic hypothesis*, which holds that certain mothers are "schizophrenogenic"; that is, the emotions displayed by the mothers of many schizophrenic children are said to be the *cause* of the child's disturbance. In point of fact, this hypothesis is based simply on an observed correlation between a mother's emotions when she is seen by a clinician and her child's deviant behavior. On logical grounds alone, there is no reason for concluding that maternal emotions are the cause; they might just as well be the *effect* of having to deal with a deviant child on a daily basis for many years. In a study bearing on this psychogenic hypothesis, Waxler and Mishler (1971) found that parents of a schizophrenic child behaved in the same manner toward their normal children as they did toward their schizophrenic child. Why then did the normal children not become schizophrenic? The answer must be that parental behavior patterns by themselves are not the cause of childhood schizophrenia.

Evidence has been mounting in favor of a *genetic hypothesis* of childhood schizophrenia. Kallmann and Roth (1956) reported concordance rates of 88.2 percent for monozygotic twins but only 22.9 percent for dizygotic twins. Thus, the more twins are alike genetically, the more likely it is that if one member of the pair is schizophrenic the other member will be similarly afflicted. Once the role of genetic factors is clarified through further research, it might become possible to predict the probability of childhood schizophrenia within a given family. At that point, parents identified as being likely to produce schizophrenic children could be alerted to the risks involved and rational family planning measures could then be decided upon.

The distinction between autism and schizophrenia and the contrasting theoretical positions discussed above may eventually provide a comprehensive account of the etiology of childhood psychosis. For the present, however, the clinician, to be effective, must deal with the specific behavior problems of profoundly disturbed children rather that dwell upon the subtleties of differential diagnosis, past etiological factors, or far distant genetic solutions. In this vein, one current approach has been to view the psychotic behavior of a given child as the result of a particular reinforcement history (Ferster, 1961). A few examples will suffice to demonstrate some of the gains made in the understanding and treatment of profoundly disturbed children when their psychotic behavior is analyzed as a learned response pattern.

Many psychotic children engage in self-injurious behaviors such as head-banging, face-slapping, or self-biting. As long as a child is self-injurious, teaching is impossible. Therefore, attempts have been made to analyze self-injury so as to be able to eliminate this behavior. Lovaas, Freitag, Gold, and Kassorla (1965) demonstrated that self-injury is often maintained by the attention it receives from well-meaning adults. Thus, a girl may learn that by banging her head against the wall, she can obtain a great deal of comforting and affection from those around her. When adults are taught to ignore the head-banging and instead praise more appropriate social behaviors, the problem can often be eliminated. Carr, Newsom, and Binkoff (1976) demonstrated that self-injury sometimes functions as an escape response. Some children apparently learn to injure themselves because such behavior causes adults to stop making demands on them as in a teaching situation. When teachers are taught not to let the children interrupt or terminate a teaching session by engaging in self-injury, thus escaping the task, this behavior problem can be eliminated. Thus, depending on whether self-injury is reinforced by attention or escape, different treatment methods are called for. Occasionally, in the case of extreme self-injury that has proven refractory to other treatment methods and endangers the child's health or progress, punishment in the form of mild electric shocks or a slap is administered contingent upon the behavior. Following only a few such instances, the behavior can often be brought under control, provided more desirable behaviors are reinforced at the same time.

Once self-injury and other atavisms are brought under control, the child is ready to be taught. At this point, the psychotic child's severe behavior deficits become readily apparent. While normal children learn a great deal by observing the behavior of others, many psychotic children do not. In an important study, Lovaas, Freitas, Nelson, and Whalen (1967) taught psychotic children to learn new behaviors by observing others. Specifically, Lovaas et al. prompted each child to imitate a wide variety of simple behaviors that the therapist modeled, such as standing up, pointing, manipulating objects, and choosing one object out of a group of objects. Each imitated act was subsequently reinforced. Eventually a child could imitate a therapist's action without prompting, the first time it was modeled. At this point, the child's newly acquired mastery of imitation was used to develop more complex and useful behaviors by having the child imitate the therapist in more difficult activities such as drawing, self-help skills, and games.

Several advances have also been made in treating language problems. Lovaas (1966) taught mute, psychotic children how to imitate simple sounds and then words using a variant of the procedure just described. Once the previously mute child was able to imitate words, more complex behaviors such as labeling and abstract language could be taught thereby allowing the child to communicate effectively. Many psychotic children, of course, are not mute. Their speech, however, is marred by the presence of echolalia. Carr, Schreibman, and Lovaas (1975) demonstrated that echolalia was most likely to occur when children were presented with a question or command they did not understand. Once they were taught the appropriate response, they no longer echoed the adult. The research reviewed above thus demonstrates that many behavior problems associated with childhood psychosis can be understood and treated.

Withdrawn behavior

Much of the behavior of withdrawn children consists of escape and avoidance responses to feared objects and situations. A child who is afraid, for example, of crowds or strangers may actively avoid or leave situations containing either of these stimuli. Because of the prevalence of such situations, such a child might drastically reduce the amount of time spent in the company of other people, including children. Since children develop age-appropriate social behaviors largely as a function of interacting with their peers, it follows that withdrawn children will gradually fall behind their peers in matters of social development. Thus, it becomes important to understand and treat the fear responses that form the basis of withdrawn behavior.

There are three important mechanisms by which fears are acquired or maintained. Watson and Rayner (1920) demonstrated how, by a process of *respondent conditioning,* Albert, a normal nine-month-old child, acquired a fear of white rats. Each time Albert was shown the rat, a hammer was struck loudly against a steel bar, startling Albert and making him cry. As a consequence of several *pairings* of the sight of the rat with the loud noise, Albert soon began to cry and withdraw from the rat, an animal to which he had previously shown no fear.

Once a fear has been established in this manner, it can help maintain a variety of escape and avoidance responses, that is, withdrawal responses. Thus, a child afraid of white rats might avoid pet stores or perhaps even shopping centers containing such stores. These avoidance and escape responses in turn are strengthened by *negative reinforcement* because they have the consequence of terminating or preventing the occurrence of the feared stimulus.

Finally, fears can also be acquired through a process of *modeling* or *observational learning.* Numerous studies have demonstrated a strong correlation between parents' fears and their child's fears. Thus, a girl who repeatedly observes her mother express horror at the sight of snakes is herself likely to develop a fear of snakes.

Several treatment approaches have been used to ameliorate withdrawn behavior based on fear. In a classic study, Mary Cover Jones (1924) demonstrated the use of *counterconditioning* to eliminate a child's fear of rabbits. Jones treated the child, Peter, by feeding him his favorite foods while gradually bringing the feared rabbit closer and closer to him. Through this gradual process, Peter learned to approach the previously feared rabbit to the extent of playfully allowing the animal to nibble at his fingers.

Bandura, Grusec, and Menlove (1967), in a much-cited study, showed how *modeling* can be used to treat children's fear of dogs. One group of children received a modeling treatment whereby they watched other children fearlessly display progressively closer approaches to a dog. Children in this modeling group subsequently showed less fear of dogs than children in control groups who did not receive the modeling treatment. Further, the children in the modeling group still displayed their fearless behavior one month later during a follow-up test.

There are many instances in which a child's withdrawn behavior may not be due primarily to fear. One such instance involves a child's not interacting with other children because of a *failure to have learned relevant social skills.* Buell, Stoddard, Harris, and Baer (1968) reported the case of a preschool child who did not know how to use outdoor playground equipment and therefore interacted very little with other children. When these investigators taught the child how to use the equipment, they found a concomitant increase in the child's physical and verbal contact with the other children as well as an increase in cooperative play.

Some children may be withdrawn because their isolate behavior receives much *social reinforcement from adults.* Allen, Hart, Buell, Harris, and Wolf (1964) reported on one such case. This nursery school girl received a great deal of attention from teachers who were concerned about her lack of interaction with peers. As long as the teachers attended to her isolate behavior, she rarely interacted with other children. But when the teachers were taught to attend to the girl only when she interacted with other children but not when she played alone, her rate of playing with other children increased to a high level and was maintained over a period of many months.

Psychophysiological disorders

The term psychophysiological disorders is a description of the fact that many problems with an obvious biological basis are also influenced by psychological factors. As such, these problems overlap the domains of the clinical child psychologist and the physician.

Asthma is a condition in which there is an extensive narrowing of the bronchioles, making the exhaling of air difficult. This results in the characteristic wheezing sounds of asthmatics. There is no doubt that the condition has a biological basis. Allergens, such as pollen or dust, and respiratory infections, particularly acute bronchitis, can precipitate asthmatic attacks. Of equal interest is the observation that psychological factors such as emotional upset can also produce asthmatic attcks. In a well-known study on the psychophysiology of asthma, Purcell, Brady, Chai, Muser, Molk, Gordon, and Means (1969) divided asthmatic children into two groups based on interview data. The asthmatic attacks of children in one group were commonly precipitated by emotional arousal such as anger or anxiety whereas the attacks in the other group were not. The investigators predicted that for children whose asthma was related to emotional precipitants, there would be an improvement in their asthma following separation from their families, the improvement presumably being based on a reduction of emotional stresses mediated by the family. Children in the other group were not expected to improve. These predictions were borne out. Following separation, the children in the emotional precipitant group showed a marked improvement in their ability to expel air as well as a reduction in wheezing. No consistent changes were observed for children in the other group.

If indeed the asthmatic attacks of some children are brought on by emotional tensions, then one might expect that training such children in systematic relaxation techniques should have an ameliorative effect. Indeed, Alexander, Miklich, and Hershkoff (1972) demonstrated that such relaxation training can produce improvements in the ability of asthmatic children to expel air.

Given that a child who is gasping for air is likely to attract much parental attention, the possibility exists that some asthma may be maintained by adult's social reinforcement. In such cases, excessive parental solicitude may actually make the condition worse.

Yet other children, particularly those who have fallen behind in school because of their illness, may learn that asthmatic attacks can help them avoid or escape from aversive school situations. The resultant pattern of what Creer, Weinberg, and Molk (1974) call "malingering" can be dealt with by reducing the aversiveness of the avoided situation, as by providing remedial tutoring.

In sum, while there is no evidence that psychological factors form the original basis for asthma, such factors are often of great importance in maintaining or worsening the condition.

Epileptic seizures, in their most serious form, consist of severe convulsions brought on by pathology of the central nervous system. Organic factors involving brain diseases such as encephalitis or tumors and metabolic disorders such as hypoglycemia (low blood sugar) can precipitate seizures. In addition, psychological factors such as stress and emotional difficulties can be precipitants. Interestingly, seizures often have a predictable pattern. Zlutnick, Mayville, and Moffat (1975) described one child whose violent spasms were reliably preceded by fixed gazing at flat surfaces. They conceptualized the seizures as a *chain of responses* in which early members of the chain (i.e., fixed gazing) were discriminative stimuli for later members (i.e., violent spasms). They further reasoned that if the response of fixed gazing

CASE HISTORY

When Tommy was referred for treatment to the Child Psychological Clinic, he was eight years old and presented a pattern of fears and aversions of a three-year duration. The main fear from which most of the other fears derived was a pervasive fear of bleeding to death as a result of bodily injury. His phobic symptom developed at the age of three-and-one-half when his sister, Wendy, was born. Wendy was born physically and mentally retarded. Wendy was quite sick during her early weeks of life due to a blood disease which did not allow her blood to clot. The parents recalled trying to explain to Tommy about Wendy's condition, but it seemed only to make him afraid of bleeding to death also. At this time, Tommy was given a room by himself, whereas previously he had been sleeping in the same room as his parents. Wendy was put in his old bed so the parents could always be close to her.

Shortly after these two incidents (birth of a retarded sibling with a blood disease and removal to a new room), Tommy's symptoms developed to full scale. At first his fear was expressed by outbursts of crying at the slightest bump or cut. He did not do very much running around and playing as he was afraid of bleeding to death. Soon this fear generalized to other potentially dangerous situations such as sleeping in the dark, thunderstorms, police sirens, funeral homes, spiders, bugs, rats, monster shows, and being alone. Tommy's parents reported that he was afraid of these things because he thought he would be hurt and would bleed to death.

Concomitant with these developments, Tommy became subject to hives and asthmatic bronchitis (allergist tests negative). He had been nearly hospitalized four times in the last three years for his bronchitis. Along with these two reactions, Tommy began having restless nights and would go to his parents' bedroom two or three times a night apparently "just to see if we (parents) were there." This occurred almost every night of the week (five to seven times per week). Thus, the behavioral symptoms most obvious were the development of hives, asthmatic bronchitis, and sleepless nights. It was hypothesized that these behaviors were concomitants of Tommy's attempts to avoid the more threatening thought of bleeding to death and served as avoidance responses for him.

Other background information revealed that Tommy was the oldest child and Wendy was his only sibling. His parents were both employed. His father was manager of a car wash and worked the day shift, while his mother was a night desk clerk at a respectable motel. She worked from 11:00 p.m. to 7:00 a.m. and was home in time to get Tommy's breakfast before he left for school. He was doing satisfactory work in school.

Reprinted with permission from: T.H. Ollendick and E. Gruen, Treatment of a bodily injury, phobia with implosive therapy. *Journal of Consulting and Clinical Psychology,* 1972, *38,* 389–393.

were followed by negative consequences, the chain would be broken and the spasms would not occur. This prediction was correct. A punishment contingency (a shout of "no" and vigorous shaking) applied to the engazing sharply reduced the frequency of spasms. The work by Zlutnick et al. demonstrates how psychological principles (such as chaining and punishment) can be applied to help remediate even those problems which have a clear organic basis.

Enuresis, as a psychological disorder, refers to the involuntary discharge of urine, without evidence of organic pathology, by children who are at an age when they should be toilet trained, according to their society's norm. The most frequently encountered problem in this area is that of *nocturnal enuresis* or bedwetting. The traditional psychodynamic viewpoint is that such enuresis is the result of underlying emotional disturbances. From this it is argued that any attempt to stop the enuresis without curing the "root" emotional difficulty will result in the emergence of some new psychological problem, a process referred to as symptom substitution. Baker (1969) tested this prediction. One group of enuretic children was given a behavioral treatment referred to as the "bell-and-pad" method, originally developed by Mowrer and Mowrer (1938). This method consists of having the child sleep on a specially wired pad that sets off an alarm when the child starts to urinate. The alarm continues to sound until the child wakes up and turns it off. Once awake, the child can complete the urination by going to the toilet. Baker found that the bell-and-pad group showed significantly greater improvement than any of several control groups who had not received this treatment. Of equal importance was the finding that no symptom substitution occurred. In fact, the children treated by the bell-and-pad method became better adjusted both at home and at school following the cure of their enuresis.

DeLeon and Mandell (1966) compared several groups of enuretic children, one of which received a fairly traditional treatment based on psychodynamic principles, while another was given the bell-and-pad conditioning treatment. The success rate was 18 percent for the psychodynamic group and 86 percent for the conditioning group. On balance then, the psychodynamic viewpoint receives little empirical confirmation. The current view is that enuresis is a behavioral *deficiency* in which a behavior has not been learned or not learned well enough. Treatments that teach appropriate self-control, such as the bell-and-pad technique, are usually sufficient for ameliorating the problem.

Excessive body weight or *obesity* is a serious childhood problem. Individuals who become obese in childhood, manifesting so-called juvenile-onset obesity, are very likely to remain that way throughout their lives. In addition, their condition is more resistant to treatment than obesity that has an onset in adulthood. Despite the gravity of the problem, little information exists on the nature and treatment of childhood obesity. Metabolic factors are rarely the cause of this condition. A more common cause is frequent social reinforcement for overeating given by oversolicitous mothers. Additional factors concern the observation that obesity frequently runs in families, raising the possibility of a genetic predisposition. However, an equally plausible explanation of this phenomenon is that the condition is the result of parental modeling of overeating.

Recently, Aragona, Cassady and Drabman (1975) demonstrated that overweight children could be successfully treated through parental training and *contingency contracting*. Parents were shown how to teach their children to eat more slowly, delay meals, and leave food on the plate. The children negotiated with their parents each week for special nonfood rewards made contingent upon specific weight losses. Weight losses, though impressive, were not maintained after the termination of treatment, suggesting the need for longer periods of treatment or intermittent booster sessions.

At the other pole from obesity is a condition known as *anorexia nervosa,* a rare disorder characterized by voluntary restriction of food intake, producing extreme weight loss, sometimes resulting in death. The condition occurs primarily in females and has its usual onset at puberty. Although the cause is not known, many anorexics appear to be afraid of becoming overweight. Leitenberg, Agras, and Thomson (1968) demonstrated the successful treatment of anorexia in two hospitalized adolescents. Treatment consisted of making privileges, such as watching television or going for walks, contingent on consuming larger and larger amounts of their meals.

Chronic rumination is sometimes found in infants. It is a condition whose cause is unknown, and consists of vomiting after almost every meal. Since such children experience life-threatening weight loss, drastic treatment is required. Lang and Melamed (1969) treated such a case by delivering a few mild electric shocks to the skin of the infant each time vomiting occurred. Following this, the infant ceased ruminating and thrived.

Cross-gender behavior

Sex-typing begins in the first two years of life and is largely completed by preschool with boys exhibiting more aggressive and more gross-motor behaviors than girls, and girls preferring less competitive activities. After preschool age, deviation from expected sex-role patterns has different consequences depending on the sex of the child. Girls displaying tomboy behaviors are generally tolerated whereas "sissified" behavior on the part of boys is generally dissapproved, especially by the child's peers.

Occasionally, cross-gender behavior in boys becomes extreme. Some boys consistently display feminine mannerisms, gestures, and gait, preferring to dress and speak in an exaggeratedly feminine way. Given society's intolerance of even *slightly* effeminate behaviors on the part of males, boys displaying such extreme cross-gender behaviors are often the recipients of severe sanctions and ridicule from their peer group. Further, such boys may develop into adult transsexuals, a group whose behavior problems have proven to be most refractory to treatment (Stoller, 1968). Adult male transsexualism is highly correlated with severe depression, social ostracism, and suicide. This pattern provides a compelling reason to treat cross-gender behavior when it is displayed by young boys.

Some of the factors which may be responsible for the development of cross-gender behaviors in boys were identified in a study by Hetherington (1965). She found that in families characterized by mother-dominance, boys were more likely to imitate their mother's behavior than their father's and, in addition, these boys demonstrated a less pronounced masculine sex-role preference than boys from father-dominant families. This finding is consistent with the literature showing that children are most likely to imitate those adults who have the greatest control over dispensing reinforcers. Interestingly, the families of boys with extensive cross-gender behavior are consistently described as being mother-dominant, the father being almost totally uninvolved with his son. The mothers, at least initially, are reported to view their son's behavior as "cute," often reinforcing the child for "acting like mommy."

Independent of either parent's contributory role in cross-gender behavior, treatment research suggests parents can alter this behavior. For example, Rekers and Lovaas (1974) trained the mother of one such child to ignore or punish her son's cross-gender behaviors while at the same time praising him and giving him special privileges when he engaged in sex-appropriate behaviors. Following ten months of treatment, the child's sex-typed behaviors became normalized.

School-related problems

In a highly technological society such as ours where education is seen as the key to social mobility, the child who performs poorly at school becomes a matter of concern to both parents and teachers. Perhaps because of this, school-related problems are the most frequent reason for referring a child to professionals who deal with childhood disorders. The most commonly cited problems are those of hyperactivity, learning disabilities, and school phobia.

A child who is constantly fidgeting and moving about, who wears out toys and furniture, has difficulty completing projects or staying with games, who fights and teases, and is inattentive and impulsive is likely to be labeled as *hyperactive*. But a child need only have a few of the above characteristics to be given this label. This perhaps accounts for why many professionals believe that at least five percent of the elementary school population can be labeled as hyperactive. Given the large number of children involved, it is not surprising to find that recent research suggests that hyperactivity is not a unitary phenomenon but instead consists of numerous subgroups having different etiologies (Ross & Ross, 1976.).

Genetic factors may play an important role in producing some cases of hyperactivity. Safter (1973) studied the full and half siblings of a group of hyperactive children. The full siblings had the same biological father as the hyperactive children whereas the half siblings did not. All siblings were adopted early in life and were therefore raised apart from their hyperactive brothers or sisters. Safer found that there was a greater incidence of signs of hyperactivity in the full siblings than the half siblings. Since the full siblings were genetically more similar to the hyperactives than were the half siblings, this finding supports the notion that some forms of hyperactivity may be genetically transmitted.

Organic factors are also said to be of great importance in producing hyperactivity, so much so that the terms hyperactivity and *minimal brain dysfunction* are often used synonymously. Yet, in a recent overview of the field, Stewart and Olds (1973) estimated that less than ten percent of hyperactive children had histories suggestive of brain damage. The frequency of perinatal complications was no greater among the hyperactives than among the general population. Thus, the widespread and indiscriminate use of the term minimal brain dysfunction to describe all hyperactive children must be rejected as both misleading and, because of the implication of irreversibility, unethical.

A number of other variables capable of producing organic changes have been linked to hyperactivity. Thus, studies have been reported which found a positive correlation between hyperactivity and the following: lead poisoning resulting from the ingestion of lead-pigment paints; excessive exposure to x-rays from color television sets; and heavy maternal smoking and drinking during pregnancy. Food additives, particulary salicylates, have also been suggested as the cause of an allergic reaction that consists partly of hyperactive behavior. As an extensive review by Ross and Ross (1976) has shown, the research linking these variables to hyperactivity is often quite limited and far more work remains to be done. Therefore, the exorbitant claims that one frequently finds in the popular media purporting that someone has discovered *the* cause of hyperactivity are premature and, in any case, fail to reflect the fact the hyperactivity is a *multiply determined* behavior and not a single disease entity.

Hyperactive behavior is sometimes described as being a *reaction to interpersonal stress.* Thomas, Chess, and Birch (1968) showed that a certain number of individuals could be characterized from early infancy as having a pattern of high activity, short attention span, and negative mood. Some parents of these "difficult" children respond to the undesirable behaviors in a punitive manner and with other expressions of disapproval. Thomas, Chess, and Birch suggested that the children *react* to the stress of excessive punishment with further heightening of their undesirable behaviors. Thus, a vicious circle is established in which the hyperactivity becomes exacerbated. These investigators reported that many parents who treated such children with tolerance and consistency were able to raise them so that they did not develop behavior problems.

More recently, *developmental factors* have been implicated as a possible cause of hyperactivity. Sykes, Douglas, Weiss, and Minde (1971) demonstrated that hyperactive children performed much more poorly than their age mates on a task requiring the detection of significant stimuli in a stimulus complex. The ability to focus on those aspects of a stimulus complex that are the significant or distinctive features is called selective attention. Hyperactive children are apparently deficient in this skill. Ross (1976) has argued from studies such as this one that some hyperactive children are developmentally immature; that is, they are similar to younger children in not yet having developed the ability to sustain selective attention. The result is that they respond to large numbers of irrelevant stimuli, making them appear impulsive, distractible, and overactive. Over time, sustained selective attention does develop but, unfortunately for many hyperactive children, the eventual development of the skill is preceded by a lenghty history of academic failure that in itself has contributed to a variety of problem behaviors.

In a few cases hyperactive behavior appears to be *acquired.* In some of these instances, a high level of activity and impulsiveness attracts considerable teacher and peer attention. Although the attention is often in the form of disapproval, the child's hyperactive behaviors may nonetheless be strengthened because they represent the major means of getting attention. In other instances, hyperactivity may be an acquired escape or avoidance response. A child who has experienced repeated failure and punishment during reading lessons, for example, may well become anxious at the sight of the printed page. This child may attempt to reduce anxiety by moving away from the reading material or by constantly looking about, a pattern of behavior that may result in the label "hyperactive." Finally, some highly overactive parents may serve as models for their children. The children subsequently acquire, through observation of their parents, an excessivly active personal tempo that may occasionally be labeled as hyperactivity.

The above discussion should make it clear that it is a fallacy to attribute all hyperactivity to a single cause such as brain dysfunction. A child who is hyperactive because of lead poisoning will obviously require a different treatment than a child whose hyperactivity represents an escape response. A recognition of the multiple etiologies of hyperactivity can only serve to enhance treatment effectiveness. We shall briefly review several commonly used treatments applied to hyperactive children.

Drug treatment, especially the use of methylphenidate, has been found effective with some hyperactive children. The drug apparently suppresses overactivity and impulsivity. The result is an improvement in the child's ability to attend, particularly to routine and repetitive tasks. The critical problem with drugs is that, used alone, they can engender an attitude of passivity in the children who come to attribute all improvements in their condition to the drugs. This difficulty suggests that drug therapy be combined with other forms of treatment in which the children are active participants so that they will attribute at least some changes to their own efforts, thereby helping to promote the long-term maintenance of treatment gains.

Cognitive methods provide a form of treatment in which children are active participants. Meichenbaum and Goodman (1971) demonstrated that impulsive children could be taught to approach tasks more reflectively. They tested a number of such children before and after a training period. The tests included several subtests of the Weschler Intelligence Scale for Children (WISC) as well as the Matching Familiar Figures Test, an instrument that requires the child to identify which of six representations of a familar object matches a standard. Initially, the children performed poorly on these tests, making many errors. Next, a training period was introduced in which the children were taught to verbalize instructions to themselves to the effect that they should go slowly and carefully scan the various response alternatives. The children practiced these self-instructions on a number of training tasks that included copying patterns and reproducing designs. Following such practice, the children were again given the original set of tasks whereupon they demonstrated significant improvements compared to a group of children who had not been trained in self-instruction. Further, these gains were still evident when a follow-up test was administered one month later. Extensions of such research may well help such children to develop self-control over other areas of their behavior.

Behavioral methods involving interventions such as token programs have been demonstrated to be effective in controlling disruptive classroom behaviors. O'Leary, Becker, Evans, and Saudargas (1969) showed that the delivery of tokens (exchangeable for back-up reinforcers) contingent on desirable behavior was successful in reducing the frequency of problem behaviors in a classroom of highly disruptive children. The question of how to make such treatment gains generalize to other environments was left unanswered by this study. More recently, however, parent-training programs have been combined with classroom token systems to bring about the generalization of treatment gains to other settings.

The hyperactivity of many children is often correlated with a level of academic achievement below that expected of them given that they are not mentally subnormal and enjoy adequate educational opportunities. Such discrepancy between expected and actual academic performance often leads people to label these hyperactive children as *learning disabled* and to use the terms learning disability and hyperactivity interchangeably. Yet, one can argue that the close association between hyperactivity and learning disability is based solely on the fact that hyperactive children, by virtue of their annoying, disruptive behavior, are most likely to be referred to specialists and therefore be identified as learning disabled. Unfortunately, other children who are *not hyperactive* but nevertheless are learning disabled go unnoticed and are therefore not singled out for special help. The existence of these children should serve to remind us that hyperactivity and learning disability are *not* synonymous.

In a recent review, Ross (1976) concluded that the major problem shared by most learning-disabled children is an inability to sustain selective attention, an inability that was also implicated as a problem for some children who are labeled hyperactive. Therefore, it would appear that cognitive methods such as those discussed above would be useful in treating these children. The fact that such help exists but often goes unused underscores the importance of developing programs to identify such children who, though they are not behavior problems, nevertheless require special educational help.

Another school-related problem is that of the child who refuses to go to school. When this is due to an extreme fear of school and related stimuli, the condition is known as *school phobia*. It should be noted that not all instances of refusal represent school phobia. For example, some children have a fear of leaving home, a condition more correctly labeled *separation anxiety*. Other children are *truant;* that is, their pattern of school refusal is more closely linked to delinquency and the strong attraction of outside activities not found at school.

In the case of school phobics, the longer the child remains outside the classroom, the more work will be missed and the more likely it will thus be that the child will fail academically. Thus, a vicious circle is established since, failing academically, the child will find going to school even more aversive. Further, once a child successfully avoids going to school by, for example, complaining of physical ailments (as these children often do), the behavior problem will be further strengthened by negative reinforcement. These considerations led Kennedy (1965) to develop a treatment procedure that stressed ignoring physical complaints and insisted on rapid, if necessary, forced return to school. Using this method, Kennedy reported success in all fifty of the cases he examined without repetition of school refusal over a follow-up period which, in some cases, lasted as long as eight years.

Aggressive behavior

No society can survive for very long if the aggressive behavior of its members is out of control. For this reason, in the process of socialization, a great deal of effort is spent on teaching children to restrain aggressive behavior or at least to express it at time and place designated as appropriate for behaving aggressively. The failure to manage childhood aggression has serious long-term consequences. Robbins (1966) reported on the current psychological status of a group of adults who, thirty years earlier, had been referred to a child guidance clinic for a variety of problems. She found that those individuals who had been referred for aggression and other antisocial behavior in childhood were more likely to have serious problems as adults than individuals referred for other problems such as fears and phobias. Further, the more severe the antisocial behavior during childhood, the more likely it was that serious problems would be present in adulthood. These findings suggest that both the individual and society could be spared much suffering if effective management procedures were applied to aggressive behaviors while the individual is still a child.

In attempting to deal effectively with aggression, one must first ask what is meant by the term. Some have suggested that aggression refers to an instinctive, genetically determined state that from time to time erupts into violent behavior. There is no conclusive evidence that humans are aggressive by nature. We shall use the terms aggression and aggressive behavior as synonyms to reflect the point of view that aggression is a *response,* not a state. Given this definition, it is important to realize that when one refers to a response as aggressive one is making a social judgment involving several factors. Bandura (1973) has outlined some of these. One important factor influencing the labeling of a given behavior as aggressive concerns the *characteristics of the behavior itself.* Behaviors likely to produce aversive consequences for others, such as physical assaults or vandalism, are very apt to be judged aggressive. The *intensity of responses* is also important in that high magnitude responses are often labeled as aggressive. Thus, slamming a door is more readily judged to be aggressive than closing a door gently. If a behavior is followed by *expressions of pain and injury* from others, that behavior is very likely to be considered as aggressive. A fourth factor concerns the *characteristics of the labeler.* For example, at the beginning of the chapter, we described how a given behavior might or might not be regarded as aggressive depending on the cultural values of the individual making the judgment. A final factor pertains to the *characteristics of the aggressor* and is related to the existence of various stereotypes associated with the aggressor. For example, in some quarters, a racial stereotype might cause an individual to label vigorous play between two boys as aggressive if they were black but as healthy fun if they were white.

The complexity of the labeling process is perhaps matched only by the complexity and variety of the factors thought to be important in the acquisition and maintenance of the aggressive behavior itself. We noted that high magnitude responses were likley to be labeled as aggressive. On this basis, one might expect that an individual with a *history of reinforcement for high intensity responding* might be more likely to emit behaviors that could be characterized as aggressive. Walters and Brown (1963) carried out a study bearing on this point. They reinforced a group of boys for responding at a high intensity on a task that involved either hitting a large doll or depressing a lever. Subsequent to this training, these boys displayed more aggression, such as kicking and pushing, in a competitive game situation than a group of boys who had been previously reinforced for responding at a *low intensity* on the same tasks. Apparently, the pretraining for the first group of boys had stregthened not just the specific responses of vigorous doll-hitting or lever-pressing but also the general response characteristic of *high intensity* and it was this response characteristic that generalized to the competitive game situation. A child's reinforcement history can therefore be seen as a sufficient condition for increasing the probability that aggressive behaviors will be performed at a later time.

Frustration is a stimulus condition consisting of either delayed reinforcement or the interruption of goal-directed behavior. Frustration not only elicits an emotional arousal we call anger but it also increases response intensity. It is this latter result that so often leads people to label responses to frustration as aggression. The frequently observed association between frustration and aggression led Dollard, Doob, Miller, Mowrer, and Sears (1939) to propose that frustration is a necessary and sufficient condition for aggression to occur. At first glance, the frustration-aggression hypothesis seems very plausible. If, for example, one child is thwarted by another child from reaching a goal, a high intensity response such as pushing or hitting made by the first child will often be successful in removing the obstacle presented by the second child. Thus, in the presence of a frustration stimulus, the aggression of the first child will have been reinforced and therefore strengthened. Repeated occurrences of this kind will ensure that in the future, frustration will almost certainly be followed by aggression. There is a body of research, however, that suggests that frustration does not always result in aggression. For example, Davitz (1952) trained one group of children to interact aggressively and a second group to play "constructively." Each group was observed in a free-play situation before and after they were exposed to a frustration condition in which a film they had been promised was interrupted and candy bars which they had been given were taken away. Davitz found that the children who had been previously trained to behave aggressively, behaved aggressively, whereas those trained to behave constructively, behaved constructively. This experiment demonstrates that frustration does not inevitably evoke aggression; rather, the domant response in a child's repertoire is the response that tends to be made when frustration is encountered and that response is determined by the child's own reinforcement history.

Operant factors involving both *positive and negative reinforcement* are often critical in the acquisition and maintenance of aggressive behavior. Patterson, Littman, and Bricker (1967) elaborated upon this theme. They suggested that aggressive behaviors are relatively rare responses that emerge from a broader matrix of *assertive behaviors*. These assertive behaviors are coercive in nature. They demand a response from the social environment and carry an implied threat of further assertive responses if they are not satisfied. For example, a boy sees a toy he wants in a store and asks his mother to buy it for him. The mother ignores the child's assertive request and the child responds by making the request again but in a louder voice. The mother, wishing to avoid a scene, relents and buys the toy. With repeated experiences such as this, a mother may well shape her child's response repertoire so that it contains a high proportion of shouted demands, thus enhancing the likelihood that the child will be labeled as aggressive. *Positive reinforcement* then is important in initially shaping aggressive behavior. Patterson et al. suggest that a second factor is needed to produce the serious problem child. That factor consists of frequent exposure to high levels of aversive emotional stimulation such as fear and anger, which in turn become eliciting stimuli for aggression. These aversive states are occasionally terminated by an aggressive response and such behavior is thereby further reinforced. In this manner, the number of potential eliciting and reinforcing stimuli for aggressive behavior is greatly multiplied and the behavior thus becomes a high probability response causing adults to view the child as a serious behavior problem.

To test several aspects of the theory, Patterson and his collaborators performed an extensive, long-term observational study of aggression in nursery school children. Several important findings emerged. First, they observed that if a child attacked another child and that attack resulted in a positive reinforcer (e.g., getting the other child's toy), the aggressor was likely to repeat the same type of attack on the same child when the next occasion for aggression arises. This result demonstrates the important role positive reinforcement plays in the maintenance of aggression. A second finding was that if a passive and unassertive child who was the victim of many attacks successfully counterattacked, this typically unaggressive child would subsequently show a gradually increasing level of aggression. Since the counterattack most likely had the effect of terminating the other child's aggression, itself an aversive stimulus, it is clear that *negative reinforcement* must play an important role in the initial acquisition of such aggressive behavior. This study is significant in that it demonstrates that operant reinforcement factors, present in everyday environments such as those represented by nursery schools, serve to aid in both the acquisition and maintenance of aggressive behavior.

Observational learning is imporatant in

the acquisition of aggressive behavior. Bandura, Ross, and Ross (1961) found that children who observed an adult model engaging in a variety of novel aggressive behaviors toward a doll were more likely to display such novel behaviors subsequently than children who watched a model behave in a calm, nonaggressive manner. This demonstrates the importance of modeling in the acquisition of *new forms* of aggressive behavior. The fact that the children who observed the aggressive model also later displayed a higher overall level of aggression, which included *nonimitated* aggressive responses, demonstrates that exposure to aggressive models may also facilitate the performance of aggressive behaviors *already* in the child's repertoire.

Modeling influences may also account for the observation that parents who use frequent physical punishment to discourage their children from aggressing tend to raise aggressive children (Bandura & Walters, 1959). This paradox is partially accounted for by the fact that as the parent is punishing aggression, the parent is also providing a potent model for aggression that the child emulates in later interactions with others. A second point concerns the fact that modeling influences are often particularly powerful under conditions of high emotional arousal. Since the child is likely to be in a highly aroused state while being punished, the aggression modeled by the parent at that time is especially likely to be learned and later reproduced by the child under similar emotion-related conditions.

It is likely that *constitutional factors* also play some role in determining aggressive behavior. As noted in the discussion of hyperactivity, there are some children who appear to be born with a tendency to display a high activity level in all of their behavior (Thomas, Chess, & Birch, 1968). Since response intensity is one factor that contributes to the labeling of a child as aggressive, it follows that, other things being equal, these children stand a greater chance of being considered aggressive than children with a constitutional tendency to lower activity levels.

What can be done to treat aggressive children? Traditionally, clinicians have proceeded on the assumption that frustration is the main determinant of aggression and that therefore aggression can be controlled by removing all frustrations. One problem with this approach is that the removal of all frustrations can be accomplished, if at all, only in a highly artificial, protective environment such as an institution. Unfortunately, as soon as the child returns to the community, frustration stimuli will again be present to set off aggressive behavior. Another problem, as we have seen, is that frustration does not always produce aggression but, instead, aggression is largely maintained by reinforcing consequences such as those provided by the peer group. Since a child returning to the community from an institution will almost certainly encounter the old peer group, it is very likely that aggressive behavior will be rapidly reinstated by the positive consequences that the peer group would provide for such behavior.

A second traditional technique is based on the *catharsis hypothesis,* which holds that aggressive children have an excess of "aggressive impulses" and should be allowed to express these so that they can "blow off steam" thereby ultimately reducing the frequency of aggressive behavior. Mallick and McCandless (1966) tested this assumption in a series of experiments. They told third-grade children that they could earn money if they completed a block construction task in a specified time period. During the task, another child, who was a confederate of the experimenters, deliberately interfered with the block-building activities thereby preventing the subjects from finishing on time. This manipulation was meant to increase the level of "aggressive impulses" in the subjects. Next, one group of subjects was allowed to engage in a shooting game using a target on which was drawn a picture of a boy of the confederate's age. This game was intended to have a cathartic effect by letting the children "work off" their aggression. Another group of subjects was told to solve a series of arithmetic problems, a task which had no cathartic value. Finally, both groups of children were given the opportunity to press a button which supposedly punished the confederate by administering a shock to him. This test thus measured the level of "residual hostility." The results indicated that catharsis had no effect on aggression. Children in the catharsis and no catharisis groups both displayed high rates of punishing the confederates and the two groups did not differ from each other in this respect. Further, in another study in the series, Mallick and McCandless demonstrated that for children whose block-building activities had not been interfered with, mere verbal expression of hostility directed at the confederate (in the form of like-dislike ratings) coupled with the shooting game constituted a sufficient condition for producing increased aggression toward the confederate later on. This study suggests that adults who promote aggressive play for purpose of therapy may actually *increase* the strength of aggression rather than reduce it.

Finally, one important *behavioral* treatment method is based on the observation that aggressive behavior is maintained largely by social reinforcement from the peer group. With this consideration in mind, Burchard and Tyler (1965) treated the aggression of an adolescent delinquent boy by immediately placing him in isolation for 15 minutes following specified aggressive acts. This "time-out" procedure prevented the boy from receiving the usual peer support and his aggressive behavior declined. Typically, many aggressive children lack appropriate social skills for obtaining positive social reinforcement. Therefore, to promote long-term treatment benefits, time-out programs such as that just described must be supplemented by programs designed to teach alternative nonaggressive behaviors that will eventually compete with the aggressive behaviors.

The aggressive behavior of some children may take the form of frequent physical violence, vandalism, and stealing. Such children are likely to be labeled by legal authorities as *juvenile delinquent.* There are several types of delinquent children. One such child, the so-called *impulsive delinquent,* experiences a temporary failure of learned controls that leads him to steal, for example, perhaps only once in his life. The *unsocialized delinquent,* on the other hand, has never been taught to control antisocial behavior and is therefore likely to commit a high frequency of illegal acts. Finally, the *socially delinquent* child, usually a member of a gang, has learned to conform to the norms of the gang, norms that unfortunately are at odds with those prevailing in the larger society.

A major focus of research on delinquency centers on the examination of the family structure of delinquent children and predelinquent children, that is, children who display many of the behaviors of delinquents but have not yet come into contact with the legal authorities. Recently, behavioral psychologists have analyzed parent-child interactions in detail and found that families of aggressive boys are characterized by a pattern in which the aggression of the boys pays off frequently, in terms of the child's ability to successfully coerce parental attention by exhibiting such behavior. Time out for aggression combined with positive reinforcement for appropriate social behavior has often been successful in controlling aggression in such children. However, these same techniques applied to children whose primary problem is stealing have not been found to be very effective. This fact prompted Reid and Hendricks (1973) to analyze the family interactions of boys who steal. They found that these families, unlike those of boys whose primary problem was physical aggression, could be characterized as having an extremely low rate of exchange of positive reinforcers between parent and child. Perhaps, then, children from such families attempt to make up for the monotony of their family life by seeking excitement outside the family such as stealing or fire-setting. The paper by Reid and Hendricks is significant in that it demonstrates that different types of delinquent behavior may stem from different types of parent-child interaction. To plan effective treatment, therefore, one must take these facts into consideration. Recently, Alexander and Parsons (1973) successfully treated a group of children whose problems included stealing by teaching all family members to increase their rates of mutual positive reinforcement. The success of this study is yet another demonstration that experimental research carried out to determine the conditions under which behavioral phenomena occur can often form the basis for the effective treatment of childhood disorders.

Summary

The definition of what is a childhood disorder is largely a function of value judgments made by adults significant in the child's environment. These judgments vary with the child's age, situation, and culture. Some behavior is considered deviant because it occurs too often, other behavior because it occurs too rarely. One can thus speak of excess and deficient behavior, but the various categories of childhood disorders often contain both kinds of behavior. Childhood psychosis, for example, is manifested by such behaviors as excessive self-injury and deficient language.

There are two major categories of childhood psychosis, early infantile autism, and childhood schizophrenia. While the children in both of these categories often display similar behavior patterns, the conditions can be differentiated by a number of characteristic features. Several theories have been proposed to explain early infantile autism but none have yet been confirmed. Treatment approaches based on principles of reinforcement have been shown to be effective in modifying the behavior of these profoundly disturbed children. The same principles have provided successful treatment for withdrawn behavior, various psychophysiological disorders, such as enuresis, and gender-inappropriate behavior.

Because many of the expectations people hold for children are based on school attendance, school behavior, and school performance, psychological problems related to school are the most frequent complaints about which children are referred for professional help. Hyperactive children who move around more than adults in their environment can tolerate have been studied extensively and various explanations of their problem have been proposed. It is likely that no single theory can account for all children who are labeled as hyperactive and their problem is probably determined by a number of factors. For this reason, no one form of treatment can be expected to be effective with all of these children. A related school problem is found with children whose academic performance falls below their expected potential. They are referred to as learning disabled children, and while some of these children are sometimes also hyperactive, hyperactivity and learning disability are by no means the same.

From the point of view of adaptive interpersonal relations, aggressive behavior represents another serious problem. Aggression is best defined as a response that is labeled as aggressive on the basis of social judgments made by significant adults in the child's environment. One of the stimulus conditions to which aggressive responses are often learned is frustration. It is characterized by delay of reinforcement or the interruption of goal-directed behavior. Both positive and negative reinforcement as well as observational learning play a role in the acquisition and maintenance of aggressive behavior. Reinforcement interventions have often proven effective in the control of aggressive behavior. Juvenile delinquency is closely related to aggression in that much of the behavior deemed delinquent takes aggressive forms. Like most other categories of psychological disorders, juvenile delinquency identifies a heterogeneous group of individuals. Increased understanding of psychological disorders will only emerge when further advances are made in differentiating among the different children that carry the same label. One promising way of accomplishing such differentiation is to determine the conditions, antecedents, and consequences under which carefully specified behavior takes place.

GLOSSARY

Autism: (See *Early infantile autism*).

Back-up reinforcer: An object or event that has been previously identified as a potential reinforcer for a given individual. It is received in exchange for a specified number of tokens or points that are dispensed when the individual performs specified desirable behaviors.

Catharsis hypothesis. Based on psychoanalytic theory, this postulates that repressed aggression or other tensions must be given an outlet in order for treatment to progress.

Childhood schizophrenia: A profound psychotic disorder characterized by onset after age 5 and often manifested by bizarre social and emotional behavior, nonsensical language, perceptual distortions, and peculiar body movements.

Concordance rates: Used in genetic studies to express the proportion of cases in which the same condition is found in two people at various levels of relationship, such as unrelated individuals, parents and children, siblings, or twins.

Contingency contracting: A mutually agreed-upon set of conditions under which people agree to reinforce one another provided each engages in specified behavior.

Counterconditioning: The reduction of a maladaptive form of behavior by conditioning the individual to emit incompatible, adaptive responses to the same set of stimuli. Used in the treatment of fears in which the individual learns to make approach instead of avoidance responses to the originally feared object.

Diathesis-stress model: A theory about psychological disorders postulating that such a disorder is brought about by an interaction of a constitutional predisposition with environmental stress.

Early infantile autism: A profound psychotic disorder characterized by early onset, withdrawal from social contacts, atypical language development, and ritualistic behavior patterns.

Echolalia: A verbal repetition of the last words or phrase heard by the speaker. Often found in early infantile autism.

Hyperactivity: A descriptive term used to label motor behavior that a child's adult caretakers consider excessive.

Minimal brain dysfunction: Condition presumed to involve deviations of function of the central nervous system. Some writers believe it to be the cause of hyperactivity even in the cases in which the child has no demonstrable brain disorder.

Negative reinforcement: A reinforcing consequence that strengthens the response on which it is contingent and that is characterized by the termination of an aversive (unpleasant or painful) stimulus. Not to be confused with punishment.

Norm: A standard of development or appropriate conduct usually derived from an average based on a large group of individuals.

Observational learning: The acquisition of new behavior as a result of watching a model display such behavior.

Punishment: A response-contingent aversive (unpleasant or painful) stmulus that weakens that response. Not to be confused with negative reinforcement.

Selective attention: Perceptual focusing on that aspect of a stimulus complex that represents the distinctive feature critical for carrying out the required task.

Stimulus overselectivity: An overexclusive attention to only one aspect of a stimulus complex that may or may not be the distinctive feature critical for carrying out the required task. Often found in children with early infantile autism.

Symbiotic relationship: A mutual interdependence between mother and child wherein the child clings persistently to the mother while the mother focuses almost all of her attention on the child. Sometimes found in children with childhood schizophrenia.

MENTAL RETARDATION

DAVID BALLA
EDWARD ZIGLER

The phenomenon of mental retardation can best be seen in the context of several levels of influence, all of which will have important effects on retarded persons. The *first* of these levels of influence is that of the individual: his biological endowment, his experiences in learning, and the presence or absence of associated difficulties such as emotional disturbance, impaired vision or hearing, or motor difficulties. The *second* level is that of the family, which influences the retarded person and is in turn influenced by his presence. The *third* level is that of the near support system: schools, community agencies, and institutions. The presence and quality of these facilities have important consequences for the ultimate adaptation of the retarded individual and his family. The *fourth* level is that of the far support system: the national government and private organizations that play important roles in formulating and implementing social policy for retarded individuals. Before considering these four levels, it is necessary to discuss the definition of mental retardation and its prevalence in our society.

The definition of mental retardation

The most widely accepted definition of mental retardation is that of the American Association on Mental Deficiency: "Mental retardation refers to significantly subaverage general intellectual functioning existing concurrently with deficits in adaptive behavior, and manifested during the developmental period" (Grossman, 1973, p.5). According to this definition, "significantly subaverage intellectual functioning" means an intelligence quotient (IQ) of more than two stan-

The preparation of this paper was supported by Research Grant HD-03008 from the National Institute of Child Health and Human Development. The authors are indebted to Margaret Houghton and Peppie Weiss for their help in the preparation of this manuscript. We would also like to thank Rosa Cascione and Elizabeth Scarf for their critical readings of an earlier draft of this manuscript.

Case Description of Mental Retardation

John is a 6-year-old white child (diagnosed as Down's syndrome) who is described as aggressive and hyperactive. He is the product of an unremarkable pregnancy, and normal, uncomplicated delivery. He was the second birth of a 20-year-old, middle-class mother. Upon birth, he weighed 5 pounds and 14 ounces and was in good physical health. The diagnosis of Down's syndrome (due to translocation) was suspected and confirmed at that time.

John's early development was characterized by a failure to reach developmental milestones as expected. He rarely cried and slept almost constantly, staying awake barely long enough to be bathed and fed. Several feeding difficulties were noted, including early vomiting of milk products and a poor appetite. He was also described as a picky eater. John never crawled, but walked in a spiderlike fashion at 7 months. He sat at 8 months and walked at 14 months. His most significant delay was in the area of speech—he has never talked but is able to communicate his needs via gestures. He was toilet trained at 4 1/2 years of age.

Upon admission to a psychiatric facility at 5 years of age, John obtained an IQ of 43 on the Stanford-Binet and was observed to be highly active, aggressive, and negativistic. He failed to comply with most requests and spent much of his time aimlessly wandering around the unit. His aggressive behavior was characterized by hitting others and throwing objects. Structured educational programs and behavioral modification strategies were employed in his treatment program.

Courtesy of Thomas Ollendick

dard deviations below the average on a standard intelligence test. In practice, persons with IQ scores below 70 are typically seen as mentally retarded.

While the IQ score is extremely important in the area of mental retardation, an equally important concept is that of mental age (MA). MA refers to the extent of mental growth as measured by a standard intelligence test and is expressed in terms of years and months. In these terms IQ is defined by the formula IQ = MA/CA X 100. Thus, if a 10-year-old child scores on an intelligence test at the level of an average 7-year-old he/or she would have an IQ of 70, at the level of a four-year-old an IQ of 40, and so on. It is important to realize that mental growth is very much like physical growth. That is to say it occurs very rapidly during childhood and ceases sometime during adolescence, between 16 and 18 years of chronological age. Thus, a retarded person will not be expected to eventually "catch up" in mental growth with a person of average IQ. Rather, using the above formula with a final CA of 16, he will eventually be expected to attain an MA of between 11 and 12 years old. This MA level can be taken as the approximate upper limit of mental development of the retarded person.

Within the general range of mental retardation, four levels are usually distinguished: mild retardation (IQs 50–70), moderate (IQs 36–49), severe (IQs 20–35), and profound (IQs below 20). In special education the term educable is often used instead of mildly retarded, and trainable instead of moderately retarded.

It must be emphasized that a low IQ score by itself is not sufficient to define mental retardation. The second aspect of the definition is "deficits in adaptive behavior." According to the American Association on Mental Deficiency Manual: "Adaptive behavior is defined as the effectiveness or degree with which the individual meets the standards of personal independence and social responsibility expected of his age and cultural group" (Grossman, 1973, p.11). Adaptive behavior, of course, means different things at different ages. A four-year-old who is not toilet trained can be seen as having a deficit in adaptive behavior. An adult who cannot make change or use public transportation likewise is seen as having a deficit in adaptive behavior. If a person had a low IQ but no deficit in adaptive behavior he would not be classified as retarded. If he had an average IQ but, for example, could not use public transportation he would likewise not be classified as retarded.

Finally, the definition of mental retardation requires that the difficulties in intellectual functioning and adaptive behavior have their source somewhere in the developmental period. A thirty-year-old who became impaired because of an automobile accident would not be classified as retarded.

Difficulties with the definition of mental retardation

Arbitrariness. The IQ score given as the cut-off point for mental retardation is a matter of convention. There is nothing in the nature of mental retardation that could tell us where to draw the defining line. In point of fact, the cut-off points we mentioned above were somewhat approximate, and the precise cut-off point actually depends on the psychometric characteristics of the particular test employed. The shortcomings of this arbitrariness are most evident when society treats an arbitrary dividing line as if it were the product of divine guidance. In many states a cut-off point becomes the legal definition of mental retardation and is used to determine if an individual qualifies for a variety of services. The difficulties in rigidly relying on such a definition are apparent when we ask the question, "Does a child with an IQ of 70 really differ from a child with an IQ of 71?"

The question of cultural bias in the IQ measures

It has been reported (Mercer, 1973) that blacks and Mexican-Americans have a greater representation than expected in special education classes for retarded. Likewise, when IQ scores alone are used to define mental retardation, blacks and Mexican-Americans have more than their expected share of people identified as retarded (Mercer, 1973). Since most people assume that there are not innate cultural differences in intellectual capacity, it has been widely argued that IQ tests are culturally biased against blacks and Spanish-speaking minorities and in favor of white middle-class Americans. As Mercer has pointed out, such a bias on the IQ test has adverse consequences for many members of minority groups since they may be erroneously seen as intellectually limited and eventually come to behave that way because of inadequate access to educational opportunities. It is possible to reconcile the assumption that there are no cultural differences in intellectual functioning with the findings that a high proportion of minority group members have low IQ scores by making the distinction between competence and performance (Cole & Bruner, 1971). If this distinction is made, it can be assumed that minority groups have the same underlying competence as members of the dominant culture. As Zigler and his colleagues (Seitz, Abelson, Levine, & Zigler, 1975; Zigler & Butterfield, 1968) have indicated, performance on an IQ test reflects a combination of three factors: 1. the formal cognitive processes such as memory, reasoning, and abstracting ability that the test was designed to assess (this factor closely approximates the idea of competence); 2. Achievement factors involving knowledge about the specific content of the test; 3. motivational factors, which involve a wide range of personality variables. Indeed, Zigler, Abelson, and Seitz (1973) argued that the exceptionally low IQ scores of economically disadvantaged young children on a standard intelligence test are due to motivational factors rather than to a general intellectual deficit. These authors argued that wariness of unfamilar testers and fearfulness of testing situations led to maladaptive patterns of responding, which led to low scores on an intelligence test. They found that when economically disadvantaged children were tested and retested on the same instrument by the same examiner within a one- to two-week period, an average 10-point IQ increase was made by the children.

Social Competence. Certainly one of the reasons why the concept of social competence is currently seen as necessary for the definition of mental retardation is the possible cultural bias in IQ tests. Indeed, Mercer (1975) has empirically demonstrated that when a social competence criterion is added to the IQ score in defining mental retardation, the excess of people in minority groups identified as retarded diminishes markedly. It has also long been known that the prevalence of mental retardation is different at different age levels, being relatively low in the preschool years, reaching its peak during the school years, and declining again during the adult years. These changes in prevalence are almost certainly due to differing intellectual demands at different ages. Children may have difficulty in school work, be referred for evaluation, and identified as retarded because of their great difficulties with academic work. When they leave school, they often become self-sufficient adults who do not come in contact with any of the agencies that would identify a person as retarded. It is because of this changing prevalence with age that many have seen IQ as a single criterion for mental retardation to be inadequate. It is only if an intellectually limited person also demonstrated evidence of social incompetence that he is likely to be identified as retarded. However, the social competence aspect of the definition of retardation has also received its share of criticism. Most often the concept is seen as being impossibly vague. What is socially competent behavior in one situation may be inadequate in another. What is considered to be acceptable behavior in one subculture may be prohibited in another. In other words, a universally accepted definition of social competence has not been agreed upon (Zigler & Trickett, in press). However, in recent years there have been several efforts to quantify the concept of social competence and therby make the definition of mental retardation more precise (e.g. Nihara, Foster, Shellhass, & Leland, 1969).

The issue of prevalence

If we accept the conventional definition of mental retardation, there are approximately six million retarded persons in the United States. Almost 90 percent of these individuals are mildly retarded (Report of the President's Committee on Mental Retardation, 1967). An additional 6 percent are moderately retarded, 3.5 percent severely retarded, and 1.5 percent profoundly retarded. Mildly retarded individuals come from predominantly impoverished backgrounds and most often show no evidence of organic brain damage. The presence of moderate, severe, and profound retardation is almost always accompanied by brain damage and seems to be evenly distributed across the spectrum of socioeconomic status.

With this general background we can discuss the four levels of influence mentioned above that we see as necessary to understand the phenomenon of mental retardation.

The individual

As suggested just above, we can identify two basic types of mental retardation: 1. mental retardation associated with a known organic disorder, and 2. mental retardation in the absence of a known organic disorder. The organic type may be due to genetic disorders, brain damage, or a variety of environmental factors such as infections or exposure to toxins (e.g., lead poisoning). These many etiologies have one factor in common: in every instance examination reveals anatomical and/or physiological abnormalities.

In addition to the organic group, which forms a minority of retarded persons, there is a group most often called cultural-familial. [Recently this group has been referred to as retardation due to psychosocial disadvantage (Grossman , 1973). We will use the more traditional terminology.] The diagnosis of cultural-familial retardation is made when an examination reveals no organic cause and when the same type of retardation exists among parents and siblings. We will begin by discussing organic causes of retardation.

The organically retarded person

Genetic causes—dominant disorders. These disorders, which are rare, are inherited in families through Mendelian transmission. That is to say, the presence of the disorder in one gene is sufficient for its expression. One in two children with an affected parent would be expected to develop the disorder. Examples of dominant disorders are neurofibromatosis and tuberous sclerosis. The later disorder is characterized in its most severe form by severe mental retardation, seizures, and a group of small fibrous tumors on the face.

Recessive disorders. These disorders result from a single gene defect transmitted by the recessive mode of inheritance. When a gene is recessive both parents must carry the defective gene for the disorder to express itself. Since carriers of the gene without the disorder must also have one normal gene, the expected incidence in children with two carrier parents is one case in four births. The most widely known of these recessive disorders is phenylketonuria (PKU), which occurs in approximately one out of 13,000 live births. A failure to metabolize phenylalanine, a substance found in many foods, leads to its accumulation within the body where it is converted to phenylpyruvic acid. This substance is toxic to the developing nervous system, acting like any other poison. If untreated, the result is severe mental retardation, hyperactivity, generally unpleasant behavior, musty body odor, and often epileptic seizures. Many of the children have blond hair and blue eyes, a characteristic that is especially striking when the parents have dark hair and dark eyes.

Fortunately, PKU can be detected before all of the manifestations are obvious. Phenylpyruvic acid is present in the urine of infants with PKU and can be detected with a simple chemical test. This test is mandatory at birth in many states. Treatment of PKU consists of placing the child on a phenylalanine-free diet until at least five years of age. Although children treated with this diet do not completely equal the intellectual development of their unaffected siblings (e.g., Berman, Waisman, & Graham, 1966), the treatment is remarkedly effective in preventing severe mental retardation if the diet is started very early in life.

Cretinism. In this disorder, the individual displays mental retardation, dwarfism, thick skin and lips, and a coarse protruding tongue. These attributes were thought to be so characteristic of retarded individuals that the word "cretin" was used in the nineteenth century as a term for all of the mentally retarded. The condition results from either an inability to metabolize thyrozine hormone or a decreased secretion of thyroxine. Cretinism due to an inability to metabolize throxine is caused by a recessive gene disorder as in PKU. Cretinism can also be nongenetic, resulting from any factor that deprives the body of thyroxine. Early treatment with thyroid hormone is often effective in reducing the degree of retardation.

Galactosemia. This recessive disorder affects carbohydrate metabolism and is caused by a disorder of galactose metabolism (a milk sugar). If elimination of lactose from the diet is accomplished early enough the symptoms can be prevented from developing. If the disorder is not treated, the individual shows mental retardation, cataracts, cirrhosis, seizures, and early death.

Tay-Sachs disease. In this disorder, an abnormal or absent enzyme leads to accumulation of gangliosides in the central nervous system. It is most common in the descendants of eastern European Jews, of whom one in thirty are carriers of the defective gene as compared with one in three thousand in the general population. Usually the baby develops normally until about six months of age, when he starts to regress in development with loss of voluntary movement, blindness, spasticity, and death by three or four years. There is no known treatment for this disease. Fortunately, it can be identified prenatally through amniocentesis. Amniocentesis is a procedure in which amniotic fluid is obtained from the sac surrounding the fetus at 14–15 weeks of pregnancy. Certain tests, including a chromosome analysis, can be performed on this fluid making possible the detection of several types of organic mental retardation. If Tay-Sachs disease is detected the parent may chose whether or not to have an abortion.

Sex-linked disorders—Turner's syndrome

Several abnormalities of the sex chromosomes are associated with mental retardation. In Turner's syndrome, most commonly the individual has a single X chromosome with a second sex chromosome missing. Individuals with this disorder are phenotypically female, of short stature, and lack in sexual development. Mild mental retardation is sometimes present but it is *not* a frequent feature of the syndrome.

Klinefelter's syndrome In this disorder of the sex chromosomes the individual has two female chromosomes (XX) and one male chromosome (Y). Hypogonadism and excessive development of the mammary glands is characteristic of the syndrome. Mild mental retardation is present in 25–50 percent of those affected. In rare instances, Klinefelter's syndrome has been found with up to five X chromosomes with the retardation increasing in severity with the increasing number of extra X chromosomes (Crandall & Tarjan, 1976).

XYY syndrome. In this syndrome, an extra male sex chromosome is present. Characteristic features of this disorder have been seen to include borderline intelligence, tallness, and aggressive behavior (Jarvik, 1976). Because of the association of this syndrome and aggressive behavior, it has received a great deal of publicity and controversy. It seems clear that there is an excess of the XYY syndrome in criminals (Jarvik, 1976).

Disorders with extra chromosomes—Down's syndrome

Approximately one in every seven hundred live births results in a child suffering from Down's syndrome. The physical appearance of these children is usually so distinctive as to permit an easy diagnosis. The child typically has a small round head, upward and outward slanting eyes, a low-bridged nose, a small mouth with drooping corners, and a protruding tongue. Most Down's syndrome children are mildly to severly retarded. There is evidence (Stedman, Eichorn, Griffin, & Gooch, 1962) that Down's syndrome children raised at home attain higher IQs than those raised in institutions. However, Down's syndrome individuals do comprise about 10 percent of the institutionalized population. Since these children have some slight physical resemblance to Mongolians, to this day they are often incorrectly referred to as mongoloids.

The cause of Down's syndrome was not known until 1959 when it was discovered that individuals with the syndrome have 47 rather than the normal complement of 46 chromosomes (Lejeune, Gautier, & Turpin, 1959). Instead of two chromosomes in the twenty-first pair, these individuals have three chromosomes. For this reason Down's syndrome is sometimes referred to as trisomy-21. Genetically normal women produce Down's syndrome children. What then is the cause of the disorder? An important clue comes from the relationship that has been discovered between the age of the mother and incidence of Down's syndrome. The incidence is approximately one in two thousand at a maternal age of 20 and rises to an incidence of one in forty when the maternal age is over 45 (Crandall & Tarjan, 1976). Thus, the likelihood of producing a child with Down's syndrome appears to be related to how long the ova have been dormant. The ova are present at the time of the mother's birth and remain in a dormant state until puberty. Consequently, before fertilization the ovum has been exposed to many years of environmental insults that can damage chromosomes. Certainly the longer this exposure the more the possibility of chromosome damage. There is a greater risk of an ovum with a chromosomal abnormality in an older mother than in a younger mother. A similar age effect for fathers of Down's syndrome children has not been found (Koch, Fishler, & Melnyk, 1971).

Other chromosome abnormalities that have been detected are trisomy-18, (Edward's syndrome), trisomy-13 (Patau's syndrome), trisomy-8, and partial trisomy-15.

Environmental causes of organic mental retardation

A variety of events experienced in the prenatal and postnatal environment can also produce organic forms of mental retardation. Prenatal causative factors include faulty maternal nutrition, exposure of the mother to drugs and toxins, and maternal diseases such as syphilis or rubella. In addition, prematurity, severe lack of oxygen at the time of birth, and birth injuries can result in significant defects in intelligence. Examples of some brain damage syndromes induced by such disturbances in the physical environment include macrocephaly (abnormally large head), hydrocephaly (gross enlargement of the head caused by accumulation of cerebrospinal fluid within the cranuim), and microcephaly (abnormally small head and brain area, sometimes caused by a genetic disorder but which also may result from a variety of pre- and postnatal diseases and traumas to the developing child).

A cause of mental retardation during infancy and early childhood is head injury resulting from accidents and child abuse. Except for these, head injury is probably a rare cause of mental retardation even though many parents report that the child's difficulties began with a blow on the head. Although the incidence of mental retardation arising from child abuse is essentially unknown, it is probably greater than generally believed. It must be emphasized that many cases of mental retardation due to environmental factors could be prevented with the application of current knowledge, one example being the prevention of premature birth (Begab, 1974; Clarke & Clarke, 1977), or more effective detection and education with high risk families, as in the case of child abuse.

The mildly or nonorganically retarded person

Approximately 75 percent of all retarded individuals have no evidence of organic etiology (of the types discussed immediately above) and are often referred to as cultural-familial retarded. Unlike the organically retarded, these individuals are almost always mildly retarded with IQs above 50. This group has been the object of the most heated controversy in the area of mental retardation. The very term cultural-familial reflects the general uncertainty that exists concerning the causes of this form of retardation. Three explanations have been advanced, the environmental, the genetic, and the polygenic and interactionist views. We will discuss each of these positions.

Environmental explanation. Many workers in the mental retardation area insist that cultural-familial retardation is due solely to environmental factors. The fact that the official terminology for this form of retardation has been changed from "cultural-familial" to "retardation due to psychosocial disadvantage" suggests that the environmental view is the most popular. However, Zigler (1970) has argued against an extreme environmental view. One source of the extreme environmental view is the evidence that this type of retardation is more prevalent in the lower socioeconomic classes, especially environments characterized by extreme poverty and squalor. It has been further bolstered by a study conducted by Skeels (1966), who reported the adult status of two groups of apparently normal children with contrasting life experiences. One group was reared in an extremely barren and socially depriving orphanage, while the second had an experience with mildly retarded adoptive mothers who cared for them and became extremely attched to them after the children had been transferred from the orphanage to an institution for the retarded as house guests. As adults, all of the individuals in the group receiving the mothering were self-supporting and socially competent adults. In contrast, only one of the members of the orphanage group could be described as a socially competent adult. Indeed, a large proportion of the orphanage group were residents of institutions as adults. In another study (e.g., Garber, 1975), one group of children was given intensive environmental stimulation beginning early in life, while another group did not receive these experiences. Children in both of these groups had mothers with IQs of less than 75. At one year of age, children in both groups had equivalent above average IQs. However, by age eight, the average IQ of the children in the stimulation group was approximately 110 while the average IQ of the children in the control group was approximately 86. Perhaps the best evidence for an extreme environmental interpretation of cultural-familial mental retrdation is found in a study by Dennis (1973) of a group of children raised for different lengths of time in an institution in Lebanon before they were adopted. Children adopted before age two eventually reached average levels of intelligence. Children adopted after age two were found to have permanent intellectual deficits. Furthermore, the older the child was when adopted, the greater the deficit.

What the extreme environmentalists have failed to recognize is that very few children classified as cultural-familial retarded have experienced the gross social deprivation that characterized the orphanage children investigated by Skeels. Many children who score in the mildly retarded IQ range live in homes which, although not affluent, appear perfectly adequate in fulfilling the child's developmental needs. What is frequently found in these homes are hard-working parents who care for their children and whose only shortcomings seem to be that they themselves do not score very high on intelligence tests.

Genetic explanation. Empahsis on the genetic determination of nonorganic retardation has a long history. IN 1877, R.L. Dugdale published his geneological study of a family he called Jukes. From generation to generation Dugdale found in this family a very high incidence of criminality, pauperism, and mental retardation. Dugdale noted the poor environmental conditions in which the generations of Jukes children were raised, and felt that the incompetence of the family was due to both environmental and hereditary factors.

Another famous geneological study was conducted by Goddard (1912) who traced two lines of descent from Martin Kallikak, a Revolutionary War soldier. One line began when Kallikak sired an illegitimate child by a retarded tavern waitress. The second line began after Kallikak married a nonretarded woman from a socially recognized family. There was a high incidence of retardation, poverty, and alcoholism among the descendants in the first line. The descendants of the legitimate marriage were normal and some were of outstanding reputation. Goddard chose to ignore the environmental differences in the two lines of descent and interpreted his findings as evidence that inheritance was the overriding determinant of intelligence and social competence.

Polygenic and interactionist explanation. In view of current thinking concerning the inheritance of complex traits such as intelligence, Goddard's genetic arguments were much too simplistic. His interpretation carried the implicit view that intelligence was some single thing inherited in an all or none fashion. More recent thinking has stressed that intelligence is a polygenic trait determined by a numbr of genes each of which makes a small positive or negative contribution to the phenotype. Individually the genes are assumed to obey Mendelian laws and to have the same properties as major genes.

An illustration of polygenic inheritance of intelligence was provided by Gottesmann, (1963). For the sake of simplicity we will assume that IQ is determined by only three pairs of genes and that a person with a genotype AaBbCc has an IQ of 100. We will also assume that each gene represented by a capital letter can raise the IQ by 10 points, that the genes represented by a small letter have no influence, and that the effect of the genes are additive. The highest possible IQ in this model would be 130 for a person of genotype AABBCC, because this person has three more capital letter genes than the average person. The lowest possible IQ would be 70 for a person with genotype aabbcc, because this person has three fewer capital letter genes than the average. The fact that in reality persons can have higher or lower IQs than these values can be explained by a polygenic model if we assume that more than three gene pairs determine IQ.

The person with the genotype AaBbCc could produce eight different types of gene combinations to be passed along to his or her children (ABC, ABc, AbC, Abc, aBC, aBc, abC, abc). When two such people of AaBbCc genotypes marry there would be 64 (8 x 8) possible genotypes for their offspring. When the relative frequency of all possible genotypic values from such matings are calculated the result resembles a normal distribution. However, each phenotype appears to be distinct and separable from each other phenotype. The reason is that this distribution was built on the assumption that only three pairs of genes determine IQ. If we assume instead that there are 15 or more pairs that determine IQ the distribution would be an excellent approximation of the normal curve of IQ. Such an assumption is not far fetched since there are between 2000 and 50,000 genes in a human cell (Stern, 1960). It should be remembered from the above discussion on environmental effects on IQ that the phenotype is not merely an expression of the underlying genotype. Even if we accept that there is a large genetic contribution to intelligence, the reaction range for the phenotypic expression of intelligence is about 25 IQ points. This means that there can be a 25-point difference in intelligence test performance by the same person reared in the worst possible environment as opposed to the best possible environment (Zigler, 1976).

This polygenic and interactionist model appears to describe the inheritance of intelligence more accurately than either the extreme genetic or the extreme environmental position. The various theories differ, for example, in predicting the IQs of the children of two retarded parents. A simplistic genetic approach generates the expectation that all of the offspring should be retarded. It is interesting to note that an extreme environmental approach generates the same prediction, since if retardation is due to the poor environment provided by retarded parents, the children of such parents should be retarded. From the polygenic and interactionist model we would predict that children should show a range of intelligence with many but not all having low IQ scores. It would also be predicted that the average IQ of the offspring should be higher than that of their parents. Indeed, studies of the IQs of retarded parents and their children have provided data consistent with these predictions derived from the polygenic and interactionist model (Reed & Reed, 1965).

The polygenic model of inheritance of intelligence is applicable to all individuals who fall within the normal range of intelligence and generates an IQ distribution of approximately 50 to 150. Since for all intents and purposes the lower limit of the IQ range of the cultural-familial retarded group is approximately 50, it seems likely that this group represents the lower portion of the normal distribution of intelligence. We are not denying the importance of the environment as a factor in determining an individual's IQ score, but only asserting that biological variability guarantees a range of intelligence in which there will always be some at the lower end. If this approach were accepted, the intelligence of the cultural-familial retarded would be viewed as reflecting the same factors that determine the intelligence of brighter individuals. An individual with this type of retardation would be considered normal in the sense that he was an integral part of the distribution of intelligence produced by variation in our population's gene pool.

It should be noted that the polygenic model is not applicable to organically retarded persons, who often have IQs below 50. It has been reported (Penrose, 1963) that there are more individuals at very low IQ levels than a normal curve would predict. For these reasons we believe that considerable clarity could be brought to the area of mental retardation if we no longer thought of the distribution of population intelligence as a single continuous normal curve.

Perhaps a more appropriate representation of the distribution of intelligence would involve two curves. The intelligence of the great majority of the population, including the cultural-familial retarded, would be seen as a normal distribution with an average of 100 and a range of approximately 50 to 150. We would superimpose on this curve a second distribution having an average of approximately 36 and a range of from 0 to approximately 70. The first curve would represent the polygenic distribution of intelligence and the second would represent all those individuals whose intellectual functioning is influenced by an identifiable defect.

There is another extremely important consequence in adopting the view that the cultural-familial mentally retarded person is a normal individual of low intelligence. In terms of cognitive development these individuals would be viewed as progressing from one intellectual stage to the next in the same sequence as nonretarded people. They would of course progress from stage to stage at a slower rate than nonretarded individuals, and the final stage achieved would be lower than that achieved by the more intelligent members of the population. In terms of cognitive functioning alone, the cultural-familial retarded person with a CA of 10 and an MA of 7 would be seen as cognitively identical to an individual with a CA of 7 and an IQ of 100. The view that nonorganically retarded and normal individuals of the same MA are cognitively identical is referred to as the developmental position.

To the developmentalist it is no great surprise that individuals of 70 IQ and of 100 IQ at the same chronological age differ on a variety of tasks. These people are at different developmental levels and such differences are exactly what a developmentalist would predict. The difficulty for the developmentalist is that, even when groups of retarded and normal individuals are matched on MA, the groups of retarded individuals often do less well than the groups of normal individuals. Two different explanations for these repeated findings have been advanced. One view, which we will discuss below, is that these differences reflect a variety of experiential or motivational differences. The second view is that the cultural-familial retarded person is really not a normal individual developing at a slower rate but rather has some inherent differences and, at every level of development, has some difference in his physiological or cognitive structure. These hypothesized differences are then viewed as producing differences in behavior even in those cases where the MA is the same.

Difference positions

An early difference position which has had an impact on the training and treatment of retarded persons was proposed by Lewin (1936) and Kounin (1941a,). This position sprang from the common observation that retarded individuals are often more perserverative and stereotyped in their behavior than are normal individuals. Lewin and Kounin developed a theory of cognitive rigidity in the retarded that they felt accounted for the behaviorally observed rigid behaviors. Other investigators have asserted that retarded individuals do not effectively use verbal means to guide their behavior; in other words, that they have a verbal mediation deficit. This position has been closely associated with the Russian psychologist, Luria (e.g., 1963). Ellis (1963) has proposed that retarded individuals have a deficit in short-term memory, a deficit that seems to be confined to secondary memory and reflects the lack of effective use of rehersal strategies (Ellis, 1970). Retarded individuals have also been seen as suffering from an attention deficit. That is to say, they have more difficulties than do normal individuals in attending to the relevant aspects of a learning situation (Fisher & Zeaman, 1973; Zeaman & House, 1963). An information processing deficit has also been proposed as characterizing retarded individuals. For example, Spitz (1973) has found that mature mildly retarded persons can remember much less information given at once than the average adult. It should be noted that experimental evidence has been presented in support of all of these theories although, as will be seen below, many of the findings are open to alternative explanations.

Motivational factors in the performance of retarded individuals

As mentioned above, adherents of the developmental approach would interpret the many findings of deficits in the behavior of retarded individuals differently than would the difference theorists. The behavior of retarded persons is not seen as the consequence of low intelligence alone, but rather as also reflecting experiential history and motivational factors exactly as in normal people. The developmentalist sees the retarded individual as a complex person whose behavior is explained by the same laws that apply to the behavior of normal individuals. Many of the behavioral differences observed between MA-matched retarded and nonretarded groups are seen as reflecting experiential and motivational differences between the two groups. Several such experiential and motivational factors influencing the behavior of retarded persons have been identified.

Social deprivation. It has been repeatedly found that the behavior of institutionalized retarded individuals is related to preinstitutional social deprivation (e.g., Clarke & Clarek, 1954; Zigler, 1961). In our own work we have defined social deprivation as including a lack of continuity of care by parents and other caretakers, an excessive desire by parents to institutionalize their child, impoverished economical circumstances, and a family history of marital discord, mental illness, abuse and/or neglect. Each of these factors has been found to exist relatively independently of the other factors. Social deprivation has been found to affect a variety of behaviors. For example, highly deprived retarded children have been found to be more verbally dependent and more wary than less deprived children (Ball, Butterfield, & Zigler, 1974). Perhaps the largest body of research has shown that social deprivation can result in a heightened motivation to interact with a supportive adult (Balla et al., 1974; Balla, Kossan, & Zigler, 1976; Zigler, 1961; Zigler & Balla, 1972; Zigler, Balla, & Butterfield, 1968). This heightened motivation to interact with an adult is consistent with the frequent observation that retarded people often excessively seek attention and support from adults.

It should be noted that heightened motivation for adult attention has been used as an indicator of an imporant aspect of normal child development, namely, dependency. Thus, we might conclude that a general consequence of social deprivation is overdependency. It is hard to overemphasize the role of such overdependency in the behavior of the retarded. Given some minimal intellectual level, the shift from dependency to independence is perhaps the single most important factor that enables the retarded to become self-sustaining members of society.

Some indication of the pervasiveness of the atypical dependency of institutionalized retarded persons can be found in a study by Zigler and Balla (1972). Normal and retarded children of three MA levels—approximately 7, 9, and 12—were compared in terms of their motivation for adult attention. In keeping with the general developmental progression from helplessness and dependence to autonomy and independence, both retarded and normal children of higher MAs were found to be less motivated for adult support than those of lower MAs. However, at every MA level the retarded children were more dependent than the nonretarded children. The disparity in dependency was just as great at the upper as at the lower developmental levels. Indeed, the older retarded group was almost twice as dependent as the youngest normal group.

Positive and negative reaction tendencies. A phenomenon that seems to be at odds with the retarded individual's increased desire for adult support has also been observed; namely, retarded childred are often wary and reluctant to interact with adults. Indeed, in several experiments it has been shown that social deprivation results both in a heightened motivation to interact with supportive adults (positive raction tendency) and a reluctance or wariness to do so (negative reaction tendency) (Harter & Zigler, 1968; Shallenberger & Zigler, 1961; Weaver, 1966; Weaver, Balla, & Zigler, 1971). Weaver (1966) examined the negative reaction tendencies of a group of noninstitutionalized retarded children who had extremely poor records of academic, social, and health adjustment. The children were either praised or criticized for performing on certain tasks and then were tested on a measure of positive and negative reaction tendencies. He found that, over a series of trials, the children who were praised displayed increased positive reaction tendencies while the children who were criticized became more wary.

In a second study (Weaver et al., 1971), experimental condition effects like those discovered previously were found for institutionalized retarded children. These investigators also found that institutionalized retarded children were more motivated to receive the reinforcement of an adult, but were more wary of doing so than either the noninstitutionalized retarded or nonretarded children. It has also been found that institutionalized retarded individuals suffer from a generalized wariness of strangers, regardless of whether the strangers are adults or peers (Harter & Zigler, 1968). That socially depriving experiences can cause a generalized and persistent wariness of adults was indicated by the finding (Balla, Kossan, & Zigler, 1976) that after approximately eight years of institutional experience, retarded individuals with a history of high preinstitutional social deprivation were still more wary than less deprived individuals.

Failure in the performance of the retarded. Another factor that has frequently been observed as affecting performance of retarded individuals is their high expectancy of failure in problem-solving situations. This failure expectancy has been seen as consequence of a history of frequent confrontations with tasks with which retarded persons are ill-equipped to deal. The experimental work employing the expectancy of failure has proceeded in two directions. The first has been an attempt to document the pervasiveness of feelings of failure in retarded persons. The work of Cromwell (1963) and his colleagues has lent support to the general position that retarded individuals have a higher expectancy of failure than normal individuals. In a further series of studies (MacMillan, 1969; MacMillan & Keogh, 1971; MacMillan & Knopf, 1971), the experimenter prevented children from finishing several tasks and subsequently asked why the tasks were not completed. In all of these studies the retarded children consistently blamed themselves for not finishing the tasks, while nonretarded children did not blame themselves.

The second line of research has focused on the effects of success and failure expectancies on actual problem-solving behavior. The problem typically used is one where 100 percent success is impossible and the kind of behavior observed is whether the subjects are willing to settle for less than 100 percent success (low expectancy of success) or behave in such a way that they believe they can achieve 100 percent success in their problem-solving efforts (high expectancy of success). With this task, retarded children have been found to have a lower expectancy of success than children of average intelligence (Gruen & Zigler, 1968; Stevenson & Zigler, 1958). Ollendick, Balla, and Zigler (1971) studied groups of retarded children. In one group the children worked with block designs, puzzles, and mazes on three successive days. Everything the children did resulted in success. Another group of children also worked on similar tasks but everything they did resulted in failure. Both groups' expectancies of success were then observed. It was found that success experiences resulted in a higher expectancy of success and failure experiences in a lower expectancy of success. From these data, it seems plausible that low expectancies of success observed in retarded individuals are based on long histories of success and failure rather than being indicative of some cognitive difference.

The reinforcer hierarchy. Due to experiential factors the retarded individual's motivation for different kinds of incentives may differ from that of normal individuals of the same MA. In other words, the position of various reinforcers in the reinforcer hierarchy may differ in retarded and nonretarded individuals. Much of the experimental work on the reinforcer hierarchy has focused on tangible and intangible reinforcement. It has been argued that certain factors in the histories of retarded children cause them to be less responsive to intangible reinforcement than are nonretarded individuals of the same MA (Zigler, 1962; Zigler & deLabry, 1962; Zigler & Unell, 1962). This work is of special importance, since intangible reinforcement (information that a response is correct) is the most immediate and frequently dispensed reinforcement in real-life tasks. When such a reinforcer is used in experimental studies comparing retarded and nonretarded individuals, any group differences found might be attributable not to differences in intellectual capacity, but rather to the different values that such reinforcement might have for the two types of individuals. Indeed, it has been demonstrated that problem-solving success in groups of normal and retarded individuals of equivalent MAs did not differ when a tangible reinforcement was used (Stevenson & Zigler, 1957; Zigler & deLabry, 1962; Zigler & Unell, 1962), but that the retarded did less well than the normal children when an intangible reinforcement condition was used (Zigler & deLabry, 1962). However, although retarded children as a group may value being correct less than do normal children as a group, this may not hold true for any particular child. The crucial factor is not being retarded per se, but rather the particular social learning experiences of the child (Byck, 1968).

In more recent work, attention has shifted to the more general phenomenon of the intrinsic reinforcement that inheres in being correct regardless of whether or not the person is reinforced for such correctness. This shift in orientation owes much to White's (1959) formulation concerning the pervasive influence of the effectance or mastery motive. There can be little question that White's effectance concept provides a framework for a variety of behaviors that appear very central in the individual's behavioral repertoire (e.g., the desire for optimal levels of sensory stimulation, manipulation, exploration, and curiosity). As with the case of tangible reinforcers, the strength of the effectance motive may be different for retarded and nonretarded children. Evidence on this point was provided by Harter and Zigler (1974). These authors devised four puzzles that measured different aspects of effectance motivation: curiosity, mastery for the sake of competence, preference for challenging or nonchallenging tasks, and variation-seeking on a puzzle task. On all of these aspects of the effectance motive, intellectually average children demonstrated more effectance motivation than retarded children. Institutionalized retarded children were also less curious than noninstitutionalized retarded children. In summary, retarded children seem to be both less responsive to intangible reinforcers and less motivated by intrinsic motives than normal children of equivalent MA.

Outerdirectedness. Retarded persons have also often been observed to use external cues excessively to guide their behavior and solve problems, rather than to rely on their own cognitive resources. This problem-solving style has been referred to as outerdirectedness (Achenbach & Zigler, 1968; Balla, Styfco, & Zigler, 1971; Sanders, Zigler, & Butterfield, 1968; Turnure & Zigler, 1964; Yando & Zigler, 1971). Three factors have been discussed as important in determining the child's degree of outerdirectedness—the general level of cognitive development, the relative incidence of success the person has experienced when employing his cognitive resources in problem-solving situations, and the extent of the individual's attachment to adults, (Balla, Kossan, & Zigler, 1976; Zigler & Abelson, 1975). Either too little or too much imitation of adults is viewed as a negative psychological indicator. Some intermediate level of imitation is viewed as a positive developmental phenomenon, reflecting the individual's healthy attachment to adults and responsivity to adult cues that can be used in problem-solving efforts. In general, both retarded and normal children of lower MA levels have been found to be more outerdirected (Balla, Styfco, & Zigler, 1971). Consistent with the success-failure aspect of the outerdirectedness formulation, independent of MA level, retarded children have been found to be more outerdirected than normal children of the same MA. Institutionalized retarded children have been found to be less outerdirected than noninstitutionalized retarded children when they were asked to solve cognitive problems with a clear right or wrong answer (Achenbach & Zigler, 1968). This finding is consistent with the outerdirectedness formulation in that institutionalized retarded individuals, as a result of living in a protected environment geared to their intellectual level, have fewer failure experiences than the noninstitutionalized retarded. However, on a nondemanding task with no clear right or wrong answer, institutionalized retarded individuals have been found to be more outerdirected than noninstitutionalized retarded individuals, presumably reflecting demands for conformity by the institution staff (Lustman, Balla, & Zigler, 1977). Finally, there is some evidence that individuals who have not formed healthy attachments to adult caretakers will have an atypically low level of outerdirectedness (Balla et al., 1976). These investigators found that institutionalized retarded individuals whose caretakers had negative attitudes concerning them were less outerdirected than those whose caretakers had positive attitudes about them. Thus, individuals who are responded to in a negative manner may learn to ignore the cues provided by adults and become less imitative.

The family

From the above discussion of the effects of social deprivation on the behavior of retarded individuals, it should be clear that the family and the type of experience that the child has in the family context have a profound effect upon the development of a retarded individual. That is to say that there is a reciprocal interaction between the retarded child and his family. In this section we shall consider the effects on the family of the presence of a retarded offspring. It is often asserted that families with retarded children have problems lasting as long as the life of their child (e.g., Robinson & Robinson, 1976). This emphasis on the inevitability of difficulties is probably an overstatement. It seems plausible that many parents of cultural-familial retarded children would not see their child as different or deviant and that his presence would be very much like that of any other child. It is when there is a large discrepancy between the IQ levels of the parents and child, most often because of organic retardation, that the major problems arise.

Roos (1963) described several typical reactions of parents to having a retarded child. One was loss of self-esteem because of interpreting the presence of a retarded child as a defect in one's self. Parents may also experience shame, often leading to social withdrawal. A heightened ambivalence toward the child is another common response. That is to say, parents may at times reject their child because of his or her irritating behavior, or lack of progress, and then because of guilt become overprotective. Many parents also experience chronic sorrow, which Roos sees as a nonpathological reaction to having a retarded child. Some parents become excessively self-sacrificing and abandon all personal pleasures for their child. In such families the child may become the total focus of interest and other family members may suffer accordingly.

Farber (e.g., 1975) has described a series of phases that a family with a severely retarded member may go through. According to him these are a series of adaptations, each of which is more extreme. It is not inevitable that every family go through all these phases and they may stop at any point when a successful adaptation is reached. The first phase is labeling, when the child is seen by the family as retarded and there is a realization that traditional family roles may change. Next comes a normalization phase in which the family attempts to maintain a normal set of roles. The family maintains a facade of normality to the outside world and seeks to maintain relationships with normal families. In the mobilization phase families intensify the effort they give to family demands while still, however, claiming normality as a family. If the adaptations made in these phases are not successful the family enters the revisionist phase, in which age and sex standards in the organization of family roles are changed. For example, a normal adolescent female may assume the role of the primary caretaker. If this phase is reached the family can no longer maintain a facade of normality and often isolates itself from community involvement. The next, polarization, essentially involves the family behaving so as not to get in each other's way. Pathological or even delusional belief may not be challenged in the interest of maintaining some kind of family coherence. If all else fails the elimination phase is reached, where the offending member is expelled from the family. This quite often represents institutionalization of the retarded child. It is interesting to note, however, that Farber has found that other family members may be eliminated. The parents may divorce or a normal sibling may be sent to live with a relative.

It has been reported that having a retarded sibling by no means always has adverse consequences for children. Grossman (1973) found that about half of a group of college students who had a retarded sibling had essentially profited from the experience, in that they were more tolerant and compassionate than other young adults. However, many others did suffer from the experience, especially in families where the siblings had unusual responsibilities for child care.

The near support system

How successfully a retarded person or his family copes with his problems, of course, heavily depends on the extent and quality of services provided by the near support system—schools, institutions, and health care facilities. In this section we will discuss some educational and institutional aspects of the care of retarded persons. Such a discussion cannot be understood without reference to the predominant ideology in the area of mental retardation today—normalization. This concept has been defined as "utilization of means which are as culturally normative as possible in order to establish and/or maintain personal behaviors and characteristics which are as culturally normative as possible" (Wolfensberger, 1972, p. 28). This concept has been so widely accepted that many of the predominant thrusts in programs design for retarded individuals can be seen as an attempt to provide environments for retarded persons that are as normalized as possible.

Special education and mainstreaming

For many years the preferred educational arrangement for the teaching of mildly and moderately retarded children living at home has been self-contained special education classrooms where the retarded person has little contact with his nonretarded peers. More recently this practice has been questioned for two reasons. It has been argued that such a system stigmatizes the retarded individual and adds to his feelings of being different and inferior. The general effectiveness of special education has also been questioned (e.g., Dunn, 1968). Consequently, mainstreaming has become an increasingly widespread educational practice. Mainstreaming means nothing more than placing retarded children in regular classes to the greatest extent possible. Such placements can range from the complete integration of retarded children into regular classes to mainstreaming in nonacademic areas such as music and physical education to the provision of resource rooms to provide special help in certain academic areas.

While the concept of mainstreaming has met with widespread acceptance, the research on its consequences has yielded mixed results. In academic areas it appears that mainstreamed children do as well as children in special classes, but there is little evidence that mainstreaming is more effective. The expectation that mainstreamed retarded children would be less stigmatized by their peers has not been borne out. In the majority of the research it has been found that mainstreamed retarded children are less well accepted by their peers than are children in self-contained special education classes (Goodman, Gottlieb, & Harrison, 1972; Gottlieb & Budoff, 1973; Iano, Ayers, Heller, McGettigan, & Walker, 1974). However, it has also been reported that mildly retarded urban children were more accepted by their peers than nonretarded children while suburban mildly retarded children were less accepted by their peers than nonretarded children when placed in regular classes with resource room backkup (Bruininks, Rynders, & Gross, 1974).

In at least one study the expectancy of failure discussed above has been investigated in mainstreamed and special-class retarded children. Gruen, Ottinger, and Ollendick (1974) found that retarded children from mainstreamed classes had higher expectancies of failure than retarded children in special classes. It seems plausible that the high expectancy of failure stemmed from a history of repeated failures.

Institutions for the retarded

As with the quesiton of mainstreaming in special education, the normalization ideology has figured prominantly in current social policy concerning institutions for retarded individuals. The first institutions for the retarded, established in the late 1800s, were quite optimistic in their outlook and had the goal of training their residents so that they could return to their communities as self-sufficient persons. For a variety of reasons, including the fact that the original goals were not met, a second philosophy achieved dominance for roughly the first half of the twentieth century. Large custodial facilities were built far from population centers with the result that the residents had little involvement with their community and nonretarded people probably had even less contact with the retarded. In the early 1960s this model of the large central institution was increasingly questioned, and in recent years the predominant thrust of social policy concerning institutions for the retarded has heavily favored small, community-based facilities and deemphasized large, central institutions. The dissatisfaction with large, central institutions seems to have come from several sources. One certainly has been the widespread acceptance of the normalization concept. Application of the normalization principle would require residential facilities to be small and located within communities. Another source has been the documentation of dehumanizing conditions in some large central institutions (e.g., Blatt, 1970; Blatt & Kaplan, 1966). The fact that large central institutions were typically built far from population centers made continued contact with residents by their parents and other community members inordinately difficult (e.g., Sarason, Zitnay, & Grossman, 1971). Finally, the courts have asserted the rights of retarded individuals to include "the right to the least restrictive conditions necessary" (*Wyatt vs. Stickney et al., 1972*). It is interesting to note that this deemphaisis of the large, central institution and the acceptance of small, community-based facilities have evolved despite the fact that very little research has been done on the issue of what determines institutional adequacy. There is little question that before the advent of the small, community-based institution the predominant position was that institutions had extremely negative and monolithic effects. Support for this view came from studies indicating that the institutionalized retarded were less developmentally advanced than supposedly comparable groups of noninstitutionalized retarded individuals (Badt, 1958; Carr, 1970; Centerwall & Centerwall, 1960; Harter, 1967; Iscoe & McCann, 1965; Kaufman, 1963; Lyle, 1959; 1960 a,b; Shipe & Shotwell, 1965; Stedman et al., 1962). However, other reports have shown that institutionalization may also have beneficial effects. Several longitudinal studies have shown an overall increase in IQ for institutionalized retarded children. Institutionalization has also been found to be related to an increase in the retarded child's autonomy, to a language advantage, and to a movement toward less verbal dependency, less outerdirectedness, and more variability in behavior (Balla & Zigler, 1975; Balla, Butterfield, & Zigler, 1974; Clarke & Clarke, 1953, 1954; Mueller & Weaver, 1964; Yando & Zigler, 1971; Zigler, Balla, & Butterfield, 1968).

In many of these studies on the effects of institutionalization even the most simple description of the institutional environment was missing. Thus, it is impossible to reconcile inconsistent findings. The work that has been done in comparing different institutions for their effects on the actual behavior of the retarded has sometimes indicated that differences can be striking (Klaber & Butterfield, 1968; Klaber, Butterfield, & Gould, 1969). Findings (e.g., Butterfield & Zigler, 1965) of differences even across large institutions in the residents' responsiveness to a supportive adult and change in IQ following institutionalization lend credence to the argument (e.g., Balla, 1976; Cleland, 1965) that the particular social-psychological characteristics and practices of institutions that may affect the behavior and development of the residents should be closely investigated.

In an initial effort in this direction, Balla et al. (1974) studied residents in four widely geographically separate institutions for the retarded. Measures of MA, IQ, responsiveness to adult support, verbal dependency, wariness of adults, outerdirectedness, and behavior variability were obtained. In an effort to provide a more detailed characterization of the institutions than in previous studies, several demographic measures of the institutions were also obtained: size, number of residents per living unit, cost per resident per day, employee turnover rate, number of attendants per resident, number of professional staff per resident, and the extent of volunteer services. The subjective impressions of the institutions were also noted. Surprisingly, neither subjective impressions of the institutions nor the objective demographic characteristics were found to be related to the resident's behavioral development.

Balla et al. (1976) conducted a study of residents in five community-based facilities in two large central institutions in a northeastern state. The community-based centers ranged in size from 12 to 290 patients, while the average size of the large central institutions was over 1,500 patients. No differences in behavior were found between persons residing in central institutions and persons residing in the community-based centers. There were also no behavioral differences between persons residing in the largest regional center with a population of 290 and the smallest regional center with a population of 12. The behavior of the residents in all of the institutions was similar.

Complicating the question of the effects of institutional experience still further are the finding that one and the same institution can have different effects on the residents depending on their preinstitutional social deprivation (Balla, Butterfield, & Zigler, 1974; Balla & Zigler, 1975; Clarke & Clarke, 1953; 1954; Yando & Zigler, 1971; Zigler & Balla, 1972; Zigler, Balla & Butterfield, 1968). Clarke and Clarke (1954) found that the greatest increase in IQ scores following institutionalization occurred in those children who came from the worst homes. Findings of several longitudinal studies (Balla & Zigler, 1975; Zigler et al., 1968; Zigler & Williams, 1963) indicated that institutionalization was more socially depriving for individuals from relatively supportive home environments than for those from highly socially depriving environments. Balla et al. (1974) reported a number of findings indicating that the child's preinstitutional social deprivation played an important part in determining his behavior while institutionalized. Other findings of this longitudinal cross-institutional study indicated that the particular course of development displayed by a child was a function of both the child's history of preinstitutional social deprivation and of the particular institution in which he resided.

The effects of institutionalization on the behavior of the retarded are also undoubtedly related to length of institutionalization as well as gender and diagnosis. Balla, McCarthy, and Zigler (1971) found that children institutionalized when they were younger were less wary than those institutionalized when they were older. Ollendick et al. (1971) found higher expectancies of failure in males than females. In summary, the question of the effects of institutions on the behavior of the retarded has proven to be an extremely complex issue; there is little evidence to indicate that small, community-based facilities are more effective than the large institutions they were meant to replace.

However, the issue of actual behavioral effects is only one aspect of the question of what kind of residential facility is most effective. Perhaps of equal importance is the issue of quality of life. Retarded individuals have a right to humane care and treatment whether or not such treatment ultimately results in improved growth and development. In investigations concerned with quality of life it has generally been found that small, community-based facilities are more adequate. The English investigators King, Raynes, and Tizard (1971) investigated resident care practices in three types of institutions. They contrasted institution-oriented practices at one extreme and resident-oriented practices at the other. For example, if a resident was not permitted to have personal possessions, this would be considered an institution-oriented practice. If he were permitted to have visitors at any time rather than only at certain times or on certain days, it would be seen as a resident-oriented practice. These investigators found care practices to be more resident-oriented in small community-based facilities than in large central institutions.

McCormick, Balla, and Zigler (1975), utilizing the technique of King et al. (1971) , conducted a study of resident care practices in institutions in the United States and in a Scandanavian country. Large central institutions, regional centers, and group homes were investigated. Striking differences in care practices were found in living units from the different types of institutions, differences that were obtained in both countries. Large central institutions were characterized by the most institution-oriented care practices and group homes by the most resident-oriented care practices with regional centers between these extremes. Thus, in general, the quality of life seems to be better in small, community-based facilities than in large, central institutions. However, while it may be true that large is bad, this does not mean that small is good. Edgerton (1975) has reported that many small group homes are just as inadequate and inhumane as the large institutions.

Other treatment methods for retarded individuals

When the traditional services provided by the near support system are not available or are seen as inadequate, parents may choose to use less conventional ways of treating their child's retardation. Proponents of these less conventional treatment methods often claim dramatic results for individuals who have participated in them. Since parents of retarded children are particularly vulnerable to any claims that their child might be significantly helped, these treatments have often gained much popularity and publicity. Several drug therapies have been in vogue from time to time for the treatment of Down's syndrome: glutamic acid, thyroid extracts, pituitary extract, large doses of vitamins, and siccacells. Turkel (1961) has devised a "U" series of medications, which is a mixture of about 48 vitamins, minerals, enzymes, and common drugs, which he claims corrects the genetic flaw in Down's syndrome. All of these treatments for Down's syndrome have been shown not to be effective in controlled studies (Share, 1976). Indeed, Freeman (1970) has described the siccacell therapy as "an expensive form of quackery" (p. 338).

An especially longlasting and prominent treatment for the retarded has been that developed at the Institutes for Achievement of Human Potential (e.g., Doman, 1974). Basic to this treatment method is the application of a variety of sensory and motor experiences directed toward improving "neurological organization." Although there are many components to this treatment, the most widely known and publicized are patterning, creeping, and crawling. When a child is patterned, several adults simultaneously manipulate the limbs and head in a rhythmic fashion for a specified time period. Proponents of this treatment method also require that the child creep and/or crawl for specified time periods. It is felt that neurological organization must be imposed on the brain and that very primitive actions, such as creeping and crawling, must be successfully mastered or remastered before it is possible to master more advanced functions. This treatment is noteworthy for its intensity. Many adults are required for the treatment of each child and treatment goes on for many hours a day, every day of the year.

Since an early positive report on the success of this method in an uncontrolled study (Doman, Spitz, Zucman, Delacato, & Doman, 1960), the treatment has been a focus of considerable controversy. A number of behavioral and medical scientists have presented papers questioning both the theory and the value of the treatment method (e.g., Cohen, Birch, & Taft, 1970; Freeman, 1967; Glass & Robbins, 1967). Recently, two controlled studies have been done utilizing variations of this treatment method. In one (Neman, Roos, McCann, Menolascino, & Heal, 1975), a limited number of positive results was reported. The conclusions of this study have been questioned in two independent reviews (*Challenge,* 1973; Zigler & Seitz, 1975). In the other study (Sparrow & Zigler, 1977) no evidence was found that the treatment was more effective than simple attention and support. It seems most reasonable to conclude that the value of the treatment method has not been demonstrated in controlled scientific studies.

The far support system

The policies of the state and national governments and of organizations concerned with retarded persons will affect near support systems, the family, and the individual retarded person. There has been, without question, a vast improvement in almost every aspect of services for retarded people in the past 20 years. It could be convincingly argued that actions within the far support system have been largely responsible for this change. The concern and interest of President John F. Kennedy in mental retardation almost certainly led to a favorable change in public attitudes. During the Kennedy administration, the National Institute of Child Health and Human Development was established, an agency that has sponsored much research in the area of mental retardation.

The National Association for Retarded Citizens (NARC) has also played a considerable role in the favorable change for retarded persons. This organization, founded in 1950, had a membership of approximately 250,000 in 1974 (Roos, 1975). Early in this organization's existence, it concentrated on providing service programs for retarded individuals, and indeed became a major provider of direct service. More recently, the emphasis of NARC has shifted from the provision of direct service to advocacy for the retarded. The concept of advocacy has many facets and is difficult to define precisely (Zigler, 1977). However, good examples of the concept can be found in recent litigation concerning the rights of the retarded, litigation in which the NARC has been deeply involved. This litigation has been in three major areas: the right to treatment in residential facilities, the right to education for all retarded children, and the responsibility of states to provide funds for their education, and the procedures for identification and placement of mildly retarded children in special education classes.

The major case on the right to treatment issue was *Wyatt vs. Stickney et al.*, (1972), in which evidence was presented that the Partlow State School in Alabama was a depriving custodial facility incapable of providing treatment for its clients. The judge in this case issued a decree essentially supporting the obligation of the state to provide treatment for retarded reisdents. On the right to education issue, the practice of schools of excluding severely and profoundly retarded children from public education programs was challenged in *Pennsylvania Association for Retarded Children (PARC) vs. Commonwealth of Pennsylvania* (1972). In a consent decree signed by both parties in this case, the state agreed to locate all children of schoolage not in school, to provide medical and psychological evaluations to determine the most appropriate placement, and to place each child located and evaluated in a free public program. Recently, the United States Congress has passed a law (PL94-142) directing that no child be excluded from a public education. Consequently, the education of severely and profoundly retarded children is now the responsibility of the public school system. In the area of placement procedures it has been argued that children placed in special education classes are denied equal educational opportunity and that the quality of special classes is lower than that of regular classes. In the state of California, at least, Mexican-American children were overrepresented in special education classes, and in *Dianea vs. State Board of Education* (1970), it was argued that this overrepresentation was due to low test scores because of experiential and/or language differences, and that the low scores did not indicate mental retardation but simply different cultural backgrounds. Again, this case was settled out of court when it was agreed that all children whose primary language was other than English would be tested in both English and the primary language, that the children would not be examined on such tests as vocabulary, general information, and other "unfair" verbal tests, and that Mexican-American and Chinese-American children already in classes for the mentally retarded would be retested in their primary language and reevaluated only on nonverbal tests (Roos, DeYoung, & Cohen, 1971). Litigation and advocacy for the retarded will almost certainly continue and may well lead to further great changes in the lives of retarded persons.

Summary

Mental retardation refers to significantly subaverage intellectual functioning (an IQ of more than two standard deviations below the average on a standard intelligence test) along with deficits in adaptive behavior. Two groups of retarded people are usually distinguished: those with no evidence of organic brain damage, the cultural-familial; and those with identifiable physiological and/or anatomical abnormalities, the organically retarded. Approximately 75 percent of the retarded population has no evidence of organic brain damage. There are many causes of organic mental retardation including genetics, brain injury, and a variety of environmental factors such as exposure to toxins. The behavior of retarded people is not a function of low intelligence alone, but also reflects differences in motivation from persons of average intelligence and such other factors as the effects of the family, of schooling and in some cases insitutionalization. The most influential current philosophy for the treatment of the retarded is that of "normalization," the use of the most culturally normative means as possible in the establishment and maintenance of culturally normative behaviors.

GLOSSARY

Adaptive behavior: The effectiveness or degree with which the individual meets the standards of personal independence and social responsibility expected of his age and cultural group" (Grossman, 1973, p. 11). Deficits in adaptive behavior are necessary for the classification of mental retardation.

Amniocentesis: A procedure in which anmiotic fluid surrounding the fetus is obtained early in pregnancy. It is possible to detect chromosomal abnormalities from this fluid and thereby identify several types of organic mental retardation early in pregnancy.

Cultural-familial retardation: Mild retardation with no evidence or organic brain damage and with a history of mental retardation in other family members. Recently this form of retardation has been referred to as "retardation due to psycho-social disadvantage."

Down's syndrome: A form of mental retardation induced by three chromosomes rather than two in the 21st pair (trisomy 21). Persons with Down's syndrome are usually moderately retarded. Sometimes incorrectly referred to as mongolism.

Genotype: The genetic constitution of an organism, not necessarily overtly manifested.

Intelligence quotient (IQ): The ratio of mental growth as measured by a standard test of intelligence to chronological age. In these terms, IQ = MA/CA x 100.

Mainstreaming: The educational practice of placing retarded children in regular classes to the greatest extent possible.

Mental age: The score on an individual standard intelligence test expressed in years and months. It is seen as a measure of the extent of mental growth.

Mild mental retardation: Retardation with IQ scores falling approximately between 50 and 70. In education, "educable" is often used as a synonym.

Moderate mental retardation: Retardation with IQ scores falling approximately between 36 and 49. In education, "trainable" is often used as a synonym.

Normalization: As defined by Wolfensberger (1972, p. 28), "utilization of means which are as culturally normative as possible in order to establish and/or maintain personal behaviors and characteristics which are as culturally normative as possible".

Organic mental retardation: A general term referring to any type of mental retardation where there is a detectable anatomical and/or physiological abnormality. Such retardation may be due to genetic disorders, brain damage, or a number of environmental factors.

Phenotype: In genetics, the characteristics that actually appear in an organism.

Phenylketonuria (PKU): A recessive genetic disorder caused by the failure to metabolize phenylalanine resulting usually in severe mental retardation. Mental retardation can be prevented by treatment with a phenylalanine-free diet.

Polygenic inheritance: Inheritance that is determined by the action of many genes all affecting the same characteristic.

Profound mental retardation: Retardation with IQ scores falling below 20.

Severe mental retardation: Retardation with IQ scores falling approximately between 20 and 35.

four

TREATMENT

The range of treatments for behavior labeled dysfunctional is considerable. Just as there are many theoretical notions as to how abnormal behavior develops, there are many approaches for dealing with the signs and symptoms of psychopathology. With some problems a traditional verbal psychotherapy may be used. With others a more contemporary behavioral therapy strategy may be followed. In still others treatment may consist of the administration of drugs and other somatic approaches such as electroconvulsive therapy. At times the individual who is labeled abnormal and given a formal psychiatric diagnosis may be hospitalized, where combinations of the above treatments may be administered. The present chapters reflect the state of the art with respect to the treatment and management of dysfunctional behavior.

Dianna Hartley and Hans H. Strupp (Chapter 18) provide an overview of the verbal psychotherapies currently being applied in clinical practice. The many styles of therapists (from nondirective to directive) are considered, with attention directed to correctly matching the right therapist for the right patient. Cyril M. Franks and David B. Abrams (Chapter 19) outline specific strategies that are subsumed under the general label of behavior therapy. The authors stress that behavior therapy is primarily a method for approaching the study and treatment of aberrant behavior. The rigor and scientific underpinnings of the method are underscored. Donald W. Goodwin (Chapter 20) provides a description of the biological approach to treatment. Considered are the use of drugs (major and minor tranquilizers, antidepressants), electroconvulsive therapy, and the now infrequently used psychosurgical methods. Alan F. Fontana (Chapter 21) looks at the role of the mental hospital as a method of treatment and as the tool of society. Attempts to make the large mental hospital more therapeutic (e.g., milieu therapy) and less custodial are examined. Finally, Sol L. Garfield (Chapter 22) puts into perspective the psychological treatments of abnormal behavior by evaluating current trends. Garfield reviews the innovative developments of the last 30 years and the many scientific attempts to evaluate the efficacy of psychotherapeutic techniques that have evolved.

Bethlehem Hospital (Bedlam).
Engraving from *The Rake's Progress* by William Hogarth (1697–1764).

A charlatan of the seventeenth century pretending to remove stones from a woman's head to cure headaches.

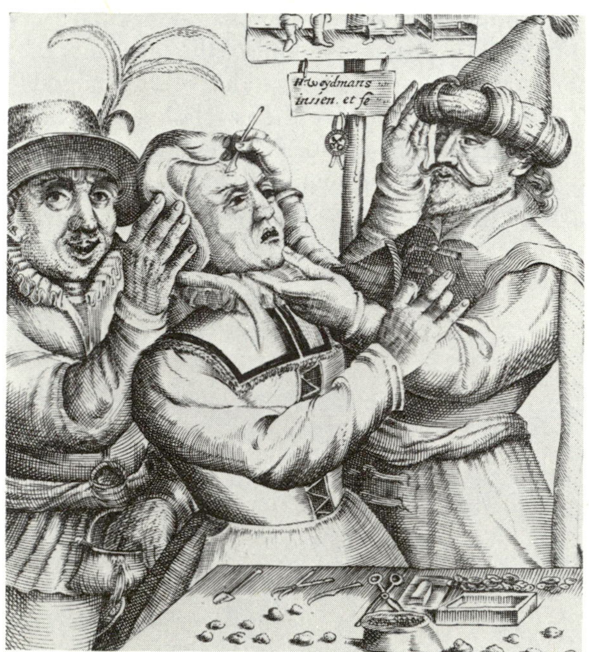

A whirling bed and whirling chair, illustration from *Traité sur l'aliénation mentale. . . ,* Amsterdam, 1826.

Shell-shocked soldiers fishing at an American Red Cross hospital at Blois, France. During the First World War, this was experimental psychiatric therapy.

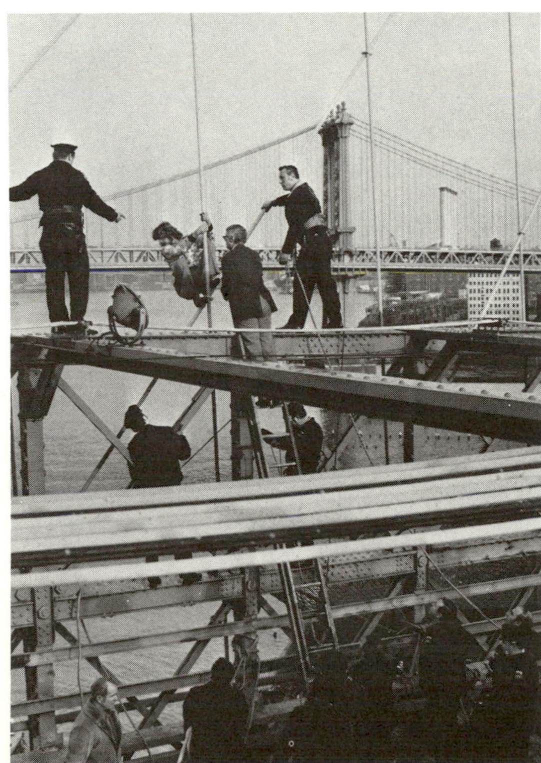

A psychiatric social worker persuading a young man not to commit suicide.

VERBAL PSYCHOTHERAPIES

DIANNA HARTLEY
HANS H. STRUPP

Most of us feel bewildered and confused when we try to understand modern psychotherapy, the "talking cure." Ideas about how to help people with psychological problems even outnumber speculations about what caused the problems originally. Indeed, the broad range of theories and techniques that come under the heading of psychotherapy appear to have little in common. Great diversity also marks those who practice: therapists vary in personal style, philosophical leanings, training, and professional activities. Those persons who manifest a tremendous assortment of problems with their families, their jobs, their friends, and themselves turn to psychotherapists for help. Some claim that therapy is most useful in dealing with many of life's dilemmas, while others assert that it is virtually useless. On one hand, a mixture of awe, fear, and puzzlement greets the disclosure that someone is in therapy; on the other, therapists are frequently lampooned in popular magazines like the *New Yorker*. What is psychotherapy? What do psychotherapists do? How do they do it? Who benefits from psychotherapy? In what ways does it help? What are the risks?

What is psychotherapy?

Before describing current psychotherapeutic practices, we should establish a basic understanding of what we mean by psychotherapy. Without attempting a formal definition, it may be said that psychotherapy is an interpersonal process designed to modify feelings, cognitions, attitudes, and behaviors that have proven troublesome to the person seeking help from a trained clinician. There is considerable controversy whether and to what extent psychotherapy differs from other human relationships in which one person helps another to solve a personal problem. However, as ordinarily understood, the psychotherapist is a trained professional person who has acquired special skills.

The historical roots of psychotherapy extend into a wide variety of areas, from ancient medicine, philosophy, religion, faith healing, and hypnotism to modern biology, medicine and social science. The notion that some forms of suffering and unhappiness have no clear physical or social causes developed long before recorded history. In many cultures, those who differed significantly from their peers in certain ways were seen as possessed by magical or evil spirits and were treated by priests, shamans, or medicine men in highly emotional ceremonies. As early as the fifth century B.C., the Greek physician Hippocrates urged that mental illness be studied and treated scientifically. Through the strong influence of religion and the disrepute of science in the Middle Ages, this idea was largely eclipsed, but reemerged later with the ascendance of the so-called medical model of mental illness as a disease to be treated by physicians like any other disease.

The emergence of psychotherapy as a unique form of healing can be traced to Franz Anton Mesmer in the eighteenth century, who claimed he could cure certain symptoms by putting patients into a trance state. Although his theories and techniques were soon discredited and rejected, mesmerism was a forerunner of hypnotism, which in turn is recognized as the precursor of psychotherapy as we know it through its influence on Sigmund Freud. Using hypnosis, Freud and Joseph Breuer observed that many of their patients had developed symptoms that symbolically expressed an attempt to resolve conflicts rooted in "forgotten" traumatic experiences of the past (Breuer & Freud, 1895). Freud pursued these observations and developed psychoanalysis, a theory of human nature and a form of treatment in which personal histories are examined in detail and childhood experiences are relived with the therapist. This treatment process results in a restructuring of the patient's experience and leads to improved functioning and adaptation. Since these discoveries toward the end of the last century, many innovators have so altered the basic techniques that the Freudian influence is all but unrecognizable. However, all verbal psychotherapies, and behavioral therapies as well, involve repeated emotionally charged interactions with a therapist in which patients or clients learn more about their own feelings, attitudes, and behavior.

In broadest terms, psychotherapy is concerned with personality and behavior change. The person who seeks help for a psychological problem desires change—he or she wants to feel or act differently, and the psychotherapist agrees to assist in achieving this goal. The major issues in psychotherapy relate to *what* is to be changed and *how* change can be brought about. The first part of the question entails definition of the *problem* for which the patient is seeking help (e.g., depression, marital difficulties, shyness, nailbiting, sexual dysfunctions, existential anxiety); the second pertains to the process and techniques by means of which change is effected (e.g., support, ventilation of feelings, interpretations). Ideally, one would like to be able to say that, given Problem X, the optimal approach is Technique Y. In practice, as the reader will discover, things are rarely so simple or straightforward; on the contrary, since human problems are extraordinarily complex, so are the issues facing the therapist who attempts to deal with these difficulties in therapeutic ways. For the same reason it is unlikely that there will ever be a single optimal approach to the solution of a psychological problem.

Psychotherapy is often described as "treatment," and since medical terminology (e.g., patient, therapist, diagnosis, etiology) has traditionally been used, the analogy of a physician ministering to a passive patient readily springs to mind. By contrast, it is important to stress that psychotherapy has at best only a superficial resemblance to this model. More accurately, psychotherapy is a *collaborative* endeavor or a partnership, in which the patient is expected to play an active part. In practice this means that the patient must gradually become more autonomous, more self-directing, and more responsible for feelings, beliefs, and actions. The process of therapy is designed not to change the patient but to help the patient make the desired changes.

In this sense, psychotherapy is a learning process and the role of the therapist is analogous to that of a teacher. The primary assumption of all psychotherapies is that feelings, cognitions, attitudes, and behavior (both adaptive and maladaptive) are products of a person's life experience—that is, they have been *learned.* If something has been learned, then it can be unlearned and relearned in a new context. Where learning is impossible (for example, in conditions attributable to genetic or biochemical factors), psychotherapy has little to offer. Similarly, if the disturbance is solely due to factors in the person's social milieu (poverty, oppression, imprisonment) or if change is imposed from outside the patient (e.g., referral by a court or school system), psychotherapists encounter great difficulties. Thus, psychotherapy works best if a patient desires change of his or her own accord and is motivated to work toward it, if the environment in which he or she lives tolerates the possibility of change, and if the inner obstacles to learning (defenses and rigidities of character) are not insurmountable.

No single definition of psychotherapy has found universal acceptance. Depending upon the therapist's theoretical orientation and other factors, psychotherapy is seen as a "psychosocial treatment," as a special form of education, or as a means of promoting personality growth and self-actualization, to cite but a few divergent views. Most therapists, including some behavior therapists (Wilson & Evans, 1977), agree, however, that psychotherapy involves a unique human relationship and techniques for relieving distress and establishing conditions for learning and for personal growth.

Who benefits from psychotherapy?

The single most important characteristic of individuals who decide to consult a psychotherapist is that they are troubled. At times they may be unaware of the cause of their suffering and unhappiness. More often, they have identified a set of circumstances they view as accounting for their disturbance. Typically, they are dissatisfied with their life, complain of troublesome feelings, or see difficulties with some aspect of their behavior. Many have tried various "home remedies" for combating their difficulties, without notable success. The patient's goals might be to "feel better," to "act differently," or to "stop" a pattern of behavior. Along with various problems, most patients experience a lack of "will power" and a sense of helplessness. Blame may be attributed to the behavior of other persons or the social environment. Life events seem to be out of the control of the patient. Often it is not possible to bring about the changes to which the patient aspires, at least not in the manner desired. While the patient ostensibly desires change of a certain kind, he or she is unwittingly committed to maintaining the status quo and actively opposes change. For example, a patient may express a wish to become more assertive, while basically searching for a human relationship that allows passivity and dependency. In any case, the patient's problem often is not what it appears to be, and redefinitions of the problem and the goals of therapy may be indicated.

Most patients approach therapy with mixed feelings. They feel both frightened and hopeful: frightened that something terrible will be discovered, that friends and relatives will think the worst, that therapy will be just one more failure experience, but hopeful that finally an expert will understand and help, that life can be changed. It is this hope, combined with faith and trust in therapy and in the therapist, that provides the early positive force for the initiation of a therapy relationship. Patients vary greatly in the extent to which they are able to form a trusting, intimate relationship. This difference may account for much of the variation in treatment outcomes. Usually patients who have a greater "ego strength"—that is, those who are more easily able to cope with everyday stress, to form good relationships, to meet their needs in their environment, and to be aware of what is going on around them as well as of their own internal process—are likely to benefit more from the verbal psychotherapies.

What does a psychotherapist do?

Psychotherapy is currently practiced by members of numerous professions, including psychiatrists, clinical psychologists, psychiatric social workers, nurses, and pastoral counselors. In the nineteenth century when psychotherapy first emerged as treatment for so-called nervous and mental diseases, its practice was a medical art, restricted to psychiatrists. Around the middle of this century many other professions gained entry into the field as a result of the growing demand for psychotherapeutic services, coupled with a redefinition of the earlier disease model. Today psychotherapy is the generic term for psychological interventions designed to ameliorate emotional or behavioral problems of various kinds. Contemporary psychotherapy is characterized by a diversity of theoretical orientations (e.g., psychodynamic, client-centered, rational-emotive, Gestalt) and treatment modalities (individual, group, family, marital). Theories and techniques of behavior therapy, which have become prominent during the past few decades, are usually differentiated form psychotherapy although behavioral interventions are clearly psychological, and many of the same general curative processes occur in both kinds of therapy. The lack of consensus concerning the role and function of the therapist reflects major disagreements about the purpose of psychotherapy, the goals of treatment, and how therapeutic change is brought about. Most professionals agree that a therapist must acquire special skills, but they do not agree on the nature of these skills or how to perfect them. Consequently, training programs for psychotherapists differ markedly in content, breadth, and duration.

In any event, the therapist engages in a raltionship with the patient and brings personal influence to bear upon that relationship. Of course, both the patient's and the therapist's personalities determine the character and quality of their interaction, but the therapist defines the framework of the relationship and determines to a large extent how the relationship shall be used to achieve particular therapeutic ends. There is still a lively debate about whether the therapist determines the outcome of therapy primarily by personal qualities or whether the outcome is ultimately a function of the techniques employed. We may find that both sets of variables contribute significantly but in varying combinations, depending in part upon patient characteristics. Clearly the *personal qualities* or the therapist must be an important factor in the equation (Parloff, Waskow, & Wolfe, 1978).

Whatever his or her theoretical orientation or professional affiliation, a good therapist performs certain tasks. The most important of these is listening with unswerving attention, compassionate concern, and genuine effort to understand the patient's personal meanings, without responding in terms of one's own feelings of the moment or according to social convention. The good therapist maintains steadfastly the goal of the patient's integrity and self-betterment, and acts only to relieve suffering and to enhance understanding.

Finally, it is important to examine how the professional therapist differs from other helpful persons. Most significantly, the therapist creates a *professional* rather than a *personal* relationship with the patient. While the patient may be lonely and in need of a friend, it is not the task of the therapist to fulfill this need, but rather to facilitate the patient's interpersonal relationships with others and to encourage more adaptive, effective, and independent action. Thus, therapists avoid undue emotional involvement with patients, a stance that is frequently contrary to the patient's wishes. On the other hand, this relative detachment allows the therapist to be more objective about the patient's difficulties. Even more important, it enables the patient to communicate more freely without having to be concerned about the therapist's personal reactions to material that ordinarily might evoke shame, fear, anger, and retaliation. By trusting the therapist and the safety of the therapeutic situation, patients can often begin to tackle other troublesome problems. The professional therapist's stance of acceptance, respect, understanding, helpfulness, and warmth, coupled with deliberate efforts not to critize, pass judgment, or react emotionally to provocations, creates a framework and an atmosphere unmatched by any other human relationship.

How does psychotherapy work?

While psychotherapy takes many different forms, it always involves change in personality and behavior, including feelings, thoughts, and actions, with the goal being the client's increased autonomy and independence. Thus, the process has often been described as one of "reparenting," in which the therapist helps the client to become a more mature adult. Most theories that guide psychotherapy assume that suffering is related in some way to immaturity—dependence, lack of competence, and the inability to realize one's goals. Problems that are amenable to psychotherapy are those that are in some way the product of past experience. That is, the person has learned faulty techniques for coping with life in this culture or has not acquired the capacities necessary to deal effectively with his or her world. In addition to these learning or developmental deficiencies, most people who seek psychotherapy find themselves enmeshed in present-day situational difficulties beyond their coping resources. Another assumption is that appropriate learning experiences, the use of certain techniques within the context of a certain kind of relationship, can influence the individual in the direction of better life adaptation. Minimally, the aim of therapy is cessation of the currently experienced stress; maximally, the therapist seeks to reconstruct the personality itself in order that it may endure greater hardships and deal more creatively with the world.

Later in this chapter we will look briefly at some of the methodologies developed to accomplish these objectives. Reader responses to the different orientations will understandably vary. Some orientations will sound productive and powerful, others implausible or ineffective. Various schools of psychotherapy have been organized by innovative thinkers, who in turn have attracted followers. Those who identify with a particular approach rarely see objectively the disadvantages of their own or the advantages of other orientations. Because therapeutic impact depends in part on the faith, hope, and trust engendered by the therapist's enthusiastic commitment to his or her technical operations, this is perhaps as it should be. In general, the proponents of all systems of psychotherapy credit their successes to more or less *specific* operations they claim are uniquely effective. So far, however, it has not been possible to show that one technique is clearly superior to another, even under reasonably controlled conditions (e.g., Luborsky, Singer, & Luborsky, 1975; Sloane, Staples, Cristol, Yorkston, & Whipple, 1975). The commonly accepted finding is that approximately two-thirds of neurotic patients who enter outpatient psychotherapy of whatever description show noticeable improvement (Garfield, 1978; Bergin & Lambert, 1978). Finally, it often turns out that initial claims for a new technique cannot be sustained when the accumulating evidence is critically examined.

An alternative hypothesis has been advanced (Frank, 1973; Strupp, 1973) that asserts that psychotherapeutic change is predominantly a function of factors common to all therapeutic approaches, brought to bear in the human relationship between the patient and the healer. The proponents of this hypothesis hold that a person, defined by himself or others as a patient, suffers from demoralization and a sense of hopelessness. Consequently, any benign human influence is likely to boost his or her morale, which in turn is registered as "improvement." Primary ingredients of these common nonspecific factors include: understanding, respect, interest, encouragement, acceptance, forgiveness—in short, the kinds of human qualities that since time immemorial have been considered effective in lifting the human spirit.

Frank (1973) identifies another important common factor in all psychotherapies, namely, their tendency to operate in terms of a conceptual scheme and specific procedures thought to be beneficial. While the contents of the schemes and the procedures differ among therapies, they have common morale-building functions. They combat the patient's demoralization by providing an explanation, acceptable to both patient and therapist, for his hitherto inexplicable feelings and behavior. This process removes the mystery from the patient's suffering and eventually replaces it with hope.

Frank's formulation implies that training in and enthusiasm for a special theory and method may increase the effectiveness of therapists. In contrast, nonprofessional helpers may lack belief in a coherent system or rationale and, hence, be less effective. This hypothesis also underscores the continuity between faith healers, shamans, and modern psychotherapists. While the latter may operate on the basis of highly sophisticated scientific theories (by contemporary standards), the function of these theories may intrinsically be no different from the most primitive rationale undergirding a faith healer's efforts. In both instances "techniques" of whatever description are inseparable from the therapist's belief system, which in successful therapy is accepted and integrated by the patient. Some patients, of course, may be more receptive to, and thus more likely to benefit from, the therapist's manipulations than others.

While the hypothesis of nonspecific factors may be correct, it is still possible that *some* technical operations may be superior to others with particular patinets, particular problems, and under particular circumstances (Strupp, 1973). Such claims are made, for example, by therapists who are interested in the treatment of sexual dysfunctions (cf., Kaplan, 1974) and by behavior therapists who have tackled a wide range of behavior disorders (Marks, 1978). As yet, many of these claims are untested, and a great deal of research needs to be done to document that specific techniques are uniquely effective.

The therapeutic alliance. Because no therapeutic approach has been established as superior to others, many theoreticians and researchers have turned their attention to the search for those common elements that could be resonsible for the benefits seen to accrue in all therapies. The most prominent of these common factors is the therapeutic alliance, a two-way commitment in which each participant performs according to an unwritten agreement. In recent years, many theorists have identified the working relationship between patient and therapist as a major therapeutic force (e.g., Greenson, 1967; Langs, 1973; Menninger & Holtzman, 1973).

As Freud developed psychoanalytic therapy, he recognized that the patient must become an active partner who collaborates with the therapist in achieving a therapeutic result. He postulated that the reasonable and rational part of the patient's personality forms an alliance and identifies with the therapist's efforts in analyzing and understanding the irrational aspects. The therapeutic relationship can be seen as composed of a "real" relationship (that is, the relationship between two adults, one of whom desires therapeutic change) and a "transference" relationship (represented by continual but unwitting efforts on the patient's part to reenact his or her neurotic conflicts with the therapist).

To the extent that factors within the patient or the therapist interfere with the establishment of a productive therapeutic alliance, therapeutic progress will be retarded or even vitiated. Premature termination or intractable dependency on the therapist are instances of such failures. It is also well known that patients who have relatively intact and strong egos have a better chance of succeeding in analytic therapy (Appelbaum, 1977; Horwitz, 1974; Kernberg, 1976) and probably in other forms of therapy as well.

While superficially resembling any good human relationship the therapeutic alliance provides a unique starting point for the patient's growing identification with the therapist. This point has been stressed by the proponents of "object relations" theory (Fairbairn, 1952; Guntrip, 1971; Kernberg, 1976; Winnicott, 1968) who are spearheading advances in psychoanalytic theory. "Object relations" refers to interpersonal relationships with important human figures in the environment. According to these authors, the "internalization" of the therapist as a "good object" is crucial for significant psychotherapeutic change. Since the internalization of "bad objects" has made the patient "ill," therapy succeeds to the extent that the therapist can become a "good object." However, because the patient tends to remain loyal to the early objects of childhood, defending them against modification, therapy inevitably becomes a struggle. Even from his cursory sketch, it is apparent that the patient's amenability to therapy, that is, the ability to form a therapeutic alliance, is importantly determined by early object relations.

How is psychotherapy conducted?

Although the actual course of therapy varies with therapist, client, and theoretical orientation, a general sequential process unfolds in all psychotherapy relationships. The elements in the sequence may not always occur in the same order and are not given equal attention by all therapists. However, some awareness of how psychotherapy may generally be expected to proceed may be useful.

The initial phase. Psychotherapy begins when an individual comes for help and participates with the therapist in deciding whether psychotherapy is the kind of help needed. The first phase of the treatment involves assessing the nature of the problems and what the client wants to change. This phase may last one session or (in classical analysis) may require weeks. The therapist conducts evaluation interviews by identifying the current presenting problems as the client sees them, exploring in depth the background of these problems, beginning to understand the client as a whole person, and, finally, arriving at an adequate working formulation of the client and the client's problems. Therapists vary in how much and what kind of information they require for an adequate working formulation. They also differ in how definitive they prefer initial formulations to be before they propose a treatment contract. Patients also present a broad range: some talk freely and rapidly, others slowly and hesitantly; some keep to the point, others ramble; some have a few focal complaints, others are diffusely unhappy. All these factors affect the length of the initial phase of therapy.

In deciding whether or not to enter a psychotherapy relationship, a therapist considers the client's appropriateness for the particular therapy he or she practices. For dynamic therapies, the major criteria are motivation for psychotherapy, tendencies toward self-exploration and self-disclosure, and general integration of personality despite difficulties. Although it is possible for unmotivated, unreflective, untalkative, or poorly integrated people to profit from therapy, these variables often determine the extent to which they become engaged in the process and benefit from it.

If the therapist and patient mutually decide they can work together toward certain goals using the techniques of psychotherapy, a "contract" is made and the beginnings of a positive therapeutic alliance exist. Ideally, the relationship begins with an explicit agreement about how meetings will be arranged, what their respective roles will be, how fees will be paid, and the nature of the goals toward which they will work.

The middle phase. After the period of assessment and agreement on a contract, psychotherapy enters its middle and usually longest phase. During this time, the client and therapist do the major portion of their work in gaining a clearer understanding of the problems and their sources and in moving toward more constructive resolution of conflicts. During this phase the therapist's major responsibilities are to help the client talk, to understand what the client reveals, and to share this understanding with the client in such a way that it becomes a meaningful part of his or her life. The client's task is to explore as clearly and honestly as possible all thoughts, feelings, actions, and circumstances related to the problems dealt with, and to be open to the therapist's interventions. However, as they proceed, interferences with the therapeutic process may be expected. Although variation is again the hallmark, all dynamic therapies make some reference to the phenomena of resistance, transference, and countertransference, as well as interpretation and working through.

After a number of sessions, a therapist shifts the focus of therapy from learning about the client to helping the client learn about himself. Common therapist interventions include silent listening, asking questions, clarifying communications, and confronting contradictions. The main tool for communicating such understanding is *interpretation.* Simply put, interpretations are comments designed to reorganize or recast something the client has said, done, or experienced in a way that points to features of feelings, cognitions, or behavior he or she has not previously recognized. Interpretations often enhance self-understanding by expanding awareness of thoughts and feelings, and thus help the client to restructure cognitive and affective experience, modify behavior patterns, and achieve greater freedom of action.

Because learning almost always requires more than one trial, we are not surprised that people do not immediately change the first time they hear an interpretation—even an accurate, well-timed one. The views of oneself and one's place in the world have been reinforced by years of experience and cannot rapidly be altered. Usually, alternative points of view must be repeated by the therapist on several occasions before the client accepts their plausibility and undergoes therapeutic change. This process of repetition, called *working through,* establishes the validity of an interpretation and extends its applicability to new events that later come under consideration. Sequentially, clients are able to see a maladaptive thought or behavior pattern in therapy with the therapist's help, then become aware of the pattern soon after it has occurred, and finally recognize it in ongoing behavior, at which time they can make a choice about whether to continue it. Although the learning process can be an arduous one for both therapist and client, it is only when the client is able to recognize patterns and make choices in ongoing situations that therapeutic change has occurred.

Inevitably in the course of therapy, a time comes when the client, although still desirous of help and trustful of the therapist to provide it, paradoxically is reluctant or unable to participate in treatment according to the conditions established in the initial phase. People seem to have an instinct to avoid certain changes and kinds of awareness. Various defenses interfere with the process of communication, exploration, and understanding. This phenomenon, *resistance,* is not conscious obstinacy, but rather is itself an event to understand and work through. It is easy to see how therapy can be perceived as a threat to the niche one has created for oneself and an attack on a way of life. Frequently clients are unable to perceive alternative choices, and cling desperately to the self-concept they have adopted over the years. The same customary methods used for warding off anxiety and pain in life, *defense mechanisms,* are used to avoid the anxiety and pain of therapy. Good therapists use resistances as another tool for understanding the person. By confronting the defensive function of certain behaviors and presenting alternatives, a therapist expresses confidence in the client's ability to grow and change despite anxiety.

The complex concept of *transference* is the pivot upon which psychodynamic therapy turns. Basically, transference refers to the tendency to apply feelings, attitudes, or impulses experienced toward previous significant figures in the person's life to current figures whom they do not realistically fit. It exists to some extent in all interpersonal relationships, but is more pronounced in those whose conflicts were not satisfactorily resolved as they moved through the various periods of maturation. It is particularly exacerbated by the treatment situation where the therapist adopts a relatively passive, neutral role vis-à-vis the client and encourages the free, honest reporting of all thoughts and feelings. The client unwittingly recreates with the therapist the very conflict that was not resolved earlier in relationships with parents and others. In other words, the client suffers from what was in the past an interpersonal conflict perhaps with the parents, which became an internalized, intrapsychic conflict. The therapeutic situation reverses the process and transforms the intrapsychic or internal conflict once more into an interpersonal one with the therapist, in a context where every effort is made to achieve a new, more adaptive solution. Reliving the conflict in the present is the core of all dynamic therapies. However, it is common for the strong positive or negative emotion generated by the conflict and directed toward the therapist to interfere with the accomplishment of the therapeutic task, and thus to serve as a form of resistance.

Therapists, like all of us, also have tendencies or attitudes not realistically justified by the other person's behavior or the therapy relationship. These processes again have their roots in unconscious needs, ingrained patterns, and conflicting feelings. When these attitudes interfere with the therapeutic task, they are called *countertransferences*. Like transference, countertransference can be either positive or negative, or it may reflect the ambivalence of the therapist. On the one hand, a therapist may feel omnipotent, overconcerned, or totally responsible for the client, develop a strong emotional interest in the client, or otherwise treat him or her as "special." On the other hand, a therapist may become hostile and reject a client, withdraw from exploration of certain areas because of anxiety, or subtly undermine the therapy. Either extreme—or oscillations from one to the other—disrupts the therapeutic relationship and can adversely affect the client. Such negative reactions, however, can be reversed and used in the service of therapeutic exploration. To the extent that the therapist becomes aware of irrational personal reactions and to the extent that the client has contributed to their occurrence, it is possible for therapist and client to explore the problem. This way of handling a potentially harmful situation usually strengthens the relationship and serves as a good model of honest communication.

The termination phase. One of the most difficult areas in psychotherapy is deciding when to end the relationship. Once we recognize the impossibility of perfect self-awareness or "fully functioning" behavior, no concrete guidelines for determining when one no longer needs therapy exist. Weiner (1975) suggests three criteria: 1. Substantial progress is seen by both client and therapist, 2. the client is capable of continuing the progress alone, and 3. the transference relationship has been resolved. It is important to keep in mind that the goal of therapy is not just to solve certain problems, but to teach a method or process of self-examination that continues throughout life. When the client is productively active in various spheres of life and striving toward understanding, love, and work in a self-fulfilling way, termination of psychotherapy can be considered. This phase of therapy offers opportunities to work through such issues as separation, loss, and independence.

With this overall view of what psychotherapy entails for the client or patient, for the therapist, and for the relationship into which they enter, we turn our attention to a more detailed examination of specific approaches to therapy.

Individual psychotherapy

From among the ever increasing number of approaches to individual psychotherapy, we have chosen to examine more closely representatives of traditional and innovative analytic, humanistic, existential, and cognitive orientations. The interested reader may consult basic sources or other secondary references such as those by Patterson (1973) or Sahakian (1976).

Psychoanalytic therapy

Classical psychoanalysis. We have already seen that Freud developed psychoanalysis as an intensive long-term procedure for gaining conscious access to repressed memories, motives, conflicts, and anxieties stemming from problems in early psychosexual development and for facilitating their resolution in the light of adult reality. The difficult task of describing psychoanalysis is complicated by inaccurate conceptions based on movies, television, novels, and magazines. The three basic tools of the analyst are free association, dream analysis, and the interpretation of transferences and resistances. Having discussed this last concept above, we turn now to description of the first two.

The fundamental rule of analysis is that the person being treated must say whatever comes to mind without censoring it, no matter how personal, painful, or trivial it may seem at the moment. To facilitate this process, called *free association,* the individual relaxes on a couch with the analyst out of sight in order not to distract or disrupt the flow of thoughts. As the patient reports all thoughts as they occur, the statements made are seen as related in meaningful ways to preceding ones, and to prior thoughts and actions. The interrelationships in the stream of thoughts, feelings, and wishes provide the therapist valuable clues about the structure of the individual's personality. These clues are then synthesized and become part of the understanding communicated to the patient.

Another important procedure is dream analysis. Dreams, "the royal road to the unconscious," and the feelings associated with them are considered especially revealing because repressive defenses are lowered in sleep. Dream analysis begins with the manifest content, the dream as it is recalled by the dreamer. Since some emotions are so unacceptable that they cannot even be revealed openly in dreams, they appear in symbolic or disguised form. The task of the therapist is to uncover the meaning of the latent content of the dream by analyzing and interpreting the symbols that appear.

Other analytic therapies. As Freud's work attracted increasing attention, he acquired a circle of disciples, some of whom came to disagree with his theoretical views. In a number of instances these theoretical diverges produced modifications in techniques. Many of the important contributors to psychoanalytic theory and practice such as Adler, Horney, and Sullivan placed increasing emphasis on sociocultural and environmental factors that they felt had been insufficiently stressed by Freud. Taking particular issue with Freud's biological orientation and emphasis on instinctual drives, a group of theorists who have come to be called "ego psychologists" detailed human adaptive functions and constructive forces in the struggle to achieve competence, mastery, and identity (e.g., Hartmann, 1964; Rapaport, 1951; Schafer, 1976). The emphasis of this approach is on understanding how the perceptual, cognitive, and affective spheres of existence organize and utilize internal and external stimuli.

Carl Jung was a close associate of Freud who later parted company with him and formulated his own theory of personality called *analytical psychology* (Jung, 1966, 1971), which is more mystical than most theories and deemphasizes sexuality as a central theme. Essentially, Jungian therapy consists of uncovering "complexes," each individual's agglomeration of associations, that have tensions and energies of their own. The basic tools are interpretations of dreams, fantasies, and artistic productions, which are studied carefully, as religious texts are studied. Jungians also hold that individuals hold the key to decoding their own unconscious and give credence to self-interpretations.

Alfred Adler, another early student of Freud, broke away and developed his theory of *individual psychology* (Adler, 1964). His social psychological model is based on the assumption that people are motivated primarily by social urges, relate cooperatively with others, and place social welfare above selfish interests. He also conceived people being motivated by ideals and expectations of the future more than by experiences of the past. According to Ansbacher and Ansbacher (1956), Adlerian therapy has three objectives. The first is understanding the life style of the client, the specific problem situation, and the meaning of the presenting symptoms. The second involves communication of this understanding in a way that leads to acceptance of the interpretation despite initial resistance, usually by rational argument. A final goal is strengthening social interest by giving an opportunity to cooperate in the joint task of treatment and by reparenting, that is, reinterpreting society as to a child. Alderian therapy differs in the kind of explanations used, and in the activity level of the therapist, who immediately draws connections and gives advice rather than deliberating and analyzing.

One of the best known of the neo-Freudians is Erik Erikson (1964, 1968), whose stages of ego development are elaborations of Freud's psychosexual stages. For Erikson, the mentally healthy individual has an ego equipped to meet the challenges of life while the anxieties of the abnormal person persist into adulthood, undermining security and identity. Therapy, for Erikson, represents at least a meaningful moratorium in which the therapist guides the client through lost life stages, beginning with building the trust and confidence not gained in childhood. He urges mutuality in the relationship, stressing that the therapist is teaching another person to be self-observant. His ideas are representative of "ego psychology" with its concern with conflict-free functions, coping and cognitive processes, and stage sequences.

Humanistic and existential approaches

Many psychotherapists reject the classical psychoanalytic model and behavioral approaches to psychotherapy. Humanistic psychology, the "third force" as it has been called by Maslow, focuses on each person as a self-fulfilling organism who has choice, will power, self-awareness, and aspirations.

Client-centered counseling. The primary objective of this form of therapy (Rogers, 1951, 1961) is to create conditions that foster self-acceptance and inherent growth potentialities. Troubled individuals are seen as essentially good, but hampered by anxiety of self-evaluation which leads to *incongruence,* or actions not in accordance with feelings and attitudes one actually experiences. The therapist creates an atmosphere in which the client feels empathically understood (i.e., the therapist puts himself or herself in the psychological frame of reference of the client and knows how the client feels) and unconditionally accepted as a whole person. The client is thus freed to explore real feelings and thoughts that were inconsistent with the previous self-concept, and to become a better integrated person. The therapist does not direct the therapy by asking questions, giving advice, or offering interpretations. Rather, the main technique is *reflection,* which consists of sensing the client's meaning and putting it into words as clearly as possible. The idea that "the therapist knows best" is rejected in favor of clarifying the client's own feelings and attitudes in such a way as to promote self-awareness, personal growth, and positive action. Clients are encouraged to assume major responsibility for their own interpretations and their own decisions.

Client-centered therapy is perhaps more adequate as an approach to viewing persons who suffer from problems in living than as a set of techniques for effecting personality and behavior change. Its emphasis on the worth of the individual in an age that obscures this value is altogether wholesome and desirable. However, its popularity and influence have lost momentum in recent years for several reasons. First, its utility is confined to a limited segment of clients who are relatively well-functioning and who already have the resources to permit them to use a positive human relationship for their own growth. Unfortunately, most of the people seen by psychotherapists have had such negative interpersonal experiences that they have difficulty recognizing and utilizing a benign relationship. Secondly, the rise of behavioral and other newer approaches paralleled the decline of Rogers's own personal leadership. Thirdly, Rogers and many other client-centered therapists have turned to work with encounter groups composed of "normal" individuals who wish to increase their sensitivity and become more open in their dealings with peers.

Gestalt therapy. F.S. Perls, the founder of Gestalt therapy, was trained in and influenced by psychoanalysis, but rejected many of its tenets. He adopted a "Gestalt" approach, which advocates a holistic analysis of psychological phenomena based on the idea that a whole person is more than just the sum of physical, psychological, or social functions (Perls, 1969; Perls, Hefferline, & Goodman, 1965). Gestalt techniques include a wide range of "exercises" designed to increase awareness of repressed needs. For example, a role reversal may be used by having a shy patient boast of accomplishments, or a typically assumed role may be elaborated and exaggerated to make it more visible. Often clients carry on dialogues between parts of their personalities or play various persons or objects in dreams. Seemingly casual observations are repeated until the underlying emotion is expressed. The therapist takes an active role in identifying perceptual blocks that blind the client to real feelings and forcing attention to stimuli previously blocked out. The focus of the therapy is the here and now. Intellectual understanding of causes underlying behavior is considered unimportant and useless, since only the present can be changed, not the past. Instead, intellectualizing is seen as avoidance of responsibility for present actions. The Gestalt therapist is interested primarily in the client's failure to be aware of needs or of immediate environmental stimuli. In practice, this means concentrated effort is focused on actual behaviors executed during the therapy session.

Group work, as an adjunct or substitute for individual therapy, is conducted along similar lines. The therapist actively insists that members express their true feelings toward each other and prevents members from slipping into stereotypical social roles that prevent personal awareness. Many of the same techniques are used as in individual therapy.

Gestalt therapy draws upon psychoanalytic teachings but seeks to overcome the heavy emphasis on verbal expression. More than most, Gestalt therapists insist that directly experienced emotion in the present forms the bedrock of all therapeutic change. Most writings and clinical examples focus on brief encounters in workshops and demonstrations, making it hard to know how this therapy proceeds over long-term cases (see Fagan & Shepherd, 1970; Polster & Polster, 1973). The seeming simplicity and potency of the techniques give them considerable appeal, especially among young therapists. Probably for this reason they are often adapted for occasional use by therapists of different persuasions.

Existential therapy. Although existential therapists have undergone traditional professional training, they are strongly influenced in their view of human nature by such philosophers as Husserl, Heidegger, Kierkegaard, Jaspers, and Sartre. Binswanger (1963), Boss (1963), Frankl (1967), and May (May, Angel, & Ellenberger, 1958) have been prominent in translating existential ideas into therapeutic techniques. The proponents of this approach share an orientation toward understanding the nature and meaning of the individual's existence, while using a wide variety of techniques, primarily derived from psychoanalysis.

A central theme is that human existence includes freedom, choice, and responsibility based on capacities for consciousness and self-consciousness. This ability to choose also produces existential guilt. The inescapability of death gives meaning to life and also contributes existential or normal anxiety.

People are seen as inextricably related to others and to the world. They grow and develop through encounters in which the past is transcended and future choices are optimized. Unfortunately, such encounters are rare and modern man is alienated from world, others, and self.

The therapist's tasks are to relate to the client as a partner in an encounter founded on trust, openness, and respect and to see that the client makes responsible choices. Through choice, awareness, and acceptance of responsibility, people can become what they want to become and gain authentic selfhood. Since existential neurosis involves the loss of life's meaning, the aim of therapy is that the client experience existence as real. Each client's malady is unique; it is essential to understand the subjective world of each person without preconceived theoretical notions.

Cognitive psychotherapies

Proponents of cognitive therapies have in common a belief that faulty attitudes and thought patterns underlie many emotional and behavioral disturbances. They choose to intervene in the thinking process, to change attitudes, and to redefine problems and meanings. Rather than focus on the emotional aspects of the patient or explore deeper significance of problems, they act in the present to change the patient's perspectives on the world and his or her place in it.

Rational-emotive therapy. Albert Ellis (1973), the founder and primary spokesman for rational-emotive therapy (RET), describes psychological problems as arising from misperceptions, mistaken cognitions, under— and overreactions to normal stimuli, and habitually dysfunctional behavior patterns. RET stresses a highly active cognitive orientation, with the basic assumption that "emotional" reactions are caused by conscious or unconscious evaluations and interpretations of situations. Although people should be encouraged to feed appropriate emotions, there are no legitimate reasons for people to make themselves upset or disturbed in inappropriate or self-defeating ways.

The cognitive part of the theory and practice has been spelled out by Ellis as a sequence of events, A-B-C-D-E. At point A is an activity or agent the patient becomes disturbed about. B represents beliefs, which may be rational or irrational, that is, overgeneralized. These beliefs lead to point C, the rational or irrational consequences of the belief. Irrational consequences include such disturbances as anxiety, self-hatred, depression, and rage. These feelings lead then to a cycle of failure, nonproductivity, and further despair. The vicious circle can be broken by therapeutic Ds and Es. D represents disputing the irrational beliefs and replacing them with more reasonable responses. Through consistent questioning and challenging of these beliefs, the cognitive and behavioral effects (E) can be changed, and the defeating cycle replaced by a more fulfilling one.

In addition to the cognitive challenges, rational-emotive therapy also uses behavioral techniques in the form of homework assignments that encourage the client step-by-step to overcome fears and perform anxiety-producing tasks. A third emphasis is on emotional release. Clients are encouraged to express their feeling openly, no matter how painful. The philosophy, which is actively taught, is that no human being is condemned for what they are or what they feel. The emphasis is on self-esteem and self-acceptance, without regard for the opinions of others.

Reality therapy. Rejecting the concept of mental illness, and emphasizing responsibility for behavior, William Glasser (1965) developed a system of psychotherapy called reality therapy. He saw all patients as denying and distorting the reality of the world around them. Successful therapy, therefore, results in recognition that reality exists and that needs must be met within that framework. Essentially, reality is achieved by fulfilling two primary needs: that of loving and being loved by another person, and that of feeling worthwhile to oneself and others. Responsibility, another basic concept of reality therapy, is defined as the ability to fulfill one's needs in a way that does not deprive others of the ability to fulfill their needs.

Practitioners of reality therapy stress several differences from other conventional therapists. The patient must become involved as a responsible person, not using "illness" as an excuse for behavior. The time frame employed is the present and future, since the past cannot be changed, nor is it seen as a necessary limitation. Therapists are open and self-disclosing with their patients, rejecting notions of transference. Conflict and unconscious motivation are not recognized as determinants of behavior. Morality of choices and issues of right and wrong are emphasized, along with active teaching of better ways to find satisfactory patterns of behavior. Thus, personal involvement and an emphasis on responsible behavior rather than on emotions are the hallmarks of reality therapy. Patients are encouraged to make better alternative plans for their lives, to commit themselves to those plans, to accept no excuse for failure, and to discipline themselves. These activities are thought to produce maturity, respect, love, and a sense of identity in the place of loneliness, failure, and psychological distress.

Short-term psychotherapy

One of the serious criticisms leveled at Freud and the early psychoanalysts was the expense of their therapy, its length, and the sacrifices demanded of the patient as well as the therapist. The pressures for the development of forms of treatment that are effective, efficient, humane, and widely applicable have steadily mounted as society seeks solutions to its multifarious human problems. Various forms of behavior therapy have partly been a product of this challenge. Dynamically oriented therapists, despite some early significant contributions (Alexander & French, 1946), have been slow to respond. Yet, progress is being made and it is safe to predict that short-term psychotherapy will receive increasing attention in the coming years. Reasons for this prognostication are not difficult to find. Most forms of psychotherapy, whether or not they are specifically designated as "short-term," are in fact time-limited. It has long been known that in clinical practice the average length of therapy is only a few sessions (Garfield, 1978). Time-limited psychotherapy appears to produce results as good as those of unlimited therapy (Luborsky et al., 1975).

While there are undoubtedly cases in which prolonged therapeutic efforts are indicated, for most patients unlimited psychotherapy is not practical. Thus in most instances the professional community and society are forced to settle for the achievement of more limited goals. In terms of patient expectations, resources, motivation, and reality considerations, it is essential to develop psychotherapies that yield significant returns in the shortest possible time and with the least expense. Traditional forms of psychotherapy require painstaking and persistent self-exploration of the patient's feelings and neurotic patterns, followed by the gradual development of insights and improved adaptation. This process is increasingly being recognized as inappropriate to the needs of a great many individuals who enlist the services of a psychotherapist.

In brief psychotherapy the therapist takes a much more active stance, sets more modest goals, takes greater responsibility for becoming a "moving force" in the therapeutic encounter, actively plans and implements interventions (as opposed to waiting for the gradual emergence of "problems" in the transference and their resolution in that context), and actively resists the temptation to broaden the therapeutic objectives once limited goals have been reached. At the present time, few therapists (especially those trained in traditional therapy) are equipped to assume the role of an "active change agent" along the lines sketched above.

Finally, it is important to call attention to a potentially serious paradox faced by short-term (as well as other forms of) psychotherapy. A potentially successful patient is expected to meet a set of criteria (personality characteristics) that are precisely those that a good many applicants for therapeutic services do not possess. To illustrate, Sifneos (1972) and Malan (1976), among others, have asserted that patients should have: (a) the ability to recognize that symptoms are psychologically determined rather than external or situationally determined, (b) a tendency to introspect, (c) a willingness to participate actively in the treatment, (d) curiosity about themselves, (e) willingness to explore and change, (f) realistic expectations in the sense of not demanding instant relief, and (g) a willingness to make reasonable sacrifices.

This paradox has given rise to the allegation that psychotherapy is most successful with those patients who need it the least. At the same time, it is becoming increasingly apparent that a sizable segment of the population may not be able to profit from the forms of psychotherapy or behavior therapy that have been developed so far. Largely, they are unable to participate actively and effectively in the therapeutic regimen, either because their ego resources are deficient or because their personalities present serious resistances to therapy. From another perspective, this may underscore the inherent incompatibility between the medical and the psychotherapeutic model. Psychotherapy basically demands the patient's active collaboration in his cure, and it can do little for individuals who expect to be passively ministered to. Psychotherapy, in the final analysis, must lead to self-help.

Psychotherapy with couples, families, and groups

We have seen that many theorists of personality and psychotherapy view problems as originating in or exacerbated by interpersonal communication within the family, in intimate relationships, or with peers. Recently, attention has been given to developing methods for intervening more directly into these social systems rather than treating the individuals within them separately. Thus, mental-health and counseling centers, hospitals, and private practitioners are now treating couples, entire families, and groups.

Marital or couples therapy

Frequently when one partner of a troubled relationship seeks individual therapy, the marital balance becomes even more precarious, as that person's views of self and of the relationship change. For that reason, therapeutic effort is often better focused directly on the interplay between the partners rather than on their individual lives. Typically, the partners are seen together or jointly by one therapist or a cotherapist team with the goal of clarifying and improving the interactions and communications between them, using a wide range of concepts and procedures. Growing out of the areas of family therapy, individual therapy, and marriage counseling, "couples therapy" is coming into wide use for those who are married, as well as for those involved in intimate relationships without marriage. A common source of a couple's problems lies in divergent role expectations regarding responsibility, dominance, autonomy, affection, or other areas. Previously harmonious marriages may be disrupted when circumstances preclude the simultaneous meeting of both sets of needs. Intimacy fosters anger, frustration, and anxiety as well as love. Many couples need help in coping with these negative feelings constructively. The recent questioning of traditional sex roles has placed strains on marriages structured in terms of male dominance.

Problems in couples frequently center on unsatisfactory sexual relations. Masters and Johnson (1970) developed a form of brief behavioral sex therapy aimed at making sex more exciting and satisfying. Using their ideas but expanding upon them, Helen S. Kaplan (1974) presented a form of sex therapy based more on psychodynamic principles. Sex therapists recognize that sexual disharmony may result from conflict in other realms, and vary in the extent to which they work also with interpersonal issues. All agree, however, that sexual inadequacy results from tension between partners and that both partners should participate simultaneously in the treatment program.

Family therapy

Family therapy evolved from two directions, clinical practice and basic research. Child guidance clinics and other mental-health facilities found that a large number of clients had relapses when they returned to their homes. As a result, they began working with other family members separately. Gradually, techniques of *conjoint family therapy* evolved with all family members being seen by the same therapist or cotherapist team (Minuchin, 1974; Satir, 1967). The other major impetus for family therapy was studies of psychopathology and communication patterns in families with a schizophrenic member (Mishler & Waxler, 1976).

Family therapy is usually undertaken when the "identified patient," typically a child, is so enmeshed in pathological family processes that individual treatment is likely to be ineffective. Although some families do come seeking help for the family as a unit, more often they are motivated primarily to change the symptomatic member. For that reason, the first task of the family therapist is to encourage all members to see themselves as active participants in the system that produced, maintains, or in some way deals with the problem. Indications for family therapy are usually family crises, conflicts along generational lines, or value conflicts within the family. This mode of therapy is particularly beneficial when the focal problem involves a young adult or adolescent separating from the family (Korchin, 1976). In the initial phase of family therapy, the therapist seeks to discover how the presenting problem is related to the network of relations in the family and how members might participate. Attempts are made to include all relevant family members, including grandparents or collateral relatives who are involved in the family life.

Beyond these initial considerations, we again find tremendous variety in the long-term goals and in the processes by which goals are attained. Therapists may focus on improving the functioning of the identified patient, clarifying communication patterns, facilitating the free expression of feelings, or many other outcomes. Many family therapists, originally trained in individual dynamics and therapy, maintain attention on one member with others seen as a context for that person. Recently, training and practice in family therapy has focused around the system-oriented approaches of Satir (1967), Haley (1971), and Minuchin (1974). Therapists also vary along a dimension called *reactors* or *conductors* (Beels & Ferber, 1972). Reactors are more nondirective and passive, while conductors actively organize the sessions, assign tasks to family members, ask probing questions, and teach. Although family therapy has grown rapidly in the last decade, many practitioners were not specifically trained for interventions at that level. Additionally, the basis of theory and technique is incompletely developed and research on which to base judgments about relative effectiveness is virtually nonexistent.

Group psychotherapy

Although group methods of psychotherapy existed early in this century, the main impetus for their use came after World War II when clinicians were faced with vastly increased pressure for clinical services. Groups were conducted for a time by therapists trained in one-to-one methods, and were often seen as necessary but inferior substitutes. Now, however, group therapy is recognized as a distinctive, valuable treatment in its own right, utilizing change mechanisms of a different order, which are better adapted to the needs of certain persons. In the last two decades, there has been an explosion of group experiences available to nonpatient populations, and the boundary between therapy and personal growth groups has been blurred, sometimes to the detriment of individual participants (Hartley, Roback, &

Abramowitz, 1976). Here, we will consider the nature of group intervention and therapeutic change in the context of more traditional group therapeutic experiences designed to help those with significant emotional distress. Readers interested in more innovative group methods are referred to Rogers (1970), Schutz (1967), or Ruitenbeek (1970).

A therapy group usually consists of six to ten members, with eight usually considered the optimal number. Sessions are generally conducted in an open circle so that all members can see each other, and last one and one-half to two hours. Cotherapist teams are common, with either an older and a younger therapist or a male and a female. Closed groups continue with only those initially started. Open groups admit new members to replace those who drop out. Groups may be heterogeneous, in terms of age, sex, cultural background or clinical condition; or they may be homogeneous, as in women's groups or adolescent groups where the common characteristic is the focus of concern.

Whatever the formal structure, group participants become intimate strangers engaged with each other in a small social system. Yalom (1975) has proposed that the curative, change-producing properties of all groups may ultimately be the same, an assertion that parallels that of Frank (1973) and Strupp (1972, 1973) for individual therapy. Group therapists are as varied in their conceptual systems, personal styles, and technical operations as are individual therapists (Parloff, 1968). Yalom (1975), however, points to one characteristic of group therapy that is consistent: the therapist is only indirectly an agent of change. The primary curative factors are the group members who accept, support, and teach each other while providing hope, the experience of universality, and opportunities for altruism. The role of the therapist is to aid in creating and maintaining the group culture.

Upon joining a therapy group, a person finds that others also suffer fears, anxieties, inadequacies, and self-doubts. This discovery relieves feelings of isolation and shame engendered by living in a society of apparently well-functioning, happy people. Seeing others in distress allows some perspective on one's own suffering and generates hope for relief. Later, the accomplishment of any member in mastering a problem becomes a source of encouragement for all. Great importance is attached to the factor of *group cohesiveness,* by which is meant the sense of solidarity, relatedness, or "we-ness" that binds the members together. Yalom compares group cohesiveness to the therapeutic alliance in individual therapy as a primary curative factor. This broader concept includes the relationship between each group member and the therapist, the relationships among members, and the feeling of attachment each member feels toward the group as a whole. Another important therapeutic element lies in the unique potential for interpersonal learning, as members are reexposed to emotional situations that they could not handle in the past. With more manageable conditions and group feedback, distortions and self-deceits become vividy apparent. Group members see disparities between attitudes and actions clearly, but also give the support necessary for trying out new behaviors that decrease that disparity. Thus group therapy, while not replacing other modalities, offers unique opportunities for healing.

Summary

We have seen in this chapter that verbal psychotherapies vary greatly along many dimensions. The formal structure of the therapy may include only a therapist and a patient, or may include cotherapy teams working with groups or families. Sessions are usually 50–60 minutes in length, but marathon sessions lasting many hours are increasingly popular. A patient may be seen four or five times a week, or only once a month; and treatment may last a few weeks or several years. In addition to these external variables, therapy styles diverge in many ways. Some therapists are active to the point of dominance, while others are so passive that they seem detached and remote. Some theories encourage the gratification of patient desires for intimacy including physical touching, while other suggest the frustration of all wishes. One therapist may take over a patient's life giving a great deal of support, guidance, and advice; another will refuse to indicate any preference at all in the patient's decision-making processes. Interventions are aimed at deep unconscious processes in some therapies and at rational daily activities in others. A patient may be asked to free associate or report dreams and fantasies, or merely to report progress toward behavioral goals.

Unfortunately, we know very little about which therapies work best for which people. Response to therapy is limited by the kind of individual who is the therapist and the one who is the patient or client. Personality variables of both people augment or negate the techniques suggested by the theoretical system within which they work. The decision of which therapy for which patient depends on the presenting problem. A situational crisis in a person with a usual good adjustment will probably respond well to a short-term, active, present-centered approach. But a person who experiences persistent, urgent, repetitive drives from unresolved childish needs and conflicts, and who feels overwhelmed by the struggles of daily life will probably benefit most from a long-term reconstructive approach. People learn best in a vast variety of ways; therapists teach best by an equal diversity of methods. Although a good therapist is, above all, flexible enough to meet the needs of the patients he or she treats, no one can be equally effective with all problems. Thus, the secret of good therapy seems to be in the unique match between a therapist and a patient who are compatible, communicate effectively with each other, and who are able to commit themselves to the collaborative task of overcoming the obstacles to the patient's growth.

GLOSSARY

Analytic psychology: Jung's system of psychology that minimizes the role of sexuality and past experience and emphasizes instead a religious, mystical factor and preparation for the future.

Client-centered or nondirective therapy: Therapy based on the ideas of Carl Rogers that the client possesses inherent potentialities for growth that are released by the therapists listening and reflecting the client's own feelings.

Common or nonspecific factors: Those ingredients found in all therapy relationships that serve to improve the patient's morale and foster hope. These include understanding, respect, encouragement, as well as a plausible explanation for the suffering and for the cure.

Conjoint therapy: Therapy in which marital partners or entire families are seen together in sessions focused on the interplay between individuals, rather than on their individual lives.

Countertransference: A therapist's feelings and emotional reactions to a patient that tend to interfere with objectivity and complicate the therapeutic relationships.

Ego psychology: The study of adaptation to the environmental and internal stimuli, focused on creative and constructive forces in the struggle to achieve a sense of mastery and identity as well as pathological adaptations.

Free association: The uninhibited sequence of ideas elicited by an analytic therapist with no hampering or directive interventions given to the patient.

Group cohesiveness: In group therapy, the working relationship that binds the members together and creates a feeling of solidarity and relatedness.

Individual psychology: The point of view established by Alfred Adler, which emphasized the urge for superiority and inferiority feelings, and compensatory goals.

Interpretation: The formulation of the meaning or significance of the patient's thought and behavior patterns and the translation of this understanding into a form to be communicated to the patient in order to enhance self-awareness.

Resistance: Conscious or unconscious opposition to therapy or to the changes in life style presented in therapy; it usually takes the form of the typically used defense mechanisms of the patient.

Therapeutic alliance: The commitment between a therapist and patient in which they work together in an atmosphere of mutual respect toward the achievement of the goals of therapy.

Transference: The displacement of either positive or negative feelings, thoughts, and wishes from a person in the past onto a current person who has come to represent the past figure, particularly onto a therapist in analytically oriented psychotherapy.

Working through: The repetition of interpretations and extension of their application to various phases of the patient's life with the goal of freeing the patient to make choices based on self-understanding.

BEHAVIOR THERAPY

CYRIL M. FRANKS
DAVID B. ABRAMS

Behavior therapy began as an attempt to provide S-R learning theory alternatives to the current intrapsychic medical models. As the field expanded, its limits became increasingly difficult to define, and it now connotes an approach rather than a set of narrowly defined techniques. In no way is behavior therapy to be regarded as a closed, unitary system. Strategies, techniques, and even theoretical concepts are diverse. What all forms of behavior therapy have in common is the methodology of behavioral analysis, operational definition, and empirical evaluation. Equally important, a humanistic concern for the individual is an integral component of good behavior therapy (Franks, 1977a; Franks & Brady, 1970). Furthermore, modern behavior therapy, departs increasingly from the radical S-R behaviorism of an earlier decade (Franks & Wilson, 1976, 1977, 1978).

Content and methodology are closely linked to a variety of allied fields: social-learning theory (Bandura, 1969, 1977a); classical and operant conditioning (Eysenck, 1960; Skinner, 1953); cognitive, developmental, and educational psychology (Achenbach, 1974; Beck, 1976; Mahoney, 1974; O'Leary & O'Leary, 1976) and experimental social psychology (Johnson & Matross, 1977). Applications include such diverse areas as the treatment of psychotic and neurotic disturbances (O'Leary & Wilson, 1976); biofeedback and behavioral medicine (Barber, DiCara, Kamiya, Miller, Shapiro, & Stoyva, 1976); community psychology (Nietzel, Winett, MacDonald, & Davidson, 1977); childhood disorders (O'Leary & O'Leary, 1976); the treatment of addictive behaviors; and marital and sex therapy (O'Leary & Wilson, 1975).

Behavior therapists view human functioning as a series of complex interactions between organism and environment. It is assumed that all behavior is determined and that, at least in principle, relationships follow predictable patterns. These relationships can be within the individual, between individuals, or between the individual and any aspect of the total environment. The behavior therapist seeks to determine precisely what variables are responsible for originating or maintaining maladaptive patterns of behavior. Behavior extends to covert (cognitive) processes as well as overt (observable) activities. Treatment involves the rearrangement of physical, psychological, and social controlling variables.

Overview and evolution

The impact of behavior therapy on the mental-health profession has been both profound and controversial. While polemics have happily declined, sharp differences of opinion between behavior therapists and others still persist (e.g., Eysenck, 1970; Locke, 1971). One concern centers around philosophical issues such as free will versus determinism (Breger & McGaugh, 1965; Skinner, 1975; Wann, 1966). Another relates to clinical practice. It is still occasionally suggested that behavior therapists are manipulative, impervious to cognitive processes, and superficial. (See Mahoney, 1974, 1977, for a detailed discussion and refutation of these matters.)

While behavior modification has been practiced for thousands of years, its formalization is relatively recent (Franks, 1969b). At the turn of this century, the work of Pavlov on classical conditioning and Watson, Thorndike, Hull, and Skinner on behaviorism, learning theory, and operant conditioning laid the foundations for the application of conditioning principles to human problems. Examples include Watson and Rayner's (1920) demonstration of an experimentally induced phobia in Albert B., and Mary Cover Jones's (1924) treatment of children's phobias by pairing desirable food with the feared object. The feared object (stimulus) was moved closer and closer to the child on successive occassions until the positive responses associated with eating replaced the original fear responses elicited by the object (counterconditioning).

It was not until the 1950s that behavior therapy emerged as a formal approach (Wolpe, 1958, and Lazarus, 1958, in South Africa; Eysenck, 1959, in England; Salter, 1949 and Lindsley, Skinner & Solomon, 1953, in the United States). Early definitions were based on 1. S-R theory, 2. acceptance only of observable, quantifiable behavior, and 3. a rejection of mentalism in any shape or form. These strategies were especially successful with selected target populations such as retarded children and phobic clients (cf. Ullmann & Krasner, 1965).

During the late 1960s, emphasis shifted toward cognition (Lazarus, 1966). In 1969, Bandura's social-learning theory achieved prominence. The explicit incorporation of cognitive mediational variables into the behavior therapy framework, together with the addition of the principles of modeling to those of classical and operant conditioning, set the stage for the emphasis upon cognitive, symbolic, and self-regulatory mechanisms of the seventies (Bandura, 1974, 1977a). If the debatable assumption that similar laws apply to covert as well as overt processes holds, then private events, images, and thoughts can be explored and manipulated in the same manner as overt behaviors (cf. Kanfer & Karoly, 1972; Mahoney & Thoresen, 1974; Thoresen & Mahoney, 1974).

In emphasizing that a person is both agent and object of change, contemporary social-learning theory highlights the self-directive nature of human behavior. Bandura's (1977b) analysis of expectations of self-efficacy extends social learning theory yet further. Efficacy expectations may be modified by performance-based feedback (e.g., modeling), vicarious information (e.g., symbolic modeling), verbal persuasion (e.g., traditional psychotherapy), or physiological change (e.g., systematic desensitization). According to Bandura, modification of self-efficacy determines both initial motivational and long-term maintenance strategies for coping with anxiety-provoking situations.

As behavior therapy matured, different interest groups arose. The so-called applied behavior analysts (Skinnerian) still remain essentially atheoretical and true to the principles of radical behaviorism in that they focus upon external (overt) behavior (see Kazdin, 1975a, for a more comprehensive review of this position). Lazarus (1976) is the archetype of an empirical, technically eclectic orientation, which accepts cognitive and other mediational processes. These processes overlap considerably with, but are not limited to, social-learning theory or even to behavior therapy. Wolpe's monumental 1958 book offered the first useful alternative to traditional psychotherapy. While his mediational model is firmly wedded to the principles of conditioning and the methodology of the behavioral scientist, it also acknowledges and makes use of such concepts and processes as imagery, anxiety, and cognition. The prevailing cognitive trend in behavior therapy is characterized by the writings of Beck (1976), Goldfried and Davison (1976), Mahoney (1974), and Meichenbaum (1977).

Most behavior therapists now concur that every clinical interaction constitutes an "experiment" in which therapist and client work together to bring out and modify the specific variables that maintain the problem behavior. Of perhaps equal importance is the emphasis upon self-control, contractual agreement, accountability, and ethical principles. This is the definition of behavior therapy currently endorsed by the Association for Advancement of Behavior Therapy (AABT):

> Behavior therapy involves primarily the application of principles derived from research in experimental and social psychology for the alleviation of human suffering and the enhancement of human functioning. Behavior therapy emphasizes a systematic evaluation of the effectiveness of these applications. Behavior therapy involves environmental change and social interaction rather than the direct alteration of bodily processes by biological procedures. The aim is primarily educational. The techniques facilitate improved self-control. In the conduct of behavior therapy, a contractual agreement is usually negotiated, in which mutually agreeable goals and procedures are specified. Responsible practitioners using behavior approaches are guided by generally accepted ethical principles. (Franks & Wilson, 1975, p. 2)

The behavior therapy approach: assessment, intervention, and research strategies

We will begin with certain conceptual matters pertaining to behavioral as contrasted with traditional personality assessment and the relationships between assessment and treatment. Next, we will examine selected methods of behavioral assessment, such as self-report, direct observation in naturalistic settings, and psychophysiological techniques. This will lead to a discussion of treatment and research strategies in the intervention process.

Behavioral versus traditional assessment

While behavioral and traditional assessment are concerned with the production of reliable and valid data, data gathering processes are different. This is because both goals and underlying assumptions are different. Goldfried and Kent (1972) conveniently summarize three major differences.

First, both psychodynamic and psychometric (trait) approaches to assessment infer some underlying construct to account for the consistency of an individual's behavior. Thus, the primary goal of traditional assessment, which views behavior as a sign of these hypothetical constructs, is to provide information for understanding "what is really going on" beyond the individual's awareness. The goal of behavioral assessment is to identify relationships between behavior and environmental factors (both within and outside the individual) to determine what controlling variables (contingencies) maintain the behavior.

Second, it follows that the selection of procedures differs radically. Traditional assessment is not overly concerned with test content or response items per se, since it is the inferences about hypothesized underlying causes that are important. Behavior is presumed to reflect stable personality characteristics that are relatively independent of the specific situational context. In contrast, the behavioral approach is concerned with specific relationships that have meaning in themselves and it is important to sample and describe each situation directly.

Third, behavioral assessment is primarily concerned with the determination of specific treatment programs, whereas the concern of traditional assessment is with global diagnostic categories prior to treatment (see Ciminero, 1977).

The approach taken in behavioral assessment depends, in part, upon the meaning given to the term personality and its role in understanding behavior (Mischel, 1977). Mischel (1968) regards behavior as situation specific rather than based upon all-pervasive personality traits. In contrast, Eysenck (1967) accepts the concept of stable personality organization or dimensions. For example, a child could be quiet and passive at home and hyperactive at school (situation specific behavior). Giving the child a global trait label such as "extraverted" implies that the child's behavior is relatively consistent across situations.

Mischel (1973) has described a special class of behaviors that exhibit relative stability across several situations. These "person variables" (we might call them personal variables) are the products of an individual's social learning history, memories of past experiences, images, and emotional reactions. They influence behavior by introducing subjective distortions into an individual's appraisal of his or her interactons with the environment. For example, a depressed client might persist in regarding himself as totally useless and worthless even though no one else sees him that way. He may be devaluing his selfworth because of past experiences that no longer apply. An adequate behavioral assessment anticipates a reciprocal interaction between personal variables and situations (Goldfried & Sprafkin, 1974).

The special methodology of behavioral assessment generates additional problems. Foremost among these is that of reactivity. Reactivity refers to a deviation from the normal frequency of occurrence of behavior as a result of assessment. For example, the deviation may be a result of a client's awareness of being observed. Reactivity may either be measured, minimized, or usefully incorporated into the treatment process.

Assessment strategies

The functional analysis of behavior (behavioral assessment) involves a determination of the environmental and cognitive variables that maintain the maladaptive patterns. The alteration of a variable that is functionally related to the maladaptive pattern should produce an observable change in that pattern. For example, temper tantrums may gain a child the attention of his father. If the frequency of tantrums alters as a result of father ignoring the tantrums and attending to other desirable behaviors, then a functional relationship has been demonstrated. One way of pinpointing the functional relationship is by observation of the stimulus conditions following and/or preceding the problematic pattern (antecedents and consequents).

Behavioral assessment means different things to different people. Yates (1975) classifies behavioral assessment into four categories: behavioral analysis (Goldfried & Pomerantz, 1968; Goldfried & D'Zurilla, 1969); behavioral diagnosis (Kanfer & Saslow, 1969); the modality profile of Lazarus (1973, 1976); and the operant, atheoretical orientation of the applied behavior analysts (Baer, Wolf, & Risley, 1968; Bijou, Peterson, Harris, Allen, & Johnston, 1969; Risley, 1970).

Clients function in a world of economic, biological, psychological, and social subsystems. The potential range of an individual's behavioral repertoire is determined, on the one hand, by biological, social and intellectual skills and, on the other, by the past history of rewards, punishers, and modeling experiences. The behavior therapist must investigate each of these subsystems before deciding upon their relative importance to diagnosis and treatment. Greater emphasis is generally placed upon currently maintaining variables than upon historical antecedents.

Kanfer and Saslow's (1969) approach is based upon the interview. They offer comprehensive guidelines for behavioral assessment. Three essential questions have to be answered: 1. Which specific behavior patterns require changes in their frequencies of occurrence: their intensities, their durations, or the conditions under which they occur? 2. Under what conditions was the behavior acquired and what factors are currently maintaining it? and 3. What are the best practical means to produce the desired changes? We might add to this list a fourth important function of behavioral assessment—the evaluation of treatment outcome.

To isolate primary problematic behavior patterns, Kanfer and Saslow suggest that initial attempts to describe the problem consider three broad categories of behavior: excesses, deficits, and assets. *Behavioral excesses* are operationally defined as that class of behaviors described by the client as problematic because of their excessive frequency, intensity, or duration when the socially tolerated frequency approaches zero (e.g., exhibitionism or alcoholism). *Behavioral deficits* are defined as a lack of desired behaviors, which fail to occur with sufficient frequency, with adequate intensity, in appropriate form, or when socially expected (e.g., impotence or social withdrawal). *Behavioral assets* are nonproblematic behaviors that may be used as building blocks for new skills. Natural talents provide a good starting point for behavior change and for improving self-confidence and motivation.

After specification of excesses, deficits, and assets, Kanfer and Saslow recommend that assessment cover the following areas: 1. A clarification of the problem situation, i.e., the context in which and the conditions under which the behavior occurs; motivational analysis in which variables (positive or negative reinforcers) that may be maintaining the problem behavior or that may be useful in shaping more appropriate behaviors are specified; developmental analysis, in which biological, sociological, and behavioral changes over time are examined; 2. an analysis of self-control and cognitive variables; an analysis of social relationships, in which significant others and their effects on the client are specified; 3. an analysis of the socio-cultural-physical environments in which cultural norms and environmental constraints and resources are explored.

Another set of guidelines for assessment is proposed by Lazarus (1973, 1976). The acronym BASIC ID stands for *b*ehavior (e.g., compulsive rituals, tics, avoidance), *a*ffect, (e.g., anxiety, anger, depression), *s*ensation (e.g., palpitations, tension, hyperventilation), *i*magery (e.g., emotive images, fantasies, traumatic memories), *c*ognition (e.g., self-statements, ruminations), *i*nterpersonal relations (e.g., social skills, assertiveness, marital adjustment) and *d*rugs (the physiological biochemical substrate and the need for medication). These seven modalities form a treatment framework for the analysis of functionally related variables. Ignoring modalities could result in incomplete treatment or relapse. The following case, adapted from Lazarus (1973) illustrates the multimodal approach to assessment and intervention. It will be noticed that assessment and intervention form part of an ongoing, closely related process.

In conducting a behavioral assessment, "How?" "When?" "Where?" and "Under what circumstances?" are more appropriate questions than the traditional "why?" For example, a child may be referred to the therapist because of "conduct problems" in the classroom. After screening for learning disabilities or pertinent physical factors, the behavior therapist might ask "What specific behaviors are indicative of the 'conduct problem'?" "With whom?" (specific teachers, parents, peers), "What happened immediately before and after these events?" and so on.

Private or covert behaviors that cannot be observed by anyone other than the client (e.g., obsessive thoughts, urges to expose oneself, eat, smoke, or drink) may be self-monitored. Self-monitoring can then be continued during treatment to provide an ongoing evaluation of progress (Ciminero, Nelson, & Lipinski, 1977). Self-report data may also be gathered by means of paper-and-pencil surveys, checklists or inventories. Common inventories include fear survey schedules (Geer, 1965), assertiveness scales (Rathus, 1973), and marital inventories (Stuart & Stuart, 1972). Imagery techniques, such as asking the client to imagine or recreate past events, may also be used as assessment devices (Lazarus, 1976).

Additionally, assessment may be based upon direct observation in the natural environment (Mariotto & Paul, 1974; Tharp & Wetzel, 1969). Recording may be carried out by a professional, parent, sibling, spouse, or teacher. Behavior may also be observed in semi-naturalistic settings such as the clinic or laboratory. A number of specialized approaches have been developed to reduce bias and reactivity. For example, observers may employ random time-sampling techniques, usually with more than one trained observer to record the same target behavior (S. Johnson & Bolstad, 1973; Kent & Foster, 1977).

Psychophysiological assessment is another way to acquire information. Objective indices of drug usage and alcohol comsumption may be obtained by means of urine analysis or breathalyzer tests. Direct indices of emotional arousal—such as cardiovascular responses, muscle tension, or skin temperature—are important for certain forms of treatment (cf. Barlow, 1977; Borkovec, Weerts, & Bernstein, 1977). Psychophysiological assessment is particularly germane to the therapeutic intervention known as biofeedback. In biofeedback, the client is provided with continuous monitoring of selected psychophysiological states (e.g., alpha rhythm or blood pressure). In this way, the feedback information provided to the client eventually enables him or her to control physiological processes over which he or she previously had no control or of which he or she was unaware. An extended discussion of biofeedback is beyond the scope of the present chapter.

The nature of the client-therapist relationship may well be an integral component of the assessment process. For the psychoanalyst, what goes on inside the consulting room is subtly but inevitably related to life outside. For the behavior therapist, this may or may not be true, and it is necessary to evaluate the relevancy of each specific facet of the client-therapist relationship with respect to its implications for generalization (Wilson & Evans, 1977).

To sum up, specificity, objectivity, and operational definition are the hallmarks of behavioral assessment. The behavior therapist uses his or her professional knowledge and experience to delineate high priority problem areas, to decide on additional assessment devices or techniques, to evaluate his or her personal biases, to assess the quality of the client-therapist relationship, to monitor the on-going therapeutic process, and to evaluate outcome. No decision or assessment conclusion is irrevocable; at any future point in therapy a reevaluation based on new evidence may take place.

Intervention strategies

With certain limitations, the methodology of behavior therapists is similar to that of other scientists. First comes detailed observation of pertinent variables. Plausible hypotheses are generated about possible patterns governing relationships between these variables and their consequences. Predictions are derived from these hypotheses and strategies developed for their investigation within the therapeutic situation. The ensuing data are then used to evaluate, refine, modify, or even reject the original hypotheses. This self-corrective procedure ensures maximally efficient progress toward the therapeutic goals.

As part of this process, a client-therapist contract is negotiated as soon after the assessment phase as possible. Together, the therapist and client formulate goals that seem best suited to serve the client's interests. Wherever possible, treatment goals and techniques are made explicit and reasonable dates for progress evaluation are incorporated into the contract. As new information

Case Illustration

Mary Ann, aged 24, was diagnosed as a chronic undifferentiated schizophrenic. Shortly after her third admission to a mental hospital, her parents referred her for treatment. According to the hospital reports, her prognosis was poor. She was overweight, apathetic, and withdrawn, but against a background of lethargic indfference, one would detect an ephemeral smile, a sparkle of humor, a sudden glow of warmth, a witty remark, an apposite comment, a poignant revelation. She was heavily medicated (Trilafon 8 mg. t.i.d., Vivactil 10 mg. t.i.d., Cogentin 2 mg. b.d.), and throughout the course of therapy she continued seeing a psychiatrist once a month who adjusted her intake of drugs.

A life history questionnaire, followed by an initial interview, revealed that well-intentioned but misguided parents had created a breeding ground for guilty attitudes, especially in matters pertaining to sex. Moreover, an older sister, five years her senior, had aggravated the situation "by tormenting me from the day I was born." Her vulnerability to peer pressure during puberty had rendered her prone to "everything but heroin." Nevertheless, she had excelled at school, and her first noticeable breakdown occurred at age 18, shortly after graduating from high school. "I was on a religious kick and kept hearing voices." Her second hospital admission followed a suicidal gesture at age 21, and her third admission was heralded by her sister's sudden demise soon after the patient turned 24.

Since she was a mine of sexual misinformation, her uncertainties and conflicts with regard to sex became an obvious area for therapeutic intervention. The book *Sex Without Guilt* by Albert Ellis (1965 Grove Press edition) served as a useful springboard toward the correction of more basic areas of sexual uncertainty and anxiety. Meanwhile, careful questioning revealed the Modality Profile given below.

During the course of therapy, as more data emerged and as a clearer picture of the patient became apparent, the Modality Profile was constantly revised. Therapy was mainly a process of devising ways and means to remedy Mary Ann's shortcomings and problem areas throughout the basic modalities. In other words, a wide array of therapeutic methods drawn from numerous disciplines was applied but, to remain theoretically consistent, the active ingredients of every technique were sought within the province of social learning theory.

The array of therapeutic methods selected to restructure her life included behavior therapy techniques such as desensitization, assertive training, role-playing, and modeling, but additional procedures were employed such as time projection, cognitive restructuring, eidetic imagery, and exaggerated role-taking. Mary Ann was also seen with her parents for eight sessions, and was in a group for 30 weeks. During the course of therapy she became engaged and was seen with her fiance for premarital counseling for several sessions. The treatment period covered the span of 13 months, at the end of which time she was coping admirably without medication and has continued to do so now for more than a year.

MODALITY	PROBLEM	PROPOSED TREATMENT
Behavior	Inappropriate withdrawal responses	Assertive training
	Frequent crying	Nonreinforcement
	Unkempt appearance	Grooming instructions
	Excessive eating	Low calorie regimen
	Negative self-statements	Positive self-talk assignments
	Poor eye contact	Rehearsal techniques
	Mumbling of words with poor voice projection	Verbal projection exercises
	Avoidance of heterosexual situations	Re-education and desensitization

Affect	Unable to express overt anger	Role playing
	Frequent anxiety	Relaxation training and reassurance
	Absence of enthuaism and spontaneous joy	Positive imagery procedures
	Panic attacks (Usually precipitated by criticism from authority figures)	Desensitization and assertive training
	Suicidal feelings	Time projection techniques
	Emptiness and aloneness	General relationship building
Sensation	Stomach spasms	Abdominal breathing and relaxing
	Out of touch with most sensual pleasures	Sensate focus method
	Tension in jaw and neck	Differential relaxation
	Frequent lower back pains	Orthopedic exercises
	Inner tremors	Gendlin's focusing method
Imagery	Distressing scenes of sister's funeral	Desensitization
	Mother's angry face shouting "you fool!"	Empty chair technique
	Performing fellatio on God	Blow up technique (implosion)
	Recurring dreams about airplane bombings	Eidetic imagery invoking feelings of being safe
Cognition	Irrational self-talk: "I am evil." "I must suffer." "Sex is dirty." "I am inferior."	Deliberate rational disputation and corrective self-talk
	Syllogistic reasoning, overgeneralization	Parsing of irrational sentences
	Sexual misinformation	Sexual education
Interpersonal relationships	Characterized by childlike dependence	Specific self-sufficiency assignments
	Easily exploited/submissive	Assertive training
	Overly suspicious	Exaggerated role taking
	Secondary gains from parental concern	Explain reinforcement principles to parents and try to enlist their help
	Manipulative tendencies	Training in direct and confrontative behaviors

Reprinted with minor editing by permission of Arnold A Lazarus and the publishers, Williams & Wilkins.

emerges, the contract should be reappraised. At all times, informed consent, ethical constraints, and accountbility enter into the formulation of the contract. This ensures both comsumer protection and a minimum of undue therapist influence.

The responsive (and responsible) behavior therapist is often faced with the need to balance the long-term and more rigorous methodology of behavioral science against the more immediate and pressing requirements of the current situation. It is here that clinical sophistication and experience become particularly important. For example, depending on the circumstances, the therapist may become more supportive, alter the pace of therapy, or focus on the client-therapist relationship.

Maintenance of gains acquired during treatment and generalization to the client's everyday life are important components of effective behavior therapy. In psychotherapy, relapse implies insufficient or inadequate treatment and subsequent therapy continues to focus on the intrapsychic conditions that were originally presumed to underlie the presenting problem. A behavior therapist takes a different point of view. Maintenance and generalization problems may be governed by a variety of additional factors. It is the task of the behavior therapist to determine the nature of these controlling variables and the circumstances under which they operate. The setting in which the behavior occurs may be important with respect to the generalization and maintenance of treatment produced improvement (Stokes & Baer, 1977). For example, treatment within the confines of an institution may be of little use in the real world unless specific self-coping strategies are programmed in to facilitate the transition. Different behaviors may vary in their susceptibility to generalization or maintenance. For example, a newly acquired behavior that is highly reinforcing, such as sexual gratification, is usually easier to maintain than another behavior that is less reinforcing, such as the making of assertive responses to unreasonable requests. Effort and persistence at a task may also be influenced by efficacy expectations, and the degree to which the client perceives him/herself to be his/her own agent (Bandura, 1977b). A variety of strategies are available for developing and strengthening self-control, independence, and other self-coping repertoires (e.g., D'Zurilla & Goldfried, 1971; Goldfried & Davison, 1976; Mahoney & Thoresen, 1974).

The intervention strategies outlined above are sometimes to be tempered by the exigencies of real life. It is rarely possible to be a purist when confronted by a desperate parent pleading for immediate help, however deficient this might be. Nevertheless, the strategies outlined above are ideals toward which we can strive, even as we recognize their inherent practical limitations (Franks, 1969a).

Research strategies

Process and outcome evaluation are the two major research issues in behavior therapy. Process research pertains to the investigation of changes that take place during the treatment process and to the study of the ingredients involved in these changes. Outcome research is concerned with the evaluation of therapy following termination; for example, whether systematic desensitization produces results superior to those obtained by a particular drug in the treatment of specific disorders.

This dichotomy between process and outcome research is more apparent than real. Evaluation of active ingredients and their effectiveness during treatment is really an intermediate measure of eventual outcome. A comprehensive evaluation of therapy entails systematic study of both facets of what is really one problem area (see Kazdin & Wilson, 1978).

A variety of research strategies may be employed to investigate these problems. These include conventional group and correlational methods as well as single-subject designs (cf. Hersen & Barlow, 1976; Franks & Wilson, 1976, 1977). The most common single subject designs are the reversal or ABAB design (Hersen & Barlow, 1976) and the multiple baseline design (Marks & Gelder, 1967). Both depend upon the objective recording of changes in one or more target behaviors when treatment variables are systematically applied and/or withdrawn in fixed sequences. Both are useful to the research scientist in that they aid the analysis of effects that could be easily masked in the more conventional group design. (Sidman, 1960).

It is sometimes advantageous to conduct research in an artificially contrived situation rather than working with the target population directly. This is known as analogue research. Sometimes, there is little or no alternative. For example, certain disorders are rare and it might take years to gather a large enough sample. Similarly, there are many occasions when it becomes impossible to examine a theoretical model involving comparative studies of various types of aversion therapy in human subjects. And assigning clients to a control group when a probably effective treatment is known to exist is clearly unethical. The college sophomore or the white rat, the most common subjects of analogue investigations, can yield data that are of value as long as they are used appropriately and with caution (Bernstein & Paul, 1971).

Behavior therapy and other orientations: some contrasts and misconceptions

We move now from the general to the particular, from a discussion of philosophical attitudes and overall strategies to a discussion of conceptual differences, specific techniques, case examples, and application in selected problem areas.

There are fundamental differences between behavior therapy and other orientations, particularly psychoanalysis. For example, according to psychoanalytic theory, the symptom is primarily a manifestation of some deep-seated underlying cause: If the symptom alone is treated, other manifestations of the underlying problem will assuredly emerge. In this respect, psychoanalysis borrows heavily from the medical model, where the concept of a symptom is usually very appropriate. The term underlying refers to variables that are supposed to be within the unconscious and are therefore characterized by the phrase "deep-seated."

By contrast, a behavior therapist thinks in terms of the maintaining or eliciting stimuli and hence searches for controlling variables regardless of whether or not they lie inside or outside the organism. Thus, the concept of the symptom is not part of the language system of the behavior therapist and "symptoms substitution" as such cannot occur. However, it would be foolish to pretend that deviant behavior, once successfully treated, never returns or that its place is not taken by another equally undesirable behavior. But the explanation is to be sought elsewhere—in an incomplete behavioral assessment, in secondary problematic behavior masked until the primary problem is successfully eliminated, in changing personal or environmental circumstances impinging upon the client.

At this stage, the reader might perhaps feel that behavior therapy as described is little different from good eclectic psychotherapy. Lazarus (1976) goes so far as to suggest that the flexible behavior therapist should be free to use any technique, regardless of theoretical underpinning, or lack thereof, as long as it has the benefit of some empirical support. While such a position may be of immediate practical utility under certain limited circumstances, it is inadequate as a research strategy. A virtually unlimited number of clinical techniques may be conjured up and it becomes impossible to validate them all or to decide which should be given priority. A guiding theoretical framework such as social learning theory enables the investigator to generate testable predictions. In the long run, such a strategy is more likely to advance both the theory and practice of behavior therapy than the more immediately clinically appealing notion of technical eclecticism.

By now we hope we have done much to assuage the major misconceptions about behavior therapy: that behavior therapy has to be simplistic; that it is based entirely upon animal learning models; that it is effective only in ameliorating presenting symptoms; that it ignores underlying pathology; that anyone can set up a behavior therapy program with little or no specialized expertise; and that it is manipulative, unethical, and insensitive to freedom of choice (see also Franks, 1965). If some of these misconceptions still prevail, it should not be assumed that behavior therapists are entirely free of responsibility. Behavior therapists are also fallible. Fortunately, the behavior of behavior therapists can also be modified. Accountability, sensitivity to data, and appropriate reactions to constructive criticism are also part of the hallmark of modern day behavior therapy.

Some behavior therapy techniques

In the words of Yates (1975), behavior therapy is more a methodological prescription than a grab bag of techniques. A purveyor of behavioral techniques does not a behavior therpist make. Nevertheless, it is techniques that bring about behavior change and it is to techniques that we address ourselves next.

Fear reduction and behavior deficits

Systematic desensitization. In systematic desensitization, as usually practiced, the therapist first establishes the client's major anxiety-producing themes. Next, a hierarchy of items within the central theme is constructed in a graded sequence from least to most anxiety provoking. The therapist relaxes the client (Bernstein & Borkovec, 1973) and asks him or her to imagine the least anxiety-provoking item in the hierarchy. The aim is to maintain a relaxed state while imagining the anxiety-provoking scene. Once relaxation is achieved, the next item in the hierarchy is presented and the method repeated until the most anxiety-arousing item in the hierarchy can be visualized with minimal anxiety arousal.

There are many variations on the basic systematic desensitization theme, e.g., taped desensitization, self-controlled desensitization, and group desensitization (cf. Goldfried & Davison, 1976). Although a few "old school" behavior therapists employ systematic desensitization routinely, most clinicians use it only after appropriate assessment and in conjunction with other techniques.

According to Wolpe's (1958) original formulation, systematic desensitization may be accounted for in terms of counterconditioning ("the conditioned substitution of relaxation for anxiety"). Many alternative, and equally plausible, explanations have since been posited and the complex theoretical, methodological, and clinical issues at stake are still far from resolved (cf. Davison & Wilson, 1973; Kazdin & Wilcoxon, 1976). Whatever the method, the clinical worth of desensitization is beyond question (cf. Franks & Wilson, 1976, 1977).

Assertion training. This is primarily intended to reduce interpersonal anxiety. Many people are unable to express either positive or negative feelings and thereby suffer debilitating anxiety in social encounters. A client may be unable to respond in his or her own best interest in situations where he or she is being treated unjustly.

Socially inhibited clients are encouraged to express their feelings directly, appropriately, and assertively. Simulation of real-life situations in the consulting room by means of role-playing or modeling may be employed (Kazdin, 1975; McFall & Twentyman, 1973). The truly assertive individual behaves in a responsible manner by noting the difference between assertive and aggressive responses, and thinking of the consequences of his or her behavior. The ultimate aim is to give the client "emotional freedom of expression" for both positive and negative emotions (Lazarus, 1971). Generalization may be enhanced by cognitive restructuring techniques such as positive self-statements (Glass, Gottman, & Shmurak, 1976).

Cognitive restructuring methods

Rational emotive therapy (RET). Ellis (1977) is the major figure in the field of cognitive restructing techniques. His system of rational-emotive therapy (RET) stems back to the philosophic writings of the ancient Greek and Roman stoics, in particular Epictetus and Marcus Aurelius. People do not directly react emotionally or behaviorally to the events encountered in their lives: they cause their own reactions by the ways they evaluate or interpret these events. According to Ellis, people who entertain any of his 11 fundamental irrational beliefs are likely to engage in maladaptive activities. As a result of their inappropriate belief systems, they are apt to be very anxious. One such belief is that there is invariably a right, precise, and perfect solution to each problem and that it is *catastrophic* if this correct solution is not found (Ellis, 1962, p. 87). This type of thinking leads to overperfectionistic standards or goals that are unlikely to be realized very often. The individual is then likely to view himself as a worthless and useless human being.

Through RET the therapist attempts to restructure maladaptive thought patterns so that realistic, attainable goals are set and feelings of self-worth retained. For the therapist, one of the more difficult tasks is to decide on the best approach for "teaching" the client that there is a need to relabel situations more rationally. This requires a careful integration of intellectual explanations (of a kind that can be easily understood by the client) and also a series of practical, behavioral excercises for developing new rational coping strategies. When skill deficits prevent the client from eliminating his irrational beliefs, role playing, assertive training, and so forth may also be required.

Problem solving training. We are constantly confronted with ever-changing problem situations. Training in effective problem solving behavior can provide means of dealing with many stressful challenges. This may be thought of as a form of self-control or independence training, which reduces feelings of helplessness or of being overwhelmed (D'Zurilla & Goldfried, 1971; Goldfried & Davison, 1975).

Problem solving training eases the client's independence from his or her therapist. It can readily be applied to most individuals, normal and abnormal. For example: Meichenbaum and Cameron (1973) and Siegal and Spivak (1976) worked with hospitalized schizophrenics; and Camp (1975) with children. Indeed, Mahoney (1974) goes so far as to view all psychotherapy in such terms. The aim of psychotherapy, according to Mahoney, is to educate the client as an "effective personal scientist" who is able to resolve problems satisfactorily and with a sense of mastery.

Self-control. Self-control provides another source of cognitive restructuring. The sequence includes self-monitoring, self-evaluation of performance, comparison with self-imposed standards, and subsequent self-reward or punishment for behaviors that meet or fail to meet the criteria. Under normal circumstances, appropriate self-imposed standards arise during the formative years as a result of complex social learning and modeling experiences. When these are inappropriate, it becomes the therapist's task to teach his client more adaptive procedures and sequences.

Self-control techniques have proved especially useful with addictive behaviors such as obesity, alcoholism, and smoking (Jeffery, 1975; Jeffery, Wing, & Stunkard, 1978; Mahoney, Moura, & Wade, 1973). Obsessive ruminations have been successfully treated using self-punishment techniques such as thought stopping (Cautela, 1969) or self-administered aversive consequences. Covert sensitization, covert extinction, and covert modeling (Cautela, 1969; Foreyt & Hagan, 1973; Kazdin, 1974) are also effective with some clients. In Susskind's (1970) idealized self-image procedure (ISI), the client and the therapist discuss and agree upon a realistic, appropriate, and attainable self-coping image. For example, an obese and unkempt person might see him/herself as relatively thinner and better groomed, or an insecure but knowledgeable teacher might see him/herself as a competent and assured classroom instructor. By a method of graded approximations involving various behavioral techniques, the client is trained to superimpose the desirable image upon his or her current self-image. He/she is encouraged to act, feel, and see him/herself becoming more like the ideal image, and to behave accordingly.

Techniques based upon operant conditioning strategies

Before discussing techniques, certain conceptual clarifications are necessary. The customary distinctions between operant and classical conditioning are too well known to list here, and even these distinctions become blurred in the light of recent suggestions that reduce generic differences to irreconcilable extremes (Franks & Wilson, 1976; Ray &

Brown, 1976). Be this as it may, there are certain fundamentals of operant conditioning that still need to be underscored, in particular the principles of reinforcement, punishment, and extinction.

According to the principle of reinforcement, a stimulus that depends upon an operant response maintains or increases the probability of future response. There are two subdivisions of reinforcement. Positive reinforcement refers to an increase in the frequency of a desired response that is followed by the presentation of the reinforcing stimulus. Negative reinforcement refers to an increase in the frequency of a desired response that is followed by the removal of an aversive stimulus. This latter situation is sometimes known as escape or avoidance conditioning (performing a task to terminate or postpone unpleasant consequences). Punishment involves a decrease in the probability of an undesired operant response occurring in the future. It may be subdivided into two classes: presentation of an aversive event or the removal of a reinforcing event, both of which result in a decrease in the probability of the undesired response being emitted in the future. The principle of reinforcement always refers to an increase in response frequency and punishment to a decrease in response frequency. A reinforcer refers to the consequent event and should not be confused with the principle itself (reinforcement). Extinction refers to the phenomenon whereby a response that was previously reinforced is no longer reinforced. It differs from punishment even though the net result in both instances is a decrease in the frequency of the response.

In complex human behavior, reward and punishment serve both incentive (satisfiers or arousers) and informational (messenger) functions. They act as carriers of information that can be integrated into memory in an abstract manner. Police and prisons convey messages about lawless behavior. The probability of being apprehended by the police (punished) immediately after (contingent upon) exhibiting lawless behavior (theft, rape, murder) determines the frequency with which the behavior occurs in our culture (functional relationship between behavior and its consequences).

Additional concepts are readily derived from these three fundamental principles. Complex behavioral sequences may be described and modified using such methods as shaping, the Premack principle, stimulus generalization, discrimination learning, chaining, reinforcement schedules, secondary reinforcement, and learning sets (for further details, see Kazdin, 1975a; Rachlin, 1970).

Operant principles are best employed under conditions of high environmental control. They are especially useful in institutions and with children, and may be used to develop skills in severly retarded or withdrawn individuals. In cases of severe deficit, the principle of "shaping" or successive approximation is employed. The desired behavior is broken down into small steps (e.g., going to the drawer, taking out a shirt, unfolding it, putting one arm in). Successive approximations are contingently reinforced until the total integrated behavior is acquired. This method may be utilized for more complex tasks such as the teaching of rudimentary language skills to autistic children (Lovaas, 1977).

For teaching language to nonverbal children, the following operant shaping sequence is typically employed. First the child is trained to attend to the teacher. Extended eye contact is then established by reinforcing any spontaneous eye contact that occurs, using smiles, praise or material rewards as reinforcers. A spoken command or prompt such as "look at me" may also be employed, in which case the reinforcement is forthcoming only if eye contact is made within five seconds of the prompt. Since the prompt serves to cue the behavior by acting as a signal, it is referred to as a discriminative stimulus. Once established, the reward schedule for attending behavior is "thinned" (partial reinforcement) to facilitate generalization and maintenance in the natural environment (Kozloff, 1973).

The second goal is the establishment of

nonverbal imitating behaviors. Initially, the child is taught gross motor imitative behavior such as clapping or touching toes. These gross movements are gradually refined to more subtle activities until eventually the child is able to model small movements around the mouth. These techniques may also be used to develop complex imitative behaviors; for example, Lovaas, Freitas, Nelson, and Whalen (1967) developed drawing, printing, self-care skills, and other preschool games in schizophrenic children. The ability to follow commands, another important aspect of language development, is also related to the ability to imitate.

The third step in the sequence, training verbal imitation, relies on four principles: reward all vocalizations; reward vocalization occuring within six seconds of the model's vocalization; reward vocalization within six seconds that approximate the sound of the model; introduce a new sound randomly interspersed with the sound from the previous step. After verbal imitation has been well established by this procedure, functional language is introduced.

Other applications of operant principles include the improvement of teaching methods by the use of computer-assisted instruction (Atkinson, 1968), programmed instruction and teaching machines (Skinner, 1963), programs for parents with learning-disabled children (Lovitt, 1975; Ryback & Staats, 1970), and methods for classroom management (O'Leary & O'Leary, 1976). Teachers may increase the participation of socially withdrawn children, improve concentration and attention span, and decrease disruptive behavior patterns (O'Leary & O'Leary, 1976).

Hyperactivity, a childhood disorder characterized by overactivity, restlessness, distractibility, and short attention span, has received considerable attention from behavioral therapists. An alternative treatment is the use of central nervous system stimulant drugs (e.g., Ritalin). Although temporarily effective, adverse side effects and poor long-term prognosis are not unusual with such agents. Chemotherapy is a passive treatment in that skill deficits and maladaptive patterns are either masked or suppressed, and the possibility of developing alternative adaptive behaviors is rarely taken into consideration. Specific behavioral restructuring programs are usually required either as alternatives or in addition to drug therapy alone. Behavior therapists may also employ response suppression techniques such as time out, response cost, or contingent verbal reprimands (O'Leary & O'Leary, 1976). A number of well designed drug-free behavioral intervention programs for hyperactive children are currently in progress (e.g. Alabiso, 1975; Ayllon, Layman, & Kandel, 1975) and preliminary reports are encouraging.

One of the more sophisticated and controversial innovations is the token economy (Atthowe, 1973; Franks & Wilson, 1976; Kazdin, 1977). Tokens (symbolic rewards) provide freedom of choice for participants but also serve training functions in that they can be given contingently upon specific behavior (such as sharing in group projects). Gradually, the token system is "faded out" in hopes that the intrinsic rewards of everyday life will come to maintain the newly acquired skills in the patient.

The token economy is not merely a strategy for delivering positive reinforcers for particular behaviors. It is a major procedure, to be employed only after careful consideration of implications and alternatives, carefully tailored to the needs of the situation and, if necessary, used in conjunction with other behavioral (or even nonbehavioral) procedures. Token economies have been successfully employed with such diverse groups as retardates, psychiatric patients, normal schoolchildren, delinquents, adult offenders, drug addicts, alcoholics, and families. More recently, the use of token economies is being extended to community and social programs, such as energy conservation and pollution control (Nietzel, Winett, MacDonald, & Davison,1977).

It has been suggested that token methods are akin to "bribery" and that they undermine the "true meaning" of doing something for "its own sake." (For a spirited debate on

In addition to general tension, multiple phobias and numerous "psychosomatic" problems, Mrs. M., a 49-year-old physician's wife, suffered from chronic depression which periodically became quite severe, causing her on three occasions to attempt suicide. She had undergone psychotherapy for three and a half years during which time she had been hospitalized briefly once and had been prescribed antidepressant drugs. Electroshock, however, had not been recommended by her psychiatrist. Neither the patient nor her husband thought the drugs had been beneficial, and Mrs. M. stopped taking them with her psychiatrist's consent after about 2 months trial. Mrs. M. terminated psychotherapy approximately 6 months before the writer's first meeting with her. Although she thought her psychiatrist had helped see her through some difficult times she had grown discouraged at her lack of progress.

Following a detailed behavioral analysis of her problems, a behavior therapy program involving multiple techniques was developed for her treatment. Systematic desensitization was decided upon for her many "phobias"; conditioned relaxation responses for certain of her psychosomatic complaints; behavior rehearsal, assertive training and reinforcement by therapist time of a series of increasingly more demanding tasks to reinstate social behaviors. Finally, marital counseling based on operant principles was planned to deal with conflicts with her husband. It seemed to the writer that success of the total program might depend to a large extent upon early alleviation of the patient's debilitating depression. Toward this end, Homme's extension of Premack's Differential Probability Hypothesis to the control of coverants was called upon.

Mrs. M. was asked to describe herself by a series of single words or phrases. Her responses were all negative. It was pointed out to her that if a person had only self-denigrating thoughts about herself it would be difficult for her not to be depressed. Therefore, we were going to substitute positive thoughts about herself for the negative ones. With agonizing slowness and much therapist prompting, Mrs. M. managed to find six positive statements she could entertain about herself. (With those patients who fail to see anything positive about themselves, it may be necessary for the therapist to reflect honestly good points that he sees in the patient—thus to start the list for her.) The six statements were printed in large letters on a sheet of note paper and in somewhat smaller letters on a card which was trimmed to fit inside the cellophane wrapper of her cigarette package. Mrs. M. was then informed how, according to Premack's hypothesis, a behavior (in her case, thinking positive thoughts about herself) could be increased by being paired with a behavior of higher probability of occurrence (smoking cigarettes in her case). She was told always to read one or two of the 6 positive items before smoking a cigarette. She was to do this without exception, which would require considerable conscious effort on her part. Whenever she put her cigarettes down for any length of time she was to place them on the sheet of note paper bearing the list of items. When carrying the pack of cigarettes around, the list would be available on the card. In addition, she was to add positive items to the list as they occurred to her.

Mrs. M. carried out the instructions faithfully and, within a week, her depression had lifted considerably; moreover, she had increased the number of positive items to 14. After the second week, she reported that she felt better about herself than she had in years. She now had 21 items on her list. The positive thoughts, she said, popped into her head even when she was not smoking or about to smoke.

Because of Mrs. M.'s obviously improved spirits implementation of her total treatment program was initiated at this time.

Mrs. M. was seen individually for 35 sessions and with her husband for an additional six sessions. In the 3 years which have elapsed since her termination of behavior therapy, the writer has been able to follow Mrs. M.'s adjustment rather carefully. She has become active in volunteer work for political and mental health causes, is considered an excellent hostess and enjoys a wide circle of friends. She reports that she has not suffered any serious depression during this time and considers herself a relatively happy person. She admits to bolstering her spirits by thinking good thoughts on those infrequent occasions when she is "down," but has made no systematic use of the Homme technique since the early weeks of behavior therapy.

this issue see Ford & Foster, 1976.) This general criticism, leveled at many operant intervention methods, is based upon misunderstanding. The basic aim of any operant behavioral program, including the token economy, is to make explicit those implicit environmental contingencies that usually shape behavior for most people. Children, for example, are constantly socialized in the accepted norms of our culture by receiving praise from their parents for being "good" boys or girls.

Space does not permit coverage of all, or even most, operant techniques. Some common methods that have been omitted include creativity development (Goetz & Baer, 1973; Meichenbaum, 1974), response cost (Kazdin, 1977), enuresis treatment methods (Foxx & Azrin, 1973), time-out procedures (Leitenberg, 1965), reinforcement menus (Homme, 1965), stimulus control and errorless learning (Terrace, 1966), and fading and prompting (Barlow & Agras, 1973). A summary of these and other techniques may be found in Kanfer and Goldstein (1975) and O'Leary and Wilson (1975).

The following case study by Todd (1972) of the treatment of a woman with chronic, severe depression is of interest on several accounts: multifaceted intervention procedures are employed, cognitive and operant procedures go hand in hand, and the disorder treated is by no means the simple behavioral malfunction that some critics consider all that behavior therapy is good for.

Behavior therapy in specific problem areas

Sexual inadequacy and deviance

According to behavior therapists, sexual inadequacy is brought about by a combination of limited sexual education, communication deficits, and learned negative emotional reactions (e.g., fear, anxiety, or guilt). The necessary correctives depend upon reeducation, the provision of accurate information, and graded communication exercises designed to reduce uncertainty and fear of performance.

After round-table discussion with ther therapists, the couple is instructed in "sensate focus" exercises in which they learn to relax together in private and to communicate to each other what feels good both physically and psychologically. This exploration of pleasnt bodily sensations, initially restricted to nongenital areas, then moves on to include nondemanding genital stimulation. Specific behavioral techniques such as role playing, orgasmic reconditioning, and masturbation training are later introduced as needed to help with individual problems (e.g., erectile or orgasmic dysfunction, dyspareunia, vaginismus, low sex drive).

Vaginismus (involuntary contraction of the vaginal musculature prior to penetration) may be treated by the method of successive approximations. Physical problems having been ruled out, the client and her partner are relaxed and instructed in the various sensate focus exercises as outlined above. The client is then asked to insert a series of progressively larger vaginal dilators and instructed not to move on to the next size until she feels perfectly comfortable. When appropriate, these exercises are repeated with her partner inserting the dilators. Eventually, penile insertion is attempted and intercourse resumed (see Masters & Johnson, 1970).

It is possible to treat many forms of sexual deviance by aversion conditioning coupled with other behavior therapy procedures provided that acceptable alternative behaviors are generated. Aversion conditioning has been successfully employed in the treatment of sadism (Davison, 1968), exhibitionism (Evans, 1970), pedophilia (Barlow, Leitenberg, & Agras, 1969) and transvestism (Marks & Gelder, 1967). It should be noted that whether or not the behavior therapist is justified in the correction of sexual deviation, even in the voluntary patient, remains a matter of lively and ongoing controversy (Franks & Wilson, 1976). We do *not* include either male or female homosexuality in our list of sexual deviations as such. Whether one should ever attempt to alter the direction of another individual's sexual orientation is another unresolved issue at this time. There is one school of behavioral thought that insists that such an attempted realignment is *never* appropriate (Davison, 1977).

The addictive behaviors

The addictive behaviors (alcoholism, obesity, smoking, and drug abuse) are notoriously difficult to treat. Virtually every conceivable form of psychiatric intervention has been tried and found wanting (O'Leary & Wilson, 1975). Nevertheless, multifaceted behavioral treatment seems to offer considerable promise. Innovative programs for the treatment of such problems as alcoholism (Briddell & Nathan, 1976), obesity (Mahoney, 1975), smoking (Bernstein & McAlister, 1976), and drug abuse (Callner, 1975) are constantly being evolved. To illustrate these developments we will focus upon alcoholism.

Neither the disease concept of alcoholism nor the loss-of-control theory (Jellinek, 1960) stand up to research scrutiny (e.g., Marlatt, Demming & Reid, 1973; Sobell & Sobell, 1973). Social learning theory offers viable explanatory alternatives. Techniques available for treatment include aversion therapy, operant conditioning, controlled drinking, stress inoculation, job skills, and assertiveness training (cf. Hedberg & Campbell, 1974; Sobell & Sobell, 1976). Throughout, the behavioral emphasis is upon objective evaluation of the functional relationships between alcohol comsumption and behavior (Briddell & Nathan, 1976). Cognitive appraisal of the individual's life situation is also important (Higgins & Marlatt, 1975).

Expectation and belief can be more potent than the actual effects of the alcohol. Many a high school gathering has been enlivened by a lot of ginger ale and a dash of bourbon masquerading as a drinking orgy. Considerable research has been directed toward the exploration of beliefs as they relate to the physiological effects of alcohol. It is not only the pharmacological effects of alcohol that trigger off the "characteristic" loss of control over behavior; the beliefs surrounding the effects of alcohol and amount ingested can be of at least equal importance (Lang, Goeckner, Adesso, &Marlatt, 1975; Wilson & Abrams, 1977).

For some alcoholics, controlled social drinking may be a more realistic treatment goal than total abstinence (Hamburg, 1975; Lloyd & Salzberg, 1975). This involves training the drinker to monitor the cues that identify his or her blood alcohol (intoxication) level. The next step is the institution of self-control strategies to limit drinking to a reasonable level. It must be stressed that investigation of controlled drinking is still in the experimental stage and should be regarded as the treatment of choice only in very special circumstances (Franks, 1977b).

Ethical and related issues in behavior therapy

By and large, the ethics of behavior therapists are no different from those of any other segment of the mental health profession. Individual rights have to be protected at all levels and for all concerned—children, adults, outpatients, voluntary residents of institutions, incarcerated individuals, and employees. Informed consent, avoidance of unnecessary deception in research, accountability, licensing, and professional training are all issues of major significance to behavior therapists and their professional organizations (cf. Davison & Stuart, 1975; Franks & Wilson, 1976, 1977, 1978; Stolz, 1978).

A commonly leveled criticism of behavior

therapy is that its directive nature leads to undue client manipulation. To this we would point out that some form of social influence is recognized and inevitable in all forms of psychotherapy. Unlike many other practitioners, the behavior therapist attempts to cope with this problem in the following ways: *First,* accountability is stressed at all levels—to the patient directly, to professional peers, and to other responsible individuals. This is accomplished by making the goals of therapy explicit, by establishing at the onset a mutually agreed upon formal contract with the client, setting forth these goals, how they are to be accomplished, and the probable time periods involved. *Second,* the goals and contract are subject to mutual review and modification as the course of treatment proceeds. *Third,* no technique is employed that has not been empirically validated and carefully evaluated with respect to optimal suitability for that particular situation. According to the guiding "principle of least intervention," the technique of choice must be the one that involves minimum client discomfort or possibility of adverse consequences. *Fourth,* no therapy is regarded as complete without the benefits of careful outcome evaluation. This serves several purposes: assessment of short- and long-term overall success; elimination of specific errors and refinement of techniques; the provision of future clinical and research directions.

Behavior therapy is characterized by sensitivity to data, replicability, impartiality, and total openness. What the behavior therapist does and why he does it are made explicit to all. There can be no mystique and no secret. Perhaps of equal importance, good behavior therapy is characterized by those humanistic values common to all the helping professions.

Particular controversy exists with respect to the use of aversion procedures. The uninformed public, and even some misinformed professionals, sometimes equate behavior therapy with aversion conditioning and even with such obviously unrelated procedures as brain surgery and electroconvulsive therapy (ECT). Brain surgery and ECT have absolutely nothing to do with behavior therapy, and aversion conditioning is but one of the many procedures available. Actually, aversion conditioning is one of the least effective procedures; it is rarely used and then only after consideration of all other alternatives and with stringent precautions. Furthermore, even when aversion conditioning is employed, it is never used in isolation. It is always conceptualized as part of an overall mutltifaceted program that stresses alternative positive programs calculated to give the client greater control of his or her own behavior (self-management) and increased freedom with respect to the options available. Films such as *A Clockwork Orange* are good theater, but are scientifically unsound. They perpetuate common misconceptions with respect to the "mysterious power" of conditioning and the misguided or even sinister intents of behavior therapists (Franks, 1977a).

Summary

In this chapter we have attempted to outline the nature of behavior therapy—its many roots and its current status. Although behavior therapists by now evidence a common core of shared strategies and ways of thinking about clinical problems, we view behavior therapy primarily as methodological prescription, an approach to the study and modification of maladaptive psychosocial activities based upon the methodology of the behavioral scientist. It is not a series of techniques. As such, there can be no entity known as behavior therapy to be meaningfully compared with specific therapies derived from other orientations. What is appropriate is to compare specific behavioral techniques or programs with other behavioral programs or with other procedures such as psychoanalytic therapy or specific drug treatments. But in the long run, it is the rigor of behavior therapy as a methodology that is more likely to contribute to its professional and scientific viability rather than its therapeutic successes, no matter how spectacular.

GLOSSARY

Assertion training: A behavioral treatment procedure designed to remove social inhibitions and interpersonal inadequacies; helping a client to openly express feelings of approval and disapproval.

Aversion conditioning: The therapeutic procedure of systematically and repeatedly pairing an aversive stimulus (e.g., electric shock) with the occurrence of thoughts, feelings, or behaviors that a client deems undesirable and wishes to eliminate.

Baseline: The frequence of a behavior prior to the introduction of an experimental or treatment intervention.

Behavioral assessment: Sampling an individual's current thoughts, feelings, and overt behavior in their situational context.

Behavior rehearsal: A behavioral treatment technique in which a client practices or rehearses a novel or problem action in the therapeutic situation. The therapist usually models the behavior and coaches the client how best to perform.

Classical conditioning: A form of learning in which a neutral stimulus (CS) that is repeatedly associated with another stimulus (UCS) comes to elicit by itself the response that initially occurred only when the UCS was present.

Cognitive restructuring: A behavior therapy procedure designed to modify the nature of a client's perceptions and thoughts about important life events so that his behavior changes.

Conditioning: The process by which an association between a stimulus and a response is learned; conditioning usually refers to either of two procedures known as classical conditioning and operant conditioning, respectively.

Contingency: The extent to which the occurrence of one event is dependent upon the occurrence of another event.

Control group: Subjects in an experiment for whom the critical independent variable is not manipulated; a basis for comparison with the experimental group for whom the independent variable is manipulated.

Counterconditioning: The displacement of a particular conditioned response by the establishment of an incompatible conditioned response to the same stimulus.

Covert sensitiztion: A form of aversion therapy in which imagined representations of undesirable activities or feelings are repeatedly associated with symbolically induced sensations of nausea or disgust.

Desensitization: A therapeutic procedure aimed at reducing anxiety in which an individual is sequentially exposed to a series of real life or imagined situations that he or she finds increasingly more fearful. Also known as systematic desensitization.

Escape conditioning: A form of instrumental conditioning in which the subject's responses terminate a noxious stimulus.

Extinction: The disruption of an association between a stimulus and a response.

Fading: The gradual removal of prompts or cues until a response is under the control of the training stimulus.

Generalization: The occurrence of a learned response in the presence of stimulus conditions that differ from those that existed during the establishment of the response.

Maintenance: The continued occurrence of a learned response, especially after a treatment intervention program has been discontinued.

Mediational processes: Inferred cognitive or affective (emotional) processes that intervene between an observable stimulus and response.

Modeling: Learning through observation and imitation of other's behavior.

Operant conditioning: Increasing or decreasing the occurrence of a given behavior by systematically manipulating the consequences of that behavior.

Premack principle: Increasing the frequency of a low probability response by making a high probability behavior contingent on its occurrence.

Punishment: The reduction of the future probability of a response as a result of immediate delivery of a stimulus for that response.

Reinforcement: The presentation of a reward or removal of an aversive stimulus following a resonse, such that the probability of that response recurring is increased.

Reliability: The degree to which a test, measurement, or classification procedure produces the same observation each time it is applied.

Self-monitoring: The systematic recording, charting, and/or display of information relevant to behavior that is the target of self-directed change (e.g., counting daily caloric intake).

Shaping: Modifying operant behavior by reinforcing only those variations in responding that deviate in a direction desired by the experimenter or therapist.

Single subject methodology (n = 1) The use of the individual as his or her own control; behavioral change is assessed relative to the individual's own behavior and not that of a separate control group. Examples include the reversal (ABAB) and multiple baseline designs.

Target behavior: A behavior that is the primary focus of a behavioral intervention program.

Technical eclecticism: The use of any technique, derived from any system, without necessarily subscribing to the theoretical systems from which the technique comes, provided that it has empirical support.

Token reinforcement: A procedure in which some evaluation or feedback is frequently given regarding behavior in the form of ratings, points, or chips that are exchangeable for some reward.

Trait theory: The theory that personality is best described in terms of the global scores that an individual obtains on different scales representing traits or personality dimensions.

Validity: The extent to which a procedure actually measures what it purports to measure; the extent to which predictions can be accurately made about a client's future behavior on the basis of test results, diagnosis or other pertinent data.

20

BIOLOGICAL PSYCHIATRY

DONALD W. GOODWIN

When the term biological psychiatry is used today, it usually refers to one or both of the following: 1. theories that psychiatric illnesses have a biochemical basis, and 2. use of drugs or other physical means to treat mental illness. Biological psychiatry is also used in a third sense.It refers to "organic" or "descriptive psychiatry," often with the implication that biological psychiatrists "reduce" all of human behavior to neurons firing and glands secreting as contrasted with "humanistic" approaches that "respect people as unique products of complex social, psychological, and biological interaction." When used in this sense, biological becomes a straw man: an abstraction to be contrasted with those other abstractions, "psychological" and "social." In truth, thoughts, feelings, and acts—including social acts—logically are just as biological as a firing nerve or a secreting gland. No scientific discussion of social insects would subdivide their behavior into biological versus nonbiological. Logically, the opposite of biological is spiritual rather than psychological or social.

Nevertheless, terms are shaped by usage, and it is true that some theories of abnormal behavior emphasize biochemistry and some treatments of abnormal behavior emphasize chemical and other physical interventions. Even in this narrow and perhaps legitimate sense, the term is sometimes abused. For example, when used as synonymous with "organic," it is often implied that biochemical theories of abnormal behavior are proven. In fact, leaving aside instances of mental illness that can be directly traced to brain damage or other physical derangement, no biochemical theory of psychiatric illness has been confirmed, although there are some promising leads (Segal, Yager, & Sullivan, 1976).

Furthermore, while there is evidence that physical intervention, medicinal and otherwise, does relieve symptoms in certain psychiatric illnesses, there is no evidence of cure. Nor should the fact that some drugs relieve psychiatric symptoms be construed as necessarily meaning the symptoms are chemical in origin. A tranquilizer may dispel stage fright sufficiently to permit the person to perform, without biochemical abnormalities causing the stage fright (early childhood experiences make much better sense).

Similarly, when biological psychiatry is called "descriptive" or "Kraepelinan" (referring to Emil Kraepelin, an early "biological" psychiatrist), this often reflects a dislike for attempts to classify abnormal behavior, again because it seems dehumanizing and betrays a lack of "compassion" for suffering people. "Descriptive" psychiatry also is used to imply that the person interested in describing the *phenomena* of disturbed behavior is uninterested in explaining *why* the person is disturbed. The "descriptive psychiatrist" is often accused—sometimes justifiably—of lacking proper respect for untested (often untestable) psychological theories. Again, "descriptive" becomes a straw man. There is no reason why a psychiatrist cannot be interested in classification (called diagnosis) and also be interested in speculating about causation. The fact is that classification almost always precedes discovery of causation and without classification (however arbitrary) communication between professionals is impossible (Woodruff, Goodwin, & Guze, 1974).

Historically, biological psychiatry, as defined in the nonderogatory sense, represents the oldest form of psychiatry. Hippocrates, Galen, and other physicians of antiquity assumed that physical changes in the body were responsible for aberrent behavior, even if the changes were due to supernatural or demonic forces. Psychopharmacology (the use of drugs for psychiatric conditions) has been in vogue since earliest recorded history. Hundreds of years before the birth of Christ, deranged individuals were treated with drugs such as hellbore, confined in dark rooms, beaten, and roughly handled to bring them to their senses. However, physical intervention was often accompanied by psychological treatment, such as diversion, and magical treatment, carried out in temples. (The patient went to the priest with an offering and slept the night in the temple. God appeared while he was asleep and cured him [Fish, 1964].) Today it is common practice to combine psychotherapy or behavior therapy with medication; they are in no way incompatible.

Well into the twentieth century, the belief was almost universal that what we call psychiatric illnesses reflected derangements in the physical organism. Throughout the eighteenth and nineteenth centuries these derangements were generally held to be hereditary. One of the earliest observations about the major psychiatric illnesses, such as schizophrenia and manic depressive disease, was that they ran in families. This of course does not mean they were hereditary (speaking French also runs in families), but the assumption that they were still was common. It was only with the advent of the social work movement and the influence of Freudian and other psychological theories in the 1920s and 1930s that psychological and social factors were held responsible for aberrent behavior.

The environmentalist movement almost totally dominated the psychiatric scene in America (less so in Europe and Russia) until the mid-1950s, when new drugs were introduced that appeared to have beneficial effects in psychiatric conditions. As their effectiveness came to be accepted, there was renewed interest in possible physical and biochemical causations of mental illness. Twin studies and other means of separating "nature" from "nurture" have convinced many investigators that environmental factors *alone* cannot account for the major psychiatric illnesses.

However, it should again be emphasized that there is no direct, incontrovertible proof that biochemical abnormalities underlie any of the so-called functional mental illnesses. This is not to deny that many clinicians and investigators *believe* biochemistry is the explanation for mental illness, but the data required to prove this are still lacking. Given the enormous complexity of the brain, and our still crude techniques for studying brain chemistry, the lack of confirmation is understandable.

Moreover, biochemical theories at least lend themselves to scientific testing, which cannot often be said of psychological theories. They lend themselves much easier to scientific study in the sense that drugs can be compared to inert substances (placebos) and definitive conclusions can be drawn. By contrast, evaluation of verbal therapies suffers from the lack of uniformity of therapists, so that controlled double blind studies (studies where bias can be avoided) are impossible. Through the last several thousand years, innumerable treatments involving physical and chemical intervention have been attempted, and in time all of were discarded. Something called the "Hawthorne" effect should be mentioned here. This refers to the phenomenon whereby any new treatment in psychiatry is viewed by its exponents with enthusiasm and this enthusiasm alone seems to produce temporary beneficial changes. Further experience with the treatment leads to a waning of enthusiasm with a corresponding drop in effectiveness. One reason why almost *any* treatment benefits some people is that the course of most psychiatric illnesses is variable, marked by spontaneous cessation of symptoms without any treatment, or a good deal of fluctuation where a person is chronically ill but worse at some times than others. Therefore, some patients respond favorably to any treatment at any given time, not because of the treatment but because their condition is characterized by spontaneous remissions (the relief of symptoms without professional intervention).

Overwhelmingly, the most popular physical intervention in psychiatric conditions today involves the use of drugs, almost all of which were developed since the early 1950s. Chief emphasis in this chapter, therefore, will be on drug therapy, with brief sections devoted to other kinds of physical intervention still occasionally used.

Sedative-hypnotics

Drugs that sedate also produce sleep (hypnosis), depending on dosage. Hence the term sedative-hypnotics. There is wide variability in individual response to all drugs, including these (Matheson & Davison, 1972). Therefore, a dose of a sedative-hypnotic that produces mild calming or anxiety reducing effects in one person may produce sleep in another.

Before the synthesis of the first barbiturates a century ago, the most commonly used sedative-hypnotics were morphine and its chemical relatives from the poppy plant, and extracts from *Cannabis sativa,* the hemp source of marihuana. Morphine of course is best known as a pain killer, but it also produces sedation and sleep and was prescribed by physicians for this purpose.

These morphinelike drugs were also widely used without prescriptions, since there were no legal restraints on their availability until the Harrison Act of 1914. One of the most popular preparations of poppy-derived drugs was tincture of opium (laudanum). Data are not available about the use of these compounds, but there is no question that it was widespread, with most of the patent medicines of the day (or at least those for "nerves"), containing morphine derivatives, cannabis derivatives, and alcohol. Use of the morphine derivatives undoubtedly produced physical addiction in many people.

Alcohol is also a sedative-hypnotic in that it calms in small doses and produces sleep in large doses. Other sedative-hypnotics available at the turn of the century were chloral hydrate, bromide, and paraldehyde. All were widely used and presumably abused. Like the most popular sedative-hypnotics of the twentieth century—barbiturates—they also produced elevation of mood (euphoria), which contributed to their popularity and abuse potential. One of the advantages of the more recently developed antianxiety drugs (see below) is that they are relatively weak euphoriants and, presumably as a result, less subject to abuse.

The common salts, potassium and sodium bromide, came into use in the nineteenth century as a sedative-hypnotic at about the same time a number of compounds were being synthesized that had sedative-hypnotic properties. These included chloral hydrate, which was related to chloroform and which became notorious as a "Mickey Finn" when combined with alcohol. Paraldehyde was also introduced in the second half of the nineteenth century, a semisynthetic compound derived from a breakdown product of alcohol. All were used in medicine as well as being freely available "across the counter." All produced not only sedation and sleep but psychological and physical addiction, emphasizing a point seldom made today. Drug abuse in this country has a very long history; and lacking comparative epidemiological data, one is justified in assuming that there may be no more drug abuse today (and possibly less) than existed 100 years ago.

It was the synthesis of barbiturates from urea (a constitutent of urine) in 1882 that produced a family of sedative-hypnotics that pushed aside their competitors to become the most popular and widely used drugs of this type in the twentieth century.

Barbiturates are divided into long-acting and short-acting forms. Representative of the long-acting form is phenobarbital, introduced early in the twentieth century. Short-acting barbiturates were introduced in the 1930s, the most popular being pentobarbital (Nembutal) and secobarbital (Seconal). The long-acting barbiturates are slowly absorbed into the blood stream and slowly eliminated. As long as 12 to 18 hours after the drug has been taken, perhaps half of the drug is still in the body. By contrast, short-acting barbiturates are quickly absorbed and rapidly eliminated, so that their peak action comes at 30 minutes to one hour and they may be almost completely eliminated from the body within six to eight hours. This difference in elimination rates has important implications for abuse potential for this reason.

Drugs in the sedative-hypnotic class that are rapidly eliminated have a greater abuse potential than members of the same class that are slowly eliminated (Goodman & Gilman, 1970). The shorter acting drugs also produce more euphoria. Originally phenobarbital was found to be effective for epilepsy and was not identified primarily as a sedative-hypnotic. For twenty years it was virtually the only barbiturate available and not considered to have an abuse potential. It produced little euphoria and epileptics were not prone to increase the dosage to obtain the same effect (i.e., tolerance did not occur).

When the shorter acting barbiturates became available, it soon became apparent that they were effective sedative-hypnotics, but not very useful in the control of epilepsy because tolerance *did* occur, with epileptic patients required to increase the dosage in order to maintain an antiepileptic effect. Within a few years, it also became apparent that the shorter-acting barbiturates had a marked potential for abuse. A sizeable proportion of people using the drugs found they had to increase the dosage to obtain the same effect, whether the desired effect was sleep or sedation. They became addicted to the drug in both the pharmacological and psychological sense (see glossary). Tolerance rapidly developed and patients were taking ten or fifteen times more of the drug than was originally needed for sleep or sedation. In fact, one way to determine whether a patient was abusing barbiturates was to give him the usual sleep-producing dose. If he showed no sign of drowsiness, it was clear that he had acquired tolerance either to barbiturates or to closely related drugs (e.g., chloral hydrate and paraldehyde).

After using the short-acting barbiturates in high dosage for a few days to a few weeks, the patient would develop a withdrawal syndrome after stopping or reducing use of the drug. The syndrome is almost identical to that seen in alcohol withdrawal, characterized by shakiness, hallucinations, convulsions, and delirium. Occasionally the withdrawal syndrome was fatal, but usually subsided in five to ten days and could promptly be relieved by administration of barbiturates. In other words, it fully met the definition of "withdrawal" in that the drug that produced the withdrawal symptoms also relieved the symptoms.

Phenobarbital is still widely used in the treatment of epilepsy, but there is growing sentiment that the shorter acting barbiturates no longer have a legitimate place in medicine. The reasons are as follows:

1. Patients become rapidly tolerant to both the sedative and sleep producing effects of the drug. After two weeks of using a short acting barbiturate for sleep, the drug loses its sleep-producing power (through tolerance) and any insomnia relieving effects produced thereafter are due to placebo effect (see glossary). In short, barbiturates are not very effective sedatives or hypnotics for long periods. (Kagen, Harwood, Rickels, Rudzek, & Sorer, 1975).

2. Short-acting barbiturates are potentially addictive. Most people who use them do *not* become addicted, as most people who drink alcohol do not become alcoholic. However, barbiturates are at least as addictive as alcohol, perhaps more so, and over the past 30 years many have become addicted. This has occurred both through indiscriminate prescriptions from physicians and, more recently, from the availability of barbiturates "on the street." Short-acting barbiturates and a number of related compounds constitute what are known as "downers" and became part of the illicit drug culture. They are frequently used with other drugs (polydrug use), especially "uppers" like amphetamines. (Brecher, 1972)

3. Overdose of barbituratelike drugs is a common (perhaps the most common) method of suicide. One reason this might be expected is that insomnia (for which barbiturates are still widely prescribed) is associated with depression and depression with suicide. As with alcohol, they produce death by suppressing the respiratory center in the brain stem.

4. A new class of drugs has been developed in the past 20 years (see next section) that has many advantages over barbiturates and lack some disadvantages. These drugs, called benzodiazepines, produce little euphoria and are "suicide proof." It is virtually impossible to ingest enough of these drugs to result in death. Like phenobarbital, they are slowly excreted and not associated with euphoria, which probably explains why they have less abuse potential than do the short-acting barbiturates and other sedative-hypnotics. (Greenblat & Shader, 1974)

There is talk about withdrawing barbiturates from the market, but no agreement as yet. For one thing, there are patients with such severe insomnia that it does not respond to any other medication. Also, small amounts of barbiturates are often added to other medications in treating headache and gastrointestinal problems. The combinations are believed effective and seem to have a low abuse potential.

In summary, since the mid-nineteenth century, twenty or more sedative-hypnotic drugs have been synthesized. These include chloral hydrate, paraldehyde, and the barbiturates. In recent years a number of sleep medications have been developed by chemically modifying the basic barbiturate molecule. All of these man-made drugs have features in common. They all produce rapid tolerance as well as cross tolerance (i.e., tolerance to one of these drugs produces tolerance to the others). Ingestion of large amounts of these drugs may result in death and sustained heavy use results in withdrawal symptoms, including potentially fatal convulsions.

All have been diverted to "street use" and are part of the polydrug culture. There is now question whether there is a legitimate place in medicine for any of these drugs. Those who advocate removing the drugs from the market generally hold that the benzodiazapines, discussed below, are superior and that the older sedative-hypnotics are no longer needed.

Anti-anxiety drugs

Sedative-hypnotic drugs have an anxiety-reducing or "tranquilizing" effect, but ordinarily the dosage required to produce the effect also causes drowsiness and some impairment in thinking and concentration. In the 1950s two new types of drugs were developed that appeared to *selectively* reduce anxiety at dosage levels that did not produce much if any drowsiness or impaired concentration. In large enough amounts these drugs will cause drowziness and sleep, yet, the person can be easily awakened and become fully alert, an important advantage that is not present with sedative-hypnotic drugs.

The new anxiety-reducing agents (sometimes called minor tranquilizers) fall into two categories. The first consists of a drug called meprobamate (best known by its trade name Miltown). The second consists of closely related compounds called benzodiazepines. As with the "major tranquilizers" (the phenothiazines, to be discussed next) and the recently developed antidepressant drugs, meprobamate and the benzodiazapines were discovered by chance. In both cases chemists were searching for better muscle relaxants and discovered that these variants of older drugs not only relaxed muscles but also selectively reduced anxiety without causing drowsiness. (There is enormous individual variation in response to *all* drugs, and the assertion that these drugs do not cause drowsiness is not applicable to all users.)

Meprobamate was popular in the late 1950s and early 1960s, but was gradually supplanted by the benzodiazapines, which by the middle 1970s represented the largest selling prescription drugs in Western societies. One reason meprobamate waned in popularity was that many users became abusers; they took more than the prescribed dose, not only to reduce anxiety but also to achieve a barbituratelike euphoria. As more and more cases of meprobamate addiction were reported—including reports of withdrawal convulsions—physicians turned to the new benzodiazapines (Librium and Valium are the two best known trade names). There are five of these drugs available on the market, and one other of similar chemical structure is prescribed for sleep. The drugs are believed to have a relatively low abuse potential due to a selective effect on anxiety unaccompanied by euphoria. Abuse has been reported where individuals become highly tolerant to the drugs and take them in large quantities, and there have been reports of withdrawal convulsions, but given the millions of prescriptions written for these drugs yearly, abuse seems infrequent.

Benzodiazapines also have other advantages. The lethal dose is so high that apparently no one has succeeded in killing himself or herself with the drugs alone. As noted earlier, suicide is an important consideration when any drug is prescribed for anxiety or insomnia, since both are depressive symptoms and most suicides are committed by persons with depression. Benzodiazapines are also widely used as muscle relaxants and have potent anticonvulsive activity. As drugs for epilepsy, benzodiazapines are at lease as useful as phenobarbital, but with one disadvantage: they cost more.

Benzodiazapines, like phenobarbital, another drug with a low abuse potential, are slowly eliminated from the body. Eighteen to 24 hours after most benzodiazapine drugs have been taken, at least half of the drug is still present in the body. In other words, a single dose of the drug continues to have effects throughout most of a day. If taken several times during the day the drug accumulates in the body until, after about a week, a steady state exists where the absorption and elimination rates are equalized (Garattini, Mussini, & Randall, 1973).

One interesting aspect of the benzodiazepines is their "taming" effect on animals. When injected into animals by dart guns, the animals become tame and manageable without necessarily being asleep. Even if they are asleep, they can easily be aroused. Whether benzodiazapines have a similar "taming" or antiaggressive effect on humans is not certain.

Antipsychotic drugs

Attempts to synthesize a superior antihistamine drug in the early 1950s led to the observation that some of these modified versions of older antihistamines calmed agitated patients. Antihistamines have mild tranquilizing effects and some are prescribed for this purpose. However, the new modified version of these drugs had little antihistamine effect but pronounced tranquilizing effects. The tranquilization differed from that produced by meprobamate and the benzodiazapines in that further observation indicated that the revamped antihistaminelike drugs (called *phenothiazines*) were not so much effective in relieving anxiety as they were in reducing psychotic symptoms. Psychosis refers to hallucinations, delusions, or scrambled thought patterns—commonly known as "craziness." These symptoms are most commonly seen in schizophrenia and mania (although they also may occur in organic brain disease and severe depressions).

The first of the phenothiazines to be investigated for its antipsychotic effects was chlorpromazine (Thorazine was the American trade name). By the mid-1950s, it was recognized that chlorpromazine was probably the most effective drug ever discovered for relieving psychotic symptoms, and it became the "drug of choice" for schizophrenia and mania. Its closest competitor at the time was reserpine, a botanical popular in India as a folk medicine for nervous complaints. Reserpine was quickly judged to be an inferior antipsychotic drug but continues to be prescribed for hypertension (in some individuals it may also cause severe depressions).

The success of chlorpromazine launched a flurry of activity in the pharmaceutical industry to develop even more effective antipsychotic drugs. Most of these have consisted of minor variations of chlorpromazine. A few other antipsychotic agents of different chemical structure have been synthesized, but they appear to have almost identical actions as the phenothiazines and will be considered here as *phenothiazinelike drugs* (AMA Department of Drugs, 1977).

While there are a score or more of phenothiazinelike drugs on the market, there is no convincing evidence that one phenothiazine is superior to another. They differ mainly in side effects. All, in fact, have serious side effects, which limit their usefulness. In selecting a phenothiazine for a particular patient, the clinician ofter does so with side effects in mind.

The most common side effects consist of symptoms similar to those seen in Parkinson's disease. These consist of involuntary movements ranging from trembling hands to jerking movements of the limbs, as well as muscular rigidity, difficulty with speech and gait, and an expressionless face. Chewing motions and tongue protrusions as well as sedation and a marked reduction in blood pressure are common.

The phenothiazines can be divided into three groups based on their side effects. There is the chlorpromazine group, which produces sedation and is useful for agitated patients, but also produces hypotension and Parkinsonian symptoms. A second group produces little hypotension or sedation, but severe Parkinsonian symptoms. The third group produces almost no Parkinsonian symptoms, but has moderate hypotensive and sedative effects. Because Parkinsonian symptoms are the most troublesome side effects, the latter group is often prescribed for outpatients, while the group that produces little or no reduction in blood pressure is often given to older patients who may have heart disease or other conditions where a lowering of blood pressure could be dangerous.

The phenothiazines are not curative; once the patient is withdrawn from medication, his or her symptoms usually return. As a result, phenothiazines are given to schizophrenic patients over long periods, often in high doses. (Mania is an episodic disorder, for which the phenothiazines rarely need to be given for long periods. Moreover, lithium is now the preferred treatment for most manics.)

Until recently, long-term use of phenothiazines was considered relatively innocuous, and they were prescribed to schizophrenic patients as insulin is prescribed for diabetics. In the past few years, a serious and sometimes fatal Parkinsonian syndrome has been described called "tardive dyskinesia," which results occasionally from prolonged use of phenothiazines. The current practice is to discontinue phenothiazines intermittently in the hope that a "drug holiday" will prevent the development of tardive dyskinesia.

Despite their limitations, large credit is given to the phenothiazines for a major revolution in psychiatry since the mid-1950s. This has consisted of radically lowering the mental hospital population and releasing large numbers of schizophrenic patients into the community. The results have not entirely been a blessing, since they can sometimes be a burden on the community or to their families, and they often are readmitted for short periods to hospitals. Nevertheless, the drugs have given hope where no hope existed before and have greatly changed mental hospital practices and attitudes toward the "incurably insane."

Antidepressant drugs

There are two major classes of antidepressant drugs, although most drugs mentioned in this chapter may provide temporary relief of depressed mood. The two classes are the *monoamine oxidase inhibitors* (MAOI's) and *tricyclic antidepressants* (Jarvik, 1977).

The MAOIs are an exception to the rule that most drugs developed in the last 25 years for psychiatric patients have been discovered by accident. The MAOIs were the logical outcome of an observation and a theory. The observation was that monoamine oxidase inhibitors increase norepinephrine in the brain. The theory was that lowered norepinephrine was the cause of depression. The theory now appears simplistic at best and may have no relevance to depression. Disillusionment with the theory has been paralleled by a failure to convincingly show that MAOIs relieve depression. Some studies indicate that they do, but others indicate that they do not, and most of the evidence for their usefulness is based on individual clinical experience (known as anecdotal evidence).

Apart from the lack of evidence showing their effectiveness, another reason MAOIs have fallen in disfavor has been the elaborate dietary restrictions patients must obey to prevent possible fatal reactions to the drugs. These include avoidance of certain cheeses, wines, yeast, and other substances that contain a chemical that causes an abrupt rise in blood pressure.

Most clinicians prescribe MAOIs only when the other major class of antidepressants—the tricyclics—have failed. Some clinicians believe that MAOIs are superior to tricyclics for certain rather poorly defined depressions, where obsessions and phobias may dominate the clinical picture.

Tricyclic antidepressants are one more example of useful drugs being discovered in the process of trying to improve upon other drugs. Clinical trials with new versions of the phenothiazines led to the observation that they were not very useful for treating psychoses but seemed to relieve depressive symptoms. (The term tricyclic refers to their chemical structure, which has a three-ring core.) Since their antidepressant properties were observed in the early 1960s, numerous studies have borne out their effectiveness in treating the classical forms of depression (what used to be called manic depressive psychosis—depressed type—and is now called primary affective disorder). It is not clear whether the drugs are as useful in treating "reactive" or "secondary" depressions that occur in patients who have other psychiatric illnesses or have experienced traumatic situations.

In order to show the effectiveness of tricyclics (or any antidepressant), it is necessary to have a comparison group of patients who receive a placebo (inert substance), where neither the investigator nor the patient knows whether the patient is receiving the active drug or the placebo (see chapter 3). This is known as a controlled double blind study and is essential in studying the effect of drugs on illnesses that are episodic (as most depressions are) and usually end spontaneously without any therapeutic intervention. Controlled double blind studies usually show that tricyclics are about 15 percent superior to the placebo group, not a very impressive gap but one that cannot be explained by chance alone. A typical study might show that 85 percent of patients on tricyclics improve in one month compared to 70 percent of patients on placebo. Based on their own clinical experience, most psychiatrists feel that tricyclics are better than the studies would indicate, the explanation being that the studies probably included many patients without "true" affective disorders. At any rate, the tricyclics are widely prescribed and with a good deal of optimism on the part of the physician.

One disadvantage of the tricyclics is that patients often must take the drug for several weeks before improvement occurs. Tricyclics have side effects also, usually occurring in the first few weeks of treatment. These include sleepiness, tremor, sexual difficulties (such as slow ejaculation) and, on rare occasions, disturbances of the heart rhythm.

When death from tricyclics occurs from overdosage, it is usually due to the drug's effect on the heart. As with the phenothiazines, side effects are uneven from antidepressant to antidepressant. Since there is little evidence that one tricyclic is superior to any other with regard to effectiveness, side effects are again often the guide to a physician's choice of a particular tricyclic. For example, amitriptyline (Elavil) produces drowsiness, at least for a time. This can be an advantage if the patient has insomnia and Elavil is often prescribed at bedtime to relieve insomnia, as well as depression. Imipramine (Tofranil) has more stimulating effects and may be the drug of choice for "retarded" depressions marked by slowness of speech and sluggishness in general.

The tricyclic drugs are slowly eliminated and a single dose at bedtime is often sufficient to relieve depressive symptoms through the following day. For reasons no one understands, the side effects tend to fade as the antidepressant effects become evident. For this reason, no tricyclic can be called a failure until tried for at least a month.

Lithium

In 1949 an Australian psychiatrist discovered that lithium salts appeared to relieve the symptoms of mania, including hyperactivity, grandiosity, insomnia, and rapid speech. The discovery went largely unnoticed for some 15 years, one reason possibly being that drug companies had little interest in marketing a natural element. Then, in the mid-1960s, controlled double blind studies were conducted, showing that lithium not only relieved the acute symptoms of mania but also appeared to prevent future attacks of mania. There is even some evidence that lithium prevents attacks of depression, although this is still questionable. Not only is lithium widely prescribed for mania but also for other conditions, such as alcoholism and acute forms of schizophrenia, where its usefulness remains unknown.

Unlike sodium salts, lithium salts are dangerous. In fact, it was tried as a sodium substitute briefly during the second World War, and caused death. It has to be given in carefully titrated doses, while monitoring blood to assure that the lithium concentration does not approach dangerous levels. Death from lithium, however, has been quite rare, and usually occurs in people who have heart disease. (Like tricyclics, lithium can produce disturbances in the heart's rhythm.) Even in safe, therapeutic doses, lithium has side effects, most noticeably tremor.

Lithium is now marketed by drug companies and represents one of the few specific treatments in psychiatry (specific in the sense that certain keys are specific for certain locks). Many scientists believe that once we understand how lithium relieves manic symptoms we will be closer to understanding manic-depressive disease.

Stimulant drugs

Amphetamines were synthesized in the early 1930s in an attempt to discover superior drugs for asthma. Similar in structure and activity to compounds produced normally by the adrenal gland, they have pronounced effects on the cardiovascular system and central nervous system. However, they were first used because of their ability to constrict blood vessels and thus reduce nasal congestion when inhaled. The popular Benzedrine inhalers of the 1930s and 1940s were, in a sense, one of the first modern street drugs. By removing the Benzedrine strip from the inhaler and chewing it, a person could obtain euphoria and self-confidence.

Drug companies, recognizing the potential market for drugs with these virtues, then made amphetamines available in tablet form. Since amphetamines depress appetite they are widely prescribed for weight problems, although their effectiveness over the long run is doubtful. During World War II they were used by pilots and others in the military exposed to danger and fatigue. They were also popular among college students who found they were useful for staying up all night to cram for examinations. It was not until the youth drug culture emerged in the 1960s that the abuse potential of amphetamines was fully realized. There had been epidemics of amphetamine abuse reported in Japan and Sweden, but relatively few Americans apparently abused the drug (possibly because of the jitteriness and insomnia associated with its use, which made taking the drug regularly in excess "hardly worth it").

The practice of injecting amphetamines intravenously started in the 1960s and resulted in the well-known speed freak who became addicted to amphetamines. Repeated use of amphetamines produces rapid tolerance to the drug, so that users can tolerate manyfold times the amount that a first user could tolerate. After the euphoria and orgasmic "rush" from injecting amphetamine (rushes also occur after heroin injections, but it is not clear how they are similar), the user experiences withdrawal symptoms, mainly depression and listlessness.

Whether amphetamines should continue to be prescribed is a matter of debate. They are useful in the treatment of narcolepsy (a condition where the patient falls asleep uncontrollably) and also in the "hyperactive child syndrome." Also available for the latter two conditions is methylphenidate (Ritalin), a more recently synthesized stimulant with an abuse potential probably similar to that of amphetamines.

Some years ago it was discovered that heavy, regular use of amphetamines produces a condition indistiguishable from schizophrenia. The user has auditory hallucinations and persecutory delusions with intact memory and intellectual functioning (Hollister, 1968). Before this was known, many heavy amphetamine users were mistakenly diagnosed as schizophrenic.

Some clinicians still feel that amphetamines may be useful for mild depression, and this may be true. There has been a great deal of emotion generated about their use and abuse, and quite possibly the abuse has been exaggerated. Apart from members of the youth drug culture, apparently only a small minority (possibly less that 1 percent) of adults for whom the drug is prescribed take the drug in large enough doses to produce psychological and physical addiction.

One dangerous thing about amphetamines is the temptation they produce to use other drugs such as barbiturates, which counteract the undesirable stimulant effects of the amphetamine. Alteration of "uppers" and "downers" produces a vicious cycle that has been disastrous for many.

Megavitamins

B vitamins in huge doses have been given to schizophrenics and alcoholics with claims of dramatic success. Controlled double blind studies have not confirmed their usefulness for either condition.

Electroconvulsive Therapy

In the early 1930s it was observed that fewer epileptics were schizophrenic than would be expected in the general population. The observation turned out to be erroneous, but before this was learned, chemicals that produce convulsions were given to schizophrenic patients. Further experience indicated that chemically produced convulsions were not useful for schizophrenia, but did relieve severe depressions.

In 1939 two Italian clinicians introduced electroconvulsive therapy (ECT) and reported that it was superior to chemically produced convulsions in relieving depression. Since then, ECT has been widely used and there is substantial evidence from studies and clinical experience that ECT does help many depressed patients (Fink, Ketz, McGaugh, & Williams, 1974).

The studies, in fact, show that ECT is sometimes superior to antidepressant drugs. Nevertheless, clinicians today almost always give antidepressant drugs before ECT on the grounds that the drugs can be prescribed to outpatients, whereas ECT is most conveniently and safely conducted in a hospital. Also, the drugs are thought to have fewer side effects. Temporary memory loss is the most conspicuous side effect of ECT, a side effect that does not occur with drug therapy. However, the memory loss is almost always limited to the period during which the patient receives the convulsive therapy and does not lead to subsequent impairment. This is assuming that a limited number of treatments—nowadays no more than 10 or 15—are given. In former times ECT was often given much more frequently (sometimes several treatments per day), and memory impairment was frequent and severe.

Other than effect on memory, however, ECT is a relatively benign therapy with probably fewer risks than many drugs for depression. For some patients with severe depression it is undoubtedly the "treatment of choice" since it produces rapid and dramatic improvement. For these patients the currently strong anti-ECT movement is unfortunate.

Psychosurgery

There is also strong sentiment against psychosurgery, much of it justifiable. Unquestionably, lobotomy—the severing of fibers to the frontal lobes and other parts of the brain—was grossly overused for a number of years after its introduction in the late 1930s. Large numbers of psychiatric patients—many undiagnosed or poorly diagnosed—underwent this operation, many emerging with severe brain damage and crippling personality changes. There is no way of knowing how many had self-limited episodic illnesses from which they would have recovered eventually, but the numbers, tragically, no doubt are sizeable.

Very little psychosurgery is currently being done. Perhaps, as is the case of electroconvulsive therapy, too little is being done. The surgical techniques for performing the operation have been improved and refined, and few patients who undergo the operation have deteriorated personalities or signs of brain damage (Kalinowsky & Hippius, 1969). And for a small group of totally incapacitated obsessional and depressed patients who respond to no other treatment, psychosurgery may be their only hope for recovery. Unlike megavitamins, for example, there *is* a substantial body of evidence that the newer surgical techniques do help a small minority of patients.

Summary

Biological psychiatry refers to the practice of using drugs or other physical means to treat mental illnesses. (The term is also applied to theories of why people become mentally ill, but this is discussed in earlier chapters.) The use of drugs and other physical means to treat mental illness dates back to antiquity, but only in recent years have several classes of drugs been developed that appear truly effective in relieving the symptoms of certain psychiatric illnesses, if not curing them. These drugs are the phenothiazine and phenothiazinelike agents for psychotic states (such as schizophrenia and mania) and the benzodiazepines for anxiety states. In addition, lithium salts have been shown effective in the treatment of mania.

Prior to the discovery of these treatments in the 1950s, barbiturates and barbituratelike drugs were widely used to relieve anxiety and insomnia, but they also produced euphoria and were widely abused. The amphetamines and other stimulant drugs, while perhaps still medically useful for certain conditions, also lend themselves to abuse. Electroconvulsive therapy, while widely accepted as an effective treatment for depression, is seldom used today unless drugs fail to relieve depression. Psychosurgery, once widely used for depressive and obsessional states, is seldom used today, despite improved surgical techniques.

Drugs and other physical treatments are in no way incompatible with psychotherapy, behavior therapy, or other treatments that do not involve altering body chemistry. On the contrary, drugs are very commonly prescribed by psychotherapists, and psychiatrists who specialize in psychopharmacology almost always combine drugs with some form of "talking therapy."

GLOSSARY

Amitriptyline: An antidepressant drug of the tricyclic class.

Amphetamines: Stimulant drugs used in the treatment of narcolepsy, mild depression, and the hyperactive syndrome, and also widely used and abused illicitly.

Benzodiazepines: A class of drugs widely used in the treatment of anxiety states.

Electroconvulsive therapy: A treatment for severe depressions that involves applying a small current of electricity to the brain, resulting in epilepticlike convulsions.

Imipramine: An antidepressant drug of the tricyclic class.

Lithium: An element found useful in the treatment of mania.

Meprobamate: A type of drug used for treating anxiety which has a considerable abuse potential.

Methylphenidate: A drug with amphetaminelike actions often used for the hyperactive child syndrome.

Monomine oxidase inhibitors: A class of drugs used for the treatment of depression.

Parkinson's disease: A disorder characterized by involuntary movements, including tremor, disturbances of emotional expression, and difficulties in walking.

Phenothiazines: Drugs used in the treatment of schizophrenia, mania, and other psychotic disorders.

Physical addiction: Abusing drugs to the extent that tolerance (more and more of the drug must be used to obtain the original effects) and withdrawal symptoms occur when the drug is withdrawn.

Placebo: Inert substances used in drug studies to determine whether the drug is effective.

Psychological addiction: A behavioral pattern of convulsive drug abuse, characterized by overwhelming involvement with the use of a drug, the securing of its supply, and a high tendency to relapse after withdrawal.

Psychosis: Any disorder characterized by hallucinations, delusions, or disorganization of thought patterns.

Psychosurgery: A rarely used procedure whereby fibers leading to the frontal lobes or other parts of the brain are surgically severed to relieve severe depressive, anxiety, or obsessional illnesses.

Reserpine: A rarely used drug for schizophrenia.

Sedative-hypnotics: Drugs such as barbiturates, chloral hydrate, and paraldehyde used both for reducing anxiety and producing sleep.

Tricyclic antidepressants: Drugs widely used in the treatment of depression.

21

MENTAL ILLNESS AND THE MENTAL HOSPITAL

ALAN F. FONTANA

The mental hospital is many things to society. In fact it is as many things as is mental illness, for the mental hospital is the opposite side of the coin to mental illness. Where mental illness is disorganization and dangerousness, the mental hospital is social control and protection; where mental illness is poverty and social marginality, the mental hospital is custody and refuge; and where mental illness is emotional distress and social disconnectedness, the mental hospital is treatment and rehabilitation. And, just as most behavioral manifestations of mental illness represent more than one of these aspects, so most activities of the mental hospital serve more than one of these functions. As we shall see, this is particularly true for those activities called treatment and rehabilitation. This parallel between the conceptions of the mental hospital and mental illness is not fortuitous but is logically necessary, because the mental hospital is society's main response to mental illness.

Definitions

In this chapter I will be using the terms mental illness, mental hospital, and patient as general terms of reference. It is useful at the beginning to mention some of the complexities encompassed by such usage. Mental illness and related terms such as insanity and schizophrenia are used here solely as descriptive labels for certain forms of behavior. No implications are intended for etiology or for internal conditions, psychological or physiological.

The term mental hospital will be used to refer to all psychiatric hospitals as well as psychiatric units of general hospitals. However, the generalizations will apply most closely to the large, public psychiatric hospitals; more selectively they will apply to the smaller, private psychiatric hospitals and to the psychiatric services of general hospitals.

"Patient" will be used to indicate any person admitted to a mental hospital. There are two major distinctions to be made concerning patients: acute-chronic and schizophrenic-nonschizophrenic. *Acute* patients are those who have been hospitalized up to one year (up to two years according to some definitions), and *chronic* patients are those who have been hospitalized continuously for two years or more. Approximately three-quarters of the chronic patients are diagnosed as schizophrenic. Thus, it is no accident that chronic and schizophrenic patients comprise the groups of patients most often studied. These distinctions and others will be made as they constitute important qualifications to the general conclusions drawn.

Organization of the large, public mental hospital

Most of the research into both the workings of the mental hospital and the nature of schizophrenia has been conducted in the large, public psychiatric hospital. The large public mental hospital houses 80 percent of all people hospitalized for mental illness at any given time. Psychiatric services of general hospitals account for an additional 18 percent, with the final two percent resident in private mental hospitals (Joint Commission on Mental Illness and Health, 1961).

Typically, public mental hospitals have a well-defined status and power hierarchy, usually autocratic in its mode of functioning: that is, communication flows in only one direction—down. At the top is the hospital administration, followed by the medical staff, the psychological and social work staffs, the nursing staff, and, at the bottom, the ward attendants. There is a wide gulf between the professional staff (the first four groups) and the patients. Most patients are from the lower socioeconomic levels, while the professional staff is from the higher levels; and there is relatively little personal contact between most patients and the professional staff. The attendants occupy a status between professional staff and patients, often feeling estranged from both. As staff, the attendants share the privileges and powers denied to patients; but they are closer to patients socioeconomically, and they have substantially more personal contact with patients than does the professional staff.

The public mental hospital is divided into a relatively small part where most resources are allocated for the treatment of acute and promising patients, and a much larger part where minimal resources are allocated for the custody of chronic and unpromising patients. Open and closed (locked) wards exist in both parts, although generally wards are kept open if possible. Some acute wards are closed because of new patients' agitation and/or unwillingness to be in the hospital. Some chronic wards are closed because of some patients' recalcitrant unmanageability. Most new admissions are cycled through the treatment part and are discharged. Thirty to 40 percent return to the hospital within six months, 40–50 percent return within one year, and 65–75 percent return within 3–5 years (Anthony, Buell, Scharatt, & Althoff, 1972). These high rates of return have led to the characterization of the mental hospital as a "revolving door" for most patients. Among functionally psychotic patients, approximately 20 percent of first admissions (Bott, 1976) and from 20 to 75 percent of both first admissions and readmissions are not discharged but are transferred to the custodial part of the hospital (Paul, 1969). Thus, although chronic patients constitute a minority of new admissions, they constitute approximately two-thirds of the patient population in the hospital at any one time (Paul, 1969).

Major functions of the mental hospital

Of the three major functions served by the mental hospital, social control has been society's earliest and most constant concern. The other functions of custody and treatment have varied in their importance to society. Let us start, then, with an examination of the nature of these functions, and follow with a historical account of their problems.

Social control and protection

The control of deviance and the protection of society has historically been society's major interest in establishing and maintaining mental hospitals. The Joint Commission on Mental Illness and Health (1961, p.58) stated this point well:

> People do seem to feel sorry for them (mental patients); but in the balance, they do not feel as sorry as they do relieved to have out of the way persons whose behavior disturbs and offends them.

Any society must set limits to individual expression to achieve at least a minimal level of order and predictability in its members' dealings with each other. Without these normative expectations for behavior, the fundamental bases for communal living would be swept away. Some normative expectations are codified as laws, and society has evolved an elaborate enforcement and judicial system for dealing with violations. But there are other normative expectations, such as "making sense," that are so pervasive that they are taken for granted and are not codified. Violations of such expectations are alarming, obnoxious, and disruptive, but not illegal. Society's solution is to declare them pathological and to remove a person, if necessary, in order to purge the carrier of pathology from the body of society.

Removal of the person not only terminates the immediate disruption and discomfort felt by other members of society, but it is also a more pervasive and fundamental function for society as well. In sociological terms, it reaffirms the definition and validity of the normative expectations for all members (Scheff, 1966); and in psychiatric terms, it locates "madness" in the removed person and reassures those left in society that they are "sane" (Bott, 1976). This act of definition, for example, has often been cited as a major obstacle to involving the families of persons diagnosed as schizophrenic in any kind of treatment where it is suggested that they may bear some responsibility for the person's disordered behavior (Bott, 1976; Langsley, Puttman, & Swank, 1969; Scott & Ashworth, 1967). The same act of definition also often serves a function for the patient. Especially in the case of voluntary admission, the patient has agreed to come to the hospital and to allow the label of the "sick one" to be applied to him. Clinical observations suggest that, for some people, it is less frightening to them to take on the label of "sick one" themselves than to chance having a parent or sibling take on the label (Bott, 1976; Scott & Ashworth, 1967).

The social control function of the mental hospital is seen most clearly in the practice of involuntary commitment, where a person may be legally confined against his or her will for an indeterminate length of time. Despite the move away from this practice in recent years, the annual rate of involuntary commitment is still substantially greater than the rate of voluntary admission (Peck, 1975; Zwerling, Karasu, Plutchik, & Kellerman, 1975). Comparisons of voluntarily admitted and involuntarily committed patients reveal different types of problematic (mentally ill) behavior prior to hospitalization (Gove & Fain, 1977; Zwerling et al., 1975). The voluntarily admitted are more often anxious, depressed, or bothered by physical problems, whereas the involuntarily committed are more often agitated, hyperactive, or assaultive. However, there is no difference in the psychopathological severity of the behavior as judged psychiatrically between the two groups of patients (Zwerling et al., 1975). Further, the involuntarily committed spend a longer time in the hospital (Gove & Fain, 1977; Zwerling et al., 1975). Thus, it is not primarily the psychopathological severity of behavior but rather the type of behavior which leads society to take action unilaterally against a person. If the person's behavioral disorder causes him personal misery that does not intrude upon the affairs of others, society generally allows him or her to come in and go out of the hospital at his or her own discretion. But if the behavioral disorder is threatening or disruptive to others, society overrides his or her wishes and confines the person.

Custody and refuge

A second major function served by the mental hospital is custody, from the perspective of society, and refuge, from the perspective of patients. Society expects that at least the basic requirements of living—food, shelter, and clothing—will be provided to all patients. However, societal toleration of barely subsistence levels for these basics, despite frequent exposés, indicates that a humane level has not always been an integral part of the expectation. Albert Deutsch (1948) has presented a particularly graphic pictorial as well as literary documentaion of the kinds of institutions referred to by the Joint Commission on Mental Illness and Health (1961) as "human dumps." Although most of the worst abuses have been corrected in recent years, the legacy of overcrowding, understaffing, inactivity, and inattention, known as "custodialism," is still with us, as this recent description of a large public mental hospital by Fowlkes (1975) testifies:

> The original hospital building, which houses half of all the patients, is a gloomy, fortress-like structure with barred windows. Inside, tiny rooms once intended for single occupancy are now double bedrooms; beds are also lined up in rows against the walls of vast rooms originally meant for use as solariums and infirmaries. Furnishings are sparse, air is close, paint is peeling, and the urine and disinfectant smells of the decades have soaked into walls and floors and mingle to make a permanent stench. Although occasional happenings of a sensationalist nature are often associated with mental hospitals, the true picture of hospital life is relentlessly passive and inert. For patients on the back or locked wards, life means being locked in, locked up, or tied down. Life on these wards is literally in a perpetual state of suspended animation. Patients elsewhere in the hospital who are less deteriorated, or who are more "manageable" through the heavy use of drugs, have more freedom and are seemingly more active in a physical sense. However, the quality of the activity is aimless and repetitive and is prompted by no particular motivation or encouragement to do anything or go anywhere. People travel incessantly the same route day after day; others stare vacantly at (frequently unfocused) television pictures, or pace the floor, or rock ceaselessly back and forth, or repeat gestures and phrases for hours on end, or sit, or sleep. (p. 56)

Many investigators have pointed out that custodialism has a deteriorating effect on patients behavior, so that much of the "symptomatic" behavior observed among patients is attributable more to their hospital environment than to their individual psychopathology. Patient adaptation to a custodial environment has variously been called "institutionalism"(Wing, 1962), "chronicity" (Sommer & Withey, 1961), and the "social breakdown syndrome" (American Public Health Association, 1962; Zusman, 1967). Each of these conceptions emphasizes that pressures are exerted on the new patient to adopt the role of long-term inmate, and that the pressures increase as the length of hospitalization increases. These pressures derive largely from the staff's desires to carry out their tasks in a manner most efficient and convenient for themselves. Patients are dealt with as objects to be processed rather than as people with whom to interact. Sommer and Withey explicitly identify transfer from an acute treatment ward to a chronic custodial ward as a particularly crucial point in the "chain of chronicity." But the pressures do not work uniformly on all patients. Zusman and Wing point to the importance of certain patients' characterological susceptibility to the pressures of acculturation. Wing notes that schizophrenics are particularly vulnerable, comprising 75 percent of long-term patients. Zusman, more generally, identifies as vulnerable those people who are deficient in self-esteem and/or in social interactional skills or desires.

As stultifying and dehumanizing as custodialism is, it would be a mistake to conclude that it continues to exist only because society tolerates it. Custodialism also continues to exist because there are some patients who not only accept it, but who actively prefer it to life outside the institution (Belknap, 1956;

Dunham & Weinberg, 1960; Fontana & Corey, 1970; Kantor & Gelineau, 1965; Levinson & Gallagher, 1964; Rowland, 1939). The most readily identifiable of these patients are those who appear essentially normal in their behavior while in the hospital. They often perform work for the hospital in the laundry, in the kitchen, or on the grounds, or they help the attendants by cleaning the wards or by managing other patients. By and large, they prefer to live on open wards so that they have the freedom to circulate around the hospital grounds as they please. Generally, they are quiet and go unnoticed except when their mode of adaptation to the hospital is threatened, as with transfer to another ward or discharge to the community. They are adept at either minimizing or calling attention to their symptomatology as it serves their purposes in maintaining the adaptation that they have worked out. Variously known as chronics, "crocks" and "institutional cures," they become progressively less interested in leaving the hospital the longer they are hospitalized (Goldman, 1965; Wing, 1962). And, according to Wing's (1962) study, the length of stay was independent of severity of symptomatology.

But why would patients choose to stay in such a place as a custodial hospital? Is it because the hospital seems so desirable, or is it because the outside community seems so undesirable? Clinical observation and empirical investigation of patients attitudes suggest that the latter is more often the case (Gordon & Groth, 1961; Simon, 1965a). Patients choosing to stay in the hospital are more socially marginal than those choosing to leave; that is, the stayers are older, less educated, and possess lower job skills (Nadler, Barrett, Miller, Lea, & Mosier, 1967). Thus the custodial mental hospital serves the function of a refuge for many patients.

Treatment and rehabilitation

The third major function served by the mental hospital is the treatment/rehabilitation of patients. This is the function most prized by the professional staff, so much so that the staff often forgets that the hospital performs other functions for society (Galioni, Notman, Stanton, & Williams, 1969). Following the model of outpatient psychotherapy, the professional staff has traditionally preferred to provide treatment that is highly verbal, emphasizes self-exploration of feelings, and aspires to promote "personality change." In the case of hospitals that serve as training sites for psychiatrists, patients are selectively admitted or turned away according to the staff's perception of them as good candidates for such treatment (Levinson, Merrifield, & Berg, 1967; Wood, Rakusin, & Morse, 1965). This treatment orientation puts the staff at odds with low socioeconomic patients who make up most of the patient population in public hospitals. These patients either want the staff to remove their distress through medications or through other means requiring little active involvement on their part (Hornstra, Lubin, Lewis, & Willis, 1972; Polak, 1970); or they are actively uninterested in participating in treatment at all (Joint Commission on Mental Illness and Health, 1961).

The discrepancy between the treatment preferences and aspirations of the professional staff and those of most public hospital patients is frustrating to the staff, at times infuriatingly so. This is particularly true when the staff is trying to treat patients who want to use the hospital as a refuge. As Simon (1965b, p. 72) has put it: "If truth be told, the discharge of a patient is almost always therapeutic for a hospital and its staff; it need not *necessarily* be therapeutic for any particular patient." The common fate of virtually all treatment programs designed to persuade, cajole, induce, or seduce chronic patients to leave the hospital voluntarily is either a high rate of rehospitalization (Anthony, Buell, Scharatt, & Althoff, 1972; Erickson, 1975; Paul, 1969), or a stalemate within the hospital where patients maintain their participation at a level just short of accepting discharge (Fontana & Corey, 1970; Ludwig & Farrelly, 1966). In the latter case, patients support one another in maintaining a stalemate by what Ludwig and

Farrelly (1966) have called the "code of chronicity." Eventually, the staff wearies of the struggle, grows apathetic toward rehabilitative goals, and withdraws its emotional investment in the program and its personal involvement with patients (Joint Commission on Mental Illness and Health, 1961)—in short, the staff becomes burnt out and develops "chronic staffrenia" (Ludwig & Farrelly, 1967). When and if staff expectations stabilize at this level of custodialism, the caretaking activities that remain constitute what is officially known as "continued treatment."

Just as custody can masquerade as treatment, so can social control. Interventions that were conceptualized and initiated as treatments often come to be seen as very effective controlling techniques (Galioni, Notman, Stanton, & Williams, 1957). Treatments such as seclusion, restraints, transfer to a closed ward, and even electroshock have been cited as actions that attendants have used to threaten and enforce obedience among patients under their care (Belknap, 1956; Dunham & Weinberg, 1960; Goffman, 1961). The use of these actions for management purposes has been relatively easy to justify as treatment because the traditional psychiatric view is that all patient behavior in the hospital is a reflection of the state of their individual psychopathology. Since this view gives no consideration to a hospital environment that might account for such behavior, all problem behavior (defined according to hospital criteria) is taken as a manifestation of patient psychopathology.

Involuntary commitment, too, has been justified as a treatment function. As civil libertarian challenges to involuntary commitment have increased, it has been defended on the basis of the person's "right to treatment" (Peck, 1975; Roth, 1977). The argument is that it would be a deprivation of a person's rights not to provide him with treatment that he presumably would voluntarily choose if he had the judgmental capacity to do so. This illustrates how far-reaching and elastic the arguments for the function of treatment can be made, and how intertwined they can be with the functions of control and custody.

But the overlap between treatment and social control is even more fundamental than any or all of these examples would suggest. The criterion for admission to a mental hospital is deviance from a broad range of largely uncodified social norms, and the criterion for release is conformity to these social norms. "Adjustment" is taken as the hallmark of successful treatment—adjustment first to the ward, then to the hospital, and finally to the outside world. Societal norms and expectations are often conceptualized as "reality," which the patient must learn to face. As much as most hospital professional staff members dislike their social control obligations, they cannot avoid them. When patients want (or can be induced to want) what society wants (or is willing to accept) for them, social control fades as an issue. But one need only let the staff support a patient's pursuit of that which society prohibits to see the limits of society's tolerance. For in the final analysis, society demands adequate protection, expects safe custody, and hopes for successful treatment.

Early history

We can obtain a better idea of the nature and strength of society's interests in having the mental hospital serve these particular functions in the particular ways that it does by tracing the history of the mental hospital in the United States. In colonial America of the late seventeenth century, there were no institutions for the mentally ill. In fact, the concept of mental illness itself was nonexistent. Deviance was considered to be due either to sinfulness (as a mark of punishment by God or of possession by the devil) or to willful violation of social norms (laziness or criminality). Society attempted to control a wide range of deviance (including that which we now call mental illness) by punishment, either by whipping, ridicule (the stocks), or, failing these, expulsion into the forest.

In the eighteenth century, as more towns were established and the distance between them decreased, each town constructed a house of correction, workhouse, or almshouse for the confinement of its pauper citizens. No distinction was made between the behaviorally disordered poor and the behaviorally nondisordered poor. Society, while accepting responsibility for the custody of its poor, limited its custodial obligation to providing subsistence support. Medical treatments for the behaviorally disordered included purging with enemas, bleeding, induced vomiting, blistering the scalp, and some holdovers from the days of witchcraft—near-drowning, spinning in a chair, and others (Joint Commission on Mental Illness and Health, 1961). The idea was to shock the person out of his "insanity," that is, out of his descent to his lower animal nature, and to induce him to rise to his human sensibilities.

Moral treatment

The close of the eighteenth century (1792) saw the introduction of a dramatically new approach to the mentally ill, pioneered by Phillippe Pinel in France and by William Tuke in England. These men rejected the view of the day that the insane were people who had degenerated to an animal level and who could only be caged, chained, or beaten. Instead, they assumed that disordered behavior represented an exaggeration of normal behavior that occurred under stress, and that given a kindly but firm environment the natural curative powers inherent in the person would assert themselves and the person would return to his normal state. The proper role of the superintendent and his staff was to set an example of socially appropriate behavior for patients to emulate. These ideas and practices became known as "moral treatment," and were brought over to America by Quaker followers of William Tuke in the early years of the nineteenth century. Several private and state hospitals were organized along the lines of moral treatment. The following passages from Charles Dickens' *American Notes* captures the patrician air of guidance and compassion for which these hospitals were known:

> Every patient in this asylum sits down to dinner every day with a knife and fork; and in the midst of them sits the gentleman, (the superintendent). Once a week they have a ball, in which the Doctor and his family, with all the nurses and attendants, take an active part. Immense politeness and good-breeding are observed throughout. They all take their tone from the Doctor; and he moves a very Chesterfield among the company. (Quoted in The Joint Commission on Mental Illness and Health, 1961, p. 31)

Impressive discharge rates (70% of first admissions) and rehospitalization rates (20% of first admissions) were recorded (Bockoven, 1956), although the comparability of either patient characteristics or follow-up procedures to present day patient populations and methodologies is not known. However, in its theoretical essentials, moral treatment was the forerunner of modern conceptions of the therapeutic community (Jones, 1953) and milieu therapy (Cumming & Cumming, 1962).

Despite the successes of moral treatment, its influence was short-lived, and by the second half of the nineteenth century at least three factors had combined to bring about its fall: overcrowding, immigration, and lack of proselytizing (Bockoven, 1956). Hospitals for moral treatment were small institutions and were reserved for the middle and upper classes. The working and lower-class insane were still sent to almshouses and jails. Dorothea Dix had been compaigning long and hard for the extension of hospital care and treatment to the insane poor. By the middle of the nineteenth century, her campaign succeeded in convincing several of the states to make such care and treatment available to all their citizens. The towns, eager to transfer the tax burden for care from themselves to the states, transfered large numbers of the indigent and aged to the state hospitals. For their part, the states failed to match the magnanimity of their intentions with the magnanimity of their fiscal appropriations. Thus, poverty and mental illness were again merged and were combined with old age as conditions for mental hospitalization. This period initiated conditions of overcrowding from which state hospitals are only now beginning to recover.

The second factor contributing to the downfall of moral treatment was the great influx of immigrants from Ireland during the middle 1800s, many of whom were sent to state hospitals as indigent and/or insane. The cultural and economic differences between the "genteel," upper-class hospital superintendents and the "uncultured," immigrant and lower-class patients became an unbridgeable gulf. Superintendents complained of the flood of "beast-like" individuals sent to their hospitals and threw up their hands in despair.

The third major factor in the decline of moral treatment was the failure of the pioneers to train successors in sufficient numbers to spread and carry on their work. Thus, even within the private hospitals, there was no robust, growing cadre of enthusiatic and competent followers to carry on the tradition in the face of a new intellectual thrust from Europe.

Genetic inferiority and lesions of the brain

That new intellectual thrust drew its strength from the discovery of the connection between general paresis and tertiary syphilis. Taking general paresis as a model, lesions of the brain were postulated to constitute a general etiological condition for insanity. In the absence of a clearly definable pathogen such as a spirochete, an unspecified genetic inferiority was adduced to be the causal agent. Further, genetic inferiority was held to lead to an inevitable degeneration that was incurable. The physical basis of the theory and the aura of science surrounding it had a great appeal to the academic community in general and to the medical profession in particular.

As Zusman (1967) has put it, the ascendence of genetic inferiority and the decline of moral treatment ushered in "the age of the cataloguers of psychopathology," notable among them, Emil Kraepelin. Kraepelin separated the "curable" from the "incurable" insane, relegating those whom we now call schizophrenic to the latter category under the label, dementia praecox. The idea of incurability was appealing to a society angered at, frustrated by, and fearful of certain of its members. It thereby rationalized a progressive cycle of increased overcrowding, reduced expenditures, and dehumanized care. By focusing only upon the person and by ignoring his environment, the behavioral deterioration and regression that these practices fostered were themselves taken as further evidence for the view that dementia praecox had an inevitable downhill course which no treatment could halt.

Stigma

The pernicious social effects of this doctrine of genetic inferiority are hard to overestimate. The presumed incurability justified offering people no treatment and no thought of discharge. The presumed intrinsic and inevitable degeneration justified a quality of care more befitting animals than humans. The legacy of hopelessness and subhuman inferiority has had a major impact upon the stigmatization that society visits upon mental patients. Not only are the mentally ill considered to be dangerous and unpredictable, but they are also viewed as weak, dirty, and worthless (Nunnally, 1961). Moreover, the biggest change in negative attitudes toward a person occurs when it is learned that the person is being treated by a psychiatrist or is hospitalized in a mental hospital, that is, when these actions certify to the public that the person is mentally ill (Cumming & Cumming, 1957; Phillips, 1963, 1967). Equally interesting was Phillips's finding that a person who was described as behaving normally but who was seeking help from a psychiatrist or a mental hospital was rejected *more* than a person who was described as behaving like a simple schizophrenic but who was seeking no help. Thus, within certain bounds, seeking psychiatric help can be more stigmatizing itself than is behaving strangely (even psychotically, according to professional experts).

Finally, in its most subtle form, this doctrine has served to insulate the thinking of many professionals, often self-protectively. There is the tendency for clinical staff to automatically attribute instances of a patient's improvement to the treatment program and to the staff's efforts; whereas there is an equally strong tendency to attribute instances of a patient's lack of improvement to the severity and intractability of the psychopathology. In the experimental realm, there is the tendency to accept less that normal performances as a relevant example of deficit associated with psychopathology; while there is the countervailing tendency to reject normal or better performances as an irrelevant or trivial example of a patient's capacity. Such a view guarantees the imperviousness of presumed inferiority to modification.

Emergence of a new intellectual climate

The doctrine of genetic inferiority and incurability held sway over mental hospital practices for almost 100 years, and dominated psychiatric thinking for some 80 years. It was not until the 1930s that a new intellectual climate in Europe found its way to America to contest its dominance (Zusman, 1967). The return of hopefulness was paved by the work of Sigmund Freud and Eugen Bleuler. Freud's work countered the pessimistic orientation of the Kraepelinian view by postulating symbolic meanings and psychosocial origins of symptoms, not only for neuroses but for psychoses as well. Bleuler's work contested the idea of incurability for dementia praecox by questioning its homogeneity as a condition. He proposed, instead, that it consisted of a group of conditions, some of which frequently showed remission. Subsequent experience has supported Eugen Bleuler's observations. Manfred Bleuler (1976) has reported that the psychotic behavior of approximately two-thirds of schizophrenic patients stabilizes with no subsequent deterioration after five years.

World War II

While these ideas started the intellectual ferment necessary for the development of a new psychiatric doctrine, it required the conditions of World War II to begin to mobilize society (specifically the Federal government) to large-scale action. Two developments were especially influential: the widespread use that the Armed Services made of "neuropsychiatric" screening criteria, and the large number of medical discharges from military service granted on the basis of neuropsychiatric disability. This official recognition of psychiatric difficulties meant that society had an obligation to those who had "broken down" while fighting for its protection; and substantial funds were committed after World War II to the expansion of psychiatric services under the direction of the Veterans Administration. This recognition also raised the public consciousness concerning psychiatric disturbance in the civilian population; and the National Institute of Mental Health was created in 1946, initially for research and training, and later for the development of treatment services.

The hospital as environmental context

Shortly after World War II, particularly in the 1950s, sociologists became interested in mental hospitals and conducted several intensive naturalistic observational studies. Sociologists explicitly rejected the medical model, along with the ideas that mental illness was qualitatively different from other kinds of deviance; that mental patients were qualitatively different from other kinds of inmates; that hospital staff were qualitatively different from other kinds of administrators, professionals, and employees; and that the mental hospital was qualitatively different from other kinds of bureaucratic organizations. This viewpoint enabled them to analyze not only the relations between the mental hospital and society, but, within the hospital, the relations among staff groups and between staff groups and patients (Belknap, 1956; Caudill, 1958; Dunham & Weinberg, 1960; Goffman, 1961; Stanton & Schwartz, 1954). By focusing upon the functions that various practices and procedures served and by identifying the ways that these satisfied different group interests and goals, they were able to go beyond both a mere description of practices and procedures and an acceptance of conventional and unconvincing rationales. Their main contribution was to detail the iatrogenic, or illness-producing, features of the hospital environment. This theme has attracted much attention from students of the mental hospital and has generated a wealth of empirical research.

Overcrowding and understaffing

Belknap (1956) showed how political pressure to accept the indigent, the aged, and the retarded, as well as the mentally ill, continually undermined attempts by hospital administrators and professional staff to develop either a coherent statement as to the rehabilitative problems they faced or a clear rationale as to the treatment programs that were needed. Additionally, continual political pressure to accept both ever increasing numbers of patients and ever decreasing per capita budgets meant that personal attention to patients was increasingly sacrificed to inflexibility and impersonality in the pursuit of operational efficiency (Belknap, 1956). In fact, these pressures could be seen to seriously exacerbate tendencies of this nature inherent in bureaucratic organizations (Kahne, 1959). Subsequent empirical studies of hospital size and staff-to-patient ratio verified the deleterious effects of overcrowding and understaffing upon the release of patients from the hospital (Gurel, 1964; Smith & King, 1975; Ullmann, 1967).

Attendants as guards and therapists

Conditions of overcrowding and understaffing were cited also as major factors in the development and reinforcement of dehumanizing perceptions and behaviors on the part of the attendants (Belknap, 1956; Dunham & Weinberg, 1960). They are in charge of 100 to 200 patients considered hopeless by administrative and professional staff, charged with the tasks of maintaining behavioral order and physical cleanliness with virtually no help from other hospital staff, given little or no training, paid extremely low wages, and drawn from people already in economically or socially desperate straits. It is little wonder that the attendants have often been authoritarian, exploitative, coercive, sometimes brutal, and generally antitherapeutic in their dealings with patients. While leveling these criticisms himself, Belknap (1956) showed how the professional staff has often exploited the attendants, all the while needing them, to avoid recognizing and dealing with the problems of care and order that ultimately are its responsibility.

Observers pointed out that the professional staff jealously reserved the prestigious activity of treatment to itself (Belknap, 1956; Dunham & Weinberg, 1960). They noted the incongruity in the fact that while the attendants had the most contact with patients, they had the least to do with their treatment. In contrast, the professional staff had the least contact with patients, but had the most to do with their treatment. Influenced by the psychoanalytic theory of individual psychopathology, "enlightened" professional staff had become preoccupied with the patient's hour of psychotherapy each day to the neglect of the "other 23 hours" (Stanton & Schwartz, 1954).

Ellsworth (1968) has carried the criticism of the professional staff even further by describing its resistance to acceptance of the attendant as a competent treater of patients. Despite an elaborate and well-controlled demonstration study in which attendants were shown to be effective therapists, particularly for chronic schizophrenic patients, the expanded role for attendants was allowed to atrophy and disappear following completion of the study (and the investigator's departure from the hospital). In Ellsworth's opinion, the demonstration program was allowed to die by professional staff because the successful performance by the attendants posed too great a threat to the professionals' self-images and job-duties as especially knowledgeable and indispensable treaters of patients.

Custodialism and humanism

Belknap (1956) pointed to the set of expectations and pressures that explained why attendants could be expected to be authoritarian and dehumanizing, but it was Gilbert and Levison (1956, 1957) who first noted that these attitudes formed an ideology that explained and justified the practices of control and neglect to the hospital staff. These investigators also showed that the attitudes were found in all groups in the hospital, and warned that the custodial orientation should not necessarily be considered "bad" in all respects, nor should its opposite, the humanistic orientation, automatically be considered "good."

Gilbert and Levinson's (1956) initial scale to measure custodial and humanistic orientations gave rise to a number of scales extending and modifying their original effort. Among the most carefully developed and most widely adopted of these are the Opinions about Mental Illness Scale (Cohen & Struening, 1962), the Ward Atmosphere Scale (Moos & Houts, 1968), and the Perception of Ward Scale (Ellsworth & Maroney, 1972). Although these subsequent scales each contain several components, the major dimension running through them can still be seen to be custodialism with its emphasis on authoritarianism, restrictiveness, order, and control at one end, and humanism with its emphasis on expression of feelings, personal involvement, spontaneity, and autonomy at the other end.

Custodial-humanistic staff attitudes and ward atmospheres have been found to be related to size and staffing. Small wards or hospitals and those with a high staff-to-patient ratio typically have humanistic orientation and, conversely, large units and those with a low staff-to-patient ratio usually have a custodial orientation (Cohen & Struening, 1965; Moos, 1972). Attempts to go beyond size and staffing in order to discover the particular staff attitudes and ward atmospheres related to good and poor treatment outcomes have met with limited success thus far. The results do not fall into any simple pattern that can be readily summarized. It is likely that the achievement of detailed replicable findings will have to depend upon the specification of critical distinctions among patient characteristics, environmental contexts, and program goals that are only partially recognized at the present time.

Two general conclusions can be drawn. The first is that attitudinal and atmospheric factors have frequently been found to be associated with results inside the hospital, but only rarely with those outside the hospital. For example, nonauthoritarian and nonrestrictive attitudes on the part of the staff have been found to be associated with early release from the hospital, but not with successful community stay once released (Cohen & Struening, 1964; Smith & King, 1975). Similarly, an accepting and interpersonally involving ward atmosphere has been found to be associated with high patient satisfaction with hospitalization and liking for the staff (Moos & Houts, 1970) and with a low rate of dropout from hospital treatment (Moos & Schwartz, 1972; Spiegel & Younger 1972);, but this ward atmosphere has been found to be associated weakly, at best, with length of stay in the community and quality of community adjustment (Ellsworth & Maroney, 1972; Ellsworth, Maroney, Klett, Gordon & Gunn, 1971; Moos & Schwartz, 1972; Moos, Shelton & Petty, 1973; Spiegel & Younger, 1972).

The second general conclusion is that, true to the warning of Gilbert and Levinson (1957), "humanistic" factors are not always associated with "good" outcomes or "custodial-restrictive" factors to "bad" outcomes (Ellsworth, 1965; Smith & King, 1975). Adult status (that is, provision for privacy, security of personal effects, and personal decision making for eating and sleeping) has been found to be *negatively* related to symptom reduction in the hospital (Kellam, Goldberg, Schooler, Berman, & Shmelzer, 1967).

This same study found high staffing (although not high staff-patient contact) to be related to low symptom reduction also. High release rates have tended to be associated with high staff control (Moos & Schwartz, 1972) and low patient autonomy (Ellsworth et al., 1971). Finally, high patient autonomy has been found to be related to poor symptomatic adjustment in the community (Smith & King, 1975). Findings such as these suggest that under some conditions, restriction can foster preparedness for community living, and that under some conditions, humanism can foster dependence on the hospital. Any categorization of given attitudes, atmospheres, or outcomes as good or bad is a harmful oversimplification.

Iatrogenesis of individual and collective disturbance

Sociological and social psychiatric collaboration during the 1950s yielded some of the most intriguing observations of all concerning the iatrogenic problems (problems caused by the hospital itself) of the mental hospital. They are intriguing both for their careful attention to individual units of behavior and for their applicability to all mental hospitals, large or small, public or private. These observations were that much of the individual and collective disturbance among patients on a ward is a function of a lack of consensus and a concomitant rivalry among different staff and/or patient members and groups (Stanton & Schwartz, 1954). Disturbance refers to the various forms of agitated, excited, hyperactive, or assaultive behavior viewed by the staff as pathological. When manifested by a single patient, these behaviors have very often been traced to a difference of opinion between two patients regarding a staff member or between two staff members regarding a patient—a process referred to as triangulation. In the former type, the disagreement usually involves a dispute between two patients as to which one the staff member likes or loves more. In the latter type, the disagreement most often concerns a difference of opinion regarding the management of a given patient between two staff members who both have responsibility for that patient's care. The dispute usually revolves around the issue of whether the patient should be treated according to ward rules like all other patients or whether the patient should be exempted from certain ward rules because of his or her particular problems. Exemption from ward rules is usually defended by its proponents as individualized attention and criticized by its opponents as indulgence or special treatment. When the two staff members cannot agree, but continue to feel strongly about the disagreement, they stop discussing it with one another and proceed to convey their contradictory messages and expectations to the patient. The patient protests, at first verbally and then behaviorally, by "acting out" in an agitated way.

This conception of individual disturbances provides the basis for the conception of collective disturbance. Usually an issue arises that disrupts an established and valued policy concerning the operation of the ward. The issue often originates from outside the ward as in the case of pressure from the hospital administration. Or it may arise from an innovation that a powerful staff member or subgroup of the staff has either been urging or started to implement. In any event, when the staff opinion is divided, subgroups form and they stop discussing the issue with each other. Tacit alliances are formed with patient groups, and each "side" pursues its mutually contradictory goals. Tension escalates until some event triggers widespread agitation and excitement, that is, a collective disturbance. The basic theoretical outline for disturbances of these types was given initially by Stanton and Schwartz (1954), and similar observations have been reported by other investigators (Caudill, 1958; Miller, 1957; Stotland & Kobler, 1965; Strauss, Schatzman, Bucher, Ehrlich, & Sabshin, 1964). However, as plausible as these ideas sound, it should be borne in mind that all the evidence, original as well as supporting, has been generated from observations constructed after the fact. Probably because of the complexity of the topic, there has not yet been an adequate test of the ideas.

Hospital adaptation and impression management

During the 1950s, sociologists also turned their attention to the mental hospital's function as a refuge for patients. They pointed out that many patients, particularly long-term patients, had created a comfortable way of life at the hospital and did not want to leave (Belknap, 1956; Dunham & Weinberg, 1960; Goffman, 1961; Stanton & Schwartz, 1954). They observed that such patients often displayed symptomatic behavior as it served their purposes in maintaining their chosen adaptation to the hospital. While such display includes conscious faking and malingering, it is not limited to such ploys. Rather it includes both the calculated and extreme efforts of the con artist and the more automatic and muted efforts employed by most patients.

These and closely related observations subsequently (Artiss, 1959; Haley, 1965; Sadow & Suslick, 1961; Towbin, 1966) challenged the traditional view of chronic schizophrenic patients as persons who are out of contact with the reality of their social environment. Goffman (1959) proposed the term impression management to describe a person's differential presentation of favorable or unfavorable aspects of him/herself to others in order to influence the impression made. A number of studies of this phenomenon among mental patients were conducted, and they indicated that schizophrenic behavior is more that just incidentally related to circumstances in the social environment.

My associates and I (Fontana & Gessner, 1969; Fontana & Klein, 1968; Fontana, Klein, Lewis & Levine, 1968) and Braginsky and his colleagues (Braginsky & Braginsky 1967; Braginsky, Braginsky, & Ring, 1969; Braginsky, Grosse, & Ring, 1966), working primarily with schizophrenic patients, each conducted a series of studies examining the circumstances surrounding shifts in patient behavior toward and away from pathology. These studies showed that schizophrenic patients increased and decreased pathological behavior in order to create an impression compatible with their goals for hospital living. For example, patients who wished to leave the hospital or avoid an unwanted transfer presented themselves as healthier than usual, while patients who wanted to stay in the ward presented themselves as sicker than usual.

While patients in these studies were not asked directly about their intentions, there is evidence that patients recognize not only the existence but also the efficacy of altering their symptomatic behavior. In a pair of studies, Sherman demonstrated that patients believe that they can successfully achieve the goals of remaining in or leaving the hospital through manipulating the impression they make on their doctors (Sherman, 1974; Sherman, Sprafkin, & Higgins, 1974).

These studies led Braginsky and me, among others, to conclude that schizophrenic patients were not out of contact with their social environment—they were just as capable as people in general, but they had developed life styles and modes of expression different from, but not necessarily inferior to, those of the dominant society.

Subsequent studies point to the need for a modification of this position. Other investigators have confirmed the existence of impression management among schizophrenic patients, but they have not found it to exist equally strongly among all subgroups of these patients, nor to exist strongly enough to eliminate all differences in behavior between patients and nonpatients (Kelly, Farina, & Mosher, 1971; Price, 1972; Sherman, Trief, & Sprafkin, 1975; Watson, 1972, 1973, 1975). One confounding factor in some of these studies has been the lack of a clear distinction between patients' verbal descriptions of psychopathological experiences and their overt behavioral manifestations of psychopathology. But, it is likely that our initial proposal overestimated the abilities of schizophrenic patients, particularly chronic schizophrenic patients. A more valid and defensible set of conclusions is that they are people who are more socially aware and more socially capable than they have traditionally been given credit for being, that they may have the potential for becoming as capable as other people, but that their current abilities are more limited in many areas than those of people in general. The major contribution of this area of research has been to bring into clearer focus the fact that much of the chronic schizophrenic's "pathological" behavior is more reflective of his attempts to attain his goals through influencing others than it is reflective of a biochemical disorder or intrapsychic conflict only incidentally related to the circumstances of his social environment.

The labeling theory of mental illness

To go along with their observations, sociologists developed a theory of mental illness called the societal reaction or labeling theory of mental illness (Lemert, 1951). More precisely, labeling theory is a general theory of deviance applied to mental illness as well as to other social phenomena identified solely by their behavioral manifestations. The crucial notion in this theory is that behavioral deviance is confirmed as an entity when it is named or labeled. Thus, mental illness is held to have no real existence in and of itself, but is considered to exist only insofar as society reacts to certain forms of deviant behavior by labeling, categorizing, and setting them apart.

The performers of deviant behavior are similarly labeled as a particular kind of people who do *that*, or who act *that* way. A rationale is evolved to explain why *those* people act *that* way. The rationale generates a set of expectations as to how the labeled deviant will behave, and the deviant experiences social pressure to confirm the expectations. To the extent that the deviant succumbs to this pressure and exhibits the expected behavior, he or she confirms the validity of the label and becomes "locked into" a deviant role. Society creates a social position, such as mental patient, for the person. The final hardening of these processes into a deviant identity occurs when the person changes his self-concept to bring it into line with the cues and feedback that he has been receiving from others.

It is understandable that sociologists would develop a theory along the lines of societal reaction and labeling, given their interests in the ways that social institutions serve the goals of people as society rather than people as individuals. The theory does have heuristic value in organizing our understanding of the influence of many social forces upon the individual with regard to mental illness. However, as investigators observed the processing of people by courts and by mental hospitals, several developed a sympathy for the deviant to the point of an ideological "championing of the underdog" and a "debunking of the overdog" (e.g., Goffman, 1961; Scheff, 1966). The mentally ill deviant were claimed to be initially no more deviant than anyone else. Mental patients were unfortunate victims of uncaring, intolerant, or overly frightened segments of society that were more powerful than them and that segregated and degraded them for their own comfort and selfish ends. Mental-health professionals were either naive and unwitting dupes of society or were society's misguided but willing partners in victimization.

The extremity of this extension of labeling theory has been criticized by Gove (1970). He points out that the public is generally loathe to label someone mentally ill, often going to great lengths to avoid doing so; that as a rule psychiatrists do not automatically recommend involuntary commitment, generally doing so in less than half of the cases they are called upon to examine; and that only a small portion of hospitalized persons become chronic patients. Lying at the crux of the overextension of the societal reaction perspective has been a blurring of primary and secondary deviance, with a concomitant dismissal of the importance of the former. Primary deviance is that behavior leading to the societal reaction, while secondary deviance is behavior that is a confirmatory response by the person to the expectations of deviance having once been labeled. It is clear that labeling theory in no way addresses the circumstances of occurrence of primary deviance; therefore, primary deviance must be assumed to be either ephemeral or inconsequential for the sole explanation to reside with secondary deviance. In recent years, Goffman (1969) and Scheff (1975) have modified their earlier positions so as to credit primary deviance with a much larger and more problematic role in accounting for the phenomena called mental illness.

Recent developments

The decade of the 1950s saw the introduction of biochemical and psychosocial technologies that were to have dramatic effects on the mental hospital and the mentally ill.

Tranquilizing medications

A biochemical revolution was ushered in with the introduction of phenothiazine and phenothiazine-derivative (tranquilizing) drugs in the mid-1950s. These medications drastically reduced patients' agitated and bizarre behaviors, rendering them more approachable and manageable (Cole, Goldberg, & Davis, 1966; Davis, 1965). Patients became more lucid in their interactions with others, and staff had less need to restrain patients with jackets, straps, packs, and seclusion rooms.

The use of tranquilizing medications is accompanied by much ambivalance among mental health professionals. While granting the calming and antipsychotic effects of these medications, there is concern that they may be used (or overused) for the convenience of the staff and for society in managing patients rather than treating them. Moreover, no etiological links to patient's behavioral disorders have been discovered for these medications thus far. A common saying is that tranquilizers do not cure symptoms but only control them. The control of symptoms might be accepted comfortably as a sufficient contribution in and of itself, were it not for the occurrence of substantial side-effects in some patients (Crane, 1968; Kennedy, Hershon, & McGuire, 1971) and unexplained deaths in others (Hollister & Kosek, 1965; Moore & Book, 1970). Although several studies have concluded that the withdrawal of long-term maintenance dosages of phenothiazine drugs leads to a recurrence of symptoms (Caffey et al., 1964; Prien, Cole & Bilkin, 1969), methodological flaws regarding double-blind procedures, attrition of treatment groups, and reliability of measuring instruments have limited the confidence to be placed in this conclusion (Tobias & MacDonald, 1974). Further, other studies have shown that only minimal reliance need be placed on tranquilizing medications for chronic patients if there is an active psychosocial treatment program operating at the same time (Paul & Lentz, 1977). In summary, there is little doubt that tranquilizing medications have immediate and dramatic calming and antipsychotic effects; there is still disagreement, however, as to their most appropriate long-term use.

Humanizing the milieu

As the harm wrought by custodial impersonality and neglect became more widely recognized and society became more receptive to supporting attempts to counteract it, mental hospital administrators and professional staff focused their energies on trying to make the patient's total hospital environment therapeutic. The values and goals of moral treatment were rediscovered, extended, and rationalized in contemporary terminology as the therapeutic community (Jones, 1953) or milieu therapy (Cumming & Cumming, 1962). Around the same time, the principles of learning as derived from experimental psychology were applied to the resocialization of chronic mental patients in the form of the token economy (Ayllon & Azrin, 1968). Under this approach, patients were reinforced or "paid" for the performance of desired behaviors with tokens, which could then be redeemed for cigarettes, candy, and special privileges. Combinations of the milieu and learning approaches appeared in the form of step-programs in which patient groups were charged with both resocializing and rewarding their patient members (Fairweather, 1964). Despite their theoretical and technological differences, all these programs were aimed at structuring the social environment so that life in the hospital would itself be therapeutic. There is little doubt that these psychosocial programs can make the hospital environment a much more humane place to be.

At the same time, however, the bulk of the gains in milieu programs occurred within the first few weeks and represent the reversal of deplorable behavioral deterioration due to past custodialism rather than the acquisition of new social skills. Moreover, the behavioral improvement is difficult to maintain, so that subsequent reversion to lower levels of functioning is common. Social-learning programs fare somewhat better however. The token economy has not only been able to maintain the immediate improvement, but it has been able to increase it over time (Paul & Lentz, 1977). Despite their effects on behavior inside the hospital, none of these programs has demonstrated widespread efficacy in preventing rehospitalization or in improving the quality of patient adjustment in the community (Anthony, Buell, Scharatt, & Althoff, 1972; Erickson, 1975).

Aftercare and community placement

A major reason for the failure of most psychosocial programs to prepare chronic patients adequately for successful living in the community is that there has not been a continuity of care and support extending from life in the hospital to life in the community. Typically, hospital staff have "referred" patients to community agencies without involving themselves in the process once the paperwork has been completed. Aftercare programs such as halfway houses, day treatment centers, and sheltered workshops have helped to keep those patients who participated in them in the community, but only a fraction of all patients referred (approximately 10%) have actually participated (Anthony et al., 1972; Vitale, 1962). Community Mental Health Centers (CMHCs) have not been of much help with this population either. Experience with the CMHCs indicates that they have typically been run on the model of the acute services of a hospital. Whatever their success with acute and/or nonpsychotic patients, they have not only been ineffective with chronic patients, but they have actively rejected them (Kirk & Thierrien, 1975; Kraft, Binner, & Dickey, 1967; Lamb & Goertzel, 1972). In short, hospital censuses have fallen but readmissions have increased. The long-term chronic patient has become the "revolving-door" chronic patient.

The quality of life for many chronic patients who have stayed in the community (or for many chronic patients while they have stayed in the community) has been described as little different from life in the hospital (Kirk & Thierrien, 1975; Lamb & Goertzel, 1971). The foster or boarding home setting, where community residents are paid to take patients in and look after them, is a particularly vulnerable target for the criticism that the back wards of the hospital have been moved into the back rooms of the community. A recent study has found, however, that the social functioning of foster home patients, after four months in the community, was better than a matched group still in the hospital (Linn, Caffey, Klett, & Hogarty, 1977). Whether these results are typical and whether they will hold up over a longer period is as yet unknown. But the quality of life in the community does depend upon the nature and extent of social stimulation and support in the patients' lives. Specifically, Lamb and Goertzel (1971, 1972) found that randomly assigned chronic patients living in "low expectation" homes, such as foster homes, function at a lower level socially than do chronic patients living in "high expectation" homes, such as halfway houses, sheltered workshops, or the houses of family or friends.

The efficacy of continuity of care and support in the community has been demonstrated recently by the thorough, controlled comparison of milieu, social-learning, and traditional chemotherapy programs carried out by Paul and Lentz (1977). First, they arranged for released patients to obtain social support in the community either from another individual or from the staff of a boarding home. Then they provided for patients to be personally accompanied and introduced to their new surroundings. Finally, they arranged for direct support to patients and/or consultation to their boarding home staffs for several months after their release. Such aftercare was instrumental in maintaining virtually all patients in the community during the 18-month follow-up period. However, it must be noted that the adjustment of patients in the two psychosocial programs declined from the level in the hospital at the time of release to the level achieved by patients in the traditional chemotherapy program. Paul and Lentz speculate that if the staff involvement with patients in the boarding homes could have been carried out to the same extent and in the same manner as it was in the hospital, patients would have maintained their higher levels of adjustment. This speculation points to a major unresolved issue among professionals today regarding the nature of appropriate aspirations for the chronically mentally ill.

The age-old problem

Just what constitutes appropriate aspirations is not a new problem but is rather a restatement of the age-old problem with the chronically mentally ill in the light of current experiences. Custody is the major aspect of the problem currently remaining in achieving a humane adjustment in the community. The problem of social control has largely been solved, because chronic schizophrenia represents a stabilization of schizophrenic behavior that is closer to eccentricity than to psychosis. Eccentricity is generally tolerable to society if the eccentric support themselves financially and manage their lives otherwise unobtrusively. However, attempts to return the eccentric schizophrenic to the community on their own as self-supporting, self-reliant citizens have failed repeatedly (Gurel, 1970; Lamb, 1968; Miller, 1967; Schooler, Goldberg, Boothe, & Cole, 1967). In general, chronic schizophrenic patients are people who either cannot or will not take custody of themselves. As we have seen, if there are no other individuals in their environment to take custody of them, society has traditionally done so by returning them to the large, public mental hospital.

The past history of dehumanization and the ever present potential for iatrogenic effects in the mental hospital have made the option of long-term hospitalization an anathema to most mental health professionals. Currently, two approaches are being advocated. There are those who assume that chronic schizophrenics have the potential for taking full custody of their own lives and that it is possible to devise treatment and rehabilitation programs to enable them to realize this potential. These professionals stress the need to move treatment and rehabilitation services out into the community (Atthowe, 1973; Lehrer & Lanoil, 1977). The plan is that these services will be *transitional* in nature, eventually enabling the person to become able and willing to manage his affairs in an independent living situation. Others assume that chronic schizophrenics have a limited capacity for taking custody of themselves and that this limited capacity will continue to be impervious to our best efforts at treatment and rehabilitation (Cumming, 1963; Fairweather, Sanders, Maynard, & Cressler, 1969). They stress the need for a wide range of both residential and nonresidential services in the community, sufficient to fully supplement patients' limitations in supporting and caring for themselves. Under this plan, such services would be *permanently* extended to those who are both chronically schizophrenic and socially marginal.

These two choices place mental health professionals and society in a dilemma. The provision of transitional treatment and rehabilitation services holds open the hope of achieving a more satisfying life and nonstigmatized status in society, but it flies in the face of repeated failure with this group of people. To provide permanent custody in the community holds promise as a technically feasible alternative to permanent custody in a mental hospital, but it faces much opposition from society and would consign this group to a second-class and thus, necessarily, a stigmatized status. The President's Commission on Mental Health (1978) tries to avoid the disadvantages of either choice by endorsing both. The Commission's *Report to the President* advocated maintaining the aspiration for effective transitional programs through the continuation of research and demonstration projects, while at the same time starting the implementation of permanent custody in the community through the establishment of support services for income maintenance, education, housing, vocational training, and mental and physical health care.

Abolishing mental hospitalization, then, will not abolish the problem of chronic mental illness because the mental hospitals, at their worst, did not originate the problem, they only exacerbated it. The problem has been returned to the community where it originated. One can only hope that society will allow the community to devise more humane solutions than it allowed the mental hospital to devise. For regardless of the approach taken, the behaviors of people who are both chronically schizophrenic and socially marginal continues to pose one of our most perplexing social problems, in conceptualizing what is wrong as well as in deciding what to do.

Summary

The mental hospital, primarily the large public mental hospital, has historically served and continues to serve three major functions for society. In order of importance to society, these are control and protection, custody and refuge, and treatment and rehabilitation. Society demands that the mental hospital aid in controlling certain deviant behaviors that are not codified as unlawful but that threaten to undermine the normative behavioral expectations essential either to society's safety or to its coherent operation. Further, society extends subsistence support and safe custody to those whom it removes from its midst. Some persons adapt to their removal to the hospital by seeking to make it a refuge. With regard to treatment and rehabilitation, society hopes to: 1. change people's tendency to behave deviantly so that there will be no need for a recurrence of social control or custody once they have been released, and 2. prevent people from using the hospital for their own ends by making an indefinite refuge of it. Benefits to patients themselves, aside from the benefits to society, are worthwhile but secondary in importance as far as society is concerned.

Tracing the development of the mental hospital historically showed that the three functions arose, merged with one another and changed over time in response to wider social conditions. In particular, the historical account revealed the cyclical nature of society's belief in and support of treatment and rehabilitation: starting with a strong orientation toward punishment in the seventeenth and eighteenth centuries; proceeding to a firm but compassionate approach in the form of moral treatment in the early nineteenth century; deteriorating to hopelessness and neglect from the mid-nineteenth to the early twentieth century; and finally, rebounding with more concern, hopefulness, and commitment of resources in the current epoch than at any other time.

Sociological analyses of the hospital environment in the 1950s called attention to the iatrogenic problems (caused by the hospital itself) of many of the traditional policies and practices of the mental hospital. Overcrowding and understaffing have been linked to poor treatment outcome; attendants have been shown to have potential as effective therapists as well as guards; custodialism and humanism have been identified as major ideologies that permeate staff attitudes and ward atmospheres; the social process of triangulation has been observed as a precipitant of individual and collective disturbance among patients; chronic schizophrenic patients have been discovered capable of impression management in furthering their chosen adaptation to the hospital; and one alternative to the medical view of mental illness has been developed in the form of labeling theory.

Several types of treatment programs have been designed to counteract the iatrogenic potential of the mental hospital. In various ways, they have attempted to structure the hospital environment so that a patient's experience in the hospital would be therapeutic. These programs have yielded two general results. First, they have been effective in modifying patient's behavior in the hospital. Second, they have achieved only limited generalization to patient behavior outside the hospital. These results are particularly applicable to chronic schizophrenic patients, who continue to pose one of the oldest unsolved problems in the entire field of mental illness/mental hospitalization. Current attempts at solving the problem of chronic schizophrenia focus upon moving treatment and rehabilitation out of the hospital and into the community. Voices from less optimistic quarters advocate moving custody out of the hospital and into the community. Developments along this front will make interesting watching during the next few years.

GLOSSARY

Aftercare: A general term for treatment and rehabilitation services provided to patients immediately following their release from the hospital; designed to serve as a continuation of hospital treatment and rehabilitation although not necessarily of the same type(s).

Authoritarianism: An attitudinal and behavioral orientation characterized by submissiveness to superiors, dominance over subordinates, strict regulation of one's own and others' behavior according to legal rules and conventional norms, discomfort with emotional expressiveness and spontaneity, idealization of one's own group and blaming other groups.

Chemotherapy: Treatment by chemical mean, as in the use of medications and drugs.

Collective disturbance: Excited, agitated, destructive or assaultive behavior manifested by patients acting in concert with one another.

Custodialism: An attitudinal and behavioral orientation characterized by a heavy premium placed upon order and control; by impersonal, aloof, and emotionally distant interaction with patients; and by a view of patients as defective people lacking in fully human potential. Closely akin to authoritarianism.

Deviance: Any behavior that deviates from social norms and distinguished as either primary or secondary deviance; primary deviance is deviance that occurs before the person has been labeled a deviant and as such has many and diverse origins, whereas secondary deviance is deviance that occurs in response to and as a confirmation of being labeled deviant.

Eccentricity: Behavior that is on the borderline between what society considers normative and deviant; generally referred to as "odd" or "strange" and, as such, is accorded cautious acceptance by society.

Humanism: An attitudinal and behavioral orientation characterized by an emphasis on emotional expression and innovation, by interested, warm, and personally involving interaction with patients, and by a toleration of deviance and a view of patients as fully human people; most often cited as the antithesis of custodialism.

Iatrogenesis: The initiation of new symptoms or the exacerbation of existing symptoms as a consequence of certain hospital procedures themselves; the production of illness by the hospital itself.

Impression management: The practice of presenting either favorable or unfavorable aspects of oneself to another person or persons in order to influence the impression made.

Insanity: Formerly used to refer to severe forms of mental illness now referred to as psychoses; currently a legal term used to denote mental incompetence and therefore lack of legal accountability.

Institutionalization: An iatrogenic consequence of hospitalization whereby the patient becomes dependent upon the hospital environment, preferring to live in the hospital rather than in the community; also referred to as institutionalism, chronicity, social breakdown syndrome, and hospitalitis.

Labeling theory: A theory of the social processes by which unsystematized and transient instances of primary deviance are systematized and preserved in the form of secondary deviance; also referred to as the societal reaction theory or perspective.

Moral treatment: An approach to the mentally ill in the United States during the first half of the nineteenth century that held that the patient was a person who was only temporarily deranged from his fully human state; based as it was upon a tolerance for deviance, a compassion for patients, and a hopefulness for remission, moral treatment was an early forerunner of the major social and environmental treatment programs in hospitals today.

Social marginality: Possession of limited social or vocational skills, financial resources, or interpersonal supports, making the maintenance of an adequate social adjustment continually precarious.

Stigma: A characteristic marking a person as being different from other people in a negative, derogatory, way and implying less than fully human status.

Triangulation: Disagreement between two individuals or groups concerning a third individual or group; potentially leading to individual or collective disturbance if the disagreement is not resolved but is nevertheless acted upon by the two parties in relation to the third party.

Ward atmosphere: The social and emotional climate of a ward environment; determined primarily by the emotional quality of patient-staff interactions, the structural nature of the treatment program, and the organizational arrangements for maintenance of the ward as a social system.

22

PSYCHOLOGICAL TREATMENTS OF ABNORMAL BEHAVIOR: PERSPECTIVE AND TRENDS

SOL L. GARFIELD

As has been evident in the preceding pages, the area of abnormal behavior is a multi-faceted and complex one. The varieties of abnormal behavior are diverse and the apparent causes range from possible inherited and genetic factors to psychological and social ones. To fully understand the behaviors and complexities involved, one must draw upon many fields of knowledge, most of which are becoming increasingly specialized. Furthermore, in spite of the advances in knowledge and the immense increase in the published literature on deviant behavior, there are still important gaps in our knowledge concerning the possible causes, classification, and treatment of disordered behavior. Because of this, conflicting theories and explanations of abnormal behavior exist, as well as a diversity of procedures devised to treat and ameliorate such conditions.

In the area of treatment, such diverse procedures as drugs, electric shock, surgery, institutionalization, and a variety of psychological approaches have been used for many types of disordered behavior, and each has had its body of loyal adherents and advocates. An adequate appraisal of this multitude of procedures is beyond the scope of this chapter. Instead, the focus of the present chapter will be an appraisal of recent trends in the area of treatments primarily psychological in nature. These have been referred to as psychotherapy or behavior therapy.

Before discussing some of the current developments in psychotherapy, it is worthwhile to step back a bit and to appraise some of the events that have preceded and influenced the current situation. The precise period of time to utilize as a basis for achieving some perspective on current and emergent trends in the treatment of psychological disorders is purely arbitrary and one can take a long or short perspective. However, there have been periods that have been characterized by increased activity and interest in mental health, by new ideas and innovations, and by expansion of treatment procedures. The period since World War II was one such historical period and, consequently, we shall take a quick look at some of the important events that have occurred since that time and have contributed to subsequent developments.

Developments in the postwar period

The years immediately following the war were filled with many important developments for the fields engaged in working with psychologically disturbed individuals—clinical psychology, psychiatry, social work, and nursing. To describe these developments even for the specialty of clinical psychology would take more space that is feasible here, and the interested reader is referred elsewhere (Garfield, 1965, 1971, 1974). However, some of the most important events can be alluded to briefly.

The large number of psychiatric casualties resulting from the war and the inadequate number of professional workers available for their care and treatment led to an increased awareness of the problems faced by those with psychological disorders. This awareness was also accompanied by demands that something be done to improve the situation. As a result, new and expanded programs of training were developed in the country, federal legislation was enacted to support such training as well as research, and evaluations were made of existing treatment facilities and institutions. Among the developments which can be noted were the creation of the National Institute of Mental Health to support training and research, the setting up of formal training programs in clinical psychology, the increase in the number of psychologists (the American Psychological Association has increased from around 4,000 members in 1945 to over 50,000 at the present time), the development of community mental health centers, a critical attitude toward the isolated state hospitals, and increased awareness of the importance of the prevention of disturbed behavior, and the emergence of many new and different types of psychotherapeutic interventions.

Consequently, the past 30 years or so have been a period of many new and frequently exciting changes in the mental health field. Among these developments was an increased interest in psychotherapy. The increase in output of individuals capable of engaging in psychotherapeutic activities, the increased emphasis on community and outpatient treatment, and the growing popularity of such psychological procedures led to a decided expansion of psychotherapeutic activities. Whereas the primary activity of clinical psychologists in the early 1950s was diagnostic testing, by the 1960s and 1970s psychotherapy had taken over (Garfield & Kurtz, 1976; Kelly, 1961), and to many had become synonymous with clinical psychology (a distortion that nevertheless influenced many young men and women to seek careers as clinical psychologists).

During the early part of the postwar period the predominant influence in psychotherapy was the psychoanalytic or psychodynamic one. In addition to the theoretical views of Freud, those of others such as Sullivan (1953) and Horney (1939) were also influential. In a survey of clinical psychologists reported by Kelly in 1961, approximately 41 percent of those surveyed identified themselves with such theoretical views. While the work of Carl Rogers (1942, 1951) was also influential among psychologists, particularly in terms of research on psychotherapy, his influence was much less. Furthermore, the latter's impact on psychiatry and social work was even more limited, whereas the psychodynamic views appeared to be the dominant ones.

Very briefly, the predominance of psychoanalytic and related views in psychotherapy had certain effects. The client's or patient's complaints or behaviors were viewed as symptoms, and dealing directly with them was seen as superficial treatment that would bring only temporary improvement and result in the appearance of other "substitute" symptoms. The cause of disturbed behavior was to be found in repressed conflicts about which the client was unaware. Therapy was directed to the uncovering and bringing to awareness the "cause" of the individual's disturbance. As a result, psychotherapy was viewed as a process requiring a relatively long time. It also appeared to require a patient who had sufficient motivation and personal resources to engage in this long and demanding procedure of self-appraisal and the attainment of insight into one's difficulties.

As the field of psychotherapy continued to expand in the 1950s and 1960s, certain changes within the field were also apparent. The influence of psychodynamic views seemed gradually to diminish, and a variety of other views and approaches to psychotherapy made their appearances on the treatment scene. The reasons for this are undoubtedly many and there is no objective way of assessing their actual importance. However, one can offer some possible explanations that appear to have some surface validity. Several will be offered here as tentative or possible explanations for this development.

One possible reason is a dissatisfaction that at least a number of psychotherapists experienced with their use of traditional psychodynamic psychotherapeutic approaches. Several bits of evidence may be presented with regard to this possibility. One is that not all prospective clients respond well to such an approach to psychotherapy. As indicated in psychoanalytic writings (Freud, 1950; Strupp, 1973), and as already mentioned, it takes a certain kind of client to persevere with the lengthy process of self-exploration required by psychodynamic psychotherapy. Not all individuals who are experiencing disturbed behavior or discomfort are willing or able to endure this process. Traditionally, a candidate for such therapy, particularly psychoanalysis, has to be highly motivated, intelligent, verbal, reasonably well educated, and have sufficient financial resources. Furthermore, many therapists and clinics are highly selective in whom they will accept for treatment (Garfield, 1978; Kadushin, 1969). Consequently, many individuals do not meet the requirements. They are either rejected for treatment, or if they are accepted, a large number prematurely drop out of treatment. (Garfield, 1978).

Another more direct bit of evidence on the decline of traditional psychodynamic views is that the percentage of psychotherapists who adhere to such views about treatment has noticeably diminished in recent years. Whereas the earlier survey of clinical psychologists reported that 41 percent of clinical psychologists identified themselves as analytic or psychodynamic in orientation (Kelly, 1961), a more recent survey found only 19 percent identifying themselves in this way (Garfield & Kurtz, 1976). In addition, an increased trend toward eclecticism in psychotherapy revealed in the latter survey also indicates a desire on the part of many psychotherapists to utilize a variety of procedures that can be more readily adapted to the needs of the individual client (Garfield & Kurtz, 1977).

Another possible reason for the trend being discussed has been an increased sensitivity on the part of many mental health workers to the many underprivileged segments of our society who were not served or helped by the more traditional forms of psychotherapy. The relatively less educated individuals from the lower socioeconomic groups have generally not been seen as desirable candidates for long-term psychodynamic psychotherapy and have also manifested the highest drop-out rates from such therapies when it has been offered to them. Consequently, a number of socially minded and innovative clinicians have attempted to modify traditional psychotherapeutic approaches and to devise newer procedures to better meet the needs of such individuals. We shall say more about such developments later in the chapter.

Still another possible influence on what has taken place may be linked to the developments that have occurred with regard to the behavior therapies. This type of therapy, deriving from learning theory and experimental psychology, has had a decided impact on the field of psychotherapy during the past 15 to 20 years. Presenting a theoretical stance completely opposite to that of the conventional "uncovering" psychodynamic therapies, behavior therapy has had significant expansion. This orientation, as noted in Chapter 19, focuses primarily on observable behavior and not on postulated internal dynamic mechanisms and constructs. Instead of trying to bring unconscious and repressed conflicts into awareness as a means of helping the client, the emphasis is on changing the disturbed behavior of the client. Behavioral pathology is viewed as a product of previous faulty learning, and in essence the individual has to learn different and more effective behaviors for coping adequately with his social situation.

Besides presenting a very different orientation and approach to problems of behavior change, the behavior therapists have also had a significant impact on the existing field of psychological therapy and treatment. They have emphasized research and subjected their work to continuous evaluation and scrutiny, something not very frequent in most other approaches. Thus, they were able to provide research evidence in support of their procedures. Furthermore, in contrast to most of the traditional psychodynamic psychotherapies, which tended to be lengthy in duration, usually requiring several years for completion, the behavioral therapies usually required only a few months for completion. The variable of time is an important one in terms of both social and economic consideration.

Finally, one other development is also worthy of mention in describing the changes that have occurred in the field of psychotherapy. This concerns the relative increase in research in this area in recent years. Before 1950, there was very little published research on this topic and what was available was of rather poor quality. Research on outcome in psychotherapy, for example, suffered from an absence of controlled studies and was based mainly on a therapist's judgment of improvement. Since therapists are not exactly impartial judges of their own therapy, such research left much to be desired.

In 1952, the British psychologist Hans Eysenck published a scathing critique of the effectiveness of psychoanalytic therapy and other conventional psychotherapies, and stirred up considerable controversy. Among other things, he attempted to show that psychotherapy was no more effective than no psychotherapy at all and that clinical psychologists, consequently, should not be trained in such an ineffective procedure! As might be imagined, Eysenck's paper drew a number of defensive and critical responses from other psychologists and the controversy has continued on and off over the years. The interested reader can examine accounts of it in other publications (Bergin, 1971; Bergin & Lambert, 1978; Eysenck, 1966; Garfield, 1974). Eysenck's critical comments, however, did draw attention to the need for adequate research and, whether directly related to his criticisms or not, there has been a noticeable increase in research since that time, of which the research of behavior therapists is one important contribution of a much wider development.

While the research in psychotherapy during the past 20 years or so has covered many different aspects, only a few selected aspects will be discussed here in terms of their probable impact on the changes that have occurred in psychotherapy. One noticeable feature was the lack of systematic evaluative research on the effectiveness of traditional long-term psychotherapy. Psychoanalysts, in particular, did not contribute much in the way of research to justify the claims made for the effectiveness of their psychotherapy (Luborsky & Spence, 1971). By contrast, client-centered or Rogerian psychotherapists and, later, the behavior therapists were actively engaged in various types of research on the effectiveness of their forms of therapy. Furthermore, as already noted, they were publishing positive results on therapies that generally required much less time than the traditional psychodynamic therapies. In addition, several studies of traditional or eclectic psychotherapy conducted in clinical settings tended to produce some unexpected results. For example, as mentioned previously, a number of studies indicated that a large percentage of patients who began psychotherapy in outpatient clinics dropped out of therapy after only a few interviews (Garfield, 1978). Additional research also showed that a significantly large number of those who terminated therapy prematurely were individuals who tended to come from the lower socioeconomic strata. In other words, traditional approaches to therapy did not seem to be well suited to such prospective clients. These findings, as indicated earlier, led a number of individuals to attempt to devise procedures better suited to such clients or patients.

One very important source of the increase in research on psychotherapy and on the need for evidence to support rival claims concerning therapeutic effectiveness was undoubtedly related to the expansion of the involvement of psychologists in this field. Prior to 1950, psychologists were not very active in the area of psychotherapy and there were relatively few clinical psychologists with training and experience in psychotherapy. However, in the past 30 years, clinical psychology has grown rapidly and there has been a serious interest in the practice of psychotherapy. Furthermore, because of their training in research, psychologists have played the leading role in the increased development of research in psychotherapy. Thus, the emergence of clinical psychology as a distinctive and recognized scientifically oriented profession in the broad field of mental health has had a decided impact on psychological treatment.

The current scene

As we have noted, a number of events have occurred that have influenced and changed traditional views of psychotherapy and behavior change. While some of the developments described can be viewed as positive in terms of sensitivity to social needs and an increase in research, the overall situation at the present time is far from satisfactory. Other trends are also discernable, and in this section an attempt will be made to discuss some of the more interesting and potentially important features of the current scene. In the following sections, I will attempt to appraise the implications of current trends, to discuss some of the innovative attempts that have been made to meet social needs, and to speculate about the future.

When one attempts to survey the current situation in psychotherapy, one tends to be faced with many different competing and often conflicting developments. As noted previously, there has been a marked increase in research. At the same time, there has been an increase in the appearance of many new forms of psychotherapy, most of which have reported little or no research on their effectiveness, and some of which appear to be esoteric or even erotic forms of therapy. According to a recent report from the National Institute of Mental Health (1975), there are over 130 different types of psychotherapy. While experimentation with new forms of therapy may be viewed as desirable, the lack of any rigorous testing of the effectiveness of these forms of psychotherapy raises a number of serious questions. Are they all potentially successful and helpful forms of psychotherapy? Are any of them potentially dangerous or harmful? Are they suitable for all types of potential clients and for all types of abnormal behavior? Without adequate testing or appraisal, one is faced with the situation of accepting them on some basis other than empirical demonstration of their effectiveness. This is not a particularly desirable state of affairs on both scientific and ethical grounds. One should ordinarily not accept a form of treatment on the basis of unverified claims or the enthusiasm of its advocates. The situation is certainly very different when it comes to putting drugs on the market for public use. This area is regulated by the Food and Drug Administration and new drugs that appear promising have to go through a series of experimental and clinical trials before they are judged as acceptable for regular clinical use. Unfortunately, there is nothing comparable to the FDA in the field of psychotherapy.

We therefore have a situation where a

large variety of psychological treatments are being offered to the public without much preliminary testing to show that they are both effective and reasonably safe treatments. Psychotherapists themselves select certain types of therapy on bases other than the proven merit of the therapies selected. Instead, it would appear as if the type of therapy is chosen on the basis of faith, indoctrination, personal appeal, current popularity, chance, or something approaching religious conversion. At the same time, some of the lesser researched therapies are written about in popular style and published in paperbacks appealing to large numbers of individuals, a number of whom may then seek out these forms of psychotherapy.

In addition to the proliferation of psychotherapies, there are two other somewhat related developments that are sources of concern. These pertain to the two questions, What is psychotherapy? and Who are to be designated as psychotherapists? It is difficult to give an adequate and precise definition of psychotherapy. For example, do counseling and the giving of advice qualify as psychotherapy? Are encounter groups, marathon groups, and "rap sessions" to be viewed as forms of group psychotherapy? Are marital or divorce counseling forms of therapy? Do college dormitory counselors perform psychotherapy? One's answers to such questions will be influenced both by one's view of psychotherapy and by an analysis of what takes place in the individual instance, and in the absence of a clear and accepted definition, such answers are not easily secured.

The above problem is also related to deciding who can perform psychotherapy. Thirty-five years ago the answer seemed relatively simple. The traditional mental health professionals—psychiatrist, clinical psychologist, and psychiatric social worker—were the main recognized purveyors of psychotherapeutic services, even though there were jurisdictional disputes among them. However, the situation today is vastly different. Counseling psychology has developed as a professional speciality whose differentiation from clinical psychology becomes increasingly blurred. In addition, there are various types of counselors who appear to provide some services of a psychotherapeutic nature, such as marital counselors, pastoral counselors, guidance counselors, vocational counselors, and rehabilitation counselors. Nurses, particularly psychiatric nurses engage in psychotherapy, including behavior therapy, and various types of group sessions are led on hospital wards by occupational therapists, psychiatric aids, and related personnel. In the 1960s, we also witnessed a variety of innovative programs to train diverse "nonprofessional" therapists (Garfield, 1969, 1974). A number of community mental health centers also attempted to train members of minority groups to become "indigenous" mental health workers and counselors. A variety of encounter and self-awareness groups were also led by individuals with very diverse backgrounds of training or no training at all!

Thus, various kinds of activities, some of which are labeled psychotherapy and others which go by various other names, are begin offered to the public by various and diverse kinds of practitioners. Little systematic evaluation is conducted on most of what takes place, there are no guidelines for deciding what is useful or harmful, fads appear to be prominent, and there is both enthusiasm and confusion in the air. Consequently, it seems worthwhile to examine more closely some of the developments visible in the current scene.

Styles, fads, and discontent

From a situation where there was a more or less dominant view of psychotherapy, the psychodynamic one, and just a relatively small number of therapeutic approaches, we have progressed today to a bewildering display of diversity. As already indicated, both favorable and negative aspects of this development can be discerned.

Although the scientific and professional arena is considered to be quite different from that of the public arena, both are affected to some degree by social forces within the larger society and culture. Thus, styles and fads become popular in both science and society. It is a prevailing belief, however, that certain canons of procedure and ethics exert some controls in the sciences and professions. Thus, there are certain prescribed procedures for carrying out and reporting research, and one who transgresses by distorting data or "fudging" results is usually ostracized or severely reprimanded in some way. The same holds true for the practice of a profession (Garfield, 1974). One who takes undue advantage of a patient or makes false claims about the service he/she offers may lose his/her professional standing or be prohibited from further practice of the profession. However, despite these conventions, we currently have an unusual situation in the area of psychotherapy, but one that is not unique to our own times (Zilboorg & Henry, 1941). We have many therapies that have not been tested or investigated by means of research and we have a variety of practitioners who do not appear to be members of the established mental health professions. What are some of the possible reasons for this state of affairs?

There are undoubtedly many reasons, and they probably vary for different individuals. As we have already noted, traditional psychotherapies were not particularly effective for many people and were not positively viewed by them. They took a long time, were expensive, made certain demands on the client, and were based on theories and used procedures that some people did not accept. Furthermore, many segments of our population were fearful of exposing themselves to "shrinks" and believed that it signified that they were crazy (Hollingshead & Redlich, 1958). This was particularly true of those in the lower socioeconomic strata. In addition, those who were referred or who sought out treatment had expectations about treatment at variance with those of the professional therapists they saw. They tended to see the therapist as a doctor who would find out what was wrong with them and then tell them what to do. Instead, they encountered a therapist who expected them to talk about themselves and "do all the work." Furthermore, they expected the treatment to be relatively brief, whereas their therapists had very different expectations. For example, in one study of individuals who expressed positive attitudes towards psychotherapy and on the average had completed high school, 73 percent expected to see definite improvement by the fifth session and 70 percent expected that therapy would last 10 sessions or less (Garfield & Wolpin, 1963), expectations not necessarily shared by their therapists.

Such findings have led to some positive assessment of problems, as well as innovations in practice to handle these problems, and these will be discussed in the next section. However, such attempts did not appreciably impede some of the developments referred to earlier. What appeared in the 1960s were a variety of approaches that differed from conventional procedures in a number of ways. Particularly evident in such developments as encounter and marathon groups, as well as some of the other newer forms of therapy, was an emphasis on full expression of feelings and openness. While such emphasis can be viewed as reactions to social conventions, as well as to psychotherapies that tended to deemphasize the expression of feelings and openness, they may be viewed also as overreactions. In any event, the popularity of "groups" of all kinds, some of which by conventional standards would be viewed as exotic or erotic, was increasingly apparent. The appearance of "nude marathons," as well as the report of casualties resulting from some marathon groups (Lieberman, Yalom, & Miles, 1973), led to concern on the part of many psychologists and psychiatrists that sensationalism was being fostered and that susceptible and fragile individuals could be harmed. While there is no adequate basis for evaluating the state of such groups today, it seems to me that the popularity of such groups is already beginning to decline, while at the same time new therapies are evident that emphasize similar values, but in a more restrained manner.

At the present time, however, there are

numerous pseudo-therapies and "self-enhancement" groups vying for public popularity. While some of these approaches are used by professional mental health workers, many are offered to the public by individuals with varying nonprofessional backgrounds. Furthermore, such activities are neither formally designated as psychotherapy nor are they directed at individuals who would be categorized as "patients" suffering from psychological disorders. Rather, they emphasize awareness, getting in touch with one's feelings, personal growth, and increasing one's potential. They would thus appear to be appealing to a different clientele, although it is difficult to make sound judgments on this matter. Certainly, it seems plausible that at least a number of individuals who are experiencing personal problems may be attracted to such procedures because they may be viewed as carrying less stigma than seeing a mental health professional and also because some of them, such as marathon groups, last for only a week-end or so. However, to the extent that such "therapies" or groups are provided by individuals relatively untrained and unknowledgeable about behavioral pathology, and that adequate diagnostic screening is not performed, the possibility exists that some individuals may be harmed. This seems particularly likely if either the group leader or other group members engage in strongly confrontative behavior, as some individuals are poorly equipped to withstand such attacks on their adequacy and self-esteem (Lieberman et al., 1973).

There seems to be little question that material about psychotherapy, groups, and related procedures have a much wider audience and appeal than has ever been true before. Popular accounts in the press, on television programs, and in paperbacks have catered to this interest and stimulated it. In addition, almost every week a new form of therapy or group approach seems to appear. Some receive enthusiastic accounts in newspaper columns, while others become best sellers in paperback form. Some of my colleagues and I, for example, were rather surprised and even slightly embarrassed by the widespread publicity given to a local university report of conventional behavior therapy that was conducted by some of our students for individuals with anxiety about public speaking. Actually, we attempted to get some local publicity in order that our students would be able to secure sufficient clients for their research projects. The report was picked up by the local press, then by a television station, and eventually carried to many parts of the country. In this instance, we received more requests for help than we could handle. This incident reflects the need for psychological services, the interest the news media have for this topic, the impact of the public news media, and the fact that most individuals who seek help do not insist on evidence concerning the effectiveness of the therapy they seek out. Thus, fads and temporary popularity are a fact of the current scene with new "therapies" constantly making their appearance.

Where such trends will lead is very difficult to predict. In contrast to the past, where some charismatic healers would only have an impact on a relatively small number of people, our increased means of communication allows particular views or movements to have an impact on large numbers of people. The possibilities, of course, are there for positive influence as well as negative, although the media clearly prefer sensational accounts over less interesting material such as reports of research. Stricter regulation of who practices psychotherapy might improve the situation since it would tend to curb the obvious quack and the untrained. However, this would by no means do away with the problem, for even many "qualified" therapists utilize basically untested procedures. Malpractice suits also may not be effective, although they have clearly had an impact on raising the costs of malpractice insurance. In the final analysis, improved and effective therapeutic procedures, evaluated by means of systematic research, seem to be the most plausible and desirable development. Because research on psychotherapy is a difficult and complex undertaking as well as a recent development, we currently have relatively few definitive results. This accounts in part for the current situation and is analogous to comparable developments in the field of medicine (Group for the Advancement of Psychiatry, 1975). However, when really effective treatment results are secured for a particular form of treatment, the competing treatments usually tend to be discarded. It should be evident, therefore, that we have some way to go in the field of psychotherapy before our problems will be resolved. However, there have also been positive developments in recent years and we can turn our attention next to some of them.

Meeting social needs for services

As indicated earlier in this chapter, the big increase in mental health personnel and services occurred after World War II. A number of surveys and studies indicated not only a shortage of such services, but also an inequality in the availability of such services. Probably the most important of these was the report of the Joint Commission on Mental Illness and Health (1961), a high level commission appointed by the United States Congress to conduct an intensive study of mental illness and its treatment. A number of important problems and recommendations were highlighted in this report.

One problem was the shortage of professional mental health personnel. For example, in 1960 when there were about 160 million people in the U.S., there were approximately 12,000 psychiatrists and perhaps about 6,000 clinical psychologists. This was a ratio of one psychiatrist to every 13,000 people and only one clinical psychologist for every 26,000 persons. In addition, these individuals were not distributed geographically in an equal manner. The large urban centers of population tend to have a disproportionally large number of psychiatrists and psychologists. Also, services are not distributed equally among the different social classes in our society. Those who are economically well-off can secure the services they need or desire, whereas the poor generally are not able to do so. For example, in a survey of psychiatric treatment in the New Haven, Connecticut area, Hollingshead and Redlich (1958) found that the most intensive and long-term psychotherapy was provided almost exclusively by private psychiatrists to patients in the middle and upper socioeconomic classes. Individuals in the lower classes, however, tended more frequently to receive diagnoses of schizophrenia and to be treated in state hospitals, institutions that generally have staff shortages and more limited personnel. Similar findings were also reported in other surveys conducted for the Joint Commission.

In addition to both a shortage of professional resources for providing needed services and an unequal distribution of services, some related problems were also apparent. One is that it is difficult to increase greatly the supply of professional personnel since long periods of training are required and the training is expensive. If one includes premedical training, medical school, internship and three years of residency training, it requires 11 to 12 years to turn out a psychiatrist. Similarly it requires an average of 9 to 10 years to receive a Ph.D. in clinical psychology. Thus, increasing the supply of conventionally trained mental health personnel requires a long-term perspective and greatly increased funds for training.

Another aspect commented upon earlier, is that some traditional forms of psychotherapy also require long periods of time. Psychoanalysis, for example, requires three to five sessions per week for several years. Apart from other considerations, psychoanalysis and psychodynamically oriented therapies are rather expensive forms of therapy, and most people cannot afford such treatment. Furthermore, it appeared as if those who were not in the greatest need of treatment received the most time-consuming and expensive treatment. "In sum, then, psychoanalysis is adapted neither to the treatment of the psychoses nor to mass application of any kind. It is principally effective for a limited number of carefully selected patients who are not totally incapacitated by their illness and do not require hospitalization" (Joint Commission on Mental Illness and Health, 1961, p.80).

As a result of their study, the Joint Commission made a number of recommendations, a few of which can be mentioned here. One was that there should be increased federal support for research on mental health. In the long run, research that may shed light on the causes of abnormal behavior and lead to possible programs aimed at preventing such behavior is the most effective procedure for alleviating personal distress. Research on more effective and efficient forms of therapy is also very worthwhile. There were also recommendations for increasing training in the mental health area including programs at different levels of skills, as well as providing special training and consultation for physicians and clergymen. The latter aspect was mentioned because a survey conducted under the auspices of the Joint Commission indicated that over two-thirds of the individuals with personal problems tended to consult clergymen and physicians, whereas only 18 percent consulted psychologists or psychiatrists (Gurin, Veroff, & Fields, 1960). Another recommendation was that mental health services be provided in the community in which the individual lives, instead of in rather distant and isolated institutions that tend to weaken the ties between the disturbed individual and his family and community.

As a result of these recommendations, Congress authorized funds to implement them. We shall comment only on one such authorization: the Community Mental Health Centers Act of 1963. This act provided funds to the states to help construct community mental health centers. Communities were defined as catchment areas of 75,000 to 200,000 persons. Later, funds were also provided for staffing these centers and five essential services were specified. These were: 1. inpatient care 2. outpatient care 3. partial hospitalization 4. emergency 24-hour service, and 5. consultation and education for related groups in the community. The latter were desired for community agencies and members of various professions in order to link the center more closely with other agencies and care givers, and to facilitate the early detection and possible prevention of mental health problems.

While the legislation and financial support for the community mental health program led to the setting up of several hundred centers, not all of them developed really novel and innovative programs to better meet the needs of the people in their catchment area. Many of them continued to provide the same traditional procedures as before. A survey of mental health activities for the City of Boston, reported by Ryan in 1969, illustrates that all of the former ills of mental health treatment have not been overcome. A few of the findings are of interest.

One such finding was that approximately 150 individuals per 1,000 of the population were identified by some source as being emotionally or behaviorally disturbed. Of these, it is estimated that only about nine will actually apply for treatment at one of the psychiatric outpatient clinics in the Boston area. Furthermore, of the nine who apply, only four may be accepted for treatment. Of the total 150 persons who are judged to have problems, an additional 5 or 6 will manifest such disturbed behavior that they will be sent to a mental hospital. Only one of the 150 will be treated by a psychiatrist in private practice. Thus, only 10 or 11 of the 150 individuals deemed to be in possible need of treatment will receive some kind of care from professional mental health workers. The remainder will, for the most part, be cared for by the family physician, social agencies, and the clergy. While perhaps two-thirds of the cases requiring help will be taken care of in some fashion by the total caretakers mentioned above, with only a small number being seen by mental health workers, the remaining one-third will receive no services at all. "realistically, nothing is 'left over' to help this one-third of the disturbed population. There is no place, there are no people, there is no time available to them" (Ryan, 1969, p. 12).

The other side of the picture presented by Ryan in his survey of mental health activities in Boston is that those individuals who receive treatment from psychiatrists appear to be a very select group. Most of them are relatively young, two-thirds are females, 80 percent have received some college education, and they tend to be in the middle and upper classes. "about one-quarter of these patients, that is of all Bostonians receiving private psychiatric treatment, are college educated, young women who live within an area of less than 100 blocks" (Ryan, 1969, p. 15).

Thus, the Boston survey points up the continuing need for psychological and psychiatric services for large sections of the population, as well as the inequality of treatment that still appears to exist. However, while the problems and obstacles have not been overcome, several important developments have occurred in response to such problems and a few of them will be mentioned here.

Reference was made earlier to the fact that lower-class individuals did not appear to meet some of the criteria judged suitable for long-term psychotherapy and that they dropped out of therapy in significant numbers. Thus, beyond the matter of the scarcity of resources, the problem appeared to be compounded by the premature departure of such (as well as other) individuals when they actually started therapy, as well as their frequent refusal of such therapy (Garfield, 1978). As a consequence, a number of attempts have been made to overcome this and related problems. One such attempt has been referred to as pretherapy training (Heitler, 1976). The purpose of such training is to help prepare the potential client for the psychotherapy to be received, and in some instances also, to prepare therapists to modify their approach. Various types of pretraining procedures have been developed. Some provide a general exposition of therapy and what one should anticipate in terms of the expected behavior of therapist and patient alike (Hoehn-Saric, Frank, Imber, Nash, Stone, & Battle, 1964). Some have used a tape-recording of a "good" therapy session (Truax & Carkhuff, 1967), while some have developed a role-induction film specifically for lower-class patients (Strupp & Bloxom, 1973). While the results have not always been uniformly successful, these represent some innovative attempts to better prepare patients for psychotherapy, and in some instances, therapists as well (Baum & Felzer, 1964; Jacobs, Charles, Jacobs, Weinstein, & Mann, 1972) in order to reduce premature termination and to improve outcome.

Still another development worthy of note concerns the use of brief and time-limited therapies. Many possible factors have contributed here. Probably the most important have been professional concerns with being able to provide more service to a larger number of people in need of help, providing therapy more in line with the expectations of those seeking help, and the recognition of the importance of therapeutic intervention at times of crisis. It is obvious that by using therapies of brief duration, clinics and therapists can see many more patients than would be the case with long-term therapies. A therapist can work with 10 individuals if treatment lasts 10 sessions instead of with one if 100 sessions are required. Furthermore, a large number of those seeking help expect and want treatment to last only a relatively brief period of time. Thus, brief therapies are congruent with these expectations of the client and more cooperation and less premature termination might be anticipated. The view has also been advanced that most individuals seek treatment when some state of crisis in their lives has been reached and when they are in a heightened state of arousal. It has also been hypothesized that this represents an optimum time for initiating therapy (Butcher & Maudal, 1976). The individual is motivated to seek help and to change, and therapeutic efforts at such a time can be used most constructively. If the client can be helped to cope with and resolve the crisis situation, he/she can return to a normal level of functioning in a relatively short time. If, however, treatment is delayed, the individual may lose the motivation for treatment, and the disturbance may tend to become more fixed and more resistant to change. Thus, treatment undertaken at the time of crisis may turn out to be the most worthwhile.

For the reasons already mentioned, a number of clinics have attempted to provide emergency treatment and to forego such procedures as lengthy intake interviews and staff conferences before a decision as to acceptance for treatment is reached. Instead, walk-in clinics will see clients almost immediately and the initial interview also becomes the start of treatment. In addition, these forms of therapy are planned to be brief. Their aim is to help the individual over the period of crisis and to restore him/her to the precrisis level of functioning. In about two-thirds of the cases, according to some reports, individuals are helped sufficiently to resume their normal role in the family and community, a rate of improvement that compares favorably with other and longer types of therapy (Butcher & Koss, 1978; Harris, Kalis, & Freeman, 1963). Those patients who do not respond to this type of therapy can be continued for longer periods or referred for other types of treatment.

While the various forms of brief therapy may differ in some ways, they appear to have certain things in common. There is more concern with the current situation of the client and correspondingly less attention is paid to past events. The therapist also tends to be more active and directive in the briefer therapies than is true of the older forms of therapy. In addition, there is more emphasis on the conscious aspects of the individual's problems and on strengths and personality assets. There also appears to be a greater emphasis on activities outside of the therapy hour such as the use of therapeutic tasks, homework, and the like. While such other therapies as behavior therapy tend to be relatively brief and to have many of the features described for the briefer therapies, they differ in terms of having a different theoretical orientation and to some extent also in terms of the procedures used.

Thus, brief therapies have been one type of response to the clear need for making psychotherapeutic services more readily available to more people and particularly for the more underprivileged segments of society. Furthermore, although some have expressed concern that the lower classes will be receiving an inferior or diluted form of treatment (Heitler, 1973), this fear does not appear to be justified by the results secured in comparisons of brief therapy with more conventional unlimited psychotherapy (Gurman & Kniskern, 1978; Luborsky, Singer, & Luborsky, 1975). Most comparisons have shown comparable improvement rates for the two types of therapy and, since time is an important variable, the briefer therapies would appear to be more efficient. Additional research on this matter with long-term follow-up studies would be of real value.

There is also an additional point that deserves specific emphasis. This pertains to the possible value of brief therapy in preventing more serious behavioral disturbance. The idea here is that many people encounter crises in their lives at certain critical times. While a large number of these persons are able to overcome and resolve these crises, such as loss of a loved one or loss of a job, some are overwhelmed and become immobilized. If these individuals are seen and helped at the time of crisis, the issues can be resolved more quickly and chronic maladjustive behavior prevented. This appears to be an important feature of at least some of the brief therapies, and the rationale seems quite plausible. From the social point of view, attempts to prevent serious disturbance would be most desirable, for in the long run, prevention can do more to ameliorate suffering than can increased efforts at treatment.

One other aspect of the movement aimed at increasing psychotherapeutic services to meet the needs of those with psychological difficulties should also be mentioned here. This pertains to the training and use of "nonprofessional" therapists, an important but controversial development. If professional manpower is limited and it is difficult to increase the supply to any great extent, one strategy is to deploy our current manpower as efficiently as possible. One way of doing this would be to use qualified professionals to train and then to supervise other less highly skilled personnel in carrying out certain designated clinical activities. With professionals to supervise their work, individuals can be selected and trained to carry out certain types of interviewing, counseling, and behavior therapy. While such persons would not have full professional responsibility for the overall treatment of the case, there are many therapeutic functions that they could be delegated to carry out. It is also believed by some that individuals selected from the neighborhood in which the clinic operates and from which most of its clients are drawn would be better able to establish rapport and communication with these clients since they have a common background and comparable set of values (Garfield, 1969).

A number of programs to train various kinds of new mental health workers have been developed in recent years and some brief reference can be made to a few of them for illustrative purposes. In one of the best known of these programs, eight college-educated, middle-aged housewives were selected from 49 applicants to be trained as psychotherapists. They were given an intensive program of training on a half-time basis for a period of two years and were systematically evaluated during their training and for several years thereafter (Rioch, 1967; Rioch, Elkes, & Flint, 1965). Few psychotherapists have been as closely evaluated as were these eight women, and on the basis of several criteria, they performed as well as the average professional (Freeman & Golann, 1965; Magoon & Golann, 1966). After graduation, all of these women were employed in regular professional settings.

Various other programs have also been developed. Some hospitals have developed programs lasting from six months to one year to train "psychiatric technicians" or "social interaction therapists." In one mental health center in the Southwest, the entire staff with the exception of the director was composed of nonprofessional personnel who were trained and supervised by professional psychologists and psychiatrists. Besides these more unique programs, many colleges and junior colleges have developed two-year programs leading to an Associate of Arts degree in some phase of mental health work.

While these and other programs have represented sincere and innovative attempts to respond to evident mental health needs, they have not developed without some stresses and controversy. Although such programs could not have been started without the support and cooperation of many professional mental health workers, they have not always been viewed positively by some professionals who have been concerned about the quality of the services offered, as well as the possible threat to their own professional well being. Some initially enthusiastic programs have had severe difficulties and some have gradually been terminated or replaced. The issue of community control in some centers has also led to political struggles between the professional staff and the nonprofessionals or with the community representatives on the center's board. Problems have also existed for the nonprofessionals in that they lacked a specific occupational identity, as well as a career ladder for occupational advancement. Nevertheless, it does appear that with proper selection, training, and supervision, such workers can perform a number of specific treatment activities that tend in the long run to increase the availability of mental health care to those with behavioral disturbance. Perhaps it should also be pointed out that such individuals who receive training for specific activities and function in public mental health centers under professional supervision should not be confused with poorly or inadequately trained individuals who offer their services directly to the public under a variety of designations such as group leader, awareness workshop leader, psychic healer, and the like.

Research on psychotherapy

Let us now shift our perspective and look more closely at another aspect of psychological treatment that has been mentioned several times previously, namely, research on psychotherapy. While most clinical practitioners are very much interested in working with individuals or groups of clients and in learning about therapeutic procedures, they manifest relatively little interest in matters of research. Among psychotherapists, psychologists make up the largest group of those who are actively involved in carrying out research investigations of psychotherapy. Nevertheless, most clinical psychologists resemble their psychotherapeutic colleagues in other professions in having little to do with research and being relatively little influenced by research findings. This, in fact, accounts for some of the current trends discussed earlier.

As was also mentioned previously, psychotherapists tend to choose their theoretical orientation and procedures on the basis of personal preferences of different sorts rather than on the basis of empirical evidence demonstrating the efficacy of their particular approach. A number of therapists also are convinced personally that they help most of their patients, that the results are obvious, and that research is unnecessary. They may not have the same confidence in the work of some of their colleagues, but of the worth of their own therapy they appear to have little doubt. Such views, obviously, do not provide an encouraging climate for research.

Regardless of how some therapists view the matter, at some point in the future there will be an increased demand from the public or sectors within it to demonstrate that specific forms of treatment are indeed effective, and not harmful. This has certainly been the case with regard to drugs and various ingredients used in the preparation and preservation of food products. In the field of psychotherapy, such investigations have been carried out with reference to only a few forms of psychotherapy, particularly the behavior therapies, client-centered therapy, and some variants of psychodynamic therapy. Before discussing this further, however, let us examine some of the problems and difficulties in conducting research on psychotherapy.

There are several reasons why research in the area of psychotherapy has been difficult. As already noted, clinicians generally have not been interested in pursuing or collaborating in research investigations that attempted to evaluate the effectiveness of psychotherapy, particularly their own therapy. Besides this, there is the complexity of the therapeutic process, the time required to collect data, particularly in long-term psychotherapy, and problems of securing adequate control groups and meaningful criteria of outcome. Clearly, evaluating the effectiveness of psychotherapy is no simple task. At a minimum, one must consider client variables (such as social class and degree of disturbance), therapist variables (personality, experience, skill), the interaction between these two sets of variables, and adequate measures of appraising change. All of these have presented difficulties for investigators of psychotherapy and have led to inconsistencies in research findings and difficulties in interpreting the published results (Garfield & Bergin, 1978). While this is not the place to attempt a detailed presentation of research on psychotherapy outcome, it will be worthwhile to examine further some of the problems and findings in this area.

Ideally, if one is conducting research on a given subject, it would be well to have a defined population or sample of subjects so that the results secured could be generalized to other comparable groups. Until very recently, this has not been the case in psychotherapy research. Instead of having a group of patients with very similar disorders with comparable degrees of disturbance and chronicity of disturbance, studies have been conducted with very heterogeneous groups of patients. Some clients conceivably are minimally disturbed, the onset of symptoms is recent, they are motivated to seek treatment, and they have a favorable family or life situation. In contrast, others may display the opposite characteristics and circumstances. Thus, to include these two very different groups of clients in one sample for research purposes may seriously cloud or limit the results secured. Similarly, the therapists in one setting may range from very good to very poor, use different procedures, and have varying amounts of experience. Again, conclusions and generalizations are difficult. It is also conceivable that some patients may respond better to one type of therapist or procedure than to others. Such considerations obviously complicate research and have been responsible in part for some of the inconsistencies and ambiguities in past research.

Another critical problem concerns the means of appraising outcome in psychotherapy. To the extent that different forms of therapy may have different goals or objectives, it may be difficult to compare their relative effectiveness. However, there are other difficulties here, for some outcomes can be evaluated relatively objectively, whereas others cannot. If a patient has a severe fear of flying, the success of treatment can be appraised rather directly by observing the patient's behavior after treatment. If subsequent to therapy the patient actually takes airplane trips with minimal discomfort, the treatment can be considered successful. If he/she cannot, then the treatment has failed. In this instance, the outcome of therapy can be reasonably appraised without difficulty and there would be high agreement among independent judges of the outcome. However, if the goal of treatment is an improved marital relationship, increased happiness, self-actualization, or general personality reconstruction, the matter of evaluating outcome is more difficult. How do we judge positive change in such instances? One most likely would have to break down the overall objective into more specific behaviors or attributes, and these in turn would have to be recorded in some systematic fashion before therapy was begun and again at regular intervals after therapy was completed. This, sad to relate, is infrequently done. What more typically occurs is that global judgments of improvement are made by the therapist and/or the patient at the end of therapy, and these become the criteria of outcome.

While there is some plausibility in ascertaining the client's appraisal of therapy since he/she is the consumer, there are also some reasons for not relying exclusively on such judgments as measures of outcome, at least as they have commonly been secured. One aspect is that the client is asked to make a judgment comparing how he/she is today as compared with how he/she was at the beginning of therapy. Memory, as well as personal factors, may influence or distort such judgments. It would be preferable to have the client rate his/her feelings and behaviors just prior to therapy, at certain times during therapy, and again at certain intervals after therapy has been completed. The same would apply in the case of judgments of improvement provided by the therapist. Besides this aspect, there are other possible factors to consider. The patient may feel under some obligation to see at least some positive change or improvement for the time, money, and effort spent for therapy, and he/she may also feel positive toward the therapist's efforts on his/her behalf. Factors unrelated to therapy may have also contributed to some change in the patient. Thus, while the patient's evaluation of therapy may be of some value and interest, it is far from a perfect or valid measure of improvement.

The therapist's evaluation of therapy made at the end of treatment is even more suspect. Therapists have a need to feel their efforts are worthwhile and that their training and expertise have not been in vain. It is also a subjective matter in which it is possible for the therapist to note changes that may not have been of primary importance to the client. For example, while the client's behavior may show little change, the client may have secured some understanding of the possible factors that have lead to the disturbed behavior, or he/she may have learned to accept his/her fate and live with his/her problems. Thus, from the therapist's view, some improvement is judged to have taken place. The fact that the therapist may view matters quite differently from the client or from that of other less involved observers is supported by results of several studies. In one study, for example, therapists' global ratings of improvement correlated only .21 with those made by the patients and .13 with ratings made by independent judges (Sloane, Staples, Cristol, Yorkston, & Whipple, 1975). In another study, a nonsignificant correlation of .10 was obtained between therapists' and clients' ratings of change (Horenstein, Houston, & Holmes, 1973).

While therapists' global ratings of improvement made at the end of therapy are thus open to some question, they have been the most frequently used measure of outcome because they are usually the easiest to obtain. Getting better appraisals of outcome is a more difficult and complex matter. However, if we are to secure worthwhile answers to our questions about the effectiveness of the various psychotherapies we have no other alternative. Consequently, let us look at what is involved in attempting more adequate appraisals of psychotherapy.

First, we must use measures that have reasonable levels of reliability and validity. Second, the measures must relate to the variables we supposedly are interested in appraising. If an individual seeks psychotherapy because of depression, or anxiousness, or shyness, or any one of a number of things, our instruments must be measures of the variables at issue. If other variables are deemed to be theoretically important and related to the problems presented by the patient, then these should be clearly specified prior to the initiation of therapy and adequate measures of them secured. Furthermore, since some appraisals of the same variables may not be highly correlated, as indicated in our previous discussion of therapists' and clients' ratings of improvement, as well as in other research (Cartwright, Kirtner, & Fiske, 1963; Garfield, Prager, & Bergin, 1971), it is important to use a variety of different kinds of measures. Among these would be observations of actual behavior, self-report inventories, and performance measures as appropriate to the problem being treated. Special kinds of problems might require the devising of specific methods of evaluation suitable for the problems at hand.

As should be evident by now, evaluating the effectiveness of psychotherapy is a complicated task but one that is clearly necessary. Furthermore, there is a growing awareness on the part of researchers in this area of the limitations of past research and the need for better designed and better controlled studies. Little has been said thus far about the matter of adequate research design and the need for proper control groups since most readers have received some instruction about these topics in their introductory courses. However, a few very important points are worth emphasizing. Since individuals may improve without treatment if a crisis situation gets resolved or something positive takes place outside of therapy, rates of improvement are essentially meaningless without some form of control group as a means of comparison. Also, if a control group is formed it is important that the patients be selected in a random manner for assignment to either the control or treatment groups or that they be closely matched on the variables of importance. Otherwise, the changes secured may be unduly influenced by by initial differences in the two groups. This, perhaps, is an obvious consideration, but it is not always observed. There are, however, some other considerations that have been increasingly emphasized by researchers in recent years.

One problem concerns the type and adequacy of the control group to be used. There are several possibilities that have been employed in recent years. There is, of course, a no-treatment group that is easy to formulate theoretically but harder to arrange in practice. Besides the ethical issue of withholding treatment from those in need, it is also difficult to keep people on a no-treatment basis. If they have to wait for a long period they may seek treatment elsewhere or refuse to comply with the demands of the study.

Another variant is a wait-list control group, in which individuals are promised therapy at some time in the future but are temporarily maintained as a control group.

Another aspect of this problem pertains to the fact that simply seeking and receiving some type of treatment from a healer may be responsible for much of the improvement the client perceives rather than the specific features of the therapy being given. For example, in the field of pharmacology a new drug may be compared with a placebo. If both the drug and the placebo result in similar degrees of improvement, then the improvement can be ascribed to the act of pill taking and the belief the patient has that he/she is receiving medication, rather than to the medication itself. A similar view has recently influenced the field of psychotherapy so that some researchers feel it is important to devise and use a special control group sometimes referred to as a "attention-placebo control group" (Gottman & Markman, 1978; Paul, 1967). In essence, this is a pseudo type of psychotherapy designed to look like therapy, but which is simply a more general discussion or contact with a therapist. A similar number of sessions is provided to control for the number of sessions in the "real" psychotherapy. One of the obvious difficulties here is devising a suitable and creditable placebo-attention control procedure.

Other problems in research have to do with selecting representative and clearly defined samples of particular kinds of behavioral disorders to be treated with clearly defined therapeutic procedures that may be particularly effective with these disorders. As already indicated, not all problems will necessarily respond to the same type of therapy. In the past, most of the psychotherapies, with the possible exception of the behavioral therapies, have been what the present writer has termed universal therapies. They were supposedly good for all disorders or a broad range of disorders. During the past decade or so, there has been an increasing recognition of this problem but much remains to be done in terms of future research. Our ultimate question is what kinds of therapeutic procedures are most effective when administered by what types of therapists to what kinds of patients?

Finally, something can be said about the types of therapists and clients used in research. We have already referred to some of the problems pertaining to the types of clients used in previous studies. An additional point has reference to the fact that many studies, particularly those involving behavior therapy, have used college students and volunteers, many of whom do not have serious pathology and who differ from the patients seen in actual clinical settings. In a similar fashion, a certain amount of research has been "analogue" research, that is, research procedures set up to resemble psychotherapy procedures but which are condensed and contrived versions of the latter. If these procedures and these clients are not comparable to those in "real life," then there is serious question concerning whether the results obtained can be applied to real clinical settings.

The issue of what kinds of psychotherapists are used in research studies is another aspect of this problem. In many studies student therapists and inexperienced therapists generally have been used, and again one may question whether this type of approach limits the value of the findings obtained. Since the adequacy of the therapist presumably may influence the results secured, this is not merely an academic question. Furthermore, some research has indicated a small but significant relationship between the length of the therapist's experience and the patient's continuation in psychotherapy (Baekeland & Lundwall, 1975).

Thus, research on psychotherapy is a complex matter and early research attempts were limited by many deficiencies. Nevertheless, the need for research is clearly apparent and researchers today, profiting from our previous experience, are more aware of the difficulties as well as more knowledgeable about the requisites of good research. While the difficulties remain, they are not insurmountable, and the level of research has improved in recent years (Garfield & Bergin, 1978). It has taken time for a greater acceptance of the need for sound research in psychotherapy to take hold, but progress has been made and we can anticipate that this will increase in the future. We can also expect that the diversity of schools of psychotherapy will diminish as research findings increase and we become more knowledgeable about what factors or procedures actually facilitate change in different groups of patients. The fact that we have so many different kinds of psychotherapy may well indicate, as it did in medicine, that we are at a very early stage of development and that when research demonstrates a truly effective treatment for particular kinds of problems, the less effective competing treatments will gradually disappear.

It is my view that psychotherapy is currently at an early stage of development. Once we know more about what procedures are truly effective or ineffective, we can begin to fashion fewer and more effective treatments for specific disorders. It is conceivable also that many of the apparently different psychotherapies of today may actually rely on the same variables for at least part of the success they claim to achieve. Instead of the specific aspects that each school emphasizes, it may well be that features that are *common to most approaches,* such as expectations for being helped, having someone to unburden oneself to in times of stress, being given some reasonable explanation for one's difficulties, being exposed to one's problems, and receiving suggestions and support for doing something about one's difficulties may actually be the variables of importance. A clearer specification and investigation of such variables may be of decided worth in advancing our knowledge of what is really therapeutic in psychotherapy.

In any event, while predictions and speculations may be of some interest, the final test or answer is what actually comes to happen. Optimism is based on some of the changes that have occurred in recent years in response to the need for psychotherapeutic services, as well as on the evident increase in both the quantity and quality of research. These do offer some reasonable hope for the future.

Summary

In this chapter I have discussed some of the developments that have taken place with regard to the psychological treatment of abnormal behavior. Particularly in the past 30 years or so, a number of interesting and important changes have occurred in the field of psychotherapy and behavior change. Not only has there been evident a greater interest in providing more abundant and efficient treatment resources for those in need, but there have also been some significant changes in conceptualizations and procedures in psychotherapy. The more traditional psychodynamic views of psychotherapy have appeared to decline in popularity and a number of newer and briefer therapies have emerged on the scene.

Along with the developments just mentioned, two other developments were also noted. One was the proliferation of psychotherapeutic approaches in recent years, many of which have received little or no systematic research appraisal. The other, in contrast to what has just been stated, was the gradual increase in the quantity and quality of research. In spite of the latter, we still have many gaps in our understanding of the psychotherapeutic process and there is a clear need for much additional and well designed research investigation to increase our knowledge of what variables really lead to positive change in psychotherapy.

Finally, a significant portion of the chapter described the complexities encountered in designing and carrying out systematic studies in psychotherapy. Some of the deficiencies in previous research were commented upon as well as some of the basic requisites required for evaluating psychotherapy. The view was advanced that psychotherapy is currently at an early stage of development, and that as we learn more about the conditions that facilitate change, we can expect the number of therapies in existence currently to gradually diminish. As practice becomes more solidly based on empirical evidence, we can also anticipate that the less effective therapeutic procedures will gradually be replaced by more effective ones.

GLOSSARY

Analogue research: Research carried out in a laboratory or other manipulated situation that attempts to reproduce in more isolated form the variables thought to be operating in the real life or clinical situation. In this way more control can be exerted over the variables of interest.

Attention-placebo: A designation used to describe a particular kind of control group in research on psychotherapy. Since the mere receiving of attention from a healer or being given a placebo (inert pill or medication) may have an effect on the client, the use of such a control group allows the investigator to compare these effects to those secured by the actual treatments being appraised.

Client-centered psychotherapy: An approach to psychotherapy developed by Carl R. Rogers that emphasizes the client's potentialities for change and the importance of the personal qualities of the therapist.

Clinical psychology: An area of specialization within the field of psychology primarily concerned with human adjustment and maladjustment. The clinical psychologist's activities include assessment, psychotherapy, and research on abnormal behavior.

Counseling psychology: As differentiated from clinical psychology, a speciality within psychology that is more concerned with "normal" problems of adjustment than with disordered behavior. Traditionally also concerned with educational and vocational problems, but there is considerable overlap with clinical psychology in terms of psychological treatment.

Eclecticism: Refers to the use or amalgamation of different theoretical views or procedures instead of adhering to only one view or set of procedures.

Global ratings of outcome: Generally refers to a single overall judgment or rating of outcome made at the end of therapy. Usually, terms such as recovered, very much improved, and improved are used.

Marathon groups: A form of encounter or quasi-therapy group that meets for a sustained period of time, most frequently over a weekend with time off for meals and sleep.

Placebo response: This initially had reference to the response of the individual to the administration of a pill or medicine that was pharmacologically inert or inactive. The meaning has been broadened to include responses influenced by factors other than the specific treatment being administered. In medicine, responses caused by interpersonal or psychological variables may be termed placebo responses.

Psychiatry: The specialty area of medicine concerned with nervous and mental "disease." Psychiatrists in their activities overlap those performed by clinical psychologists to some degree, but as physicians, psychiatrists can utilize drugs and somatic treatments.

Reliability: Usually refers to the consistency of measures or evaluation techniques. A reliable measure is one that gives consistent results.

Substitute symptoms: Supposedly, symptoms that appear because treatment has been directed at the presenting symptoms of the client and not at the underlying causes of the symptoms. Research data tend not to give it much support.

Time-limited psychotherapy: Usually brief psychotherapy in which the number of sessions is fixed and announced to the client at the beginning of therapy.

Universal therapies: A term used by the present author to designate psychotherapies that overtly or by implication claim to be effective for almost all psychosocial disorders.

Validity: In reference to methods of appraisal, pertains to how well a given measure actually measures what it is supposed to measure.

REFERENCES

Chapter 1

Angel, C., Leach, B.E., Martens, S., Cohen, M., & Heath, R. Serum oxidation tests in schizophrenic and normal subjects. *Archives of Neurology and Psychiatry,* 1957, *78,* 500–504.

Ban, T. *Recent advances in the biology of schizophrenia.* Springfield, Ill.: Charles C Thomas, 1973.

Bateson, G., Jackson, D.D., Haley, J., & Weakland, J. Toward a theory of schizophrenia. *Behavioral Science,* 1956, *1,* 251–264.

Braginsky, B.M., Braginsky, D.D., & Ring, K. *Methods of madness: The mental hospital as a last resort.* New York: Holt, Rinehart, & Winston, 1969.

Buss, A.H. *Psychopathology.* New York: Wiley, 1966.

Caldwell, B.M. The effects of infant care. In M.L. Hoffman & L.W. Hoffman (Eds.), *Review of child development research* (Volume 1). New York: Russell Sage Foundation, 1964.

Durkheim, E. Anomic types of suicide. In S.N. Eisenstadt (Ed.), *Comparative social problems.* New York: Free Press, 1964.

Ferster, C.B. Classification of behavioral pathology. In L. Krasner & L.P. Ullmann (Eds.), *Research in behavior modification.* New York: Holt, Rinehart, & Winston, 1965.

Fontana, A. Familial etiology of schizophrenia: Is a scientific methodology possible? *Psychological Bulletin,* 1966, *66,* 214–227.

Greenberg, D.J., Scott, S.B., Pisa, A., & Friesen, D.D. Beyond the token economy: A comparison of two contingency programs. *Journal of Consulting and Clinical Psychology,* 1975, *43,* 498–503.

Hall, C.S., & Lindzey, G. *Theories of personality* (2nd edition). New York: Wiley, 1970.

Hersen, M. Historical perspectives in behavioral assessment. In M. Hersen & A.S. Bellack (Eds.), *Behavioral assessment: A practical handbook.* Oxford: Pergamon, 1976.

Heston, L.L. Psychiatric disorders in foster home reared childred of schizophrenic mothers. *British Journal of Psychiatry,* 1966, *112,* 819–825.

Hovey, H.B. The questionable vaidity of some assumed antecedents of mental illness. *Journal of Clinical Psychology,* 1959, *15,* 270–272.

Jahode, M. Toward a social psychology of mental health. In A.M. Rose (Ed.), *Mental health and mental disorder.* New York: Norton, 1955.

Jahoda, M. *Current concepts of positive mental health.* New York: Basic Books, 1958.

Katz, M.M., Cole, J.O., & Lowery, H.A. Nonspecificity of diagnosis of paranoid schizophrenia. *Archives of General Psychiatry,* 1964, *11,* 197–202.

Kazdin, A.E. Assessing the clinical or applied significance of behavior change through social validation. *Behavior Modification,* 1977, *1,* 427–452.

Kazdin, A.E., & Wilson, G.T. *Evaluation of behavior therapy: Issues, evidence, and research strategies.* Cambridge, Mass.: Ballinger, 1978.

Kent, R.N., & O'Leary, K.D. A controlled evaluation of behavior modification with conduct problem children. *Journal of Consulting and Clinical Psychology,* 1976, *44,* 586–596.

Kety, S.S., Rosenthal, D., Wender, P.H., & Schulsinger, F. Mental illness in the biological and adoptive families of adopted schizophrenics. *American Journal of Psychiatry,* 1971, *128,* 302–306.

Lejeune, J. Down's syndrome explained as error in meiotic process. *Roche Reports,* 1970, *7,* 1–2.

Mosher, L.R., & Gunderson, J.G. Special report: Schizophrenia, 1972. *Schizophrenia Bulletin,* 1973, *7,* 12–52.

Nathan, P.E. Alcoholism. In H. Leitenberg (Ed.), *Handbook of behavior modification and behavior therapy.* Englewood Cliffs, N.J.: Prentice-Hall, 1976.

Nunnally, J.C., Jr. *Popular conceptions of mental health.* New York: Holt, Rinehart, & Winston, 1961.

Rogers, C.R. *Counseling and psychotherapy.* Boston: Houghton Mifflin, 1942.

Rogers, C.R. *Client-centered therapy.* Boston: Houghton Mifflin, 1951.

Salzinger, K. *Schizophrenia: Behavioral aspects.* New York: Wiley, 1973.

Scheff, T.J. *Being mentally ill: A sociological theory.* Chicago: Aldine, 1966.

Scott, W.A. Research definitions of mental health and illness. *Psychological Bulletin,* 1958, *55,* 29–45.

Sewell, W.H. Infant training and the personality of the child. *American Journal of Sociology,* 1952, *58,* 150–159.

Sloane, R.B., Staples, F.R., Cristol, A.H., Yorkston, N.J., & Whipple, K. *Psychotherapy versus behavior therapy.* Cambridge, Mass.: Harvard University Press, 1975.

Srole, L., Langner, T.S., Michael, S.T., Opler, M.K., & Rennie, T.A.C. *Mental health in the metropolis: The midtown Manhattan study.* New York: McGraw-Hill, 1962.

Szasz, T.S. *The myth of mental illness: Foundations of a theory of personal conduct.* New York: Hoeber-Harper, 1961.

Weschsler, H., Solomon, L., & Kramer, B.M. (Eds.), *Social psychology and mental health.* New York: Holt, Rinehart, & Winston, 1970.

Zilboorg, G., & Henry, G. *A history of medical psychology.* New York: Norton, 1941.

Zubin, J. Classification of the behavior disorders. In P.R. Farnsworth, O. McNemar, & Q. McNemar (Eds.), *Annual review of psychology* (Vol. 18). Palo Alto, Calif.: Annual Reviews, 1967.

Chapter 2

Alexander, F.G., & Selesnick, S.T. *The history of psychiatry: An evaluation of psychiatric thought and practice from prehistoric times to the present.* New York: Harper & Row, 1966.

Blashfield, R.K., & Draguns, J.G. Evaluative criteria for psychiatric classification. *Journal of Abnormal Psychology,* 1976, *85,* 140–150.

Brill, H. Psychiatric diagnosis, nomenclature, and classification. In B.B. Wolman (Ed.), *Handbook of clinical psychology.* New York: McGraw-Hill, 1965.

Caplan, R.B. *Psychiatry and the community in nineteenth century America.* New York: Basic Books, 1969.

Feighner, J.P., Robins, E., Guze, S.B., Woodruff, R.A., Winokur, G., & Munoz, R. Diagnostic criteria for use in psychiatric research. *Archives of General Psychiatry,* 1972, *26,* 57–63.

Freedman, A.M., Kaplan, H.I., & Sadock, B.J. *Modern synopsis of comprehensive textbook of psychiatry.* Baltimore: Williams & Wilkins, 1972.

Hoch, P.H., & Zubin, J. (Eds.). *Current problems in psychiatric diagnosis.* New York: Grune & Stratton, 1953.

Howells, J.G. (Ed.). *World history of psychiatry.* New York: Brunner/Mazel, 1975.

Hunt, W.A., Wittson, C.L., & Hunt, E.B. Military performance of a group of marginal neuropsychiatric cases. *American Journal of Psychiatry,* 1952, *109,* 168–171.

Hunt, W.A., Wittson, C.L., & Hunt, E.B. A theoretical and practical analysis of the diagnostic process. In P.H. Hoch & J. Zubin (Eds.). *Current problems in psychiatric diagnosis.* New York: Grune & Stratton, 1953.

Laing, R.D. *The politics of experience.* London: Pelican Books, 1967.

Matarazzo, J.D. The interview: Its reliability and validity in psychiatric diagnosis. In B.B. Wolman (Ed.), *Clinical diagnosis of mental disorders: A handbook.* New York: Plenum, 1979.

Meehl, P. Schizotaxia, schizotypy, schizophrenia. *American Psychologist,* 1962, *17,* 827–838.

Murphy, J.M. Psychiatric labeling in cross-cultural perspective. *Science,* 1976, *191,* 1019–1028.

Neaman, J.S. *Suggestion of the devil, the origins of madness.* Garden City, N.Y.: Anchor Press/Doubleday, 1975.

Plato (Timaeus). In *Plato, Timaeus, and Critias.* (H.D.V. Lee, trans.) London: Penguin Books, 1971.

Reisman, J.M. A history of clinical psychology. New York: Wiley, 1976.

Rogers, C. *Client-centered therapy.* Boston: Riverside Press, 1951.

Smith, S. (Ed.), *Psychological testing and the Mind of the Tester.* Proceedings of the scientific conference held in honor of the Menninger Foundation's 50th anniversary, Oct 10–11, 1975; *Bulletin of the Menninger Clinic,* 1976, *40.*, 565–572.

Spitzer, R.L., Sheeney, M., & Endicott, J. DMS-III: Guiding principles. In V.M. Rakoff, H.C. Stancer, & H.B. Kedward (Eds.), *Psychiatric diagnosis.* New York: Brunner/Mazel, 1977.

Sokal, R.R. Classification: Purposes, principles, progress, prospects. *Science,* 1974, *185,* 1115–1123.

Stainbrook, E. Some historical determinants of contemporary diagnostic and etiological thinking in psychiatry. In P.H. Hoch & J. Zubin (Eds.), *Current problems in psychiatric diagnosis.* Grune & Stratton, 1953.

Szasz, T.S. *The myth of mental illness: Foundations of a theory of personal conduct.* New York: Hoeber-Harper, 1961.

Szasz, T.S. *Law, liberty, and psychiatry.* New York: Macmillan, 1963.

Townsend, J.J. Labeling theory. *Science,* 1977, *1966,* 480–482.

Zilboorg, G., & Henry, G.W. *A history of medical psychology.* New York: Norton, 1941.

Zubin, J., Salzinger, K., Fleiss, J.L., Gurland, B., Spitzer, R.L., Endicott, J., & Sutton, S. Biometric approach to psychopathology. *Annual Review of Psychology,* 1975, *26,* 621–671.

Chapter 3

Agras, S., Sylvester, D., & Oliveau, D. The epidemiology of common fears and phobias. *Comprehensive Psychiatry,* 1969, *10,* 151–156.

Allen, M.G. Twin studies of affective illness. *Archives of General Psychiatry,* 1976, *33,* 1476–1478.

Austin, N.K., Liberman, R.P., King, L.W., & DeRisi, W.J. A comparative evaluation of two day hospitals. *Journal of Nervous and Mental Disease,* 1976, *163,* 253–262.

Beck, A.T., Ward, C.H., Mendelsohn, M., Mock, J., & Erbaugh, J. An inventory for measuring depression. *Archives of General Psychiatry,* 1961, *4,* 561–571.

Bornstein, M.R., Bellack, A.S., & Hersen, M. Social-skills training for unassertive children: A multiple-baseline analysis. *Journal of Applied Behavior Analysis,* 1977, *10,* 183–196.

Coble, P., Foster, F.G., & Kupfer, D.J. Electroencephalographic sleep diagnosis of primary depression. *Archives of General Psychiatry,* 1976, *33,* 1124–1127.

Eisler, R.M., Hersen, M., Miller, P.M., & Blanchard, E.B. Situational determinants of assertive behaviors. *Journal of Consulting and Clinical Psychology,* 1975, *43,* 330–340.

Elkin, T.E., Hersen, M., Eisler, R.M., & Williams, J.G. Modification of caloric intake in anorexia nervosa: An experimental analysis. *Psychological Reports,* 1973, *32,* 75–78.

Epstein, L.H., Hersen, M., & Hemphill, D.P. Music feedback as a treatment for tension headache: An experimental case study. *Journal of Behavior Therapy and Experimental Psychiatry,* 1974, *5,* 59–63.

Geer, J.H. The development of a scale to measure fear. *Behaviour Research and Therapy,* 1965, *3,* 45–53.

Goodwin, D.W., Schulsinger, F., Hermansen, L., Guze, S.B., & Winokur, G. Alcoholic problems in adoptees raised apart from alcoholic biological parents. *Archives of General Psychiatrty, 1973, 28,* 238–243.

Hall, R.V., Fox, R., Willard, D., Goldsmith, L., Emerson, M., Owen, M., Davis, F., & Porcia, E. The teacher as observer and experimenter in the modification of disputing and talking-out behaviors. *Journal of Applied Behavior Analysis,* 1971, *4,* 141–149.

Hathaway, S.R., & McKinley, J.C. *Minnesota Multiphasic Personality Inventory: Manual for administration and scoring.* New York: Psychological Corporation, 1967.

Hersen, M. Personality characteristics of nightmare sufferers. *Journal of Nervous and Mental Disease,* 1971, *153,* 27–31 (a).

Hersen, M. Fear scale norms for an inpatient

population. *Journal of Clinical Psychology,* 1971, *27,* 375–378 (b).

Hersen, M., & Barlow, D.H. *Single-case experimental designs: Strategies for studying behavior change.* New York: Pergamon, 1976.

Hersen, M., & Bellack, A.S. (Eds.). *Behavioral assessment: A practical handbook.* NewYork: Pergamon, 1976.

Hersen, M., Levine, J., & Church, A. Parameters of the spiral affect-effect in organics, schizophrenics, and normals. *Journal of Genetic Psychology,* 1972, *120,* 177–187.

Hersen, M., Miller, P.M., & Eisler, R.M. Interactions between alcoholics and their wives: A descriptive analysis of verbal and nonverbal behavior. *Quarterly Journal of Studies on Alcohol,* 1973, *34,* 516–520.

Hogarty, G.E. Informant ratings of community adjustment. In I.E. Waskow & M.B. Parloff (Eds.), *Psychotherapy change measures: Report of the clinical research branch, NIMH outcome measures project.* Washington, D.C.: U.S. Government Printing Office, 1975.

Hollingshead, A.B., & Redlich, F.C. *Social class and mental illness.* New York: Wiley, 1958.

Holzman, P.S., Kringlen, E., Levy, D.L., Proctor, L.R., Haberman, S.J., & Yasillo, N.J. Abnormal-pursuit eye movements in schizophrenia: Evidence for a genetic indicator. *Archives of General Psychiatry,* 1977, *34,* 802–805.

Katkin, E.S., & Hoffman, L.S. Sex differences and self-report of fear: A psychophysiological assessment. *Journal of Abnormal Psychology,* 1976, *85,* 607–610.

Katz, M., & Lyerly, S. Methods of measuring adjustment and social behavior in the community: I. Rationale, description, discriminative validity and scale development. *Psychological Reports,* 1963, *13,* 503–535.

Kazdin, A.E. Statistical analysis for single case experimental designs. In M. Hersen & D.H. Barlow, *Single-case experimental designs: Strategies for studying behavior change.* New York: Pergamon, 1976.

Kazdin, A.E. Assessing the clinical or applied importance of behavior change through social validation. *Behavior Modification,* 1977, *1,* 427–452.

Kupfer, D.J., Foster, F.G., Detre, T.P., & Himmelhoch, J. Sleep EEG and motor activity as indicators in affective states. *Neuropsychobiology,* 1975, *1,* 296–303.

Lacey, J.I. The evaluation of autonomic responses: Toward a general solution. *Annals of the New York Academy of Sciences,* 1956, *67,* 123–164.

Lacey, J.I. & Van Lehn, R. Differential emphasis in somatic response to stress. *Psychosomatic Medicine,* 1952, *4,* 71–81.

Langner, T.S., & Michael, S.T. *Life stress and mental health.* New York: Macmillan, 1963.

Liberman, R.P., Teigen, J., Patterson, R., & Baker, V. Reducing delusional speech in chronic paranoid schizophrenics. *Journal of Applied Behavior Analysis,* 1973, *6,* 57–64.

Lubin, B. Adjective checklists for the measurement of depression. *Archives of General Psychiatry,* 1965, *12,* 57–62.

Matarazzo, J.D. *Wechsler's measurement and appraisal of adult intelligence.* Baltimore: Williams & Wilkins, 1972.

Miller, P.M., Hersen, M., Eisler, R.M., & Hilsman, G. Effects of social stress on operant drinking of alcoholics and social drinkers. *Behaviour Research and Therapy,* 1974, *12,* 65–72.

Miller, P.M., Hersen, M., Eisler, R.M., & Watts, J.G. Contingent reinforcement of lowered blood/alcoholic levels in an outpatient chronic alcoholic. *Behaviour Research and Therapy,* 1974, *12,* 261–263.

Mills, H.L., Agras, W.S., Barlow, D.H., & Mills, J.R. Compulsive rituals treated by response prevention: An experimental analysis. *Archives of General Psychiatry,* 1973, *28,* 524–529.

O'Connor, R.D. Relative efficacy of modeling, shaping, and the combined procedures for modification of social withdrawal. *Journal of Abnormal Psychology,* 1972, *79,* 327–334.

Reich, L., Weiss, B.L., Coble, P., McPartland, R., & Kupfer, D.J. Sleep disturbance in schizophrenia. *Archives of General Psychiatry,* 1975, *32,* 51–55.

Rosenthal, R. *Experimenter effects in behavioral research.* New York: Appleton-Century-Crofts, 1966.

Saccuzzo, D.P., & Miller, S. Critical interstimulus interval in delusional schizophrenics and normals. *Journal of Abnormal Psychology,* 1977, *86,* 261–266.

Sloane, R.B., Staples, F.R., Cristol, A.H., Yorkston, N.J., & Whipple, K. Patient characteristics and outcome in psychotherapy and behavior therapy. *Journal of Consulting and Clinical Psychology,* 1976, *44,* 330–339.

Spitzer, R.L., & Endicott, J. Assessment of outcome by independent clinical evaluators. In

I.E. Waskow & M.B. Parloff (Eds.), *Psychotherapy change measures: Report of the clinical research branch, NIMH outcome measures project.* Washington, D.C.: U.S. Government Printing Office, 1975.

Stabenau, J.R. Genetic and other factors in schizophrenic, manic-depressive, and schizoaffective psychoses. *Journal of Nervous and Mental Disease,* 1977, *164,* 149–167.

Turner, S.M. Hersen, M., & Alford, H. Effects of massed practice and meprobamate on spasmodic torticollis: An experimental analysis. *Behaviour Research and Therapy,* 1974, *12,* 259–260.

Winer, B.I. *Statistical principles in experimental design.* New York: McGraw-Hill, 1962.

Wolpe, J., & Lazarus, A.A. *Behavior therapy techniques.* New York: Pergamon, 1966.

Chapter 4

Asarnow, R.F., Steffy, R.A., MacCrimmon, D.J., & Cleghorn, J.M. An attentional assessment of foster children at risk for schizophrenia. *Journal of Abnormal Psychology,* 1977, *86,* 267–275.

Baekgaard, W., Nyborg, H., & Nielsen, J. Neuroticism and extraversion in Turner's Syndrome. *Journal of Abnormal Psychology, 1978, 87,* 583–586.

Federman, D.D. *Abnormal sexual development.* Philadelphia: Saunders, 1967.

Fischer, M. Psychoses in the offspring of schizophrenic monozygotic twins and their normal co-twins. *British Journal of Psychiatry,* 1971, *118,* 43–52.

Fulker, D.W. A biometrical genetic approach to intelligence and schizophrenia. *Social Biology,* 1973, *20,* 266–270.

Gottesman, I.I., & Shields, J. Contributions of twin studies to perspectives on schizophrenia. In B.A. Maher (Ed.), *Progress in experimental personality research* (Vol.3). New York: Academic Press, 1966.

Hampson, J.J. Determinants of psychosexual orientation. In F.A. Beach (Ed.), *Sex and behavior.* New York: Wiley, 1965.

Hampson, J.L., Hampson, J.G., & Money, J. The syndrome of gonadal dysgenesis (ovarian agenesis) and male chromosomal pattern in girls and women: Psychologic studies. *Bulletin Johns Hopkins Hospital,* 1955, *97,* 207–226.

Harvey, J., Judge, C., & Wiener, S. Familial X-linked mental retardation with an X chromosome abnormality. *Journal of Medical Genetics,* 1977, *14,* 46–50.

Heston, L.L., & Denny, D. Interactions between early life experience and biological factors in schizophrenia. In D. Rosenthal & S.S. Kety (Eds.), *The transmission of schizophrenia.* New York: Pergamon, 1968.

Horn, J.M., Loehlin, J.C., & Willerman, L. IQ correlations obtained in the Texas Adoption Study. Cited in J.C. DeFries & R. Plomin, Behavioral genetics. *Annual Review of Psychology,* 1978, *29,* 496.

Horn, J.M., Willerman, L., & Loehlin, J.C. *Heritability of intelligence: Evidence from the Texas Adoption Project.* Presented at annual meetings of the Behavior Genetics Association, Louisville, Ky., April 1977.

Hsai, D.Y.Y. The hereditary metabolic diseases. In J. Hirsch (Ed.), *Behavior genetic analysis.* New York: McGraw-Hill, 1967.

Huntley, R.M.C. Heritability of intelligence. In J.E. Meade & A.S. Parkes (Eds.), *Genetic and environmental factors in human ability.* Edinburgh, Scotland: Oliver & Boyd, 1966.

Karlsson, J.L. *The biologic basis of schizophrenia.* Springfield, Ill.: Charles C Thomas, 1966.

Kety, S.S., Rosenthal, D., Wender, P.H., & Schulsinger, F. The types and prevalence of mental illness in the biological and adoptive families of adopted schizophrenics. In D. Rosenthal & S.S. Kety (Eds.), *The transmission of schizophrenia.* New York: Pergamon, 1968.

Kety, S.S., Rosenthal, D., Wender, P.H., Schulsinger, F., & Jacobsen, B. Mental illness in the biological and adaptive families of adopted individuals who have become schizophrenic: A preliminary report based on psychiatric interviews. In R.R. Fieve, D. Rosenthal, & H. Brill (Eds.), *Genetic research in psychiatry.* Baltimore: Johns Hopkins University Press, 1975.

Lehrke, R.G. Sex-linkage: A biological basis for greater male variability in intelligence. In R.T. Osborne, C.E. Noble, & N. Wegl (Eds.), *Human variation: The biopsychology of age, race, and sex.* New York: Academic Press, 1978.

Lyle, O.E., & Gottesman, I.I. Premorbid psychometric indicators of the gene for Huntington's Disease. *Journal of Consulting and Clinical Psychology,* 1977, *45,* 1011–1022.

Macalpine, I., & Hunter, R. The "insanity" of King George III: A classic case of porphyria. *British Medical Journal,* 1966, *1,* 65–71.

Macalpine, I., & Hunter, R. Porphyria and King George III. *Scientific American,* 1969, *221,* 38–46.

Macalpine, I., Hunter, R., & Rimington, C. Porphyria in the royal houses of Stuart, Hanover, and Prussia: A follow-up study of George III's illness. *British Medical Journal,* 1968, *1,* 7–18.

Meehl, P.E. Schizotaxia, schizotypy, schizophrenia. *American Psychologist,* 1962, *17,* 827–838.

Money, J. Psychosexual differentiation. In J. Money (Ed.), *Sex research: New developments.* New York: Holt, Rinehart, & Winston, 1965.

Money, J. Cognitive deficits in Turner's Syndrome. In S.G. Vandenberg (Ed.), *Progress in human behavior genetics.* Baltimore: Johns Hopkins University Press, 1968.

Munsinger, H. The adopted child's IQ: A critical review. *Psychological Bulletin,* 1975, *82,* 623–659.

Myrianthropolus, N.C. Huntington's chorea. *Journal of Medical Genetics,* 1966, *3,* 298–314.

Neale, J.M., McIntyre, C.W., Fox, R., & Cromwell, R.L. Span of apprehension in acute schizophrenics. *Journal of Abnormal Psychology,* 1969, *74,* 593–596.

Nielsen, J., Nyborg, H., & Dahl. G. *Turner's Syndrome Acta Jutlandica* (Medicine Series 21, Aarhus Universitet), 1977, *65.*

Nyborg, H., & Nielsen, J. Sex chromosome abnormalities and cognitive performance: III. Field dependence, frame dependence and failing development of perceptual stability in girls with Turner's Syndrome. *Journal of Psychology,* 1977, *96,* 205–211.

Pollin, W. The pathogenesis of schizophrenia. *Archives of General Psychiatry,* 1972, *27,* 29–37.

Porter, I.H. *Heredity and disease.* New York: McGraw-Hill, 1968.

Potegal, M. A note on spatial-motor deficits inpatients with Huntington's Disease: A test of hypothesis. *Neuropsychologia,* 1971, *9,* 233–235.

Rose, R.J. In search of schizotypy: Heritable variation in the span of apprehension. Unpublished manuscript, Indiana University, 1978.

Rose, R.J., Harris, E.L., Christian, J.C., & Nance, W.E. Genetic variance in nonverbal intelligence: Evidence from the MZ half-sib model. *Science,* 1979, *205,* 1153–1154.

Rosenthal, D. *Genetic theory and abnormal behavior.* New York: McGraw-Hill, 1970.

Rosenthal, D., Wender, P.H., Kety, S.S., Schulsinger, F., Welner, J., & Ostergaard, L. Schizophrenics' offspring reared in adoptive homes. In D. Rosenthal & S.S. Kety (Eds.), *The transmission of schizophrenia.* New York: Pergamon, 1968.

Shields, F., & Slater, E. Genetic aspects of schizophrenia. *British Journal of Hospital Medicine,* 1967, *1,* 579–591.

Slater, E. A review of earlier evidence on genetic factors in schizophrenia. In D. Rosenthal & S.S. Kety (Eds.), *The transmission of schizophrenia.* New York: Pergamon, 1968.

Slater, E., & Cowie, V.A. *The genetics of mental disorders.* London: Oxford University Press, 1971.

Witkin, H.A., & Mednick, S. Criminality in XYY and XXY men. *Science,* 1976, *193,* 547–555.

Zerbin-Rudin, E. Endogene Psychosen. In P.E. Becker (Ed.), *Human Genetik, ein kurses Handbuck* (Vol.2). Stuttgart, W. Germany: Thieme, 1967.

Chapter 5

Abel, E.L. *Drugs and behavior: A primer in neuropsychopharmacology.* New York: Wiley, 1974.

Goth, A. *Medical pharmacology.* St. Louis: C.V. Mosley, 1974.

Guyton, A.C. *Textbook of medical physiology,* 4th Ed., Philadelphia: W.B. Saunders, 1971.

Milner, P.M. *Physiological psychology.* New York: Holt, Rinehart & Winston, 1970.

Morgan, C.T. *Physiological psychology.* New York: McGraw-Hill, 1965.

Morgan, C.T., & Stellar, E. *Physiological psychology.* New York: McGraw-Hill, 1965.

Stevens, C.F. *Neurophysiology: A primer.* New York: Wiley, 1966.

Chapter 6

Andrew, R.J. The origin and evolution of the calls and facial expressions of the primates. *Behavior,* 1963, *20,* 1–109.

Arco, C.M.B. *Response-dependent and response-independent social stimulation of neonatal social visual behavior.* Unpublished masters thesis, West Virginia University, 1977.

Arglye, M. & Dean, J. Eye contact, distance, and affiliation. *Sociometry,* 1965, *28,* 289–304.

Baer, D.M. The control of developmental processes: Why wait? In J.R. Nesselroade & H.W. Reese (Eds.), *Life-span developmental psychology: Methodological issues.* New York: Academic Press, 1973.

Baer, D.M., Rowbury, T.G., & Goetz, E.M. Behavioral traps in the preschool: A proposal for research. In A.D. Pick (Ed.), *Minnesota symposia on child psychology* (Vol.10). Minneapolis: University of Minnesota Press, 1976.

Baltes, P.B., Reese, H.W., & Nesselroade, J.R. *Life-span developmental psychology: Introduction to research methods.* Monterey, Calif.: Brooks/Cole, 1977.

Bijou, S.W., & Baer, D.M. *Child development: II. Universal stage of infancy.* New York: Appleton-Century-Crofts, 1965.

Bloom, L., Lightbrown, P., & Hood, L. Structure and variation in child language. *Monographs of the Society for Research in Child Development* 1975 *40,* (2, Serial No. 160).

Bowes, W.A., Jr., Brackbill, Y., Conway, E., & Steinschneider, A. The effects of obstetrical medication on fetus and infant. *Monographs of the Society for Research in Child Development,* 1970, *35,* (4, Serial No. 137).

Brackbill, Y. Extinction of the smiling response in infants as a function of reinforcement schedule. *Child Development,* 1958, *29,* 115–124.

Braine, M.D.S. The ontogeny of English phrase structure: The first phase. *Language,* 1963, *39,* 1–13.

Braine, M.D.S. Children's first word combinations. *Monographs of the Society for Research in Child Development,* 1976, *41,* (1, Serial No. 164).

Braine, M.D.S., Heimer, C.B., Wortis, H., & Freedman, A.M. Factors associated with impairment of the early development of prematures. *Monographs of the Society for Research in Child Development,* 1966, *31,* (4, Serial No. 106).

Brainerd, C.J. Judgments and explanations as criteria for the presence of cognitive structures. *Psychological Bulletin,* 1973, *79,* 172–179.

Brainerd, C.J. Postmortem on judgments, explanations, and Piagetian cognitive structures. *Psychological Bulletin,* 1974, *81,* 70–71.

Brown, A.L. The development of memory: Knowing, knowing about knowing, and knowing how to know. In H.W. Reese (Ed.), *Advances in child development and behavior* (Vol. 10). New York: Academic Press, 1975.

Brown, A.L. Development, schooling, and the acquisition of knowledge about knowledge. In R.C. Anderson, R.J. Spiro, & W.E. Montague (Eds.), *Schooling and the acquisition of knowledge.* Hillsdale, N.J.: Lawrence Erlbaum Associates, 1978. (Cited in M. Perlmutter & G. Lange A developmental analysis of recall-recognition distinctions. In P.A. Ornstein (Ed.), *Memory development in children.* Hillsdale, N.J.: Lawrence Erlbaum Associates, 1978.)

Brown, R., & Fraser, C. The acquisition of syntax. In U. Bellugi & R. Brown (Eds.), The acquisition of language. *Monographs of the Society for Research in Child Development,* 1964, *29* (1,Whole No. 92), 43–79.

Butterfield, E.C., Wambold, C., & Belmont, J.M. On the theory and practice of improving short-term memory. *American Journal of Mental Deficiency,* 1973, *77,* 654–669.

Chandler, M.J. Social cognition: A selective review of current research. In W.F. Overton & J.M. Gallagher (Eds,), *Knowledge and development: I. Advances in research and theory.* New York: Plenum, 1977.

Chandler, M.J., Seifer, R., & Woffey, E. *Black and white magic: The "extinction" of conserving responses as a function of experimenter credibility.* Paper presented at the annual meeting of the Piaget Society, Philadelphia, June 1977.

Eimas, P.D. Attentional processes (with editorial insertions). In H.W. Reese & L.P. Lipsitt (Eds.), *Experimental child psychology.* New York: Academic Press, 1970.

Eimas, P.D. Speech perception in early infancy. In L.B. Cohen & P. Salapatek (Eds.), *Infant perception: From sensation to cognition.* New York: Academic Press, 1975.

Eimas, P.D., & Tartter, V.C. On the development of speech perception: Mechanisms and analogies. In H.W. Reese & L.P. Lipsitt (Eds.), *Advances in child development and behavior* (Vol. 13). New York: Academic Press, 1978.

Elkind, D. Cognitive development. In H.W. Reese & L.P. Lipsitt (Eds.), *Experimental child psychology.* New York: Academic Press, 1970.

Endler, N.S., Boulter, L.R., & Osser, H. Infancy, early experience, and critical periods: Introduction and commentary. In N.S. Endler, L.R. Boulter, & H. Osser (Eds.), *Contemporary issues in developmental psychology*

(2nd ed.). New York: Holt, Rinehart, & Winston, 1976.

Erikson, E.H. *Childhood and society* (2nd ed.). New York: Norton, 1963.

Etzel, B.C., Leblanc, J.M., & Baer, D.M. Preface. In B.C. Etzel, J.M. LeBlanc, & D.M. Baer (Eds.), *New developments in behavioral research: Theory, method, and application.* Hillsdale, N.J.: Lawrence Erlbaum Associates, 1977.

Fitzgerald, H.E., & Brackbill, Y. Classical conditioning in infancy: Development and constraints. *Psychological Bulletin,* 1976, *83,* 353–376.

Flavell, J.H. Developmental studies of mediated memory. In H.W. Reese & L.P. Lipsitt (Eds.), *Advances in child development and behavior* (Vol.5). New York: Academic Press, 1970.

Flavell, J.H. *Cognitive development.* Englewood Cliffs, N.J.: Prentice-Hall, 1977.

Gesell, A. The ontogenesis of infant behavior. In L. Carmichael (Ed.), *Manual of child psychology* (2nd ed.). New York: Wiley, 1954.

Hagen, J.W., Jongeward, R.H., Jr., & Kail, R.V., Jr. Cognitive perspectives on the development of memory. In H.W. Reese (Ed.), *Advances in child development and behavior* (Vol. 10). New York: Academic Press, 1975.

Hayhurst, H. Some errors of young children in producing passive sentences. *Journal of Verbal Learning and Verbal Behavior,* 1967, *6,* 634–640.

Herrera, G. Effects of nutritional supplementation and early education on physical and cognitive development. In R.R. Turner & H.W. Reese (Eds.), *Life-span developmental psychology: Intervention.* New York: Academic Press, 1978.

Hunter, W.S. The delayed reaction in animals and children. *Behavior Monographs,* 1913, *2* (1, Whole No. 6).

Jonas, G. *Stuttering: The disorder of many theories.* New York: Farrar, Straus & Giroux, 1977.

Katchadourian, H. *The biology of adolescence.* San Francisco: Freeman, 1977.

Kaye, H. Sensory processes. In H.W. Reese & L.P. Lipsitt (Eds.), *Experimental child psychology.* New York: Academic Press, 1970.

Kendler, T.S. An ontogeny of mediational deficiency. *Child Development,* 1972, *43,* 1–17.

Kendler, T.S., & Kendler, H.H. Experimental analysis of inferential behavior in children. In L.P. Lipsitt & C.C. Spiker (Eds.), *Advances in child development and behavior* (Vol.3). New York: Academic Press, 1967.

Klein, R.E. *Malnutrition, poverty, and the development of mental abilities in rural eastern Guatemala.* Paper presented at the meeting of the International Society for the Study of Behavioural Development, Guildford, England, July 1975.

Kohlberg, L. Continuities in childhood and adult moral development revisited. In P.B. Baltes & K.W. Schaie (Eds.), *Life-span developmental psychology: Personality and socialization.* New York: Academic Press, 1973.

Kron, R.E. Instrumental conditioning of nutritive sucking behavior in the newborn. *Recent Advances in Biological Psychiatry,* 1966, *9,* 295–300.

Levine, M. (Ed.). *A cognitive theory of learning.* Hillsdale, N.J.: Lawrence Erlbaum Associates, 1975.

Lipsitt, L.P., & Reese, H.W. *Child development.* Glenview, Ill.: Scott, Foresman, 1978.

McAllister, D.E. The effects of various kinds of relevant verbal pretraining on subsequent motor performance. *Journal of Experimental Psychology,* 1953, *46,* 329–336.

McCandless, B.R. Socialization. In H.W. Reese & L.P. Lipsitt (Eds.), *Experimental child psychology.* New York: Academic Press, 1970.

McCandless, B.R., & Trotter, R.J. *Children: Behavior and development* (3rd ed.) . New York: Holt, Rinehart & Winston, 1977.

Millar, W.S. Operant acquisition of social behaviors in infancy: Basic problems and constraints. In H.W. Reese (Ed.), *Advances in child development and behavior* (Vol. 11). New York: Academic Press, 1976.

Miller, S.A. Extinction of Piagetian concepts: An updating. *Merrill-Palmer Quarterly,* 1976, *22,* 257–281.

Miller, W., & Ervin, S. The development of grammar in child language. In U. Bellugi & R. Brown (Eds.), The acquisition of language. *Monographs of the Society for the Research in Child Development,* 1964, *29*(1, Whole No. 92), 9–34.

Moore, R.Y. Mental impairment. In H.W. Reese & L.P. Lipsitt (Eds.), *Experimental child psychology.* New York: Academic Press, 1970.

Mussen, P.H., Conger, J.J., & Kagan, J. *Child development and personality* (4th ed.). New York: Harper & Row, 1974.

Myers, N.A., & Perlmutter, M. Memory in the years from two to five. In P.A. Ornstein (Ed.), *Memory development in children.*

Hillsdale, N.J.: Lawrence Erlbaum Associates, 1978.

Naeye, R.L., Blanc, W., & Paul, C. Effects of maternal nutrition on the human fetus. *Pediatrics,* 1973, *52,* 494–503.

Newman, B.M. & Newman, P.R. *Development through life.* Homewood, Ill.: Dorsey, 1975.

Paivio, A. *Imagery and verbal processes.* New York: Holt, Rinehart, & Winston, 1971.

Palermo, D.S. Language acquisition. In H.W. Reese & L.P. Lipsitt (Eds.), *Experimental child psychology.* New York: Academic Press, 1970.

Papalia, D.E. & Olds, S.W. *A child's world.* New York: McGraw-Hill, 1975.

Phillips, J.L., Jr. *The origins of intellect: Piaget's theory* (2nd ed.). San Francisco: Freeman, 1975.

Piaget, J. *On the development of memory and identity.* Barre, Mass.: Clark University Press and Barre Publishers, 1968.

Piaget, J., & Inhelder, B. *The psychology of the child.* New York: Basic Books, 1969.

Piaget, J., & Inhelder, B. *Memory and intelligence* (A.J. Pomerans, trans.). New York: Basic Books, 1973.

Razran, G.H.S. Conditioned responses in children. *Archives of Psychology.* 1933, *148,* 720.

Reese, H.W. Attitudes toward the opposite sex in late childhood. *Merrill-Palmer Quarterly,* 1966, *12,* 157–163.

Reese, H.W. *The perception of stimulus reactions: Discrimination learning and transposition.* New York: Academic Press, 1968.

Reese, H.W. *Basic learning processes in childhood.* New York: Holt, Rinehart, & Winston, 1976.

Reese, H.W. Imagery and associative memory. In R.V. Kail, Jr. & J.W. Hagen (Eds.), *Perspectives on the development of memory and cognition.* Hillsdale, N.J.: Lawrence Erlbaum Associates, 1977.

Reese, H.W., & Porges, S.W. Development of learning processes. In V. Hamilton & M.D. Vernon (Eds.), *The development of cognitive processes.* London: Academic Press, 1976.

Reese, H.W., & Schach, M.L. Comment of Brainerd's criteria for cognitive structures. *Psychological Bulletin,* 1974, *81,* 67–69.

Rheingold, H.L., & Eckerman, C.O. Fear of the stranger: A critical examination. In H.W. Reese (Ed.), *Advances in child development and behavior* (Vol. 8). New York: Academic Press, 1973.

Rheingold, H.L., Gewirtz, J.L., & Ross, H.W. Social conditioning of vocalizations in the infant. *Journal of Comparative and Physiological Psychology,* 1959, *52,* 68–73.

Risley, T.R. The development and maintenance of language: An operant model. In B.C. Etzel, J.M. LeBlanc, & D.M. Baer (Eds.), *New developments in behavioral research: Theory, method, and application.* Hillsdale, N.J.: Lawrence Erlbaum Associates, 1977.

Seligman, M.E.P. On the generality of the laws of learning. *Psychological Review,* 1970, *77,* 406–418.

Siqueland, E.R. Basic learning processes: I. Classical conditioning. In H.W. Reese & L.P. Lipsitt (Eds.), *Experimental child psychology.* New York: Academic Press, 1970. (a)

Siqueland, E.R. Instrumental conditioning in infants. In H.W. Reese & L.P. Lipsitt (Eds.), *Experimental child psychology.* New York: Academic Press, 1970. (b)

Sorensen, R.C. *Adolescent sexuality in contemporary America: Personal values and sexual behavior, ages 13–219.* New York: World Publishing, 1973.

Stein, Z., Susser, M. Saenger, G., & Marolla, F. Nutrition and mental performance. *Science,* 1972, *178,* 708–712.

Steiner, J.E. Human facial expressions in response to taste and smell stimulation. In H.W. Reese & L.P. Lipsitt (Eds.), *Advances in child development and behavior* (Vol. 13). New York: Academic Press, 1978.

Strean, L.P., & Peer, L.A. Stress as an etiological factor in the development of cleft palate. *Plastic and Reconstructive Surgery,* 1956, *18,* 1–8.

Thorpe, L.P. *Child psychology and development* (2nd ed.). New York: Ronald Press, 1955.

Titchener, E.B. *Lectures on the experimental psychology of the thought processes.* New York: Macmillan, 1909.

Vore, D.H. *Prenatal nutrition and post-natal intellectual development.* Paper presented at the annual meeting of the Society for Research and Child Development, Minneapolis, April 1971.

Watson, R.I. *Psychology of the child* (2nd ed.). New York: Wiley, 1965.

Wellman, H.M., Ritter, K., & Flavell, J.H. Deliberate memory behavior in the delayed reactions of very young children. *Developmental Psychology,* 1975, *11,* 780–787.

White, K.M., & Speisman, J.C. *Adolescence.* Monterey, Calif.: Brooks/Cole, 1977.

White, S.H. Evidence for a hierarchical arrangement of learning processes. In L.P. Lipsitt & C.C. Spiker (Eds.), *Advances in child development and behavior* (Vol.2). New York: Academic Press, 1965.

White, S.H. The learning theory tradition and child psychology. In P.H. Mussen (Ed.), *Carmichael's manual of child psychology* (3rd ed., Vol. 1). New York: Wiley, 1970.

Will, J.A., Self, P.A., & Datan, N. Maternal behavior and perceived sex of infant. *American Journal of Orthopsychiatry,* 1976, *46,* 135–139

Wolff, P.H. Observations on the early development of smiling. In B.M. Foss (Ed.), *Determinants of infant behavior* (Vol.2). New York: Wiley, 1963.

Yuille, J.C., & Catchpole, M.J. The effects of delay and imagery training on the recall and recognition of object pairs. *Journal of Experimental Child Psychology,* 1974, *17,* 474–481.

Zaporozhets, A.V., & Elkonin, D.B. (Eds.). *The psychology of preschool children* (J. Shybut & S. Symon, trans.). Cambridge, Mass.: M.I.T. Press, 1971.

Chapter 7

Atchley, R.C. *The social forces in later life: An introduction to social gerontology* (2nd ed.). Belmont, Calif.: Wadsworth, 1977.

Baltes, P.B. Longitudinal and cross-sectional sequences in the study of age and generation effects. *Human Development,* 1968, *11,* 145–171.

Baltes, P.B. *Life-span developmental psychology: Observations on method and theory.* Paper presented at the annual meeting of the American Psychological Association, San Francisco, August 1977.

Baltes, P.B., Cornelius, S.W., & Nesselroade, J.R. Cohort effects in developmental psychology: Theoretical and methodological perspectives. In W.A. Collins (Ed.), *Minnesota symposium on child psychology* (Vol. 11). Minneapolis: Institute of Child Development, University of Minnesota, 1976.

Baltes, P.B. & Labouvie, G.V. Adult development of intellectual performance: Description, explanation, and modification. In D. Eisdorfer & M.P. Lawton (Eds.), *The psychology of adult development and aging.* Washington, D.C.: American Psychological Association, 1973.

Bem, S. The measurement of psychological androgyny. *Journal of Consulting and Clinical Psychology,* 1974, *42,* 155–162.

Bengtson, V.L. *The social psychology of aging.* New York: Bobbs-Merrill, 1973.

Bennett, R., & Eckman, J. Attitudes toward aging: A critical examination of recent literature and implications for future research. In C. Eisdorfer & M.P. Lawton (Eds.), *The psychology of adult development and aging.* Washington, D.C.: American Psychological Association, 1973.

Birren, J.E. Psychophysiological relations. In J.E. Birren, R.N. Butler, S.W. Greenhouse, L. Sokoloff, & M.R. Yarrow (Eds.), *Human aging: A biological and behavioral study.* Washington, D.C.: U.S. Government Printing Office, 1963.

Birren, J.E. Increments and decrements in the intellectual status of the aged. *Psychiatric Research Reports,* 1968, *23,* 207–214.

Birren, J.E. Age and decision strategies. In A.T. Welford & J.E. Birren (Eds.), *Interdisciplinary topics in gerontology,* (Vol.4). Basel, Switzerland: S. Karger, 1969.

Birren, J.E. Toward an experimental psychology of aging. *American Psychologist,* 1970, *25,* 124–135.

Block, J.H. Conceptions of sex role: Some cross-cultural and longitudinal perspectives. *American Psychologist,* 1973, *28,* 512–526.

Botwinick, J. *Cognitive processes in maturity and old age.* New York: Springer, 1967.

Botwinick, J. *Aging and behavior.* New York: Springer, 1973.

Botwinick, J. Intellectual abilities. In J.E. Birren & K.W. Schaie (Eds.), *Handbook of the psychology of aging.* New York: Van Nostrand Reinhold, 1977.

Botwinick, J., & Thompson, L.W. Cardiac functioning and reaction time in relation to age. *Journal of Genetic Psychology,* 1971, *119,* 127–132.

Brent, S.B. Individual specialization, collective adaptation, and rate of environmental change: A dialectical relationship between ontogeny and phylogeny. *Human Development,* in press.

Buck-Morss, S. Socioeconomic bias in Piaget's theory and its implication for cross-culture studies. *Human Development,* 1975, *18,* 35–49.

Buehler, C. *Der menschliche Lebenslauf als psychologisches Problem.* Leipzig, E. Germany, 1933.

Cattell, R.B. Theory of fluid and crystallized intelligence: A critical experiment. *Journal of Educational Psychology,* 1963, *54,* 1–22.

Chown, S.M. Age and the rigidities. *Journal of Gerontology,* 1961, *16,* 353–362.

Clayton, V. Erikson's theory of human development as it applies to the aged: Wisdom as contradictive cognition. *Human Development,* 1975, *18,* 119–128.

Coelho, G.V., Hamburg, D.A., & Adams, J.E. *Coping and adaptation.* New York: Basic Books, 1974.

Comfort, A. *The biology of senescence.* London: Routledge & Kegan Paul, 1956.

Conger, J.J. *Adolescence and youth: Psychological development in a changing world.* New York: Harper & Row, 1973.

Cowgill, D.O., & Holmes, L.O. *Aging and modernization.* New York: Appleton-Century-Crofts, 1972.

Cumming, E. & Henry, W.H. *The process of disengagement.* New York: Basic Books, 1961.

Dohrenwend, B.P., & Dohrenwend, B.S. The conceptualization and measurement of stressful life events: An overview. In J.S. Strauss, H.M. Babigan, & M. Roff (Eds.), *Proceedings of conference on methods of longitudinal research in psychopathology.* New York: Plenum, 1977.

Dowd, J.J. Aging as exchange: A preface to theory. *Journal of Gerontology,* 1975, *30,* 584–594.

Eisdorfer, C. The implications of research for medical practice. *Gerontologist,* 1970, *10,* 62–67.

Eisdorfer, C., & Stotsky, B.A. Intervention, treatment, and rehabilitation of psychiatric disorders. In J.E. Birren & K.W. Schaie (Eds.), *Handbook of the psychology of aging.* New York: Van Nostrand Reinhold, 1977.

Eisdorfer, C., & Wilkie, F. Intellectual changes with advancing age. In L.F. Jarvik, C. Eisdorfer, & J.C. Blum (Eds.), *Intellectual functioning in adults.* New York: Springer, 1973.

Eisdorfer, C., & Wilkie, F. Stress, disease, aging and behavior. In J.E. Birren & K.W. Schaie (Eds.), *Handbook of the psychology of aging.* New York: Van Nostrand Reinhold, 1977.

Elder, G.H., Jr. Age differentiation and the life course. *Annual Review of Sociology,* 1975 *1,* 165–190.

Erikson, E.H. Generativity and ego integrity. In B.L. Neugarten (Ed.), *Middle age and aging,* Chicago: University of Chicago Press, 1968

Feldman, S.S. Sex-role concept and sex-role attitudes: Enduring personality characteristics or adaptations to changing life situations? *Developmental Psychology,* in press.

Finch, C.E., & Hayflick, L. (Eds.), *Handbook of the biology of aging.* New York: Van Nostrand Reinhold, 1977.

Flavell, J.H. Cognitive changes in adulthood. In P.B. Baltes & L.R. Goulet (Eds.), *Life-span developmental psychology.* New York: Academic Press, 1970.

Goulet, L.R. The interfaces of acquisition: Models and methods for studying the active, developing organism. In J.R. Nesselroade & H.W. Reese (Eds.), *Life-span developmental psychology: Methodological issues.* New York: Academic Press, 1973.

Gutmann, D.L. Parenthood: Key to the comparative psychology of the life cycle? In N. Datan & L. Ginsberg (Eds.), *Life-span developmental psychology: Normative life crises.* New York: Academic Press, 1975.

Havighurst, R.J. *Developmental tasks and education.* New York: David McKay, 1972.

Havighurst, R.J. Neugarten, B.L. & Tobin, S.S. Disengagement and patterns of aging. In B.L. Neugarten (Ed.), *Middle age and aging.* Chicago: University of Chicago Press, 1968.

Hefner, R., Rebecca, M., & Oleshansky, B. Development of sex-role transcendence. *Human Development,* 1975, *18,* 143–158.

Heilbrun, A.B., Jr. Identification and behavioral ineffectiveness during late adolescence. In E.D. Evans (Ed.), *Adolescents: Readings in behavior and development.* New York: Holt, Rinehart & Winston, 1970.

Hertzog, C., Gribbin, K., & Schaie, K.W. *The influence of cardio-vascular disease and hypertension on intellectual stability.* Paper presented at the annual meeting of the Gerontological Society, Louisville, Ky., October 1975.

Hoffman, L.W. Changes in family roles, socialization and sex differences. *American Psychologists,* 1977, *32,* 644–657.

Holmes, T.H., & Masuda, M. Life change and illness susceptibility. In B.S. Dohrenwend & B.P. Dohrenwend (Eds.), *Stressful life events: Their nature and effects.* New York: Wiley, 1974.

Holmes, T.H., & Rahe, R.H. The social readjustment rating scale. *Journal of Psychosomatic Research,* 1967, *11,* 213–218.

Horn, J.L., & Cattell, R.B. Refinement and test of the fluid and crystallized intelligence. *Journal of Educational Psychology,* 1966, *57,* 253–270.

Horn, J.L. Organization of data on life-span development of human abilities. In L.R. Goulet & P.B. Baltes (Eds.), *Life-span developmental psychology.* New York: Academic Press, 1970.

Horn, J.L. Human abilities: A review of research and theory in the early 1970's. *Annual Review of Psychology,* 1976, *27,* 437–485.

Horn, J.L., & Cattell, R.B. Refinement and test of the fluid and crystallized intelligence. *Journal of Educational Psychology,* 1966, *57,* 253–270.

Horn, J.L. & Cattell, R.B. Age differences in fluid and crystallized intelligence. *Acta Psychologica,* 1967, *26,* 107–129.

Horner, M.S. Femininity and successful achievement: A basic inconsistency. In J.M. Bardwick et. al. (Eds.), *Feminine personality and conflict.* Belmont, Calif.: Brooks/Cole, 1970.

Jaccoby, A.P. Transition to parenthood: A reassessment. *Journal of Marriage and the Family,* 1969, *31,* 720–727.

Jarvik, L.F., & Cohen, D. A biobehavioral approach to intellectual changes with aging. In C. Eisdorfer & M.P. Lawton (Eds.), *The psychology of adult development and aging.* Washington, D.C.: American Psychological Association, 1973.

Jarvik, L.F., Eisdorfer, C., & Blum, J.C. (Eds.), *Intellectual functioning in adults.* New York: Springer, 1973.

Jenkins, J.J. Second discussant's comments: What's left to say? *Human Development,* 1971, *14,* 279–286.

Jung, C.G. *Modern man in search of a soul.* New York: Harcourt, Brace, & World, 1933.

Kohn, M. *Class and conformity: A study in values.* Homewood, Ill.: Dorsey Press, 1969.

Kuhlen, R.G. Age and intelligence: The significance of cultural change in longitudinal vs. cross-sectional findings. In B.L. Neugarten (Ed.), *Middle age and aging.* Chicago: University of Chicago Press, 1968.

Kuhlen, R.G. Personality change with age. In P. Worchel & D. Byrne (Eds.), *Personality change.* New York: Wiley, 1964.

Labouvie-Vief, G. Adult cognitive development: In search of alternative interpretations. *Merrill-Palmer,* in press.

Labouvie-Vief, G., & Chandler, M. Cognitive development and life-span developmental theory: Idealistic versus contextual perspectives. In P.B. Baltes (Ed.), *Life-span development and behavior.* New York: Academic Press, 1978.

Lawton, M.P., & Nahemow, L. Ecology and the aging process. In C. Eisdorfer & M.P. Lawton (Eds.), *The psychology of adult development and aging.* Washington, D.C.: American Psychological Association, 1973.

Lehr, U. Zur Problematik des Menschen im reiferen Erwachsenenalter. *Probleme und Ergebnisse der Psychologie,* 1966, *16.*

Levinson, D.J., Darrow, C.M., Klein, E.B., Levinson, M.H., & McKee, B. The psychosocial development of men in early adulthood and the mid-life transition. In D.F. Ricks, A. Thomas, & M. Roff (Eds.), *Life history research in psychopathology,* (Vol. 3). Minneapolis: University of Minnesota Press, 1974.

Livson, F. *Sex differences in personality development in the middle adult: A longitudinal study.* Paper presented at the 28th annual meeting of the Gerontological Society, Louiville, Ky., October 1975.

Loewe, H. *Lernpsychologie: Einfuehrung in die Lernpsychologie des Erwachsenenalters.* Berlin: Deutscher Verlag der Wissenschaften, 1977.

Looft, W.R., & Charles, D.C. Egocentrism and social interaction in young and old adults. *Aging and Human Development,* 1971, *2,* 21–28.

Lopata, H.Z. Widowhood: Societal factors in life-span disruptions and alternatives. In N. Datan & L.H. Ginsberg (Eds.), *Life-span developmental psychology: Normative life crises.* New York: Academic Press, 1975.

Lowenthal, M.F. Toward a sociological theory of change in adulthood and old age. In J.E. Birren & K.W. Schaie (Eds.), *Handbook of the psychology of aging.* New York: Van Nostrand Reinhold, 1977.

Lowenthal, M.F., & Chiriboga, D. Social stress and adaptation: Toward a life-course perspective. In C. Eisdorfer & M.P. Lawton (Eds.), *The psychology of adult development and aging.* Washington, D.C.: American Psychological Association, 1973.

Lynn, D.B. *Parental and sex-role identification: A theoretical formulation.* Berkley: McCutchan, 1969.

Maas, H.S., & Kuypers, J.A. *From thirty to seventy.* San Francisco: Jossey-Bass, 1974.

MacDonald, M.L., & Butler, A.K. Reversal of helplessness: Producing walking behavior in wheel chair residents using behavior modification procedures. *Journal of Gerontology,* 1974, *29,* 97–101.

Masters, W.H., & Johnson, V.E. Human sexual

response: The aging female and the aging male. In B.L. Neugarten (Ed.), *Middle age and aging.* Chicago: University of Chicago Press, 1968.

Mead, M. *Culture and commitment: A study of the generation gap.* New York: Doubleday, 1970.

Money, J., & Ehrhardt, A.A. *Man and woman, boy and girl.* Baltimore: Johns Hopkins University Press, 1972.

Monge, R.H. *Age differences in dogmaticism and anxiety from the 20's to 70's.* Unpublished manuscript, Syracuse University, 1972.

Mussen, P.H. Long-term consequents of masculinity of interests in adolescence. *Journal of Consulting Psychology,* 1962, *26,* 435–440.

Neugarten, B.L. Personality changes in the aged. *Catholic Psychological Record,* 1965, *3,* 9–17.

Neugarten, B.L. Personality and aging. In J.E. Birren & K.W. Schaie (Eds.), *Handbook of the psychology of aging.* New York: Van Nostrand Reinhold, 1977.

Neugarten, B.L., Crotty, W.J., & Tobin, S.S. Personality types in an aged population. In B.L. Neugarten (Ed.), *Personality in middle and late life.* New York: Atherton, 1964.

Neugarten, B.L., & Hagestad, G.O. Age and the life course. In R.H. Binstock & E. Shanas (Eds.), *Handbook of aging and the social sciences.* New York: Van Nostrand Reinhold, 1976.

Neugarten, B.L., Havighurst, R.J., & Tobin, S.S. Personality and patterns of aging. In B.L. Neugarten (Ed.), *Middle age and aging.* Chicago: University of Chicago Press, 1968.

Neugarten, B.L., Moore, J.W., & Lowe, J.C. Age norms, age constraints, and adult socialization. *American Journal of Sociology,* 1965, *70,* 710–717.

Nydegger, C.N. *Late and early fathers.* Paper presented at the 1973 annual meeting of the Gerontological Society, Miami, 1973

Papalia, D.E., & Del Vento Bielby, D. Cognitive functioning in middle and old adults: A review of research based on Piaget's theory. *Human Development,* 1974, *17,* 424–443.

Pearlin, L.I. Sex roles and depression. In N. Datan & L.H. Ginsberg (Eds.), *Life-span developmental psychology: Normative life crises.* New York: Academic Press, 1975

Perry, W.G. *Forms of intellectual and ethical development in the college years.* New York: Holt, Rinehart, & Winston, 1970.

Piaget, J. Intellectual evolution from adolescence to adulthood. *Human Development,* 1972, *15,* 1–12.

Reese, H.W. Life-span models of memory. *Gerontologist,* 1973, *13,* 472–478.

Reese, H.W. The development of memory: Life-span perspectives. In H.W. Reese (Ed.), *Advances in child development and behavior.* (Vol.11). New York: Academic Press, 1976.

Riegel, K.F. Personality theory and aging. In J.E. Birren (Ed.), *Handbook of aging and the individual.* Chicago: University of Chicago Press, 1959.

Riegel, K.F. Dialectic operations: The final period of cognitive development. *Human Development,* 1973, *16,* 346–370.

Riegel, K.F. History of psychological gerontology. In J.E. Birren & K.W. Schaie (Eds.), *Handbook of the psychology of aging.* New York: Van Nostrand Reinhold, 1977.

Riegel, K.F., & Riegel, R.M. A study on changes of attitude and interest during the later years of life. *Vita Humana,* 1960, *3,* 177–206.

Riegel, K.F., & Riegel, R.M. Development, drop, and death. *Developmental Psychology,* 1972, *6,* 306–319.

Rowland, K.F. Environmental events predicting death for the elderly. *Psychological Bulletin,* 1977, *84,* 349–372.

Schaie, K.W. Rigidity-flexibility and intelligence: A cross-sectional study of the adult life span from 20 to 70 years. *Psychological Monographs,* 1958, *72,* (9, Whole No. 462).

Schaie, K.W. A general model for the study of developmental problems. *Psychological Bulletin,* 1965, *64,* 92–107.

Schaie, K.W. Translations in gerontology: From lab to life: Intellectual functioning. *American Psychologist,* 1974, *29,* 802–807.

Schaie, K.W. Toward a stage theory of adult development. *International Journal of Aging and Adulthood Development,* in press.

Schaie, K.W., & Labouvie-Vief, G. Generational versus ontogenetic components of change in adult cognitive behavior: A fourteen-year cross-sequential study. *Developmental Psychology,* 1974, *10,* 305–320.

Schaie, K.W., & Parham, I.A. Stability of adult personality: Fact or fable? *Journal of Personality and Social Psychology,* 1976, *34,* 146–158.

Sedney, M.A. *Process of sex-role development during life crises in middle-aged women.* Paper presented at the 1977 annual meeting of the American Psychological Association, San Francisco, August 1977.

Selye, H. *The stress of life.* New York: McGraw-Hill, 1956.

Sheehy, G. *Passages: Predictable crises of adult life.* New York: Dutton, 1976.

Shock, N.W. Biological theories of aging. In J.E. Birren & K.W. Schaie (Eds.), *Handbook of the psychology of aging.* New York: Van Nostrand Reinhold, 1977.

Sofer, C. *Man in mid-career.* New York: Cambridge University Press, 1970.

Tanner, J.M. Sequence, tempo and individual variation in growth and development of boys and girls aged twelve to sixteen. In J. Kagan & R. Coles (Eds.), *Twelve to sixteen: Early adolescence.* New York: Norton, 1972.

Treas, J. Aging and the family. In D.S. Woodruff & J.E. Birren (Eds.), *Aging: Scientific perspectives and social issues.* New York: D. Van Nostrand, 1975.

Urberg, K.A., & Labouvie-Vief, G. Conceptualizations of sex-roles: A life span developmental study. *Developmental Psychology,* 1976, *12,* 15–23.

Walsh, D.A., & Baldwin, M. *Age differences in semantic memory.* Paper presented at the 1977 annual meeting of the American Psychological Association, San Francisco, August 1977.

Wang, H.S. Cerebral correlates of intellectual functioning in senescence. In L.F. Jarvik, C. Eisdorfer, & J.E. Blum (Eds.), *Intellectual functioning in adults.* New York: Springer, 1973.

Watson, J.A., & Kivett, V.R. Influences on the life satisfaction of older fathers. *The Family Coordinator,* 1976, *4,* 482–488.

Weg, R.B. Changing physiology of aging: Normal and pathological. In D.S. Woodruff & J.E. Birren (Eds.), *Aging: Scientific perspectives and social issues.* New York: D. Van Nostrand, 1975.

Werner, H. *Comparative psychology of mental development.* New York: International Universities Press, 1948.

Woodruff, D.S. A physiological perspective on the psychology of aging, In D.S. Woodruff & J.E. Birren (Eds.), *Aging: Scientific perspectives and social issues.* New York: D.Van Nostrand, 1975.

Woodruff, D.S., & Birren, J.E. Age changes and cohort differences in personality. *Developmental Psychology,* 1972, *6,* 252–259.

Zaks, P.M., & Labouvie-Vief, G. *Training of role taking in elderly nursing home patients.* Paper presented at the 1977 annual meeting of the American Psychological Association, San Francisco, August 1977.

Chapter 8

Agras, S., Sylvester, D., & Oliveau, D. The epidemiology of common fears and phobias. *Comprehensive Psychiatry,* 1969, *10,* 151–156.

Bandura, A. *Principles of behavior modification.* New York: Holt, Rinehart, & Winston, 1969.

Bandura, A. Self-efficacy: Toward a unifying theory of behavioral change. *Psychological Review,* 1977, *84,* 191–215.

Bellack, A.S., & Hersen, M. *Behavior modification: An introductory textbook.* Baltimore: Williams & Wilkins, 1977.

Blanchard, E.B., & Hersen, M. Behavioral treatment of hysterical neurosis: Symptom substitution and symptom return reconsidered. *Psychiatry,* 1976, *39,* 118–129.

Carver, C.S., & Blaney, P.H. Avoidance behavior and perceived arousal. *Motivation and Emotion,* 1977, *1,* 61–73.

Franks, C.M., & Wilson, G.T. (Eds.), *Annual review of behavior therapy: Theory and practice:* (Vol.4). New York: Brunner/Mazel, 1976.

Hall, C.S., & Lindzey, G. *Theories of personality* (2nd ed.). New York: Wiley, 1970.

Kanfer, F.H., Karoly, P., & Newman, A. Reduction of children's fear of the dark by competence-related and situational threat-related verbal cues. *Journal of Consulting and Clinical Psychology,* 1975, *43,* 251–258.

Lang, P.J. The application of psychological methods to the study of psychotherapy and behavior modification. In A.E. Bergin & S.L. Garfield (Eds.), *Handbook of psychotherapy and behavior change.* New York: Wiley. 1971.

Ludwig, A.M., Brandsma, J.M., Wilbur, C.B., Bendfeldt, F., & Jameson, D.H. The objective study of a multiple personality. *Archives of General Psychiatry,* 1972, *26,* 298–310.

Marks, I.M. The origins of phobic states. *American Journal of Psychotherapy,* 1970, *24,* 652–676.

Marks, I.M. Phobias and obsessions: Clinical phenomena in search of a laboratory model. In J.D. Maser & M.E.P. Seligman (Eds.), *Psychopathology: Experimental models.* San Francisco: Freeman, 1977.

Martin, B. *Anxiety and neurotic disorders.* New York: Wiley, 1971.

Martin, B., & Sroufe, L.A. Anxiety. In C.G. Costello (Ed.), *Symptoms of psychopathology: A handbook.* New York: Wiley, 1970.

Miller, N.E. Studies of fear as an acquired drive: I. Fear as motivation and fear reduction as reinforcement in the learning of new responses. *Journal of Experimental Psychology,* 1948, *38,* 89–101.

Morris, D. *The naked ape.* New York: Dell, 1967.

Munford, P.R., Reardon, D., Liberman, R.P., & Allen, L. Behavioral treatment of hysterical coughing and mutism: A case study. *Journal of Consulting and Clinical Psychology,* 1976, *44,* 1008–1014.

Rachman, S. Primary obsessional slowness. *Behaviour Research and Therapy,* 1974, *12,* 9–18.

Rachman, S. Obsessional-compulsive checking. *Behaviour Research and Therapy,* 1976, *14,* 269–278.

Rachman, S. The passing of the two-stage theory of fear and avoidance: Fresh possibilities. *Behaviour Research and Therapy,* 1976, *14,* 125–132. (b)

Rachman, S., DeSilva, P., & Röper, G. The spontaneous decay of compulsive urges. *Behaviour Research and Therapy,* 1976, *14,* 445–453.

Rachman, S., & Seligman, M.E.P. Unprepared phobias: "Be prepared." *Behaviour Research and Therapy,* 1976, *14,* 333–338.

Seligman, M.E.P., & Hager, J. *The biological boundaries of learning.* New York: Appleton-Century-Crofts, 1972.

Slater, E., & Glithero, E. A follow-up of patients diagnosed as suffering from hysteria. *Journal of Psychosomatic Research,* 1965, *9,* 9–13.

Spielberger, C.D. Theory and research on anxiety. In C.D. Spielberger (Ed.), *Anxiety and behavior.* New York: Academic Press, 1966.

Spielberger, C.D., Gorsuch, R.L., & Luschene, R.E. *Manual for the State-Trait Anxiety Inventory.* Palo Alto, Calif.: Consulting Psychologist Press, 1970.

Spitzer, R.L., Sheehy, M., & Endicott, J. DSM-III: Guiding principles. In V.M. Rakoff, H.C. Stancer, & H.B. Kedward (Eds.), *Psychiatric diagnosis.* New York: Brunner/Mazel, 1977.

Sternbach, R.A. *Principles of psychophysiology.* New York: Academic Press, 1966.

Szpiler, J.A., & Epstein, S. Availability of an avoidance response as related to autonomic arousal. *Journal of Abnormal Psychology,* 1976, *85,* 73–82.

Taylor, J.A. A personality scale of manifest anxiety. *Journal of Abnormal Psychology,* 1953, *48,* 285–290.

Thomas, A., Chess, S., Birch, H.G., Hertzig, M.E., & Korn, S. *Behavioral individuality in early childhood.* New York: N.Y.U. Press, 1963.

Wade, T.C., Malloy, T.E., & Proctor, S. Imaginal correlates of self-reported fear and avoidance behavior. *Behaviour Research and Therapy,* 1977, *15,* 17–22.

Watson, D., & Friend, R. Measurement of social-evaluative anxiety. *Journal of Consulting and Clinical Psychology,* 1969, *33,* 448–457.

Woodruff, R.A., Goodwin, D.W., & Guze, S.B. *Psychiatric diagnosis.* New York: Oxford University Press, 1974.

Zubin, J. Classification of the behavior disorders. *Annual Review of Psychology,* 1967, *18,* 373–401.

Chapter 9

Abraham, K. Notes on the psychoanalytic investigation and treatment of manic-depressive insanity and allied conditions (1911). In W. Gaylin (Ed.), *The meaning of despair.* New York: Science House, 1968.

American Psychiatric Association. Draft of *Diagnostic and statistical manual of mental disorders, (DSM-III)* (3rd ed.) Washington, D.C.: American Psychiatric Association, 1977.

Bart, P. Depression: A sociological theory. In P. Roman & H. Trice (Eds.), *Explorations in psychiatric sociology.* Philadelphia: Davis, 1974.

Beck, A.T. *Depression: Causes and treatment.* Philadelphia: University of Pennsylvania Press, 1973.

Beck, A.T. *Cognitive therapy and the emotional disorders.* New York: International Universities Press, 1976.

Bibring, E. The mechanism of depression (1953). In P. Greenacre (Ed.), *Affective disorders.* New York: International Universities Press, 1965.

Bowlby, J. *Separation.* New York: Basic Books, 1973.

Clayton, P.J., Halikas, J.A., & Maurice, W.L. The depression of widowhood. *British Journal of Psychiatry,* 1972, *120,* 71–78.

Cole, J.O., & Davis, J.M. Antidepressant drugs. In A.M. Freedman, H.I. Kaplan, & B.J. Sadock (Eds.), *Comprehensive textbook of psychiatry.* Baltimore: Williams & Wilkins, 1975.

Fink, M., Kety, S., McGaugh, J., & Williams,

T.A. (Eds.), *Psychobiology of convulsive therapy*. Washington, D.C.: Winston, 1974.

Freud, S. Mourning and melancholia (1917). In E. Jones (Ed.), *The collected papers of Sigmund Freud*. New York: Basic Books, 1959.

Helgason, T. Epidemiology of mental disorders in Iceland. *Acta Psychiatrica Scandinavica,* 1964, *40,* (Supp. 173).

Hollender, M. *The practice of psychoanalytic psychotherapy*. New York: Grune & Stratton, 1965.

Kraepelin, E. *Manic depressive insanity and paranoia*. New York: Arno, 1896.

Lewinsohn, P.M. The behavioral study and treatment of depression. In M. Hersen, R.M. Eisler, & P.M. Miller (Eds.), *Progress in behavior modification* (Vol. 1). New York: Academic Press, 1975.

Lewinsohn, P.M., Biglan, A., & Zeiss, A. Behavioral treatment of depression. In P. Davidson (Ed.), *Behavioral management of anxiety, depression, and pain*. New York: Brunner/Mazel, 1976.

Maier, S.F. & Seligman, M.E.P. Learned helplessness: The evidence. *Journal of Experimental Psychology* (General), 1976, *103,* 3–46.

Mendels, J. *Concepts of depression*. New York: Wiley, 1970.

Mendels, J. (Ed.). *The psychobiology of depression*. New York: Spectrum, 1975.

Mendels, J., & Cochrane, C. The nosology of depression: The endogenous-reactive concept. *American Journal of Psychiatry,* 1968, *124,* (May Suppl.).

Mendelson, M. *Psychoanalytic concepts of depression*. New York: Spectrum, 1974.

Paykel, E.S., Myers, J.K., Dienelt, M.N., Klerman, G.L., Lindenthal, J.J., & Pepper, M. Life events and depression. *Archives of General Psychiatry,* 1969, *21,* 753–760.

Perris, C. A study of bipolar (manic-depressive) and unipolar recurrent depressive psychoses. *Acta Psychiatrica Scandinavica,* 1966, *42,* (Suppl. 194).

Robins, E., Gassner, S., Kayes, J., Wilkinson, R.H., Jr., & Murphy, G.E. The communication of suicidal intent: A study of 134 consecutive cases of successful (completed) suicide. *American Journal of Psychiatry,* 1959, *115,* 724–733.

Robins, E., & Guze, S.B. Classification of affective disorders: The primary-secondary, endogenous-reactive, and the neurotic-psychotic concepts. In T.A. Williams, M.M. Katz, & J.A. Shields (Eds.), *Recent advances in the psychobiology of the depressive illnesses*. Washington, D.C.: U.S. Government Printing Office, 1972.

Schless, A.P., & Mendels, J. Life stress and psychopathology. *Psychiatry Digest,* 1977, *38,* 24–35.

Schuyler, D. *The depressive spectrum*. New York: Jason Aronson, 1974.

Schwartz, G.E., Fair, P.L., Salt, P., Mandel, M.R., & Klerman, G.L. Facial muscle patterning to affective imagery in depressed and non-depressed patients. *Science,* 1976, *192,* 489–491.

Seligman, M.E.P. *Helplessness: On depression, development, and death*. San Francisco: Freeman, 1975.

Slater, E., & Cowie, V. *The genetics of mental disorders*. New York: Oxford University Press, 1971.

Spitz, R.A. Anaclitic depression. *Psychoanalytic Study of the Child,* 1946, *2,* 313–342.

Taylor, M.A., & Abrams, R. Manic states: A genetic study of early and late onset affective disorders. *American Journal of Psychiatry,* 1973, *28,* 656–658.

Weissman, M., & Paykel, E. *The depressed woman*. Chicago: University of Chicago Press, 1974.

Winokur, G. The types of affective disorder. *Journal of Nervous and Mental Disease,* 1973, *156,* 82–96.

Wolpert, E.A. (Ed.), *Manic depressive illness*. New York: International Universities Press, 1977.

Chapter 10

Ader, R. The role of developmental factors in susceptibility to disease. In Z.J. Lipowski, D.R. Lipsitt, & P.C. Whybrow (Eds.), *Psychosomatic medicine: Current trends and clinical applications*. New York: Oxford University Press, 1977.

Alexander, F. *Psychosomatic medicine*. New York: Norton, 1950.

Alexander, F., French, T.M., & Pollock, G.H. (Eds.). *Psychosomatic specificity: I. Experimental study and results*. Chicago: University of Chicago Press, 1968.

American Psychiatric Association. *Diagnostic and statistical manual of mental disorders* (2nd ed.). Washington, D.C.: American Psychiatric Association, 1968.

Ax, A.F. Editorial. *Psychophysiology,* 1964, *1,* 1–3.

Barber, T.X. *LSD, marihuana, yoga and hypnosis.* Chicago: Aldine, 1970.

Beatty, J., & Legewie, H. (Eds.). *Biofeedback and behavior.* New York: Plenum, 1977.

Benson, H., Greenwood, M.M. & Klemchuk, H. The relaxation response: Psychophysiologic aspects and clinical application. In Z.J. Lipowski, D.R. Lipsitt, & P.C. Whybrow (Eds.), *Psychosomatic medicine: Current trends and clinical applications.* New York: Oxford University Press, 1977.

Brudny, J., Korein, J., Grynbaum, B.B., Friedmann, L.W., Weinstein, S., Sachs-Frankel, G., & Belandres, P.V. EMG feedback therapy: Review of treatment of 114 patients. *Archives of Physical Medicine and Rehabilitation,* 1976, *57,* 55–61.

Budzynski, T.H., Stoyva, J.M., Alder, C.S., & Mullaney, D.J. EMG biofeedback and tension headache: A controlled outcome study. *Psychosomatic Medicine,* 1973, *35,* 484–496.

Cohen, D.H., & Obrist, P.A. Interactions between behavior and the cardiovascular system. *Circulation Research,* 1975, *37,* 693–706.

Davis, M.H., Saunders, D.B., Creer, T.L., & Chai, H. Relaxation training facilitated by biofeedback apparatus as a supplemental treatment in bronchial asthma. *Journal of Psychosomatic Research,* 1973, *17,* 121–128.

Davison, G.C., & Neale, J.M. *Abnormal psychology: An experimental clinical approach.* New York: Wiley, 1974.

Dekker, E., Pelse, H.E., & Groen, J. Conditioning as a cause of asthmatic attcks. *Journal of Psychosomatic Research,* 1957, *2,* 97–108.

Eastwood, M.R. Epidemiological studies in psychosomatic medicine. In Z.J. Lipowski, D.R. Lipsitt, & P.C. Whybrow (Eds.), *Psychosomatic medicine: Current trends and clinical applications.* New York: Oxford University Press, 1977.

Engel, B.T. Response specificity. In N.S. Greenfield & R.A. Sternbach (Eds.), *Handbook of psychophysiology.* New York: Holt, Rinehart, & Winston, 1972.

Engel, B.T., & Bleecker, E.R. Application of operant conditioning techniques to the control of the cardiac arrhythmias. In P.A. Obrist, A.H. Black, J. Brener, & L.V. DiCara (Eds.), *Cardiovascular psychophysiology.* Chicago: Aldine, 1974.

Frankel, F.H. Hypnosis as a treatment method in psychosomatic medicine. In Z.J. Lipowski, D.R. Lipsitt, & P.C. Whybrow (Eds.), *Psychosomatic medicine: Current trends and clinical applications.* New York: Oxford University Press, 1977.

Freis, E.D. The clinical spectrum of essential hypertension. *Archives of Internal Medicine,* 1974, *133,* 982–987.

Friar, L.R., & Beatty, J. Migraine: Management by trained control of vasoconstriction. *Journal of Consulting and Clinical Psychology,* 1976, *44,* 46–53.

Friedman, M. *Pathogenesis of coronary artery disease.* New York: McGraw-Hill, 1969.

Friedman, M., & Rosenman, R.H. Association of specific overt behavior pattern with blood and cardiovascular findings. *Journal of the American Medical Association,* 1959, *169,* 1286–1296.

Friedman, M., & Rosenman, R.H. *Type A behavior and your heart.* New York: Knopf, 1974.

Graham, D.T. Psychosomatic medicine. In N.S. Greenfield & R.A. Sternbach (Eds.), *Handbook of psychophysiology.* New York: Holt, Rinehart, & Winston, 1972.

Gutmann, M.C., & Benson, H. Interaction of environmental factors and systemic arterial blood pressure: A review. *Medicine,* 1971, *50,* 543–553.

Harris, A.H., & Brady, J.V. Long-term studies of cardiovascular control in primates. In G.E. Schwartz & J. Beatty (Eds.), *Biofeedback: Theory and research.* New York: Academic Press, 1977.

Harris, A.H., Findley, J.D., & Brady, J.V. Instrumental conditioning of blood pressure elevations in the baboon. *Conditional Reflex,* 1971, *6,* 215–226.

Harris, A.H., Goldstein, D.S., & Brady, J.V. Visceral learning: Cardiovascular conditioning in primates. In J. Beatty & H. Legewie (Eds.), *Biofeedback and behavior.* New York: Plenum, 1977.

Haynes, S.N., Moseley, D., & McGowan, W.T. Relaxation training and biofeedback in the reduction of frontalis muscle tension. *Psychophysiology,* 1975, *12,* 547–552.

Hill, E. *Bronchial reactions to selected psychological stimuli and concomitant autonomic activity of asthmatic children.* Unpublished doctoral dissertation, Department of Psychology, State University of New York at Buffalo, 1975.

Hinkle, L.E., Jr. The concept of "stress" in the biological and social sciences. In Z.J. Lipowski, D.R. Lipsitt, & P.C. Whybrow (Eds.), *Psychosomatic medicine: Curren trends and clinical applications*. New York: Oxford University Press, 1977.

Jacobson, E. *Progressive relaxation* (2nd ed.). Chicago: University of Chicago Press, 1938.

Jenkins, C.D., Zyzanski, S.J., & Rosenman, R.H. Progress toward validation of a computer scored test of the Type A coronary-prone behavior pattern. *Psychosomatic Medicine,* 1971, *36,* 344–351.

Julius, S., & Esler, M. Autonomic nervous cardiovascular regulation in borderline hypertension. *American Journal of Cardiology,* 1975, *36,* 685–696.

Julius, S., & Schork, M.A. Borderline hypertension—A critical review. *Journal of Chronic Diseases,* 1971, *23,* 723–754.

Katkin, E.S., Fitzgerald, C.R., & Shapiro, D. Clinical applications of biofeedback: Current status and future prospects. In H.L. Pick, H.W. Leibowitz, J.E. Singer, A. Steinschneider, & H.W. Stevenson (Eds.), *Psychology: From research to practice.* New York: Plenum, 1978.

Katkin, E.S., & Murray, E.N. Instrumental conditioning of autonomically mediated behavior: Theoretical and methodological issues. *Psychological Bulletin,* 1968, *70,* 52–68.

Kiely, W.F. From the symbolic stimulus to the pathophysiological response: Neurophysiological mechanisms. In Z.J. Lipowski, D.R. Lipsitt, & P.C. Whybrow (Eds.), *Psychosomatic medicine: Current trends and clinical applications.* New York: Oxford University Press, 1977.

Kimmel, E., & Kimmel, H.D. A replication of operant conditioning of the GSR. *Journal of Experimental Psychology,* 1963, *65,* 212–213.

Lachman, S.J. *Psychosomatic disorders: A behavioristic interpretation.* New York: Wiley, 1972.

Lazarus, R.S. Psychological stress and coping in adaptation and illness. In Z.J. Lipowski, D.R. Lipsitt, & P.C. Whybrow (Eds.), *Psychosomatic medicine: Current trends and clinical applications.* New York: Oxford University Press, 1977.

Lipowski, Z.J. Physical illness and psychopathology. In Z.J. Lipowski, D.R. Lipsitt, & P.C. Whybrow (Eds.), *Psychosomatic medicine: Current trends and clinical applications.* New York: Oxford University Press, 1977. (a)

Lipowski, Z.J. Psychosomatic medicine in the seventies: An overview. *Amerian Journal of Psychiatry,* 1977, *134,* 233–244. (b)

Miller, N.E. Learning of visceral and glandular responses. *Science,* 1969, *163,* 434–445.

Miller, N.E. Clinical applications of biofeedback: Voluntary control of heart rate, rhythm, blood pressure. In H.I. Russek (Ed.), *New horizons in cardiovascular practice.* Baltimore: University Park Press, 1975.

Miller, N.E. & Dworkin, B.R. Critical issues in therapeutic applications of biofeedback. In G.E. Schwartz & J. Beatty (Eds.), *Biofeedback: Theory and research.* New York: Academic Press, 1977.

Minuchin, S., Baker, L., Rosman, B.L., Liebman, R., Milman, L., & Todd, T.C. A conceptual model of psychosomatic illness in children: Family organization and family therapy. *Archives of General Psychiatry,* 1975, *32,* 1031–1038.

Moos, R.H. Determinants of physiological responses to symbolic stimuli: The role of the social environment. In Z.J. Lipowski, D.R. Lipsitt, & P.C. Whybrow (Eds.), *Psychosomatic medicine: Current trends and clinical applications.* New York: Oxford University Press, 1977.

Purcell, K., Brady, K., Chai, H., Muser, J., Molk, L., Gordon, N., & Means, J. The effect on asthma in children of experimental separation from the family. *Psychosomatic Medicine,* 1969, *31,* 144–164.

Purcell, K., & Weiss, J.H. Asthma. In C.G. Costello (Ed.), *Symptoms of psychopathology: A handbook.* New York: Wiley, 1970.

Rahe, R.H. Epidemiological studies of life change and illness. In Z.J. Lipowski, D.R. Lipsitt, & P.C. Whybrow (Eds.), *Psychosomatic medicine: Current trends and clinical applications.* New York: Oxford University Press, 1977.

Rees, L. The significance of parental attitudes in childhood asthma. *Journal of Psychosomatic Research,* 1963, *7,* 181–190.

Roessler, R., & Engel, B.T. The current status of the concepts of physiological response specificity and activation. In Z.J. Lipowski, D.R. Lipsitt, & P.C. Whybrow (Eds.), *Psychosomatic medicine: Current trends and clinical applications.* New York: Oxford University Press, 1977.

Schwartz, G.E. Voluntary control of human cardiovascular integration and differentiation through feedback and reward. *Science,* 1972, *175,* 90–93.

Schwartz, G.E., & Beatty, J. (Eds.). *Biofeedback: Theory and research.* New York: Academic Press, 1977.

Shapiro, A.P., Redmond, D.P., McDonald, R.H., Jr., & Gaylor, M. Relationships of perception, cognition, suggestion and operant conditioning in essential hypertension. *Progress in Brain Research,* 1975, *42,* 299–312.

Shapiro, D., Crider, A.B., & Tursky, B. Differentiation of an autonomic response through operant reinforcement. *Psychonomic Science,* 1964, *1,* 147–148.

Shapiro, D., Mainardi, J.A., & Surwit, R.S. Biofeedback and self-regulation in essential hypertension. In G.E. Schwartz & J. Beatty (Eds.), *Biofeedback: Theory and research.* New York: Academic Press, 1977.

Shapiro, D., & Surwit, R.S. Operant conditioning: A new theoretical approach in psychosomatic medicine. *International Journal of Psychiatry in Medicine,* 1974, *5,* 377–387.

Shapiro, D., & Surwit, R.S. Learned control of physiological function and disease. In H. Leitenberg (Ed.), *Handbook of behavior modification and behavior therapy.* Englewood Cliffs, N.J.: Prentice-Hall, 1976.

Shapiro, D., Tursky, B., & Schwartz, G.E. Differentiation of heart rate and systolic blood pressure in man by operant conditioning. *Psychosomatic Medicine,* 1970, *32,* 417–423.

Skinner, B.F. *The behavior of organisms: An experimental analysis.* New York: Appleton-Century, 1938.

Solomon, P., & Patch, V.D. *Handbook of psychiatry.* Los Altos, Calif.: Lange, 1971.

Sterman, M.B. Clinical implications of EEG biofeedback training: A critical appraisal. In G.E. Schwartz & J. Beatty (Eds.), *Biofeedback: Theory and research.* New York: Academic Press, 1977.

Stoyva, J. Self-regulation and the stress-related disorders: A perspective on biofeedback. In D.I. Mostofsky (Ed.), *Behavior control and modification of physiological activity.* Englewood Cliffs, N.J.: Prentice-Hall, 1976.

Vachon, L., & Rich, E.S., Jr. Visceral learning in asthma. *Psychosomatic Medicine,* 1976, *38,* 122–130.

Weiner, H. Lessons taught by experimental high blood pressure research. *Psychosomatic Medicine,* 1976, *38,* 297–299.

Woolfolk, R.L. Psychophysiological correlates of meditation. *Archives of General Psychiatry,* 1975, *32,* 1326–1333.

Chapter 11

Alexander, F.G., & Selesmick, S.T. *The history of psychiatry.* New York: New American Library, 1966.

Andreasen, N.C. Scale for the assessment of thought, language, and communication (TLC). Mimeographed paper, 1978.

Bateson, G., Jackson, D.D., Haley, J., & Weakland, J. Toward a theory of schizophrenia. *Behavioral Science,* 1956, *1,* 251–264.

Beels, C.C. Family and social management of schizophrenia. *Schizophrenia Bulletin,* 1975, *13,* 97–118.

Benjamin, J.D. A method for distinguishing and evaluating formal thinking disorders in schizophrenia. In J.S. Kasanin (Ed.), *Language and thought in schizophrenia.* Berkeley: University of California Press, 1944.

Blaney, P.H. Two studies on the language behavior of schizophrenics. *Journal of Abnormal Psychology,* 1974, *83,* 23–31.

Bleuler, E. *Dementia praecox or the group of schizophrenias.* J. Zinkin, trans., New York: International Universities Press, 1950.

Cameron, N. Experimental analysis of schizophrenic thinking. In J.S. Kasanin (Ed.), *Language and thought in schizophrenia.* Berkeley: University of California Press, 1944.

Center for Studies of Schizophrenia. *Schizophrenia: Is there an answer?* Washington, D.C.: U.S. Government Printing Office, 1972.

Chapman, L.J. Distractibility in the conceptual performance of schizophrenics. *Journal of Abnormal and Social Psychology,* 1956, *53,* 286–291.

Chapman, L.J., & Chapman, J.P. *Disordered thought in schizophrenia.* New York: Appleton-Century-Crofts, 1973.

Chapple, E.D. The standard experimental (stress) interview as used in interaction chronograph investigations. *Human Organization,* 1953, *12,* 23–32.

Chapple, E.D., Chapple, M.F., Wood, L.A., Miklowitz, A., Kline, N.S., & Saunders, J.C. Interaction chronograph method for analysis of differences between schizophrenics and controls. *Archives of General Psychiatry,* 1960, *3,* 160–167.

Clark, W.C. The "psyche" in psychophysics: A sensory-decision theory analysis of the effect of instructions on flicker sensitivity and response bias. *Psychological Bulletin,* 1966, *65,* 358–366.

Clark, W.C., Brown, J.C., & Rutschmann, J. Flicker sensitivity and response bias in psychiatric patients and normal subjects. *Journal of Abnormal Psychology,* 1967, *72,* 35–42.

Cohen, B.D. Referent communication in schizophrenia: The perseverative-chaining model. In K. Salzinger (Ed.), *Psychology in progress. Annals of the New York Academy of Sciences,* 1976, *270,* 124–140.

Cohen, B.D. Referent communication disturbances in schizophrenia. In S. Schwartz (Ed.), *Language and cognition in schizophrenia.* Hillsale, N.J.: Lawrence Erlbaum Associates, 1978.

Cohen, B.D., & Camhi, J. Schizophrenic performance in a word-communication task. *Journal of Abnormal Psychology,* 1967, *72,* 240–246.

Committee on Nomenclature and Statistics. *Diagnostic and statistical manual: Mental disorders.* Washington,D.C.: American Psychiatric Association, 1952.

Crider, A., Maher, B., & Grinspoon, L. The effect of sensory input on the reaction time of schizophrenic patients of good and poor premorbid history. *Psychonomic Science,* 1965, *2,* 47–48.

Cromwell, R.L., & Dokecki, P.R. Schizophrenic language: A disattention interpretation. In S. Rosenberg & J.H. Koplin (Eds.), *Developments in applied psycholinguistics research.* New York: Macmillan, 1968.

Davis, J.M. Overview: Maintenance therapy in psychiatry: 1.Schizophrenia. *American Journal of Psychiatry,* 1975, *132,* 1237–1245.

DeSilva, W.P., & Hemsley, D.R. The influence of context on language perception in schizophrenia. *British Journal of Social and Clinical Psychology,* 1977, *16,* 337–345.

Dohrenwend, B.S., & Dohrenwend, B.P. (Eds.). *Stressful life events.* New York: Wiley, 1974.

Domerus, E. von. The specific laws of logic in schizophrenia. In J.S. Kasanin (Ed.), *Language and thought in schizophrenia.* Berkeley: University of California Press, 1944.

Erlenmeyer-Kimling, L. A prospective study of children at risk for schizophrenia: Methodological considerations and some preliminary findings. In R.D. Wirt, G. Winokur, & M. Roff (Eds.), *Life history reseach in psychopathology.* (Vol. IV), Minneapolis: University of Minnesota Press, 1975.

Fairbanks, H. Studies in language behavior: II. The quantitative differentiation of samples of spoken language. *Psychological Monographs,* 1944, *56* (No. 2, Whole No. 255), 19–38.

Feldstein, S., & Jaffe, J. Vocabulary diversity of schizophrenics and normals. *Journal of Speech and Hearing Research,* 1962, *5,* 76–78.

Flor-Henry, P. Lateralized temporal-limbic dysfunction and psychopathology. In S.R. Harnad, H.D. Steklis, & J. Lancaster (Eds.), *Origins and evolution of language and speech. Annals of the New York Academy of Sciences,* 1976, *280,* 777–795.

Gardos, G., & Cole, J.O. Maintenance antipsychotic therapy: Is the cure worse than the disease? *American Journal of Psychiatry,* 1976, *133,* 32–36.

Garmezy, N. The prediction of performance in schizophrenia. In P. Hoch & J. Zubin (Eds.), *Psychopathology of schizophrenia.* New York: Grune & Stratton, 1966.

Goldstein, K. Methodological approach to the study of schizophrenic thought disorder. In J.D. Kasanin (Ed.), *Language and thought in schizophrenia.* Berkeley: University of California Press, 1944.

Goodstein, L.D., Guertin, W.H., & Blackburn, H.L. Effects of social motivational variables on choice reaction time of schizophrenics. *Journal of Abnormal and Social Psychology,* 1961, *62,* 24–27.

Gottschalk, L.A. Theory and application of a verbal method of measuring transient psychologic states. In K. Salzinger & S. Salzinger (Eds.), *Research in verbal behavior and some neurophysiological implications.* New York: Academic Press, 1967.

Gottschalk, L.A., & Gleser, G. *The measurement of psychological states through the content analysis of verbal behavior.* Berkeley: University of California Press, 1969.

Hakerem, G., & Lidsky, A. Characteristics of pupillary reactivity in psychiatric patients and normal controls. In M.L. Kietzman, S. Sutton, & J. Zubin (Eds.), *Experimental approaches to psychopathology.* New York: Academic Press, 1975.

Hakerem, G., Sutton, S., & Zubin, J. Pupillary reactions to light in schizophrenic patients and normals. In H.E. Whipple (Ed.), *Can psychopathology be measured? Annals of the New York Academy of Sciences,* 1964, *105,* 820–831.

Hammer, M., & Salzinger, K. Some formal characteristics of schizophrenic speech as a measure of social deviance. *Annals of the New*

York Academy of Sciences*, 1964, *105*, 861–889.

Helzer, J.E., Clayton, P.J., Pambakian, R., Reich, T., Woodruff, R.A., Jr., & Reveley, M.A. Reliability of psychiatric diagnosis: II. The test/retest reliability of diagnostic classification. *Archives of General Psychiatry*, 1977, *34*, 136–141.

Hersen, M., & Bellack, A.S. *Behavioral assessment*. New York: Pergamon, 1976. (a)

Hersen, M., & Bellack, A.S. A multiple-baseline analysis of social-skills training in chronic schizophrenics. *Journal of Applied Behavior Analysis*, 1976, *9*, 239–245. (b)

Kallmann, F.J. The genetic theory of schizophrenia. An analysis of 691 schizophrenic twin index families. *American Journal of Psychiatry*, 1946, *103*, 309–322.

Kasanin, J.S. (Ed.), *Language and thought in schizophrenia*. Berkeley: University of California Press, 1944.

Kazdin, A.E. Behavior modification and the "treatment of schizophrenia." In P.A. Magaro (Ed.), *The construction of madness*. London: Pergamon, 1976.

King, H.E. Psychomotor correlates of behavior disorder. In M.L. Kietzman, S. Sutton, & J. Zubin (Eds.), *Experimental approaches to psychopathology*. New York: Academic Press, 1975.

Klein, E.B., Cicchetti, D., & Spohn, H. A test of the censure-deficit model and its relation to premorbidity in the performance of schizophrenics. *Journal of Abnormal Psychology*, 1967, *72*, 174–181.

Kraepelin, E. *Dementia praecox and paraphrenia*. R.M. Barclay, trans., G.M. Robertson, Ed. Edinburgh: E & S Livingstone, 1919.

Kristofferson, M.W. Shifting attention between modalities: A comparison of schizophrenics and normals. *Journal of Abnormal Psychology*, 1967, *72*, 388–394.

Laffal, J. The contextual associates of sun and god in Schreber's autobiography. *Journal of Abnormal and Social Psychology*, 1960, *61*, 474–479.

Laffal, J. Changes in the language of a schizophrenic patient during psychotherapy. *Journal of Abnormal and Social Psychology*, 1961, *63*, 422–427.

Laffal, J. *Pathological and normal language*. New York: Atherton, 1965.

Landis, C., & Bolles, M.M. *Textbook of abnormal psychology*. New York: Macmillan, 1950.

Liberman, R.P. Behavior modification of schizophrenia. In W.J. DiScipio (Ed.), *Behavioral treatment of psychotic illness*. New York: Behavioral Publications, 1974.

Maher, B.A., McKean, K.O., & McLaughlin, B. Studies in psychotic language. In P.J. Stone, D.C. Dunphy, M.S. Smith, & D.M. Ogilvie (Eds.), *The general inquirer: A computer approach to content analysis*. Cambridge, Mass.: M.I.T. Press, 1966.

Mann, M.B. Studies in language behavior: III. The quantitative differentiation of samples of written language. *Psychological Monographs*, 1944, *56*, 41–74.

Meadow, A., Greenblatt, M., Levine, J., & Solomon, H.C. The discomfort-relief quotient as a measure of tension and adjustment. *Journal of Abnormal and Social Psychology*, 1952, *47*, 658–661.

Mednick, S.A., & Schulsinger, F. Some premorbid characteristics related to breakdown in children with schizophrenic mothers. In D. Rosenthal & S.S. Kety (Eds.), *The transmission of schizophrenia*. New York: Pergamon, 1968.

Mednick, S.A., & Schulsinger, F. A learning theory of schizophrenia: Thirteen years later. In M. Hammer, K. Salzinger, & S. Sutton (Eds.), *Psychopathology: Contributions from the social, behavioral, and biological sciences*. New York: Wiley, 1973.

Moon, A.F., Mefferd, R.B., Jr., Weiland, B.A., Pokorny, A.D., & Falconer, G.A. Perceptual dysfunction as a determinant of schizophrenic word associations. *Journal of Nervous and Mental Disease*, 1968, *146*, 80–84.

O'Kelley, L.I. & Muckler, F.A. *Introduction to psychopathology*. Englewood Cliffs, N.J.: Prentice-Hall, 1955.

Oltmanns, T.F., Ohayon, J., & Neale, J.M. Distractibility in schizophrenia: The effect of anti-psychotic medication and diagnostic criteria. *Journal of Psychiatric Research*, in press.

Oltmanns, T.F., & Neale, J.M. Distractibility in relation to other aspects of schizophrenic disorder. In S. Schwartz (Ed.), *Language and cognition in schizophrenics*. Hillsdale, N.J.: Lawrence Erlbaum Associates, 1978.

Paul, G.L., & Lentz, R.J. *Psychosocial treatment of chronic mental patients*. Cambridge, Mass.: Harvard University Press, 1977.

Payne, R.W. The measurement and significance of overinclusive thinking and retardation in schizophrenic patients. In P. Hoch & J. Zubin (Eds.), *Psychopathology of schizophrenia.* New York: Grune & Stratton, 1966.

Peastrel, A.L. Studies in efficiency: Semantic generalization in schizophrenia. *Journal of Abnormal and Social Psychology,* 1964, *69,* 444–449.

Professional Staff of the U.S.–U.K. Cross-national Project. The diagnosis and psychopathology of schizophrenia in New York and London. *Schizophrenia Bulletin,* 1974, *11,* 80–102.

Rochester, S.R., & Martin, J.R. *Discourse of the schizophrenic speaker.* New York: Plenum, in press.

Romano, J. The central core of madness. In L.C. Wynne, R.L. Cromwell, & S. Matthysse (Eds.), *The nature of schizophrenia.* New York: Wiley, 1978.

Rosenbaum, G., MacKavey, W.R., & Grisell, J.L. Effects of biological and social motivation on schizophrenic reaction time. *Journal of Abnormal and Social Psychology,* 1957, *54,* 364–368.

Rosenthal, D. *Genetic theory and abnormal behavior.* New York: McGraw-Hill, 1970.

Salzinger, K. Shift in judgment of weights as a function of anchoring stimuli and instructions in early schizophrenics and normals. *Journal of Abnormal and Social Psychology,* 1957, *55,* 43–49.

Salzinger, K. The immediacy hypothesis and schizophrenia. In H.M. Yaker, H. Osmond, & F. Cheek (Eds.),*The future of time.* Garden City, N.Y.: Doubleday, 1971 (a)

Salzinger, K. An hypothesis about schizophrenic behavior. *American Journal of Psychotherapy,* 1971, *25,* 601–614. (b)

Salzinger, K. *Schizophrenia: Behavioral aspects.* New York: Wiley, 1973.

Salzinger, K. *But is it good for the patients?* Paper presented at the American Psychological Association Meetings, San Francisco, August 1977.

Salzinger, K. A behavioral analysis of diagnosis. In R.L. Spitzer & D.F. Klein (Eds.), *Critical issues in psychiatric diagnosis.* New York: Raven Press, 1978. (a)

Salzinger, K. *The behavioral mechanism to explain abnormal behavior.* Paper presented at the New York Academy of Sciences, New York City, April 1978. (b)

Salzinger, K. Language behavior. In A.C. Catania & T.A. Brigham (Eds.), *Handbook of applied behavior analysis: Social and instructional processes.* New York: Irvington/Naiburg, 1978.

Salzinger, K., & Pisoni, S. Reinforcement of affect responses of schizophrenics during the clinical interview. *Journal of Abnormal and Social Psychology,* 1958, *57,* 84–90.

Salzinger, K., & Pisoni, S. Reinforcement of verbal affect resonses of normal subjects during the interview. *Journal of Abnormal and Social Psychology,* 1960, *60,* 127–130.

Salzinger, K., & Pisoni, S. Some parameters of the conditioning of verbal affect responses in schizophrenic subjects. *Journal of Abnormal and Social Psychology,* 1961, *63,* 511–516.

Salzinger, K., Pisoni, S., Feldman, R.S., & Bacon, P.M. *The effect of drugs on verbal behavior.* Presented at the American Association for the Advancement of Science Symposium, Denver, 1961.

Salzinger, K., Portnoy, S., & Feldman, R.S. Experimental manipulation of continuous speech in schizophrenic patients. *Journal of Abnormal and Social Psychology,* 1964, *68,* 508–516. (a)

Salzinger, K., Portnoy, S., & Feldman, R.S. Verbal behavior of schizophrenic and normal subjects. *Annals of the New York Academy of Sciences,* 1964, *105,* 845–860.

Salzinger, K. Portnoy, S., & Feldman, R.S. Verbal behavior in schizophrenics and some comments toward a theory of schizophrenia. In P. Hoch & J. Zubin (Eds.), *Psychopathology of schizophrenia.* New York: Grune & Stratton, 1966.

Salzinger, K., Portnoy, S., & Feldman, R.S. *The communicability of essays contrary to their authors' beliefs.* Paper presented at American Psychological Association Convention, Montreal, 1973.

Salzinger, K., Portnoy, S., & Feldman, R.S. Communicability deficit in schizophrenics resulting from a more general deficit. In S. Schwartz (Ed.), *Language and cognition in schizophrenia.* Hillsdale, N.J.: Lawrence Erlbaum Associates, 1978.

Salzinger, K., Portnoy, S., Pisoni, D.B., & Feldman, R.S. The immediacy hypothesis and response-produced stimuli in schizophrenic speech. *Journal of Abnormal Psychology,* 1970, *76,* 258–264.

Salzinger, K., & Salzinger, S. Behavior theory for the study of psychopathology. In M. Hammer, K. Salzinger & S. Sutton (Eds.), *Psychopathology: Contributions from the social, behavioral, and biological sciences.* New York: Wiley, 1973.

Saslow, G., & Matarazzo, J.D. A technique for studying changes in interview behavior. In E.A. Rubinstein & M.B. Parloff (Eds.), *Research in psychotherapy,* Washington, D.C.: American Psychological Association, 1959.

Schacht, T., & Nathan, P.E. But is it good for the psychologists? Appraisal and status of DSM-III. *American Psychologist,* 1977, *32,* 1017–1025.

Segal, J. (Ed.) *Research in the service of mental health.* Rockville, Md.: NIMH, Washington, D.C.: U.S. Government Printing Office, 1975.

Shagass, C., & Overton, D.A. Measurement of cerebral "excitability" characteristics in relation to psychopathology. In M.L. Kietzman, S. Sutton, & J. Zubin (Eds.), *Experimental approaches to psychopathology.* New York: Academic Press, 1975.

Shakow, D. The nature of deterioration in schizophrenic conditions. *Nervous and Mental Disease Monographs,* (No. *70*). New York: Coolidge Foundation, 1946.

Shakow, D. Segmental set: A theory of the formal psychological deficit in schizophrenia. *Archives of General Psychiatry,* 1962, *6,* 1–17.

Shimkunas, A. Hemispheric asymmetry and schizophrenic thought disorder. In S. Schwartz (Ed.), *Language and cognition in schizophrenia.* New York: Lawrence Erlbaum Associates, 1978.

Silverman, J. Variations in cognitive control and psychophysiological defense in the schizophrenias. *Psychosomatic Medicine,* 1967, *29,* 225–251.

Smith, K., Pumphrey, M.W., & Hall, J.C. The "last straw": The decisive incident resulting in the request for hospitalization in 100 schizophrenic patients. *American Journal of Psychiatry,* 1963, *120,* 228–233.

Snyder, S.H. *Madness and the brain.* New York: McGraw-Hill, 1974.

Spitzer, R.L., & Fleiss, J.L. A re-analysis of the reliability of psychiatric diagnosis. *British Journal of Psychiatry,* 1974, *125,* 341–347.

Sutton, S., Hakerem, G., Zubin, J., & Portnoy, M. The effect of shift of sensory modality on serial reaction time: A comparison of schizophrenics and normals. *American Journal of Psychology,* 1961, *74,* 224–232.

Sutton, S., & Zubin, J. Effect of sequence on reaction time in schizophrenia. In A.T. Welford & J.E. Birren (Eds.), *Behavior, aging and the nervous system.* Springfield, III.: Charles C Thomas, 1965.

Task Force on Nomenclature and Statistics. *DSM-III draft.* New York: Biometrics Research, 1977.

Taylor, W.L. Cloze procedure: A new tool for measuring readability. *Journalism Quarterly,* 1953, *30,* 415–433.

Tobias, L.L., & MacDonald, M.L. Withdrawal of maintenance drugs with long-term hospitalized mental patients: A critical review. *Psychological Bulletin,* 1974, *81,* 107–125.

Ullmann, L.P., & Krasner, L. *A psychological approach to abnormal behavior.* Englewood Cliffs, N.J.: Prentice-Hall, 1975.

Venables, P.H. Input dysfunction in schizophrenia. In B.A. Maher (Ed.), *Progress in experimental personality research,* (Vol. 1). New York: Academic Press, 1964.

Vetter, H.J. *Language behavior in schizophrenia.* Springfield, III.: Charles C Thomas, 1968.

Vetter, H.J. Psychopathology and atypical language development. In D. Aaronson & R.W. Rieber (Eds.), *Developmental psycholinguistics and communication disorders. Annals of the New York Academy of Sciences,* 1975, *263,* 140–155.

Vigotsky, L.S. Thought in schizophrenia. *Archives of Neurology and Psychiatry,* 1934, *31,* 1063–1077.

Waldbaum, J.K., Sutton, S., & Kerr, J. Shift of sensory modality and reaction time in schizophrenia. In M.L. Kietzman, S. Sutton, & J. Zubin (Eds.), *Experimental approaches to psychopathology.* New York: Academic Press, 1975.

Weaver, L.A., Jr., & Brooks, G.W. The use of psychomotor tests in predicting the potential of chronic schizophrenics. *Journal of Neuropsychiatry,* 1964, *5,* 170–180.

Whitehorn, J.C. & Zipf, G.K. Schizophrenic language. *Archives of Neurology and Psychiatry,* 1943, *49,* 831–851.

Woods, W.L. Language study in schizophrenia. *Journal of Nervous and Mental Disease,* 1938, *87,* 290–316.

Wurster, S.A. Effects of anchoring on weight judgments of normals and schizophrenics. *Journal of Personality and Social Psychology,* 1965, *1,* 274–278.

Wynne, L.C., With the assistance of Singer, M.T. Bartko, J.T., & Toohey, M.T., Schizophrenics and their families: Research on parental communication. In J.M. Tanner (Ed.), *De-*

velopments in psychiatric research. London: Hodder & Stoughton, 1977.

Yates, A.J. Psychological deficit. *Annual Review of Psychology,* 1966, *17,* 111–144.

Yozawitz, A. *Central auditory processing of speech and non-speech stimuli in affective psychotics and schizophrenics: A neuropsychological investigation.* Unpublished doctoral dissertation, City University of New York, 1977.

Zahn, T.P., Rosenthal, D., & Shakow, D. Reaction time in schizophrenic and normal subjects in relation to the sequence of series of regular preparatory intervals. *Journal of Abnormal and Social Psychology,* 1961, *63,* 161–168.

Zahn, T.P., Rosenthal, D., & Shakow, D. Effects of irregular preparatory intervals on reaction time in schizophrenia. *Journal of Abnormal and Social Psychology,* 1963, *67,* 44–52.

Zax, M., & Stricker, G. *Patterns of psychopathology: Case studies of behavioral dysfunction.* New York: Macmillan, 1963.

Zubin, J. Classification of the behavior disorders. *Annual Review of Psychology,* 1967, *18,* 373–406.

Zubin, J. Problem of attention in schizophrenia. In M.L. Kietzman, S. Sutton, & J. Zubin (Eds.), *Experimental approaches to psychopathology,* New York: Academic Press, 1975.

Zubin, J. Ther role of vulnerability in the etiology of schizophrenic episodes. In L.J. West & D.E. Flinn (Eds.), *Treatment of schizophrenia.* New York: Grune & Stratton, 1976.

Zubin, J. But is it good for science? *The Clinical Psychologist,* 1977–78, *31,* 1–7.

Zubin, J., & Gurland, B.J. The U.S.–U.K. project on diagnosis of the mental disorders. In L.L. Adler (Ed.), *Issues in cross-cultural research. Annals of the New York Academy of Sciences,* 1977, *285,* 676–686.

Zubin, J., Salzinger, K., Fleiss, J.L., Gurland, B., Spitzer, R.L., Endicott, J., & Sutton, S. Biometric approach to psychopathology: Abnormal and clinical psychology—statistical, epidemiological, and diagnostic approaches. *Annual Review of Psychology,* 1975, *26,* 621–671.

Chapter 12

Task Force on Nomenclature and Statistics. *Diagnostic and statistical manual of mental disorders* (3rd ed. draft). Washington, D.C.: American Psychiatric Association, 1978.

Beach, F.A., Hebb, D.O., Morgn, C.T. & Nissen, H.W. *The neuropsychology of Lashley,* New York: McGraw-Hill, 1960.

Benton, A.L. Constructional apraxia: Some unanswered questions. In A.L. Benton (Ed.), *Contributions to clinical neuropsychology.* Chicago: Aldine, 1969.

Butters, N., & Cermak, L.S. Some analyses of amnesic syndromes in brain-damaged patients. In R.L. Isaacson & K.H. Pribram (Eds.), *The hippocampus,* (Vol. 2), New York: Plenum, 1975.

Butters, N., & Cermak, L.S. Neuropsychological studies of alcoholic Korsakoff patients. In G. Goldstein & C. Neuringer (Eds.), *Empirical studies of alcoholism,* Cambridge, Mass.: Ballinger, 1976.

Committee on Nomenclature and Statistics. *Diagnostic and statistical manual on mental disorders.* Washington, D.C.: American Psychiatric Association, 1968.

Gazzaniga, M.S., Bogen, J.E., & Sperry, R.W. Laterality effects in somesthesis following cerebral commisurotomy in man. *Neuropsychologia,* 1963, *1,* 209–215.

Goldstein, G., & Neuringer, C. *Empirical studies of alcoholism.* Cambridge, Mass.: Ballinger, 1976.

Goldstein, G., & Shelly, C.H. Neuropsychological diagnosis of multiple sclerosis in a neuropsychiatric setting. *Journal of Nervous and Mental Disease,* 1974, *158,* 280–290.

Goldstein, K., & Scheerer, M. Abstract and concrete behavior: An experimental study with special tests. *Psychological Monographs,* 1941, *53* (2, Whole No. 239).

Goodglass, H., & Kaplan, E. *The assessment of aphasia and related disorders.* Philadelphia: Lea & Febiger, 1972.

Halstead, W.C. *Brain and intelligence: A quantitative study of the frontal lobes.* Chicago: University of Chicago Press, 1947.

Klove, H., & Matthews, C.G. Neuropsychological studies of patients with epilepsy. In R.M. Reitan & L.A. Davison (Eds.), *Clinical neuropsychology: Current status and applications.* New York: Winston-Wiley, 1974.

Levy, J. Psychobiological implications of bilateral asymmetry. In S.J. Dimond & J.G. Beaumont (Eds.), *Hemisphere function in the human brain.* London: Elek Science, 1974.

Lezak, M.D. *Neuropsychological assessment.* New York: Oxford University Press, 1976.

Milner, B. Amnesia following operation on the temporal lobes. In C.W.M. Whitty & O.L.

Zangwill (Eds.), *Amnesia.* London: Butterworths, 1966.

Milner, B. Memory and the medial temporal regions of the brain. In K.H. Pribram & D.E. Broadbent (Eds.), *Biology of memory.* New York: Academic Press, 1970.

Newcombe, F. Selective deficits after focal cerebral injury. In S.J. Dimond & J.G. Beaumont (Eds.), *Hemisphere function in the human brain.* London: Elek Science, 1974

Reitan, R.M., Reed, J.C., & Dyken, M.L. Cognitive, psychomotor and motor correlates of multiple sclerosis. *Journal of Nervous and Mental Disease,* 1971, *153,* 218–224.

Schilder, P. Localization of the body image (postural model of the body). *Research publications of the Association for Nervous and Mental Disease,* 1932, *13,* 466–484.

Teuber, H.L. Some alterations in behavior after cerebral lesions in man. *Evolution of nervous control.* Wshington, D.C.: American Association for the Advancement of Science, 1959.

Weinstein, E.A., & Kahn, R.L. *Denial of illness: Symbolic and physiological aspects.* Springfield, Ill.: Charles C Thomas, 1955.

Weinstein, E.A., & Kahn, R.L. Symbolic reorganization in brain injuries. In S. Arieti (Ed.), *American handbook of psychiatry,* (Vol. I). New York: Basic Books, 1959.

Chapter 13

Armor, D.J., Polick, J.M., & Stambul, H.B. *Alcoholism and treatment* (Report #R-1739-NIAA). Santa Monica, Calif.: Rand, 1976.

Bebbington, P.E. The efficacy of Alcoholics Anonymous: The elusiveness of hard data. *British Journal of Psychiatry,* 1976, *128,* 572–580.

Blachly, P.H. An "electric needle" for aversive conditioning of the needle ritual. *International Journal of Addictions,* 1970, *6,* 327–328.

Blum, E.M., & Blum, R.H. *Alcoholism: Modern psychological approaches to treatment.* San Francisco: Jossey-Bass, 1972.

Briddell, D.W., & Nathan, P.E. Behavior assessment and modification with alcoholics: Current status and future trends. In M. Hersen, R.M. Eisler, & P.M. Miller (Eds.), *Progress in behavior modification* (Vol. 2). New York: Academic Press, 1976.

Caddy, G.R. Blood alcohol concentration discrimination training: Development and current status. In G.A. Marlatt & P.E. Nathan (Eds.), *Behavioral approaches to alcoholism.* New Brunswick, N.J.: Rutgers Center of Alcohol Studies, 1977.

Cadoret, R.J. Genetic determinants of alcoholism. In R.E. Tarter & A.A. Sugerman (Eds.), *Alcoholism: Interdisciplinary approaches to an enduring problem.* Reading, Mass.: Addison-Wesley, 1976.

Cahalan, D. *Problem drinkers.* San Francisco: Jossey-Bass, 1970.

Cahalan, D., Cisin, I.H., & Crossley, H. *American drinking practices.* New Brunswick, N.J.: Rutgers Center of Alcohol Studies, 1969.

Cahalan, D., & Room, R. *Problem drinking among American men.* New Brunswick, N.J.: Rutgers Center of Alcohol Studies, 1974.

Cappell, H. An evaluation of tension models of alcohol consumption. In R.J. Gibbons, Y. Israel, H. Kalant, R.E. Popham, W. Schmidt, & R.G. Smart (Eds.), *Research advances in alcohol and drug problems* (Vol. 2). New York: Wiley, 1975.

Caudill, B.D. & Marlatt, G.A. Modeling influences in social drinking: An experimental analogue. *Journal of Consulting and Clinical Psychology,* 1975, *43,* 405–415.

Chaney, E.F., O'Leary, M.R., & Marlatt, G.A. *Skill training with alcoholics.* Unpublished manuscript, University of Washington, 1978.

Commission of Inquiry into the Non-Medical Use of Drugs, *Final report.* Ottawa: Information Canada, 1973.

Conger, J.J. The effects of alcohol on conflict behavior in the albino rat. *Quarterly Journal of Studies on Alcohol,* 1951, *12,* 1–29.

Conger, J.J. Alcoholism: Theory, problem and challenge: II. Reinforcement theory and the dynamics of alcoholism. *Quarterly Journal of Studies on Alcohol,* 1956, *17,* 291–324.

Coombs, R.H. *Junkies and straights.* Lexington, Mass.: Lexington Books, 1975.

Copemann, C.D. Drug addiction: I. A theoretical framework for behavior therapy. *Psychological Reports,* 1975, *37,* 947–958.

Cruz-Coke, R. Genetic aspects of alcoholism. In Y. Israel & J. Mardones (Eds.), *Biological basis of alcoholism* New York: Wiley, 1971.

Davies, V.E., & Walsh, M.J. Effect of ethanol on neuroamine metabolism. In Y. Israel & J. Mardones (Eds.), *Biological basis of alcoholism* New York: Wiley, 1971.

Davis, W.M., & Smith, S.G. Role of conditioned

reinforcers in the initiation, maintenance, and extinction of drug-seeking behavior. *Pavlovian Journal,* 1976, *11,* 222–236.

Dole, V.P., & Nyswander, M.E. Rehabilitation of heroin addicts after blockade with methadone. *New York State Journal of Medicine,* 1966, *66,* 2011–2017.

Droppa, D.C. Behavioral treatment of drug addiction: A review and analysis. *International Journal of Addictions,* 1973, *8,* 143–161.

DuPont, R.L. Profile of a heroin-addiction epidemic. *New England Journal of Medicine,* 1971, *285,* 320–324.

Engle, K.B., & Williams, T.K. Effect of an ounce of vodka on alcoholics' desire for alcohol. *Quarterly Journal of Studies on Alcohol,* 1972, *33,* 1099–1105.

Freund, G. Diseases of the nervous system associated with alcoholism. In R.E. Tarter & A.A. Sugerman (Eds.), *Alcoholism: Interdisciplinary approaches to an enduring problem.* Reading, Mass.: Addison-Wesley, 1976.

Goodwin, D.W., Crane, J.B., & Guze, S.B. Alcoholic "blackouts": A review and clinical study of 100 alcoholics. *American Journal of Psychiatry,* 1969, *126,* 77–84.

Gross, M.M., & Hastey, J.M. Sleep disturbances in alcoholism. In R.E. Tarter, & A.A. Sugerman (Eds.), *Alcoholism: Interdisciplinary approaches to an enduring problem.* Reading, Mass.: Addison-Wesley, 1976.

Hamburg, S. Behavior therapy in alcoholism: A critical review of broad-spectrum approaches. *Journal of Studies on Alcohol,* 1975, *36,* 69–87.

Hershon, H. Alcoholism and the concept of disease. *British Journal of Addiction.* 1974, *69,* 123–131.

Higgins, R.L. & Marlatt, G.A. The effects of anxiety arousal upon the consumption of alcohol by alcoholics and social drinkers. *Journal of Consulting and Clinical Psychology,* 1973, *41,* 426–433.

Higgins, R.L. & Marlatt, G.A. Fear of interpersonal evaluation as a determinant of alcohol consumption in male social drinkers. *Journal of Abnormal Psychology,* 1975, *84,* 644–651.

Hill, H.E. Haertzen, C.A., & Davis, H. An MMPI factor analytic study of alcoholics, narcotic addicts and criminals. *Quarterly Journal of Studies on Alcohol,* 1962, *23,* 411–431.

Himmelsbach, C.K., & Small, L.F. Clinical studies of drug addiction: II "Rossium" treatment of drug addiction. (With a report on the chemistry of "Rossium". Suppl. 125 to the Public Health Reports). Washington, D.C.: U.S. Government Printing Office, 1937.

Jacobson, G.R., *Diagnosis and assessment of alcohol abuse and alcohol* Washington, D.C.: National Institute on Alcohol Abuse and Alcoholism, 1975.

Jellinek, E.M. Phases of alcohol addiction. *Quarterly Journal of Studies on Alcohol,* 1952, *13,* 673–684.

Jellinek, E.M. *The disease concept of alcoholism.* New Brunswick, N.J.: Hillhouse Press, 1960.

Jones, K.L., Smith, D.W., Ulleland, C.N. & Streissguth, A.P. *Pattern of malformation in offspring of chronic alcoholic mothers.* Lancet, 1973, *1,* 1267–1271.

Keller, M. On the loss-of-control phenomenon in alcoholism. *British Journal of Addiction,* 1972, *67,* 153–166.

Keller, M. A nonbehaviorist's view of the behavioral problem with alcoholism. In P.E. Nathan, G.A. Marlatt, & T. Løberg (Eds.), *Experimental and behavioral approaches to alcoholism.* New york: Plenum, 1978.

Korsten, M.A., & Lieber, C.D. Medical complications of alcoholism: Hepatic studies. In R.E. Tarter & A.A. Sugerman (Eds.), *Alcoholism: Interdisciplinary approaches to an enduring problem.* Reading, Mass.: Addison-Wesley, 1976.

Layard, J.C. Morphine. *Atlantic Monthly,* 1874, *33,* 697–712.

Lemere, F. What causes alcoholism? *Journal of Clinical Psychopathology,* 1956, *17,* 202–206.

Lieber, C.S. Ethanol and the liver. In P.G. Bourne & R. Fox (Eds.), *Alcoholism: Progress in research and treatment.* New York: Academic Press, 1973.

Lied, E.R., & Marlatt, G.A. *Modeling as a determinant of alcohol consumption: Effects of subject sex and prior drinking distory.* Unpublished manuscript, University of Washington, 1978.

Light, D. Costs and benefits of alcohol consumption. *Society,* September/October, 1975.

Lindesmith, A.R. *Addiction and opiates.* Chicago: Aldine, 1968.

Lloyd, R.W. & Salzberg, H.C. Controlled social drinking: An alternative to abstinence as a treatment goal for some alcohol abusers. *Psychological Bulletin,* 1975, *82,* 815–842.

Lovibond, S.H., & Caddy, G.R. Discriminated aversive control in the moderation of alcoholics' drinking behavior. *Behavior Therapy,* 1970, *1,* 437–444.

Maisto, S.A., Lauerman, R., & Adesso, V.J. A

comparison of two experimental studies investigating the role of cognitive factors in excessive drinking. *Journal of Studies on Alcohol,* 1977, *38,* 145–149.

Manson, M.P. A psychometric determination of alcoholic addiction. *American Journal of Psychiatry,* 1949, *106,* 199–205.

Marlatt, G.A. Alcohol, stress and cognitive control. In I.G. Sarason & C.D. Spielberger (Eds.), *Stress and anxiety* (Vol 3). Washington, D.C.: Hemisphere (Wiley), 1976. (a)

Marlatt, G.A. The drinking profile: A questionnaire for the behavioral assessment of alcoholism. In E.J. Mash & L.C. Terdal (Eds.), *Behavior therapy assessment: Diagnosis and evaluation.* New York: Springer, 1976. (b)

Marlatt, G.A. Behavioral assessment of social drinking and alcoholism. In G.A. Marlatt & P.E. Nathan (Eds.), *Behavioral approaches to alcoholism.* New Brunswick, N.J.: Rutgers Center of Alcohol Studies, 1977.

Marlatt, G.A. Craving for alcohol, loss of control and relapse: A cognitive-behavioral analysis. In P.E Nathan, G.A. Marlatt, & T. Løberg (Eds.), *Experimental and behavioral approaches to alcoholism.* New York: Plenum, 1978.

Marlatt, G.A., Demming, B., & Reid, J.B. Loss of control drinking in alcoholics: An experimental analogue. *Journal of Abnormal Psychology,* 1973, *81,* 233–241.

Marlatt, G.A., Kosturn, C.F., & Lang, A.R. Provocation to anger and opportunity for retaliation as determinants of alcohol consumption in social drinkers. *Journal of Abnormal Psychology,* 1975, *84,* 652–659.

Marlatt, G.A., & Marques, J.K. Meditation, self-control, and alcohol use. In R.B. Stuart (Ed.), *Behavioral self management: Strategies and outcomes.* New York: Brunner/Mazel, 1977.

Marlatt, G.A., & Nathan, P.E. (Eds.), *Behavioral approaches to alcoholism.* New Brunswick, N.J.: Rutgers Center of Alcohol Studies, 1977.

Mattison, J.B. Morphinism in medical men. *Journal of the American Medical Association,* 1894, *23,* 186–188.

Maurer, D.W., & Vogel, V.H. *Narcotics and narcotic addiction.* Springfield, Ill.: Charles C Thomas, 1973.

McClearn, G.L. The genetic aspects of alcoholism. In P.G. Bourne & R. Fox (Eds.), *Alcoholism: Progress in research and treatment.* New York: Academic Press, 1973.

McClelland, D.C., Davis, W.M., Kalin, R., & Wanner, E. *The drinking man.* New York: Free Press, 1972.

Mello, N.K. Some aspects of the behavioral pharmacology of alcohol. In D.H. Efron (Ed.), *Psychopharmacology: A review of progress, 1957–1967.* (Public Health Service Publication No. 1836). Washington, D.C.: U.S. Government Printing Office. 1968.

Miller, P.M. Behavioral assessment in alcoholism research and treatment: Current techniques. *International Journal of the Addictions,* 1973, *8,* 831–837.

Miller, P.M. *Behavioral treatment of alcoholism.* New York: Pergamon, 1976.

Miller, P.M. Alternative skills training in alcoholism treatment. In P.E. Nathan, G.A. Marlatt, & T. Løberg (Eds.), *Experimental and behavioral approaches to alcoholism.* New York: Plenum, 1978.

Miller, P.M., & Mastria, M.A. *Alternatives to alcohol abuse: A social learning model.* Champaign, Ill.: Research Press, 1977.

Miller, W.R. Alcoholism scales and objective assessment methods: A review. *Psychological Bulletin,* 1976, *83,* 649–674.

Miller, W.R., & Caddy, G.R. Abstinence and controlled drinking in the treatment of problem drinkers. *Journal of Studies on Alcohol,* 1977, *38,* 986–1003.

Miller, W.R., & Marlatt, G.A. The Banff Skiism Screening Test: An instrument for assessing degree of addiction. *Addictive Behaviors,* 1977, *2,* 81–82.

Miller, W.R., & Munoz, R.F. *How to control your drinking.* Englewood Cliffs, N.J.: Prentice-Hall, 1976.

Myerson, R.M. Effects of alcohol on cardiac and muscular function. In Y. Israel & J. Mardones (Eds.), *Biological basis of alcoholism.* New York: Wiley, 1971.

Nathan, P.E. Alcoholism. In H. Leitenberg (Ed.), *Handbook of behavior modification and behavior therapy.* Englewood Cliffs, N.J.: Prentice-Hall, 1976.

Nathan, P.E. Studies in blood-alcohol level discrimination. In P.E. Nathan, G.A. Marlatt, & T. Løberg (Eds.), *Experimental and behavioral approaches to alcoholism.* New York: Plenum, 1978.

Nathan, P.E., & Briddell, D.W. Behavioral assessment and treatment of alcoholism. In B. Kissin & H. Begleiter (Eds.), *The biology of alcoholism.* (Vol.5). New York: Plenum, 1977.

Nathan, P.E., Marlatt, G.A., & Løberg, T. *Ex-*

perimental and behavioral approaches to alcoholism. New York: Plenum, 1978.

Nathan, P.E., & O'Brien, J.S. An experimental analysis of the behavior of alcoholics and nonalcoholics during prolonged experimental drinking. *Behavior Therapy,* 1971, *2,* 455–476.

National Council on Alcoholism. Criteria for the diagnosis of alcoholism. *American Journal of Psychiatry,* 1972, *129,* 127–135.

National Institute on Alcohol Abuse and Alcoholism. *Alcohol and health* (First, second, and third reports to the U.S. Congress). Washington, D.C.: Department of Health, Education, and Welfare, 1971, 1974, and 1977.

O'Brien, C.P. Experimental analysis of conditioning factors in human narcotic addiction. *Pharmacological Reviews,* 1976, *27,* 533–543.

Orford, J., & Hawker, A. Note on the ordering of onset of symptoms in alcohol dependence. *Psychological Medicine,* 1974, *4,* 281–288.

Pattison, E.M. Nonabstinent drinking goals in the treatment of alcoholism. *Archives of General Psychiatry,* 1976, *33,* 923–930.

Plaut, T.F. *Alcohol problems: A report to the nation by the Cooperative Commission on the Study of Alcoholism.* New York: Oxford Universtiy Press, 1967.

Pomerleau, O., Pertschuk, M., & Stinnett, J. A critical examination of some current assumptions in the treatment of alcoholism. *Journal of Studies on Alcohol,* 1976, *37,* 849–867.

Randolph, T. The descriptive features of food addiction: Addictive eating and drinking. *Quarterly Journal of Studies on Alcohol,* 1956, *17,* 198–224.

Ray, O.S. *Drugs, society, and human behavior.* St. Louis: Mosby, 1974.

Reid, J.B. The study of drinking in natural settings. In G.A. Marlatt & P.E. Nathan (Eds.), *Behavioral approaches to alcoholism.* New Brunswick, N.J.: Rutgers Center of Alcohol Studies, 1977.

Restak, R. The brain makes its own narcotics. *Saturday Review,* March 5, 1977.

Robins, L.N. *Veterans' drug use three years after Vietnam.* St. Louis: Department of Psychiatry, Washington University School of Medicine (mimeograph), 1976.

Rush, B. *An inquiry into the effects of ardent spirits upon the human body and mind* (1785). Brookfield: Merriam (8th ed.), 1814.

Russell, J.A., & Mehrabian, A. The mediating role of emotions in alcohol use. *Journal of Studies on Alcohol,* 1975, *36,* 1508–1536.

Selzer, M.L. The Michigan Alcoholism Screening Test: The quest for a new diagnostic instrument. *American Journal of Psychiatry,* 1971, *127,* 89–94.

Siegler, M., Osmond, H., & Newell, S. Models of alcoholism. *Quarterly Journal of Studies on Alcohol,* 1968, *29,* 571–591.

Snyder, S.H. Opiate receptors and internal opiates. *Scientific American,* March 1977.

Sobell, M.B., & Sobell, L.C. Individualized behavior therapy for alcoholics. *Behavior Therapy,* 1973, *4,* 49–72.

Sobell, M.B., & Sobell, L.C. Second year treatment outcome of alcoholics treated by individualized behavior therapy: Results. *Behaviour Research and Therapy,* 1976, *14,* 195–215.

Sobell, M.B., & Sobell, L.C. *Behavioral treatment of alcohol problems: Individualized therapy and controlled drinking.* New York: Plenum, 1978.

Solomon, R.L. An opponent-process theory of acquired motivation: IV. The affective dynamics of addiction. In J. Maser & M.E.P. Seligman (Eds.), *Psychopathology: Experimental models.* San Francisco: W.H. Freeman, 1977.

Solomon, R.L. & Corbit, J.D. An opponent-process theory of motivation: I. Temporal dynamics of affect. *Psychological Review,* 1974, *81,* 119–145.

Szasz, T. *Ceremonial chemistry.* New York: Anchor Press/Doubleday, 1974.

Tarter, R.E. Empirical investigations of psychological deficit. In R.E. Tarter & A.A. Sugerman (Eds.), *Alcoholism: Interdisciplinary approaches to an enduring problem.* Reading, Mass.: Addison-Wesley, 1976.

Tarter, R.E., & Schneider, D.U. Models and theories of alcoholism. In R.A. Tarter & A.A. Sugerman (Eds.), *Alcoholism: Interdisciplinary approaches to an enduring problem.* Reading, Mass.: Addison-Wesley, 1976.

Tintera, J., & Lovell, H. Endocrine treatment of alcoholism. *Geriatrics,* 1949, *4,* 274–280.

Trainor, D. Brain opiates may play important role in therapy. *The Journal,* June 1, 1977.

Verden, P., & Shatterly, D. Alcoholism research and resistance to understanding the compulsive drinker. *Mental Hygiene,* 1971, *55,* 331–336.

Weil, A. *The natural mind.* Boston: Houghton Mifflin, 1972.

Wilson, G.T. Alcoholism and aversion therpay: Issues, ethics and evidence. In G.A. Marlatt

& P.E. Nathan (Eds.), *Behavioral approaches to alcoholism.* New Brunswick, N.J.: Rutgers Center of Alcohol Studies, 1977.

World Health Organization, *Expert committee on drugs liable to produce addiction: Second report,* (Technical report series no. 21). Geneva: World Health Organization, 1950.

Chapter 14

Abel, G.G. Personal communication, June 12, 1975

Abel, G.G., Barlow, D.H., & Blanchard, E.B. *Developing heterosexual arousal by altering masturbatory fantasies: A controlled study.* Paper presented to the 7th Annual Convention of Association for Advancement of Behavior Therapy, Miami, December 1973.

Abel, G.G., Barlow, D.H., Blanchard, E.B., & Guild, D. *The components of rapists' sexual arousal.* Paper presented at the annual meeting of the American Psychiatric Association, Anaheim, Calif., May 1975.

Abel, G.G., Barlow, D.H., Blanchard, E.B. & Mavissakalian, M. *The relationship of aggressive cues to the sexual arousal of rapists.* Paper presented at the American Psychological Association, New Orleans, September 1974.

Abel, G.G., & Blanchard, E.B. The measurement and generation of sexual arousal in male sexual deviates. In M. Hersen, R.M. Eisler, & P.M. Miller (Eds.), *Progress in behavior modification* (Vol. 2). New York: Academic Press, 1976.

Abel, G.G., Levis, D.J., & Clancy, J. Aversion therapy applied to taped sequences of deviant behavior in exhibitionism and other sexual deviations: A preliminary report. *Journal of Behavior Therapy and Experimental Psychiatry,* 1970, *1,* 59–66.

American Medical Association Committee on Human Sexuality. *Human sexuality.* Washington, D.C.: American Medical Association, 1972.

Annon, J.S. *The extension of learning principles to the analysis and treatment of sexual problems.* (Doctoral dissertation, University of Hawaii, 1971 *Dissertation Abstracts International,* 1971, *32,* (6-B), 3627. (University Microfilms No. 72-290, 570.)

Annon, J.S. The therapeutic use of masturbation in the treatment of sexual disorders. In R.D. Rubin, J.P. Brady, & J.D. Hendeson (Eds.), *Advances in behavior therapy* (Vol. 4). New York: Academic Press, 1973.

Annon, J.S. *The behavioral treatment of sexual problems: Intensive therapy.* Honolulu: Enabling Systems, 1975.

Annon, J.S. *The behavioral treatment of sexual problems: Brief therapy.* New York: Harper & Row, 1976.

Annon, J.S., & Robinson, C.H. Sex therapies—peer and self-counseling. In W.E. Johnson (Ed.), *Sex in life.* New York: William C. Brown, 1978 (a)

Annon, J.S., & Robinson, C.H. The use of vicarious learning in the treatment of sexual concerns. In J. LoPiccolo, & L. LoPiccolo (Eds.), *Handbook of sex therapy.* New York: Plenum, 1978. (b)

Bandura, A. *Principles of behavior modification.* New York: Holt, Rinehart, & Winston, 1969.

Barker, J.C. Behaviour therapy for transvestism: A comparison of pharmacological and electrical aversion techniques. *British Journal of Psychiatry,* 1965, *111,* 268–276.

Barlow, D.H. Assessment of sexual behavior. In A.R. Ciminero, K.S. Calhoun, & H.E. Adams (Eds.), *Handbook of behavioral assessment.* New York: Wiley, 1977.

Barlow, D.H., Agras, W.S., & Raynolds, E.J. *Direct and indirect modifications of gender specific motor behavior in a transsexual.* Paper presented at the 80th Annual Meeting of the American Psychological Association, Honolulu, 1972.

Barlow, D.H., Reynolds, E.J., & Agras, W.S. Gender identity change in a transsexual. *Archives of General Psychiatry,* 1973, *28,* 569–576.

Barnett, W. *Sexual freedom and the Constitution: An inquiry into the constitutionality of repressive sex laws.* Albuquerque: University of New Mexico Press, 1973.

Beach, F.A. Cross-species comparisons and the human heritage. *Archives of Sexual Behavior,* 1976, *5,* 469–485.

Begelman, D.A. Ethical and legal issues in behavior modification. In M. Hersen, R.M. Eisler, & P.M. Miller (Eds.), *Progress in behavior modification* (Vol. 1). New York: Academic Press, 1975.

Belt, B.G. Some organic causes of impotence. *Medical Aspects of Human Sexualtiy,* 1973, *7,* 152.

Bethell, M.F. A rare manifestation of festishism. *Archives of Sexual Behavior,* 1974, *3,* 301–302.

Bieber, I. A discussion of "Homosexuality: The ethical challenge." *Journal of Consulting and Clinical Psychology,* 1976, *44,* 163–166.

Bond, I.K., & Hutchison, H.C. Application of reciprocal inhibition therapy to exhibitionism. *Canadian Medical Association Journal,* 1960, *83,* 23–25.

Brown, J.S. A behavioral analysis of masochism. *Journal of Experimental Research in Personality,* 1965, *1,* 65–70.

Buss, A.H. *Psychopathology.* New York: Wiley, 1966.

Chevalier-Skolnikoff, S. Homosexual behavior in a laboratory group of stumptail monkeys (Macaca arctoides): Forms, contexts, and possible social functions. *Archives of Sexual Behavior,* 1976, *5,* 511–527.

Conrad, S.R., & Wincze, J.P. Orgasmic reconditioning: A controlled study of its effects upon the sexual arousal and behavior of adult male homosexuals. *Behavior Therapy,* 1976, *7,* 155–166.

Curran, D., & Parr, D. Homosexuality: An analysis of 100 male cases. *British Medical Journal,* 1957, *1,* 797–811.

Davison, G.C. Homosexualtiy: The ethical challenge. *Journal of Consulting and Clinical Psychology,* 1976, *44,* 157–162.

DeRiver, J.P. *Crime and the sexual psychopath.* Springfield, Ill.: Charles C Thomas, 1958.

Epstein, A.W. The fetish object: Phylogenetic considerations. *Archives of Sexual Behavior,* 1975, *4,* 303–308.

Eysenck, H.J., & Rachman, S. *The causes and cures of neurosis.* San Diego: Robert A. Knapp, 1965.

Feingold, L. An illustration of the behavioral therapy approach in the treatment of social and sexual problems. *Pennsylvania Psychiatric Quarterly,* 1966, *6,* 3–19.

Feldman, M.P., & MacCulloch, M.J. *Homosexual behavior: Therapy and assessment.* New York: Pergamon, 1971.

Ferinden, W.E., & Tugender, H.S. *A handbook of hypno-operant therapy and other behavior therapy techniques* (Manual No. 2). New Jersey: Power Publishers, 1972.

Ford, C.S., & Beach, F.A. *Patterns of sexual behavior.* New York: Harper & Brothers, 1951.

Franks, C.M. Reflections upon the treatment of sexual disorders by the behavioral clinician: A historical comparison with the treatment of the alcoholic. *Journal of Sex Research,* 1967, *3,* 212–222.

Friedman, L.J. *Virgin wives: A study of unconsummated marriages.* Springfield, Ill.: Charles C Thomas, 1962.

Gagnon, J.H., & Simon, W. *Sexual conduct: The social sources of human sexuality.* Chicago: Aldine, 1973.

Gambrill, E.D. *Behavior modification: Handbook of assessment, intervention, and evaluation.* San Francisco: Jossey-Bass, 1977.

Gaupp, L.A., Stern, R.M., & Ratliff, R.G. The use of aversion-relief procedures in the treatment of a case of voyeurism. *Behavior Therapy,* 1971, *2,* 585–588.

Goldfried, M.R., & Linehan, M.M. Basic issues in behavioral assessment. In A.R. Ciminero, K.S. Calhoun, & H.E. Adams (Eds.), *Handbook of behavioral assessment.* New York: Wiley, 1977.

Green, R., & Money, J. (Eds.). *Trans-sexualism and sex reassignment.* Baltimore: Johns Hopkins University Press, 1969.

Greenblatt, R.B., & McNamara, V.P. Endocrinology of human sexuality. In B.J. Sadock, H.I. Kaplan, & A.M. Freedman (Eds.), *The sexual experience.* Baltimore: Williams & Wilkins, 1976.

Halleck, S.L. Another response to "Homosexuality: The ethical challenge." *Journal of Consulting and Clinical Psychology,* 1976, *44,* 167–170.

Haslam, M.T. The treatment of psychogenic dyspareunia by reciprocal inhiition. *British Journal of Psychiatry,* 1965, *111,* 280–282.

Heiman, J.R. Women's sexual arousal: The physiology of erotica. *Psychology Today,* 1975, *8* (11), 91–94.

Herink, R. (Ed.). *Psychotherapy handbook.* New York: Jason Aronson, in press.

Hunt, M. *Sexual behavior in the 1970's.* Chicago: Playboy Press, 1974.

Kinsey, A.C., Pomeroy, W.B., & Martin, C.E. *Sexual behavior in the human male.* Philadelphia: Saunders, 1948.

Kinsey, A.C., Pomeroy, W.B., Martin, C.E., & Gebhard, P.H. *Sexual behavior in the human female.* Philadelphia: Saunders, 1953.

Lazarus, A.A. In support of technical eclecticism. *Psychological Reports,* 1967, *21,* 415–416.

Lazarus, A.A., & Serber, M. Is systematic desensitization being misapplied? *Psychological Reports,* 1968, *23,* 215–218.

Lester, D. *Unusual sexual behavior: The standard deviations.* Springfield, Ill.: Charles C Thomas, 1975.

Marks, I.M., Rachman, S., & Gelder, M.G.

Method for assessment of aversion treatment in fetishism with masochism. *Behaviour Research and Therapy,* 1965, *3,* 253–258.

Masters, W.H., & Johnson, V.E. *Human sexual response.* Boston: Little, Brown, 1966

Masters, W.H., & Johnson, V.E. *Human sexual inadequacy.* Boston: Little, Brown, 1970.

Mathis, H.I. Instating sexual adequacy in a disabled exhibitionist. *Psychotherapy: Theory, Research and Practice,* 1975, *12,* 97–100.

McConaghy, N. Penile response conditioning and its relationship to aversion therapy in homosexuals. *Behavior Therapy,* 1970, *1,* 213–221.

McGuire, R.J., Carlisle, J.M., & Young, B.G. Sexual deviation as conditioned behavior: A hypothesis. *Behaviour Research and Therapy,* 1965, *2,* 185–190.

McGuire, R.J., & Vallance, M. Aversion therapy by electric shock: A simple technique. *British Medical Journal,* 1964, *1,* 151–153.

Mead, M. *Sex and temperament.* New York: New American Library, 1935.

Meyer, V., & Chesser, E.S. *Behavior therapy in clinical psychiatry.* New York: Science House, 1970.

Miller, H. The deviant imagination: Can you imagine? *Contemporary Psychology,* 1976, *21,* 804–805.

Money, J. & Ehrhardt, A.A. *Man & woman, boy & girl: The differentiation and dimorphism of gender identity from conception to maturity.* Baltimore: Johns Hopkins University Press, 1972.

Money, J., Jobaris, R., & Furth, G. Apotemnophilia: Two cases of self-demand amputation as a paraphilia. *Journal of Sex Research,* 1977, *13,* 115–125.

Ovesey, L., & Meyers, H. Retarded ejaculation: Psychodynamics and psychotherapy, *American Journal of Psychotherapy,* 1968, *22,* 185–201.

Pauly, I.B. Female transsexualism: Part I. *Archives of Sexual Behavior.* 1974, *3,* 487–507. (a)

Pauly, I.B. Female transsexualism: Part II. *Archives of Sexual Behavior.* 1974, *3,* 509–526. (b)

Pinard, G., & Lamontagne, Y. Electrical aversion, aversion relief and sexual retraining in treatment of fetishism with masochism. *Journal of Behavior Therapy and Experimental Psychiatry,* 1976, *7,* 71–74.

Pomeroy, W.B. Homosexuality. In R.W. Weltage (Ed.), *The same sex: An appraisal of homosexuality.* Boston: Pilgrim Press, 1969.

Proctor, E.B., Wagner, N.N., & Butler, J.C. *The differentiation of male and female orgasm: An experimental study.* Paper presented at the annual meeting of the American Psychological Association, Montreal, September 1973.

Quinsey, V.L., Steinman, G.M., Bergersen, S.G., & Holmes, T.F. Penile circumference, skin conductance, and ranking responses of child molesters and "normals" to sexual and nonsexual visual stimuli. *Behavior Therapy,* 1975, *6,* 213–219.

Rachman, S. Aversion therapy: Chemical or electrical? *Behaviour Research and Therapy,* 1965, *2,* 289–299.

Rachman, S. Sexual fetishism: An experimental analogue. *Psychological Record,* 1966, *16,* 293–296.

Rachman, S. & Hodgson, R.J. Experimentally-induced "Sexual fetishism": Replication and development. *Psychological Record,* 1968, *18,* 25–27.

Reinisch, J.M. Fetal hormones, the brain, and human sex differences: A heuristic, integrative review of the recent literature. *Archives of Sexual Behavior,* 1974, *3,* 51–90.

Rekers, G.A., & Lovaas, O.L. Behavioral treatment of deviant sex-role behaviors in a male child. *Journal of Applied Behavioral Analysis,* 1974, *7,* 173–190.

Rekers, G.A., & Varni, J.W. Self-monitoring and self-reinforcement processes in a pretranssexual boy. *Behaviour Research and Therapy,* 1977, *15,* 177–180.

Robinson, C.H. *The effects of observational learning on the masturbation patterns of pre-orgasmic females.* Paper presented at the annual meeting of the Society for the Scientific Study of Sex, Las Vegas, November 1974. (a)

Robinson, C.H. The effects of observational learning on sexual behaviors and attitudes in orgasmic dysfunctional women. (Doctoral dissertation, University of Hawaii, 1974.) *Dissertation Abstracts International,* 1975, *35* (9-B). (University Microfilms No. 75-5040, 221.) (b)

Roen, P.R. Impotence: A concise review. *New York State Journal of Medicine,* 1965, *65,* 2576–2582.

Sagarin, E. Incest: Problems of definition and frequency. *Journal of Sex Research,* 1977, *13,* 126–135.

Sandler, J. Masochism: An empirical analysis. *Psychological Bulletin,* 1964, *62,* 197–204.

Semans, J.H. Premature ejaculation: A new approach. *Southern Medical Journal,* 1956, *49,* 353–362.

Serber, M. *Shame aversion therapy: A new aversive technique with sexual deviants.* Film demonstration presented at the meeting of the Association for Advancement of Behavior Therapy, Miami, September 1970.

Shenken, L.I. Some clinical and psychopathological aspects of bestiality. *Journal of Nervous and Mental Disease,* 1964, *139,* 137–142.

Shoor, M., Speed, M.H., & Bartelt, C. Syndrome of the adolescent child molester. *American Journal of Psychiatry,* 1966, *122,* 783–789.

Smith, S., & Guthrie, E. Exhibitionism. *Journal of Abnormal and Social Psychology,* 922, *17,* 206–209.

Smithfield, A.P. *Compulsive sex practices* (Vols. 1 & 2). San Diego: Academy Press, 1970.

Socarides, C.W. *The overt homosexual.* New York: Grune & Stratton, 1968. (a)

Socarides, C.W. A provisional theory of setiology in male homosexuality. *International Journal of Psychoanalysis,* 1968, *49,* 27–37. (b)

Staats, A.W., & Staats, C.K. *Complex human behavior: A systematic extension of learning principles.* New York: Holt, Rinehart, & Winston, 1963.

Stevenson, I., & Wolpe, J. Recovery from sexual deviations through overcoming non-sexual neurotic responses. *American Journal of Psychiatry,* 1960, *116,* 737–742.

Stoudenmire, J. Behavioral treatment of voyeurism and possible symptom substitution. *Psychotherapy: Theory Research and Practice,* 1973, *10,* 328–333.

Tennent, G., Bancroft, J., & Case, J. The control of deviant sexual behavior by drugs: A double-blind controlled study of benperidol, chlorpromazine, and placebo. *Archives of Sexual Behavior,* 1974, *3,* 261–271.

Thayler, V. A new look at bestiality. *Sexology,* 1977, *43* (9), 18–22.

Ullmann, L.P., & Krasner, L. (Eds.), *Case studies in behavior modification.* New York: Holt, Rinehart, & Winston, 1965.

Ullmann, L.P., & Krasner, L. *A psychological approach to abnormal behavior* (2nd. ed.). Englewood Cliffs, N.J.: Prentice-Hall, 1975.

Vance, E.B., & Wagner, N.N. Written descriptions of orgasm: A study of sex differences. *Archives of Sexual Behavior,* 1976, *5,* 87–98.

Wolpe, J. *Psychotherapy by reciprocal inhibition.* Stanford, Calif.: Stanford University Press, 1958.

Yates, A.J. *Behavior therapy.* New York: Wiley, 1970.

Chapter 15

Adams, S. Evaluation: A way out of rhetoric. In R. Mattison, T. Palmer & S. Adams (Eds.), *Rehabilitation, recidivism and research.* Hackensack, N.J.: National Council on Crime & Delinquency, 1976.

Bandura, A. *Aggression: A social learning approach.* Englewood Cliffs, N.J.: Prentice-Hall, 1973.

Bandura, A., and Walters, R.H. *Adolescent aggression.* New York: Ronald Press, 1959.

Bazelon, D.L. Psychologists in corrections: Are they doing good for the offender or well for themselves? In S.L. Brodsky (Ed.), *Psychologists in the criminal justice system.* Carbondale, Ill.: Southern Illinois University Press, 1973.

Cloward, R.A. & Ohlin, L.E. *Delinquency and opportunity.* Glencoe, Ill.: Free Press, 1960.

Cohen, H., & Filipczak, J. *A new learning environment.* San Francisco: Jossey-Bass, 1971.

Eysenck, H.J. The development of moral values in children: The contribution of learning theory. *British Journal of Educational Psychology,* 1960, *30,* 11–21.

Feldman, M.P. *Criminal behavior: A psychological analysis.* New York: Wiley, 1977.

Flad and Associates, Inc. *Six year master plan: Wisconsin correctional system.* Madison, Wisc.: Flad and Associates, 1977.

Freedman, B.J. *An analysis of social behavioral skill deficits in delinquent and non-delinquent adolescent boys.* Unpublished doctoral dissertation, University of Wisconsin, 1974.

Friedlander, K. *The psychoanalytic approach to juvenile delinquency.* Oxford: Alden Press, 1967.

Glaser, D. *Routinizing evaluation: Getting feedback on effectiveness of crime and delinquency programs.* Rockville, Md.: National Institute of Mental Health, Center for Studies of Crime and Delinquency, 1974.

Glueck, S., & Glueck, E. *Physique and delinquency.* New York: Harper & Brothers, 1956.

Goodrick, D., Vigdal, G., & Sutton, D. Emerging directions in alcohol treatment: New hope for the problem drinking offender. *Offender Rehabilitation,* 1976, *1,* 57–66.

Goring, C. *The English convict: A statistical study.* London: His Majesty's Stationery Office, 1913.

Halleck, S. Juvenile delinquents: "Sick" or "bad?" *Social Work,* 1962, *7,* 58–61.

Halleck, S. *Psychiatry and the dilemmas of crime.* New York: Harper & Row, 1967.

Hare, R.D. *Psychopathy: Theory and research.* New York: Wiley, 1970.

Hooten, E.A. *Crime and the man.* Cambridge, Mass.: Harvard University Press, 1939.

Jenkins, R.L. Psychiatric syndromes in children and their relation to family background *American Journal of Orthopsychiatry,* 1966, *36,* 450–457.

Jenkins, R.L., & Hewitt, L. Types of personality structure encountered in child guidance clinics. *American Journal of Orthopsychiatry,* 1944, *14,* 84–94.

Lerner, K. *A study of some basic assumptions from the I-level theory of delinquency.* Unpublished doctoral dissertation, Purdue University, 1971.

Lipton, D., Martinson, R.M., & Wilks, J. *The effectiveness of correctional treatment.* New York: Praeger, 1975.

Lombroso, C. *Crime: Its causes and remedies.* Boston: Little, Brown, 1918.

Martinson, R. What works?: Questions and answers about prison reform. *Public Interest,* 1974, *35,* 22–54.

McFall, R. Personal communication, 1977.

Megargee, E.I. Undercontrolled and overcontrolled personality types in extreme antisocial aggression. *Psychological Monographs,* 1966, *80,* (No. 611).

Megargee, E.I. *Crime and delinquency.* Morristown, N.J.: General Learning Press, 1975.

Megargee, E.I. The need for a new classification system. *Criminal Justice and Behavior,* 1977, *4,* 107–114. (a)

Megargee, E.I. Directions for further research. *Criminal Justice and Behavior,* 1977, *4,* 211–216. (b)

Megargee, E.I. A new classification system for criminal offenders. *Criminal Justice and Behavior,* 1977, *4,* 107–216. (c)

Merton, R. Social structure and anomie. *American Sociological Review,* 1938, *3,* 672–682.

Montague, M.F.A. The biologist looks at crime. *Annals of the American Academy of Political and Social Science,* 1941, *217,* 46–57.

National Institute of Mental Health. *Graduated release.* Washington, D.C.: U.S. Government Printing Office, 1971.

Pacht, A.R. (Ed.). *Key issue study.* Unpublished report, Wisconsin Division of Corrections, 1972.

Pacht, A. & Halleck, S. Development of mental health programs in corrections. *Crime and Delinquency,* 1966, *12,* 1–8.

Pacht, A., Halleck, S., & Ehrmann, J. Diagnosis and treatment of the sex offender: A nine year study. *American Journal of Psychiatry,* 1962, *118,* 802–808.

Palmer, T.B. California's community treatment program for delinquent adolescents. *Journal of Research in Crime and Delinquency* 1971, *8,* 74–92.

Palmer, T.B. The community treatment project in perspective: 1961–1973. *Youth Authority Quarterly,* 1973, *26,* 29–43.

Palmer, T.B. Martinson revisited. *Journal of Research in Crime and Delinquency,* 1975, *12,* 133–152.

Phillips, E.L., Wolf, M., Fixsen, D., & Bailey, J. The Achievement Place model: A community-based, family style, behavior modification program for predelinquents. In E. Ribes-Inesta & A. Bandura (Eds.), *Analysis of delinquency and aggression.* New York: Wiley, 1976.

President's Commission on Law Enforcement and Administration of Justice, *The challenge of crime in a free society* Washington, D.C.: U.S. Government Printing Office, 1967.

Quay, H.C. Personality dimensions in delinquent males as inferred from the factor analysis of behavior ratings. *Journal of Research in Crime and Delinquency.* 1964, *1,* 33–37.

Quay, H.C. & Parsons, L.B. *The differential behavioral classification of the juvenile offender.* Washington, D.C.: Bureau of Prisons, U.S. Department of Justice, 1970.

Quay, H.C., & Peterson, D.R. A brief scale for juvenile delinquency. *Journal of Clinical Psychology* 1967, *45,* 139–142.

Rans, L. *Population profiles: Iowa Women's Reformatory. 1918–1975.* Pittsburgh: Entropy Limited, 1976.

Redl, F., & Wineman, D. *Children who hate.* Glencoe, Ill.: Free Press, 1951.

Schellhardt, T.D. Can chocolate turn you into a criminal? Some experts say so. *Wall Street Journal,* June 2, 1977.

Sheehan, S. Annals of crime: A prison and a prisoner. *The New Yorker,* Oct. 1977, pp. 46–99.

Sheldon, W.H. *Varieties of delinquent youth.* New York: Harper & Brothers, 1949.

Simon, R.J. *Women and crime.* Lexington, Mass.: D.C. Heath, 1975.

Sullivan, C.E., Grant, M.Q., & Grant, J.D. The development of interpersonal maturity: Applications to delinquency. *Psychiatry,* 1957, *20,* 373–385.

Sutherland, E. *Principles of criminology,* (4th ed). Philadelphia: Lippincott, 1947.

Ullmann, L.P., & Krasner, L. *Psychological approaches to abnormal behavior* (2nd ed.). Englewood Cliffs, N.J.: Prentice-Hall, 1975.

U.S. Department of Justice, Federal Bureau of Investigation. *Crime in the United States, 1976.* Washington, D.C.: U.S. Government Printing Office, 1977.

Warren, M. *Interpersonal maturity level classification: Juvenile diagnosis & treatment of low, middle, and high maturity delinquents.* California Youth Authority (Mimeographed report), 1966.

Wilson, J.Q. *Thinking about crime.* New York: Basic Books, 1975.

Chapter 16

Alexander, A.B., Miklich, D.R., & Hershkoff, H. The immediate effects of systematic relaxation training on peak expiratory flow rates in asthmatic children. *Psychosomatic Medicine,* 1972, *34,* 388–394.

Alexander, J.F., & Parsons, B.V. Short-term behavioral intervention with delinquent families: Impact on family process and recidivism. *Journal of Abnormal Psychology,* 1973, *81,* 219–226.

Allen, K.E., Hart, B.M., Buell, J.S., Harris, F.R., & Wolf, M.M. Effects of social reinforcement on isolate behavior of a nursery school child. *Child Development,* 1964, *35,* 511–518.

Aragona, J., Cassady, J., & Drabman, R.S. Treating overweight children through parental training and contingency contracting. *Journal of Applied Behavior Analysis,* 1975, *8,* 269–278.

Baker, B.L. Symptom treatment and symptom substitution in enuresis. *Journal of Abnormal Psychology,* 1969, *74,* 42–49.

Bandura, A. *Aggression: A social learning analysis.* Englewood Cliffs, N.J.: Prentice-Hall, 1973.

Bandura, A., Grusec, J.E., & Menlove, F.L. Vicarious extinction of avoidance behavior. *Journal of Personality and Social Psychology,* 1967, *5,* 16–23.

Bandura, A., Ross, D., & Ross, S.A. Transmission of aggression through imitation of aggressive models. *Journal of Abnormal and Social Psychology,* 1961, *63,* 575–582.

Bandura, A., & Walters, R.H. *Adolescent aggression.* New York: Ronald Press, 1959.

Bettleheim, B. *The empty fortress.* New York: Free Press, 1967.

Buell, J., Stoddard, P., Harris, F.R., & Baer, D.M. Collateral social development accompanying reinforcement of outdoor play in a preschool child. *Journal of Applied Behavior Analysis,* 1968, *1,* 167–173.

Burchard, J., & Tyler, V.O., Jr. The modification of delinquent behavior through operant conditioning. *Behaviour Research and Therapy,* 1965, *2,* 245–250.

Carr, E.G., Newsom, C.D., & Binkoff, J.A. Stimulus control of self-destructive behavior in a psychotic child. *Journal of Abnormal Child Psychology,* 1976, *4,* 139–153.

Carr, E.G., Schreibman, L., & Lovaas, O.I. Control of echolalic speech in psychotic children. *Journal of Abnormal Child Psychology,* 1975, *3,* 331–351.

Creer, T.L. Weinberg, E., & Molk, L. Managing a hospital behavior problem: Malingering. *Journal of Behaviour Therapy & Experimental Psychiatry,* 1974, *5,* 259–262.

Davitz, J.R. The effects of previous training on postfrustration behavior. *Journal of Abnormal and Social Psychology,* 1952, *47,* 309–315.

DeLeon, G., & Mandell, W. A comparison of conditioning and psychotherapy in the treatment of functional enuresis. *Journal of Clinical Psychology,* 1966, *22,* 326–330.

Dollard, J., Doob, L.W., Miller, N.E., Mowrer, O.H., & Sears, R.R. *Frustration and aggression.* New Haven: Yale University Press, 1939.

Ferster, C.B. Positive reinforcement and behavioral deficits of autistic children. *Child Development,* 1961, *32,* 437–456.

Gardner, R., & Heider, K.G. *Gardens of war: Life and death in the New Guina stone age.* New York: Random House, 1969.

Hetherington, E.M. A developmental study of the effects of sex of the dominant parent on sex-role preference, identification, and imitation in children. *Journal of Personality and Social Psychology,* 1965, *2,* 188–194.

Jones, M.C. A laboratory study of fear: The case of Peter. *Pediatrics Seminar,* 1924, *31,* 308–315.

Kallman, F.J., & Roth, B. Genetic aspects of preadolescent schizophrenia. *American Journal of Psychiatry,* 1956, *112,* 599–606.

Kanner, L. Problems of nosology and psychodynamics in early infantile autism. *American Journal of Orthopsychiatry,* 1949, *19,* 416–426.

Kennedy, W.A. School phobia: Rapid treatment of fifty cases. *Journal of Abnormal Psychology,* 1965, *70,* 285–289.

Lang, P.J., & Melamed, B.G. Avoidance conditioning therapy of an infant with chronic ruminative vomiting: Case report. *Journal of Abnormal Psychology,* 1969, *74,* 1–8.

Leitenberg, H., Agras, S., & Thomson, L.E. A sequential analysis of the effect of selective positive reinforcement in modifying anorexia nervosa. *Behaviour Research and Therapy,* 1968, *6,* 211–218.

Levy, R.I. On getting angry in the Society Islands. In W. Caudill and T.Y. Lin (Eds.), *Mental health research in Asia and the Pacific.* Honolulu: East-West Center Press, 1969.

Lovaas, O.I. A program for the establishment of speech in psychotic children. In J.K. Wing (Ed.), *Early childhood autism.* Oxford: Pergamon, 1966.

Lovaas, O.I., Freitag, G., Gold, V.J., & Kassorla, I.C. Experimental studies in childhood schizophrenia: Analysis of self-destructive behavior. *Journal of Experimental Child Psychology,* 1965, *2,* 67–84.

Lovaas, O.I., Freitas, L., Nelson, K., & Whalen, C. The establishment of imitation and its use for the development of complex behavior in schizophrenic children. *Behaviour Research and Therapy,* 1967, *5,* 171–181.

Lovaas, O.I., Schreibman, L., Koegel, R., & Rehm, R. Selective responding by autistic children to multiple sensory input. *Journal of Abnormal Psychology,* 1971, *77,* 211–222.

Mallick, S.K. & McCandless, B.R. A study of catharsis of aggression. *Journal of Personality and Social Psychology,* 1966, *4,* 591–596.

Meichenbaum, D.H., & Goodman, J. Training impulsive children to talk to themselves: A means of developing self-control. *Journal of Abnormal Psychology,* 1971, *77,* 115–125.

Mowrer, O.H., & Mowrer, W.M. Enuresis: A method for its study and treatment. *American Journal of Orthopsychiatry,* 1938, *8,* 436–459.

O'Leary, K.D., Becker, W.C., Evans, M.B., & Sandargas, R.A. A token reinforcement program in a public school: A replication and systematic analysis. *Journal of Applied Behavior Analysis,* 1969, *2,* 3–13.

Patterson, G.R., Littman, R.A., & Bricker, W. Assertive behavior in children: A step toward a theory of aggression. *Monographs of the Society for Research in Child Development,* 1967, *32,* (No. 5. Whole No. 113).

Purcell, K., Brady, K., Chai, H., Muser, J., Molk, L., Gordon, N., & Means, J. The effect on asthma in children of experimental separation from the family. *Psychosomatic Medicine,* 1969, *31,* 144–164.

Reid, J.B., & Hendricks, A.F.C.J. Preliminary analysis of the effectiveness of direct home intervention for the treatment of predelinquent boys who steal. In L. Hamerlynck, L. Handy, & E. Mash (Eds.), *Behavioral change: Methodology, concepts, and practice.* Champaign, Ill.: Research Press, 1973.

Rekers, G.A., & Lovaas, O.I. Behavioral treatment of deviant sex-role behaviors in a male child. *Journal of Applied Behavior Analysis,* 1974, *7,* 173–190.

Rimland, B. *Infantile autism.* New York: Appleton-Century-Crofts, 1964.

Robbins, L.N. *Deviant children grow up: A sociological and psychiatric study of sociopathic personality.* Baltimore: Williams & Wilkins, 1966.

Ross, A.O. *Psychological aspects of learning disabilities and reading disorders.* New York: McGraw-Hill, 1976.

Ross, D.M., & Ross, S.A. *Hyperactivity: Research, theory, action.* New York: Wiley, 1976.

Safer, D.J. A familial factor in minimal brain dysfunction. *Behavior Genetics,* 1973, *3,* 175–186.

Schover, L.R., & Newsom, C.D. Overselectivity, developmental level, and overtraining in autistic and normal children. *Journal of Abnormal Child Psychology,* 1976, *4,* 289–298.

Stewart, M.A., & Olds, S.W. *Raising a hyperactive child.* New York: Harper & Row, 1973.

Stoller, R.J. *Sex and gender.* New York: Science House, 1968.

Sykes, D.H., Douglas, V.I., Weiss, G., & Minde, K.K. Attention in hyperactive children and the effects of methylphenidate (Ritalin). *Journal of Child Psychology and Psychiatry,* 1971, *12,* 129–139.

Thomas, A., Chess, S., & Birch, H.G. *Temperament and behavior disorders in children.* New York: N.Y.U. Press, 1968.

Walters, R.H., & Brown, M. Studies of reinforcement of aggression: III. Transfer of responses to an interpersonal situation. *Child Development,* 1963, *34,* 563–571.

Watson, J.B., & Rayner, R. Conditional emotional reactions. *Journal of Experimental Psychology,* 1920, *3,* 1–14.

Waxler, N.E., & Mishler, E.G. Parental interaction with schizophrenic children and well siblings. *Archives of General Psychiatry,* 1971, *25,* 223–231.

Zaslow, R.W., & Breger, L. A theory and treatment of autism. In L. Breger (Ed.), *Clinical cognitive psychology.* Englewood Cliffs, N.J.: Prentice-Hall, 1969.

Zlutnick, S., Mayville, W.J., & Moffat, S. Modification of seizure disorders: The interruption of behavioral chains. *Journal of Applied Behavior Analysis,* 1975, *8,* 1–12.

Chapter 17

Achenbach, T., & Zigler, E. Cue-learning and problem-learning strategies in normal and retarded children. *Child Development,* 1968, *3,* 827–848.

Badt, M.I. Level of abstraction in vocabulary definitions of mentally retarded school children. *American Journal of Mental Deficiency,* 1958, *63,* 241–246

Balla, D.A. Relationship of institution size to quality of care: A review of the literature. *American Journal of Mental Deficiency,* 1976, *81,* 117–124.

Balla, D., Butterfield, E.C., & Zigler, E. Effects of institutionalization on retarded children: A longitudinal cross-institutional investigation. *American Journal of Mental Deficiency,* 1974, *78,* 530–549.

Balla, D., Kossan, N., & Zigler, E. *Effects of pre-institutional history and institutionalization on the behavior of the retarded.* Unpublished manuscript, Yale University, 1976.

Balla, D., McCarthy, E., & Zigler, E. Some correlates of negative reaction tendencies in institutionalized retarded children. *Journal of Psychology,* 1971, *79,* 77–84.

Balla, D., Styfco, S.J., & Zigler, E. Use of the opposition concept and outerdirectedness in intellectually-average, familial retarded, and organically retarded children. *American Journal of Mental Deficiency,* 1971, *75,* 663–680.

Balla, D., & Zigler, E. Pre-institutional social deprivation and responsiveness to social reinforcement in institutionalized retarded individuals: A six-year follow-up study. *American Journal of Mental Deficiency,* 1975, *80,* 228–230.

Begab, M. The major dilemma of mental retardation: Shall we prevent it? (Some social implications of research in mental retardation.) *American Journal of Mental Deficiency,* 1974, *78,* 519–529.

Berman, P., Waisman, H., & Grahm, F. Intelligence in treated phenylketonuric children: A developmental study. *Child Development,* 1966, *37,* 731–747.

Blatt, B. *Exodus from pandemonium.* Boston: Allyn & Bacon, 1970.

Blatt, B., & Kaplan, F. *Christmas in purgatory.* Boston: Allyn & Bacon, 1966.

Bruininks, R.H., Rynders, J.E., & Gross, J.C. Social acceptance of mildly retarded pupils in resource rooms and regular classes. *American Journal of Mental Deficiency,* 1974, *78,* 377–383.

Butterfield, E.C., & Zigler, E. The influence of differing institutional social climates on the effectiveness of social reinforcement in the mentally retarded. *American Journal of Mental Deficiency,* 1965, *70,* 48–56.

Byck, M. Cognitive differences among diagnostic groups of retardates. *American Journal of Mental Deficiency,* 1968, *73,* 97–101.

Carr, J. Mental and motor development in young mongol children. *Journal of Mental Deficiency Research,* 1970, *14,* 205–220.

Centerwall, S.A., & Centerwall, W.R. A study of children with mongolism reared in the home compared to those reared away from the home. *Pediatrics,* 1960, *25,* 678–685.

Challenge. Editorial. September-October 1973, p.2.

Clarke, A.D.B., & Clarke, A.M. How constant is the IQ? *Lancet,* 1953, *265,* 877–880.

Clarke, A.D.B., & Clarke, A.M. Cognitive changes in the feebleminded. *British Journal of Psychology,* 1954, *45,* 173–179.

Clarke, A.D.B. & Clarke, A.M. Prospects for prevention and amelioration of mental retardation: A guest editorial. *American Journal of Mental Deficiency,* 1977, *81* (6), 523–533.

Cleland, C. Evidence on the relationship between size and institutional effectiveness: A review and an analysis. *American Journal of Mental Deficiency,* 1965, *70,* 423–431.

Cohen, H.J., Birch, H.G., & Taft, L.T. Some considerations for evaluating the Doman-Delacato "patterning" method. *Pediatrics,* 1970 *45* (2), 302–414.

Cole, M., & Bruner, J.S. Cultural differences and inferences about psychological processes. *American Psychologist,* 1971, *26,* 867–876.

Crandall, B.F., & Tarjan, G. Genetics of mental retardation. In M.A. Sperber & L.G. Jarvik

(Eds.), *Psychiatry and genetics: Psychological, ethical, and legal considerations.* New York: Basic Books, 1976.

Cromwell, R.L. A social learning approach to mental retardation. In N.R. Ellis (Ed.), *Handbook of mental deficiency.* New York: McGraw-Hill, 1963.

Dennis, W. *Children of the creche.* New York: Appleton-Century-Crofts, 1973.

Doman, G. *What to do about your brain-injured child.* Garden City, N.Y.: Doubleday, 1974.

Doman, R.J., Spitz, E.B., Zucman, E., Delacato, C.H., & Doman, G. Children with severe brain injuries. *Journal of the American Medical Association,* 1960, *174,* 257–262.

Dugdale, R.L. *The Jukes: A study of crime, pauperism, disease, and heredity.* New York: Putnam, 1877.

Dunn, L. Special education for the mildly retarded: Is much of it justifiable? *Exceptional Children,* 1968, *35,* 5–22.

Edgerton, R.B. Issues relating to the quality of life among mentally retarded persons. In M.J. Begab & S.A. Richardson (Eds.), *The mentally retarded and society: A social science perspective.* Baltimore: University Park Press, 1975.

Ellis, N.R. The stimulus trace and behavioral inadequacy. In N.R. Ellis (Ed.), *Handbook of mental deficiency.* New York: McGraw-Hill, 1963.

Ellis, N.R. Memory processes in retardates and normals. In N.R. Ellis (Ed.), *International review of research in mental retardation* (Vol. 4). New York: Academic Press, 1970.

Farber, B. Family adaptations to severely mentally retarded children. In M.J. Begab & S.H. Richardson (Eds.), *The mentally retarded and society: A social science perspective.* Baltimore: University Park Press, 1975.

Fisher, M.A., & Zeaman, D. An attention-retention theory of retardate discrimination learning. In N.R. Ellis (Ed.), *International review of research in mental retardation* (Vol. 6). New York: Academic Press, 1973.

Freeman, R.D. Controversy over "patterning" as a treatment for brain damage in children. *Journal of the American Medical Association,* 1967, *202,* 385–388.

Freeman, R. Psychopharmacology and the retarded child. In F. Menolascino (Ed.), *Psychiatric approaches to mental retardation.* New York: Basic Books, 1970.

Garber, H.L. Intervention in infancy: A developmental approach. In M.J. Begab & S.A. Richardson (Eds.), *The mentally retarded and society: A social science perspective.* Baltimore: University Park Press, 1975.

Glass, G.V., & Robbins, M.P. Neurological organization and reading. *Reading Research Quarterly,* 1967, *3,* 7–52.

Goddard, H.H. *The Kallikak family.* New York: Macmillan, 1912.

Goodman, H., Gottlieb, J., & Harrison, R.H. Social acceptance of EMRs integrated into a nongraded elementary school. *American Journal of Mental Deficiency,* 1972, *76,* 412–417.

Gottlieb, J., & Budoff, M. Social acceptability of retarded children in nongraded schools differing in architecture. *American Journal of Mental Deficiency,* 1973, *78,* 15–19.

Gottesman, I. Genetic aspects of intelligent behavior. In N.R. Ellis (Ed.), *Handbook of mental deficiency.* New York: McGraw-Hill, 1963.

Grossman, H. (Ed.). *Manual on terminology and classification in mental retardation, 1973 revision.* Washington, D.C.: American Association on Mental Deficiency, 1973.

Gruen, G., Ottinger, D., & Ollendick, H. Probability learning in retarded children with differing histories of success and failure in school. *American Journal of Mental Deficiency,* 1975, *79,* 417–423.

Gruen, G. & Zigler, E. Expectancy of success and the probability learning of middle-class, lower-class, and retarded children. *Journal of Abnormal Psychology,* 1968, *73,* 343–352.

Harter, S. Mental age, IQ, and motivational factors in the discrimination learning set performance of normal and retarded children. *Journal of Experimental Child Psychology,* 1967, *5,* 123–141.

Harter, S., & Zigler, E. Effectiveness of adult and peer reinforcement on the performance of institutionalized and noninstitutionalized retardates. *Journal of Abnormal Psychology,* 1968, *73,* 144–149.

Harter, S., & Zigler, E. The assessment of effectance motivation in normal and retarded children. *Developmental Psychology,* 1974, *10,* 169–180.

Iano, R.P., Ayers, D., Heller, H.B., McGettingan, J.F., & Walker, V.S. Sociometric status of retarded children in an integrative program. *Exceptional Children,* 1974, *40,* 267–271.

Iscoe, I., & McCann, G. Perception of an emotional continuum by older and younger mental retardates. *Journal of Personality and Social Psychology,* 1965, *1,* 383–385.

Jarvik. L.F. Genetic modes of transmission relevant to psychopathology. In M.A. Sperber & L.F. Jarvik (Eds.), *Psychiatry and genetics: Psychosocial, ethical, and legal considerations.* New York: Basic Books, 1976.

Kaufman, M. The formation of a learning set in institutionalized and noninstitutionalized mental defectives. *American Journal of Mental Deficiency,* 1963, *67,* 601–605.

King, R.D., Raynes, N.V., & Tizard, J. *Patterns of residential care: Sociological studies in institutions for handicapped children.* London: Routledge & Kegan Paul, 1971.

Klaber, M.M., & Butterfield, E.C. Stereotyped rocking—A measure of institution and ward effectiveness. *American Journal of Mental Deficiency,* 1968, *73,* 13–20.

Klaber, M.M., Butterfield, E.C., & Gould, L. Responsiveness to social reinforcement among institutionalized retarded children. *American Journal of Mental Deficiency,* 1969, *73,* 890–895.

Koch, R., Fishler, K., & Melnyk, J. Chromosomal anomalies in causation: Down's syndrome. In R. Koch & J.C. Dobson (Eds.), *The mentally retarded child and his family: A multidisciplinary handbook.* New York: Brunner/Mazel, 1971

Kounin, J. Experimental studies of rigidity: I. The measurement of rigidity in normal and feebleminded persons. *Character and Personality,* 1941, *9,* 251–272. (a)

Kounin, J. Experimental studies of rigidity: II. The explanatory power of the concept of rigidity as applies to feeblemindedness. *Character and Personality,* 1941, *9,* 273–282. (b)

Lejeune, J., Gautier, M., & Turpin, R. Le mongolisme. Premier example d'aberration autosomique humaine. *Annèe Genetique,* 1959, *1,* 41.

Lewin, K. *A dynamic theory of personality.* New York: McGraw-Hill, 1936.

Luria, A.R. Psychological studies of mental deficiency in the Soviet Union. In N.R. Ellis (Ed.), *Handbook of mental deficiency.* New York: McGraw-Hill, 1963.

Lustman, N.M., Balla, D., & Zigler, E. *Imitation in institutionalized and noninstitutionalized retarded childred and in children of average intellect.* Unpublished manuscript, Yale University, 1977.

Lyle, J.G. The effect of an institution environment on the verbal development of imbecile children: I. Verbal intelligence. *Journal of Mental Deficiency Research,* 1959, *3,* 122–128.

Lyle, J.G. The effect of an institution upon the verbal development of imbecile children: II. Speech and language. *Journal of Mental Deficiency Research,* 1960 *4,* 1–13. (a)

Lyle, J.G. The effect of an institution environment upon the verbal development of imbecile children: III. The Brooklands residential family unit. *Journal of Mental Deficiency Research,* 1960, *4,* 14–23. (b)

MacMillan, D.L. Motivational differences: Cultural-familial retardates vs. normal subjects on expectancy for failure. *American Journal of Mental Deficiency,* 1969, *74,* 254–258.

MacMillan, D.L., & Keogh, B.K. Normal and retarded children's expectancy for failure. *Developmental Psychology,* 1971, *4,* 343–348.

MacMillan, D.L., & Knopf, E.D. Effect of instructional set on perceptions of event outcomes by EMR and nonretarded children. *American Journal of Mental Deficiency,* 1971, *76,* 185–189.

McCormick, M., Balla, D., & Zigler, E. Resident-care practices in institutions for retarded persons: A cross-institutional, cross-cultural study. *American Journal of Mental Deficiency,* 1975, *80,* 1–17.

Mercer, J.R. *Labelling the mentally retarded.* Berkeley: University of California Press, 1973.

Mercer, J.R. Psychological assessment and the rights of children. In N. Hobbs (Ed.), *Issues in the classification of children.* San Francisco: Jossey-Bass, 1975.

Mueller, M.W., & Weaver, S.J. Psycholinguistic abilities of institutionalized and noninstitutionalized trainable mental retardates. *American Journal of Mental Deficiency,* 1964, *68,* 775–783.

Neman, R., Roos, P., McCann, B., Menolascino, R., & Heal, L. Experimental evaluation of sensorimotor patterning used with mentally retarded children. *American Journal of Mental Deficiency,* 1975, *79,* 372–384.

Nihara, K., Foster, R., Shellhass, M., & Leland, H. *AAMD Adaptive Behavior Scales.* Washington, D.C.: American Association on Mental Deficiency, 1969.

Ollendick, T., Balla, D., & Zigler, E. Expectancy of success and the probability learning of retarded children. *Journal of Abnormal Psychology,* 1971, *77,* 275–281.

Pennsylvania Association for Retarded children vs.

Commonwealth of Pennsylvania. 343F. Supp. 279 (E.D., Pa.), 1972.

Penrose, L.S. *The biology of mental deficiency*. London: Sidgwick & Jackson, 1963.

President's Committee on Mental Retardation. *MR 67: A first report to the President on the nation's progress and remaining great needs in the campaign to combat mental retardation*. Washington, D.C.: Superintendent of Documents, U.S. Government Printing Office, 1967.

Reed, E.W., & Reed, S. *Mental retardation: A family study*. Philadelphia: Saunders, 1965.

Robinson, H.R., & Robinson, N. *The mentally retarded child: A psychological approach*. New York: McGraw-Hill, 1976.

Roos, P. Psychological counseling with parents of retarded children. *Mental Retardation*, 1963, *1*, 345–350.

Roos, P. Parents and families of the mentally retarded. In J.M. Kauffman & J.S. Payne (Eds.), *Mental retardation: Introduction and personal perspectives*. Columbus, Ohio: Merrill, 1975.

Roos, S.L., DeYoung, H.G. & Cohen, J.S. Confrontation: Special education placement and the law. *Exceptional Children*, 1971, *38*, 5–12.

Sanders, B., Zigler, E., & Butterfield, E.C. Outerdirectedness in the discrimination learning of normal and mentally retarded children. *Journal of Abnormal Psychology*, 1968, *73*, 368–375.

Sarason, S., Zitnay, G., & Grossman, F. *The creation of a community setting*. Syracuse: Syracuse University Division of Special Education and Rehabilitation and the Center on Human Policy, 1971.

Seitz, V., Abelson, W.D., Levine, E., & Zigler, E. Effects of place of testing on the Peabody Picture Vocabulary Test scores of disadvantaged Head Start and non-Head Start children. *Child Development*, 1975, *46*, 481–486.

Shallenberger, P., & Zigler, E. Rigidity, negative reaction tendencies, and cosatiation effects in normal and feebleminded children. *Journal of Abnormal and Social Psychology*, 1961, *63*, 20–26.

Share,J.B. Review of drug treatment for Down's syndrome persons. *American Journal of Mental Deficiency, 1976, 80*, 388–393.

Shipe, E., & Shotwell, A.M. Effect of out-of-home care on mongoloid children: A continuation study. *American Journal of Mental Deficiency*, 1965, *69*, 649–652.

Skeels, H.M. Adult status of children with contrasting early life experiences. *Monographs of the Society for Research in Child Development*, 1966, *31* (3, Serial No. 105).

Sparrow, S., & Zigler, E. *An evaluation of the effects of a sensorimotor patterning treatment on the behavior of seriously retarded children*. Unpublished manuscript, Yale University, 1977.

Spitz, H.H. The channel capacity of educable mental retardates. In D.K. Routh (Ed.), *The experimental psychology of mental retardation*. Chicago: Aldine, 1973.

Stedman, D.J., Eichorn, D.H., Griffin, J., & Gooch, B. *A comparative study of growth and development trends of institutionalized and noninstitutionalized retarded children: A summary report*. Paper read at AAMD National Convention, New YOrk, 1962.

Stern, C. *Principles of human genetics*. (2nd ed.). San Francisco: Freeman, 1960.

Stevenson, H.W., & Zigler, E. Discrimination learning and rigidity in normal and feebleminded individuals. *Journal of Personality*, 1957, *25*, 699–711.

Stevenson, H.W., & Zigler, E. Probability learning in children *Journal of Experimental Psychology*, 1958, *56*, 185–192.

Turkel, H. Medical treatment of mongoloids. *Exerpta Medica. International Congress, Series #43, Second International Congress on Mental Retardation*, 77, Vienna, 1961.

Turnure, J.E., & Zigler, E. Outer-directedness in the problem-solving of normal and retarded children. *Journal of Abnormal and Social Psychology*, 1964, *69*, 427–436.

Weaver, S.J. *The effects of motivation-hygiene orientation and interpersonal reaction tendencies in intellectually subnormal children*. Unpublished doctoral dissertation, George Peabody College for Teachers, 1966.

Weaver, S.J., Balla, D., & Zigler, E. Social approach and avoidance tendencies of institutionalized retarded and noninstitutionalized retarded and normal children. *Journal of Experimental Research in Personality*, 1971, *5*, 98–110.

White, R.W. Motivation reconsidered: The concept of competence. *Psychological Review*, 1959, *66* 297–332.

Wolfensberger, W. *The principle of normalization in human services*. Toronto: National Institute on Mental Retardation, 1972.

Wyatt vs. Stickney, et al. Civil Action No. 3195-N, Adequate habilitation for the mentally retarded. District Court of the United States for Middle District of Alabama, Northern Division, February 28, 1972.

Yando, R., & Zigler, E. Outerdirectedness in the problem-solving of institutionalized and non-institutionalized normal and retarded children. *Developmental Psychology,* 1971, *4,* 277–288.

Zeaman, D., & House, B.J. The role of attention in retardate discrimination learning. In N.R. Ellis (Ed.), *Handbook of mental deficiency.* New York: McGraw-Hill, 1963.

Zigler, E. Social deprivation and rigidity in the performance of feebleminded children. *Journal of Abnormal and Social Psychology,* 1961, *62,* 413–421.

Zigler, E. Rigidity in the feebleminded. In E. Trapp & P. Himelstein (Eds.), *Readings on the exceptional child.* New York: Appleton-Century-Crofts, 1962.

Zigler, E. The nature-nurture issue reconsidered: A discussion of Uzgiris' paper. In H.C. Haywood (Ed.), *Social-cultural aspects of mental retardation.* New York: Appleton-Century-Crofts, 1970.

Zigler, E. Head Start: Not a program but an evolving concept. In J.D. Andrews (Ed.), *Early childhood education: It's an art! It's a science!* Washington, D.C.: The National Association for the Education of Young Children, 1976.

Zigler, E. dealing with retardation. *Science,* 1977, *196,* 1192–1194.

Zigler, E., & Abelson, W. *Is an intervention program necessary in order to improve economically disadvantaged children's IQ scores?* Unpublished manuscript, Yale University, 1975.

Zigler, E., Abelson, W.D., & Seitz, V. Motivational factors in the performance of economically disadvantaged children on the Peabody Picture Vocabulary Test. *Child Development,* 1973, *44,* 294–303.

Zigler, E., & Balla, D. Developmental course of responsiveness to social reinforcement in normal children and institutionalized retarded children. *Developmental Psychology,* 1972, *6,* 66–73.

Zigler, E., Balla, D., & Butterfield, E.C. A longitudinal investigation of the relationship between preinstitutional social deprivation and social motivation in institutionalized retardates. *Journal of Personality and Social Psychology,* 1968, *10,* 437–445.

Zigler, E., & Butterfield, E.C. Motivational aspects of changes in IQ test performance of culturally deprived nursery school children. *Child Development, 1968, 39,* 1–14.

Zigler, E., Butterfield, E.C. & Capobianco, F. Institutionalization and the effectiveness of social reinforcement: A five- and eight-year follow-up study. *Developmental Psychology,* 1970, *3,* 255–263.

Zigler, E., & DeLabry, J. Concept-switching in middle-class, lower-class, and retarded children. *Journal of Abnormal and Social Psychology, 1962, 65,* 267–273.

Zigler, E., & Seitz, V. On "an experimental evaluation of sensori-motor patterning": A critique. *American Journal of Mental Deficiency,* 1975, *79,* 483–492.

Zigler, E., & Trickett, P.K. IQ, social competence and evaluation of early childhood intervention programs. *American Psychologist,* in press.

Zigler, E., & Unell, E. Concept-switching in normal and feebleminded children as a function of reinforcement. *American Journal of Mental Deficiency,* 1962, *66,* 651–657.

Zigler, E., & Williams, J. Institutionalization and the effectiveness of social reinforcement: A three-year follow-up study. *Journal of Abnormal and Social Psychology,* 1963, *66,* 197–205.

Chapter 18

Adler, A. *Superiority and social interest.* Evanston, Ill.: Northwestern University Press, 1964.

Alexander, F., & French, T. *Psychoanalytic therapy.* New York: Ronald Press, 1946.

Ansbacher, H.L. & Ansbacher, R.R. *The individual psychology of Alfred Adler.* New York: Basic Books, 1956.

Appelbaum, S. *The anatomy of change.* New York: Plenum, 1977.

Beels, C., & Ferber, A. What family therapists do. In A. Ferber, M. Mendelsohn, & A. Napier (Eds.), *The book of family therapy.* New York: Science House, 1972.

Bergin, A.E. & Lambert, M. The evaluation of therapeutic outcomes. In S.L. Garfield, & A.E. Bergin (Eds.), *Handbook of psychotherapy and behavior change* (2nd ed.). New York: Wiley, 1978.

Binswanger, L. *Being-in-the-world.* New York: Basic Books, 1963.

Boss, M. *Psychoanalysis and daseinsanalysis.* New York: Basic Books, 1963.

Breuer, J., & Freud, S. *Studies on hysteria.* New York: Basic Books, 1957. (Original, 1985.)

Ellis, A. *Humanistic psychotherapy: A rational-emotive approach.* New York: Julian Press, 1973.

Erikson, E. *Insight and responsibility.* New York: W W Norton, 1964.

Erikson, E. *Identity: Youth and crisis.* New York: W W Norton, 1968.

Fagan, J., & Sheperd, I.L. (Eds.). *Gestalt therapy now.* Palo Alto, Calif.: Science and Behavior Books, 1970.

Faribairn, R. *Object relations theory of the personality.* New York: Basic Books, 1952.

Frank, J.D. *Persuasion and healing* (2nd ed.). Baltimore: Johns Hopkins University Press, 1973.

Frank, J.D. Therapeutic components of psychotherapy. *Journal of Nervous and Mental Disease,* 1974, *159,* 325–342.

Frankl, V. *Psychotherapy and existentialism: Selected papers on logotherapy.* New York: Washington Square Press, 1967.

Garfield, S.L. Resarch on client variables in psychotherapy. In S.L. Garfield & A.E. Bergin (Eds.), *Handbook of psychotherapy and behavior change* (2nd ed.). New York: Wiley, 1978.

Glasser, W. *Reality therapy.* New York: Harper & Row, 1965.

Goldstein, A.P. *Therapist-patient expectancies in psychotherapy.* New York: Pergamon, 1962.

Greenson, R. *The technique and practice of psychoanalysis.* New York: International Universities Press, 1967.

Guntrip, H. *Psychoanalytic theory, therapy, and the self.* New York: Basic Books, 1971.

Haley, J. *Changing families: A family therapy reader.* New York: Grune & Stratton, 1971.

Hartley, D., Roback, H.B., & Abramowitz, S.I. Deterioration effects in encounter groups. *American Psychologist,* 1976, *31,* 247–255.

Hartmann, H. *Essays on ego psychology.* New York: International Universities Press, 1964.

Horwitz, L. *Clinical prediction in psychotherapy.* New York: Jason Aronson, 1974.

Jung, C.G. *Two essays on analytical psychology.* Princeton: Princeton University Press, 1966.

Jung, C.G. *The portable Jung.* New York: Viking, 1971.

Kaplan, H.S. *The new sex therapy: Active treatment of sexual dysfunctions.* New York: Brunner/Mazel, 1974.

Kernberg, O. *Borderline conditions and pathological narcissism.* New York: Jason Aronson, 1975.

Kernberg, O.F. Some methodological and strategic issues in psychotherapy research: Research implications of the Menninger Foundation's Psychotherapy Research Project. In R.L. Spitzer and D.F. Klein (Eds.), *Evaluation of psychological therapies.* Baltimore: Johns Hopkins University Press, 1976.

Korchin, S.J. *Modern clinical psychology.* New York: Basic Books, 1976.

Langs, R. *The technique of psychoanalytic psychotherapy.* New York: Jacon Aronson, 1973.

Luborsky, L., Singer, B., & Luborsky, L. Comparative studies of psychotherapies: Is it true that "Everyone has won and all must have prizes?" *Archives of General Psychiatry,* 1975, *32,* 995–1008.

Malan, D.H. *Toward the validation of dynamic psychotherapy: A replication.* New York: Plenum, 1976.

Marks, I. Behavioral psychotherapy of adult neurosis. In S.L. Garfield & A.E. Bergin (Eds.), *Handbook of psychotherapy and behavior change* (2nd ed.). New York: Wiley, 1978.

Masters, W.H. & Johnson, V.E. *Human sexual inadequacy.* Boston: Little, Brown, 1970.

May, L., Angel, E., & Ellenberger, H.E. (Eds.). *Existence: A new dimension in psychiatry and psychology.* New York: Basic Books, 1958.

Menninger, K.A. & Holtzman, P.S. *Theory of psychoanalytic techniques* (2nd ed.). New York: Basic Books, 1973.

Minuchin, S. *Families and family therapy.* Cambridge, Mass.: Harvard University Press, 1974.

Mishler, E.G. & Waxler, N.E. *Interaction in families.* New York: Wiley, 1976.

Parloff, M.B. Analytic group psychotherapy. In J. Marmor (Ed.), *Modern psychoanalysis.* New York: Basic Books, 1968.

Parloff, M., Waskow, I., & Wolfe, B. Research on therapist variables in relation to process and outcome. In S.L. Garfield, & A.E. Bergin (Eds.), *Handbook of psychotherapy and behavior change* (2nd ed.). New York: Wiley, 1978.

Patterson, C.H. *Theories of counseling and psychotherapy.* New York: Harper & Row, 1973.

Perls, F.S. *Gestalt therapy verbatim.* Lafayette, Calif.: Real People Press, 1969.

Perls, F.S., Hefferline, R.F., & Goodman, P. *Gestalt therapy* (2nd ed.). New York: Julian Press, 1965.

Polster, E., & Polster, M. *Gestalt therapy integrated.* New York: Brunner/Mazel, 1973.

Rapaport, D. (Ed.). *Organization and pathology of thought.* New York: Columbia University Press, 1951.

Rogers, C.R. *Client-centered therapy.* Boston: Houghton Mifflin, 1951.

Rogers, C.R. *On becoming a person.* Boston: Houghton Mifflin, 1961.

Rogers, C.R. *Carl Rogers on encounter groups.* New York: Harper & Row, 1970.

Ruitenbeek, H.M. *The new group therapies.* New York: Avon Books, 1970.

Sahakian, W.S. *Psychotherapy and counseling* (2nd ed.). Chicago: Rand McNally, 1976.

Satir, V. *Conjoint family therapy* (2nd ed.). Palo Alto, Calif.: Science and Behavior Books, 1967.

Schafer, R. *A new language for psychoanalysis.* New Haven: Yale University Press, 1976.

Schultz, W.C. *Joy.* New York: Grove, 1967.

Sifneos, D. *Short-term psychotherapy and emotional crisis.* Cambridge, Mass.: Harvard University Press, 1972.

Sloane, R.B., Staples, F.R., Cristol, A.H., Yorkston, N.J., & Whipple, K. *Psychotherapy versus behavior therapy.* Cambridge, Mass.: Harvard University Press, 1975.

Strupp, H.H. On the technology of psychotherapy. *Archives of General Psychiatry, 1972 26,* 270–278.

Strupp, H.H. Toward a reformulation of the psychotherapeutic influence. *International Journal of Psychiatry,* 1973, *11,* 263–327.

Weiner, I.B. *Principles of psychotherapy.* New York: Wiley, 1975.

Wilson, G.T., & Evans, I.M. The therapist-client relationship in behavior therapy. In A.S. Gurman, & A.M. Razin (Eds.), *The therapist's contribution to effective treatment: An empirical assessment.* New York: Pergamon, 1977.

Winnicott, D. *The family and individual development.* London: Tavistock, 1968.

Yalom, I.D. *The theory and practice of group psychotherapy* (2nd ed.). New York: Basic Books, 1975.

Chapter 19

Achenbach, T.M. *Developmental psychology.* New York: Ronald Press, 1974.

Alabiso, F. Operant control of attention behavior: A treatment for hyperactivity. *Behavior Therapy,* 1975, *6,* 39–43.

Atkinson, R.C. Computerized instruction and the learning process. *American Psychologist,* 1968, *23,* 225–239.

Atthowe, J.M. Token economies come of age. *Behavior Therapy,* 1973, *4,* 646–654.

Ayllon, T., Layman, D., & Kandel, H.J. A behavioral-educational alternative to drug control of hyperactive children. *Journal of Applied Behavior Analysis,* 1975, *8,* 137–146.

Baer, D., Wolf, M., & Risley, T. Some current dimensions of applied behavior analysis. *Journal of Applied Behavior Analysis,* 1968, *1,* 91–97.

Bandura, A. *Principles of behavior modification.* New York: Holt, Rhinehart, & Winston, 1969.

Bandura, A. Behavior theory and the models of man. *American Psychologist,* 1974, *29,* 859–869.

Bandura, A. *Social learning theory.* Englewood Cliffs, N.J.: Prentice-Hall, 1977. (a)

Bandura, A. Self-efficacy: Toward a unifying theory of behavioral change. *Psychological Review,* 1977, *84,* 191–215. (b)

Barber, T., DiCara, L., Kamiya, J., Miller, N., Shapiro, D., & Stoyva, J. (Eds.), *Biofeedback and self-control.* Chicago: Aldine, 1976.

Barlow, D.H. Assessment of sexual behavior. In A.R. Ciminero, K.S. Calhoun, & H.E. Adams (Eds.), *Handbook of behavioral assessment.* New York: Wiley, 1977.

Barlow, D.H. & Agras, W.S. Fading to increase heterosexual responsiveness in homosexuals. *Journal of Applied and Behavior Analysis,* 1973, *6,* 355–366.

Barlow, D.H., Leitenberg, H., & Agras, W.J. The experimental control of sexual deviation through manipulation of the noxious sense in covert sensitization. *Journal of Abnormal Psychology,* 1969, *74,* 596–601.

Beck, A.T. *Cognitive therapy and the emotional disorders.* New York: International Universities Press, 1976.

Bernstein, D.A., & Borkovec, T.D. *Progressive relaxation training.* Champaign, Ill.: Research Press, 1973.

Bernstein, D.A., & McAllister, A. The modification of smoking behavior: Progress and problems. *Addictive Behaviors,* 1976, *1,* 89–102.

Bernstein, D.A., & Paul, G.L. Some comments on therapy analogue research with small animal "phobias." *Journal of Behavior Therapy and Experimental Psychiatry,* 1971, *2,* 225–237.

Bijou, S.W., Peterson, R.F., Harris, F.R., Allen, K.E., & Johnston, M.S. Methodology for experimental studies of young children in natural settings. *Psychological Record,* 1969, *19,* 177–210.

Borkovec, T., Weerts, T., & Bernstein, T. Assessment of anxiety. In A. Ciminero, K.S. Calhoun, & H.E. Adams (Eds.), *Handbook of behavioral assessment.* New York: Wiley, 1977.

Breger, L., & McGaugh, J. Critique and reformulation of "learning theory" approaches to psychotherapy and neurosis. *Psychological Bulletin,* 1965, *63,* 338–358.

Briddell, D.W., & Nathan, P.E. Behavior assessment and modification with alcoholics: Current status and future trends. In M. Hersen, R.M. Eisler, and P.M. Miller (Eds.), *Progress in behavior modification,* (Vol. 2). New York: Academic Press, 1976.

Callner, D.A. Behavioral treatment approaches to drug abuse: A critical review of the research. *Psychological Bulletin,* 1975, *82,* 143–164.

Camp, B. *Verbal mediation in young aggressive boys.* Unpublished manuscript, University of Colorado School of Medicine, 1975.

Cautela, J.R. Behavior therapy and self-control: Techniques and implications. In C.M. Franks (Ed.), *Behavior therapy: Appraisal and status.* New York: McGraw-Hill, 1969.

Ciminero, A.R. Behavioral assessment: An overview. In A.R. Ciminero, K.S. Calhoun, & H.E. Adams (Eds.), *Handbook of behavioral assessment.* New York: Wiley, 1977.

Ciminero, A.R., Nelson, R.O., & Lipinski, D.P. Self-monitoring procedures. In A.R. Ciminero, K.S. Calhoun, & H.E. Adams (Eds.), *Handbook of behavioral assessment.* New York: Wiley, 1977.

Davison, G.C. Elimination of a sadistic fantasy by a client-controlled counterconditioning technique. *Journal of Abnormal Psychology,* 1968, *73,* 84–90.

Davison, G.C. Homosexuality: The ethical challenge. *Journal of Homosexuality,* 1977, *2,* 195–204.

Davison, G.C., & Stuart, R.B. Behavior therapy and civil liberties. *American Psychologist,* 1975, *30,* 755–763.

Davison, G.C., & Wilson, G.T. Processes of fear reduction in systematic desensitization: Cognitive and social reinforcement factors in humans. *Behavior Therapy,* 1973, *4,* 1–21.

D'Zurilla, T., & Goldfried, M.R. Problem solving and behavior modification. *Journal of Abnormal Psychology,* 1971, *78,* 107–126.

Ellis, A. *Reason and emotion in psychotherapy.* New York: Lyle Stuart, 1962.

Ellis, A. (Ed.). *Handbook of rational-emotive therapy.* New York: Springer, 1977.

Evans, D.R. Subjective variables and treatment effects in aversive therapy. *Behaviour Research and Therapy,* 1970, *8,* 147–152.

Eysenck, H.J. Learning theory and behaviour therapy. *Journal of Mental Science,* 1959, *105,* 61–75.

Eysenck, H.J. (Ed.), *Behaviour therapy and the neuroses.* London: Pergamon, 1960.

Eysenck, H.J. *The biological basis of personality.* Springfield, Ill.: Charles C Thomas, 1967.

Eysenck, H.J. Behavior therapy and its critics. *Journal of Behavior Therapy and Experimental Psychiatry,* 1970, *1,* 5–15.

Ford, J.D., & Foster, S.L. Extrinsic incentives and token-based programs: A re-evaluation. *American Psychologist,* 1976, *31,* 87–90.

Foreyt, J.P., & Hagan, R.L. Covert sensitization: Conditioning and suggestion? *Journal of Abnormal Psychology,* 1973,*82,* 17–23.

Foxx, R., & Azrin, N. Dry pants: A rapid method of toilet training children. *Behaviour Research and Therapy,* 1973, *11,* 435–442.

Franks, C.M. Behavior therapy, psychology and the psychiatrist. Contributions, evaluation and overview. *American Journal of Orthopsychiatry,* 1965, *35,* 145–151.

Franks, C.M. The practitioner as behavioral scientist—myth, wishful thinking or reality! *New Jersey Psychologist,* 1969, *19,* 4–8. (a)

Franks, C.M. (Ed.). *Behavior therapy: Appraisal and status.* New York: McGraw-Hill, 1969. (b)

Franks, C.M. Clockwork orange revisited: Travesty and truth about aversive conditioning. In O.L. McCabe (Ed.), *Psychotherapy and behavior change.* New York: Grune & Stratton, 1977. (a)

Franks, C.M. The case for controlled drinking. (Review of W.R. Miller & R.F. Muñoz. *How to control your drinking. Englewood Cliffs, N.J.: Prentice-Hall, 1976.) Contemporary Psychology,* 1977, *22,* 668–669. (b)

Franks, C.M., & Brady, J.P. What is behavior therapy and why a new journal? *Behavior Therapy,* 1970, *1,* 1–3.

Franks, C.M., & Wilson, G.T. (Eds.). Annual review of behavior therapy: Theory and practice. (Vol.3). New York: Brunner/Mazel, 1975.

Franks, C.M., & Wilson, G.T. (Eds.), *Annual review of behavior therapy: Theory and practice.* (Vol. 4). New York: Brunner/Mazel, 1976.

Franks, C.M., & Wilson, G.T. (Eds.), *Annual review of behavior therapy: Theory and practice.* (Vol.5). New York: Brunner/Mazel, 1977.

Franks, C.M., & Wilson, G.T. (Eds.). *Annual review of behavior therapy: Theory and practice.* (Vol. 6). New York: Brunner/Mazel, 1978.

Geer, J.H. The development of a scale to measure fear. *Behaviour Research and Therapy,* 1965, *3,* 45–53.

Glass, C.R., Gottman, J.M., & Shmurak, S.H. Response acquisition and cognitive self-statement modification approaches to dating skills. *Journal of Counseling Psychology,* 1976, *23,* 520–526.

Goetz, E., & Baer, D. Social control of form diversity and the emergence of new forms in children's blockbuilding. *Journal of Applied Behavior Analysis,* 1973, *6,* 241–250.

Goldfried, M.R., & Davison, G.C. *Clinical behavior therapy.* New York: Holt, Rinehart, & Winston, 1976.

Goldfried, M.R., & D'Zurilla, T.J. A behavior analytic model for assessing competence. In C.D. Spielberger (Ed.), *Current topics in clinical and community psychology.* New York: Academic Press, 1969.

Goldfried, M.R., & Kent, R.N. Traditional versus behavioral personality assessment: A comparison of methodological and theoretical assumptions. *Psychological Bulletin,* 1972, *77,* 409–420.

Goldfried, M.R., & Pomerantz, D. Role of assessment in behavior modification. *Psychological Reports,* 1968, *23,* 75–87.

Goldfried, M.R., & Sprafkin, J.N. *Behavioral personality assessment.* Morristown, N.J.: General Learning Press, 1974.

Hamburg, S. Behavior therapy in alcoholism: A critical review of broad-spectrum approaches. *Journal of Studies on Alcohol,* 1975, *36,* 69–87.

Hedberg, A.G., & Campbell, L. A comparison of four behavioral treatments of alcoholism. *Journal of Behavior Therapy and Experimental Psychiatry,* 1974, *5,* 251–256.

Hersen. M., & Barlow, D. *Single-case experimental designs: Strategies for studying behavior change.* New York: Pergamon, 1976.

Higgins, R., & Marlatt, G.A. Fear of interpersonal evaluation as a determinant of alcohol consumption in male social drinkers. *Journal of Abnormal Psychology,* 1975, *84,* 644–665.

Homme, L.E. Perspectives in psychology—XXIV control of coverants: The operants of the mind. *Psychological Record,* 1965, *15,* 501–511.

Jeffery, D.B. Treatment of evaluation issues in research on addictive behaviors. *Addictive Behaviors,* 1975, *1,* 23–36.

Jeffery, R.W., Wing, R.R. & Stunkard, A.J. Behavioral treatment of obesity: The state of the art in 1976. *Behavior Therapy,* 1978, *9,* 189–199.

Jellinek, E.M. *The disease concept of alcoholism.* New Haven: Hillhouse Press, 1960.

Johnson, D.W., & Matross, R. Interpersonal influence in psychotherapy. In A.S. Gurman & A.M. Razin (Eds.), *The therapist's contribution to effective psychotherapy: An empirical approach.* New York: Pergamon, 1977.

Johnson, S., & Bolstad, O. Methodological issues in naturalistic observation: Some problems and solutions for field research. In L.A. Hamerlynck, L.C. Handy, E.J. Mash (Eds.), *Behavior change: methodology, concepts and practice.* Champaign, Ill.: Research Press, 1973.

Jones, M.C. The elimination of children's fears. *Journal of Experimental Psychology,* 1924, *7,* 382–390.

Kanfer, F.H., & Goldstein, A.P. (Eds.), *Helping people change.* New York: Pergamon, 1975.

Kanfer, F., & Karoly, P. Self-control: A behavioristic excursion into the lion's den. *Behavior Therapy,* 1972, *3,* 398–416.

Kanfer, F., & Saslow, G. Behavioral diagnosis. In C.M. Franks (Ed.), *Behavior therapy: Appraisal and status.* New York: McGraw-Hill, 1969.

Kazdin, A.E. Effects of covert modeling and model reinforcement of assertive behavior. *Journal of Abnormal Psychology,* 1974, *83,* 240–252.

Kazdin, A.E. *Behavior modification in applied settings.* Homewood, Ill.: Dorsey Press, 1975. (a)

Kazdin, A.E. Covert modeling, imagery assessment, and assertive behavior. *Journal of Consulting and Clinical Psychology,* 1975, *43,* 716–724. (b)

Kazdin, A.E. *The token economy: A review and evaluation.* New York: Plenum, 1977.

Kazdin, A.E., & Wilcoxon, L.A. Systematic desensitization and non-specific treatment effects: A methodological evaluation. *Psychological Bulletin,* 1976, *83,* 729–758.

Kazdin, A.E., & Wilson, G.T. *Evaluation of behavior therapy: Issues, evidence and research strategies.* Cambridge, Mass.: Ballinger, 1978.

Kent, R., & Foster, S. Direct observational procedures: Methodological issues in naturalistic settings. In A. Ciminero, K.S. Calhoun, & H.E. Adams (Eds.), *Handbook of behavioral assessment.* New York: Wiley, 1977.

Kosloff, M. *Reaching the autistic child: A parent training program.* Champaign, Ill.: Research Press, 1973.

Lang, A.R., Goeckner, D.J., Adesso, V.J., & Marlatt, G.A. Effects of alcohol on aggression in male social drinkers. *Journal of Abnormal Psychology,* 1975, *84,* 508–518.

Lazarus, A.A. New methods in psychotherapy: A case study. *South African Medical Journal,* 1958, *32,* 660–664.

Lazarus, A.A. Broad spectrum behavior therapy and the treatment of agoraphobia. *Behaviour Research and Therapy,* 1966, *4,* 95–97.

Lazarus, A.A. *Behavior therapy and beyond.* New York: McGraw-Hill, 1971.

Lazarus, A.A. Multimodal behavior therapy: Treating the "Basic Id." *Journal of Nervous and Mental Disease,* 1973, *156,* 404–411.

Lazarus, A.A. *Multimodal behavior therapy.* New York: Springer, 1976.

Leitenberg, H. Is time-out from positive reinforcement an aversive event? A review of experimental evidence. *Psychological Bulletin,* 1965, *64,* 428–441.

Lindsley, O.R., Skinner, B.F., & Solomon, H.C. *Studies in behavior therapy. Status report 1.* Waltham, Mass.: Metropolitan State Hosspital, 1953.

Lloyd, R.W., Jr., & Salzberg, H.C. Controlled social drinking: An alternative to abstinence as a treatment goal for some alcohol abusers. *Psychological Bulletin,* 1975, *82,* 815–842.

Locke, E.A. Is "behavior therapy" behavioristic? (An analysis of Wolpe's psychotherapeutic methods.) *Psychological Bulletin,* 1971, *76,* 318–327.

Lovaas, O.I. *The autistic child.* New York: Irvington, 1977.

Lovaas, O.I., Freitas, L., Nelson, K., & Whalen, C. The establishment of imitation and its use for the development of complex behavior in schizophrenic children. *Behaviour Research and Therapy,* 1967, *5,* 171–182.

Lovitt, T.C. Applied behavior analysis and learning disabilities; Specific research recommendations and suggestions. *Journal of Learning Disabilities,* 1975, *8,* 33–50.

Mahoney, M.J. *Cognition and behavior modification.* Cambridge, Mass.: Ballinger, 1974.

Mahoney, M.J. The obese eating style: Bites, beliefs, and behavior modification. *Addictive Behaviors,* 1975, *1,* 47–53.

Mahoney, M.J. Reflections on the cognitive-learning trend in psychotherapy. *American Psychologist,* 1977, *32,* 5–13.

Mahoney, M.J., Moura, N., & Wade, T. The relative efficacy of self-reward, self-punishment, and self-monitoring: Techniques for weight loss. *Journal of Consulting and Clinical Psychology,* 1973, *40,* 404–407.

Mahoney, M.J., & Thoresen, C. (Eds.), *Self-control: Power to the person.* Monterey, Calif.: Brooks/Cole, 1974.

Mariotto, J.J., & Paul, G.L. A multimethod validation of the inpatient multidimensional psychiatric scale with chronically institutionalized patients. *Journal of Consulting and Clinical Psychology,* 1974, *42,* 497–508.

Marks, I.M., & Gelder, M.G. Transvestism and fetishism: Clinical and psychological changes during faradic aversion. *British Journal of Psychiatry,* 1967, *113,* 711–729.

Marlatt, G.A., Demming, B., & Reid, J.B. Loss of control drinking in alcoholics: An experimental analogue. *Journal of Abnormal Psychology,* 1973, *81,* 233–241.

Masters, W.H., & Johnson, V.E. *Human sexual inadequacy.* Boston: Little, Brown, 1970.

McFall, R., & Twentyman, C.T. Four experiments on the relative contributions of rehearsal, modeling, and coaching to assertion training. *Journal of Abnormal Psychology,* 1973, *81,* 199–218.

Meichenbaum, D.H. *Cognitive behavior modification.* Morristown, N.J.: General Learning Press, 1974.

Meichenbaum, D.H. A cognitive behavior modification assessment approach. In M. Hersen & A. Bellack (Eds.), *Behavioral assessment: A practical approach.* Oxford: Pergamon, 1977.

Meichenbaum, D.H., & Cameron, R. Training schizophrenics to talk to themselves: A means of developing attentional controls. *Behavior Therapy,* 1973, *4,* 515–534.

Mischel, W. *Personality and assessment.* New York: Wiley, 1968.

Mischel, W. Towards a cognitive social learning reconceptualization of personality. *Psychological Review,* 1973, *80,* 252–283.

Mischel, W. On the future of personality measurement. *American Psychologist,* 1977, *32,* 246–254.

Nietzel, M.T., Winnett, R.A., MacDonald, M.L. & Davidson, W.S. *Behavioral approaches to community psychology.* New York: Pergamon, 1977.

O'Leary, D.K., & O'Leary, S. *Classroom management: The successful use of behavior modification,* (2nd ed.). New York: Pergamon, 1976.

O'Leary, D.K., & Wilson, G.T. *Behavior therapy: Application and outcome.* Englewood Cliffs, N.J.: Prentice-Hall, 1975.

Rachlin, J. *Introduction to modern behaviorism.* San Francisco: Freeman, 1970.

Rathus, S. Instigation of assertive behavior through videotape-mediated assertive models and directed practice. *Behaviour Research and Therapy,* 1973, *11,* 57–66.

Ray, R.D., & Brown, D.A. The behavioral specificity of stimulation: A systems approach to procedural distinctions of classical and instrumental conditioning. *Pavolovian Journal of Biological Science,* 1976, *11,* 3–23.

Risley, T.R. Behavior modification: An experimental-therapeutic endeavor. In L.A. Hannerlynck, P.O. Davidson, & L.E. Acker (Eds.), *Behavior modification and ideal mental health services.* Calgary, Canada: University of Calgary Press, 1970.

Ryback, D., & Staats, A.W. Parents as behavior therapy technicians in treating reading deficits (dyslexia). *Journal of Behavior therapy and Experimental Psychiatry,* 1970, *1,* 109–119.

Salter, A. *Conditioned reflex therapy.* New York: Farrar, Straus, 1949.

Sidman, M. *Tactics of scientific research.* New York: Basic Books, 1960.

Siegal, J., & Spivack, G. A new therapy program for chronic patients. *Behavior Therapy,* 1976, *7,* 129–130.

Skinner, B.F. *Science and human behavior.* New York: Macmillan, 1953.

Skinner, B.F. Behaviorism at fifty. *Science,* 1963, *140,* 951–958.

Skinner, B.F. The steep and thorny way to a science of behavior. *American Psychologist,* 1975, *30,* 42–49.

Sobell, M.B., & Sobell, L.C. Individualized therapy for alcoholics. *Behavior Therapy,* 1973, *4,* 49–72.

Sobell, M.B., & Sobell, L.C. Second year treatment outcome of alcoholics treated by individualized behavior therapy: Results. *Behaviour Research and Therapy,* 1976, *14,* 195–216.

Stokes, T.F., & Baer, D.M. An implicit technology of generalization. *Journal of Applied Behavior Analysis,* 1977, *10,* 349–367.

Stolz, S.B. & Associates. *Ethical Issues in Behavior Modification.* San Francisco: Jossey-Bass, 1978.

Stuart, R.B. & Stuart, F. *Marital pre-counseling inventory.* Champaign, Ill.: Research Press, 1972.

Susskind, D.J. The idealized self-image (ISI): A new technique in confidence training. *Behavior Therapy,* 1970, *1,* 538–541.

Terrace, H.S. Stimulus control. In W.K. Honig (Ed.), *Operant behavior: Areas of research and application.* New York: Appleton-Century-Crofts, 1966.

Tharp, R.G., & Wetzel, R.J. *Behavior modification in the natural environment.* New York: Academic Press, 1969.

Thoresen, T., & Mahoney, M.J. *Behavioral self-control.* New York: Holt, Rinehart & Winston, 1974.

Todd, F.J. Coverant control of self-evaluative responses in the treatment of depression: A new use for an old principle. *Behavior Therapy,* 1972, *3,* 91–94.

Ullmann, L.P., & Krasner, L. (Eds.), *Case studies in behavior modification.* New York: Holt, Rinehart & Winston, 1965.

Wann, T.W. (Ed.). *Behaviorism and phenomenology.* Chicago, Ill.: University of Chicago Press, 1966.

Watson, J.B., & Rayner, R. Conditioned emotional reactions. *Journal of Experimental Psychology,* 1920, *3,* 1–14.

Wilson, G.T., & Abrams, D.B. Effects of alcohol on social anxiety and physiological arousal: Cognitive versus pharmacological processes. *Cognitive Research and Therapy,* 1977, *1,* 195–210.

Wilson, G.T., & Evans, I.M. The therapist-client relationship in behavior therapy. In A.S. Gurman & A.M. Razin (Eds.), *The therapist's contribution to effective psychotherapy: An empirical approach.* New York: Pergamon, 1977.

Wolpe, J. *Psychotherapy by reciprocal inhibition.* Stanford, Calif.: Stanford University Press, 1958.

Yates, A.J. *Theory and practice in behavior therapy.* New York: Wiley, 1975.

Chapter 20

AMA Department of Drugs. *AMA drug evaluation.* Littleton, Mass.: Publishing Sciences Group, 1977.

Brecher, E.M., & the editors of *Consumer Reports. Licit and illicit drugs.* Boston: Little, Brown, 1972.

Fink, M., Kety, S., McGaugh, J., & Williams, T. *Psychobiology of convulsive therapy.* New York: Wiley, 1974.

Fish, F. *An outline of psychiatry for students and practitioners.* Briston, Eng.: John Wright, 1964.

Garattini, S., Mussini, E., & Randall, O. (Eds.), *The benzodiazepines.* New York: Raven Press, 1973.

Goodman, L.S., & Gilman, A. *The pharmacological basis of therapeutics.* London: Macmillan, 1970.

Greenblatt, D., & Shader, R. *Benzodiazepines in clinical practice.* New York: Raven Press, 1974.

Hollister, L.E. *Chemical psychoses, LSD, and related drugs.* Springfield, Ill.: Charles C Thomas, 1968.

Jarvik, M.E. *Psychopharmacology in the practice of medicine.* New York: Appleton-Century-Crofts, 1977.

Kagan, F., Harwood, T., Rickels, K., Rudzik, A.D., & Sorer, H. *Hypnotics.* New York: Spectrum, 1975.

Kalinowsky, L.B., & Hippius, H. *Pharmacological convulsive and other somatic treatments in psychiatry.* New York: Grune & Stratton, 1969.

Matheson, D.W., & Davison, M.A. *The behavioral effects of drugs.* New York: Holt, Rinehart, & Winston, 1972.

Segal, D.S., Yager, J., & Sullivan, J.L. *Foundations of biochemical psychiatry.* Boston: Butterworth, 1976.

Woodruff, R.A., Goodwin, D.W., & Guze, S.B. *Psychiatric diagnosis.* New York: Oxford University Press, 1974.

Chapter 21

American Public Health Association. *Mental disorders: A guide to control methods.* New York: American Public Health Association, 1962.

Anthony, W.A., Buell, G.J., Scharratt, S., & Althoff, M.E. Efficacy of psychiatric rehabilitation. *Psychological Bulletin,* 1972, *78,* 447–456.

Artiss, K.L. (Ed.). *The symptom as communication in schizophrenia.* New York: Grune & Stratton, 1959.

Atthowe, J.M., Jr. Behavior innovation and persistence. *American Psychologist,* 1973, *28,* 34–41.

Ayllon, T., & Azrin, N.H. *The token economy: A motivational system for therapy and rehabilitation.* New York: Appleton-Century-Crofts, 1968.

Belknap, I. *Human problems of a state mental hospital.* New York: McGraw-Hill, 1956.

Bleuler, M. The long-term course of the schizophrenic psychoses. In R. Cancro (Ed.), *Annual review of the schizophrenic syndrome 1974–5,* (Vol. 4). New York: Brunner/Mazel, 1976.

Bockoven, J.S. Moral treatment in American psychiatry. *Journal of Nervous and Mental disease,* 1956, *124,* 167–194, 292–321.

Bott, E. Hospital and society. *British Journal of Medical Psychology,* 1976, *49,* 97–140.

Braginsky, B.M., & Braginsky, D.D. Schizophrenic patients in the psychiatric interview: An experimental study of their effectiveness at manipulation. *Journal of Consulting Psychology,* 1967, *31,* 543–547.

Braginsky, B.M., Braginsky, D.D., & Ring, K. *Methods of madness. The mental hospital as a last resort.* New York: Holt, Rinehart, & Winston, 1969.

Braginsky, B.M., Grosse, M., & Ring, K. Controlling outcomes through impression-management: An experimental study of the manipulative tactics of mental patients. *Journal of Consulting Psychology,* 1966, *30,* 295–300.

Caffey, E.M., Jr., Diamond, L.S., Frank, T.V., Grasberger, J.C., Herman, L., Klett, C.J., & Rothstein, C. Discontinuation or reduction of chemotherapy in chronic schizophrenics. *Journal of Chronic Disease,* 1964, *17,* 347–358.

Caudill, W. *The psychiatric hospital as a small society.* Cambridge, Mass.: Harvard University Press, 1958.

Cohen, J. & Struening, E.L. Opinions about mental illness in the personnel of two large mental hospitals. *Journal of Abnormal and Social Psychology,* 1962, *64,* 349–360.

Cohen, J., & Struening, E.L. Opinions about mental illness: Hospital social atmosphere profiles and their relevance to effectiveness.

Journal of Consulting Psychology, 1964, *28*, 291–298.

Cole, J.O., Goldberg, S.C. & Davis, J.M. Drugs in the treatment of psychoses: Controlled studies. In J. Solomon (Ed.), *Psychiatric drugs*. New York: Grune & Stratton, 1966.

Crane, G.E. Tardive dyskinesia in patients treated with major neuroleptics: A review of the literature. *American Jouranl of Psychiatry*, 1968, *124*, 40–48.

Cumming, E., & Cumming, J. *Closed ranks*. Cambridge: Harvard University Press, 1957.

Cumming, J. The inadequacy syndrome. *Psychiatric Quarterly*, 1963, *37*, 723–733.

Cumming, J., & Cumming, E. *Ego and milieu: Theory and practice of environmental therapy*. New York: Atherton, 1962.

Davis, J.M. Efficacy of tranquilizing and antidepressant drugs. *Archives of General Psychiatry*, 1965, *13*, 552–572.

Deutsch, A. *The shame of the states*. New York: Harcourt, Brace, 1948.

Dunham, H.W., & Weinberg, S.K. *The culture of the state mental hospital*. Detroit: Wayne State University Press, 1960.

Ellsworth, R.B. A behavioral study of staff attitudes toward mental illness. *Journal of Abnormal Psychology*, 1965, *70*, 194–200.

Ellsworth, R.B. *Nonprofessionals in psychiatric rehabilitation*. New York: Appleton-Century-Crofts, 1968.

Ellsworth, R.B., & Maroney, R. Characteristics of psychiatric programs and their effects on patients' adjustment. *Journal of Consulting and Clinical Psychology*, 1972, *39*, 436–447.

Ellsworth, R.B., Maroney, R., Klett, W., Gordon, H., & Gunn, R. Milieu characteristics of successful psychiatric treatment programs. *American Journal of Orthopsychiatry*, 1971, *41*, 427–441.

Erickson, R.C. Outcome studies in mental hospitals: A review. *Psychological Bulletin*, 1975, *82*, 519–540.

Fairweather, G.W. *Social psychology in treating mental illness: An experimental approach*. New York: Wiley, 1964.

Fairweather, G.W., Sanders, D.H., Maynard, H., & Cressler, D.C. *Community life for the mentally ill: An alternative to institutional care*. Chicago: Aldine, 1969.

Fontana, A.F., & Corey, M. Culture conflict in the treatment of "mental illness" and the central role of patient leader. *Journal of Consulting and Clinical Psychology*, 1970, *34*, 244–249.

Fontana, A.F., & Gessner, T. Patients' goals and the manifestation of psychopathology. *Journal of Consulting and Clinical Psychology*, 1969, *33*, 247–253.

Fontana, A.F., & Klein, E.B. Self-presentation and the schizophrenic "deficit." *Journal of Consulting and Clinical Psychology*, 1968, *32*, 250–256.

Fontana, A.F., Klein, E.B., Lewis, E., & Levine, L. Presentation of self in mental illness. *Journal of Consulting and Clinical Psychology*, 1968, *32*, 110–119.

Fowlkes, M.R. Business as usual—at the state mental hospital. *Psychiatry*, 1975, *38*, 55–64.

Galioni, E.F., Notman, R.R., Stanton, A.H., & Williams, R.H. The nature and purposes of mental hospital wards. In M. Greenblatt, D.J. Levinson, & R.H. Williams (Eds.), *The patient and the mental hospital*. Glencoe, Ill.: Free Press, 1957.

Gilbert, D.C., & Levinson, D.J. Ideology, personality, and institutional policy in the mental hospital. *Journal of Abnormal and Social Psychology*, 1956, *53*, 263–271.

Gilbert, D.C., & Levinson, D.J. "Custodialism and humanism" in mental hospital structure and in staff ideology. In M. Greenblatt, D.J. Levinson, & R.H. Williams (Eds.), *The patient and the mental hospital*. Glencoe, Ill.: Free Press, 1957.

Goffman, E. *The presentation of self in everyday life*. New York: Doubleday, 1959.

Goffman, E. *Asylums: Essays on the social situation of mental patients and other inmates*. Garden City, N.Y.:Doubleday, 1961.

Goffman, E. The insanity of place. *Psychiatry*, 1969, *32*, 357–388.

Goldman, A.R. Wanting to leave or to stay in a mental hospital. Incidence and correlates. *Journal of Clinical Psychology*, 1965, *21*, 317–322.

Gordon, H.L., & Groth, C. Mental patients wanting to stay in the hospital. Attitudes. *Archives of General Psychiatry*, 1961, *4*, 124–130.

Gove, W.R. Societal reaction as an explanation of mental illness: An evaluation. *American Sociological Review*, 1970, *35*, 873–884.

Gove, W.R., & Fain, T. A comparison of voluntary and committed psychiatric patients. *Archives of General Psychiatry*, 1977, *34*, 669–676.

Gurel, L. Correlates of psychiatric hospital effectiveness. *Factors in mental hospital effectiveness* (Intramural report 64–5). Washington,

D.C.: Psychiatric Evaluation Project, Veterans Administration Hospital, 1964.

Gurel, L. A ten-year perspective on outcome in functional psychosis. *Highlights of the fifteenth annual conference.* Washington, D.C.: Veterans Administration Cooperative Studies in Psychiatry, 1970.

Haley, J. The art of being schizophrenic. *Voices,* 1965, *1,* 133–147.

Hollister, L.E., & Kosek, J.C. Sudden deaths during treatment with phenothiazine derivatives. *Journal of the American Medical Association,* 1965, *192,* 1035–1038.

Hornstra, R.K., Lubin, B., Lewis, R.V., & Willis, B.S. Worlds apart: Patients and professionals. *Archives of General Psychiatry,* 1972, *27,* 553–557.

Joint Commission on Mental Illness and Health. *Action for mental health.* New York: Basic Books, 1961.

Jones, M. *The therapeutic community.* New York: Basic Books, 1953.

Kahne, M.J. Bureaucratic structure and impersonal experience in mental hospitals. *Psychiatry,* 1959, *22,* 363–375.

Kantor, D., & Gelineau, V. Social processes in support of chronic deviance. *International Journal of Social Psychiatry,* 1965, *11,* 280–289.

Kellam, S.G., Goldberg, S.C., Schooler, N.R., Berman, A., & Shmelzer, J.L. Ward atmosphere and outcome of treatment of acute schizophrenia. *Journal of Psychiatric Research,* 1967, *5,* 145–163.

Kelly, F.S., Farina, A., & Mosher, D.L. Ability of schizophrenic women to create a favorable or unfavorable impression on an interviewer. *Journal of Consulting and Clinical Psychology, 1971, 36,* 404–409.

Kennedy, P.F., Hershon, H.I., & McGuire, R.J. Extra-pyramidal disorders after prolonged phenothiazine therapy, including a factor analytic study of clinical features. *British Journal of Psychiatry,* 1971, *118,* 509–518.

Kirk, S.A., & Therrien, M.E. Community mental health myths and the fate of former hospitalized patients. *Psychiatry,* 1975, *38,* 209–217.

Kraft, A.M., Binner, P.R., & Dickey, B.A. The community mental health program and the longer-stay patient. *Archives of General Psychiatry,* 1967, *16,* 64–70.

Lamb, H.R. Release of chronic psychiatric patients into the community. *Archives of General Psychiatry,* 1968, *19,* 38–44.

Lamb, H.R., & Goertzel, V. Discharged mental patients—are they really in the community? *Archives of General Psychiatry,* 1971, *24,* 29–34.

Lamb, H.R., & Goertzel, V. The demise of the state hospital—a premature obituary? *Archives of General Psychiatry,* 1972, *26,* 489–495.

Langsley, D.G., Pittman, F.S., & Swank, G.E. Family crises in schizophrenics and other mental patients. *Journal of Nervous and Mental Disease,* 1969, *149,* 270–276.

Lehrer, P., & Lanoil, J. Natural reinforcement in a psychiatric rehabilitation program. *Schizophrenia Bulletin,* 1977, *3,* 297–302.

Lemert, E.M. *Social pathology.* New York: McGraw-Hill, 1951.

Levinson, D.J., & Gallagher, E.B. *Patienthood in the mental hospital.* Boston: Houghton Mifflin, 1964.

Levinson, D.J., Merrifield, J., & Berg, K. Becoming a patient. *Archives of General Psychiatry,* 1967, *17,* 385–406.

Linn, M.W., Caffey, E.M., Klett, C.J., & Hogarty, G. Hospital vs. community (foster) care for psychiatric patients. *Archives of General Psychiatry,* 1977, *34,* 78–83.

Ludwig, A.M., & Farrelly, F. The code of chronicity. *Archives of General Psychiatry,* 1966, *15,* 562–568.

Ludwig, A.M., & Farrelly, F. The weapons of insanity. *American Journal of Psychotherapy,* 1967, *21,* 737–749.

Miller, D.H. Retrospective analysis of posthospital mental patients' worlds. *Journal of Health and Social Behavior,* 1967, *8,* 136–140.

Miller, D.H. The etiology of an outbreak of delinquency in a group of hospitalized adolescents. In M. Greenblatt, D.J. Levinson, & R.H. Williams (Eds.), *The patient and the mental hospital.* Glencoe, Ill.: Free Press, 1957.

Moore, M.T., & Book, M.H. Sudden death in phenothiazine therapy: A clinicopathologic study of twelve cases. *Psychiatric Quarterly,* 1970, *44,* 389–402.

Moos, R. Size, staffing and pychiatric ward treatment environments. *Archives of General Psychiatry,* 1972, *26,* 414–418.

Moos, R., & Houts, P. The assessment of the social atmospheres of psychiatric wards. *Journal of Abnormal Psychology,* 1968, *73,* 595–604.

Moos, R., & Houts, P. Differential effects of the social atmospheres of psychiatric wards. *Human Relations,* 1970, *23,* 47–60.

Moos, R., & Schwartz, J. Treatment environment

and treatment outcome. *Journal of Nervous and Mental Disease,* 1972, *154,* 264–275.

Moos, R.H., Shelton, R., & Petty, C. Perceived ward climate and treatment outcome. *Journal of Abnormal Psychology,* 1973, *82,* 291–298.

Nadler, S., Barrett, E.M., Miller, D., Lea, M.E., & Mosier, J. Patients who choose to live in the hospital. *International Journal of Social Psychiatry,* 1967, *13,* 150–157.

Nunnally, J.C. *Popular conceptions of mental health.* New York: Holt, Rinehart, & Winston, 1961.

Paul, G.L. The chronic mental patient: Current status—future directions. *Psychological Bulletin,* 1969, *71,* 81–94.

Paul, G.L., & Lentz, R.J. *Psychosocial treatment of chronic mental patients.* Cambridge, Mass.: Harvard University Press, 1977.

Peck, C.L. Current legislative issues concerning the right to refuse versus the right to choose hospitalization and treatment. *Psychiatry,* 1975, *38,* 303–317.

Phillips, D.L. Rejection: A possible consequence of seeking help for mental disorders. *American Sociological Review,* 1963, *28,* 963–972.

Phillips, D.L. Identification of mental illness: Its consequences for rejection. *Community Mental Health Journal,* 1967, *3,* 262–266.

Polak, P. Patterns of discord. Goals of patients, therapists, and community members. *Archives of General Psychiatry,* 1970, *23,* 277–283.

President's Commission on Mental Helath. *Report to the President.* (Vol.1). Washington, D.C.: U.S. Government Printing Office, 1978.

Price, R.H. Psychological deficit versus impression management in schizophrenic word association performance. *Journal of Abnormal Psychology,* 1972, *79,* 132–137.

Prien, R.F., Cole, J.O., & Bilkin, N.F. Relapse in chronic schizophrenics following abrupt withdrawal of tranquilizing medication. *British Journal of Psychiatry,* 1969, *115,* 679–686.

Roth, L.H. Involuntary civil commitment: The right to treatment and the right to refuse treatment. *Psychiatric Annals,* 1977, *7,* 244–257.

Rowland, H. Friendship patterns in a state mental hospital. *Psychiatry,* 1939, *2,* 363–373.

Sadow, L. & Suslick, A. Simulation of a previous psychotic state. *Archives of General Psychiatry,* 1961, *4,* 452–458.

Scheff, T.J. *Being mentally ill: A sociological theory.* Chicago: Aldine, 1966.

Scheff, T.J. (Ed.). *Labeling madness.* Englewood Cliffs, N.J.: Prentice-Hall, 1975.

Schooler, N.R., Goldberg, S.C., Boothe, H., & Cole, J.O. One year after discharge: Community adjustment of schizophrenic patients. *American Journal of Psychiatry,* 1967, *123,* 986–995.

Scott, R.D., & Ashworth, P.L. "Closure" at the first schizophrenic breakdown: A family study. *British Journal of Medical Psychology,* 1967, *40,* 109–145.

Sherman, M. Impression management: Patient perceptions of the efficacy of psychiatric self-presentation. *Journal of Abnormal Psychology,* 1974, *83,* 459–462.

Sherman, M., Sprafkin, R., & Higgins, K. Perceived efficacy and interpersonal impact of impression management among psychiatric patients. *Journal of Abnormal Psychology,* 1974, *83,* 440–445.

Sherman, M., Trief, P., & Sprafkin, R. Impression management in the psychiatric interview: Quality, style, and individual differences. *Journal of Consulting and Clinical Psychology,* 1975, *43,* 867–871.

Simon, W.B. On reluctance to leave the public mental hospital. *Psychiatry,* 1965, *28,* 145–156. (a)

Simon, W.B. A skeptic's view of the mental illness game or: An old state hospital hand's jaundiced look at progress. *Mental Hygiene,* 1965, *49,* 69–73. (b)

Simon, W.B. Some problems in helping patients in public mental hospitals. *Mental Hygiene,* 1969, *53,* 428–432.

Smith, C.G., & King, J.A. *Mental hospitals. A study in organizational effectiveness.* Lexington, Mass.: D.C. Heath, 1975.

Sommer, R., & Withey, G. The chain of chronicity. *American Journal of Psychiatry,* 1961, *118,* 111–117.

Speigel, D., & Younger, J.B. Ward climate and community stay of psychiatric patients. *Journal of Consulting and Clinical Psychology,* 1972, *39,* 62–69.

Stanton, A.H., & Schwartz, M.S. *The mental hospital: A study of institutional participation in psychiatric illness and treatment.* New York: Basic Books, 1954.

Stotland, E., & Kobler, A.L. *Life and death of a mental hospital.* Seattle: University of Washington Press, 1965.

Strauss, A., Schatzman, L., Bucher, R., Ehrlich, D., & Sabshin, M. *Psychiatric ideologies and institutions.* Glencoe, Ill.: Free Press, 1964.

Tobias, L.L., & MacDonald, M.L. Withdrawal of maintenance drugs with long-term hospitalized mental patients: A critical review. *Psychological Bulletin,* 1974, *81,* 107–125.

Towbin, A.P. Understanding the mentally deranged. *Journal of Existentialism,* 1966, *7,* 63–84.

Ullmann, L.P. *Institution and outcome: A comparative study of psychiatric hospitals.* New York: Pergamon, 1967.

Vitale, J.H. Mental hospital therapy: A review and integration. In J.H. Masserman (Ed.), *Current psychiatric therapies* (Vol. 2). New York: Grune & Stratton, 1962.

Watson, C.G. Roles of impression management in the interview, self-report, and cognitive behavior of schizophrenics. *Journal of Consulting and Clinical Psychology,* 1972, *38,* 452–456.

Watson, C.G. Conspicuous psychotic behavior as a manipulative tool. *Journal of Clinical Psychology,* 1973, *29,* 3–7.

Watson, C.G. Impression management ability in psychiatric hospital samples and normals. *Journal of Consulting and Clinical Psychology,* 1975, *43,* 540–545.

Wing, J.K. Institutionalism in mental hospitals. *British Journal of Social and Clinical Psychology,* 1962, *1,* 38–51.

Wood, E.C., Rakusin, J.M., & Morse, E. Resident psychiatrist in the admitting office. A man in conflict. *Archives of General Psychiatry,* 1965, *13,* 54–61.

Zusman, J. Some explanations of the changing appearance of psychotic patients: Antecedents of the social breakdown syndrome concept. *International Journal of Psychiatry,* 1967, *3,* 216–237.

Zwerling, I., Karasu, T., Plutchik, R., & Kellerman, S. A comparison of voluntary and involuntary patients in a state hospital. *American Journal of Orthopsychiatry,* 1975, *45,* 81–87.

Chapter 22

Baekeland, F., & Lundwall, L. Dropping out of treatment: A critical review. *Psychological Bulletin,* 1975, *82,* 738–783.

Baum, O.E., & Felzer, S.B. Activity in initial interviews with lower class patients. *Archives of General Psychiatry,* 1964, *10,* 345–353.

Bergin, A.E. The evaluation of therapeutic outcomes. In A.E. Bergin & S.L. Garfield (Eds.), *Handbook of psychotherapy and behavior change.* New York: Wiley, 1971.

Bergin, A.E. & Lambert, M.J. The evaluation of therapeutic outcomes. In S.L. Garfield and A.E. Bergin (Eds.), *Handbook of psychotherapy and behavior change.* (2nd ed.). New York: Wiley, 1978.

Butcher, J.N., & Koss, M.P. Research on brief and crisis-oriented therapies. In S.L. Garfield & A.E. Bergin (Eds.), *Handbook of psychotherapy and behavior change* (2nd ed.). New York: Wiley, 1978.

Butcher, J.N., & Maudal, G.R. Crisis intervention. In I.B. Weiner (Ed.), *Clinical methods in psychology.* New York: Wiley, 1976.

Cartwright, D.S., Kirtner, W.L., & Fiske, D.W. Methods factors in changes associated with psychotherapy. *Journal of Abnormal and Social Psychology,* 1963, *66,* 164–175.

Eysenck, H.J. The effects of psychotherapy: An evaluation. *Journal of Consulting Psychology,* 1952, *16,* 319–324.

Eysenck, H.J. *The effects of psychotherapy.* New York: International Science Press, 1966.

Freeman, R.W., & Golann, S.E. *Third-year evaluations by co-workers of Mental Health Counselors.* Paper presented at the American Psychological Association Convention, Chicago, September 1965.

Freud, S. *Collected papers* (Vol. 2). London: Hogarth Press and the Institute of Psychoanalysis, 1950.

Garfield, S.L. Historical introduction to clinical psychology. In B.B. Wolman (Ed.), *Handbook of clinical psychology.* New York: McGraw-Hill, 1965.

Garfield, S.L. New developments in the preparation of counselors. *Community Mental Health Journal,* 1969, *5,* 240–246.

Garfield, S.L. *Clinical psychology: Definition and overview.* New York: General Learning Press, 1971.

Garfield, S.L. *Clinical psychology: The study of personality and behavior.* Chicago: Aldine, 1974.

Garfield, S.L. Research on client variables in psychotherapy. In S.L. Garfield & A.E. Bergin (Eds.), *Handbook of psychotherapy and behavior change* (2nd ed.). New York: Wiley, 1978.

Garfield, S.L., & Bergin, A.W. (Eds.), *Handbook of psychotherapy and behavior change* (2nd ed.). New York: Wiley, 1978.

Garfield, S.L., & Kurtz, R. Clinical psychologists in the 1970's. *American Psychologist,* 1976, *31,* 1–9.

Garfield, S.L., & Kurtz, M. A study of eclectic

views. *Journal of Consulting and Clinical Psychology,* 1977, *45,* 78–83.

Garfield, S.L. Prager, R.A., & Bergin, A.E. Evaluation of outcome in psychotherapy. *Journal of Consulting and Clinical Psychology,* 1971, *37,* 307–313.

Garfield, S.L., & Wolpin, M. Expectations regarding psychotherapy. *Journal of Nervous and Mental Disease,* 1963, *137,* 353–362.

Gottman, J.M., & Markman, H.J. Experimental designs in psychotherapy research. In S.L. Garfield & A.E. Bergin (Eds.), *Handbook of psychotherapy and behavior change* (2nd ed.). New York: Wiley, 1978.

Group for the Advancement of Psychiatry. *Pharmacotherapy and psychotherapy: Paradoxes, problems and progress.* New York: American Psychiatric Association, 1975.

Gurin, G., Veroff, J., & Fields, S. *Americans view their mental health.* New York: Basic Books, 1960.

Gurman, A.S., & Kniskern, D.P. Research on marital and family therapy: Progress, perspective, and prospect. In S.L. Garfield & A.E. Bergin (Eds.), *Handbook of psychotherapy and behavior change: An empirical analysis* (2nd ed.). New York: Wiley, 1978.

Harris, M.R., Kalis, B.L., & Freeman, E.H. Precipitating stress: An approach to brief therapy. *American Journal of Psychotherapy,* 1963, *17,* 465–471.

Heitler, J.B. Preparation of lower-class patients for expressive group psychotherapy. *Journal of Consulting and Clinical Psychology,* 1973, *41,* 251–260.

Heitler, J.B. Preparatory techniques in initiating expressive psychotherapy with lower-class, unsophisticated patients. *Psychological Bulletin,* 1976, *83,* 339–352.

Hoehn-Saric, R., Frank, J.D., Imber, S.D., Nash, E.H., Stone, A.R., & Battle, C.C. Systematic preparation of patients for psychotherapy: I. Effects on therapy behavior and outcome. *Journal of Psychiatric Research,* 1964, *2,* 267–281.

Hollingshead, A.B., & Redlich, F.C. *Social class and mental illness: A community study.* New York: Wiley, 1958.

Horenstein, D., Houston, B., & Holmes, D. Clients', therapists', and judges' evaluations of psychotherapy. *Journal of Counseling Psychology,* 1973, *20,* 149–153.

Horney, K. *New ways in psychoanalysis.* New York: Norton, 1939.

Jacobs, D., Charles, E., Jacobs, T., Weinstein, H., & Mann, D. Preparation for treatment of the disadvantaged patient: Effects on disposition and outcome. *American Journal of Orthopsychiatry,* 1972, *42,* 666–674.

Joint Commission on Mental Illness and Health. *Action for mental health.* New York: Basic Books, 1961.

Kadushin, D. *Why people go to psychiatrists.* New York: Atherton, 1969.

Kelly, E.L. Clinical psychology—1960: Report of survey findings. *American Psychological Association, Division of Clinical Psychology Newsletter,* 1961, *14* (1), 1–11.

Lieberman, M.A., Yalom, I.D., & Miles, M.B. *Encounter groups: First facts.* New York: Basic Books, 1973.

Luborsky, L., Singer, B., & Luborsky, L. Comparative studies in psychotherapy: Is it true that everyone has won and all must have prizes? *Archives of General Psychiatry,* 1975, *32,* 995–1008.

Luborsky, L., & Spence, D.P. Quantitative research on psychoanalytic therapy. In A.E. Bergin & S.L. Garfield (Eds.), *Handbook of psychotherapy and behavior change.* New York: Wiley, 1971.

Magoon, T.M., & Golann, S.E. Nontraditionally trained women as mental health counselors/psychotherapist. *Personnel and Guidance Journal,* 1966, *44,* 788–793.

Paul, G.L. Strategy of outcome research in psychotherapy. *Journal of Consulting Psychology,* 1967, *31,* 109–118.

Report of Research Task Force of the National Institute of Mental Health. *Research in the Service of Mental Health* U.S. Government Printing Office, (DHEW Publication No. (ADM) 75-236.) Rockville, Md.: 1975.

Rioch, M.J. Pilot projects in training mental health counselors. In E.L. Cowen, E.A. Gardner, & M. Zax (Eds.), *Emergent approaches to mental health problems.* New York: Appleton-Century-Crofts, 1967.

Rioch, M.J., Elkes, C., & Flint, A.A. National Institute of Mental Health project in training mental health counselors. Washington, D.C.: Dept. of H.E.W. Public Health Service Publication No. 1254, 1965.

Rogers, C.R. *Counseling and psychotherapy.* Boston: Houghton Mifflin, 1942.

Rogers, C.R. *Client-centered therapy.* Boston: Houghton Mifflin, 1951.

Ryan, W. (Ed.). *Distress in the city.* Cleveland: Case Western Reserve University Press, 1969.

Sloane, R.B., Staples, F.R., Cristol, A.H., Yorkston, N.J., & Whipple, K. *Psychotherapy versus behavior therapy*. Cambridge, Mass.: Harvard University Press, 1975.

Strupp, H.H. On the basic ingredients of psychotherapy. *Journal of Consulting and Clinical Psychology,* 1973, *41,* 1–8.

Strupp, H.H., & Bloxom, A.L. Preparing lower-class patients for group psychotherapy: Development and evaluation of a role-induction film. *Journal of Consulting and Clinical Psychology,* 1973, *41,* 373–384.

Sullivan, H.S. *The interpersonal theory of psychiatry*. New York: Norton, 1953.

Truax, C.B., & Carkhuff, R.R. *Toward effective counseling and psychotherapy*. Chicago: Aldine, 1967.

Zilboorg, G., & Henry, G.W. *A history of medical psychology*. New York: Norton, 1941.

AUTHOR INDEX

SUBJECT INDEX